ARTIFICIAL INTELLIGENCE and TUTORING SYSTEMS

Computational and Cognitive Approaches to the Communication of Knowledge

ARTIFICIAL INTELLIGENCE and TUTORING SYSTEMS,

Computational and Cognitive Approaches to the Communication of Knowledge

BY

Etienne Wenger

University of California, Irvine

FOREWORD BY

John Seely Brown

Xerox Palo Alto Research Center

and

James Greeno

University of California, Berkeley

MORGAN KAUFMANN PUBLISHERS, INC.
95 FIRST STREET
LOS ALTOS, CALIFORNIA 94022

Editor and President   *Michael B. Morgan*
Production Manager   *Jennifer M. Ballentine*
Production Assistant   *Todd R. Armstrong*
Composition   *The Font Factory*
Book Design   *Beverly Kennon-Kelley*
Cover Design   *Irene Imfeld*
Illustrations   *Matthew Bennett*
Copyediting   *Adam Cornford*

Figure credits can be found following the Bibliography.

Library of Congress Cataloging-in-Publication Data

Wenger, Etienne, 1952-
    Artificial intelligence and tutoring systems.

    "January 12, 1987."
    Bibliography: p.
    Includes index.
    1. Artificial intelligence—Data processing.
2. Computer-assisted instruction. 3. Knowledge,
Theory of. I. Title. II. Title: Tutoring systems.
Q336.W46 1987   006.3   87–3170
ISBN 0–934613-26-5

ISBN 0-934613-26-5

A mes parents
Alfred et Liliane Wenger

Foreword

It is always a pleasure to introduce a fine book by a young author. Etienne Wenger's *Artificial Intelligence and Tutoring Systems* is the fruit of an ambitious effort that has succeeded remarkably well. In this book, Wenger has taken on the task of reviewing the state of the art and science of intelligent tutoring systems. The result is a work that provides a new level of conceptual coherence and analytic structure to ITS research, thereby helping to define the field as a legitimate, and potentially very important, scientific and technological domain.

Let's consider Wenger's accomplishments in turn. To start with, he has given us an insightful review of AI-based instructional systems. His treatment will be valuable as an introductory text, for it provides informative descriptions of each system as a whole and useful comparisons of significant features. In doing so, he has also conveyed a sense of the intellectual history of the field, for he shows how specific features of tutoring programs resulted from theoretical and practical attempts to address system deficiencies. As an example, Wenger's excellent discussions of mental models show how they emerged as a response to system failures to handle certain kinds of communication tasks. Wenger also gives an exceptionally penetrating discussion of diagnostic systems, showing the respective advantages and disadvantages of top-down (model-driven) and bottom-up (data-driven) methods of student modeling.

But this book is no mere catalog of programs and techniques. Most significantly from our point of view, he has also laid out a provocative framework for analyzing and comparing intelligent tutoring systems. This framework addresses fundamental scientific issues concerning the nature of knowledge, learning, and communication, which are at the heart of ITS design. It is relative to this framework that Wenger's discussions reveal how research on intelligent tutoring systems contributes not only to the fields of artificial intelligence and education, but also to basic scientific problems in linguistics, psychology, and philosophy.

Wenger's framework for understanding intelligent tutoring systems centers on the notion of communicable knowledge. In this view, the primary function of a tutoring system is as a vehicle of communication. In developing this notion, Wenger makes very productive use of an epistemological assumption, developed by Philip Kitcher, that knowledge is warranted belief. Wenger takes a warrant for a belief to be the set of experential or conceptual episodes provided by the system that give rise to the belief and justify it for a particular person. The key notion is that knowledge can only be communicated—and therefore learned— through the mediation of warrants that connect with the individual's present understanding. It therefore becomes crucial that system designers pay close attention to the various kinds of warrants for belief (e.g., causal, functional, teleological) and to the various ways that these justifications become manifest, ranging from sequences of experiences to verbal explanations. Wenger's framework unifies a number of issues surrounding knowledge communication in ITS, including the problem of explanations—a topic frequently alluded to but all too often finessed in expert systems research.

One emerges from this book with an altered vision of intelligent tutoring systems in which informed presentational schemes—presentational schemes based on knowledge about the warranting conditions for new beliefs—play a newly important role. Wenger's epistemological view and theoretical framework together expand the universe of intelligent tutoring systems, building conceptual links between systems that demonstrate their processes of reasoning explicitly, that enable students to reflect on their own reasoning, and that provide rich environments for exploratory learning. Thus, tutoring programs that have emphasized methods as diverse as interaction with computational experts, coaching, and free exploration are interpretable within a single, coherent conceptual framework.

But we believe that there is more to Wenger's accomplishment than its manifest contribution to ITS theory. The rapid pace of technological and social change and the growth of information have created pressing new educational needs. It is no longer appropriate to think of education as transpiring solely in school or between the ages of six and eighteen. Instead, it is imperative that people acquire the cognitive and interactional skills necessary for self-directed, life-long learning. We believe that this agenda requires an examination of fundamental assumptions about knowledge and learning, a fresh look at alternatives to the didacticism that currently dominates our educational system, and the development of new kinds of educational resources. The expanded view of the requirements of successful knowledge communication implicit in Wenger's framework begins to address several of the issues that will be important to this reformulation of educational means and ends. Wenger's work has obvious implications for the development not only of instructional systems per se, but also of information systems more generally. But the implications of this work extend even beyond that. We believe that a better understanding of the nature of knowledge and its warrants will result in increased attention to the social and physical contexts in which learning takes place, as these often determine the situational characteristics that bring about growth in knowledge. Wenger's analytic framework and his focus on learning as a process of communication will contribute significantly to inquiry into the various ways that individuals come to know, either articulately or tacitly, in a range of everyday situations, including free exploration, apprenticeship, collaboration, and reflection.

Wenger's book is a particularly timely contribution. It could not have been written as recently as five years ago, since a critical mass of information about intelligent tutoring systems sufficient for this kind of conceptual analysis had not yet developed. Nor could it have been written five years from now, for by then there will be too much material to review in the thorough manner employed here. *Artificial Intelligence and Tutoring Systems*, therefore, stands as a unique document revealing a young field's accomplishments and, more importantly, its promise at an important threshold of development.

John Seely Brown, Xerox Palo Alto Research Center
James G. Greeno, University of California, Berkeley

Acknowledgments

This book was not a planned project; it could not have been. It grew out of research I was doing as a graduate student at the University of California at Irvine, and surreptitiously became "the book." In the process of making room for this new entity and bringing the project to completion, many people had to go out of their way: it is my great pleasure to thank them all here and to give explicit recognition to some of them.

I want to thank Susan Chipman and Michael Shafto of the Personnel and Training Division of the Office of Naval Research and Dorothy Fischer of the Joseph Fischer Foundation for their appreciation for my work. The ONR contract N00014-85-K-0373 provided some financial support, and an award from the Fischer Foundation helped with student fees. The University also awarded me several tuition fellowships. I gratefully acknowledge the support of these organizations.

I want to thank everyone in the Department of Information and Computer Science at UCI for the friendly atmosphere and for the sophisticated and reliable working environment I have enjoyed while writing. Some people deserve special mention: the department's chair, John King, who on several occasions made exceptional use of his administrative talents to allow me to continue working on this project free of other worries; my advisor, Dennis Kibler, who as a scholar believed in me through the endless saga of the book and fended for me whenever the reasonable opinion was expressed that graduate students should just concentrate on finishing their dissertations and getting out; my office mate, Rogers Hall, faithful friend and delightful intellectual companion, who I know would have preferred me to move on to other projects with him, but who never showed impatience as I remained absorbed in my writing.

I want to thank the book's reviewers for taking time out of their busy schedules to comment on the draft: Jeffrey Bonar, Lewis Johnson, Bob London, Derek Sleeman, and Kurt VanLehn. I also want to thank Adam Cornford for his careful copyediting. Michael Morgan and Jennifer Ballentine of Morgan Kaufmann Publishers have been just what I expected from my editors: dedicated to the intellectual and physical quality of the book, and very concerned with my every opinion and with my personal experience of the whole process. It is still somewhat hard for me to believe that such fine scientists and visionary thinkers as John Seely Brown and Jim Greeno would care to write a foreword to anything I wrote. But knowing that they have, I can only thank them wholeheartedly; such honor is probably my greatest surprise in this adventure.

I want to thank my parents, to whom this book is dedicated, not only for their encouragement and support ever since I went back to studying, but more generally for always taking parenting as seriously as they have. I know their love and dedication is a key to what I have become, and the prominence of their names in this book is a small token of my gratitude.

I want to thank my wonderful wife Paula. Her love and support have given me endless reasons to dedicate this book to her, including her candid but firm insistence that this honor should just go to my parents. Such tender paradoxes, only the heart knows how to resolve. With just more love.

And I want to thank my son Jad for carrying around the young beauty of his soul. One day, as I was grabbing the folder containing the precious manuscript on my busy way out, he said to me with his two-and-a-half-year-old innocence: "You want me to write it for you, your book?" In your own simple way, Jad, you have, and through you, this book is silently dedicated to all the children—young and old—who grow up in this world: may you always see learning as the greatest game in life, yet never as a reason to lose what you already know.

Etienne Wenger

Contents

Part II   A panorama: people, ideas, and systems

Chapter 9   More on student modeling: toward domain-independent mechanisms 185

Part III A synopsis: the state of the art

Contents

Part I

A first glance: introducing the field

There has been a surge of interest in computer-based instructional systems that display some degree of intelligence. These "intelligent tutoring systems" are seen as a promising avenue by many educators and training specialists, as worthy challenges by researchers, and even as revealing testbeds for cognitive theories by psychologists. Such an interest parallels the wave of excitement rising around the field of artificial intelligence (AI), and is also amplified by a renewed concern for educational issues in both public education and technical training. This combination of factors, which has kindled the sympathy of research funding agencies, has sparked the creation of a number of important research projects.

Ever since computers were first introduced as information-processing machines that might one day become widely available, their enormous potential for educational use has been recognized and heralded, generally with enthusiasm, sometimes with apprehension. Although the vision of computers in education has a long history, we will not go into details here; the reader is referred to the literature listed in the bibliographical notes at the end of Chapter 1. In short, the first attempts at creating educational software have had mixed results. Projects have often done more to reveal problems than to fulfill promises, with respect to both their technical and pedagogical performances and their integration into the larger context of educational institutions (O'Shea and Self, 1983). The story has by no means come to an end, fortunately, and efforts continue in spite of some bad press. However, the difficulty of producing good-quality material has left a sense of uncertainty sometimes bordering on disillusion. Undoubtedly, this very disappointment with unsophisticated programs has attracted attention to ideas from artificial intelligence: as premature as the promise of AI may seem at times, it is perceived as bringing new hopes to an old dream.

This book presents the field of research combining the "new hopes" of artificial intelligence and the old dream of tutoring systems. It is divided into three distinct parts:

- Part I is an introduction to both the book and the field. This "first glance" spans two chapters. Chapter 1 identifies what is unique about the research and methodology of the field, and introduces central themes underlying the book. Chapter 2 describes general components of tutoring systems in terms of corresponding communication issues. In the process, it equips the reader with some concepts and terminology necessary for following subsequent discussions.

- Part II is a panoramic technical survey of the research conducted since the field's first systems in the early seventies. It is organized around individual projects and along historical lines. It is intended both to provide a useful reference to the work that has shaped the field and to give a sense of the evolution of ideas whereby principles are emerging.

- Part III returns to a synoptic presentation organized around issues, complementing the historical development of Part II with an orthogonal viewpoint centered on major conceptual themes. Drawing on examples from the technical descriptions of Part II, it attempts to provide a coherent discussion that highlights emerging principles and open questions while articulating distinctions helpful for further research.

Relating these various viewpoints will require numerous cross-references. To help the reader, both author and subject indexes are provided; these thorough indexes should also be helpful when the book is used as a reference. In addition, chapters in Parts I and II end with summaries, and most chapters are followed by some bibliographical notes.

Chapter 1

Knowledge
communication systems

For historical reasons, much of the research in the field of educational software involving artificial intelligence has been conducted under the name of "ICAI." This acronym stands for "Intelligent Computer-Aided Instruction," a phrase that evolved out of the name "Computer-Aided Instruction" (CAI) commonly given the use of computers in education. More recently, "ICAI" has often been replaced by the acronym "ITS," for "Intelligent Tutoring Systems" (Sleeman and Brown, 1982). In this book, I prefer to use this latter acronym to distinguish instructional systems involving artificial intelligence from more traditional approaches, which will simply be referred to as CAI. This preference is motivated by a claim that, in many ways, the significance of the shift in research methodology goes beyond the addition of an "I" to CAI.

3

1.1   Implicit versus explicit encoding of knowledge

The purpose of this chapter is to give the reader a sense of the field's identity by outlining its goals, its methodology, and its relation to other fields. To this end, let us start with a contrast between CAI and ITS, since both enterprises share the goal of producing instructional systems.

Educational software engineering: encoding of decisions

Traditional CAI programs are statically organized receptacles structured to embody both the domain and the pedagogical knowledge of expert teachers. In this sense, the use of computers in CAI is reminiscent of the view of books as containers for the knowledge of authors. Books have facilities like lines, pages, sections, chapters, a table of contents, an index, and even figures, all of which are tools for organizing the presentation of knowledge and ideas. Authors have both some knowledge in some domain, which has to be communicated, and some knowledge about book writing, which they apply to take advantage of these facilities. However, one does not expect a book to have dynamic access to the knowledge it contains so that it can answer unexpected questions from the reader or draw new relevant inferences. Nor does one expect that the book be able to modify its presentation on the fly to adapt itself to a reader's specific needs.

Note that a book can be quite sophisticated and support various levels of reading, inviting the advanced reader to skip certain sections or providing a glossary and cross-references between sections. Yet everything has to be set in advance by the author within the fixed constraints of the printed medium, no matter how sophisticated the details may become. In the same way, the task of creating educational material in the CAI approach can be an extremely sophisticated process of translating a teacher's pedagogical decisions into a program. However, all the circumstances in which decisions are necessary have to be anticipated, so that appropriate code can be written to capture these decisions. The strength of this traditional CAI approach resides in the paradigm's ability to take direct advantage of the pedagogical experience of human teachers and to reflect this expertise straightforwardly in the behavior of programs without an articulation of its underlying principles.

Various directions of research efforts can be identified within the traditional CAI paradigm. Some researchers are actually producing new course material using available programming facilities (e.g., Bork, 1980). Others are creating and refining generic sets of tools for course authors, like specialized *authoring languages* or *authoring environments* intended to facilitate the writing of educational software (PLATO: CERL, 1977;

TICCIT: Alderman, 1979).   This work also includes the development of sophisticated computer graphics and of various hardware facilities that extend the communication function of the computer. In addition, specific software-engineering methods are being investigated in an effort to optimize the process of translating the pedagogical decisions made by experts into the framework of computer-based systems (TICCIT: Bunderson, 1974; Bork, 1981, 1986a).

Artificial intelligence: explicit encoding of knowledge

For research on instructional systems involving artificial intelligence, the purpose is not to provide a software-engineering framework within which experts can compose instructional interactions by representing their decisions in the form of programs. Rather, the purpose is to capture the very knowledge that allows experts to compose an instructional interaction in the first place. Instead of decisions resulting from some knowledge, it is the knowledge itself that is explicitly represented so that it can be used in computer-based systems. It is then the responsibility of programs to compose instructional interactions dynamically, making decisions by reference to the knowledge with which they have been provided.

Obviously, there is no strict dividing line between the two types of programs; actual systems will lie on a continuum between completely fixed pre-programming and perfect autonomy. On the one hand, more sophisticated CAI systems are given some autonomous capabilities: for instance, they can generate exercises (Uhr, 1969) or adapt the level of difficulty to some measure of the student's performance (Park and Tennyson, 1983). On the other hand, models of expertise produced by artificial intelligence vary greatly in their generality, that is, in the degree to which knowledge underlying specific decisions is made explicit. In fact, we will see that ITS research is still far from the ideal goal of a system capable of entirely autonomous pedagogical reasoning, purely on the basis of primitive principles, in domain knowledge as well as in pedagogical expertise. Whether this goal can be fully reached at all, or how soon, or to what extent it is desirable, are still matters of speculation reflecting the state of the entire field of artificial intelligence.

Nevertheless, the difference is crucial. In particular, transferring the expertise as opposed to the decisions of experts creates the possibility that systems make decisions not anticipated by these experts, whose knowledge has been handed over in a "raw" state to be used by autonomous processes. Indeed, the teaching style of intelligent tutoring systems may end up differing from that of human teachers in significant ways so as to take advantage of the characteristics of machines. For instance, while computers are usually weak at improvisation, they tend to outperform people in the precision and completeness of their use of available information.

It is not my intention here to conjure the somewhat eerie vision of computers replacing human teachers because they do a "better job." I personally do not believe that computers compete with human teachers in any real sense, or that they can or should replace people in instructional settings. Teaching as a social act simply involves too many dimensions beyond the exact processing of information for which computers are made, and at which they can excel. But consider again the example of books: they have certainly outperformed people in the precision and permanence of their memory, and the reliability of their patience. For this reason, they have been invaluable to humankind. Now imagine active books that can interact with the reader to communicate knowledge at the appropriate level, selectively highlighting the interconnectedness and ramifications of items, recalling relevant information, probing understanding, explaining difficult areas in more depth, skipping over seemingly known material ... intelligent knowledge communication systems are indeed an attractive dream.

1.2 Knowledge communication

Because of this emphasis on actually giving systems access to a representation of the knowledge that they attempt to communicate, I will often call these systems *knowledge communication systems*. The notion of knowledge communication provides some interesting perspectives on the subject. From the standpoint of artificial intelligence, it implies a view of pedagogical activities as the manifestation of a more general capability of intelligent systems. From the standpoint of education, knowledge communication does not carry the social connotations that teaching[1] does, yet the concept of communication suggests a system of symbols and conventions and a cooperative interaction whereby information is shared. From the standpoint of this book, the composition of the phrase reflects the duality inherent to the field's main research themes: intertwined investigations of communication processes and of the nature of knowledge.

In fact, because of the perspective it provides, the notion of *knowledge communication* will be a central theme of this book. For the purpose of

---

[1] Although I personally like the idea of leaving the term "teaching" to refer to a relation binding two human beings, a relation that I consider one of the deepest and noblest that can exist, the term will often be used in connection with computers in this book, almost inevitably, along with "knowledge," "reasoning," and other anthropomorphic metaphors typical of AI jargon.

our presentation, knowledge communication is defined as *the ability to cause and/or support the acquisition of one's knowledge by someone else, via a restricted set of communication operations.* A few points about this definition are worth noting. First, the specification of a restricted set of communication operations, such as a language, screen graphics, or a set of exercises, excludes both the direct inspection and the complete transfer of internal states. Second, this notion of knowledge communication is very broad in that it includes very indirect ways of having one's knowledge acquired by someone else. With this definition, we will see that all the critical issues pertaining to ITS are issues involved in the intelligent communication of knowledge. Finally, I have abstained from attempting to define knowledge or communication. Such definitions would stand in contradiction to the claim that the enterprise described here is intrinsically bound to an inquiry into the nature of these concepts.

1.3 Practical and theoretical implications

Although there is a hope that eventually the explicit encoding of domain and pedagogical knowledge will give rise to more intelligent, adaptive, and effective behavior on the part of systems, I want to suggest that the shift from the programming of decisions to the programming of knowledge is in itself the main distinctive feature of educational systems involving artificial intelligence. Thus, even if the distinction between systems in CAI and those in ITS cannot always be made with clear-cut behavioral criteria (Bork, 1986b), the overall methodological shift is radical. As a result, the primary goal becomes a computational understanding of processes of knowledge communication rather than an optimization of the production of systems. Of central importance then is the notion of *model*: model of the domain, model of the student, and model of communication processes (Clancey, 1986b). Let us briefly review some practical and theoretical implications of this methodological shift.

Toward a cognitively oriented form of software engineering

For the design of useful instructional systems, the shift to building explicit computational models of domain and pedagogical expertise introduces a cognitive orientation that broadens the scope of the enterprise. It is in sharp contrast with the behaviorist views characteristic of early notions of programmed teaching (Skinner, 1968). In fact, we will see in Part II that the lessons learned in the field so far keep suggesting a need to place epistemological, cognitive, and pedagogical issues before the mass production of instructional artifacts or the creation of authoring languages. Note that this does not mean that the design of systems has to be postponed; in fact, design is an intrinsic part of the field's methodology, and has been a critical catalyst in the articulation of processes that has led to the field's main contributions. Rather, it means that the enterprise needs to become concerned with profound questions about the nature of knowledge, communication, learning, and understanding.

A practical consequence of the fact that the design of generic tools is not just a technological matter is that intelligent tutoring systems remain difficult to build. The most successful projects described in this book have required years of work by talented people, and have often gone through several generations of prototype systems involving major reconsiderations of approach. Few of these systems have left the laboratory. These comments are not pessimistic. Teaching *is* difficult, and the fact that designing intelligent tutoring systems requires such a deep understanding of the processes involved may well be a sign that we have found a methodology whereby we can start attacking general issues in a systematic way.

It is interesting to note that ITS is defined here in methodological and epistemological terms, but not in terms of educational philosophies. In fact, as will become clear in the survey of Part II, many educational attitudes are represented in the field and are viewed as sharing similar problems. Traditionally, the advocates of the educational use of computers have proposed two different types of application. Some view the computer as a device for the delivery of instruction and for the monitoring of guided practice. In seeking ways to break out of this paradigm with its tendency to produce somewhat inflexible tutorial programs, a number of researchers have attempted to use the computer in a more open-ended way, as an interactive tool in an environment designed for exploratory learning (Papert, 1980). Not only are the contributions of artificial intelligence relevant to both approaches, but an argument of this book will be that many of the same issues are involved in the design of both types of systems when they are viewed as vehicles for the communication of knowledge (see Section 19.2).

Toward a communication-oriented epistemology

As a scientific enterprise, the field of artificial intelligence can be loosely described as the study of principles of computational intelligence as manifested in man-made systems. In this context, the notion of knowledge communication as a general capability of intelligent systems has a special significance. In fact, underlying this book is a claim that, unlike numerous possible application domains for AI, knowledge communication is not a mere application of AI techniques. Rather, the study of knowledge communication is presented as an integral part of the study of intelligence, much like problem solving or learning.

The most obvious—though circumstantial—support for this view is the fact that knowledge communication is a widespread intelligent behavior, which is interesting in itself. Indeed, if human beings are considered as good examples of intelligent systems, knowledge communication is a critical ability, possessed to some degree by most people. From this perspective, we will see that knowledge communication as a computational process has an unusual ability to push AI investigations forward because it requires the combination of techniques from various subareas. But the real argument is perhaps more subtle and more fundamental. It is based on the conjecture that communication and knowledge affect one another in a deep way, so that the study of one inevitably involves concerns for the other. For the argument to be of interest, it is not necessary to adopt the extreme position that they determine or limit one another; one need simply assume that they are inextricably involved in a complex process of mutual influence.

We will come back to this issue in more detail toward the end of the book, after the survey of research projects has provided some cases that corroborate the importance of this dialectical phenomenon. Indeed, a theme that will surface again and again is that the goal of communicating knowledge with explicit representations in instructional systems has led researchers to undertake very fundamental investigations into the nature of knowledge and into the characteristics that make it communicable. These investigations have in turn given rise to important insights into issues of knowledge representation, reasoning, and learning central to artificial intelligence. In fact, some of these investigations have been among AI's most significant developments; they establish intelligent knowledge communication as a fundamental research direction in artificial intelligence, when it has usually been considered as an application.

1.4   An interdisciplinary enterprise

Because of the many dimensions involved in the creation of knowledge communications systems, the field is inherently interdisciplinary. From a research perspective, this point cannot be emphasized enough (Brown and Greeno, 1984). Thus, even though the vision of individualized tutoring systems is still central, the field should be viewed not merely as an extension of CAI, but as a crossroads where researchers from a variety of backgrounds find common interests. In this sense, even the AI perspective emphasized in this chapter is too narrow, since progress in intelligent knowledge communication is tightly linked to the development of many other fields of research. In fact, several researchers whose work is covered in this book have their primary research interests in these other fields. Like AI, these related disciplines both contribute to and benefit from advancements in knowledge communication systems, and one hopes that this will inspire more interdisciplinary cooperation in the future. Here, we briefly mention the disciplines whose impact seems most significant, without claiming to be exhaustive.

With their interest in human intelligence, *epistemology, psychology,* and *cognitive science* are linked to research in automated knowledge communication much in the same way that AI is. However, they deal with issues specific to human cognition, which are essential ingredients of successful communication with people but are often absent from AI work. As these researchers seek to understand and build models of how people know, how they learn, and how both experts and novices perform in various domains, their findings are crucial to the explicit representations of human knowledge required for knowledge communication systems. Conversely, we will see that some psychologists have incorporated the purposes and methodologies of ITS into their research and have found instructional systems to be good research tools in the development of cognitive theories.

Obviously, *education* and *educational psychology* are very closely related research areas, in their attempts to capture the constituents of pedagogical expertise, to gather a corpus of useful empirical techniques, and to produce useful instructional artifacts. In return, the episte- mological attitude adopted for computational approaches provides new opportunities to study curricula and teaching strategies. Eventually, the explicit computational models of pedagogical expertise developed for knowledge communication systems make both theoretical and practical contributions to research in education. In reality, however, ties be- tween the educational community and ITS researchers have been rather tenuous. This situation—which has prompted some concerns among educators (Suppes, 1979)—seems to be changing quite rapidly.

The notion of knowledge communication as presented here also brings forward the relevance of other fields concerned with communi- cation. These clearly include *linguistics.* Linguistic research is relevant at two levels. First, there is much interest in endowing intelligent tutoring systems with some capacity to understand and use natural languages. Second, most speech acts can be viewed in a very broad sense as a form of knowledge communication. Thus, although ITS research concentrates on situations where there are long-term intentions to cause modifications to the state of knowledge of interlocutors, there remains a large overlap between the two fields: for instance, the articulation of tacit conventions such as conversational postulates, or the use of models of participants. *Anthropology* is another related field, inasmuch as the study of cognitive processes central to designing explicit models of knowledge communication cannot isolate itself from the cultural fabric and situational dimension in which interactions are to take place and in which knowledge evolves (Suchman, 1987; Lave, in press).

Finally, in the area of *human-computer interaction*, principles of knowledge communication are also pertinent to a number of situations where a computer-based system has to interact with people, and where increased "intelligence" on the system's part can improve the flow of information. Such situations include help systems, user interfaces, and database retrieval systems. In the case of expert systems, they also include explanations and justifications to users as well as processes of knowledge acquisition for development and maintenance. These aspects are not explicitly treated in this book, since each of them is a topic by itself. However, because of the common interest in knowledge communication processes, it is fairly safe to predict that the progression toward more sophisticated interactive systems will bring these areas continually closer, and will make the investigations described and the principles outlined in this book increasingly relevant.

Summary and conclusion

In sum, the field has been presented as an attempt to produce computational models of interactive knowledge communication. In many ways this introduction to the field simply reflects its ties to artificial intelligence. This is true not only of the explicit encoding of knowledge, but also to a large extent of the relevance of multiple disciplines. The chapter also reflects the dual purpose of AI enterprises, where a science of intelligence coexists with an engineering discipline. This dual purpose will underlie the presentation of the whole book. Since science and engineering in this field are clearly not independent, I will not go out of my way to treat them in distinct sections. While different people may be more interested in one perspective than the other because of different personal objectives, it is healthy for both sides to remember that both undertakings advance hand in hand. In a comparison with more traditional CAI efforts at building useful instructional systems, the close interplay of a computational theory of knowledge communication with the engineering enterprise can in fact be viewed as the truly distinctive feature of the emerging field this book is about.

Bibliographical notes

General references to CAI work abound. Many central issues of CAI are covered in a very good review by Suppes (1979), and more recently in books by Bork (1981, 1986a). Famous large projects and final reports include PLATO (CERL, 1977), TICCIT (Alderman, 1979), the Stanford

CAI project (Suppes, 1981), and the British NPD (Hooper, 1977). Sophisticated aspects of adaptive CAI are reviewed by Park and Tennyson (1983); their adaptive instructional system MAIS (Tennyson et al., 1984) exemplifies well the gray area between CAI and ITS. The concept of learning environment is discussed by Papert (1980) and that of learning tool by Goldberg (1979). A good entry point into the general topic of computer-based learning is the book by O'Shea and Self (1983); it contains many references and an interesting historical summary of computer use in education. General references for ITS are given in the bibliographical notes of Chapter 2.

A collection on mental models edited by Gentner and Stevens (1983) contains good examples of the cognitive perspectives adopted by many ITS researchers. The challenges to some of these views presented by anthropologists Suchman (1987) and Lave (in press) open new dimensions for reflecting on and designing AI-based instructional systems. For a more direct challenge to ITS and its use of the computer metaphor for cognition, see the bibliographical notes of Chapter 14.

As to educational research, the collections edited by Chipman et al. (1985), and by Glaser (1978, 1982, 1987) contain many relevant articles with an emphasis on cognitively oriented approaches. Relevant studies also come from researchers primarily interested in group instruction: Bloom (1984) documents the effectiveness of one-to-one tutoring, and Palincsar and Brown (1984) show the importance of having a model of the target competence that can perform the actual task with students.

Barr et al. (1979) discuss the general notion of transfer of expertise underlying both expert and tutoring systems. The issue of explanations for expert systems is addressed by Swartout (1981), Neches et al. (1985), and Hasling et al. (1984) (see Chapter 12). A number of interesting papers on human-computer interaction can be found in a book on user-centered system design edited by Norman and Draper (1986) and in a recent collection including a section on models of computer users (Baecker and Buxton, 1987).

An exhaustive bibliography of related themes is clearly impossible; the few useful pointers given here and later are merely representative of all the potentially relevant literature. In this regard, this book concentrates on an in-depth analysis of the ITS enterprise—and even that has produced a rather voluminous bibliography. This focus has, I think, resulted in a useful book to serve as a text for a course on knowledge communication systems, as an introduction to the subject, or as a reference. However, a single book can hardly do justice to the interdisciplinary nature of the field.

Chapter 2

Basic issues

Before we start describing actual projects that attempt to design knowledge communication systems, it is useful to consider briefly a few issues basic to the topic. When we speak about knowledge communication in this book, we refer primarily to an instructional situation, involving a *tutoring system*—or a human teacher—and a *student*; the object of communication is *knowledge* or *expertise* in some *domain*. However, as mentioned before, many of the issues discussed here can be generalized to other situations in which intelligent knowledge communication is required.

This chapter is merely introductory: it presents issues that have become traditional in the context of ITS research, but is not intended as a discussion of these issues. I have chosen to postpone such a discussion until Part III so that it can build on the descriptions of projects.[1] For this initial presentation, we follow a natural division of the task of knowledge communication into four distinct components, each corresponding to a distinct section: domain expertise, model of the student, communication strategies or pedagogical expertise, and interface with the student. Similar divisions have been proposed by Hartley and Sleeman (1973), Laubsch (1975), Burton and Brown (1976), and Carr and Goldstein (1977). Though projects often concentrate on some of these issues at the expense of others, most researchers have identified these distinct functions in essentially the same way.

2.1 Domain knowledge: the object of communication

In the transition between CAI and ITS, the knowledge of the subject matter is historically the first aspect of a teacher's expertise to have been explicitly represented in systems. In traditional CAI, the expertise to be conveyed is contained in prestored presentation blocks, sometimes called *frames*, which are designed by an expert teacher and are simply displayed to the student under given conditions. In knowledge communication systems, there is a special module, often called the *expert*, that contains a representation of the knowledge to be communicated. In most cases, this representation of the subject matter is not only a description of the various concepts and skills that the student is to acquire, as in a curriculum, but an actual *model*, which can perform in the domain and thus provide the system with a *dynamic* form of expertise.

The functions of the expert module

The expert module fulfills a double function. On the one hand, it acts as the *source* for the knowledge to be presented. This includes generating explanations and responses to the student as well as tasks and questions. On the other hand, the expert module serves as a *standard* for evaluating the student's performance. For this function, it must be able to generate solutions to problems in the same context as the student does so that their respective answers can be compared. If the tutoring system is to guide the student in solving problems, the expert module must also generate sensible solution paths so that intermediate steps can be compared. Perhaps most important, it must be able to generate *multiple* possible solution paths, rather than just the single one required for models of expertise constructed solely for performance purposes.

---

[1] Since this chapter is primarily meant to provide the conceptual vocabulary for Part II, the advanced reader may elect to skip it.

In its function as a standard, the expert module can also be used to assess the student's overall progress. This requires the establishment of a *measure* that can compare knowledge—in a form of what educators have called "criterion-referenced measurement" (Hambleton, 1984). When this type of global comparison is possible, the expert module can be said to constitute an explicit representation of the *teaching goal*. Here, knowledge communication systems differ substantially from CAI programs. Because of the explicit representation of the knowledge to be conveyed, the teaching goals embodied by the expert module can be expressed in terms of the knowledge itself. Otherwise, teaching goals can only be expressed in terms either of exercises to go through, with the hope that knowledge will be acquired in the process, or of thresholds on a grading scale for measuring the student's performance.

Aspects of communicability

Mere expertise will not usually be sufficient to support pedagogical decisions. Unlike performance, the communication process is organized around *learning*: that is, around the successful integration of new material and new experiences into the student's existing body of knowledge. This requires pieces of information that are specifically used for pedagogical purposes, although by nature they belong to the domain. For instance, prerequisite relations and measures of relative difficulty are crucial to flexibility in assembling instructional sequences. Other pedagogically oriented pieces of domain knowledge include rationales for explanations in terms of goals and causes, as well as conceptual or taxonomic relations between pieces of knowledge that facilitate the use of analogies and abstractions.

With respect to learning, the nature of the expert model itself is crucial. Even when the expert is a distinct module capable of reproducing expertise, its internal structure may be more or less open to inspection, and more or less able to support explanations of its actions and conclusions. In fact, the *communicability* of models of expertise is a theme that will surface continually in this book. Expert modules can be classified along a spectrum ranging from completely opaque or "black-box" representations, whereby only final results are available, to fully transparent or "glass-box" ones, whereby each reasoning step can be inspected and interpreted. Furthermore, whether opaque or transparent, the expert module may achieve its performance with methods that vary in their degree of similarity to the ones used by human experts. Both aspects, *transparency* and *psychological plausibility*, affect the degree of *articulation* of the model of expertise, and the support that the expert module provides for communication processes.

Finally and crucially, the expert module by necessity embodies a specific view of the domain. The representation language it uses and the concepts it takes as atomic primitives are choices made by the designer that bias the entire presentation. If the student does not share basic tenets of this view, communication can be compromised, both because the student does not understand the instruction and because the system cannot interpret the student's behavior in terms of its own knowledge. Although human teachers also have their own views of their domain, good teachers have an unmatched ability to perceive the student's view and to adapt their behavior accordingly. This issue touches upon fundamental limitations inherent in the notion of "model" and central to the problem of knowledge representation in artificial intelligence. Because of its deep pedagogical implications, it is particularly relevant to the design of knowledge communication systems.

2.2   Student model: the recipient of communication

No intelligent communication can take place without a certain under-standing of the recipient. Thus, along with the idea of explicitly repre-senting the knowledge to be conveyed came the idea of doing the same with the student, in the form of a *student model*. Ideally, this model should include all the aspects of the student's behavior and knowledge that have repercussions for his performance and learning. However, the task of constructing such a student model is obviously not a simple one for computer-based systems. In fact, it is even difficult for people, who have much more in common with their fellow interlocutors than do silicon machines. An additional handicap of computers is that their *communication channel* is very restricted, usually a keyboard and a screen, whereas people combine data from a wide variety of sources, like voice effects or facial expressions. Fortunately, a perfectly accurate model of the student along all dimensions is not a sine qua non for reasonable pedagogical decisions, but even building a partial model that provides the required information is a challenge for computer-based systems.

The student model: information

The adaptability of an instructional system, obviously, is largely deter-mined by the coverage and accuracy of the information contained in its student model. In fact, the idea of a student model is not new (Fletcher, 1975). With an AI-based model of expertise that can perform in the domain, it becomes possible to infer unobservable aspects of the student's behavior in order to produce an *interpretation* of his actions and to reconstruct the *knowledge* that has given rise to these actions. These two types of information support detailed pedagogical decisions in guiding the student's problem solving and in organizing his learning experiences, respectively.

A model of the student's knowledge is likely to be formed out of the system's representation of the target expertise. Accordingly, a student model can include a *distinct evaluation* of the mastery of each element of the knowledge to be acquired, in contrast with the overall measures of performance often used in traditional CAI. The student's state of knowledge can then be compared with the knowledge of the expert module in terms of these distinct evaluations, and instruction adapted to exercise portions of the model shown to be weak.

However, incorrect or suboptimal behavior does not always proceed from incomplete knowledge. It can also be due to *incorrect versions* of the target knowledge. Therefore, a more informative student model is able to provide an explicit representation of the student's incorrect versions of the target expertise so that remedial actions can be taken. Furthermore, a student model can contain *explanatory information* about the genesis of these incorrect pieces of knowledge. To this end, incorrect knowledge must be represented so as to reflect the process by which errors arise. Errors can be traced back to the original learning process or to deeper misconceptions either within the subject matter or in a related area. This type of information is of course crucial to effective long-term remediation.

The student model: representation

Models can also vary in the language they use to describe the student. For this purpose, the language designed to represent the system's expertise is a useful core, but is often insufficient. Extensions to accommodate incorrect knowledge can take various forms. One solution is to construct the student model from the *primitives* of a language for the domain that spans both correct and incorrect knowledge. The hope is that the granularity of these primitives is so fine that all misconceptions as well as the correct version can be modeled by appropriate combinations of primitives. Thus the language does not in itself carry information about correctness. This approach is the more "purist" in that, theoretically at least, it does not require that all errors be anticipated. In practice, however, it can be very difficult to define a language that accounts for all observed errors with a consistent set of primitives that is small enough for the search to be tractable.

In the face of these difficulties, another solution is to gather a great deal of information about likely *errors and misconceptions* for a given domain and a given population of students and to include these observed distortions as primitives of the modeling language. The system then selects from its models of correct and incorrect knowledge elements the ones that account for the student's behavior. While theoretically limited in scope, this enumerative approach has the practical advantage that the knowledge about the likelihood of errors it incorporates can be derived empirically or obtained from expert teachers. By generating diagnostic expectations, this knowledge focuses the search for a student model on previously observed behavior patterns. For current applications, the laborious development of such "catalogs" of errors for various domains is an important activity of designers.

Beyond the representation of expertise, special descriptive languages may also need to be developed if models are to include information about individual students that is not part of domain expertise (e.g., "this student is a third grader"). In this regard, an important feature of a student model is that of being *executable* or *runnable*. An executable student model can be run to yield exact predictions about the behavior of a particular student in a particular context. This simulation allows the verification of precise hypotheses as to the nature of a student's misconceptions.

The diagnostic process: accounting for data

The process of forming and updating the student model by analyzing data made available to the system is often called *diagnosis*. Numerical values grading performance can mostly be updated with some simple statistical computations. In contrast, detailed diagnosis usually requires search, whether the system is trying to reconstruct a goal structure to interpret the student's behavior or attempting to model his knowledge. Indeed, the task somewhat resembles both automated theory formation (where a theory must be built to account for some data) and some aspects of automatic programming (where a program must be built to account for some behavior). In general, these are very hard AI problems, which involve the formulation and evaluation of competing hypotheses.

As behavior must be traced to problem-solving decisions and to the influence of individual correct and incorrect knowledge elements, diagnosis faces an instance of an ubiquitous problem in automated theory formation: the assignment of credit and blame for successes and failures to individual decision points. The direction of the process depends on the nature of problem solving in the domain: interpretation of the student's actions can proceed in a top-down fashion, as for instance when there are few ways of implementing a given goal, or in a bottom-up fashion, as when single steps have only few possible interpretations. Moreover, depending on the modeling language available, the search for a student model can be model-driven—that is, a model is perturbed to account for the data—or data-driven if a model is constructed from primitive building blocks.

In pedagogical diagnosis, the search spaces representing the possible student models are frequently very large—increasingly so as models become more sophisticated. Observable behavior is in most cases only the tip of the iceberg and results from complex internal processes and structures that must be inferred. In addition, it has been observed that multiple misconceptions can interact to generate very unexpected behaviors, including the correct one. Finally, the interactive setup imposes real-time constraints on the amount of searching that can be done. Thus, making search processes fit for on-line use—or even marginally tractable—usually requires a number of clever heuristic decisions.

Regardless of the exact approach to the search problem, it is important to consider how the diagnostic process deals with the presence of *noise* in the data. Burton and Brown (1979b) identify three sources of noise that complicate diagnosis. First, the modeling language is almost inevitably a simplification of the complex processes of human reasoning and decision making. Therefore, the student model will always be an approximation of the actual student. Second, students are never perfectly consistent: they have performance lapses for a wide variety of reasons, and sometimes they are just lucky. Finally, learning itself brings noise into the data: hypotheses about the student that were accurate in a given knowledge state may soon no longer be so because learning has occurred, sometimes in very indirect ways. A few methods have been proposed for coping at least partially with these noise factors. Some of these methods are purely statistical while others attempt to take into account extraneous factors, like the cognitive load that a problem imposes on the student or special situations in which an irregularity in behavior is likely to occur.

Finally, diagnostic processes can vary in the *type of information* that is made available to them, even within the narrow scope of what a computer can process. It may be important to know something about the relevant teaching the student has received so far, or about his general background. During the session, some systems are allowed to take overt, *active* steps for diagnostic purposes in addition to conducting *passive* observation. For instance, they can present a problem so as to discriminate between two hypotheses in the student model. Perhaps most significant along this line is the extent to which the diagnostic process involves the student directly, by asking him to evaluate his understanding or to explain his behavior. We have seen that purely *inferential* diagnosis, which excludes the student, is a very difficult task. But a purely *interactive* approach suffers from the fact that people are not always good at explaining their own mental processes, and are sometimes altogether mistaken about them. An additional though less fundamental obstacle is natural-language processing where the current state of the art limits the possibilities for verbal exchanges with computers.

2.3 Pedagogical knowledge: the skill of communication

The pedagogical decisions embodied in the branching mechanisms and the contents of presentation frames found in good CAI programs reflect a large amount of knowledge about how to communicate knowledge. Until recently, the idea that this pedagogical knowledge could be explicitly represented in tutoring systems has been paid less attention than the representation of the subject matter. In fact, in many of the systems presented in Part II, the pedagogical knowledge is deeply buried in the various pieces of code that control the tutorial interaction. Historically, early interest in the representation of pedagogical knowledge mostly grew from existing CAI or educational traditions as part of an effort to refine sequencing algorithms for instructional programs.

Systems will differ in the extent to which pedagogical knowledge is made explicit in identifiable *pedagogical* or *didactic* modules.[2] In this regard, didactic decisions, instead of simply being hard-coded, can be derived from the interactions of specialized *rules* or from similar knowledge structures meant to represent the system's pedagogical expertise. In an ideally transparent system, this expertise can even be stored in the form of general *principles* expressed declaratively and interpreted into actual decisions. Explicit representations of pedagogical knowledge create the potential for systems to adapt and improve their strategies over time, and for components to be reused in other domains.

Didactic decisions are made by references to the student model and to the model of domain knowledge. At the *global* level, these decisions affect the sequences of instructional episodes. Taking advantage of the curricular information included in the representation of the subject matter, the didactic module adapts its presentation of topics to the needs of individual students. At the *local* level, the module determines when an intervention is desirable, whether or not the student should be interrupted in an activity, and what could and should be said or presented at any given time. This includes *guidance* in the performance of activities, *explanations* of phenomena and processes, and *remediation*.

All these decisions are subtle. The order and manner in which topics are treated can produce very different learning experiences. In tutorial guidance, it is sometimes more effective to let the student search for a while than always to interrupt him. On the other hand, left completely to himself, the student will often get stuck or lost. Successful learning depends on a wide variety of factors, and the most informationally accurate tutoring system is nonetheless defeated if it destroys the student's personal motivation or sense of discovery. Pedagogy is an art that requires a great versatility: it is probably itself more complex and more difficult than most of the subject matters to whose teaching it is applied. In fact, precise specifications of the essential constituents of this expertise do not exist (Ohlsson, 1987a). It is not surprising, therefore, that instructional

---

[2]The word "didactic" will be used to contrast pedagogical interventions with diagnostic processes, which are also a type of pedagogical activity. In this book, the term "didactic" does not have any pedantic or moralizing connotations, nor is it associated with classroom lecturing.

systems are not yet assigned very substantial parts of the pedagogical decision process.

Pedagogical decisions are made in the context of an instructional environment that determines the degrees of control over the activity and over the instructional interaction possessed respectively by the tutorial system and by the student. While there is now interest in systems that vary their degree of control according to some criteria of optimality (Barzilay, 1984), this issue has traditionally been a design decision. Some systems *monitor* the student's activity very closely, adapting their actions to the student's responses but never relinquishing control. In *mixed-initiative* dialogues, the control is shared by the student and the system as they exchange questions and answers. The system must be able to respond to the student, but it can also ask questions whose answers help it understand what the student is trying to do, or what he knows. In *guided-discovery learning* or *coached activities*, the student is in full control of the activity, and the only way the system can direct the course of action is by modifying the environment. This self-imposed unobtrusiveness makes the diagnostic process difficult, but the existence of an independent activity allows the coach to remain silent in case of doubt.

2.4   Interface: the form of communication

Whereas the pedagogical module decides the timeliness and content of didactic actions, the interface module takes care of their final form. More generally, this module processes the flow of communication in and out. In both directions, it translates between the system's internal representation and an *interface language* understandable to the student. Although the interface operates in close cooperation with both the diagnostic and the didactic modules, its decisions are of a different nature and require a different type of knowledge. It is therefore useful to identify the interface as a distinct component.

At first sight, the role of the interface may seem ancillary, but it would be a mistake to consider it a secondary component in instructional contexts. Its practical importance in the success of knowledge communication can be understood at two levels. First, in finalizing the form in which a system presents a topic, the interface can make this presentation more or less understandable. Because the interface is also the final form in which a system presents itself, such qualities as ease of use and attractiveness can be crucial to the students' acceptance of the system. Second, progress in media technology provides increasingly sophisticated tools whose communicative power can drive the design of the entire system.

An aspect of the interface issue traditionally connected with AI research is the processing of *natural language,* whose use can free the interaction from the contrived character of traditional computer interfaces. Text understanding is a notably difficult task, plagued with problems such as incompleteness, anaphoral references, and contextual inferences. Although text generation would seem easier, actually translating a piece of knowledge into an explanation is no small feat. Even from the purely syntactic perspective, it is a challenge for a computer to generate a text that does not seem redundant or contrived to people. Although the free use of natural language still belongs to the future, actual systems vary in their ability to deal with verbal utterances. For the input, interfaces range from the use of fixed menus with multiple-choice answers to a fairly free treatment of a pseudo-natural language. For the output, they range from the mere display of prestored pieces of text typical of CAI to the use of fairly complex generic frames. Within these limits, flexibility varies according to the granularity of the pieces of knowledge with which individual pieces of text are associated.

As a counterweight to technical difficulties, the restricted conceptual context in which the verbal communication takes place can facilitate the design of natural-language interfaces for practical instructional systems. This allows restricted versions of natural-language processors to be used. In this regard, Burton and Brown (1979a) note that the interface must not only be robust and efficient so as to become unobtrusive, but also be able to present a clear picture of the system's capabilities. Unless the student precisely perceives the extent to which the system can respond to his input, his interaction will be hampered either by too difficult queries or by suboptimal use of the facilities. Although this problem is common to all types of interactive software, systems that seem to manifest some intelligence tend to draw unrealistic expectations from naive users.

The treatment of text is increasingly supplemented and even sometimes essentially replaced by the use of computer graphics. The design of graphic interfaces presents delicate problems of its own. In addition to the fact that such design is a laborious process, the use of graphic displays for communication purposes requires much sensitivity to a variety of human factors, and to the view of the domain that the displays present.

The knowledge required for the translation function of the interface has been represented explicitly in instructional systems for some time, for instance in the form of parsing mechanisms. However, the idea of actively using knowledge about the expressiveness of the interface in the communication process is only now surfacing as the intelligent management of the screen and other media comes to be understood as a communication skill. We will see that some researchers are thinking of automating certain interface decisions by incorporating knowledge about interface principles into their systems.

Summary and conclusion

Of course, the boundaries between the components defined in this chapter are not always sharp. For instance, decisions at the level of the interface can take on a pedagogical significance, and evaluations of the student's answers can be shared between the expert and the diagnostic module. Furthermore, these various tasks need not correspond to distinct modules in an actual system. Nevertheless, such distinctions reflect a useful level of abstraction, and these four components of knowledge communication systems constitute a traditional division of labor in the field. Figure 2.1 summarizes some of the issues we have mentioned in connection with each component.

The center of the figure contrasts design decisions with knowledge. In keeping with the theme of the previous chapter, each component involves trade-offs between decisions made by designers and decisions made by systems themselves. For instance, a ready-made curriculum can be included in the representation of domain knowledge. In contrast, a system can be set up to plan its own curriculum, taking advantage of the explicit representation of teaching goals, of the student model, and of prerequisite relations provided by an adequate model of expertise. In general, as knowledge is made more explicit, more responsibility for the communication process is placed on the system, which is required to make decisions traditionally made by designers. From a practical standpoint, these dynamic decisions are meant to imply increasing degrees of adaptability and are expected to produce flexible educational tools that can sensibly individualize their communication of knowledge. If the dream of intelligent knowledge communication systems can be achieved to some reasonable extent, the enterprise whose first stumbling steps are described in this book may well be among the most valuable contributions of artificial intelligence to society.

Bibliographical notes

The collection of papers edited by Sleeman and Brown (1982) is a classic; an extension of a special 1979 issue of the *International Journal of Man-Machine Studies*, this collection was the first book specifically on intelligent tutoring systems and is still a good reference for many systems presented in Part II. Several new collections of papers cover more recent work: two of them contain reports from workshops (Lawler and Yazdani, 1987; Self, in press), and one centers on the theme of learning issues (Mandl and Lesgold, 1987). Several other collections are forthcoming.

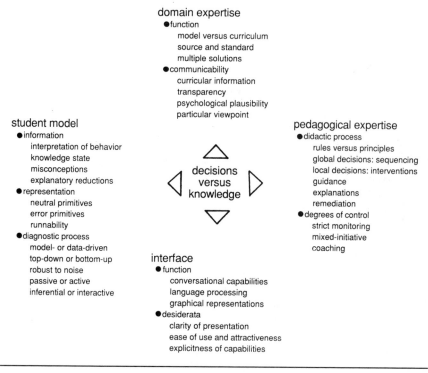

domain expertise
- function
    model versus curriculum
    source and standard
    multiple solutions
- communicability
    curricular information
    transparency
    psychological plausibility
    particular viewpoint

student model
- information
    interpretation of behavior
    knowledge state
    misconceptions
    explanatory reductions
- representation
    neutral primitives
    error primitives
    runnability
- diagnostic process
    model- or data-driven
    top-down or bottom-up
    robust to noise
    passive or active
    inferential or interactive

decisions
versus
knowledge

pedagogical expertise
- didactic process
    rules versus principles
    global decisions: sequencing
    local decisions: interventions
    guidance
    explanations
    remediation
- degrees of control
    strict monitoring
    mixed-initiative
    coaching

interface
- function
    conversational capabilities
    language processing
    graphical representations
- desiderata
    clarity of presentation
    ease of use and attractiveness
    explicitness of capabilities

Figure 2.1 Some basic issues in knowledge communication: a summary.

A number of overview papers are also available. A collection of short articles on specific topics and systems can be found in (Clancey et al., 1982); it is a good introduction written for a fairly general audience. As a nontechnical introduction to a number of topics covered here, the book by O'Shea and Self (1983) is suitable for an audience unfamiliar with AI or even with computers. The main perspective is that of implications for education.

The overview of CAI by Suppes (1979) includes a critical look at ICAI's first decade. A short report on ICAI by Roberts and Park (1983) is specifically written as an introduction for a CAI audience. Sleeman (1983b) gives a brief review of methodological considerations for ITS, illustrated with some examples.

Fletcher (1985) provides a good summary of systems and issues, including lists and tables, intended for professionals in technical training. Dede (1986, 1987) discusses broad research issues faced by the field and possible social implications; his high-level perspective is appropriate for planners and management.

Official briefings on the field (Brown and Goldstein, 1977; Brown and Greeno, 1984) outline its philosophy and provide good assessments of progress and prospects. Goldstein and Papert (1977) explore the educational value of epistemological investigations inherent in artificial intelligence research. As a spokesman for the field's visions, Brown (1983a, 1983b, 1985) discusses many innovative concepts. Clancey's overview (1986b) is intended for a rather sophisticated audience: it provides an insightful reflection on the notion of "qualitative model" as an underlying theme for ITS.

A panorama:
people, ideas, and systems

Now that we have briefly looked at some basic issues, we are ready to set out on a guided tour of specific research projects. The notion of a guided tour has two relevant connotations. First, a guided tour evokes the image of someone enlivening the visit with comments and viewpoints. Thus, as we look at the different projects, I will augment purely descriptive reports with discussions. Like a tour guide, I will play different roles, acting sometimes as a historian, sometimes as an analyst, sometimes as a critic. Since a survey needs to be thought-provoking to be really useful, I will freely express personal opinions and ideas. Like the remarks of a tour guide on the work of some famous architect, however, my comments should be viewed as an effort to induce a deeper perception of important issues rather than as a claim that I understand anything better than the researchers themselves. It is always easy to make comments in retrospect, but the real credit goes to those who do the work.

The second connotation evoked by a guided tour is that of a succession of points of interest where visitors stop to marvel for a while before moving on. As the tour proceeds, the understanding of important themes emerges from visits to a number of sites. In this sense, the notion of a tour suggests an approach to understanding a field of research. For a young field such as the one we survey, it seems most instructive to look at what people involved in the field do, what they are interested in, and how their work and ideas evolve.

In keeping with this goal of conveying a sense of the field's conceptual history by highlighting the evolution of ideas, a single project is always presented in one block, even if it spans a long period of time and goes through profound changes. In fact, a number of chapters start with very early work and end with current developments. Usually we follow the research through its successive phases without anticipating conclusions so as to better appreciate its evolution. As a secondary constraint, work done on related themes or with similar approaches tends to be clustered together. These broad organizing themes include: mental models (3–5), pedagogical strategies as extensions of CAI approaches (6–7), diagnosis (8–10: procedural skills; 11: plan analysis), rule-based expert systems and cognitive models (12–13). Finally, a somewhat chronological order is maintained so that influences across projects can be highlighted with a minimum of forward references.

Though the resulting organization is an attempt at satisfying numerous constraints simultaneously, the linear sequence of a panoramic tour has to emphasize some aspects at the cost of others. After this historical panorama, we will be ready to return to a synthetic style for the synopsis that is Part III. When presentations are organized around conceptual issues, as in Parts I and III, they provide a synthetic but somewhat static view of a field. In particular, these conceptual presentations require that the discussion of projects that address multiple issues be split among sections. For Part II, the intention behind the organization around evolving research projects is to give the reader a more dynamic sense of the whole enterprise.

Chapter 3

Tutorial dialogues: from semantic nets to mental models

For the purpose of this book, we will consider that ITS research really started as a distinct approach with a dissertation by Jaime Carbonell (1970a) and with his system, SCHOLAR, now considered a classic. It would be wrong, however, to assume that Carbonell was alone in thinking along these lines at the time (Wexler, 1970). This first chapter of our panorama describes Carbonell's pioneering work as well as the long tradition of ITS research that it spawned at BBN,[1] where Carbonell developed his system.

As the title indicates, this chapter combines two different—though constantly interacting—themes: the goal of producing tutorial dialogues

---

[1] Bolt Beranek and Newman Inc., a research laboratory in Cambridge, Massachusetts.

and an investigation of principles for representing the knowledge to be conveyed. On the one hand, communication strategies must be expressed in terms of representational abstractions. On the other hand, the requirements of communication direct research efforts to the nature of domain knowledge and of reasoning mechanisms that can support communication processes. After these themes interact in the context of systems such as SCHOLAR and WHY, the investigation of mental representations even predominates. Chapter 5 describes two recent projects that continue this line of research.

3.1   SCHOLAR: launching a new paradigm

In his landmark paper entitled "AI in CAI: an artificial-intelligence approach to computer-assisted instruction," Carbonell (1970b) defines the difference between what he calls *frame-oriented* CAI and the new paradigm he was then proposing under the name of *information-structure-oriented* CAI. These two approaches correspond in many ways to what in Part I we called respectively traditional CAI and ITS. The use of the word *frame-oriented* to describe the CAI systems then prevalent refers to the prestored instructional units, often called frames, in which CAI encodes lessons prepared by a human expert. These units contain small portions of the curriculum and are successively displayed on the screen for presentation and questions. Their exact sequence is determined by fixed branching decisions based on a predefined set of possible answers expected from the student. Identifying some shortcomings of this approach, Carbonell stresses the need to anticipate all possible interactions: not only unexpected answers from the student, but— even more important in Carbonell's opinion—unexpected questions the student may want to ask.

In contrast, he presents his *information-structure-oriented* paradigm. This name alludes to the representational scheme in which he proposes to cast the domain knowledge possessed by the system. At that time Quillian (1968) was developing his notion of *semantic networks* as a general structure for knowledge representation, and Carbonell was apparently quite thrilled by the idea. He mentions his belief that semantic networks are an accurate model of the way people store and access information. Under this assumption, he envisions systems that could hold *mixed-initiative dialogues* with students, responding to their questions by traversing the network, and asking them questions so as to convey the contents of the network to them interactively. He claims that this is the way a human teacher uses his own knowledge representation to generate tutorial sessions of explanations and questions.

In addition to his own interest in machine-based mixed-initiative dialogues, Carbonell sees other good reasons why his paradigm holds great promise. In particular, he mentions that building a frame-oriented system can be a rather tedious job for a teacher who has to program all the details of the interaction. On the contrary, the task of putting together a knowledge structure and defining teaching strategies is both challenging and instructive. To substantiate his claim, Carbonell even describes interactive development tools that he suggests should be made available to support the construction of this new type of system. Although the idea was perhaps premature, since the design of intelligent tutoring systems is still a very difficult task today, Carbonell already sees that the design process enforces a good conceptualization of the subject; he predicts that research on knowledge structures and corresponding tutorial strategies will give rise to insights beneficial not only to CAI but to education in general. As we proceed, the themes of this book should demonstrate the accuracy of his vision.

A system to conduct tutorial dialogues

As a practical example of an information-structure-oriented system, Carbonell presents SCHOLAR, a tutoring system that can conduct a mixed-initiative dialogue with a student. Let us consider SCHOLAR's four components, as defined in Part I.

The system's knowledge of the subject matter, the geography of South America,[2] is represented in a semantic network whose nodes stand for geographical objects and concepts, as illustrated in Figure 3.1. Since these objects and concepts are organized in a partial hierarchy with relations like superpart, superconcept, and superattribute, some simple inferences can be made by propagation of inherited properties via these hierarchical links. For instance, the system can conclude that Santiago is in South America since Santiago is in Chile and Chile is in South America. In addition, the system can determine the semantic relation between two nodes by following their respective paths up the hierarchy until a common node is found. For instance, it can find that Santiago and Buenos Aires are both South American cities. These inferences are used to answer specific questions by the student.

In his presentation of a new paradigm for instructional systems, Carbonell is very concerned with issues of diagnosis and stresses the advantage of having a representation of the knowledge "not far from" that possessed by the student. Speculating that the full semantic net could be used to model the student's knowledge, he suggests starting

---

[2]Where Carbonell came from.

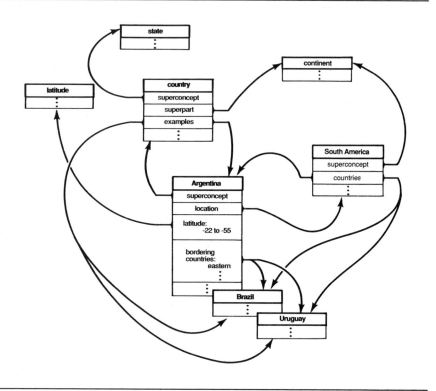

Figure 3.1 A portion of SCHOLAR's semantic net (after Carbonell, 1970b).

with the complete network to model the perfect student and progressively perturbing it to reflect the student's actual performance, deleting and even modifying nodes and links. Certainly his claim that the automated diagnosis of misconceptions will be "feasible in a near future" (Carbonell, 1970b, p. 199) may seem somewhat naive in view of the difficulties that subsequent research has revealed. However, SCHOLAR's student model in terms of evaluations attached to the individual concepts of a modular representation of expertise constitutes an early version of what has later been called the "overlay" method (see Section 7.4.2). Of course, in the case of SCHOLAR, there is certainly no complex diagnostic process taking place, since nodes are marked on the basis of statements by the student. Nevertheless, Carbonell's ideas about diagnosis were quite revolutionary and on the mark if placed in their historical context.

SCHOLAR's tutorial strategies are fairly primitive, consisting mainly of local topic selections. For instance, the student is allowed to ask vague questions such as "Tell me something about Peru." Since this type of question requires more than straight retrieval and inference, SCHOLAR must be able to determine which information is most relevant. The notion of distance between nodes in the network gives some indication of relevance, but it is not quite sufficient to characterize subjective relevance. For this purpose, numerical tags are attached to individual nodes and to their various attributes. These relevance tags also provide some guidance to SCHOLAR in selecting topics, for instance in formulating questions, when the system is given the initiative. Apart from these tags, however, tutorial strategies basically rely on random choices. Therefore, in spite of a simple agenda mechanism used to record covered topics and bias the strategies toward choosing a topic that the student has mentioned before, the basic randomness of topic selection gives SCHOLAR's dialogues a somewhat disconnected flavor, as can be seen in the excerpt presented in Figure 3.2.

This excerpt also demonstrates the linguistic capabilities of the system's interface. The language is a restricted subset of English, limited to simple sentences. Text is generated by sentence and question templates that are filled in with information from the network. The parsing of student questions follows the same principle in reverse, while the parsing of student answers is done by matching keywords from a list dynamically generated from the network for each question. This means that SCHOLAR does not understand wrong answers, and therefore cannot extract diagnostic information from them. As an interesting detail, note that the student can request a change of control mode for the dialogue (in the figure, by typing 'Q/A'). By means of this facility, the student can request the system to merely answer her questions, to conduct a mixed-initiative dialogue, or to take the lead and ask questions.

As a generic system for the teaching of knowledge represented with semantic nets, SCHOLAR has not been used very widely, except for an intelligent on-line consultant for a text editor called NLS-SCHOLAR (Grignetti et al., 1975). This is partly because semantic nets do present some fundamental limitations, like the difficulty of representing procedural knowledge. Even in geography, dynamic systems such as meteorological processes seem to exceed these nets' representational capabilities. Also, more recent research on semantic nets has shown that the inheritance of properties in conceptual hierarchies is a complex problem in general (Woods, 1975; Brachman and Levesque, 1985).

Nonetheless, SCHOLAR is a background for much of the research described in this chapter. Furthermore, the separation of tutorial capabilities from domain knowledge and the expression of dialogue management tasks in terms of general representational abstractions have become methodological principles central to the research covered in this book. In this sense, SCHOLAR can be considered historically as the first ITS project, and its significance as a milestone for the whole field cannot be overstated.

⋮

SCHOLAR: Approx what is the area of Brazil?

Student: 2,500,000 square miles.

SCHOLAR: Wrong. Please indicate if the following statement is correct: the area of Paraguay is approx 47,432 square miles.

Student: What is the area of Brazil?

SCHOLAR: The area of Brazil is approx 3,600,000 square miles. Now answer the question you didn't answer before.

Student: False.

SCHOLAR: Rephrase your statement. I can't understand it.

Student: Incorrect.

SCHOLAR: Very good. The area of Paraguay is approx 157,000 square miles. The language in Brazil is French. Right or wrong?

Student: Wrong.

SCHOLAR: You are correct. The language in Brazil is Portuguese. Is it true that the capital in Brazil is Brazilia?

Student: Yes.

SCHOLAR: That's fine. Approx what is the population in Brazil?

Student: 60,000,000.

SCHOLAR: Approximately true, but a more exact value is 70,000,000. What is Brazil?

Student: Tell me about Peru.

SCHOLAR: Wait a minute. I am checking my files. Let's proceed now. Peru is a country. It is in South America. The population is approx 7,000,000 people. The capital is Lima. Now answer the question you didn't answer before.

Student: Q/A.

SCHOLAR: Do you want to change the general mode of the interaction to Q/A? Please answer Y or N.

Student: Y

SCHOLAR: OK, Mr. Jones. Let's go ahead.

Student: Please, tell me more about Peru.

SCHOLAR: The area of Peru is approx 480,000 square miles. The language is Spanish.

Student: How many ...

⋮

Figure 3.2 Excerpt from a dialogue with SCHOLAR (Carbonell, 1970b).

© 1970, IEEE. Reprinted, with permission, from *IEEE Transactions on Man-Machine Systems*, Vol. MMS-11, No. 4, pp. 190–202.

3.2 Natural reasoning and tutorial dialogues

When SCHOLAR was compared with human tutors, it was found to have two important areas that were in obvious need of further improvement. One area was the extent of the inferences it was able to make within the representational framework of semantic nets. The other concerned the tutorial strategies necessary to conduct a coherent and effective dialogue. Although these two research directions spawned in the context of the SCHOLAR project deal with apparently very distinct problems, they turned out to be related when they eventually converged on an interest in the Socratic method for guiding a student's reasoning process.[3]

3.2.1 Natural reasoning: plausible inferences

Although the original version of SCHOLAR had some interesting inferential capabilities, these compared poorly with people's reasoning, called here *natural reasoning*. In particular, SCHOLAR was unable to do the kind of *plausible* reasoning that people rely on to cope with incomplete knowledge. Therefore, the system's ability to answer questions like a human tutor was limited; it would simply state its ignorance in situations where people would have made a good guess. In an effort to get a grasp on the nature of human reasoning, the research group (Carbonell and Collins, 1973; Collins et al., 1975a) set out to study the methods people use to draw plausible inferences. In this section, we summarize these observations in connection with possible extensions to SCHOLAR's inference mechanisms.

Techniques supported by simple extensions to SCHOLAR

Some of the techniques to which people were observed to resort can be implemented with amazingly simple extensions to SCHOLAR. A semantic net, or a portion of a semantic net, can be viewed as a set of objects and relations. A set can be *closed*, when all of its members are known, or *open* otherwise. In this context, reasoning strategies will differ considerably according to whether the domain is closed or open. Because sets are delimited by reference to some concepts that determine membership, and because most concepts in the real world

---

[3]Unfortunately, Jaime Carbonell died suddenly in 1973, and never saw the project evolve that far. Allan Collins has continued this effort, later joined by Albert Stevens.

are relatively vague, dealing with real domains will mostly necessitate making inferences from incomplete knowledge.

Since it is in general impossible to represent explicitly the sets of false or irrelevant relations, negative inferences constitute an important class of inferences dealing with open sets. *Contradiction* is commonly used by people to make negative inferences. Computationally, some inferences by contradiction can be achieved by the addition of two types of markers in a semantic net. First, a pair of relations can be marked as being mutually exclusive. For instance, a given object cannot be a city and a river, though it can be a city and a capital. Secondly, exhaustive sets can be marked as closed. This ensures that properties of subparts collectively imply the same properties for the whole. For instance, if no country on a continent is known to produce sugar, then it can be inferred that the continent does not produce sugar, provided the available set of its countries is marked as closed.

Less certain conclusions can be drawn by making *assumptions*. For instance, one can assume uniqueness for certain relations. In this way, if a country's language is Spanish, then it cannot be French, assuming that a country only has one language. One can also use a form of "inverse induction" that Carbonell and Collins call the *lack-of-knowledge* strategy. This strategy, which people apparently often resort to, assumes a relatively even distribution of information across the database. It is best illustrated by an example. If oil is not on the list of Uruguay's products, this does not necessarily imply that Uruguay does not produce oil at all, since the database may be incomplete. Furthermore, there is no list of the goods that a country does not produce. However, if oil is listed for other similar countries for which the overall depth of information does not significantly differ, Uruguay most likely does not produce oil, because if it did, this would probably be known.

In the structure of SCHOLAR's semantic network, there are already facilities to support the lack-of-knowledge strategy. The concept hierarchy can be used to collect objects similar to the original one: they must be its siblings with respect to a common superordinate. Now the depth of knowledge can be measured by the numerical relevance tags associated with information. In our example, if oil is mentioned for another country—say Venezuela—with a relevance-tag value at which something else is known for Uruguay, this is an indication that oil is not produced in Uruguay.

More complex inference techniques

While the techniques we have just described can be implemented on a semantic net with fairly simple mechanisms, there are other forms of reasoning that are central to question answering but that would require much more complex extensions to SCHOLAR. First, facts known by people do not always have simple true or false values, and the solution suggested for SCHOLAR was to add *uncertainty* tags to facts in the network. However, reasoning with uncertainty poses a complex problem because there must be some way to propagate the values representing levels of certainty through the inference process. This propagation of beliefs is really nontrivial and is still an important research issue in AI today. Since no such mechanism was proposed for SCHOLAR, it is unlikely that mere tags could have sufficed.

Secondly, the authors describe an inference technique they call *functional* analysis. This technique involves an analysis of the factors on which some hypothesis depends. For instance, SCHOLAR has been given the ability to infer a region's climate by considering its location. However, this type of causal reasoning is quite complex in general, and the nature of the mechanisms it requires is still an object of research today. While the other types of reasoning described here are mainly useful for answering questions, functional analysis can give rise to very interesting forms of tutorial dialogues in which the tutor guides the student's inferences. In the course of experimental dialogues conducted by the authors to investigate these different forms of reasoning, it was observed that students not only learn facts, but more important, learn how to index functional knowledge around concepts so as to facilitate subsequent inferences. It seems that this observation was crucial in the group's ensuing decision to concentrate on the Socratic method for teaching causal reasoning.

3.2.2   An inquiry into the nature of tutorial dialogues

To improve on SCHOLAR's ability to conduct tutorial dialogues, Collins et al. (1975b) decide to analyze the protocols of such dialogues with human tutors in order to extract some elements of these tutors' strategies. This approach is similar to the successful use of protocol analysis by Newell and Simon (1972) in their study of human problem solving, with the difference that the protocol is now the product of the activity itself, rather than a verbalization added onto it. The idea is first to *analyze* natural dialogues, then to *synthesize* the findings by implementing them in a system like SCHOLAR. From a methodological point of view, Collins et al. claim that combining analysis of human data with synthesis into a computational model provides access to the available expertise (through the analysis) while keeping the focus on relevant information (for the synthesis). Although this first study of tutorial dialogues does not result in a complete theory of mixed-initiative tutoring, it addresses central issues concerning strategies exhibited by human tutors but unknown

---

RULE 1

When the topic is an attribute (e.g., geographical features), select the most important unused value under the current topic.

When the topic is a value (e.g., South America), select the most important attribute and value under the current topic.

Context affects this selection by temporarily increasing the importance of topics that are related to the previous topic discussed.

Figure 3.3 Example of a rule for topic selection (Collins et al., 1975b).

to SCHOLAR. These include the selection of topics to be discussed or reviewed, the interweaving of questions and presentation, and the correction of errors. Some of these observations are translated into modifications of SCHOLAR, so that its behavior better approximates that of human tutors.

While the first version of SCHOLAR relies heavily on randomness to select new topics, the new version includes heuristic rules to direct this selection. These rules, an example of which is given in Figure 3.3, are extracted from observations of human tutors, but in keeping with SCHOLAR's principles, they are expressed in terms of relevance tags and other aspects of the knowledge representation. Selected topics for discussion or review are entered onto an agenda with a time allowance proportional to their importance. The agenda now plays a central role in the unfolding of the dialogue. While discussing a topic, the tutor pushes other topics onto the agenda either because they are related or because they have been mentioned by the student. When time has elapsed or when the current topic is exhausted, the tutor moves to the next topic on the agenda. Although the reviewing of topics was found to be an important aspect of human tutoring (Collins et al., 1975b), there is no specific strategy added to SCHOLAR for this purpose, apart from the fact that topics tend to reappear in different contexts.

An important extension is some capability to parse and discuss errors. In the new version of SCHOLAR, a separate module handles detected errors by reporting factors that distinguish the student's answer from the correct one, as illustrated in Figure 3.4. Note that there is still no sophisticated student model. To avoid redundancies, SCHOLAR simply remembers which questions the student has answered correctly so that it can skip over them. Since SCHOLAR does not form a good student model, it must always start a new topic with some questions so as to build on the student's responses. This is in contrast to human tutors, who were observed to introduce a new topic with a phase of pure presentation when they thought the student did not know anything about it (Collins et al.,

⋮

SCHOLAR: The eastern and central plain of Argentina is --
Student: Chaco.
SCHOLAR: No.
            The northern plain of Argentina is the Chaco. The
            eastern and central plain of Argentina is the Pampas.
Student: Is the Chaco in Chile?
SCHOLAR: No.
            The Chaco is in Argentina, Paraguay, and Bolivia, not
            in Chile.
Student: Are the Andes a region in Chile?
SCHOLAR: Well, you're almost right.
            More specifically, a region of Chile is the Southern
            Andes.

⋮

**Figure 3.4 Example of output from the new answer evaluation module
(Collins et al., 1975b).**

1975b). However, this is only possible on the basis of information about the student's general knowledge.

3.3   WHY: the Socratic method

When combined, the studies of natural reasoning and of tutorial dialogues led to research on the Socratic method for teaching reasoning through dialogues. In the Socratic method, the tutor does not teach a subject by direct exposition, but leads the student by successive questions to formulate general principles on the basis of individual cases, to examine the validity of her own hypotheses, to discover contradictions, and finally to extract correct inferences from the facts she knows. The initial purpose of this research was to come up with the set of rules a Socratic tutor follows to achieve his goal through a succession of local decisions—though, as we will see, the interest soon included other topics dealing with the representation of expertise. Because facts in geography are not tightly bound by causal relations, and because functional analysis as we have described it above plays such an important role in Socratic dialogues, meteorology was chosen as a new domain. More specifically, the tutorial dialogues investigate the processes leading to rainfall.

RULE 6: Form a general rule for an insufficient factor.

IF the student gives an explanation of one or more factors that are not sufficient,

THEN formulate a general rule asserting that the factors given are sufficient **and** ask the student if the rule is true.

Reason for use
to force the student to pay attention to other causal factors.

Example
If the student gives water as the reason why they grow rice in China, ask him "Do you think any place with enough water can grow rice?"

Figure 3.5 An example of a rule for Socratic tutoring.
© Adapted from "Processes in acquiring knowledge," by A. Collins, in *Schooling and the Acquisition of Knowledge*, Hillsdale, NJ: Erlbaum. © 1977 by Lawrence Associates, Inc.; reprinted with permission.

Toward a computational model of Socratic tutorial strategies

After analyzing further tutorial dialogues, Collins (1977) presents a set of two dozen rules which seem to embody the local decisions made by Socratic tutors in conducting their dialogues. These decisions aim at inducing both the formulation of hypotheses and the testing of these hypotheses in a predictive fashion. Collins' production rules, an example of which is given in Figure 3.5, have as condition the last response of the student in relation to the tutor's knowledge, and as action what the tutor should ask or propose next. An important point for the evolution of the project is that these individual rules can be organized into larger categories, which form a taxonomy of Socratic techniques (e.g., entrapment, as defined below). In this regard, although this classification is not yet reflected in this initial rule-based model, note how Collins gives for each rule an explanation of the purpose motivating its use and connecting it to a more general strategy.

The rule presented in Figure 3.5 illustrates the way the Socratic method leads the student to find errors or contradictions by *entrapping* her in the consequences of her own conclusions. If the student agrees with the overgeneral rule presented, the tutor will then come up with a known *counterexample*, thus forcing the student to correct the course of her reasoning by considering other factors. If the student does not agree with the overgeneral rule, the same effect will be achieved by asking her why she disagrees. The fourth question of the dialogue presented in Figure 3.6 is an example of an application of this rule.

The compilation of this corpus of rules—which was later refined to comprise about 60 rules (Collins and Stevens, 1982)—is important for two reasons. On the one hand, it is the first attempt at capturing a complete, sophisticated tutorial strategy into a general process model. On the other hand, the Socratic method which the rules attempt to capture is a central concept for individualized instruction. By involving the student in an active inquiry process, the tutor teaches facts and causal relations in the domain as well as associated reasoning skills which make the knowledge extendible. Of course, the basic reasoning skills thus acquired are also generally applicable.

A system implementing the Socratic method

Collins' set of tutorial rules was used to construct an experimental Socratic tutoring system for rainfall processes called WHY (Stevens and Collins, 1977). In this system, the domain knowledge is no longer contained in a semantic net, which would not be very fit for the representation of processes. Instead, the knowledge about rainfall is stored in a hierarchy of *scripts* that represent stereotypical sequences of events. These fixed sequences are to capture both the temporal and the causal relations between events in a way that is easily amenable to inspection. The generation of questions and the evaluation of the student's answers are based on these scripts. The nested nature of the script hierarchy provides an organized view of the knowledge, with more general scripts giving overall sequences of events and more detailed scripts accounting for intermediate causal chains relating these events. The system can exploit this hierarchy to cover the subject starting from a general understanding and moving toward a more and more detailed description of the process.

Figure 3.6 presents a sample of an actual dialogue with WHY. Although the language and the format are still reminiscent of SCHOLAR, and the actual natural-language processing capabilities are still relatively simple, one can clearly perceive the strategic element missing in SCHOLAR. In fact, the excerpt presented in the figure is quite coherent and could have been conducted by a human tutor. However, in the course of such a dialogue, the system does not build a global student model; its diagnostic capability is limited to independent evaluations of responses. As a consequence, the coherence of the dialogue with respect to pedagogical adaptability is a local characteristic. In this regard, some fundamental capabilities of human Socratic tutors were found to be missing in WHY, and we discuss the ensuing research in the next section.

3.4 From local strategies to multiple mental models

Two major weaknesses of the system WHY and its rules for Socratic tutoring were to give rise to further research. First, the global tutorial

⋮

WHY: Do you think the Amazon jungle has heavy rainfall or light rainfall?
>   *(Rule 1: Ask for a prediction about a particular case.)*

Student: Heavy rainfall

WHY: Why does the Amazon have heavy rainfall?
>   *(Rule 2: Ask for prior cause.)*

Student: Because it's near the Atlantic

WHY: Yes, the Amazon jungle is near the equatorial Atlantic. How does that affect rainfall in the Amazon jungle?
>   *(Rule 3: Ask for intermediate cause.)*

Student: The water in the current is warm

⋮

WHY: Do you think that any place with mountains has heavy rainfall?
>   *(Rule 6: Form a general rule for an insufficient cause.)*

Student: Yes

WHY: Southern California has mountains. Why doesn't Southern California have heavy rainfall?
>   *(Rule 7: Pick a counter-example for an insufficient cause, and Rule 2: Ask for prior causes)*

⋮

**Figure 3.6 Excerpt from a sample dialogue with WHY
(Stevens and Collins, 1977).**

goals often pursued by human tutors, such as the correction of a pervasive misconception, are ignored in the local applicability conditions of the rules. Second, the script-based representation is not really sufficient either to explain the mechanisms involved in the rainfall process or to diagnose and correct the student's misconceptions. We address these two issues in this section.

3.4.1 Considering global goals

In an attempt to evaluate Collins' set of rules as a prescriptive theory of Socratic tutoring, Resnick (1977) points out that the motivations for the usage of a rule, given by Collins in the form of comments (see Figure 3.3), could be incorporated into the condition of the corresponding rule. The presence of these additional constraints would have two advantages. First, it would help resolve conflicts that occur when multiple actions are associated with the same condition, as can happen with the original set of rules. Second, it would have the intuitively desirable effect of introducing references to the overall purpose of the tutor in the selection of actions.

Although this idea points to the right direction, it turns out that the motivations given by Collins for the usage of rules are merely justifications for their use with respect to local techniques. In this sense, they do not capture the kinds of "higher-order goals" that seem to be guiding human tutors in their decisions. To discover what these higher-order goals are and how they influence tutorial strategies, Stevens and Collins (1977, 1982) again analyze protocols of tutorial sessions, but this time they ask the tutors to comment on their strategies as they communicate with students via a computer terminal. They are requested to justify their decisions both in terms of goals and in terms of their perception of the student's knowledge. In the case of rainfall, the actions of human tutors clearly follow two top-level goals: to refine the student's *causal model*, and to tune the *procedures* that manage this model so as to extract predictions from it.

While pursuing these top-level goals, tutors are found to generate two subgoals which correspond to two distinct types of episodes occurring in the dialogues: diagnosing and correcting. *Diagnosis* turns out to be a rather sophisticated process of tracing surface errors to deeper misconceptions. The strategies for *correction* can be classified into categories which correspond to different types of errors. The five types of "conceptual errors" identified by the authors in dialogues about rainfall range from mere factual errors, which can be corrected by straight statements, to erroneous reasoning strategies such as premature conclusions, whose correction requires complex interactions. This classification of error types is also interesting because human tutors seem to use this classification to give priorities to correction episodes. Indeed, when multiple errors are present, they appear to push correction episodes onto an agenda in a consistent order determined by the types of these errors.

Although rules could probably be formulated to capture the pursuit of high-level goals, the authors merely present their findings as a theory. There are additional difficulties involved in the development of practical Socratic tutoring systems implementing this theory. The most fundamental obstacle is that the decisions taken at the level of these goal-directed episodes are based on a thorough interactive diagnosis of misconceptions. Stevens and Collins admit that this complex diagnostic process is currently not well understood. In addition, its implementation would require natural-language understanding capabilities beyond those available.

3.4.2　Domain knowledge: multiple viewpoints

Complex diagnostic strategies and the pursuit of global tutorial goals also make additional requirements of the model of domain knowledge that was perceived as a weakness of the original version of WHY. Stevens et al. (1979) remark that the script-based representation is limited to the linear relations between events. Although this linear sequence of causal and temporal relation is important, it only captures global aspects of processes like rainfall. A second important aspect is the *functional* perspective.

The functional perspective: a second viewpoint on physical processes

This perspective considers the various elements involved in processes, and their functions in the interactions that give rise to various events. Viewing these elements as individual *actors*, the functional perspective describes the *roles* they play in processes. For example, in the rainfall process, an air mass is an actor whose role is to act as a source of rainwater. In addition, these actors have attributes that are *factors* influencing the extent to which the roles of actors are manifested. For instance, the temperature and altitude of an air mass are crucial factors in its role as a source of rainwater. Finally, important *functional relations* hold between factors, and explain the *results* of processes. In our example, the temperature of an air mass is inversely related to its altitude, and therefore the rising of the mass will result in its cooling.

While the exact details of the functional perspective are interesting, they are not the main point here. What is important to see is that this perspective represents a *viewpoint* not captured by the temporal and causal sequences cast as scripts. Rather than discarding the script viewpoint as insufficient, Stevens et al. advocate the coexistence of different but complementary viewpoints. Although both viewpoints describe the same phenomena, their respective emphases are different. Since they highlight different aspects of processes, they will lead to different presentations of the subject and to the perception of different misconceptions.

As to the impact these two viewpoints can have on the shaping of the tutorial dialogue, the script viewpoint tends to influence the sequencing of major teaching episodes, whereas the functional viewpoint tends to guide local interactions. Indeed, human tutors are observed to follow temporal and causal links in traversing a curriculum. In contrast, when they detect an error in the form of mispredictions, they often do not address the error directly; rather, they use the functional model to interactively correct the underlying misconception that led to the observed misprediction. In capturing these two aspects of a Socratic tutor's role, the delineation of these two different viewpoints is an important pedagogical insight. As a perception of different mental representations of physical processes, it is a contribution to our understanding of common-sense reasoning.

Additional open issues in domain-specific knowledge

Although the addition of the functional viewpoint to WHY would constitute an important extension, there are additional open problems to designing a complete Socratic tutor. One of them is that tutorial expertise must include information about specific misconceptions people often develop in a particular domain, as well as processes and strategies to handle them. Indeed, many misconceptions are domain-specific and shared by many individuals, and this speaks in favor of a model-driven approach to diagnosis. But misconceptions present common patterns and thus can often be traced to deeper misconceptions, like overgeneralizations or cheap metaphors. This could warrant a more data-driven approach. At any rate, each type of conceptual error must be approached with a specific strategy, and this knowledge must be part of the tutor. Knowledge about misconceptions must be coupled with a powerful diagnostic process, since there is no simple mapping between misconceptions and surface manifestations. Unfortunately, the authors remain cautiously silent on the nature of these diagnostic processes, which are probably made even more complicated by the presence of multiple viewpoints.

Another open problem is that there are many more viewpoints than just the two mentioned here. Indeed, when Stevens et al. analyzed actual dialogues in terms of these two viewpoints, they found that almost half the statements dealt with other representational viewpoints, such as spatial structures, description of physical principles, and explication of metaphors (often requiring knowledge from other domains). It is also unclear how these viewpoints interact and how they are integrated into a unified conceptualization of the domain, a question that Stevens and Collins decided to investigate further. This is the subject of the next section.

3.4.3   From multiple viewpoints to multiple mental models

The interplay of multiple viewpoints on a physical process naturally leads to the notion of mental models. In this context, a mental model can be defined as an internal representation of a physical system used by a person or a program to reason about processes involving that system. The difference between a model and a viewpoint is that the model is runnable as a form of partial simulation that yields predictive power. Compared to fixed scripts, models have the advantage that they can be run to consider alternatives, whereas in scripts all alternatives must be explicitly represented. Because the simulation involves objects and their roles, mental models also include the functional viewpoint in a natural way.

Learning about physical processes viewed as model tuning

In a first study of the concepts people have of meteorological processes, Stevens and Collins (1980) find four different models:

- At the planetary level, there is a model of *climates*, which describes global water and air currents and their influences on climates;

- Associated with climates is a model of the *water cycle*, in which masses of air absorb water, transport it, and release it as rain;

- The water-cycle model refers to a *macroscopic functional* model of evaporation, very similar to the functional viewpoint, with factors like temperature and humidity;

- Finally, there is a *microscopic* simulation model of evaporation, which accounts for particles colliding and leaving water at the surface.

These models suggest that the understanding of complex systems hinges to a great extent on an ability to use different models and to map between them.

For each of these models, Stevens and Collins describe stages of refinement indicating further learning. In this paradigm for the representation of physical systems, they define learning as "largely a process of refining models so that they correspond better with the real world" (p. 183). Although they do not give more concrete criteria for the quality of the model in terms of intrinsic features and define progress only in terms of output, they do list some operations that can be applied to refining a model; these include changing, deleting or adding, and generalizing or differentiating parts of it. Pedagogically, this view recommends a constant confrontation of the model's predictions with the outcome of the real system, a central technique of the Socratic method. From a diagnostic standpoint, the view suggests that misconceptions must be traced to imprecisions in the underlying models and in the mappings between them.

Componential views of mental models

An interesting development of this research is the notion of components of a mental model. Concentrating only on the evaporation process, Collins and Gentner (1983) analyze the hierarchy of models people possess. Again they find that different levels exist in the simulation model. At the top level, they find the *functional* model described earlier. This functional model is based on an *aggregate* model, which deals with the behaviors of groups of similar particles forming entities like a gas or a liquid. Finally, the behavior of these aggregate entities can be explained in terms of an underlying *molecular* model. This study emphasizes the hierarchical relations between models. Like scripts with subscripts, models support one another in a "reductionistic" fashion where some relations in one model can be explained in terms of another, lower-level model.

Each level in turn can be viewed as a combination of *component models*. For instance, Collins (1985b) observes that the molecular model of evaporation consists of five subprocess components, including among others the behavior of water molecules both in water and in the air. For each subprocess, he describes a few component models that seem to cover the viewpoints of most subjects. Figure 3.7 shows the various component models that subjects were found to have for the behavior of water molecules in water and in the air. Note how most component models are associated with an analogy to an extraneous concept. The same division into subprocesses, in which various component models represent different views, is reported for other domains such as electrical circuits and heating systems. In this context, the global mental model of an individual student can be viewed as a combination of different component models for each subprocess.

From a pedagogical standpoint, these studies are moving toward a formalization of the diagnosis and correction of mental models. Because models are layered hierarchically, teaching can be viewed as a process of probing the student's models at successively deeper levels. Then, because models can be understood in terms of a combination of components, it is possible to analyze the type of views commonly encountered for each component and to establish catalogs of model components for various domains. Diagnosis can then recognize misconceptions in terms of faulty components or of bad combinations, and correction can involve strategies specific to types of faulty components.

Unfortunately, this research on mental models has not yet produced computational systems that implement these views, let alone systems that teach these models interactively. This would require precise languages and processes to support the mental simulations for which these models are useful. However, the interest in mental models is relatively

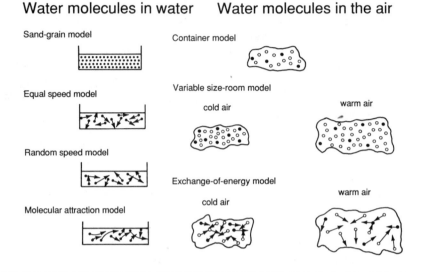

Figure 3.7 Different component models used for evaporation processes (Collins, 1985b).

new in AI as well as in cognitive psychology, and the development of representational schemes for mental models is an active area of research. The next two chapters will cover some of these developments.

Summary and conclusion

The line of research we have just discussed has been conducted under the banners of artificial intelligence and of psychology. It is interesting both for the important contributions it has produced and because it is quite paradigmatic of the field's development.

SCHOLAR was a breakthrough in launching the field. With its domain knowledge represented with a semantic net, it makes use of inference procedures to conduct a simple tutorial interaction. Discourse management tasks are expressed in terms of representational abstractions. The ensuing focus on natural reasoning and tutorial strategies has resulted in the definition of a few effective but computationally tractable techniques for reasoning with incomplete knowledge and for improving the coherence of dialogues. The combination of analysis and synthesis as a technique for studying and implementing communication processes is a basic methodological principle of the field.

The project WHY has probably not been given the recognition it deserves in the literature, maybe because it has remained largely theoretical. Yet as a first attempt at capturing a complete tutorial strategy as complex as the Socratic method in a concise, rule-based computational model, it is also a breakthrough. While the design of WHY uncovered many difficult issues that are still objects of research today, the system has also provided ground for further investigation of the interactions between the goals of Socratic tutors and their representation of domain knowledge.

The research on multiple representational viewpoints and mental models is continuing at BBN, and is also receiving much attention in both artificial intelligence and psychology. It is hoped that this research will lead to a clearer definition of representational schemes and processes that can support the use of such models in automated reasoning and subsequently in active knowledge communication. Because the componential view of mental models addresses issues of their construction, it is a first step toward understanding how such models can be diagnosed and corrected. In particular, it invites the fascinating question of how the Socratic method can now be tied to a theory of mental models.

From the perspective of the evolution of ideas, this whole research trajectory is quite interesting. It started with the straightforward inferences and simple tutorial strategies of SCHOLAR; however, the goal of building a Socratic tutor led to the current concern with mental models, and thence to the complex didactic strategies and diagnostic processes that teaching these models will eventually require. Throughout its evolution, this research demonstrates a constant interaction between issues of pedagogical strategies and of knowledge representation. Such an interaction is typical of the field and will be noticed repeatedly during this survey. In this sense, the projects of this chapter exemplify well the role of catalyst that interest in intelligent knowledge communication plays in the investigation of computational intelligence in general.

Bibliographical notes

The paper by Carbonell (1970b) is a classic well worth reading. The paper by Wexler (1970), whose doctoral work was in many ways similar to Carbonell's but evolved out of a CAI tradition, will help the reader understand better the historical context in which Carbonell made his statements.

Grignetti et al. (1975) present NLS-SCHOLAR, an interesting attempt to use the SCHOLAR framework for teaching a different type of knowledge. NLS-SCHOLAR is built on top of a text editor (NLS) and acts as an "assistant and tutor" for users. The system's semantic net contains both declarative and procedural knowledge about the functions of the editor. NLS-SCHOLAR's learning-by-doing philosophy is more in line with that of the SOPHIE project (see next chapter) from which it also derives its improved natural-language capabilities. A number of experimentations with the SCHOLAR framework are discussed in (Collins and Grignetti, 1975).

Extensions to SCHOLAR's inference mechanisms are described in (Collins et al., 1975a), and the analysis/synthesis approach to the study of tutorial strategies is covered in (Collins et al., 1975b). Both papers provide numerous examples of the capabilities under consideration as exhibited both by people and by computers.

The initial set of rules for Socratic dialogues that was formulated as a result these studies can be found in (Collins, 1977); the article is followed by the comments made by Resnick (1977). WHY is discussed in a condensed conference paper (Stevens and Collins, 1977), which mainly concentrates on the goals pursued by Socratic tutors. The best reference for this part of the project is a longer book chapter by Collins and Stevens (1982) describing their study of the Socratic method (also called *inquiry teaching*); this description includes the full set of rules for Socratic dialogues. A summary can be found in (Collins, 1985a), and applications to other domains are discussed in (Collins and Stevens, 1983). Stevens, Collins, and Goldin (1979) discuss issues of diagnosis with a study of common misconceptions about rainfall processes. Stevens and Collins (1980) describe the multiple models subjects use in reasoning about rainfall; concentrating on evaporation, Collins and Gentner (1983) study hierarchical relations between models, and Collins (1985b) presents the notion of component models.

Chapter 4

SOPHIE:
from quantitative
to qualitative simulation

The SOPHIE project is in many ways reminiscent of SCHOLAR and its subsequent developments. SOPHIE is also a milestone for the field, but whereas SCHOLAR was instrumental in setting the field's basic themes and goals, SOPHIE did much to establish it as a respectable subarea in the eyes of the AI community. Like SCHOLAR, SOPHIE generated a long and diverse line of research: while the SOPHIE project itself went through three successive phases spanning more than five years, its roots go back to the early seventies, and the research it spawned is still going on today. Finally, as we will see, both projects eventually led to very similar research interests.

4.1   Simulation: dialogues and learning environments

Like Carbonell, SOPHIE's designers John Seely Brown and Richard Burton were originally interested in tutorial dialogues, and their first project as a team at UCI[1] is a "question-answering system for mixed-initiative CAI" (Brown et al., 1973). Unlike Carbonell's, however, their central representational scheme for domain knowledge is a simulation model rather than a semantic network, because the system focuses on qualitative models of processes rather than on the organization of facts. Indeed, simulation-based reasoning will be the central theme of the whole SOPHIE project.

4.1.1   The METEOROLOGY tutor: question answering

The domain chosen for this first mixed-initiative tutorial system is meteorology, the domain later adopted for WHY. However, instead of the scripts used in WHY, the causal knowledge about processes is represented in finite-state automata in which sequences of events are simulated by transitions between states. The individual automata representing different meteorological processes are united into one "dynamic process model," and transition conditions are augmented with global predicates that refer explicitly to assumptions constituting the context of questions; hence, the automata look like *augmented transition networks* (ATN), as can be seen in Figure 4.1. This figure shows the automaton representing the condition of the air, with its three states and its transition conditions. In addition to this process model, factual information about meteorological concepts is contained in a semantic net, which is used to answer the student's questions in the style of SCHOLAR.

Figure 4.2 presents some answers given by the METEOROLOGY tutor to questions about both facts and processes. Questions are parsed by keyword matching. For the generation of answers to questions about processes, small units of text are associated with each state in the various automata, and sentences are constructed by simple concatenation of these text elements, with the addition of a few transition words. In spite of this crude natural-language interface, one can see how qualitative state descriptions, such as "increase" or "supersaturated," are used to compose complete paragraphs whose coherence derives from the underlying simulation of the process. Note that this simulation is primarily

---

[1]University of California at Irvine.

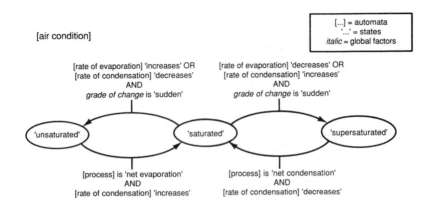

**Figure 4.1 An automaton for the condition of the air
(after Brown et al., 1973).**

qualitative, that is, based on state transitions; if required by the form of the question, quantitative information is introduced after the fact with additional computations.

These temporal/causal descriptions are based on an inference tree built dynamically by simulation of the question on the model. The state of the appropriate automaton is set to reflect the question (e.g., second question in Figure 4.2), or a global assumption is modified (e.g., third question in Figure 4.2). Then enabled transitions are propagated throughout the model, and recorded in an inference tree whose branches stand for different causal chains. This inference tree need not always be traversed from the root to the leaves as it is to generate the answers given in Figure 4.2; it can be used to answer various types of questions requiring that a causal path be established between two events. For instance, searching the inference tree allows the system to determine whether "relative humidity decreases when the temperature drops."

To insure that the simulation proceeds by coherent global states and without infinite loops, transitions standing for instantaneous changes in condition are given priority over transitions standing for advances in time. In other words, real time is frozen until causal relations have been fully propagated. This distinction between transitions due to time-bound processes and transitions due to functional relations turns out to be crucial to a coherent notion of causality, and will reappear in various forms in

Factual question:

Question: Is it true that fog is a form of precipitation?

Answer: No, fog is an example of condensation.

Questions about processes:

⋮

Question: (What happens if the air temperature decreases to 20 degrees and there are no condensation nuclei)

Answer: The (humidity of saturation)(decrease) from 24 to 17 mm Hg because (air temperature)(decrease). The (relative humidity)(increase) from 100 to 180 % because (humidity of saturation)(decrease) and (gradient of change)(sudden). The (water temperature) (decrease) from 25 to 20 degrees because (air temperature) (decrease). The (rate of evaporation) (decrease) from 24 to 17 mm Hg because (water temperature) (decrease). Then the (air condition)(supersaturated) because (rate of evaporation)(decrease) and (gradient of change) (sudden).

Question: (Suppose the pressure decrease gradually)

Answer: The (absolute humidity)(decrease) because ...

Figure 4.2 Answers given by the METEOROLOGY tutor (after Brown et al., 1973).

©1973, IEEE. Reprinted, with permission, from *IEEE Transactions on Systems, Man and Cybernetics*, 3, pp. 248–257.

later efforts to develop computational models of causal reasoning.[2] The relevance of this early attempt at capturing causality is thus both historical and technical. First, the METEOROLOGY tutor provides a demonstration of feasibility: its dynamic generation of explanations on the basis of a simulation-based representational scheme motivates the development of SOPHIE. Second, it provides a starting point for later work on qualitative models.

---

[2]The distinction is a precursor of the distinctions between real and mythical time in ENVISION theory (Section 4.6; and Section 5.2.1, footnote 8), and between direct and indirect influences in QP theory (Section 5.1.4).

4.1.2 A reactive learning environment for troubleshooting

In SOPHIE (SOPHisticated Instructional Environment) the pedagogical purpose is different: it is not so much to imitate a dialogue with a human teacher as to provide a *reactive learning environment* in which the student can try his ideas, have them critiqued, and receive advice. This notion of a reactive learning environment is an important paradigm for the contributions of artificial intelligence to an open-ended use of computers in educational settings. Brown et al. (1982) suggest that computer technology can be used to make experimentation both "easier" and "safer" by simulating environments that capitalize on the motivational value of exploratory problem-solving activities. AI-based supervision can then be provided to make sure that students learn from their experimentation.

SOPHIE's educational role is that of a "lab" where the student has a chance to apply his knowledge and receive informed feedback. The domain is the troubleshooting of electronic circuits. Since the problem-solving activity revolves around a model of a circuit whose components can be faulted, troubleshooting means performing a series of measurements to propose and test hypotheses concerning the location and nature of the fault. Not only does the student have a chance to apply his theoretical knowledge of electronic laws to understanding the "causality underlying circuit mechanisms," but he also acquires general troubleshooting strategies.

Soon after starting on the SOPHIE project, Brown and Burton moved to BBN to join forces with Carbonell and the SCHOLAR group. The idea was to combine their respective inference mechanisms. Together with the proximity of the AI lab at MIT,[3] which had another ITS research group, that made the Boston area an interesting concentration of ITS activity for a few years. The last stage of the research described in this chapter is being done at Xerox PARC.[4]

4.2 Natural-language interface: semantic grammars

Before turning to SOPHIE's simulation-based reasoning, we should describe another very important contribution of the project: the natural-language capabilities of SOPHIE's interface. Burton and Brown (1979a) define four goals that motivated various stages in the construction of

---

[3]Massachusetts Institute of Technology in Cambridge, Massachusetts.

[4]Xerox Palo Alto Research Center in Palo Alto, California.

SOPHIE's interface, and which provide a useful set of criteria for the design of instructional interfaces in general:

- *Efficiency*: the student should not have to wait for the parser to complete its task, since resulting interruptions in thought processes can be costly in terms of memory failures and loss of interest.

- *Habitability*: within its domain, the system should accommodate the range of ways in which students are likely to express the same ideas. Indeed, it was observed not only that there is a great variety in the expression even of very simple requests, but also that people are not very good at rephrasing their thoughts; thus it is important for the interface to accept the student's first wording.

- *Robustness with ambiguities*: a system should not expect each sentence to be complete and unambiguous, as people gain much communication power and conciseness in assuming contextual inferences on the part of their interlocutors.

- *Self-tutoring*: natural language allows students to concentrate on the subject rather than on the idiosyncrasies of a formal language. However, it was also observed that people who interact in natural languages with an apparently intelligent system tend to expect it to exhibit human conversational capabilities (Burton, 1976). On the other hand, students may not think of certain options offered by a system. The interface should therefore make suggestions and handle unacceptable inputs in such a way as to clarify the scope of possible interactions.

Efficiency and habitability: semantic parsing

Up to that time, the understanding of natural-language input fell into two extreme categories. At one extreme was *keyword matching*, which affords a lot of flexibility but does not provide a precise understanding of the text. At the other extreme was *syntactic parsing*, which reflects the exact structure of the input sentences but allows no flexibility. The notion of *semantic grammars*, proposed by Burton in his dissertation (1975, 1976), was to provide a desirable middle path for SOPHIE's parsing mechanisms. For greater conciseness of definition and ease of development in cases involving more complex input sentences, the grammar implemented with proceduralized rules was later replaced by the formalism of augmented transition networks *(semantic ATN's)*, compiled for efficiency (Burton and Brown, 1979a).

The basic idea of a semantic grammar is to have rules decompose global categories into lower-level constituents as in a regular syntactic grammar. But whereas a regular grammar decomposes syntactic categories—say, a sentence into noun and verb phrases—a semantic grammar decomposes semantic categories, that is, domain concepts, into their constituents. In the case of SOPHIE for instance, a semantic grammar would decompose a notion like measurement into other semantic categories like the location and the quantity of the measurement:

$$<measurement>::=<measurable\ quantity><preposition><location>$$

This semantic decomposition is recursively repeated down to the different ways elementary concepts can be expressed in English. For instance, a given quantity will eventually become a number with the specification of a unit.

While the introduction of semantic information into the parsing mechanisms requires that the domain be limited and well-defined, it has a number of advantages over purely syntactic stratagems. First, it allows the habitability of the interface to be defined precisely with respect to the expressivity required for the domain rather than with universal language constructs. Second, the semantic categories afford more predictive power during parsing, thus increasing efficiency and the ability to recognize extraneous or missing words and phrases.

A robust interface

In SOPHIE, the internal meaning of all sentences consists of operations to be performed, expressed as functions with arguments. This is true of instructions the student gives to the system as well as questions he asks, since questions can be translated into operations that retrieve the answer. In this context, the semantic parser is designed to produce exactly the system's internal interpretation of the request: a functional form instantiated to the extent that values for the function and for its arguments were provided in the input sentence. Some system parameters determine the degree of fuzziness allowed in parsing each semantic category by prescribing, for instance, the number of words that can be skipped if they do not fit into the grammatical definition of the current category.

When anaphoral references and ellipses occur, the parser simply returns a functional form that is only partially instantiated. Then the context of the dialogue is searched backward for semantically compatible values to be supplied for missing arguments or missing function names. This allows the system's interface to handle incomplete but contextually meaningful questions such as those found in the extract from an actual dialogue with SOPHIE shown in Figure 4.3. Note how SOPHIE uses deeply semantic information to disambiguate words (e.g., "between"). The dialogue also illustrates attempts by the system to uncover its

      ⋮

Student: Now what is the outpt?

SOPHIE: (outpt ⇒ output) The output voltage is 1.2 volts.
If you are not sure whether a value is correct, you can ask ``Is that value correct?''

> *After a spelling correction, the word "output" is disambiguated as meaning "output voltage." Then SOPHIE informs the student about one of its facilities.*

Student: Is that right?

SOPHIE: In a working circuit the output voltage is 30.1 volts. That value is incorrect.

> *Resolution of anaphora: "that" refers to the value of the previous measurement.*

Student: What is the voltage between the current limiting transistor and the constant current source?

SOPHIE: The voltage at N4 is 2.48 volts.

> *"Between" is construed as referring to a specific point at which the voltage is measured with respect to ground, an interpretation explicitly indicated to the student.*

Student: What is it between there and the base of Q6?

SOPHIE: The voltage between N4 and N5 is 1.28 volts.

> *Here "it" refers to the voltage and "there" refers to N4. Note that "between" has to be treated differently because the two nodes are explicit now.*

Student: Is there any ripple in the voltage at the base of Q4?

SOPHIE: I'm sorry, I do not handle AC characteristics.

> *Using the keyword "ripple," SOPHIE recognizes that the student is moving to an area that it is unable to handle. This capability avoids much frustration for the student, who may otherwise try to rephrase his query, thinking that the system just could not handle his wording.*

Student: What is the base current of Q3?

SOPHIE: The base current of Q3 is 12 microamps.

Student: Thru the emitter?

SOPHIE: The emitter current of Q3 is −.26 milliamps.

Student: Q4

SOPHIE: The emitter current of Q4 is −.26 milliamps.

> *This sequence illustrates the way SOPHIE handles ellipses, that is, sentences where the student only expresses the piece of his thought that is different from the previous context. Note how "Thru the emitter?" cannot be resolved syntactically as could "The emitter current?". Note also how both functions and arguments can be completed. Again, SOPHIE gives its full interpretation.*

Student: If C2 were leaky, what would the voltage across it be?

> *Here, the referent to "it" occurs earlier in the same sentence.*

      ⋮

Figure 4.3 Examples of input sentences correctly handled by SOPHIE (after Burton and Brown, 1979a).

facilities to the student and to respond to inputs it cannot handle with general statements about the scope of its capabilities. The latter is done at the parsing level with keywords, and also at the level of internal modules with lists of common misconceptions.

Viewed as an engineering undertaking, this approach to natural-language understanding has produced an unusually robust interface, which goes a long way toward satisfying the four criteria defined above. It provides fast and correct responses to most queries on a continuum from full sentences for novices to short abbreviations for more advanced users. After being tuned during hours of experimental use of SOPHIE, the interface can reportedly "handle nearly all sentences generated by users who have had a few minutes of exposure to the system" (p. 693, Brown et al., 1975a). However, this implementation is only meant to handle single queries without any complex grammatical constructs.

While semantic grammars as presented have no particular claim to psychological validity, their compilation of syntax and semantics does support a very humanlike handling of simple language input. They achieve this largely by taking advantage of the limited scope in which the interactions take place, since they make ample use of domain-specific knowledge. Apparently, human listeners also apply a great deal of specific knowledge during text understanding. At any rate, the techniques are widely applicable to tutoring systems, which tend to operate within a rather restricted, well-defined conceptual territory.

4.3 SOPHIE-I: simulation-based inferences

SOPHIE-I (Brown et al., 1974, 1975a; Brown and Burton, 1975) is not meant to function as a complete source of instruction, but rather as an automated lab built around a simulated circuit, with an instructor providing intelligent critiques. Since it does not take many pedagogical initiatives, its pedagogical expertise is minimal. In fact, it does not have a student model, nor does it possess an explicit knowledge of active troubleshooting strategies. The lab instructor uses its knowledge mainly to respond with meaningful feedback, whether the student is asking a question, proposing a hypothesis, or attempting a new measurement. Besides its remarkable linguistic capabilities described above, the interest of SOPHIE-I resides in its use of multiple representations of its domain knowledge to provide an "efficient and robust" inference engine. The different representations are *simulation-based* with a mathematical model of the circuit, *procedural* with a set of "intelligent" specialists using the model, and *declarative* with a semantic net of facts.

SOPHIE's instructional tasks

Once a fault, which can be of varying degrees of difficulty, has been inserted into the circuit for the student to debug, the procedural specialists of the inference engine answer specific requests and queries by setting up appropriate experiments on a general circuit simulator based on the circuit's mathematical model. These specialists take care of four distinct tasks.

The first task is to *answer hypothetical questions* about the consequences of an action or event, such as "What would happen to this component if that was done?" Different specialists determine under which boundary conditions the experiments must be set up in order to be meaningful, interpret the output of the simulation, and finally iteratively propagate the possible violations of circuit constraints that the hypothetical action may have generated (e.g., a blown-up component).

The second task is to *evaluate hypotheses.* Although the system knows the correct answer—since it inserted the fault in the circuit— merely comparing a student hypothesis with the actual fault would not differentiate between a well-reasoned conclusion and a wild guess. In order to evaluate the current hypothesis, the tutor needs to know whether it is consistent with the set of measurements performed by the student up to that point. To this end, SOPHIE keeps a record of these past measurements, which it replays on a temporary version of the circuit simulating the hypothesis. As old and new measurements are compared, the hypothesis evaluator classifies these measurements as contradicting, supporting, or independent of the current hypothesis. For pedagogical purposes, finding a contradicting measurement provides a counterexample to the hypothesis.

Third, if the student is really lost, it may be necessary to *list all the possible hypotheses* consistent with the set of measurements performed so far. For this rather complex task, the generate-and-test technique is applied: first an overgeneral list of underspecified hypotheses is proposed on the basis of rule-based heuristics; then the list is pruned by simulations of single, instantiated hypotheses on the circuit.

The last and most complex inference task to be performed is to *evaluate a new measurement* proposed by the student. What must be determined is how much information the measurement provides that could not have been logically derived from existing measurements. Because this task is similar to the task of verifying the independence of a set of axioms, a similar approach is taken: the hypothesis generator described in the last paragraph is asked to generate all consistent hypotheses with and without the new measurement. If the sets of hypotheses are different, the new measurement is not redundant.

        ⋮

Student: What could be wrong?

SOPHIE: Here are some faults which explain the measurements you observed:

      the beta of Q3 is low

      the beta of Q4 is low

      or R22 has the wrong resistance

Student: What would the output voltage be if the beta of Q3 were 8?

SOPHIE: If the beta of Q3 were 8 under the present setting, the output voltage would be 10.5 volts. In a working circuit it is 19.9 volts.

Student: Is the emitter current of Q4 correct?

SOPHIE: The emitter current of Q4 is -61 milliamps. In a working circuit the emitter current of Q4 is -49 milliamps. That value seems to be incorrect.

Student: Could R22 be low?

SOPHIE: Is it OK if I use 25 ohms for the resistance of R22?

Student: Yes

SOPHIE: That fault agrees with all of the measurements you have made.

        ⋮

Figure 4.4 Illustrations of some of SOPHIE-I's inference capabilities (Brown et al., 1975a).

    Figure 4.4 presents an excerpt from a dialogue with SOPHIE-I where three of the four tasks mentioned above are required. The student's first question requests a list of hypotheses, whereas the second one presents a hypothetical situation whose consequences must be determined. The third question merely retrieves facts, although in two different contexts and with an evaluation of what "correct" is in this case. Finally, the student proposes a hypothesis which must be evaluated under his current set of measurements. Note how SOPHIE must interpret the word "low" appropriately by choosing an actual value to set up its experiment.

The value of quantitative simulations

In a more recent paper, Brown et al. (1982) reflect on the use of quantitative simulation for making inferences and see it as a double-edged sword. On the one hand, the simulation provides a lot of leverage to the inference process, because large amounts of knowledge are encoded in the model and brought to bear via the simulation. On the other hand, this embedded knowledge is often based on implicit assumptions and empirical decisions on the part of the model's designers, which may be very subtle. For instance, the formulas used to run the simulation may only be valid for certain classes of inputs. If these assumptions are not made "explicit and checkable," they can easily be violated when the simulation involves faults.

For teaching purposes, the main drawback of quantitative simulation is its inability to give a full account of the causality underlying its inferences. Causality is pedagogically important because it is the main ingredient of the kinds of explanations human students can understand. In a troubleshooting context, causality, more than information content, drives the diagnostic reasoning and the decision to perform measurements. The shortcomings of quantitative simulation for instructional systems like SOPHIE motivate much of the further research presented in the coming sections.

4.4   SOPHIE-II: an articulate expert

SOPHIE-II (Brown et al., 1976) is not yet an attempt to deal with the fundamental limitations of quantitative simulation mentioned above; rather, it is an improvement of the pedagogical setup in which SOPHIE-I's simulated lab is used. As we have seen, SOPHIE-I exclusively provides a reactive environment and does not take didactic initiatives. In SOPHIE-II, a troubleshooting expert is added to the simulated lab. Although this expert cannot follow the student in his own approach, it can demonstrate troubleshooting *strategies*, given a faulted circuit. For the demonstration, the student is requested to select a function block to be faulted. He can then watch the expert reason out the location of the fault. Figure 4.5 shows an excerpt from a demonstration performed by SOPHIE-II. As an interesting motivational detail of the setup, note how the student is involved in the process by the questions the expert asks as it demonstrates its troubleshooting strategies. Note also the role played by a computer-based "referee" that makes explicit use of SOPHIE-I's simulated lab to rectify incorrect predictions made by the student. This limited participation encourages the student to start using SOPHIE-I on his own.

In contrast with SOPHIE-I's approach, the troubleshooting expert reasons qualitatively, making causally meaningful measurements and explaining its strategic decisions as it proceeds. Although the dialogues generated are quite impressive, the troubleshooting expert is not unusually sophisticated from an AI standpoint, since it merely follows

$\vdots$

SOPHIE-II: How does the OUTPUT CURRENT of the CONSTANT CURRENT
SOURCE compare with a working circuit?

Student: OK

SOPHIE-II: The current source is working then. The modules now
left are CL, VL, OPF and DARL. I think I will make my
next measurement on the Darlington amplifier. I want
to know whether the BASE CURRENT of Q4 is OK.

Student: HELP

Referee: Let's use SOPHIE to find the answer.

>> Is the base current of Q4 OK?

SOPHIE-I: The base current of Q4 is 0.0 amps, which seems to
be incorrect because in a working circuit it is .031
milliamps.

Referee: So, you see, the BASE CURRENT of Q4 is LOW in the
faulted circuit. Let's go on ...

SOPHIE-II: Low input current to the Darlington amplifier would
certainly result in lower than normal voltage at
its output under moderate current loads. I think
then, the Darlington amplifier is OK, since it is
following its input. Now, since we have already seen
that the CCS output current is OK, perhaps either the
current limiter or the voltage limiter must be drawing
excessive current from the CCS.

$\vdots$

**Figure 4.5 Excerpt of a troubleshooting session with SOPHIE-II's expert
(Brown et al., 1976).**

a parameterized decision tree in which multiple levels of prestored
explanations are attached to each node. During a demonstration, these
explanatory frames are instantiated to produce dialogues such as the
one presented in Figure 4.5. What is advocated here is an articulate
representation of the expertise to be conveyed in qualitative and causal
terms, but the limitations of the fixed decision tree do not allow the
system to follow and coach the student in his own troubleshooting
process. SOPHIE-III will attempt to fill this gap with a more flexible
representation of the expertise. Nevertheless, SOPHIE-II is pedagogically
significant: it adds a new dimension to the lab session, whereby the

student's personal experimentation now alternates with observation of expert behavior actively involving his understanding of the circuit. The combination of these two types of instructional exposure in the same environment provides a powerful pedagogical setup, since the student is able to watch the expert troubleshoot the very faults he has to deal with.

SOPHIE-I and II in actual use

When SOPHIE-II became operational, it was actually used for a short course in electronic troubleshooting with both its demonstration and its "lab" capabilities. One interesting variation, which provided a good learning experience, was a game that SOPHIE was programmed to monitor. Two players would take turns inserting a fault into the circuit for their opponent to diagnose. To encourage the "inserter" to envision the consequences of faults and to choose faults he could understand, the scoring algorithm would also ask him to predict the results of measurements performed by the "diagnoser." When two teams of two partners were playing, the debates between partners about the next move offered a rare opportunity to observe without interference the kind of strategic argumentation that underlies decision making. One major advantage of this type of naturally occurring interactive protocol is that people not only argue for the decisions they make, but also— crucially—against decisions they discard. The authors claim that this latter information, readily available here, is actually quite difficult to obtain through more classical protocol paradigms.

4.5 SOPHIE-III: humanlike reasoning

Unlike SOPHIE-II, SOPHIE-III (Brown et al., 1982) attacks the problem of reconsidering SOPHIE-I's reasoning style and representational scheme organized around a quantitative simulation. Although SOPHIE-I's inferential capabilities are outstanding (it would often outperform its designers), its approaches to problems are sometimes so foreign to human reasoning that their pedagogical leverage is seriously limited. As an example of a powerful but pedagogically inadequate inference mechanism, recall the method used in SOPHIE-I for evaluating the redundancy of measurements. Although generating all possible hypotheses is an extremely powerful technique, it makes no use of the kind of causal reasoning performed by human troubleshooters. Therefore it makes no distinction between logically obvious redundancies, which can simply be stated, and more obscure, albeit correct ones, which require complex explanations. For teaching purposes, such powerful conclusions are of little value if they cannot be justified in terms that the student can relate to.

Whereas SOPHIE-I concentrates on providing a "reactive" environment, which responds primarily from the perspective of the domain, the inference engine of SOPHIE-III is designed to be the core of a pedagogically "active" environment, which centers on the learning needs of a student. It was meant to support learner-oriented activities such as coaching and student modeling, while still allowing the student to take the initiative.

4.5.1 Paradigmatic systems: the BLOCKS tutor

Because of the complexity of the domain of electronics, separate projects were also started for the purpose of investigating various related issues in simpler domains. The coaching of problem-solving activities was explored in WEST, student modeling in BUGGY, and information-theoretic troubleshooting in the BLOCKS tutor. WEST and BUGGY became projects of their own and are covered in coming chapters.

The BLOCKS tutor (Brown and Burton, 1978b) is based on a game in manipulatory mathematics that uses the concept of *attribute blocks* (Greenes et al., 1972) to exercise the student's deductive abilities of the type necessary for troubleshooting. In the game as implemented, a block is defined by three attributes: its *size* (large or small), its *color* (red, yellow, green, or blue), and its *shape* (triangle, square, circle, or diamond). In the setup shown in Figure 4.6, card A and card B each state one attribute value (e.g., large) or the negation of a value (e.g., not blue). Thus they each define a set of blocks. These two sets, with their union and their intersection, define four areas as shown in the diagram. The contents of the two cards are not shown to the student, who must deduce them by a sequence of queries. For each query, he chooses one block and asks the system in which of the four areas the block should be placed according to the cards' contents. If each new block is chosen judiciously, knowing where it belongs narrows the range of possible values for the cards until these values are uniquely determined. The skill of the game is then to select blocks whose placement is expected to provide a maximum of information about the cards. This is analogous to selecting optimal measurements in troubleshooting.

The dialogue excerpt presented in Figure 4.6 demonstrates the main capabilities of the BLOCKS tutor. Note how the annotated interventions require deductions that would be quite difficult for a human tutor, who would probably respond mostly 'yes' or 'no' according to the actual values of the cards. However, because the underlying deductions are based on strategic rules likely to be used by people for the domain, BLOCKS is able

$\vdots$

BLOCKS: Welcome to the attribute blocks world. Two cards have been chosen. Choose a block.

Student: LARGE YELLOW SQUARE.

> *Usually abbreviated LYS.*

BLOCKS: Put the LARGE YELLOW SQUARE in area 3.

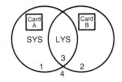

Student: SMALL YELLOW SQUARE.

BLOCKS: Put the SMALL YELLOW SQUARE in area 1. You should be able to deduce card B now.

> *BLOCKS notices that there is only one possibility left for card B.*

Student: Is card B LARGE?

BLOCKS: That's correct.

Student: Is card A SMALL?

BLOCKS: No. If card A were SMALL, then the LARGE YELLOW SQUARE which is in area 3 would be outside of loop A.

> *BLOCKS finds a counterexample to dismiss an inconsistent conjecture.*

Student: LARGE YELLOW DIAMOND.

BLOCKS: Put the LARGE YELLOW DIAMOND in area 3.

Student: Is card A YELLOW?

BLOCKS: It could be, but it could also be NOT RED, NOT GREEN, NOT BLUE, NOT CIRCLE or NOT TRIANGLE.

> *The fact is that card A is YELLOW, but BLOCKS responds with a 'maybe', noticing that there are still other possibilities according to the evidence available to the student.*

$\vdots$

Student: SMALL YELLOW DIAMOND.

BLOCKS: Could you tell me some possibilities for card A?

Student: YELLOW and NOT CIRCLE.

> *In this last sequence, the student has proposed a redundant block that does not split his set of hypotheses. Therefore, BLOCKS takes the initiative and goes through a short dialogue to make the student aware of this fact.*

BLOCKS: Would the SMALL YELLOW DIAMOND go inside or outside of a loop which had a card value YELLOW?

Student: Inside.

BLOCKS: Right. Would the SMALL YELLOW DIAMOND go inside or outside of a loop which had a card value NOT CIRCLE?

Student: Inside.

BLOCKS: Right. So the SMALL YELLOW DIAMOND goes inside of loop A no matter which of those values card A has. Put the SMALL YELLOW DIAMOND in area 1.

$\vdots$

Figure 4.6 A dialogue with the BLOCKS tutor (Brown and Burton, 1978b).

to provide reasons for its statements in terms the student can understand. In the second half of the dialogue, for instance, when BLOCKS points out the redundancy of the student's block (his "measurement" in SOPHIE's terminology), it can actually lead him to appreciate why his block could not provide any new information, given his current set of hypotheses. This interactive "entrapment" is typical of the Socratic style adopted for the tutor.

Admittedly, the interventions of BLOCKS are still somewhat oppressive, since its tutoring module does not possess any subtle pedagogical principles dealing with motivational and other related issues. These aspects were to be investigated in the context of WEST (see Chapter 7). In fact, a preliminary controlled evaluation of the BLOCKS tutor's instructional effectiveness yielded negative results (Gallagher, 1981).

Nevertheless, BLOCKS is an insightful study of troubleshooting strategies based on optimization of expected information, and the interactive treatment of these strategic issues gives an idea of the type of dialogue envisaged for future versions of SOPHIE. Indeed, the methodological intent behind the spawning of such focused projects was to isolate specific issues to be explored in the context of carefully chosen domains with different "paradigmatic systems." These prototypes allow initial experimentation with one aspect of interest while simplifying others. If the interesting characteristics of these experimental domains scale up, the prototypes may eventually be merged into one complete system.

4.5.2 Toward humanlike reasoning in electronics

Even though the combination of all the facilities of BLOCKS, WEST, and BUGGY in SOPHIE has not been implemented, the goal of supporting a variety of pedagogical tasks guided the conception of SOPHIE-III's reasoning engine for electronic troubleshooting, whose design is based on observations of the techniques used by both experts and students.

Let us look briefly at this new reasoning engine, referring the reader to the paper by Brown et al. (1982) for a complete technical discussion. SOPHIE-III's expertise is divided into troubleshooting expertise and electronics expertise, each implemented in a separate module.

The *troubleshooting expert* works on top of the electronics expert. It is a small circuit-independent expert system whose knowledge, accessible for tutorial purposes, concerns the management of a set of hypotheses in a troubleshooting context. In order to eliminate candidates from the set of possible faults, it proposes new measurements according to both the electronics expert's deductions and general troubleshooting strategies of the type explored with the BLOCKS tutor.

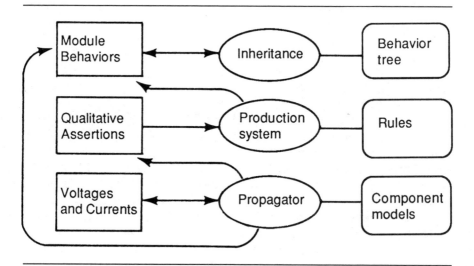

Figure 4.7 Diagram of the electronics expert (Brown et al., 1982).

The *electronics expert* functions at three levels, which are illustrated in Figure 4.7. For each level, the rightmost column indicates the type of knowledge used, the center column shows the reasoning mechanism applied, and the leftmost column contains the factual information supplied as input. At the local level of the circuit's components (the bottom of the diagram), the electronics expert applies general knowledge of the principles of electronics to propagate quantitative information about voltages and currents across components. These local inferences, expressed as quantitative ranges, are then translated into qualitative assertions for a rule-based system that infers the behavior of the circuit's modules. Finally, at the global level (the top of the diagram), the electronics expert uses circuit-specific knowledge to analyze the circuit in terms of the behavior of logical modules. The circuit-specific knowledge is represented as a *behavior tree* which is central to the expert's reasoning capabilities. The behavior tree, a small sample of which is shown in Figure 4.8, is a network whose nodes represent module behaviors and whose links represent structural relations and interactions between modules liable to spread faults through the system. Therefore, module behaviors can be propagated through these links as a form of simulation in terms of qualitative descriptions of behavior.

To record the efforts of these different types of reasoners in a unified way, a common language is used to insert each deduction into a database along with relevant assumptions and justifications. These explicit statements of all assumptions and justifications accompanying

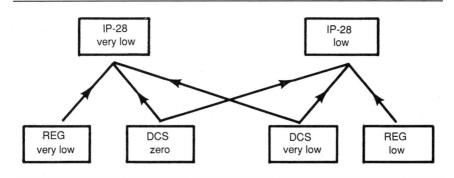

Figure 4.8 Small portion of SOPHIE-III's behavior tree (Brown et al., 1982).

each deduction are what the troubleshooting expert uses in its decision process, and are also intended to support the generation of explanations.

Further problems with SOPHIE-III

In spite of SOPHIE-III's flexibility and humanlike reasoning, there are two important areas, both central concerns in artificial intelligence, where the authors see challenging problems to motivate further research. The first problem pertains to the basic assumptions on which the representation and reasoning are based. Assumptions such as a single fault to be searched for are good working heuristics for troubleshooting, but are often violated in real situations. Similarly, mental representations of physical systems often fail to predict actual behavior in extreme cases or when faults are present. When assumptions are thus violated, it must be possible to retract them. However, properly handling the retraction of assumptions and its impact on inferences is notably difficult and requires complex mechanisms known as *truth-maintenance systems* (Doyle, 1979; de Kleer, 1986).

The second problematic area mentioned by Brown et al. is the encoding of the circuit-specific knowledge, originally implicitly present in SOPHIE-I's quantitative simulator, and now contained in SOPHIE-III's production rules and behavior tree. In spite of all efforts to formalize their representation and to restrict their use, the somewhat ad hoc rules and structural links containing this knowledge are a poor substitute for a general-purpose causal model of the circuit, as apparently used both by experts and students. In fact, issues of assumptions and of mental models of physical systems are closely related. In the next section, we describe the research on such models that Brown has been doing since then with Johan de Kleer, whose doctoral dissertation was on the subject of causal reasoning (de Kleer, 1979), and who participated in the last phase of SOPHIE's development.

4.6   Mental models: qualitative reasoning

Although the study of mental models of physical systems described here is not directly related to the construction of a specific instructional system, it is appropriate to delineate the general direction of this research, for a number of reasons. First, it was largely motivated by SOPHIE's educational purpose. Furthermore, it can be viewed as a development of the early work on qualitative simulations with automata in the METEOROLOGY tutor. Finally, quite apart from the fact that this research is conducted by people obviously interested in building instructional systems, it will certainly have important pedagogical implications, since it focuses on the formation as well as the use of causal models. The topic is of central importance for education in general and for the design of tutoring systems in particular.

Function from structure: envisioning

De Kleer and Brown (1981, 1982, 1983) call the type of models in which they are interested *mechanistic mental models*, though they are often simply referred to as *causal* or *qualitative* models because they are based on causal reasoning in qualitative terms. These are the models people use to think about physical devices: in particular, to infer the functioning of a device from knowledge of its structure. Such inference is exemplified by SOPHIE-III's need to understand an electronic circuit where each component has some known properties, and where the function of the whole circuit results from the structural relations between those components. Rather than the ad hoc descriptions used in SOPHIE-III, de Kleer and Brown would like to propose a principled framework within which a large class of models can be represented.

To be useful, such a framework should fulfill two essential conditions. First, the models it produces should be *robust*: that is, their predictions should remain in correspondence with the behavior of the actual system even in unusual circumstances, such as when parts are modified or faults inserted. Second, the framework should address the issue of the *learnability* of models. It turns out that both issues have to do with the explicit handling of assumptions. Indeed, according to the theory and in keeping with the conclusions of SOPHIE-III, the fragility of mechanistic mental models stems primarily from implicit assumptions, violations of which break the correspondence between model and actual system.

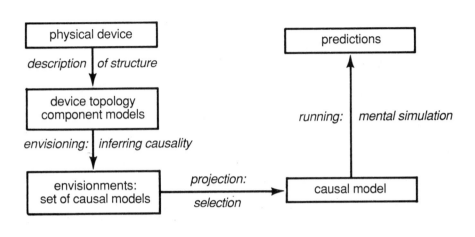

Figure 4.9 Phases in the process of qualitative simulation.

Qualitative simulation is commonly held to involve only the mental manipulation of a set of inputs to yield predictions. In contrast, because of its emphasis on assumptions, de Kleer and Brown's theory divides the process into two distinct phases: the construction of causal models, and their use in specific simulations. Expressed in terms of the knowledge of SOPHIE-III, this would mean that behavior trees are now constructed dynamically so that their assumptions can be made explicit. Figure 4.9 delineates the progression from the device to the resulting predictions with boxes standing for data structures and arrows for processes.

Figure 4.10 provides a simple instance of this progression with the construction of a causal model for a buzzer. First, the topology of the physical device is represented in terms of its components, their interconnections, as well as their known behaviors in response to inputs. Then, from this structural device topology, a form of inference termed *envisioning* is applied to construct *causal models* (also called *envisionments*) that link the components with respect to their behaviors. Envisioning describes the device in terms of component states: it deals with changes in these states and their consequences for the states of other components. Finally, a causal model can be mentally *run* on specific inputs to yield predictions by propagation of behavior through the causal links.

Note how this type of modeling process, which has been implemented in a computer program called ENVISION, allows more than simply running the model on different inputs. Because its primary task is the explicit construction of causal models from the structure of the device, the modeling process can take into account modifications to the components as well as to the inputs. This is crucial for the knowledge

a) device

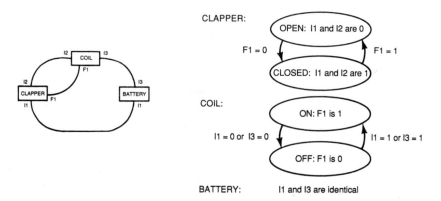

b) Device topology and component models

(F1 = magnetic field   I1, I2, I3 = electrical connections)

CLAPPER:

OPEN: I1 and I2 are 0

F1 = 0   F1 = 1

CLOSED: I1 and I2 are 1

COIL:

ON: F1 is 1

I1 = 0 or I3 = 0   I1 = 1 or I3 = 1

OFF: F1 is 0

BATTERY: I1 and I3 are identical

c) causal model

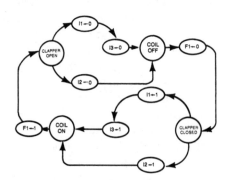

Figure 4.10 Construction of a causal model for a buzzer

Adapted from "Assumptions and ambiguities in mechanistic mental models," by J. de Kleer and J. S. Brown, in *Mental Models*, Hillsdale, NJ: Erlbaum. ©1983 Lawrence Erlbaum Associates, Inc., reprinted with permission.

that underlies troubleshooting, and constitutes an important requirement of the theory. In this view, the key to deep understanding lies as much in the *relation* between the structure and the causal model as it does within the causal model itself. Indeed, envisioning not only creates the causal model, but does it in a way that makes the relation between the two understandable. In this sense, it goes beyond the ordinary notion of qualitative simulation to focus on the explicit manipulation of assumptions.

Principled construction of causal models: robustness and learning

Envisioning extracts causality from structural descriptions by examining the local interactions between components as it propagates state transitions through the device. Since the behavior of these components is not necessarily uniquely defined by purely qualitative descriptions of attributes and states or by structure alone, envisioning must keep track of the possible variants produced on the basis of differing assumptions. This is why, in Figure 4.9, the process of envisioning is described as resulting in a *set* of causal models, one of which has to be selected with additional information about specific cases. For instance, in the buzzer of Figure 4.10, when the coil is on, the clapper will open only if the pull of the magnetic field is stronger than that of the spring. Retracting this assumption gives rise to two models: one that buzzes and one that does not. Selecting one model over the other for simulating a particular case requires either quantitative information or observation of the device's global functioning (i.e., whether or not it buzzes).

This last point reveals some key insights into the nature of robust mechanistic mental models. An important distinction needs to be made between *device-specific assumptions*, by which models become ad hoc, and *class-wide assumptions*, which are necessary for modeling, but can be made explicit a priori because they apply to entire classes of devices. This leads to the formulation of principles for model construction. Inasmuch as the structural modeling language of the theory describes the device's components in terms of *states* and *transitions*, it is quite reminiscent of the automata used in the METEOROLOGY tutor. However, components are now defined in a context-free fashion and do not refer to each other. To this end, their behavior is described strictly *locally*, that is, solely with respect to *conduits* that connect them to the rest of the device.[5]

Strict adherence to the *locality* principle is one way to comply with a more general principle, perhaps the most fundamental one uncovered

---

[5]Note that here model components are always physical parts, whereas the METEOROLOGY tutor's automata can describe processes or parameters (see Section 5.1.4 about QP theory, which develops this latter approach).

by de Kleer and Brown. The principle, which they call *no function in structure*, states that the description of the behaviors of individual components should not assume the functioning of the whole device or even of other parts of the device. If this principle is violated, then it becomes difficult to prove that the model's predictions were not built into the structural description in the first place. Furthermore, these violations would severely impair a model's ability to simulate certain faults, since the insertion of a fault might modify the context in which components operate. This might then invalidate the original description of components' behaviors, hence render any prediction yielded by the model suspect.

While the principle is clearly important, building models that perfectly abide by it turns out to be extremely difficult.[6] Each time further assumptions are retracted, the envisioning process becomes more complex. In fact, when mechanistic models are taught, de Kleer and Brown recommend using *sequences of explanatory models* whereby implicit assumptions of function or context are progressively retracted from the structural description. Since one can never be absolutely sure that all assumptions have been identified, the contribution of the principle to the issue of learning is to indicate in which *direction* the understanding of a model should evolve to achieve robust understanding.

Prescriptive and descriptive theories

At this point, it might be useful to situate the contribution of de Kleer and Brown in the context of the surging interest in mental models. In contrast with most psychological approaches to the subject, theirs does not attempt to capture the way people in general use mental models; rather, it aims to formalize the informal, qualitative reasoning of experts with a language and calculus for constructing causal models. In this sense their theory is one of competence, not of performance. They are concerned with pedagogical issues, in particular explanations, but purely from a prescriptive standpoint: their work pertains to the representation of expertise rather than the diagnosis of misconceptions—the latter being more of a central concern of Stevens and Collins—although principles of robustness turn out be useful in defining classes of errors that violate them.

In their concentration on a mechanistic formalism and on robustness, de Kleer and Brown have to ignore some important aspects, uncovered by more descriptive studies with a psychological focus, like the

---

[6]For instance, the example given in Figure 4.10 violates the principle since the clapper's closing is assumed to make the current flow (I1 and I2 are 1)—something that happens only if the clapper is on a loop with a working battery.

use of multiple models derived from metaphors. Another problem in modeling human performance is the isolation of the processes shown in Figure 4.10, which does not allow for their interaction. Although the distinctions between them are important theoretical contributions, little space is left for exploratory investigations and feedback from the environment if processes cannot be interleaved or merged. Finally, Hollan and Hutchins (1984) have expressed some reservations about the use of purely qualitative models, drawing attention to other forms of reasoning with models of physical systems that involve estimates of magnitude.

The strength of de Kleer and Brown's approach, when compared to more descriptive treatments like Stevens and Collins', resides in its attempt at formalizing the representations and processes involved in constructing and using mental models, so that phenomena can be captured in computational terms. The systematic concern with assumptions has defined a spectrum of modeling capabilities, and has produced an intrinsic measure of a model's quality that characterizes learnability in terms of representational criteria rather than merely in terms of performance. If a model is only evaluated according to the precision of its predictions, then modifications required for improvement are not well defined: learning can only take place through an undirected generate-and-test search or with the help of ad hoc heuristics.

Qualitative physics

For the purpose of this book, what we have said so far should suffice to give the reader a sense of how the work on SOPHIE has evolved and how the current research can affect the way physical processes are taught. Our brief treatment, however, does not do justice to the extent and significance of this work, and the reader is referred to the papers mentioned for more information. Recently, the research has taken on a more general and ambitious character; de Kleer and Brown (1984; Brown and de Kleer, 1984) have set out to devise a "framework for a qualitative physics" as an alternative to the usual mathematically based physics. They want to extend the ENVISION theory[7] to include all physical processes. If the physical world is viewed as a collection of mechanistic devices whose behaviors can be causally reduced to the interactions between their components, then common-sense reasoning about physical processes can be considered as the manipulation of a huge qualitative causal model.

---

[7] To facilitate references in this book, we will call this work the ENVISION theory, even though ENVISION is the name of one program only, and not an official name for the whole theory.

In contrast, classical physics only provides quantitative constraints in the form of equations, which the authors claim can neither support suggestive explanations nor give rise to insights, because they do not carry causal information. One goal of this new theory is to define qualitative equivalents to the classical notion of differential and integral calculus by combining the use of qualitative equations (called *confluences*) with the envisioning process. In short, de Kleer and Brown are trying to develop a series of concepts and principles that support a qualitative representation of the world capable of inferences, predictions, and explanations via a "qualitative causal calculus."

Summary and conclusion

We have followed the history of a multifaceted investigation into the use of simulation models for knowledge communication, starting with finite automata and leading to the notion of a qualitative physics. A number of important contributions to the field were made in the course of this investigation, and three other projects, two of which will be described later, were spawned in the process. SOPHIE-I is now considered a classic in the field. On the one hand, its intelligent use of a circuit model makes it appear knowledgeable in its domain. On the other hand, its powerful natural-language capabilities due to its semantic grammar make it appear knowledgeable in communication. The result is an instructional system that did much to render the ITS enterprise credible. With the addition of a demonstration module, SOPHIE-II extends the system's pedagogical value by allowing the student to see an expert perform on the same problems in the same environment. The whole setup was actually used for a short course.

SOPHIE-III has not produced an instructional system, but its theme has inspired recent projects, in particular the ones described in the next chapter. More generally, this work on qualitative reasoning is of seminal importance for the research on mental models. In this regard, the evolution of the SOPHIE project can be viewed as a search for the right ingredients of "cognitive fidelity" in modeling expert reasoning. SOPHIE-I abandons the automata of the METEOROLOGY tutor to take advantage of mathematically based computational formalisms, which place the emphasis on physically faithful simulations. In an effort to gain cognitive fidelity, SOPHIE-III moves away from the structurally isomorphic representations of quantitative simulations to concentrate on mental models, but in some sense it goes too far and becomes too specialized to a given form of reasoning in the context of a specific task. Envisioning reintroduces structure, but in qualitative terms: it makes causal models more general by relating them explicitly to structure and by providing a calculus for moving between levels. The subtlety of the process is that, in any given situation, the model of an expert may be very similar to that of a novice, but because elaborate envisioning makes assumptions explicit, the expert's model is actually more robust. I must admit to a sense of excitement about this subject. In the context of the contrast between encoding decisions and encoding knowledge outlined in Part I, this notion of reasoning from "first principles" is a step toward purer forms of artificial intelligence. We will return to this theme in Part III.

Having seen the SOPHIE project's evolution from the early simulations to the recent research on a qualitative physics, we can better appreciate how it parallels the evolution from SCHOLAR's semantic nets to multiple mental models. Again we find that the requirements of communication have motivated an epistemological investigation of models of domain knowledge. And again we find that the result of that investigation has ramifications not only for the task of communication, but also for an understanding of fundamental reasoning processes. In fact, much of the recent trend of concern for mental models of physical processes, both in artificial intelligence and cognitive science, can be traced to research issues related to knowledge communication. In particular, the two lines of research we have covered so far have played a central role. Thus, the theme of knowledge communication as an integral part of an investigation of intelligence has already found supportive evidence in two of the most important research projects in the history of the field.

Bibliographical notes

In addition to Burton's dissertation (Burton, 1975), two technical reports discuss the concept of semantic parsing (Burton, 1976; Burton and Brown, 1977). A more recent, and more available, book chapter by Burton and Brown (1979a) provides a good discussion of issues of interface and semantic parsing. The reader interested in parsing natural language for instruction may want to read the paper by Weischedel, Voge, and James (1978). Though admittedly a prototype, their GERMAN tutor is fairly sophisticated. Unlike Burton's semantic parser, this system separates syntactic and semantic issues. Thus, it can deal both with syntactic errors—by using an extended ATN to recognize and signal errors—and with semantic matters of language usage and text comprehension—by referring to a limited world model.

The BLOCKS tutor is described in (Brown and Burton, 1978b), and Gallagher (1981) reports on a formal evaluation of the tutor's effectiveness in fostering problem-solving skills in students. Although the study was too short to be conclusive,[8] and although BLOCKS was in fact never meant to be a complete tutoring system, Gallagher's is one of the very rare attempts to evaluate an intelligent tutoring system formally, in the educational tradition. Perhaps the experiment's most significant result was to suggest the importance of making sure that students cannot avoid problem-solving efforts by somehow eliciting the answer from the system.

The early paper by Brown, Burton, and Zdybel (1973) on the METEOROLOGY tutor is an interesting historical landmark. Two thorough reports on SOPHIE-I are available: (Brown, Burton, and Bell, (1975a) focuses on the pedagogical capabilities and (Brown and Burton, 1975) on representational issues. A good overview is given in (Brown, 1977). The reference for SOPHIE-III is the paper by Brown, Burton, and de Kleer (1982); though rather long and difficult, this seminal paper reveals some of the more subtle aspects of the development of SOPHIE-III, and also briefly covers the first two versions of SOPHIE. The pedagogical philosophy of SOPHIE-II is discussed in a recent review of the project by Brown and Burton (1986).

For mechanistic mental models, the reference is (de Kleer and Brown, 1983), and for the research on qualitative physics, (de Kleer and Brown, 1984). The book in which this last paper appears (Bobrow, 1984) is a broad survey of AI work on qualitative models. A good overview of the recent research on mental models of physical processes is provided by de Kleer (in press).

---

[8]BLOCKS advocates a fairly sophisticated strategy, which is likely to interfere with students' problem solving at first.

Chapter **5**

Interactive simulations: communicating mental models

After seeing how research interests that originated with WHY and SOPHIE ended up converging, we continue on the theme of mental models with two recent projects that attempt to communicate these models. In order to create a learning environment based on an interactive simulation, STEAMER concentrates on the interface and on the graphic rendition of a model. QUEST pursues a similar goal, but uses an internal representation of qualitative models to generate explanations; QUEST also addresses developmental issues. Since both projects directly or indirectly involve people from the WHY team, and since most of the research described here has been conducted at BBN, this chapter could be viewed as a historical continuation of Chapter 3. However, it was essential to cover the SOPHIE project first because of the fundamental influence of de Kleer and Brown's work on the two projects.

5.1   STEAMER: simulation and abstraction

The STEAMER project started in the late seventies as a joint venture involving a number of researchers: principally James Hollan and Mike Williams from NPRDC,[1] and Albert Stevens, Bruce Roberts, and Ken Forbus from BBN. Alongside the work on ENVISION theory and the theoretical interest in mental models generated by WHY, STEAMER constitutes an attempt to make use of the concept in an instructional context involving a complex device. Even though computational formalisms for the representation of mental models were not ripe for direct use in tutorial systems, the notion had matured enough to become one of the project's central themes.

5.1.1   Manipulable simulation of a steam plant

STEAMER is an instructional tool for training engineers who will operate large ships. The steam propulsion plants of these ships are extremely complex physical systems, and it takes engineers years of training to acquire the necessary expertise. Admittedly, the ultimate purpose of the training is to learn to perform the vast collection of procedures associated with both normal and abnormal operating conditions. However, Williams, Hollan, and Stevens (1981) see two reasons why this involves forming a mental model of the plant and understanding related engineering principles: the number of procedures is too large for rote memorization, and the handling of casualties among components is likely to require the invention of entirely novel procedures. This training is thus a prime example of the acquisition of a sophisticated mental model.

The vehicle used to support students' development of an accurate mental model is that of an *interactive, inspectable simulation* based on computer graphics. STEAMER displays a running model of the propulsion plant via a language of animated icons, which allow the student to form a mental model and to learn procedures by manipulating this simulated plant. Figure 5.1 shows the system as seen by the student, with one color monitor for the simulation and another terminal for written interactions. The display on the left screen has been blown up; it presents a top-level view of the steam plant. The various indicators appearing in the display are connected to an underlying quantitative model and are updated as the simulation proceeds. They may also be set to specific

---

[1] Naval Personnel Research and Development Center, in San Diego.

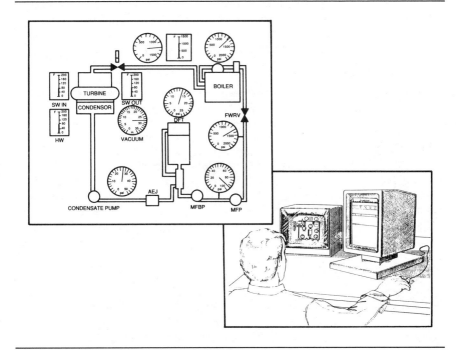

Figure 5.1 A top-level view of a propulsion plant as presented
by STEAMER (after Stevens, 1982).

values by the student, who can then observe the consequences of her
manipulations.   A hierarchical decomposition of the model allows the
student to explore subsystems in further details.   With the use of a
mouse[2] to set indicators and select from menus, students reportedly
require almost no special introduction before they can start experimenting
with the system (Stevens et al., 1983).

On the pragmatic side, much effort has been invested in developing
generic graphic and design tools for supporting the generation of interactive graphic simulations by nonprogrammers (Stevens et al., 1983).
The idea was to produce a system that instructors could easily tailor
to their needs and extend.   This resulted in the design of an object-
oriented graphics editor that manipulates icons representing objects such
as gauges, pipes, and flows.   There are also facilities for connecting
these objects to the variables of an underlying quantitative model and
for associating procedures with objects. With these facilities and tools, a

---

[2] A hand-held device, shown in Figure 5.1, with which the user can point to areas of the
screen by moving an arrow across the display.

large proportion of the learning environment for steam propulsion plants known as the STEAMER system has been built by a nonprogrammer propulsion expert. Apparently, STEAMER has been well received when used for actual training at the Great Lakes Naval Training Center.

5.1.2   Tutorial capabilities: the use of abstractions

For learning about such a system as complex as a steam plant, students need some tutorial guidance that complements free manipulations. The original plan was to augment STEAMER's simulation with pedagogical capabilities covering plant operating procedures, basic engineering principles, and explanations about plant functioning. Two modules were completed: a tutorial module that provides feedback during the execution of known procedures, and a "minilab" for exploring the structure of specific components.

Explanations of procedures: abstract objects

Observations of expert explanations revealed a "deep and complex" knowledge about the system, which was never explicitly captured in STEAMER. However, with respect to explaining procedures, these observations suggested three important points for the design of a tutorial module (Stevens and Roberts, 1983):

- specific components are described in terms of *abstract devices* (e.g., a turbine is an instance of a steam chamber with drains);

- advice is given in terms of *abstract procedures* executed on these abstract devices (e.g., open the drains before admitting steam into a chamber);

- *rationales* for the ordering of steps in procedures are established by references to *engineering principles* couched in terms of these abstractions (e.g., if drains are not opened first, water can mix with steam and be projected through pipes at high speed, causing ...).

In STEAMER, the student can be asked to execute a given procedure by selecting successive steps from a menu. When applied to the design of a tutor for this task, the use of abstractions as described above provides leverage, allowing a fairly simple scheme to generate pedagogically sound explanations. First, relatively few abstract devices and associated procedures need be represented internally in order to cover the large number of actual operations. Second, if a procedure is represented as a collection of steps with ordering relations referring to basic principles, then the student can be given feedback on her procedure both in general terms and with a practical example made even more concrete by the simulation (see Section 7.2 for the general notion of "issues and examples"). The tutor can also easily monitor which principles the student violates and which ones she knows.

Structure of components: abstract functionality

For occasions when a student wants to understand the structure of a control component in details, STEAMER has a facility called the *feedback minilab* (Forbus, 1984a), where simulated devices can be assembled and tested. On the minilab's screen, the student has a menu of icons representing abstract functions typical of control devices, such as measuring subcomponents or comparators. She can select these abstract components and assemble them on the screen to construct her own control devices. The minilab is then able to generate code from subcomponent specifications to produce a simulation program for the device. Hence, once a controller has been constructed graphically in this way, it can be integrated into a simulation so that its effects on the embedding system can be observed.

Figure 5.2 shows the minilab[3] after the student has constructed the device shown in the middle of the screen on the right. As implemented, the minilab has limited tutorial capabilities: it can critique the student's device by locating common bugs and recognizing some instances of known devices. Its pedagogical significance lies in its definition of abstract components in terms that allow simulated devices to be built. It is very important for students to acquire this vocabulary of functional abstractions, and the minilab helps root the abstractions' meaning in direct experiments.

5.1.3 Inspectable simulations: conceptual fidelity

The use of graphic abstractions has a number of practical advantages for making models of physical systems such as a steam plant inspectable: there is no opaque material, components are not distributed spatially, and parameters can be displayed even though no actual instrumentation exists. The student can even become aware of transient phenomena by stopping the simulation or by single-stepping through procedures to gain

---

[3] In the actual minilab, the graphics appear separately. In Figure 5.2, icons have been inserted in the text screen for conciseness. The abstract functions corresponding to available icons are listed above them in the black area.

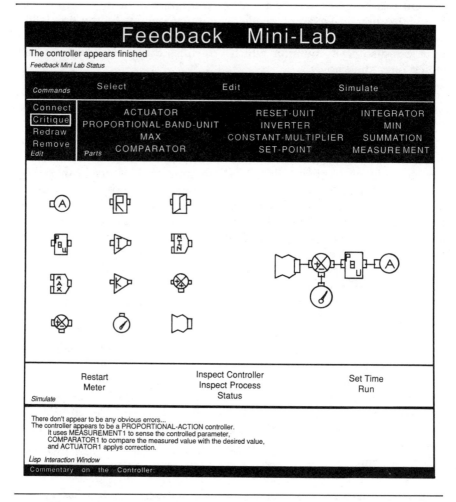

Figure 5.2 A view of the minilab facilities (after Forbus, 1984a).

a detailed understanding of their effects on the system. Furthermore, she can create hypothetical situations by inserting faults into various components.

Mental models are also abstractions. In this regard, Hollan et al. (1984) emphasize that the view of the propulsion plant presented by STEAMER's simulation is meant to reflect less an exact physical model than a mental model as used by an expert. They call this effort to render a conceptual rather than a physical view the principle of *conceptual fidelity*: a simulation model is conceptually faithful to the extent that its presentation illustrates the conceptual abstractions that experts seem to use in reasoning about a system, rather than the system itself. As an

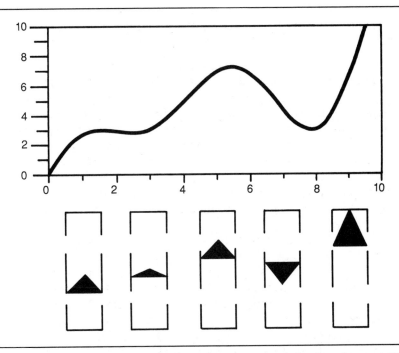

**Figure 5.3 STEAMER's icons indicating the rate of change of a quantity
(Hollan et al., 1984).**

example, Figure 5.3 shows the icons displayed by STEAMER to depict
a variable's rate of change, a kind of data typically difficult to represent
with traditional gauges, but crucial to expert reasoning. The pedagogical
claim is that running a conceptually faithful simulation can be considered
a form of *continuous explanation*, since it reflects an expert's view of
phenomena.

Of course, a complete explanation requires an articulation of causal
and functional relations in addition to the use of conceptual abstractions.
Nevertheless, the design of conceptually faithful simulations, even at the
level of the interface as in STEAMER, does require an understanding of
what constitutes a qualitative model and of how it is used to support
reasoning processes. To gain this understanding, Williams, Hollan, and
Stevens (1983) investigate the mental models used by subjects to reason
about a simple physical device. In consonance with the conclusions of
Collins and Gentner, they suggest that qualitative reasoning involves the
interaction of multiple models, each able to contribute a complementary
aspect to the global understanding. Hence, conceptual fidelity may
require the fusion of a number of mental models into the representation
of a physical system.

5.1.4   From graphic abstractions to qualitative processes

Even though the STEAMER project is directly inspired by AI research in its investigation of the pedagogical use of abstractions and simulations, the theoretical research on mental models and conceptual fidelity has not yet found an explicit AI incarnation there. The underlying model is purely mathematical; it is converted into qualitative concepts solely by means of the graphic representational schemes and associated procedures. STEAMER, therefore, cannot be said to possess the mental model of a propulsion system that it is trying to teach. It merely provides an inspectable abstract view of a quantitative model. In this sense, it shares many of SOPHIE-I's pedagogical limitations, particularly with respect to causal explanations.

However, the issue of explaining complex systems was a fascinating part of STEAMER's original research agenda, and interest in qualitative reasoning and explanations of systems and processes has permeated the whole project. Even if it has never found realization in the implemented system, this interest has motivated a number of related studies (Forbus and Stevens, 1981; Stevens and Steinberg, 1981; Weld, 1983). Along these lines, a member of the research team, Ken Forbus (1984b), has undertaken to investigate in a general way the kind of qualitative reasoning involved in human thinking; he is interested in the way people think about physical processes like the transfer of heat in a steam plant. This investigation has resulted in his Qualitative Process (QP) theory, regarded as a seminal piece of AI research on the representation of mental models of the world.

While a detailed description of QP theory is beyond the scope of this book, the most instructive way to give a brief introduction is to compare it with ENVISION theory. Indeed, the two theories pay attention to complementary aspects of physical phenomena. In ENVISION, the ontological primitives are physical entities. The physics of confluences defines the possible behaviors of these entities under various circumstances, and processes are emergent properties derived from the interactions that propagate state changes among connected entities. In contrast, QP theory concentrates on processes as primitive sources of change. As shown in Figure 5.4, a *process* is defined by certain enabling conditions, by relations between some of the individual entities involved in the process, and by the influence of the process on some of these entities. Thus, activated processes influence physical entities— either *directly*, or *indirectly* by relational coupling—and the states of such entities are emergent properties determined by the combined action of the processes that influence them.

Process heat-flow

Individuals:
> source: an object, Has-Quantity(source, heat)
> destination: an object, Has-Quantity(destination, heat)
> path: a Heat-Path, Has-Connection(path, source, destination)
>
> *Individuals are physical entities and processes involved in the process under consideration. The process heat-flow involves three physical entities: a source of heat, a destination for heat, and a conductive path. As described here, the heat-flow process does not involve other processes as components.*

Preconditions:
> Heat-Aligned(path)
>
> *Preconditions enable the process but are independent of the process itself: here, heat must be able to flow though the path for the process to be possible.*

Quantity Conditions:
> A[temperature(source)] > A[temperature(source)]
>
> *Quantity conditions also enable the process but are inherent in the process: here, the temperature of the source must be greater than the temperature of the destination for the process to be active.*

Relations:
> Let flow-rate be a quantity: A[flow-rate] > ZERO
> flow-rate α_{Q+} (temperature(source) − temperature(destination))
>
> *Flow-rate is "qualitatively proportional" to the difference between the temperature of the source and the temperature of the destination; it is "positively" proportional to the difference in that it increases and decreases with it.*

> [temperature(source) α_{Q+} heat(source)]
> [temperature(destination) α_{Q+} heat(destination)]
>
> *These two relations, not explicitly stated in the original, have been added here in this specific form to make the process description self-contained (otherwise, heat-flow never stops). In general, the relation between temperature and heat is of course more complex.*

Influences:
> I−(heat(source), A[flow-rate])
> I+(heat(destination), A[flow-rate])
>
> *The heat of the source is negatively influenced by the amount of flow-rate whereas the heat of the destination is positively influenced by the amount of flow-rate.*

**Figure 5.4 The description of a process of heat transfer
(after Forbus, 1984b).**

The crucial distinction between direct and indirect influences induces a partial ordering on dependencies with respect to the origin of changes. Furthermore, neither influences nor proportional relations are commutative. Note that it is the responsibility of designers to encode these relations properly; they cannot be generated by the system the way envisionments are. Nevertheless, the resulting directionality naturally gives rise to qualitative descriptions that are in line with an intuitive notion of causality. This is possible because, in consonance with the notion of conceptual fidelity, QP theory provides tools for describing a perception of the world. Its vocabulary of primitives centers on situations (called *views*), and on processes that transform these situations. Processes and situations are perceptual abstractions to which a witness attributes historical relevance. QP thus reflects an effort to account for phenomena by means of general abstractions. Envisioning, on the other hand, tries to ground conceptual interpretations in physical structure: that is, in realities that are independent of perception. Its efforts to account for phenomena, therefore, will tend to be reductionistic, to look for structural invariants that provide a mechanistic explanation of behavior.

In sum, QP theory attempts to provide a language for encoding causality as perceived by people in general—a form of naive physics—whereas ENVISION theory attempts to provide a modeling framework for reproducing causality from structure—more in line with the concerns of experts and scientists. With respect to knowledge representation, the two approaches constitute complementary viewpoints: information distributed in one is localized in the other (de Kleer, in press). With respect to knowledge communication, these approaches constitute complementary ingredients of the ability to explain: conceptual abstractions as opposed to reductionistic grounding. This theme is further discussed in Chapter 15.

5.2   QUEST: progressions of qualitative models

QUEST (Qualitative Understanding of Electrical System Troubleshooting) is a new project being conducted at BBN by Barbara White and John Frederiksen. Like STEAMER, it is pursuing the line of research on mental models with a pedagogical application. It also shares with STEAMER the practical goal of building a learning environment centered on interactive graphic simulation for instruction about physical devices. In fact, before joining BBN, Barbara White had done her doctoral dissertation in the context of the LOGO project[4] on the subject of learning environments based on computer games. She had built a navigational game for

---

[4]See Section 7.1.

Newtonian mechanics that allowed children to refine their understanding of concepts such as "force" or "acceleration" by pushing objects in a simulated world (White, 1981). Like STEAMER, this game was based on graphic animation, but lacked an internal representation of the domain model to be communicated.

In QUEST, the principle of conceptual fidelity is carried beyond the interface into the internal representation in order to address the issue of explanations. In this sense, the project is continuing the research line of WHY even more directly than did STEAMER. Knowledge about the device—an electrical circuit—is represented internally as a qualitative model. Not only is there interest in using a qualitative model directly for instructional purposes, but the project investigates the existence of multiple models for a domain, another theme of WHY.

QUEST can also be viewed as a descendant of SOPHIE for two reasons. First, the internal representation of models uses a causal calculus based on device components that is directly influenced by de Kleer and Brown's research on qualitative reasoning. The second link is the similarity between domains and between pedagogical approaches. As in SOPHIE, the project's goal is to provide the student with a reactive learning environment in which she can solve circuit problems. In QUEST, however, graphic simulations and causal explanations of circuit behavior play a prominent role because of the emphasis placed on supporting the student's development of runnable models of electrical circuits. The goal is for the student to understand the general principles governing the behavior of these circuits so as to be able to predict the states of components and perform a small set of troubleshooting operations. To this end, the environment is to be flexible enough to allow the student to build and modify circuits while still receiving explanations of component states and demonstrations of troubleshooting.

5.2.1 Mental models: a developmental approach

White and Frederiksen build on many ideas from AI research on mental models and qualitative reasoning. However, their concern with the subject is more directly pedagogical, and their approach decidedly developmental. The theme of their work is to investigate successions of mental models that correspond to increasing levels of expertise about the principles of the domain rather than about a given device. Thus a mental model is seen as a *generic model* that can handle devices of a given level of complexity with a given level of sophistication.

These developmental progressions serve as foundations for the design of instructional systems that are explicitly geared toward transitions between models. A crucial notion here is that of *upward compatibility*, whereby early models are formed with a view to enabling later transformations: a lower-level models is adequate for a restricted set of circuit problems, but can be extended and refined with a minimum of reconsideration. The pedagogical motivation for such progressions imposes additional constraints: at one end, efforts are made to build on pre-existing knowledge, and at the other to take into consideration the purpose for which a model is acquired.

Differences between models

Some concepts for a typology of mental models are emerging from this developmental approach. White and Frederiksen (1986b) identify three dimensions along which models differ, and which determine different kinds of questions models can answer about the corresponding devices: the type, the order, and the degree of a model.[5]

- *Type*: the three types of models that White and Frederiksen are mostly concerned with are *qualitative, proportional* (using pseudo-quantitative constructs such as "greater than"), and *quantitative*. In addition to these causal/behavioral models, they also mention other types such as *structural* and *functional* (dealing with the functions of components, for instance with respect to accomplishing design intentions).

  In accord with de Kleer and Brown (1984), White and Frederiksen emphasize the importance of qualitative models as support for causal explanations. Considering both the novice and the expert, they take exception to the approach of traditional physics curricula, which emphasize the use of quantitative constraints. On the one hand, these methods are not easily connected to students' existing intuitions about physical phenomena. On the other, recent studies of problem solving have revealed that a phase of qualitative reasoning always precedes the application of quantitative methods by experts (Larkin et al., 1980; Chi et al., 1981). Thus an important pedagogical goal of the project is to create a curriculum in which situations and problems both require and motivate the use of qualitative reasoning.

  In accord with Forbus (1984b), White and Frederiksen also stress the need for maintaining *causal consistency*—that is, the need for causality to have a consistent direction. This is in contrast with the

---

[5]White and Frederiksen (1986abc) do not explicitly present the type of a model as a dimension along with order and degree. However, the notion is not new, and it underlies their discussion so clearly that its elevation to the status of an explicit dimension here is in keeping with their view.

constraints provided by equations, which lack such directionality. For instance, the algebraic formulation of a law such as $I = \frac{V}{R}$ does not enforce the important understanding that the electromotive force measured as voltage causes current, not vice versa. The fact that this understanding is consistent with finer-grained models of physical phenomena in electricity demonstrates the importance of causal consistency for upward compatibility. Redundant versions of constraints, as provided by algebraic manipulations, should thus be introduced individually in compliance with causal consistency. In the case of Ohm's law, determining voltage on the basis of current must be perceived as backward reasoning along causal chains.

- *Order*: the order of a model reflects the order of the derivatives that are used to describe changes. Thus, in the domain of electricity, a zero-order model only reasons with the presence or absence of voltages or currents, and with dramatic changes such as those caused by a switch; a first-order model can deal with variations in voltages or resistance; a second-order model is concerned with the rate of change; and so on.

  The primary motive for this decomposition into successive orders is pedagogical,[6] in that increments of complexity in terms of order support upward compatibility and generate interesting simplifications. White and Frederiksen argue for the pedagogical significance of zero-order qualitative models in reasoning about electrical circuits like the one presented in Figure 5.5. For the novice, this order provides a needed context for learning to use basic concepts like "circuit" or "conductivity." Such models also allow fairly sophisticated forms of problem solving, including troubleshooting for opens and shorts. Once these concepts have been mastered, first-order considerations can then be introduced without contradictions and be seen as a way to answer additional questions. According to White and Frederiksen, quantitative constraints should not be taught until they can be rooted in qualitative reasoning, and motivated by its limitations—for instance, in determining states of equilibrium.

- *Degree*: the degree of a model stands for its level of elaboration. Thus, within a type and an order, models can increase in sophistication by taking additional constraints into consideration. The concept of elaboration can be better understood in the light of White and Frederiksen's view of a mental model as a generic conceptualization

---

[6]There is also a subtle conceptual motive for this segregation, which is to acknowledge that higher-order qualitative models often assume a quantitative scale for the previous order, for instance by allowing multiple increments to have a cumulative effect (White and Frederiksen, 1986b).

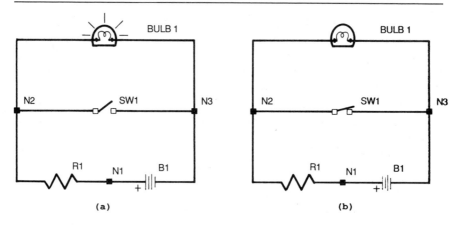

"In order for the bulb to light, there must be a voltage
drop across it. There is a device in parallel with the
bulb, the switch. Two devices in parallel have the same
voltage drop across them. Voltage drop is directly proportional to resistance: If there is no resistance, there
can be no voltage drop. Since the switch has no
resistance, there is no voltage drop across the switch.
Thus, there is no voltage drop across the light, so the
light will be off ."

**Figure 5.5 A circuit amenable to zero-order qualitative reasoning
(White and Frederiksen, 1986c).**

for a class of devices.   They see three main components to a
model:

1. *Structural information* is modeled after the representation used
   for ENVISION theory, including device topology and component
   models.   In QUEST, this circuit-specific information abides by
   the no-function-in-structure principle, in that components cannot
   refer explicitly to the states of other components or the functioning
   of the whole device. However, the way in which state transitions
   in components can affect the embedding system is different, as
   we will see shortly.

2. *Simulation and explanation principles* do not abide by the locality
   principle, but explicitly include domain-specific concepts with
   global implications. Circuit principles make use of notions such
   as "conductive path," as illustrated by the principle stated in
   Figure 5.6.   Note how such principles contrast with the single simulation principle of ENVISION theory, which is domain-
   independent and local: the two ports of a connector must have
   the same value. Thus, in ENVISION theory, components only

Zero-order voltage rule:

> **IF** there is at least one conductive path to the negative side of a voltage source from one port of the device (a return path),
>
> **and IF** there is a conductive path from another port of the device to the positive side of that voltage source (a feed path),
>
> **and IF** there is no non-resistive path branching from any point on that "feed" path to any point on any "return" path,
>
> **THEN** the device has a voltage applied to that pair of ports.

Figure 5.6 A circuit principle (after White and Frederiksen, 1986b).

affect global behavior by modifying the values of their ports. In QUEST, they modify not port values but state descriptors, which can be inspected by simulation and explanation principles that infer the values of ports. These state descriptors use domain-specific concepts such as "degree of conductivity" or "source of voltage." However, principles and state descriptors are all device-independent.

For simulations and explanations, the bridge between global concepts and local component descriptions is provided by a *topological search* process through which components can determine their states (e.g., they can find out whether there is a conductive path between a port and a voltage source). This process is similar to envisioning in that it is triggered by components and roots simulation and causality in local information about component states. The difference is that the search is driven by domain-specific concepts like "conductive loop," which describe phenomena emerging from component interactions and influencing their states, and are thus reminiscent of processes à la QP theory. This combination allows explanations to articulate domain principles beyond the functioning of a given device while still elucidating specific behaviors.[7]

3. *Control structures* are required for managing the simulation process: real-time intervals alternate with the propagation of causal

---

[7]There is a price for this use of non-local principles: causal explanations may require additional principles to disambiguate exact causal relations between components when more than one component has changed state in the previous evaluation cycle (e.g., if a bulb turns on, which other component enabled a voltage to be applied to it?).

relations, whereby components reevaluate their states in cycles until the simulation stabilizes in one global state.[8]

Further degrees of elaboration may involve increases in sophistication in all three aspects of the model: more elaborated reasoning may require more detailed component models, additional or refined principles, and/or more complex control structures.

Understanding and learning

Viewing learning about a domain as a progression of models is a natural consequence of this taxonomy of models. As the student learns, her model becomes more elaborated—changes in degree—by including further constraints. More radical transitions take place when a new order or a new type is introduced.

However, this should not suggest that there is a complete ordering of models along a progression that cycles through degrees, orders, and types. White and Frederiksen caution that true expertise cannot be assessed by a single ability such as that of predicting states. In their view, deep understanding does not consist of a single model, but is characterized by the coexistence of a set of complementary models that vary along the dimensions defined above. Of particular importance then is the ability to integrate models of various types and orders into a flexible understanding of the domain. This is a theme of ENVISION theory: via envisioning expertise integrates structural and causal models. This emphasis on the interplay of various conceptualizations is also in consonance with the notion of multiple viewpoints proposed by Stevens et al. (1979). How these various conceptualizations of the domain are related and are selected for dealing with various circumstances is still a topic for further research.

5.2.2 A learning environment for zero-order qualitative models

White and Frederiksen have implemented a learning environment based on a progression of zero-order qualitative models for electrical circuits such as the one shown in Figure 5.5. The successive models have increasing degrees of elaboration and represent one possible learning

---

[8]This succession of instantaneous causal effects is called *mythical time* in ENVISION theory (de Kleer and Brown, 1984). It induces an ordering on simultaneous events that elicits causality.

path. Evolving in parallel with device models is a sequence of troubleshooting algorithms for locating opens and shorts to ground. The progression of models can be used in multiple ways to support tutorial actions and to model the student. When a student is assumed to be at one model in the progression, the tutoring system can select problems that will induce a transition to the next model—that is, problems that can be solved by the transformed model but not by the current one. Explanations can also be pruned to concentrate on the differences between the current model and the next; this is reminiscent of the way sequences of models in planning nets concentrate on "crucial ideas" (see Section 8.4.1).

This adaptability supports a number of learning modes, allowing the student to be exposed to a variety of experiences. Two learning modes are possible when the system is in control: the student can be given problems and receive help only when in trouble (*problem-driven* mode); or she can be shown some demonstrations first, followed by exercises (*example-driven* mode). QUEST uses a variety of problem types: predicting the behavior of components, designing or modifying circuits to exhibit certain behaviors, listing faults consistent with some behavior, and locating faults. All these problems involve the use of runnable models and troubleshooting, and are indexed according to models in the underlying progression. For a given transition to a new model, however, it turned out that problems requiring the use of a transformed model were not all equally able to induce proper extensions. Thus they had to be further classified as prototypical problems, extreme examples, counterexamples, potential bug generators, and bug correctors. With this indexing of problems according to models, the student can be allowed to choose which topic she wants to learn about next, thus building her own curriculum (*student-directed* mode).

Adherence to the no-function-in-structure principle is also a crucial feature of the internal representation. As a pedagogical target, it induces models that are robust and general; as support for tutorial activities, it affords a high degree of flexibility. Because the internal representation of qualitative models is based on principles and descriptions of device components that are circuit-independent, QUEST can handle any circuit, given a topological description. Moreover, it does so within the competence of a specified degree of elaboration. Hence, there can even be an *open-ended exploration* mode: the student can build circuits and experiment with them while still receiving tutorial assistance, explanations, and demonstrations from the system.

To support this variety of interaction modes, the learning environment offers the student a number of facilities. First, at any point, the student can request an explanation of some observed behavior or a demonstration of problem solving and troubleshooting. Verbal explanations, produced by a speech synthesizer,[9] are combined with graphic animations of a circuit schematic on the visual display. This allows the student to see the behavior of components simulated as it is explained (see Figure 5.5). Also available are a circuit editor for modifying and building circuits or for introducing faults, and some troubleshooting facilities, such as a test light and temporary disconnections of subcircuits.

The system in practice: evaluation and comments

These facilities make for a rather sophisticated learning environment, which has undergone some preliminary testing with middle-school students. In pretests, these children had been found to be genuine novices lacking key concepts and exhibiting "serious misconceptions" about electrical circuits. Moreover, they did not have any troubleshooting experience. After five days of interacting individually with QUEST for one hour per day, "all seven students were able to make accurate predictions about circuit behavior and could troubleshoot for opens and shorts to ground in series circuits. They went from getting all the pretest questions wrong to getting all eight correct on the post-test" (White and Frederiksen, 1986b, p. 60). Though more thorough testing is required, the prospects seem very good.

The tests have also revealed some interesting weaknesses. The variety of problem-solving situations in which students needed help calls for more levels of explanation beyond the two available. This includes the ability both to give shorter summaries for pointed questions and to explain phenomena in greater depth, particularly in relation to the physical models of components. For teaching troubleshooting, the inventiveness exhibited by some students also calls for a more flexible algorithm based on principles rather than on fixed rules.

An interesting point about this experiment is that students were very conservative with the freedom allowed by the environment. They went with the proposed curriculum, using mostly the problem-driven and occasionally the example-driven mode, and usually doing all problems at every stage even though they had the prerogative of requesting a move to a new topic once they had mastered the current one. Whether this conservatism is due to the prevalent attitude in traditional school settings or to some feature of the experiment, it suggests that sophisticated environments such as QUEST will need to educate students explicitly about possible learning strategies.

---

[9]In the demonstration I saw, I found the monotonous voice of the synthesizer rather unpleasant, but was told that children do not mind it.

Progressions of models and knowledge communication

On the outset, students were told that there would be a new model in the system with the passage to a new topic. They were therefore motivated to acquire this model, and indeed, in subsequent interviews, their reasoning was found to be very similar to that of the last model seen. In fact, White and Frederiksen (1986c) claim that, when there was a discrepancy, "differences between the students' mental models and those that we were trying to teach were not due to the inevitability of misconceptions, but rather, were due to limitations of the learning environment." For them, it is therefore more important to refine the progressions of mental models and associated problem selection than to concentrate on diagnostic and remedial activities.

Of course, the curricular freedom allowed the student may thwart the process and yield misconceptions that will have to be repaired. It is also important to remember that the development of mental models in QUEST is targeted at effectiveness in a restricted set of problem-solving skills. Students also need to develop models of electricity as a physical phenomenon (Haertel, 1987). The central questions of integration of multiple conceptualizations, mentioned by White and Frederiksen as a key to deep understanding, is not yet addressed seriously—in particular, the issue of the meaning of concepts in electricity in the context of the student's model of the world. This conceptual integration almost inevitably involves an interactive process whereby analogies to existing concepts are tuned and implicit assumptions exposed.

Nevertheless, the claim is an important one for the field to consider: it reflects a belief that correct teaching tools based on adequate representations of knowledge could prevent misconceptions altogether. This viewpoint revives in a new context some of the highest hopes that motivated behaviorists' interest in programmed learning (Skinner, 1968). With respect to the topic of this book, the hypothesis can have very deep implications. In its mildest form, it points to the obvious necessity to make every effort to avoid the formation of misconceptions. In its most extreme form, it touches upon the very meaning of knowledge communication as an interactive process between two intelligent entities.

Summary and conclusion

The concept of mental model permeates this chapter. The abstract nature of mental models gives rise to the notion of conceptual fidelity in representing physical systems. In STEAMER, this principle governs the design of a graphic interface that makes the mental model of a complex steam plant inspectable for instructional purposes. The theme of abstraction also informs the tutorial facilities that were designed on top of STEAMER.

Since conceptual fidelity is applied only to the interface, the research on mental models has demonstrated its relevance to the design of useful artifacts even before its own results have matured to the point at which they can be directly implemented. Practically, STEAMER is important because it has stimulated much interest in the development of object-oriented graphic simulations for training (e.g., Munro et al., 1985; Woolf et al., 1986). Not only do these simulations provide trainees with rather realistic experiences that the cost of actual systems may otherwise prohibit, but conceptual fidelity combined with interaction adds a further pedagogical dimension. According to Stevens et al. (1983), "it is difficult to describe, in a way that can be truly appreciated, just how effective this interactive inspectable simulation can be."

STEAMER has also inspired theoretical investigations into the notion of qualitative reasoning and explanations, leading to the formulation of Qualitative Process theory. The parallel with SOPHIE holds interest beyond mere historical evolution. A comparison between QP and ENVI-SION theories has revealed two complementary ontologies: one is based on physical systems and their components viewed as devices; the other is based on physical processes and situations. We have suggested that these two positions also reflect different but complementary views on what it means to explain.

In QUEST, the issue of explanations based on qualitative models reaches the point at which research finds a direct application in a learning environment centered on a simulated circuit. The simulation is basically component-oriented, but it does provide some of the advantages of process-oriented simulations by incorporating some higher-level concepts with which to guide the evaluations of component states. While locality in a strict sense is not preserved, the no-function-in-structure is complied with because component descriptions need not be directly committed to specific values for ports. Instead, they use domain-specific concepts such as conductivity that inform simulation principles about their treatment of input. This is a crucial difference, which resolves some difficulties with the representation used in ENVISION theory (see footnote 6 in Section 4.6); however, this nonlocality requires a restricted domain and fairly straightforward devices when compared to the complex feedback mechanisms to which ENVISION theory has been applied.

From a pedagogical standpoint, the resulting system is capable of cogent explanations without sacrificing flexibility. In fact, the learning environment is so flexible that a number of learning modes are supported, including exploratory modes by which the student enjoys a great deal of control. The theme of the project is to develop progressions of mental models, which define possible curricula and around which problems and explanations can be organized. The need to differentiate between models has produced helpful classificatory dimensions. The extent to which these progressions can become programmed learning paths that obviate the need for diagnosis and remediation becomes an important question for theories of knowledge communication.

Bibliographical notes

There is no complete overview of the STEAMER project in the open literature. The most often cited reference is the overview paper by Hollan, Hutchins, and Weitzman (1984), which concentrates on the graphic aspect, and discusses conceptual fidelity. This bias reflects the more recent direction taken by these researchers who want to produce a general theory of the use of graphic interfaces to allow "direct manipulations" (Hutchins et al., 1985; Hollan et al., 1986). Stevens, Roberts, and Stead (1983) more specifically report on STEAMER's graphic editor. The tutorial capabilities are described in (Stevens and Roberts, 1983). An early overview of the project's agenda can be found in (Williams, Hollan, and Stevens, 1981).

Forbus and Stevens (1981) report on the early use of STEAMER's simulation to explicate the functioning of devices in detail. The general nature of explanations in connection with simulations is also investigated by Weld (1983). Stevens and Steinberg (1981) develop a typology of explanations derived from an analysis of instruction manuals. STEAMER's minilab is described in (Forbus, 1984a). The reference for QP theory is a long but worthwhile article by Forbus (1984b). For a comparison of various approaches to qualitative modeling, see (de Kleer, in press).

An interesting reflection on the issue of mental models in training is proposed by Rouse and Morris (1985). Recent work inspired by STEAMER includes the graphic authoring system of the IMTS project (Intelligent Maintenance Training System), discussed in (Munro et al., 1985; Towne et al., 1987), and the RECOVERY BOILER tutor, a simulation-based training system for emergency responses, presented in (Woolf et al., 1986).

Early papers by White and Frederiksen (1984, 1985) introduce the QUEST model. For a complete description of the learning environment, see one of the two reports (White and Frederiksen, 1986a and b), (1986b) being the most comprehensive. A good summary is provided by a conference paper (White and Frederiksen, 1986c). White's dissertation (1981) presents her work on Newtonian physics, a domain to which she intends to apply the notion of model progression.

The reader interested in the development of mental models may want to look at some related work. DiSessa (1983) explains the evolution of common-sense models of physical phenomena in terms of phenomenological primitives (e.g., result is effort "over" resistance), and in terms of the circumstances in which these primitives are called upon to explain the world. Haertel (1987) provides an insightful discussion of pedagogical issues involved in providing students with accurate qualitative models of electricity. The reader specifically interested in electrical circuits may also want to read about the THEVENIN project (Joobbani and Talukdar, 1985), an attempt to build a tutoring system for electrical circuit analysis. Another system, MHO, is presented in the next chapter.

Chapter 6

Existing CAI traditions: other early contributions

This chapter presents some contributions by two separate lines of research whose early ties to the field evolved out of established CAI traditions. Both projects had been in existence before SCHOLAR came out, and they made their contributions via their own natural development as they were trying to make their systems more sophisticated. This has often resulted in an interest in sophisticated algorithms for pedagogical decisions with less emphasis on models of the target expertise.

One line of research, conducted at the Institute for Mathematical Studies in the Social Sciences at Stanford University (IMSSS), was geared toward the production of complete curricula for use in real settings. The other, at the University of Leeds in England, led to interest in the automation of intelligent teaching decisions.

6.1   Early attempts to tailor problem-solving experiences

IMSSS has had a long tradition of research in educational computer use with the inspiration of Patrick Suppes; systems have been developed for teaching in such varied domains as logic, axiomatic mathematics, and foreign languages. IMSSS researchers have also attacked some important practical questions, like computer speech generation with their system MISS (for Micro-programmed Speech Synthesizer). In spite of its central importance to the development of CAI, much of this work is not directly relevant to the purpose of this book, and the reader is referred to a collection of papers for further information (Suppes, 1981).

Even though the three systems developed at IMSSS and covered in this section may not seem very typical of the ITS paradigm, they have had some direct influence on the field. We will survey EXCHECK, a proof checker that uses natural inference methods, and two systems primarily concerned with selecting appropriate exercises from a pool of prestored problems. The first one is a tutor for symbolic integration that represents domain knowledge by means of numerical methods. The second one is a tutor for novice programmers that optimizes the sequencing of programming tasks with a symbolic representation of a curriculum. Without going into details, we should also mention the LOGIC course, based on a first-order logic theorem prover (Goldberg and Suppes, 1976), which has been used extensively at Stanford, and a grading system that applies some natural-language processing principles to check the syntactic correctness of German sentences in a test (Levine, 1981). A distinguishing feature of projects conducted at IMSSS is the attention given to large experiments with systems in teaching contexts, and to gathering and analyzing data about their performance.

6.1.1   EXCHECK: understanding natural proof procedures

Like the LOGIC course, EXCHECK has formed the core of an undergraduate course at Stanford for many years (McDonald, 1981). It is thus one of the rare systems described in this book that have actually gone beyond the experimental stage to be used regularly for instruction. Although this is quite remarkable, it should be mentioned that EXCHECK lacks a number of the features of intelligent tutoring systems mentioned in Part I. Its curriculum in axiomatic set theory is built in as a predefined succession of lessons through which the student goes, interacting with the system as he constructs the proofs attached as exercises to each lesson. EXCHECK follows the student's proof locally, but it does not form a global model of the student; nor does it have pedagogical strategies to make its interventions contextually relevant and effective. It communicates with the student via a simple formal language of abbreviations that does not require complex processing. Figure 6.1 presents a proof done by a student with EXCHECK as well as the informal summary produced by the system.

Natural proof procedures: a learning environment with informed feedback

The interest of EXCHECK for our purpose lies in its attempt to follow the student's proof in terms of natural procedures that closely reflect the human approach to theorem proving (Smith et al., 1975; Smith and Blaine, 1976). These procedures are quite different from the logically and syntactically detailed—but semantically "boring"—inference mechanisms resorted to by typical computer-based theorem provers. People are more interested in merely stating the central ideas of a proof. Thus, as a proof checker for instructional use, EXCHECK must be able to understand a human student's informal reasoning in the course of a proof, including the use of well-understood lemmas and the skipping of "obvious" steps.

The inference procedures implemented in EXCHECK (Blaine, 1981) are the result of a careful analysis of informal mathematical reasoning. Informal reasoning may not seem amenable to mechanical verifications; however, the definition of these procedures shows that such reasoning can be cast in terms of operators that are manipulable in a logically rigorous way. Because the operators are few, the students can state their intentions to the system in a simple and natural language. Yet these operators represent procedures much more complex than the simple inference steps of logic-based theorem provers. In particular, they must have access to some domain-specific knowledge required to extract the central ideas of proofs. In practice, they are implemented as macro-operators on an underlying first-order logic theorem prover.

Although it has a fixed curriculum, EXCHECK allows some freedom in the sequence of exercises traversed by students. In addition to following the proofs required in the fixed lessons, EXCHECK can supervise exercises that require the student to construct sets when given a membership condition. EXCHECK can also be used in a *play* mode where the student can try to prove any formula or theorem that falls within the subject matter covered in the curriculum. These capabilities reflect the proof checker's flexibility.

While EXCHECK's proof-building operators are primarily used to communicate the steps of a proof to the system, they also constitute the building blocks of a model of informal mathematical reasoning for the domain of axiomatic set theory. Blaine and Smith (1977) view an explicit definition of such models as an important contribution to

EXCHECK: `Derive:   If A ⊂ B then ¬(B ⊆ A)`

> *The student is asked to derive a simple theorem. EXCHECK will complete the student's input to save typing; this is indicated in all capitals.*

Student: `hyp (1)`

EXCHECK: `A ⊂ B`

> *The hypothesis of the theorem is assumed. The goal is automatically reset to the consequent of the theorem.*

Student: `raa`

> *The student begins an indirect proof; the command 'raa' is a mnemonic for reductio ad absurdum.*

EXCHECK: `assume (2) B ⊆ A`

> *The program assumes the negation of the current goal. The goal is now any contradiction.*

Student: `1defINITION`

EXCHECK: `Number or Name?`

Student: `proPER SUBSET`

EXCHECK: `1 Df. proper subset (3) A ⊆ B and A ≠ B`

> *The definition of proper subset is applied to line 1.*

Student: `2,3estABLISH`

Student: `B = A`

EXCHECK: `2,3 Establish (4) B = A`

> *The student asks the theorem prover to check the simple set-theoretic inference.*

Student: `3,4conTRADICTION`

EXCHECK: `Using`

Student: `ok`

> *The student indicates that lines 3 and 4 lead to a contradiction.*

EXCHECK: `3,4 Contradiction (5) B ¬⊆ A`

> *EXCHECK returns the negation of assumption 2.*

Student: `qed`

EXCHECK: `Correct`

> *EXCHECK accepts the derivation; it also prints out the following review of the proof for the student to keep a clear picture of what has been done:*

```
Derive:   If A ⊂ B then ¬(B ⊆ A)
Assume (1) A ⊂ B
By raa show:  ¬(B ⊆ A)
Assume (2) B ⊆ A
From 1, by definition of proper subset,
    (3) A ⊆ B and A ≠ B
From 2,3 it follows that (4) A = B
3,4 lead to a contradiction; hence, assumption 2 is
    false:  (5) ¬(B ⊆ A)
```

**Figure 6.1 A simple proof understood by EXCHECK
(Blaine, 1982).**

AI by ITS researchers involved with complex curricula, where much knowledge about reasoning processes has been accumulated in various domains. In this sense, EXCHECK has a definite ITS flavor, although the complete models of expertise and learning that Blaine and Smith talk about are still largely implicit in EXCHECK's predefined curriculum. Thus EXCHECK cannot be said to possess the knowledge of its domain in enough depth to teach it. Like SOPHIE-I, it provides an interface to an opaque underlying representation; this results in a friendly environment for students, who can receive intelligent—albeit local—feedback, and have their work verified in terms they can understand. For the domain of mathematical proofs, this is a nontrivial achievement.

6.1.2 A probabilistic model for judgmental knowledge

The doctoral dissertation that Ralph Kimball (1973, 1982) completed in the early seventies was ahead of its time in its use of an interaction between domain knowledge and a student model to guide the construction of a teaching sequence. Judging by how infrequently it is referred to in other work, however, it did not receive the recognition it deserves. The purpose of this tutor is to communicate its judgmental knowledge while the student is solving a sequence of example problems selected from a fixed archive. The domain is symbolic integration,[1] chosen precisely because the expertise needed for solving problems is of a judgmental nature (versus algorithmic for, say, arithmetic). Yet because this knowledge is well documented, it is possible to group problems into classes for which certain approaches can be recommended.

Numerical representation of expertise

The INTEGRATION tutor has an unusual way of using probabilistic values to represent judgmental knowledge. Domain expertise is represented as a matrix that relates all problem classes to all solution methods. Each matrix element is a value indicating the probability of applying a given problem-solving approach to a given problem class, thus generating a subproblem in a new class. Of course it is assumed that the student uses the same classification for problems as does the expert, and that the student knows the different approaches (e.g., integration by parts). But within this probabilistic representation of expertise, the system can be

---

[1]For easy reference, this tutoring system will be called the INTEGRATION tutor in this book, though this is not an official name.

said to have an explicit characterization of the teaching goal in the form of a matrix representing expertise. The student's state of knowledge is represented as a similar matrix, whose values can readily be compared to those of the expert.

New problems are selected on the basis of a metric for the difference between the student's and the expert's respective approaches. Since this metric is tuned to favor the selection of problems for which the expected distance between the two approaches is maximal, topics are chosen in a "breadth-first" rather than in a focused fashion. As far as teaching strategies are concerned, all the tutor can do is to give advice according to its own approach probabilities. However, it momentarily accepts unexpected or unusual approaches proposed by the student, the mean and variance of problem length (number of steps) determining a time threshold. In addition, an "alarm" threshold leads to occasional remedial phases, which take the form of a problem solved by the expert. Figure 6.2 presents an excerpt from a session with the INTEGRATION tutor. The simple language interface basically consists of multiple-choice questions. This is possible because the tutor always maintains full control over the interaction.

For diagnosis, the system simply updates the probabilities in the student's matrix with methods from probability theory. When problem classes occur for the first time, ad hoc heuristics generate a seed probability. Kimball claims that the probabilistic approach allows precise measurements of student learning revealing its discontinuities. He suggests that the identification of these discontinuities, which are apparently associated with failures, is an important pedagogical task. Kimball goes into a lengthy technical argument to support the applicability of his probabilistic approach to modeling the student, mainly from the standpoint of the independence of the probabilities associated with the various approaches. Many of his concerns actually apply to other modular representations, such as rule-based ones, used more recently for student modeling.

Learning by adapting probabilistic values

A unique feature of the INTEGRATION tutor is that its domain expertise can improve in the course of a tutorial session. If the student's approach leads to a better solution than the trace stored in the expert's archive, the system adopts the student's solution as its standard: hence the label of *self-improving* sometimes given this tutor. Surprisingly, students who actually experimented with the system contributed many improvements to the expert's archive, which Kimball had thought to represent a level of expertise well beyond theirs. It even turned out that many contributions came from "average" students, a strong argument in favor of tutors with a capacity to learn while teaching.

$\vdots$

Tutor: Ok, Ruth, our integral is $\int X\log(X)dX$. What shall we do to solve it?

Student: sub

Tutor: Can you think of a substitution? (Yes, Help or Exit)

Student: yes

Tutor: Let U =

Student: log(X)

Tutor: Ok, Ruth, we will let $U = \log(X)$. Thus $X = e^U$ and $dX = e^U\, dU$ which we substituted into the integrand. Our new integral is now $\int Ue^{2U}\, dU$. Please type Good, Bad or Giveup:

Student: bad

Tutor: Can you think of a substitution? (Yes, Help or Exit)

Student: help

Tutor: I can't find a suitable substitution. Will exit ...
Ok, Ruth, our integral is $\int X\log(X)dX$. What shall we do to solve it?

Student: help

Tutor: I suggest you try integration by parts. What shall we do to solve it?

Student: parts

Tutor: Integration by parts! We shall use the notation $\int UdV = UV - \int VdU$. Can you think of a choice for U? (Yes, Help or Exit)

Student: help

Tutor: How about letting $U = \log(X)$.

$\vdots$

Figure 6.2 Excerpt from a session with the INTEGRATION tutor (Kimball, 1982).

Though this simple learning ability is an attractive feature, its very simplicity is also symptomatic of the restricted knowledge content of the representation of expertise. Although Kimball's matrices can certainly model the external behavior manifested by knowledge in the domain, the probabilistic values are totally ignorant of the large sets of reasons and beliefs they summarize. In some ways, these reasons and beliefs are more important for real expertise than the behavior they generate; thus it is doubtful that probabilities by themselves can support intelligent knowledge communication.

As a matter of fact, we will see later that this selection of a solution method for a problem is an instance of a more general problem-solving paradigm, called *classification* by Clancey (see Chapter 12). Clancey found that even the rules of an expert system are an insufficiently detailed representation of problem-solving knowledge for the purposes of an instructional system. Here explanations are even more compromised, since probabilities merely reproduce the results obtained from the processing of such rules. However, the dialogue in Figure 6.2 suggests that, in practice, a reasonable tutorial interaction can be achieved with probabilities as long as explanations are not required.

6.1.3   BIP: curriculum information networks

BIP (for Basic Instructional Program) is presented as a "problem-solving laboratory" for introductory programming classes (Barr et al., 1976). It attempts to individualize the sequence of instruction via the appropriate selection of successive tasks from a pool of 100 sample problems. In contrast with Kimball's distance metric on probabilistic values, BIP bases its selection on information contained in a network, called the Curriculum Information Network (CIN), that relates tasks in the curriculum to issues in the domain knowledge.

BIP-I: layered curriculum organization

A simplified portion of BIP-I's curriculum information network is displayed in Figure 6.3. The curriculum is divided into three conceptual layers. At the top are central issues of expertise, called *techniques*, which must be ordered in advance according to the prerequisite relation. In practice this is often a simple linear ordering, but the network representation allows for more complex hierarchies. These techniques are composed of lower-level knowledge units called *skills*. The sets of skills corresponding to the various techniques are neither internally ordered nor mutually disjoint. Finally, skills are related to various tasks that exercise them.

In BIP-I, the student model is defined only in terms of the skills, though in general other levels could be used as well. Associated with each skill is a pair of numerical values. One value stands for the system's estimate of the student's mastery of the skill and is updated by very simple techniques according to his performance on each task. The other stands for the student's own estimate of his understanding and is updated in the course of a short interview following each exercise. Since problem selection takes both values into account, this is an interesting, albeit simple, combination of inferential and interactive diagnosis.

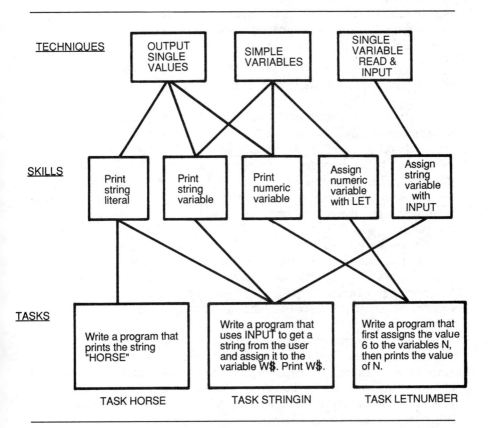

Figure 6.3 A simplified portion of BIP-I's CIN (Barr et al., 1976).

The problem selection performed by BIP-I is a fairly straightforward optimization process. The method is first to construct the set of the skills to be exercised according to the curriculum's hierarchy and the student model. Then another set is constructed to contain the skills that may be included in a problem because they are sufficiently mastered. Finally, the goal is to find the problem that exercises the greatest number of skills in the required set without including any skills beyond the student's reach. Further discrimination is afforded by the order of the techniques to which the skills under consideration are attached, the priority being of course given to early skills. If no problem can be found for a given combination of skills, then a "hole" in the curriculum has been uncovered, requiring the addition of a new problem.

In the tradition of the IMSSS, BIP-I's task selection strategy was tested in controlled experiments, in which it was compared in actual use to a version of the same tutor that employed the predetermined branching typical of CAI. Apparently, both groups of students scored equally well on the post-test, but data collected on-line during instruction showed a "significant improvement" in the quality of the learning process for the BIP-I group, in that the number of problems successfully completed was substantially higher.

BIP-II: pedagogically organized information

BIP-II (Wescourt, Beard, and Gould, 1977) refines and augments the information contained in the curriculum information network. The skills required for one technique are still grouped into sets, but this time, instead of being unordered, these sets are themselves organized as networks. The skills are connected by links representing pedagogical information in addition to prerequisite relations, including analogical relations, class-object relations, functional dependencies, and relative difficulty.

To avoid redundancies, however, these relations are not entered directly into the CIN. Instead they are contained in a second network whose nodes are the primitive elements of the domain. In this approach to teaching programming in Basic, the nodes represent syntactic language constructs. These primitive elements are linked according to the relations listed above. Figure 6.4 presents a simplified portion of such a network of primitive elements for Basic. Since the skills in BIP-II are described in terms of these primitive elements, they inherit the relations linking their respective constituents. For instance, a skill that requires a conditional control structure is harder than a skill that only requires an unconditional one, since the two structures are linked by a pointer indicating increasing difficulty, as shown in the figure.

The system's other aspects are basically the same as in BIP-I, particularly the task selection procedure, which uses the same set-based approach. Of course, because of the refined representation of the curriculum, it can be more precise in its construction of the set of skills that need exercising. Apparently the sequences proposed by BIP-II are significantly different from those proposed by the selection procedure of BIP-I, especially if the student performs well initially. Although the authors mention the leverage that the new links provide in inferring the student's knowledge, their real potential for use in diagnosis and remediation has not been explored.

Problem-solving guidance: limited diagnostic information

As an intelligent programming tutor, BIP is admittedly incomplete. The only form of advice it can give the student consists of hints stored with the different tasks, since it has no knowledge of design, coding or debugging. Furthermore, its feedback to the student is limited by its

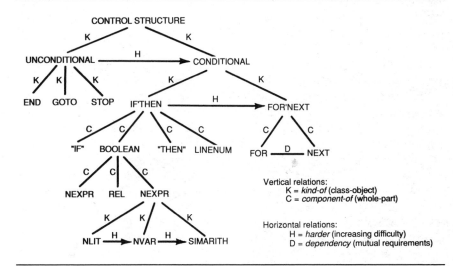

**Figure 6.4 Portion of the network of syntactic elements in Basic
(Wescourt et al., 1977).**

inability to diagnose logical errors. When a program has been completed,
BIP simply tests it on a set of input/output pairs without any analysis of
the algorithm, as do systems presented in Chapter 11. After a syntactic
match on keywords has revealed the use or absence of certain constructs
designated as necessary or forbidden for the task, the student is merely
informed about language constructs that should or shouldn't have been
used.

6.2 Pedagogical experiments: teaching expertise

In England, there has always been much interest in the educational use
of computers. The Open University, for instance, has for some time
been running large experiments with distributed computer-based courses.
While SCHOLAR was being developed at BBN, a group at the Computer-
based Learning Project at the University of Leeds was coming to similar
conclusions after working on advanced CAI systems for teaching medical
diagnosis and arithmetic operations. In a paper that could be considered
the British counterpart of Carbonell's classic, Hartley and Sleeman (1973)
try to define some characteristics of "intelligent teaching systems." Their
central theme is the generation of intelligent pedagogical decisions. Like
Carbonell, Hartley and Sleeman propose a taxonomy of instructional

programs; but whereas Carbonell's distinction is essentially based on the separate representation of domain knowledge, Hartley and Sleeman's classification into four classes concentrates on features of the teaching process.

Hartley and Sleeman's *prestructured* systems correspond to Carbonell's frame-oriented ones. But between traditional CAI and ITS, they see the intermediate type of *generative* systems which are programmed to generate tasks by piecing problems together in a simple way. Finally, they divide intelligent tutoring systems into two nondisjoint categories. In *adaptive* systems, instructional actions to be performed are selected under the guidance of means-end rules and according to heuristic teaching strategies. Some of these systems are even classified as *self-improving* because they refine their knowledge by evaluating their own performance. Possible improvements can cover domain knowledge (e.g., the INTEGRATION tutor), or teaching strategies (see the QUADRATIC tutor in this section), in which case they can be either general or specific to particular students.

Further work by Sleeman on student models will be described in Chapter 9. Here we report on some pioneering work by two of his students, who investigate the teaching process with two complementary approaches. Tim O'Shea is interested in the design of self-improving systems that monitor their own performance, and John Self attempts to define teaching decisions formally in terms of a student model. More recently, O'Shea and Self (1983) teamed up to write a book on educational implications of AI research (see bibliographical notes of Chapter 1).

6.2.1   Self-improving tutors: tuning strategies empirically

O'Shea and Sleeman (1973) observe that, while intelligent tutoring systems often have the advantage of an explicit set of tutorial strategies, these strategies are always fixed. This leaves no room for improvement by the system itself even though the progress of students does provide feedback on the teaching performance. The tutor we describe here was constructed by O'Shea for his doctoral dissertation (1979a, 1979b)[2] as a first attempt at giving a tutoring system some ability to set up experiments using variations of its strategies and to adopt those that seem to produce the best results. After briefly outlining the tutor itself to provide the necessary background, we concentrate on its self-improving mechanisms.

---

[2] Although the publication dates are recent, the actual work was done in the early seventies.

The QUADRATIC tutor

The domain is the solution of simple quadratic equations[3] of the form $x^2 + c = bx$, whose answers can be obtained by clever guesses and with the help of a few rules. These rules are simple applications of Vieta's general root theorem, which states that b is the sum of the equation's two solutions and that c is their product. The tutor presents example problems on the basis of which students are to discover and master the rules. Figure 6.5 shows an excerpt from a session with the QUADRATIC tutor. Besides the self-improving capabilities, an accomplishment worth mentioning even for this simple domain is that students in the experiments apparently enjoyed learning with the system very much, and improved their performances dramatically.

The tutor has two tasks: it must select appropriate examples from an archive of problems, then tutor the student by providing him with comments and hints, and possibly by interrupting him if he takes too long. For these tasks, the system considers three sources of information: its task difficulty matrix, its student model, and its tutorial strategies. The *task difficulty matrix* is used in the selection of new problems. It relates specific features in a problem to well-defined teaching goals, like the need to practice an individual rule. It is fixed for the domain. The *student model* is a set of hypotheses about the student's current mastery of each of the few rules he must learn plus some combinations of them (a diagnostic scheme called an overlay in Section 7.4.2); it is regularly updated. The *teaching strategies* are the core of the tutor, and they are represented as a set of production rules, a representation chosen because such declarative schemes are more amenable to automatic manipulation.

Self-improvement by experimentation

The self-improvement facilities deal only with the teaching strategies and tune parameters that govern trade-offs between conflicting goals in the teaching task. For instance, when generating a sequence of examples, one must not only reinforce acquired rules by presenting confirming examples, but also push towards the discovery of new rules by presenting situations in which the old rules do not apply. Other parameters that can be modified include the frequency of encouraging remarks, the number of guesses allowed before the system gives out the solution, and other limits on the tutor's patience. Finally, the system can monitor the effort

---

[3]For easy reference, we will call this system the QUADRATIC tutor in this book, although this is not an official name.

⋮

Tutor: Consider the equation $x^2 + 18 = 19x$. Guess the answers.

Student: 3

Tutor: Nope, keep trying.

Student: 6,12,2,3

Tutor: Nope, keep trying.

Student: 4,5,6,7,8,9,10

Tutor: You are not trying to think of any rules to help you. We will look at another example. Try to find a rule. The right answers are in fact 1 and 18. Consider the equation $x^2 + 48 = 19x$. Guess the answers.

Student: 1,18,12,48,19,64,9,2

Tutor: Nope

Student: 3

Tutor: That's right. See if you can get the other answer.

Student: 6

Tutor: Nope, keep trying.

Student: 3

Tutor: Yes, but you have guessed that correctly before

Student: 15,18,9,1

Tutor: Nope. That's a lot of guesses. Let's try another example. The right answers are in fact 3 and 16

⋮

Figure 6.5 Excerpt from a session with the QUADRATIC tutor (O'Shea, 1979b).

it expends in optimizing its performance by varying the time it spends on two teaching tasks: forming a more or less accurate student model by testing diagnostic hypotheses, and generating more or less appropriate examples by matching problem features with pedagogical requirements.

For improvements to be possible, not only is it necessary to have an explicit and modular representation of the strategies, but the *tutorial objectives* must also be clearly defined. The instructional experiments embodied in the variations of the system's parameters revolve around four distinct tutorial goals:

1. to increase the number of students completing the session;

2. to improve their scores on the post-test;

3. to decrease the time taken by students to learn all four rules and their combinations;

4. to decrease the computer time used in the process.

The foundation for the experimentation process is a *database of assertions* which O'Shea calls a "theory of instruction" for the domain.   Each assertion in the database indicates the expected results of a specific experimental modification performed on the production rules. Results are expressed in terms of possible or definite effects on teaching performance with respect to one goal. For instance, an assertion could say that spending more resources on selecting appropriate problems might improve the performance of students on the post-test. Thus these assertions represent a corpus of possibly useful experiments.

After choosing one of the four goals, the system selects all the assertions that propose modifications leading to a possible improvement with respect to that goal; then it executes the changes these assertions suggest. Statistical tests evaluate the variations in performance caused by the modifications, with respect to each of the four goals. The overall improvement of the system is then computed as a linear function of the goals' respective variations. If a significant improvement is achieved, the modifications are adopted. In addition, as a form of learning involving some serendipity, new assertions are added to the original database to record the effects of the experiment on the different goals. In this way, not only does the system improve, but its ability to set up experiments is also extended. Obviously, it must have had a minimal number of assertions to start with. Figure 6.6 gives an overview of the flow of information through the self-improving component.

Empirical versus analytical learning

The experiments with modifications of the teaching strategies yielded results that were encouraging but not extremely significant in view of the possibly insufficient statistical evaluations that were used. According to O'Shea, optimal sequences of experiments turned out to be difficult to determine because modifications are not independent of one another. In particular, the database of assertions ignores interactions between the modifications made to the production rules on the one hand, and the certainty values of its assertions on the other. It may well happen that an assertion predicting a certain result from a change in strategies is no longer true after some other modifications have been performed. In light of these difficulties, O'Shea suggests that this self-improving mechanism may be best suited for a scheme whereby the system sets up its experiments in cooperation with human teachers.

It is worthwhile spending some time considering this self-improving paradigm because it is of considerable generality as a learning mecha-

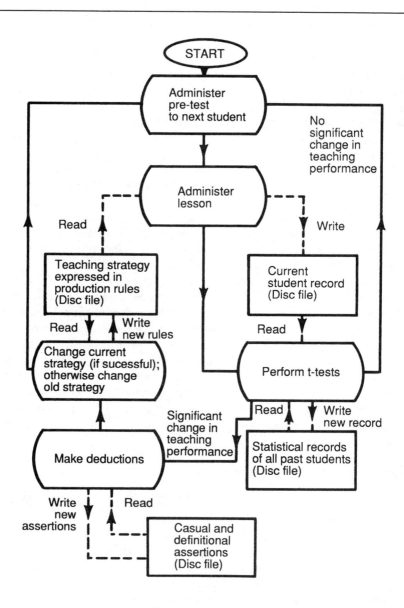

Figure 6.6 Schematic diagram of the self-improving component (O'Shea, 1979b).

nism. Although it is based on earlier work in AI, O'Shea's notion of recording the results of learning with assertions that can themselves induce further learning is an interesting contribution. It has a very attractive "bootstrapping" flavor unusual in machine learning. Another central characteristic is that the learning taking place via the self-improving mechanisms is purely empirical. Indeed, it is guided only by statistical evaluations of the results of experiments, never by a causal analysis, since it is not based on an explicit learning theory accounting for the student's discovery process.

With a representation of tutorial strategies in the form of rules— rather than of general principles—learning is empirical because it is impossible to reason about rules without knowing the principles they embody. This is probably the most fundamental limitation of the system, and could well explain such difficulties as its inability to detect interactions between experiments. Its empirical nature is also the reason it cannot generate qualitatively new behaviors, but only tune existing strategies. Now this observation does not mean that O'Shea's approach is invalid. Much research in the field of education is by necessity empirical, because current learning theories fail to account precisely for many essential ingredients of human knowledge acquisition. In this context, such experiments can yield very useful results. Therefore, O'Shea's attempt at automating a process that is difficult even for people is an important contribution, but it must be placed in proper perspective to be understood. When he says that his database of assertions represents a "theory of instruction" for the domain, it is even better than that—it is a theory that contains the seeds of its own evolution. Essentially, however, it is an empirical theory of instruction.

6.2.2   Concept teaching: a formal analytical approach

Quite a few years before the idea was actually applied in systems such as BUGGY and LMS (see coming chapters), Self had already proposed a procedural paradigm for the student model. At that time, the student's state of knowledge was usually recorded as an evaluation of performance and was represented by sets of numerical registers, by stochastic models, or by tags as in SCHOLAR. In contrast, Self (1974) stresses the advantages of implementing a student model as a set of programs that would be able to predict observed answers. He mentions possible improvements in the quality of feedback and remedial actions made possible by an explicit representation of the student's procedure. He also suggests that task difficulty could then be measured from the student's perspective in terms of the complexity of the required procedure. This could be derived from a comparison of the student model with the expert. Finally, the system's teaching objectives could be explicitly stated in terms of the expected content of the student model.

The program Self offers as an example is a small, admittedly rudimentary version of a Socratic tutor. Self acknowledges some of the problems that a procedural model presents, including its potentially poor descriptive value and the difficulty of comparing programs and defining measures. In fact, current runnable student models do not really follow Self's vision since maintaining a purely procedural model dynamically can be equivalent to automatic programming, a notoriously difficult AI problem. Nevertheless, these ideas were ahead of their time and have had much influence on later research.

Teaching and learning models

Self's vision of formalizing teaching in terms of a student model is given a sharp focus in his work on concept teaching (Self, 1977). Unfortunately, this elegant piece of research has not been given the recognition it deserves, in spite of its unique AI flavor. It differs from other projects by being a formal experiment on teaching rather than a teaching system. The domain is the acquisition of simple conjunctive concepts in a relational language close to first-order logic. An example of the concepts taught by Self's system would be $R(x) \wedge \neg T(y)$ ("There is a rectangle and no triangle").[4] The target concept is taught through successive variable-free examples classified as positive or negative instances. For example, the tutor could say that $R(a) \wedge T(b)$ ("There is a rectangle a and a triangle b") is a negative example. Since the order in which the sequence of instances is presented greatly influences the time the student takes to converge on the correct concept, the idea is for the teacher to use a learning model to optimize its selection of examples.

First, Self presents a *concept learning program*. The program takes as input the classified examples in the sequence, then forms a bounded set of weighted hypotheses, and manages this set until it reduces to a singleton containing the correct concept. This is a rather standard AI learning system, except that the management of the set of hypotheses is conducted by heuristic operators rather than by a formal learning theory. In reality, the teaching sequence consists not of single instances but of small sets of instances from which the learning program selects one. Thus, the learning program is given the unusual ability to select the instance with the greatest expected information content with respect to its current hypotheses.

---

[4]By established conventions, x and y are variables, whereas a and b are constants.

Now, the only duty of the corresponding *concept teaching program* is to select the small sets to be presented at each iteration from a pool of prestored classified instances. Its objective is to find the sequence that will minimize the time elapsed between the presentation of the first instances and the last error in classification. To this end, it maintains a model of the student's set of hypotheses (exactly how the model is inferred is left unspecified). In addition to a definition of the target concept, it is given a model of its student's learning mechanisms. Hence it can select the instances by which its learning model would minimize the difference between its student model's set of hypotheses and the correct concept. This difference must be computed according to some distance measure, which can be very difficult to determine. Of course, the teaching system's effectiveness will depend not only on the quality of this measure, but also on the accuracy of its learning model and of its model of the student's set of hypotheses.

The value of formal experiments

Self's system remains a laboratory experiment: it admittedly operates in an unrealistic toy domain, and does not address many difficult issues, notably diagnosis. The selection of examples is of course only one small subtask in the process of teaching, and Self's program does not interact with the student at all. Because it merely selects instances from a small repertoire, it can exhaustively search this repertoire each time. It does not attempt to generate optimal tasks given a goal and a student model. It also makes the simplifying assumption that the student's strategies in managing its set of hypotheses are fixed. This greatly simplifies the modeling task, and allows the optimization of the teaching sequence to be determined by object-level considerations only. Most important, the learning takes place in a complete vacuum, as is typical of early work in machine learning. Concepts are acquired in isolation from their semantic implications and their connections to a large body of existing knowledge.

As a developing field, however, ITS needs more of this type of laboratory work. Because the pragmatic needs that motivate ITS research are very concrete and immediate, formal experiments tend to look useless. In the long run, however, research on a precise definition of teaching in computational terms is as important as engineering feats. In Self's system, the explicit representation of the teaching goal and the explicit relation of the student model to that goal via a learning model give an interesting computational definition of optimal teaching actions. Although it is not presented as a self-improving system, Self's program contrasts with O'Shea's in that the tutor has access to a formal learning model. Thus its search for optimal teaching actions is analytical rather than being based on empirical experiments. Of course, its analysis is quite rudimentary, since it is an exhaustive search. It only deals with a toy domain, generating simplistic actions, and it only considers the information-theoretic content of examples. But long before expert systems made AI attractive to practical users, seminal research was done in the closed worlds of small blocks and theorem-provers.

Summary and conclusion

The projects at IMSSS were motivated more by interest in educational issues than in artificial intelligence. This pragmatic attitude has resulted in an emphasis on testing the effectiveness of basic design decisions in real settings with statistical methods. As an early system EXCHECK is somewhat of a classic, because it has proved useful in regular classroom environments. Like SOPHIE-I, it creates an intelligent interface with a powerful but obscure model of domain expertise in an attempt to provide a learning environment in which the student can receive feedback during problem solving. To this end, it emulates human proof techniques with macro-operators that make use of a theorem prover while bringing to bear knowledge specific to the domain of proofs in set theory.

Kimball's system uses matrices of probabilistic values to represent judgmental knowledge. The simplicity of this representation has a number of advantages such as the use of probabilistic techniques to update the student model, or the possibility of establishing a distance measure between expert and student useful for selecting exercises. This simplicity also affords the capability of incorporating better moves demonstrated by students into the system's own expertise. However, all this representation seems to allow for guiding the student is a simple form of advice indicating what to do next, an issue we will return to in Part III (Chapter 15).

With its curriculum information network, BIP uses a representational scheme that is more in the AI tradition. However, BIP's curriculum is an organization of topics, not an operational model of expertise. This limits BIP's diagnostic capabilities and its usefulness as an active programming tutor. Nevertheless, BIP's central theme is an important contribution: this type of network provides a system with a complex representation of the curriculum highlighting pedagogically relevant relations between topics. By using this detailed information about conceptual relations between topics—as opposed to a simple numerical distance measure—the task of automatically constructing tailored teaching sequences looks more like pedagogical planning. In the next chapter, we will see an attempt at pushing this idea further by superimposing an information curriculum network on an operational model of expertise (Section 7.4.4).

Interest in advanced CAI at the Computer-based Learning Project at Leeds led to the definition of a framework for "intelligent teaching systems" and developed into early investigations of teaching strategies. The QUADRATIC tutor can monitor its own teaching performance and modify its rule-based strategies, adopting the ones that result in improvements with respect to its explicit goals. Pedagogical experiments are suggested by a database of possible modifications and corresponding expected results. This database itself is updated as successive experiments are conducted. Even though no dramatic improvements have been observed, this self-improving component represents a first attempt at automating an empirical form of educational research.

Taking an analytical approach in contrast with these empirical experiments, Self is interested in formalizing teaching actions in terms of a student model. He wants a student model that is predictive as well as inspectable. His "concept teaching program" even uses a learning model to construct optimal instructional sequences in an artificial domain. Because he does not address the diagnosis issue, his systems remain laboratory experiments. Nevertheless, his investigation of the use of a runnable representation of the student's knowledge in program form has started an important trend in the field.

Bibliographical notes

The work done at IMSSS in the seventies is covered in a large collection of papers edited by Suppes (1981). The paper by McDonald (1981) in this collection concentrates on an analysis of the use of EXCHECK as an instructional system, and the one by Blaine (1981) on discussions of the research on natural reasoning, also found in the paper by Smith et al. (1975). Blaine and Smith (1977) place EXCHECK in the ITS perspective and discuss the importance of dealing with the large amount of knowledge contained in an entire curriculum. For the interested reader, Trybulec and Blair (1985) present MIZAR, another computer-based proof analyzer that attempts to understand reasoning steps familiar to people.

The most available reference for the INTEGRATION tutor is (Kimball, 1982). Two short conference papers describe BIP-I (Barr, Beard, and Atkinson, 1975; Barr and Beard, 1976), but the most complete report is a journal article by Barr, Beard, and Atkinson (1976). The extensions of BIP-II are presented by Wescourt, Beard, and Gould (1977). Koffman and Perry (1976) discuss another scheme for heuristic topic selection based on a structured curriculum; they use empirically determined linear combinations of numerical parameters contained in the student model.

With its emphasis on teaching decisions, the paper by Hartley and Sleeman (1973) is an interesting counterpart to Carbonell's classic. O'Shea's dissertation has been published as a book (O'Shea, 1979a), but a more concise description of the QUADRATIC tutor is given in

(O'Shea, 1979b); a very short article concentrates on the system's rule-based framework (O'Shea, 1979c). Generalizations of the rule-based structure of the QUADRATIC tutor have led to speculations about the possibility of creating generic rule-based tools for use by nonprogrammers in constructing instructional systems (O'Shea et al., 1984; Heines and O'Shea, 1985).

The paper by Self (1974) on procedural student models is another classic. His experiments with concept teaching are described in (Self, 1977). Both papers are fairly technical. In a more casual paper, Self (1979) lists some difficult open problem with the notion of AI-based student model. Self (1985a, 1985b) has been coordinating a project at the universities of Lancaster and Leeds whose central theme gives an even more central role to the student model. The project's purpose is to investigate the paradigm of guided-discovery learning as opposed to straight teaching. As in concept teaching, a learning model is included in the student model, but this time it is not used to select teaching actions. Instead, it should be sophisticated enough to learn along with the student. The hope is that the model will then be able to form a knowledge representation similar to that developed by the student. In this way, the system should be able to provide some guidance to the student in his own discovery process rather than impose a predetermined view of the domain.

Chapter 7

Learning environments: coaching ongoing activities

Although advocates of the use of artificial intelligence for instructional systems often argue from the alleged rigidity of CAI, the image of inflexible drill-oriented programs they present is in many cases undeserved. An especially promising paradigm that does not fit this caricatural description is the design of open-ended learning environments mentioned in the introduction of this book. In this chapter, we consider two important contributions of artificial intelligence to the effectiveness of learning environments. On the one hand, we briefly consider some ways in which AI concepts can influence the design of such environments, using the LOGO project as an example. On the other, we discuss the construction of automated coaches that provide unobtrusive assistance while the student is involved in independent learning. We cover WEST and WUSOR, two early projects concerned with the design of coaching systems. Finally, we outline some recent work combining the various themes presented here.

In both WEST and WUSOR, the ongoing activity is a game. However, game environments are chosen merely for their conceptual simplicity and intrinsic motivational value—the principles discussed here are applicable to any independent learning activity. Though games are attractive contexts for discovery learning, students involved in educational games often overlook learning opportunities and get stuck on "plateaus" of proficiency. Making them aware of further possibilities is the task of a coach: his purpose is not to lecture, but to foster the learning inherent in the activity itself by pointing out existing learning opportunities and by transforming failures into learning experiences. With the rapid proliferation of computer games on the market, computer-based coaching may soon become an important paradigm for practical knowledge communication systems, in what Goldstein and Carr (1977) call "an athletic paradigm for intellectual education."

However, the art of coaching is subtle: interventions must be effective in preventing plateaus without destroying interest in the activity. Coaching differs from other tutoring situations like mixed-initiative dialogues in that the student is always in complete control of the activity. The problem of responding correctly to the student is replaced by that of interrupting her at the right time with the right comments. As we have mentioned, the diagnostic task is difficult because it must take place behind the scenes, but the coach can also adopt a conservative attitude and simply remain silent when it is in doubt. Note that the assumptions and principles of computer-based coaches are relevant to an important class of knowledge communication systems in computer science, often called "intelligent help systems" (Breuker, in press). These systems can intervene to help the user of another system when the use of available facilities does not seem optimal.

7.1 LOGO: knowledge communication as learning

The topic of computer-based learning environments is vast. It includes pedagogical issues such as the trade-off between self-pacing and efficiency, epistemological issues such as the choice of presentation artifacts for domain knowledge, and implementational issues such as the design of graphic displays. A repeated conclusion from practical experience with these environments in practice is that students tend to require some additional assistance or guidance to take full advantage of their exposure.

A thorough treatment of the topic of computer-based learning environments is beyond the scope of this chapter. Furthermore, a number of related issues are addressed indirectly in connection with various projects described in this book. Nevertheless, before turning to specific coaching systems, it is appropriate to take a brief look at one of the earliest and most publicized—if controversial—projects centered on the concept of computer-based learning environment.

Admittedly, the LOGO project (Papert, 1980) is usually not viewed as part of ITS history. However, there are good reasons for mentioning it here. Although LOGO does not use AI programming to build tutoring systems, the whole project is deeply influenced by AI concepts and methodologies. Indeed, it was initiated and conducted at MIT's AI lab by Seymour Papert, also known for his work on self-organizing systems (Minsky and Papert, 1969). Furthermore, WEST and WUSOR were both designed in the Boston area, and there was much communication and mutual influence between the three projects. Finally, we will see that LOGO's philosophy bears an interesting relation to central themes of this book.

LOGO: programming as a discovery tool

Papert was deeply influenced by Piaget's ideas, and therefore the fundamental concept underlying LOGO is essentially epistemological: Papert suggests that it is more important to help children learn how to develop and debug their own theories than it is to teach them theories we consider correct. In LOGO, the basic method is to use the computer as a universal experimental simulator that learners can manipulate to explore concepts. Because programming requires an explicit and inspectable definition of ideas, it is viewed as an exercise by which students are involved in forming computational models of their developing concepts, thus becoming their own epistemologists (Papert, 1972a, 1972b).

Although its approach is not tied to any domain, LOGO is mainly known for its applications in the exploratory learning of mathematics. In particular, the programmable "turtle" for the study of geometry has become famous. The turtle is a simple wheeled device bearing a pen, which can be programmed to move across a sheet of paper to draw geometrical figures. The idea is that a child who can discover how to program the turtle to draw, say, a triangle gains a very practical notion of what a triangle is. However, the use of the turtle is not limited to such simple geometrical concepts, and its power to "reify" concepts has been exploited to give students a personal experience of very advanced mathematical concepts (Abelson and diSessa, 1980). Now that LOGO has become fairly widespread, its concepts have found many application domains beyond mathematics.

Knowledge communication as a learning process

In addition to the mutual influence between projects mentioned above, there are more fundamental reasons why I think that LOGO should be discussed briefly here. First, its pedagogical claims widen the scope of the contributions computers can make to education. Papert suggests not only that the LOGO approach helps develop concepts that are deeply rooted in personal experience, but also that the notion that theories—like programs—have to be debugged can give children a more positive image of themselves as intellectual agents: learning naturally involves a process of trial and error (Papert, 1980). In this sense, the concept of *search*, central to artificial intelligence, takes on a very profound and practical pedagogical significance.

Furthermore, the educational philosophy underlying LOGO provides a different perspective on a central theme of this book. We are interested in the epistemological investigations of domain expertise that researchers undertake for computer-based knowledge communication. Symmetrically, LOGO takes advantage of the epistemological requirements of computational representations to help students formulate concepts. It is in some sense precisely the other side of the coin: you can only express what you know well, and you get to know well what you try to express. My impression is that we have only begun to appreciate the intellectual significance of this dialectical enterprise. Computer-based knowledge communication requires a clear formulation of the knowledge in question; similarly, programming, viewed as a form of knowledge communication, constitutes a learning process by which knowledge becomes explicit.

7.2 WEST: relevance and memorability of interventions

The WEST project was initiated in the context of SOPHIE, which was originally meant to include a troubleshooting coach. Since the domain of electronics seemed too complex for a first computer-based investigation of the art of coaching, the domain chosen for that purpose was the educational computer game "How the WEST was won," developed for the PLATO Elementary Mathematics Project.[1] This domain is still in keeping with the concept of reactive learning environment central to SOPHIE, but requires much simpler skills.

"How the WEST was won." The purpose of the game is to exercise arithmetic skills. Players are involved in a race to their home town, as shown on the display of Figure 7.1. When their turn comes, they are given three random numbers by the spinners on the right; with

---

[1]PLATO, one of the largest CAI projects ever undertaken, involves the development of sophisticated course authoring tools and of a variety of educational materials.

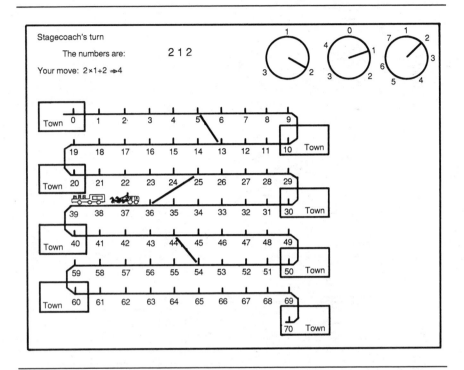

Figure 7.1 The game "How the West was won" (Burton and Brown, 1979b).

these numbers, they have to compose an arithmetic expression that involves two different operators and that determines the number of spaces they can move. However, the game is so designed that getting the largest number is not always the best strategy, because of shortcuts and the possibility of bumping backward an opponent who is not in a town. Thus, players are encouraged to explore different ways of combining the numbers with arithmetic operators. In consonance with the observations of other projects, Resnick (1975) had noticed that most students playing the game would soon get stuck in fixed patterns—hence miss the opportunity to practice arithmetic on a variety of expressions—if better moves were not pointed out to them from time to time: the game was begging for a coach.

7.2.1   Tutoring with issues and examples

Burton and Brown (1976) propose a general paradigm for computer-based coaching, which they call *issues and examples*, and whose basic

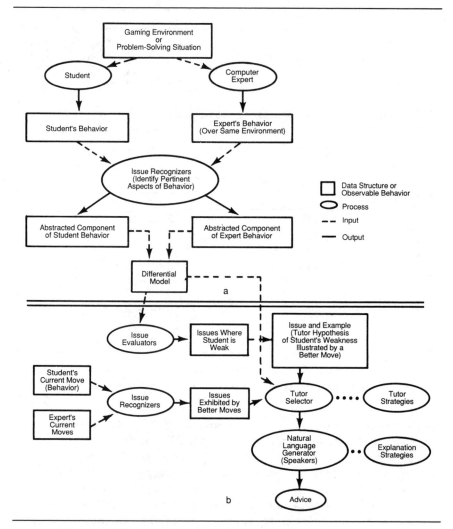

**Figure 7.2 Information flow diagram of the modeler/tutor
(Burton and Brown, 1979b).**

architecture is summarized in the information flow diagram of Figure 7.2.
The purpose of this paradigm is to make the interventions of the coach
both *relevant* and *memorable*. The knowledge to be conveyed is described
as a set of issues, which are presented to the student as they become
relevant to the game, along with concrete examples pertaining to her
current move. Finding relevant issues and appropriate examples hinges
on the notion of *differential modeling*, whereby the student's behavior is
analyzed and recorded in relation to the expert's choices for the same

$\vdots$

Bob is at 54 -- the COMPUTER is at 40.

WEST: It's MY turn ... Spinners are 2 4 2 My expression is:
2+(4/2) which gives ME 4
I took a SHORTCUT
I bumped YOU
the COMPUTER is at 54 -- Bob is at 40.

WEST: It's YOUR turn ... Spinners are: 1 2 2 What arithmetic
expression did you form?

Student: 1+2*2

WEST: What number does that give you?

Student: 5

WEST: You don't seem to be bumping very much. Bumps are hard to
get but they are usually a good idea. One good example
would be the expression: (1*2)+2, which would give you a
SHORTCUT and a BUMP!! So you could have been at 54 while
I would have ended up at 40. Bob is at 45 -- the COMPUTER
is at 54.

$\vdots$

**Figure 7.3 Excerpt from a dialogue with WEST
(Burton and Brown, 1976).**

circumstances. Because of the game's random nature, it is impossible to predict ahead of time which skills will be necessary. Therefore, the student's mastery of the various issues cannot be determined by their absolute occurrences in her play, but only by comparison with an expert's decisions for the same moves.

When it is the student's turn to play, the expert generates an ordered list of all the possible moves. If the student's expression does not yield the expert's optimal move, the diagnostic process starts. First, the student's move is analyzed by *issue recognizers* to determine which issues were used. Next, all the expert's moves that are better than the student's are also analyzed by the same recognizers, to produce a list of issues the student failed to apply. Finally, these issues are evaluated in the existing differential student model to find one in which the student is known to be weak.

If one such issue is found, it can be presented to the student: both abstractly, using a piece of prestored text, and concretely, using the expert's better move as an example. Figure 7.3 shows an excerpt from a sample dialogue between a student and WEST where a weakness is addressed. Note that the system has decided to concentrate on the issue of bumps only. If there are many issues that the student has failed to apply and in which she is weak, an ordering has to be imposed according to some criterion. This criterion can be a pedagogical strategy, like an emphasis on focus or on diversity, or it can be a structured curriculum à la BIP. In WEST, there is no facility for presenting multiple related issues together when they tend to interact (e.g., subtraction and moving backward), although Burton and Brown feel it would sometimes be useful.

In addition to helping select relevant topics, the differences between the lists of issues respectively applied by the student and the expert also provide information for updating the student model. In WEST, the differential model records how often each issue was used appropriately and how often it was overlooked. There is no notion of erroneous issues. An example of a student model is displayed in Figure 7.4; the model shows weaknesses in bumps, parentheses, and various types of expressions. Note that updating the student model is made nontrivial by "noise," due to inconsistencies in the student's behavior, and to ambiguities over which issues are responsible for suboptimal moves. This topic is treated in further details in Section 17.3. Pedagogically, WEST adopts a cautious attitude and intervenes only when there is good evidence for a weakness (see Principle 1 in Figure 7.5).

In sum, the issues-and-examples paradigm proposes a mechanism for determining when and how knowledge could be presented by a coach to motivate learning in the performance of an activity. If there is evidence of weaknesses, critical issues are mentioned when the student has just failed to use them, that is, in the context of moves she has just been thinking about. That makes the issues relevant. Then they are introduced with the help of concrete examples in the form of better solutions for the current moves. At that time, the student perceives them as crucial to successfully completing the activity. That makes them memorable.

The role of WEST's expert

Two remarks about the role of the expert module in the issues-and-examples paradigm are in order. The first point is that the expert needs a global strategy to determine optimality when ordering moves (in the case of WEST, the default strategy is maximizing the distance ahead of the opponent). Of course it is quite possible that the student is following a different strategy. If this strategy is valid, Burton and Brown suggest that the expert should adopt it; otherwise, the tutor should intervene to correct the student. As can be seen in Figure 7.4, an issue of strategy is included in the student model, in addition to arithmetic and game skills. The use of a different strategy is hypothesized when a student consistently chooses suboptimal moves without manifesting obvious weaknesses in

ARITHMETIC
SKILLS

EXPRESSIONS	(A+B)×C	(A×B)+C	(A+B)-C	(A×B)/C	A/(B×C)	A×(B-C)	(A×B)-C
Moves	1	3	-	-	-	-	-
Best	-	1	-	-	-	-	-
Fair	-	1	-	-	-	-	1
Poor	-	1	-	1	-	-	-
Miss	2	1	1	1	1	1	-

PARENTHESES	Need & Use	Use Any Way	No Use	None & Miss
	1	-	8	4

SPIN-ORDER	Good	Poor
Original	2	3
Reverse	-	1
Decreasing	1	-
Increasing	-	-
Other	2	-

GAME
SKILLS

SPECIALS	Took	Missed
Town	3	2
Bump	-	1
Shortcut	-	-

DIRECTION	Good	Poor	Was / best
Forward	5	4	9
Backward	-	-	-

STRATEGIES

STRATEGIES	Max Delta	Max Dist	Max Number	Specials	Other
	3	4	2	3	4

**Figure 7.4 A student model constructed by WEST
(after Burton and Brown, 1979b).**

related issues. Since WEST's domain is limited, available strategies can be exhaustively listed, and tested to see whether any of them can explain the student's moves (although Burton and Brown (1979b) did find one player who had adopted a strategy unknown to WEST). In more open domains, diagnosing strategies can be extremely difficult.

The second point is that the expert does not need to use the issues, or even to know about them, since its moves are analyzed by the same diagnostic procedures as are the student's (see top half of Figure 7.2). In fact, in the case of WEST, the expert's technique is simply to generate all the possible expressions and simulate the corresponding moves on the board. This is an interesting example of the cooperation of two representations for the same domain expertise. One is not psychologically

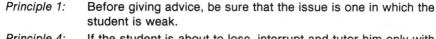

Principle 1:	Before giving advice, be sure that the issue is one in which the student is weak.
Principle 4:	If the student is about to lose, interrupt and tutor him only with moves that will keep him from losing.
Principle 5:	Do not tutor on two consecutive moves, no matter what.
Principle 9:	Always have the computer expert play an optimal game.
Principle 10:	If the student asks for help, provide several levels of hints:

        (1) Isolate a weakness and directly address it.

        (2) Delineate the space of possible moves at this point in the game.

        (3) Select the optimal move and tell the student why it is.

        (4) Describe how to make that optimal move.

Figure 7.5 Examples of coaching principles (Burton and Brown, 1979b).

plausible, but is powerful. The other, here with no performing power, is able to provide justifications in "teachable" terms. Of course, there is a trade-off between the advantage of having an opaque expert— usually more efficient—and the complexity of analyzing a move. In some domains, the analysis may prove prohibitive; then the expert must be implemented in terms of the pedagogical issues so that they are directly reflected in its moves.

7.2.2   Pedagogical principles for coaching

While the mechanisms described above can determine optimal coaching opportunities from the perspective of the ongoing activity, they do not cover motivational factors. The coach must still exercise pedagogi-cal judgment to exploit these opportunities properly from the human learner's perspective. To this end, Burton and Brown (1979b) try to capture the pedagogical strategy underlying skilled coaching in a learning environment. They come up with a list of a dozen general principles, which they do not claim as exhaustive. These principles provide both theoretical justifications for the mechanisms of issues and examples, and heuristic pedagogical guidance in dealing with the student when using this paradigm. Figure 7.5 lists a few of these principles. Note that in WEST these principles are not represented in this declarative form. They are merely embodied in the design of the tutorial module, where they are enacted by a process of "deliberation" between competing specialists voting to determine the system's interventions.

WEST in actual use: an encouraging success

In controlled experiments with WEST in elementary schools, students in the coached group exhibited "a considerably greater variety of patterns" in the expressions they formed. Furthermore, they even "enjoyed playing the game considerably more than the uncoached group" (Burton and Brown, 1979b, p. 98 of the reprint). Although the authors do not have a definite explanation for this observation, the fact that the presence of the coach somehow added excitement to the activity is rather remarkable. At any rate, these results are quite encouraging: they show that the coach really succeeded in fostering learning without any adverse effect on the fun of the game.

WEST's influence on the field has been very significant, and the system is still a reference for researchers today; however, the tutor itself has not been used after the few months of preliminary experiments, as far as I know. While this may be due to the cost of the machine on which WEST was originally developed, I hope that the recent increase in the power of cheap microcomputers will broaden the interest in such systems. Considering the number of worthless computer games available on the market, it is a shame that a carefully designed program like WEST, which actually reached a functional stage, should remain a laboratory experiment.

7.3   The design of learning environments

In WEST, the coach has no control over the environment, although Burton and Brown mention the possibility of tinkering with the generation of random numbers to fit some learning needs. For instance, a pedagogical principle says that the expert should always play optimally to serve as an example; but if a student is becoming discouraged and needs a chance to win, the computer could simply be given bad numbers. When necessary, spinners could also be tampered with to generate pedagogically useful examples. In general, it is likely that a coach will have the power to modify the environment in order to create good learning conditions.

Fischer, Brown, and Burton (1978; Burton, Brown, and Fischer, 1984) propose a paradigm for the design of optimal learning environments, which they call *increasingly complex microworlds*. The concept of microworlds created for educational purposes with the computer as a universal simulator is already the central theme of LOGO. Fischer et al. set out to formalize the notion of a succession of microworlds where the modifications at each step are meant to support learning. The idea is to start with a simplified world and to have a coach progressively add new dimensions of complexity that require an increasing mastery of basic skills. Fischer et al. present skiing instruction as a pedagogical success model that has made use of microworlds. Over the years, skiing instruction has become safer and surprisingly effective. According to the authors, the key to this success is the definition of progressive learning phases: instructors have combined technological advances with pedagogical cleverness to provide useful simplified versions of the skill.

Toward a theory of pedagogical simplification

The formulation of a theory of pedagogical simplification has to address two issues. First, the areas open to simplification must be identified, as well as the nature of possible and useful modifications. Then potential problems in scaling up from a simple to a more complex microworld must be anticipated so that the coach can make transitions smooth and effective. In this regard, progressions of mental models of the type discussed in Chapter 5 should prove invaluable. Indeed, these progressions are constructed on the basis of explicit criteria, such as the order of a model, which can be viewed as simplification principles for the domain.

Fischer et al. see three general aspects of a task that can be simplified: the expectations of performance, the equipment involved, and the environment. In their example of skiing, this could mean, for instance, doing very simple turns, with shorter skis, on a gentle slope, respectively. Selecting the best simplifications is not a trivial task. The authors note that the simplified skill must be in some ways "isomorphic" to the real one so that scaling up corresponds to a simple incremental mapping. Oversimplification can be counterproductive both because it may give rise to unexpected difficulties (e.g., turning on an almost flat slope), and because it may present too distorted a view of the task.

Of course, any simplification is likely to cause inappropriate generalizations on the part of the student. It becomes the duty of the coach to foresee and diagnose these errors, and to help the student correct them through the sequence of microworlds. In contrast with QUEST, the idea is not so much to avoid erroneous conclusions as it is to make errors *constructive*. If the environment is such that errors generate enough feedback for the student to recognize, understand, and correct them, they can become important learning points. This is reminiscent of LOGO's view of theory formation through the trial and error process of program design and debugging.

This theory is not presented as complete. A more detailed study should be conducted to investigate the nature of useful simplifications in each area and the types of misgeneralization they are likely to generate.

In addition, there are modifications, like the use of bad numbers in WEST, that do not deal directly with task complexity but with other pedagogical factors such as motivation. Next, corresponding coaching principles have to be laid out. Actually, this is an important area of research, since the principle of simplification pervades the process of curriculum construction, which need to be automated to some degree in instructional systems.

7.4 WUSOR: toward learner-oriented models of expertise

The WUSOR project first started as a class project for a course in educational technology at MIT. It later evolved into a full research project by Ira Goldstein and his student Brian Carr. As a coach for an independent learning activity, WUSOR was certainly influenced by LOGO's concepts since Goldstein had long been involved in the LOGO project, but the main initial inspiration was apparently provided by the work on WEST conducted at nearby BBN. However, the primary focus in WUSOR is not so much on pedagogical principles as on issues of representation for the skill to be taught, with an attempt to include in this representation information about the learner that can support pedagogical tasks.

WUMPUS: logical and probabilistic reasoning.   WUSOR is a coach for the computer game WUMPUS (Yob, 1975). This computer game takes the player through successive caves in a warren where the terrible Wumpus is hiding. In addition to the Wumpus, other dangers are lurking: namely deadly pits, and bats that grab the player and drop her in a random cave. Whenever the player reaches a new cave, she is given a list of the neighboring caves. She also receives some warnings when applicable: a draft or a squeak reveals the presence of a pit or a bat, respectively, in an unspecified neighboring cave; the Wumpus itself can be smelled up to two caves away. The player moves by selecting the neighboring cave she wants to visit next. To win the game, she must shoot one of her five arrows into the Wumpus' lair. She can lose by falling into a pit, by walking into the Wumpus' lair, or by using up her arrows without scoring any hits. Figure 7.6 shows a snapshot of a "display" version of the game after the player has visited caves 15 and 4.

In deciding which neighboring cave to visit next, the player must exercise logical and probabilistic reasoning to draw inferences from the signals she has received so far. Because time limits can be imposed, she must also exhibit decision and planning skills in the context of a trade-off between safety and inquisitiveness.

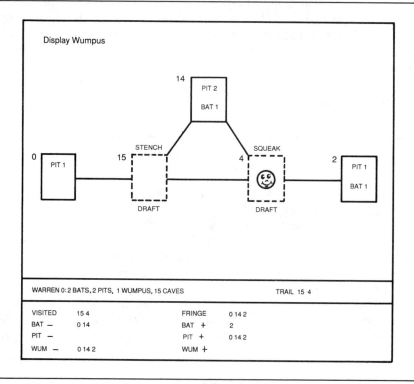

Figure 7.6 The WUMPUS game state after two moves (after Goldstein, 1979).

7.4.1 WUSOR-I: an expert-based coach

The first version of the coach, WUSOR-I (Stansfield, Carr, and Goldstein, 1976), consists solely of an expert and an advisor. In the *expert*, the domain knowledge is represented in the form of production rules. These rules are organized into specialists for each danger, which cooperate to classify all possible moves and select the best one. So as always to play from the student's point of view, the expert keeps a record of the information gathered so far. The expertise consists of heuristic rules for approximate probabilities, rather than lengthy computations; this is not only for efficiency, but—more important—because this approach is more in line with that of human players.

The *advisor* module does not have any tutorial strategies; it intervenes each time the student has not chosen the optimal move according to the expert's classification. Associated with each move category and with each rule is a specific set of explanations that are delivered to the student. The advisor does not maintain a student model, and players are simply requested to rate themselves on a four-point scale at the beginning of the game. This rudimentary form of self-evaluation influences the kind of explanations given, and leads to the suppression of some expert rules, thereby preventing beginners from being flooded with advanced material.

Unlike WEST, WUSOR-I does not attempt to diagnose the student's state of knowledge and to adapt its interventions accordingly. As a coach, therefore, WUSOR-I is quite unsophisticated. Its interest lies in its emphasis on the representation of the game-playing skill, which contrasts with WEST's in a fundamental way. Inasmuch as each rule can be considered as one issue, the rule-based representation has the same modularity as the decomposition of the knowledge into issues. However, unlike WEST's black-box expert, WUSOR-I's expert is itself built out of these rules. Hence, it explicitly contains the issues to be conveyed and uses them for its performance. This pedagogical transparency of the representation of expertise will have important implications for the subsequent developments towards a more elaborate tutor.

7.4.2 Overlays: a rule-based paradigm for student modeling

The main improvement that WUSOR-I needed was the addition of a detailed student model. In the process of designing WUSOR-II, Carr and Goldstein (1977) propose their *overlay* theory of student modeling, which has become a standard paradigm in ITS.

The overlay architecture

The overlay paradigm is applicable whenever the expertise can be expressed as a set of rules. Basically, it is quite similar to WEST's differential modeling, which inspired it. It also attaches individual evaluations to single units of the knowledge by comparing the student's behavior with the expert's. But since these units are now parts of the expert itself, the student's state of knowledge is viewed as a subset of the expert's knowledge: hence the term "overlay." As in WEST, the evaluation of a single rule numerically indicates the frequency of its correct use. It is recorded as the ratio of the number of times it was appropriate to the number of times it was correctly applied. But whereas in WEST's differential model, the complete history is kept and is analyzed each time by an ad hoc procedural specialist, the overlay model has a single critic that determines when an individual skill can be considered as acquired. For this decision, it analyzes the history of the variations in the evaluation parameters for that skill. Thus it is meant to detect inconsistencies and discontinuities, and to act cautiously if the history of a skill indicates constant changes.

The overlay theory also defines multiple sources of evidence available to the diagnostic module for its update of the overlay model:

- *Implicit* evidence is derived from a comparison of the student's behavior with the expert's decision, and is the kind used in WEST's differential model. It requires the ability to relate a given behavior to a specific set of skills.

- *Structural* evidence is retrieved from a syllabus in the form of a network of dependencies and relative complexities among the skills, along the lines of BIP's Curriculum Information Network. This network provides the notion of a *frontier* of the student's knowledge, where teaching should concentrate. Since it is where learning is likely to occur, variations taking place far from the frontier should be treated with caution.

  Note that this form of "frontier teaching" is well suited for procedural skills where building blocks of the expertise are added successively. For teaching complex interconnected subjects such as those involving multiple mental models, a web covering the entire domain is gradually refined, and the frontier must be defined as a level of depth or refinement in the student's current model.

- *Explicit* evidence is derived from additional interactions with the student, either indirectly by specific test cases built to evaluate hypotheses, or interactively by questions.

- *Background* evidence provides performance estimates for initializing the overlay.

The overlay student model is integrated into a complete rule-based architecture for an intelligent tutor, illustrated in the diagram of Figure 7.7. The *expert* with its *rules of skill* can suggest and analyze moves. The diagnostic module, here called the *psychologist*, builds and updates the student model using its *rules of evidence*. The *tutor*, with its *rules of explanation*, prunes the full report of the expert to tailor its intervention to the student according to the model maintained by the psychologist. Finally, *rules of language* are applied to create a proper interface in the form of a *speaker* and a *listener*. Within this architecture, Carr and Goldstein envision a more elaborate overlay model that includes the student's receptivity to various tutoring strategies. Whereas her domain knowledge is hypothesized as an overlay of the rules of the expert, her learning preferences can be described as an overlay of the rules of the tutor. In updating this part of the model, the diagnostic module has to rate the various tutorial rules according to their perceived effectiveness with individual students.

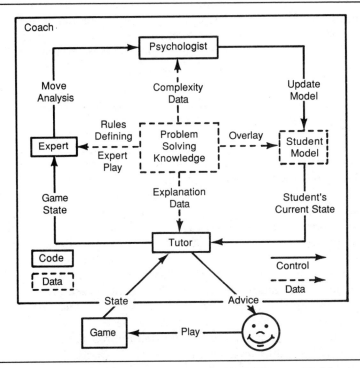

Figure 7.7 The "overlay" architecture for coaching systems (Goldstein, 1982).

Limitations of the overlay paradigm

There are two important limitations to the overlay student model. The first is an instance of the general problem of expertise representation, amplified here because the student's knowledge is viewed as a subset of the expert's. The overlay model will fail if the domain allows for multiple problem-solving paradigms and if the student follows one that the expert is not programmed to know, possibly making good moves that the expert system would consider non-optimal. Dealing with multiple paradigms would require a "meta-expert"—a set of different experts among which the system would choose the appropriate model. Note that WEST does that when it adopts the student's strategy.

The second difficulty is specific to the overlay modeling paradigm. In some ways, the overlay's evaluation of single rules is similar to the tags used in SCHOLAR to indicate the acquisition of pieces of factual information. However, errors in procedural knowledge are more complex than gaps in factual knowledge. The overlay assumes that suboptimal behavior is caused only by the insufficient mastery of individual skills, and that distortions in the correct skills do not occur. This is admittedly an unrealistic simplification because, in most domains, student modeling will require that incorrect rules and inappropriate applications of correct rules be specifically described. In fact, studying and cataloging common errors for specific domains have been important concerns of more recent research efforts in student modeling, as will be seen in coming chapters.

7.4.3 The overlay theory in WUSOR-II

The incorporation of many aspects of the overlay theory into WUSOR-II (Carr, 1977) represents a definite move toward a learner-oriented tutor, both for the student model and for the representation of expertise. Whereas the student's knowledge is a real overlay model, her learning preferences are only represented by a set of three registers indicating her need for repetition, her degree of forgetfulness, and her receptivity to advice. As a form of curriculum, the representation of game expertise is now organized into five successive phases, ranging from basic rules of the game to logical and finally to probabilistic rules (see Figure 7.9). The coach will not proceed to the next phase before the student has mastered certain fundamental skills in the current one. This is an important departure from the unsegmented rule-based approach, since the domain knowledge, while still exclusively representing expertise, is structured so as to reflect the standpoint of the learner.

Figure 7.8 presents an excerpt from an interaction with WUSOR-II. This dialogue actually corresponds to the situation shown in Figure 7.6. An interesting feature of a rule-based student model is that it is runnable using a suitable interpreter. Although WUSOR-II was tested with many students in informal experiments, the coach was mostly tuned with the help of a synthetic student, SYNDIE, whose knowledge was an overlay of the system's rules. The notion of a synthetic student presupposes a number of assumptions that limit its use as a general testbed (Ihrie, 1978). In particular, the overlay student learns by discrete steps corresponding to the addition of rules; this rather static style fails to reflect the gradual mastery of concepts by human students. Nevertheless, SYNDIE turned out to be quite useful in the preliminary debugging process, where it revealed many of the coach's inadequacies.

7.4.4 WUSOR-III: the genetic graph

The *genetic graph* (Goldstein, 1978, 1979), conceived for WUSOR-III, furthers the movement toward a learner-oriented knowledge represen-tation begun with WUSOR-II. To this end, it combines the concept of

.
.
.

WUSOR: Hi Mary. There are 15 caves, 2 bats, 2 pits, and 1
Wumpus. You are now at cave 15 with neighbors 4, 14,
and 0. Brrr! There is a draft. You are near a pit. What a
stench! The Wumpus is near! What now?

Student: 4

WUSOR: You are now at cave 4 with neighbors 15, 14, and 2. Brrr!
There is a draft. Squeak! A bat is near. What now?

Student: 14

WUSOR: Mary, it isn't necessary to take such large risks with
pits. One of caves 2 and 14 contains a pit. Likewise,
one of caves 0 and 14 contains a pit. This is multiple
evidence of a pit in cave 14 which makes it likely that
cave 14 contains a pit. It is less likely that cave 0
contains a pit. Hence, Mary, we might want to explore
cave 0 instead. Do you want to take back your move?

.
.
.

**Figure 7.8 Excerpt from a game with WUSOR-II
(Goldstein and Carr, 1977).**

overlay on a rule-based representation of domain knowledge with a
learner-oriented set of links reminiscent of BIP-II's extended Curriculum
Information Network. The word *genetic* refers to Piaget's notion of
genetic epistemology because this representation attempts to capture the
evolutionary nature of knowledge. The word *graph* is used because the
evolutionary relations between pieces of knowledge are expressed as links
in a network. A section of the genetic graph for the WUMPUS game is
shown in Figure 7.9.

Like BIP-II's network, the genetic graph represents elementary subskills (i.e., individual rules) as nodes connected by links representing their
evolutionary relations, such as *generalization* or *analogy*. The links for
relative difficulty correspond to the phases of WUSOR-II, except that
more difficult rules are now explicitly viewed as *refinements* of specific
easier ones. Inspired by Brown and Burton's then recent BUGGY model
(covered in the next chapter), Goldstein also augments the graph with
the possibility of including incorrect versions of rules connected to the
corresponding correct ones by explicit *deviation* links. These buggy rules
are to provide the representation of incorrect skills missing in the original
overlay paradigm.

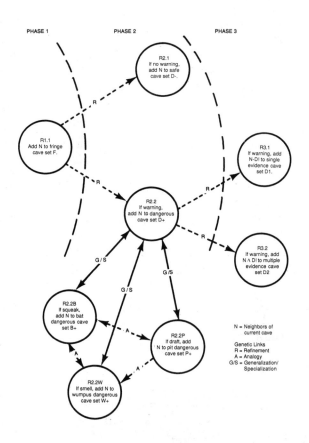

Figure 7.9 A region of WUSOR's genetic graph (Goldstein, 1979).

The topology of the graph: a source of pedagogical information

For modeling purposes, the student's knowledge can be represented as an *overlay on the nodes* of the genetic graph, including correct and incorrect rules. Arguably, the numerous evolutionary links connecting subskills constitute a partial learning theory for the domain and could thus guide the search for a plausible model. In addition, Goldstein suggests that the student's individual learning history can be modeled as an *overlay on the links* of the genetic graph. This is useful because different explanation strategies can be associated with the different types of evolutionary links. Figure 7.10 shows an example of the variations on an explanation that are warranted by different types of links for WUSOR's intervention in

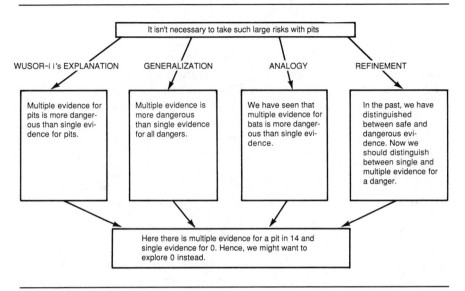

Figure 7.10 Explanations corresponding to different types of links (Goldstein, 1979).

Figure 7.8. The overlay on the links then supports pedagogical actions that view learning as a process of building upon existing knowledge. Thus, with the genetic graph, the notion of a learning frontier defined by the overlay model is even more useful. Not only does a learning frontier provide a focus for both teaching and diagnosing, but now it also provides explicit evolutionary connections between specific new skills and specific existing knowledge.

Goldstein also mentions various measures that could be defined using the topology of the genetic graph. For instance, the student's degree of belief or of confidence in a newly acquired skill could be connected to the number and types of links that have been made explicit. More generally, the density of links connecting a given node to the rest of the graph could also be used as a measure of the skill's integration, with the idea that isolated skills might be more difficult to acquire. Goldstein does not fully explore these topological considerations, but they may potentially provide syntactic equivalents for notions like difficulty and confidence, which have been traditionally regarded as subjective and vague. With computational definitions for these measures, automated curriculum construction could be given clearer criteria and directions. For instance, the concept of simplified microworlds mentioned in the last section could be made more concrete.

Representing problem-solving expertise for teaching

Goldstein (1980) suggests that for teachable models of expertise the inclusion of evolutionary information is only one of a number of additional areas that need to be considered beyond the design of an operational model. Also relevant are the *data structures* manipulated by students to represent problem states. In WUSOR, different inferences are facilitated by maps of the warren and by tables and lists. The "display" version of the game shown in Figure 7.6 constitutes an effort to deal with this aspect by offering players multiple representational facilities for recording information (see also Section 14.4). Finally, Goldstein mentions the need for some measures of the *cognitive load* imposed on the student by various tasks, which in WUSOR is simply implemented with respect to the number and types of objects in the warren.

WUSOR-III was never fully implemented, and the genetic graph remained an idea, although versions of the concept have been used in more recent systems. Of course, evolutionary links stand for complex learning processes, but do not fully capture these processes in the genetic graph as it is presented. For instance, the statement that an analogical link exists between two concepts says little about the value of the analogy, the conditions under which it is applicable, and the conceptual mapping relevant to it. Furthermore, learning is always viewed as a set of local additions and refinements, with no allowance for major reconceptualizations. On the practical side, an obvious question is whether it is realistic to assume the existence of a complete static graph for complex domains. Although Goldstein claims that it would be easy to build a dynamic version of the genetic graph, in which links and nodes are created "on the fly", there is no evidence that this is feasible for such complex domains. Nevertheless, the notion of a learner-oriented model of domain knowledge is important and deserves more attention.

7.5   Architectures organized around curricula

A number of related themes have been introduced in this chapter, including coaching ongoing activities, exploratory microworlds, curricula of pedagogical issues, and learning-oriented representations of expertise. These ideas form the core of a new project conducted by the ITS Group, a team of researchers at LRDC.[2] By building on these themes and bringing these ideas together, they hope to uncover general principles for the design of intelligent tutoring systems and to implement these principles

---

[2] Learning Research and Development Center at the University of Pittsburgh.

into reusable tutoring architectures. Thus, although much of this work is still under development, it is appropriate to conclude the chapter by briefly outlining the project's approach.

The question of curriculum design for instructional systems and the automation of dynamic curriculum adaptation are natural interests for LRDC, given its background in educational research and task analysis. In fact, the project's emphasis is not on constructing computational performance models for the domain, but on developing frameworks in which to cast a curriculum consisting of pedagogical "issues" à la WEST. As in the genetic graph, the purpose is to structure the set of issues in order to support pedagogical decisions. However, the ITS Group's effort goes beyond the mere use of genetic links: the organization of knowledge is to include explicit connections to a hierarchy of curricular goals, so that complete curricula involving multiple lessons can be accommodated.

7.5.1 The bite-sized architecture

The practical context for this study of curriculum-centered representations is the concept of a *bite-sized tutoring architecture* (Bonar, 1985c; Bonar et al., 1986). Instead of organizing tutoring systems around functional components, such as a diagnostic or an expert module, this type of architecture organizes the system around pedagogical issues, called *bites*. Each bite is itself a miniature system focused on a specific piece of the subject matter. In addition to some domain knowledge, it includes:

- knowledge about its *conceptual* relations to other bites, such as part/whole, class/subclass, or analogical relations;

- knowledge about its *curricular* relations to other bites, such as pre- and postrequisites, so that it can trigger remedial actions;

- indication about the *student's mastery* of its part of the subject matter (a miniature student model, which in conjunction with other bites forms a type of overlay);

- the ability to *diagnose* the student's use and disuse of this knowledge by taking the blame for suboptimal actions;

- the ability to generate *problems* that involve the use of this knowledge;

- the ability to generate *instructional interventions* related to this knowledge.

Note that the functional components still exist, but that they are distributed across the representation of the curriculum. In keeping with the object-oriented programming style that inspired the concept, the various bites can share common components and procedures so that duplication of information is avoided. Of course, the lack of central pedagogical control requires additional machinery in order to implement coherent strategies; in return, however, it is possible to adopt a variety of instructional modes with minimal modifications to the knowledge base. For generic architectures, the modularity of this object-oriented scheme affords flexibility in reusing portions of systems for other domains; exactly how far systems can be reused is determined by the degree of commonality between domains and tutorial approaches.

SMITHTOWN (Shute and Glaser, 1986; Shute and Bonar, 1986) is a system for teaching economics, which combines a microworld for exploratory learning with a bite-sized tutoring module. The student is presented with a simulated town; she can vary parameters such as the supply or the price of certain goods to study the modifications induced in other parameters. Figure 7.11 shows a snapshot of SMITHTOWN's "notebook" facility, which allows the student to record her experiments. The system implements two simultaneous pedagogical intentions: teaching principles of economics and teaching general investigative behaviors. Bites at the economics level monitor which laws the student is discovering, supplying the name of the new concept when she makes a relevant hypothesis. If the student flounders excessively, the system can become more directive and suggest experiments according to a curriculum that organizes the domain bites. Bites for investigative behaviors monitor various skills of scientific inquiry such as the ability to collect and record data in a systematic way. At this level, the system acts as a coach, but it does not address inquiry skills directly, since these bites constitute a sort of metacurriculum. Instead, it advises the student in her investigation of the domain, employing different levels of hints as in WEST.

7.5.2   Curriculum organization and steering testing

From a conceptual perspective, Lesgold (1987) suggests that the representation of a curriculum for a tutoring system should be organized into layers, as shown in Figure 7.12. Each layer provides a different type of pedagogical information. At the bottom, in the *knowledge layer*, the subject matter is decomposed into distinct issues, which are linked into a network in the style of the genetic graph; this level would correspond to SMITHTOWN's bites in economics. In the *curriculum layer*, pedagogical goals and subgoals organize the subject matter into successive lessons by pointing down to the knowledge layer. SMITHTOWN uses this type of knowledge to guide the floundering student. Viewing this level as distinct from the knowledge level allows a system to include multiple curricular viewpoints on the same knowledge, each of which

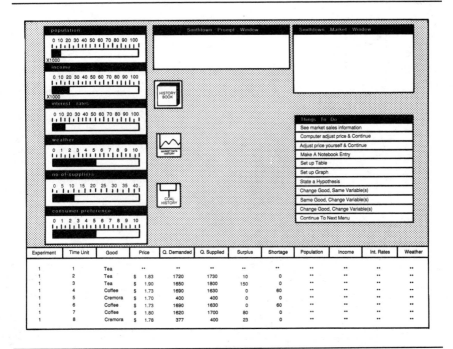

Experiment	Time Unit	Good	Price	Q. Demanded	Q. Supplied	Surplus	Shortage	Population	Income	Int. Rates	Weather
1	1	Tea	**	**	**	**	**	**	**	**	**
1	2	Tea	$ 1.83	1720	1730	10	0	**	**	**	**
1	3	Tea	$ 1.90	1650	1800	150	0	**	**	**	**
1	4	Coffee	$ 1.73	1690	1630	0	60	**	**	**	**
1	5	Cremora	$ 1.70	400	400	0	0	**	**	**	**
1	6	Coffee	$ 1.73	1690	1630	0	60	**	**	**	**
1	7	Coffee	$ 1.80	1620	1700	80	0	**	**	**	**
1	8	Cremora	$ 1.78	377	400	23	0	**	**	**	**

Figure 7.11 Recording data in SMITHTOWN (Shute and Bonar, 1986).

partitions the subject matter in a different way. The top layer deals with "metacognitive" skills, like learning abilities or SMITHTOWN's inquiry skills, and general aptitudes like mathematical reasoning: hence the name *aptitude layer*. The concepts used in this layer are closer to the general terms that teachers often use to evaluate students. Information at this level induces modifications in the way the curriculum is organized, which in turn influence the presentation of knowledge. In some cases—as in SMITHTOWN—these aptitudes themselves can become part of the curriculum. Such emphasis on metacognitive issues is an important theme of the project (Glaser, 1984).

The organization of the curriculum is useful for both didactic and diagnostic purposes. MHO (Lesgold et al., 1987) is a system for learning principles of electricity that supports both free exploration and guided problem solving. Its tutoring component exploits the curriculum organization to implement the concept of *steering testing*. When it takes control of the interaction, MHO dynamically generates tasks—electrical circuits and questions about them—that have to fulfill two conditions. First, observing the student's performance on each task should maximize the information made available concerning possible changes in her knowledge state. Second, each task should concentrate on elements of the

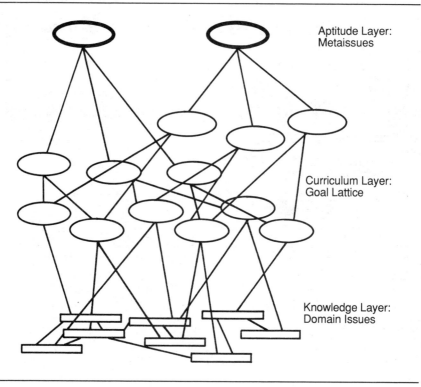

Figure 7.12 Layered curriculum representation (Lesgold, 1987).

curriculum that are in the current focus so that diagnostic information can direct the course of instruction.

In addition to the three layers described above, intelligent task generation requires a further type of knowledge called *treatment* knowledge (Lesgold et al., 1987). Treatment knowledge—also represented as bites in MHO—deals with various situations in which the same domain knowledge must be used; it involves information about problem types and formats and about their probable influence on the student's performance. Thus, in the network in Figure 7.12, it would be at the same level as, but distinct from, the curriculum layer.

The student model is represented as an overlay on the curriculum, each bite containing a separate evaluation of mastery. Much as a frontier can be defined on a genetic graph, the idea is to define regions of interest in the curriculum, where changes in knowledge are likely to take place. To this end, MHO uses rather straightforward heuristics that combine information about the curriculum's structure with information about the stability and mastery level of the student's knowledge of various bites. For each task, these bites post *constraints* that the generated problem should attempt to fulfill. For instance, an "arithmetic" bite at the aptitude level may request that the problem not involve difficult calculations, because the student's apparent weakness in arithmetic might then mask her knowledge of the domain.

MHO's heuristically derived tasks are primarily composed for their diagnostic value, that is, for their ability to test selected aspects of the student's knowledge. However, because they lie at the frontier of her knowledge, and because this frontier is defined in a structured curriculum, these are likely to have didactic value as well. In situations in which this assumption proves true, steering testing should be able to combine testing and teaching to produce highly adaptive instructional sequences.

In conclusion, it is worth repeating that this distributed approach to subject-matter representation emphasizes the notion of *lesson* rather than that of *model* as a reservoir of domain knowledge. As in BIP, the system's ability to demonstrate the target expertise is therefore given less importance than its ability to make pedagogical decisions. In this regard, this approach sharply contrasts with the progressions of mental models used in QUEST. MHO is based on a hierarchy of declarative principles concerning electrical circuits; it concentrates on task generation for guiding the student's discovery of these individual relations (e.g., Ohm's law) rather than on complete explanations of circuit behavior.

Summary and conclusion

Computer-based learning environments are relevant to the topic of this book at two levels. Artificial intelligence can contribute concrete conceptualizations to enhance the communicative power of these environments. Learning environments that incorporate concepts from artificial intelligence are a fascinating prospect further discussed in Section 19.2. Here, we have mentioned the LOGO project, and viewed its concentration on programming as the use of knowledge communication for learning purposes. Furthermore, the concept of increasingly complex microworlds formalizes the design of learning environments in which a coach progressively retracts principled simplifications until the target level of difficulty becomes teachable. There is an interesting parallel between this concept and that of progressions of models used in QUEST.

Given that students using automated learning environments tend to need assistance, another contribution of AI is the design of intelligent coaching systems that enhance the learning process by turning critical experiences into learning opportunities. WEST was the first system in this class. It has contributed the concept of differential modeling and that of teaching via issues and examples, whereby the coach detects the relevance of issues and illustrates them with an appropriate example. In addition, a number of general coaching principles followed in the design of WEST have been outlined. Not least among the system's contributions is its success in a short period of classroom use, which revealed that children both improved their learning and enjoyed being coached.

The WUSOR project concentrates less on pedagogical strategies than on the model of domain knowledge required for coaching. The notion of overlay, a refinement of WEST's differential model, is widely used in the field to refer to a student model expressed as a subset of a complete model of expertise. In a move from expert-oriented to learner-oriented representations of expertise, the model of domain knowledge has evolved from the unsegmented rule-based expert of WUSOR-I to the epistemological concerns of the genetic graph. According to Goldstein, this move involves a number of dimensions, including:

- an explicit representation of evolutionary links that reflect processes involved in the acquisition of a skill;

- a study of data structures useful in representing problems;

- measures of complexity and estimates of cognitive load for problem-solving tasks.

This evolution is again illustrative of the constraints that knowledge communication imposes on knowledge representation. Here however, the emphasis is not only on the nature of expert reasoning processes, but mainly on the learner's perspective.

Current work at LRDC's ITS Group builds on many ideas introduced in this chapter and the previous one, with the goal of producing generic frameworks for the design of tutoring systems. The bite-sized architecture organizes tutoring functions around a decomposition of domain expertise into curriculum units reminiscent of WEST's issues. The prevalent paradigm for a number of prototypical systems under development at LRDC is to use these autonomous tutoring units called bites to guide the student's interaction with a microworld that illustrates the domain principles to be understood. The bite-sized architecture serves as a context for articulating principles of curriculum organization. This organization in turn supports an implementation of the concept of steering testing, which combines diagnostic and didactic purposes into adaptive sequences of heuristically generated tasks.

Steering testing successfully integrates a number of themes developed in the last two chapters: it supplements sequencing optimization à la BIP with diagnostic information based on issues à la WEST, in the context of a learner-oriented organization of knowledge à la genetic graph. In this sense, steering testing in a bite-sized architecture is the epitome of a curriculum-oriented perspective on knowledge communication systems that has permeated these two chapters. The view of expertise as a curriculum, with its pedagogical emphasis, contrasts with the view of expertise as a model, with its epistemological and cognitive emphasis. Of course, the two views are not incompatible; in fact, weaving them together is one of the field's most promising challenges.

Bibliographical notes

The reader interested in the philosophy of LOGO and in computer-based learning environments in general is encouraged to read the book by Papert (1980). The book by Abelson and diSessa (1980) is a fascinating journey into geometry illustrating the power of the LOGO approach for communicating difficult abstract concepts. The idea of manipulable microworlds central to LOGO has been attracting the attention of people interested in AI (Howe, 1979), especially in Europe where these environments often involve learning activities based on the AI concept of "logic programming" (Yazdani, 1984). The recent collection edited by Lawler and Yazdani (1987) includes a large section on learning environments.

Burton, Brown, and Fischer (1984), in a revised version of (Fischer et al., 1978), explore the concept of increasing complexity in sequences of microworlds, and Fischer (1987) presents an application of the concept to the design of a programming environment.

The most available discussion of WEST is (Burton and Brown, 1979b). WUSOR's overlay paradigm is presented in a conference paper by Carr and Goldstein (1977), and the concept of the genetic graph is investigated by Goldstein (1979). Goldstein (1980) provides a good overview of the entire WUSOR project. Breuker (1987) describes EUROHELP, a recent project—conducted in the context of the European ESPRIT program—that applies the coaching paradigm to an intelligent help system.

The interest in metacognitive issues at LRDC is based on work by Glaser (1984). The bite-sized architecture is presented in (Bonar et al., 1986), but is also discussed in (Bonar, 1985) and (Cosic, 1985). Shute and Glaser (1986) report on SMITHTOWN; a shorter conference paper is also available (Shute and Bonar, 1986). Lesgold (1987) introduces the notion of information layers for curriculum representation. Steering testing and MHO are discussed in (Lesgold et al., 1987). LRDC's ITS Group is investigating the architectural principles presented here with other prototypical systems in such diverse domains as arithmetic (Bonar, 1985c), electricity in a previous version of MHO called OHM (Cosic, 1985), and optics (Reimann, 1986).

Another tutoring system developed at the University of Pittsburgh, largely in the context of LRDC, is SPIRIT (Barzilay, 1984, 1985); it deals with basic concepts and practice problems in probability theory. SPIRIT combines a number of techniques discussed in this book, including a rule-based didactic module à la GUIDON (see Chapter 12), error analysis and association with likely misconceptions à la MENO-II (see Section 11.4), and an object-oriented approach to student modeling reminiscent of the bite-sized architecture. One of the project's main theme is the effective integration of these components, with a view to implementing a global pedagogical strategy; this interest in pedagogical principles extends the research line of WEST. In this regard, SPIRIT's most distinctive feature is the integration of two didactic subcomponents, the "tutor" and the "mentor," which enable SPIRIT to vary its didactic strategy on the basis of its student model, switching between unobtrusive coaching and directive tutoring.

Chapter 8

Bugs in procedural skills: the 'buggy repair step' story

Like WEST, the study described in this chapter was spawned in the context of the SOPHIE project. Again, the choice of domain is motivated by its simplicity compared to electronics, but this study investigates diagnosis rather than coaching strategies. Recall that WEST's differential student model, like WUSOR-II's overlay, views the student's knowledge state as a subset of issues comprising the correct skill. There is no provision for defining incorrectly encoded issues that the student may have acquired. To make this provision possible, the study covered here concentrates on the notion of *bug*. This term, borrowed from computer programming jargon, has become a buzzword among people interested in student models; it refers to errors internalized by the student that are explicitly represented in the student model. Bugs are usually procedural or localized errors rather than deep, pervasive misconceptions. The study of the bugs commonly encountered by a student population in a domain is often called a *theory of bugs*.

This chapter covers the evolution of a long project that started with BUGGY, a purely descriptive theory of bugs whereby the model enumerates observable bugs. We also present DEBUGGY, which extends this model into a diagnostic system. Thereafter, we discuss REPAIR and STEP theories, which attempt to provide "generative bug stories" to explain the genesis of observed bugs in terms of underlying cognitive models.

8.1 BUGGY: an enumerative theory of bugs

The development of BUGGY began with the analysis of protocols produced by students who were solving problems requiring algebraic manipulations (Brown et al., 1975b). Later, to avoid obscuring the analysis with algebra's numerous rules and to take advantage of available data, Brown and Burton (1978a) decided to explore their modeling paradigm in the domain of arithmetic skills. More specifically, the BUGGY project has come to be generally associated with place-value subtraction.

8.1.1 A modular representation of subskills

The preliminary studies of students performing algebra had revealed the need for a special representational scheme for procedural skills such that any constituent of the skill that can be mislearned is represented independently. This scheme was to support the design of a *diagnostic model*: that is, a model of the student's current skill that would reflect its exact composition of correct and incorrect elementary subskills. These specifications led to the adoption of the *procedural network* as a representational mechanism for diagnostic models (Brown et al., 1977b). A procedural network for a skill is a decomposition of that skill into subprocedures which are linked together in a lattice of subgoals. Figure 8.1 shows a procedural network for subtraction. The links stand for the procedure-calling relation, down to a set of primitive actions. A procedural network is executable, and can thus be run on a set of problems to model the skill that it represents. Its structure is also inspectable in that, unlike a flat set of rules, it uses well-defined subprocedure calls.

A diagnostic modeling scheme based on a procedural network contains all the necessary subskills for the global skill, as well as all the possible buggy variants (or *bugs*) of each subskill. It can replace an

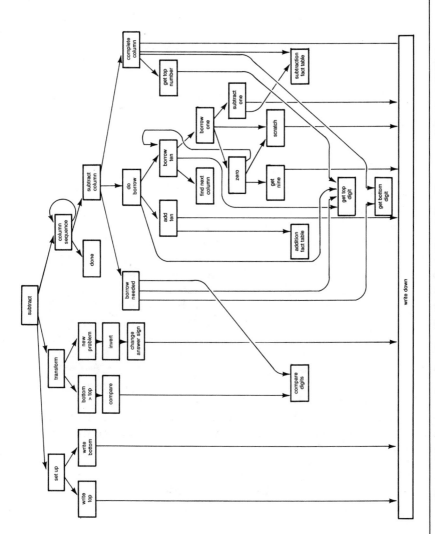

Figure 8.1 A procedural network for subtraction (after Brown and Burton, 1978a).

143	The student subtracts the smaller digit in each column from the larger digit regardless of
-28	which is on top.
125	

143
-28
125
The student subtracts the smaller digit in each column from the larger digit regardless of which is on top.

143
-28
125
When the student needs to borrow, he adds 10 to the top digit of the current column without subtracting 1 from the next column to the left.

1300
-522
878
When borrowing from a column whose top digit is 0, the student writes 9 but does not continue borrowing from the column to the left of the 0.

140
-21
121
Whenever the top digit in a column is 0, the student writes the bottom digit in the answer, i.e., $0-N=N$.

Figure 8.2 Examples of bugs in subtraction procedures (Brown and Burton, 1978a).

individual subskill in the procedural network by one of its bugs, and thus attempt to reproduce a student's incorrect behavior. If such a faulted network does obtain the same answers as the student on a sufficient set of problems, the bugs that have replaced their correct siblings in the network are then posited as being those possessed by the student. Such an instantiation of the subprocedure calls, which actually models the student in a *deterministic* fashion, is considered a *deep-structure model*: it explains the student's incorrect behavior in terms of a set of exact internalized errors, rather than of, say, a probabilistic estimate of correct and incorrect answers such as is typical of stochastic models. When presenting the examples of bugs in subtraction procedures shown in Figure 8.2, Brown and Burton actually invite readers to try to discover the bugs themselves first, in order better to appreciate the difficulty of the task. Note, for instance, that the first two lines show two different bugs that produce the same answer.

Limitations of enumerative theories of bugs

With this deterministic approach to accounting for errors, the precise information about the nature of internalized bugs contained in the deep structure is very helpful for pedagogical purposes. In this sense, BUGGY's diagnostic model is a real milestone in the research on student modeling. However, we should mention two important limitations of the paradigm. First, it is clear that the modeling capability of the network hinges on a proper decomposition of the skill to a granularity level at which each single bug can be isolated as a variant of a separate procedure. In general, this will require in-depth analysis both of the domain and of actual performances by large numbers of students. Even then, the fixed library of bugs will limit the modeling power of the system to student errors it knows about.

The second limitation is perhaps more fundamental because of its repercussions for remediation. While BUGGY's procedural network is able to single out bugs in the student's procedure, it does not attempt to explain them. In the representational language of procedural networks, any buggy subprocedure is only related to the correct one by virtue of carrying out the same subgoal, that is, of being called in the same circumstances. Apart from that, they are two individual pieces of code: the language has no facility for explicitly representing the semantic nature of the deviation a bug stands for, let alone explaining how it was generated. After describing some implemented systems based on the BUGGY paradigm, we will turn to some research that was undertaken to address these two limitations.

8.1.2 The nature of bugs in procedural skills

The idea of a diagnostic model assumes that, in problems that require procedural skills, mistakes are due to the correct execution of an incorrect procedure, and not to an inability to follow an otherwise correct procedure. In fact, in the process of decomposing arithmetic skills and defining libraries of bugs to account for existing data, Brown and Burton found that many students manifest a nearly perfect consistency in following incorrect procedures. Since this discovery confirms the intuition underlying the notion of diagnostic model—and contradicts the widely held belief that students who make mistakes are simply not good at following procedures—a game was devised on the BUGGY model to train teachers in analyzing student errors.

In this game, the program instantiates a simple bug in the diagnostic model and asks a team of teachers to discover it. They are to make up problems and submit them for the buggy model to solve, until they can single out the bug. As in SOPHIE-II's game, the team format is helpful in getting participants to articulate their strategies and hypotheses. Indeed, experimentation with the game revealed that people are not very good at giving precise procedural descriptions verbally, as can be seen in Figure 8.3, which shows a session with BUGGY in the domain of addition. Apparently, student teachers found the game illuminating in that what looked at first like a completely random behavior could eventually be

BUGGY: Welcome to Buggy. I have chosen a bug.
Here is an example of the bug.
```
 17
+ 5
 13
```
Now you can give me problems to determine the bug.

Team:
```
18    43
+ 6   +79
```

BUGGY: 15   23

Team: Got the bug! Student adds the number to be carried in the last column worked in.

This cryptic description is typical of those observed. The team is trying to say that if a column adds to more than 9, the unit digit and the carry digit are added together and written as the answer for that column. BUGGY does not attempt to understand the English descriptions, but heuristically generates five problems on which the players may test their hypothesis. The generation of these problems involves some knowledge about the manifestations of individual bugs.

BUGGY: Here are some problems to test your theory about the bug. What is:
```
 21
+39
```

Team: 51

BUGGY: That's not the bug I have. Using my bug:
```
 21
+39
 15
```
Try giving me more examples ...

The first hypothesis did account for the observed behavior. Unfortunately, it is not the student's bug.

Team:
```
  51    99    68
+1707   +99   + 9
```

BUGGY: 21   36   23

The team needs to try problems of a greater diversity. This highlights the importance of considering a variety of hypotheses before positing a diagnosis. Notice the possibly humorous, probably disastrous results that would have transpired if the team had stopped earlier and tried to tutor the student on the basis of their initial belief.

Team: Got the bug! The student is adding all the digits together.

BUGGY: Here are some problems to test your theory about the bug. What are:
```
33    1091    8     28    90
+99   +  60   +34   +70   + 6
```

Team: 24   17   15   17   15

BUGGY: Very good. My description of the bug is: The student always sums up all the digits, with no regard to columns.

Figure 8.3 A BUGGY game with teacher students
(after Brown and Burton, 1978a).

traced to a consistent buggy procedure. Moreover, exposure to the game significantly improved their ability to detect error patterns (Brown et al., 1977a).

A similar result was achieved when the game was tried in a classroom with seventh and eighth graders. This "role reversal," in which students did the diagnosing, had a rather interesting effect. At first, students would find the program's mistakes really "dumb," but after some exposure, they would realize that there was always a systematic explanation for its behavior; they became less judgmental once they saw that surface errors revealed deeper bugs. Brown and Burton find this result "particularly exciting, since it paves the way for students to see their own faulty behavior not as being a sign of their own stupidity, but as a source of data about their own errors" (Brown and Burton, 1978a, p. 172).

8.2 DEBUGGY: a diagnostic system

Burton (1982) describes DEBUGGY, a sophisticated diagnostic system extending the BUGGY model. He discusses the issues of search strategies and inconsistent data involved in inferring the deep-structure model from problems solved by students. Two versions of DEBUGGY are presented: an off-line version, which analyzes tests taken by students, and an on-line version, IDEBUGGY, which diagnoses the student's procedure incrementally while giving him new problems to solve.

8.2.1 Off-line diagnosis: heuristic search strategies

To construct the student model as an individualized procedural network, the simplest method that comes to mind is of course generate-and-test: each bug in turn replaces a subprocedure in the correct model, until a bug is found with which the model reproduces all the student's answers on the problem set. In reality, however, the situation is complicated by the need to deal with compound bugs, whereby primitive bugs combine to manifest in ways that can be quite nontrivial. A study of subtraction problems (VanLehn, 1982) shows that 37% of the students manifest multiple bugs, sometimes as many as four together. Even though the number of primitive bugs is often limited (about 110 observed bugs for subtraction), trying all combinations, even only up to four, will generate too large a search space for exhaustive testing.

To make the search computationally tractable, DEBUGGY assumes that the simple bugs that interact to form multiple ones can also be detected individually. This means that there exists at least one problem in which either the simple bugs appear in isolation or the complex bug is consistent with their individual manifestations. On this assumption, the generate-and-test method is first used to construct an *initial hypothesis space*. Every primitive bug is tested, plus a few very common combinations, and only those for which there is evidence in the data are kept. The initial hypothesis space is further reduced by eliminations of certain overlaps in coverage, with preference for multiple over single evidence. Next, the bugs in this initial hypothesis space are combined, and every combination that explains more than its parts is retained in the set of hypotheses. DEBUGGY limits compounding by barring some bug-specific incompatibilities and by retaining only one combination when two are deemed equivalent (e.g., two orderings of independent bugs). This combining of hypotheses is repeated until a perfect model is obtained or until a predetermined threshold of complexity for multiple bugs is reached.

For the domain of subtraction, this method was tried on large sets of data with good results. The same techniques can be applied to other domains, provided it is reasonable to assume that primitive bugs always manifest individually in problem sets.

8.2.2   Coercions: a model-driven analysis of noisy data

A further consideration is that students are never perfectly consistent with their own procedures, so that it is not realistic to expect perfect matches. In addition to purely careless mistakes, certain domain-specific performance *slips* tend to occur frequently. To deal with this noise, Burton adopts a technique he calls *coercion*. Basically, a coercion is an attempted rational justification for the discrepancies between a hypothesis and part of the data. The justification is proposed with respect to known common performance slips, which are introduced into a hypothesized model to force a match with the data. For the domain of subtraction, coercions naturally include errors in basic facts (e.g., $6 - 4 = 3$), but Burton also considers variations in applying a procedure that are likely to occur in limit cases (e.g., in the rightmost and leftmost columns, which are often perceived differently by students). In addition, some likely inconsistencies in performance are associated with specific bugs.

Of course, coercions must be used with caution, lest all hypotheses be made to look good. Burton notes that any behavior in subtraction could be explained with enough errors in basic facts. Hence, coercions can only be applied to discriminate between hypotheses that are otherwise well supported by the data, and it is essential to devise a good system of penalties to constrain the effects of any coercions that are not consistent throughout the test.

At any rate, coercions do not account for all the noise, and the best hypothesis must still be selected through a final classification according to some general criteria of quality such as data coverage and simplicity of hypotheses. Even then, a significant proportion of students had to be classified as "undiagnosed"—about a third of students with errors—because DEBUGGY could not reliably account for their behavior. This proportion is apparently fairly stable across samples of the student population, even when the proportion of students with errors varies. The fact that bugs and slips do not suffice to diagnose the application of procedural skills is an important result, which seems to reveal some fundamental limitations of bug-level analyses (VanLehn, 1982). In the context of the BUGGY project, this observation helped motivate the development of more sophisticated models such as REPAIR theory.

Coercions and bugs

Note that the similarity between coercions and bugs is striking. They both introduce deviations into a procedural model on the basis of some expectations concerning likely errors. In general, the exact distinction between coercions and bugs is open to discussion, although in the case of DEBUGGY it is well justified by Burton. Because of this similarity, it is interesting to wonder whether the scheme used for coercions could also be applied for other bugs. Instead of introducing the effects of known classes of performance slips into the model, as do coercions, one could introduce the effects of common misconceptions about the domain, with a similar penalty system. This might provide a way of explaining bugs in terms of more general underlying misconceptions. As we will see, further research on generative models for bugs has attempted something similar, but only in terms of learning processes. The reduction of bugs to misconceptions in an underlying model of the domain is still mostly an open research area.

In conclusion, while the notion of coercions is not a panacea, it is a very important contribution to student modeling. In fact, very little work has been done on the issue of noisy data in ITS; most systems simply resolve the difficulty with some form of unsophisticated numerical averaging. In contrast, Burton openly addresses the issue, and his coercions are a form of *model-driven* analysis of noise. As such, they make extensive use of the domain's semantics and allow specific knowledge about performance to be brought to bear, unlike purely statistical methods. Their applicability extends beyond the design of instructional diagnostic systems to other AI tasks involving data analysis and partial matches, like theory formation, machine learning, and analogical reasoning.

- generate a simple problem;

- generate a problem that splits between the bugs in the current set of active hypotheses;

- allow more-obscure bugs as hypotheses;

- create more hypotheses by extending (compounding) the current ones;

- reconsider previously suspended hypotheses;

- propose a diagnosis;

- give up.

Figure 8.4 Summary of tasks available for selection by IDEBUGGY (Burton, 1982).

8.2.3 IDEBUGGY: an on-line version

Since the version of DEBUGGY just described operates off-line and requires all the data at once, it can be used to correct entire tests, but cannot be used to tutor. This motivated the design of an interactive version, IDEBUGGY, also described by Burton (1982). The difficulty with the on-line setup is that the system cannot spend much time computing between problems (although Burton does not mention taking advantage of the time when the student is thinking and the system is waiting for some input). In IDEBUGGY, to limit and optimize the use of time, a heuristically guided controller chooses among the different tasks that are possible at any point, such as the ones listed in Figure 8.4. Then it activates small independent modules to perform specific actions. In this way, the control is never committed to any single function for a long period of time. At a high level, IDEBUGGY must deal with two alternating tasks: generating problems and managing the space of hypotheses.

Problem generation

The fact that the system can intelligently generate new problems in the course of diagnosis is an important advantage of the on-line setup, since these problems can be designed to discriminate among competing hypotheses. To compose new discriminatory subtraction problems, a generate-and-test strategy is adopted. With each primitive bug is associated a heuristic problem generator that is made to meet certain conditions in the generated problem, like having a zero on top or the same digit twice in one column. Because of the possibility of noise, an additional stratagem adopted in IDEBUGGY is to vary past problems slightly, for instance by changing numbers, to ensure that the diagnostic information they have provided is not due to performance slips.

When a number of problems have been generated heuristically to involve the bugs hypothesized by the currently competing models, they are first solved internally by each of these models. If different answers are produced, the problems are able to discriminate between competitors and are submitted to the student; otherwise more problems are generated. There has to be a threshold on this generation of problems since internally differing hypotheses may be *logically equivalent*, that is, may always manifest with the same answers—something the system has no way to detect syntactically. Beyond the threshold, hypotheses are considered equivalent unless a later problem happens to discriminate between them.

Managing the space of hypotheses

Since the student's answers are only progressively available, the set of hypotheses the system must manage can be too large to be considered in its entirety at every move. In IDEBUGGY, there are two measures aimed at limiting the search space. First, although no hypothesis is ever completely forgotten, only a small set is kept active. In the course of the session, hypotheses are "suspended" as they mispredict the student's answers, to be recalled later only if the active ones become relatively worse. Second, primitive bugs are ordered from common to obscure; the more obscure ones are tried only later, when the more common ones have failed. Single hypotheses are also combined into compound ones gradually as the current set reveals itself unable to model the student. Finally, coercions are applied to promising hypotheses until only one hypothesis remains and is proposed as the diagnosis.

There is little report on the actual use of IDEBUGGY. The interplay between the advantage of being able to generate diagnostic problems and the difficulty of having to respond quickly requires a greater recourse to heuristic control. As a result of this heuristic character, it is somewhat difficult to ascertain whether the scheme used here will diagnose bugs in a reasonable number of problems in general, and Burton does not provide any demonstration. Nevertheless, general engineering principles for the design of on-line diagnosis are proposed: shorter lifespan of individual tasks, suspension and recall of hypotheses from and to a current set, and gradual introduction of complexity according to likely relevance.

8.2.4   Diagnostic tests and the notion of subskill

We have seen that the off-line version of DEBUGGY has been tested extensively on real data, reportedly with much success. However, not surprisingly, its diagnostic power is limited by the quality of the test used by the students. Brown and Burton (1978a) suggest that the art of test design can be made both more formal and more meaningful by the existence of a theory of bugs for the domain.

From an engineering standpoint, Brown and Burton propose to use the BUGGY model to define a measure of the *diagnosticity* of a test. A test of high diagnosticity is designed to manifest the possible bugs individually, and to do so in enough different circumstances to determine bugs' consistency quite reliably. Brown and Burton's idea is to partition the set of bugs into equivalence classes where the equivalence relation is that the bugs produce the same answers on all the problems in the test. With this measure, an ideal test is one for which each bug is in its own partition. Burton (1982, p. 172) reports using a program based on this idea to produce a "test capable of distinguishing among 1200 compound bugs with only 12 problems!" The test used in practice actually had 20 problems, so that individual bugs and compounds would be invoked enough times for their consistency to be determined.

From a pedagogical standpoint, Brown and Burton note that grading based on the number and type of bugs or misconceptions manifested in a test would be fairer and more amenable to proper remediation than usual grading schemes based on the number of right and wrong answers. Since this proposal for more informative grading is backed by a practical method and puts to good pedagogical use the ability of computers to deal precisely with complex information, I hope that it will have an impact beyond the research laboratory. However, more proofs of feasibility to publicize this type of knowledge-oriented testing may be required before it can be widely adopted, since constructing theories of bugs is a very laborious process.

Primitive subskills: a formal definition

An important concept for the design of diagnostic tests is that of a *primitive subskill*. This concept is also critical for curriculum construction, especially if the process is automated as in BIP. For a given domain the exact set of these subskills can be extremely difficult to define. Equipped with the tools of the BUGGY model, Burton (1982) suggests that a partition of the theory of bugs be used to define a primitive subskill as "any isolatable part of the skill that it is possible to mislearn" (p. 177). More formally, the set of all observable bugs is partitioned under the equivalence relation of giving wrong answers on the same problems, considering all possible problems. Then a primitive subskill is an equivalence class in this partition; in other words, it is a part of the skill that corresponds to bugs manifesting in exactly the same problems. In practice, one need only consider a finite number of problems.

This definition is elegant because it captures subskills as the smallest units of knowledge that can be individually mislearned in a purely empirical way, independent of any representation of the "correct" skill. As a consequence, it can take into account misperceptions of the domain that are unlikely to have any correspondence in a representation of this correct skill, such as that held by a student who was found to skip columns with equal digits when borrowing. It follows that the decomposition of the skill with this definition is likely to provide a much finer granularity than one that starts with a representation of a correct version. Place-value subtraction with borrowing, for instance, turns out to involve as many as 58 subskills.

8.3 REPAIR theory: a generative theory of bugs

The BUGGY model can diagnose a procedure in terms of a set of primitive subskills and their variants, but we have seen that it has no way of automatically deriving its primitive bugs from the correct skill. In the overlay model, for instance, a student's suboptimal behavior is modeled by a syntactic simplification of the expert skill in that some units of knowledge are simply ignored. In Chapter 10, we will see another modeling language by Young and O'Shea in which distortions of the original subskill correspond to some syntactic manipulations of the representation. In contrast with these syntactic modifications, further work on the BUGGY project is based on the assumption that observed bugs are determined by the cognitive architecture that produces them. In other words, these deviations cannot be explained, let alone automatically generated, without a theory of how people form misconceptions and invent ways of dealing with them when they give rise to problematic situations.

REPAIR theory is proposed by John Seely Brown and Kurt VanLehn (1980) as an information-processing model of the *rational genesis* of bugs. It builds on BUGGY's extensive data to achieve the explanatory power lacking in its diagnostic models. Much as bugs in the BUGGY model are meant to account for systematic errors that students are observed to make, REPAIR theory is meant to provide procedures and constraints that will account for the appearance of the bugs observed and not of others. In the REPAIR model, the formation of bugs is described as the result of "complex, intentional actions reflecting mistaken beliefs about the skill"

(p. 380). Unlike computers, students become inventive when their actions are blocked by a situation their current knowledge has not prepared them to handle. When incomplete knowledge leads to an *impasse*, that is, a point where a necessary action violates a constraint, they attempt a *repair*, that is, a local piece of problem solving that will allow them to continue in spite of the impasse.

The whole theory is based on the interplay of impasses and repairs, in that surface bugs as observed in BUGGY are now derived from various chains of impasse-repair episodes. Thus, a manifested bug is different from the distortion of the student's internalized procedure that leads to an impasse. In other words, from the standpoint of a model of the student's knowledge, an observed bug is now reduced to the application of an incorrect procedure, called the student's *core procedure*, which gives rise to the impasse-repair process manifesting as a bug à la BUGGY. This reduction has obvious implications for in-depth remediation, since tutorial interventions can address the core procedure directly. Figure 8.5 shows a hypothetical example of the types of "bug stories" that serve as targets for the theory: here the faulty core procedure does not modify zeroes when borrowing across them.

8.3.1   Representation of procedural skills

Since the nodes in BUGGY's procedural networks are treated as black boxes, the language does not provide any formalism for expressing the internal differences between a correct subskill and one of its buggy variants. In a move to refine the granularity of procedural networks while retaining the subgoaling hierarchy, Brown and VanLehn propose to represent the skill with a *generalized AND/OR graph* (GAO graph). Because the internal representation is no longer a diagnostic convenience, but is instrumental for explaining how bugs are generated, VanLehn (1981, 1983a) goes to great lengths to justify all the representational decisions in cognitive terms. Although some details of the argumentation fail to convince me, it is rare in AI that such care is taken to uncover and support all assumptions and decisions, and to acknowledge the profound and critical implications of the representation for the quality and the validity of a model. For this book, we cannot go into all the details, but the interested reader is encouraged to look at VanLehn's papers.

Essentially, the basic mechanism of a GAO graph is that of a production system, with the advantages of the finely grained formalism of production rules. But this production system is interpreted with a goal stack of interspersed AND and OR goals that provide the representation with an explicit control structure. In addition, some notion of scope is afforded by a focus of attention that can be shifted with the generation of

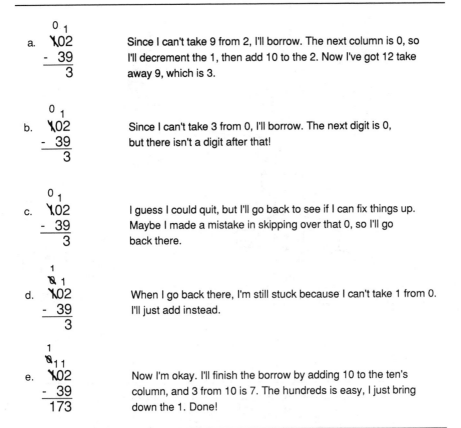

a.
$$\begin{array}{r} 0\ _1 \\ \cancel{1}02 \\ -\ 39 \\ \hline 3 \end{array}$$

Since I can't take 9 from 2, I'll borrow. The next column is 0, so I'll decrement the 1, then add 10 to the 2. Now I've got 12 take away 9, which is 3.

b.
$$\begin{array}{r} 0\ _1 \\ \cancel{1}02 \\ -\ 39 \\ \hline 3 \end{array}$$

Since I can't take 3 from 0, I'll borrow. The next digit is 0, but there isn't a digit after that!

c.
$$\begin{array}{r} 0\ _1 \\ \cancel{1}02 \\ -\ 39 \\ \hline 3 \end{array}$$

I guess I could quit, but I'll go back to see if I can fix things up. Maybe I made a mistake in skipping over that 0, so I'll go back there.

d.
$$\begin{array}{r} 1 \\ \cancel{0}\ _1 \\ \cancel{1}02 \\ -\ 39 \\ \hline 3 \end{array}$$

When I go back there, I'm still stuck because I can't take 1 from 0. I'll just add instead.

e.
$$\begin{array}{r} 1 \\ \cancel{0}\ _1\ _1 \\ \cancel{1}02 \\ -\ 39 \\ \hline 173 \end{array}$$

Now I'm okay. I'll finish the borrow by adding 10 to the ten's column, and 3 from 10 is 7. The hundreds is easy, I just bring down the 1. Done!

Figure 8.5 An example of a "bug story" (VanLehn, 1981).

subgoals. A simplified GAO graph for a correct subtraction procedure is displayed in Figure 8.6. Each node consists of a few rules that implement a goal. AND goals are in boxes: their subgoals are sequential steps executed in order. OR goals are in ellipses: their subgoals are choices, one of which is selected for execution. Note how the regular alternation of AND and OR goals makes every sequence and decision point explicit.

8.3.2 Mechanisms for the generation of bugs

Within the GAO graph, an impasse is a situation in which no legal rule applies. When an impasse is reached, the flow of control switches from the rule interpreter to a local problem solver, which attempts a repair. In accordance with some careful empirical investigations of actual repairs,

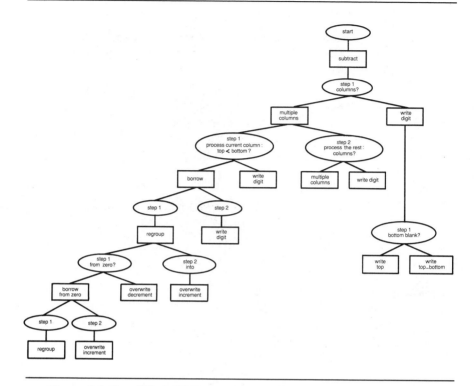

**Figure 8.6 Simplified GAO graph for a correct subtraction procedure
(after VanLehn, 1983a).**

the scope of the problem solver is limited to the current execution state, so that repairs are only applied to the process state of the rule interpreter, but not to the rule structure or the subtraction problem. As a result, any form of look-ahead is excluded, with the consequence that, as soon as the repair has been applied and control has returned to the interpreter, a new impasse may be generated. Such chains of impasses, illustrated in Figure 8.5, are frequently observed in practice, and they are always short. This principle of locality of repairs is central to the theory because it rules out major reconsiderations of the procedure during execution. Repairs are viewed only as small temporary patches performed within the confines of the rule interpreter so as to allow the execution to proceed. They are not in themselves a form of learning.

Because of this locality, the repairing process is viewed as a property of a general-purpose reasoning engine which interprets core procedures, that is, as a property of the architecture of the human mind. As a consequence, the theory has to argue for the psychological validity of its rule interpreter in terms of the plausibility of the bugs it generates. To this end, it includes a number of principles governing the generation and filtering of repairs and impasses.

Generative principles for repairs and impasses

Three basic principles constrain the types of problem-solving heuristics actually allowed in the theory to account for more data with additional repairs. Since repair mechanisms are assumed to be part of a general-purpose reasoning engine, the first principle is that they be *domain-independent* rather than based on some domain-specific singularity. They must be instances of general problem-solving strategies such as skipping a step, backing up to a previous choice point, or replacing an operation by an analogous one used in similar circumstances. Applications of these last two repairs are illustrated in Figure 8.5, steps c. and d., respectively. The second principle reflects the locality of the problem solver in requiring that repairs be *small*, consisting of one primitive action or known subgoal.

The third constraint on the addition of new repair heuristics is provided by the *independence principle* of impasses and repairs. This is a natural consequence of the first principle, since repairs are domain-independent properties of the interpreter and impasses are caused by faulty core procedures, which are domain-specific. Therefore, in generating bugs, impasses and repairs are considered as orthogonal, in the sense that any repair can potentially be applied to any impasse to generate different bugs. Of course not all pairings of any repair with any impasse are interesting. In this regard, the independence principle states that any new repair, added to the theory to generate certain observed bugs, must also produce bugs that actually occur in the data or are highly plausible when it combines with all existing impasses to which it is legally applicable. In this way, it is not possible to add ad hoc rules just to explain one bug.

For the model to be complete, there is also a need for generative principles that modify the original skill so as to produce the *core procedures* that lead to impasses. The mechanism used by Brown and VanLehn for simplifying or distorting a procedure represented as a GAO graph is that of deleting rules: the *deletion principle*. The absence of one rule causes the interpreter to fire another one instead—usually, but not always, leading to an impasse. If no impasse is reached, the bug generated is a repairless one, and is equivalent to the type generated in models based on syntactic manipulations. If an impasse is reached, the stage is set for a repair.

Filtering principles for impasses and repairs

In practice, the deletion of certain rules generates core procedures that are psychologically very unlikely; hence a few filtering principles must augment the scheme so as to block the deletion in these specific cases.

The intent of these *blocking principles* is to enforce assumptions about plausible learning and forgetting processes. As a simplification principle, deletion, which is syntactic in nature, is not meant to reflect the way students arrive at incomplete versions of the skill, but merely to generate impasses that can occur and require repairs. Since this principle was merely chosen as a useful theoretical assumption, the authors view it as the least satisfactory part of the theory. In fact, they suspect that it is largely responsible for the theory's inadequacies. A complete theory of bug formation needs a validated model of the way distortions of the skill arise in the context of learning, and this motivates further developments of the theory described in later sections.

In addition to the principles that block rule deletion under certain conditions, there need also be filtering principles for repairs so as to avoid the generation of implausible bugs in some cases. Of course, many repairs are discarded before they are actually used because their very application to an impasse immediately violates the preconditions of some rule they involve. Nevertheless, a number of the repairs absolutely required for covering the data would generate absurd bugs when legally paired with certain impasses. To veto the use of repairs in these cases, the theory includes a set of *critics*. However, critics must represent knowledge of general constraints in the domain in the form of regularities that students can be assumed to have abstracted from observation. An example of a critic for subtraction states that the general form of solutions precludes the presence of blanks in the middle of the number in the answer.

8.3.3 Explanatory power and observational coverage

An interesting observation is that ignoring a critic, like ignoring a rule, can lead to a new impasse, which impasse in turn can combine with any repair to generate a new bug. Because of this possibility, the set of critics cannot just be extended at will to fit the data, but must be carefully determined so that no unobserved bugs are generated. Note that this constraint is similar to the one limiting the addition of new repairs. In fact, these two constraints are illustrative of the way Brown and VanLehn ensure that the theories they build are not just ad hoc computational models "tailored" to fit some data. There must be global principles that propagate the consequences of local modifications throughout the model. Without these ripple effects, called the *entailments* of changes, a model is just a program cleverly constructed to reproduce some behavior: it does not explicitly contain the reasons that make it a better model than another completely different program with the same output. As a result, it lacks explanatory power altogether. We will come back to this point because this care in designing an explanatory model is an important contribution

	impasses	repairs
generative principles	• rule deletion	• domain-independent heuristics
	• ignoring critics	• locality of problem-solving
applicability constraints	• deletion applies to any rule unless blocked	• repairs apply to any impasse unless filtered
filtering principles	• blocking principles	• rule preconditions • critics
constraints on filters	• blocking principles reflect learning	• critics are general domain regularities

Figure 8.7 Summary of principles governing the use of impasses and repairs in REPAIR theory.

to the research on information-processing models of human cognition in general. Principles governing the use of impasses and repairs in REPAIR theory are summarized in Figure 8.7.

This first version of a generative theory failed to reproduce a fairly large portion of the observed bugs. As we mentioned, the deletion principle is seen as the main culprit. However, REPAIR theory did predict several unobserved bugs which were subsequently observed. Furthermore it correctly predicted a phenomenon that it was not originally meant to explain, but that was later observed as quite common: *bug migration*. Apparently, bugs exhibited by one student sometimes vary between tests and even in the same test. The theory actually suggests that students, who do not usually seem to retain in long-term memory the local patches they perform, may well apply different repairs when presented with the same impasse. The data confirmed that migration takes place inside of classes of bugs caused by the same impasses. Therefore, although bugs are not always stable, they can nevertheless be accounted for in a systematic way. Such serendipity certainly provides strong supporting evidence for the fundamental principles of a theory.

8.4 STEP theory: a learning model of bug generation

We have seen that REPAIR theory does not attempt to explain or model the genesis of a student's core procedure, but instead uses the deletion principle to perturb the correct skill so that an impasse is generated. Because this is a mere syntactic manipulation, a few somewhat ad hoc guidelines must prevent the deletion of certain rules.   Although the deletion principle does constrain the form of incorrect procedures by maintaining the structure of the correct one, a better model of impasse generation requires a theory of how procedural skills are acquired through the kind of teaching sequences children encounter in schools (VanLehn, 1981).   VanLehn's doctoral dissertation (1983a, 1983b) is an impressive attempt at coupling the principles of REPAIR theory with such a model. The name "STEP theory" highlights the central role played by successive lessons in incrementally transforming functional subsets of the skill into its complete version.   This emphasis on knowledge as the result of a communication process clearly sets this work apart from other AI models of skill acquisition, which mainly concentrate on the effect of practice on performance.   It also makes it particularly interesting in the context of this book.

8.4.1   Planning nets: teleological reasoning

Before we present the current form of STEP theory, a bit of history is in order; an initial direction of research deserves some attention even though it was abandoned.   Furthermore, the motives for the decision to change direction are interesting for our understanding of the current theory.   In trying to model the way students build incorrect procedures, it is reasonable to assume initially that they perceive the *teleology* of the procedures (that is, the goals of its steps), but that erroneous *teleological rationalizations* lead them to choose forms of the skill that differ from the intended one.   A study adopting this perspective would concentrate on the way students "understand" procedures.   An interesting issue in this regard is the use of manipulative models such as Dienes blocks or abaci, included in some curricula.   These models are intended to impart some semantic understanding of procedures to students, and require an analogical transfer to the target procedure.

As a first step toward such a study, VanLehn and Brown (1980) propose the mechanism of *planning nets* for representing the meaning of procedures from a teleological perspective.   As illustrated in Figure 8.8, a planning net is a directed graph.   Nodes contain increasingly expanded flow charts that represent the partial design stages of a procedure being synthesized from first principles.   Links[1] stand both for domain-dependent constraints the procedure must comply with regarding the

---

[1]In the example of the figure, the exact meaning of the cryptic labels on the links is not important: they refer to a detailed example in the paper. Splitting branches indicate that two constraints can be dealt with independently.

operation, the representation, or the physical substrate, and for general planning and derivational heuristics used to resolve violations of constraints. Two nodes are linked if applying a constraint or a heuristic to the procedure of the first one leads to the new version of the second one. The last node of the graph is the complete procedure.

The name "planning nets" refers to these planning intentions, explicitly represented along with the procedure. The teleological knowledge provided by this planning information gives a coherent view of how successive parts of the procedure combine to accomplish the procedure's purpose. The authors argue that this is the kind of information experts use to draw analogies between procedures. Actually, the design of the representational scheme was originally intended to account for the ability to recognize these analogical relations. Analogies, viewed as structure-preserving mappings between these semantically enriched representations, are to play an important role in the acquisition of the skill.

From a pedagogical standpoint, the successive nodes of a planning net constitute learning stages whereby the ontology of a procedure can guide the development of teaching sequences. Indeed, the relation between two procedures is defined in terms of a formal mapping determining their teleological differences: hence, the notion of planning nets supports operational definitions of principles such as those listed in Figure 8.9, which govern the derivation of optimal sequences of example procedures. The key to these natural teleologically oriented explanations is to introduce the teleology of a procedure in an incremental, monotonic, and connected progression. To this end, one has to find pairs of models of the procedure both to *manifest* the implications of successive constraints and to *motivate* the requirements they impose on the design. Thus, the transition from one model to the next is made to highlight the succession of *crucial ideas* that constitute the foundation of the skill and justify the shape of the final procedure.

As an example, VanLehn and Brown (1980) present a detailed explanatory sequence for the standard subtraction procedure whose 19 successive models illustrate no less than 18 constraints derived from the application of an efficiency metric. I have to admit that the explanation has clarified my own understanding of a procedure I thought I understood well. By requiring the replay of design decisions, the construction of planning nets forces assumptions to be made explicit in a way that is reminiscent of efforts to eliminate function from structure in ENVISION theory. This similarity is generalized in Chapter 15.

Although, as we will see, the ideas presented here did not seem suitable for providing an explanatory framework for BUGGY's data, they may still be applicable as a prescriptive model for more sophisticated forms of learning and teaching. Indeed, the information about design contained in planning nets captures a rich notion of expertise necessary for effective instruction in complex domains. For instance, the formalism

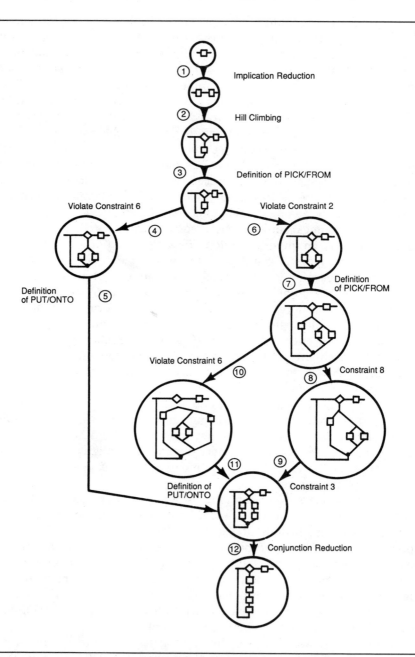

Figure 8.8 A planning net for a simple procedure.
Adapted from "Planning nets: A representation for formalizing analogies and semantic models of procedural skills," by K. VanLehn and J. S. Brown, in *Aptitude, Learning and Instruction: Cognitive Process Analyses*, Hillsdale, NJ: Erlbaum. ©1980 by Lawrence Erlbaum Associates, Inc.; reprinted with permission.

Incrementality: for each constraint, there should exist a pair of exemplary procedures, illustrating respectively the absence and the presence of the constraint.

Progression: each transition between two versions of the procedure should illustrate an improvement according to a measure of quality such as an efficiency metric.

Tightness: each pair of procedures in the sequence should illustrate at least one constraint.

Nonredundancy: constraints should not be introduced or removed twice.

Monotonicity: optimally, constraints should only be added.

Figure 8.9 Some principles of teleological explanations

Adapted from "Planning nets: A representation for formalizing analogies and semantic models of procedural skills," by K. VanLehn and J. S. Brown, in *Aptitude, Learning and Instruction: Cognitive Process Analyses*, Hillsdale, NJ: Erlbaum. ©1980 by Lawrence Erlbaum Associates, Inc.; reprinted with permission.

of planning nets helps to motivate the use of semantic supports of an analogical nature, and to uncover or foresee potential problems. In this sense, this work is interestingly related to the concept of increasingly complex microworlds discussed in Section 7.3. It provides this concept with a more precise definition of the important notion of pedagogically useful simplification. In addition, the approach is particularly appropriate for discovery-based learning, since its perspective on learning is rooted in teleological reasoning within the domain, independently of teaching actions. Because another direction was eventually chosen, the various implications of using planning nets were not fully explored. Nonetheless, this research on teleology-oriented teaching has great potential and certainly deserves further effort. It will be used as an example on numerous occasions in Part III.

8.4.2   The nature of learning in procedural skills

In the context of REPAIR theory, it turned out that the teleological approach was unrealistic for a descriptive model of classroom learning of arithmetic procedures. According to the theory, repairs performed by students are local, temporary patches, not the debugging of their core procedure that an understanding of teleological semantics would permit. Moreover, the empirical data on bugs seem to indicate that students do not use semantic criteria such as teleological understanding in selecting among possible alternative generalizations while forming their core procedure.

The teaching sequence: supporting inductive learning

Instead of looking within the domain for explanations of how incorrect procedures are formed, VanLehn turns to the teaching sequence. He finds that there are tacit conventions that teachers follow when introducing procedural skills such as subtraction, and corresponding tacit expectations that students have when being taught. These conventions are analogous to the *felicity conditions* that linguists have observed to tacitly govern conversations and to facilitate inferences by the listener. Felicity conditions for the teaching of procedures are the basic constituents of STEP theory, and we will briefly describe each of them. From the learner's standpoint, they constitute pedagogical solutions to problems that plague *inductive learning from examples*, which, according to VanLehn, is the form of learning that students apply to building their core procedures in conventional arithmetic curricula.

- Proper induction requires a *minimal set of examples*. Therefore, the first felicity condition states that the examples and exercises of each lesson are sufficient to fully induce the part of the procedure taught in that lesson. When this felicity condition is not strictly adhered to— as sometimes happens—unlucky students are led to induce incorrect core procedures that are nonetheless consistent with the teaching they have received.

- Induction from examples has always been confronted with the problem of *disjunctions*. If one allows unrestrained use of disjunctions, then one can always trivially take as one possible generalization the disjunction of all instances encountered so far. If one disallows disjunctions, then the concept description language must be able to describe every possible intermediate generalization. To solve this dilemma, the second felicity condition states that students are only presented with at most *one disjunction per lesson*. For instance, the cases of borrowing from nonzero digits and from zero will be taught in separate lessons since they are two branches of a decision point, that is, a disjunction.

- Induction is also made difficult when an unlimited number of *invisible objects* can participate in the generalizations. When presented with the example $f(4, 2) = 6$, one can induce that f is an addition, but 6 could also be obtained by $f(x, y) = x \times y - y$. Both functions are consistent with the example with the difference that the second one introduces the invisible object 8 as an intermediate result. The third felicity condition states that in introductory lessons, all the work is shown in the examples, in other words, invisible objects are banned.

- While the three felicity conditions mentioned above have been consistently confirmed in observations of actual textbooks, VanLehn mentions a fourth one without claiming that it is more than plausible.

The condition states that new subparts of the procedures can be added on by mere *assimilation* in the Piagetian sense, that is, without a restructuring of the procedure learned so far. For instance, learning borrowing from zero will not fundamentally change the borrowing procedure previously presented; it will merely add a new disjunction.

Induction from examples: a source of mislearning

Certainly these felicity conditions reflect good pedagogical common sense, and viewing them in the framework of learning by induction from examples gives an elegant justification for their existence. However, it seems hard to believe that students learn procedures using only induction from examples, both because it is too difficult and because it is too narrow-minded. While textbooks do not usually contain detailed descriptions of procedures—that's VanLehn's main argument—teachers do go through them carefully in class. In fact, I suspect that VanLehn's model, which is built on the assumption of pure inductive learning, is at once too powerful and too narrow with respect to learning mechanisms to be a complete cognitive model. Were it fully accurate, a much larger number of students would not be able to learn arithmetic at all.

However, this does not necessarily invalidate the model with respect to bug formation. Indeed, it is likely that the part of the learning where bugs develop is in the piece of unguided induction that the student actually performs to make up for incomplete—or incompletely understood— demonstrations. Unfortunately, felicity conditions must then be justified in vaguer terms like memory organization and reconstructive memory retrieval as well as learning processes. In the rest of this presentation, we will abide by VanLehn's assumption.

8.4.3 SIERRA: a model of the generation of core procedures

In addition to their pedagogical interest, these felicity conditions provide a focused framework for the specifications of a learning model based on the principles of STEP theory. The purpose is to replace the deletion principle of REPAIR theory by a plausible mechanism for the generation of buggy core procedures. SIERRA (VanLehn, 1987) is a computational model that combines the principles of both theories.

The learning model

At the top level, SIERRA consists of two modules, each corresponding to one of the underlying theories. A *learning module* based on AI techniques

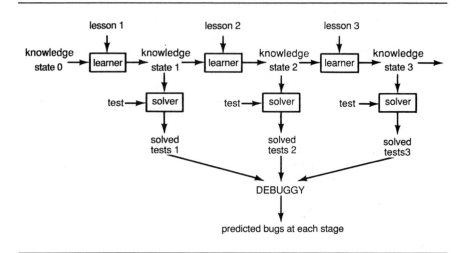

Figure 8.10 Top-level diagram of SIERRA's operations (VanLehn, 1983a).

for inductive learning follows the framework of STEP theory to form core procedures. Then a *problem-solving module* follows a version of REPAIR theory to generate bugs. The spatial knowledge needed to parse problems is captured in a *grammar* provided as pre-existing background knowledge.

Figure 8.10 gives a high-level description of the way SIERRA operates to predict bugs. The model takes as input an initial knowledge state and a lesson sequence, where each lesson contains worked examples and exercises in compliance with the felicity conditions. To learn procedures, SIERRA builds a GAO graph by parsing worked examples found in textbooks and by doing the exercises provided with each lesson. Note how the regular alternation of AND and OR nodes allows new subprocedures to be added incrementally to the graph; the condition that only one disjunctive chunk is learned per lesson prescribes that only one branch of an OR goal is added to the graph at each stage. After each lesson, the learning module produces a new knowledge state, which is fed to the solving module. In the context of a diagnostic test, the solving module applies its repairs to all possible impasses in the current knowledge state, and generates a set of solved tests that is fed to DEBUGGY.

Sources of impasses

Apart from problems that require skills in lessons the learner has not yet seen, there are three main sources of impasses in SIERRA. One is *mistaken or excessive generalization* from the set of examples: the learner is biased to find the maximally general precondition for the applicability of a disjunction's branch. An example of overgeneralization is a student who always borrows after having consistently seen examples requiring borrowing. *Overspecificity* can also create impasses by making matches impossible: the learner is biased to find the maximally specific conditions when retrieving an object. An example of overspecificity is a student who thinks that one must borrow from a column that is both adjacent to the current one and the leftmost because all examples so far were two-column problems. If borrowing is required when there is more than one column left to do, an impasse is generated. Finally, to account for incomplete learning or partial forgetting of a single subprocedure, the *deletion* of rules is retained. However, deletion is now limited to rules within the description of a single procedural unit, or, in syntactic terms, rules under an AND goal in the GAO graph. This restriction, while still imperfect for empirical coverage, is more general than individual blocking principles, and does not interfere with learning the procedure as would the addition of marks on undeletable rules.

The problems posed by critics are admittedly not resolved by STEP theory. The main difficulty is that critics vary among individuals; thus, explaining their acquisition would require a theory that could account in detail for individual differences in the acquisition of general guidelines for the domain. This is beyond the current theory.

8.4.4   Coverage and validation: competitive argumentation

A formal experiment was designed to evaluate the coverage of the model. SIERRA was given the sequence of lessons from an actual textbook used by a control group of students in their classes. The successive sets of bugs produced by SIERRA were then compared to those discovered by DEBUGGY in similar tests taken by the students after the same lessons. Not unexpectedly, the empirical coverage was much better than with past theories (REPAIR, and Young and O'Shea's described in Section 10.2), although still incomplete.

However, VanLehn rightly points out that mere empirical coverage is only a partial evaluation of a theory, mainly useful for comparing two theories. Especially in the case of complex information-processing models, "there is a trade-off between empirical adequacy and explanatory adequacy. If the model can be too easily tailored, then it is the theorist, not the theory, that is doing the explaining. The theory per se has little explanatory value." (VanLehn, 1983a, p. 71).

In fact, VanLehn spends very little of his voluminous dissertation on demonstrating the coverage of his theory. Most of his effort goes into underlining its principled construction. First, he traces the performance of his model to a restricted set of sufficient principles, emphasizing that his design is transparent with respect to them. Second, he argues that these principles are necessary to the theory for empirical and explanatory adequacy by comparing them with potential competitors in what he calls *competitive argumentation*. In this context, it becomes essential to have well-defined processes by which modifications to the underlying principles propagate through the theory, via the kind of global constraints called entailments in REPAIR theory. VanLehn is now advocating his competitive argumentation as a general methodology for validating AI-based theories of human cognition (VanLehn et al., 1984). One of his central claims is that the contributions of a solid argumentation may well outlive the theory it was meant to support.

Competitive argumentation: the role of assumptions

In spite of its scientific elegance, this kind of rigor is not without dangers. The need to fit a large number of facts into a unified framework may tempt one to force the argumentation and to find farfetched a posteriori justifications. Maintaining the falsifiability of a theory with clearly enunciated principles is an ideal scientific goal, but it cannot override plausibility and objectivity. Nature may not always be theoretically aesthetic. In this sense, argumentation can be an extremely subtle process: it hinges on basic assumptions that limit the scope and validity of conclusions in ways that are not always easy to recognize. For instance, VanLehn (1983a) argues at one point that people must learn recursively (e.g., borrowing across zeroes). His argument in favor of recursion uses the fact that learning nonrecursive control structures such as loops would require too many disjunctions, thus violating a felicity condition. The proof is rigorous and fits elegantly within the framework of the theory, making it easy to overlook the fact that it is only valid if loops are not considered as primitives in the language. The argument then hinges on an arbitrary decision about the granularity level of representational primitives.

A more fundamental issue worth discussing here is the methodological approach adopted in deriving the model: the empirical basis is the set of bugs that students acquire and exhibit, which are readily observable with the BUGGY model, rather than problem-solving processes, which are indeed difficult to observe. By attempting to cover the set of observable bugs in its entirety while avoiding all unobservable ones, REPAIR and STEP theories find a broad base of tangible constraints that have repercussions for basic hypotheses about human cognition via the entailments of models.

While the reliability of these empirical constraints endows the theories with credibility, the limited perspective they embody also calls for some caution. For instance, consider the decision to abandon a model of teleological reasoning in favor of a simple form of inductive learning. Personally, I strongly doubt that teleological understanding is completely absent from learning in the classroom, as VanLehn claims it is. In this case, I suspect that VanLehn reached his conclusions because of the methodological decision to consider bugs as the only source of data, as opposed to the behavior of "bug-free" students. On the basis of this bug-oriented information, the observer is biased toward students who do not apply teleological rationalizations when forming their procedures or when doing repairs. It may well be that many students do in fact understand the teleology of procedures to various degrees and do apply sound rationalizations, but that their behavior is not covered by a database of systematic bugs. One may claim that there is no need to worry about successful students; yet their behavior is important for prescriptive purposes, since a study of behavior biased toward the pathological may lead to inappropriate conclusions about the remedial actions required.

Methodological considerations

Rather than invalidating VanLehn's contributions, these controversies illustrate the type of subtleties involved in constructing computer-based models of human behavior, and show that the path he has chosen is as difficult as it is scientifically necessary. Although rigorous theories and proofs are not final validations, they are research tools useful for laying bare important assumptions on which they are based, so that further research can then directly proceed with investigations of these assumptions. In fact, discussions of the kind presented above are a tribute to this research just because they are possible. Indeed, artificial intelligence is a young science, and many of its results have been quite unprincipled. Discussions and justifications of design decisions have often been rather loose, to the point where there is sometimes hardly anything to argue about. VanLehn's care in stripping his model naked and arguing for every one of its basic principles comes as a breath of fresh air, and—one hopes—as an example that will be followed.

Although VanLehn presents his competitive argumentation as a methodology for AI models of cognition, his claims and ideas have relevance to AI in general, where the need to track down the "source of power" in programs is now being recognized (Lenat and Brown, 1984). Of course, a large proportion of AI theories do not attempt to cover empirical data obtained from the observation of human cognition; but they do claim to support an intended intelligent behavior that can fulfill the same function as data. As with cognitive models, it is then crucial to demonstrate which principles support this behavior, and to justify why they are essential. Since we are interested in models of knowledge intended for communication with people, such methodological considerations are certainly extremely relevant to this book.

Summary and conclusion

BUGGY was a milestone for the field in attempting to include an explicit representation of incorrect knowledge in a runnable student model. The notion of "bug" has highlighted the diagnostic importance of internalized errors that manifest in the work of students in a variety of ways. Thus, even if the behavior seems inconsistent at first, some regular patterns can be recognized by an analysis at the right level. For the design of instructional systems, BUGGY has demonstrated the usefulness and the feasibility of gathering a complete catalog of common errors for a given domain. Undoubtedly, constructing these enumerations of bugs does require large investments of time and effort, and this may restrict their use to limited domains. In fact, in some nonprocedural domains such a task may be altogether infeasible. Nonetheless, there are numerous candidate domains that are central educational concerns of our time and for which detailed theories of bugs would be very useful. A significant but often overlooked contribution of the BUGGY project is the way it defines the diagnosticity of tests and the notion of subskill in terms of a collection of observable bugs. Thus, a beneficial side effect of developing a theory of bugs is that it usually induces insights into the nature of the skill under consideration.

As a piece of engineering, DEBUGGY has demonstrated the feasibility of a robust diagnostic system based on a theory of bugs. However, its contribution goes beyond the engineering feat, with principles for organizing search processes and for providing on-line diagnosis. Of particular interest is the notion of coercion, which brings knowledge about likely irregularities in behavior to bear on the treatment of noisy data. This is in sharp contrast with the usual statistical methods applied to this difficult problem.

REPAIR and STEP theories take on a definite psychological bent in their attempt to explain the generation of surface bugs by reducing their occurrence to the student's application of an underlying core procedure. Indeed, the process leads to the postulation of principles about the way the mind learns and interprets procedures; the model includes both problem-solving repairs and learning mechanisms. These principles are then argued for in terms of explanatory power with respect to the data about observed bugs. Of special relevance to the theme of this book is the emphasis on the effects of a teaching sequence. Indeed, viewing a skill as the result of knowledge communication requires the study of learning to assume that a number of felicity conditions govern the communication process.

An understanding of the origin of bugs has crucial implications for remedial action, as well as for the development of pedagogical strategies that endeavor to avoid the generation of these bugs in the first place.

For instance, the learning operators of SIERRA put requirements on the types of examples presented, and the enforcement of these constraints by a learning model could improve the quality of textbooks. However, the decision to use a syntactically oriented inductive learning scheme may limit the pedagogical implications of the model. By ignoring the effects of deeper misconceptions, it may not get to the essence of a skill and really touch upon the qualities that make successful students acquire and retain correct knowledge in a systematic way. These qualities should be the focus of educational efforts. In this regard, the research on planning nets proposes an alternative worth pursuing.

We have also dwelt on the methodological contributions of REPAIR and STEP theories because such concerns for the principled design of computational models are essential in research on knowledge communication. While VanLehn gets much of the credit for making competitive argumentation a systematic methodology, his dissertation extends a long tradition of AI research rooted in scientific rigor, where the concept has progressively matured.

Originating with the SOPHIE project, this line of research has now branched into two directions. One is the research on mental models and qualitative reasoning with its emphasis on knowledge representation, but with the same quest for formalism and principles. It deals with domain expertise in the teaching process, and adopts an AI approach. The other direction is this research on problem-solving and learning models, which evolved from BUGGY to the point of postulating architectural properties of the human mind. With its emphasis on diagnosis and on psychological validity, it is an investigation of some learner-oriented aspects of teaching, and adopts an approach in line with the more formal aspects of cognitive science. The complementarity of these two fronts of research reflects the prescriptive and descriptive concerns in knowledge communication processes, which have to create a bridge between some knowledge and a learner.

Bibliographical notes

For the BUGGY model, the paper by Brown and Burton (1978a) is the best reference. More details about the BUGGY game are given in (Brown et al., 1977a). A complete catalog of bugs with some diagnostic tests and remediation suggestions can be found in a manual intended for school teachers who participated in experiments (Friend and Burton, 1980). Burton (1982) presents DEBUGGY and IDEBUGGY; he also discusses the notion of subskill. VanLehn (1982) gives a detailed account of the empirical studies conducted to test DEBUGGY and to investigate the concept of bug-level analysis; this paper documents some of the motivations for the development of REPAIR theory.

REPAIR theory is fully described in (Brown and VanLehn, 1980); this paper is a classic, which includes interesting methodological considerations. A shorter paper on REPAIR theory is available (Brown and VanLehn, 1982), but it reports on an earlier stage of the theory's development in spite of the later publication date.

A brief description of STEP theory can be found in (VanLehn, 1983b). SIERRA is discussed as a learning model in (VanLehn, 1987). For the interested reader, VanLehn's dissertation (1983a) is recommended in spite of its length; though detailed, it is accessible and explicitly made for multiple levels of reading. Also recommended, but much shorter, is a discussion of competitive argumentation as a scientific methodology by VanLehn, Brown, and Greeno (1984).

The work on planning nets is discussed in an important paper by VanLehn and Brown (1980); in appendix, a complete example of teleological explanation for a subtraction procedure is given. Brown (1983a) briefly reports on ARITHMEKIT, an experimental reactive environment developed to let children explore various subtraction algorithms; the system's use of multiple number representations embodies some of the principles of the planning net view. The reader interested in this issue may also want to look at studies by Lauren Resnick (1982): her analysis of some of BUGGY's subtraction bugs emphasizes a contrast between syntax and semantics, in an attempt to associate bugs with difficulties in linking the two. The ensuing investigation of the use of semantic principles for remediation by "mapping instruction" (Resnick and Omanson, 1987) is very much in line with the work on planning nets.

Chapter 9

More on student modeling: toward domain-independent mechanisms

Continuing on the theme of the previous chapter, we describe the research on student models carried out by Derek Sleeman and some of his students. Since Sleeman had been instrumental in starting ITS research at the University of Leeds (see Section 6.2), a large part of this work was done in England, except for a few years at Stanford University. After an early system that performs interactive diagnosis (PSM/ACE), this research on student modeling turns to issues of diagnostic inferences (LMS/PIXIE) and presents some interesting parallels with and divergences from the evolution of the BUGGY project. Finally, a proposed improvement of overlay modeling is discussed (UMFE).

9.1 PSM/ACE: interactive diagnosis

Inspired by the success of AI programs like DENDRAL (Buchanan et al., 1969), which can perform complex theory formation tasks in chemistry, Sleeman, with his own background as a chemist, decides to explore the possibility of using similar programs for teaching purposes. Observing students trying to infer simple molecular structures from nuclear magnetic resonance spectra, he notices that their main difficulty is in understanding the algorithm they are using to form hypotheses from the data and evaluate them. They fail to see why a decision leads to a contradiction, and they find it difficult to backtrack correctly to earlier decision points. Although they are familiar with the depth-first search algorithm they use, they do not understand it well enough to apply it properly.

The Problem-Solving Monitor (PSM) (Sleeman 1975, 1977) is a system that attempts to provide assistance and explanations at crucial points during the application of the algorithm. The hope is that students will understand the algorithm better if they can see how the system handles difficult situations. PSM can describe the current search space, show why certain choices are impossible, and demonstrate the backtracking process. The excerpt from a session with PSM presented in Figure 9.1 illustrates some types of assistance provided by the system. Although the management of a search space is an AI problem, this first version provides assistance in a rather straightforward manner, by keeping track of the portion of the search tree explored by the student so far and using specialized modules for explanations. The system intervenes upon request and there is no need for teaching strategies or a student model.

Following explanations of the student's reasoning

Further leverage is provided by the definition of a formal language for the domain that can describe the steps taken by the algorithm. The system can then generate a trace of its actions, which need only be translated into natural language for the student. Although this extends the generality of the original monitoring scheme, explanations still do not require sophisticated processes. The real interest of the formal language is that it provides a medium useful for recording and following the student's reasoning. Based on this idea, a later version of the monitor (called ACE for Analyzer of Complex Explanations) allows students to propose justifications for their decisions in a subset of English (Sleeman, 1977; Sleeman and Hendley, 1979). These explanations are then translated into the formal language, and compared to the trace produced internally by the system on the same problem. The comparison is performed by a

---

PSM: In our notation, (the expanded form of) the spectrum of your molecule is ((3 2)(3 2)(2 5)(2 4)(2 3)(2 2)). (C 7 H 14 0) *(Molecular formula)*

⋮

Student: ((H)(CH3)(3 2)) *(Head of the molecule)*

PSM: Correct

Student: (help)

PSM: Good. You have discovered the head of the molecule. So far you have identified ((CH3)). Also we know that the peak for the last group is (3 2). The previous group has 0 interacting protons: therefore the next group must have 2 interacting protons. Choose appropriate groups from those remaining. And of course we know the peak will be split by at least 3 hydrogens: i.e., those on the current group.

Student: ((J)(H)(CH2)(2 4)) *(Join a new group)*

PSM: No.

Student: (explain)

PSM: Your group was OK. Well, if we had such a group it would have to be followed by a group with 1 interacting protons. No such group exists in remaining spectra.

Student: ((J)(H)(CH2)(2 5)) *(New hypothesis)*

PSM: Correct

Student: (summary)

PSM: Head of molecule ((CH3)(CH2)). Peak for the last group is (2 5). Remaining molecular formula is (C 5 H 9 0). Spectra (expanded form) still to be explained ((3 2)(2 4)(2 3)(2 2)).

⋮

Figure 9.1 Excerpt from a session with PSM (Sleeman, 1975).

domain-specific algorithm that generates comments similar to those given by PSM.

The definition of a special internal language to represent informal reasoning and follow a sequence of arguments is somewhat similar to EXCHECK's treatment of proofs, although ACE's language is based on a grammar rather than on logical macro-operators. This gives the student more freedom of expression. The translation of her statements into the formal language is done with a semantic grammar, as defined by Burton and used in SOPHIE. The elements of the formal language that record the traces internally constitute the semantic categories to be looked for (such as facts, equations, and deductions), organized into successive arguments. In this case, the parser has the interesting ability to interact with the student when it encounters difficulties, asking for specific corrections until it can satisfy its expectations.

For the system to be really "friendly," robust natural-language capabilities are not sufficient. Indeed, people do not always give complete arguments for each reasoning step, but skip arguments that have been mentioned before or that seem obvious. As in EXCHECK, the comparison between the two traces must be more than a simple match, since students' explanations will usually not be completely rigorous, albeit informally correct. Therefore, ACE's comparison algorithm accepts some partial matches and looks at previous statements for missing arguments. It uses the grammar of its internal language to map between various forms of the arguments (e.g., the different orders of premises and conclusions) and its expectations about the final solution to guide the search of the context. Figure 9.2 gives an idea of the type of dialogue of which ACE is capable. It shows how ACE can follow the formation and rejection of hypotheses typical of depth-first search, and illustrates some reconstruction of arguments.

Domain knowledge and understanding of explanations

Inasmuch as it analyzes a partial model of the student's reasoning, ACE does perform a local type of diagnosis. Its most outstanding feature is its complete reliance on the student's own explanations. In fact, ACE is to my knowledge the only diagnostic system that is purely interactive. While EXCHECK can follow a proof, it cannot understand a student's justifications for her decisions. Although ACE's reasoning abilities are still quite rudimentary, any success in understanding and evaluating justifications given by a student is significant in view of the enormous problems encountered by inferential modelers.

Admittedly, ACE leaves many questions unsolved. In particular, it can only understand explanations that are stated in terms of the facts and deductions that it uses. In reality, ACE can only comment on missing or incomplete arguments, but cannot deal with arguments that are altogether wrong, irrelevant, or reliant on global knowledge of the domain. In this sense, its matching of traces embodies a fairly narrow definition of what it means to "understand" the student's explanations. Of course, this fundamental limitation is an instance of a general problem inherent in any knowledge representation. But in the case of a system that claims to understand explanations, it becomes a central issue.

⋮

ACE: Please input your statements:

Student: The next group is CO with a null peak and then the next group could be CH2 with a (2 4) peak, but there is no peak with area 4 so it could be CH2 with the (2 5) peak, but again there is no peak with this area.

ACE: The meaning extracted from your argument is:
The next group is CO with a peak (0 0).
The next group is CH2 with a peak (2 4).
No peak with appropriate area.
The next group is CH2 with a peak (2 5).
No peak with appropriate area.
Is it what you intended?

Student: Yes.

ACE: Please input your statements:

Student: So the next group must be CH2 (2 2). This could then be followed by CH2 with a splitting of 5 and an interaction of 2 but this would be followed by a CH3 group which would take the (3 2) peak which would terminate the chain leaving some atoms.

ACE: (Confirms its translation of the statement: skipped)

Student: So the CH2 group must take the (2 4) peak and then we have CH2 (2 5) and finally a methyl group which has the (3 2) peak which completes the answer.

ACE: (Confirms its translation of the statement: skipped)

Student: Argument completed.

⋮

ACE: We are now considering:
The next group is CO with a peak (0 0).
The next group is CH2 with a peak (2 2).
The next group is CH2 with a peak (2 4).
The next group is CH2 with a peak (2 5).
The next group is CH3 with a peak (3 2).
This is the solution.
An argument we have reconstructed from the partial one you gave. Is it what you intended?

Student: Yes.

ACE: This argument is completely correct. Do you wish to see the reasoning chains you did not explore?

⋮

**Figure 9.2 Excerpt from a dialogue with ACE
(Sleeman and Hendley, 1979).**

As a possible improvement for future systems, Sleeman and Hendley suggest employing a single data structure for both execution and pedagogical use to replace the canned formal language statements currently attached to ACE's procedural steps. The idea is that the executable algorithm should be fully inspectable so that it can be used directly for comparisons with the student's statements and for explanations, and so that it can be explored by the student in as much detail as required. However, the real issues in interacting with the student are probably deeper. Recent research on the use of rule-based systems for instructional purposes has revealed that inspectable structures (i.e., individual rules) are not the final solution (see, for instance, Chapter 12). In this sense, interactive diagnosis touches upon fundamental limitations of most current AI systems, which do not have a first-hand knowledge of their domain. As a consequence, they cannot evaluate the truth of assertions by tracing them back to a model of the domain's first principles.

9.2   LMS: inferential diagnosis with rules and mal-rules

For unreported reasons, the ACE project was not pursued further. Instead, Sleeman started to work on an inferential diagnostic system for procedural skills as found in arithmetic and algebra. His system is called LMS, for Leeds Modeling System.

9.2.1   Representing procedural skills with production systems

Like BUGGY, LMS is built on a modular representation for subskills and their buggy variants, but instead of using a procedural network, Sleeman represents the student's procedure as an ordered set of production rules. When interpreted, this production system becomes an executable model. Interpretation here means cycling through the rules and applying at each cycle the first rule whose conditions are satisfied until no more rules can be applied. Using ordering to decide which rule should be applied next can capture simple notions such as the precedence of operators. However, it does not explicitly capture higher-level control heuristics that are often useful in solving algebraic equations, like the goal of collecting or isolating the variables (Bundy, 1983, ch. 12). Ordering was apparently chosen not so much for reasons of psychological validity as because it can be easily interpreted by people like teachers who might not be familiar with more complex conflict resolution schemes. Figure 9.3a presents LMS's production rules for algebra. The levels indicated here correspond to the rules' order in the teaching sequence and not to their order of application. An individual model is then an ordered list of these rules.

Note that this use of production rules is very similar to that of subskills in procedural networks, but fundamentally different from the use of production rules in REPAIR theory. Here, rules are never deleted. Instead, bugs are represented as variants of the correct rules. These variants, called *mal-rules*, can be inserted into the production system to model the student in the same way that bugs are inserted into BUGGY's network. Figure 9.3b lists a few mal-rules used for algebra that correspond to correct rules directly above them (but with M's prefixed to their names). Mal-rules always have the same conditions as the corresponding correct rule so that they will be called in the same circumstances, but they can have arbitrarily different action-sides so as to generate bugs. As in BUGGY, there is no syntactic mechanism in the language for explicitly representing the nature of the deviations between correct and incorrect actions. The exception is the way control errors are handled. These errors are modeled by an incorrect ordering rather than by modifications to the rules' conditions, and thus have a simple syntactic equivalent. Figure 9.3c shows two pairs of partial models solving the same equations. In the first pair, the bug is represented by a difference in rule order; in the second pair, the first rule is replaced by a mal-rule.

9.2.2 Containing the combinatorics of the modeling task

As in DEBUGGY, diagnosis infers from a student's answers to a problem set which rules and mal-rules compose her procedure. Since rules are applied in order, the diagnostic process must also specify the order of rules and mal-rules selected for the model. The combinatorics inherent in such an inductive problem generate a very large search space even for simple skills, and much of the early work on LMS deals with this issue. While Burton uses heuristic assumptions to avoid searching the whole space, Sleeman attempts to organize the search systematically. A first version of LMS (Sleeman and Smith, 1981) decomposes the modeling process into a sequence of partial models, in which rules are introduced one at a time in the order indicated in Figure 9.3a. The model's incremental construction is meant to reflect learning in the context of an instructional sequence. Once a partial model has been inferred, the subsequent one is built by addition of the next rule or one of its mal-rules at the correct or an incorrect place in the ordered set. With some heuristics that further reduce the number of places in a model at which a new rule can be inserted, the number of possible models becomes manageable for exhaustive search.

a. Rules for the algebra domain (evaluate form and slightly stylized)

RULE NAME	LEVEL	CONDITION−SET	ACTION
FIN2	1	(SHD X = M/N)	(SHD (M N)) or (SHD evaluated)
SOLVE	2	(SHD M∗X = N)	(SHD X = N/M) or (SHD INFINITY)
ADDSUB	3	(lhs M +|− N rhs)	(lhs [evaluated] rhs)
MULT	4	(lhs M∗N rhs)	(lhs [evaluated] rhs)
XADDSUB	5	(lhs M∗X +|− N∗X rhs)	(lhs (M +|− N)∗X rhs)
NtoRHS	6	(lhs +|− M = rhs)	(lhs = rhs −|+ M)
REARRANGE	7	(lhs +|− M +|− N∗X rhs)	(lhs +|− N∗X +|− M rhs)
XtoLHS	8	(lhs = +|− M∗X rhs)	(lhs −|+ M∗X = rhs)
BRA1	9	(lhs < N > rhs)	(lhs N rhs)
BRA2	10	(lhs M ∗ <N∗X +|− P> rhs)	(lhs M∗N∗X +|− M∗P rhs)

M, N and P are integers; lhs, rhs, *etc.*, are general patterns (which may be null); +\|− means either + or − may occur; SHD indicates the String Head; and < and > represent standard "algebraic brackets."

b. Some mal−rules for the domain (using the same conventions as above)

RULE NAME	LEVEL	CONDITION−SET	ACTION
M.SOLVE	2	(SHD M∗X = N)	(SHD X = M/N) or (SHD INFINITY)
M.NtoRHS	6	(lhs +|− M = rhs)	(lhs = rhs +|− M)
M2.NtoRHS	6	(lhs1 +|− M lhs2 = rhs)	(lhs1 +|− lhs2 = rhs +|− M)
M.XtoLHS	8	(lhs = +|− M∗X rhs)	(lhs +|− M∗X = rhs)
M1.BRA	10	(lhs M ∗ <N∗X +|− P> rhs)	(lhs M∗N∗X +|− P rhs)
M2.BRA	10	(lhs M ∗ <N∗X +|− P> rhs)	(lhs M∗N∗X +|− M +|− P rhs)

c. Pairs of correct and "buggy" models executing typical tasks (The first line gives the initial state and all subsequent lines give the rule that fires, and the resulting state.)

	2X = 3 ∗ 4 + 5			2X = 3 ∗ 4 + 5
MULT	2X = 12 + 5		ADDSUB	2X = 3 ∗ 9
ADDSUB	2X = 17		MULT	2X = 27
SOLVE	X = 17/2		SOLVE	X = 27/2
FIN2	(17/2)		FIN2	(27/2)

    i) Shows (MULT ADDSUB SOLVE FIN2) and (ADDSUB MULT SOLVE FIN2) solving 2X = 3 ∗ 4 + 5.

	2X + 5 = 9			2X + 5 = 9
NtoRHS	2X = 9 − 5		M.NtoRHS	2X = 9 + 5
ADDSUB	2X = 4		ADDSUB	2X = 14
SOLVE	X = 2/1		SOLVE	X = 7/1
FIN2	(2)		FIN2	(7)

    ii) Shows (NtoRHS ADDSUB SOLVE FIN2) and (M.NtoRHS ADDSUB SOLVE FIN2) solving 2X + 5 = 9.

Figure 9.3 Rules and mal−rules used by LMS for algebra (after Sleeman, 1983a).

However, the assumption that earlier partial models are not modified by the addition of a new rule had to be retracted following experiments with students. As it turned out, rules that have been applied correctly on simple problems are sometimes replaced by a mal-rule in more complex situations. This is an important observation for diagnosis because it shows that subskills cannot be considered independently in a simple incremental fashion. Interactions between parts of the knowledge during learning and the cognitive load generated by more advanced problems must also be taken into account. This requires a complex modeling apparatus, and no diagnostic process to date can give an explicit account of such interactions.

In LMS, reconsidering former models brings back the problem of a large search space. Within his ordered rule-based framework, Sleeman (1982a, 1983a) proposes a domain-independent syntactic analysis of the conditions of rules that reveals many models as redundant. For instance, if two rules can never apply to the same situation, then their order is unimportant. Not only can this analysis of rule interactions be performed by static observation of the rule set, but further leverage is obtained if the problem set is known in advance. Given a set of rules and mal-rules and a set of problems, LMS takes advantage of such observation to first generate off-line a complete set of *nonredundant models*. Admittedly, even the set of nonredundant models will grow very large if the number of rules increases, and for less simple domains, further measures will be necessary. But in the case of LMS, the set of nonredundant models is manageable. The on-line program merely selects one of these models by matching the answers they generate on the problem set with those of the student. Noise is dealt with by simple statistical techniques for finding the best fit, and there is no equivalent to DEBUGGY's coercions.

9.2.3 Automated test generation

A useful feature of the rule-based framework is that rules constitute natural building blocks for constructing problems that test whether a student has mastered the rules in question. Sleeman (1981, 1983a) suggests using the rules *in the opposite direction*: starting from the answer and generating a problem template by working backward. For instance, if one rule says that $nX = m \rightarrow X = \frac{m}{n}$, then applying it backward to $X = \frac{2}{3}$ generates the problem $3X = 2$. While the inversion method works to discriminate between models with different rules and mal-rules, generating a problem to discriminate between two orderings requires more effort. Sleeman proposes an algorithm for merging the respective problem templates of two rules in such a way that order can be tested. While accommodating one template to include the other, the algorithm makes sure that the rules' conditions interact so that both rules apply to certain situations where their order of application matters.

The ability to generate a problem set for diagnostic purposes allows the diagnostic process to focus on particular rules, and to propose discriminatory problems for competing models. Unlike IDEBUGGY's specialized test generators, Sleeman's mechanisms have the advantage of being domain-independent and generally applicable to rule-based representations. However, unforeseen interactions between rules may still create ambiguities, and Sleeman does not really address the issue of building large tests. In particular, he does not give criteria that would allow an automatic evaluation of a specific test's diagnostic power. Hence, it is not clear that in domains with large numbers of rules, his task generation system would be able to construct a complete diagnostic test of reasonable length.

9.3 PIXIE: generating mal-rules

While early experiments with LMS had exhibited a fairly good coverage of observed errors in the domain of algebraic equations, more recent field work revealed wide gaps in LMS's ability to account for faulty behavior in the same domain (Sleeman, 1984a). Because of the age difference between the two groups, and because the mal-rules used had been designed for the first group, Sleeman suspects the fixed set of mal-rules as the main culprit. Further work on PIXIE (LMS's new name now that Sleeman has left Leeds) concentrates on generative mechanisms for mal-rules. Although this move is similar to the transition between BUGGY and REPAIR theory, PIXIE's initial emphasis is on the pragmatic needs of student modeling rather than on general cognitive theories. Its generative mechanisms are primarily meant to automate the data-driven generation of mal-rules, in hope that this will allow PIXIE to break out of the limitations of diagnosis based on a predefined catalog of bugs.

9.3.1 Diagnosis by reconstruction

The first mechanism suggested by Sleeman (1982b) is a set of domain-specific abstract bug types derived from observation of mal-rules. These schemata can be instantiated to produce many specific mal-rules. Sleeman gives the example of a student who was simply leaving the unknown alone to the left of the equal sign, and adding all the numbers to the right without distinctions between isolated numbers and coefficients. For example, the equation $3x + 4x = 2$ would become $x + x = 3 + 4 + 2$.

Interestingly, the student claimed that she was following the teacher's instruction of isolating the unknown! In this case, different mal-rules could be formed by instantiating the same schema with different cumulative operations for the numbers moved to the righthand side.

Sleeman also mentions inserting perturbations into the student's procedure, including the deletion of parts used in other theories. Unfortunately, all these mechanisms are somewhat underspecified, and it is not clear how Sleeman thinks they should be implemented. The problem is that they do not fit in any underlying framework. Since they are not integrated into a broader theory, they are underconstrained: there are no principles to contain the search space or to prevent the generation of implausible mal-rules. We will see that this is a fundamental difficulty of methods based on syntactic manipulations.

In a different vein, Sleeman (1982b) also suggests a truly data-driven algorithm to infer new mal-rules. Given a problem and the student's answer to it, this algorithm uses a heuristic search to bridge the two with a sequence of operations. An example of its attempt to reconstruct the student's solution process is displayed in Figure 9.4. It should be read from the bottom up, whereas the student's hypothesized solution process goes top down. Starting with the student's answer, the algorithm uses rules and mal-rules in reverse sequence (as it does for the problem generation task mentioned earlier), working backward toward the given problem. It applies heuristics to decompose numbers into operands of arithmetic operations. Then it looks ahead to find an instantiation of the decomposition likely to lead to the numbers appearing in the given problem. When no available transformation applies to completing the path, PIXIE *hypothesizes a new mal-rule*, which is exactly the transformation needed to fill the gap. Apparently, this algorithm has been implemented and has rediscovered some mal-rules, although it is not quite clear how the search is guided. More important, the program does not seem to have any way of preventing the inference of transformations that are psychologically implausible or at the wrong level of granularity. Again, this is due to the absence of a cognitive framework.

Toward remedial dialogues

Despite these deficiencies the reconstruction mechanism is rather interesting, and work on this type of reconstructive diagnosis is worth pursuing. Indeed, it has the unique feature of combining a model-driven process with a truly data-driven extension, in that it posits as mal-rules the student's *actual steps* when it cannot account for them with its existing model. While the current algorithm was only used in isolated cases, it could be made to consider larger amounts of data, and thereby to propose only mal-rules that have crossed a threshold of

g) $3X + 5 = 6$
     $\implies$ Inference step: positing the mal−rule $mX \rightarrow X + m$
f) $X + 3 + 5 = 6$
     $\Longleftarrow$ *Instantiate to left handside of target equation*
e) $X + [8 - n] + [n] = 6$
     $\Longleftarrow$ *Apply heuristic decomposition*
d) $X + 8 = 6$
     $\Longleftarrow$ *Use the rule NtoRHS backward*
         (NtoRHS moves isolated numbers to the right handside)
c) $X = -8 + 6$
     $\Longleftarrow$ *Instantiate to right handside of target equation*
b) $X = [-2 - n] + [n]$
     $\Longleftarrow$ *Apply heuristic decomposition*
a) $X = -2$

Figure 9.4 Inference of the mal−rule "mX $\rightarrow$ X + m" by reconstruction (after Sleeman, 1982b).

observational support. The algorithm might be applied to interactive diagnosis, where its reconstruction capabilities could be used to guide the dialogue. In fact, this last idea has a great deal of potential because even young students (ages 11–14) seem to be able to speak about their own approach. Indeed, in the interviews that followed his experiments, Sleeman (1984b) found all the students to be very articulate about their procedures, a finding in contrast with the observations of the BUGGY team. If this is really the case, then the purely inferential path to student modeling may be uselessly difficult for this class of teaching situations, and solutions halfway between ACE and PIXIE/LMS may be more promising. The reconstruction mechanism would then be a good candidate for the inferential core of a mixed diagnostic process because its data-driven extension enables it to accept unexpected statements and its model-driven basis incorporates an incrementally evolving theory of bugs.

Sleeman sees PIXIE's use in remediation as the next step. He wants to observe remedial actions taken by human teachers on the basis of PIXIE's model of the student's misconceptions. His hope is to capture their strategies into a system involving PIXIE. Indeed, moving to remediation is an important step in the modeling process. Not only is it the real test of the quality and utility of a student model, but it can also guide further research by determining more precisely the type of model actually required. Furthermore, I believe that interactive diagnostic processes of the type mentioned in the previous paragraph will include partial or tentative remedial actions early on; eventually, in many teaching situations, diagnosis and remediation will be tightly interwoven into one dialogue, as they are in the Socratic method.

9.3.2   Student interviews: toward a generative theory of bugs

For remediation purposes, the cognitive validity and explanatory power of student models take on a greater importance. Sleeman has spent much time analyzing student interviews that followed field experiments with PIXIE/LMS. A detailed report of the findings is beyond the scope of this book; the reader is referred to (Sleeman, 1984b). However, it is worth mentioning that interviews turned out to be a very useful method for understanding student approaches to algebra.

Misgeneralization as a generative principle

From these interviews emerged a classification of errors into two groups and the description of corresponding generative mechanisms. Consistent errors that manifest procedural bugs are classified as either manipulative or parsing mal-rules. *Manipulative mal-rules* can be generated by deletion or replacement of part of a rule's action, and correspond to the deletion bugs of REPAIR theory. Sleeman claims that manipulative mal-rules occur at the time of application: rules are known, but misapplied. *Parsing mal-rules* stem from severe misconceptions about the subject domain and the notation used, or about prerequisite knowledge. Their origin is deeply rooted in the learning process. In some cases, they are so fundamental that they may not even be viewed as variants of correct rules. Obviously, each type of error requires very different kinds of remedial action.

To explain the emergence of parsing mal-rules, Sleeman (1984a, 1984c) suggests the mechanism of *misgeneralization*. Unfortunately, he has not yet included this mechanism into a broader learning model, where its extent could be defined in computational terms. At any rate, he sets out to compare it with the mechanisms of REPAIR/STEP theory, claiming that misgeneralization, like the pairing of impasses with different repairs, explains the phenomenon of bug migration. Apparently, there is evidence that many algebra students have several applicable rules for the same situations because of incorrect generalizations. These overlapping rules all compete in their procedure, and their choosing different rules at different times would indeed account for bug migration.

In his competitive argumentation, VanLehn (1983a) discards misgeneralization as a basic mechanism for the REPAIR/STEP model on both observational and explanatory grounds. He claims not only that it would generate unobserved bugs but that it ascribes almost unrestricted learning power to the student. In reality, STEP theory does use misgeneralization in generating core procedures, but only in the very restricted context of straightforward induction from examples. As we have seen, STEP theory assumes that induction is based not on teleological understanding but on a mere effort to account well for observed examples. In contrast, Sleeman's notion of misgeneralization does include teleological reasoning as a central force, since the learning is viewed as constantly involving active theory building. This view is thus more in line with Matz's ideas about generalization and extrapolation from past knowledge presented in Section 10.1.

The attitude of the learner: a controversy

These different views reveal fundamentally different assumptions concerning the attitude of the learner, which may at least partly be due to differences in domains and age groups studied. The assumption of syntactic learning in STEP theory could stem from a predominant attitude in early learning in arithmetic, whereas learning in algebra may require the formation of some sort of teleological model. However, there is also a contrast between the methodologies adopted to gather data in the two projects. REPAIR/STEP is based on a collection of observed bugs, whereas Sleeman conducts interviews with students. Although there is no definite proof of the influence of these methodologies on the conclusions, the correlation is striking.

In his presentation, Sleeman is careful to point out that neither mechanism is exclusive, suggesting that misgeneralization be considered at the learning stage and repairs at the application stage. Even if it turns out that the two processes can usually be associated respectively with these two stages, it is still essential to note that they primarily reflect different depths in the domain model used by students for dealing with new situations. A given student's attitude will probably vary and range somewhere between perfect theorizing and blind patching, according to circumstances such as learning environment, age, interest level, or external pressure. In short, what seems to be required is a broader, possibly composite, generative theory of bugs.

9.4   UMFE: a generic modeling subsystem

A project of a different kind—though still concerned with diagnosis—is an attempt to build a domain-independent modeling subsystem, called UMFE for "User Modeling Front End" (Sleeman, 1984d). The purpose is to create a generic front end to be coupled to a complex system. When this host system is trying to communicate some information to the user in response to a query, the front end would filter the response according to its model of the user's knowledge and translate it into an understandable form. Although UMFE is merely an experiment with a simple *overlay* model, its extension to the overlay paradigm is worth discussing briefly since it represents an effort to make interactive diagnosis as concise as possible.

The propagation of diagnostic information

As is usual in an overlay, UMFE takes as input a list of domain concepts and forms its user model by tagging individual concepts to indicate the degree to which it "believes" a concept is known. The extension to the paradigm is that these concepts are not treated as independent pieces of knowledge from a diagnostic standpoint. In addition to the list of concepts, UMFE is given ratings reflecting their relative difficulty and importance, together with a set of inference rules that explicitly prescribe how diagnostic information about the user's knowledge can be propagated through the list of concepts. These rules are also rated to indicate the certainty of their inference. For instance, a system designer could decide that if the user knows someone's last name, the user is likely to know that person's first name with a certainty factor of 70%, but her middle name with only 15%. Note that UMFE does not possess general rules of its own, and thus that a new set of rules has to be defined extensionally for each domain and for each class of users.

Figure 9.5 gives an example of a query to a medical database[1] via UMFE. In the context of a query to the host system, UMFE's task is to ask the user a minimal number of relevant questions to implicitly infer as much information as possible about her likely state of knowledge. Then it filters the output from the host system accordingly, so that the response does not rely on concepts marked as unknown. Thus, UMFE has three sources of evidence from which to assess the user's understanding of each concept in its model: the initial rates given as inputs, the user's statements, and the inferences asserted by its consistency rules. Since information from these different sources can be contradictory, a system like UMFE must be able to resolve conflicts. For this task, the current version uses a straightforward ranking of reliability among information sources. In addition, some thresholds of inconsistency cause it to rely solely on the user's statements. Ideally, however, UMFE should be able to make use of its knowledge to weigh the value of its information and thus attempt to recover from inconsistencies, possibly by updating its rules and rates.

---

[1] The database of NEOMYCIN (see Chapter 12).

:

User: What is the connection between CRYPTOCOCCUS and
INFECTIOUS-PROCESS?

UMFE: In this context do you understand the significance of
MENINGITIS -- Please type YES or NO: <u>YES</u>
In this context do you understand the significance of
FUNGAL-MENINGITIS -- Please type YES or NO: <u>YES</u>
In this context do you understand the significance of
CRYPTOCOCCUS -- Please type YES or NO: <u>YES</u>

INFECTIOUS-PROCESS ⇒ MENINGITIS ⇒ FUNGAL-MENINGITIS
⇒ CRYPTOCOCCUS

> *The concepts in the overlay model are now tagged as follows (the sources of evidence
> are the concept rates (implicit), the inference rules (explicit) and the user):*
> INFECTIOUS-PROCESS: *known* (explicit, implicit)
> MENINGITIS: *known* (explicit, user)
> FUNGAL-MENINGITIS: *known* (explicit, explicit, user)
> CRYPTOCOCCUS: *known* (explicit, user)
> COCCIDIOIDES: *known* (explicit)

User: What is the connection between COCCICIOIDES and
INFECTIOUS-PROCESS?

UMFE: INFECTIOUS-PROCESS ⇒ MENINGITIS ⇒ FUNGAL-MENINGITIS
⇒ CRYPTOCOCCUS

:

**Figure 9.5 A dialogue with a database monitored by UMFE
(after Sleeman, 1984d).**

A prototype: limitations and possibilities

Admittedly, the current version of UMFE is only a rudimentary prototype
that will require many refinements and extensions before it is of practical
use. Sleeman suggests replacing the ternary values of concept tags in
the overlay ("known," "unknown," or "no-information") with continuous
degrees of likelihood. He also sees that a fixed set of explicit inference
rules imposes a uniform conceptualization on modeling; yet, to model a
particular user, it may be necessary to select between various candidate
sets of rules. To account for learning or for uneven distribution of the
user's expertise, it may also be useful to apply different rules at different
times or in different parts of the database.

There are other central issues that should also be given some thought
for systems similar to UMFE. For instance, UMFE has no sophisticated
mechanism for propagating certainty factors, which is done by simple

multiplications. In today's AI systems, the propagation of uncertainty through a corpus of inference rules is a nontrivial problem, particularly the handling of multiple evidences. Also, when UMFE probes the user, it merely performs a binary search on the difficulty level of concepts. It asks first about an average concept and moves towards easier or more difficult ones according to the user's response. It does not try to optimize the number of questions it asks by analyzing their informational value with respect to its propagation mechanisms. In addition to its interest as a general problem in interactive modeling, such optimization would represent a very practical improvement for the use of UMFE in complex domains.

While the issues we have seen merely require extensions to the current version of the overlay model, there seems to be a more fundamental difficulty in generalizing the "front end" concept. So far, UMFE has only been applied to simple factual knowledge retrieved from the database of a medical expert system, so that all the answers it has had to handle are simple chains of the type shown in Figure 9.5. In this context, when it has to convey an explanation to the user, it can just filter out unknown concepts and skip them. This may be a workable solution in such elementary cases; for more complex explanations, however, the host system's output may have to be reworded completely to retain its sense. The need to understand a given concept's role in the overall explanation will require that the modeling subsystem interact with the main system in more complex ways. Of course, UMFE's current limitations are of the sort inherent in any prototype. We indicate them only because they give rise to general considerations and motivate further research. At any rate, the idea of a generic modeling subsystem that takes explicit propagation mechanisms as input has many potential applications in instructional and other settings.

Summary and conclusion

Sleeman's investigation of the diagnostic task is very diverse. The general thrust of this work is to devise domain-independent mechanisms that provide frameworks for constructing tutoring systems (Sleeman, 1987).

In ACE, the emphasis is on interactive diagnosis. Unlike WHY, which extracts information about the student's knowledge by asking questions, ACE merely follows the student's explanations to match statements to the trace of an internal problem solver. Although this attitude allows more freedom of expression, we have seen that ACE still requires a lot of cooperativeness on the part of the student.

LMS, which reflects a move toward inferential diagnosis, is reminiscent of BUGGY in that its mal-rules are used very much as buggy subskills are: a student model is composed in a model-driven fashion as a combination of rules and mal-rules. In fact, the term "mal-rule" is often used as an alternative to the diagnostic notion of "bug." In LMS, the use of rule ordering gives a syntactic equivalent to control errors resulting from the misapplication of an otherwise correct subskill. Production rules can also be inverted to generate problems that test their use. Perhaps the most interesting contribution of this work is PIXIE's notion of generating mal-rules by heuristic backward reconstruction of the problem-solving process. When a step cannot be accounted for by the current model of rules and mal-rules, the student's step is posited as a new mal-rule in a form of data-driven diagnosis. The difficulty of this purely data-driven method is that it lacks constraints to prevent the generation of undesirable mal-rules.

Continuing on the theme of REPAIR and STEP theories, Sleeman is also concerned with the mechanisms that participate in the generation of bugs. Interviewing students rather than attempting to account for an enumerative theory of bugs, he views the student as a more active learning agent involved in theory formation. In this view, reasoned mis-generalization is considered as the main generative principle accounting for erroneous procedures. Although no computational model has evolved out of these ideas, they have made for some interesting controversies.

Finally, a contribution to the engineering of diagnostic systems is the concept of explicit rules for propagating diagnostic information through a student model. The propagation mechanism capitalizes on the connectedness of knowledge elements that UMFE's diagnostic rules try to capture. Unfortunately, general principles for designing the set of inference rules and for avoiding a fully extensional definition of propagational mechanisms have not been investigated. Although UMFE, as a prototype implementation of the idea, is a fairly rudimentary system, the notion that a body of knowledge is more than a set of independent pieces of information is an important dimension for the overlay paradigm.

Bibliographical notes

The early Problem-Solving Monitor is described in (Sleeman, 1975) and its successor, ACE, in (Sleeman and Hendley, 1979). Sleeman (1983a) gives a good overview of the evolution of LMS and the issue of test generation; more details about early versions can be found in (Sleeman and Smith, 1981) and about test generation in (Sleeman, 1981). Sleeman (1982b) presents mechanisms for mal-rule generation. The possibility of using PIXIE as a general ITS paradigm is explored in (Sleeman, 1987). A good overall discussion of interviews with algebra students is given in (Sleeman, 1984b). For use of the same methodology in investigating other domains (programming), see (Sleeman et al., 1984) and (Putnam et al., 1984). Misgeneralization and the distinction between manipulative and parsing mal-rules are discussed in (Sleeman, 1984c). UMFE is presented in (Sleeman, 1984d).

For the reader specifically interested in algebra, there are other systems for the domain of algebraic equation solving. When compared to PIXIE, these systems put less emphasis on manipulative rules and related mal-rules and pay more attention to solution strategies of the type articulated by Bundy (1983, chap. 12). The papers by Lantz et al. (1983) presents a tutor that conducts a simple dialogue with the student; the system gives hints and executes the student's commands, letting her concentrate on strategic decisions by taking care of the details of operator application. McArthur (1987) discusses GED, an interface to be used as a problem-solving tool for algebra; in the tutor being designed in connection with this interface, a central feature is the explicit representation of strategic knowledge and its use to generate solution traces that students understand easily (McArthur et al., 1987). See also Section 10.1 and ALGEBRALAND in Section 14.4.

Chapter 10

Bug reconstruction: beyond libraries of bugs

The concept of "diagnostic model" developed for BUGGY inspired several research projects on student modeling. Some of these projects are direct responses that propose alternative methods of solving the same problem, and some merely share the same or a related goal. In the previous chapter, we saw Sleeman's work on his notion of mal-rules, including his attempts at reconstructing bugs. In this chapter, we look at three additional projects that in one way or another shed additional light on important issues centering on the reconstruction of bugs.

First, we briefly present some research conducted at MIT by Marilyn Matz on the genesis of misconceptions. Next, we consider a rule-based representation of procedures proposed by Richard Young and Tim O'Shea in England as an alternative to procedural networks. Their scheme has the advantage that distortions of the correct skill diagnosed as bugs have syntactic correspondents in the representation. Finally, we discuss a

205

very different type of diagnostic system designed at CMU[1] by Patrick Langley and Stellan Ohlsson, who apply machine learning techniques to generating student models, and more generally cognitive models, without a pre-existing library of bugs.

10.1   Extending past knowledge with general operators

The research of Matz (1982) is very relevant to the controversy about mislearning operators presented in the last chapter. She studies bug generation by concentrating on the influence of past knowledge. In consonance with REPAIR and STEP theories, she bases her study of errors in high-school algebra on the notion of an active, inventive learner. She would agree with Brown and VanLehn that actions leading to incorrect solutions are of general applicability (recall that this is a constraint on repairs), but she argues that they are not basically different from the inventive actions that lead to correct extensions of old knowledge. In contrast with the notion of repair-generated errors, Matz views errors that are not mere performance slips as "the results of reasonable, though unsuccessful, attempts to adapt previously acquired knowledge to a new situation" (1982, p. 25). Errors arise when *generally useful extrapolation techniques* are applied to a pool of *base knowledge*, either because the specific techniques do not apply in a particular case, or because the base knowledge is insufficient.

In this context, Matz suggests that some power to predict the types of errors that learners of a given domain are likely to make can be derived from studying the types of extrapolation techniques people resort to. On the basis of observed errors, she proposes a taxonomy of extrapolation techniques applicable to algebra: these include the standard concept of *generalization*, and frequently observed assumptions of *linearity*, whereby a known operator is applied to subparts independently and the partial results combined linearly. Figure 10.1 illustrates the concept of linearity by presenting some examples of the correct and incorrect applications of an extrapolation operator called "generalized distribution." To explain expert-novice differences, Matz claims that misapplications of extrapolation techniques are often due to the way novices match rules to a problem. They merely use feature-level correspondences that lead to pattern replacements, while experts apply schemata that allow more complex replacements based on a structural view of the problem. This claim is in consonance with other studies of expert-novice differences (e.g., Larkin, 1983).

---

[1] Carnegie-Mellon University in Pittsburgh, Pennsylvania.

Correct applications	Incorrect applications
$a(b + c) = ab + ac$	$a(b \times c) \Rightarrow ab \times ac$
$\frac{b+c}{a} = \frac{b}{a} + \frac{c}{a}$	$\frac{a}{b+c} \Rightarrow \frac{a}{b} + \frac{a}{c}$
$\sqrt[n]{a \times b} = \sqrt[n]{a} \times \sqrt[n]{b}$	$\sqrt[n]{a + b} \Rightarrow \sqrt[n]{a} + \sqrt[n]{b}$
$(a \times b)^n = a^n \times b^n$	$(a + b)^n \Rightarrow a^n + b^n$
	$2^{(a+b)} \Rightarrow 2^a + 2^b$
	$2^{(a \times b)} \Rightarrow 2^a \times 2^b$

Figure 10.1 Extrapolation by linearity assumption: generalized distribution (Matz, 1982).

Also important for predicting misconceptions are domain-specific differences between otherwise related domains, which Matz illustrates with the transition from arithmetic to algebra. On the one hand, procedures can have new forms: in algebra, problem solving involves planning rather than mere algorithms. This gives rise to new complications such as the need to understand the goal and evaluate progress during problem solving. On the other hand, new concepts are introduced, like the use of variables; and old concepts take on new meanings, like equality, which becomes a constraining relation between two distinct expressions (e.g., $3x + 3 = 2x + 7$) rather than a tautology indicating that an equality-preserving transformation or operation has taken place (e.g., $3 + 5 = 8$, or, more subtly: $4(x + 3) = 4x + 12$).

Although this work has not evolved into a computational model, it interestingly contrasts with other approaches because it explicitly assumes that the student involved in learning brings existing knowledge to bear in trying to deal with new situation. Not only does it attempt to account for these influences rather than considering learning in an epistemic vacuum; but it articulates operators that are used for extending the applicability of existing knowledge. Inasmuch as it unifies learning and mislearning mechanisms, it is a step toward merging correct and incorrect performance and learning into a unified theory.

10.2 Syntactic manipulations on production systems

In place of the procedural network of BUGGY, Young and O'Shea (1978, 1981) propose to take advantage of the expressive power of production systems in order to model subtraction procedures. Note that their use of production rules is fundamentally different from that of Sleeman, who is interested in representing and recognizing known bugs. Since Young and O'Shea are interested in explaining bugs, their use of production rules is similar to the GAO graphs of REPAIR theory.[2] Young and O'Shea's idea is to take advantage of the modular nature of the production system formalism so as to decompose the skill to a granularity level at which deviations can be expressed by simple syntactic manipulations. Thus, single operations are represented as production rules at a lower granularity level than bugs or mal-rules. Figure 10.2 shows a portion of Young and O'Shea's production system for a correct subtraction procedure. Primitive operators are marked with an asterisk.

In this format, a faulty procedure is modeled by modification of one or more rules in the correct set of productions. Since each rule has a condition and an action, there are four ways in which a rule can be modified: it can be missing altogether, or it can have a wrong condition, a wrong action, or both. However, in practice, most of the observed errors can simply be ascribed to missing rules. In order to model certain recurring erroneous patterns, Young and O'Shea also allow the addition of specific (mal-)rules (e.g., to model number facts involving zero, they add the mal-rule $0 - N = N$). Apparently, the production system language has given a fairly good empirical coverage. In addition to the authors' own corpus of data, the language was also tested on BUGGY's most frequent bugs with good results.

Note how the successful application of rule deletion is due to an ingenious exploitation of the granularity level of production rules. Young and O'Shea's production system uses a standard rule interpreter based on conflict resolution principles and rule ordering, as opposed to an explicit control structure such as the goal stack of REPAIR theory. Without an explicit representation of control, the actual control mechanisms that determine sequences of operations in the procedure are implicitly contained in the rules themselves, which can even assert conditions to trigger other rules (e.g., FD or B2A in the figure). The result is a finely grained decomposition of the procedure into various rules that correspond individually to primitive operations and to their sequencing relations, so that both control and operations can be affected by simple modifications to the set of rules.

---

[2] However, Young and O'Shea conceived their scheme before REPAIR theory came out, possibly influencing Brown and VanLehn in their selection of a new representation.

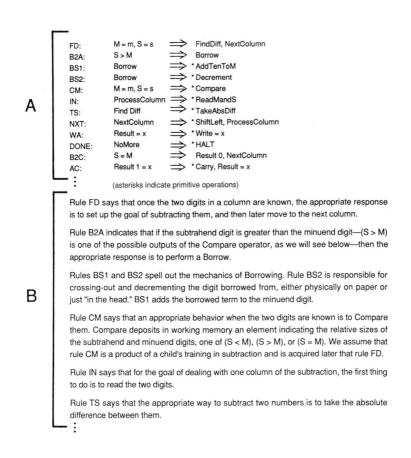

FD:	M = m, S = s	⟹	FindDiff, NextColumn
B2A:	S > M	⟹	Borrow
BS1:	Borrow	⟹	* AddTenToM
BS2:	Borrow	⟹	* Decrement
CM:	M = m, S = s	⟹	* Compare
IN:	ProcessColumn	⟹	* ReadMandS
TS:	Find Diff	⟹	* TakeAbsDiff
NXT:	NextColumn	⟹	* ShiftLeft, ProcessColumn
WA:	Result = x	⟹	* Write = x
DONE:	NoMore	⟹	* HALT
B2C:	S = M	⟹	Result 0, NextColumn
AC:	Result 1 = x	⟹	* Carry, Result = x

⋮

(asterisks indicate primitive operations)

Rule FD says that once the two digits in a column are known, the appropriate response is to set up the goal of subtracting them, and then later move to the next column.

Rule B2A indicates that if the subtrahend digit is greater than the minuend digit—(S > M) is one of the possible outputs of the Compare operator, as we will see below—then the appropriate response is to perform a Borrow.

Rules BS1 and BS2 spell out the mechanics of Borrowing. Rule BS2 is responsible for crossing-out and decrementing the digit borrowed from, either physically on paper or just "in the head." BS1 adds the borrowed term to the minuend digit.

Rule CM says that an appropriate behavior when the two digits are known is to Compare them. Compare deposits in working memory an element indicating the relative sizes of the subtrahend and minuend digits, one of (S < M), (S > M), or (S = M). We assume that rule CM is a product of a child's training in subtraction and is acquired later that rule FD.

Rule IN says that for the goal of dealing with one column of the subtraction, the first thing to do is to read the two digits.

Rule TS says that the appropriate way to subtract two numbers is to take the absolute difference between them.

⋮

Figure 10.2 Production system for subtraction (Young and O'Shea, 1981).

Syntactic manipulations: practical and theoretical limitations

When compared with BUGGY's representation, the main advantage of this type of production system for modeling bugs is that the relation of the faulty knowledge to the correct one usually corresponds to syntactic manipulations of the representation. In contrast, we have noted that bugs have to be programmed and inserted into procedural networks without a supporting representational mechanism to account for the nature of the deviation.

At first sight, this feature should give some leverage for automated student modeling, yet Young and O'Shea do not propose a diagnostic system using their representation. In fact, building such a system would present severe difficulties. Two different approaches are possible: the modifications to the set of rules that should be considered in modeling could be given in advance by designers; or else they could be generated by the modeling system by means of syntactic manipulations. In the first case, the system would be equivalent to DEBUGGY in that the same limitations and problems would be encountered—a fixed set of bugs, a combinatorial search, and the difficulty of dealing with noisy data. If the modifications were not given but were generated automatically, the limitation of a fixed set of bugs would be deferred to another level: the extent to which the representation's syntax supports modifications that model observed behavior. In this respect, for these production systems, the good empirical coverage gives a favorable indication.

However, a more fundamental limitation of models based merely on syntactic manipulations of the representation would then be uncovered in the form of the unmanageable search space they generate. Indeed, the representation's very flexibility, which allows it to account for many errors, is also its downfall, in that the search for a buggy model is unconstrained. Apart from a few loose stylistic recommendations, the model does not include constraints as to which rules can be deleted, which conditions and actions can be modified and to what extent, and which specific incorrect rules can be added. Not that such constraints do not exist: in reality, students do not make certain errors. The problem is that these constraints fall outside of the representational scheme used by Young and O'Shea, and therefore cannot be expressed within the model. In contrast, recall that an underlying theme of REPAIR/STEP theory is the attempt to include within the computational model the constraints that govern modifications to the procedure. In this regard, it is methodologically crucial to try to model the generation of all observed bugs, but not of implausible ones. Concentrating on frequent bugs provides a good coverage in terms of the proportion of errors that are reproduced; yet including rare bugs provides important constraints for a general model of bug generation linked to assumptions about human cognition. In sum, an improvement in expressive power such as the one afforded by Young and O'Shea's language over BUGGY's procedural networks is only a partial contribution to a better understanding of the deviations manifested as bugs.

10.3   ACM: machine learning techniques for diagnosis

The Automated Cognitive Modeling system (ACM) presented by Langley and Ohlsson (1984) proposes a unique approach to the diagnostic task, which eliminates the need for a "library of bugs." Interestingly, ACM takes advantage of the modular nature of production systems in a way very similar to Young and O'Shea's. However, Langley and Ohlsson resolve some of the difficulties we have just mentioned by placing their production system within a more formal framework that specifies the structure of individual rules. Perhaps because of their interest in machine learning, Langley and Ohlsson view the task of modeling a student's procedure as an instance of a learning problem within this framework. With their background in psychology, however, they actually present their system as a general tool for constructing cognitive models, although they describe it mainly in the context of bug detection in procedural skills. The domain used as an example is place-value subtraction, with a view to reconstructing BUGGY's set of bugs.

Machine learning techniques for diagnosis

Machine learning techniques were initially formulated to enable computer-based systems to acquire correct concepts and procedures. For instance, in a paradigm known as *learning from examples*, a system is given examples of a concept or behavior to be learned, and develops an internal representation that allows its own output to be consistent with the set of given examples. As implemented in many systems, however, this form of learning is completely driven by the examples on which the learning is based, without any a priori notion of correctness for the domain. The only goal is consistency with the set of examples. Hence, provided that the primitives in the description language are sufficiently refined, correct as well as incorrect behaviors can be learned by the same process. That means that if a person's answers on a set of problems are considered as the output of an internalized procedure, techniques for learning procedures from examples of input/output can be applied to forming a model of this procedure consistent with the observed behavior. By now the reader has probably noticed that this is exactly the task of diagnostic programs such as DEBUGGY and LMS.

   Note that the recourse to techniques for learning from examples advocated in ACM is fundamentally different from the use of similar mechanisms in STEP theory and in the SIERRA model. In VanLehn's system, the learning techniques are used to model the way students actually learn their procedure from a set of correct examples in an instructional sequence. Some bugs may be generated in the resulting procedure by an insufficient set of examples or by failures of the learning process. In ACM, there is no attempt to model human learning. Instead, the purpose is purely diagnostic: to induce the student's procedure from observation of his correct and incorrect results independently of how the procedure was learned in the first place. There is no notion of mislearning, and errors in the procedure merely reflect errors in the examples. Because ACM infers a procedure from primitive operators given the procedure's input and output, its task is a simple form of automatic programming.

10.3.1   ACM's modeling process

As in Young and O'Shea's model, the assumption behind ACM is that the student's procedure can be represented as a production system. But this time, in line with a long tradition of cognitive modeling at CMU (Newell and Simon, 1972), the production system is placed in the framework of a *problem space*: a domain is formalized in terms both of a language for describing problem states and of a set of very general primitive operators for moving from one state to another. In this framework, the diagnostic task can be simplified by a uniform definition of the structure of production rules. In ACM, all rules are formed by the coupling of one of these operators with a description of the problem states to which it should be applied. If a procedure is represented as such a production system, and if a given problem space has been assumed, two distinct procedures for the same domain differ in the conditions that recommend the applications of the primitive operators to given states. For instance, a missing operator is simply modeled by some "never" condition. The problem of inferring a model of a student's procedure is now reduced to that of finding, for each individual operator in the problem space, applicability conditions consistent with the student's use of these operators.

Given a student's answers on a set of problems, the process requires three phases. First, a problem space must be defined. This stage is not automated in ACM, since it touches upon fundamental issues in knowledge representation; the problem space is defined by the designers for a target student population (Figure 10.3 lists the operators currently used for subtraction). Second, given a problem space, ACM has to determine which sequences of operators have led to the student's answers. These *solution paths* provide a pool of examples of operator applications. Finally, ACM has to infer applicability conditions that will reproduce these sequences on the same problems. Once inferred, these applicability conditions explain the student's behavior with regard to the operators in the problem space; thus, they constitute the student model. Because a student's conditions for a given operator can be readily compared with the correct ones, the model can be easily understood by those who have to interpret it.

Path hypotheses: diagnostic and psychological heuristics

Originally, the method by which ACM found a solution path was simply an exhaustive search, whereby each primitive operator was tried on each

Add-Ten(number, row, column) Takes the number in a row and column and replaces it with that number plus ten.

Decrement(number, row, column) Takes the number in a row and column and replaces it with that number minus one.

Find-Difference(number1, number2, column) Takes the two numbers in the same column and writes the difference of the two as the result for that column.

Find-Top(column) Takes a number from the top row of column and writes that number as the result for that column.

Shift-Column(column) Takes the column which is both focused on and being processed and shifts both focus of attention and processing to the column on its left.

Shift-Left(column) Takes the column which is focused on and shifts the focus of attention to the column on its left.

Shift-Right(column) Takes the column which is focused on and shifts the focus of attention to the column on its right.

Figure 10.3 Primitive operators for subtraction.
Adapted from "Rules and principles in cognitive diagnosis," by P. Langley, J. Wogulis, and S. Ohlsson, in *Diagnostic Monitoring of Skill and Knowledge Acquisition*, Hillsdale, NJ: Erlbaum. ©1987 by Lawrence Erlbaum Associates, Inc.; reprinted with permission.

state moving forward from the problem. The only form of pruning was to abandon a branch of the search as soon as the result yielded for a column was different from the student's digit. Furthermore, each problem was treated in isolation. This presented two difficulties: the search space could be very large, and there could be many possible paths for a given solution. Recent versions of ACM (Langley, Wogulis, and Ohlsson, 1987) make use of heuristics to reduce the search space, and—as we will see shortly—combine the search for solution paths with the formation of a global model.

ACM's *diagnostic heuristics* take the form of additional conditions to the legal definitions of operators, so that implausible applications are immediately pruned without generating new search paths. In addition, the depth-first search algorithm does not consider paths that are substantially longer than the correct procedure. This heuristic is based on the assumption that most subtraction bugs stem from simplifications of the skill that implicate fewer operator applications. Note that this may be tied to the view of the domain imposed by the granularity level of the problem space: to account for rare bugs, REPAIR theory has to posit an

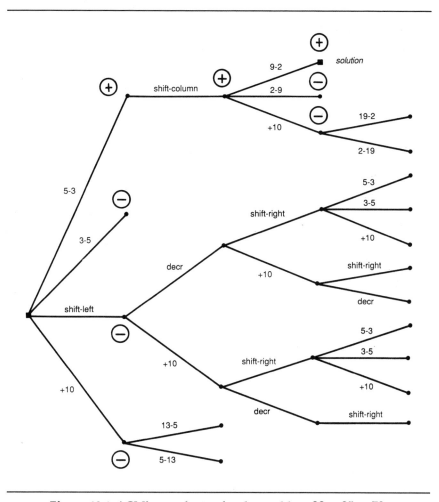

Figure 10.4 ACM's search tree for the problem $93 - 25 = 72$.
Adapted from "Rules and principles in cognitive diagnosis," by P. Langley, J. Wogulis, and S. Ohlsson, in *Diagnostic Monitoring of Skill and Knowledge Acquisition*, Hillsdale, NJ: Erlbaum. ©1987 by Lawrence Erlbaum Associates, Inc.; reprinted with permission.

additional problem space, with repair mechanisms in contradiction with this assumption. Figure 10.4 shows a search tree generated when ACM was determining the student's path for the problem $93 - 25 = 72$. With the bug exhibited here, the student never borrows but instead always subtracts the smaller from the larger digit in every column, regardless of their relative positions.

Although these diagnostic heuristics have been helpful in practice, they remain largely domain-specific and ad hoc, and they are admittedly a weak part of the system. A backward reconstruction similar to Sleeman's (see previous chapter) might solve some of these problems, but the more general issue of finding and selecting good path hypotheses remains. To address this question, Ohlsson and Langley (1987) investigate the notion of a *Diagnostic Path Finder* (DPF), a domain-independent system that formulates plausible path hypotheses. To this end, DPF constructs paths by searching the set of all possible operator instantiations. Its best-first algorithm evaluates paths by means of a combination of general heuristics for the "goodness" of psychological hypotheses. These *psychological heuristics* are listed in Figure 10.5. They have two functions. During hypothesis formation, they can be used to prune highly implausible paths, for instance, floundering or redundant ones. During hypothesis selection, they provide criteria for comparisons between competing paths by giving priority to those that require less severe assumptions. The list in Figure 10.5 is admittedly tentative and incomplete. According to Ohlsson and Langley, an obstacle to this research direction is that psychology has not yet come up with very detailed definitions of what makes a "good" psychological hypothesis. Nevertheless, even though DPF has not yet lived up to its promise in practice, it is a very interesting development of ACM. It has the potential of providing the diagnostic paradigm with constraints that fulfill the apparently contradictory requirements of being both general and rich in information.

Inferring production rules: learning from examples

To infer the production system that models the student's procedure, ACM applies a technique known as *learning from solution paths* (Sleeman, Langley and Mitchell, 1982). For each operator in the problem space, any instance of the operator that lies on the student's solution path is labeled positive, and any instance that leads one step away from the path is labeled negative. On the search tree of Figure 10.4, these labels are indicated by "+" and "−" respectively. With this labeling, which classifies problem states with respect to the operator under consideration, any appropriate technique for *learning from examples* (Michalski et al., 1986) can be used to characterize the set of states to which the student applies the operator. In diagnostic terms, this characterization of problem states stands for the student's concept of the operator's applicability. When condition-action rules have been built in this way for each operator, the result is a production system that will reproduce the student's behavior on the same data. Figure 10.6 presents the production system generated by ACM in the case of the student of Figure 10.4. Additional conditions given at the outset are shown in square brackets. This is a very simple example in which ACM needs to infer only one condition, marked with an arrow. In accordance with the student's bug, ACM has learned to

---

Assumptions excluding implausible paths

Causal closure: The arguments to each operator on the path are available when the operator is applied.

Purposefulness: There are no superfluous steps, in that intermediate results are used by subsequent operators.

No duplication: Available results are not rederived.

Criteria for comparing competing hypotheses (in order of importance)

Memory load: Paths that implicate smaller memory load are preferred.

Subgoals: Paths that satisfy more subgoals are preferred.

Productivity: Paths that have a higher ratio of satisfied subgoals to operator applications are preferred.

Minimal error: Paths that make minimal assumptions about errors are preferred (in terms of similarity to the correct path rather than number of bugs à la DEBUGGY).

Minimal length: Shorter paths are preferred, other things being equal.

Figure 10.5 Some "psychological heuristics" for path hypotheses (Ohlsson and Langley, 1987).

apply the "find-difference" operator in such a way that the smaller digit is always subtracted from the "greater," without any condition that the digit being subtracted from be above. ACM has also correctly eliminated all operators related to borrowing by finding only negative instances for them.

The exact method adopted for this learning task in ACM has changed substantially over the project's history, as efforts were made to deal with noise in the data. Currently, ACM constructs characterizations of problem states for operator applicability by piecing together sets of conditions, using statistical computations (χ^2) to select the most discriminating, yet simple descriptions. Not only does this statistical approach tolerate noisy data, but it can produce an evaluation of the final model. Note that ACM may be able to carry over noise in the data to the model it produces. In contrast with DEBUGGY, which has to make choices when presented with noise, ACM could produce a model with a certain amount of indetermination, that is, with incomplete conditions for operators, resulting in multiple possible behaviors. This is because production systems are not limited to the representation of procedural knowledge. Thus, ACM's method may be extendible to less restricted domains, provided they can be formalized with a problem space.

Find-Difference

IF *number-a* is in *column-a* and *row-a*,
and *number-b* is in *column-a* and *row-b*,
[and you are processing *column-a*],
[and you are focused on *column-a*],
[and there is no result for *column-a*],

$\rightarrow$ and *number-a* is greater than or equal to *number-b*,

THEN write the difference between *number-a* and *number-b*
as the result for *column-a*.

Shift-Column

IF you are processing *column-a*,
and you are focused on *column-a*,
and *column-b* is to the left of *column-a*,
[and there is a result for *column-a*],

THEN shift your focus from *column-a* to *column-b*,
and process *column-b*.

Find-Top

IF *number-a* is in *column-a* and *row-a*,
and *row-a* is above *row-b*,
[and you are processing *column-a*],
[and there is no result for *column-a*],
[and you are focused on *column-a*],
[and there is no number in *column-a* and *row-b*],

THEN write *number-a* as the result for *column-a*.

Figure 10.6 Production system for the "smaller-from-larger" bug

Adapted from "Rules and principles in cognitive diagnosis," by P. Langley, J. Wogulis, and S. Ohlsson, in *Diagnostic Monitoring of Skill and Knowledge Acquisition*, Hillsdale, NJ: Erlbaum. ©1987 by Lawrence Erlbaum Associates, Inc.; reprinted with permission.

Another development of recent versions is that path finding and rule building are now interleaved. ACM builds production systems for hypothesized paths as each problem is being analyzed. This incremental method has the advantage that path finding for subsequent problems can use the developing rules to direct its search by assuming that the path to be found must be consistent with at least one of the rule sets generated so far. In this way, indetermination is reduced with each new piece of data until a fixed procedure is established. If no path consistent with any current rule set can be found, ACM posits that bug migration has taken place and starts to learn a *new* procedure. Note that this approach implies an interpretation of the phenomenon of bug migration very different from

REPAIR theory's. In fact, although ACM can recognize bug migration, it does not suggest any explanation for it. This is because it is not an attempt to produce a generative account of bugs: the diagnostic models constructed by ACM are closer to those of DEBUGGY, in that they merely provide descriptions of student behavior.

10.4   Primitive operators versus bugs

Even though ACM does not explain bugs, its machine learning approach makes its diagnosis fundamentally different from that of other systems like DEBUGGY and LMS. Because the need for libraries of bugs is eliminated, the correct behavior is not considered the initial state from which bugs are variants. Instead, all procedures are constructed from the same set of primitive domain elements, independently of a predefined model of correct or incorrect behavior. The resulting data-driven flavor of the diagnostic process is ACM's most distinctive feature. Admittedly, the use of various heuristics to guide the search for a plausible solution path often requires prior knowledge of the correct path, but the primitive operators that model the student's path are still neutral with regard to correctness.

Bug reconstruction: low granularity of primitives

As far as efficiency is concerned, Langley, Ohlsson, and Sage (1984) claim that basing modeling on primitive operators rather than on bugs has the advantage that the number of co-occurring bugs does not increase the search space. It is true that this has been a major problem for other systems, and that the size of ACM's search space is only a function of the number of operators and of the complexity of the state description language.   However, it remains to be shown that the likelihood of numerous bugs co-occurring is more problematic than the need for a large number of operators. Indeed, an important limit on the generalization of ACM to complex domains is that the search space explodes with the number of operators and the size of state descriptions. Of course, more complex domains will also generate larger libraries of bugs, but without the need for the same low granularity level.

A crucial reason bug catalogs are often preferred is that predefined bugs make it easier to bring additional knowledge to bear. For instance, ACM's modeling process is ignorant of the teaching context—central in STEP theory—and there is no obvious way to make it take this type of information into account. In contrast, since IDEBUGGY considers bugs in a certain order, it would be straightforward to use information from STEP theory to generate orderings that reflect individual students' exposure to different lessons. In general, data-driven approaches à la ACM seem to proceed in a vacuum because the task of reconstructing errors without incorrect operators necessitates decomposing the domain representation to a granularity at which a lot of knowledge about semantic constraints is lost. Thus, while the low granularity affords greater flexibility for capturing unforeseen errors, it leaves the search undirected. This is why the research on psychological heuristics associated with DPF is so interesting; it attempts to remedy this lack of knowledge with general principles, not only concerning the domain, but mainly concerning human cognition.

Defining the right primitives

Theoretically, ACM's reconstructive approach is more open-ended than its model-driven counterparts in that it is not limited by a fixed, enumerative theory of bugs. Furthermore, established libraries tend to concentrate on frequently observed bugs. Because these bugs are already well-known, they may not be the most interesting for teachers or for cognitive psychologists. Of course, central assumptions are made when primitives for a domain are defined. Indeed, the whole scheme is based on the assumption that bugs do not occur inside these primitives, but only in the conditions for their applicability. Thus, while ACM's problem space does not include a model of correctness for the domain, it does include another type of model: a set of assumptions on what the student's primitives are. Even though the system's diagnostic power will largely depend on the choices involved in defining primitives, the authors argue that these assumptions are less constraining than a library of predefined bugs.

However, to reproduce BUGGY's descriptions in a unified framework, the ACM project has had to concentrate on creating production systems for the ten most common bugs only. These limitations are apparently mostly due to the difficulty of defining the correct set of primitives for the domain. In fact, ACM's problem space has changed a great deal over the project's history. In general, the task seems so complex that it may be the downfall of the approach for many applications. Of course, building a theory of bugs is not exactly easy either, and the development of the BUGGY model was described as a long and laborious process. Nevertheless, a library of bugs has the practical advantage of not being committed to a single problem space, and therefore it can include a wider variety of bugs without generating an unmanageable search space. In decomposing domain knowledge for reconstructive diagnosis, there is a subtle trade-off between the goal of accounting for all errors with finely grained primitives and the necessity of limiting the number of operators. In the light of Matz's research presented earlier, some operators outside the problem domain may also be required, since a student's procedure is integrated into a larger body of knowledge.

As a partial solution to this problem, Langley et al. (1984) suggest that ACM could have access to a number of problem spaces at different levels of granularity, and could search for the level at which the student's bugs can be described. Rather than searching for a model in one given problem space with one description language, ACM would search among problem spaces, generating new sets of operators by expanding operators in terms of lower-level primitives. For reasons of parsimony, a student should be modeled at the highest level at which all his bugs can be described, although higher-level bugs should always be describable in terms of their lower-level components. Of course, such a search would probably turn out to be very expensive, if at all feasible, and the authors do not venture to propose solutions. Furthermore, a language for the decomposition of operators must still be defined, not to mention new state descriptors. Should further work confirm the value of reconstructive diagnosis, the idea might be best suited for automated tools to assist people in constructing problem spaces.

From a practical perspective, coming up with the description language needed by ACM is an interesting and informative exercise, even if it does not have the psychological depth of generative theories. Note that, according to Burton's definition of subskills, the process may require an exploration of the space of bugs. Nevertheless, since it aims at building a model of the behavioral primitives of a domain, it is likely to provide insights into the nature of this domain. In this sense, defining a problem space may produce representational primitives useful for other functions of a tutoring system, for instance, building blocks for curriculum design.

Summary and conclusion

In this chapter, we have been interested in mechanisms that contribute to the automated reconstruction of bugs. Albeit theoretical, Matz's study is very relevant. To explain errors in early algebra, she specifies the notion of mislearning using a small number of operators that have the unique feature of connecting the genesis of misconceptions to past knowledge. In a diagnostic system, these operators could be crucial to an evolutionary student model whereby bugs are reconstructed from interactions between new and existing knowledge.

Young and O'Shea demonstrate the diagnostic leverage provided by the clever use of production systems to decompose skills into fine-grained components. This results in a representation language with some expressive power for describing the nature of deviations diagnosed as bugs. However, we have noted the lack of constraints associated with purely syntactic manipulations and the need to bring to bear information about manipulations that correspond to observable behavior.

ACM approaches the reconstruction task elegantly with the use of concepts from psychology and machine learning. By casting their representation of the domain in the framework of a problem space, Langley and Ohlsson separate primitive operators from their applicability conditions. Then they use machine learning techniques to infer the student's procedure from the data. Since the conditions that recommend operator applications can be heuristic, similar techniques could be used for nonprocedural domains. However, the task of formalizing a domain into a manageable problem space has turned out to be very difficult, even for a simple domain such as subtraction.

In spite of its limited performance, ACM is an important contribution to the diagnosis of procedural skills, as an alternative to the model-driven approaches found in BUGGY and LMS. The broader context of a problem space gives a semantic support to the notion of bugs missing in Young and O'Shea's manipulations. Thus within the production system framework, ACM can be said to automatically generate explanations of a student's bugs in terms of the description of a problem space. Of course, because there is no learning or performance model, these explanations are purely descriptive: they do not include the type of genetic information central to the STEP/REPAIR model.

Compared to PIXIE's reconstruction of solution paths, ACM reflects different choices in the trade-off between generality and specific constraints. On the one hand, ACM relies on well-defined general mechanisms that are truly domain-independent in that they do not make use of domain-specific knowledge other than the description of the problem space given as input. In contrast, PIXIE relies heavily on decomposition heuristics and look-ahead instantiations to direct the search, but must find equivalents if the scheme is to be applied to other domains. On the other hand, the inference step of Sleeman's reconstruction is perhaps more purely data-driven in the sense that mal-rules are posited without a priori definitions of operators. However, this freedom can lead to inappropriate inferences, since the nature and granularity of new mal-rules are not constrained.

Finally, in defining psychological heuristics to guide ACM's selection of plausible solution paths, the notion of a domain-independent diagnostic path finder has the potential of becoming a significant contribution of the ACM project. If a set of general heuristics could be devised for defining the characteristics of "good" psychological hypotheses, they would constitute very useful diagnostic tools. In fact, inasmuch as Matz's extrapolation operators summarize her analyses of human learning, the common theme is one of general diagnostic operators extracted from psychological observations.

In sum, this chapter has uncovered two themes central to diagnostic bug reconstruction. On the one hand, there is a need for expressive languages in which to represent the domains under consideration. On the other hand, diagnosis requires the formulation of general principles or heuristics which constrain this expressiveness with information about psychological plausibility.

Bibliographical notes

The research on mislearning operators is described in (Matz, 1982), and in full detail in (Matz, 1980). The more recent paper by Young and O'Shea (1981) is the most available discussion of their use of production systems.

The first official version of ACM is described in a technical report by Langley, Ohlsson, and Sage (1984), which is condensed in a conference paper (Langley and Ohlsson, 1984). Ohlsson and Langley (1987) discuss the research on the Diagnostic Path Finder (DPF). The best reference for ACM is a recent paper by Langley, Wogulis, and Ohlsson (1987). In addition to a comprehensive description of the current system, the paper includes a discussion of ideas for further research. The theme is to replace the behavioral descriptions of faulty solution paths in terms of misapplied operators by accounts of the violations of principles inherent in a given faulty solution. Such diagnostic reports would likely lead to remediation at the level of general misconceptions rather than at that of specific bugs.

Chapter 11

Problem solving and design: diagnostic plan analysis

Most of the research we have covered in the last few chapters deals with diagnosis in the context of purely procedural skills. From a diagnostic standpoint, this type of skill has the advantage that there is a small number of known sequences of operations for reaching a given solution. Problem-solving and planning domains present a different situation because of the number of choices involved in the construction of a solution. Early on, people concerned with the design of tutoring systems for such domains had realized the need for a diagnostic module capable of following the student's planning decisions (Goldstein, 1974; Koffman and Blount, 1975; Ruth, 1976). These early systems revealed issues in the monitoring of problem solving on which researchers are still working today.

In this chapter, we consider a number of projects that deal with diagnostic and tutoring issues in problem-solving contexts: the FLOW tutor, the SPADE project, the MACSYMA ADVISOR, and some systems developed in the context of the MENO project, including BRIDGE, PROUST, and MENO-TUTOR. Literature references to some other systems are given in the bibliographical notes. In most cases, the subject matter happens to be the design of some form of computer program. However, this is only incidental, and the ideas we describe are applicable to any problem-solving domain in which constructing solutions involves some planning.

11.1   The FLOW tutor: structured memory organization

The first project we look at was undertaken by Donald Gentner and Donald Norman at the Center for Human Information Processing (CHIP) at UCSD.[1] These two psychologists actually turned to the task of building an intelligent tutor in order to test and explore their theories about human memory organization. Recently, they have joined forces with some researchers working on STEAMER to found a common research project. They study issues related to instructional systems with the same emphasis on the notion of "manipulable interface" that was already present in STEAMER (Hollan et al., 1986).

Teaching strategies expressed in terms of schemata

One main tenet of Norman and Gentner's cognitive theory (Norman et al., 1976) is that memory is organized as a network of *schemata* or prototype concepts. They define a schema as a named frame with a list of slots that can be instantiated with values. Since values for slots can be pointers to other schemata, memory can be viewed as a semantic network of connected schemata. This is called an *active structural network* so as to convey the idea that it can contain both procedural and factual knowledge. Unfortunately, the theory does not exactly specify the learning mechanisms that build and later tune these structures, nor the processes that interpret and use them. Nevertheless, in this view of memory organization, the aim of teaching can be defined as fostering the construction of these networks by supporting the acquisition of new schemata, the connection of new schemata to existing ones, and the revision of incorrect ones. Two types of pedagogical strategy can be derived from these structural characteristics, contrasting in the kinds of intermediate knowledge states they generate:

---

[1]University of California at San Diego.

- in *linear* teaching, the network grows by increments consisting of full nodes. This is similar to the notion of frontier teaching in the genetic graph.

- in *web* teaching (Norman, 1973, 1976), a skeleton network covering the entire subject matter is introduced first (i.e., a form of overview). Then successive increments consist of increasingly complete levels of detail. Here, the frontier of learning determines the depth rather than the breadth of knowledge.

Tutors built on top of active structural networks

To investigate further the ramifications of their theories, Gentner and Norman have started to build two tutors: one for factual knowledge and the other for procedural knowledge. For both tutors, the idea was to have a computer-based system and a human teacher cooperate at first, and thence to progressively implement the system so that it would take over the human teacher's functions. Unfortunately, their two tutors never reached the points at which tutorial principles were followed by the part that was implemented.

For factual knowledge, they represent the history of the American Civil War as a network of event-schemata in which events are causally linked (Norman, 1976). To interact with the student, the system travels along the links, supporting interactions very similar to SCHOLAR's. Actually, by the available description, it is difficult to see what this system does that a modified version of SCHOLAR could not do, since SCHOLAR is also based on a semantic net representation of factual knowledge.

For procedural knowledge, the domain is FLOW, a very simple programming language that can be learned in a matter of a few hours (Gentner et al., 1974; Gentner and Norman, 1977; Gentner, 1977, 1979). Here the active structural network is used to represent programming knowledge and to interpret the student's programs in terms of this knowledge. The schemata are organized hierarchically: at the top are elementary sections of the instructional booklet that the student follows, and at the bottom are the keys that she can press. The system's interpretation of a program takes the form of a tree, which connects the individual characters of the program text entered by the student to a schema of functional specifications. Figure 11.1 shows one schema used by the FLOW tutor along with one of its descendants. This schema corresponds to the FLOW statement 030 DISPLAY "JEAN"; current instantiations are in bold characters, and names of existing schemata are preceded by an asterisk.

The FLOW tutor's diagnostic mechanism takes advantage of the hierarchical organization of schemata to give an interpretation of the

---

*Display-quoted-string-1932

schema:	**display-quoted-string**	*(prototype schema)*
statement number:	**030**	*(pointer to the code)*
value:	**JEAN**	*(parameter)*
status:	**satisfied**	*(status in the search for links)*
host:	***display-1911**	*(parent in the hierarchy)*
element:	***d-1937**	*(child in the hierarchy)*
element:	***quoted-string-1941**	*(schema below)*

*Quoted-string-1941

schema:	**quoted-string**	
value:	**JEAN**	
status:	**observed**	
host:	***display-quoted-string-1932**	*(schema above)*
element:	***quote-1946**	
element:	***character-string-1951**	
element:	***quote-1955**	

Figure 11.1 Linked schemata used by the FLOW tutor (Gentner, 1977).

student's program. As the tutor observes every character entered by the student, high-level schemata make predictions about likely next keystrokes and, when predictions are not met, low-level schemata search for possible interpretations. These schemata trigger possible hierarchical *parents*, which are placed on an agenda. When these parents are in turn activated, they look for further confirmation in the lower schemata and for their own parent. Therefore the programming knowledge of the system is actually contained in the links between schemata.

Since buggy schemata for common errors are included in the hierarchy to catch mistakes, FLOW's knowledge representation can be considered a precursor of later theories of bugs. Furthermore, inasmuch as the relations between schemata can be viewed as planning knowledge, this is an early attempt at using a hierarchical set of "planning" methods to diagnose problem-solving activities. The interplay of top-down expectations and bottom-up reconstruction is also a common feature of a number of diagnostic plan analyzers that will be described in coming sections. However, the FLOW tutor can hardly be said to analyze plans since FLOW programs are all extremely simple.

For unreported reasons, the FLOW tutor project was abandoned before significant results could be achieved in terms of usable systems. This is unfortunate, because the idea of building tutors around a theory of memory organization is very interesting. Ironically, although Gentner and Norman seem to favor the concept of web teaching strategy, which is of their own formulation, their work on tutoring systems does not directly reflect this preference. Yet the hierarchical organization of knowledge in both domains could be exploited. In history, global events are connected by intermediate causal links, and in programming, high-level concepts are implemented in terms of more primitive constructs. Still both systems traverse their curriculum in a linear fashion. Thus a central question, fascinating in the context of a cognitive theory of memory organization, remains largely unaddressed: how could a theory of memory and learning be used to make a system adapt its overall pedagogical strategies?

11.2 SPADE: toward a tutor based on a theory of design

The SPADE project grew out of LOGO as a way to concentrate on the problem solving performed in the process of program design, and to conceive a tutor that could provide guidance to students in their programming attempts. This section first outlines the theory of design that was to serve as a foundation for the construction of such a tutor. Then it describes an interactive programming editor that makes use of some of these ideas.

11.2.1 Ideas for a theory of design

After being involved with LOGO for some time, Goldstein (1974, 1975) presents MYCROFT, a debugging aid for small LOGO programs. Using annotated plans as models, the system is able to interpret simple picture programs. It can even suggest corrections if it has found discrepancies between the program and a propositional description of the intended figure. For its task, it uses its knowledge of plans and debugging techniques coupled with much information specific to the geometrical domain. In spite of these debugging capabilities, MYCROFT does not include the kind of problem-solving knowledge necessary for a programming tutor. This is the theme of the SPADE project (Structured Planning And DEbugging) that Goldstein undertook with his student Mark Miller (Goldstein and Miller, 1976b; Miller and Goldstein, 1976a, 1977a). SPADE builds on many of MYCROFT's ideas, but is much more ambitious in both scope and goal. Here, the purpose is to build a programming tutor based on a general theory of planning and debugging that would capture the essential ingredients of the program design experience (Goldstein and Miller, 1976a). Although the ultimate goal of constructing a complete learning environment was never fully realized, the results achieved in the process are interesting in their own right.

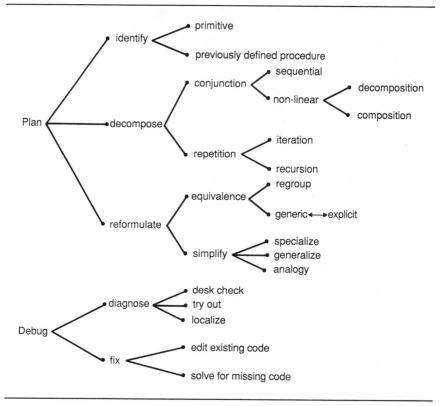

Figure 11.2 Partial taxonomies for planning and debugging (Miller, 1979).

A linguistic view of the design process

The first requirement for a computational theory of behavior is to define a formalism in which the theory can be cast. Not quite satisfied with the flat nature of the production systems used by Newell and Simon (1972), Goldstein and Miller borrow a formalism from linguistics to suggest *context-free grammars* for modeling the problem-solving process. They feel that the hierarchical organization of grammar rules makes for a more structured model, in which rewrite rules will stand for planning decisions, and the lexicon will consist of the programmer's observable actions. The vocabulary used to describe the different stages of the problem-solving process is based on a taxonomy of concepts involved in both planning and debugging, with the hope that both aspects can be captured in a unified theory. Figure 11.2 gives an idea of the kinds of concept taxonomies used in SPADE for planning and debugging.

Of course, the authors admit that context-free grammars present all sorts of limitations that will have to be dealt with. For instance, the *top-down* view of problem solving that these grammars embody is a substantial simplification in that it ignores the benefits of bottom-up exploration. In a first phase, however, the advantage of having a structured organization of problem-solving knowledge outweighs this limitation, although later experimentations with the implemented portion of the project revealed the central importance of exploration.

Another issue is that problem-solving decisions are not really context-free: they depend on the *semantics* of the problem, like the expected form of the solution, and on *pragmatic* considerations, like the existence of reusable code. These global factors can be incorporated into the theory if the context-free grammars are extended with mechanisms found in augmented transition networks (ATN), another formalism used for parsing languages. Though the core of an ATN is a finite-state automaton (computationally equivalent to a context-free grammar), local conditions for transitions between states can be augmented with global predicates. In a formalism they call PATN (for Planning ATN) Miller and Goldstein (1977a) use a set of global registers to contain problem-specific parameters (e.g., the problem description) and use global assertions associated with arcs in the parse tree to include pragmatic information (e.g., testing for the existence of a library subroutine).

Diagnostic concerns: parsing protocols with PATN

In addition to its value as a performance model for pedagogical guidance, PATN was also to be used for diagnostic purposes. PAZATN is an interactive Protocol AnalyZer (Miller and Goldstein, 1976c), which cooperates with an expert to parse protocols of actual problem-solving sessions. It relies on a PATN parser to come up with hypotheses for the planning strategies applied by the programmer. When presented with the protocol of a problem-solving session, the PATN parser produces a set of possible derivation trees whose branches are annotated with global considerations. PAZATN then selects the most likely hypothesis. However, from a diagnostic standpoint, PAZATN seems to ignore the difficult issue of recognizing and diagnosing errors in the plan whether they are due to incorrect planning actions or to the incorrect application of correct planning actions.

As a representation of problem-solving knowledge, a grammar embodies a certain view of the process. Hence, the design of a grammar must make strong assumptions about the planning process applied by the student. To account for individual differences, Miller and Goldstein (1977b) propose to perturb an archetypical grammar representing expert knowledge into a tailored grammar representing the student's planning knowledge. This is equivalent to inferring her language of primitive actions and decisions, and addresses the fundamental issue of domain representation in an interesting way since the learning of grammars is an active research issue. However, methods and constraints to make search for an individual grammar manageable are unfortunately left unspecified, leaving the idea unsupported.

11.2.2 SPADE-0: a plan-based editor

In contrast with the theoretical ideas presented above, SPADE-0 (Miller and Goldstein, 1976b; Miller, 1979) is a first step toward implementing a tutoring system based on the theory. However, this initial stage of implementation is really a *plan-oriented programming editor* rather than a complete tutor. In this sense, it bears some resemblance to the PROGRAMMER'S APPRENTICE, also developed at MIT in the same period with a software engineering rather than a pedagogical bent (Rich and Shrobe, 1976; Rich, 1984).

The purpose of SPADE-0's editor is to encourage good design strategies by making decision processes explicit. To this end, it interacts with the student mainly through questions and answers in terms of plans, debugging techniques, choices among next possible steps, and design alternatives. It uses the vocabulary developed for the formal model, with words like "decompose" or "reformulate." It also includes concepts for the episodes of a program, like the "setup" or the "interface." Only at the lowest level does it deal with actual code. The fact that the user must learn this specialized vocabulary can be seen both as a difficulty and as an advantage. On the one hand it requires extra work, but on the other it forces a dialogue at the problem-solving level within the structure of a formal theory, rather than at the level of the syntax of a programming language.

Figure 11.3 contains an excerpt from a programming session with SPADE-0. Note that the purely top-down, left-to-right design process of the theory is not imposed on the student, who can start in the middle of the tree of Figure 11.2 ("SEQUENTIAL"), and can postpone parts of the problem ("later"). In fact, experiments with the system have revealed that programmers do not follow a strict top-down method, but usually make design decisions "in that order which minimizes the probable scope of future modifications" (Miller, 1979, p. 127). The student's planning decisions are recorded in a decision tree that represents a developmental history of the program. The editor functions as a bookkeeper, updating this tree and allowing the student to access, expand, or revise any node, as illustrated by the last interaction in Figure 11.3. In this way, the process of refining the plan into a program is explicitly viewed as a succession of trials and repairs, very much in the theory-building tradition of LOGO. A partial rule-based model of task-independent problem-solving expertise

⋮

SPADE-0: OK. What name for the procedure you wish to plan today?

Student: WW

SPADE-0: What type of plan would you like to use?

    A. Identify as previously solved problem.

    B. Decompose into sub-problems.

    C. Reformulate into alternative problem.

Student: SEQUENTIAL

> *SPADE-0 recognizes the response as a specialization of one of the items on the menu, and does not force the student to articulate each level according to the top-down taxonomy of Figure 11.2.*

SPADE-0: OK. I am assuming PLAN → DECOMPOSE → SEQUENTIAL.
What are the main steps in this sequential plan?

Student: WELL POLE ROOF

SPADE-0: Do you want to include a SETUP step?

Student: Later.

> *The tutor notices that the student's plan does not include the usual setup preamble. The response "later" causes SPADE-0 to mark this part of the plan with a warning.*

SPADE-0: OK, John. I am postponing the SETUP of WW until later.
What now?

Student: Go to the second interface of the sequential plan.

> *In its internal plan, SPADE-0 has placed optional interfaces between the main steps given by the student. After this request, the editor will be positioned between POLE and ROOF.*

SPADE-0: Do you want to include this optional interface?

Student: Yes.

⋮

**Figure 11.3 Excerpt from a programming session with SPADE-0
(Miller, 1979).**

gives the editor a limited capability to advise the student on which step to take next. However, Miller describes these tutoring capabilities as rather ad hoc, and SPADE-0 does not build individual student models.

An experimental didactic system

Since SPADE-0 was conceived only as an experimental "limited didactic system," many extensions would have been necessary for the project to become a full-size tutor that took advantage of all the machinery of the theory. SPADE-1 and SPADE-2 were to include task-specific guidance derived from the problem description, inference of the student's plan from incomplete protocol information, and a full student model (probably in the form of an individualized PATN grammar). However, it seems that these successors were never realized, apparently more because of changes in the personal lives of the authors than because the research itself came to a dead end.

Because SPADE remained so speculative, it did not have the impact it might otherwise have had. Indeed, the underlying theme of formalizing the expertise to be taught as a performance theory was an early anticipation of the methodological conclusions reached by numerous other projects. The important insight that automated tutoring has to be based on a thorough epistemological study of the domain is a reflection of concerns central to LOGO. So, while in some ways SPADE moves away from LOGO's principle of discovery learning, it is faithful to its tradition of a deeply epistemological approach to knowledge communication; this fidelity is well reflected in the way SPADE-0 interacts with the student in terms of elements of its problem-solving theory. Indeed, a remarkable feature of SPADE-0 is that the theory is not only a background that supports the tutoring but is brought to the foreground in the interaction with the student. This high-level dialogue is well in line with LOGO's Piagetian view of the student as epistemologist.

11.3   The MACSYMA ADVISOR: plans and beliefs

Like SPADE, the ADVISOR built by Michael Genesereth (1977, 1978) for his doctoral dissertation, deals with the use of plans in a problem-solving context. Here, however, the goal is not to build a tutor but an *on-line consultant*, geared towards providing a reactive environment with intelligent feedback à la SOPHIE. The ADVISOR's domain is the complex mathematical package MACSYMA. Users can define sequences of mathematical operations for MACSYMA to perform, but they often need help. The user questions most commonly encountered in protocols of human consultants can be divided into five types of requests. The user is asking for:

- *directions*: "How do I construct a matrix?"

- *factual information*: "What are the arguments of the function COEFF?"

- *verification of facts*: "Is it the case that RATSIMP can be used for expanding with respect to a variable?"

- *explanation of method*: "How does MACSYMA invert a matrix?"

- *explanation of behavior*: "Why did this operation return 0?"

In the ADVISOR, each type of question is handled by a specialized module. The sources of information available are a semantic-net representation of declarative knowledge with some inferential capabilities, and a problem-solving model (called MUSER, for MACSYMA User). Even though most of these modules were implemented, the ADVISOR is only an experimental system that lacks an interface and never reached the point of being made available to MACSYMA users.

Since the ADVISOR is merely helping the user in her problem-solving attempt rather than teaching her, understanding the user's approach well is critical for aligning comments or corrections. Therefore, much effort was directed toward designing the MUSER model and using this model to interpret the user's actions. The fifth type of question—explanation of behavior—is particularly delicate and important. Indeed, novices are often puzzled by results returned by MACSYMA because they are unfamiliar with the semantics of MACSYMA's operations. When a user asks for help in such cases, the ADVISOR needs to give a form of feedback that reflects a context broader than merely that of the current operation. In contrast with the usual local error messages and on-line help systems, it is to act as an intelligent consultant: it must be able to explicate unexpected responses in terms of the user's actual intentions and to provide appropriate advice.

Figure 11.4 shows a consultation in which the ADVISOR is asked to explain MACSYMA's behavior, given the user's goal and the event that violated her expectation. The ADVISOR needs to infer the user's approach by analyzing a trace of the preceding operations. As in SPADE, the problem is one of recognizing a plan by observing problem-solving actions. In the ADVISOR, the process has two interesting features: it allows the ADVISOR to infer misconceptions in the user's mental model of MACSYMA and to interact with the user directly in terms of these misconceptions.

The dependency graph: a plan annotated with assumptions

Whereas a plan is implicitly defined in SPADE's linguistic theory as the derivation tree resulting from the parsing, Genesereth (1982) starts by formalizing the notion of a plan as a *dependency graph*. As in SPADE's plans, the user's observed actions are justified in terms of a hierarchy of planning decisions; again, mental operations, which deal with beliefs and decisions, are distinct from actions, which deal with domain objects. Here, however, mental operations are annotated with assumptions about their applicability, their input, and their expected effects. These annotations stand for beliefs about MACSYMA's operations held by the user. The MUSER model's mental operations are a set of annotated planning methods, which the user is assumed to be employing in interacting

$\vdots$

MACSYMA: $X^2 - Z(X+XY-YZ)$ (D6)

User: (A:COEFF(D6,X,2), B:COEFF(D6,X,1), C:COEFF(D6,X,0))   (C7)

(-B + SQRT(B^2- 4AC)) / 2A   (C8)

MACSYMA: 0   (D8)

User: Help

> *In spite of the cryptic language—already simplified for this figure—one can recognize that the user is trying to solve a quadratic equation, first by extracting the coefficients, and then by applying the quadratic formula. However, the result is incorrect because MACSYMA's COEFF operation requires that the formula given as argument be expanded before the call. The following consultation was given by the ADVISOR, except that it has been translated into English since the implementation does not have natural-language facilities.*

User: I was trying to solve D6 for X, and I got 0.

ADVISOR: Did you expect COEFF to return the coefficient of D6?

> *The ADVISOR is querying the user concerning his beliefs about COEFF, which it suspects to be incorrect.*

User: Yes, doesn't it?

ADVISOR: COEFF(Expression, Variable, Power) returns the correct coefficient of Variable^{Power} in Expression only if Expression is expanded with respect to Variable. Perhaps you should use RATCOEFF.

> *The ADVISOR suggests the use of a version of COEFF that does not need expanded expressions. Although there are more elegant ways to circumvent the use of COEFF with completely different approaches (e.g., factorization), the ADVISOR selects RATCOEFF because it constitutes the minimal change to the user's plan.*

User: Ok, thanks. Bye.

$\vdots$

Figure 11.4 A consultation with the MACSYMA ADVISOR (Genesereth, 1982).

with MACSYMA. Thus, a dependency graph can be considered a proof that a sequence of actions achieves a goal, with respect to a model of MACSYMA's operations and a model of problem solving.

Like Miller and Goldstein, Genesereth views plan recognition as an instance of a parsing problem: the trace of the user's actions is like a sentence that must be parsed in terms of the fixed set of planning methods. However, Genesereth ignores the semantic and pragmatic considerations expressed in PATN. Instead, the ADVISOR concentrates on the relation between the user's goal and her beliefs about MACSYMA. To this end, the ADVISOR's parser considers two key factors in addition to its set of planning methods: the constraints provided by the dataflow between operations and the subgoals generated by previous operations. The dataflow between the operations must be propagated up through the planning methods as the dependency graph is constructed, whereas subgoal expectations must be propagated down. These constraints, along with some heuristics, guide the associations of subgoals and methods that structure the graph in an alternation of bottom-up recognition and top-down expectation.

Inferring misconceptions and interactive diagnosis

This propagation of dataflow constraints between planning methods is crucial to inferring misconceptions. Here is how it works: as the plan is being formed bottom-up, these constraints climb the derivation tree; when they reach an assumption or a retrieval operation, they provide information about the user's beliefs and the contents of her database. The ADVISOR can then search for modifications to these assumptions that will be consistent with these propagated constraints and will complete the parsing process. This is a powerful scheme, which does not require a priori knowledge of expected misconceptions. In practice, the ADVISOR's database includes a few prestored misconceptions that are incorporated into planning methods, but Genesereth (1982) claims that this model-driven recognition of common misconceptions is done only for efficiency. In general, the mechanisms of dataflow propagation is sufficient. Of course, this assumes that MUSER's set of planning methods covers the user's and that all errors are due to misconceptions about MACSYMA and not to buggy planning methods.

Inferring the user's beliefs about the domain allows the ADVISOR not only to provide pointed remediation, but also to involve the user in choosing between competing hypotheses, once possible plans have been identified. In fact, interaction with the user plays an important role in the diagnosis, and supplements purely inferential processes with direct interactive feedback even before all possible candidate plans have been considered. In contrast with the SPADE-0 editor, the ADVISOR does not try to enforce reasoning about plans by interacting with the user in terms of a planning vocabulary. On the contrary, it completely avoids talking directly about plans in esoteric terms, since it merely uses them as a diagnostic tool. Instead, after selecting a likely candidate plan heuristically, it directly asks the user about her beliefs concerning operations in the domain of MACSYMA, as suggested by assumptions explicitly mentioned in the plan. The ADVISOR's first question in Figure 11.4 is an example of this type of hypothesis confirmation. Should the user have answered differently, the ADVISOR would have tried another plan.

This interactive approach to confirming diagnosis is attractive for two reasons. First, it involves the user early in the process. Second, it keeps the dialogue at the level of beliefs, where misconceptions are thought to occur, hiding the actual diagnostic process from the user. Once the ADVISOR has detected and confirmed misconceptions, it can correct them and offer the user the alternative most closely in line with her own plan.

Unfortunately, the ADVISOR has only been tested with knowledge of three different problems, and must therefore be viewed as a feasibility study. At this level it was successful, since it was able to reconstruct plans in the simple cases with which it was presented; but doubts persist about its generality, since even within a single domain like MACSYMA, the set of user beliefs is not easily bounded. Nevertheless, tracing errors back to deeper misconceptions is very important pedagogically. Many requests for explanations of behavior are disguised requests for corrections to a mental model that gave rise to a misprediction, and projects that can claim to have addressed this difficult issue are rare.

11.4   MENO: debugging and tutoring

The MENO project started in the late seventies at the University of Massachusetts at Amherst, as an ambitious attempt to build an intelligent tutor for novice Pascal programmers. The project's goals were to diagnose nonsyntactic errors in simple programs, to connect these bugs to underlying misconceptions, and to tutor the student with respect to these misconceptions. After the first system, MENO-II (briefly described below), the project branched into a number of directions leading to different doctoral dissertations. These are surveyed in the following sections. Jeff Bonar undertook an analysis of models of loop constructs possessed by novice programmers (Bonar, 1985a). Elliot Soloway moved to Yale, where he and Lewis Johnson attacked the bug diagnosis problem from a new angle, in a system called PROUST (Johnson, 1986). Beverly Woolf and David McDonald worked on the remedial aspects, with an interest in dialogue management for a generic tutoring module called MENO-TUTOR (Woolf, 1984).

11.4.1   MENO-II: error-oriented program analysis

MENO-II (Soloway et al., 1981, 1983a) is a diagnostic system that specializes in the analysis of loops and related variables (e.g., control variables or accumulation sums). It concentrates on the goals of detecting bugs and of relating them to underlying misconceptions. First, the "Bug Finder" parses a student's program into a parse tree that is matched against a simple description of the solution. This is done with the help of specialized knowledge about types of loops and corresponding plans, as well as a library of known bug types. If a bug is discovered, it is then analyzed by a set of specific inference routines that suggest possible underlying misconceptions. This does not require very sophisticated reasoning since MENO-II's known misconceptions are organized in a network and are directly associated with the bugs listed in the library. If multiple misconceptions are plausible for a given bug, they are all reported. Figure 11.5 presents an excerpt from an analysis produced by MENO-II. Note that in addition to reporting the results of the analysis, the tutoring component provides some correcting statements, which are simply stored in connection with the bugs known to MENO-II.

When tested in the context of an actual introductory course, MENO-II's relatively simple matching scheme, which ignores the process of program development and issues of control and dataflow, failed to correctly diagnose a large portion of bugs in student programs. In retrospect, Soloway and Johnson (1984) attribute these difficulties to a lack of careful empirical studies of actual student programs and error types, and to the absence of a plausible theory of how programmers program. Because it analyzes bugs locally in a context-independent fashion by means of simple template matches, MENO-II was simply unprepared to cope with the complexity of the programming process and with the extraordinary variability in programs and errors that subsequent investigations revealed.

11.4.2 The knowledge of novice programmers

Their confidence "only a bit shaken" (Soloway and Johnson, 1984, p. 57), Soloway and his colleagues set out to conduct the empirical studies and build the theory of programming knowledge that were lacking in MENO-II (Soloway and Ehrlich, 1984; Spohrer et al., 1985). In these investigations of programming expertise centering on the concept of iterative loops, the researchers consider the knowledge that novices bring to bear on the task of designing programs. This latter includes not only their burgeoning knowledge about programming, but also the knowledge they apply naturally when thinking about iterative plans and communicating instructions for iterative tasks in their native language. Since such studies provide a deeper understanding of the difficulties novices encounter, they have implications beyond the design of tutoring systems. For instance, they can guide the design of more "natural" programming languages that take advantage of existing tendencies (Soloway et al., 1983b). They can

---

Problem: Read in a set of integers and print out their average. Stop reading numbers when the number 99999 is seen. Do NOT include the 99999 in the average.

Student's program

```
1 program Average (input,output);

2 var Sum, Count, Data:  integer;

3    Avg:  real;

4 begin

5    Sum:= 0;

6    Count:= 0;

7    read (Data);

8    while Data <> 99999 do

9      begin

10       Sum:= Sum + Data;

11       Count:= Count + 1;

12       Data:= Data + 1;

13     end;

14   Avg:= Sum / Count;

15   writeln('The average is ',Avg);

16 end.
```

MENO-II's comments

Data is the New Value Variable
Count is the Counter Variable
Sum is the Running Total Variable

You modified Data by adding Data to 1 (line 12) Whereas ... you should modify the New Value Variable by calling the read procedure: read(Data).

Two misconceptions can be associated with this bug:

1. You might be thinking that the single call to the read procedure (read(Data)) at the top of your program is enough to define a variable which will always be read from the terminal. In fact, you need to call the read function a second time in your program to read additional values.

2. You might be thinking that Data is like Count, in that adding 1 to a variable will retrieve the next value. The computer does not know to interpret + 1 in the former case as a read.

Figure 11.5 Comments produced by MENO-II (Soloway et al., 1983a).

---

also suggest the construction of better curricula in computer programming (Soloway et al., 1982; Soloway, 1986).

Toward a generative theory of bugs for looping plans

Of special relevance after our extensive discussion of theories of bugs for procedural skills is a study of the mechanisms that generate conceptual errors in novice programmers (Bonar, 1985a, 1985b; Bonar and Soloway, 1985). To understand the difficulties these novices encounter, Bonar and Soloway observe people describing tasks "step by step" using natural language, as for instance when giving directions or instructions. They compare subjects who describe an iterative task in natural language with others who attempt to program an isomorphic task in a formal computer-programming language such as Pascal. The units of analysis are problem-solving schemata—or plans—which play a central role in both the informal realm of linguistic descriptions and the formal realm of computer programming. The theme of the research is that there exist close but sometimes deceptive resemblances between natural linguistic procedures and the formal plans required in using a programming language. Links can be found at two levels. At the *functional* level, both types of description provide instructions for tasks involving similar actions, such as iterations or conditional choices. At the *surface* level, both tend to use similar vocabulary and syntax even though the functional semantics of shared terms may have very limited overlap. As grounds for transfer, these relations both facilitate understanding and memorization and create confusion.

As a first step toward a generative theory of bugs for programming constructs, Bonar and Soloway study the influence of these functional and syntactic relations on programming errors committed by novices. The program shown in Figure 11.6 is typical of the class of behaviors they attempt to analyze. In this solution to the averaging problem of Figure 11.5, consider the loop delimited by the word "Repeat" at line 14 and the condition "until ..." at line 21. The student defines this loop by describing the first two steps of the iterative process, and then expects the program to generalize correctly, and to repeat the same procedure until some condition becomes true. Although incorrect in Pascal, this way of describing iterative tasks is very common in natural language, where the description of a few steps is followed with an utterance such as "and so on." Thus, while this program is probably too buggy for any syntactically oriented program-analysis system to make sense of, it reflects a misconception on the student's part that is both identifiable and explainable if one considers transfers from pre-existing knowledge.

From these analyses, Bonar and Soloway (1985) present a tentative catalog of *bug generators* for novice programming.[2] In the style of REPAIR theory, these bug generators combine a "patch" with an impasse, though the absence of a complete model makes the definitions of both phenomena less precise. Many of these patching heuristics involve the misapplication of existing knowledge in a related domain, in a fashion reminiscent of Matz's extrapolation operators. For instance, when confronted with an impasse in their programming efforts, novices tend to resort to their knowledge of plan descriptions in natural language. In line 22 of Figure 11.6, the word "then" is used illegally to intro-duce the instructions to be executed following the loop. In this case, the word "then" has a very specific usage in Pascal, in the construct "if ... then ... else ... ", whereas in English it can be widely used to indicate a sequence. This bug would be explained with a general operator that interprets programming constructs as natural-language constructs.

These abstract bug types are admittedly not complete generative explanations, and much more work is required before a full generative theory is available. At this point, there is no computational model of the

---

[2]Note that the word "bug" here is used in its original sense of error in a computer program.

```
        ⋮
 9    Read;
10    Readln;
11    Sentinel := 99999
12    N := 0;
13    S := 0;
14  Repeat
15    Read;
16    Readln;
17    Sum := 0
18    N := 1
19    Sum:= I + Next I
20    N := 2
21    until I = 99999
22    then Average = Sum/N
23    Writeln ('Average':= 0);
24  END.
```

Figure 11.6 A very buggy program with explainable misconceptions
Adapted from "Pre-programming knowledge: A major source of misconceptions in novice programmers," by J. G. Bonar and E. M. Soloway, *Human-Computer Interaction*, Hillsdale NJ: Erlbaum. ©1985 by Lawrence Erlbaum Associates, Inc.; reprinted with permission.

behavior, nor is there an automated diagnostic system that can generate these explanations. Nevertheless, the theory's current form is interesting in the context of this book in that it hints at the requirements for theories of bugs in nonprocedural domains. Indeed, there is an important gap between the procedural domains of the theories of bugs we have seen so far and the complex reasoning involved in learning how to program. In problem-solving contexts, the notion of impasse has to be distinguished from regular subgoal setting, and repair-oriented inventiveness from normal search processes. In consonance with attempts to define impasses and repairs in terms of new problem spaces (Laird et al., 1986), this research includes the application of knowledge from related domains in its explanation of how novices cope with situations in which their domain-specific knowledge is insufficient.

BRIDGE: from natural language to programming

On the assumption that novices reason primarily with natural-language constructs, the findings of the analyses just described suggest that a student learning to program must develop new "mental models" of iterative plans, models that comply with the formalism of computer programming.

In fact, Bonar (1985b) argues that there are increasingly detailed stages in the way one can define a plan, moving from a mere restatement of the problem in natural language to a detailed, runnable program. BRIDGE (Bonar and Weil, 1985) is a tutoring system that takes advantage of these observations to help students make the necessary transitions. The theme is to find natural evolving stages in the development of plans, and to articulate each stage explicitly as the student designs a program. Let us illustrate the four stages traversed by BRIDGE with typical phrases pertaining to the averaging problem of Figure 11.5:

1. nonprocedural *restatement:*   "compute the average of"
                                            "a set of integers"
2. description in terms of *aggregates:*   "sum all the integers"
                                            "count them"
3. *sample step* description: "add the next integer to"
                                            "the sum and so on until"
                                            " 99999 is seen"
4. *programming language specification:*   "repeat"
                                            "read in an integer"

Figure 11.7 shows some snapshots of an interaction with BRIDGE. In Figure 11.7a, the student is currently at Level 2, where inputs are described in terms of data aggregates and where the notion of a loop is not yet required. At the next stage, the student is asked to define the operations for a sample step, and finally these operations are incorporated into a structured loop. The four levels containing the plans required at each stage of the "averaging" problem are shown at the top of the screen. Plans that the student has dealt with are indicated in reverse video (white on black).

The interface with the student avoids problems of natural-language processing by the use of a set of *informal programming languages,* which associate with each planning phase a number of typical expressions derived from the analyses described in the previous section. Menus of phrases, such as "Sum up ..." and " ... the integers," are presented on the screen for the student to select from in composing sentences. Informal programs at each level are then formed by different combinations of these sentences. The use of these key phrases allows the tutor to recognize not only what portion of the target program the student is working on, but also at which stage in the theory of planning knowledge she is forming a plan. In this way, tutoring can be adapted to help the student complete the current level and move to the next one.

This setup has diagnostic value in that it allows the student to express clearly intermediate stages in problem solving; in this way, the tutor does not have to perform very complex analyses. It also has didactic value in that the student is taken step by step from her understanding of the problem in natural linguistic terms to the development of a program.

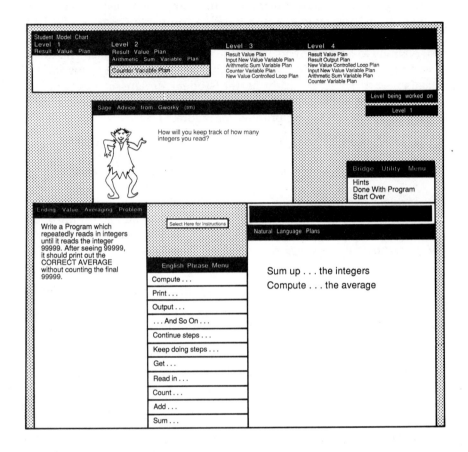

Figure 11.7a The BRIDGE tutor in early stages of the planning process (Bonar and Weil, 1985).

Thus, daily linguistic knowledge about task descriptions can be brought to bear for instructional purposes in an effort to integrate programming expertise with existing knowledge.

After the fourth level has been completed (as it is on the left of Figure 11.7b), the student moves to a new phase during which she constructs a visual solution by piecing individual plans together. This plan-level phase makes external use of plans that are similar to those used internally by PROUST, described in the next section. In this regard, it is interesting to compare Figure 11.7b with Figure 11.10. Figure 11.7b shows two stages in the formation of the visual, plan-level solution. Note

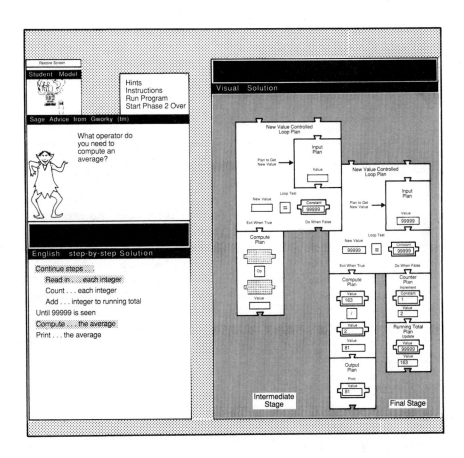

Figure 11.7b Phase 2: piecing plans together (intermediate and final stages).

that the final construction on the very right can be run on actual inputs, with the computed values being shown in the boxes. Only then will the tutor guide the student through a translation of her program structure into a target programming language such as Pascal. In this last phase, the formal plans required to implement each operation are individually converted into sequences of statements, which are then merged into a program.

BRIDGE needs more exposure to students to determine whether they find the framework overly confining, since they are forced through a planning process that they may or may not find natural. The most interesting feature of this experimental system—which is admittedly not very sophisticated from an AI standpoint—is that it provides another example of an environment explicitly articulating an underlying study of performance in the domain. As in SPADE's plan-based editor, the theory is brought to the foreground to become an instrument of communication between the tutor and the student. In the case of BRIDGE, the vocabulary not only deals with performance, but follows a study oriented toward the genesis of programming knowledge.

11.4.3   PROUST: intention-based diagnosis

"Remembering blunders past," Soloway and Johnson (1984) work on a new system called PROUST in which they reconsider the problem of program analysis in the light of the careful investigations of programming spawned by MENO-II's difficulties.   While BRIDGE brings this new understanding to the foreground in the tutorial session, as SPADE does, PROUST uses it in the background for diagnostic purposes, more as the ADVISOR does. Soloway and Johnson are less interested in explaining the origins of misconceptions in programming knowledge with a generative theory of bugs than in reconstructing a plausible program-design process so as to provide a problem-specific context for the recognition and discussion of bugs.

The importance of intentions

To motivate their approach, Johnson and Soloway (1984a, 1984b) argue that diagnostic methods that look for bugs in programs merely by inspecting the code cannot cope with a wide variety of programs. Indeed, such methods fail to recognize that nonsyntactic bugs are not an intrinsic property of the faulty program, but reside in the relation between the programmer's intentions and their realization in the code. Not only is code inspection insufficient, but even plan-recognition techniques, when used in isolation as in SPADE and the ADVISOR, are easily thrown off by faulty code, and by complex interactions between various goals and between the different plans that implement them. In contrast, the gist of *intention-based* program analysis is a comparison of intended functions and structures to actual ones. Underlying PROUST's approach to diagnosis is a view of the design process that distinguishes between three levels. First, the problem specifications give rise to an agenda of *goals* and *subgoals*. These in turn lead to the selection of *plans*, which are finally implemented as *code*. By considering all three levels, not only does this approach make the analysis less susceptible to misinterpreting

Original problem statement

Noah needs to keep track of rainfall in the New Haven area in order to determine when to launch his ark. Write a Pascal program that will help him do this. The program should prompt the user to input numbers from the terminal; each input stands for the amount of rainfall in New Haven for one day. Note: since rainfall cannot be negative, the program should reject negative input. Your program should compute the following statistics from this data:

1. the average rainfall per day;

2. the number of rainy days;

3. the number of valid inputs (excluding any invalid data that might have been read in);

4. the maximum amount of rain that fell on any one day.

The program should read data until the user types 99999; this is a sentinel value signaling the end of input. Do not include the 99999 in the calculations. Assume that if the input value is non-negative and not equal to 99999, then it is valid input data.

Problem statement as input to PROUST (slightly simplified for readability)

Objects:

 ?DailyRain is of the class ''scalar measurement''

Goals:

 Sentinel-controlled input sequence (?DailyRain, 99999)

 Loop input validation (?DailyRain, ?DailyRain < 0)

 Output (Average (?DailyRain))

 Output (Count (?DailyRain))

 Output (Guarded count (?DailyRain))

 Output (Maximum (?DailyRain))

Figure 11.8 The "rainfall" problem with its formal rendition (Johnson, 1986).

---

unusual code, but it also produces more meaningful bug reports for a student struggling with a programming assignment.

 The exact set of intentions underlying a program is usually not available as data, but must be reconstructed on the basis of evidence provided by the problem specifications given to the programmer and by the program proposed as a solution. The "rainfall" problem shown in Figure 11.8 is a typical example of the programming assignments

PROUST can deal with. Included in the figure is the formal description of the problem given to PROUST as input along with the student program to be analyzed: as the problem-description language stands, composing these formal specifications for an assignment can be fairly complex and does require some familiarity with PROUST's design.

Given this information, PROUST searches for the most plausible *interpretation* of the program with respect to the specifications. To this end, it needs to infer a plausible design process that replays the programmer's intentions. Hence, the theme of PROUST's method is *analysis by synthesis*. The method combines reconstruction of intentions with detection of bugs. Both must occur together, because bugs can lead to misinterpretations of intentions, and intentions are necessary to distinguish bugs from unusual but correct code.

An interpretation can be seen as a sophisticated kind of parse tree since it is defined as a mapping of the code onto the specifications via a hierarchical goal structure for the program. The space of possible interpretations in which PROUST conducts its search is organized into three layers according to the design stages mentioned above. At the top are the various possible decompositions of the specifications into goals and subgoals, then the plans that could be selected as implementation methods for each one, and finally the different ways in which plans can match the code. In view of the wide variability of novice programs and of the possibility of bugs at all three levels, the interpretation space is quite large even for relatively simple programs.

PROUST's knowledge base and interpretation process

To master this search space, PROUST relies on a detailed knowledge base providing information about the types of program it is expected to encounter. Although this knowledge parallels that required for actual design, it does not constitute an attempt to reproduce the design process that novices follow. Instead, it is specifically geared toward interpretation, combining expert knowledge about programming with knowledge about likely novice errors. The main components of PROUST's knowledge base are as follows:

- *Goals and object classes*: PROUST has information about the goals and objects mentioned in its problem specifications and the ways in which they can be implemented or reformulated (Figure 11.9 shows an example of a goal useful for the rainfall problem). In addition, PROUST knows about implicit goals and objects that have to be inferred, and thus can sometimes be omitted in the problem statement. Finally, it possesses heuristic rules that can detect likely goal interactions and generate new goal expectations in connection with certain errors.

Instance of:	read and process
Form:	sentinel-controlled input sequence (?New, ?Stop)
Main segment:	main loop
Main variable:	?New
Name phrase:	"sentinel-controlled loop"
Outer control plan:	yes
Implementations:	Sentinel process-read while
	Sentinel read-process while
	Sentinel process-read repeat
	Sentinel read-process repeat
	Bogus yes-no plan
	Bogus counter-controlled loop

**Figure 11.9 The goal "Sentinel-controlled input sequence"
(Johnson, 1986).**

- *Plans*: PROUST has a list of plans indexed by the goals they achieve. As can be seen in the simple examples used in Figure 11.10, the abstraction level of these plans is fairly low in that their templates are quite close to actual code. This is due to the need to catch low-level bugs; too much information about the code is lost when a program is translated into an abstract description. To assist in bug detection, the list also includes some buggy plans and some information about misapplications of correct plans.

- *Code*: Such detailed plans often match the code only partially. To deal with these *plan differences*, PROUST applies two types of rule that are somewhat reminiscent of DEBUGGY's coercions:

  o *transformation rules* of the type used in code optimizers, which preserve equivalence between two versions of a piece of code. These rules adapt the plan so as to repair the match.

  o *bug rules* that explain mismatches by hypothesizing a bug of a known type. These bugs are to be reported to the student.

  Since a number of these plan-difference rules can chain to resolve a given mismatch, their use is controlled by a metric for the quality of matches.

With this knowledge, PROUST tries to construct an interpretation for the program to be analyzed. Starting with a goal agenda derived from the problem specifications, PROUST selects successive goals for

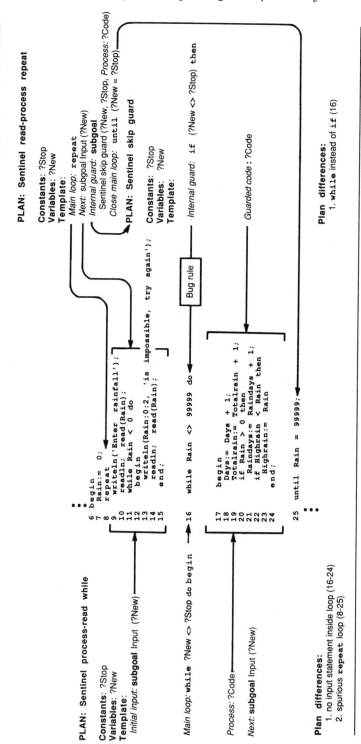

Figure 11.10 Two competing hypotheses for a buggy program (after Johnson, 1986).

analysis, though not necessarily in the order in which they were attacked by the student. To optimize its depth-first generation of a plausible goal decomposition, it gives priority to global control structures that maximize the coherence of its growing interpretation. For instance, in Figure 11.9, the slot "outer control plan" indicates that this goal is a good candidate with which to start the search. After performing any applicable reformulation or elaboration in terms of other goals (e.g., when two goals share a counter to be incremented), PROUST searches for corresponding implementations for which there is evidence in the code. Note that these may in turn generate new subgoals to be entered on the agenda, as illustrated in Figure 11.10.

Hypothesized plans are then evaluated according to how well they match the code, and how well they fit in the context of the overall interpretation. Attempts are also made to resolve partial mismatches with bug or transformation rules. A few internal critics watch for inconsistent hypotheses. Finally, in a form of differential diagnosis, competing hypotheses are compared to one another, at the bottom as to how much code they can explain, and at the top as to how severe they assume the student's misconceptions to be. The best one explains the most data with the most conservative assumptions. Figure 11.10 presents an example of a buggy solution to the rainfall problem being analyzed by PROUST. In this case, there are two loops involving a comparison with the sentinel 99999, at line 16 and at lines 8–25 respectively. Since both hypotheses shown in the figure produce only partial matches, PROUST has to decide which of the two loops was intended as the main loop. Because plan differences on the left reflect more severe errors, PROUST selects the outer loop, resolving the mismatch by positing that the student intended the "while" loop to be an "if." Note how differential diagnosis in terms of larger structures supports the inference of a nontrivial bug, which would be difficult to assert with the same confidence otherwise.

Although this case provides a clear and concise example of differential diagnosis involving bugs, construction of a reasonable interpretation is not restricted to the inference of such local intentions. In some programs, especially in incorrect or poorly written ones, goals can be realized indirectly in the code via obscure interactions between goals and their respective plans. For instance, checks for valid inputs can be spread throughout the program and can even include compensating actions that undo former computations. In these complex cases, the goal decomposition both influences and depends on the selection of plans. This means that various goal structures must be tried with various plans until a coherent interpretation is generated. Selecting among competing hypotheses then requires a sophisticated ability both to reason about goals and to form various models of the programmer's intentions so that differential diagnosis in terms of these models can finally select the most plausible interpretation.

⋮

PROUST: Now reporting MINOR bug in the SETUP part of your
program: The initialization at line 7 appears to be
unnecessary. The statement in question is:
   RAIN:= 0

(To continue, please press carriage return)

PROUST: Now reporting CRITICAL bug in the CONTROL part of your
program:

You used a WHILE statement at line 19 where you should
have used an IF. WHILE and IF are not equivalent in this
context; using WHILE in place of IF results in an
infinite loop.

The statement in question is:
   WHILE RAIN <> 99999 DO ...

(To continue, please press carriage return)

⋮

**Figure 11.11 PROUST's bug report for the program shown above
(Johnson, 1987b).**

PROUST used in real settings

After it has converged on one interpretation, PROUST evaluates its own
reliability by measuring how fully it accounts for elements of the code
and the specifications, and by applying its internal critics to detect flaws
remaining in its final interpretation. If it is not fully confident, it discards
uncertain portions of its analysis and warns the student about the incompleteness of its interpretation. Then it sorts bugs to be reported, trying to
group them so that it can point to common underlying misconceptions.
Figure 11.11 shows an excerpt from PROUST's bug report for the program
displayed in Figure 11.10. For the second bug, simpler code analyzers that
ignore intentions would probably just report the infinite loop, distracting
the student from her actual mistake of choosing the "while" loop in
the first place. Johnson (1986) reports, however, that in actual settings
some students found PROUST's explanations somewhat difficult to use,
suggesting the need for an active tutoring module.
   PROUST was tested on the first syntactically correct versions of
the rainfall program produced by 206 students. Eighty-nine percent
of these programs contained bugs. PROUST was fully confident about

its interpretation in 81% of cases, and found only 4% of the programs impossible to comprehend. Overall, it correctly detected 78% of the total of 795 bugs (however, the hit rate was 94% if one considers only analyses that gave PROUST full confidence). Although a fair number of "false alarms" were generated,[3] this performance is reportedly comparable to that of human teaching assistants (Soloway and Johnson, 1984). Results were less impressive on a more complex problem (50% of full analyses and 64% of correctly detected bugs), warranting further testing and refinement. Apparently, PROUST runs into problems because more complex assignments leave more design decisions to students, who then have to elaborate the problem requirements creatively. On PROUST's part, less detailed specifications require a greater ability to infer goal decompositions primarily from the code. Since such bottom-up analyses are extremely difficult, Johnson (1987b) is now considering ways of allowing students to discuss their intentions explicitly with the diagnostic system.

In comparison with other program analyzers described in this chapter, PROUST's main contribution is its handling of multiple goals. The FLOW tutor, SPADE, and the ADVISOR assume that all the operations to be accounted for can be reduced to a single high-level goal via a simple hierarchy. This assumption is possible because they only deal with very simple programs. In real programming tasks, even those presented in introductory courses, the specifications generate multiple, often interacting, goals. By addressing this issue, PROUST's explicit reconstruction of the programmer's intentions constitutes an important advance whose ramifications are not limited to computer programming. Of course, whether PROUST's current approach will be able to cope with large classes of problems remains to be seen. We have just mentioned some difficulties that result from its reliance on specifications to guide its reasoning about goals. An additional problem with PROUST's primarily top-down approach is in the way it recognizes programming structures. Because of its limited ability to perceive functional intent by inspection, it is still overly dependent on syntactic clues, such as the comparison with a prescribed sentinel in Figure 11.10.

Nevertheless, PROUST couples serious engineering concerns with the investigations of program design that followed MENO-II, reaching a point where the theory may well be able to handle real tasks. PROUST's reasoning in terms of intentions not only gives leverage to diagnosis, but provides the kind of information needed for effective remedial action. With this depth of analysis, a tutoring module based on PROUST, now in development at Yale (Littman et al., 1986), should be able to point to

---

[3]Eighty-six false alarms for 622 detected bugs.

the cause rather than the manifestation of bugs and to address remedial issues in the context of the student's apparent intentions.

11.4.4   MENO-TUTOR: strategies for tutorial discourses

Complementing the diagnostic abilities of PROUST, MENO-TUTOR (Woolf and McDonald, 1984a, 1984b; Woolf, 1984) begins to address the issue of remediation. It attempts to capture the discourse strategies observed in human tutors who strive to be sensitive to their listeners (Woolf and McDonald, 1983). While this work is similar to and inspired by the study of Socratic dialogues in WHY, the current focus of the research is not so much on defining individual rules as on designing a coherent framework for representing and organizing elements of a discourse strategy. MENO-TUTOR attempts to formalize the type of discourse procedures developed earlier for GUIDON (see next chapter). This domain-independent discourse strategy is to be coupled with a domain-specific language generator that implements the strategic decisions by means of utterances constructed from a database of domain knowledge.

The discourse management network: articulate tutorial strategies

The strategy is cast in what the authors call a *discourse management network*, which is a kind of augmented transition network. The nodes or states correspond to tutorial actions that constitute the basic components of a theory of tutorial dialogues. These states are hierarchically organized into three strategic layers that make the pedagogical decision process more transparent. MENO-TUTOR's network of 40 states is shown in Figure 11.12. The links indicate hierarchical dependencies whereby actions at one level are possible refinements of the actions at the level above. For instance, suppose that the system is in the interactive tutoring mode at the pedagogical level, and that an incorrect answer from the student has triggered the strategic action of teaching her some piece of data. Many actions at the tactical level can then be chosen to accomplish this, such as giving a corrective statement for her answer, making a general statement about some relevant facts, or questioning the causal dependencies underlying her assertion.

The arcs of the discourse management network, which are *not* shown in the figure, define the sequences of states normally traversed by the tutor. When the action corresponding to one state has been completed, the outcome of the tutorial episode activates one arc that moves the focus from the current action to the next. From a pedagogical perspective, these transitions correspond to default tutorial decisions based on local considerations.

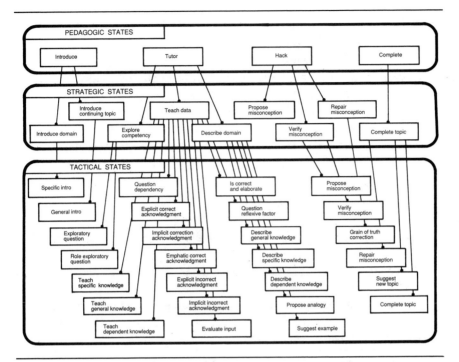

Figure 11.12 The discourse management network of MENO-TUTOR (Woolf and McDonald, 1984b).

Supplementing the default decisions represented by these arcs is a collection of *metarules* (rules about how to use rules) that can move the focus to any state in the network when their conditions are satisfied. The interventions of these metarules can preempt the default path at any stage; they represent major changes in the focus of the discourse that are warranted by the global context of the dialogue. Hence, the activation conditions that trigger metarules include elements of three global models (similar to those formerly used in GUIDON, as described in the next chapter): the student model, the discourse model containing a summarized history of the dialogue, and the domain model recording the coverage of topics. Figure 11.13 gives two examples of metarules used by MENO-TUTOR in connection with a Socratic dialogue on rainfalls.

The performance of MENO-TUTOR as an exploration tool

So far, MENO-TUTOR has been tested in two domains: rainfall processes—the domain of WHY—in which most of the basic work was

Strategic metarule S1-Explore
  from: teach-data
  to: explore-competency
  Description: Moves the tutor to begin a series of shallow questions about a variety of topics.
  Activation: The present topic is complete and the tutor has little confidence in its assessment of the student's knowledge.
  Behavior: Generates an expository shift from detailed examination of a variety of topics on the threshold of the student's knowledge.

Tactical metarule T6-A.Implicit
  from: explicit-incorrect-acknowledgment
  to: implicit-incorrect-acknowledgment
  Description: Moves the tutor to utter a brief acknowledgment of an incorrect answer.
  Activation: The wrong answer threshold has been reached and the student seems confused.
  Behavior: Shifts the discourse from an explicit correction of the student's answer to a response that recognizes, but does not dwell on, the incorrect answer.

**Figure 11.13 Examples of tutorial metarules
(Woolf and McDonald, 1984a).**

done; and Pascal programs, the original domain of MENO. In both domains, the language generators were shallow and the domain database small, because the natural-language interface had not yet been given much attention. The next step is to build these additional components so that the scheme can be tested in more complex contexts. Figure 11.14 shows a dialogue produced by MENO-TUTOR for the buggy program in Figure 11.5. Note how the tutor first adopts an interactive approach: it explores the competency of the student with two general questions to make sure that student and tutor share the same vocabulary. Once it is sure that the student understands the basics of looping constructs, MENO-TUTOR verifies her exact misconception with the next two questions. Finally, it attempts to repair her misconception with the tactic called "grain of truth correction," reinforcing what is correct about the student's thinking before proposing the required refinement.

From an engineering standpoint, it is worth noting that MENO-TUTOR achieves an interesting modularity, which makes for a clean framework for implementation. First, it separates discourse strategies from domain knowledge and language generation—although the exact nature of the interface between these parts has not yet been well defined.

Tutor: Do you know that DATA, in line 8, is a control variable for the WHILE loop?

Student: Yes

Tutor: Does that mean that DATA should be
a) Initiated before the loop?
b) Added into Sum within the loop?
c) Modified within the loop?
d) Both a) and c)

Student: C

Tutor: You seem to understand about the control variable of the WHILE loop. Now let us talk about some other command statements. What do you think READ(DATA) in line 7 does with the value of DATA?
a) Reads all the values of DATA at one time.
b) Reads in a single value of DATA.
c) Assigns several new input values to DATA.

Student: A

Tutor: Then do you think that DATA:= DATA + 1 updates the next of those values?

Student: Yes

Tutor: There is your misconception. Adding one is a common way to step through a range of values. But it cannot apply here because your READ instruction in line 7 retrieves only a single value. You should replace line 12 by a second call to READ(DATA).

Figure 11.14 MENO-TUTOR's remediation for programming misconceptions (Woolf and McDonald, 1984b).

Then, within the strategy, it deals with local decisions and global changes of context using different mechanisms, which are connected by their references to the same discourse management network.

The main purpose of MENO-TUTOR is to serve as a generic tool for exploring various tutorial strategies. The hierarchical network provides a set of tutorial primitives with default sequences, so that a variety of pedagogical approaches can be generated by the addition of different metarules. Although the dialogues generated in the tests were all very short, they were able to cover small topics in many different but coherent ways when different sets of metarules were tried. This ability to maintain coherence under changes of metarules is largely attributable to the articulation of tutorial discourse management provided by MENO-TUTOR's primitives. It is this ability that makes the scheme a good candidate as a testbed for exploring the space of discourse strategies. However, the articulation is only behavioral: there is still no mechanism to explicitly represent the communication principles on which decisions are based and interpret them in specific dialogue situations. These principles are still merely embodied by the set of arcs and metarules.

Summary and conclusion

This chapter has covered a number of systems that attempt to construct interpretations of students' solutions in problem-solving contexts. The types of solutions analyzed by these systems result from a planning process whereby goals are implemented as sequences of actions. In diagnosis all these systems make use of some form of hierarchical organization of known methods or plans, with which they build a structure that connects solutions to goals: the FLOW tutor utilizes schemata organized in an active structural network, SPADE views a plan as a parse tree, the ADVISOR constructs a dependency graph, and PROUST attaches plans to a goal hierarchy.

The search process that arrives at the final structure is usually bidirectional. The FLOW tutor works on-line and uses an interplay of expectations and confirmations. Although SPADE has not been implemented as a diagnostic system, its linguistic view of plans as parse trees suggests a variety of parsing techniques. The ADVISOR builds its dependency graph in a bidirectional fashion, propagating constraints derived from dataflow information. PROUST proceeds in two phases. First, it constructs an initial set of hypotheses in a mostly top-down search, then it performs a differential analysis that takes into account the interplay of intentions from above and the coverage of data from below, along with the severity of hypothesized errors.

Each system has its specialty. The FLOW tutor performs its analysis on-line, although its model of programming is rudimentary. SPADE incorporates global aspects of the design process, which bring to bear constraints external to purely hierarchical planning. Because these semantic and pragmatic considerations are certainly part of a general theory of design, it would be interesting to investigate their importance for recognizing and understanding errors. The ADVISOR seeks to infer the user's beliefs about the domain and to engage in a dialogue in terms of these beliefs. Finally, PROUST is able to cope with interactions between multiple goals, and has shown promise in real instructional settings.

To detect errors, the FLOW tutor triggers buggy schemata, and PROUST uses buggy plans as well as bug rules that resolve plan differences during the matching process. MENO-II and PROUST both hypothesize misconceptions about the domain heuristically, using prestored catalogs. In contrast, the ADVISOR can infer a restricted class of mistaken beliefs directly from the data. In this regard, the ADVISOR and PROUST have addressed two crucial, related issues. In general, the way a student's domain beliefs and intentions interact to manifest in complex solutions is a fascinating question, which still requires much research.

BRIDGE is based on a study of misconceptions about the programming domain which takes into consideration the linguistic knowledge novices bring to learning computer programming. This work has not yet given rise to a diagnostic system. Instead, BRIDGE uses the concepts developed in the study to create a supportive learning environment for novices. In this chapter, we have again seen how the design of AI-based instructional systems motivates a variety of domain analyses and empirical investigations. The results of these studies are useful both in the background, for internal computation—as in the ADVISOR or PROUST—and in the foreground, for pedagogical purposes—as in SPADE-0 and BRIDGE.

The MENO project has also evolved into a study of tutorial dialogues reminiscent of WHY's Socratic rules. In MENO-TUTOR, domain-independent discourse strategies are organized in a discourse management network: that is, a hierarchical augmented transition network divided into layers of abstractions. States represent tutorial primitives, and local strategies are set off by transitions between these states. In addition to these local decisions, the scheme has facilities for specifying metarules that can change the context when the global discourse situation warrants it. This has resulted in short dialogues that remain coherent despite changes in global strategy.

Bibliographical notes

The most available report on the FLOW tutor is a book chapter by Gentner (1979), which includes general comments about the design of tutoring systems. Technical reports provide more details on the Civil War tutor (Norman, 1976) and the FLOW tutor (Gentner and Norman, 1977).

A full understanding of the SPADE project requires the reading of a number of technical reports cited in Section 11.2. Condensed conference papers summarize the theory of design (Miller and Goldstein, 1977a) and discuss the use of grammars for intelligent tutoring systems (Miller and Goldstein, 1977b). The article by Miller (1982) provides a good retrospective account, which concentrates on the editor SPADE-0. Goldstein and Grimson (1977) describe PONTIUS-0, a short-lived project to build a coach for a flight simulator. Instead of a grammar à la SPADE, the flying skill is represented as production rules—as used in WUSOR—with planning, rationales, and other higher-level knowledge as annotations on these rules. This extension to the theory even includes some aspects of learning in the domain, since the metalevel information contained in these annotations is meant both to provide control and to support automated self-corrections.

Unfortunately, little literature is available on the MACSYMA ADVISOR. Short of bravely diving into Genesereth's dissertation (1978), one can only try to infer as much as possible about the consulting capabilities of this complex system from a one-page abstract (Genesereth, 1977). The use of the dependency graph for inferring misconceptions is discussed in a book chapter (Genesereth, 1982).

The best reference for MENO-II is (Soloway et al., 1983a). Many articles on subsequent empirical and prescriptive studies of programming are cited in Section 11.4.2, and many can also be found in a recent collection (Soloway and Iyengar, 1986). Bonar's dissertation (1985a) on bug generators for novice programmers is summarized in (Bonar and Soloway, 1985). BRIDGE is described in an article on the concept of informal programming languages (Bonar and Weil, 1985).

As to PROUST, Johnson's dissertation has been published in book form (1986) for the reader who wants a very detailed account of how the system works and performs. A condensed version is available as an article (Johnson, 1987a). Johnson (1987b) summarizes the main points and explores avenues for further research. Johnson and Soloway (1985) present a simplified version of PROUST called Micro-PROUST. Sebrechts et al. (1987) report on encouraging experiments with GIDE, an application of PROUST's approach to other domains (e.g., statistics).

MENO-TUTOR is fully described in Woolf's dissertation (1984); it is summarized in (Woolf and McDonald, 1984b), a good description that includes some detailed examples of how dialogues are produced. As a foundation for the design of a complete programming tutor, Littman et al. (1986) report on further analyses of human tutoring for remedial advice to novice programmers. The purpose of this last study is to detect regularities in the way these tutors evaluate bugs in student programs and subsequently select some of these bugs for remediation.

Some systems that address issues related to this chapter are covered later in the book: IMAGE and ODYSSEUS (Chapter 12) and the LISP tutor (Chapter 13). Some other related systems will not be covered in detail. MALT (for MAchine Language Tutor) (Koffman and Blount, 1975) is an early attempt at individualizing the tutoring of programming for students learning machine language; it has limited analytical capabilities. An early program analyzer based on the notion of plan recognition and intended for instructional applications is described in (Ruth, 1976). LAURA (Adam and Laurent, 1980) performs its analysis by comparing programs represented as graphs.

A recent doctoral dissertation by William Murray (1986) presents TALUS, a system that uses a different approach from that adopted for projects covered in this chapter. TALUS does not use planning knowledge, but analyzes programs by *verification*. The analysis is performed in two phases. First, TALUS attempts to recognize the student's algorithm by comparing her program to known algorithms for the problem. This selection employs a formal description language and heuristic matches. Then TALUS uses heuristics and formal proof methods to assess the equivalence of the student's program to the stored version of the algorithm. By successively decomposing the program into equivalence assertions, it is able to locate faulty code and to propose replacements. As far as dealing with variability and bugs is concerned, TALUS' performance on programs written in a restricted subset of Lisp compares favorably to PROUST's. TALUS is also described in a short conference paper (Murray, 1985) and in an article that condenses the dissertation (Murray, 1987).

Chapter 12

GUIDON:
the epistemology
of an expert system

There are good reasons existing expert systems seem to offer an ideal basis on which to build tutorial programs, other than the obvious fact that they embody large amounts of expert knowledge. One advantage of these systems is the usual separation of a knowledge base of production rules from the procedural interpreter that uses them. This allows access to rather finely-grained, modular pieces of knowledge, which are expressed declaratively and can often be understood independently. In addition, explanation facilities have been developed to justify the behavior of some systems. They can trace the chains of inferences, thus offering explanations of both how the reasoning has led to the conclusions the system proposes, and why the system needs certain pieces of information when it requests data from the user.

An example of a program possessing these characteristics is MYCIN, one of the earliest and best-known expert systems. MYCIN, whose original conception was in fact inspired by SCHOLAR's dialogue capabilities (Clancey, 1986a), had been developed at the Heuristic Programming Project at Stanford in the mid-seventies as an expert consultation system in the diagnosis of bacterial infections (Shortliffe, 1976): it seemed like the perfect candidate for extension into a knowledge-based tutorial system. Practically, there was a need for ways to expose medical students to a wider variety of cases than those encountered in their clinical experiences. As a further motivation, the domain-independent infrastructure of MYCIN, its reasoning engine, had been extracted and made into a generic system called EMYCIN (van Melle, 1979), which had been tested for applicability in various domains. The hope was that a tutor built for MYCIN would be able to handle any EMYCIN domain with a minimum of modifications, and that the principles underlying such a tutor would even be applicable to expert systems in general.

William Clancey undertook the task of building a tutorial system on top of MYCIN for his doctoral dissertation; this chapter covers three phases of the project, including GUIDON, NEOMYCIN, and GUIDON2. Clancey's research showed that things were not quite as they seemed, and led to very important findings for the design of both expert and instructional systems. Indeed, the project gave rise to a fascinating inquiry into epistemological questions related to knowledge communication. This inquiry, which continues today, has produced some of the most spectacular demonstrations of the field's ability to bring to light fundamental AI research issues.

12.1   GUIDON: a tutor on top of MYCIN

Even if an expert system has good explanation capabilities, it can only justify its actions passively. To be able to actively present knowledge, a tutoring system needs additional machinery to select instructional material, to be sensitive to the student and to conduct an effective interaction. GUIDON (Clancey, 1979a, 1979b, 1979c, 1983c, 1987a) is a tutor built on top of MYCIN, with the following goals:

- assessing the pedagogical usefulness of MYCIN's knowledge base;

- uncovering the additional knowledge a tutoring system would require;

- attempting to express tutorial strategies in domain-independent terms.

Although its existing rules are used differently in tutoring, MYCIN itself is not modified for this first version of GUIDON. The rule base and the consulting facilities serve as a core, which is extended with new capabilities and other augmentations to produce an active tutor.

RULE 507

IF   (1) The infection which requires therapy is meningitis,
(2) Organisms were not seen in the stain of the culture,
(3) The type of infection is bacterial,
(4) The patient does not have a head injury defect, and
(5) The age of the patient is between 15 years and 55 years

THEN   The organisms that might be causing the infection are
diplococcus-pneumoniae (.75) and neisseria-meningitidis (.74)

Figure 12.1 A typical MYCIN rule (Clancey et al., 1984).

12.1.1   Tutorial context: the case method

The pedagogical presentation strategy adopted for GUIDON's presentation is the *case method*: a mixed-initiative dialogue concentrates on successive specific cases so as to convey MYCIN's knowledge to students in a realistic problem-solving context.   Because the student's actual diagnosis of cases culled from medical archives helps focus the dialogue, the case method is reminiscent both of the Socratic method and of the "issues and examples" of WEST. GUIDON's purpose is to guide the student's reasoning as a Socratic tutor does. To this end, it uses MYCIN's approximately 450 rules as "issues" that can be presented by means of concrete examples when relevant to the case at hand.   A typical rule from MYCIN's knowledge base is shown in Figure 12.1.   Note that rules have numerical "certainty factors" (CF) that grade the certainty of their inferences, but that they do not articulate how the heterogeneous premises combine to imply the conclusions. This will turn out to be a crucial issue.

Once a case has been selected and described by GUIDON, the student acts as a diagnostician, asking questions to gather important data and proposing hypotheses. In the style of WEST's differential modeling, the student's behavior is compared to the expert behavior proposed by MYCIN in the same context. The tutorial program intervenes when the student asks for help or when his actions are suboptimal. For instance, GUIDON will suggest steps for the student to take or warn him that his questions are irrelevant to the case at hand. Figure 12.2 presents an excerpt from a dialogue with GUIDON in which the student proposes a hypothesis. The program can understand simple sentences and a list of standardized options that act like commands (e.g., "help," "details," "justify," "summary," etc.). Output sentences are constructed from a store of primitive phrases. Since the student is allowed to take the initiative

After presentation of relevant case data ...

Student: I think that the organisms present are Diplococcus-pneumoniae, Pseudomonas-aeruginosa, and Neisseria-meningitidis.

GUIDON: Good. The age of the patient gives evidence for concluding that Diplococcus-pneumoniae might be present (Rule 507—*see Figure 12.1*). The fact that the patient has been seriously burned is good reason to suspect Pseudomonas-aeruginosa (Rule 578). Both conclusions apply because the infection which requires therapy is meningitis, no organisms were seen on a gram stain of the culture, and the type of infection is bacterial.

The age of the patient also leads one to suspect Neisseria-meningitidis (Rule 507). Do the fact that the infection was acquired while the patient was hospitalized and information about diseases to which the patient has been exposed support this conclusion?

Student: No.

GUIDON: Right. This would be a good reason to rule out Neisseria-meningitidis (Rule 561). What facts about this case tell you that the organisms which might be present are E. coli and Klebsiella-pneumoniae?

Student: Help

The student was expected to describe each factor with a phrase, one per line. Help is provided with a list of all relevant factors for the current goal.

GUIDON: Choose from:

1. The patient does not have a TB risk factor and the patient's x-ray is not abnormal
2. Ottitis-media and Epigolottitis are not among the diagnoses consistent with the patient's clinical history
3. The white count (WBC) from the patient's peripheral CBC is less than 2.5 thousand
4. The infection was acquired while the patient was hospitalized
5. The patient was seriously burned
6. None of these

Student: 1 3 4

GUIDON: You're right about the WBC (Rule 557) and the evidence gained from the fact that the infection was acquired while the patient was hospitalized (Rule 545). However, the lack of a TB risk factor and a normal x-ray is weak evidence that Mycobacterium-TB is not one of the organisms which might be present (Rule 160).

The menu items are derived from the rules covering the hypothesis, some of which are shown in Figure 12.4. They are selected to force the student to reveal his understanding. When the student incorrectly chooses 1, GUIDON tells him how MYCIN has used this particular piece of evidence.

⋮

Figure 12.2 An excerpt from a dialogue with GUIDON: gathering data (Clancey, 1979c).

and to change the topic, GUIDON must be able to respond intelligently by maintaining a record of the context of the interaction.

12.1.2   Modularity: domain and pedagogical expertise

In design terms, the central theme of GUIDON is the complete separation of domain knowledge from pedagogical knowledge. This modularity between these two basic types of expertise is motivated both by the engineering need to have a clean design and by a desire to maintain a high degree of generality. The separation allows for various experiments with different strategies; it also makes the tutor easily adaptable to other domains. This section first describes the main extensions to the original production system that were deemed necessary for tutoring purposes. Then it presents the distinct tutorial module.

Additional layers of domain knowledge

MYCIN reasons backward from hypotheses, starting with possible diagnostics and setting up successive subgoals down to available evidence. In Rule 507 presented in Figure 12.1, for instance, each of the five conditions can become a subgoal if it is not an available piece of information. Subgoals can be fulfilled by the conclusions of other rules or by inquiries to the user. For tutorial purposes, GUIDON needs not only final conclusions from MYCIN, but also information about this entire reasoning process. To this end, the conclusions MYCIN communicates to GUIDON are extended with a full trace of inferences in the form of an AND/OR tree, including an explicit mention of the goal accomplished by each rule. Because this tree contains all information relevant to the case at hand, readily organized according to logical dependency, it constitutes the foundation for conducting the dialogue. It allows the tutorial module to see all the knowledge the expert has used to deal with the case, and exactly where this knowledge is brought to bear in the reasoning process. It also shows the points at which the expert had to request further information. The tutor can then follow its tutorial strategies to select matters it wants to bring to the student's attention.

However, this performance report, which is available almost without extensions in MYCIN, does not contain all the domain knowledge needed for tutoring purposes. To support the explanations given by GUIDON, various *annotations*, such as pieces of canned text justifying inferences or pointers to medical publications, had to be attached to individual rules in MYCIN. In addition, the tutor needs some *abstract metaknowledge* about the rules themselves and how they are represented, so that it can reason

---

T-RULE 2.04

IF   (1) The number of factors appearing in the domain rule that
      need to be asked by the student is equal to 0, and
   (2) The number of subgoals remaining to be determined
      before the domain rule can be applied is equal to 1

THEN   (1) Say: subgoal suggestion
   (2) Discuss the (sub)goal with the student in a goal-directed
      mode [Procedure001]
   (3) Wrap up the discussion of the domain being considered
      [Procedure017]

**Figure 12.3 An example of tutorial rule for presentation
(Clancey, 1979c).**

about them. Extensions in this direction had already been investigated
in MYCIN for automating the rule acquisition process (Davis, 1978).
GUIDON must know the constituents and the structure of rules because
many tutorial decisions depend on the forms of rules under consideration,
and on an analysis of their instantiation, as can be seen in Figure 12.3.
Finally, another useful source of information is provided by *generic rule
schemata* for types of related rules. These create an explanatory context
in which a rule can be presented. Redundancy can be avoided if the
description of a rule is limited to the key factors that distinguish it from
others of its type.

The tutorial module: a distinct expert system

Though, as mentioned earlier, GUIDON's tutorial module is completely
separate from MYCIN, it is also a rule-based system with a very similar
rule structure. While we have just seen that it knows about the form
of knowledge representation in MYCIN, its rules never mention any
fact specific to MYCIN's domain. Hence, the modular separation of
knowledge exists at the semantic as well as at the design level. The
tutoring component can thus be viewed as a small expert system of its
own, with about 200 rules. Its domain of expertise is the management
of a tutorial interaction following the case method, in the context of a
MYCIN-like representation of the expertise to be taught (i.e., EMYCIN).
   To adapt the dialogue to the specific needs of a given teaching
session, the tutorial production system maintains and refers to a separate
database of facts relevant to the interaction. This database, called the
communication model, comprises three different parts:

- The *student model* is formed as an overlay on the set of domain rules. GUIDON does not use buggy rules to interpret the student's actions, nor does it attempt to describe his behavior in terms of higher-order strategies. In addition to the regular assessment of overall mastery, GUIDON's overlay uses two local values per rule to indicate its belief that the student could apply the rule in a given circumstance and its belief that he actually did apply it to produce his current statements. These three values heuristically feed into one another as the student model is updated:

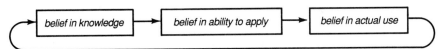

- The *case syllabus* contains information collected from an expert about the relative importance of topics, and serves to determine future topics to be covered.

- The *focus record* keeps track of the global context of the dialogue in a set of registers so as to ensure a certain continuity.

GUIDON's *tutorial rules* embody knowledge about discourse procedures and dialogue patterns, and about updating processes for the communication model. They are organized as packets dealing with specific goals; this arrangement makes for longer tutorial sequences than responding to the student only with local interventions. Tutorial rules address the basic issues of finding opportunities to intervene, selecting relevant information, and presenting it. When GUIDON takes the initiative or responds to a request for help, it must, among other things, determine the interest of specific MYCIN rules according to their relevance to the case, their status in the student model, and their intrinsic importance in the corpus of knowledge. Then it must select a mode of presentation and choose the format for asking specific questions. One of GUIDON's tutorial rules appears in Figure 12.3. It recommends a procedure for the discussion of a domain rule that needs only one of its subgoals confirmed before it can be applied. The tutorial rule suggests considering this last subgoal using a specific presentation procedure, and then discussing the domain rule's conclusion using another procedure.

An important task of the tutorial module is to respond to the student's hypotheses and guide him toward understanding how they fit with known information. To this end, the rule packets that maintain the overlay student model perform some fairly sophisticated diagnostic reasoning. When the student proposes a hypothesis, GUIDON must explore the domain knowledge he may have brought to bear to produce it. Since the mapping between hypotheses and rules can be complex, the system must estimate which parts of this knowledge have most

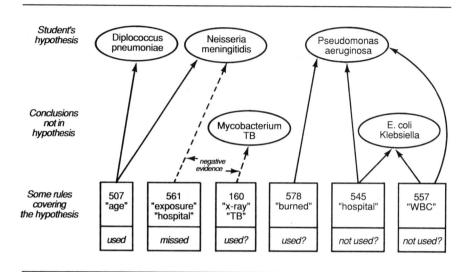

Figure 12.4 Some rules covering the student's hypothesis
(after Clancey, 1979c).

likely been applied by the student to constructing his hypothesis. As
can be seen in Figure 12.4, multiple rules can provide positive and
negative evidence for a single hypothesis, and a single rule can support
or contradict multiple hypotheses.

The network in Figure 12.4 deserves a short technical explanation
since it actually corresponds to the dialogue of Figure 12.2. For instance,
in its first question, GUIDON believes that the student has overlooked
negative evidence against Neisseria meningitidis provided by Rule 561,
and brings this point to his attention. For the use of the rule-based
representation, this network illustrates the type of information provided
to the tutor when a hypothesis propounded by the student is evaluated
against the expert system's conclusions. Drawing additional evidence
from its overlay model, GUIDON applies tutorial rules of the form shown
in Figure 12.5 to analyze such networks. In the situation shown in
Figure 12.4, this particular tutorial rule has applied to domain rules 545
and 557, since some of their conclusions are not in the propounded
hypothesis. This leads the tutor to suspect that the student has not considered them and motivates GUIDON's second question in the dialogue.

12.1.3   GUIDON and MYCIN: rule-based representations

The pedagogical goal of GUIDON is to impart MYCIN's rules to a
student. Such a goal assumes that these rules represent the necessary

---

T-RULE 6.05

IF (1) The student's hypothesis does include values that can be concluded by this domain rule, as well as others, and

(2) The hypothesis does not include values that can only be concluded by this domain rule, and

(3) Some other values concluded by this domain rule are missing from the hypothesis

THEN Define the belief that the domain rule was considered by the student to be -0.70.

Figure 12.5 An example of tutorial rule for student modeling (Clancey, 1979c).

expertise for the task of medical diagnosis and that students will find them useful. Given this assumption, the rule-based scheme of GUIDON's tutorial module performs well and produces very reasonable dialogues with fairly long strategic sequences. In this sense, GUIDON has demonstrated the possibility of using knowledge engineering techniques to build a sophisticated tutoring system whose strategies are expressed solely in terms of the rule-based representational scheme in which domain expertise is cast.

Because tutorial rules were reportedly built incrementally by successive case studies (Clancey, 1986a), the way many expert systems are developed, GUIDON's tutorial strategies are less articulate than those of MENO-TUTOR's discourse management network, which are expressed in terms of tutorial primitives. Moreover, its pedagogical principles are not made explicit, though some of them can be articulated retrospectively (Clancey, 1983c). As a consequence, attempts to use GUIDON for other domains where EMYCIN had been tried were somewhat less successful pedagogically. These domains include pulmonary diseases, psychopharmaceutical prescriptions, and structural analysis.[1] According to Clancey, problems are due to the difference in the breadth and depth of inference trees: the dialogue management expert is not able to adapt the level of discourse to different granularity levels for domain rules (Clancey et al., 1984). Nevertheless, from an engineering standpoint, making the transition to these new domains by replacing GUIDON's knowledge base was remarkably easy (Clancey, 1986a).

---

[1]The systems providing the knowledge bases were PUFF, HEADMED and SACON, respectively.

MYCIN's rules as domain expertise for tutoring

The assessment of MYCIN's knowledge base as a pedagogical resource yielded a different but no less significant result. Remember that GUIDON is not explicitly concerned, either in its interventions or in its student model, with the reasoning strategies of medical diagnosis. Apparently, this turned out to be a severe limitation for its pedagogical goal at two levels:

- As support for managing the dialogue: if a student followed a diagnostic strategy different from MYCIN's top-down search through the hierarchy of diseases, GUIDON would reject reasonable hypotheses. In the short excerpt in Figure 12.6, for instance, the student is using the knowledge encoded in Rule 507 (displayed in Figure 12.1) to make a reasonable guess outright. In its dependence on MYCIN, GUIDON cannot take into account the fact that the rule's key causal factor is the patient's age, and that other clauses are there merely for control purposes. Hence, it flatly rejects the student's suggestion at this point, since MYCIN, with its purely top-down approach, cannot consider Rule 507 before other clauses have been established.[2]

- As elements of the curriculum: students who used GUIDON in field experiments found it hard to understand and remember MYCIN's rules. The reason is again that the strategies and knowledge organization they embody are not made explicit, but are built in, resulting in heterogeneous rule structures. Hence, students could not really make sense of these rules so as to integrate them into a useful body of knowledge (Clancey, 1984a).

Some light can be shed on these difficulties by consideration of the methodology adopted for designing MYCIN and acquiring its expertise. The interviews with experts that preceded the coding had primarily aimed at extracting the technical details of expert knowledge necessary to reach performance within the rule-based framework. There had been no attempt to identify, let alone capture in the system, the problem-solving framework and the medical knowledge that gave meaning to the contents of rules. Although some of this knowledge was subsequently added for GUIDON's benefit in the form of canned annotations, it was still not sufficiently integrated into the system's model of expertise to make up for the obscurity of domain rules.

---

[2]See also GUIDON's first comment in Figure 12.2: "Both conclusions apply because . . ."

⋮

The student has offered to state a partial solution

GUIDON: What are the organisms which might be causing the infection?

Student: Neisseria-meningitidis.

GUIDON: What facts about this case tell you that Neisseria-meningitidis is one of the organisms which might be causing the infection?

Student: Age

GUIDON: The fact that the age of patient 538 is 34 years is not evidence for the conclusion that Neisseria-meningitidis is one of the organisms which might be causing the infection.
Do you have a question?

⋮

Figure 12.6 GUIDON rejects a reasonable hypothesis (Clancey, 1986a).

12.2 NEOMYCIN: reconfiguring the expert knowledge

In order to remedy GUIDON's shortcomings, Clancey and his team set out to uncover the ingredients that were obviously missing. To this end, they started to collect detailed protocols of the whole diagnostic process as conducted by experts and to observe teachers articulating their reasoning while helping students. This effort revealed such fundamental differences in knowledge organization and in strategy between human experts and MYCIN that the mere cleanup anticipated was not going to be sufficient. Instead, what was required was a complete reconfiguration, to obtain an explicit model of "diagnostic thinking" (Clancey, 1984a). This led to the design of NEOMYCIN.

Before we elaborate, it is important to underline that the decision to reconfigure MYCIN does not imply that MYCIN's diagnostic or medical expertise is fundamentally insufficient. MYCIN's performance in its domain is thought to be comparable to that of faculty members at Stanford's School of Medicine. Thus, the knowledge is there, but the rules represent *compiled expertise*, molded into a machine-efficient framework. It is this compiled nature of the rules that makes them too obscure for students. In this sense, the reconfiguration of MYCIN into NEOMYCIN can be viewed as an effort to "decompile" the expertise and capture different aspects of the underlying knowledge through explicit counterparts in the expert system.

12.2.1   NEOMYCIN: a model of diagnostic thinking

A detailed description of NEOMYCIN's rather complex diagnostic apparatus is out of place here. It can be found in (Clancey and Letsinger, 1981) and in (Clancey, 1983b). However, it is appropriate to present the main ideas of the modifications undertaken, because they indicate general issues involved in the shift from a performance-oriented design to a knowledge-engineering approach centered on communicability.

Explicit control mechanisms: articulating the reasoning strategy

One of the most revealing processes in the design of NEOMYCIN was the observation of tutorial sessions with a physician reputed to be a good teacher. Surprisingly, his explanations were in large part not specific to the medical domain. For instance, he would ask a student working on a case to justify the extent to which a particular request for data helped him discriminate between his currently active hypotheses. What became clear is that students were not just given rules about what to do, but that domain-specific information was placed in the context of an explicit reasoning strategy, which was described in general terms revolving around the management a set of hypotheses.

As a result, the most fundamental novelty in NEOMYCIN is the separation of strategic knowledge from domain facts and rules. Instead of MYCIN's interpreter, which repeatedly cycles through the rules to move backward from successive goals to the data, the control structure is now a domain-independent set of metarules that explicitly represent a hierarchically organized *reasoning strategy* for medical diagnosis. It is called a *metastrategy* because it is itself an expert system, in the strategic domain, used to control another expert system in the object domain. With about 75 rules in NEOMYCIN, this strategy-based control structure creates tasks to manage a space of hypotheses. Its knowledge deals with abstract notions like forming a hypothesis space, grouping hypotheses into more general classes, or refining them into special cases to confirm them against the data. Figure 12.7 gives an idea of the spectrum of strategic concepts the system applies, and Figure 12.8 describes the general format of individual metarules.

This notion of a set of hypotheses is important because MYCIN has no awareness of the concept of hypothesis as it moves from goals to subgoals trying to find values for various parameters. In NEOMYCIN,

Figure 12.7 NEOMYCIN's explicit diagnostic strategy (after Clancey, 1986a).

all currently active hypotheses are contained in a new data structure, the *differential*, intended as an equivalent to human working memory; this gives the system some controllable breadth of focus. Figure 12.8 shows an example of NEOMYCIN's strategic metarules dealing with the differential. This explicit management of hypotheses allows the kind of *compiled associations* by which experts heuristically trigger hypotheses from data (see, for instance, Figure 12.6) and quickly move from one hypothesis to another, cutting across hierarchies of logical dependency to avoid exhaustive search.

In considering Figure 12.8, note how MYCIN's chaining of domain rules via subgoals has been replaced by the chaining of metarules via diagnostic tasks. In NEOMYCIN, all domain inferences and data requests take place under the control of the metastrategy, which applies domain rules. As a consequence, there is no need for the reasoning to move strictly backward, exhausting a fixed set of successive candidate conclusions, as it does in MYCIN. Instead, the system can move forward and propose hypotheses from the data, while still keeping a reasonable focus. According to Clancey and Letsinger (1981, p. 831), it is precisely

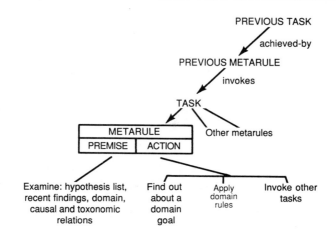

METARULE 397 (for the task "group and differentiate")

IF There are two items on the differential that differ in some disease process feature

THEN Ask a question that differentiates between these two kinds of processes.

Figure 12.8 Abstract format and specific example of metarule (Hasling et al., 1984).

"NEOMYCIN's forward, non-exhaustive reasoning and management of a space of hypotheses" that make its strategy more humanlike. The scheme has a number of advantages:

- Backward chaining only makes sense when the set of possible conclusions is small. With its new configuration, NEOMYCIN has been expanded to cover a wider range of diseases that could be confused with meningitis.

- The existence of an explicit differential allows the system's focus to move in a logical way, making meaningful transitions that correspond to competing hypotheses. Clancey claims a decrease in the number of questions NEOMYCIN asks the user, as well as an improvement in their relevance to a physician's view of the problem. This had been an important issue for MYCIN, whose exhaustive search method generates question sequences that often seem erratic to medical professionals unaware of its inner mechanisms.

- Bottom-up hypotheses of the type proposed by the student in Figure 12.6 can be accepted and entered into the differential to be elaborated later.

- Justifications and explanations can be given in terms of strategic goals and tasks with respect to specific hypotheses (Hasling et al., 1984). An example of strategic explanation can be found in the explanation window in Figure 12.12. Contrast Statement 4.0, which conveys a domain rule, with Statement 5.0, which explains a strategic intention.

Knowledge organization: articulating the epistemological structure

Not only is the interpreter expressed in terms of an explicit reasoning strategy, but the knowledge base containing the domain rules is reconfigured so that its structure provides the type of abstract information necessary to instantiate this strategy. To this end, MYCIN's rules are cleaned up with regard to their strategic and domain content. The first task is to rid them of the strategic information embedded in the form of additional clauses and clause orderings in rule premises. For instance, in MYCIN, various rules dealing with alcoholism would each put an additional condition on the patient's age to ensure that the system does not ask whether a child is an alcoholic.[3] These conditions are ordered so that the system checks for the age first. In NEOMYCIN, the fact that children are not usually alcoholics is made into a separate rule, and the fact that general conditions must be checked before more specific ones becomes an explicit reasoning strategy.

Beyond the excision of embedded control, domain knowledge is further organized into coherent epistemic categories for distinct types of information such as general principles, common world realities, definitional and taxonomic relations, causal relations, and heuristic rules. When these are grouped into abstract structures that the metastrategy can reason about, semantically meaningful channels can be created to guide the access to rules. In keeping with the performance of human experts, who can access their rules in multiple but meaningfully focused ways according to context, NEOMYCIN's rule base is overlaid with a set of orthogonal viewpoints through which the strategy can index the rules, as illustrated in Figure 12.9. These viewpoints are abstract structures with an explicit semantic significance, and act like windows giving access to the knowledge base. As an example of such a viewpoint, the hierarchy of etiological relations between disorders (specializations of causes) implicit

---

[3]Note how this use of age for control purposes differs from Rule 507's use of age as direct causal factor, even though both clauses are represented in a uniform fashion in MYCIN.

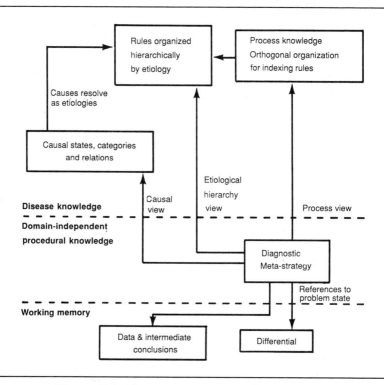

Figure 12.9 Abstract components of NEOMYCIN

Adapted from "Methodology for building an intelligent tutoring system," by W. J. Clancey, in *Methods and Tactics in Cognitive Science*, Hillsdale, NJ: Erlbaum. ©1984 by Lawrence Erlbaum Associates, Inc.; reprinted with permission.

in MYCIN has been extracted from its rules (e.g., clauses 1 to 3 in Rule 507, Figure 12.1). It has become a separate structure that points to relevant rules (see Figure 12.12 for a partial display). However, the same rules can also be accessed via the knowledge of processes associated with specific disorders. As hypotheses are generated, triggered, enabled, confirmed, or ruled out, these various access channels are crucial to support the variety of reasoning tasks and focusing strategies by which data and conclusions can be connected.

12.2.2   The significance of NEOMYCIN's reconfiguration

The shift from MYCIN to NEOMYCIN is another—perhaps the clearest— example of an epistemological investigation into the nature of knowledge instigated by a need to communicate. Here we see GUIDON, one of the most sophisticated intelligent tutors ever built, unable to teach successfully because its expertise is compiled into an obscure representational scheme. We see that it is not a matter of the quantity of knowledge, since MYCIN's powerful knowledge base was even augmented with numerous additional sources of information. The problem is really one of epistemological organization.

As in GUIDON, the conclusion at the design level is a call for explicit and separate representation of the types of knowledge involved. However, whereas in GUIDON the separation is between domain knowledge and pedagogical knowledge, here the distinction is more subtle: it applies to all aspects of the domain knowledge itself. Viewed in knowledge-engineering terms, the decompilation process explodes the representation of knowledge into distinct categories. As these categories are disentangled and isolated, semantically based mechanisms are provided to support references and access between them. Thus, while GUIDON expresses tutoring strategies in terms of an abstract representational scheme, NEOMYCIN separates the reasoning strategy and expresses it abstractly, in terms of tasks that manipulate specific types of information.

Whether or not the results of the decompilation are directly translated into material presented to the student, this clear articulation of all the constituents of human expertise is essential both for generating lessons and explanations and for forming and using a student model. Inasmuch as procedurally embedded knowledge cannot be articulated, a merely performance-oriented performance scheme is unlikely to be adequate for communication purposes. Knowledge communication requires a form of *epistemological mapping* whereby the system's representation of knowledge and processes reflects the human approach to the domain. Exactly how complete and detailed a psychological model is practically necessary remains to be established for individual cases. In this regard, Clancey (1984a) stresses that the decompilation does not necessarily reflect the way knowledge is actually used by experts in their daily practice. Rather, it constitutes a viewpoint on their understanding to which they can resort in dealing with novel situations. This level is useful for communication because it deals with knowledge in such a way that it can be integrated in a general model of the domain (see Chapter 15).

This redesign of the tutor's base of expertise is perceived as so essential that Clancey (1984a, 1984b, 1986a) proposes this type of epistemological investigation as a methodological principle for the construction of expert tutorial systems. The approach has both didactic and diagnostic implications since the presentation of knowledge is formulated according to the expert system's reasoning, and the student model is hypothesized as an overlay on its expertise. Moreover, inasmuch as conceptual transparency is an essential quality of maintainable and self-explanatory AI systems, the design considerations covered in this section have practical implications that reach far beyond instructional applications. On the one hand, design and modifications are simplified because separating knowledge from its use obviates the redundant encoding of strategic information. On the other hand, since most future expert systems will be incorporated into larger structures where the decision-making process will also include human beings, the ability to justify reasoning processes and interact with users in terms they can relate to will be crucial. For further treatment of this aspect of the work on NEOMYCIN, the reader is referred to (Clancey, 1983a, 1983b) and (Hasling et al., 1984).

12.3   GUIDON2: tutoring systems for classification tasks

One reason a complete knowledge communication system based on the new consultation program is somewhat slow in coming is that Clancey wants to develop a generic tutoring paradigm for the whole class of problem solvers typified by NEOMYCIN, in keeping with the original idea of GUIDON's domain-independent tutorial module. Remembering the lesson of GUIDON, he wants to make sure that such a system is based on a thorough understanding of the problem-solving process it is meant to convey.

12.3.1   HERACLES: a heuristic classification system

To this end, Clancey (1984c, 1985) has focused on the definition of the class of problem solvers that perform what he calls *heuristic classification*. The purpose of this type of system is always to classify a given case according to a predetermined taxonomy by relating some features of the data to descriptions of the candidate categories. Clancey reports that under careful scrutiny, the problem-solving paradigm of heuristic classification covers an unexpectedly large number of very diverse systems that can nonetheless be seen to follow a unifying principle. In addition to diagnostic and troubleshooting expert systems that must recognize known malfunctions from symptoms, this includes all the problem solvers that must select from a fixed set of solution methods to handle specific situations. Heuristic classification is opposed to *constructive problem solving* in which solutions must be assembled from a collection of primitive operations. Figure 12.10 presents the abstract structure of the heuristic classification method as revealed by the decompilation of NEOMYCIN. In consonance with the theme of the preceding section, note how the diagram makes a natural distinction between vertical moves using *structural* knowledge about the domain, such as definitions

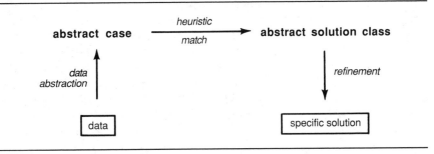

Figure 12.10 The abstract structure of the method of heuristic classification (after Clancey, 1985).

or generalizations, and horizontal moves which reflect *problem-solving* knowledge about the domain, such as heuristic associations.

As a system that performs heuristic classification, NEOMYCIN can be mapped onto this abstract framework, with the advantage that its reasoning strategy has been made explicit. Much as EMYCIN captures the domain-independent aspects of MYCIN, HERACLES is a generic *heuristic classification system* that captures the domain-independent mechanisms of NEOMYCIN. This includes a reasoning strategy, expressed as metarules and tasks, and a language of relations between objects, which organize domain knowledge so that it can be reasoned about in abstract terms.

Particularly revealing is the difference in the types of abstraction that define the two systems: while EMYCIN is defined in terms of a specific type of implementation (i.e., rule-based representation with backward chaining), HERACLES is defined in terms of an abstract class of problem-solving methods (i.e., those based on heuristic classification). Communication purposes have played a central role in the emergence of this crucial difference because implementation-oriented frameworks are not informative enough about the nature of processes for the communication mechanisms that depend on them. However, for generic tools in general, it is important to note that this difference also has deep knowledge-engineering implications, which are too seldom appreciated.

12.3.2 Diagnosing heuristic classification

The pedagogical ramifications of NEOMYCIN's decompilation are being explored with instructional systems based on the problem-solving model of HERACLES. While current implementations still concentrate on the medical domain of NEOMYCIN, the generality of the underlying base of expertise with respect to problem classes promises wide applicability for the concepts being developed. In this context, this section and the next briefly consider a number of systems that, although still under construction, illustrate the kind of pedagogical leverage provided by a decompiled model of expertise. They already attest to the significance of the conceptual evolution that has paralleled the decompilation process.

We start with two programs that attempt to take advantage of the framework of HERACLES to interpret the actions of a student who is performing heuristic classification. Both systems use the explicit representation of strategic knowledge to "parse" the student's observable actions, mostly data requests, in terms of the hierarchy of strategic tasks.

IMAGE: interpretations for tutoring purposes

IMAGE (London and Clancey, 1982) is presented as a plan recognizer along the lines of those described in Chapter 11. Although HERACLES itself is not a planning system in that its decisions are local, its behavior can be interpreted in terms of global plans with hierarchical decompositions of goals into tasks and subtasks. Designed for use on-line, IMAGE proceeds incrementally, updating both a local partial plan and its global interpretation of the student's approach after each observable action. The eventual student model is an overlay on both strategic and domain-specific knowledge.

To reconstruct the student's plan in terms of strategic tasks known to HERACLES, IMAGE uses a bidirectional approach, called *predictions and descriptions*, very reminiscent of the FLOW tutor's interweaving of expectations and confirmations. From the top down, the expertise of HERACLES is applied to predict actions the student is likely to take next according to his currently hypothesized plan. It is advantageous to generate initial hypotheses in this model-driven fashion because of the large number of possible interpretations of a single step in domains such as medical diagnosis. Only if these predictions fail to account for the data does a bottom-up search start in an attempt to find a plausible description of the student's step. The bottom-up search uses heuristics like the one shown in Figure 12.11 to make sense of the student's moves by associating his observed actions with known strategic concepts. The reconstruction process turns out to be useful mainly when the student makes a sudden change of topic that HERACLES could not foresee.

To avoid as often as possible the lengthy search involved in the bottom-up construction of a description, the prediction generator produces multiple expectations, ranked by their preferability according to HERACLES; one of these expectations can then be selected to account for the student's step. Although there is no equivalent to this ranking in the bottom-up search, recent versions include an explicit representation of plan-based errors. Since the set of ranked expectations contains information about alternatives favored by the expert, it can also be used

---

RULE 20 (Refined hypothesis)

IF Some untested hypotheses that are closely relevant to student's data query are related as causal or "taxonomic" descendants of any member of his set of active hypotheses,

THEN Assume he is "refining" an active hypothesis; if it can be pinpointed to one hypothesis, then consider "refining" that node in the student model.

Figure 12.11 A reconstruction heuristic in IMAGE
(London and Clancey, 1982).

to evaluate the student's action and guide the subsequent presentation of advice by the tutoring module. This use of strategic expertise to generate multiple ranked predictions about the student's next action is both efficient and informative. When combined with the formation of a global plan, it allows the tutor to compare and discuss various strategies.

As a diagnostic component, IMAGE emphasizes the interpretation of actions with a view to advising and tutoring the student during problem solving. Thus it concentrates on recognizing strategic approaches and their repercussions for the application and presentation of knowledge. In this direction, IMAGE's most unusual feature is an attempt to deal with the multiple ways in which knowledge can be accessed in HERACLES/NEOMYCIN by providing various explanations of, or viewpoints on, the student's behavior (London, 1986; see also Section 16.3.1). The possibility of suggesting a corresponding variety of tutorial actions is quite fascinating.

ODYSSEUS: knowledge acquisition and student modeling as a learning task

ODYSSEUS (Wilkins et al., 1986; Wilkins, 1986) makes use of the strategic knowledge of HERACLES to construct interpretations of the student's actions, much as does IMAGE. However, the emphasis is different. In ODYSSEUS, the ultimate goal is to modify the domain-specific knowledge base in an effort to produce a student model that accounts for behavior. In fact, the system's original purpose is to apply machine learning techniques to automating the later stages of knowledge acquisition in expert systems. To this end, ODYSSEUS tries to identify missing or incorrect relations in the knowledge base by observing an expert's behavior. Then it attempts corresponding extensions and repairs. This setup, often called a *learning apprentice* in AI (Mitchell et al., 1985), can also be used to model a student's knowledge by reconstruction, much as learning techniques are used in ACM.

With its emphasis on interpretation and tutorial discussions, IMAGE is primarily model-driven. With its emphasis on reconstruction of a student model, ODYSSEUS is primarily data-driven; it builds "lines of reasoning" to account for each action from the bottom up, resorting to search more liberally. These various lines of reasoning are then compared and evaluated by a learning "critic" that analyzes them on the basis of various sources of information, including:

- *Simulations of HERACLES* that provide the dynamic status of parameters useful in evaluating interpretations (for instance, lines of reasoning that rederive known results can be eliminated);

- *Heuristic preference rules* gathered from experts and favoring certain approaches;

- A *student model* that records the student's strategic style;

- *Measures of distance* to HERACLES' preferred strategy;

- *Measures of coherence* of the resulting global interpretation.

Note that many of these criteria and their applications are reminiscent of the diagnostic heuristics used by ACM's diagnostic path finder, which performs a similar bottom-up reconstruction of sequences of operators. Although—unlike ACM—ODYSSEUS has access to intermediate steps, the situation is complicated by the fact that domain relations and facts can be composed to produce compiled relations, for instance by the fusion of chains of inferences, so that path reconstruction requires a dynamic analysis of the knowledge base. Actual learning occurs when no interpretation is deemed satisfactory, and ODYSSEUS attempts to hypothesize entirely new domain relations until an interpretation can be given that satisfies the critic. Finally, the knowledge base is modified accordingly.

The decompiled nature of expertise in HERACLES is central to ODYSSEUS in several ways. First, the reasoning strategy, which is assumed to be shared by the student and is therefore never reconsidered, is used as a pivot to infer domain relations in the knowledge base. This is reminiscent of the MACSYMA ADVISOR's use of planning methods. Second, the language of abstract relations in HERACLES constrains the search for new relations. Finally, ODYSSEUS' learning modules can themselves be viewed as performing heuristic classification with respect to possible interpretations of observed actions, and possible modifications of the knowledge base. Thus they can be implemented as HERACLES systems, with the possibility that they can improve their own knowledge.

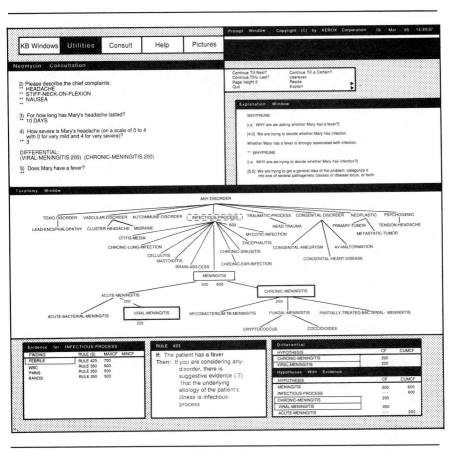

Figure 12.12 A GUIDON-WATCH display during a consultation (after Richer and Clancey, 1985).

©1985, IEEE. Reprinted, with permission, from *IEEE Computer Graphics and Applications*, Vol. 5, No. 11, pp. 51–64.

12.3.3   Teaching heuristic classification

With HERACLES as a computational model of classification competence, the current effort on GUIDON2 (Clancey, 1984d) is to create a family of complementary instructional modules. The systems briefly outlined below each specialize in various aspects of the learning process, offering a spectrum of pedagogical tools to fit the student's needs.

- **GUIDON-WATCH** (Richer and Clancey, 1985) is an advanced interface that takes advantage of the possibility of graphic animation and multiple windows in modern workstations to make the reasoning strategy of HERACLES inspectable by the student. These demonstrations of problem solving enable the student to gain some understanding of the overall structure of strategies for heuristic classification tasks. On the screen display, the reasoning strategy is dynamically superimposed by means of visual indicators on the knowledge structures it accesses. Figure 12.12 shows a snapshot of GUIDON-WATCH during a medical consultation. Boxes and shades are drawn around facts and rules under consideration and the different windows can provide multiple viewpoints on the same object. Note how NEOMYCIN has already triggered fairly specific hypotheses, which it is now trying to confirm.

In the context of GUIDON-WATCH, some attempts are made to automate aspects of screen management, such as decisions about the optimal sizes of windows, their contents, and their removal from the display. Although this direction has not been pushed very far, it represents a step toward the use of AI techniques to encode presentation principles for the interface.

- **GUIDON-MANAGE** is a problem-solving environment in the style of ALGEBRALAND (see Section 14.4), where the student manipulates a set of operators whose detailed problem-solving effects are implemented by the system (Clancey, 1987b). Interestingly, these operators are expressed in terms of a *patient-specific model*, a causal graph linking conclusions to findings. Figure 12.13 presents an example of such a graph in which two hypotheses are still disconnected. With this notation, which shows explicitly how hypotheses account for facts, diagnosis can be viewed as the progressive extension of such a graph until it is fully connected: that is, as a model-building activity (Clancey, 1986a, 1986b; see also Section 14.4).

- **GUIDON-DEBUG** (Clancey et al., 1986; Clancey, 1987b) is an experimental module that allows the student to modify the knowledge base by critiquing problem-solving sessions, for instance by suggesting an additional question. The interface to the expert system is provided by ODYSSEUS. With this module, the student is able to appreciate how domain knowledge is organized to support instantiations of the reasoning strategy and how it affects the course of the diagnostic process. By introducing into the knowledge base bugs that the student must correct (e.g., a missing relation), the system can enforce the learning of very specific pieces of knowledge. However, preliminary experiments have shown the need for a tutorial program to assist students in this activity. As a consequence, the effort has shifted to the design of an advanced explanation component (Clancey, 1987b).

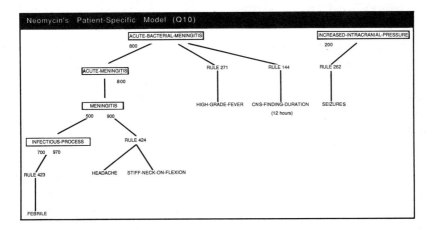

Figure 12.13 Graphical representation of a patient-specific model (Clancey, 1986b).

Reproduced, with permission, from the *Annual Review of Computer Science*, Vol.1, ©1986 by Annual Reviews Inc.

The evolution of the model of expertise is deeply intertwined with an evolution in the perception of curricular goals, which consisted initially of MYCIN's rules. GUIDON2's purpose is to explicate a reasoning strategy for heuristic classification and to place the acquisition of the necessary domain knowledge in this context. With the use of visual displays, the management of a space of hypotheses can even be viewed—and possibly formalized—as the construction of a static causal model for the case under consideration.

The significance of the project's evolution has only begun to be manifest in instructional systems, and there is still much to be done. The potential—merely suggested by the systems mentioned in this section—is exciting. Indeed, from a uniform set of compiled rules, what has emerged is a rich array of concepts and viewpoints constituting varied tools for teaching heuristic classification at multiple levels of abstraction.

Furthermore, the way in which the reasoning strategy serves as a pivot to deal with a model of domain knowledge is central to the form of learning that GUIDON2 tries to address (Clancey, 1987b). This parallel between knowledge engineering and learning, which underlies both ODYSSEUS and GUIDON-DEBUG, has deep pedagogical implications. It suggests a learning model that is rooted in epistemological considerations and explicitly concerned with the construction of a model of expertise.

Summary and conclusion

The GUIDON project is unique in its attempt to turn an existing expert system for a complex task into an intelligent tutor. The main contribution of GUIDON's first version is the identification and separate treatment of the different types of knowledge that must be made available in order for a tutor to function effectively. On the one hand, with respect to domain knowledge, performance expertise is augmented with support information and metalevel abstractions. On the other hand, pedagogical expertise is explicitly represented in the form of a distinct expert system whose rules refer only to the general representational scheme in which the domain expertise is cast—never to the domain contents. Thus, the tutorial expert system is ideally domain-independent, although some experiments with other domains still suggest a lack of pedagogical flexibility.

While the rule-based implementation of the tutorial module is quite successful, the use of MYCIN as a source of domain expertise is more problematic. Because MYCIN's approach is not psychologically plausible and its implicit reasoning strategy is inflexible, GUIDON has difficulty in following students. For similar reasons, students have difficulty in absorbing MYCIN's expertise. The attempt to anchor general knowledge communication mechanisms in EMYCIN's representation reveals the limitations of compiled production systems for instructional purposes. Though rule preconditions are meant to describe the applicability of pieces of knowledge, they do not explicate the strategic context into which the rule fits. For a representation of expertise to support general communication processes, the representational framework must make the epistemological organization of expertise explicit by means of identifiable counterparts at the syntactic level.

As a consequence, the project's focus turns to the core of expert knowledge left untouched in GUIDON, and NEOMYCIN is designed. The emerging principles are a separation of knowledge from the procedures that use it, and a corresponding organization of knowledge into explicit abstract categories. This investigation of the nature of MYCIN's expertise for communication purposes results in a new model of diagnostic thinking whose significance can be viewed from a number of perspectives.

From the perspective of our understanding of expert reasoning, this investigation leads to the identification of the method of heuristic classification and results in a framework within which the problem-solving behavior of various systems can be understood as following the same principle. This theoretical framework is supplemented with a computational model for a large class of problem solvers that perform heuristic classification, with a clear articulation of the constituents of expertise. Describing HERACLES as a generic system with respect to a class of problem-solving strategies suggests an epistemological basis for the definition of knowledge-engineering tools.

From the perspective of the design of knowledge communication systems, a methodology with three essential stages is emerging. First, it recommends a careful, epistemologically oriented study of the domain, which may involve the analysis of both expert and student protocols. This phase is followed by the construction of a validated model of expertise that captures all epistemological distinctions. Finally, an attempt is made to design instructional systems. It is important to strive to express communication processes separately from their domain contents because the abstractions required to connect the two feed back into the perception of the domain, providing additional descriptive capabilities that may warrant further iterations through the whole process. Herein lies a key to the significance of the field. If the reader has not forgotten the introductory remarks of Part I and the conclusions of numerous other projects described earlier, the theme underlying the evolution of GUIDON's model of expertise from MYCIN to HERACLES should already seem familiar, though this is probably its most articulate instance. Now its engineering ramifications are formalized as a methodology.

From the perspective of GUIDON's pedagogical goals, the shift from the specific rules of one expert system to the reasoning strategy underlying a large class of problem solvers produces organizing principles for domain knowledge. In diagnosis, this explicit strategy provides both flexibility in the recognition of problem-solving behavior for following the student and a context for inferring his knowledge. Based on the diversified representational capabilities of HERACLES, GUIDON2 is a family of instructional modules that specialize in complementary aspects of the learning process. The learning model that is emerging is one that draws on the parallel between the epistemological concerns of knowledge engineering and the active model building of students. This suggests that artificial intelligence can play an important educational role by supplying tools that support this view of the student.

Bibliographical notes

A good overview of GUIDON is provided in (Clancey, 1983c), and with more technical details in (Clancey, 1979c). Clancey (1987a) has recently published a revised version of his dissertation as a book. The paper by Clancey, Shortliffe, and Buchanan (1984) discusses GUIDON from the perspective of medical CAI.

The first report on NEOMYCIN is a conference paper (Clancey and Letsinger, 1981). The new explanation facilities made possible by the reconfiguration are presented in (Hasling, Clancey, and Rennels, 1984), a revised version of (Hasling, 1983). The importance of explicit control knowledge for knowledge engineering and explanation capabilities is discussed briefly in (Clancey, 1983a) and at length in (Clancey, 1983b). Further methodological considerations specific to tutoring systems and to psychologically plausible models of reasoning can be found in an overview paper (Clancey, 1984a).

The concept of classification problem solving was initially presented in a short conference paper (Clancey, 1984c), but the interested reader will prefer the longer article (Clancey, 1985); this important paper examines heuristic classification as a general problem-solving paradigm—captured by HERACLES—and proposes an analysis of expert systems in terms of such paradigms.

The most up-to-date document on ODYSSEUS available as of this writing is a technical report by Wilkins (1986). An early version of IMAGE is described in (London and Clancey, 1982), but the interested reader is encouraged to obtain more recent reports. In presenting the development of IMAGE, London's thesis proposal (1986) contains some insightful discussions of both student modeling systems and models of expertise. GUIDON-WATCH is described in (Richer and Clancey, 1985), and GUIDON-DEBUG in a working paper by Clancey et al. (1986). A recent paper by Clancey (1987b) outlines the directions taken by the GUIDON2 project and discusses some educational implications of knowledge engineering when viewed as a learning model.

Two recent overviews by Clancey summarize the understanding gained in the course of the project. In the more entertaining one, Clancey (1986a) adopts a historical perspective, with personal anecdotes highlighting the transitions between various phases. More ambitious and more difficult—but highly recommended—is a theoretical overview of the use of models in knowledge communication (Clancey, 1986b).

Chapter 13

ACTP:
a marriage with
cognitive psychology

John Anderson and his research group at Carnegie-Mellon University entered the ITS stage through an interesting side door. Like the researchers involved in developing the FLOW tutor, they are psychologists seeking challenging testbeds for their theories. This unusual side door may well end up evolving into a main entrance because it hinges on an insightful realization of the mutual dependence of knowledge communication systems and cognitive science. Anderson had been working for many years on ACT (Adaptive Control of Thought), a general theory of cognition with a particular emphasis on skill acquisition (Anderson, 1983). As a recent version, ACT* (ACT-star), had finally satisfied many of its author's initial ambitions, the group turned to the construction of intelligent tutoring systems both as a challenging application domain and as a proving ground for the validity of their theoretical claims. They have started a special interdisciplinary project involving both psychologists and computer scientists at CMU: the Advanced Computer Tutoring Project (ACTP).

13.1 Cognitive theories and pedagogy

Anderson (1984) sees the symbiotic relation between cognitive psychology and ITS as a necessary one. On the one hand, only well-understood performance and learning models can provide the clear objectives and principles necessary to make tutoring systems precise and effective. On the other hand, these systems provide a reliable testbed for the theories from which they draw their underlying principles. Anderson even suggests that some aspects of cognition can only be investigated by observation of the learning capabilities they support. He argues his point with an analogy to computer programming. The input/output is not an absolute criterion of the language in which a program is written, since many languages can produce the same final behavior with the same efficiency. What is more informative about the language is the ease with which specific modifications may be made to the program under consideration. In human cognition, the most common form of internal modification is learning, and therefore the study of learning should be particularly revealing of cognitive structures. As environments for the investigation of learning capabilities, intelligent tutoring systems are at once flexible and predictable, two qualities which make them attractive experimentation tools.

The underlying cognitive model: a brief overview

Because the design of ACTP's tutors is based on the cognitive model provided by ACT* theory, we will set the stage with a brief description of some of its basic tenets. Since ACT* is a large theory, the reader should be aware that we concentrate only on those aspects necessary for our discussion of the tutoring systems, and that even there our treatment is exceedingly succinct. For a complete coverage, the reader is referred to (Anderson, 1983). Recently, the "goal-restricted production system architecture" of the theory has been implemented as a more compact computer model called GRAPES (Anderson et al., 1984a; Sauers and Farrell, 1982), which serves as a learning model for the tutoring systems.

The theory's first assumption is that cognitive functions can be represented as sets of *production rules*. GRAPES steers away from the classical production systems of CMU, in that productions are strictly interpreted within a hierarchical goal structure, somewhat reminiscent of the AND/OR graphs of REPAIR theory. In other words, the use of a production rule is determined both by the state of the system and by the current goals. As we will see, this explicit goal structure is important for tutoring purposes.

The second central assumption concerns the mechanisms of the learning model. The idea is that knowledge is first acquired declaratively through instruction, and that it has to be converted and reorganized into procedures through experience. Only then can it be usefully reflected in behavior. The basic learning mechanism is called *knowledge compilation*. It can take two forms: *proceduralization*, in which a general piece of knowledge is converted into a specific production to apply to a special class of cases, and *rule composition*, in which a few rules used in sequence to achieve a goal are collapsed into a single rule that combines their effects.

A third important assumption for teaching concerns the size of memories. Since the individual rules do not disappear after they participate in composition, there is assumedly no limit on the size of long-term memory. By contrast, working memory is bounded in order to reflect human learning abilities by confining the size of possible new productions.

When compared with VanLehn's STEP learning model, the GRAPES model and the whole ACT project claim much broader generality, since they are presented as a unified cognitive architecture. Indeed, ACT* has successfully modeled aspects of human skill acquisition in various domains, including language. However, GRAPES does not attempt to account for bugs in the same data-oriented fashion as VanLehn's work. In addition, it does not specify the relation between the learner and the teacher with the precision of STEP theory. Like the STEP model, however, it accounts for skill acquisition in the absence of, or in isolation from, a rich understanding of the domain. But whereas VanLehn deliberately discards teleological reasoning during learning and states this as an assumption of his model, Anderson does not clearly define the scope of his theory. We will come back to this last point later.

An investigation of tutoring strategies

To complement the foundation provided by the cognitive theory, McKendree et al. (1984) observe the techniques used by good human tutors in providing guidance during problem solving. Tutors are observed to spend most of their time clarifying misconceptions and redirecting the course of the problem-solving effort by setting new goals. To accomplish this, they use a small repertoire of well-defined strategies, including reminding or statement of facts, analogy, and decomposition or simplification of problems. Their actions, however, are usually indirect, in the form of hints. In particular, the tutors never seem to state explicitly the productions that have to be learned. Perhaps surprisingly, since production rules are claimed to be the representation of the skill, the theoretical framework supports the use of such indirect strategies. Indeed, the mechanisms for accessing and tuning productions suggest that they should not be learned declaratively, but rather should be compiled by the learner during problem solving, if they are to be properly understood, integrated, and later recalled and adapted.

This study of human tutoring techniques attempts to do for problem-solving guidance what Collins has done for Socratic dialogues, although on a much less detailed and ambitious scale. Interestingly, the existence of a specific learning model gives a slightly different context to the study because strategies can often be understood in terms of the model. The techniques that were observed are still in the form of a catalog and have not yet been structured into an explicit and coherent computational model, as tutorial discourse management has been in MENO-TUTOR. As a result, these techniques have not yet been directly incorporated into the tutoring systems as explicit tutorial strategies, even though they have influenced the design.

13.2   Tutoring systems based on theoretical principles

Anderson has built two tutoring systems so far: one for proofs in high-school geometry, the GEOMETRY tutor, with Franklin Boyle (Boyle and Anderson, 1984; Anderson et al., 1985b) and the other for Lisp programming, the LISP tutor, with Robert Farrell and Brian Reiser (Farrell et al., 1984b; Reiser et al., 1985). For lack of a better name, we will refer to these systems as ACTP's tutors. Here, we will concentrate on the LISP tutor[1] because it is better documented in the open literature, but both systems embody the same underlying ideas. Since ACTP's tutors are built to reflect principles dictated by the learning theory, our presentation will be organized along the dimensions defined by these principles (Anderson et al., 1984b).

Problem solving as a tutorial context

The learning mechanism of *knowledge compilation* suggests the basic pedagogical principle that instruction for skill acquisition should be for the most part given in a *problem-solving context* rather than in separate lectures. This way, declarative knowledge can be converted into useful

---

[1] The LISP tutor is also known as GREATERP, a Lisp predicate whose spelling stands for Goal-Restricted Environment for Tutoring and Educational Research on Programming.

productions immediately. Learning is enhanced because the problem-solving context provides a set of conditions for encoding the applicability of the knowledge and its relevance to problem-solving goals. This is the idea of learning by doing. Furthermore, lenient guidance during problem solving allows the student to make the *successive approximations* necessary to progressively form and refine her productions. Finally, students taught individually by a human tutor were found to learn approximately four times as efficiently as in a class situation (Reiser et al., 1985; Bloom, 1984). Hence, ACTP's tutors function as individualized problem-solving guides.

To present knowledge in a problem-solving context, the tutor must be able to communicate with the student in terms of the various tasks required for constructing a proof or designing a computer program (Brooks, 1977). In the CMU jargon (see Section 10.3.1), these tasks are viewed as different *problem spaces* in which production rules must be selected for following and guiding the student. Early papers (Farrell et al., 1984a) report that the LISP tutor can function in four distinct problem spaces to cover issues of design and of coding: means-end analysis for sequences of operations, problem decomposition, case analysis, and Lisp coding. More recent reports combine the first three to distinguish between only two tutorial modes: planning and coding (Reiser et al., 1985).

In any case, this ability to change problem space according to the needs of the student is a very interesting feature, whose importance has not been explicitly recognized in former systems. It is implicit in SPADE, which is able to talk in terms both of plans and of code, and in BRIDGE's planning levels. NEOMYCIN also functions at different conceptual levels, with its distinct categories of knowledge: the reasoning strategy, for instance, can be viewed as a distinct problem space.

Ideal and buggy models: goal-restricted production systems

As in GUIDON, the *production rules* of the GRAPES model of Lisp programming are the units of knowledge the tutor is trying to communicate. After we have insisted so much on the difficulties caused by MYCIN's rule-based representation, the reader may be surprised by this decision. However, in GUIDON, the problem was not with the rule-based language itself, but with the contents of the rules. In GRAPES, rules are not part of an existing expert system. Instead, they are merely a modular representation language to encode cognitive processes. The LISP tutor's 325 rules were designed after numerous problem-solving protocols had been analyzed, and the primitive rules of novice programming do not summarize large amounts of expert knowledge. They are made to correspond as closely as possible to conceptual units that novices can relate to and remember. In addition to the *ideal model* represented by

A. Ideal rule for the merging of two lists in Lisp

IF   The goal is to combine LIST1 and LIST2 into a single list,
and LIST1 and LIST2 are both of the type list,

THEN   Use the function APPEND,
and set subgoals to code LIST1 and LIST2.

B. Buggy rule related to the rule above, suggesting an incorrect function

IF   The goal is to combine LIST1 and LIST2 into a single list,
and LIST1 and LIST2 are both of the type list,

THEN   Use the function LIST,
and set subgoals to code LIST1 and LIST2.

Figure 13.1 A rule and a buggy variant from the LISP tutor's
knowledge base (Reiser et al., 1985).

correct rules, the tutor's knowledge base also contains a *buggy model* whose 475 mal-rules are buggy variants of the ideal model's rules (Anderson et al., 1985a).[2] Figure 13.1 shows one rule from the LISP tutor's knowledge base, along with a buggy variant.

The combination of the ideal and buggy models, as well as the presence of much redundancy in each one, makes for a generic model that should be able to simulate a wide variety of correct and incorrect behaviors for the domain. To avoid excessive search in interpreting the student's steps and to prevent the tutor from giving advice beyond the student's level, advanced rules are turned off in the early stages, as they are in WUSOR. In ACTP's tutors, each lesson actually makes use of a different rule set, especially tailored to the needs of its specific level. While this sequence of rule sets, each limited to the expertise of the ideal student at the corresponding level, is a simple yet powerful way to align the representation of expertise to the curriculum, it risks making rules so specific that they lose their value as pedagogical targets. Consider the sample rule in Figure 13.2, actually used by the LISP tutor in a lesson about recursion: while it can be very useful as an engineering device in guiding the student in the context of one lesson, it is so precisely tailored to a specific type of recursion problems that it seems hardly desirable to have students acquire it.

---

[2]In more recent versions, the total number of rules has grown to over 1,200 (Anderson and Skwarecki, 1986).

Recursive functions

   IF   The goal is to code a recursive function, FUNCTION, with an integer argument, INTEGER

THEN   Use a conditional structure and set as subgoals
(1) to code the terminating condition when INTEGER is 0, and
(2) to code the recursive case of FUNCTION(INTEGER − 1).

Figure 13.2 A highly tailored rule for Lisp programming
©1985 by AAAS. Reprinted, with permission, from *Science*, Vol. 228, No. 4698, pp. 456–462.

As we have mentioned, an important characteristic of production rules in the GRAPES model is that they are applied in the framework of an explicit goal structure; note how each rule in the figures explicitly refers to a goal. For instruction in a problem-solving context, this focus on goals has several benefits. First, at the local level, it allows the tutor always to relate its explanations to the current situation and to present the rules in a context where their relevance to problem-solving goals is clear. Moreover, on a more global level, it makes the decomposition of the problem into a hierarchy of goals and subgoals explicit; hence, the student can remember it along with the actual form of the resulting Lisp function. However, in a comparison with NEOMYCIN's explicit representation of strategy, Clancey (1986b) notes that this type of goal structure tends to explicate goals in problem-specific rather than in strategic terms.

Finally, we should briefly mention a proposition that makes an interesting use of the learning theory (Anderson et al., 1984b). It addresses the granularity of primitive rules, a crucial question since rules are used to recognize the student's steps as well as to guide them. In this proposition, the mechanism of rule compilation is called upon to play an active role in the representation of expertise. On the assumption that it is the actual learning mechanism, rule composition can be applied to adapt the domain primitives as the student is learning. Whereas Langley and Ohlsson were considering searching for the right language by decomposing operators for ACM, the mechanism of rule composition can change the granularity level of expertise by combining existing rules. According to the theory, these composite rules are precisely what the student is meant to learn, and if they become the new primitives, the granularity level has been updated.

In the existing systems, this dynamic adaptive process is unnecessary because a new rule set is hand-crafted for each lesson. However, since the tutor is following the student's problem solving very closely, it is not inconceivable that a tractable search for composite rules could

---

The tutor's response to the use of LIST instead of APPEND

LISP tutor: You should combine the first list and the second
list, but LIST is not the right function. If you
LIST together (a b c) and (x y z), for example, you
will get ((a b c) (x y z)) instead of (a b c x y z).
LIST just wraps parens around its arguments.

**Figure 13.3 Explanation associated with the buggy rule
shown earlier (Reiser et al., 1985).**

be performed during diagnosis or as a background process during the
interaction. In fact, it would be fascinating to find out to what extent this
application of the learning theory is able to replace the somewhat ad hoc
construction of tailored rule sets. We will discuss some other aspects of
this idea at the end of this chapter.

Tutorial interventions: immediate feedback

Because the mechanism of *knowledge compilation* is triggered by the successful application of productions in the achievement of a goal, it does not
support useful learning during a lengthy exploration of erroneous paths.
This suggests another pedagogical principle: the necessity of *immediate
feedback* on errors. In addition to being confirmed by actual experiments
with students (Lewis and Anderson, 1985), the adoption of this principle
is corroborated by the need for a learning process to blame errors on some
specific decision points. If feedback is delayed, precise blame assignment
is made much more difficult, in that it requires an analysis of the solution
path. The current learning theory, as implemented in ACTP's tutors, is
not equipped to provide support for such a reflexive analysis by students.

    To provide feedback, ACTP's tutors monitor every keystroke by
the student and intervene as soon as they perceive a meaningful error. Of course, there are important exceptions to this principle because
exploration is sometimes crucial to understanding. For instance, the
GEOMETRY tutor will let the student explore a correct but fruitless path
of inference until she seems to be really floundering. Tutorial rules
associated with both ideal and buggy rules provide the student with
various levels of explanation. Figure 13.3 presents an example of an
explanation associated with the buggy rule shown earlier. Note that
these tutorial rules are not equivalent to GUIDON's: they merely trigger
explanations and do not embody a tutorial strategy. There is not much
information about how the control module for the simple pedagogical
strategy of ACTP's tutors is actually implemented.

Like the FLOW tutor and IMAGE, ACTP's tutors use the expertise of their problem solver to predict the steps the student will take. While a student is working on a problem, the problem solver generates all the possible next steps, both correct and incorrect, according to its database of rules. They are compared to the student's step, and the rule that matches it is selected as an interpretation of her action. If the tutor cannot give a model-driven interpretation of the student's step, there is no attempt to reconstruct her plan from the bottom up. Instead, the tutor signals that it does not understand the last input, and after a predetermined threshold in the number of trials, it simply suggests the best next step according to its ideal model. Anderson (1984) calls this tutoring technique *model tracing*, to express the fact that the student is made to follow the system's model quite closely. Indeed, this name well reflects its completely model-driven approach to both diagnosis and guidance.

In addition to pedagogical justifications, model tracing has the useful feature for diagnosis that the student never strays far from a correct solution. Thus the search for a student model is always limited to one local rule or mal-rule whose output has to match the student's step. This simple classificatory technique proved inadequate for the analysis of entire programs in MENO-II, but may well be fit for such local diagnosis in the context of the highly directive guidance typical of ACTP's tutors. In this case, the student's goal and plan are usually known because the planning mode allows the student to indicate nonobvious choices explicitly to the tutor via simple menus. Of course, there remains the problem of producing a rule base large enough to cover multiple possible paths and expected errors.

Although Farrell et al. (1984a, 1984b) describe their student modeling paradigm as "interactive," it is not really interactive in the sense that we have given the word in Part I, since the diagnostic process almost never directly involves the student, except for very occasional goal disambiguations. According to our taxonomy, its interpretation of the student's steps by means of comparison with ideal and buggy rules is *inferential*. The word "dynamic" used by Reiser et al. (1985) better expresses the fact that diagnosis is done immediately, as the student works; it results in local corrections for the problem under consideration, and in an incremental overlay on the ideal and buggy models of the student's knowledge.

The attractive simplification of the diagnostic task afforded by model tracing's straightforward scheme might cast a doubt on the need for more complex program analyzers. However, such immediate feedback is likely to be useful only in the early stages of learning how to program and for relatively simple programming tasks. Indeed, it completely ignores the crucial skill of debugging, since the student is never allowed to really go wrong. In actual programming situations, important errors are usually discovered only after an unsuccessful execution. Of course, it is possible to include in the curriculum special lessons to address debugging issues specifically, while adopting the same directive strategy based on a model of debugging (Kessler and Anderson, 1986).

Nevertheless, it remains to be seen whether such model-driven lessons can replace the experience of designing and refining one's own program until it is correct, since problem-solving models that do justice to the versatility of human cognition are still beyond our reach. In spite of the much greater complexity and difficulty of their diagnostic task, systems like PROUST have the advantage that they can provide feedback without imposing an approach to programming. Past the early stages of learning the syntax and semantics of a specific language, finding and refining one's own planning and programming style becomes the predominant concern. Trade-offs between these approaches are further discussed in Section 17.4.

Interface: dealing with working memory limitations

As we have seen, the limited size of working memory is an important factor in the learning theory. Practically, this limited size is believed to severely hamper human learning; recovering from working memory failures has been observed to consume much time and effort (Anderson et al., 1984a; Anderson and Jeffries, 1985). This suggests that a tutor could provide valuable assistance by trying to *minimize the load on working memory*. The claim is that unloading working memory allows the student to concentrate all her efforts on crucial problems and thus to learn faster.

To this end, ACTP's tutors maintain a great deal of contextual information on the screen. Furthermore, they offer the student a set of reminding functions (keys) that allow her to recall elements of the problem-solving context and of the knowledge she has acquired so far. Figure 13.4 presents two snapshots of an interaction between the LISP tutor and a student who is trying to program a factorial function. We have seen that in providing guidance in the different problem spaces, ACTP's tutors explicitly conform to the hierarchical goal structure of the theory of problem solving. In the first snapshot, note how the current goal stack is displayed by the LISP tutor as a support to the student's memory, and how the LISP tutor communicates with the student by means of a planning vocabulary of goals and subgoals reminiscent of the SPADE editor. In this way, the goal context of the student's actions is always available on the screen.

The first snapshot also shows the structural editor used by the LISP tutor. This editor takes care of most of the syntactic details of the language, like parentheses and the structure of Lisp function definitions. The claim is again that such a powerful editor allows students to focus on

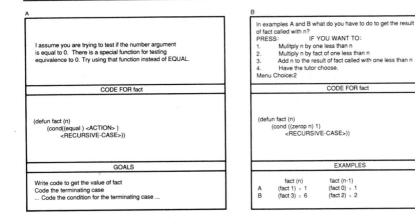

Figure 13.4 Two snapshots of an interaction with the LISP tutor
©1985 by AAAS. Reprinted, with permission, from *Science*, Vol. 228, No. 4698, pp. 456–462.

conceptual difficulties. Apparently, their final ability to deal with syntax is not impaired (Reiser et al., 1985).

The second snapshot shows the tutor in planning mode; it guides—and follows—the student's planning by presenting choices and by proposing examples for her to work out. Menus are used to simplify the communication interface with the student.

13.3 Field evaluation of ACTP's tutors

Few projects presented in this panorama have resulted in systems complete enough to be evaluated in actual instructional settings. Both the GEOMETRY and the LISP tutors, however, have been tested with real students, in experimental settings and in actual classrooms. So far, the results are very encouraging.

Three high-school students of different general aptitudes were involved in a preliminary test of the GEOMETRY tutor. All three reached a good level of proficiency, and even reported liking geometry after studying it with the tutor. This a very impressive result given geometry's usually poor rating as a subject matter. Of course, this success may be largely attributable to the insightful use of a proof graph that provides a concrete representation of the concept of proof. Figure 13.5 shows three snapshots of a proof constructed with the GEOMETRY tutor. In the initial state, the theorem to be proved is at the top and the premises are at the bottom. The proof graph, completed in the final state, highlights the structure of the proof in that it progressively leads the student to connect the conclusion with the premises by means of both backward and forward inference paths. This structured representation contrasts with the usual sequences of statements. As will be discussed further in Section 14.4, the educational paradigm of ITS strongly motivates such pedagogical insights by requiring a computational view of the target behavior.

In a controlled experiment with the LISP tutor, two groups of 10 students were given the same lectures, but only one group used the tutor for the exercises. The tutored students reportedly spent 30% less time on the problems than those working on their own, but scored 43% better on the post-test (Anderson et al., 1985a). The LISP tutor is also used for a one-semester course at CMU: "typical results showed students scored one letter grade higher on final written tests when they worked with the tutor" (Anderson and Skwarecki, 1986, p. 846). In these scores, it appears that the presence of the tutor is more significant for the performance of poor students (Anderson et al., 1985a); from a social standpoint, this is again very encouraging.

As to the tutor's directive attitude, it does not seem to disturb complete novices, but tends to arouse some impatience in advanced students who have had previous programming experience. In this regard, the project is actively trying to remedy the tutor's inflexibility (Anderson and Skwarecki, 1986). In new versions of the LISP tutor, still under development, the problem-solving models are based on a new architecture, the PUPS production system (Anderson and Thompson, 1986), whose control mechanisms are more flexible than those of the GRAPES model. With this architecture, model tracing does not need to impose a top-down, left-to-right approach to programming: the student can move around the program to expand any unfinished portion.

With increased flexibility comes the issue of efficiency. The project is designing a tutoring architecture whereby efficiency need not be sacrificed: the idea is to compile in advance all the tutorial interactions made possible by the model, much as it is done in PIXIE. The PUPS problem solver is presented with a programming exercise and uses its correct and buggy rules to generate a *solution trace*, that is, a data structure representing all the code—correct and incorrect—that the model can possibly recognize for the given exercise. The solution trace keeps a reasonable size by abstracting noncritical ordering relations and combinatoric redundancies. During this generative process, both tutorial interventions and pointers to possible corrections are attached to these pieces of code. The result is essentially a CAI program, which is automatically generated by a complex and flexible AI-based system without time constraints, but runs efficiently on-line by retrieving from the solution trace the prefabricated interventions associated with the student's code.

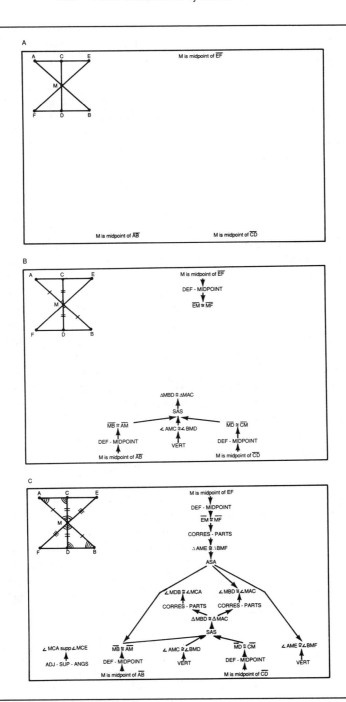

Figure 13.5 Three snapshots of the construction of a proof graph (Anderson et al., 1985b).

13.4   Skill acquisition and expertise

Recall the claim by Anderson et al. that the mechanism of rule composition could be applied to address the problem of granularity level in knowledge representation. Since the mechanism has not been used dynamically, whether or not collapsing rules without modifying the underlying conceptual language is a sufficient solution to the granularity issue remains an open question. I believe that it is at best a partial solution because it only considers one aspect of learning, namely the creation of larger operators. This brings us to a central issue in understanding the work of Anderson and his colleagues: the difference between skill acquisition and the broader notion of acquisition of expertise. As we approach the end of our tour of existing systems, it is appropriate to take a good look at this fundamental question because it is relevant not only to knowledge communication, but to artificial intelligence in general. It also introduces some important themes of Part III.

First, let us notice that the term "knowledge compilation" used by Anderson is the exact opposite of the term knowledge "decompilation" used by Clancey in NEOMYCIN. Yet both denote the passage to an improved stage of expertise.[3] This seems to indicate that there are at least two directions in the learning process. On the one hand, experts become better at doing what they do, but on the other they also acquire a better understanding of their domain. They build procedural chunks out of single rules in order to become efficient, but at the same time they gain a more detailed sense of the intermediate causal links that single rules summarize.

Whereas skill acquisition can be tested by straightforward performance measures, expertise is a much more subtle notion: it implies an in-depth understanding of the domain that includes, but goes beyond, mere performance. In addition to applying rules, experts develop and refine a model of their domain that supports their reasoning, their use of rules, and their ability to communicate their knowledge. As a consequence, expertise must also be evaluated by the capacity to handle novel situations, to reconsider and explain the validity of rules, and to reason about the domain from first principles, using mental simulation techniques such as envisioning rather than rules.

---

[3] Admittedly, decompilation as presented in NEOMYCIN is a knowledge-engineering concept rather than a learning mechanism. However, decompilation is motivated by a need to support learning, and in GUIDON2, it becomes an integral part of the learning process.

A symptomatic example of the perspective adopted by Anderson and his group is provided by their treatment of analogy as a reasoning and learning mechanism (Anderson et al., 1984b; Pirolli et al., 1984).[4] During the analysis of protocols produced by students learning to program in Lisp, it was observed that analogy with examples plays a central role mainly in the early stages of learning. Anderson et al. (1984a) call this form of transfer *structural analogy* because it maps the structure of a past piece of code onto the new problem by a mere replacement of individual elements. As the theory predicts, such simple structural analogy between programs is apparently less relied upon by advanced students, because they have constructed specific productions through knowledge compilation. There is a certain controversy in the literature about the educational value of analogy (Hall, 1986a). On this issue, Anderson et al. (1984b) warn against some dangers in its use after observing students who program by structural analogy with examples, without forming general rules. While the authors have good reasons to favor instead the promotion of domain-specific operators (compiled productions), they agree that operators are difficult to communicate and to encode without recourse to examples.

Let us now attempt to understand this treatment of analogy in light of a view of expertise that is limited to skill acquisition. First, the preference of advanced programmers for compiled operators may simply reflect the fact that they are less often presented with really novel situations. Second, structural analogy that uses an old piece of code as a template for the composition of a new one is a very weak form of analogy. It is in contrast with the rich view of analogy formalized by VanLehn and Brown (1980) in the work on planning nets mentioned earlier. They claim that experts build analogies between procedures by mapping between their *deep structures*—in their case, the underlying planning information. Thus, while simple structural analogy between procedural forms has to be replaced by operators for the acquisition of mere skills, one could argue that the contrary is true of more powerful forms of analogy for the acquisition of expertise. As a general mechanism for discovering regularities, analogy takes advantage of a rich representation of knowledge to transfer information across domains, to connect new and old information, and to integrate both via generalization when applicable. This would suggest that experts are more apt to resort to analogy because they can draw on richer stores of knowledge. Pedagogically speaking, what seems to emerge is that analogy should be encouraged and carefully

---

[4]As this book is going to press, the group's stand on the analogy issue is changing substantially (Anderson and Thompson, 1986). However, the following discussion is intended to uncover interesting questions, which are general enough to remain important despite the evolution of individual opinions.

guided when used, rather than be banned as a learning tool. This would ensure the progressive formation of appropriate general rules while preserving the expressive power of examples.

This prevalence of a structural form of analogy that must be abandoned during learning is quite symptomatic of a notion of skill acquisition isolated from a richer understanding of the domain. We should add that this view is typical of many information-processing models of learning. Two factors seem able to explain this bias. First is the need to simplify assumptions in the early stages of research. Second is the influence of psychology, which has traditionally preferred to consider easily measurable manifestations of learning like reaction times rather than complex changes in information structures. Along these lines, AI research at CMU has often viewed learning as an emergent property of performance: problem-solving models are augmented with simple recording mechanisms, such as rule composition or chunking (Laird et al., 1986).

Now, skill acquisition is certainly a necessary aspect of the acquisition of expertise. In this sense it is an important aspect of learning that must be studied and supported by curricula. It may even be the best place to start, and should therefore have a prominent place in both the cognitive and the educational research lines. Nevertheless, it is important to keep a proper perspective when it comes to general terms like "architecture of cognition" used for ACT*. Skill acquisition is not equivalent to the acquisition of expertise. Even Lisp programming already seems too complex a task to be considered a mere skill beyond a very elementary stage. In the context of a symbiotic relation between cognitive science and knowledge communication systems, setting clear goals is crucial, because the prescriptive pedagogical principles that arise out of a single viewpoint cannot necessarily be generalized to all educational settings.

Summary and conclusion

Within the scope of their outlook, Anderson and his group have produced impressive results. First, their ACT theory, which presents a unified view of cognitive processes across faculties, has had a profound impact on cognitive science, a discussion of which is beyond the scope of this book. Then their idea of basing the design principles of their computer-based tutors on a large cognitive theory is extremely promising for knowledge communication systems and will certainly become a widespread paradigm.

From a psychological perspective, tutoring systems are viewed as experimental tools. With respect to the claim that ACTP's systems are good testbeds for learning theories, their high directiveness is a mixed blessing. On the one hand, their success in the context of model tracing may be an indication that the underlying model indeed corresponds to what people do or ought to do. On the other hand, this high directiveness tends to elicit such a specific behavior that its emergence may say little about general processes.

From a pedagogical perspective, this directiveness means that the model-driven paradigm for computer-based tutoring that emerges from these systems will be best suited for instruction to novices in well-structured domains. This is in keeping with the concentration of the theory on skill acquisition. In this regard, it is interesting to compare ACTP with the GUIDON project. GUIDON starts with an expert system with which to explore knowledge communication issues, and GUIDON2's learning model, derived from knowledge-engineering practice, concentrates on epistemological concerns. The resulting use of AI in instruction aims at providing tools to support this type of articulate learning. By contrast, ACTP starts with a learning model; its emphasis on skill acquisition results in highly directive tutoring systems, whose ability to recognize and guide problem solving is based on cognitive experiments and on computational models of behavior. These two lines of research, with their sharply contrasting learning models, represent different directions in exploring the potential contributions of AI to computer use in education.

From an ITS perspective, the model-driven paradigm of ACTP's tutors places them somewhat toward the CAI end of the spectrum, in spite of their cognitive foundation. Indeed, the pedagogical complexity has to be rather exactly foreseen by the designers; it has to be hand-crafted into a program of largely predefined actions that requires a fairly constrained interaction. Though ACTP's recent efforts are increasing the paradigm's flexibility, the notion of a compiled ITS corroborates the CAI flavor of this approach to knowledge communication.

From a software-engineering perspective, the underlying tutoring architecture mainly derives its power from the modularity of rule-based programming: with descriptions of behavior in terms of rules, pedagogical actions can be triggered by the student's steps through a simple matching process. It is interesting to note that this architecture could even in some cases be used in the absence of a complete model of performance for the domain.[5] As a matter of fact, complete models for general programming tasks do not exist, hence the hand-crafted specificity of the LISP tutor.

These last remarks, made from the standpoint of ITS research, do not in any way tarnish the merits of ACTP's tutors. They are a necessary

---

[5]There are notable exceptions to this, like the GEOMETRY tutor's ability to ask its performance model whether an inference path is fruitful.

part of this book since we are interested in understanding the theoretical significance of contributions. In this regard, the main theme here is the synergism of ITS and cognitive psychology. ACTP has demonstrated that research in cognitive psychology can produce very useful insights into both domain-specific problems and general principles for ITS. From a pragmatic standpoint, ACTP has brought ITS as close to practical applications as it has ever been: both the GEOMETRY and the LISP tutors have been used in classrooms, and the recent attempt to produce compiled versions will allow tutoring systems to run on machines that are more widely available. In fact, the LISP tutor is now marketed commercially. Even at the cost of some simplifications, this is a welcome achievement.

Bibliographical notes

The reference for ACT theory is the book by Anderson (1983). The GRAPES model and its application to the study of Lisp programming are described in (Anderson, Farrell, and Sauers, 1984a). Anderson (1984) discusses the relation between cognitive psychology and ITS, and Anderson et al. (1984b) present some principles for tutoring systems derived from cognitive theories. McKendree et al. (1984) report on observations of human tutors. Lewis and Anderson (1985) discuss a study of learning in which an important variable was the delay of feedback; interestingly, this study favors intentional learning activities rather than the unconscious compilation mechanisms typical of ACT theory.

Early versions of the LISP tutor are presented in (Farrell et al., 1984a, 1984b). A fairly nontechnical article introduces both tutors (Anderson, Boyle, and Reiser, 1985a), and another concentrates on the LISP tutor (Anderson and Reiser, 1985). Detailed coverage is provided in conference papers: (Reiser, Anderson, and Farrell, 1985) for the LISP tutor, and (Anderson, Boyle, and Yost, 1985b) for the GEOMETRY tutor. The project's new directions are outlined in (Anderson and Skwarecki, 1986), and a model of novice program debugging for use in extending the LISP tutor is presented in (Kessler and Anderson, 1986).

A synopsis:
the state of the art

After surveying individual research projects in some depth, we are now ready to return to a discussion organized around conceptual issues. Enlarging on topics raised in Part I, this third part attempts to summarize various contributions described in Part II and to merge them into a coherent view of the body of knowledge accumulated by the field so far. Another important goal is to identify interesting directions and to provide conceptual foundations for further research.[1]

As we move along, the reader should remain aware that many of the points we bring up are still open questions, and that the purpose of this

---

[1] To illustrate these presentations, the coming chapters make extensive use of references to projects covered in Part II, assuming that the reader is now somewhat familiar with them. The text will not be loaded down with redundant references to the literature. The reader is referred to the relevant sections of Part II, where all references are carefully given. In most cases, the use of the index at the end of the book will make cross-references easy to follow. Otherwise, explicit pointers will be provided.

synoptic recapitulation is to outline emerging directions in an evolving paradigm still largely shaped by the intuitions of individual researchers. Nonetheless, it is a significant achievement for a young field to have identified some important questions and trade-offs. Rather than constituting a theory, therefore, this third part develops a taxonomy of interesting issues relevant to both researchers and practitioners. Combining scientific and engineering viewpoints, it introduces concepts and distinctions useful for approaching the topic and for thinking about problems. The conceptual cement unifying the presentation of lessons learned, solutions proposed, and issues of interest is provided by central research themes.

Part III still basically abides by the fourfold division of communication tasks presented in Part I: domain expertise, student models, pedagogical strategies and instructional interface. However, Part III's organization is meant to reflect a deeper view of the primary concerns of the field, as conveyed by the two terms of the phrase "knowledge communication." The first three chapters (14 to 16) concentrate on "knowledge" and deal with what will be called the *model of communicable knowledge*. The last three chapters (17 to 19) concentrate on *models of communication processes*. The idea is that the four tasks mentioned above are organized around a model of knowledge in the domain, which provides a resource for communication processes, including models of the subject matter and of the student. In this view, communication processes form an additional layer around the model of communicable knowledge, as illustrated in the following diagram:

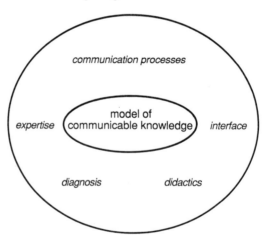

The notion of a model of communicable knowledge is important in bringing forward *communicability* as a general characteristic of models. The fact that it somewhat blurs the distinction between student models and models of expertise is revealing in this regard: for instance, the ability for a model to adopt various viewpoints will be presented as critical to communicability (see Section 16.3). As a methodological necessity, the definition of expertise for current computational models has to be reduced to a narrower set of criteria than would be expected of human experts. In particular, the ability to communicate expertise, usually taken for granted in human experts, is ignored in most current AI models. The next three chapters can thus be viewed as an attempt to understand some of the ramifications of communicability as a primary criterion of success for models of expertise. That this is a very significant contribution of ITS to artificial intelligence is a central claim of this book.

In contrast with object-level performance, communicability must accommodate a wider range of uses for a given model, depending on the view of knowledge communication embodied in the embedding system. This includes the demonstration and explanation of expertise in tutoring and its recognition and assessment in the interpretation of the student's behavior. In the first half of Part III, we discuss some issues of communicability from three perspectives: the *computer* as a representational medium, the *domain* as a subject matter, and the *student* as a source of variability in the models of expertise that need to be considered.

The discussion then moves to the topic of communication processes, which are presented as an alternation between perception and action. *Diagnostic* and *didactic* activities are covered in two different chapters. These models of pedagogical activities lead naturally to a view of the computer as a communication agent and to a view of the field's purpose as the creation of computational models of interactive knowledge communication. This view is summarized in the last chapter in the context of an abstract architecture for knowledge communication systems. Finally, the Epilogue returns to some themes introduced in Chapter 1 concerning the relation between knowledge and communication.

Chapter 14

The computer

One of the foremost characteristics of the models of communicable knowledge discussed in this book is that they are implemented on computer systems. In this chapter, we focus on the significance of the computer as a representational *medium* for the knowledge to be communicated and consider the extent to which knowledge can be captured in different parts of a system. We discuss a number of concepts, such as epistemic fidelity, process models, and reification, so as to characterize some unique ways in which computer-based implementations of models that involve artificial intelligence can support knowledge communication. Finally, we introduce the notion of communication environment as a backdrop for thinking about the implications of having a machine represent the knowledge people eventually have to learn.

14.1   Representational mappings: epistemic fidelity

For the purposes of this discussion, let us define a *representation* of knowledge very broadly, as a *mapping* of knowledge into a physical medium. It is useful to be able to speak about the knowledge that is the source of this mapping, and we will use the adjective *epistemic* to refer to this "disembodied" level. Whether such an epistemic level really exists in some Platonic sense is not the point here. The claim is, rather, that the distinction between the epistemic and the representational levels is *useful* in designing and evaluating models of communicable knowledge.

Two facets of knowledge representation: internal and external

Viewed as a representational medium for the knowledge to be communicated, a computer system consists of two types of hardware: the *internal* hardware, the information-processing engine, and the *external* hardware, the interface devices with which the student actually interacts. This division is of course obvious and relevant for any computer system, but the distinction it makes between the computer's functions is especially important for knowledge communication systems. In fact it is a distinction between two forms of representation for the knowledge to be conveyed; we will simply call these the *internal* and *external* representations, respectively. Admittedly, interface design has not traditionally been considered a form of knowledge representation, and this terminology takes some liberties with the strict computational meaning of representation. However, this perspective is a useful one for tutoring systems. Indeed, not only does the interface language map meaning onto a system of symbols, but this "external representation" can actually compete with the internal representation as a vessel for domain knowledge. This suggests the triangular relations displayed in Figure 14.1.

Epistemic fidelity of representational mappings

From a design standpoint, the perspective of two distinct mappings suggests that different degrees of emphasis can be placed on each representation. However, the degree to which they are actually independent is a central issue. Consider the case of the canned explanations used in numerous systems. They include epistemic elements that are not just a clever external representation of the domain model available to the system; rather, they constitute additional conceptual entities that do not have even remote counterparts in the system's internal representation, but are drawn directly from the epistemic level. Although it is tempting to associate these explanations with the tutorial component because of

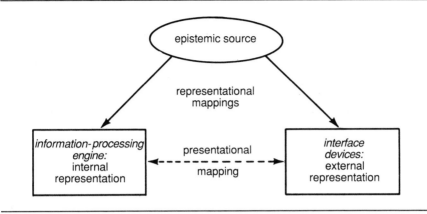

Figure 14.1 The source of representational mappings

their pedagogical nature, they logically belong to the interface, since the knowledge they contain is for presentation only.

In other words, the interface becomes epistemically removed from the system's actual domain expertise to the degree that it takes advantage of the student's ability to read more into its presentations than the system is aware of. Contrast, for instance, the icons of GUIDON-WATCH, which merely highlight internal processes, with those of STEAMER, which illustrate concepts not available to the system's internal model. Conversely, the external representation can ignore important internal reasoning processes that are therefore not communicated to the student. In later versions of SCHOLAR, fairly subtle forms of reasoning allow the system to answer questions in the absence of complete information; but these reasoning processes, though an important aspect of expertise, lack any external representation, and thus remain hidden from the student.

In these circumstances, it makes sense to speak about the *epistemic fidelity* of a representational mapping. The term refers to the degree of completeness to which the physical realization of a representation brings a rendition of the expertise as defined at the epistemic level. In attempts to understand a tutoring system, the *relative* epistemic fidelity of internal and external representations is a useful concept. It compares the domain knowledge available to the internal model with the knowledge stored in presentation units of the interface language. In other words, it compares the portions of the epistemic model that act respectively as sources for the two mappings.

In fact, on the spectrum between frame-based CAI and futuristic knowledge communication systems, this notion of relative epistemic fidelity provides an interesting measure of a system's "intelligence" with respect to domain knowledge. Figure 14.2 illustrates three points on

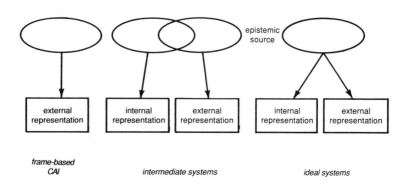

Figure 14.2 Epistemic fidelity of representational mappings.

this spectrum. In purely frame-based CAI, there is hardly any internal representation of domain expertise. The information-processing engine is merely used as a driver for the external representation, which contains all the knowledge to be conveyed. In most of the systems described in this book and in systems of the near future, there is some degree of overlap between the two sources. Finally, in ideally "intelligent" knowledge communication systems, the interface is strictly an external representation of the expertise that the system possesses internally. This has important pedagogical ramifications. When internal and external representations achieve the same granularity level of epistemic fidelity, the system can fully control the pedagogical meaning of each communication step and can also monitor its effects. Thus, relative epistemic fidelity gives a sense of the extent to which the system can take active responsibility for its communication of knowledge.

14.2 Internal representation: the power of process models

The internal representation achieves a high degree of epistemic fidelity by taking advantage of the computer's information-processing engine. In early systems, two aspects of this potential were realized for knowledge communication. In SCHOLAR, Carbonell explored the ability of computer-based representations to handle the nonlinearity of declarative knowledge: that is, their ability to reflect actively its interconnectedness with representational structures. In the METEOROLOGY tutor, Brown et al. explored the potential of an information-processing engine to represent and simulate processes.

When these two capabilities of information-processing engines are combined, they make it possible to include in communication systems *process models* of the expertise to be conveyed. In fact, being based on implemented process models of the subject matter has become an essential characteristic of the systems we have described. Unlike stochastic models, which only reproduce some quantitative aspects of the external behavior under consideration, process models actually simulate the processes that give rise to this behavior. Hence, they become an important aspect of communicability.

Process models and pedagogical activities

The existence of process models of expertise has a double impact on diagnosis. First, the student's problem-solving activities can be followed by the system and readily compared to the internal model's decisions by *differential modeling*. This is a crucial ability for instruction *in situ*. Second, the internal representation supplies a language for constructing a student model that can actually be run and tested on problems.

In the representation of the subject matter, process models have been used to simulate two types of processes. First, they have been used to model the phenomena the student has to understand, such as electronic circuits in SOPHIE or rainfall in WHY. In many cases, the student can be given some first-hand experience with the subject matter, as in STEAMER's simulation of a steam plant. Simulation can render phenomena with a vividness that fosters the development of accurate mental models by the student. Inasmuch as the internal representation is epistemically faithful, these process models even support a type of instruction that can begin to address directly the student's models of the world.

The second—and perhaps even more significant—use of process models has been in the computational rendition of parts of the actual reasoning process the student is expected to learn to perform, as in NEOMYCIN or in ACTP's tutors. These process models not only capture the knowledge necessary for the target behavior, as do the frames of CAI systems; they also simulate the use of this knowledge in the solution of relevant problems. As a consequence, the system can communicate knowledge, not only in the abstract, but in actual use, as for instance in the demonstrations of SOPHIE-II or GUIDON-WATCH, and in the on-line problem-solving guidance of numerous tutors.

Of course, the two uses of process models can coexist, as in SOPHIE-III and QUEST, which include both a model of the circuit and a troubleshooting expert. This combination is articulated in the concept of envisioning whereby understanding a system resides in a problem-solving process that maps causality and structure. The need for this mapping highlights the shortcomings of mere simulations as ways of explaining phenomena: the student is still left with the responsibility for producing a reasonable account of her observations (Brown and Burton, 1986; Section 18.4). As the integration of these two types of knowledge is better understood, process models allow new forms of explanations that support the development of robust mental models by combining simulations of phenomena and demonstrations of related reasoning processes.

The possibility of communicating knowledge in use, or situated knowledge, has been seen as one of the most promising contributions of artificial intelligence to the design of instructional systems (Brown and Burton, 1986). Recent advances in educational research suggest that a crucial aspect of successful instruction is the ability to model expert behavior *in situ* for the student. Informed by this model, the student becomes involved in activities, at first with the support of a pedagogical "scaffolding" provided by the instructor, who progressively "fades" out as he hands over the responsibility to the student. Electronic versions of this form of "apprenticeship" become possible with computer-based process models of expertise (Collins and al., in press).

14.3 External representation: the power of interfaces

To achieve epistemic fidelity, the external representation takes advantage of the flexibility and expressive potential of various interface devices. Its pedagogical role is brought to the foreground by recent advances in the production of high-resolution displays and of data-storage facilities, such as videodiscs, that support the large amount of information required to drive rich visual and auditory presentations. For instance, GUIDON-WATCH makes clever use of visual indicators such as multiple windows, shading, and graphical icons to convey a rather complex reasoning process.

Because of its use of powerful media, the external representation does not always play the ancillary role traditionally associated with user interfaces. In fact, it can be the *driving force* of system design. From this perspective, the GUIDON project has gone the traditional road by constructing an internal model first, then augmenting it with visual displays in GUIDON-WATCH. In contrast, STEAMER has progressed in the other direction. After a useful external representation had been designed, research efforts turned to the internal model that supports the interface: the intention behind QP theory was to incorporate the conceptual contents of the visual displays into the internal representation, so that the system's pedagogical activities and responsibilities could be extended.

Functions of external representations

In mapping the model of expertise onto systems of symbols the student can readily grasp, the external representation both takes advantage of existing communication conventions, such as natural languages, and introduces new ones, such as the use of a mouse. In general, there is a trade-off between the need to take advantage of existing communication tools and the need to be effective in the context of computer-based interfaces. On the one hand, the medium has specific possibilities and limitations; on the other, the interface itself should not impose such a learning load that it obstructs the learning of the target expertise.

As a *mediating device*, the interface not only translates the flow of communication, but prevents breakdowns in the process. Inasmuch as the system makes use of communication tools whose full implications are beyond its grasp, the external representation should make clear the extent of the system's capabilities; otherwise, communication is likely to break down because of wild interpretations and excessive or insufficient expectations. For instance, natural languages already have a role in the student's world, so that their use tends to bring to bear her full linguistic capabilities (Burton and Brown, 1979a).

As a *problem-solving environment*, the interface can support the student in her task, allowing her to concentrate on important aspects of learning. A good case in point is the way the LISP tutor reduces student memory failures by means of a context window where information about currently active goals is maintained; we have seen that it also uses a structured editor that takes care of syntactic details. Such auxiliary functions can be crucial to the success of a tutoring system.

As a *communication medium*, the interface needs to facilitate interpretation of the system's behavior so that the student is able to reconstruct the model of expertise at the epistemic level. Hence, the design of the external representation needs to be rooted in a deep understanding of the domain. In STEAMER, most of the pedagogical "intelligence" of the system resides in this direct mapping. Since interfaces expand the domain model's communicability and provide leverage for learning, their design is a pedagogical task. Actually, the interface language can rival the generation of active communication steps in pedagogical importance.

14.4 Process model and interface: reification

The coexistence of both a process model and an interface that possess the same degree of epistemic fidelity opens the possibility of making processes inspectable. The idea is to transform implicit or unobservable phenomena into objects that can be visualized and studied. This process of *reification* (Brown, 1983b, 1985; Collins and Brown, 1987) is useful to the student in problem solving because the inspection of an "audit trail" of her decisions acts as a form of cognitive mirror. It is also useful for simulations of phenomena and demonstrations of expertise.

Graphic simulations can reify aspects of external processes that are not immediately inspectable, thus helping the student to construct valid interpretations and robust mental models. For instance, a simulation can visualize the nature, properties, and functions of objects in the world; it can also bring to life hidden "objects" like rates or forces as well as relations like equality or proportionality. There is evidence that such *conceptual entities* and their perception as objects are vital to the development of problem-solving expertise (Greeno, 1983; Larkin, 1983). In fact, the explicit reification of conceptual entities forms the core of what STEAMER's designers have called the conceptual fidelity[1] of their simulation.

Similarly, reasoning processes can be reified as structured visual displays on the screen, so that these processes can also become objects of study. To illustrate this concept, Brown (1983b) presents AL-GEBRALAND, an experimental problem-solving environment for high-school algebra that implements the reification of mental processes. This "computer-based exercise book" is intended to help "kids learn more from the actual doing of the homework" (p. 54). On the screen display from ALGEBRALAND shown in Figure 14.3, note how the system keeps and structures an audit trail of the search space explored by the student as she applies the manipulation operators in the menu. This trail highlights crucial decision points and dead ends, and can reveal the multiplicity of correct solution paths.

The proof graphs used in the GEOMETRY tutor are another example of useful reification (see Figure 13.5). Here, a proof is clearly shown as a path between axioms and theorem, and certain actions are clearly shown to be fruitless because their results lie on incomplete paths. This use of a graphic stratagem to elucidate the structure of geometry proofs may turn out to be as helpful to students as the tutor's interventions. Note again how the emphasis is on the total process of completing the proof rather than on the final product, and how clever use of graphics is combined with a deep understanding of the structure of the domain at the epistemic level.

By placing the emphasis not only on the *product* of reasoning, but on the entire thought *process*, reification favors deeper forms of learning that

---

[1]Note that conceptual fidelity is different from what we have called epistemic fidelity. Conceptual fidelity refers to the adoption of a conceptual perspective (what Greeno [1983] calls an "ontology"), while epistemic fidelity more generally refers to the completeness of a rendition of expertise.

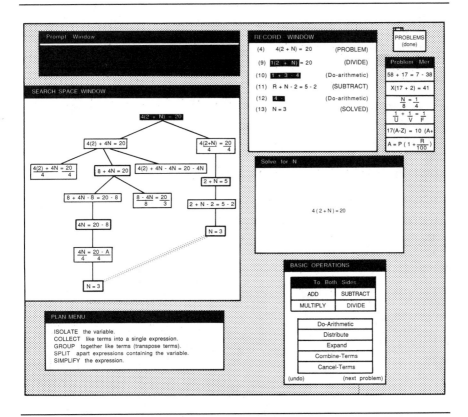

Figure 14.3 The reification of problem-solving processes in ALGEBRALAND (after Brown, 1983b).

are rooted in reflexive recapitulations of mental processes (Brown, 1983b). Some features of ALGEBRALAND are critical in this regard. First, the system facilitates problem solving by implementing operators for the student. This also minimizes the cost associated with errors; moreover, the search tree makes recovery easy. The student is thus encouraged to generate multiple problem-solving traces. Second, these traces can be studied, compared, and even augmented after the fact. For instance, the "plan menu" shown on the lower left of the screen in Figure 14.3 can be used by students to annotate their problem-solving traces with strategic justifications.

Foss (1987a) observed that students who reviewed their problem-solving traces with ALGEBRALAND acquired general skills for detecting errors and recovering from them, as well as for avoiding errors. These skills were found useful in subsequent problem solving done without the system. Such ability to make constructive use of errant solutions sheds a new light on the issue of delayed feedback: the long-term benefits of reflexive analysis—in terms of both understanding and retention— may indeed outweigh the inefficiencies often associated with discovery learning (Foss, 1987b).

Reification and notation

Viewed as a pedagogical target, reification often constitutes an attempt to create a written notation for a process. Not only does such notation support student visualization of processes, but it also makes it easier for the student to communicate her intentions to the system. In ALGEBRALAND, the student can request the system to return to a former decision point for reconsideration by indicating a location directly on the search tree. In the GEOMETRY tutor, a large part of the interaction consists of mouse clicks that indicate points on the proof graph at which the student wishes to perform some operation. One important consequence is that learning the interface is no longer separated from learning the subject matter. Instead, there is synergism between them.

Clancey (1986b) remarks that the existence or nonexistence of a written notation for problem-solving is a defining characteristic of a domain. When a notation exists, problem solving can be formalized as manipulations of this notation, in a form of *written calculus* for the domain. Clancey contrasts subtraction, whose well-defined written calculus makes operations essentially syntactic, to medical diagnosis, for which no widely accepted notational conventions exist. However, in GUIDON-WATCH and GUIDON-MANAGE, both of which attempt to reify heuristic classification tasks in medical diagnosis, some notation for the domain is developed, in the form of a causal graph representing a "patient-specific model." This notation allows some aspects of the diagnostic process to be formalized as operations on the graph, and the quality of solutions to be evaluated with respect to the form of the graph. In Figure 12.13, where such a graph is displayed, note how part of the derivation process is recorded in the final product with rule numbers.

The existence of a written calculus has repercussions both for the design of process models of expertise and for instruction in general. With its emphasis on the representation of processes as well as of products, reification calls for a new type of notation. As a step towards creating written notations for domains and processes that traditionally lack them, this research, driven by the design of knowledge communication systems, can contribute significantly to the way problem solving is understood in various domains.

14.5   Representational commitments

If computer-based representations of subject matter and of reasoning processes are to be used as the basis for communication, it is appropriate to close this chapter with some questions about what these representations mean to knowledge communication. The themes introduced here will be developed further in the Epilogue. Such questions are particularly relevant if expertise can be reified via a computer-based representation. Is it justified to expect anything that deserves the name of communication? What is the cognitive significance of representational commitments? More specifically, in the design of a given knowledge communication system, how literally is the expertise as represented in a computer meant to be conveyed?

Almost by definition, of course, knowledge communication as we have described it is never literal, since it implies the use of a restricted set of communication operations. Because the thoughts of human interlocutors cannot be inspected, recipients must interpret communication by a process of reconstruction, and there is always some uncertainty about the similarity of the knowledge possessed by each participant. No teacher instructs a student at the neural level, indicating which sets of neurons should fire and in which sequences. Instead, there is a *communication environment* that defines common reference points; in this environment, the goal is not so much literal exposition as it is effective reconstruction. Communication thus creates what are essentially *equivalence classes* of models of knowledge within which communication is possible and useful. Disparities within one such class are overcome by an interactive process of breakdowns and repairs.

Philosophically, this situation can be viewed as extremely fortunate, in spite of all legitimate attempts to create unequivocal languages. Indeed, the freedom of ultimately having to interpret communication in a personal and unique way is, I think, well worth the trouble of having to constantly repair misunderstandings. Equally important, however, is the fact that both the constraints and the structure of the communication environment can themselves enrich the content of communication. For instance, the operators used in the audit trails of the reification of some mental processes are not meant to render literally the events that actually took place in the student's head. In most cases, such a claim would be extremely naive. Rather, these operators are communication tools that, once assimilated, support ways of thinking about processes that are useful in constructing models of one's own performance.

These notions of communication environment and related equivalence classes of models are essential to situating the pedagogical role of AI-based systems. Not only are these notions critical for the philosophical validation of the concept of a knowledge communication system, but the study of communication environments involving computers has very practical design implications. These notions also clarify this book's use of the phrase "model of communicable knowledge." Strictly speaking, a model of communicable knowledge is not the same thing as a model of expertise, though we will often use the terms interchangeably. Whereas models of expertise with claims to psychological validity emphasize the importance of representational commitments, which are meant to account for behavior, models of communicable knowledge place the emphasis on effectiveness within a communication environment.

At this point, the reader may reasonably start to wonder whether models of communicable knowledge differ fundamentally from books or from the frames of CAI systems, which also perform within a communication environment where meaning can be attributed in a reconstructive fashion. In the systems considered in this book, the emphasis is placed on the *functionality* of knowledge within a process model that can perform in the domain. In this sense, though functionality can be captured at various levels of epistemic fidelity, these systems can be said to have access to the knowledge they communicate. However, because these functional models are used and interpreted within the perspective and the purposes of a communication environment, there need be no claim that this is exactly the knowledge the student will eventually acquire.

This divergence in focus in no way diminishes the mutual relevance of models of human cognition and models of knowledge communication processes, a central theme of this book. In fact, an interesting prospect is that this mutual relevance may even lead to the definition of expanded or altogether novel communication environments. Nevertheless, downplaying representational commitments in favor of the requirements of a communication environment frees the field from some of the debate on the computational metaphor for human cognition. Communication environments can be redefined to accommodate the computer as a participant. This broadens the range of possibilities and makes a wider variety of research directions in artificial intelligence and other disciplines pragmatically relevant. Finally, the medium's ability to mimic the contents of the message constitutes a subtle communication power; hence, an explicit awareness of the notion of communication environment can be helpful in producing systems that take advantage of computational metaphors without conveying an impoverished view of the expertise.

Bibliographical notes

Collins, Brown, and Newman (in press) argue that a number of recently proposed educational methods have in common an apprenticeship approach to learning: the expert *models* the *actual* task at first, then involves the student and progressively fades away to let the student take over.

Greeno (1983) discusses the importance of domain ontologies for models of problem solving; he defines a domain ontology as a specification of which representational terms receive the status of object as opposed to the mere status of property. Brown (1983b) discusses the concept of reification, emphasizing process rather final product. Ideas about reification are also treated in more general terms in (Brown, 1983b), and on a short paper on computers viewed as "ideas amplifiers" (Brown, 1985). Collins and Brown (1987) discuss the reflective forms of learning made possible via reification, whether students review their own performance or compare it with an expert's. Foss (1987a) reports on experiments with ALGEBRALAND concerning implications of reflective recapitulation for developing self-corrective abilities; she also studies the effect this type of problem solving on retention (Foss, 1987b).

Dreyfus and Dreyfus (1986) take a strong stand against reification, which they argue is dangerously likely to generate misperceptions about the nature of expertise by ignoring the central role of intuition. Thus, they suggest that the use of computers for instruction be limited to drill and practice in the early stages of learning. Their book extends on themes presented in an earlier article (Dreyfus and Dreyfus, 1984).

Chapter 15

The domain

While the communicability of models is a concern that permeates the entire book, this chapter concentrates on models of expertise: it introduces or sharpens some concepts and distinctions that are useful in considering the issue of communicability from the perspective of domain knowledge. Because the actual relevance of some of these definitions will be established progressively as they resurface in different contexts, this chapter will avoid repetition by remaining mostly descriptive and by laying foundations without always going over their relevance in full detail. Although providing all forward pointers would be too cumbersome, particularly relevant elaborations of the topic in more specific contexts can be found in Sections 16.2.3, 16.4.2, 17.2, 18.2, 18.4 and 20.4.

15.1   Communicability in epistemic terms

Taking full advantage of the computational medium without excessive
contamination of the contents of communication calls for a sense of the
communicability of models at the *epistemic level*. Under the influence of
AI research, an epistemic study of domain expertise puts the emphasis on
the functionality of the constituents of various aspects of this expertise,
but defers overly specific representational commitments to concentrate
on the role of a model in a communication environment. In this book,
the notion of epistemic level is therefore tightly connected to that of
communication environment.[1]

Scope of expertise: completeness

The goal of having an implemented process model of expertise is an
interesting constraint for the definition of the subject matter. For a
model to be operational, knowledge cannot be merely enunciated and
explained: it must be put to work. Thus, all the knowledge critical to the
target behavior has to be captured in the model of expertise, including
the knowledge required for appropriately using knowledge. The fact
that this model must be able to solve the same problems the student
will eventually learn to solve ensures that, at some level of epistemic
fidelity, it is complete. The importance of this fact is corroborated by
experiences in knowledge engineering that have revealed the difficulty
of extracting accurate information from experts in a form that can be
made operational. These experiences take on pedagogical relevance when
knowledge engineering becomes a form of task analysis for the design of
knowledge communication systems.

At the other extreme, one can of course wonder to what extent
intelligent teaching does require a detailed coverage of all the knowledge the student is supposed to acquire. For instance, a Socratic tutor
theoretically need not know all the answers beforehand, but must be
able to guide a student's own exploration. The role of guide as opposed
to that of provider of information requires a mastery of principles about
using and acquiring knowledge rather than a mastery of specific facts.
This rather fascinating notion suggests a different type of computerized
assistance for human learning. Existing systems that implement Socratic
tutoring do not follow such ideal versions of the method, which would
require an understanding of reasoning processes and a perception of

---

[1] A similar concept is defined by Newell (1982) who argues for the existence of a knowledge
level in information-processing terms; our emphasis on a communication environment,
however, is a profound epistemological difference.

the student's approach far beyond the capabilities of current student modeling systems. True Socratic tutoring requires the ability to "learn along" with the student, and such powerful learning models are not yet available for nontrivial domains.[2] Recent research in machine learning has developed the concept of *learning apprentice* (Mitchell et al., 1985; Wilkins et al., 1986), which is quite relevant. However, these learning apprentices learn by observing experts whose actions they then try to explain internally in order to deduce the relevant information, and to this end, they actually need large amounts of domain-specific knowledge. Thus it is not clear that Socratic guidance requires any less knowledge than do other types of tutoring.

Relevance: articulation and compilation of expertise

While adequate performance provides a good test of a model's completeness, it is not a guarantee that the knowledge is in a form relevant to students. The field has had to face this conclusion on numerous occasions, and the evolution of some of the major projects described in Part II, such as WHY, SOPHIE, and GUIDON, has been driven by a quest for various aspects of communicability.

Kitcher (1983) defines intellectual knowledge as *warranted belief*, where the "warrant" for a belief is a set of specific experiential episodes that have given rise to the belief and that justify it to a particular person. An important point of this definition, which makes it quite relevant to our topic, is that although beliefs are often warranted with respect to other beliefs, the actual warrant is a *process*, not just a collection of beliefs. Accordingly, knowledge communication generates or modifies beliefs, and the communication process has to warrant these beliefs for the recipient of communication.

It is relevant to distinguish here between two types of knowledge that we will call *compiled* and *articulate*. While articulateness is not a trait of expertise necessary for mere performance, it becomes important when the goal is to support a communication process that warrants beliefs. To some extent, the ability to warrant beliefs could even be said to define the concept of articulateness as used here. Obviously the distinction is not hard and fast, and the two terms define a spectrum of models. However, it has turned out to be so important for the field that it will constitute the backdrop for the rest of the chapter. In the coming sections, we sharpen the definition of these two concepts by detailing the types of features they cover. Figure 15.1 presents a summary of the issues that are considered.

---

[2] Though the INTEGRATION tutor is able to learn from the student, it does not learn along with him. This more difficult approach is being explored by Self et al. (bibliographical notes in Chapter 6).

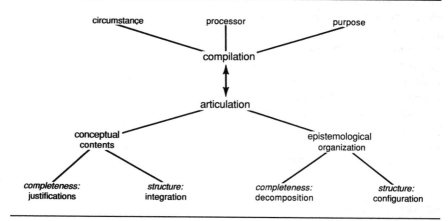

Figure 15.1 Compilation and articulation.

15.2   Compiled knowledge

We will consider knowledge to be in a compiled form when it has become so specialized to a specific use as to have lost transparency and generality. For simplicity, we will speak of the state of being compiled independently of the process by which the state was reached; for instance, a machine-language program is in a compiled form even if it was written directly in machine language. Strictly speaking, this interpretation weakens the concept—since almost any form of knowledge could be viewed as compiled with respect to a possible underlying theory—but this does not make it less useful for our purpose. Knowledge about the world and knowledge of reasoning processes can both be in a compiled form for a variety of reasons:

- *Specific circumstances*: specialized knowledge can be formed to deal with recurring situations. For models of the world, it takes the form of superficial causal/temporal relations between states; for reasoning processes the form of situation-specific condition/action pairs. In ACT* theory, for instance, knowledge compilation is a form of automatization that generates efficient behavior for specific classes of circumstances.

- *Specific processor*: knowledge can also be specialized for the processor that uses it. In MYCIN, for instance, the production rules are designed for a specific rule interpreter that performs simple backward-chaining reasoning. Similarly, the quantitative relations of numerical simulations in SOPHIE-I and STEAMER are devised for interpretation by straightforward numerical operations. Formulas and equations are generally a compiled form of knowledge about the physical world useful for the derivation of results, usually quantitative, by formal computation. Likewise, procedures are compiled so that results can be obtained by predetermined sequences of "syntactic" manipulations.

- *Specific purpose*: knowledge can be compiled for specific types of activities, whether for efficiency, or because more sophisticated forms of expertise are unnecessary or inapplicable. For instance, a physicist teaches her child that the switch turns on the light, ignoring all she knows about electricity, because the child does not have the background to understand the complex processes involved.   As diagnostic knowledge, the bugs of BUGGY are in a compiled form for the purpose of efficient recognition.

The degree of compilation is also relevant. The probabilistic representation of judgmental knowledge used in the INTEGRATION tutor is an example of a highly compiled model of knowledge in the simulation of expert performance. Indeed, the numerical links between problem classes and solution methods carry no information whatever about the mathematical reasons why a given solution method works best for a given problem class. In fact, these quantities are representationally equivalent to the production rules with numerical weights used in MYCIN, which also summarize deeper reasoning unavailable to the model. However, whereas the reasoning chains that lead to one visible decision in MYCIN involve numerous rules, each matrix value in the INTEGRATION tutor corresponds to one final decision. In this sense, these matrices are more compiled than typical production systems.

Many existing systems are based on compiled forms of knowledge. The power of compiled knowledge is that it can be highly efficient and simple to apply to specific situations for which it is intended. Although such efficiency and simplicity are often achieved at the expense of adaptability and generality, it would be wrong to conclude that compiled knowledge is useless for instructional purposes. As a typical example of a system based on compiled knowledge, the INTEGRATION tutor is able to perform many pedagogical tasks reasonably well: it can evaluate steps and model the student, direct problem solving with suggestions, select problems to optimize learning according to its student model, solve examples step by step for the student to follow, and learn when presented with a better solution. All this makes for a fairly adaptive interaction. However, beliefs tend to be presented without much direct support for learning, and the warranting process must come from *external* sources such as a problem-solving context or prestored explanations.

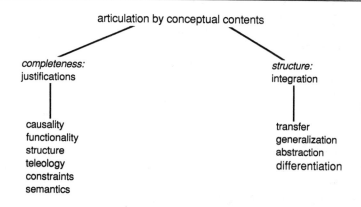

completeness:
justifications

causality
functionality
structure
teleology
constraints
semantics

structure:
integration

transfer
generalization
abstraction
differentiation

Figure 15.2 Articulation by contents.

15.3   Conceptual articulation: contents

In discussing the articulation of knowledge, we will consider two dimensions: the *content* of a model, or the extent of its knowledge viewed as a collection of interconnected beliefs, and the *organization* of this knowledge, that is, the way these beliefs are combined to describe various aspects of expertise. On the one hand, articulation by content involves conceptual issues typified by the retraction of assumptions central to the later phases of the SOPHIE project. On the other hand, organization has to do with the creation of explicit descriptors which convey the epistemological structure of expertise, as illustrated by the decompilation of NEOMYCIN.

In this section, we first consider how additional beliefs and additional relations in the content of the model can help provide increased levels of articulation. As shown in Figure 15.2, the topic is treated in two subsections: the first one deals with the completeness of the model with respect to conceptual support, the second with the degree to which knowledge is integrated into connected conceptual structures.

15.3.1   Articulation by justifications: toward first principles

One way to articulate knowledge is to augment the model with information that explicitly provides the missing justifications for surface beliefs. This type of articulation requires additional knowledge in the form of deeper beliefs or models of *first principles*, to which the compiled beliefs can be reduced in a process that warrants them. Models of external phenomena and models of reasoning can both be augmented in this way. However, it is interesting to note that the two types of models can provide justifications for one another. Reasoning and problem-solving decisions are often justified in terms of processes in the world. Conversely, as we will see, artificial systems must often be understood in terms of the reasoning processes involved in their design. Below are some types of justifications studied in projects described in Part II. For one reason or another, each form of articulation has been deemed relevant for various communication purposes.

- *Causality*: detailed accounts of causality are central to justification in terms of first principles and seem to pervade human reasoning about processes. The notion of causality underlies all the research on mental models and qualitative reasoning. Indeed, qualitative reasoning can be viewed as addressing a subset of the distinctions and relations covered by quantitative reasoning, selected for their causal relevance. In addition to constituting a particular type of understanding, causal descriptions also serve as intermediate perspectives for accessing knowledge about device behavior and functionality that involves the context of use (de Kleer, in press) (WHY, SOPHIE, ENVISION, QP theory, QUEST).

- *Structure* enables causality, and a causal model which is not anchored in structure is fragile because it has to be based on assumptions. In troubleshooting, for instance, a student must understand how structural faults modify causal relations and consequently behavior. The envisioning process reflects an effort to free the representation from preconceptions about the global behavior of the system under consideration, and, eventually, to understand this behavior fully in terms of structural relations. The ability to translate between structural and causal descriptions is thus viewed as a key to understanding physical systems (SOPHIE, ENVISION, QUEST).

- *Functionality* augments a model with information about the roles played by various agents and factors in transitions between states, which are viewed as the results of complex interactions. In WHY, the functional perspective was meant to explain the temporal and causal sequences captured in scripts, and was introduced because human tutors had been observed to correct mispredictions by providing remediation at the functional level. At a finer level, functionality arises out of causality, and in many cases participates in teleology.

- *Teleology* places functionality in the context of actual purposes. As a source of justifications, it fundamentally differs from causality in its attention to goals. Both justify a phenomenon: causality justifies it as the result of a process, teleology as a means to an end. Linguistically, both answer the question "why"—the former in the sense of "how come" and the latter in the sense of "what for." For instance, planning nets capture the teleological information that justifies the structure of a procedure in terms of the functions fulfilled by its components in accomplishing its purpose.

- *Constraints* are tightly related to teleology in explicating the structure of procedures, in that they highlight both the difficulties to be resolved in attaining a goal and the limitations of the means available for doing so. In that they capture information about teleology and constraints, planning nets are not only applicable to the representation of procedures, but to all the systems that Simon (1969) calls "artificial." The word artificial here means "resulting from a design," where the notion of design is defined very broadly as a set of constraints on the structure of an entity arising from the interactions of its goals with its environment. This extends the relevance of planning nets—and their pedagogical implications (Section 18.3.2)—from the realm of procedures, for which they were originally proposed, to a very large class of objects.

- *Definitional semantics*: articulating the definitional conventions that underlie concepts is admittedly a rather different type of articulation than the types described above, since it involves the communication process itself. However, it is important to mention it here because it would be wrong to believe that justifications only derive from grounding models in realities external to communication processes. Clarifying definitions and their semantic fields is a central part of the articulation of knowledge, because the usefulness and power of models are tied to conceptual vehicles—largely inherited from communication—that participate in knowledge representation. Recognizing that justifications must deal with communication tools is based on a crucial understanding that communication processes become part of the acquired knowledge, a theme further developed in Section 20.4. Some simple examples found in existing systems are the corrections of misbeliefs in the MACSYMA ADVISOR and the study of overlaps between natural and formal languages in BRIDGE.

Of course, justifications of surface beliefs involve additional beliefs that may in turn require justifications such as finer-grained causal relations. In fact, all forms of articulation mentioned above interact at various levels to provide justifications for one another. For instance, structure and functionality enable causality, but can be justified teleologically in terms of constraints emerging from causal relations. This recursive quality of justifications is illustrated by the hierarchies of mental models proposed by Collins and Gentner, where each new model explains the previous one in a reductionistic fashion. The concept of articulation in terms of "first principles," therefore, can be defined only relatively: it indicates a direction for the depth of knowledge rather than an absolute threshold.

Certainly, how much depth is necessary is a practical question which has to do with the goals and constraints of instructional settings. Deeper knowledge does not automatically improve performance and can even hamper it in some cases (Rouse and Morris, 1985). Hence, the theme of this section should not be construed to be "the deeper the better." Whether or not justifications in terms of first principles are directly useful for performance, however, they support a different type of learning. The articulation of the underlying planning net of a procedure, for instance, creates a meaningful context for integrating the procedure into memory, for reconstructing details at recall time, and even for acquiring other procedures by highlighting nontrivial similarities for analogical reasoning purposes. Similarly, all the research dealing with the various forms of articulation of knowledge described above has been essentially motivated by knowledge communication requirements: warranting beliefs, organizing instruction, and perceiving the sources of errors and misconceptions.

15.3.2   Articulation by integration

Learning does not take place in a vacuum, and existing knowledge is inevitably, and for the most part profitably, brought to bear first in efforts to cope with novel situations. In their study of schema acquisition (in the same line of work as the FLOW tutor), Rumelhart and Norman (1981) report that both successes and weaknesses in students' understanding of a word processor are largely determined by analogies they draw with familiar objects like typewriters, file cards, or tape recorders. They suggest that these extraneous models brought to bear in the formation of a new schema have "a far more important role than the formal instruction received" (p. 355) and that instruction should deal with these models directly to ensure that the proper understanding is attained with a maximum of useful transfer and a minimum of interferences. The integration of knowledge requires processes of transfer, abstraction, generalization, and differentiation by which existing knowledge with established warrants plays a crucial role in warranting new beliefs. In this light, the knowledge required for effective communication expands well beyond the subject matter to include general information about the world and the ways people see and understand it.

In practice, encoding large amounts of knowledge in a readily available format is still a challenge for both hardware and design reasons. Thus there are inevitable limitations on the epistemic fidelity of the system with respect to processes of knowledge integration in learning because of the variety of student backgrounds and because of the intractable richness of flexible forms of transfer. In this broad sense, current computer-based tutors are of necessity poor in knowledge when compared with even the most ignorant student, and there is a need to foresee accurately what extraneous knowledge is likely to be relevant. Furthermore, just having additional knowledge in the system is not sufficient. In this regard, computational studies of knowledge integration processes such as analogical reasoning and of their role in learning (Hall, 1986ab) have not yet found systematic applications in tutoring systems.[3]

15.3.3   Conceptual contents: concluding remarks

Supporting the warranting of beliefs may require knowledge beyond the subject matter per se, both inside and outside the domain. The extent of this additional knowledge is determined by the instructional role the tutor is expected to play in the context of the student's developing understanding. As students are likely to bring to bear large banks of extraneous knowledge not accessible to the computer, methods for conveying an accurate perception of this role must be devised. Similarly, the retraction of assumptions inherent in the producing justifications can be a bottomless process (Winograd and Flores, 1986); however, within the practical purposes of a communication environment, it is not inconceivable for a system to contain all the knowledge of first principles relevant to the instruction of a given student population.

Research on complex forms of reasoning as described in this section is fascinating because purely compiled knowledge with its inability to deal with novel situations always seems somehow "borrowed" from an expert. This fascination for models of first principles and for integrated conceptualizations surely has to do with some intuition we have about what it means to be autonomously intelligent. In fact, the ability to reason from first principles is often linked to a notion of "real" knowledge, probably because our own understanding of the world initially grows out of direct perception via the senses. Admittedly, what it really means to be "intelligent" or to "understand" something can be viewed as philosophical questions with which artificial intelligence is somewhat reluctant to concern itself other than from the standpoint of its own assumptions and goals. There are often legitimate pragmatic reasons for this, and to some degree, the notion of a communication environment does dissolve these concerns for our purposes. Nevertheless, when systems, even indirectly, take responsibility for the form of the knowledge

---

[3]But there is some interest in these issues, for instance in the context of a German project working on a tutor for Lisp (Weber et al., 1986; Wender, 1987).

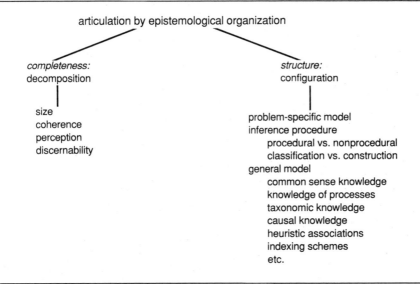

articulation by epistemological organization

completeness:
decomposition

size
coherence
perception
discernability

structure:
configuration

problem-specific model
inference procedure
   procedural vs. nonprocedural
   classification vs. construction
general model
   common sense knowledge
   knowledge of processes
   taxonomic knowledge
   causal knowledge
   heuristic associations
   indexing schemes
   etc.

Figure 15.3 Articulation by organization.

people acquire, the epistemic fidelity that hinges on these concerns takes on a very compelling and practical importance.

15.4   Epistemological articulation: organization

The redesign of MYCIN as part of the GUIDON project addresses the need for a subtler articulation that involves the organizational structure of the model of communicable knowledge. Unlike mere performance criteria, which consider only the final result, communication purposes are very sensitive to this internal organization, since they deal directly with intermediate steps. In this section, as summarized in Figure 15.3, we are interested in two related aspects of epistemological organization: *decomposition* into primitive units and *configuration* of these units into the explicit components of a model.

15.4.1   Articulation by decomposition

As illustrated by the composition operator of ACT* theory or the matrices of the INTEGRATION tutor, compiled knowledge tends to collapse series of decisions into larger units of reasoning. The level at which primitive units of knowledge best support the communication process is crucial to determine. For instance, a large proportion of the efforts invested in the construction of the BUGGY model, and in a different form in ACM, was dedicated to defining individual subskills in subtraction. The idea was to decompose the domain into useful chunks by uncovering "natural" boundaries between primitive components of the overall skill.

The curriculum view: learnable units

The presentation of a subject matter in *assimilable increments* can be considered as a form of felicity condition that is justified in terms of learning requirements. The mere *size* of such increments is defined with respect to the limits of static memory structures. But size alone is not a sufficient criterion; learnability is also determined by the conceptual context in which a unit of knowledge has to be assimilated. Hence, memory structures should not be viewed as static, but as reflecting an understanding of the domain. Complementing size is a notion of *conceptual coherence* with respect to this understanding. In prescribing that a communicable primitive should only contain information of a single kind, coherence is essential for the configuration of models discussed below.

In its pedagogical implications, the notion of assimilable units is reminiscent of VanLehn's idea of "one disjunct per lesson," a felicity condition that dictates the conceptual size of a lesson. Of course, a "lesson" defines an island in a curriculum at a different level than the type of primitives we are discussing. But if the word "lesson," with its social connotations, is replaced by the phrase "single learning episode," with its cognitive connotations, then criteria such as conceptual size and coherence can be viewed as variants of VanLehn's condition: they define a granularity level at which communicable primitives are conceptually small and homogeneous enough to be learned as single units. The concept of "one disjunct" could then correspond to that of a single index in a dynamic memory structure.

The diagnostic view: perceptual units

Most of the examples we have seen of decompositions of expertise into communicable units, such as the issues in WEST, the rules in WUSOR, the schemata in FLOW, or the planning steps in SPADE, essentially reflect the intuition of the systems' authors about what the primitive constituents of a curriculum should be for their domain and for their target student population. However, diagnostic requirements shed additional light on the issue by bringing to bear students' perception of the domain. Indeed, the primitives that correspond to the perceptual units used by students in a domain may not always be intuitively obvious or easy to determine a priori. A case in point is the design of the BUGGY model, where students were found to make a number of distinctions between subskills that investigators had not foreseen: for instance, skills such as subtracting $m - 0$ and $m - m$ were perceived by children as very different from the more general $m - n$ (Burton, 1982).

For this reason, Burton adopts a more formal approach, one that is independent of a representation of the correct skill and uses only data about errors and possible exercise problems in determining primitive subskills. He defines these primitives as the smallest units of knowledge that can be individually mislearned. Formally, as we have seen, they are determined by equivalence classes in an equivalence relation on all possible bugs with respect to diagnostic discernability. Intuitively, the idea of this very clever definition is that the complete skill can in some sense be articulated as the avoidance of all possible errors on all possible problems. Thus, if a further distinction was possible and practically relevant, there would exist at least one test problem that could discriminate between erroneous subskills at this finer level by manifesting a bug. These finer constituents of the skill would then become primitive subskills and perceptual units in themselves.

Of course, it may be difficult to apply such a formal definition to complex domains, where skills may involve multiple forms of knowledge and where various levels of abstraction may be simultaneously required. In addition, the definition considers a skill in isolation from its conceptual significance in a broader curricular context. Nevertheless, some important conclusions relevant to our purpose can be drawn from this insightful scheme.

- First, diagnostic purposes put additional constraints on the decomposition of the domain in that the more intuitive criteria of learnability may not capture some distinctions in the way students perceive the domain, and thus may not provide evidence for determining these perceptual primitives. This has the consequence that some aspects of expertise related to these perceptual primitives—aspects that are critical from the perspective of students—may never be made explicit parts of the model of communicable knowledge, perhaps because they are simply too obvious to designers.

- Second, because errors reveal what one has to know in order to avoid them, they are a crucial source of data, with the advantage of being often more reliably observable than competing sources of information. Note that in contrast to the learnable units described above, perceptual units do not necessarily become explicit parts of the actual curriculum, but they do provide constraints on the design of optimal teaching sequences.

- Finally, the usefulness of a fine granularity in the model of communicable knowledge is fundamentally limited by whatever granularity of distinctions is made possible by the diagnostic data available in the communication environment.

15.4.2 Articulation by configuration

Decomposition is a prerequisite to configuration. Many projects have addressed the issue of the configuration of models of communicable knowledge, by representing control structures (e.g., procedural networks in BUGGY, explicit goal structures in REPAIR and in ACT) and by separating types of knowledge (e.g., arithmetic, game-specific, and strategic issues in WEST; general planning knowledge, problem-specific knowledge, and pragmatic design decisions in SPADE; layers of programming expertise with separate tiers in PROUST and multiple problem spaces in the LISP tutor). Yet NEOMYCIN remains the most illuminating example of epistemic configuration for purposes of articulation. In fact, its themes are so important that it is worth restating them in general terms as emerging principles.

Recall that in MYCIN, the knowledge of physicians had been compiled into rules designed to perform diagnosis within a simple backward-chaining control structure. As a consequence, when students were found to have difficulties learning with GUIDON, it was conjectured that they were not so much dismayed by a lack of explanations in terms of first principles (some explanations were even included in the form of canned text associated with individual rules) as by the blending of different kinds of knowledge that was required to produce the expected behavior within a machine-efficient framework. This made it difficult for students to integrate these rules into their own conceptual framework.

In this context, the main thrust of NEOMYCIN's decompilation is a reconfiguration of the model. Once compiled chunks of existing knowledge have been exploded into conceptually coherent units, the objective of configuration is to organize them into distinct *epistemic categories* representing functional and conceptual constituents of expertise. In contrast with justifications in terms of first principles, which incorporate additional knowledge into a model, configuration adds additional descriptors that articulate its epistemological organization. When these epistemic categories are set up as distinct knowledge structures, corresponding access channels for different types of knowledge can be designed so that the use of knowledge by the process model explicitly reflects the roles played by various aspects of expertise in the overall problem-solving effort.

In a recent article, Clancey (1986b) summarizes this decompilation of knowledge as a separation between "what is true" and "what to do." He proposes an abstract view of problem solving that distinguishes between the *general model*, the *inference procedure* and the *problem-specific model* (see Figure 15.1). Problem solving takes place when the inference procedure applies the domain-specific knowledge contained in the general model to manipulating the problem-specific model into the form that constitutes a solution. For instance, a physician uses reasoning strategies to call upon her medical knowledge (see Figure 12.9) in forming and refining a diagnostic model of the patient that should eventually explain all observed symptoms as coherently as possible (see Figure 12.13).

An explicit and epistemically faithful representation of the inference procedure is crucial to the articulation of process models because it allows processes to be understood in terms of general functions, such as those of HERACLES/NEOMYCIN's metastrategy (see Figure 12.7). Clancey (1986b) calls these models *functional*, in contrast with purely *behavioral* simulations where functions are only implicit in the behavior simulated. These functions can be viewed abstractly as model-manipulation operators for constructing problem-specific models, in contrast with goal structures, which only capture purpose in problem-specific terms. The explicit identification of these functions provides a descriptive vocabulary anchored in a process model; the generality of this vocabulary is useful both for explanations (Hasling et al., 1984) and for diagnosis (e.g., IMAGE's use of NEOMYCIN).

Parallel but distinct design processes for the general model and the inference procedure work in synergy. On the one hand, the abstract conceptual structure of the general model constrains the form of the inference procedure, which must make use of natural distinctions and thus reflect this structure. On the other hand, the functions of the inference procedure—as derived, say, from interviews with experts— suggest further distinctions between categories in the general model through patterns in the use of knowledge (see Figure 15.1 for some examples). The idea is to uncover abstract relations between entities that are procedurally treated in similar ways, and to restate the model in terms of these relations (Clancey, 1986a).

In fact, this definition of epistemic categories by the cognitive role of knowledge becomes increasingly relevant to design as the inference procedure becomes nontrivial. Ultimately, viewed as a form of *meta-knowledge*, the inference procedure can itself be viewed as a problem-solving process with its own general model and inference procedure. If practically warranted, such a recursive stratification of reasoning control provides further levels of articulation.

15.4.3   Epistemological organization: concluding remarks

By way of summary, Figure 15.4 classifies some of the high-level distinctions mentioned above along two dimensions. The lines represent different degrees of specificity with respect to the domain, and the

	structural knowledge	**problem-solving knowledge**
problem-specific	problem model	problem decomposition
domain-specific	domain model	heuristic rules and associations
domain-independent	world model	reasoning strategy

Figure 15.4 High-level categories of a problem-solving model.

columns oppose the notion of a model as a conceptualization to that of problem-solving knowledge geared toward specific results. Though we have spoken mainly of models of reasoning because of NEOMYCIN's example, a large portion of the discussion also applies to models of external phenomena, and the same improvements in generality and flexibility can be achieved. In QUEST, White and Frederiksen make similar distinctions for models of electrical circuits: structural descriptions (problem-specific), simulation and explanation principles (domain-specific), and control structures (domain-independent).

The pedagogical advantage of an articulate decomposition and configuration of the model of communicable knowledge is that distinct components of expertise can be taught separately. When taught explicitly and in parallel, they can provide learning platforms for each other. Because information is separated from the way it is used, it can be applied in multiple contexts and its role in each can be made explicit.

For the design of models of communicable knowledge, the abstract descriptors of epistemological articulation have two important functions. First, they serve as anchors into the domain for general communication mechanisms. Second, they provide additional modeling tools for new generations of models of expertise. From a methodological standpoint, these two functions highlight the importance of research on knowledge communication systems as a catalyst in the articulation process. NEOMYCIN would probably never have existed were it not for Clancey's attempt to build a domain-independent tutorial module on top of MYCIN. Indeed, the goal of designing computational tutorial components with *general* pedagogical strategies acts as a driving force because generality requires such abstract anchors.

15.5 The paradox of articulation

The various types of articulation discussed in this chapter reflect two forces. One—illustrated by the notion of configuration—is linguistic or epistemological. From this perspective, articulation creates epistemic objects to describe phenomena: it strives for increased descriptive power and enriches the vocabulary with new distinctions that capture useful patterns. The other force—illustrated by the notion of justification—is mechanistic. From this perspective, articulation reduces phenomena to mechanisms involving lower-level invariants and to logical implications: it retracts assumptions to account for the world in terms of structure, goals, and constraints; it strives for robustness and for simplicity of principles. This duality is also well illustrated by the contrast between the mechanistic models of ENVISION theory and the rich causal descriptions of QP theory (see Section 5.1.4). For a very specific domain, QUEST appears to have successfully combined advantages of both.

These two forces in articulation often work synergetically. For instance, NEOMYCIN's explicit reasoning, which describes abstract patterns of behavior, captures the functionality of operators and thus provides a framework for expressing the teleological significance of individual actions. Conversely, the no-function-in-structure principle cleans up the configuration of the model and leads to the distinct categories articulated in QUEST. However, a subtle point is that these two forces can also conflict: models with increased expressive power can lose explanatory value, and mechanistic reductions can lose cultural relevance. The use of abstract descriptors can replace the full understanding of their semantic foundations and then constitute a source of assumptions as descriptors themselves become linguistic objects that can be manipulated at a more syntactic level. Conversely, first principles ignore complex patterns that can be central to a useful perception of the world.[4] The evolution from SOPHIE-I to SOPHIE-III and to ENVISION theory can be seen as corrections to problems of these types. Producing models that are both robust and expressive, both general and relevant, is an exciting challenge, central not only to knowledge communication systems, but to AI, psychology, and education.

15.6 Articulation versus compilation

Compiled and articulate forms of knowledge require trade-offs because they support different abilities and present different problems. The various types of articulation we have presented implicate a view of expertise as a *structured set of multiple collections of interconnected beliefs* interacting in nontrivial ways to generate behavior. Since the complex fabric of conceptual relations is made explicit, the very process of weaving new beliefs into this complex fabric helps provide warrants for them.

---

[4]For related issues in models of communication processes, see Section 16.4.2 and Section 17.5 (footnote 5).

	compiled	**articulate**
conceptual contents	overlapping (redundant)	independent (non-redundant)
explicit relations	isolated	connected
acquisition	discrete	integrated
sources of warrant	external	intrinsic
application	direct	by interpretation
efficiency	high	low
adaptability	low	high
modifiability/extensibility	low	high
support for transfer	low	high

Figure 15.5 Contrasts between compiled and articulate knowledge.

Because articulate knowledge tends to include justifications in both causal and teleological terms, it can be revised dynamically and adapted to novel situations.

In contrast, units of compiled knowledge tend to be isolated and ready to use efficiently. This apparent isolation due to specialization hides the fact that implicit conceptual knowledge tends to be spread redundantly across the boundaries of these units, whereas units of articulate knowledge tend to be more coherent and to overlap less. Isolation allows learning and performance to take place without a complete understanding of the domain, but renders the warranting of compiled knowledge more difficult and more dependent on external sources of confirmation. Adaptations and extensions are thus difficult without the help of a teacher. Figure 15.5 summarizes some contrasting characteristics of compiled versus articulate knowledge.

While articulate models of expertise gain generality from their ability to isolate the constituents of expertise from their various manifestations, they tend to be very complex, difficult to build, and computationally inefficient. However, speed can be critical for on-line tutors. Sometimes, conflicts between efficiency and articulateness can be circumvented by the construction of sophisticated *interpretation modules,* as in SOPHIE-I. A related solution is the coexistence of *multiple models* with various degrees of articulation, such as WEST's double representation of expertise or the compiler used in recent versions of HERACLES/NEOMYCIN (Clancey, 1986a). This suggests that articulation and compilation are not mutually exclusive. Indeed, human experts often exhibit an amazing ability to combine highly compiled and highly articulate knowledge, and to move from one to the other with great ease.

In this context, the level of articulation required for effectiveness in a communication environment is not necessarily a cognitively faithful reflection of the way that knowledge is applied by people or experts in practice. Thus, the degree to which models are articulated must be carefully determined according to a system's instructional role, the pedagogical goals and teaching methods prevalent in the context in which it is used, and the sophistication and motivation of students. Arithmetic for pupils in elementary schools (BUGGY) or elementary programming for computer-novice humanities students (the LISP tutor) are both different from, say, medical diagnosis for advanced students in medical schools (GUIDON). Making the level of articulation a pragmatic design decision based on effectiveness within a communication environment also highlights the fact that articulation is in reality never complete.

Finally, in the same line, it is worth repeating that, as demonstrated by MYCIN's performances, articulation of any kind is not a requirement for the performance of AI systems as long as active communication is not an essential part of their function. However, the practical relevance of this research to AI is not limited to instructional settings since articulation has ramifications for a number of nonpedagogical issues such as maintenance, modifiability, generality, and the acquisition of knowledge from human experts (a different kind of communication process). Perhaps most important for the eventual usefulness of complex AI systems is the ability to justify behavior and decisions to human users effectively.

From a pedagogical perspective, having to produce a complete process model of expertise that can be useful in a communication environment, having to ensure some degree of articulation, and having to provide expressive reifications of processes together constitute a stringent set of requirements which have an unusual potential for generating insights and for opening new perspectives on what it means to perform in a domain. In fact, Collins et al. (in press) have found the introduction of new, more realistic, more operational perspectives on various domains to be a common trait of a number of recent successes in educational research. In this regard, the nature of research in artificial intelligence is to approach a domain in operational terms, and the vocabulary of concepts that this approach produces can be used to present students with an applicable understanding of performance in that domain. In conclusion, the fact that good teachers and good knowledge engineers may indeed have epistemological perspicacity in common is an exciting revelation for the field.

Chapter 16

The student

In the last chapter, some aspects of the model of communicable knowledge were discussed, but only from the standpoint of the final expertise. Here, we are concerned with variants of expertise as possessed by a student involved in learning. These variants are described as *knowledge states*. We have already started on the topic unofficially in that the level of compilation and the level of articulation can be considered as two dimensions of variability between knowledge states. Although we have contrasted articulation and compilation for exposition purposes, they can coexist as two forms of expertise. The sections of this chapter discuss further dimensions of variability in knowledge states: scope, incorrect knowledge, and a more subtle notion of viewpoints.

16.1   Scope of expertise

Since the student has to acquire knowledge in assimilable increments, the scope of her expertise will grow progressively. Such differences in scope have prompted the representation of a model's scope as an *overlay*: expertise is decomposed into independent components that become orthogonal dimensions of variability in knowledge and a system of markings is superimposed on the model of expertise to indicate the level of mastery of these individual units of knowledge. The subsets thus defined inherit the essential characteristics of the full model. Overlays provide a simple mechanism to determine candidate areas for pedagogical action. Still in common use today, the concept has a long history in the field, starting as early as SCHOLAR in which individual facts are tagged as known or unknown. Later it was applied to modular representations of problem-solving expertise, such as issues in WEST and rules in WUSOR.

The evolution of the WUSOR project, which centered on the concept of overlay, suggests that overlays are advantageously used in connection with a *genetic organization* of knowledge. First, in WUSOR-II, rules are organized in groups ordered according to levels of difficulty. Then, under the influence of BIP's Curriculum Information Network, plans for WUSOR-III produce the concept of a genetic graph in which explicit links between pairs of rules indicate genetic relations: that is, the aspects of the learning process that are relevant to acquiring one rule if the other is known. By including prerequisite as well as other relations, genetic organization generalizes the notion of prerequisite hierarchies studied in educational research (Resnick, 1973). Statically embedded in the graph is a form of *learning model* for the domain, or rather a class of potential learning models. Thus combining a genetic organization with an overlay gives rise to the important concept of a *learning frontier* that determines the boundaries of the student's knowledge and suggests a focus for pedagogical activities.

The overlay technique has primarily been used in connection with production systems whose performance tends to degrade gradually when rules are removed, so that the subsets delineated by overlay are still runnable. Because these rules usually represent isolated units of compiled knowledge, learning may be viewed as a process of discrete accumulation. Furthermore, the flat organization of these compiled rules allows the use of a single frontier. As articulation brings more structure to the components of expertise, more complex stratagems will have to be devised to capture different aspects of learning that are sources of trade-offs in instruction, such as depth versus coverage or strategic versus object-level expertise.

16.2   Incorrect knowledge

Under the strict overlay[1] paradigm, variations in knowledge states result from incompleteness, but never from incorrectness.   Note that this distinction may depend on the level of decomposition.   For instance, Young and O'Shea have shown that a number of subtraction bugs could be accounted for by rule deletion in an appropriately fine-grained production system. However, there is ample evidence that inappropriate behavior often stems from existing but incorrect versions of pieces of knowledge or even from incorrect beliefs that bear no relation to the correct expertise, so that information about which deviations to expect in a domain plays an important role in a tutor's ability to communicate knowledge (Stevens et al., 1979).

The study of epistemic deviations observed in a specific domain has usually been called a *theory of bugs,* and we have adopted this terminology in this book because of its prior usage in the field. The term is not strictly appropriate, however, in that many of these "theories" turn out to be essentially descriptive rather than explanatory, and in that the notion of "bug" tends to be associated with internalized procedural errors as opposed to factual errors or deep misconceptions. In this book, the term "theory of bugs" is used in a general way to refer to any study of epistemic deviations of any type for a given domain and student population.

16.2.1   Different types of theories of bugs

Because it is crucial to perceive the student's knowledge exactly, theories of bugs have received a fair amount of attention in spite of their relatively short history. Indeed, they were even the central research topic of several projects covered in Part II. Three different basic types of theories of bugs emerging from this research are defined below. Figure 16.1 presents a classification of some existing examples of theories of bugs. Since actual systems often combine characteristics from more than one type, the classification is done in two passes: the main classification (rows) is refined with additional distinctions (columns) along the same dimensions. Hence, pure examples of each type are on the diagonal.

---

[1]The term overlay has come to be associated mainly with systems that do not explicitly represent faulty knowledge, an approach we will call the *strict overlay;* the overlay technique, however, can be applied to models containing "buggy" elements (e.g., a genetic graph's deviation links, ACTP's tutors), an approach we will call the *extended overlay.*

	enumerative	reconstructive	generative
enumerative	ACTP: extensionally defined list of observable errors	DEBUGGY, LMS: combination of enumerated bugs that reconstruct observed errors	MENO-II: enumerated errors recognized and attributed to enumerated misconceptions
reconstructive	PROUST: reconstructs design intentions using a library of buggy plans	ACM, PIXIE, ADVISOR: reconstruct bugs from a language of neutral primitives	Young & O'Shea: incorrect procedures reconstructed with manipulations that explain the nature of bugs
generative	Bonar & Soloway: library of abstract bug generators to explain the origins of observed errors	REPAIR: generates bugs by replaying the inventive handling of impasses	REPAIR/STEP, Matz: reduction of the occurrence of bugs to mislearning

Figure 16.1 Types of theories of bugs.
(See text for explanations.)

Enumerative theories of bugs

In most existing systems that address the issue, theories of bugs are *enumerative* in that they take the form of *catalogs* or *libraries* of commonly observable deviations, which are individually recognized as underlying the student's behavior. These bugs could be purely descriptive—for instance, if WEST were to include incorrect issues—but they are usually represented as pieces of a process model such as subprocedures, mal-rules, or incorrect plans. Thus they can be inserted in a student model to generate runnable variants as in BUGGY, or used to "parse" the student's actions as in MENO or PROUST; in either case, bugs can be diagnosed in a model-driven, top-down fashion.

A further distinction between theories is whether or not primitive bugs can be combined to provide an explanation of observed errors. There are relatively few purely enumerative theories of bugs that allow diagnosis by simple generate-and-test mechanisms, as in ACTP's tutors. When individual bugs can be combined, they produce combinatorially large search spaces (e.g., DEBUGGY, LMS), thus requiring the use of heuristics for diagnosis. Furthermore, co-occurring bugs can interact and hide the usual symptoms of their singular occurrence. Nevertheless, enumerative theories of bugs have proved quite useful because they support model-driven forms of diagnosis and because their characterizations of errors can be used as triggers for prestored remedial actions. However, in addition to the obvious problem of the fixed size, the unstructured enumeration of observable bugs may not be practical for all domains, as will be discussed shortly.

Reconstructive theories of bugs

A few systems attempt to escape the limitations of a fixed catalog of bugs by reconstructing internalized bugs on the basis of observed errors, usually in a data-driven, bottom-up fashion. In its pure form, the reconstruction of deviations differs from the combination of enumerated bugs in that the building blocks it uses are neutral with respect to correctness. They constitute a representational language at a *finer granularity level of decomposition*, which defines a space of possible models, both correct and incorrect. In ACM, this space is defined by the coupling of problem state descriptions with primitive operators. The MACSYMA ADVISOR has a language of assertions about dataflow with which to fill slots in a parse tree. PIXIE's reconstructive process is somewhat different: it simply hypothesizes new mal-rules using the student's own steps when these steps cannot be accounted for with existing rules.

These theories of bugs need to be built around some form of performance model that provides a context for reconstructing observed bugs, either by simulation of a solution path, as in ACM, or by replay of problem-solving rationales, as in PROUST's treatment of intentions. Interestingly, with purely reconstructive theories of bugs à la ACM, the model of performance is so dominant that it theoretically subsumes the need for any enumerative theory of bugs. All the constraints are provided by the description of the problem space. This approach requires a very carefully designed language if it is to describe all observable bugs in a domain. As a consequence, from a practical standpoint, purely reconstructive theories of bugs still have to prove their feasibility in terms of coverage and generality. At any rate, reconstructive mechanisms can be extremely useful when combined with an enumerative theory. In PIXIE, they dynamically extend the coverage of the library of mal-rules. In PROUST, they operate on top of a database of buggy plans so as to bring to bear constraints derived from a model of performance.

Generative theories of bugs

Both enumerative and reconstructive theories of bugs are essentially concerned with the detection of errors as they are manifested in the student's behavior. Just as the validity of compiled rules can be reduced to justifications in terms of first principles, surface manifestations of errors can usually be traced back to some underlying misconceptions or to the mislearning of some aspect of knowledge. A *generative* theory of bugs attempts to capture this reducible quality of errors in an effort to understand the student's difficulties in the wider context of her reasoning and learning processes. Generative theories of bugs not only possess a language capable of expressing surface bugs and defining a space of variants of the target knowledge, as do reconstructive theories, but they include psychologically plausible *mechanisms* that explain these bugs in terms of their generation process.

The modeling of generation processes has important pedagogical implications. The shift to PROUST, for instance, has the primary consequence that the diagnostic mechanism used in MENO-II is fundamentally modified, but there is no attempt at using a process model to explain why a faulty plan is in the library or is possessed by the student. In contrast, REPAIR/STEP theory provides a framework for explaining the genesis of bugs in learning and in problem-solving, but it intentionally does so independently of a specific context or of a particular diagnostic method. As a consequence, the detection techniques of DEBUGGY are basically left unchanged. However, even though the incorporation of such dynamic generative theories into a complete tutoring system has never been tried, process models of bugs are a rich source of information. For instance, used in connection with reconstruction mechanisms, they could provide further evidence for diagnostic hypotheses. Most important, they open new possibilities for remediation (see Section 18.3.3). But even if the explanations yielded by generative theories cannot be computed dynamically on-line, theoretical results can be incorporated in compiled forms in instructional systems to support in-depth remediation, to prevent the occurrence of bugs, and to diagnose generative patterns using more static recognition schemes.

16.2.2 Trade-offs between types of theories of bugs

Constructing any of these three types of theories of bugs is a major undertaking for all but the most trivial domains; it requires large investments of time and effort, as shown by the detailed analysis of a very large database of worked problems needed for BUGGY/REPAIR/STEP, the tests and interviews with students needed for LMS, and the analysis of protocols of problem-solving sessions needed for ACTP's tutors. In ACM, tuning the problem space is reported to have been a painstaking process (Langley, private communication), and the investigation of students' programming errors undertaken for MENO/PROUST has by itself led to numerous publications.

In this regard, the modularity of enumerative lists of bugs is a major design advantage. Freed from the constraints of a unified model, such as a problem space or a fixed architecture, these libraries can be built one bug at a time by purely *empirical* observation of student errors. Furthermore, even completely idiosyncratic bugs can be added as they are uncovered, without problematic consequences for the rest of the theory. The price of these advantages is that the coverage of such enumerative theories is fixed and their explanatory value limited.

The design of the other two types presents a very different picture since they require the construction of a unified *modeling framework*. Hence, they cannot be extended in the same simple fashion, by discrete empirical increments. The dynamic predictive power of these non-enumerative theories stems from constraining relations between their parts, and the need to cover certain idiosyncratic errors can make these models very difficult to build. In REPAIR/STEP theory, considering the full range of observed bugs in subtraction even leads to fundamental assertions about human cognition.

If the constraints are relaxed, the coverage of models tends to become excessive. In reconstructive theories, this leads to a proliferation of competing hypotheses that weakens the value of diagnostic results. In generative theories, constraint relaxation decreases the explanatory power of the generative stories produced for observed errors. These trade-offs place reconstructive and generative theories at the cutting edge of modeling techniques in psychology and AI. In practice, the research leading to all the existing non-enumerative theories of bugs has been based on data provided by enumerative libraries. Of course, not all bugs need be observed initially; for instance, RE-PAIR theory predicted unobserved bugs that appeared in additional data.

New theories of bugs, of any type, are much needed and can constitute important contributions to the field. Also needed is a methodology for building such theories and for combining the respective advantages of different types. Enumerative theories will probably be prevalent in practice in the near future because they demand less of the design process in the current state of the art. But even when process models of bugs come of pedagogical age, the kind of empirical knowledge about observable errors that bug libraries can contain will still be needed. Indeed, it is unlikely that even the best models will be able to cover all the numerous and subtle factors involved in human errors. In addition, efficiency will probably warrant the use of more compiled representations for recognizing common errors.

However, non-enumerative theories deserve attention not only because of the open-ended nature of their coverage, but also because of the additional support they give in setting a context for pedagogical processes, as will be discussed in coming chapters. Furthermore, notions like repairs and impasses, or like ACM's psychological heuristics, are of general interest. Indeed, these investigations are likely to result in widely applicable contributions both to the construction of instructional systems and to the study of human reasoning.

16.2.3   Bugs and misconceptions: compilation and articulation

Notions such as bugs, mal-rules, buggy rules, and even—to a large
extent—incorrect planning methods, have been used in connection with
theories of bugs for mostly compiled knowledge. Just as the acquisition
processes for compiled and articulate forms of knowledge are different,
so are the deviations that are likely to be encountered. Here we consider
the respective natures of typical deviations in compiled and articulate
contexts by comparing their generative processes.

Compiled knowledge: mislearning and forgetting

REPAIR/STEP theory explicitly assumes that conceptual models in arithmetic have a negligible influence on the bug-generating mechanism.
Instead, for the formation of erroneous core procedures, the theory
exclusively considers failures of a general inductive learning scheme
to extract all the correct information from a teaching sequence. When
the application of such buggy procedures leads students to impasses,
manifested bugs are generated by repairs, which are always instances
of domain-independent problem-solving heuristics, rather than reasoning
about the principles of the domain. Such an assumption is quite extreme,
but, as we have seen, it is carefully argued for in terms of available data.
   According to this approach, bugs originate mostly in mislearning
and forgetting: that is, in the student's failure to follow an instructional
sequence and to organize and retain information internally, or in the
teacher's failure to present sufficiently complete and unambiguous information. Inasmuch as the acquisition and application of compiled knowledge is detached from a conceptual model of its domain, and inasmuch
as relations between pieces of knowledge are not made explicit, compiled
bugs can be considered in isolation and are reasonably amenable to the
types of theories of bugs currently prevalent in the field.
   It is important to note again that the design decisions underlying
REPAIR/STEP reflect not so much the intrinsic nature of arithmetic as a
specific approach to the domain. In fact, before VanLehn and Brown
laid down the final assumptions of their theory, they had seriously
considered the use of Dienes blocks as a model for the semantics of place-
value subtraction. The goal was to understand learning and learning
difficulties in the context of an analogical transfer between the block-
based representation and the numerical one (VanLehn and Brown, 1980).
However, although these blocks are actually used in some schools to
teach arithmetic, they seemed too semantically based to account for the
available data on bugs, which appeared to stem from a totally syntactic
approach to arithmetic. As a consequence, the articulate representation of

planning nets was abandoned in favor of a compiled form of knowledge that seemed more epistemically faithful to the approach actually taken by students.

Articulate knowledge: misconceptions

As the requirements of epistemic fidelity warrant the use of more articulate forms of knowledge, bugs tend to be replaced by misconceptions whose origins are not restricted to the instructional interaction and to forgetting. For instance, the discovery-based learning that WHY's Socratic method encourages is completely centered on an evolving model of the world; the sources of most errors are to be found in this model rather than in instructional sequences. Similarly, Matz ignores the teacher's specific interventions when she shows how arithmetic knowledge has to be revised as students move to algebra, and how a large number of errors can be understood in light of this transition. Because she views the learner as an active agent intentionally involved in theory formation, the learning operators she proposes are used to build a model of the domain rather than to follow some instruction. In her view, the sources of errors are to be found mostly in interactions between concepts, which are characteristic of articulate forms of knowledge.

In the dimension of *justifications*, misconceptions are propagated by conceptual dependencies, as in the hierarchies of models studied by Collins and Gentner, where errors at one level can be explained by misconceptions and gaps in an underlying model. In the dimension of *integration*, misconceptions develop through various forms of transfer and can even originate outside the domain. Matz concentrates on former stages in the curriculum,[2] but erroneous analogical transfer can take place from any domain. A good case in point is the "sponge analogy" reported by Stevens et al. (1979) to influence reasoning in meteorology. As an air mass rises, it expands. The sponge analogy, frequently used by Stevens' subjects, would then suggest that the air mass can hold more water as a result. In reality, the opposite happens: when an air mass expands, it cools with the consequence that it can hold less water. This misleading analogy involves elements of a naive physics that are clearly outside the boundaries of expertise in meteorology.

As a model becomes epistemically organized and the configuration of knowledge separates concepts from their roles in reasoning strategies, the manifestations of misconceptions become too diversified to be captured enumeratively, and the study of deviations has to produce more general

---

[2] Similarly, Schuster (1985) describes a simple tutor in which a model of the native grammar proves helpful in understanding the errors of a student learning a second language.

descriptions. Although theories of bugs for articulate forms of knowledge still lie beyond the current state of the art, and general principles have yet to be established, some research mentioned in this book specifically addresses relevant aspects, both theoretical and empirical. These include:

- the definition of general model-building operators to whose faulty application misconceptions can be reduced (WHY, Matz, ENVISION);

- the definition of principles, such as "no function in structure," whose violations can both predict and explain errors (ENVISION);

- the study of reductionistic hierarchies of models and of the decomposition of models into components (WHY);

- the definition of abstract—albeit domain-specific—"bug generators," such as those used to capture the influence of natural language on the semantics of programming languages (MENO: Bonar and Soloway);

- the enumerative study of specific, analogy-based component models (WHY) and other specific interferences between concepts (Matz): although the subject is intractably open-ended in general, certain analogical interferences, like that of the sponge described above or that of a typewriter in learning about a word processor, may be so pervasive in some domains that information about them will be essential to successfully detecting and correcting misconceptions;

- the enumerative study of specific "conceptual bugs" and of patterns revealing deeper misconceptions (for instance, relating specific misconceptions to more abstract faults in the functional perspective, as in WHY).

In conclusion, though the compiled knowledge of most existing systems has drawn much attention to the notion of "bugs," the nature of relevant deviations is highly dependent on the level of articulation adopted for a model, and the corresponding theories of bugs are likely to take a different form. This highlights the importance of design decisions about articulation, as discussed at the conclusion of the previous chapter. Compiled bugs are isolatable, but they do not necessarily represent clean misconceptions. By contrast, misconceptions in articulate contexts manifest in multiple ways and are connected within a fabric of relations that also ties them to a global conceptualization of the domain. This issue is developed further in the coming sections.

16.3 Viewpoints

The need to place misconceptions in a broader conceptual context leads us to consider a further type of variation between knowledge states, which we will call the issue of *viewpoints*. With respect to misconceptions, the notion of viewpoint is important not only because it provides a context for diagnosis, but because it can change the understanding of what a misconception is: it can be a subtle—but pedagogically crucial—shift of focus from what is wrong to what is right in a statement, from correcting to teaching and learning.

In spite of its importance, this topic has not yet been addressed by the field in principled ways. In its full generality, the problem of viewpoints is admittedly very complex and difficult. However, restricted versions can still be very useful in instructional contexts and the topic seems ripe for more research. Hence, the main purpose of this section is to articulate various aspects of the issue, such as its extent and its relevance, in order to open up possibilities and to provide a basis for further investigations.

16.3.1 What are viewpoints?

Because the concept of viewpoint is used here very broadly, let us start with some definitions, which will be clarified by a series of examples mostly drawn from projects we have already covered. For our purposes, a viewpoint is defined as an *interpretative context*. It is determined by its *kernel* and its *scope*. The kernel of a viewpoint consists of a variable number of *keys*, which together define the interpretative context referred to as a viewpoint. Keys can be prior decisions, correct or incorrect beliefs, analogies, or assumptions that either explicitly belong to the model or must be inferred as underlying it. The scope of a viewpoint delineates its foreseeable area of relevance. Note that the exact scope of a viewpoint is rarely precisely defined a priori since viewpoints are likely to have obscure ramifications. "Foreseeable" implies that the scope of a viewpoint is some minimal area of probable applicability. In sum, a viewpoint is an interpretative context whose kernel contains critical keys to the proper understanding of entities within its scope.

The list of examples that follows is meant to provide both some concrete illustrations for this abstract definition, and some sense of its scope by outlining the beginning of a typology of viewpoints. Defined as an interpretative context, the notion of viewpoint is relevant at three levels: specific to a situation, specific to a domain, and as background.

Situation-specific viewpoints: individual solutions

Because situations can be approached—and problems solved—in different ways, the most obvious form of viewpoint is situation-specific; this
aspect has been addressed by most systems to some degree. Indeed, the
need to adapt instruction to *multiple approaches and solutions to a problem*
constitutes a fundamental difference between ordinary AI systems and
models of communicable knowledge.

- *Solutions can be constructed in multiple ways.* As the solution to
  some problem requires choices that are often equifinal, the kernel of
  the problem-specific viewpoint is dynamically constructed of critical
  problem-solving or planning *decisions* (e.g., IMAGE, PROUST, LISP
  tutor, etc.).

- *Problems can be attacked in multiple ways.* For instance, WEST can
  adopt a number of global game strategies, each of which provides
  a different context for evaluating moves. TALUS has a library of
  a number of known abstract algorithms for a specific problem and
  selects one as a reference for the interpretation of the student's
  program. Here, the kernel of a viewpoint is a global *strategy* or
  solution method.

- *Problems can be viewed in multiple ways.* The solution of problems
  in physics and mathematics often involves choices among *frames of
  reference* (e.g., coordinate systems or global concepts such as force
  or work), which provide different views of the problem and suggest
  different solution methods (Larkin, 1983). In addition, one problem
  can be viewed as if it were another via analogical reasoning, so that
  the solution of a similar problem can be brought to bear (Hall, 1986c).
  The kernels of viewpoints in these cases are *frames of reference,
  conceptual frameworks,* or *analogies.*

- *Identical decisions can have different sources.* In a recent proposal
  to extend IMAGE, London (1986) addresses a more subtle type of
  situation-specific viewpoint, brought to light by the decompilation
  of NEOMYCIN. Since NEOMYCIN's rules can be accessed from
  a number of orthogonal index schemes, similar questions can be
  triggered by very different mechanisms. For instance, a request
  for information can originate from a causal perspective because it
  is causally relevant to some current hypothesis, or from a process-
  oriented or a strategic perspective because certain types of questions
  are good to ask in a given situation. Here, the kernel of a viewpoint
  is the identification of an *epistemic category* that acts as the source of
  a problem-solving episode.

Domain-specific viewpoints: individual conceptualizations

Domains can also be approached in different ways; hence, there can be different viewpoints at the level of students' knowledge. The examples listed below illustrate some types of kernels that can generate viewpoints at this level.

- Even in the supposedly simple domain of syntactic place-value subtraction, there exist at least two widespread procedures for borrowing (Fawcett and Cummins, 1970). Some children are taught to add one to the lower digit of the adjacent column rather than to subtract one from the upper digit, as shown in the partially completed problems of Figure 16.2. Though this slight variation is equifinal, it does modify the kinds of difficulties associated with borrowing. In particular, it evades the problem of "borrowing across zeroes," at the cost of a less clean justification in terms of regroupings in the decimal representation of numbers. In this case, the keys to viewpoints are diverging *compiled design decisions* corresponding to different underlying *planning nets*.

- Various *sources of transfer* in related domains constitute interpretative contexts that create definite biases in the understanding of the target domain. For instance, Gentner and Gentner (1983) report on the different concepts of electricity generated by analogies to flows of fluids and to teeming crowds.

- Different *sets of primitives* give rise to different viewpoints. In SPADE, for instance, when Miller and Goldstein speculate that an archetypal planning grammar could possibly be mutated to correspond to the student's planning grammar, this would make the system adopt the student's viewpoint, insofar as her planning grammar represents her view of the planning task.

- Recall that STEAMER's conceptual fidelity is considered a crucial pedagogical ingredient of the simulation. The goal is to support the formation of a useful mental model under the assumption that knowledge about a phenomenon is different from a physical image of that phenomenon. We have seen that in reifying conceptual abstractions such as rate of change, the simulation creates new objects that facilitate problem solving and reasoning based on mental simulation. In this case, *ontological commitments* constitute the keys to a viewpoint on the domain.

Note that some of the topics we have discussed earlier can be considered as generating viewpoints. A case in point is the level of articulation or compilation (e.g., SOPHIE: amount of function included in structure;

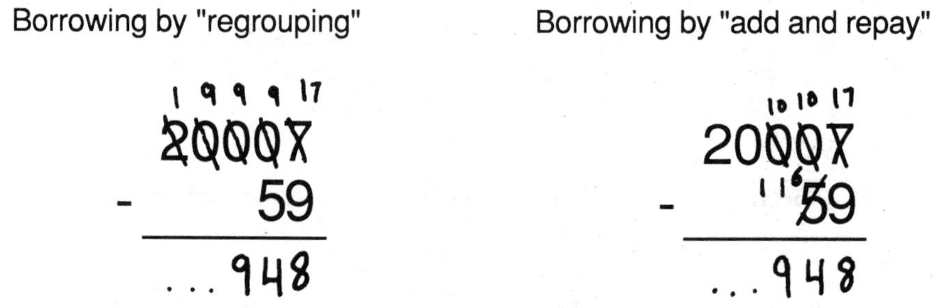

Borrowing by "regrouping"   Borrowing by "add and repay"

Figure 16.2 Two different borrowing procedures.

WHY: causal scripts versus functional explanations; REPAIR/STEP: syntactic versus semantic approaches; ACM and ACT: granularity).

Background viewpoints: individual worldviews

Learning in a domain is always tied to the background assumptions that constitute the student's worldview. The philosophy of science has paid much attention to the notion of worldview because of the role it plays in the formation of scientific theories. Laudan (1977) observes that theories always emerge in the wider context of *research traditions*. He defines a research tradition as "a set of general assumptions about the entities and processes in a domain of study, and about the appropriate methods to be used for investigating the problems and constructing the theories in that domain" (p. 81). Warranted beliefs are in some sense personal theories about the world and a person's criteria for accepting interpreted experience as a warrant for beliefs constitute an informal methodology. Hence, it is useful to view the student involved in learning as a *microcosm of the scientific community* and to apply this definition of a research tradition to the notion of a personal worldview as applied to learning in a domain. This metaphor, whose pedagogical implications are beyond the scope of this book, draws attention to the importance of background assumptions for knowledge communication—especially when articulate knowledge is being taught, a topic that is still mostly untouched.[3]

---

[3] But see Section 18.4.

Composite viewpoints

Composite viewpoints are formed when multiple viewpoints with overlapping scopes are combined by composition of their kernels. Because viewpoints can be *compatible* or *competing*, and because the simple union of kernels can lead to inconsistent viewpoints, these composition operations constitute a fascinating calculus, which is very different from logical implication and deserves to be studied seriously for process models. Not only do such compositions take obvious forms, such as the combined use of multiple, mutually incompatible analogies to illustrate one topic (Rumelhart and Norman, 1981; Burnstein, 1983), but the coexistence and interaction of viewpoints are fundamental epistemological issues that underlie the construction of warranted beliefs. An important consequence of this notion of composite viewpoints is that it makes sense to speak globally about *a person's viewpoint* in the singular.

16.3.2 Viewpoints in knowledge communication systems

The issue of viewpoints is relevant to knowledge communication systems at two levels. First, the process of system design by its very nature implies a commitment to some viewpoints because current computational models are inevitably detached from the semantics of the phenomena they are about and are therefore unable to reconsider their own design assumptions. In this context, the selection of basic viewpoints is a critical decision (e.g., perceptual units in BUGGY, ontology in STEAMER, level of articulation in REPAIR). Second, a system's ability to adopt more than one viewpoint has been recognized as a necessary form of adaptability (e.g., strategies in WEST, problem spaces in the LISP tutor). In the context of WHY, Stevens et al. (1979) conclude that "multiple representational viewpoints complicate tremendously our task of building a system to carry on reasonable tutorial interactions. Nevertheless, the step from a unitary to a multi-dimensional representation for instructional knowledge is a necessary one" (p. 24 of the reprint).

In an instructional context, the ability to adopt multiple viewpoints is useful at a number of levels:

- *Optimization of diagnosis*: it is fairly obvious that the adoption of the proper viewpoint is essential for a system to make sense of the student's input. Stevens et al. (1979) even suggest that errors are not only connected to specific viewpoints, but that they may also arise from missing viewpoints or from a difficulty in integrating multiple viewpoints. The detection of viewpoints can therefore both support and extend the diagnostic process. For instance, a student who is using the space bar to move the cursor of a word processor is clearly bringing to bear an analogy with a typewriter. The advantage of making explicit the viewpoint responsible for a bug is that it can predict unobserved bugs; it can thus facilitate the diagnostic process by guiding the interpretation of further correct and incorrect actions and by resolving ambiguities. It can also make remediation more effective by placing misconceptions in context or by distinguishing between different sources for the same surface errors. This requires a mechanism by which the keys of a viewpoint can be recognized when they manifest themselves within its scope (see also Section 17.3.3).

- *Optimization of didactic steps*: that tutorial interventions should be in line with the student's viewpoint is again obvious. In the context of IMAGE, London (1986) also suggests that selecting an optimal viewpoint is crucial because different viewpoints have different degrees of "power" with respect to the concept under discussion in the context of the student's current plan. For London, the power of a viewpoint is defined representationally as the structural complexity—the *richness*—of the concept when considered in the light of that viewpoint.

- *Instructional tools*: new light can be shed on a topic by the introduction of a new viewpoint. This is the theme of research conducted at LRDC about presenting and exercising the concept of rational number by means of multiple microworlds—the well-known scales or pies as well as some new ones—for multiple semantic interpretations of the target concept (Ohlsson, 1987b). Using the example of rational numbers, Ohlsson suggests that concepts can rarely be captured in their entirety by a single illustration, especially in abstract domains like mathematics. Thus, the design of illustrative microworlds must be based on a *semantic analysis* of the target concept so as to define the aspects that each possible microworld conveys most naturally.

- *Instructional targets*: because the student's viewpoint provides a context for interpreting experience so as to warrant beliefs, deep forms of learning often need to modify this viewpoint. As the set of beliefs evolves, the requirements of warrants broadcast modifications at various levels. Thus, the attainment of a new viewpoint can be an instructional goal in itself, although there is evidence that viewpoints can be very "resistant to change" (Clement, 1983). In contrast to the concept of an overlay, this qualitative view of learning suggests that a student's knowledge state is not just a subset of that of the expert, but the scope of a different kernel whose influence biases the interpretation of information. Modifying this kernel may require an explicit recognition of its effects on the scope (see Section 18.4.2).

Theories of viewpoints

By analogy with the concept of a theory of bugs, we might call the description and organization of relevant viewpoints for a domain and for a student population a *theory of viewpoints*. There is an interesting relation between the notion of a theory of viewpoints and the notion of epistemological and conceptual articulation.

From an epistemological perspective, a viewpoint is of course a more elusive concept that a belief or a bug. Although the keys that identify a viewpoint will often be explicit parts of the model of knowledge, the viewpoint itself tends to be an emergent property that characterizes some aspect of a knowledge state but lacks an explicit representational counterpart in the model. Therefore, the design of a theory of viewpoints may imply the creation of an additional vocabulary of descriptors to articulate these viewpoints, as in WEST's enumerative list of strategies. The trade-offs involved in this explicit representation are a general issue to be discussed shortly.

It may also be important to have a level of representation at which viewpoints can be compared and recognized as referring to the same entities. In IMAGE, for instance, decisions are viewed in the context of plans reconstructed in terms of NEOMYCIN's explicit strategy, which provide this mediating structure. In this regard, the level of articulation takes on a critical significance. For instance, at the compiled level, the two versions of the subtraction procedure mentioned above are separate entities, but the respective underlying planning nets represent a level of articulation at which the common goals can be recognized. The idea of a space of planning nets consisting of various sequences of increasingly complex versions of a common target procedure is actually suggested by VanLehn and Brown (1980). All these sequences must comply with a small set of principles intended to ensure that any sequence tightly follows a teleological interpretation of the procedure. A space of planning nets can thus be thought of as a space of possible viewpoints on a procedure—or on any "artificial" object—in which different planning decisions can be compared and recognized as responding to similar constraints. (Note that this is very similar to the way PROUST recognizes the equivalence of programs.)   More generally, compiled knowledge requires a lot of redundancy for representing multiple viewpoints (e.g., multiple rules in the LISP tutor). With more articulate knowledge, the keys to viewpoints can be isolated so that viewpoints can be identified by their minimal characteristics and thus more readily compared.

16.4   Knowledge states

We have now identified a number of dimensions of variability between knowledge states. Viewed as a succession of transitions between knowledge states, learning is a multifaceted activity that can involve all these dimensions, so that a change in the scope of the general model, the correction of a deviation, or the modification of a viewpoint constitute equally valid, but epistemically different, forms of learning. Articulating one's knowledge can be as significant as correcting some misconception, and reorganizing primitives into larger chunks for efficiency can be as important as acquiring some new concept. Each of these dimensions, therefore, may be useful to capture in a tutoring system because of their ramifications for pedagogical purposes (see Figure 18.6).

16.4.1   Knowledge states: structural and genetic constraints

The dimensions of variability considered by a tutoring system determine the set of distinctions between knowledge states deemed relevant. However, distinctions without constraints may not suffice to define a useful and manageable space of possible models. For instance, in the context of an overlay where each subset is a priori equally probable, we have seen that the organization of the genetic graph provides a region of likely transitions between states. In addition to these *genetic* constraints that deal with consistency between knowledge states over time, there can be *structural* constraints that impose consistency within a knowledge state. A very simple version of structural constraints on knowledge states underlies the extensions to the overlay paradigm proposed in UMFE. *Consistency rules* can be defined that broadcast information about the mastery of one concept to related concepts throughout the database in order to discard implausible knowledge states. As knowledge states become more complex and more organized, such structural constraints need not always be stated extensionally, but can be defined in terms of abstract relations. They can also link different dimensions of variability, for instance when bugs are keys to viewpoints which in turn predict the likelihood of further bugs.

The actual importance of these constraints obviously depends on a number of factors, such as the domain, the instructional setting, and the level of articulation. Anderson (1985, private communication) reports that empirical observations do not suggest the existence of much pedagogical correlation between the compiled rules of the LISP tutor, in that the level of mastery of any one rule does not seem to be significantly predictive of the level of mastery of any other. In contrast, MYCIN's decompilation revealed that there were pedagogically significant conceptual connections underlying its individual rules. When structural and genetic constraints are relevant, they can considerably reduce the number of knowledge states that must be considered as possible student models, since information about one aspect of the model can be broadcast to determine other aspects and to focus attention. Similarly, constraints can be exploited to amplify the effect of instruction and to determine optimal learning paths whereby the length of the instruction process is minimized and the student's knowledge is maximized at any point in the process.

16.4.2 Representing variations: classification versus emergence

In this chapter, we have been concerned with differences between knowledge states; this brings up the general issue of how to represent distinctions so that they are useful in the context of a tutoring system. Trade-offs of interest are whether or not distinctions have to be anticipated, whether or not variations still result in a runnable process model, and whether or not distinctions can be easily identified and used for the purpose of the system. This representational issue, mentioned in the context of bugs and viewpoints, is actually relevant to all dimensions of variability. It is distinct from, albeit clearly related to, the processing issue of model-driven versus data-driven diagnosis. In a process model of expertise, variations between knowledge states can be represented in two general ways: by *emergence*, with implicit differences between models, or by *classification* (Clancey, 1986b), with specific and explicit representational descriptors.

A central characteristic of classification is the existence of a system of predefined categories. For instance, with an enumerative theory of bugs, the student can be classified as possessing one or more of the enumerated bugs. Because classification models need not actually possess the characteristics they describe, they allow the inclusion of higher-order assertions about knowledge states in the student model. Another consequence is that the detail level of their accounts is very variable. Their complexity can range from a single value, such as a grade on a scale describing a student's performance, or a single assertion, such as the existence of a viewpoint, to a multi-level explanation, such as a medical diagnostic that assigns causes to a patient's symptoms. Whether or not a classification model is runnable for simulation purposes depends on the nature of the target categories: that is, whether they are purely descriptive, as in WEST, or components of a process model, as in WUSOR or BUGGY. A student model is often a mixture of both classification and emergence. For example, in an overlay model, there is a process of classification with respect to each unit of knowledge viewed as a dimension of variability; globally, however, the exact subset representing the student at any point is an emergent property in that there are no explicit categories to describe one subset in relation to another.

The definition of categories focuses the model on features that are deemed relevant for the system's purposes. Because these categories reflect the expected use of the model, additional knowledge can be associated with them, to be brought to bear once a classification has been established. For instance, if a viewpoint is explicitly represented as a classification category, it can be hypothesized as soon as a small number of keys have been recognized, thereby suggesting other keys that are likely to be observed. It is even possible for a classification to trigger default assumptions that can augment actual observations. Inasmuch as categories focus the attention on distinctions of interest, it is also fairly straightforward to associate didactic knowledge with classification categories, just as specific treatments can be associated with known diseases.

In contrast, emergent characteristics need not be anticipated and are therefore not limited to expected cases. Because they must be reconstructed, they tend to give more detailed accounts of the variations they stand for. However, when variations in knowledge states are emergent properties of the model, they may not be easily usable in a tutoring system. For instance, some misconceptions only manifest themselves through patterns, and it is very difficult to recognize the presence of a pattern of behavior without the use of predefined descriptors that can be primed as the pattern manifests over time. Note that this is independent of the quality of a model as a simulation of the student: a connectionist student model in the form of a neural net may be very precise as a simulation, yet it may not yield much information useful for achieving effectiveness within a communication environment.[4] Some global pedagogical functions, such as the optimizations of exercise selection performed by BIP or by the INTEGRATION tutor, do make some use of emergent properties. However, the subset of expertise represented as an overlay is usually not considered globally for didactic decisions. In general, taking advantage of emergent properties of the student model for didactic purposes requires a type of dynamic adaptability which is mostly beyond the capabilities of current systems. Yet there are interesting prospects for research, as discussed in Section 18.3.3.

16.4.3 Theories of knowledge states: knowledge communication

In keeping with our terminology, let us globally refer to the description of relevant knowledge states for a domain and a student population

---

[4] Of course, any symbolic student model can be said to involve some form of classification since it uses a vocabulary of discrete functions to describe the student. The issue is one of decomposition: that is, whether the classification takes place at the level of interest (e.g, one bug, one viewpoint, etc.).

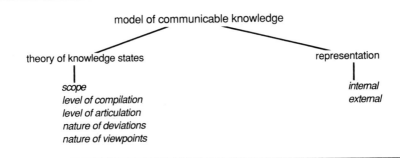

Figure 16.3 Dimensions of variability between knowledge states.

as a *theory of knowledge states*. As summarized in Figure 16.3, the construction of a model of communicable knowledge involves defining a theory of knowledge states and designing a representation. In the coming chapters, as we consider the computer as a communication agent, rather than as a mere medium, we will assume the existence of such a model of communicable knowledge. This does not necessarily include all the dimensions we have covered, but presupposes the definition of identifiable states, which can be recognized—whether by classification or by emergence—and serve as the basis for pedagogical decisions. In other words, the coming discussions cover a wide spectrum of knowledge communication systems whose actual power will be largely determined by the quality of their models of communicable knowledge. Obviously, a model of communicable knowledge need not be static, but is itself likely to be modified by communication processes.

When learning is viewed as successive transitions between knowledge states, the purpose of teaching is accordingly to facilitate the student's traversal of the space of knowledge states by means of a variety of instructional actions. This definition of teaching involves two basic types of activity, which are primary loci of pedagogical expertise: attempts at perceiving the student's current knowledge state and attempts at causing or supporting a transition to a new state—which may or may not be known in advance to the system.[5] In the course of an instructional session, this implies an alternation between *diagnostic* steps and *didactic* steps.

---

[5]Leaving this option open is important to free the definition from commitments to an educational philosophy.

Chapter 17

Diagnosis

The word *diagnosis* has been used to refer to pedagogical activities aiming at collecting and inferring information about the student or his actions. Because this task often involves the construction of a student model, these activities have also been called *student modeling*. In this chapter, we adhere to the more general term diagnosis, because some of the activities we describe do not result in what is usually called a student model. On the other hand, diagnosis should not be construed as the mere detection of bugs. Etymologically, the word simply means "to know thoroughly," but is perhaps better understood here as "to know sufficiently" given the pragmatic and necessarily approximate nature of the task.

To set the stage, let us start this chapter with some fundamental distinctions and some terminology. First, diagnostic tasks are varied in nature and can be viewed from various perspectives, some of which correspond to distinct tasks or phases:

- *Inferences*: diagnosis reconstructs internal processes and states on the basis of observable behavior, either "bottom-up," assembling primitives from the data, or "top-down," testing variations in a model. This inferential view highlights the fundamental assumption that internal states produce behavior in a *deterministic* fashion, so that it makes sense to posit reasoning chains, knowledge structures, and various internal states to *account* for observed behavior.

- *Interpretation*: diagnosis makes sense of observations and inferences by placing them in context. It deals with viewpoints and goals. The interpretative view highlights the pedagogical need to understand the student before helping him. To this end, diagnosis generates plausible rationalizations and problem-solving stories to *explain* observations and inferences.

- *Classification*: diagnosis makes relevant distinctions to enable different actions. From this perspective, the purpose is to *characterize* or *evaluate* observations and inferences according to expectations.

When considering diagnostic activities, it is also useful to distinguish between three levels at which information can be relevant for pedagogical purposes. Figure 17.1 will provide a background for the definition of these levels. The diagram, which is only meant as a general framework for our discussion, describes very abstractly how knowledge determines behavior via cognitive processes in the student.

The behavioral level. The first level, *behavioral diagnosis*, only deals with behavior and the product of behavior, without trying to perceive the knowledge state involved in its generation. It is illustrated by the bottom two lines of Figure 17.1. A number of systems are actually only concerned with this level, although it would be wrong to conclude that they require less sophistication. At this behavioral level, it is useful to distinguish between *observable* behavior, which consists of external actions such as typing an answer, and *unobservable* behavior, which is purely an internal mental process—or at least which the computer cannot observe. In this context, unobservable behavior is the use of knowledge in a reasoning chain, which is viewed as distinct from knowledge itself.[1]

---

[1] The difference between unobservable behavior and knowledge can be subtle and may only make sense in the context of a communication environment. At the neural level, one can indeed wonder if there is anything meaningfully identifiable but unobservable behavior.

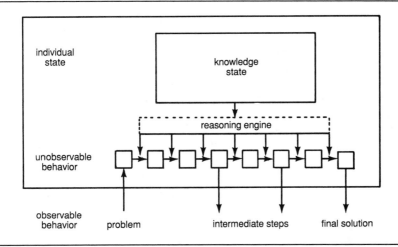

Figure 17.1 An abstract cognitive framework for diagnosis.

The epistemic level. The second level, *epistemic diagnosis*, deals with the student's knowledge state, including aspects of both his model of the domain (general model) and his strategic knowledge (inference procedure). Ideally, this involves variability along all the dimensions discussed in the last chapter, although not much will be said here about the level of articulation or the student's viewpoint, which for the most part have not been addressed by existing systems.

The individual level. The third level deals with everything else. Since this level is concerned with the individual whose behavior and knowledge are of interest to the first two, and since it includes a wide variety of aspects, let us just call it the level of *individual diagnosis*. Positing this level as an explicit area of interest has the advantage of supporting a view of the student, not only as a recipient of communicable knowledge, but as an agent with an identity of his own, engaged in an active learning process. The most immediate consequence of this view is that collecting information about this agent's individual characteristics can be a productive diagnostic activity. Since the individual level has not received much attention so far, we will not say much about it in this chapter; we will mention the subject mainly as an area for further research. In order to make the notion more precise, let us list some aspects of diagnosis that fall under the categories of this level:

- *architectural*: to become a simulation model, a knowledge state must be "incarnated" within a cognitive architecture, as was done in REPAIR and ACT theories. The assumptions and parameters of this architecture can become subject to diagnosis.

- *learning*: a learning model can be included in the student model to follow or anticipate the student's acquisition of knowledge, as in Self's Concept Teaching system. Learning styles can then become a concern as they were—albeit statically—in the overlay on the links of WUSOR-III's genetic graph.

- *stereotypical*: personality traits and individual preferences can be valuable in selecting topics and presentation styles—for instance, a preference for visual or textual displays. A related example is a system by Elaine Rich (1979) called GRUNDY, which performs some of the functions of a library consultant. It attempts to build simple personal profiles of people in order to recommend books they would probably enjoy reading. It uses a language of attributes to describe readers' tastes, background, educational status, and other characteristics relevant to a library consultant. The different values potentially taken by these attributes are organized into *stereotypes*, which can be activated by the user's responses to questions posed by the system, and which generate default values for attributes not yet mentioned.

- *motivational*: this includes parameters such as the levels of interest, overload, or tiredness that may warrant temporary changes in instructional style and pace. Though never subjected to diagnosis, these aspects have been important concerns in the design of a number of systems.

- *circumstantial*: it may be useful to understand the influence of the environment on the signals the system receives from the student. This includes some special events that distract the student or otherwise modify his performance, such as the intervention of a teacher or the help of a friend. It also includes problems the student may experience with the environment, independently of his interaction with the system.

- *intentional*: this covers the viewpoint of the student, not with respect to the subject matter, but with respect to the meaning of the tutorial interaction. In this regard, experiments with WEST provide us with an interesting anecdote. Some children enjoyed the interventions of the coach so much that they abandoned the goal of winning the game and tried instead to get the tutor to speak as often as possible (Burton and Brown, 1979b).

- *reflexive*: the model the student has of himself in the context of a domain and of an instructional interaction is a very interesting topic, briefly touched upon in Section 18.4.3.

- *reciprocal*: ITS research has been very concerned with the model that the system constructs of the student, but hardly at all with the model that the student forms of the system. The latter has been more of a concern for researchers in man-machine interaction who want to understand difficulties that users encounter in dealing with unfamiliar aspects of computer systems. This issue can be quite important for instructional systems, since designers have to make critical assumptions in this regard, some of which may need to be retracted. Furthermore, as the relation between a student and a tutoring system begins to be viewed as one of communication, the significance of reciprocal models will need to be recognized and the student's input will need to be interpreted in light of this type of information.

In general, though the individual level has not been subjected to on-line diagnosis, assumptions about it have played some role in the design of diagnostic systems, and a view of a student model with three distinct levels will help to make these assumptions more explicit. Note that while the language for diagnosis at the behavioral and epistemic levels is usually provided by the model of communicable knowledge, individual diagnosis requires a specialized, largely domain-independent vocabulary, which the field still needs to investigate.

Organization of the chapter

The rest of this chapter is divided into five sections. The first two sections consider diagnostic schemes at the behavioral and epistemic levels respectively. Some of the difficulties involved in diagnosis are addressed in a separate section on "noise," which presents some sources of discrepancies between diagnostic conclusions and reality, and some techniques used to deal with these discrepancies. Then comes a section on the collection and extent of available data, followed by some concluding remarks on the nature and necessity of diagnosis.

17.1   Behavioral diagnosis

Figure 17.2 gives an overview of some diagnostic activities that can be performed at the behavioral level, along with exemplary systems. The figure also provides an organizer for the topics of this section. The main distinction is between systems that deal only with observable behavior and systems that infer aspects of unobservable behavior.

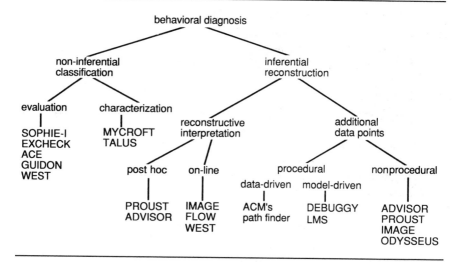

behavioral diagnosis

non-inferential classification

inferential reconstruction

evaluation

SOPHIE-I
EXCHECK
ACE
GUIDON
WEST

characterization

MYCROFT
TALUS

reconstructive interpretation

additional data points

post hoc

PROUST
ADVISOR

on-line

IMAGE
FLOW
WEST

procedural

data-driven

ACM's
path finder

model-driven

DEBUGGY
LMS

nonprocedural

ADVISOR
PROUST
IMAGE
ODYSSEUS

Figure 17.2 Taxonomy of behavioral diagnostic processes.

17.1.1 Noninferential evaluation

A number of systems attempt to give the student direct informed feedback at the behavioral level without inferences of a modeling nature—though they do perform other types of inferences of a diagnostic nature. They derive their classificatory capabilities from a powerful representation of knowledge about *correctness* in their domain. For instance, in order to *evaluate* the student's input, SOPHIE-I has access to a circuit simulator and to some knowledge about optimal measurements, EXCHECK applies a theorem prover, and ACE refers to an internal set of correct reasoning steps. In systems that perform program analysis, the student's input is not only evaluated, but exact errors are *characterized*. In these cases, the touchstone often consists of a set of correct or incorrect program descriptions: annotated plans in MYCROFT, augmented parse trees in MENO-II, and definitions of algorithms in TALUS (see also Ruth, 1976).

In addition to knowledge about correctness, the evaluations performed by these systems require rather complex *interpretation* processes by which the student's responses can be matched against the standards. This includes interpreting statements from the perspective of the student, as in SOPHIE-I and GUIDON, which must always evaluate hypotheses with respect to the data known to the student. WEST even infers the underlying strategic viewpoint in order to perform the proper evaluation of moves (that is why WEST is on two branches in the tree of Figure 17.2; see also Section 17.3.3).

Interpretation also includes conversion into a testable form. For instance, in attempting to show that two versions of an algorithm are equivalent, TALUS translates programs into an abstract description language and uses a heuristic counterexample generator in addition to its theorem prover. SOPHIE-I also uses quite sophisticated heuristics to set up simulation experiments on its model of the circuit. When it verifies a hypothesis given by the student in general qualitative terms (e.g., "the beta of the transistor is too low"), it must choose actual values to plug into the model so as to reliably confirm or disconfirm the hypothesis. This setup process is more than a simple translation into quantitative terms: it requires knowledge about the diagnostic meaning of a critical experiment, such as its boundary conditions.

In all these examples, evaluation involves both an explicit standard and a fairly complex comparison scheme that usually requires nontrivial domain knowledge. However, note that evaluation is performed by analysis, independently of the knowledge and processes by which people generate correct and incorrect solutions. In evaluations by frame-based CAI programs, which also ignore solution paths, the compiled matching schemes of branching strategies hide the complexity of the actual evaluation process. What distinguishes the systems mentioned above is the *complexity and explicitness* of the knowledge about correctness that they apply in their analyses, and the much greater flexibility afforded by the dynamic application of this knowledge.

17.1.2 Inference of unobservable behavior

The inference of unobservable behavior moves up one level in the diagram of Figure 17.1. It differs from the analyses described above in the attention it pays to problem-solving processes; actually, it constitutes a different use of AI, requiring modeling capabilities such as a theory of bugs. These inferences can be motivated by the requirements of complex behavioral interpretations and/or by the need to have more data points for the subsequent task of inferring a knowledge state. In the first case, the emphasis is on the product (the problem-specific model); and in the second, it is on the process.

Reconstructive interpretation of dynamically constructed solutions

In problem-solving domains, the dynamic construction of a goal structure often determines not only the correctness but the shape of the final output. Solutions, therefore, tend to be complex objects whose form cannot be understood independently of the path by which they were produced; consequently, behavioral interpretation and evaluation require the reconstruction of problem-solving rationales, an idealized form of "solution path."

Interestingly, the diagnostic approach commonly used for this purpose applies a general strategy that Brown, Collins, and Harris (1978) suggest underlies a very wide variety of interpretative activities, ranging from story understanding to the analysis of electronic circuits. They claim that the key mechanism for this type of interpretative understanding is reconstructive problem solving in terms of goals and plans. They give the example of one of Aesop's fables and demonstrate that the only way to understand the fable is to reconstruct the main character's problem solving. Likewise, their observations of both experts and students reveal that the analysis of electronic circuits involves reconstructing both the designer's intentions and the realization of these intentions as hierarchies of plans.

The diagnostic modules that implement this type of reconstructive interpretation for pedagogical purposes typically have access to a library of plans (also called methods, rules, or schemata) that decompose goals into subgoals down to primitive actions. This often includes incorrect methods for interpreting faulty solutions (e.g., PROUST, FLOW). For the diagnostic process, these systems all adopt some form of bidirectional search in their attempt to connect the student's input to some goals with a coherent planning structure. In many respects, their interpretation of data is reminiscent of parsing. They alternate between model-driven confirmation and data-driven recognition of plans and goals, as illustrated in Figure 17.3. As described in more detail in Part II, individual systems make some variants to this basic paradigm, either to fulfill specific requirements that interfere with the simple construction of a hierarchical structure (global and external constraints in SPADE, multiple interacting goals in PROUST, collapsed chains of inferences in ODYSSEUS), or to account for suboptimal solutions (completion of parse in the MACSYMA ADVISOR, ranked expectations in IMAGE).

Because the planning methods are organized hierarchically, the bidirectional search affords much diagnostic leverage by generating expectations, which can then be confirmed in the data. Some systems are purely *reconstructive*, taking only the final product as input. In this context, the structure of the solution provides most of the constraints for constructing an interpretation that involves a tight goal structure and minimal assumptions about errors. Other systems build the goal structure as they follow the student's problem solving. This *interpretative* setup provides additional constraints but has different requirements (see Section 17.4). Recall that IMAGE uses a first level of interpretation provided by NEOMYCIN's functional descriptors, on top of which it reconstructs the student's plan by means of successive observations. At the extreme of this spectrum is the model tracing of ACTP's tutors, where

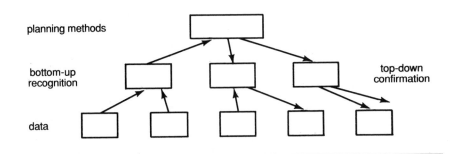

Figure 17.3 Bidirectional search through a hierarchy of plans.

the reconstruction of the student's goal structure is built into the step-by-step interpretation of behavior, requiring practically no search.

Inferred behavior as data for epistemic diagnosis: solution processes

In procedural domains, the form of the final solution is less dependent on the process. As a result, evaluation is straightforward, and behavioral reconstruction is a prerequisite to inferring the student's knowledge state, i.e., his internalized procedure. Although there is also a goal structure that underlies procedures (that is what planning nets for subtraction are meant to capture), it need not be dynamically constructed during problem solving: it has been frozen into a fixed sequence of operations, and is only useful for understanding the resulting procedure. If the system is interested in the student's procedure but not in his understanding of the procedure, it need only reconstruct the sequence of primitive operations that leads to the student's answer.

This process relies on different sources of constraints. In model-driven diagnosis, as in DEBUGGY, constraints are provided by the correct procedure, by assumptions of minimal errors, and by heuristics about bug compounds. In the data-driven reconstruction of ACM's path finder, the notion of minimal errors is less straightforward and requires the use of heuristics about the plausibility of solution paths. Moreover, since the result of diagnosis is a knowledge state, and since knowledge states are fairly stable over time, ambiguities in the reconstruction of these behavioral sequences can also be handled by multiple observations of problem-solution pairs.

In nonprocedural domains, where models of problem solving are incomplete, diagnostic interpretation as discussed above must use a mixture of knowledge about the problem-solving process, whose elements could potentially be constituents of a knowledge state, and of knowledge about correctness in the domain. For instance, in PROUST, the heuristics about likely goal interactions are diagnostic in nature and are not likely to belong to a student's knowledge state, whereas the plans from the library should ideally be plans that students know about and use. Thus, the reconstructive interpretations described above can also provide material for epistemic diagnosis, which in turn constrains interpretation across observations.

The use of inferred behavior as data for epistemic diagnosis differs somewhat from mere interpretation, in that there is a claim that the reconstructed operations represent the ones used by the student. In fact, an actual solution path may include backtracking and abandoned search paths, which cannot be reconstructed post hoc but may be important for inferring a complete knowledge state. This argues in favor of additional observations (but see Section 17.4). In procedural domains, reconstructed solution paths can reasonably be viewed as actual sequences of operations, since no search is assumed to be involved—although some of these assumptions are retracted in the context of REPAIR theory.

17.2 Epistemic diagnosis

To discuss diagnosis at the epistemic level, it is useful to distinguish three phases in the inference of a knowledge state, as shown in Figure 17.4. The first task is to determine which knowledge elements have been directly involved in the available account of behavior, a task we will call the *direct assignment of credit and blame*. The other two tasks have received less attention: we will label as *structural consistency* the broadcast of repercussions of this direct recognition on the rest of the knowledge state, and as *longitudinal consistency* the update of the existing student model according to new information. Again, the figure provides an organizer for the topics of this section.

17.2.1 Direct assignment of credit and blame

The purpose of the direct assignment of credit and blame is to discover both which knowledge, correct or incorrect, has been used to produce behavior, and which relevant knowledge has been overlooked. While the former only requires the availability of a modeling language, the latter requires some form of *differential modeling*, whereby the knowledge used by the student can be compared to that which the expert would have used (e.g., WEST, GUIDON).

The methods adopted to extract epistemic information from behavior can be classified into three basic categories: *model tracing*, which follows

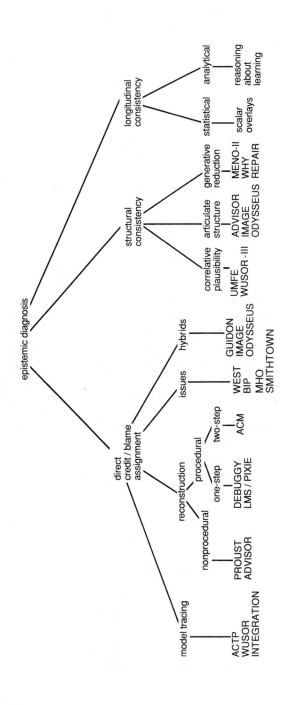

Figure 17.4 The phases of epistemic diagnosis.

observable behavior; *reconstruction*, which requires the inference of unobservable behavior; and the use of *issues*, which can detach the recognition process from the modeling of behavior. These three approaches vary in at least three dimensions of pedagogical importance:

- the level of articulation of the knowledge they can infer;

- the degree to which they capture the role of knowledge in behavior, and to which they are, consequently, able to reproduce this behavior;

- the extent to which they require detailed diagnostic data in the form of behavioral observation.

Some of the difficulties involved in this phase are further discussed in the next section on the issue of noise in available data.

Model tracing

The idea behind model tracing is to create a close correspondence between units of the internal model and single steps of observable behavior. The required tuning of granularity can affect the design of the interface (see Section 17.4) as well as that of the internal model. Recall that knowledge compilation in ACT* theory transforms declarative knowledge into a rule format that is directly usable for performance. As a consequence, compiled problem-solving knowledge, though it is a form of knowledge, maps directly onto behavior, unlike a concept or a principle, which must be interpreted before it can manifest itself in behavior. Thus *knowledge compilation* is really the core principle of the model-tracing paradigm; in fact, compiled knowledge is the only form of expertise represented in ACTP's tutors as implemented, whether or not other forms of knowledge were ever made explicit in the design process.

Because compiled knowledge can summarize chains of reasoning of arbitrary complexity as more coarsely grained rules, the need to infer unobservable steps is avoided. Being very close to observable behavior, compiled knowledge allows direct comparisons of the student's input with single steps of the system's internal model. In this sense, model tracing is at the border between behavioral and epistemic diagnosis. In fact, it merges the two phases into one matching process, which simultaneously assigns credit and blame for behavior to internal pieces of knowledge, interprets behavior directly in terms of this compiled knowledge, and evaluates the correctness of both behavior and knowledge in terms of missing or buggy rules. The model-driven nature of this step-by-step interpretation obviously requires the availability of fully operational knowledge states, which currently exist only for very simple domains, or for simplified versions of complex ones.

Because the granularity of compiled primitives isolates behavioral errors, the model-driven matching of rules and mal-rules against the student's steps is strongly reminiscent of the lists of expected responses used in frame-based CAI. In fact, it often results in a similar directiveness. There is, however, a subtle but important difference between the two approaches. Whereas expected responses are only behavioral diagnostic devices that trigger branching decisions and remediation, the rules used in model tracing stand for beliefs supposedly held by the student, and thus are viewed as constituents of his knowledge state. Not only do they interpret local behavior, but they participate in the formation of a global student model by means of an extended overlay, which is then runnable and predictive of the student's actions. This difference significantly changes the perspective of the design process by bringing forward the cognitive aspects. Its practical importance in the operations of a system is of course determined by the extent to which this global student model is exploited for pedagogical decisions and for further diagnosis.

Reconstruction

As mentioned earlier, the reconstruction of behavior can form the basis for epistemic inferences: once a plausible reconstructive interpretation has been reached, the diagnostic process can try to discover the ramifications of this interpretation for the formation of a partial knowledge state. In DEBUGGY and LMS, behavioral operations are units of the procedure itself, so that behavioral and epistemic diagnosis are merged into a single search process.[2] Similarly, the use of planning methods can be monitored and recorded, as is done in recent versions of PROUST by extended overlay on plans from the library. In general, when epistemic elements, such as subprocedures, rules, planning methods, or concepts, participate in the reconstructed solution path, they can be primed as if they had been observed.

When assignment of credit and blame is based on reconstructed behavior, therefore, most of the diagnostic complexity is usually dealt with during the initial reconstruction process—unless behavioral and epistemic modeling languages are substantially different, as in ACM, the MACSYMA ADVISOR, or IMAGE/ODYSSEUS. In the case of ACM, the two phases are distinct: interestingly, machine-learning techniques are used, not to give a computational account of the student's learning, but to transform diagnostic reconstructions of behavior into a diagnostic description of knowledge.

Because reconstruction can capture the internal use of knowledge by mental processes that may not be easily accessible even with the

---

[2] Although algebraic manipulations are generally not considered to be strictly procedural knowledge, LMS, with its fixed order of rule applications, does treat them as procedures.

best interfaces, it can support epistemic diagnosis for high levels of *articulation*. This makes overlays as used on PROUST's plans, which capture the internal use of knowledge, potentially quite different from overlays on the rules of ACTP's tutors, even though the recording schemes for the mastery of individual elements may be fairly similar.

Issues

Model tracing and reconstruction both attempt to simulate processes in order to perform the direct assignment of credit and blame. The concept of issues, as used in WEST, in BIP, and in MHO, presents a different situation. Recall that an issue is a curriculum element whose participation in decisions can be recognized and discussed. Thus an issue can be anything of pedagogical interest to the system, even a misconception (though BIP and WEST did not include incorrect knowledge). Since issues are not directly tied to behavior, any number of them can be independently recognized as having participated or not participated in any decision. The fact that issues need not be part of a simulation makes possible the diagnosis of articulate aspects of knowledge without the stringent need to model the exact process of their participation in generating behavior. This can be particularly useful for capturing emergent properties of knowledge states such as the existence of a viewpoint.

Viewed as general diagnostic devices, issues are instances of what were earlier called *classification categories*. From a design standpoint, the flexibility of the concept of issues is very attractive, but it is not without its cost. In a model-tracing context, the diagnostic complexity lies in the design of the model's units, such as individual rules, since they must produce simple matches with the student's behavior. In epistemic diagnosis based on reconstruction, the participation of knowledge in reasoning must be carefully modeled. By contrast, the design of the issues themselves is much less constrained, but the diagnostic complexity is hidden in the need to design corresponding *classification schemes*, called "issue recognizers" in WEST. This can be a nontrivial task. One advantage, though, is that classification can make use of clues and analytical sources of evidence other than the direct role of knowledge in behavior.

Being classification categories, issues do not necessarily constitute an operational modeling language. The monitoring of dynamic problem-solving situations may thus require additional machinery for evaluating decisions—performed in WEST as a separate process, by a compiled "expert." Because the use of issues does not require the existence of operational knowledge states, diagnosis may not produce runnable student models, as is the case in both WEST and BIP. Although this is a disadvantage, the pedagogical usefulness of the focused information provided by classification may override it.   As the field turns to less-compiled forms of knowledge in the context of composite curricula, the notion of issues may well regain some popularity (as indicated by the recent work on the bite-sized architecture and curriculum structures at LRDC). Indeed, the design of general classification schemes for nontrivial pedagogical issues would certainly be considered a worthy AI activity, with challenges parallel to those found in similar systems for medical diagnosis.

Hybrid approaches

The three approaches just described are not incompatible and can actually be advantageously combined: for instance, if a system follows the student's problem solving but has a model of expertise at a finer granularity than his observable actions.   We have seen that IMAGE adopts such a composite scheme, tracing the student's actions with HERACLES/NEOMYCIN while reconstructing intermediate steps to infer his plan. GUIDON is another case in point. MYCIN's rules are part of an operational model of expertise which, for diagnostic purposes, is assumed to reflect that of the student and is used to trace his behavior. However, in this context, GUIDON's maintenance of its overlay model has the flavor of issues: it resorts to a complex classification scheme that uses multiple sources of evidence to estimate the likelihood that each relevant rule was actually applied by the student to arrive at a hypothesis.

17.2.2   Structural consistency

Additional constraints provided by the structure of knowledge states can increase the leverage of direct assignment of credit and blame.   The simplest thing one can do is to assert correlations between the likelihoods of various pieces of knowledge being mastered. With "consistency rules" à la UMFE, these correlations can be arbitrary. In WUSOR-III, they follow the genetic organization of the set of rules.   The advantage of these extensionally defined networks is that they can be designed in the absence of epistemological structure and of a model of conceptual interactions, that is, for compiled knowledge.

One of the most pedagogically meaningful aspects of diagnosis is to trace the successful or unsuccessful application of a piece of knowledge back to interactions between its conceptual constituents. MENO-II performs a simple version of this *generative reduction* with an extensionally defined network that associates diagnosed surface bugs with possible underlying misconceptions. For the general case of this reduction process, the concept of articulation is critical. Indeed, when a compiled rule à la MYCIN contains at once some elements of control, some common-sense knowledge, and some allusions to domain-specific processes, for the system to infer its mastery in an overlay has limited pedagogical significance. Not only is the rule itself insufficiently refined for its conceptual constituents to be directly identified, but the lack of epistemic structure prevents the diagnostic process from recognizing common misconceptions or missing concepts that underlie failures in the use of distinct rules.

With respect to epistemological organization, much leverage is afforded by the articulate configuration of the model into an interacting set of constituents of expertise, because the diagnosis of one supplies a context for inferring others. For instance, in the MACSYMA ADVISOR, the reconstruction of the user's derivation tree in terms of planning methods provides a structure for the inference of his understanding of MACSYMA. When the dataflow constraints propagated through this "dependency graph" reach their source, they reveal the user's beliefs about the preconditions or postconditions of primitive operations in MACSYMA. Similarly, in IMAGE and ODYSSEUS, the reconstruction of the student's strategy provides a context for attributing his decisions to specific constituents of expertise. In other words, information about the inference procedure can serve as a pivot for getting to the general model and vice versa (Clancey, 1986b). With respect to conceptual content, the explicit manipulation of assumptions is essential so that observed errors can be interpreted as violations of assumptions—assumptions that then need to be retracted.

In some sense, generative reduction can be viewed as a form of dynamic decompilation of knowledge. As such, it is intended to interpret the student's actions with inferences that support pedagogical actions of increased generality. However, such dynamic knowledge decompilation is as difficult as it is fascinating if it has to be performed by on-line inferential simulations. Given the computational complexity of pure simulation-based diagnosis à la REPAIR/STEP, on-line generative reduction may require the coexistence of multiple models of expertise, as in WEST, with different levels of articulation, so that diagnosis involves a combination of model tracing, reconstruction, and issue recognition.

17.2.3   Longitudinal consistency

In the case of an ongoing tutorial session, the update of the knowledge state takes place in the context of a continuous series of observations from which new diagnostic information has to be integrated into the existing student model.[3] To be pedagogically reliable, the updating methods involved in this stage of the diagnostic process must fulfill the contradictory requirements of being at once sensitive enough to adapt the tutor's attitude without delay, and stable enough not to be easily disturbed by local variations in performance. Because of these difficult requirements, the details of these updating methods are often derived empirically (some of these methods are discussed further in the next section). Most common is the use of scalar attributes, such as numerical weights, associated with individual elements of the knowledge state in the context of an overlay. These weights are updated by some statistical or pseudostatistical computations as knowledge manifests itself in behavior.

In his defense of the use of statistical and pseudostatistical methods for updating the student model, Kimball (1982) notes that they rely on an assumption of independence between various pieces of knowledge. If structural and genetic constraints are relevant, however, concepts cannot be understood in isolation; rather, they have to be considered as part of the history of knowledge states in which they have participated. If the update of the knowledge state derived from one observation was placed in the context of a rich view of the evolution of the student's knowledge, this would make diagnostic updating methods very similar to what AI researchers have called "truth maintenance" or "belief revision" (Doyle, 1979; de Kleer, 1986). Admittedly, such diagnostic updating methods, which combine theories of learning and belief revision in a form of "reasoning about learning," still belong to the future, though they are a fascinating research topic which is gaining some popularity (Halpern, 1986). In the meantime, the simple updating methods currently adopted tend to consider the possible effects of epistemic interdependence as noise.

17.3 Noise: sources and solutions

The issue of noise must be addressed by any realistic system performing pedagogical diagnosis. This section considers three general sources of noise, which are briefly discussed together with some proposed solutions. The first source is that the student's behavior is not consistent over time. The second is that there are inherent ambiguities in the diagnostic process. The third is that the assumptions of the model of communicable knowledge may not hold in certain situations, in which case noise itself can become a source of information.

---

[3]Ideally, this includes the recognition of patterns that manifest themselves over time. This is very difficult without explicit descriptors, however, as mentioned in Section 16.4.

17.3.1   Noise in the data: variations in behavior over time

Noise in the data can be attributed to factors at various levels. At the
behavioral level, noise is generated by local inconsistencies. Specifically, it
originates from a mismatch between behavior and knowledge: on a given
task, the student manifests a different behavior than the one his actual
knowledge state would generate in ideal conditions. These variations in
performance, which are independent of the student's knowledge, include
various types of local slips as well as circumstantial events such as
inattention or luck. Note how the sources of behavioral noise correspond
to *individual* parameters that can cause variations in behavior. At the
epistemic level, noise originates from the fact that the student's knowledge
state goes through ongoing modifications, which render earlier diagnostic results obsolete because of *learning*—or because of *unlearning* (e.g.,
forgetting or getting confused). These effects can be very subtle because
the connectedness of knowledge is likely to generate *interferences* that
cause instruction and practice to have unpredictable ramifications. On
the one hand, acquiring additional knowledge can create new confusions
in previous knowledge. On the other hand, new knowledge can clarify
or solidify previous knowledge, in a form of indirect learning.

There are no magical solutions to such a difficult diagnostic problem,
and existing proposals are few. Approaches to the issue can be classified
in terms of the three levels of diagnosis, in that different methods use
information from different levels to cope with noise as intelligently as
possible. However, there is no implied correspondence between the level
of the source of noise and the level of the solution.

Solutions of a "behavioral" character: scalar weights

Statistical or pseudostatistical methods belong to the behavioral realm
in that they attempt to integrate new information as cleverly as possible
without making use of a model of the student's knowledge. When the
mastery of a piece of knowledge is simply summarized as a ratio of the
number of times it was applied by the student to the number of times it
had been found advantageously applicable by the expert, this frequency
ratio does not record the absolute usage so as to take reinforcement into
account. In particular, it makes one successful application, which may be
due to luck, look better than eight out of ten, which is a good indication
of mastery, especially if the two failures took place early. One solution
is to maintain a history of usage of individual pieces of knowledge, with
"evaluators" gauging the reliability of the information by the stability of
data over time; this is done in WUSOR-II with a specialized program that
stamps a rule as known only when its history has stabilized, and in the

MHO tutor with heuristics for classifying issues on a scale of mastery. This notion of a history is pedagogically important in that it takes into account the *variations* in mastery as well as mastery itself.

Another solution is to accumulate reinforcement in the form of an absolute numerical weight, as ACTP's tutors do for both correct and buggy rules. The updating method modifies the old weight of a rule by adding or subtracting a fixed number for a success or a failure respectively. For the model to remain sensitive to recent variations, the fixed number can be added to, or subtracted from, only a fraction of the existing value.[4] In the context of a rule-based student model, which follows the problem solving of the student by model tracing, these numerical values provide a default ranking for resolving conflicts between applicable rules at any step.

Solutions of an "epistemic" character: genetic organization

At the epistemic level, the reliability of incoming data is assessed with the help of information derived from the contents of the knowledge state. In describing the genetic graph, Goldstein suggests that the *topology* of the space of knowledge states provides this assessment. For instance, on the assumption that the acquisition of new pieces of knowledge follows natural links connecting them to existing knowledge, the locus of learning is fairly well predicted by the *frontier* of the student's knowledge as defined on the network of these "genetic" links. Incoming data that indicate variations far behind or ahead of the current frontier are suspect; they must be considered with caution but not discarded, since learning does sometimes take place in jumps. Furthermore, in the student model itself, the confidence in the mastery of each piece of knowledge can be assessed not only on the basis of data extracted from behavior, but also in terms of the number and nature of *genetic connections* with other parts of the curriculum that have been made explicit by instruction.

Solutions of an "individual" character: modeling inconsistencies

The methods described so far all assess the validity of diagnostic information, but they do not attempt to model the generation of noise or in any way explain or predict its presence. In general, however, behavioral variations are called noise when they are caused by phenomena that are not being modeled. Since most forms of noise originate at the individual level, it is natural to wonder to what extent the possibility

---

[4]In the LISP tutor, the new weight is defined as $\frac{2}{3}$ of the existing weight $+$ or $-$ 1.

of accurate individual diagnosis could turn the treatment of noise into actual modeling.

While this is a thought for the future, an interesting example is provided by the transition from DEBUGGY to REPAIR theory. In DE-BUGGY, bug migration is a form of noise that can only be dealt with by statistical methods. However, in REPAIR theory, bug migration is explained by the fact that repairs are applied to the problem-solving process and not to knowledge itself. Therefore, when the same impasse is met a second time, nothing in the cognitive architecture prescribes that the same repair should be applied. By combining all possible repairs with a given impasse, REPAIR theory can even predict classes of bugs within which migration is likely to be observed.

Accurate modeling at the individual level may be a bit much to ask in a general sense. But even if an individual model is not able to predict the exact manifestation of noise, it may at least provide information to help predict its presence and perhaps its degree. A good case in point is again DEBUGGY, whose use of coercions we have earlier called a *model-driven* treatment of noise. The idea is to use heuristic knowledge about likely variations in performance to explain away mismatches between the student model and observed behavior. These heuristics are derived from an implicit model of perceptual and performance processes.

17.3.2   Noise in the diagnostic process: ambiguities

Because of the restricted channel of any communicative situation, the diagnostic process is inherently ambiguous. In the interpretation of observed behavior and in the inference of internal knowledge structures, choices must often be made between competing explanations in the absence of discriminating data. This is a major source of noise. Multiple rules in model tracing or multiple reasoning chains in reconstruction may reproduce the current behavior of the student. The problem is even more acute when "issues" are used without process model of reasoning. Recall that any number of issues can be simultaneously and independently recognized as participating in one decision. However, if the student does not make an optimal decision, it can be very difficult to assign blame precisely, since failure in any of the necessary issues would block the action.

Let us consider two possible solutions, whose characteristics are summarized in Figure 17.5. In the absence of decisive data, one can heuristically *select* one hypothesis. This is a good solution for mutually exclusive interpretations—in model tracing, for instance, where rules, both correct and incorrect, compete in matching single steps in behavior, and where accumulative weights can give some indication about the

	"select"	**"spread"**
hypotheses	competing and weighted	shared responsibility
recovery	weight compensation	participation in multiple contexts
focus	quick	slow
caution	less	more
instruction style	directive	unobtrusive

Figure 17.5 Two methods for the resolution of ambiguities in diagnosis.

most likely interpretation. Recovery from errors takes place as weights are updated in different contexts in which the conflict does not exist. Heuristic selection allows immediate action, and the reinforcement of accumulative weights tends to focus on perceived remediation needs quickly, in keeping with the directive attitude typical of model-tracing tutors such as ACTP's.

Alternatively, one can *spread* the credit or blame among competitors, as was done in WEST. This is a good solution for issues, since it is possible that a number of issues are simultaneously responsible for suboptimal behavior. In this alternative, the assessment of remediation requirements is slower but more certain, in keeping with the cautious attitude of an unobtrusive coach. The hope is that the real culprit(s) will participate in enough suboptimal decisions in different contexts to be singled out eventually. Of course, credit and blame need not be spread evenly. GUIDON, in fact, applies a complex heuristic strategy to individually modifying its diagnostic beliefs for each relevant rule.

17.3.3   Noise in the model of communicable knowledge

Because the model of communicable knowledge is of necessity an approximation and because it inevitably incarnates a specific viewpoint, it is itself a source of noise. Furthermore, most current modeling paradigms only capture the quantitative coverage of learning, as for instance with the notion of a learning frontier in an overlay. They ignore the qualitative effects of learning on the student's viewpoint, which is likely to vary over time.

Because the student's viewpoint can shift, noise can itself become *data* in certain cases: the presence of noise may indicate a mismatch of viewpoints between system and student—what Burton and Brown (1979b) have called the degree of *cognitive tear*. Beyond a certain threshold of cognitive tear, and if multiple viewpoints are available to a system, other viewpoints should be tried. Recall that a simple version of this stratagem has been adopted in WEST, as it monitors the use of each issue at each move. When the student's play is consistently found suboptimal without corresponding weaknesses in related issues, that is, when noise is persistent and apparently not due to the spreading of credit and blame, WEST tries to see whether different strategies for determining the best moves provide better explanations of observed behavior. In this sense, WEST can be said to use the presence of noise as data because noise is relative to a viewpoint and can lead to a revision of the viewpoint adopted by the system. This idea will become very relevant to future systems that include more sophisticated versions of theories of knowledge states with multiple viewpoints.

17.4 Sources of evidence: diagnostic data

It goes without saying that the scope and nature of available data are critical factors for the diagnostic power of a system. As mentioned earlier, computer systems are handicapped in this regard. Most indirect sources of evidence, such as facial expressions, require wider communication channels than are available to current computers. Of course, some indirect information can be made available to them. In FLOW, for instance, each keystroke is timed: the tutor applies heuristic knowledge about the natural length of pauses in human programming to detect needs for intervention. However, for diagnostic purposes, the channel's "bandwidth" is usually that of a keyboard, sometimes with a mouse. But even within this limited bandwidth, there is a wide range of possible interfaces that give access to different data, both quantitatively and qualitatively. The design of a good diagnostic interface, therefore, can be critical to the success of a diagnostic module. In this section, we consider some trade-offs involved in extensions of the channel through which diagnostic mechanisms collect evidence, either by passive observation or by overt action.

17.4.1 Diagnostic observation

In most existing systems, the communication channel for diagnosis consists of solutions to some problems or of unobtrusive observations of the student's actions in the context of the performance of a task. An appropriately designed interface, however, can ensure that the system receives a maximum of information about what the student is doing to help make its diagnosis both computationally tractable and more accurate. For instance, the programs dealing with subtraction could get information from scratch marks and their timing as they are made by the student.

Granularity of information: reification in reverse

In practice, the goal of replacing reconstruction by model tracing is one that may require a lot of ingenuity on the part of designers in addition to their pedagogical wisdom. In ACTP's tutors, artifacts like the structural editor for Lisp or the proof tree for geometry allow the student to communicate his decisions to the tutor not only in a natural, unobtrusive fashion, but also at the level of detail imposed by the interface. The model-tracing scheme depends on the granularity of information in such structured environments to avoid the inference of unobservable behavior.

Not only is the knowledge of the model compiled, but the interface is refined, until both reach the same granularity level of epistemic fidelity. In some sense, then, what we have here is the principle of reification in reverse. Thus the duality of purpose in instructional interface design is not a competition between the requirements of communication in each direction. There is often a good deal of synergism. For instance, ALGE-BRALAND's language of operators forces the student to communicate his decisions within a specified framework, but it can also provide him with a set of tools with which to understand the domain.

The price of additional diagnostic data

At first sight, an increase in diagnostic data is always desirable; the catch, however, is that additional information requires additional mechanisms, not only to collect it but also to interpret it, since observing intermediate steps is only useful if they can be understood by the system. In procedural domains such as subtraction—if ACM, for instance, was to collect information about intermediate steps—interpretation may not require unreasonable extensions, although some of the behavior hypothesized by REPAIR theory may be quite complex and hard to follow. In a nonprocedural domain like programming, the situation is more problematic. Following the development history of a nontrivial program may require much additional machinery beyond that required for a post hoc analysis.

One difficulty is that the *semantics* of intermediate steps may not be the same as the semantics of the final solution. In the context of the MENO project, we mentioned studies that show the semantic evolution from early planning to coding. This implies multiple problem spaces, an

issue that both BRIDGE and the LISP tutor try to address. Another—
related but perhaps more fundamental—difficulty is that, in complex
domains, reasoning goes through various *phases*, such as exploration or
reminding, which make intermediate steps much more difficult to understand teleologically than the final solution. While a final solution can be
analyzed behaviorally in terms of notions of correctness in the domain
and of implemented goals, the precise interpretation of intermediate steps
requires a complete model of reasoning. Without such a model, these
steps cannot be interpreted, since they reflect a process and not a product.

Consider the contrast between PROUST, which must analyze a
finished program, and the LISP tutor, which follows and guides the
student's programming step by step. Although at first sight, the diagnostic task of the LISP tutor is much easier, we have noted that its
model-tracing paradigm is only feasible when instruction is extremely
directive. Independently of other pedagogical considerations, such as a
need for immediate feedback, the tutor must make sure that the student
is always on a path known to the system. Hence, the observation of
intermediate steps provides information but imposes severe constraints
on the interaction. In contrast, PROUST leaves the student a lot more
freedom, but requires sophisticated analytical machinery to make up
for the lack of data. To palliate the current lack of general models
of the type of problem solving involved in computer programming,
the two projects have opted for different solutions at two extremes of
a spectrum: PROUST completely ignores intermediate steps, whereas
ACTP stringently constrains the domain.

17.4.2 Overt diagnostic actions

Another way to augment the power of a diagnostic module is to supplement passive observation with overt diagnostic actions. We should
distinguish between *active* diagnosis, whereby the system can test its
hypotheses, and *interactive* diagnosis, whereby the student is invited to
report on his decisions and knowledge.

Active diagnosis

There are not many examples of systems that are able to take overt
diagnostic actions when they have determined that further data is required for discriminating between the competing models that remain.
Generating these actions is indeed a difficult task. First, the defining
difference between the competing models must be determined with

sufficient precision.   Then, test problems or exercises to obtain the necessary information with a minimum of inconvenience must be selected or composed.   Finally, the diagnostic action must be inserted into the instructional sequence in an unobtrusive way, without disturbing other pedagogical parameters such as interest or continuity.   Of course, well-designed tests can also have a didactic value, an assumption central to MHO's steering-testing scheme based on constraint-posting.   In this case, the process is made very dynamic, since the student's knowledge state evolves with each test.

In purely diagnostic systems, such as IDEBUGGY and PIXIE, both of which include algorithms for generating diagnostic problems (described in Part II), the issue of merging tests with instruction is not relevant. However, it is still necessary to minimize the number of problems required to reach a diagnostic, by choosing test items that provide a maximum of information (Marshall, 1981; Doignon and Falmagne, 1985), and by deciding when two constructed hypotheses are no longer worth distinguishing (Burton, 1982).   In spite of these difficulties, active diagnosis has the advantage of being one type of extension to diagnostic communication channels that does not require additional interpretive machinery in the form of extended models.

Interactive diagnosis

With the generation of discriminatory problems, diagnosis is allowed to take active control of the instructional session; but it still does not take advantage of the communication abilities of the student, who remains largely unaware of the exact diagnostic goals underlying tutorial actions. Few systems invite the student to participate explicitly in the diagnostic process by volunteering information.   There are, of course, the simple forms of self-evaluation that WUSOR requests before a session and that BIP requests after each problem.   The LISP tutor sometimes engages in menu-driven dialogues with the student, but these dialogues are primarily didactic, even though they provide information about the student's goals.

While their communication capabilities are still rather rudimentary, some systems do perform some interactive diagnosis.   ACE attempts to understand a student's explanations of his reasoning in terms of its own internal trace; it does this somewhat passively, however, without generating precise diagnostic questions (except to clarify details of language usage).   In their restricted forms of Socratic dialogue, WHY, GUIDON, and MENO-TUTOR probe the student's knowledge by asking him to justify predictions or hypotheses in the context of specific cases.   Though untested on any reliable scale, the way the MACSYMA

ADVISOR takes advantage of the student's communication abilities is particularly interesting. In order to select the most plausible hypothesis when interpreting a sequence of operations, it does not ask the student directly about his actions and intentions in the current sequence. Instead, because it is able to hypothesize general beliefs that the student is likely to hold about MACSYMA, it can perform its interactive diagnosis with questions about these beliefs. In interactive diagnosis, this ability to consider noncompiled forms of knowledge moves the dialogue to a level of abstraction at which the student is less likely to be puzzled by the viewpoint underlying the system's questions.

As mentioned in the introduction, there are serious difficulties for the prospects of interactive diagnosis. Not only does the current state of the art set technical limitations on dialogues between computers and people, but people's accounts of their own actions and understanding can be rather incoherent and sometimes unreliable. Even if they are coherent and reliable—and the language can be processed—there remains the issue of understanding these self-reports in terms of the models that students have of the domain, of themselves, and of the system. This also includes knowledge about communication and cultural conventions that cause interlocutors to have expectations about the form of dialogues. Again, amplifications or extensions to diagnostic communication channels must be traded off against the additional knowledge required to exploit them.

Thus, even if the student is more involved in the formation of the student model, inferential diagnostic capabilities remain necessary. First, in obvious or simple cases, it is better to use inference than to bother the student with trivial questions. Second, as students are unlikely to describe their approach completely and correctly, some inferences will be needed to fill gaps and verify student statements. Third, the system needs to generate intelligent questions, and to do this it must be actively constructing a model. Last and perhaps most important for the system to understand a student's "confession" and ask the right questions, it will need a rather complete model of how misconceptions develop in the domain—the kind of model now being investigated by research on inferential diagnosis.

Nevertheless, Sleeman (1984a) has found in interviews that even fairly young students are able to speak sensibly about their own knowledge of algebraic manipulations. In addition, there may be many ways to restrict the scope of a dialogue so that it remains tractable. In fact, given the difficulty of the diagnostic task, it is somewhat surprising that existing systems do not resort more often to simple forms of interactive diagnosis involving constrained natural-language dialogues, or even menus or graphics. This is quite an interesting area for further research in the near future: not only may there be feasible solutions, but generalizable results would undoubtedly have important practical applications.

17.5 Aspects of diagnostic expertise

In essence, diagnosis can be viewed as a process of reasoning about reasoning and about learning. As a pure modeling activity, it reconstructs knowledge states responsible for observable behavior by a reversal of the individual model that has processed knowledge into actions. When the underlying model is a simple rule interpreter, the reversal is trivial: rules match behavior instead of generating it, and data from the student provide the conflict resolution scheme. With more complex views of cognition, it is usually neither possible nor practical to reverse an individual model for actual diagnosis. Not only is complete modeling beyond current capabilities in AI, but its computational costs are prohibitive. In a number of instances, useful *diagnostic heuristics* have been compiled from underlying individual models, as in ACM's path finder and DEBUGGY's coercions. As recurring patterns are identified, classification[5] can also replace emergent properties of data-driven simulations, focusing the search on relevant features and bringing to bear relevant knowledge accumulated from experience with students.

If diagnosis is construed as meaning "to know sufficiently" and if it is a very difficult task, it is worth asking how much of it is actually sufficient, even within the inherent limitations due to the availability of data. Few but the most simple diagnostic systems can currently meet the efficiency requirements of on-line diagnosis. While there are solutions which have not been fully investigated, such as preliminary off-line computations (e.g., LMS, PUPS) or a progressive scheme by which an initially coarse model is refined on demand or during waiting periods, the actual need for diagnosis is eventually a pragmatic issue determined by pedagogical factors. In fact, after a period of excitement about student models, some researchers are expressing reservations about the assumption that more is better. Ohlsson (1987a), for one, claims that the role of diagnosis should be viewed as monitoring the success of unfolding pedagogical plans. In this context, he suggests that the usefulness of diagnostic distinctions can be measured by their abilities to distinguish between possible courses of action.

Though final answers for specific cases will always be dependent on their specific contexts, the role of diagnosis in knowledge communication systems and the extent to which researchers ought to concentrate on

---

[5]Note that the introduction of classification can constitute either a process of articulation (when it augments a model with additional descriptors) or one of compilation (when it replaces modeling with recognition mechanisms). This illustrates the subtle duality inherent in the process of articulation, whereby its manipulation of assumptions and its creation of descriptors can be in conflict (see Section 15.5).

the topic are important issues. In this regard, comparisons with human teachers are usually not very illuminating. First, classroom teaching is very different from the type of tutoring performed by computer systems. Second, human private tutors and their students share extensive conversational capabilities and common backgrounds that are completely inaccessible to current computers. As a consequence, the issue of the potential role of diagnosis in computer-based tutors has to be situated in the general context of a *computational understanding of knowledge communication*. As we turn to the topic of didactic action in the next chapter, shedding some light on this issue will be one of our main goals.

Quite apart from these considerations, explicit interest in and careful study of diagnostic strategies typical of ITS have relevance beyond the design of tutoring systems. Such interest reflects a view of teaching as a communication process, one in which didactic responsibilites are deeply rooted in diagnostic perception. Given that educational research has been largely concerned with presentation methods, research on student models is an important contribution of ITS research.

Chapter 18

Didactics

The word *didactics* will be used here to refer to pedagogical activities intended to have a direct effect on the student, as opposed to diagnostic activities. This is the sense in which we have used the adjective "didactic" so far. Note that didactics is usually construed more generally, as "the art or science of teaching," which does not exclude diagnostic activities. Since there does not seem to be an English word for the particular aspect of pedagogy that didactics denotes here, I have taken the liberty of restricting the meaning of the word for the context of this book.

Implemented process models of didactics with some articulation of the expertise involved are few, and active interest in such explicit models is relatively recent. Let us recapitulate the milestones of this sparse history. On the one hand, there has been interest in algorithms for selecting or generating tasks, with early systems like the INTEGRATION tutor and BIP, and recent work on steering-testing schemes at LRDC.

On the other hand, there has been interest in principles for conducting tutorial interactions. As an early experiment, the QUADRATIC tutor can modify its own strategies, but these modifications are mainly adjustments of parameters. The design of WEST led to the articulation of pedagogical principles for coaching students involved in activities. Similarly, investigations in the context of WHY resulted in the articulation of a set of rules for Socratic teaching. In neither case, however, was the articulation operational enough to be directly interpreted by the system into actual decisions. Instead, programs had to be built that embodied, rather than interpreted, those principles. In GUIDON, the didactic module became a rule-based expert system of its own: though its tutorial rules are relatively compiled, GUIDON can deal with case-based tutoring for knowledge represented in MYCIN-like systems. More recently, MENO-TUTOR introduced the notion of a discourse management network as a general formalism for a more articulate representation of expertise in conducting tutorial dialogues.

Although there is a growing interest in computational models of didactics, the topic remains largely untended. Not least among the reasons for this neglect is the fact that human teachers' expertise is a very complex skill whose constituents are little understood. It is of course not the ambition of this chapter to propose a complete, or even a partial, theory of didactic expertise. More humbly, we elaborate on the themes we have already introduced to provide a framework in which the notion of *didactic operation* can be considered from a computational perspective. Underlying the discussion is an intention to hand over more pedagogical responsibilities to the system by putting more decisions dynamically under its control.

This chapter will be organized around four characteristic aspects of a didactic operation, as presented in Figure 18.1. Though no tutor implemented to date addresses all these aspects, they constitute good tools for thinking about didactic processes in computational terms, either in existing or in future systems, and for looking at the possible roles of diagnosis. Each aspect is the topic of a section: the *plan of action* that enacts a didactic operation, the *strategic context* in which the operation is triggered, the *decision base* that provides *constraints* and *resources* for the construction of the operation, and finally the *target level* of the student model at which the operation is aimed. In conclusion, we examine the ramifications of this framework for the respective roles of diagnosis and didactics in pedagogical processes.

18.1 Didactic operations: plans of action

A didactic operation is defined as a unit of decision in a didactic process. It is more general than a didactic intervention, in that it does not necessarily

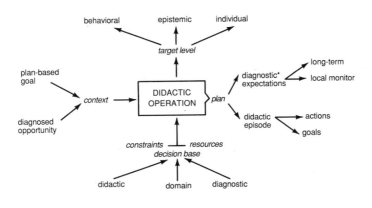

Figure 18.1 Four aspects of a didactic operation.

correspond to actions visible to the student. A good candidate framework for defining didactic operations is the concept of a *plan*, because it can be made general enough to encompass all the situations we wish to include here, from the simple prestored interventions of current systems to the dynamic knowledge communication capabilities of futuristic tutors. Recent computationally oriented discussions of pedagogical expertise that emphasize its problem-solving nature have taken similar approaches (Leinhardt and Greeno, 1986; Ohlsson, 1987a), and some systems under development implement versions of this view (Peachey and McCalla, 1986; Breuker et al., 1987; Macmillan and Sleeman, 1987).

A curriculum is quite clearly a plan; however, the concept actually applies to most didactic activities. Even a local explanation, for instance, can be considered a plan. Since an explanation rarely consists of a single conceptual element, the granularity of communicable units will require an *incremental presentation*. Viewed as a scheme to cause a transition between two knowledge states using a succession of intermediate steps, a nontrivial explanation is a plan, a kind of mini-curriculum, for leading the student along a local learning path.

In addition to generating an *episode* of actions or subgoals, a didactic operation can generate explicit *diagnostic expectations*. AI research on planning distinguishes situations in which the actual effects of operations in an episode can be predicted accurately from those in which they cannot, and in which the execution of a plan requires some monitoring (Charniak and McDermott, 1986). Because of the limitations of communication channels, the number and complexity of factors influencing the modifications of a knowledge state, and the inherently approximate nature of diagnostic information, *uncertainty is a fundamental aspect of communication*. Moreover, interactive formats have real-time constraints that may force actions before a complete picture has been computed. In this sense, strategies of knowledge communication must involve constant revision and adaptation and must interleave diagnosis with planned action. Diagnostic expectations that articulate goals and possible outcomes can be both *local*, monitoring the unfolding of the plan, and *global*, building up a long-term context and creating continuity throughout the tutorial session.

Although purely dynamic versions of didactic planning still belong to the future, the notion of a didactic plan as presented in Figure 18.1 can be useful in the design of currently feasible systems. Most didactic operations in today's tutors consist of a single basic action, such as presenting a piece of prestored text or submitting a selected problem. Since these prefabricated interventions are didactically planned during system design, the granularity of the decisions that remain to the system itself is fairly coarse. It can be refined, however, if the underlying plan or the set of expectations are made explicit to the system.

18.2   Pedagogical contexts

Instruction has goals. In general, goals can be achieved either through intentional planning activities, by which one gains control over the environment, or through the recognition of opportunities presented by the environment's resources. Most of the time, goals are best achieved by an appropriate combination of both styles. Hence, in attaining teaching goals and in generating subgoals, *opportunistic* and *plan-based* approaches define a range of pedagogical styles that vary in the system's control over the shape of the tutorial sequence. In turn, the degree of this control determines different *triggering contexts* for didactic operations and suggests different roles for diagnosis and didactics.

Opportunistic contexts

Opportunistic strategies take advantage of teaching opportunities that arise in the context of some activity or dialogue in which the student is engaged. The environment is deemed rich and structured enough for instructional goals to be eventually achieved, and the student's activities or statements provide a focus for diagnosis and for the content of tutorial interventions. Since the strategic context is loose, teaching opportunities are revealed by diagnostic information, and planning is locally focused on these opportunities. As a consequence, the presentation of the material is mainly driven by the student's interaction with the environment. Note that, as illustrated by ACTP's tutors, the adoption of an opportunistic strategy does not necessarily imply that the student is given a greater amount of freedom.

Most of the systems we have described follow some version of this opportunistic approach, which is very compatible with their compiled models of expertise. From a research standpoint, opportunistic tutors present interesting challenges, since the pedagogical expertise required for intelligent opportunistic interventions can be quite sophisticated (e.g., WEST or GUIDON). From a practical standpoint, these strategies are very well suited for teaching *in situ*, for problem-solving guidance or coaching in learning environments, especially if the tutored activities complement other kinds of teaching such as formal instruction. Furthermore, the feasibility of opportunistic tutors has been demonstrated, and some preliminary studies, provided in the context of WEST and of ACTP's tutors, indicate that experimental prototypes can already be quite effective in appropriate instructional settings.

Admittedly, the problem-solving environment often contains an implicit plan or curriculum, in the form of a pool of activities or topics, ordered or otherwise, that the interaction is expected to cover. However, opportunistic systems have little control over how the organization of instructional sessions communicates the subject matter to the student; this somewhat limits their adaptive monitoring of the student's learning and their usefulness as primary sources of instruction.

Plan-based contexts

In plan-based contexts,[1] pedagogical goals predominate. Their attainment is dynamically controlled by the system, which organizes the activity and the interaction around them. As a consequence, planning tends to be hierarchical. Although the structure of the environment and the student's behavior play a less central role, the student does not necessarily have less freedom. A plan-based context simply means that the tutor manipulates the sequences of experiences through which the student is expected to acquire the target expertise. In other words, the system plans learning events, globally or locally, even when the student enjoys a great deal of freedom within this context, and this plan provides the focus for didactic and diagnostic activities. Note how this changes the function of diagnosis from triggering interventions to monitoring an unfolding plan. Since most existing systems are essentially opportunistic, the field has paid very little attention so far to didactic planning—admittedly quite a complex subject (but see bibliographical

---

[1]It may be necessary to clarify that while the view of didactic operations as producing plans is convenient to include plan-based contexts, it does *not* imply in any way that plan-based contexts are to be preferred to, or are more general than, opportunistic ones.

notes). In most systems, if the order of topics is not predefined, diagnostic information is combined with local optimization criteria to determine good exercises or issues to attack next (e.g., BIP, MHO).

Mixed strategies: embedded contexts

Of course, both opportunistic and plan-based strategies are useful for different purposes; a system need not be committed to a single strategy, either over time or across levels of embedded contexts. Within a globally opportunistic strategy, the tutor can take control with local interventions that are strongly plan-based so as to get a focused point across to the student. Conversely, within a plan-based strategy, new goals can emerge in a completely opportunistic fashion, taking advantage of unexpected events. In fact, a complex interleaving of such embedded contexts with alternating opportunistic and plan-based strategies was observed to be characteristic of Socratic dialogues led by human tutors; this observation largely motivated the evolution of the WHY project. A similar type of alternation was also incorporated in a compiled form in the network and metarules of MENO-TUTOR (see Figure 11.12). In addition, observations of human teachers who interleave opportunistic and plan-based styles have led a number of researchers to suggest the need for some sort of internal "agenda," which would keep track of active subgoals and emergent goals and provide a complex triggering context for didactic operations (Collins et al., 1975b; Collins and Stevens, 1982; Leinhardt and Greeno, 1986).

18.3 Decision base: constraints and resources

Didactics must comply with a number of *constraints*, which ensure its effectiveness but which often imply the resolution of conflicts between various competing factors affecting decisions (e.g., the QUADRATIC tutor). In addition, didactic operations require *resources* as building material. Note that the limitation of resources is also a subtle and implicit source of constraints. The triggering context, of course, provides important constraints and resources by focusing didactic operations on recognized opportunities or prevailing plans. However, there are additional considerations on which to base decisions, and this section identifies three potential sources of both constraints and resources for systems: *didactic*, *domain-specific*, and *diagnostic* information, whose contributions are summarized in Figure 18.2.

A good case in point is WEST, a salient feature of which is the recognition of a need for further deliberation following diagnostic triggering. Though "issue recognizers" can report multiple issues as relevant,

	constraints	resources	
		local	*global*
diagnostic	relative strengths and weaknesses	integration remediation	means-ends analysis
domain	relative importance of topics	content of interventions	sequencing
didactic	pedagogical principles	tactics	strategies

Figure 18.2 Aspects of the decision base of didactic operations.

"issue evaluators" must select a single candidate for an intervention by evaluating these issues both in the context of the current student model (diagnostic source), and with respect to their individual significance for the current move (domain source). Even if an important issue has been recognized as overlooked in the current move and evaluated as weak in the student model, however, coaching principles can still oppose tutorial intervention, for instance if it would otherwise take place for two moves in a row (didactic source). In general, once an operation has been triggered in a given context, the system must still decide what to do or say, how to do or say it, or even whether to do or say anything at all. Actually, WEST can be made to report on its deliberation process: observers have been surprised to discover that there is almost always something the system might say and that it uses its didactic deliberations mostly to keep quiet!

18.3.1   Didactic base

WEST's coaching principles (see Figure 7.5) provide good examples of didactic constraints in the form of pedagogical principles and of felicity conditions that reflect the needs of students. As illustrated by the deliberation process, these constraints often interact with other requirements, both cooperating and competing with them. In the model-tracing paradigm, for instance, the need to keep the student on track is in line with the principle of immediate feedback, but prevents dynamic deliberation in applying the principle. Another type of didactic constraint is provided by sequencing schemes. Figure 18.3 shows a few sequencing principles alongside examples of projects in which they have been explored. Note that only some of the systems mentioned actually follow their respective principles with on-line topic selection capabilities.

sequencing principles	examples
simple to complex	WUSOR-II, ACTP: rules are ordered by classes of difficulty
focused to diversified	QUADRATIC tutor: acquired rules exercised in new contexts
breadth versus focus	INTEGRATION tutor: selected topic maximizes distance between expert and student
one disjunct per lesson	STEP: OR branch of AND/OR tree
web versus linear	FLOW: the links of a network indicate levels of detail versus extent of coverage
prerequisites first	BIP, WUSOR-III, MHO: selection according to prerequisites and other genetic relations
important first	SCHOLAR: importance tags
compiled to articulate	ENVISION: less function in structure
following logical structure of domain	
causal	WHY: following causal scripts
teleological	Planning nets: following successive design refinements articulating additional constraints

Figure 18.3 **A few sequencing principles explored in various projects.**

With respect to didactic resources, researchers who have adopted a "problem-solving" view of teaching activities emphasize the importance of a large repertoire of local and global didactic techniques which they call teaching "routines" and "agendas" (Leinhardt and Greeno, 1986) or "tactics" and "strategies" (Ohlsson, 1987a). These techniques can be very general (i.e., correction by counterexample), domain-specific (e.g., use of Dienes blocks for teaching decimal number representation), or even specific to classes of students (e.g., different age groups). They reflect and exploit the conventions of the communication environment, which provide both constraints and resources for didactic operations.

A wide selection of techniques makes for more precise interventions. For instance, GUIDON can choose from a variety of discourse procedures to present a rule to the student, using a rather sophisticated selection scheme. Similarly, WEST has different levels of hints for the same topics, and SOPHIE-II has multiple explanation structures grafted onto decision nodes. In WUSOR-III, there was a plan to associate different types of explanation with different types of genetic link (see Figure 7.10). Taking a rather extreme position, Ohlsson (1987a) even claims that the availability of a variety of local tactics, and of global strategies that organize the use of these tactics, is the ultimate determinant of a tutoring system's adaptability. Although he tends to ignore the importance of opportunistic strategies and of flexibility in the domain contents of interventions, he hits home when he suggests that the didactic repertoire of current systems is often poor, and that richer theories of didactic primitives are badly needed.

However, making such a theory operational for computer-based tutors is a very difficult research issue, especially if one wants to preserve its generality. Recall that the descriptive theories of WHY and WEST are not directly interpreted into actual tutorial operations, and that GUIDON's tutorial principles are highly compiled. In this sense, the dialogue management network of MENO-TUTOR (see Figure 11.12) is an interesting attempt to define some general didactic primitives for remedial interactions and to organize them into an operational framework with hierarchies of strategic and tactical states. Yet in the implementations of the scheme we described, the linguistic capabilities and domain database are rudimentary.

18.3.2   Domain base

To become applicable, most didactic strategies must be combined with the constraints provided by the structure of the domain and with the resources provided by the model of expertise. In general, the problem of merging didactic and domain knowledge dynamically—a theme of further work on MENO-TUTOR (Woolf and McDonald, 1984a)—can be quite complex. The stratagem used in GUIDON is to compile tutorial strategies into didactic packages that are domain-independent, but are specialized to a specific representational scheme for the target expertise. Didactic strategies can thus use the representational syntax as an anchor into the domain. We have noted the methodological importance of this approach in motivating the formation of abstractions (Section 15.4.3). The resulting articulation is critical to putting curriculum decisions and explanation generation under the system's control.

Sequencing information

Many of the sequencing principles listed in Figure 18.3 are instances of this required combining. Although they reflect a pedagogical standpoint, they must be implemented with information about relations between topics, such as the genetic links used in BIP and WUSOR-III. Toward the bottom of the list, the structure of the domain even becomes predominant. The links of a genetic graph define sequences that place the emphasis on domain-independent learning mechanisms (e.g., generalization, specialization, refinements, or analogy), adapting instruction to the needs of specific learning models. By contrast, principles like the "no function in structure" and articulate representations like planning nets place the emphasis on the crucial ideas of the domain, adapting instruction to different viewpoints.

Recall that with planning nets, a procedure can be represented as a series of increasingly complex versions where each step resolves a new requirement with which the procedure must comply. VanLehn and Brown suggest that the structure of underlying planning nets constitutes a framework for constructing of natural teaching sequences that provide an incremental warranting process for the student. Not only are crucial constraints brought to light one by one, in a version of "one disjunct per lesson," but the teleological information defines a natural order corresponding to a possible design. This highlights the importance of articulation as an organizing principle for learning experiences. In fact, a presentation of material according some natural *structure of the domain* can be considered as a type of felicity condition. In this sense, the model's configuration is critical, in that it allows instruction to be organized around meaningful epistemic categories rather than arbitrary rule boundaries.

Content of interventions

The processes required to assemble effective interventions on the fly are not yet well-understood: in particular, the principles involved in generating meaningful explanations that take advantage of a process model of expertise. Since most existing systems do their tutoring in opportunistic contexts with compiled representations of expertise, their process model is mainly used to follow the student and to trigger the presentation of prefabricated interventions, rather than to generate explanations. Even in this scheme, the compiled nature of the model can present some problems. In the INTEGRATION tutor, for instance, not only are chains of reasoning collapsed but the knowledge about one problem class is not contained in a single value. Instead, it is spread throughout the set of values that relate a problem class to all solution methods, so that explanations cannot be readily associated with a piece of expertise. This dissipation typical of compiled knowledge undermines the presentation of explanations and can limit on-line interventions to problem-solving hints.

As decisions become the results of explicit chains of reasoning, however, more refined explanatory frames can be associated with single pieces of expertise (e.g., rules in GUIDON or ACTP's tutors). They can thereby be assembled by a tutorial module into more flexible interventions. SOPHIE-II's troubleshooting expert is capable of rather sophisticated demonstrations, but the flexibility of its domain expertise has been sacrificed to explanatory capabilities. The predefined paths of the fixed decision tree allow designers to foresee all the ways in which a node might be reached; consequently, explanations, produced by means of predefined textual frame structures instantiated during problem solving, can refer to the context of the decisions they justify.

As decompilation reveals the locus of expertise and represents structural and strategic abstractions explicitly, didactic interventions can focus on critical concepts and can describe expertise in general terms rather than problem-specific ones (e.g., NEOMYCIN versus GUIDON, STEAMER's tutor). The problem-specific situation can then be used merely to illustrate the stated principles. Ultimately, as expertise becomes articulate, reification can become explanatory, a theme underlying GUIDON-WATCH. GUIDON2 concentrates on explanations of problem solving by combining general strategic principles with self-contained domain relations. QUEST on the other hand explains the behavior of physical systems; to this end, it articulates causality by combining the use of general principles of electricity with structural circuit models that abide by the no-function-in-structure principle.

More generally, from the standpoint of domain knowledge, articulation is the key to explanations: Figure 18.4 places the types of articulation mentioned in Chapter 15 in correspondence with possible types of explanation.

18.3.3 Diagnostic base

Once a didactic operation has been triggered, extending the use of diagnosis can provide further constraints by revealing relatively weak areas of the student's knowledge (WEST, GUIDON), by considering underlying misconceptions (MENO-II), or by determining the most appropriate viewpoint (IMAGE). Furthermore, the possibility of a student model at the individual level brings to bear a wider range of constraints for the dynamic application of pedagogical principles. In addition to these initial constraints, the student model also supplies material for constructing didactic operations, in the form of information about the student's existing knowledge and about the nature of her errors.

Tailored interventions

Even the most articulate model is insufficient for generating good explanations. Such explanations must not only satisfy didactic principles but must also take diagnostic information into account so as to tailor their content and detail level to individual students. To be appropriate from a behavioral perspective, an explanation must be in line with the student's situation-specific viewpoint. To be appropriate from an epistemic

---

justifications

  teleological accounts:
    of expertise by articulate demonstrations (SOPHIE-II)
    of design by constraints and goals (planning nets)
  causal accounts:
    of physical processes by running envisionments (ENVISION, QUEST)
    of observed symptoms by classification (NEOMYCIN)
  functional accounts:
    of the roles of relevant factors in processes by inquiry (future WHY)
    of reasoning episodes by strategic explanations (NEOMYCIN)
  structural accounts:
    of the physical substrate of causal relations by envisioning (ENVISION)
    of circuit behavior by instantiation of general principles of
      electricity (QUEST)
  semantic clarification:
    articulation of meanings and definitions (MACSYMA ADVISOR, MENO)

integration

  relations (genetic graph):
    articulation of genetic relations (e.g., generalization, refinement)
    articulation of analogical and contrasting relations
  abstractions (STEAMER):
    articulation of abstract objects by conceptually faithful reifications
    articulation of procedures in terms of abstract processes and objects

organization

    articulation of general principles (NEOMYCIN, QUEST)
    articulation of the role of knowledge in decisions by reification of
      reasoning (GUIDON-WATCH)

**Figure 18.4 Types of explanations in correspondence with types
of articulation.**

---

perspective, the explanation must be a useful summary, frequently even
an abstraction, that provides a minimal account of the information the
student is missing. In this respect, decisions about what to say and what
to skip are crucially based on diagnosis.

    Acting as a resource, diagnosis provides information about existing
knowledge. This allows the use of *contrasts and relations*, which make
didactics much more effective than purely expertise-oriented demonstrations. The system motivates additions and refinements by contrasting
them with the limitations of existing knowledge and clarifies them by
contrasting them with competing beliefs. When epistemic relations are
explicated, the understanding of both new and old knowledge is enriched
and solidified, and further abstractions can be formed. In general,

connecting new beliefs to existing ones in an incremental fashion is one of a teacher's key functions. Although knowledge integration was a theme behind the conception of the genetic graph, it is still mostly beyond the capabilities of current systems. As researchers give this topic the attention it deserves, the *global* notion of a *knowledge state* in a student model will become increasingly significant.

The value of diagnostic information as a resource is perhaps clearest in remedial situations, where contrasts with the student's behavior and knowledge are essential. WEST's principle of issues and examples and WHY's entrapment techniques both implement versions of this idea. Moreover, deeper forms of diagnosis are very useful in this regard. For instance, PROUST's reconstruction of a program's goal structure allows remediation to situate the descriptions of errors relative to the student's intentions. When generative information is available, constructing didactic operations on the basis of diagnostic results becomes completely open-ended. Indeed, generative diagnosis à la REPAIR/STEP can potentially show the student how her misconceptions arose during learning and how they have manifested themselves in problem solving; in this way, errors and misconceptions can be reduced to processes the student recognizes as incorrect. The general idea here is to use a form of reification to help the student do her own blame assignment by means of an *abstract replay* (Collins and Brown, 1987) of the genesis of errors in learning or problem-solving contexts. This use of diagnosis as a didactic resource can produce dynamic responses that engage the student to probe the system's understanding of her behavior and that foster the development of metacognitive skills.

Tailored sequences

Topic selection requires the consideration of global diagnostic information, as in the INTEGRATION tutor (distance measure over matrices), the QUADRATIC tutor (difficulty matrix relating problem features to weaknesses in the student model), BIP (optimized mixtures of mastered and weak issues in a new problem), and MHO's steering testing (global optimization under constraints posted by bites throughout the system). Inasmuch as the construction of a didactic plan lays out sequences of transitions between knowledge states toward some goal states, it is best viewed as a kind of means-end analysis, whereby differences between current and target knowledge states are successively reduced (Hartley and Sleeman, 1973; Ohlsson, 1987a).

Accordingly, a didactic plan can be seen as a succession of knowledge states—or clusters of knowledge states considered equivalent—an approach adopted in QUEST. An interesting extension of this approach is to define dimensions in which two knowledge states can differ, such as the order or the degree of a model in QUEST. Along the same lines, the notion of knowledge state presented in Chapter 16 suggests a number of such dimensions at a very general level (see Figure 16.3). For didactic purposes, these differences and their varying degrees of significance guide the planning process. By defining directions for further learning and teaching, these epistemic dimensions provide the beginnings of a framework with which to formalize topic selection in terms of differences between knowledge states.

The student model: constraints and resources

In contrast with opportunistic triggering and plan monitoring, the use of diagnostic information as constraints and resources for constructing didactic operations usually requires the system to inspect large portions of the student model. The distinction is fairly subtle, in that the formation of a global model does not necessarily imply that the model will be used as a complete state for pedagogical decisions. In fact, the didactic interventions of many systems are typically based solely on the local behavioral information provided by the match—or the absence of a match—between the model's actions and the student's. In this regard, the extent to which the student model is used globally to support didactics is an important determinant of the types of decisions a system can make and the level of responsibility it can take for the student's acquisition and integration of knowledge.

18.4　Target levels of didactic operations

So far, we have mostly spoken of didactic operations as addressing the knowledge state of the student. This is in fact far from always being the case, even when the ultimate purpose of a global operation is a transformation in knowledge state. The *target level* of a didactic operation is defined as the level of the student model—behavioral, epistemic, or individual—at which an operation seeks *immediate* modifications. Different target levels define classes of instructional capabilities and strategies. Selecting the target level, or levels, to which an operation should be addressed is an important didactic decision in itself, though not made dynamically by current systems.

18.4.1　The behavioral target level

At the behavioral level, didactic interventions guide the performance of a task without addressing internalized knowledge in any direct or

---

behavioral guidance (WEST, GUIDON, ACTP's tutor)

     specific   hints

     general   advice (form of compiled knowledge)

     errors   correction by direct or indirect indication of errors
                correction by suggestion of better solutions

exposure to behavior (compiled knowledge)

     expertise   simple demonstrations (INTEGRATION tutor)
                 traces of reasoning (GUIDON, ALGEBRALAND)

external phenomena   simulation (STEAMER)

Figure 18.5 Taxonomy of behavior-oriented didactic actions.

organized fashion. Hence, they can be constructed dynamically even when only compiled knowledge is available. Figure 18.5 lists the main types of interventions of this category. From the target level perspective, *hints* or pieces of *advice* are fundamentally different from explanations, and *corrections* likewise different from remediation, in that they only address behavior. Similarly, *simple demonstrations* and *traces of reasoning* are restricted to exposing behavior in the domain without providing other forms of support for learning. Finally, *simulations* only expose the behavior of objects: the types of instructional interaction they provide are usually targeted initially at the behavioral level, in the form of manipulations of the simulated environment. Though STEAMER is the example most familiar to the reader, it is somewhat unfair to use it here, since one theme of the project is precisely to move away from physically faithful simulations and to include epistemic elements.

Because they do not articulate justifications, such didactic operations all require a good deal of interpretation by the student in order to be converted into useful knowledge. The pedagogical assumption here is that by being repeatedly exposed to problems, students will somehow be able to acquire the correct expertise, which usually includes a conceptual understanding beyond that possessed by the system. It is very unlikely, for instance, that Kimball was hoping students would develop the form of expertise possessed by the INTEGRATION tutor. Applying their mathematical knowledge, they are expected to infer by themselves which features in a problem class make a given solution method appropriate.

Viewed as processes of knowledge communication, didactic operations targeted at the behavioral level capitalize on the fact that performing a task and being exposed to an environment constitute a good learning context, one that provides students with ample raw material for actively forming their own conceptualization of the domain. In particular, student interpretation of difficulties and errors can be turned into a learning experience, if these difficulties and errors are properly resolved. As a consequence, didactic operations targeted at the behavioral level are a very effective way of supporting the acquisition of knowledge *in situ*, provided the design of the system is conducive to the types of interpretation that can warrant beliefs.

18.4.2   The epistemic target level

At the *epistemic* level, didactic operations explicitly seek to modify the student's knowledge state, either via direct communication or via practice, by organizing specific experiences to expose the student to. At this level, explanations are central to dealing with the articulation of knowledge. Unlike behaviorally-oriented interventions, explanations explicitly supply some of the interpretations of phenomena that serve as warranting processes for the student.

Direct modifications in a knowledge state can be sought in other ways, too. Many existing systems, for instance, concentrate on the compilation of knowledge: they offer opportunities for intensive practice, sometimes organizing sequences of exercises to cause specific changes.[2] In general, modifications within the different dimensions of variability between knowledge states require different types of didactic operations. Figure 18.6 sets some classes of didactic operations alongside the epistemic dimensions with which they deal.

Here, the dimensions of a knowledge state identified in Chapter 16 provide the beginnings of a framework for a taxonomy of didactic primitives. For instance, a statement with some examples may just suffice for presenting a new assimilable fact, whereas the correction of a misconception will probably require some confrontation followed by some corrective suggestions and explanations. Modifying a viewpoint is even more involved, since the keys have to be modified via a recognition of their effects on the scope. Laudan (1977) stresses that scientific research traditions are not dismissed by direct confrontation, but are *evaluated over time* according to their ability to produce theories that solve problems *perceived* as important by the scientific community. For didactic purposes, the analogy of such traditions to a student's viewpoint (Section 16.3) suggests a need for the student to be actively *engaged* in problem solving, for her to perceive problems—perhaps even "own" them (Lave, in press). In this way, her viewpoint can be *pulled* by an iterative

---

[2]Note that pure compilation without any conceptual evolution is rare; most systems in this class supplement practice with explanatory and remedial capabilities that are tied to opportunistic strategies.

epistemic dimensions	classes of didactic operations	expected modifications
scope	statements, examples, etc. practice: varied exposure	quantitative change (assimilation) increased generality
compilation	behavioral guidance practice: focused exposure	compilation of procedures proceduralization (automatization) and composition (chunking)
articulation	explanations practice: articulate demonstrations	warranted beliefs understanding of processes
deviations	remediation practice: "confront and explain"	articulate corrections operational corrections
viewpoint	global remediation practice: "engage and pull"	qualitative change (accommodation) extended understanding

Figure 18.6 Classes of didactic operations in correspondence with epistemic dimensions.

process of uncovering current limitations and discovering new problem-solving capabilities that *demonstrate a new viewpoint's conceptual superiority*. In a retrospective discussion of SOPHIE's pedagogical philosophy, Brown and Burton (1986) suggest that computer-based tutoring systems can have an unusual power to "engage and pull" the student's knowledge state. In reactive learning environments based on simulation, problem solving incites the student to reveal her interpretation of phenomena by stating precise hypotheses: these hypotheses can then be critiqued with respect to earlier actions by an expert à la SOPHIE-I; furthermore, their full implications can be explored with the help of an expert à la SOPHIE-II, which can provide its own analysis of the same situation.

18.4.3 The individual target level

It has been observed that a large part of a school teacher's energy is spent on the management of the learning process rather than on the epistemic aspects of knowledge communication (Anderson, 1985, private communication). These management tasks actually deal with dimensions of the individual model—motivation, cognitive load, interpretation of the instructional context—that have a profound impact on learning. Although very few existing systems target didactic operations at the individual level, some strategies targeted at the individual level are often incorporated in the design of a system (e.g., attractive graphics for motivation or the LISP tutor's context window for dealing with the limits of working memory).

In contrast with WHY's Socratic strategy, which addresses issues of dialectical teaching in terms of the knowledge being discussed, WEST's coaching principles deal mainly with motivational aspects. These concerns can result in actual didactic interventions: for instance, the coach may change the odds in order to give the student a chance to win.[3] Obviously, the purpose of this action is not to communicate knowledge directly, but to maintain a close match between opponents or to change the despairing student's state of mind so that further knowledge communication is possible. Decisions to slow or increase the pace, to abandon a topic temporarily or to congratulate the student on a small success can have similar motivations. These are in fact very delicate didactic decisions.

Metacognition: reflexive models

The strategies mentioned above are didactic in their attempt to have a positive effect on the student's learning, but they are not direct forms of knowledge communication. The situation is somewhat different for pieces of metacognitive advice like requests to the student that she think longer before moving or that she analyze erroneous solutions to understand what went wrong. In WEST, for instance, the coach can suggest that the student try to learn from her opponent if the system has been continually using issues the student has failed to apply. This is a form of knowledge, though not strictly part of the subject matter. Thus, the line between the epistemic and the individual levels of the student model cannot be defined in absolute terms. Indeed, if individual dimensions such as general reasoning patterns and learning strategies become open to direct communication, they become knowledge that can be taught.

Of course, this notion of changes in *individual states* instigated by intentional communication touches upon educational issues that are beyond the scope of this book: the extent to which internal cognitive processes are amenable to the introspection that would be required for communicating them, as well as the nature of cognitive invariants and innate abilities. Nevertheless, this view has interesting implications for the individual student model: it suggests that aspects viewed as individual that become the object of direct knowledge communication

---

[3]The system cannot make intentional mistakes. It is a coaching principle of WEST that the system should always play optimally because the student can learn by observing the system's moves.

should be moved to the epistemic level, resulting in a form of reflexive theory of knowledge states.

Little has been said so far about the student's model of herself as a knowing, performing, and learning agent in an instructional environment, because little has been done in the field regarding such reflexive models. Not only is a student's reflexive model central to the success of pedagogical enterprises, because of the profound effects such models can have on learning attitudes, but a positive reflexive model with respect to learning and performing in a domain may be just as important a result of instruction as knowledge acquisition. In this regard, computer-based systems that incorporate concepts from artificial intelligence may have a unique role, one that cannot be filled by non-interactive educational tools such as books or films, or even by interactive tools that merely implement a conventional teaching strategy. Artificial intelligence is concerned with the nature of mental processes and with ways of representing them in a dynamic fashion. Insofar as representations are inspectable, the reification of these processes to support a reflexive form of learning is a very promising prospect. To what extent the effects of reification can be enhanced with an active coaching strategy on the part of a system remains to be seen.

18.5 Aspects of didactic expertise

Like diagnosis, didactics is fundamentally a process of reasoning about reasoning and learning. As a pure problem-solving activity, it schemes transitions in knowledge states within the constraints imposed by the individual level and by a limited communication channel. On the basis of such a fundamental definition, the task of creating a pedagogical bridge between a model of communicable knowledge and a model of the student is extremely difficult and computationally costly. In practice, such a basic approach is often avoided: as with other domains of expertise, applied didactic knowledge takes more compiled forms.

Along these lines, the constraints imposed by limitations from the individual level have often been crystallized into communication conventions for the tutorial environment, which can themselves be considered as independent sources of constraints. That is why felicity conditions can actually be viewed as conventions, though their origins are presumably in cognitive limitations. In the same vein, general strategies for dealing with these constraints often take the form of pedagogical principles, which can be articulated in terms of the dimensions of the individual model.

As successful resolutions to conflicting requirements are discovered, experience is crystallized into known strategies and tactics; these take the form of frozen plans that incorporate fixed sets of diagnostic expectations along with built-in mechanisms for dealing with common breakdowns. At various levels, compiled didactic knowledge takes the form of well-established curricula, of tested lesson plans, of libraries of activities and presentation techniques, or of ready-made responses for the purpose of opportunistic action. The compilation of didactic experience parallels that of diagnostic experience as compiled didactic operations can progressively be placed in heuristic correspondence with diagnostic classification categories.

Diagnosis and didactics in knowledge communication systems

One goal we set for ourselves in this chapter was to gain some understanding of the importance of diagnosis as a design and research concern by considering its role in didactic processes. We have, in sum, identified three classes of circumstances, each with different implications for the respective roles of diagnosis and didactics.

In purely opportunistic strategies, the monitored activities provide a focus for both diagnostic and didactic activities, but diagnosis is the driving force in that it reveals opportunities for tutorial interventions. Indeed, pedagogical goals are associated with diagnostic units such as issues or rules, and their attainment is monitored by differential modeling. Thus the extent to which tutoring is possible is determined by diagnosis, both quantitatively (the proportion of opportunities that are recognized) and qualitatively (the precision with which the reason for each intervention is identified). This characteristic of the opportunistic approach favors a "diagnosis-driven" design process by which the didactic module is built around the diagnostic one.

By contrast, in purely plan-based strategies, the main task of diagnosis is to monitor the implementation of teaching plans that embody pedagogical goals. These plans provide a focus for diagnostic activities in the form of predictions about future states, with the consequence that differential modeling is performed in terms of plan-based expectations. This may imply a need to explain differences in terms of plan failures so that revisions can be made. The ensuing subordination does not imply that diagnosis is less important, but it warrants a "didactics-driven" design process by which the diagnostic module is built around the didactic one.

Finally, when diagnosis provides constraints for didactic deliberation and resources for constructing tailored didactic operations, there is no simple relation of subordination in either direction: both processes work in synergy. Because didactic capabilities are not fixed but can be enriched by diagnostic resources, they do not rigidly limit the relevance of diagnosis. The power of this synergetic process has not yet been explored systematically, since it requires very dynamic didactic operations that are mostly beyond the capabilities of current systems. Nevertheless, from a research standpoint, there is no evidence that interest in deep forms of diagnosis need be curbed. On the contrary, advances on both fronts, didactics and diagnosis, seem to go hand in hand.

Bibliographical notes

Two early papers discuss an active didactic component: Hartley and Sleeman (1973) suggest the use of means-ends rules and Laubsch (1975) the use of planning techniques. Some recent computationally oriented studies of teaching expertise come from the educational perspective. Leinhardt and Greeno (1986) analyze the planning procedures and data structures used by teachers in classrooms, and Leinhardt (1985) investigates the explanatory structure of a lesson sequence. Ohlsson (1987a) speculates about some implications of these studies for the design of tutoring systems; he views these systems as problem solvers involved in planning, and lays out some design principles supported by this view.

Not until recently has the idea of didactic planning been actually implemented in systems. Peachey and McCalla (1986) present a prototypical system for teaching basic concepts in economics; the system plans a short curriculum and dynamically reconsiders its plans during application. Breuker et al. (1987) are applying planning techniques for coaching interventions in the context of their intelligent help system EUROHELP. Macmillan and Sleeman (1987) report on SIIP (for Self-Improving Instructional Planner), a generic architecture for didactic planning based on the "blackboard" paradigm. Macmillan et al. (1986) discuss a list of issues central to didactic planning.

Chapter 19

Knowledge
communication

The presentation of Part III can be seen as a circular itinerary through topics in knowledge communication, as shown in Figure 19.1. It starts with a view of the computer as a representational medium for the knowledge to be conveyed, with an emphasis on the notion of process models. Evaluating the support that various models provide for communication, Part III distinguishes between compiled and articulate forms of knowledge, and discusses several dimensions of variability between knowledge states, dimensions that allow the construction of a student model. In this context, knowledge communication can be defined as the instigation of modifications in a student's knowledge state via an alternation of diagnostic and didactic steps. These active communication functions require expertise that can also take the form of computer-based process models. In this light, the whole endeavor presented in this book

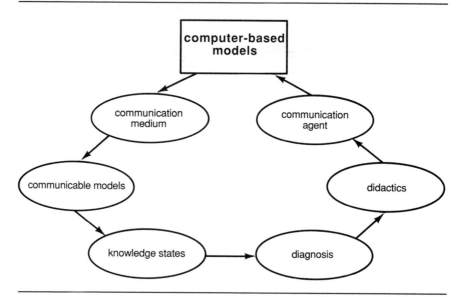

Figure 19.1 An itinerary through topics in knowledge communication.

can be considered as a series of attempts to create process models of interactive knowledge communication.

19.1   The components of knowledge communication

A convenient way to view the topics of the last five chapters as an investigation of process models of knowledge communication is to summarize these discussions with an abstract architecture, as illustrated in Figure 19.2. The different components retain the fourfold division of functions adopted so far, with the addition of a pedagogical module to provide some global coordination. The organization of all these modules around the model of communicable knowledge highlights its central role in supplying various levels of information about the domain.

19.1.1   The presentation level

Figure 19.2 distinguishes between modules in the upper and lower halves of the diagram. The two modules in the lower half do not directly take part in major pedagogical decisions. Instead, they support the communication process by making the representation of knowledge

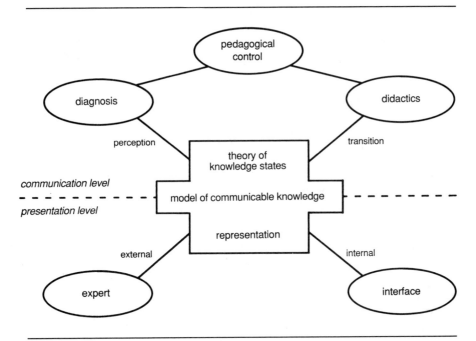

Figure 19.2 Components of an architecture for knowledge communication.

available. As the connections in the diagram illustrate, the expert and the interface modules respectively deal with the internal and external aspects of representation discussed in Chapter 14.

The expert module can either directly answer student questions, as in SCHOLAR and SOPHIE, or provide information to other modules when they need it. In WEST, for instance, the expert produces an ordered list of moves to be analyzed by pedagogical processes; in the GEOMETRY tutor, it is sometimes requested to perform proofs in order to check on the fruitfulness of a path chosen by the student. To extract useful information from the internal representation, the expert module applies general knowledge about reasoning processes (e.g., SCHOLAR) and about the meaning of information (e.g., SOPHIE), which can make it quite a complex subsystem.

In order to translate the flow of communication to and from the student, the interface module manages the devices to which the external representation is targeted. STEAMER connects dials on a display to internal variables; SOPHIE uses its semantic grammar, defined as a set of external conventions representing objects and actions in the domain, to parse the student's statements in terms of internal functions. In its management role, the interface module applies general knowledge about the way people relate to the conventions of its devices. For instance, the automated window management of GUIDON-WATCH is meant to provide an optimal compromise between the amount of information on the screen and the readability of the display. The development of such flexible, possibly domain-independent, *information presentation modules* is an active area of research in human-computer interaction, where potential roles for artificial intelligence principles are being explored (Richer and Clancey, 1985; Mackinlay, 1986). As the interface module takes on more dynamic responsibility for the presentation of instructional material, it may start to assume tasks of increasing pedagogical significance.

19.1.2   The communication level

The activities of the modules in the upper half of Figure 19.2 result in decisions that shape the course of instruction, alternating between perception and action. In their interactions with the model of communicable knowledge, diagnosis and didactics concentrate on the theory of knowledge states as it is defined in Chapter 16: the theory supplies domain-specific information with a pedagogical perspective.   These modules have both been discussed at length, with the conclusion that synergistic cooperation between the two is a key to knowledge communication. This motivates the addition of a pedagogical module to implement a coherent pedagogical strategy without the need to subordinate either module to the other.

The creation of a separate module responsible for optimizing the interplay of diagnosis and didactics makes explicit the special type of expertise involved in the overall management of pedagogical functions. This overall management includes decisions about the degree of control exercised by the system (e.g., coaching versus instructing in SPIRIT), the selection of strategic contexts (e.g., opportunistic versus plan-based contexts), the interleaving of pedagogical episodes, and the allocation of computational resources required by competing functions.   In the QUADRATIC tutor, the pedagogical module even monitors the validity of its own pedagogical principles, experimenting with possible improvements. The pedagogical module, whose expertise is neither diagnostic nor didactic in nature, reflects the global view of the knowledge communication process that a system implements.

19.1.3   The communication model

As knowledge communication unfolds over time, a system requires information about its interaction with a given student in order to maintain

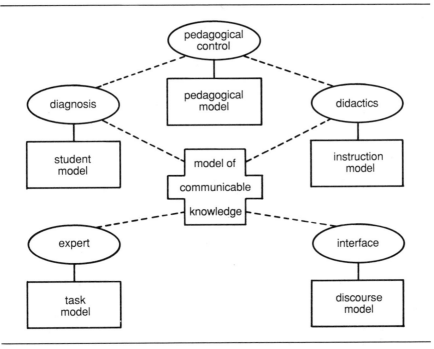

Figure 19.3 The different parts of the communication model.

consistency. The need to record this information has motivated the notion of a *communication model*, proposed in GUIDON and adopted in MENO-TUTOR. The communication model can be viewed as a student-specific database maintained by communication processes to support further decisions. It can be divided into a number of submodels, each of which is logically associated with one module of the abstract architecture shown in Figure 19.2. While these logical associations, mapped in Figure 19.3, do reflect physical interactions, they do not imply that the information contained in a submodel is for the exclusive use of the corresponding module.

- In the **task model**, the expert module keeps information about the circumstances in which a problem is posed. Although the system usually has access to final answers, evaluation and advice are often pedagogically useful only when placed in the context in which the student is making decisions. In WUSOR, for example, the system knows which caves contain dangers, but must maintain information about the warnings the student has been given so far in order to judge the quality of his moves. Similarly, GUIDON must consider which symptoms are known to the student in order to evaluate hypotheses, and SOPHIE must remember which measurements the student has made in order to critique the soundness of new measurements.

- The **discourse model** is maintained by the interface so as to resolve ambiguities and to ensure continuity in its use of conventions. For instance, the discourse model allows the system to avoid redundancies and to resolve ellipses and anaphorae. In both SOPHIE and ACE, when some information is missing, the discourse model can be searched backward for the "closest" mention of an element that could legally and logically complete the current utterance.

- The **student model** needs little introduction at this point. As we have seen, it can be descriptive or simulative, or a combination of the two. Each of its submodels—behavioral, epistemic, and individual—plays a distinct role in the continuity of the communication process.

- The **instruction model** maintained by the didactic module records important aspects of the instructional interaction with the student, such as topics that have been covered or explanations that have been given. It avoids repetitions and allows reminders; it also ensures the continuity of the session in terms of instructional actions, for instance when different levels of intervention are available for the same topic, as in SOPHIE-II's explanations or WEST's hints. In general, the instruction model is more than a sequential record of activities: it contains the current goals (as in SCHOLAR's agenda), as well as active plans. Because it can record expectations generated by didactic operations, it can support the detection and repair of breakdowns in communication.

- The **pedagogical model**, associated with the control component, keeps a record of the global strategic decisions and resulting contexts. An example of a pedagogical model is the QUADRATIC tutor's database of assertions, which keeps track of the success of pedagogical strategies and of the expected effects of modifying those strategies.

Since there can be some overlap in the information covered by the various parts of the communication model, the submodels are not necessarily disjoint in their implementations. However, they each represent fundamentally different perspectives. These distinctions can be clarified with some antinomial contrasts.

- *Task versus student*: although the task model does record problem-specific information made available to a specific student, it is important to note that it is *not* a weak form of student model at the behavioral level. Indeed, even when the task model is tailored to a given student and a given session, it does not attempt to reflect the problem-specific model possessed by the student, but only information explicitly made available via his interaction with the environment. As the student proceeds with problem solving, diagnosis updates the student model with decisions, additional inferences, and forgotten or misunderstood information, none of which are reflected in the task model. Conversely, the task model may reflect several possible decompositions of the task, only one of which has been adopted by the student.

- *Task versus instruction*: whereas the task model records problem-specific information that is available to the student from any external source, the instruction model is concerned with information given to the student with some didactic intention—information not only about the problem at hand but also about applicable expertise.

- *Student versus instruction*: whereas the student model attempts to capture the knowledge as it has been assimilated by the student, the instruction model simply records facts about the instructional interaction, regardless of its actual effect on the student. Thus each model represents a different viewpoint on the interaction, and one aspect of communication can be understood as a process of making these viewpoints agree.

- *Instruction versus pedagogical*: the instruction model keeps track of actions actually taken and of their expected results, while the pedagogical model is concerned with the global goals, strategic intentions, and principles that these actions implement.

Whether the strategic context is opportunistic or plan-based, the notion of a communication model broadens the concept of knowledge communication. Insofar as its submodels are used globally to support pedagogical decisions, it suggests a view of knowledge communication, not as the generation of isolated interventions, but as the construction of a *communication context* that is shared by the student and the system and in which the interaction develops.

19.2 Knowledge presentation

Systems like STEAMER or GUIDON-WATCH, and to some extent SOPHIE-I,[1] do not engage in active knowledge communication: rather, they simply make knowledge in their domains available to students. They can fulfill very useful pedagogical functions using almost exclusively

---

[1]SOPHIE-I can be said to perform some form of diagnosis in evaluating the student's hypotheses and measurements.

processes characteristic of the lower half of the diagram in Figure 19.2. In this sense, the dividing line of Figure 19.2 distinguishes between two classes of instructional systems involving artificial intelligence: active knowledge communication systems, which require all the functions in the diagram; and more passive systems, which require only those in the lower half, and which can be called *knowledge presentation systems*.

Although they comprise a subset of the functions of knowledge communication systems, knowledge presentation systems implement a radically different pedagogical approach. By simply making knowledge available rather than actively communicating it, they leave most of the responsibility of managing the learning process to the student, who acts as his own tutor. He is expected to have enough understanding of the domain and of his learning needs to decide what to explore or to focus on next, as well as to interpret what is presented. In this sense, knowledge presentation systems are related to microworlds, which use a restricted simulation to let students explore a domain. The difference between simulation-based microworlds and knowledge presentation systems derives from the AI component central to the latter. While a microworld environment simulates a domain under study, a knowledge presentation system simulates knowledge about this domain. The student does not explore the world: he explores knowledge about the world. STEAMER's notion of conceptual fidelity is precisely intended to capture this difference. In QUEST, for instance, the student visits conceptual models of electricity rather than simulated circuits. In GUIDON-WATCH, he directly witnesses the strategies of a reasoning process.

Because of this emphasis on knowledge, it is advantageous to view knowledge presentation systems as a subset of knowledge communication systems in spite of the difference in pedagogical approaches. This view brings to bear the notions of *communicability* and of reconstructive effectiveness within a communication environment, both of which are important regardless of the exact role the system is to play in the student's learning. In other words, knowledge presentation requires basically the same type of model of communicable knowledge as does active communication. Of course, it does not require a theory of knowledge states per se, since it is not actively involved with the student's knowledge state. However, most of the dimensions discussed earlier are relevant. For instance, a theory of viewpoints may be crucial to understanding design alternatives; and although a theory of bugs need not be incorporated into knowledge presentation systems, a study of common misconceptions may be very useful at the design stage in revealing errors that the presentation may attempt to prevent.

This kinship between the two types of systems is also corroborated by the fact that part of a knowledge communication system is potentially a knowledge presentation system. For instance, the original intent of the

STEAMER project was to produce a full tutor. Much energy went into designing the knowledge presentation part of the system, which turned out to be very useful by itself. Conversely, a knowledge presentation system is an ideal foundation on which to construct a coach or a real tutor by adding pedagogical modules that actively assist or instruct the student, a direction taken by the GUIDON project.

Knowledge presentation systems promise to be an important application area for many of the concepts presented in this book. From a design standpoint, they have the advantage of not requiring the full apparatus of active knowledge communication—with the complexity of a theory of knowledge states and the articulation of pedagogical expertise that are required for making tutoring effective. Thus such systems can take advantage of technological advances without waiting for advances on all other fronts.

From an educational standpoint, the notion of an AI-based learning environment is quite attractive. One can even envision AI-based versions of the LOGO paradigm, whereby students articulate knowledge by building AI models. Such environments provide students with the freedom to explore and a sense of control as they investigate a domain within a simulative context geared toward both operational knowledge and articulate conceptualization.

19.3 Knowledge communication

Even in the context of exploratory learning, augmenting the presentation level with active knowledge communication capabilities involving the modules of the upper half of Figure 19.2 usually extends the benefits derived from the instructional use of computer programs. Indeed, the unobtrusive interventions of a coaching component can save the student from problems typical of unguided learning such as stagnating, floundering excessively, or overlooking learning opportunities. In mixed-initiative tutoring and in more directive forms, components of active knowledge communication even move to center stage, often relegating the presentation level to supporting functions.

As a system assumes a more active pedagogical role and takes some dynamic responsibility for the student's learning, the nature of its internal model of expertise becomes crucial: this model provides the language in terms of which the systems can assess needs to adapt its actions. In this sense, intelligence at the pedagogical level is not possible without intelligence at the domain level, and the requirements of knowledge communication are more stringent that those of presentation (e.g., SOPHIE-I versus SOPHIE-III). However, with the use of nonsimulative diagnostic devices such as WEST's issues or MHO's bites, fully operational and articulate process models of domain expertise are not indispensable for constructing process models of communication functions.

Admittedly, adaptability in the best systems is rather coarse when compared to the way human teachers can weave diagnosis and didactics tightly together. The ability of teachers to move back and forth between compiled and articulate knowledge, in both diagnosis and didactics, also contrasts strikingly with current systems in which diagnosis in terms of compiled knowledge is the norm. Although these communication capabilities call for more studies of human tutoring and conversational mechanisms that are computationally oriented, the issue is more subtle. Bringing more intelligence into knowledge communication requires an understanding of the *communication environment* in which it takes place. In other words, intelligence is relative to an environment. The anthropomorphic view that more intelligence for systems means more humanlike capabilities can be as much of a distraction as it is an inspiration. Indeed, the communication environment created by two people and that created by a person and a machine are not likely to be the same, and the terms of the cooperation required for successful communication may differ in fundamental ways. Hence, computational models of knowledge communication will require new theories of knowledge communication, as computer-based systems evolve and as research in artificial intelligence and related disciplines provides more powerful models.

Chapter 20

Epilogue

This book has reported on the emergence of a research field concerned with process models of interactive knowledge communication. After this succession of possible solutions and open problems, the final verdict on how much has been accomplished is left to the reader: when some progress has been made on a very difficult issue, it is always possible to claim that very much or very little has been accomplished. Since there is no doubt that much remains to be done, let us conclude with a brief overview of potential contributions of this research, in order to provide an array of motivations for further work.

20.1 Direct outcome: useful systems

The most direct and obvious promise of the field is the production of actual systems useful for helping people acquire various forms of expertise through individualized learning. Furthermore, while most of the systems described here are tutoring systems, the technology developed for them is relevant beyond strictly instructional contexts, and can find potential applications in all kinds of computer systems that have to interact with human users.

As we have seen, AI-based instructional systems can vary greatly in the type of pedagogical approach they implement, and even in their use of the technology; they range from simulative reification to directive tutoring, from traditional problem-solving environments to BUGGY's simulations of students for teacher training. Thus, they accommodate very different learning models (e.g., GUIDON2 versus ACTP). In their use of artificial intelligence, projects can emphasize the notion of model of expertise (e.g., SOPHIE, QUEST, GUIDON) or that of appropriate response or intervention (e.g., WEST, MHO, ACTP).

The field has mainly concentrated on theoretical and technical aspects so far; however, preliminary exposures, some of which are listed in Figure 20.1, suggest that its products can be effective in realistic settings and that students tend to enjoy them. Speculations about the impact this research is likely to have on education are beyond the scope of this book. In fact, little attention has been paid to crucial practical issues—computational efficiency, robustness, speed of response, software engineering, cost effectiveness, validation by formal evaluation, and social acceptability and integration.[1] This focus reflects the fact that most systems built so far have been laboratory experiments primarily intended to demonstrate feasibility.

20.2 Indirect outcome: articulation of expertise

A recurring theme in the evolution of the projects surveyed in Part II has been an iterative search for models of expertise capable of supporting the communication of knowledge with some degree of generality. The multidimensional requirements of communicability and student modeling take the process of articulation much further than do the more straightforward

---

[1] For treatment of some of these issues, see the book by O'Shea and Self (1983) and the articles by Dede (1986, 1987).

systems	exposure
EXCHECK & LOGIC course	extensively used in university courses
BIP	used in college-level introductory programming courses;
SOPHIE-I	available over an electronic network (ARPA) for two years
SOPHIE-I & II	used in short electronics courses
WEST	used in an elementary school for four months
BUGGY	game played by teachers in training; also used by students
DEBUGGY	has diagnosed problems for thousands of students
STEAMER	used in classroom at Great Lake Naval Training Center
PROUST	used in some college introductory programming courses
GUIDON-WATCH	used in a medical school class
LISP tutor	used in college-level introductory programming courses; available commercially
GEOMETRY tutor	used for a term in a high-school class

Figure 20.1 Some experimentations with systems in actual use.

requirements of performance-oriented AI systems. An additional factor is the design of instructional interfaces oriented toward reification, which can produce notational tools for problem solving. With respect to the articulation of knowledge, Clancey (1986a) underlines the importance of the AI methodology inherited by the field: computational process models reify expertise; they can be put to work, studied, and iteratively refined as these studies produce new descriptors that become part of the model.

Quite apart from the prospect of producing useful systems, this articulation of domain expertise in the form of theories of knowledge states is itself a potentially significant contribution of the research. Similarly, the articulation of pedagogical expertise inherent in the design of general process models of knowledge communication can be useful beyond the realm of computer systems.

Interestingly, the converse is also true. Indeed, a further—less direct thus less obvious, but no less important—contribution of this research is its potential for drawing attention to aspects of expertise that cannot be easily articulated, or not at all. The difficulties that AI has run into has often resulted in a greater appreciation—and I am speaking from personal experience—for the amount of tacit knowledge that underlies both expertise and daily living. From a pedagogical standpoint, recognizing overtly the existence and significance of these unarticulated aspects can lead to a more realistic view of expertise and of the processes necessary for acquiring it.

20.3   Related research: motivation and validation

Insofar as knowledge communication touches upon fundamental epistemological, cognitive, pedagogical, linguistic, and cultural issues, it can
both motivate and validate related research.   In fact, as a research
context, knowledge communication has shown a remarkable propensity
for spawning seminal investigations. In the course of our presentation,
we have had opportunities to show the relevance of just about every area
of research in artificial intelligence; moreover, the challenge of knowledge
communication demands an unusual convergence of abilities, a fact
reflected in the complexity of some of the systems the field has produced.
Of particular interest is the ability to reason about other reasoning agents
within a communication environment.

   Occurring as it does at the crossroads of artificial intelligence, epistemology, psychology, education, linguistics, anthropology, and man-
machine studies—not to mention the subject matters themselves—this
research is inherently interdisciplinary. The complexity of the task of
knowledge communication and its universality as a manifestation of
human intelligence make computational models of the process revealing
testbeds for theories and techniques in all the disciplines involved.

20.4   Research topic: knowledge and communication

Finally, an aspect of this research that tends to be overlooked is that process models of knowledge communication are themselves a fundamental
topic of the quest for principles of intelligence. This point—alluded to in
the introduction—has received much support in our tour of projects and
merits a brief if speculative elaboration. We have observed that the quest
for communicability invariably leads to epistemological and cognitive
insights. This observation invites the conjecture that communicability
is often not just a characteristic to be imposed upon knowledge for
communication purposes, but an attribute deeply rooted in knowledge
itself. In other words, knowledge that is communicable may have unique
properties whose ramifications extend beyond communication purposes.

   An intuition about why this should be the case is derived from the
notion of a communication environment as a resource for the articulation
of knowledge. Both the generation and the interpretation of knowledge
communication can be viewed as processes of classification by which
knowledge and the use of knowledge are mapped onto and off the set
of distinctions made possible by the categories of the communication

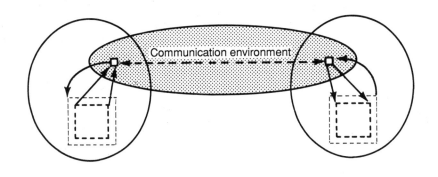

Figure 20.2 Abstract view of the process of knowledge communication.

environment.[2] Knowledge is articulated when emergent properties or unknown phenomena receive classificatory descriptions in the conceptual framework set by the communication environment. This process is amplified by the feedback obtained from diagnosis, which provides a sounding board for the articulation of knowledge. From this fundamental perspective, generation and interpretation of communication are symmetrical, as illustrated in Figure 20.2. Thus both the knowledge states involved in knowledge communication are modified: knowledge communication is viewed as a dynamic interaction between intelligent agents by which knowledge states are engaged in a process of expansion and articulation.

Note that the whole process depicted in Figure 20.2 is as important as the communication content: in bouncing back and forth between the communication environment and personal experience, the communication process establishes classification schemes required for giving meaning to the categories of this environment and for articulating new distinctions about the world. Eventually, the communication process itself is integrated into the knowledge of both the communicator and the recipient: these categories along with their classification schemes then become reasoning tools that can be used even when no communication is required.

Because these classifications carry with them the reflection of experience against the communication environment, their internal use reveals a striking connection between communication and reflexive reasoning.

---

[2]In this sense, a communication environment is similar to a language. However, a communication environment is a more general notion and is not to be confused with a set of linguistic utterances.

Along these lines, it is interesting to wonder how communication capabilities such as diagnosis and didactics might affect reasoning when they are applied reflexively. For instance, knowledge about common errors or about ways errors are likely to be generated can constitute a vital asset of expertise that takes the form of a reflexive theory of bugs. Indeed, experts often know about certain types of errors which people in general or they in particular are prone to. As a result, they can make a conscious effort to avoid these errors, and can readily detect, understand, and correct them, should they arise anyway. Similarly, theories of knowledge states applied reflexively can give rise to self-directed learning.

In the context of a quest for principles of intelligence, these remarks stimulate the conjecture that models of intelligence that are capable of sophisticated knowledge communication differ fundamentally from those that are not, in ways beyond the mere ability to communicate. In addition, the permeation of reasoning processes by the communication environment highlights the importance of a culture—in some sense, a wider communication environment—in the development of sophisticated thoughts. The fact that the development of abstract forms of intelligence may be inherently bound to the culture in which knowledge is communicated makes the study of learning and teaching within a communication environment a central concern for AI. Although it is obviously beyond the scope of this book to do more than touch upon these fascinating themes, they are mentioned here in the hope of leaving the reader with a sense of excitement about their potential scientific significance.

From a pedagogical standpoint, this emphasis on the communication process as a resource for warranting and articulating knowledge again highlights the importance of communication environments. In this respect, concepts such as process models, theories of knowledge states, reification, diagnosis, and didactics all reflect a variety of relevant research directions whereby technology converges with studies of human cognition: they suggest that systems of the type described in this book have an unusual potential for supporting interesting, perhaps quite novel, communication environments. Needless to say, we have merely scratched the surface, and much interdisciplinary research is now required. However, the prospects are promising, and the definition and investigation of these new communication environments is a worthwhile enterprise—one that can contribute to making learning at once active, entertaining, effective, and rewarding, and to gearing tomorrow's human community toward the full development of individuals.

Bibliography

Abelson, H.; and diSessa, A.A. (1980) *Turtle Geometry: The Computer as a Medium for Exploring Mathematics.* MIT Press, Cambridge, Massachusetts.

Adam, A.; and Laurent, J.-P. (1980) LAURA: a system to debug student programs. *Artificial Intelligence*, vol. 15, pp. 75–122.

Alderman, D.L. (1979) Evaluation of the TICCIT computer-assisted instructional system in the community college. *SIGCUE Bulletin*, vol. 13, no. 3, pp. 5–17.

Anderson, J.R. (1983) *The Architecture of Cognition.* Harvard University Press, Cambridge, Massachusetts.

Anderson, J.R. (1984) Cognitive psychology and intelligent tutoring. *Proceedings of the Cognitive Science Society Conference*, Boulder, Colorado, pp. 37–43.*

Anderson, J.R.; Farrell, R.G.; and Sauers, R. (1984a) Learning to program in LISP. *Cognitive Science*, vol. 8, no. 2, pp. 87–129.

Anderson, J.R.; Boyle, C.F.; Farrell, R.G.; and Reiser, B.J. (1984b) Cognitive principles in the design of computer tutors. *Proceedings of the Sixth Cognitive Science Society Conference*, Boulder, Colorado, pp. 2–8.*

Anderson, J.R.; and Jeffries, R. (1985) Novice LISP errors: undetected losses of information from working memory. *Human-Computer Interaction*, vol. 1, no. 2, pp. 107–131.

Anderson, J.R.; and Reiser, B.J. (1985) The LISP tutor. *Byte*, vol. 10, no. 4, pp. 159–175.

Anderson, J.R.; Boyle, C.F.; and Reiser, B.J. (1985a) Intelligent tutoring systems. *Science*, vol. 228, no. 4698, pp. 456–462.

Anderson, J.R.; Boyle, C.F.; and Yost, G. (1985b) The geometry tutor. *Proceedings of the International Joint Conference on Artificial Intelligence*, Los Angeles, pp. 1–7.**

Anderson, J.R.; and Skwarecki, E. (1986) The automated tutoring of introductory programming. *CACM*, vol. 29, no. 9, pp. 842–849.

Anderson, J.R.; and Thompson, R. (1986) Use of analogy in a production system architecture. *Unpublished Manuscript*, Department of Psychology, Carnegie-Mellon University, Pittsburgh, Pennsylvania.

Baecker, R.; and Buxton, W. (1987) *Readings in Human-Computer Interaction*. Morgan Kaufmann, Los Altos, California.

Barr, A.; Beard, M.; and Atkinson, R.C. (1975) Information networks for CAI curriculums. In Lecareme, O.; and Lewis, R. (Eds.) *Computers in Education*, pp. 477–482. North-Holland, Amsterdam, The Netherlands.

Barr, A.; and Beard, M. (1976) An instructional interpreter for BASIC. In Colman, R.; and Lorton, P. Jr. (Eds.) *Computer Science and Education. ACM SIGCSE Bulletin*, vol. 8, no. 1, (or *ACM SIGCUE Topics*, vol. 2), pp. 325–334.

Barr, A.; Beard, M.; and Atkinson, R.C. (1976) The computer as a tutorial laboratory: the Stanford BIP Project. *Int Jrnl Man-Machine Studies*, vol. 8, pp. 567–596.

Barr, A.; Bennett, J.S.; and Clancey, W.J. (1979) Transfer of expertise: a theme for AI research. *Working Paper HPP-79-11*. Heuristic Programming Project, Stanford University, Stanford, California.

Barzilay, A. (1984) *An expert system for tutoring probability theory*. Doctoral dissertation, University of Pittsburgh, Pittsburgh, Pennsylvania.

Barzilay, A. (1985) SPIRIT: a flexible tutoring style in an intelligent tutoring system. *Proceedings of the Second Conference on Artificial Intelligence Applications*, Miami Beach, Florida, pp. 336–341. IEEE Computer Society Press, Washington, D.C.

Blaine, L.H.; and Smith, R.L. (1977) Intelligent CAI: the role of the curriculum in suggesting computational models of reasoning. *Proceedings of the National ACM Conference*, Seattle, Washington, pp. 241–246. Association for Computing Machinery, New York.

Blaine, L.H. (1981) Programs for structured proofs. In Suppes, P. (Ed.) *University-level Computer-assisted Instruction at Stanford: 1968–1980*. Institute for Mathematical Studies in the Social Sciences, Stanford University, Stanford, California.

Blaine, L.H. (1982) EXCHECK. In Barr, A.; and Feigenbaum, E.A. (Eds.) *Handbook of Artificial Intelligence* (vol. II). Addison-Wesley, Reading, Massachusetts.

Bloom, B.S. (1984) The 2 sigma problem: the search for methods of group instruction as effective as one-to-one tutoring. *Educational Researcher*, vol. 13, pp. 4–16.

Bobrow, D.G. (Ed.) (1984) *Qualitative Reasoning about Physical Systems*. MIT Press, Cambridge, Massachusetts. (Reprint from vol. 24 of *Artificial Intelligence*; copublished with North-Holland, Amsterdam, The Netherlands.)

Bonar, J.G. (1985a) *Understanding the Bugs of Novice Programmers*. Doctoral dissertation, Department of Computer and Information Science, University of Massachusetts, Amherst, Massachusetts.

Bonar, J.G. (1985b) Mental models of programming loops. *Technical Report*. Learning Research and Development Center, University of Pittsburgh, Pittsburgh, Pennsylvania.

Bonar, J.G. (1985c) Bite-sized intelligent tutoring. *ITSG Newsletter 85-3*. Learning Research and Development Center, University of Pittsburgh, Pittsburgh, Pennsylvania.

Bonar, J.G.; and Soloway, E.M. (1985) Preprogramming knowledge: a major source of misconceptions in novice programmers. *Human-Computer Interaction*, vol. 1, no. 2, pp. 133–161.

Bonar, J.G.; and Weil, W. (1985) An informal programming language. Paper presented at the meeting *Expert Systems in Government*, October, Washington, D.C.

Bonar, J.G.; Cunningham, R.; and Schultz, J. (1986) An object-oriented architecture for intelligent tutoring. *Proceedings of the ACM Conference on Object-Oriented Programming Systems, Languages and Applications*. Association for Computing Machinery, New York.

Bork, A. (1980) Physics in the Irvine Educational Technology Center. *Computers and Education*, vol. 4, pp. 37–57.

Bork, A. (1981) *Learning with Computers*. Digital Press, Bedford, Massachusetts.

Bork, A. (1986a) *Learning with Personal Computers*. Harper and Row, New York.

Bork, A. (1986b) Nontrivial, nonintelligent computer-based learning. *Technical Report*. Educational Technology Center, University of California, Irvine, California.

Boyle, C.F.; and Anderson, J.R. (1984) Acquisition and automated instruction of geometry skills. Paper presented at the *Annual Meeting of the AERA*, New Orleans. American Educational Research Association, Washington, D.C.

Brachman, R.J.; and Levesque, H.J. (Eds.) (1985) *Readings in Knowledge Representation*. Morgan Kaufmann, Los Altos, California.

Breuker, J. (in press) Coaching in help systems. In Self, J.A. (Ed.) *Artificial Intelligence and Human Learning: Intelligent Computer-aided Instruction*. Chapman and Hall, London.

Breuker, J.; Winkels, R.; and Sandberg, J. (1987) Coaching strategies for help systems: EUROHELP. *Abstracts of the Third International Conference on Artificial Intelligence and Education*, p. 16. Learning Research and Development Center, University of Pittsburgh, Pittsburgh, Pennsylvania.

Brooks, R.E. (1977) Towards a theory of the cognitive processes in computer programming. *Int Jrnl Man-Machine Studies*, vol. 9, pp. 737–751.

Brown, J.S.; Burton, R.R.; and Zdydel, F. (1973) A model-driven question-answering system for mixed-initiative computer-assisted instruction. *IEEE Transactions on Systems, Man, and Cybernetics*, vol. 3, pp. 248–257.

Brown, J.S.; Burton, R.R.; and Bell, A.G. (1974) SOPHIE: a sophisticated instructional environment for teaching electronic troubleshooting. *BBN Report 2790*. Bolt Beranek and Newman Inc., Cambridge, Massachusetts.

Brown, J.S.; and Burton, R.R. (1975) Multiple representation of knowledge for tutorial reasoning. In Bobrow, D.; and Collins, A. (Eds.) *Representation and Understanding: Studies in Cognitive Science*. Academic Press, New York.

Brown, J.S.; Burton, R.R.; and Bell, A.G. (1975a) SOPHIE: a step towards a reactive learning environment. *Int Jrnl Man-Machine Studies*, vol. 7, pp. 675–696.

Brown, J.S.; Burton, R.R.; Miller, M.L.; de Kleer, J.; Purcell, S.; Hausman, C.L.; and Bobrow, R. (1975b) Steps toward a theoretical foundation for complex knowledge-based CAI. *BBN Report 3135 (ICAI Report 2)*. Bolt Beranek and Newman Inc., Cambridge, Massachusetts.

Brown, J.S.; Rubinstein, R.; and Burton, R.R. (1976) Reactive learning environment for computer-assisted electronics instruction. *BBN Report 3314*. Bolt Beranek and Newman Inc., Cambridge, Massachusetts.

Brown, J.S. (1977) Uses of AI and advanced computer technology in education. In Seidel, R.J.; and Rubin, M. (Eds.) *Computers and*

Communications: Implications for Education. Academic Press, New York.

Brown, J.S.; and Goldstein, I.P. (1977) *Computers in a Learning Society.* Testimony for the House Science and Technology Committee, Publication no. 23-082-0. U.S. Government Printing Office, Washington, D.C.

Brown, J.S.; Burton, R.R.; Hausman, C.L.; Goldstein, I.; Huggins, B.; and Miller, M.L. (1977a) Aspects of a theory for automated student modeling. *BBN Report 3549 (ICAI Report 4).* Bolt Beranek and Newman Inc., Cambridge, Massachusetts.

Brown, J.S.; Burton, R.R.; and Larkin, K.M. (1977b) Representing and using procedural bugs for educational purpose. *Proceedings of the National ACM Conference,* Seattle, Washington, pp. 247–255. Association for Computing Machinery, New York.

Brown, J.S.; and Burton, R.R. (1978a) Diagnostic models for procedural bugs in basic mathematical skills. *Cognitive Science,* vol. 2, pp. 155–191.

Brown, J.S.; and Burton, R.R. (1978b) A paradigmatic example of an artificially intelligent instructional system. *Int Jrnl of Man-Machine Studies,* vol. 10, pp. 323–339.

Brown, J.S.; Collins, A.; and Harris, G. (1978) Artificial Intelligence and learning strategies. In O'Neil, H. (Ed.) *Learning Strategies.* Academic Press, New York.

Brown, J.S.; and VanLehn, K. (1980). Repair theory: a generative theory of bugs in procedural skills. *Cognitive Science,* vol. 4, pp. 379–426.

Brown, J.S.; Burton, R.R.; and de Kleer, J. (1982) Pedagogical, natural language, and knowledge engineering techniques in SOPHIE I, II, and III. In Sleeman, D.H.; and Brown, J.S. (Eds.) *Intelligent Tutoring Systems.* Academic Press, London.

Brown, J.S.; and VanLehn, K. (1982) Toward a generative theory of "bugs." In Carpenter, T.; Moser, J.; and Romberg, T. (Eds.) *Addition and Subtraction: A Cognitive Perspective.* Lawrence Erlbaum Associates, Hillsdale, New Jersey.

Brown, J.S. (1983a) Learning-by-doing revisited for electronic learning environments. In White, M.A. (Ed.) *The Future of Electronic Learning.* Lawrence Erlbaum Associates, Hillsdale, New Jersey.

Brown, J.S. (1983b) Process versus product: a perspective on tools for communal and informal electronic learning. In *Report from the Learning Lab: Education in the Electronic Age,* Educational Broadcasting Corporation. (Reprinted in *Journal of Educational Computing Research* (1985), vol. 1, pp. 179–201.)

Brown, J.S.; and de Kleer, J. (1984) A framework for a qualitative physics. *Proceedings of the Sixth Cognitive Science Society Conference,* Boulder, Colorado, pp. 11–17.*

Brown, J.S.; and Greeno, J.G. (1984) Report of the research briefing panel on information technology in precollege education. In *Research Briefings 1984*. National Academy Press, Washington, D.C.

Brown, J.S. (1985) Idea amplifiers: new kinds of electronic learning. *Educational Horizons*, vol. 63, pp. 108–112.

Brown, J.S.; and Burton, R.R. (1986) Reactive learning environments for teaching electronic troubleshooting. In Rouse, W.B. (Ed.) *Advances in Man-Machine Systems Research*. JAI Press, Greenwich, Connecticut.

Buchanan, B.G.; Sutherland, G.L.; and Feigenbaum, E.A. (1969) Heuristic DENDRAL: a program for generating explanatory hypotheses in organic chemistry. In Meltzer, B.; and Michie, D. (Eds.) *Machine Intelligence*, vol. 4. Edinburgh University Press, Edinburgh, Scotland.

Bunderson, C.V. (1974) The design and production of learner-controlled courseware for the TICCIT system: a progress report. *Int Jrnl Man-Machine Studies*, vol. 6, pp. 479–492.

Bundy, A. (1983) *The Computer Modelling of Mathematical Reasoning*. Academic Press, London.

Burnstein, M. (1983) Concept formation by incremental analogical reasoning and debugging. *Proceedings of the International Machine Learning Workshop*, University of Illinois, Urbana-Champaign, Illinois.

Burton, R.R. (1975) *Semantically-centered parsing*. Doctoral dissertation, University of California, Irvine, California.

Burton, R.R. (1976) Semantic grammars: an engineering technique for constructing natural language understanding systems. *BBN Report 3453 (ICAI Report 3)*. Bolt Beranek and Newman Inc., Cambridge, Massachusetts.

Burton, R.R.; and Brown, J.S. (1976) A tutoring and student modeling paradigm for gaming environments. In Colman, R.; and Lorton, P. Jr. (Eds.) *Computer Science and Education. ACM SIGCSE Bulletin*, vol. 8, no. 1, (or *ACM SIGCUE Topics*, vol. 2), pp. 236–246.

Burton, R.R.; and Brown, J.S. (1977) Semantic grammar: a technique for constructing natural language interfaces to instructional systems. *BBN Report 3587 (ICAI Report 5)*. Bolt Beranek and Newman Inc., Cambridge, Massachusetts.

Burton, R.R.; and Brown, J.S. (1979a) Toward a natural language capability for computer-assisted instruction. In O'Neil, H. (Ed.) *Procedures for Instructional Systems Development*. Academic Press, New York.

Burton, R.R.; and Brown, J.S. (1979b) An investigation of computer coaching for informal learning activities. *Int Jrnl of Man-Machine Studies*, vol. 11, pp. 5–24. (Reprinted in Sleeman, D.H.; and Brown, J.S. (Eds.) *Intelligent Tutoring Systems*. Academic Press, London.)

Burton, R.R. (1982) Diagnosing bugs in a simple procedural skill. In Sleeman, D.H.; and Brown, J.S. (Eds.) *Intelligent Tutoring Systems.* Academic Press, London.

Burton, R.R.; Brown, J.S.; and Fischer, G. (1984) Analysis of skiing as a success model of instruction: manipulating the learning environment to enhance skill acquisition. In Rogoff, B.; and Lave, J. (Eds.) *Everyday Cognition: Its Development in Social Context.* Harvard University Press, Cambridge, Massachusetts.

Carbonell, J.R. (1970a) *Mixed-Initiative Man-Computer Instructional Dialogues.* Doctoral dissertation, Massachusetts Institute of Technology, Cambridge, Massachusetts.

Carbonell, J.R. (1970b) AI in CAI: an artificial intelligence approach to computer-assisted instruction. *IEEE Transactions on Man-Machine Systems,* vol. 11, no. 4, pp. 190–202.

Carbonell, J.R.; and Collins, A. (1973) Natural semantics in artificial intelligence. *Proceedings of the Third International Joint Conference on Artificial Intelligence,* Stanford, California, pp. 344–351.**

Carr, B. (1977) Wusor-II: a computer-aided instruction program with student modeling capabilities. *AI Lab Memo 417 (Logo Memo 45).* Massachusetts Institute of Technology, Cambridge, Massachusetts.

Carr, B.; and Goldstein, I.P. (1977) Overlays: a theory of modeling for computer-aided instruction. *AI Lab Memo 406 (Logo Memo 40).* Massachusetts Institute of Technology, Cambridge, Massachusetts.

CERL (Computer-based Education Research Laboratory) (1977) *Demonstration of the PLATO IV computer-based education system.* Final report, University of Illinois, Urbana-Champaign, Illinois.

Charniak, E.; and McDermott, D. (1986) *Introduction to Artificial Intelligence.* Addison-Wesley, Reading, Massachusetts.

Chi, M.T.H.; Feltovich, P.J.; and Glaser, R. (1981) Categorization and representation of physics problems by experts and novices. *Cognitive Science,* vol. 5, pp. 121–152.

Chipman, S.F.; Segal, J.W.; and Glaser, R. (Eds.) (1985) *Thinking and Learning Skills: Research and Open Questions* (vol. II). Lawrence Erlbaum Associates, Hillsdale, New Jersey.

Clancey, W.J. (1979a) *Transfer of rule-based expertise through a tutorial dialogue.* Doctoral dissertation, Stanford University, Stanford, California.

Clancey, W.J. (1979b) Dialogue management for rule-based tutorial. *Proceedings of the Sixth International Joint Conference on Artificial Intelligence,* Tokyo, pp. 155–161.**

Clancey, W.J. (1979c) Tutoring rules for guiding a case method dialogue. *Int Jrnl Man-Machine Studies,* vol. 11, pp. 25–49. (Reprinted in Sleeman, D.H.; and Brown, J.S. (Eds.) *Intelligent Tutoring Systems.* Academic Press, London.)

Clancey, W.J.; and Letsinger, R. (1981) NEOMYCIN: reconfiguring a rule-based expert system for application to teaching. *Proceedings of the Seventh International Joint Conference on Artificial Intelligence*, Vancouver, pp. 829–835.** (also reprinted in Clancey, W.J.; and Shortliffe, E.H. (Eds.) (1984) *Medical Artificial Intelligence: The First Decade*. Addison-Wesley, Reading, Massachusetts.)

Clancey, W.J.; Bennett, J.S.; and Cohen, P.R. (1982) Applications-oriented AI research: education. In Barr, A.; and Feigenbaum, E.A. (Eds.) *Handbook of Artificial Intelligence*. Addison-Wesley, Reading, Massachusetts.

Clancey, W.J. (1983a) The advantages of abstract control knowledge in expert system design. *Proceedings of the National Conference on Artificial Intelligence*, Washington, D.C., pp. 74–78.**

Clancey, W.J. (1983b) The epistemology of a rule-based expert system: a framework for explanation. *Artificial Intelligence*, vol. 20, no. 3, pp. 215–252. (Reprinted in Buchanan, B.G.; and Shortliffe, E.H. (Eds.) *Rule-based Expert System: The MYCIN Experiment*. Addison-Wesley, Reading, Massachusetts.)

Clancey, W.J. (1983c) GUIDON. *Journal of Computer-Based Instruction*, vol. 10, no. 1, pp. 8–14.

Clancey, W.J. (1984a) Methodology for building an intelligent tutoring system. In Kintsch, W.; Polson, P.G.; and Miller, J.R. (Eds.) *Methods and Tactics in Cognitive Science*. Lawrence Erlbaum Associates, Hillsdale, New Jersey.

Clancey, W.J. (1984b) Acquiring, representing, and evaluating a competence model of diagnosis. *HPP Memo 84-2*. Knowledge Systems Lab, Stanford University, Stanford, California. (To appear in Chi, M.T.H.; Glaser, R.; and Farr, M. (Eds.) *Contributions to the Nature of Expertise*.)

Clancey, W.J. (1984c) Classification problem solving. *Proceedings of the National Conference on Artificial Intelligence*, Austin, Texas, pp. 49–55.**

Clancey, W.J. (1984d) Teaching classification problem solving. *Proceedings of the Cognitive Science Society Conference*, Boulder, Colorado, pp. 44–46.*

Clancey, W.J.; Shortliffe, E.H.; and Buchanan, B.G. (1984) Intelligent computer-aided instruction for medical diagnosis. In Clancey, W.J.; and Shortliffe, E.H. (Eds.) *Medical Artificial Intelligence: The First Decade*. Addison-Wesley, Reading, Massachusetts.

Clancey, W.J. (1985) Heuristic classification. *Artificial Intelligence*, vol. 27, no. 3, pp. 289–350.

Clancey, W.J. (1986a) From GUIDON to NEOMYCIN and HERACLES in twenty short lessons: ONR final report 1979–1985. *AI Magazine*, vol. 7, no. 3, pp. 40–60.

Clancey, W.J. (1986b) Qualitative student models. In Traub, J.F. (Ed.) *Annual Reviews of Computer Science*, vol. 1, pp. 381–450. Annual Reviews, Inc., Palo Alto, California.

Clancey, W.J.; Richer, M.; Wilkins, D.C.; Barnhouse, S.; Kapsner, C.; Leserman, D.; Macias, J.; Merchant, A.; and Rodolitz, N. (1986) GUIDON-DEBUG: the student as knowledge engineer. *Knowledge Systems Lab Report KSL-86-34*, Department of Computer Science, Stanford University, Stanford, California.

Clancey, W.J. (1987a) *Knowledge-based Tutoring: The GUIDON Program*. MIT Press, Cambridge, Massachusetts.

Clancey, W.J. (1987b) The knowledge engineer as student: metacognitive bases for asking good questions. In Mandl, H.; and Lesgold, A.M. (Eds.) *Learning Issues for Intelligent Tutoring Systems*. Springer-Verlag, New York.

Clement, J. (1983) A conceptual model discussed by Galileo and used intuitively by physics students. In Gentner, D.; and Stevens, A.L. (Eds.) *Mental Models*. Lawrence Erlbaum Associates, Hillsdale, New Jersey.

Collins, A.; Warnock, E.H.; Aiello, N.; and Miller, M.L. (1975a) Reasoning from incomplete knowledge. In Bobrow, D.; and Collins, A. (Eds.) *Representation and Understanding: Studies in Cognitive Science*. Academic Press, New York.

Collins, A.; Warnock, E.H.; and Passafiume, J. (1975b) Analysis and synthesis of tutorial dialogues. In Bower, G. (Ed.) *The Psychology of Learning and Motivation* (vol. IX). Academic Press, New York.

Collins, A.; and Grignetti, M. (1975) Intelligent CAI. *BBN Report 3181*. Bolt Beranek and Newman Inc., Cambridge, Massachusetts.

Collins, A. (1977) Processes in Acquiring Knowledge. In Anderson, R.C.; Spiro, R.J.; and Montague, W.E. (Eds.) *Schooling and the Acquisition of Knowledge*. Lawrence Erlbaum Associates, Hillsdale, New Jersey.

Collins, A.; and Stevens, A.L. (1982) Goals and strategies for inquiry teachers. In Glaser, R. (Ed.) *Advances in Instructional Psychology* (vol. II). Lawrence Erlbaum Associates, Hillsdale, New Jersey.

Collins, A.; and Gentner, D. (1983) Multiple models of evaporation processes. *Proceedings of the Fifth Cognitive Science Society Conference.**

Collins, A.; and Stevens, A.L. (1983) A cognitive theory of interactive teaching. In Reigeluth, C.M. (Ed.) *Instructional Design Theories and Models: An Overview*. Lawrence Erlbaum Associates, Hillsdale, New Jersey.

Collins, A. (1985a) Teaching reasoning skills. In Chipman, S.F.; Segal, J.W.; and Glaser, R. (Eds.) *Thinking and Learning Skills: Research and Open Questions*. Lawrence Erlbaum Associates, Hillsdale, New Jersey.

Collins, A. (1985b) Component models of physical systems. *Proceedings of the Seventh Cognitive Society Conference*, Irvine, California, pp. 80–89.*

Collins, A.; and Brown, J.S. (1987) The computer as a tool for learning through reflection. In Mandl, H.; and Lesgold, A.M. (Eds.) *Learning Issues for Intelligent Tutoring Systems*. Springer-Verlag, New York.

Collins, A.; Brown, J.S.; and Newman, S. (in press) Cognitive apprenticeship: teaching the craft of reading, writing and mathematics. In Resnick, L.B. (Ed.) *Cognition and instruction: issues and agendas*. Lawrence Erlbaum Associates, Hillsdale, New Jersey.

Cosic, C.L. (1985) Enhanced learning by discovery. *Technical Report*. Learning Research and Development Center, University of Pittsburgh, Pittsburgh, Pennsylvania.

Davis, R. (1978) Knowledge acquisition in rule-based systems: knowledge about representations as a basis for system construction and maintenance. In Waterman, D.; and Hayes-Roth, F. (Eds.) *Pattern-directed Inference Systems*. Academic Press, New York.

Dede, C. (1986) A review and synthesis of recent research in ICAI. *Int Jrnl Man-Machine Studies*, vol. 24, pp. 329–353.

Dede, C. (1987) Implications of the possible implementation of artificial intelligence based educational devices. *Technical Report*. University of Houston, Clear Lake, Texas.

de Kleer, J. (1979) The origin and resolution of ambiguities in causal arguments. In *Proceeding of the Sixth International Joint Conference on Artificial Intelligence*, Tokyo, pp. 197–203. **

de Kleer, J.; and Brown, J.S. (1981) Mental models of physical systems and their acquisition. In Anderson, J.R. (Ed.) *Cognitive Skills and Their Acquisition*. Lawrence Erlbaum Associates, Hillsdale, New Jersey.

de Kleer, J.; and Brown, J.S. (1982) Some issues on mechanistic mental models. *Proceedings of the Fourth Cognitive Science Society Conference*.*

de Kleer, J.; and Brown, J.S. (1983) Assumptions and ambiguities in mechanistic mental models. In Gentner, D.; and Stevens, A.L. (Eds.) *Mental Models*. Lawrence Erlbaum Associates, Hillsdale, New Jersey.

de Kleer, J.; and Brown, J.S. (1984) A physics based on confluences. *Artificial Intelligence*, vol. 24, pp. 7–83. (Reprinted in Bobrow, D.G. (Ed.) *Qualitative Reasoning about Physical Systems*. MIT Press, Cambridge, Massachusetts.)

de Kleer, J. (1986) An assumption-based truth-maintenance system. *Artificial Intelligence*, vol. 28, pp. 127–162.

de Kleer, J. (in press) Qualitative physics. In *The Encyclopedia of Artificial Intelligence*. Wiley, New York.

diSessa, A.A. (1983) Phenomenology and the evolution of intuition. In Gentner, D.; and Stevens, A.L. (Eds.) *Mental Models*. Lawrence Erlbaum Associates, Hillsdale, New Jersey.

Doignon, J.-P.; and Falmagne, J.-C. (1985) Spaces for the assessment of knowledge. *Int Jrnl Man-Machine Studies*, vol. 23, pp. 175–196.

Doyle, J. (1979) A truth maintenance system. *Artificial Intelligence*, vol. 12, pp. 231–272.

Dreyfus, H.L.; and Dreyfus, S.E. (1984) Putting computers in their proper place: analysis versus intuition in the classroom. *Teacher College Record*, vol. 85, no. 4, pp. 578–601.

Dreyfus, H.L.; and Dreyfus, S.E. (1986) *Mind over Machine: Human Intuition and Expertise in the Era of the Computer*. Free Press, New York.

Farrell, R.G.; Anderson, J.R.; and Reiser, B.J. (1984a) Interactive student modeling in a computer-based LISP tutor. *Proceedings of the Sixth Cognitive Science Society Conference*, Boulder, Colorado, pp. 152–155.*

Farrell, R.G.; Anderson, J.R.; and Reiser, B.J. (1984b) An interactive computer-based tutor for LISP. *Proceedings of the National Conference on Artificial Intelligence*, Austin, Texas, pp. 106–109.**

Fawcett, H.P.; and Cummins, K.B. (1970) *The Teaching of Mathematics from Counting to Calculus*. Merrill Publishing, Columbus, Ohio.

Fischer, G.; Brown, J.S.; and Burton, R.R. (1978) Aspects of a theory of simplification, debugging, and coaching. *Proceedings of the Second Annual Conference of the Canadian Society for Computational Studies of Intelligence*, Toronto, pp. 139–145.

Fischer, G. (1987) A critic for Lisp. *Abstracts of the Third International Conference on Artificial Intelligence and Education*, p. 26. Learning Research and Development Center, University of Pittsburgh, Pittsburgh, Pennsylvania.

Fletcher, J.D. (1975) Modeling of learner in computer-based instruction. *Journal of Computer-Based Instruction*, vol. 1, pp. 118–126.

Fletcher, J.D. (1985) Intelligent instructional systems in training. In Andriole, S.J. (Ed.) *Applications in Artificial Intelligence*. Petrocelli Books, Princeton, New Jersey.

Forbus, K.; and Stevens, A.L. (1981) Using qualitative simulation to generate explanations. *BBN Report 4490*. Bolt Beranek and Newman Inc., Cambridge, Massachusetts.

Forbus, K. (1984a) An interactive laboratory for teaching control system concepts. *BBN Report 5511*. Bolt Beranek and Newman Inc., Cambridge, Massachusetts.

Forbus, K. (1984b) Qualitative process theory. *Artificial Intelligence*, vol. 24, pp. 85–168. (Reprinted in Bobrow, D.G. (Ed.) *Qualitative Reasoning about Physical Systems*. MIT Press, Cambridge, Massachusetts.)

Foss, C.L. (1987a) Learning from errors in ALGEBRALAND. *Technical Report IRL-87-0003*. Institute for Research on Learning, Palo Alto, California.

Foss, C.L. (1987b) Memory for self-derived solutions to problems. *Technical Report IRL-87-0002.* Institute for Research on Learning, Palo Alto, California.

Friend, J.E.; and Burton, R.R. (1980) *Teacher's Guide for Diagnostic Testing in Arithmetic: Subtraction.* Cognitive and Instructional Sciences, Xerox Palo Alto Research Center, Palo Alto, California.

Gallagher, J.P. (1981) The effectiveness of man-machine dialogues for teaching attribute blocks problem-solving skills with an artificial intelligence CAI system. *Instructional Science,* vol. 10, pp. 297–332.

Genesereth, M.R. (1977) An automated consultant for MACSYMA. *Proceedings of the Fifth International Joint Conference on Artificial Intelligence,* Cambridge, Massachusetts, p. 789.**

Genesereth, M.R. (1978) *Automated Consultation for Complex Computer Systems.* Doctoral dissertation, Harvard University, Cambridge, Massachusetts.

Genesereth, M.R. (1982) The role of plans in intelligent teaching systems. In Sleeman, D.H.; and Brown, J.S. (Eds.) *Intelligent Tutoring Systems.* Academic Press, London.

Gentner, D.R.; Wallen, M.R.; and Miller, P.L. (1974) A computer-based system for studies in learning. *Technical Report.* Center for Human Information Processing, University of California, San Diego, California.

Gentner, D.R. (1977) The FLOW tutor: a schema-based tutorial system. *Proceedings of the Fifth International Joint Conference on Artificial Intelligence,* Cambridge, Massachusetts, p. 787. **

Gentner, D.R.; and Norman, D.A. (1977) The flow tutor: schemas for tutoring. *Technical Report 7702.* Center for Human Information Processing, University of California, San Diego, California.

Gentner, D.R. (1979) Toward an intelligent computer tutor. In O'Neil, H. (Ed.) *Procedures for instructional systems development.* Academic Press, New York.

Gentner, D.; and Gentner, D.R. (1983) Flowing waters and teeming crowds: mental models of electricity. In Gentner, D.; and Stevens, A.L. (Eds.) *Mental Models.* Lawrence Erlbaum Associates, Hillsdale, New Jersey.

Gentner, D.; and Stevens, A.L. (Eds.) (1983) *Mental Models.* Lawrence Erlbaum Associates, Hillsdale, New Jersey.

Glaser, R. (Ed.) *Advances in Instructional Psychology.* Vol. I (1978), vol. II (1982), vol. III (1987). Lawrence Erlbaum Associates, Hillsdale, New Jersey.

Glaser, R. (1984) Education and thinking: the role of knowledge. *American Psychologist,* vol. 39, pp. 93–104.

Goldberg, A.; and Suppes, P. (1976) Computer-assisted instruction in elementary logic at the university level. *Educational Studies in Mathematics,* vol. 6, pp. 447–474.

Goldberg, A. (1979) Educational uses of a Dynabook. *Computers and Education*, vol. 3, pp. 247–266.

Goldstein, I.P. (1974) Understanding simple picture programs. *AI Lab Memo 294*. Massachusetts Institute of Technology, Cambridge, Massachusetts.

Goldstein, I.P. (1975) Summary of MYCROFT: a system for understanding simple picture programs. *Artificial Intelligence*, vol. 6, no. 3, pp. 249–288.

Goldstein, I.P.; and Miller, M.L. (1976a) AI-based personal learning environments: directions for long-term research. *AI Lab Memo 384*. Massachusetts Institute of Technology, Cambridge, Massachusetts.

Goldstein, I.P.; and Miller, M.L. (1976b) Structured planning and debugging: a linguistic theory of design. *AI Lab Memo 387*. Massachusetts Institute of Technology, Cambridge, Massachusetts.

Goldstein, I.P.; and Carr, B. (1977) The computer as coach: an athletic paradigm for intellectual education. *Proceedings of the National ACM Conference*, Seattle, Washington, pp. 227–233. Association for Computing Machinery, New York.

Goldstein, I.P.; and Grimson, E. (1977) Annotated production systems: a model for skill acquisition. *Proceedings of the Fifth International Joint Conference on Artificial Intelligence*, Cambridge, Massachusetts, pp. 311–317.**

Goldstein, I.P.; and Papert, S. (1977) Artificial intelligence, language, and the study of knowledge. *Cognitive Science*, vol. 1, no. 1, pp. 1–21.

Goldstein, I.P. (1978) The genetic graph: a representation for the evolution of procedural knowledge. *Proceedings of the Second Annual Conference of the Canadian Society for Computational Studies of Intelligence*, Toronto, pp. 100–106.

Goldstein, I.P. (1979) The genetic graph: a representation for the evolution of procedural knowledge. *Int Jrnl Man-Machine Studies*, vol. 11, pp. 51–77. (Reprinted in Sleeman, D.H.; and Brown, J.S. (Eds.) *Intelligent Tutoring Systems*. Academic Press, London.)

Goldstein, I.P. (1980) Developing a computational representation for problem-solving skills. In Tuma, D.; and Reif, F. (Eds.) *Problem Solving and Education: Issues in Teaching and Research*. Lawrence Erlbaum Associates, Hillsdale, New Jersey.

Goldstein, I.P. (1982) WUMPUS. In Barr, A.; and Feigenbaum, E. A. (Eds.) *Handbook of Artificial Intelligence* (vol. II). Addison-Wesley, Reading, Massachusetts.

Greenes, C.E; Willbutt, R.E.; and Spikell, M.A. (1972) *Problem Solving in the Mathematics Laboratory*. Prindle, Weber, and Schmidt, Inc., Boston, Massachusetts.

Greeno, J.G. (1983) Conceptual entities. In Gentner, D.; and Stevens, A.L. (Eds.) *Mental Models*. Lawrence Erlbaum Associates, Hillsdale, New Jersey.

Grignetti, M.; Hausman, C.L.; and Gould, L. (1975) An intelligent on-line assistant and tutor: NLS-SCHOLAR. *Proceedings of the National Computer Conference*, pp. 775–781.

Haertel, H. (1987) A qualitative approach to electricity. *Technical Report IRL-87-0001*. Institute for Research on Learning, Palo Alto, California.

Hall, R.P. (1986a) Understanding analogical reasoning: viewpoints from psychology and related disciplines. *Technical Report 86-10*. University of California, Irvine, California.

Hall, R.P. (1986b) Understanding analogical reasoning: computational approaches. *Technical Report 86-11*. University of California, Irvine, California. (To appear in *Artificial Intelligence*.)

Hall, R.P. (1987) When trains become hoses: justifying problem comparisons in problem solving. *Abstracts of the Third International Conference on Artificial Intelligence and Education*, p. 29. Learning Research and Development Center, University of Pittsburgh, Pittsburgh, Pennsylvania.

Halpern, J.Y. (Ed.) (1986) *Theoretical Aspects of Reasoning about Knowledge: Proceedings of the 1986 Conference*. Morgan Kaufmann, Los Altos, California.

Hambleton, R.K. (1984) Criterion-referenced measurement. In Husen, T.; and Postlethwaite, T.N. (Eds.) *International Encyclopedia of Education*. Pergamon Press, New York.

Hartley, J.R.; and Sleeman, D.H. (1973) Towards intelligent teaching systems. *Int Jrnl Man-Machine Studies*, vol. 5, pp. 215–236.

Hasling, D.W. (1983) Abstract explanations of strategy in a diagnostic consultation system. *Proceedings of the National Conference on Artificial Intelligence*, Washington, D.C., pp. 157–161.**

Hasling, D.W.; Clancey, W.J.; and Rennels, G. (1984) Strategic explanations for a diagnostic consultation system. *International Journal of Man-Machine Studies*, vol. 20, pp. 3–19. (Reprinted in Coombs, M.J. (Ed.), *Developments in Expert Systems*. Academic Press, London.)

Heines, J.M.; and O'Shea, T. (1985) The design of rule-based CAI tutorial. *Int Jrnl Man-Machine Studies*, vol. 23, pp. 1–25.

Hollan, J.D.; Hutchins, E.L.; and Weitzman, L. (1984) STEAMER: an interactive inspectable simulation-based training system. *AI Magazine*, vol. 5, no. 2, pp. 15–27.

Hollan, J.D.; and Hutchins, E.L. (1984) Reservations about qualitative models. *Proceedings of the Sixth Cognitive Science Society Conference*, Boulder, Colorado, pp. 183–187.*

Hollan, J.D.; Hutchins, E.L.; McCandless, T.P.; Rosenstein, M.; and Weitzman, L. (1986) Graphical interfaces for simulation. *Technical Report ICS-8603*. Institute for Cognitive Science, University of California, San Diego, California.

Hooper, R. (1977) *The National Development Programme in Computer-assisted Learning: Final Report of the Director.* Council for Educational Technology, London.

Howe, J.A.M. (1979) Learning through model building. In Michie, D. (Ed.) *Expert Systems in the Microelectronic Age.* Edinburgh University Press, Edinburgh, Scotland.

Hutchins, E.L.; Hollan, J.D.; and Norman, D.A. (1985) Direct manipulation interfaces. *Human-Computer Interaction,* vol. 1, pp. 311–338. (Reprinted in Norman, D.A.; and Draper, S.W. (Eds.) *User-centered Design: New Perspectives on Human-Computer Interaction.* Lawrence Erlbaum Associates, Hillsdale, New Jersey.)

Ihrie, D.W. (1978) Analysis of a synthetic student as a model of human behavior. *AI Lab Memo 477.* Massachusetts Institute of Technology, Cambridge, Massachusetts.

Johnson, W.L.; and Soloway, E.M. (1984a) PROUST: knowledge-based program debugging. *Proceedings of the Seventh International Software Engineering Conference,* Orlando, Florida, pp. 369–380.

Johnson, W.L.; and Soloway, E.M. (1984b) Intention-based diagnosis of programming errors. *Proceedings of the National Conference on Artificial Intelligence,* Austin, Texas, pp. 162–168.**

Johnson, W.L.; and Soloway, E.M. (1985) PROUST: an automatic debugger for Pascal programs. *Byte,* vol. 10, no. 4, pp. 179–190.

Johnson, W.L. (1986) *Intention-based Diagnosis of Novice Programming Errors.* Research Notes in Artificial Intelligence, Morgan Kaufmann, Los Altos, California (copublished with Pitman, London).

Johnson, W.L. (1987) Understanding and debugging novice programs. *ISI Technical Report.* Information Science Institute, Marina del Rey, California. (To appear in *Artificial Intelligence.*)

Johnson, W.L. (in press) Modeling programmers' intentions. In Self, J.A. (Ed.) *Artificial Intelligence and Human Learning: Intelligent Computer-aided Instruction.* Chapman and Hall, London.

Joobbani, R.; and Talukdar, S.N. (1985) An expert system for understanding expressions for electric circuit analysis. *Proceedings of the Ninth International Joint Conference on Artificial Intelligence,* Los Angeles, pp. 23–25.**

Kessler, C.M.; and Anderson, J.R. (1986) A model of novice debugging in LISP. In Soloway, E.M.; and Iyengar, S. (Eds.) *Empirical Studies of Programmers.* Ablex Publishing, Norwood, New Jersey.

Kimball, R. (1973) Self-optimizing computer-assisted tutoring: theory and practice. *Technical Report 206.* Psychology and Education Series; Institute of Mathematical Studies in the Social Sciences, Stanford University, Stanford, California.

Kimball, R. (1982) A self-improving tutor for symbolic integration. In Sleeman D.; and Brown, J.S. (Eds.) *Intelligent Tutoring Systems.* Academic Press, London.

Kitcher, P. (1983) *The Nature of Mathematical Knowledge.* Oxford University Press, New York.

Koffman, E.B.; and Blount, S.E. (1975) Artificial intelligence and automatic programming in CAI. *Artificial Intelligence,* vol. 6, pp. 215–234.

Koffman, E.B.; and Perry, J.M. (1976) A model for generative CAI and concept selection. *Int Jrnl Man-Machine Studies,* vol. 8, pp. 397–410.

Laird, J.; Rosenbloom, P.; and Newell, A. (1986) *Universal Subgoaling and Chunking: The Automatic Generation and Learning of Goal Hierarchies.* Kluwer Academic Publishers, Hingham, Massachusetts.

Langley, P.; and Ohlsson, S. (1984) Automated cognitive modeling. *Proceedings of the National Conference on Artificial Intelligence,* Austin, Texas, pp. 193–197.**

Langley, P.; Ohlsson, S.; and Sage, S. (1984) Machine learning approach to student modeling. *Technical Report CMU-RI-TR-84-7.* Robotics Institute, Carnegie-Mellon University, Pittsburgh, Pennsylvania.

Langley, P.; Wogulis, J.; and Ohlsson, S. (1987) Rules and principles in cognitive diagnosis. In Fredericksen, N. (Ed.) *Diagnostic Monitoring of Skill and Knowledge Acquisition.* Lawrence Erlbaum Associates, Hillsdale, New Jersey.

Lantz, B.S.; Bregar, W.S; and Farley, A.M. (1983) An intelligent CAI system for teaching equation solving. *Journal of Computer-Based Education,* vol. 3, no. 1, pp. 35–42.

Larkin, J.H.; McDermott, J.; Simon, D.P.; and Simon, H.A. (1980) Expert and novice performance in solving physics problems. *Science,* vol. 208, pp. 1335–1342.

Larkin, J.H. (1983) The role of problem representation in physics. In Gentner, D.; and Stevens, A.L. (Eds.) *Mental Models.* Lawrence Erlbaum Associates, Hillsdale, New Jersey.

Laubsch, J.H. (1975) Some thoughts about representing knowledge in instructional systems. *Proceedings of the Fourth International Joint Conference on Artificial Intelligence,* Tsibili, USSR, pp. 122–125.**

Laudan, L. (1977) *Progress and its Problems: Towards a Theory of Scientific Growth.* University of California Press, Berkeley, California.

Lave, J. (in press) *Cognition in Practice.* Cambridge University Press, Cambridge, England.

Lawler, R.; and Yazdani, M. (Eds.) (1987) *Artificial Intelligence and Education: Learning Environments and Intelligent Tutoring Systems.* Ablex Publishing, Norwood, New Jersey.

Leinhardt, G. (1985) The development of an expert explanation: an analysis of a sequence of subtraction lessons. *Technical Report.* Learning Research and Development Center, University of Pittsburgh, Pittsburgh, Pennsylvania.

Leinhardt, G.; and Greeno, J.G. (1986) The cognitive skill of teaching. *Journal of Educational Psychology,* vol. 78, no. 2, pp. 75–95.

Lenat, D.B.; and Brown, J.S. (1984) Why AM and EURISKO appear to work. *Artificial Intelligence*, vol. 22, no. 3, pp. 269–294.

Lesgold, A.M. (1987) Toward a theory of curriculum for use in designing intelligent instructional systems. In Mandl, H.; and Lesgold, A.M. (Eds.) *Learning Issues for Intelligent Tutoring Systems.* Springer-Verlag, New York.

Lesgold, A.M.; Bonar, J.G.; Ivill, J.M.; and Bowen, A. (1987) An intelligent tutoring system for electronics troubleshooting: DC-circuit understanding. *Technical Report*. Learning Research and Development Center, University of Pittsburgh, Pittsburgh, Pennsylvania. (To appear in Resnick L.B. (Ed.) *Knowing and Learning: Issues For the Cognitive Psychology of Instruction.* Lawrence Erlbaum Associates, Hillsdale, New Jersey.)

Levine, D.R. (1981) Computer-based analytic grading for German grammar instruction. In Suppes, P. (Ed.) *University-level Computer-assisted Instruction at Stanford: 1968–1980.* Institute for Mathematical Studies in the Social Sciences, Stanford University, Stanford, California.

Lewis, M.W.; and Anderson, J.R. (1985) Discrimination of operator schemata in problem solving: learning from examples. *Cognitive Psychology*, vol. 17, pp. 26–65.

Littman, D.; Pinto, J.; and Soloway, E.M. (1986) An analysis of tutorial reasoning about programming bugs. *Proceedings of the National Conference on Artificial Intelligence*, Philadelphia, pp. 320–327.**

London, R.; and Clancey, W.J. (1982) Plan recognition strategies in student modeling: prediction and description. *Proceedings of the National Conference on Artificial Intelligence*, Pittsburgh, Pennsylvania, pp. 335–338.**

London, R. (1986) Student modeling with multiple viewpoints by plan inference. *Thesis proposal*. School of Education, Stanford University, Stanford, California.

Mackinlay, J.D. (1986) *Automatic design of graphical presentations.* Doctoral dissertation (Report STAN-CS-86-1138), Stanford University, Stanford, California.

Macmillan, S.A.; Emme, D.; and Berkowitz, M. (1986) Instructional planners: lessons learned. *Technical Report*, FMC Corporation, Santa Clara, California. (To appear in Psotka, J.; Massey, D.; and Mutter, S. (Eds.) *Intelligent Tutoring Systems: Lessons Learned.* Lawrence Erlbaum Associates, Hillsdale, New Jersey.

Macmillan, S.A.; and Sleeman, D.H. (1987) An architecture for a self-improving instructional planner for intelligent tutoring systems. *Computational Intelligence*, vol. 3, no. 1.

Mandl, H.; and Lesgold, A.M. (Eds.) (1987) *Learning Issues for Intelligent Tutoring Systems.* Springer-Verlag, New York.

Marshall, S.P. (1981) Sequential item selection: optimal and heuristic policies. *Journal of Mathematical Psychology*, vol. 23, no. 2, pp. 134–152.

Matz, M. (1980) *Towards a Computational Model of Algebraic Competence.* Masters thesis, Massachusetts Institute of Technology, Cambridge, Massachusetts.

Matz, M. (1982) Towards a process model for high school algebra. In Sleeman, D.H.; and Brown, J.S. (Eds.) *Intelligent Tutoring Systems.* Academic Press, London.

McArthur, D. (1987) Developing computer tools to support performing and learning complex cognitive skills. In Berger, D.E.; Pezdek, K.; and Banks, W.P., (Eds.) *Applications of Cognitive Psychology: Computing and Education.* Lawrence Erlbaum Associates, Hillsdale, New Jersey.

McArthur, D.; Stasz, C.; and Hotta, J.Y. (1987) Learning problem-solving skills in algebra. *Journal of Educational Technology Systems*, vol. 15, no. 3, pp. 303–325.

McDonald, J. (1981) The EXCHECK CAI system. In Suppes, P. (Ed.) *University-level Computer-assisted Instruction at Stanford: 1968–1980.* Institute for Mathematical Studies in the Social Sciences, Stanford University, Stanford, California.

McKendree, J.; Reiser, B.J.; and Anderson, J.R. (1984) Tutorial goals and strategies in the instruction of programming skills. *Proceedings of the Sixth Cognitive Science Society Conference*, Boulder, Colorado, pp. 252–254.*

Michalski, R.S.; Carbonell, J.G.; and Mitchell, T.M. (Eds.) (1986) *Machine Learning: An Artificial Intelligence Approach, Vol. II.* Morgan Kaufmann, Los Altos, California.

Miller, M.L.; and Goldstein, I.P. (1976a) Parsing protocols using problem-solving grammars. *AI Lab Memo 385.* Massachusetts Institute of Technology, Cambridge, Massachusetts.

Miller, M.L.; and Goldstein, I.P. (1976b) SPADE: a grammar based editor for planning and debugging programs. *AI Lab Memo 386.* Massachusetts Institute of Technology, Cambridge, Massachusetts.

Miller, M.L.; and Goldstein, I.P. (1976c) PAZATN: a linguistic approach to automatic analysis of elementary programming protocols. *AI Lab Memo 388.* Massachusetts Institute of Technology, Cambridge, Massachusetts.

Miller, M.L.; and Goldstein, I.P. (1977a) Structured planning and debugging. *Proceedings of the Fifth International Joint Conference on Artificial Intelligence*, Cambridge, Massachusetts, pp. 773–779.**

Miller, M.L.; and Goldstein, I.P. (1977b) Problem solving grammars as formal tools for intelligent CAI. *Proceedings of the National ACM Conference*, Seattle, Washington, pp. 220–226. Association for Computing Machinery, New York.

Miller, M.L. (1979) A structured planning and debugging environment for elementary programming. *Int Jrnl Man-Machine Studies*, vol. 11, pp. 79–95. (Reprinted in Sleeman, D.H.; and Brown, J.S. (Eds.) *Intelligent Tutoring Systems*. Academic Press, London.)

Minsky, M.; and Papert, S. (1969) *Perceptrons: An Introduction to Computational Geometry*. MIT Press, Cambridge, Massachusetts.

Mitchell, T.M.; Mahadevan, S.; and Steinberg, L.I. (1985) LEAP: a learning apprentice for VLSI design. *Proceedings of the Ninth International Joint Conference on Artificial Intelligence*, Los Angeles, pp. 573–580.**

Munro, A.; Fehlig, M.R.; and Towne, D.M. (1985) Instruction intrusiveness in dynamic simulation training. *Journal of Computer-Based Instruction*, vol. 12, no. 2, pp. 50–53.

Murray, W.R. (1985) Heuristic and formal methods in automatic program debugging. *Proceedings of the Ninth International Joint Conference on Artificial Intelligence*, Los Angeles, pp. 15–19.**

Murray, W.R. (1986) *Automatic program debugging for Intelligent Tutoring Systems*. Doctoral dissertation (Technical Report AI TR86-27), University of Texas, Austin, Texas.

Murray, W.R. (1987) Automatic program debugging for intelligent tutoring systems. *Computational Intelligence*, vol. 3, no. 1.

Neches, R.; Swartout, W.R.; and Moore, J. (1985) Explainable (and maintainable) expert systems. *Proceedings of the Ninth International Joint Conference on Artificial Intelligence*, Los Angeles, pp. 382–389.**

Newell, A.; and Simon, H.A. (1972) *Human Problem Solving*. Prentice-Hall, Englewood Cliffs, New Jersey.

Newell, A. (1982) The knowledge level. *Artificial Intelligence*, vol. 18, no. 1, pp. 87–127.

Norman, D.A. (1973) Cognitive organization and learning. *Technical Report*, Center for Human Information Processing, University of California San Diego, California.

Norman, D.A. (1976) Studies of learning and self-contained educational systems. *Report 7601*, Center for Human Information Processing, University of California, San Diego, California.

Norman, D.A.; Gentner, D.; and Stevens, A.L. (1976) Comments on learning: schemata and memory organization. In Klahr, D. (Ed.) *Cognition and Instruction*. Lawrence Erlbaum Associates, Hillsdale, New Jersey.

Norman, D.A.; and Draper, S.W. (Eds.) (1986) *User-centered Design: New Perspectives on Human-Computer Interaction*. Lawrence Erlbaum Associates, Hillsdale, New Jersey.

Ohlsson, S. (1987a) Some principles of intelligent tutoring. In Lawler, R., and Yazdani, M. (Eds.) *AI and Education: Learning Environments and Intelligent Tutoring Systems*. Ablex Publishing, Norwood, New Jersey.

Ohlsson, S. (1987b) Sense and reference in the design of interactive illustrations for rational numbers.   In Lawler, R.; and Yazdani, M. (Eds.) *AI and Education: Learning Environments and Intelligent Tutoring Systems*. Ablex Publishing, Norwood, New Jersey.

Ohlsson, S.; and Langley, P. (1987) Identifying solution paths in cognitive diagnosis. In Mandl, H.; and Lesgold, A.M. (Eds.) *Learning Issues for Intelligent Tutoring Systems*. Springer-Verlag, New York.

O'Shea, T.; and Sleeman, D.H. (1973) A design for an adaptive self-improving teaching system. In Rose, J. (Ed.) *Advances in Cybernetics*. Gordon and Breach Publishers, London.

O'Shea, T. (1979a) *Self-improving Teaching Systems: an Application of Artificial Intelligence to Computer-aided Instruction*. Birkhauser Verlag, Basel.

O'Shea, T. (1979b) A self-improving quadratic tutor. *Int Jrnl Man-Machine Studies*, vol. 11, pp. 97–124. (Reprinted in Sleeman, D.H.; and Brown, J.S. (Eds.) *Intelligent Tutoring Systems*. Academic Press, London.)

O'Shea, T. (1979c) Rule-based computer tutors. In Michie, D. (Ed.) *Expert Systems in the Microelectronic Age*. Edinburgh University Press, Edinburgh, Scotland.

O'Shea, T.; and Self, J.A. (1983) *Learning and Teaching with Computers*. Prentice-Hall, Englewood Cliffs, New Jersey.

O'Shea, T.; Bornat, R.; Du Boulay, B.; Eisenstadt, M.; and Page, I. (1984) Tools for creating intelligent computer tutors. In Elithorn, A.; and Barneji, R. (Eds.) *Human and Artificial Intelligence*. North-Holland, London.

Palincsar, A.S.; and Brown, A. L. (1984) Reciprocal teaching of comprehension-fostering and comprehension-monitoring activities. *Cognition and Instruction*, vol. 1, no. 2, pp. 117–175.

Papert, S. (1972a) Teaching children thinking. *Programmed Learning and Educational Technology*, vol. 9, no. 5, pp. 245–255.

Papert, S. (1972b) Teaching children to be mathematicians versus teaching about mathematics. *International Journal of Mathematics, Education, Science, and Technology*, vol. 3, pp 249–262.

Papert, S. (1980) *Mindstorms: Children, Computers, and Powerful Ideas*. Basic Books, New York.

Park, S.I.; and Tennyson, R.D. (1983) Computer-based instructional systems for adaptive education: an review. Contemporary Education Review, vol. 2, no. 2, pp. 121–135.

Peachey, D.R.; and McCalla, G.I. (1986) Using planning techniques in intelligent tutoring systems. *Int Jrnl Man-Machine Studies*, vol. 24, pp. 77–98.

Pirolli, P.L.; Anderson, J.R.; and Farrell, R.G. (1984) Learning to program recursion. *Proceedings of the Sixth Cognitive Science Society Conference*, Boulder, Colorado, pp. 252–254.**

Putnam, R.T.; Sleeman, D.H.; Baxter, J.A.; and Kuspa, L.K. (1984) A summary of misconceptions of high-school Basic programmers. *Occasional Report no. 010.* Technology Panel: Study of Stanford and the Schools, Stanford University, Stanford, California.

Quillian, M.R. (1968) Semantic memory. In Minsky, M. (Ed.) *Semantic Information Processing.* MIT Press, Cambridge, Massachusetts.

Reimann, P. (1986) REFRACT: a microworld for geometrical optics. *Technical Report.* Learning Research and Development Center, University of Pittsburgh, Pittsburgh, Pennsylvania.

Reiser, B.J.; Anderson, J.R.; and Farrell, R.G. (1985) Dynamic student modeling in an intelligent tutor for LISP programming. *Proceedings of the Ninth International Joint Conference on Artificial Intelligence Conference,* Los Angeles, pp. 8–14.**

Resnick, C.A. (1975) *Computational Models of Learners for Computer-assisted Learning.* Doctoral dissertation, University of Illinois, Urbana-Champaign, Illinois.

Resnick, L.B. (1973) Hierarchies in children's learning: a symposium. *Instructional Science,* vol. 2, pp. 311–362.

Resnick, L.B. (1977) On holding an instructional discourse. In Anderson, R.C.; Spiro, R.J.; and Montague, W.E. (Eds.) *Schooling and the Acquisition of Knowledge.* Lawrence Erlbaum Associates, Hillsdale, New Jersey.

Resnick, L.B. (1982) Syntax and semantics in learning to subtract. In Carpenter, T.; Moser, J.; and Romberg, T. (Eds.) *Addition and Subtraction: A Cognitive Perspective.* Lawrence Erlbaum Associates, Hillsdale, New Jersey.

Resnick, L.B.; and Omanson, S.F. (1987) Learning to understand arithmetic. In Glaser, R. (Ed.) *Advances in Instructional Psychology* (vol. III). Lawrence Erlbaum Associates, Hillsdale, New Jersey.

Rich, C.; and Shrobe, H.E. (1976) Initial report on a LISP programmer's apprentice. *AI Lab Memo 354.* Massachusetts Institute of Technology, Cambridge, Massachusetts.

Rich, C. (1984) A formal representation for plans in the Programmer's Apprentice. In Brodie, M.; Mylopoulos, J.; and Schmidt, J. (Eds.) *On Conceptual Modeling.* Springer-Verlag, New York.

Rich, E. (1979) User modeling via stereotypes. *Cognitive Science,* vol. 3, pp. 355–366.

Richer, M.H.; and Clancey, W.J. (1985) GUIDON-WATCH: a graphic interface for viewing a knowledge-based system. *IEEE Computer Graphics and Applications,* vol. 5, no. 11, pp. 51–64.

Roberts, F.C.; and Park, O. (1983) Intelligent computer-assisted instruction: an explanation and overview. *Educational Technology,* vol. 23, no. 12, pp. 7–12.

Rouse, W.B.; and Morris, N.M. (1985) On looking into the black box: prospects and limits in the search for mental models. *Technical*

Report 85-2. Center for Man-machine Systems, Georgia Institute of Technology, Atlanta, Georgia.

Rumelhart, D.E.; and Norman, D.A. (1981) Analogical processes in learning. In Anderson, J.R. (Ed.) *Cognitive Skills and their Acquisition*. Lawrence Erlbaum Associates, Hillsdale, New Jersey.

Ruth, G.R. (1976) Intelligent program analysis. *Artificial Intelligence*, vol. 7, pp. 65–85.

Sauers, R.; and Farrell, R.G. (1982) GRAPES user's manual. *Technical Report ONR-82-3*. Department of Psychology, Carnegie-Mellon University, Pittsburgh, Pennsylvania.

Schuster, E. (1985) Grammars as user models. *Proceedings of the Ninth International Joint Conference on Artificial Intelligence*, Los Angeles, pp. 20–22.**

Sebrechts, M.M.; Schooler, L.J.; and Soloway, E.M. (1987) Diagnosing student errors in statistics: an empirical evaluation of GIDE. *Abstracts of the Third International Conference on Artificial Intelligence and Education*, p. 48. Learning Research and Development Center, University of Pittsburgh, Pittsburgh, Pennsylvania.

Self, J.A. (1974) Student models in computer-aided instruction. *Int Jrnl Man-Machine Studies*, vol. 6, pp. 261–276.

Self, J.A. (1977) Concept teaching. *Artificial Intelligence*, vol. 9, no. 2, pp. 197–221.

Self, J.A. (1979) Student models and artificial intelligence. *Computers and Education*, vol. 3, pp. 309–312.

Self, J.A. (1985a) A perspective on intelligent computer-assisted learning. *Journal of Computer-Assisted Learning*, vol. 1, pp. 159–166.

Self, J.A. (1985b) Application of machine learning to student modelling. *Proceedings of the Second International Conference on Artificial Intelligence and Education*, Exeter, England. (Reprinted in Lawler, R.; and Yazdani, M. (Eds.) *AI and Education: Learning Environments and Intelligent Tutoring Systems*. Ablex Publishing, Norwood, New Jersey.)

Self, J.A. (Ed.) (in press) *Artificial Intelligence and Human Learning: Intelligent Computer-aided Instruction*. Chapman and Hall, London.

Shortliffe, E.H. (1976) *Computer-based Medical Consultations: MYCIN*. American Elsevier Publishers, New York.

Shute, V.; and Bonar, J.G. (1986) An intelligent tutoring system for scientific inquiry skills. *Proceedings of the Eighth Cognitive Science Society Conference*, Amherst, Massachusetts, pp. 353–370.*

Shute, V.; and Glaser, R. (1986) An intelligent tutoring system for exploring principles of economics. *Technical Report*. Learning Research and Development Center, University of Pittsburgh, Pittsburgh, Pennsylvania.

Simon, H.A. (1969) *The Sciences of the Artificial*. MIT Press, Cambridge, Massachusetts.

Skinner, B.F. (1968) *The Technology of Teaching.* Appleton-Century-Crofts, New York.

Sleeman, D.H. (1975) A problem-solving monitor for a deductive reasoning task. *Int Jrnl Man-Machine Studies*, vol. 7, pp. 183–211.

Sleeman, D.H. (1977) A system which allows students to explore algorithms. *Proceedings of the Fifth International Joint Conference on Artificial Intelligence*, Cambridge, California, pp. 780–786.*

Sleeman, D.H.; and Hendley, R.J. (1979) ACE: a system which analyses complex explanations. *Int Jrnl Man-Machine Studies*, vol. 11, pp. 125-144. (Reprinted in Sleeman, D.H.; and Brown, J.S. (Eds.) *Intelligent Tutoring Systems.* Academic Press, London.)

Sleeman, D.H. (1981) A rule-based task generation system. *Proceedings of the Seventh International Joint Conference on Artificial Intelligence*, Vancouver, pp. 882–887.**

Sleeman, D.H.; and Smith, M.J. (1981) Modelling students' problem solving. *Artificial Intelligence*, vol. 16, pp. 171–187.

Sleeman, D.H. (1982a) Assessing aspects of competence in basic algebra. In Sleeman, D.H.; and Brown, J.S. (Eds.) *Intelligent Tutoring Systems.* Academic Press, London.

Sleeman, D.H. (1982b) Inferring (mal) rules from pupils' protocols. *Proceedings of the European Conference on Artificial Intelligence*, Orsay, France, pp. 160–164. (Also in *Proceedings of the International Machine Learning Workshop*, Illinois, 1983, pp. 221–227; and reprinted in Steels, L.; and Campbell, J.A. (Eds.) *Progress in Artificial Intelligence.* Ellis Horwood, Chichester, United Kingdom.)

Sleeman, D.H.; and Brown, J.S. (Eds.) (1982) *Intelligent Tutoring Systems.* Academic Press, London.

Sleeman, D.H.; Langley, P.; and Mitchell, T.M. (1982) Learning from solution paths: an approach to the credit assignment problem. *AI Magazine*, vol. 3, no. 1, pp. 48–52.

Sleeman, D.H. (1983a) Inferring student models for intelligent computer-aided instruction. In Michalski, R.S.; Carbonell, J.G.; and Mitchell, T.M. (Eds.) *Machine Learning: An Artificial Intelligence Approach.* Morgan Kaufmann, Palo Alto, California.

Sleeman, D.H. (1983b) Intelligent tutoring systems: a review. *Proceedings of the EdCompCon '83 Meeting*, pp. 95–101. IEEE Computer Society, Washington, D.C.

Sleeman, D.H. (1984a) Basic algebra revisited: a study with 14 year olds. *Int Jrnl Man-Machine Studies*, vol. 22, no. 2, pp. 127–150.

Sleeman, D.H. (1984b) An attempt to understand student's understanding of basic algebra. *Cognitive Science*, vol. 8, no. 4, pp. 387–412.

Sleeman, D.H. (1984c) Misgeneralization: an explanation of observed mal-rules. *Proceedings of the Sixth Cognitive Science Society Conference*, Boulder, Colorado, pp. 51–56.*

Sleeman, D.H. (1984d) A user-modelling front-end subsystem. *Int Jrnl Man-Machine Studies*, vol. 23, no. 1, pp. 71–88.

Sleeman, D.H.; Putnam, R.T.; Baxter, J.A.; and Kuspa, L.K. (1984) Pascal and high-school students: a study of misconceptions. *Occasional Report no. 009*. Technology Panel: Study of Stanford and the Schools, Stanford University, Stanford, California.

Sleeman, D.H. (1987) PIXIE: a shell for developing intelligent tutoring systems. In Lawler, R.; and Yazdani, M. (Eds.) *AI and Education: Learning Environments and Intelligent Tutoring Systems*. Ablex Publishing, Norwood, New Jersey.

Smith, R.L.; Graves, H.; Blaine, L.H.; and Marinov, V.G. (1975) Computer-assisted axiomatic mathematics: informal rigor. In Lecareme, O.; and Lewis, R. (Eds.) *Computers in Education*. North-Holland, Amsterdam, The Netherlands.

Smith, R.L.; and Blaine, L.H. (1976) A generalized system for university mathematics instruction. *ACM SIGCUE Bulletin*, vol. 1, pp. 280–288.

Soloway, E.M.; Woolf, B.P.; Rubin, E.; and Barth, P. (1981) MENO-II: an intelligent tutoring system for novice programmers. *Proceedings of the Seventh International Joint Conference on Artificial Intelligence*, Vancouver, pp. 975–977.**

Soloway, E.M.; Ehrlich, K.; Bonar, J.; and Greenspan, J. (1982) What do novices know about programming? In Shneiderman, B.; and Badre, A. (Eds.) *Directions in Human-Computer Interactions*. Ablex Publishing, Norwood, New Jersey.

Soloway, E.M.; Rubin, E.; Woolf, B.P.; Bonar, J.; and Johnson, W.L. (1983a) MENO-II: an AI-based programming tutor. *Journal of Computer-Based Instruction*, vol. 10, no. 1, pp. 20–34.

Soloway, E.M.; Bonar, J.; and Ehrlich, K. (1983b) Cognitive strategies and looping constructs: an empirical study. *CACM*, vol. 26, no. 11, pp. 853–860.

Soloway, E.M.; and Ehrlich, K. (1984) Empirical investigations of programming knowledge. *IEEE Transactions on Software Engineering*, vol. 10, pp. 595–609.

Soloway, E.M.; and Johnson, W.L. (1984) Remembrance of blunders past: a retrospective on the development of PROUST. *Proceedings of the Sixth Cognitive Science Society Conference*, Boulder, Colorado, p. 57.*

Soloway, E.M. (1986) Learning to program ¾ learning to construct mechanisms and explanations. *CACM*, vol. 29, no. 9, pp. 850–858.

Soloway, E.M.; and Iyengar, S. (Eds.) (1986) *Empirical Studies of Programmers*. Ablex Publishing, Norwood, New Jersey.

Spohrer, J.; Soloway, E.M.; and Pope, E. (1985) A goal/plan analysis of buggy Pascal programs. *Human-Computer Interaction*, vol. 1, no. 2, pp. 163–207.

Stansfield, J.C.; Carr, B.; and Goldstein, I.P. (1976) Wumpus advisor I: a first implementation of a program that tutors logical and probabilistic reasoning skills. *AI Lab Memo 381*. Massachusetts Institute of Technology, Cambridge, Massachusetts.

Stevens, A.L.; and Collins, A. (1977) The goal structure of a Socratic tutor. *Proceedings of the National ACM Conference*, Seattle, Washington, pp. 256–263. Association for Computing Machinery, New York.

Stevens, A.L.; Collins, A.; and Goldin, S. (1979) Misconceptions in students' understanding. *Int Jrnl Man-Machine Studies*, vol. 11, p. 145–156. (Reprinted in Sleeman, D.H.; and Brown, J.S. (Eds.) *Intelligent Tutoring Systems*. Academic Press, London.)

Stevens, A.L.; and Collins, A. (1980) Multiple models of a complex system. In Snow, R.; Frederico, P.; and Montague, W. (Eds.) *Aptitude, Learning, and Instruction* (vol. II). Lawrence Erlbaum Associates, Hillsdale, New Jersey.

Stevens, A.L.; and Steinberg, C. (1981) A typology of explanations and its application to intelligent computer-aided instruction. *BBN Report 4626*. Bolt Beranek and Newman Inc., Cambridge, Massachusetts.

Stevens, A.L. (1982) *Quantitative and Qualitative Simulation in Portable Training Devices*. Report to the National Academy of Sciences; Bolt Beranek and Newman Inc., Cambridge, Massachusetts

Stevens, A.L.; Roberts, B.; and Stead, L. (1983) The use of a sophisticated interface in computer-assisted instruction. *IEEE Computer Graphics and Applications*, vol. 3, March/April, pp. 25–31.

Stevens, A.L.; and Roberts, B. (1983) Quantitative and qualitative simulation in computer-based training. *Journal of Computer-Based Instruction*, vol. 10, no. 1, pp. 16–19.

Suchman, L. (1987) *Plans and Situated Actions: The Problem of Human-Machine Communication*. Cambridge University Press, Cambridge, England.

Suppes, P. (1979) Current trends in computer-assisted instruction. *Advances in Computers*, vol. 18, pp. 173–229. Academic Press, New York.

Suppes, P. (1981) *University-level Computer-assisted Instruction at Stanford: 1968–1980*. Institute for Mathematical Studies in the Social Sciences, Stanford University, Stanford, California.

Swartout, W.R. (1981) Explaining and justifying in expert consultant programs. *Proceeding of the Seventh International Joint Conference on Artificial Intelligence*, Vancouver, pp. 815–823.**

Tennyson, R.D.; Christensen, D.L.; and Park, S.I. (1984) The Minnesota adaptive instructional system: an intelligent CBI system. *Journal of Computer-Based Instruction*, vol. 11, no. 1, pp. 2–13.

Towne, D.M.; Munro, A.; Pizzini, Q.A.; and Surmon, D.S. (1987) Simulation composition tools with integrated semantics. *Abstracts of the Third International Conference on Artificial Intelligence and Education*, p. 54. Learning Research and Development Center, University of Pittsburgh, Pittsburgh, Pennsylvania.

Trybulec, A.; and Blair, H. (1985) Computer-assisted reasoning with MIZAR. *Proceedings of the Ninth International Joint Conference on Artificial Intelligence*, Los Angeles, pp. 26–28.**

Uhr, L. (1969) Teaching machine programs that generate problems as a function of interaction with students. *Proceedings of the National ACM Conference*, pp. 125–134. Association for Computing Machinery, New York.

Van Melle, W. (1979) A domain-independent production rule system for consultation programs. *Proceedings of the Sixth International Joint Conference on Artificial Intelligence*, Tokyo, pp. 923–925.**

VanLehn, K.; and Brown J. S. (1980). Planning Nets: a representation for formalizing analogies and semantic models of procedural skills. In Snow, R.; Frederico, P.; and Montague, W. (Eds.) *Aptitude, Learning, and Instruction: Cognitive Process Analyses*. Lawrence Erlbaum Associates, Hillsdale, New Jersey.

VanLehn, K. (1981) On the representation of procedures in Repair theory. *CIS Report 16*. Cognitive and Instructional Sciences Series; Xerox Palo Alto Research Center, Palo Alto, California. (Reprinted in Ginsburg, H.P. (Ed.) (1982) *The Development of Mathematical Thinking*. Academic Press, New York.)

VanLehn, K. (1982) Bugs are not enough: empirical studies of bugs, impasses and repairs in procedural skills. *Journal of Mathematical Behavior*, vol. 3, pp. 3–72. (Also available as *CIS Report 11*. Cognitive and Instructional Sciences Series; Xerox Palo Alto Research Center, Palo Alto, California.)

VanLehn, K. (1983a) *Felicity conditions for human skill acquisition: validating an AI-based theory*. Doctoral dissertation, Massachusetts Institute of Technology, Cambridge, Massachusetts. (Also available as *CIS Report 21*. Cognitive and Instructional Sciences Series; Xerox Palo Alto Research Center, Palo Alto, California.)

VanLehn, K. (1983b) Human procedural skill acquisition: theory, model, and psychological validation. *Proceedings of the National Conference on Artificial Intelligence*, Washington, D.C., pp. 420–423.**

VanLehn, K.; Brown, J.S.; and Greeno, J.G. (1984) Competitive argumentation in computational theories of cognition. In Kintsch, W.; Miller, J.; and Polson, P. (Eds.) *Methods and Tactics in Cognitive Science*. Lawrence Erlbaum Associates, Hillsdale, New Jersey.

VanLehn, K. (1987) Learning one subprocedure per lesson. *Artificial Intelligence*, vol. 31, no. 1, pp. 1–40.

Weber, G.; Waloszek, G.; and Wender, K.F. (1986) The role of episodic memory in an intelligent tutoring system. *Technical Report*, Institut für Psychologie, Technische Universität, Braunschweig, West-Germany.

Weischedel, R.M.; Voge, W.M.; and James, M. (1978) An artificial intelligence approach to language instruction. *Artificial Intelligence*, vol. 10, pp. 225–240.

Weld, D.S. (1983) Explaining complex engineered devices. *BBN Report 5489*. Bolt Beranek and Newman Inc., Cambridge, Massachusetts.

Wender, K.F. (1987) Psychological considerations for the design of tutorial systems. *Abstracts of the Third International Conference on Artificial Intelligence and Education*, p.56. Learning Research and Development Center, University of Pittsburgh, Pittsburgh, Pennsylvania.

Wescourt, K.; Beard, M.; and Gould, L. (1977) Knowledge-based adaptive curriculum sequencing for CAI: application of a network representation. *Proceedings of the National ACM Conference*, Seattle, Washington, pp. 234–240. Association for Computing Machinery, New York.

Wexler, J.D. (1970) Information networks in generative computer-assisted instruction. *IEEE Transactions on Man-Machine Systems*, vol. 11, no. 4, pp. 181–190.

White, B.Y. (1981) *Designing Computer Games to Facilitate Learning*. Doctoral dissertation (AT-TR-619, Artificial Intelligence Laboratory), Massachusetts Institute of Technology, Cambridge, Massachusetts.

White, B.Y.; and Frederiksen, J.R. (1984) Modeling expertise in troubleshooting and reasoning about simple electric circuits. *Proceedings of the Sixth Cognitive Science Society Conference*, Boulder, Colorado, pp. 337–343.*

White, B.Y.; and Frederiksen, J.R. (1985) QUEST: qualitative understanding of electrical system troubleshooting. *ACM SIGART Newsletter*, no. 93, pp. 34–37.

White, B.Y.; and Frederiksen, J.R. (1986a) Qualitative models and intelligent learning environments. In Lawler, R.; and Yazdani, M. (Eds.) *AI and Education: Learning Environments and Intelligent Tutoring Systems*. Ablex Publishing, Norwood, New Jersey.

White, B.Y.; and Frederiksen, J.R. (1986b) Progressions of qualitative models as foundations for intelligent learning environments. *BBN Report 6277*. Bolt Beranek and Newman Inc., Cambridge, Massachusetts (To appear in *Artificial Intelligence*.)

White, B.Y.; and Frederiksen, J.R. (1986c) Intelligent tutoring systems based upon qualitative model evolution. *Proceedings of the National Conference on Artificial Intelligence*, Philadelphia, pp. 313–319.**

Wilkins, D.C. (1986) Knowledge base debugging using apprenticeship learning techniques. *Proceedings of the Knowledge Acquisition for Knowledge-based Systems Workshop*, pp. 40.0–40.14. (Also available as *Knowledge Systems Lab Report KSL-86-63* (revised version). Department of Computer Science, Stanford University, Stanford, California.)

Wilkins, D.C.; Clancey, W.J.; and Buchanan, B.G. (1986) An overview of the ODYSSEUS learning apprentice. In Mitchell, T.M.; Carbonell, J.G.; and Michalski, R.S. (Eds.), *Machine Learning: A Guide to Current Research*. Academic Press, New York.

Williams, M.D.; Hollan, J.D.; and Stevens, A.L. (1981) An overview of STEAMER: an advanced computer-assisted instruction system for propulsion engineering. *Behavior Research Methods and Instrumentation*, vol. 13, no. 2, pp. 85–90.

Williams, M.D.; Hollan, J.D.; and Stevens, A.L. (1983) Human reasoning about a simple physical system. In Gentner, D.; and Stevens, A.L. (Eds.) *Mental Models*. Lawrence Erlbaum Associates, Hillsdale, New Jersey.

Winograd, T.; and Flores, C.F. (1986) *Understanding Computers and Cognition: A New Foundation for Design*. Ablex Publishing, Norwood, New Jersey.

Woods, W.A. (1975) What's in a link? In Bobrow, D.; and Collins, A. (Eds.) *Representation and Understanding: Studies in Cognitive Science*. Academic Press, New York.

Woolf, B.P.; and McDonald, D.D. (1983) Human-computer discourse in the design of a Pascal tutor. *CHI 83: Human Factors in Computer Systems*. Association for Computing Machinery, New York.

Woolf, B.P. (1984) *Context-dependent Planning in a Machine Tutor*. Doctoral dissertation, Department of Computer and Information Science, University of Massachusetts, Amherst, Massachusetts.

Woolf, B.P.; and McDonald, D.D. (1984a) Context-dependent transitions in tutoring discourse. *Proceedings of the National Conference on Artificial Intelligence*, Austin, Texas, pp. 355–361.**

Woolf, B.P.; and McDonald, D.D. (1984b) Building a computer tutor: design issues. *IEEE Computer*, vol. 17, no. 9, pp. 61–73.

Woolf, B.P.; Blegen, D.; Jansen, J.H.; and Verloop, A. (1986) Teaching a complex industrial process. *Proceedings of the National Conference on Artificial Intelligence*, Philadelphia, vol. II, pp. 722–728.**

Yazdani, M. (Ed.) (1984) *New Horizons in Educational Computing*. Wiley, New York.

Yob, G. (1975) Hunt the Wumpus. *Creative Computing*, September/October, pp. 51–54.

Young, R.M.; and O'Shea, T. (1981) Errors in children's subtraction. *Cognitive Science*, vol. 5, pp. 153–177. (Originally in *Proceedings of the Meeting of the Society for the Study of Artificial Intelligence and Simulation of Behavior*, 1978.)

---

* Available from Lawrence Erlbaum Associates, Hillsdale, New Jersey.
** Available from Morgan Kaufmann, Los Altos, California.

Figure Credits

Author Index

Underlined numbers indicate pages on which work by an author is discussed or specifically introduced with a brief description. Numbers in italic are pages in the bibliographical notes, and numbers in brackets are pages in the bibliography.

Abelson, Harold, 125, 151, [433]
Adam, Anne, 258, [433]
Aesop, 374
Aiello, Nelleke, 35–37, 50, [441]
Alderman, D.L., 5, 11, [433]
Anderson, John R., 289–304, 306, 362,
  411, [433, 434, 436, 443, 447, 449,
  450, 453]
Atkinson, Richard C., 108–109, 121, [434]

Baecker, Ronald, 12, [434]
Barnhouse, Steve, 284, 288, [441]
Barr, Avron, 12, 108–109, 121, [434]
Barth, Paul, 236–237, [456]
Barzilay, Amos, 21, 151, [434]
Baxter, Julie A., 203, [453, 456]
Beard, Marian, 108–111, 121, [434, 459]
Bell, Alan G., 59–61, 78, [436]
Bennett, James S., 12, 24, [434, 440]
Berkowitz, Melissa, 415, [449]
Blaine, Lee H., 102–104, 121, [435, 456]
Blair, Howard, 121, [458]
Blegen, Darrell, 98, 99, [460]
Bloom, Benjamin S., 12, 293, [435]
Blount, Sumner E., 223, 258, [448]
Bobrow, Daniel G., 78, [435]
Bobrow, Robert, 154, [436]
Bonar, Jeffrey G., 145–149, 151, 236–237,
  238–244, 258, 348, 354, [435, 449,
  455, 456]
Bork Alfred, 4, 5, 7, 11, [435, 436]
Bornat, Richard, 122, [452]
Bowen, Andrew, 147–148, 151, [449]
Boyle, C. Franklin, 292–301, 306, [434, 436]
Brachman, Ronald J., 33, [436]
Bregar, Williams S., 203, [448]
Breuker, Joost, 124, 151, 397, 415, [436]
Brooks, Ruven E., 293, [436]

Brown, Ann L., 12, [452]
Brown, John Seely, 3, 9, 14, 19, 22,
  23, 25, 51–77, 77–78, 79, 89, 90, 94,
  126–133, 133–135, 141, 151,
  153–183, 183–184, 206, 208, 303, 314,
  316, 317–319, 322–323, 343, 352, 361,
  370, 374, 387, 404, 407, 411, [436,
  437, 438, 439, 442, 443, 449, 455,
  458, 459]
Buchanan, Bruce G., 186, 263, 269, 281,
  287, 327, [438, 440, 460]
Bunderson, C. Victor, 5, [438]
Bundy, Alan, 190, 203, [438]
Burnstein, Mark, 359, [438]
Burton, Richard R., 14, 19, 22, 51–77,
  77–78, 126–133, 133–135, 141, 151,
  153–165, 183, 187, 191, 220, 314,
  316, 317, 337, 370, 387, 391, 411,
  [436, 437, 438, 439, 443, 444]
Buxton, William, 12, [434]

Carbonell, Jaime R. Sr., 29–37, 49, 52, 55,
  111, 121, 215, 314, [439]
Carbonell, Jaime G. Jr., 215, [450]
Carr, Brian, 14, 124, 135–140, 141, 151,
  [439, 445, 457]
Charniak, Eugene, 397, [439]
Chi, Michelene T.H., 90, [439]
Chipman, Susan F., 12, [439]
Christensen, Dean L., 12, [458]
Clancey, William J., 7, 12, 24, 25, 108, 262–
  287, 287–288, 295, 302, 320, 327,
  338, 339, 342, 363, 382, 420, 429,
  [434, 439, 440, 441, 446, 449, 454,
  460]
Clement, John, 360, [441]
Cohen, Paul R., 24, [440]

Subject Index

Pages on which an item is directly addressed are indicated in two ways: the numbers are either underlined or followed by the name of a project. Numbers in italic indicate pages in summaries or in bibliographical notes. In cross-references, multiple references are separated by semicolons; commas indicate subfields; slashes separate multiple subfields at the same level.

Abacus, 172
Abstract replay, <u>407</u>, (*see also* Reification; Reflexive model)
Abstraction, 15, <u>333</u>, 406, (*see under* Explanation, use of; *also* Functionality, abstract)
  graphic, 80–86 (STEAMER), <u>97–98</u>, 283–284 (GUIDON-WATCH), (*see also* Reification)
Accommodation, 360, <u>410–411</u>
ACE (Analyzer of Complex Explanations), <u>186–190</u>, <u>201</u>, 372, 391, 422
ACM (Automated Cognitive Modeling), <u>210–220</u>, <u>221</u>, 281, 295, 336, 348, 349, 350, 351, 358, 375, 379, 389, 393
ACT (Adaptive Control of Thought), <u>289</u>
ACT* theory, 289, <u>290–291</u>, 304, 328, 335, 338, 369, 378
Activation conditions, (*see* Preconditions)
Active diagnosis, (*see under* Diagnosis)
Active structural network, <u>224–225</u>, <u>256</u>, (*see also* schema)
Activity, (*see* Environment; Task)
Actors (in functional descriptions), 44
ACTP (Advanced Computer Tutoring Project), <u>289–306</u>, 315, 347, 348, 350, 358, 374, <u>378</u>, 380, 385, 387, <u>389</u>, 399, 402, 404, 409, 428, (*see also* GEOMETRY tutor; LISP tutor)
Adaptability, (*see under* Pedagogy; Viewpoints)
Adaptive Control of Thought, (*see* ACT)
Addition, 157–159 (BUGGY)
Adequacy, (*see under* Empirical; Explanatory)
Advanced Computer Tutoring Project, (*see* ACTP)
Advice, 106, 132, 231, <u>233</u>, 281, <u>409</u>, 421
  metacognitive, <u>412</u>
ADVISOR, (*see* MACSYMA ADVISOR)
Agenda, 33, <u>38</u>, 43, 226, <u>400</u>, 402, 422

in diagnosis, 244, 246 (PROUST)
Aggregate models, 47 (WHY)
Aggregates (of data), 241 (BRIDGE)
AI (Artificial Intelligence), 1–2, <u>8</u>, 16, 69, 277, 302, <u>334</u>, 341, 351, 381
  ITS and, (*see* Knowledge communication, AI and)
  methodology, <u>5–6</u>, <u>11</u>, 57, <u>170–171</u>, <u>179–181</u>, <u>343</u>, 413, 424, 425, 429, (*see also* Competitive argumentation; Entailments; ITS methodology; Modularity)
Alarm threshold, 106 (INTEGRATION)
Algebra, 154, 190–194 (LMS), <u>203</u>, 392
ALGEBRALAND, 284, <u>318–320</u>, 389, 409
Algorithm, (*see also* Procedure)
  recognition, 259 (TALUS), 356, 373
  teaching, 186–188 (PSM/ACE)
Allocation of resources, 38, <u>113–114</u>, <u>420</u>
Ambiguities, 57, 130, 188, 375, <u>386–387</u>, 422, (*see also* Noise)
Analogy (analogical), (*see also* Integration; Structure-preserving)
  interferences, 333, <u>353–354</u>, 360
  multiple, 75, <u>359</u>, <u>360</u>
  pedagogical value of, <u>303–304</u>, <u>333</u>
  reasoning by, <u>172–175</u>, 291, <u>303–304</u>, <u>333–334</u>, 352, 353, <u>356</u>, <u>357</u>, <u>360</u>
  relations, 15, 45, 97, 110, <u>141–144</u>, 145, 355, 403, 406
  structural, <u>303–304</u>
Analysis, (*see under* Protocol; Semantic; Bug-level; Plan; Program; Proof)
  and synthesis, <u>37</u>
  by synthesis, 246 (PROUST)
Analyzer of Complex Explanations, (*see* ACE)
Anaphora, 22, 57, 422
AND/OR graphs, 265, (*see under* GAO)
Annotations, <u>265</u>, <u>319</u>, (*see also* Production systems)
Anthropology, 10, 430

MAIS (Minnesota Adaptive Instructional System), *12*

Mal-rules, 190–198, *202,* 205, 208, *221,* 294, 349, 378, *(see also* Bugs)

manipulative versus parsing, *197*

MALT (MAchine Language Tutor), *258*

Man-machine, *(see* Human-computer)

Manipulation, *(see under* Assumptions; Interface; Mal-rules; Syntactic; Problem solving)

Mapping instruction, *184*

Matching, *(see* Bugs (in programs), rules; Coercions; Equivalence; Keyword)

Mathematical models, *(see* Quantitative)

Mathematics, 102–105 (EXCHECK), 126 (LOGO), 232, *360*

Means-end analysis, 293, 407

Media technology, 5, 21, 316

Medical diagnosis, 262–286 (GUIDON), 320, 339, 343, 381

Medium, the computer as, *311–323*

Memory, 130, 177, 216, 224–225 (FLOW), *256,* 273, 291 (ACT), 298–299, *317, 320,* 412

MENO, 236–240, 254, 348, 350, 354, 389, 406

MENO-II, *152,* 236–237, 244, 251, *256,* 297, 348, 350, 372, 381, 405

MENO-TUTOR, 252–256, *257,* 269, 292, 391, 396, 400, 403, 421

Mental models, 45–48 (WHY), *49,* 69–76 (ENVISION), *77,* 79–97 (QUEST), *97–98,* 233, 240, *315–316,* 318, 331, 357, *(see also* Causal; Qualitative; Process; Reasoning; Simulation)

perspectives on, 45–46, *47, 70, 89*

Mentor (mode), *152* (SPIRIT)

Menus, *(see under* Interface)

Metacognition (metaknowledge, metalevel reasoning, metastrategy), 146–149 (SMITHTOWN), 265–266 (GUIDON), 272–278 (NEOMYCIN), 319–320 (ALGEBRALAND), *339,* 383, 393, 407, *412–413,* 413, *430–432, (see also* Reflexive model; Strategy, reasoning)

Metarules, *253,* 255, 272, *274,* 400

Meteorology, 33, 39, 52, 353

METEOROLOGY tutor, *52–54,* 70, 73, 76, 314

Methodology, *(see under* ITS; AI; *also* Design)

MHO, *147–149,* 380, 385, 391, 400, 402, 407, 425, 428

Micro-PROUST, *258*

Microworlds, *125–126,* 146, 360, 424, *(see also* Environment)

increasingly complex, *133–135,* 175

Migration of bugs, *(see under* Bugs)

Minilab, *(see under* Feedback)

Misconceptions, 17, 44–45, *183–184,* 197, 207, *222, 353–354,* 380, 392, 407,

410, *(see under* Articulation, and; Bugs, versus; *also* Errors; Diagnosis; Remediation)

inevitability of, *97, (see also* Bugs, prevention and diagnosis)

inferring underlying, 44–45 (WHY), 233, 235–236 (ADVISOR), 237 (MENO-II), 250 (PROUST), *257,* 348, 349, *381–382,* 407, *(see also* Bugs, theories of, generative)

viewpoints and, *355, 359–360,* 362

Misgeneralization, 134, *178, 197–198,* 202, 206–207

Mislearning, 17, 165, 177–179 (SIERRA), 197–198, *206–207,* 211, 337, 348, 349, 352–354

MISS (Micro-programmed Speech Synthesizer), 102

MIT (Massachusetts Institute of Technology), 55, 125, 135, 205, 230

Mixed-initiative, *21, 30,* 37, 52, 124, 263, *(see also* Dialogues)

MIZAR, *121*

Models, *7,* 25, *(see under* Communicable knowledge; Communication, background and foreground use of; Comparing; Correspondence; Curriculum versus; Order of; Progressions of; Robustness of; Simulation versus)

types of, *(see* Aggregate; Architectural; Causal; Communication; Component; Deep-structure; Diagnostic; Discourse; Domain; First-order; Functional; General; Instruction; Intentional; Learning; Mental; Molecular; Motivational; Patient-specific; Pedagogical; Problem-specific; Process; Proportional; Qualitative; Quantitative; Reciprocal; Reflexive; Stereotypical; Stochastic; Student; Task; World; Zero-order)

typologies of, *45–48, 90–94*

Model-driven, *(see under* Diagnosis; Noise)

Model tracing, *297–298* (ACTP), 374, 378, *378–379,* 380, 382, 385, 386, 401

Modeling, *(see under* Cognitive; Syntactic manipulations versus; Syntax and semantics in; *also* Diagnosis)

Modeling-scaffolding-fading, *316, 322–323*

Modularity, 254, *265–266, 277, 286, 338–339,* 341–342, 346, 350, *(see also* Representation, abstractions; Pedagogy, domain content and)

Molecular models, 46, 47 (WHY)

Motivation, 20, 113, 124, *132–133,* 370, 391, *412*

Motivational model, *370*

Mouse, *81,* 317, 320, 388

Multiple, *(see under* Analogy; Expert module; Explanations; Hints; Representation; Solution path; Viewpoints)

Multiple-choice, *(see* Interface, menus)

S

Experiences
of
Depression

Experiences *of* Depression

∽

THEORETICAL, CLINICAL,
AND RESEARCH PERSPECTIVES

Sidney J. Blatt

AMERICAN PSYCHOLOGICAL ASSOCIATION
WASHINGTON, DC

Published by
American Psychological Association
750 First Street, NE
Washington, DC 20002
www.apa.org

To order
APA Order Department
P.O. Box 92984
Washington, DC 20090-2984
Tel: (800) 374-2721; Direct: (202) 336-5510
Fax: (202) 336-5502; TDD/TTY: (202) 336-6123
Online: www.apa.org/books/
E-mail: order@apa.org

In the U.K., Europe, Africa,
and the Middle East,
copies may be ordered from
American Psychological Association
3 Henrietta Street
Covent Garden, London
WC2E 8LU England

Typeset in Century Schoolbook by World Composition Services, Inc., Sterling, VA

Printer: United Book Press, Inc., Baltimore, MD
Cover Designer: Berg Design, Albany, NY
Technical/Production Editor: Dan Brachtesende

The opinions and statements published are the responsibility of the authors, and such opinions and statements do not necessarily represent the policies of the American Psychological Association.

Library of Congress Cataloging-in-Publication Data

Blatt, Sidney J. (Sidney Jules)
 Experiences of depression : theoretical, clinical, and research
 perspectives / Sidney J. Blatt.—1st ed.
  p. cm.
 ISBN 1-59147-095-1
  1. Depression, Mental. 2. Introjection. I. Title.

 RC537.B525 2004
 616.85′27—dc22   2003016292

British Library Cataloguing-in-Publication Data
A CIP record is available from the British Library.

Printed in the United States of America
First Edition

Dedicated to the memory of Sura Malka Blatt:
A grandmother I never knew;
but who has been with me always.

Contents

Foreword

Peter Fonagy

Anyone who picks up this book should be under no illusion. It is the work of one of the giants in our field. There are but a handful of individuals who can claim to have complete mastery of a field and to exercise this with elegance, wisdom, and creative brilliance. Sidney J. Blatt's stature as a senior psychologist in one of the world's great centers of the mind sciences is undisputed. He is also a clinical psychologist with a record of discovery and mentorship that few anywhere in the world can rival and, beyond this, a psychoanalyst with a powerful clinical and epistemological commitment to the field. What is most remarkable about Dr. Blatt is that he has simultaneously pursued each of these intellectual commitments to the highest level of excellence, measured by the native criteria of the respective disciplines. He has integrated ideas and observations from clinical psychology, cognitive science, and psychoanalysis to create something genuinely original. This has been done with great integrity, cutting no corners, resisting the temptation to arrive at half-baked generalizations and the appearance of identity on a pars pro toto principle. Blatt's contribution is genuinely interdisciplinary, in the best sense of that word. Fluent in each of the languages he uses, he moves among the clinical and normal psychology worlds and Freud's world with fluidity and remarkable grace.

The present book is a highly significant contribution summarizing and integrating almost 30 years of work on the subtypes of depression, culminating in a general model of psychopathology. The psychology of depression is one of the outstanding challenges of psychology and psychiatry. It is perhaps the single most written about disorder in both these disciplines, and rightly so given the burden of disease associated with this diagnosis (Murray & Lopez, 1996). To have made a fundamental contribution to a field of this importance is indeed a mark of greatness.

Blatt's idea is a deceptively simple one. Looked at phenomenologically, there are at least two kinds of depression. The orientation of the person with depression can be toward the other or toward the self. The discovery emerges clearly when aspects of the experience of depression are examined and has proved to be extremely robust to replication. When these findings were first made in the early 1970s, few could have guessed just how fruitful this line of research would turn out to be. Whereas the discovery was an empirical one, it immediately illuminated the clinical work of all those who have attempted to make sense of the subjective world of individuals with this diagnosis. Appreciating the distinction between anaclitic and introjective depression, like any profound insight, feels immediately obvious once genuinely taken on board. It seems almost self-evident that depression associated with dissatisfaction with oneself is different from the feeling of being unloved or uncared about, or unworthy of the love of another. It is a distinction that is of assistance in empathizing with different aspects of this complex and difficult disorder.

The contribution of the DEQ (the Depressive Experiences Questionnaire) goes significantly beyond making a categorical distinction. It turns out across literally hundreds of studies that a distinction that is made based on the factor structure of a questionnaire taps into a profound dichotomy that underpins human personality organization. Blatt's quality as a scientist shines through here. He and his coworkers were not satisfied, as many psychometricians might have been, with merely describing a vital dimension that discriminates these two groups of individuals with depression. Using a remarkable narrative instrument, Blatt and colleagues have been able to explore the mental representational system that underpins these two forms of depression. The DEQ and the ORI (Object Relations Inventory) together have facilitated the development of an important body of clinical empirical investigations in this field. It turns out that anaclitic and introjective depressed individuals have particular impairments in the development of mental representation that create specific vulnerabilities to loss and depression. The former appear to possess primarily sensorimotor-preoperational representations of caregiving figures, which leaves them with a need for direct, immediate, physical need-gratifying contact with the caregiver. They are concerned with what people can do for or to them. By contrast, individuals with introjective, self-critical depression have a representational system where a specific, perhaps excessively critical part of the object can behave as if they were the entire individual, insufficiently balanced by the amalgam of love and hate, good and bad, that makes up the human psyche. As these parts are not well integrated into a more conceptual mode of thought, this deficit, paradoxically, enables them to exercise more rigorous criticism of their own behavior and thinking than a better integrated, less fragmented mind. The strength of correspondence between the two measures is striking, but it is important to note that the measures are found to illuminate other instruments in current use.

The book reviews an enormous body of work on the relationship of childhood family experience and depression, exploring longitudinal studies of normal children, studies of children at risk, and retrospective recollections of adults. Inconsistent, intrusive or controlling, overprotective parenting is revealed as a key factor in the development of depression. The developmental origin of self-criticism is to be found in destructive parent–child relationships, where critical, judgmental, demanding, and disapproving parental attitudes, not surprisingly, perhaps, are found to lead to negative representation of self and others. By contrast, those whose depression is characterized by dependency, whose pathology is rooted in problems of interpersonal relatedness, are more likely to make suicidal gestures, show other signs of oral dependency such as substance abuse and alcohol dependence, and have chronic fears of being abandoned. Parental overprotection, manipulating the expression and availability of care and affection, may generate heightened dependency. Perhaps the interpersonal factor is less well understood relative to its counterpart, yet we immediately find that the distinction is of enormous help in understanding gender differences in psychopathology. Girls are known to show internalizing patterns, whereas boys tend to show an externalizing one.

Blatt and colleagues are able to helpfully tie in the distinction on the basis of the experiential typology of depression with the growing literature on the representation of attachment relationships. Their proposed dichotomy overlaps in a highly informative way with the Bowlby–Ainsworth–Main categorization. The idea of the dialectic between individuation on the one hand and attachment on the other as the two poles between which personality development must oscillate makes profound sense at many levels. It also helps us understand the nature of psychopathology as a failure to achieve a balance between these opposite poles. *Anaclitic pathology* (an exaggerated need for relatedness–preoccupation/entanglement) is present in dependent, histrionic or borderline personality disorder. *Introjective pathology* (an exaggerated quest for identity–dismissing or avoidant pathology) is thought to characterize schizoid, schizotypal, narcissistic, antisocial, or avoidant individuals. This is one of the few great insights that dynamic psychology has provided, and this book fully explores applications across a range of pathologies, life situations, and therapeutic experiences.

The person-centered approach of Blatt's perspective thus has the potential to greatly deepen our understanding of most forms of psychiatric disturbance, not just depression, by adding a well-thought-out and extensively empirically supported dynamic developmental standpoint. Looking at the interaction between experiences of depression and personality disorder brings helpful clarification of qualitative differences in the nature of depressive experience in different types of Axis II pathology. Depression in individuals with borderline personality disorder is characterized by emptiness; loneliness; desperation vis-à-vis attachment figures; and labile, diffuse affectivity. For nonborderline individuals with major depression, these aspects correlate negatively with the severity of depression, whereas for borderline individuals, the same symptoms correlate almost perfectly with severity within the limits of the reliability of measurement.

It is not just descriptive psychopathology that is given an additional dimension through Blatt's conceptualization. Treatment response or variability in response to treatment begins to make more sense once the experience of depression is taken into consideration. The value of Blatt's approach is in focusing our attention on the subjective world of the person experiencing psychological distress. Qualitative differences in the nature of that experience have highlighted differences in underlying mechanism, etiology, and treatment response. In the future, the person-centered approach that takes the representational world as its focus may help to refine our predictions about treatment outcomes for a variety of different types of psychological disturbance.

And indeed it is in the area of treatment and treatment development that I think the contribution of this book will be most keenly felt. Alan Kazdin and Philip Kendall (Kazdin & Kendall, 1998) proposed over four years ago that treatment research should begin with the identification of key dysfunctions associated with a particular disorder. This leads to the suggestion that there must be a conceptual link established between the method of treatment and the dysfunctional mechanism identified in connection with the disorder. It is without doubt that Blatt and his colleagues have identified and elaborated a key dysfunctional mechanism that underpins depression. It is now up to those who work in dynamic psychotherapy to build on these important discoveries and refine their treatment so that it more specifically addresses the nature of the disorder that an individual with a diagnosis of depression experiences. For too long, psychodynamic psychotherapists have luxuriated in an intellectually satisfying but practically undemanding "one size fits all" model of psychological therapy. The future of psychoanalytically oriented therapy is in the development of innovative treatment models for treatment-resistant conditions. This requires the comprehensive exploitation of what we have called the psychoanalytic knowledge base (Fonagy, 2003), which is an integration of the cumulative findings of insight-oriented psychotherapy and the psychoanalytic theory of the mind as elaborated through conceptual, empirical, and interdisciplinary research.

This book is clearly essential reading for all of us who work psychotherapeutically, regardless of orientation. We ignore knowledge concerning the experiences of our patients at our peril. It is vital reading for psychodynamic therapists who are committed to improving the way they plan and implement therapeutic interventions, particularly with depressed individuals. Here is the conceptual and empirical basis for the next generation of psychodynamic therapists for depression. Blatt offers a treatment that is closer to and more focused on the patient's experience, that is therefore more readily structured and coherently delivered, and that provides a clearer basis for training and research, both of treatment effectiveness and of the relationship of process to outcome. This is a groundbreaking volume that integrates more than a quarter of a century's work. Let us hope that it will generate a further quarter of a century's productive and fruitful research to alleviate the distress of a group of individuals whose mental health problems have not yet been solved, notwithstanding all our intensive efforts.

Acknowledgments

This book integrates clinical and empirical research that I have conducted on depression over the past 30 years in collaboration with a group of remarkable colleagues and friends: David C. Zuroff, John S. Auerbach, Susan A. Bers, Joseph P. D'Afflitti, Beth Hart, Christopher C. Henrich, Erika Homann, Gabriel P. Kuperminc, Bonnie J. Leadbeater, Patrick Luyten, Suniya S. Luthar, Celina Maroudas, Donald M. Quinlan, Carrie E. Schaffer, Golan Shahar, Shula Shichman, Robert E. Steele, Steven J. Wein, and Ada H. Zohar.

I am deeply grateful to them for the excitement of discovery that we have shared. Their contributions are a vital part of this book.

Experiences
of
Depression

Introduction

Some of the most vivid memories of my early childhood are accompanying my father each year to the cemetery, as observant Jews do early each fall, to visit the grave of his mother, who died when he was between 3 and 4 years of age. Because my father's family were recent immigrants and of very limited means, his mother had been buried at the far end of the cemetery, in what my father referred to as the "paupers' section," where the graves were very close together and often badly neglected, even though arrangements had supposedly been made for the care of some of the gravesites. The first visit to the cemetery I can recall was when I was not much older than the age at which my father lost his mother; I remember holding my father's hand and attempting to console him as he knelt and wept over his mother's grave. While weeping, my father would remove the weeds each year as he attempted to tidy up the gravesite. I also recall, at the age of 13, accompanying my mother on a long and very painful two-hour bus trip as she responded to an urgent phone call informing her that her father had just had a heart attack. I vividly remember trying to reassure and console my mother as she, correctly anticipating her father's death, grieved his loss as the bus wandered through a seemingly endless series of rural New Jersey villages before we arrived at her parents' summer home.

Thus, it is not surprising that I sought a career in clinical psychology and in psychoanalysis and that I became interested in depression, or that I became particularly sensitive in my clinical work to a type of depression associated with object loss and that I attempted to differentiate that type of depression from the more usual form of depression that derives from a harsh and punitive superego, involving intense self-criticism and feelings of worthlessness, failure, and guilt. These early life experiences probably made me particularly sensitive to an apparent contradiction and paradox in Freud's classic formulations of melancholia (1917/1957e) in which he discussed the relation of depression to an oral-incorporative, dependent, phase of libidinal development that precedes object choice, as well as to a more advanced and complex phase of psychological development that derives from the formation of the superego and the beginning resolution of the Oedipal complex and involves experiences of guilt, self-reproach, and self-punishment.

In the opening paragraph of *Mourning and Melancholia*, Freud (1917/1957e) cautiously noted that the definition of *melancholia* varies widely and that one cannot be certain if the various somatic and psychogenetic forms of melancholia can be grouped into a single entity. Thus, I was puzzled by Freud's extensive attempts, throughout his paper (Blatt, 1974, 1998), to develop a unified conceptualization of melancholia that integrates the diverse processes of both oral dependency and superego development into a single formulation. It seemed to me more appropriate to think about two different types of depression, each based on one of these two very different fundamental mechanisms of psychological development identified by Freud: (a) a depression focused primarily on interpersonal issues, such as dependency, helplessness, and feelings of loss and abandonment, and (b) a depression derived from a harsh, punitive superego that is focused primarily on self-criticism, concerns about self-worth, and feelings of failure and guilt.

In *Mourning and Melancholia*, Freud (1917/1957e) also indicated that the vulnerability to depression is a consequence of a failure to have internalized adequately the representation of a caring object because of ambivalent feelings toward the object. Loss can be fully accepted and integrated only when an adequate level of representation (i.e., object constancy) has been achieved (Blatt, 1974; Blatt, Quinlan, & Chevron, 1990). Thus, in our research, my colleagues and I have also examined the content and structural organization of mental representation of significant others in depression, based on the assumption that impairments in the representation of significant caregivers create particular vulnerability to loss and depression. Again, personal experiences probably played a pivotal role in my sensitivity to this aspect of depression (i.e., the importance of an adequate level of mental representation in dealing with object loss). At around the age of 9, I became disillusioned with my father for his failure to support me in what in retrospect I realize was a relatively minor, but a symbolically important, matter. Disappointed and angry with my father, I threatened to run away from home. I packed my bags and defiantly walked out of our house. I had walked no more than about two or three blocks when I became acutely aware that I could not remember what my mother looked like. In terror, I rapidly returned home. This intensely powerful personal experience is probably one of the primary antecedents in my lifelong professional interest in the importance of mental representation in psychological functions.

Experiences based on my beginning work as a clinical psychoanalyst when I was in training at the Western New England Psychoanalytic Institute and from empirical investigations with colleagues, undergraduate and graduate students, and postdoctoral fellows at Yale University, provided further support for my observations and speculations about the nature of depression. As I describe in detail in chapter 1, two of my four "control" (supervised) cases that were part of my early psychoanalytic training provided the primary impetus for my study of depression. Both of these patients came into analysis with primary features of depression, but one patient's depression was vividly focused on experiences of abandonment and neglect, whereas the other patient was focused on issues of guilt and concerns about self-worth (Blatt, 1974). In addition, these two patients differed in the quality of their mental representations. The patient concerned with issues of abandonment represented significant people in her life primarily around the extent to which they provided, or failed to provide, her with gratification and support. In contrast, the representations of the patient concerned with issues of guilt and self-worth were more conceptual as he struggled to integrate disparate negative and positive elements in a more organized conception of his significant others and himself.

Experiences in empirical research provided further validity for these formulations about two types of depression and the role of impaired object representation in depression that had emerged in my clinical work. Research efforts on the two types of depression were initially expressed in a doctoral dissertation completed at Yale University by Joseph P. D'Afflitti. Parts of D'Afflitti's dissertation were based on his collaboration with Donald M. Quinlan and myself in our attempt to develop a procedure for assessing life experiences associated with depression. On the basis of a general assumption that has guided much of my career in clinical psychology and psychoanalysis (see, e.g., Blatt, 1974, 1991, 1995b; Blatt & Levy, 1998; Blatt & Wild, 1976; Blatt, Wild, & Ritzler, 1975)—that various forms of psychopathology are better understood as psychological processes that emerge from disruptions of normal psychological development than as separate diseases that derive from some presumed but still-unspecified and -undocumented biological disturbance (i.e., as in the *Diagnostic and Statistical Manual of Mental Disorders*; American Psychiatric Association, 1994)—D'Afflitti, Quinlan, and I reviewed a number of major statements on depression (e.g., Freud's [1917/1957e] *Mourning and Melancholia*, Edward Bibring's [1953] *Mechanisms of Depression*, and the article *Twelve Cases of Manic–Depressive Psychosis* by Mabel Blake Cohen and colleagues [M. B. Cohen, Baker, Cohen, Fromm-Reichman, & Weigert, 1954]), to glean statements not about the symptoms of depression but about the nature of the life experiences reported by depressed patients. We developed 66 statements or items that tapped issues such as a distorted or depreciated sense of self and others, dependency, helplessness, egocentricity, fear of loss, ambivalence, difficulty dealing with anger, self-blame, guilt, loss of autonomy, and distortions of family relations. We selected these items not to assess types of depression but because they seemed to represent a wide range of experiences that were characteristic of the lives of depressed patients. These 66 statements were initially administered to a group of 128 college students—far too few participants, of course, to conduct a meaningful factor analysis of the responses to these items. Nevertheless, we conducted an initial factor analysis to see if we could identify clusters of items in the students' responses to the 66 items we had gleaned from the clinical literature. D'Afflitti came to my office one morning with the results of this initial factor analysis, discouraged by the fact that the clustering of the items into three empirically defined factors did not seem to make sense to him. On the basis of my clinical experiences with my two psychoanalytic training cases at that time, I immediately recognized that the first factor contained items primarily focused on issues of loneliness and abandonment and that the second factor comprised items focused on issues of self-definition and self-worth. On the basis of these initial findings, D'Afflitti, Quinlan, and I sought a substantially larger group of college students and found that the 66 items did indeed cluster into three primary orthogonal factors. The first factor was focused on issues of interpersonal relatedness; we labeled it *Dependency*. The second factor, which we labeled *Self-Criticism*, contained items that were focused on issues of self-definition and self-worth. In addition, a third factor emerged that contained primarily items focused on positive self-feelings; we labeled it *Efficacy* (Blatt, D'Afflitti, & Quinlan, 1976). Thus, we had serendipitously found a method for assessing the two types of depressive experiences and titled this assessment procedure the *Depressive Experiences Questionnaire* (DEQ; Blatt, D'Afflitti & Quinlan, 1979). Details of the development of the DEQ are presented in chapter 3.

The Dependency factor of the DEQ consists of items that are primarily externally directed; refer to interpersonal relations; and contain themes of abandonment, loneliness, and helplessness as well as the desire to be close to, related to, and dependent on, others. High-loading items of this factor reflect concerns about being rejected and hurting or offending people and having difficulty in managing anger and aggression for fear of losing someone. The second factor, Self-Criticism, consists of items that are more internally directed and reflect feelings of guilt, emptiness, hopelessness, dissatisfaction, and insecurity. Failure to meet expectations and standards, inability to assume responsibility, feeling threatened by change, ambivalence about self and others, and tending to assume blame and feeling critical toward oneself are all reflected in high-loading items on the Self-Criticism factor. The Efficacy factor includes items that indicate a sense of confidence about one's personal resources and capacities. Themes of high standards and personal goals; responsibility; inner strength; and feelings of independence, satisfaction, and pride in one's accomplishments are central to the items that load highly on this factor. Thus, the Efficacy factor presents a positive picture of goal-oriented strivings and feelings of accomplishment (Blatt, Quinlan, & Chevron, 1990; Schaffer & Blatt, 1990). Extensive subsequent research in a number of different countries has confirmed the stability of this factor structure of the DEQ in both adolescents and adults (e.g., Zuroff, Quinlan, & Blatt, 1990) as well as its reliability and validity (e.g., Blatt & Zuroff, 1992) in a variety of clinical and nonclinical samples. The development of the DEQ (Blatt, D'Afflitti, & Quinlan, 1976, 1979) and subsequent questionnaires that assess these two dimensions of depression (e.g., the Sociotropy–Autonomy Scale [SAS; Beck, 1983], the Personal Styles Inventory [Robins & Ladd, 1991], and the two factors of the Dysfunctional Attitudes Scale [A. N. Weissman & Beck, 1978]) have led to a very large body of research that has enriched our understanding of the nature of depression and its etiology and treatment. I review this extensive research literature in the latter half of the book (chaps. 5–7).

Empirical investigation of mental representation in depression was initiated by Stephen J. Wein in his undergraduate psychology honors thesis at Yale University. Based on our discussions in 1973–1974 about the nature of object representation in depression, Steve had the creative idea to ask a group of Yale undergraduates to write brief descriptions of their mothers and their fathers. This idea—to assess representations through briefly written descriptions—seemed like a fine idea for an undergraduate research project, but I held little hope that this simple procedure would yield significant data for more substantial investigations. I was astounded when Steve and I reviewed the descriptions he collected from Yale undergraduates. These descriptions were remarkably revealing and compelling, so much so that my first reaction was to wonder how my own children would describe me. We (Steve Wein, Donald

Quinlan, Eve Chevron, and I) developed several systematic ways to evaluate these descriptions of significant others (e.g., mother and father) and related these measures to several standard measures of depression. These initial investigations are reported in detail in chapter 4, but suffice to say at this point that the differences I had observed clinically about the quality of object representation in the two types of depression were supported by our initial study (Blatt, Wein, Chevron, & Quinlan, 1979). Steve went on to medical school and psychiatric residency after graduating from Yale and today is a supervising and training analyst at the New York Psychoanalytic Institute. Although he did not pursue a career in psychological research, Steve gave us a methodology that my colleagues, especially John Auerbach and Diana Diamond, and I have continued to explore over the last 25 years, developing methods for systematically evaluating the content and structural organization of these descriptions of self and significant others.

The development of these two research procedures derived from psychoanalytic formulations—the assessment of two types of depressive experiences and the assessment of the content and structural organization of mental representation—led to a host of investigations by a number of outstanding graduate and undergraduate students and postdoctoral fellows at Yale University, including Joseph P. D'Afflitti, Eve Chevron, Cathy MacDonald, Steven Wein, Erika Homann, Suniya Luthar, Kathleen Otero, Celina Maroudas (at the Hebrew University of Jerusalem), Carrie Schaffer, Golan Shahar, Robert E. Steele, and Susan Bers. Donald M. Quinlan, made vital contributions to the development of the DEQ. Also, David C. Zuroff, after finishing his PhD in clinical psychology at the University of Connecticut, remained briefly in New Haven from 1979–1981 and joined our depression research group. David eventually joined the faculty at McGill University, where he and his research team, including Myriam Mongrain and Darcy Santor, have made major contributions by bringing social psychological perspectives to the study of depression. Beginning in 1991, I began to explore the role of dependency and self-criticism in adolescent development in collaboration with Beth Hart, Bonnie Leadbeater, Gabriel Kuperminc, Chris Henrich, and the W. T. Grant Foundation. In July 2000, Golan Shahar, on leave from a faculty post at Bar Ilan University in Israel, joined me as a postdoctoral fellow, sponsored by the Rothchild Foundation. Previously, Shahar had done extensive research using the DEQ with Professor Beatriz Priel at the Ben Gurion University of the Negev, at Yale he began a series of creative investigations of the two types of depressive experiences, including collaborating with David Zuroff, which has added substantially to our understanding of depression. Zuroff and I (Blatt & Zuroff, 1992) summarized much of the research on the DEQ that had been conducted from this perspective until about 1991. However, this area of clinical investigation has continued to expand rapidly, and now an extensive array of findings support the validity of the distinction of the two types of depression and elaborate its importance in both clinical and nonclinical samples across a wide age range as well as across different socioeconomic, cultural, and ethnic groups. Further research, primarily in collaboration with John S. Auerbach, also indicated the important role of mental representations in various forms of psychopathology, especially depression, as well as in the therapeutic process. This book is my attempt to integrate this diverse literature of theoretical formulations, clinical examples, and a wide range of research findings indicating the importance of differentiating between these two forms of depression and how this distinction has facilitated further understanding of the etiology and clinical expression of depression. In this book I also review research on the role of impairments in mental representation in depression and their change in the therapeutic process.

Thus, the purpose of this book is to present a psychological perspective on depression and to demonstrate how observations in the psychoanalytic treatment of two depressed patients provided insight into the phenomenology of depression that has led to a wide range of clinical and empirical investigations of the etiology, clinical expression, and treatment of depression. This focus on the phenomenology rather than on the symptoms of depression alerted me and my colleagues to the important differences between a depression that is focused primarily on interpersonal relations and involves intense feelings of loneliness and fears of abandonment from a depression that is focused on issues of self-definition and involves intense feelings of failure, worthlessness, and guilt. This book is based on the fundamental assumption that depression is best understood and treated not as a biological disease that derives from a presumed but as-yet-undocumented chemical imbalance but as psychological disturbances that derive from difficult untoward life circumstances that occur both early and later in psychological development. Thus, the goal of this book is to provide an understanding of the life experiences that lead to depression with the belief that the fuller understanding of these experiences and their exploration in the psychotherapeutic process are central to the treatment of depression.

This book is an integration of clinical and theoretical perspectives on depression as well as extensive empirical investigations. These three perspectives are inextricably intertwined. Clinical observations initially led to theoretical formulations and then to empirical investigations, which in turn sharpened the level of our clinical observations. Our empirical research derived from clinical observation and theory and, likewise, our clinical experiences and theoretical formulations were influenced by our emerging empirical findings. Thus, this book has sections devoted primarily to clinical observations and theoretical formulations, whereas other sections of the book are devoted primarily to the details of empirical investigations and summaries of these findings. Some readers may find the clinical–theoretical sections (chaps. 1, 2, and 8) of greater interest, other readers may find the research sections (chaps. 3–7) more relevant, but the emphasis throughout this book is on the value of the integration of clinical, theoretical, and empirical perspectives and how each of these perspectives serves to enrich, and is enriched in turn, by these integrative efforts.

In large part, my efforts derived from, and were greatly enhanced by, my clinical experiences with patients who shared with me intimate details of their lives, and by rewarding collaborations with outstanding students and colleagues. Over the years, students and colleagues, as well as patients, have shared with me their sense of the inconsistencies and anomalies they have experienced in our attempts to understand the complex issues in depression. We have collaboratively struggled to refine our formulations, to construct more effective understanding, and to develop investigations to try to resolve these inconsistencies. Scientific and clinical progress, as Piaget (e.g., 1937/1954) noted in discussing normal development, occurs as the consequence of the recognition of anomalies and inconsistencies and through efforts to resolve these perturbations (Blatt, 1984). Thus, I am grateful to my patients, students, and colleagues for their steadfast unwillingness to settle for simple solutions to complex problems and for their demand that we seek fuller, more complete answers to these difficult issues. In addition, Golan Shahar, as well as David Zuroff, John Auerbach, Erika Homann, and Donald Quinlan, provided a critical reading of aspects of the manuscript for this book and made a number of insightful and creative suggestions for which I am grateful. I am also indebted to Joan Cricca for her dedicated, thoughtful, and painstaking efforts in preparing the manuscript and, as always, I am indebted to my wife, Ethel, for her support of these endeavors over the years.

Part I

Theoretical Formulations and Clinical Examples of Anaclitic and Introjective Depression

Introduction:

Theoretical Formulations and Clinical Examples of Anaclitic and Introjective Depression

In the two chapters in this section I present the clinical observations and theoretical formulations that led to the differentiation of two types of depressive experiences. In chapter 1, I review the classic psychoanalytic literature on depression, beginning with Freud's initial observation in 1895. Although presented in classic psychoanalytic terms, these early clinical observations and formulations provided the basis for the more contemporary articulation of two fundamental phenomenological dimensions of depression. This differentiation is based not on the symptoms of depression but on the life experiences that are central in depressive experiences. In addition, these clinical examples and this theoretical review led to my recognition of the importance of impairments in the representation of caregiving relations in these two types of depression. In this book I explore these two hypotheses about depression: that impairments in the establishment of the representation of caregiving relationships contribute to fundamentally different experiences of depression: a depression based on (a) profound feelings of loss and loneliness or (b) intense feelings of a lack of self-worth.

In chapter 2, I present a number of examples of the various ways these two types of depression can be expressed in a clinical context.

1

Two Types of Depression

The formulation of two types of depression—*anaclitic* and *introjective* depression—initially derived from two patients I saw in psychoanalysis as part of my training at the Western New England Institute for Psychoanalysis, a young man and a young woman, both diagnosed as depressed. It became clear during the analytic process, however, that remarkable differences existed between these two patients despite the similarity of their fundamental diagnosis—differences in their early life experiences, their basic character or personality style, and the nature of their depressive experiences. Also impressive were the differences in the quality of their mental representations of self and others and the nature of the reparative process that occurred in the treatment process. A brief summary of these two patients illustrates some of these differences.

Primary Clinical Examples

Anaclitic (Dependent) Depression

Helen H., a young, recently married woman, entered analysis because of recurrent and intense feelings of depression, tension, and anxiety. She was in the process of obtaining a divorce and was frightened that she would become "lonely, old, and crazy" like her mother, or that she would commit suicide. Her mother had made a serious suicide attempt when Helen was nine years old, and Helen's outstanding memory of this event was of being left behind—alone, frightened, and screaming—as they rushed her mother to the hospital. This reminded her of her own hospitalization for a tonsillectomy at age six and her feelings of being "left alone" in the darkness of the anesthesia and her fear that she would die.

Helen was never able to sleep away from home as a child, and as an adolescent she was unable to take trips out of town. She said she had married

---

This chapter incorporates material from (a) "Levels of Object Representation in Anaclitic and Introjective Depression," by S. J. Blatt, 1974, *Psychoanalytic Study of the Child, 29*, pp. 107–157. Copyright 1974 by Yale University Press. Reprinted with permission; (b) "Convergence of Psychoanalytic and Cognitive Behavioral Theories of Depression," by S. J. Blatt and C. Maroudas, 1992, *Psychoanalytic Psychology, 9*, pp. 157–190. Copyright 1992 by Erlbaum. Reprinted with permission; and (c) "Contributions of Psychoanalysis to the Understanding and Treatment of Depression," by S. J. Blatt, 1998, *Journal of the American Psychoanalytic Association, 46*, pp. 723–752. Copyright 1998 by The Analytic Press. Reprinted with permission.

in an attempt to extricate herself from a consuming and destructive relationship with what she perceived as her erratic, labile, and probably borderline psychotic mother, but after her marriage she rented an apartment within view of her mother's home. The mother called several times each day, frequently berating Helen. Although Helen was very upset by these endless calls, she could never place limits on them. She was convinced that she would be free of her mother only after her mother's death.

Helen reported that she was conceived because of her parents' wish to avoid having her father drafted for military service in the Korean War. After Helen's birth, her mother was confined to bed because of severe back pains and was unable to care for her. The mother was unable to lift and cuddle Helen, and the father assumed primary responsibility for her care and feeding. As an infant, she had eczema, and in her early teens, as she tried to leave home for summer camp, she developed psoriasis. Her parents were divorced when she was an adolescent, and she felt abandoned by her father in the divorce as well as earlier because of his frequent absence from home during her childhood, especially during evenings and weekends, when his work frequently required him to be away. She believed that she had never had a childhood and a chance to play and that she had to work for anything she wanted. She maintained that she had never seen warmth, love, or tenderness at home and that her family had never done anything together. She reported always feeling very upset when she saw a family together. For example, she abruptly ran out of a friend's engagement party in tears because of the warmth, closeness, and affection expressed by the family members of her friend. She went to her apartment and slept for more than 12 hours. At her own wedding, her parents fought, and her mother cursed her father.

Helen had great difficulty tolerating feelings of loneliness. Shortly after she separated from her husband, she became intensely involved in a long series of brief relationships, most of which lasted only a few days. She ran frantically from one brief affair to another, each time convinced that this was "the real thing," "the perfect relationship," and that she would marry again. She felt little conscious guilt or embarrassment about these brief affairs, only disappointment and feelings of having been used and abandoned. Almost without exception she chose depreciated men from lower socioeconomic and educational levels. The men were of such a nature that she was convinced that if her parents found out about these affairs, her mother would commit suicide and her father would die of a heart attack. The promiscuity had stopped several months before she began analysis with me, and she did not report any of these relationships in the screening interviews.

Almost immediately, Helen seemed to have difficulty with the demands of the analytic process. Beginning in the third hour of the analysis, she began to doze when painful issues came up. The drowsiness increased in frequency and intensity; although she struggled to stay awake so she could "benefit from analysis," she was often unable to stop herself from falling sound asleep. When awake, she often played with her eyeglasses, and it became apparent only later that she was using them as a reflecting surface, a mirror, to keep me in sight during the psychoanalytic sessions. Other indications of an association between object loss and an emphasis on vision occurred. For example, she was very proud of having earned the money to buy contact lenses; yet on the day after the assassination of President Kennedy she confused which lens was for which eye and never wore her contact lenses again.

Helen had difficulty with separations in analysis. Weekends away from work and analysis were empty and painful. She seemed unable to tolerate the loneliness, and she had frequent male visitors and numerous phone calls each night. During the first extended separation from analysis, for a month-long summer holiday, she feared she would go crazy and have to be hospitalized. She requested that she and I "keep in touch" by mail. During the summer vacation she again became frantically involved in a series of brief affairs. Each affair lasted a few days, and each time she again felt intensely in love and was convinced she was going to remarry. After being abandoned by these men, she felt used, abused, and angry. She was aware of, and frightened by, her temptation to become a prostitute.

Her sleep during the psychoanalytic sessions also seemed to be a response to the feelings of loneliness and abandonment she experienced in my silences in analysis and her inability to keep me in sight. Her sleep in analysis often had a peaceful, restful quality; she seemed to want to be held and enveloped. During the second extended separation from analysis, a two-week Christmas holiday, she joined her most recent boyfriend on a trip—the first time she had ventured out of town. On her return, she once again reported that she had fallen in love and that she was planning to get married. After a few days, she abruptly announced that she had decided to interrupt her analysis, because her boyfriend objected to it. It was only on reviewing the case record that I noted that this interruption occurred exactly nine months to the day after Helen and I had first met for the initial evaluation before entering psychoanalysis (see G. Rose, 1962). The interruption also occurred immediately after the Christmas–New Year holiday, when themes of birth and the start of a new life are prevalent in society as a reaction to the emptiness, barrenness, and darkness of the winter solstice.

During the course of her analysis, Helen reported several brief dream fragments. In one dream, there was a knock on the door, and when she answered the door, no one was there. She also had frequent nightmares of being attacked and raped, but she would not elaborate on these in any detail. She briefly mentioned a dream she had shortly before her marriage in which she awoke screaming, "Catch the baby, catch the baby before it falls from the shopping cart." In a current dream, a rat bit her hand, and in another, a boyfriend turned her over to other men to have intercourse with her. She was unable to associate to any of these dreams. She also commented that she often felt tempted to assume a fetal position when masturbating, but she was frightened by the implications of this. At one point in analysis, while following a series of thoughts about her mother, she abruptly stopped and said she felt like she was in "quicksand, being sucked in." She often expressed the thought that her mother had cast a spell over her and she was frightened that she would eventually commit suicide or at least never remarry and would become "lonely, old, and crazy" like her mother.

In terms of diagnosis, Helen seemed to have an anaclitic depression in a basically dependent or infantile narcissistic character disturbance with possibly borderline features. Her depressive concerns focused on her feelings of being unwanted, unloved, and abandoned, which she defended against by seeking direct physical and sensory contact with people, especially men. She had a desperate need to be close to people and to be in touch with them—to keep them in view. Her sadomasochistic fantasies and activities were ways of seeking intense sensory stimulation as well as expressing her rage about deprivation and abandonment. She had to seek substitutes for the failure to have internalized a sense of need-gratifying experiences and of a need-gratifying relationship, yet she constantly provoked abandonment in her indiscriminate search for someone who would provide some sense of contact and immediate need satisfaction. In numerous ways the clinical material illustrated her impaired object representations and her attempts to cope with frightening experiences of object loss and abandonment by maintaining direct, immediate, sensorimotor contact.

Introjective (Self-Critical) Depression

George L. also sought analysis because of intense feelings of depression and concerns about his increasing inability to function effectively, but he was very different from Helen. Colleagues and friends considered him to be quite successful; he had achieved genuine recognition in several high positions that most people felt required much more experience than he possessed. Although he found little meaning and satisfaction in these accomplishments, he was driven to succeed and win recognition, and he worked endlessly, to the point of exhaustion. Several years before he sought analysis, on the eve of the successful completion of a complex and highly responsible professional task on which he had been working for many months, he began to feel faint and panicky while sitting in a barber's chair. The barber's tissue around his neck seemed very tight, and he felt choked by it. As he got up he was unable to walk; he felt that his feet were not touching the ground and that he was about to topple over. For several years after this incident, his functioning continued to decline, and when he finally sought analysis he was barely able to concentrate and work.

When George was a preadolescent, his mother died from an overdose of sleeping pills, and he assumed that she had committed suicide. The mother had been hospitalized at least once several years earlier, when he was a young child, for what seemed to be a severe depression. He remembered her lying on the couch completely covered with a blanket, wearing sunglasses, and being unresponsive. He had a personal myth of himself as being simultaneously rich and poor because he was from a wealthy family that refused to provide him with funds or support. In part, however, this myth also reflected his early childhood experiences with his mother: her occasional gaiety, laughter, and singing, which alternated with periods of despondency and depression.

Shortly after George sought analysis, his father was killed in a single-car accident, and he became disorganized and acutely depressed. I referred him to once-weekly psychotherapy with another therapist to deal with his grief and his acute depression over his father's death, and after several months he returned to begin his analysis with me. He was in psychoanalysis four times per week for 4½ years, which, in retrospect at the end of treatment, he described as consisting of four phases. The first phase he described as helping him hold onto life, preventing further disorganization and possible suicide. The second phase was a time of stabilization in which he gained strength and security. He characterized the third phase as the beginning of a will to live and the belief that there was a future and that it was worth working toward. The fourth phase of analysis was a period in which he struggled with very painful issues and began the difficult process of change. Although he described his analysis in somewhat dramatic fashion, it accurately portrayed his precarious balance when he began analysis and his progressive integration.

Many hours in the first year of analysis were devoted to George's feelings of despair, anguish, guilt, and anger over the death of his parents and the tragedy of their lives. He had numerous images of death, such as seeing himself on a marble slab, being trapped, abandoned, breathless, and choking, and a dream in which he felt like a cold mechanical octopus. He was intensely interested in Hamlet and Dostoyevsky, particularly in *Crime and Punishment*, and in fact he began the initial session of his analysis with the dramatic announcement that he was Raskolnikov. He had intense feelings of guilt about his responsibility for the death of his parents, much of it associated with Oedipal strivings. He believed that love killed his mother because his parents were sleeping together the night she died. He felt sexually attracted to "older women" who were about the age of his mother when she died, and he was particularly interested in older women who needed help. He was excessively altruistic, unable to say no for fear of hurting, rejecting, or offending someone.

Throughout the analysis, George spoke of something inside, vague and unspecified, that had to come out if he were to improve. On leaving each analytic session, he automatically stated the time of the next appointment. He was frightened that there would be no tomorrow and that I would not be there. By means of this automatic phrase at the end of each analytic hour he sought to cope with his intense feelings and apprehension that life and people were unpredictable and unstable.

During the last year of analysis, just after he began to consider the possibility of termination, George began "hearing" a voice inside, a male voice, not unlike his father's, saying emphatically, "Die, boy, die." He heard this voice as he increasingly felt tempted to jump in front of a train or truck or out of a window. He spent considerable time in analysis working on his intense depressive feelings; his self-destructive impulses and behavior; his wish to die and rejoin his parents; his negative introjects, such as the voice; and his anguished feelings that somehow his sexuality had caused his mother's death. He felt empty, impotent, listless, defeated, like a "zombie" or "Dorian Gray," because people were so impressed with him, while inside he felt disturbed, corrupt, and evil. Although he felt that he had made considerable progress in his analysis and that his work was progressing well, he told a joke about a patient who died from improvement. Suicide seemed a serious possibility.

During this period, George's stepmother, a former mental health professional, called and said that she wanted to inform me that George was suicidal and that I should hospitalize him. I told her that that was a matter between George and me. In response, she said that I should be aware that if George committed suicide I would face a major malpractice suit. When George arrived the next day for his appointed hour, I asked him to sit in the chair rather than lying on the couch. I asked if he knew that his stepmother had called and was "concerned about his well-being." George indicated that he was aware that she had called. I asked him if he felt in any danger, and he assured me that he was not. I said that I had no problem with his discussing his suicidal thoughts if he would agree to notify me if and when he felt that he was in danger. With his assurance that he would, he returned to the couch, and we proceeded with our analytic work. Although he continued for some time to discuss his suicidal thoughts and impulses, no need ever arose for us to interrupt his analysis.

Throughout the analysis, George sought information about the circumstances of his mother's death. He visited the home in which they lived when she died, he went to the local newspaper to read the death notice and, later in the analysis, he actively considered for the first time trying to locate her grave. He often found it pleasant on a nice afternoon to walk through the local cemetery. Throughout this adult life he maintained an interest in a subject matter in which his mother had been actively interested and, while in analysis, he began to develop this avocation into a career. His interests were in the same specific areas as his mother's, but he went further than that; he became particularly interested in the development of this topic during the period of his mother's life. Thus, he was simultaneously involved in the area of his mother's major interest as well as in the era in which she lived. He made a major contribution in this area and eventually achieved considerable success and recognition. From an analytic point of view, one of the major functions of these interests was an attempt to reconstruct more reality-adequate representations of his mother by coming to know more fully her interests and many aspects of her life. However, George also worked to establish a differentiation from her as well. He began to explore his fears that he might be psychotic like his mother, and he wondered why he had been accepted for analysis, as it seemed unlikely that he would ever improve.

George's depression lightened after he began to express his anger toward his parents and as he began to elaborate aspects of his negative introjects, such as his identification with his mother who was severely depressed and his hearing the male voice say "Die, boy, die." He completed a major project in his new career and began to develop confidence in the future. This was vividly expressed one hour when he reported seeing a sign with the comment: "Today is the beginning of the rest of your life." He began to feel that he had been through the depths of his depression and that "things inside had come out." As he worked through his ambivalence about his parents and aspects of the termination, he began to establish a more mature basis for identification. In a letter subsequent to termination he wrote,

> I miss you very much and will always think of you with fondness and tenderness. Your courage, [and] steadfast refusal to abandon your faith in me at a time when I virtually had given up hope for myself has helped me regain some measure of self-confidence and self-respect.

George's character structure was obsessive in nature. His depression was primarily introjective in quality, with major antecedents in his difficulty resolving Oedipal issues. His depression focused around issues of guilt, blame, responsibility, and self-worth. He struggled with object loss in an intense and profound way. In analysis, he struggled to achieve a stable representation of his mother by attempting to reconstruct parts of her life and by coming to know her major area of interest and by building his new career around this interest. His progress in analysis closely paralleled his development of more conceptual and symbolic and less ambivalent, literal, and concrete representations of her.

In contrasting the two cases, Helen's concerns were more oral in nature and involved struggles around individuation and separation from a mutually devouring, consuming, and destructive relationship with her mother. Her concerns focused on feelings of being unloved and abandoned and, although there were no conscious feelings of guilt, there was considerable sadomasochistic activity and fantasy. Her object relationships were unstable and on the level of need satisfaction. They seemed insufficient to enable her to tolerate separation and object loss, and she struggled to maintain direct physical and sensory contact with people. George, in contrast, had formed identifications and was struggling primarily with superego issues, and he experienced profound feelings of guilt over his strivings. Although he was driven to succeed and win recognition and approval, he was unable to derive much satisfaction from his accomplishments. He was continually besieged by feelings of self-doubt and fears of punishment, and he dreaded criticism and disapproval. Like Helen, he had traumatic experiences of object loss but struggled to maintain his interpersonal relationships on a developmentally more advanced level. In contrast to Helen, rather than trying to maintain direct physical contact, George struggled to develop consistent and integrated representations of himself and of significant others. In treatment, his object representations were initially ambivalent, somewhat concrete, and depictive, but as his analysis progressed his representations became more differentiated, abstract, symbolic, and integrated. Although Helen and George both sought analysis primarily for intense feelings of depression related to traumatic experiences of object loss, their cases illustrate some of the differences between an anaclitic and an introjective depression.

The differences between these two patients led me to review the classic psychoanalytic literature on depression. Two predominant issues emerged in this review: (a) *the nature of depressive experiences*—whether they primarily involve themes of abandonment, loss, and a lack of gratification or themes of failure, anger, aggression, and guilt, and (b) *the nature of the mechanisms that lead to depression*—how impairments in the quality of object relationships and object representation create a vulnerability to depression.

Classic Psychoanalytic Formulations of Depression

Freud (1917/1957e) was initially cautious in *Mourning and Melancholia* about seeking a unitary formulation for the complex phenomenon of depression. He ultimately tried to understand depression by discussing it in relation to a very early developmental stage in which the infant's awareness is focused on the gratification that the caregiver provides rather than on the caregiver herself—what in psychoanalytic theory is referred to as an *oral-incorporative stage* of libidinal development that precedes object choice—as well as to a more advanced and complex phase of psychological development that derives from the formation of the superego and the beginning resolution of the Oedipal complex[1] and involves experiences of guilt, self-reproach, and self-punishment. Rather than trying to develop a unified conceptualization of melancholia that integrates the processes of oral incorporation and superego formation into a single formulation of depression, my psychoanalytic experiences with Helen and George suggested that Freud's formulations actually identify two fundamental experiences in depression that enable one to differentiate two types of depression: (a) a depression focused primarily on interpersonal issues, such as dependency, helplessness, and feelings of loss and abandonment, and (b) a depression that derives from a harsh, punitive superego that is focused primarily on self-criticism, concerns about self-worth, and feelings of failure and guilt.

The differentiation of these two types of depression based on two different types of experiences and psychological processes is consistent with many aspects of the psychoanalytic literature on depression that discusses issues of both object loss and disruptions in self-worth as central in depression. The exact role of these two psychological mechanisms and sets of issues, however, has never been precisely differentiated. Issues of loneliness and loss, as well as expressions of a harsh, punitive, critical superego (feeling guilty or worthless) were often articulated in the psychoanalytic literature, but their differential role in depression seems inconsistent and controversial. The literature seemed to suggest that both these issues occur in depression, but often in relatively independent ways.

The term *depression* has been used in the psychoanalytic literature to describe reactions to extreme experiences of deprivation in infancy (Provence & Lipton, 1962; Spitz & Wolf, 1946) and as a relatively high-level, developmental stage (H. Segal, 1964; Winnicott, 1954). *Depression* has been used to describe a character or personality style (Blatt, 1966) with an unusual susceptibility to dysphoric feelings, a vulnerability to feelings of loss and disappointment, intense need for contact and support, and a proclivity to assume blame and responsibility and to feel guilty. Depression has been discussed not only in terms of infantile feelings of abandonment and helplessness but also in terms of superego formation and the relatively advanced and complex psychological phenomenon of guilt. Rubenfine (1968), for example, considered depres-

---

[1]The Oedipal phase in psychoanalytic theory involves the child's emerging awareness of his or her role in a family matrix and his or her relationship with each parent and the relationship of the parents with each other—the beginning of triadic interpersonal structures. This capacity for triadic thinking in interpersonal relationships is structurally similar to the development of operational thought, which develops at about the same time as psychoanalysis designates the development of the Oedipal phase and which, according to Piaget (e.g., 1945/1962), involves the capacity to coordinate at least three dimensions as the child becomes capable of the cognitive operations of transformation, reversibility, and conservation (Blatt, 1983, 1995b).

sion to be primarily concerned with restoring past pleasure and as originating in a fixation to a state of narcissistic union with the mother. He saw guilt only as a consequence of the aggression felt toward the frustrating nongratifying object. Beres (1966), in contrast, stated that "an essential determinant of true depression, whether as a transient manifestation or as part of depressive illness, is a sense of guilt which carries with it the assumption of a structured superego and an internalized conflict" (p. 484). Mendelson (1960) pointed to the need to develop a broad conceptualization of depression that can integrate these various observations and theories and differentiate between the wide range of phenomena called *depression*—the normal and necessary affective state—and the various types of prolonged, recurring, and debilitating processes of clinical depression. Thus, considerable controversy existed in psychoanalytic thought about the relative role of feelings of abandonment and loss and feelings of failure and guilt in depression.

Some psychoanalytic theorists asserted that failure to maintain contact with the need-gratifying aspects of an object is of paramount importance in depression (e.g., M. B. Cohen, Baker, Cohen, Fromm-Reichman, & Weigert, 1954; Fenichel, 1945; Rado, 1928; Rochlin, 1965; H. Segal, 1964). The processes of internalization, described by Freud (1917/1957e), were viewed in part as an attempt to preserve contact with the object and to retain its love and approval (Nacht & Racamier, 1960). Thus, Freud (1917/1963, 1921/1957d, 1923/1961b) discussed the normal psychological process of internalization[2] in which the need gratification the object provided is replaced within the self by a sense of having been loved and of being lovable. Stressing the importance of this psychological process of internalization to character formation, Freud stated that the "character of the ego is a precipitate of abandoned object-cathexis and that it contains the history of those object-choices" (1923/1961b, p. 29). The result of this identification is an "alteration in character [that] has been able to survive the object-relation and in a certain sense to conserve it" (S. Freud, 1923/1961b, p. 30). However, in melancholia, "a strong fixation to the loved object. . . . [has] little power of resistance" (1917/1957e, p. 249) because of the failure of internalization to establish a mature, relatively nonambivalent, identification with the object.

Freud's initial observations about depression appeared in his correspondence with his friend and colleague, Wilhelm Fleiss, in essays titled *Draft G. Melancholia* (1895/1957b) and *Draft N* (1897/1957c), in which Freud noted that

> Hostile impulses against parents (a wish that they should die) are also an integral constituent of neuroses. . . . they are repressed at times when compassion for the parents is active—at times of their illness or death. On such occasions it is a manifestation of mourning to reproach oneself for their death (what is known as melancholia) or to punish oneself. (Freud, 1897/1957c, pp. 254–255)

In a later commentary, *Contributions to a Discussion on Suicide*, presented to the Vienna Psychoanalytic Society in April 1910, Freud (1910/1957a, p. 232)

---

[2]Piaget (1945/1962) discussed a similar process that he called *interiorization*.

noted that "The affective processes in melancholia, however, and the vicissi-tudes undergone by the libido in that condition, are totally unknown to us. Nor have we arrived at a psycho-analytic understanding of the chronic affect of mourning." Freud (1917/1957e, p. 244) subsequently attempted to clarify his understanding of depression by contrasting the clinical state of melancholia with the normal psychological processing of mourning:

> The distinguishing mental features of melancholia are a profoundly painful dejection, cessation of interest in the outside world, loss of a capacity to love, inhibition of all activity, and a lowering of self-regarding feelings to a degree that finds utterance in self-reproaches and self-revilings, and culmi-nates in a delusional expectation of punishment. This picture becomes a little more intelligible when we consider that, with one exception, the same traits are met with in mourning. The disturbance of self regard is absent in mourning; but otherwise the features are the same.

Thus, for Freud (1917/1957e), the predominant feature of melancholia, in response to object loss, is heightened self-criticism and a loss of self-respect in which "The patient represents his ego to us as worthless, incapable of any achievement and morally despicable; he reproaches himself, vilifies himself and expects to be cast out and punished" (p. 246). Freud noted further (p. 247) that "one part of the ego sets itself over against the other, judges it critically and, as it were, takes it as its object." Freud identified this "critical agency" with the conscience, what he later (Freud, 1923/1961b) formulated as the superego. He saw this critical agency as key to understanding the clinical condition of melancholia—the recognition that these "self-reproaches are re-proaches against a love object which have been shifted away from it on to the patient's own ego" (Freud, 1917/1957e, p. 248). Thus, one of the primary features of melancholia is intense ambivalence toward the object in which the hostility toward the lost object is expressed in self-reproach and self-vilification. Aggres-sion originally felt toward the rejecting or disappointing object is displaced toward the self through a process of introjection and manifests itself in self-reproach and self-hatred:

> A leading characteristic of [melancholia] . . . is a cruel self-depreciation of the ego combined with relentless self-criticism and bitter self-reproaches. . . . these reproaches apply . . . to the object and represent the ego's revenge upon it. The shadow of the object has fallen upon the ego. . . . The introjection of the object is . . . unmistakably clear. (Freud, 1921/1957d, p. 109)

Abraham (1911/1927, 1916, 1924/1949), in contrast, noted a frequent un-derlying oral preoccupation in depression. He (1924/1949) attempted to elabo-rate Freud's observations about the centrality of self-reproach and self-blame in melancholia by noting that these processes are associated with a regression to the oral stage of psychosexual development. Early and repeated frustrations in oral gratification, according to Abraham, were the source of the melancholic individual's ambivalent and hostile feelings toward the object. Sandor Rado (1928, p. 422), in an analysis of Abraham, elaborated these formulations about the importance of orality in depression:

> We find in . . . [individuals predisposed to depression] an intensely strong craving for narcissistic gratification and a very considerable narcissistic intolerance . . . even to trivial offenses and disappointments they immediately react with a fall in their self-esteem. . . . Those predisposed to depression are, moreover, wholly reliant and dependent on other people for maintaining their self-esteem, they have not attained to the level of independence where self-esteem has its foundations in the subject's own achievements and critical judgment.

In elaborating the vulnerability to narcissistic injury in depressed individuals, Rado (1928, p. 423) noted that "they cling to objects like leeches . . . and feed upon them."

Freud's seminal contribution to the study of depression, *Mourning and Melancholia* (1917/1957e), focused on superego issues and processes of internalization and identification. Freud, and many early psychoanalytic thinkers, were also influenced by Abraham's (1911/1927) attempt to link melancholia to the oral stage of libidinal development. Thus, although Edith Jacobson (1953, p. 53), from primarily an ego psychology model, considered depression primarily in terms of a pathology of the ego ideal and the self-critical superego functions, and considered the profound loss of self-esteem as the "central psychological problem of depression," she, like Freud (1917/1957e) and Abraham (1911/1927, 1916, 1924/1949), also considered the importance of early oral conflicts and an intense ambivalent dependence on, and fear of abandonment by, an ambivalently loved object in the etiology of depression.

Classic psychoanalytic theory also emphasized the similarity between depression and obsessive neuroses with its emphasis on order and control (anality) and intensely ambivalent relationships (e.g., Abraham, 1911/1927). In comparing depression and obsessive–compulsive neurosis, Abraham (1911/1927, 1924/1949) noted that ambivalence is much greater in depression, and thus the patient with depression is unable to retain a relationship with the object. Thus, Abraham (1924/1949) considered obsessive neurosis to be at a later stage, "where object love begins" (p. 432). It is

> at this point that the tendency to preserve the object begins to predominate. On the later level the conserving tendencies of retaining and controlling the object predominate, whereas on the earlier level those tendencies hostile to their object—those of destroying and losing it—come to the fore. Thus, in contrast to the depressed patient, the obsessional neurotic . . . is able to maintain contact with his object. (p. 432)

Rado (1928) also emphasized that the "process of melancholia represents an attempt at reparation (cure). . . . [Melancholia] is designed to revive the ego's self-regard" (p. 435)—"the repentant ego desires to win the forgiveness of the offended object, and as an atonement, submits to being punished by the superego" (p. 430) in a sequence of "guilt–atonement–forgiveness" (p. 425). Melanie Klein, who was influenced by both Abraham and Rado as well as Freud, formulated a developmental theory that included a "depressive position." She (1935, p. 146) noted that "According to Freud and Abraham, the fundamental process in melancholia is the loss of the love object." She also noted later (1940, p. 146) that

> the processes of introjection . . . lead to the institution inside ourselves of loved and hated objects, who are felt to be "good" and "bad," and who are interrelated with each other and with the self: that is to say, they constitute an inner world. This assembly of internalized objects becomes organized, together with the organization of ego, and in the higher strata of the mind it becomes discernable as the super-ego.

Klein (1935, p. 147) noted that a significant change takes place in the development of the infant's object relations "from a partial object-relation to the relation to the complete object." "In the earliest [paranoid–schizoid] phase the persecuting and the good objects (breasts) are kept wide apart in the child's mind. . . . With the introjection of the whole and real object, they come closer together" (1935, p. 172). With the introjection of the whole and real object in the depressive position the infant's anxieties are more concerned about the loss of the good object and the relationship with that object. "In my view, the infantile depressive position is the central position in the child's development. The normal development of the child and its capacity for love would seem to rest largely on how the ego works through this nodal position" (M. Klein, 1935, p. 174). Normal development involves a resolution of ambivalence toward the object and the eventual internalization of the good object that facilitates the child's development of self-esteem. Klein (1935, 1940) thus considered the basic experience in depression to be the failure to have established or to have lost the good internal object; the predisposition to depression derives from the failure to establish firmly a sense of relatedness to a reliable caring other— "the good internal object." According to Anna Freud (1952), the emotional involvement with absent objects can be maintained for progressively longer times with maturation; thus, mourning the "gradual process of detaching [the] libido from an internal image . . . cannot be expected to occur before object constancy . . . has been established" (A. Freud, 1965, p. 67). Loss of the object can be experienced and fully accepted only when adequate levels of representation have been established in the internalization of the need-gratifying objects. Without a capacity for object constancy, object loss can result in depression. Rochlin (1965) stressed that depression involves dread of abandonment and isolation and a continuing attempt to conserve the object. Thus, the quality of object relations and the level of internalization of object representations determine in large measure the vulnerability to depression. As I discuss later in this chapter, and again in chapter 4, colleagues and I have developed methods for assessing the developmental level (the structural organization) and the thematic content of object representations and have studied their role in depression.

Two Types of Depressive Experiences

Bibring (1953) and Fenichel (1945) both conceptualized depression as a unitary phenomenon. For Fenichel (1945), depression involved a decrease in self-esteem, whereas Bibring (1953) viewed depression as an affective reaction of helplessness to a difficult reality. Although Fenichel and Bibring each viewed depression as a unitary phenomenon, they both distinguished different developmental levels at which this experience can occur. Fenichel noted that the loss of self-esteem can occur either because of a perception that the world is empty or barren or the belief that one does not deserve anything, Fenichel stressed that feelings of inferiority in depression are frequently rooted in disappointment and humiliation:

> The content of the "injuries to infantile narcissism," which precipitate the primary depression, may vary. These injuries may be extraordinary experiences of abandonment and loneliness or they may, in especially predisposed individuals, consist in the usual and unavoidable disappointments such as the birth of siblings, experiences of minor humiliations, penis envy, or the frustrations of the Oedipus longings. (p. 404)

In an attempt to understand the archaic regulation of self-esteem in depression, Fenichel (1945) summarized the developmental stages of guilt feelings as follows:

> In the life of the infant, the stages of hunger and satiety alternate. The hungry infant remembers having been satisfied previously and tries to force the return of this state by asserting his "omnipotence" in screaming and gesticulation. Later on, the infant loses belief in his omnipotence; he projects this omnipotence onto his parents and tries to regain it through participation in their omnipotence. He needs this participation, the feeling of being loved, in the same way that previously he needed milk. Now the succession of hunger and satiety is replaced by the succession of states in which the child feels alone and therefore experiences a kind of self-depreciation—we call it annihilation—and states in which he feels loved and his self-esteem is reestablished. Still later, the ego acquires the ability to judge by anticipating the future. Then the ego creates (or rather uses) states of "minor annihilation" or small "diminutions" in self-esteem as a precaution against the possibility of a real and definite loss of narcissistic supplies. Still later, the superego develops and takes over the inner regulation of self-esteem. No longer is the feeling of being loved the sole prerequisite for well-being, but the feeling of having done the right thing is now necessary. Conscience develops its warning functions; "bad conscience" again creates states of minor annihilations or small diminutions in self-esteem to warn against the danger of definite loss of narcissistic supplies, this time from the superego. (p. 388)

In this description, Fenichel (1945) articulated at least two ways in which self-esteem is markedly diminished: (a) an early stage, in which "annihilation" and "diminutions" are caused by the unavailability of the caregiving object and its supplies, and (b) a later stage, in which the feelings of annihilation and loss of esteem are caused by the superego's judgment of having done something wrong. Thus, although Fenichel viewed depression as a unitary phenomenon involving a loss of self-esteem, he seemed to describe at least two types of depression. The first is primarily oral in nature, and emphasizes the direct availability of the object and of its narcissistic supplies. Fenichel stated that this "receptive orality" is often accompanied by a "receptive skin eroticism" and that in the last analysis the need for narcissistic supplies is the need for a union with an omnipotent mother. The second type or level of depression appears to be developmentally more advanced and involves the loss of self-esteem as a function of the vicissitudes of the resolution of the Oedipus conflict. The failure to experience appropriate approval and acceptance of assertive strivings results in feelings of inferiority and a loss of self-esteem from guilt.

Bibring (1953), like Fenichel (1945), saw depression as a unitary phenomenon but viewed depression as primarily involving the ego's awareness of helplessness in regard to its aspirations. However, Bibring also viewed these feelings of helplessness as deriving from several sources: (a) the oral level "of not being loved or not being independent"; (b) an anal level, in which the failure to achieve mastery over one's body and to find adequate means of self-assertion results in feeling dirty, unworthy, guilty, and having no control over aggressive and libidinal impulses; and (c) a phallic level, in which competitive Oedipal struggles result in feelings of helplessness about being reduced, defeated, or punished. Thus, in Bibring's unitary view of depression, feelings of helplessness may be experienced as a reaction to dependency, guilt, or failure and can derive from different developmental stages in which there are differences in ego development, object relations, and the representation of the self and others. Although Bibring and Fenichel both viewed depression as a unitary phenomenon, their formulations suggest that the differentiation of the predominance of dependency or guilt in depression may provide a meaningful basis for a refined and more precise study of the complex and perplexing phenomenon of depression.

Grinker, Miller, Sabshin, Nunn, and Nunnally (1961), in a factor analytic empirical investigation of psychiatric descriptions of patients who were depressed, identified several independent factors in depression, two of which differentiate a depression that focuses on feelings of deprivation and attempts to manipulate the world to obtain nutrients from a depression primarily concerned with feelings of guilt and restitution. Anthony (1970), in discussing masochism in adolescents, presented two brief but vivid case examples that illustrate these two types of depression. Anthony said of one patient, "Following the session, she would go home and try and continue the session on the telephone. She would 'shadow' me from my home to my office, and even followed me round a supermarket on one occasion" (p. 852). She approached the end of each session with "anxiety, depression, anger, demandingness, and a refusal to leave. . . . It was difficult terminating any session without generating a miniature depression" (p. 854). The second patient

> mentioned that she did not need to be here all the time since she carried a picture of me in her mind and was able to discuss her problems equally with this picture. "It's even better because when you're inside me like that you don't interrupt." (p. 857)

Anthony viewed the first patient as "mainly preoedipal" and her depression as "based on a marked symbiotic tie with the omnipotent, need-satisfying mother" and involving feelings of "shame, humiliation, inferiority, inadequacy, and weakness"; narcissistic object relations; orality; and dependency. The second patient he viewed as more Oedipal in nature, with a great deal of guilt and moral masochism associated with a punitive superego (p. 849). The first case illustrates the marked dependency that can occur in one type of depression, and the second case illustrates the intense struggle for internalization (introjection) that can occur in another type of depression. Anthony's two examples not only are consistent with the importance of differentiating two types of depression, but they also suggest the important differences in the quality of the object representation in these two types of depression. Schmale (1972) differentiated two types of depressive affect: helplessness and hopelessness. Helplessness is the depressive affect associated with separation and the loss of gratification; hopelessness is "associated with the castration experience" and an awareness of "unachievable acceptance" in a "wished for relationship" or in attaining a specific goal (p. 331).

Although these two types of depression may be interrelated and on a continuum, a simple, dependent anaclitic depression can be differentiated from a more complex introjective depression. I use the term *anaclitic depression* here somewhat more broadly than initially proposed by Spitz and Wolf (1946) but consistent with Freud's use of the term *anaclitic*, which he derived from the Greek term *anaclitas*, meaning to lean upon or depend on, to describe a more infantile type of object choice in which the mother is sought to soothe and provide comfort and care. This type of depression results from early disruption of the basic caregiving relationship with the primary object and can be distinguished from an introjective depression, which results from a harsh, punitive, unrelentingly critical superego that creates intense feelings of inferiority, worthlessness, guilt, and a wish for atonement (Cameron, 1963; S. Freud, 1917/1957e, 1921/1957d, 1923/1961b; E. Jacobson, 1966). I use the term *introjective depression* here to express the relationship of this type of depression to superego formation and the predominant psychological processes of introjection at this developmental phase. E. Jacobson (1954), for example, discussed introjection as a mechanism that is part of the process of building up identifications. Jacobson (1954, p. 251) spoke of an "introjective identification" with a bad object that patients set up in themselves and in which the superego becomes "punitive through reanimation of a powerful, severe, aggressive," bad, and destructive object.

Thus, the classic psychoanalytic literature on depression, consistent with my clinical experience, indicates two major independent foci in depression and maintains that these foci define two major types of disorders that are both called *depression* because they both involve intense sadness and dysphoria. These formulations, especially those of Bibring (1953) and Fenichel (1945), also suggest that depression is not just a clinical disorder but, as described in the classic psychoanalytic literature, can also be a normal—and, in fact, necessary—affective state (Bibring, 1953; Freud, 1917/1957e; Zetzel, 1960). Thus, depression can be defined as a basic affect state that can range from a relatively appropriate and transient dysphoric response to untoward life events to a severe and persisting disorder that can involve serious distortions of reality. As such, depression can vary in intensity from relatively mild to profound and from a subtle transient experience to a severely disabling clinical disorder. Depression can be a relatively appropriate response to an accurate appraisal of reality, or it can be based on severe reality distortions (Blatt, 1974).

The distinctions between two primary types of life experience that define two primary types of depression stand in contrast to the usual attempts to differentiate among types of depression based on symptomatic expressions, including the distinction between psychotic and neurotic, endogenous and exogenous (or reactive), primary and secondary, major and minor, unipolar and bipolar, and melancholia and other depressive disorders. Because of the remarkable heterogeneity of symptoms in both nonclinical and clinical samples, most of these attempts to differentiate types of depression on the basis of differences in symptoms have been relatively unsuccessful (Blatt, Quinlan, Chevron, McDonald, & Zuroff, 1982). The distinction between an anaclitic and an introjective depression proposed in this book, in contrast, articulates a reliable subtyping of depression that has demonstrated validity—a subtyping that provides continuity between normal life experiences and the factors that appear to precipitate depressive reactions. As I summarize in the sections that follow, this distinction, implicit in numerous formulations in the classic psychoanalytic literature on depression, provided the clinical and theoretical basis for a major subtyping of depression in several contemporary approaches to depression.

ANACLITIC DEPRESSION. Several classic psychoanalytic authors have discussed a "simple" form of depression in which concerns are primarily focused on the basic relationship with the mother, experiences of guilt are relatively minor, and the predominant fears are of being abandoned and unloved. Thus, this "simple," "primary," or "endogenous" form of depression has been characterized as primarily oral in nature and related to early childhood reactions to narcissistic injury, loss of love, and the fear of impoverishment and starvation (e.g., Abraham, 1911/1927, 1924/1949; Deutsch, 1933; Freud, 1917/1957e, 1926/1959; E. Jacobson, 1971; Rado, 1928; Weiss, 1944). Engel and Reichsman (1956), for example, in studying an infant with a gastric fistula, noted a phenomenon they called a *depression withdrawal reaction* that "occurred when the infant was confronted alone by a stranger and was characterized by muscular inactivity, hypotonia, and sad facial expression, decreased gastric secretion, and eventually a sleep state" (p. 428). This depressive state vanished, however, as soon as the baby was reunited with a familiar person. E. Jacobson (1971, p. 171) reported on a large group of patients with "simple depressions," who were relatively free of guilt but with intellectual and motor retardation; feelings of being dejected, detached, weary, inferior, worthless, empty, and apathetic; and having numerous physical and psychosomatic complaints.

Anaclitic (or dependent) depression is characterized by a dysphoric tone stemming from feeling unloved, unwanted, neglected, and abandoned. The individual expresses a childlike dependency; has little capacity for frustration; and desires to be fed, comforted, and soothed in a direct and immediate fashion. Early disruptions in caring relationships, consisting of deprivation, inconsistency, or overindulgence, lead to an inordinate fear of loss of love, abandonment, and impoverishment. The individual feels helpless about finding gratification for his or her hunger for love.

The primary feelings in anaclitic depression are helplessness, weakness, depletion, and being unloved. Intense wishes to be soothed and cared for, helped, fed, and protected are expressed in cries for love, feelings of hunger, oral cravings, difficulty tolerating delay and postponement, and in a desperate search to find alternate sources of gratification and feelings of satisfaction and peace (Abraham, 1924/1949; S. Freud, 1917/1957e; Lewin, 1950; Rado, 1928). Dominant are fears and apprehensions of being abandoned and a sense of helplessness in being unable to find gratification and comfort (Fenichel, 1945; E. Jacobson, 1953). Object relations are primarily incorporative (Abraham, 1924/1949; Fenichel, 1945; S. Freud, 1917/1957e; M. Klein, 1935; Rado, 1928), consuming, relatively undifferentiated, based on need gratification, and at the symbiotic and early substages of separation and individuation (Mahler, 1968). Other people are valued only for their capacity to provide immediate gratification. A sense of well-being derives from a continual supply of love and assurance. When an object is unable to provide these supplies, feelings of being unloved and helpless are provoked. With support and need gratification, a temporary sense of comfort is achieved, but satisfaction and gratification are experienced as emanating only from the object (E. Jacobson, 1971), and no internal sense of having been loved or of feeling lovable has been established.

Representation of the object involves a preoccupation with the frustration or gratification that others provide. Experiences of either narcissistic blissful union or utter depletion alternate, primarily as a function of the immediate and direct availability of others. With relatively little internalization of the experiences of gratification or of the object providing the satisfaction, the individual demands the constant visible and physical presence of objects. Separation and object loss are dealt with by primitive means, such as denial and a frantic search for substitutes. Thus, Abraham and Freud (1965, p. 339) assumed that a depression that develops early in infancy, a basic depression with oral eroticism, was a prototype for later melancholia. The individual is dominated by an inordinate fear of abandonment and an excessive vulnerability to object loss (Rochlin, 1965)[3] and has difficulty expressing anger and rage for fear of destroying the other as a source of satisfaction. Weiss (1944) described this simple form of depression as "less awake" and less involved in the external world because of the libidinal fixation on an object that is rejected but cannot be relinquished.

INTROJECTIVE DEPRESSION. Rado (1928) distinguished two routes to depression: (a) a sequence of hunger and deprivation, with awakening rage, in which there is little self–object differentiation, such as during moments of satisfaction

---

[3]Spitz and Wolf (1946) and Spitz (1965) have indicated that the origins of anaclitic depression usually occur with severe deprivation around six to eight months of age, when the infant begins to consolidate a differentiation between the primary need-gratifying person and others, but before the development of object constancy (A. Freud, 1952, 1965). The difference between severe infantile and narcissistic character disorders and schizophrenia is, in part, a function of the degree to which self–object differentiations are maintained. Severe infantile character disorders have intense symbiotic involvement but without a loss of the basic differentiation between the self and nonself (e.g., Blatt & Wild, 1976; E. Jacobson, 1954, 1964b; Mahler, 1968).

at the breast, and (b) a route characterized by themes of guilt, atonement, and forgiveness. Beres (1966) and Guntrip (1969), in contrast, have restricted the concept of depression to patients with severe conflicts with guilt. Feelings and preoccupations with themes of guilt, atonement, and forgiveness occur in a developmentally more advanced introjective depression that involves concerns of being unworthy, unlovable rather than unloved, guilty, and having failed to live up to expectations and standards (e.g., E. Jacobson, 1943, 1953; Jarvie, 1950; Zetzel, 1953, 1960). Exceedingly high ideals (E. Jacobson, 1953), an overly harsh superego, a keen sense of morality, and intense commitment, which result in constant self-scrutiny and evaluation, are the primary expressions of depression. Guilt is the result of temptations and thoughts of transgression (often related to Oedipal issues) and the sense that one has failed to live up to expectations and standards and therefore will be disapproved of and criticized. Extensive demands for perfection; a proclivity to assume blame and responsibility; and feelings of being unable to achieve approval, acceptance, and recognition all contribute to the development of depression. Intense, overstated standards, often attributed to external figures, and constant intense concerns about disapproval and punishment, lead to ambivalent and hostile feelings toward the object. The individual struggles to compensate for feelings of failure by overachieving to win approval and recognition, but usually with little lasting satisfaction. The presence of an other is important, not so much to provide need gratification but to offer approval and acceptance. Concerns are primarily related to the development of the superego and the processes of sexual identification and self-definition; often expressed in strivings and competition. The parents' conscious and unconscious attitudes and feelings about themselves and their child (e.g., M. B. Cohen et al., 1954) have important effects on the child's conscious and unconscious feelings about himself and his strivings. Zetzel's (1965) observations of major sexual identity confusion in patients with a guilty depression offer some support for the formulation that introjective depression evolves during the phallic, Oedipal phase. Depression develops at this stage, not from abandonment and neglect, but rather from markedly ambivalent, demanding, deprecatory, and hostile parent–child relationships.

Introjective (self-critical) depression is typified by punitive, harsh self-criticism; self-loathing; blame; guilt; and depression, and intense involvement in activities is designed to compensate for feelings of inferiority, worthlessness, and guilt (Blatt & Shichman, 1983). Excessive ideals, a harsh superego, and a constant drive to perform and achieve are associated with guilt and shame over not having lived up to expectations, reflecting the internalization or introjection of the values and attitudes of harsh judgmental and critical parental figure(s). Efforts are so concentrated on achievement to gain approval and to compensate for feelings of failure and inadequacy that the capacity for enjoyment is impaired. The type of person described by S. Freud (1916/1957f) as "wrecked by success" is likely to have an introjective depression in which guilt, derived from conflicts over phallic strivings and symbolic Oedipal triumphs, can paradoxically contribute to depression following success. However, success can also precipitate an anaclitic depression when the success involves the actual or imagined loss of supportive relationships.

Disturbance in both anaclitic and introjective depression can be relatively mild or reach psychotic proportions. Hypomanic reactions can also occur in both types of depression; hypomania in anaclitic depression would involve intense seeking of and clinging to relationships, whereas in an introjective depression it would involve frantic efforts to demonstrate strength, material accomplishments, power, physical attractiveness, intellectual capacity, or creativity as a way of seeking recognition and avoiding scorn, criticism, and punishment. Compensatory restitutive hypomanic reactions in introjective depression do not require direct and physical contact with an object but rather are expressed in more symbolic derivatives such as recognition, approval, and material possessions.

Introjective depression, compared with anaclitic depression, involves a higher level of psychological development with a greater capacity for internalization. The major defense, rather than denial, is introjection or identification with the aggressor, with a proclivity to assume responsibility and blame and to be harsh and critical toward the self. Object relations extend beyond immediate need satisfaction; the involvement with the object persists independent of frustration and gratification. Object relations are at the later stages of the separation–individuation process. Concerns about receiving care and nuturance are replaced by more symbolic concerns about receiving approval from an other and about the other's response to and acceptance of one's feelings of love for the object. Relationships are highly ambivalent, and the person is unable to resolve and integrate contradictory feelings. Attempts to retain the object and its potential love and approval occur through introjection—a process in which aspects of a significant other, such as his or her values and judgments, become part of the self but still feel like a foreign presence within one's thoughts. Thus, the struggles that originally were between the person and the ambivalently loved object eventually come to exist primarily within the person (S. Freud, 1917/1957e). Representations of the object and the self are more differentiated but are based on repetitive, drive-laden (often aggressive) interpersonal interactions and on exaggerated and contradictory part properties and features of the other. Because these representations are usually based on the ambivalent, hostile, and aggressive aspects of the relationship, the internalizations result in feelings of doubt, self-criticism, and guilt. The continual negative self-judgments and guilt, as well as the exaggerated and overstated representations, serve to maintain contact with the object in a vivid and hyper-cathected, albeit ambivalent, way. However, object and self-representations are at a somewhat higher developmental level in introjective depression than in anaclitic depression, as indicated by the fact that guilt requires a sense of self; a capacity to be self-reflective; and some appreciation for sequences of causality, both in assuming responsibility for an act and in considering alternate modes of atonement and reparation. Whereas introjective depression involves more advanced ego development, regression can also revive earlier conflicts and levels of organization.

Full differentiation from love objects—with individuation, emancipation, and the development of the capacity to seek new and enduring relationships—occurs with the internalizations associated with normal psychological development. Object loss can then be experienced and accepted, because adequate levels of representation have been established in the internalizations achieved in the relinquishing of infantile and Oedipal objects (Loewald, 1962; Schafer, 1968). Affectionate relationships with the parents enable the child to develop affectionate relationships with others, establish positive self-representations, and express competitive strivings with security and confidence. Disappointments can result in sadness but do not lead to sustained depression because of the internalization of a constructive and positive relationship with the primary object.

Contemporary Psychological Theories of Depression

The differentiation between an anaclitic (dependent) and an introjective (self-critical) depression (Blatt, 1974), derived from the classic psychoanalytic literature on depression, is consistent with the formulations of several other contemporary clinical investigators with different theoretical perspectives. From a psychoanalytic object-relations perspective, John Bowlby (1980, 1988b), on the basis of ethological assumptions, distinguished between *anxiously attached* and *compulsively self-reliant* individuals and how each of these individuals are vulnerable to experiences of depression. From a psychoanalytic interpersonal perspective, Silvano Arieti and Jules Bemporad (1978, 1980) differentiated between a *dominant-other* and a *dominant-goal* type of depression. Also, from a cognitive–behavioral tradition, Aaron Beck (1983) differentiated between a *sociotropic* and an *autonomous* type of depression. Thus, using different terms and based on very different theoretical assumptions, a number of contemporary investigators have also differentiated a depression based on disruptions of interpersonal relationships from a depression based on disruptions in self-esteem.

John Bowlby: An Ethological and Object-Relations Model

Bowlby focused on early parent–child interactions and their effects on subsequent personality development, including the creation of a vulnerability to psychological disturbance. In contrast to traditional psychoanalytic considerations of personality differences in terms of unconscious drives, conflicts, and defenses, Bowlby (1988b), following Adolf Meyer, emphasized the role of early interpersonal experiences in personality development. Influenced by ethological and object-relations theory, Bowlby developed a theory of attachment and separation to account for the detrimental effects of inadequate maternal care in early childhood and to explain aspects of young children's interpersonal behavior. His primary thesis is that "emotionally significant bonds between individuals have basic survival functions and therefore a primary status" (Bowlby, 1988b, p. 2). Early interpersonal relationships expressed in harmonious, tense, anxious, or even nonexistent attachment patterns influence personality development.

The initial attachment that infants form with their mother (or maternal surrogate) is independent of the need to be fed but rather is based on the need for protection. Such a bond, expressed in "attachment behavior," results "in a person attaining or maintaining proximity to some other clearly identified individual who is conceived as better able to cope with the world" (Bowlby, 1988a, p. 7). Bowlby and others, notably Ainsworth (1985), Main (e.g., Main, Kaplan, & Cassidy, 1985), and Bretherton (1985), extensively investigated attachment behavior in infants and young children. Although the expression of attachment behavior is different at various stages of development, it is expressed in some form by all individuals, especially at times of illness or fear and during periods of increased need for comfort and care. Attachment behavior is a control system constructed in an environment in which a responsive caregiver is vital for survival. The caregiver's failure to respond, whether because of physical absence or lack of sensitivity, can be stressful and even traumatic. Repeated failures can severely affect the nature of attachment bonds and psychological growth and development.

Bowlby's central thesis is that the nature of the emotional bonds developed in early childhood determines the nature of subsequent interpersonal relations and consequently personality development and mental health. "Each partner builds in his or her mind working models of self and other and of patterns of interaction that have developed between them" (Bowlby, 1988b, p. 2). These cognitive patterns, developed early in childhood, contribute significantly to the ways individuals experience and interpret their interpersonal environment.

Bowlby (1988a) highlighted the major differences between his formulations and classical psychoanalytic theory:

> Each infant is held to have his own individual array of potential pathways for personality development, which . . . include many that are compatible with mental health and also many that are incompatible. Which particular pathway he proceeds along is determined by the environment he meets with, especially the way his parents (or parent substitute) treat him, and how he responds to them. Children who have sensitive and responsive parents are enabled to develop along a healthy pathway. Those who have insensitive, unresponsive, neglectful or rejecting parents are likely to develop along a deviant pathway which is in some degree incompatible with mental health and renders them vulnerable to breakdown, should they meet with adverse events. Even so, since the course of subsequent development is not fixed, changes in the way a child is treated can shift his pathway in either a more favorable direction or a less favorable one. . . . It is this persisting potential for change that gives opportunity for effective therapy. (Bowlby, 1988a, p. 136)

Bowlby made it clear that he does not regard the infant as passing through an immutable series of developmental stages at any one of which he or she may become vulnerable to mental illness. Early experiences are highly significant, but environmental factors throughout life are also important in determining personality development and mental health.

The major types of attachment patterns discussed by Bowlby are consistent with research findings (e.g., Ainsworth, 1985; Main et al., 1985). Secure attachment is characterized by an assurance that parents will be available and responsive; the child appears confident in his or her relationship with the parents and relatively free of anxiety. Anxious–resistant (ambivalent) insecure attachment is a response to inconsistent caregiving in which the parental figure may be available and caring some of the time but at other times unresponsive and likely to use threats of abandonment as a means of control. Such children appear demanding and tense, impulsive, easily frustrated, passive, and helpless. Anxious–avoidant insecure attachment, in contrast, usually results from repeated rebuffs and rejections by the parent figure, and, in the extreme, from prolonged institutionalization. The child has little belief that he or she will receive help and comfort when needed and consequently is likely to be emotionally insulated and hostile, although, at times, also demanding of attention (Bowlby, 1988b). Longitudinal research demonstrates that these patterns of attachment observed in the first year of life describe relatively stable behavioral, cognitive, emotional, and interpersonal modes of functioning (Main et al., 1985). Securely attached infants as preschoolers are cooperative, popular with peers, and highly resilient and resourceful (Sroufe, 1983) and at age six are relaxed and friendly and converse with their parents in a free-flowing and easy manner (Main & Cassidy, 1988). Insecure avoidant infants as preschoolers appear emotionally insulated, hostile, and antisocial (Sroufe, 1983) and later tend to distance themselves from their parents and ignore their parents' initiatives in conversation (Main & Cassidy, 1988). Anxious–resistant or preoccupied insecure infants are tense and impulsive as toddlers and passive and helpless in preschool (Sroufe, 1983) and later show a mixture of insecurity and hostile behavior in interaction with their parents (Main & Cassidy, 1988). These three attachment patterns are relatively stable over time (Bretherton, 1985), even into adolescence (Elicker & Sroufe, 1992) and adulthood; they have cross-generational continuity as indicated by mothers reporting similar caring experiences with their own mothers and by the fact that pregnant women report early childhood caring experiences that are congruent with their subsequent caring behavior with their own infants (Fonagy, Steele, Moran, Steele, & Higgit, 1991; Fonagy, Steele, & Steele, 1991; Fraiberg, Adelson, & Shapiro, 1975; Main et al., 1985; Slade & Aber, 1992). These patterns of secure and insecure attachment in adults are also characterized by differences in cognitive processes as observed in the degree of cohesion and consistency of narrative reports by adults about their early life experiences (Main et al., 1985). Also, these attachment patterns have been observed in multiple cultures (e.g., George & Solomon, 1989; Grossmann, Fremmer-Bombik, Rudolph, & Grossmann, 1988; Main et al., 1985; Ricks, 1985; Zeanah, Benoit, Hirshberg, Barton, & Regan, 1991). In an integrative overview of much of the research and theory about attachment, Bowlby (1988a, 1988b) called for more detailed research to clarify how these early attachment patterns influence personality development, especially types of psychopathology, including depression.

States of depression for Bowlby are an extension of unremitting experiences of sadness that the person feels unable to change. Because sadness usually appears as a reaction to some form of loss "of a loved person or else of familiar and loved places, or of social roles" (Bowlby, 1980, p. 245), depression is regarded as intimately related to loss, both past and present. Because insecure attachments are expressions of a real or feared loss of the parental figure, either temporary or permanent, vulnerability to depression is viewed as deriving from these early insecure attachments. Although Bowlby did not discuss different types of depression in detail, he described several different personalities who, following loss, are prone to develop chronic mourning (a depressive disorder): (a) those with anxious and ambivalent relationships, (b) those prone to compulsive caregiving, and (c) those disposed to assert independence from affectional ties (Bowlby, 1980).

Freud (1917/1957e) discussed at length the relationship between anxious–ambivalent relationships and vulnerability to depression following loss. Freud's formulations are consistent primarily with the anxious–ambivalent (preoccupied) type of insecure attachment in which dependency and anxiety are coupled with hostility directed toward significant figures and fear of rejection by them. Such an attachment in childhood is characterized by a high demand for attention stemming from a hope that love will be provided, coupled with a fear of neglect or abandonment. This pattern of dependency and anxiety about abandonment is consistent with the descriptions of an anaclitic or dependent depression.

In contrast with the anxious–ambivalent (preoccupied) insecure attachment, Bowlby (1980) proposed that some adults assert independence from emotional ties as an expression of an anxious–avoidant attachment in response either to the early loss of a parent and subsequent inadequate (often institutional) care or to an unsympathetic parent who is critical and rejecting of the child's desires for love and attention. The child is often made to feel guilty for the disappearance of, or neglect by, the parental figure. As a defense against feeling unloved and isolated, the child strives to be self-reliant and, in adulthood, often becomes distant from others, showing little appreciation for, or investment in, interpersonal relatedness. Bowlby (1980, 1988a) likened this to Winnicott's description of the false self and to the traditional narcissistic personality. This description seems similar to the introjective (or self-critical) type of depression.

Bowlby (1980) also described a third group of individuals as compulsive caregivers who do not directly parallel either of two types of depression, but it is important to note a strong element of dependency in this group. Compulsive caregivers are described as being anxious and guilty about leaving home and simultaneously resent being forced to stay at home from an early age to care for a sick, disturbed, or hypochondriacal parent. These individuals are highly dependent on those they care for and they are also made to feel guilty for their parent's sickness. Thus, in response to a threat of loss, usually of the parent, these individuals feel excessively guilty and develop chronic mourning and are preoccupied with caring for the other in ways that they themselves would have liked to be cared for.

Bowlby (1980) also discussed three types of childhood experiences that create a vulnerability to depression. Some children never succeed in gaining a stable and secure relationship with parental figures despite repeated efforts to meet their parents' demands. Other children, made to feel incompetent and unlovable, come to expect all relationships to be rejecting and hostile. They remain alone and independent of affectional ties. Finally, there are children who experience the actual loss of a parent in early childhood. G. W. Brown and Harris (1978) and G. W. Brown, Bifulco, and Harris (1987) found that about 35% of women with depressive disorders in inner London had lost their mothers before their 11th birthday, as compared with only about 13% of control participants. Actual early loss of a significant figure appears to interact with attachment patterns and contribute to the development of depression in adolescence and adulthood.

Bowlby (1988a) proposed that these three types of childhood experiences create specific cognitive–affective schemas that increase the vulnerability to depression. He discussed how certain cognitive–affective schemas continue independent of the situation that initially stimulated the response. Certain information in the environment, originally prompted by implicit or explicit parental attitudes about the nature of the parent–child relationship, are organized into the working mental models of attachment relationships so the child can adapt to parental expectations and behavior, thereby maintaining contact with the parent and avoiding conflict. The child consequently is unable to reappraise concepts of the self or the parent and is unable to express certain feelings and needs that would disrupt these rules for maintaining the relationship. Persistent idiosyncratic ways of interpreting interpersonal situations derive from these earlier distorted experiences with the parents. These maladaptive mental representations of caring relationships continue into adulthood so that there is a strong "tendency for the sadness, yearning and perhaps anger . . . to be disconnected from the situation that aroused them" (Bowlby, 1980, p. 248).

Silvano Arieti and Jules Bemporad: An Interpersonal Model

Arieti and Bemporad (1978, 1980), like Bowlby, have emphasized the role of early interpersonal relationships in personality development and the creation of vulnerability to psychological disturbance. Their interpersonal orientation parallels many aspects of Bowlby's attachment theory. Like Bowlby, they did not distinguish between forms of depression according to psychiatric classifications but rather considered both mild and severe depression in terms of childhood experiences and differences in personality style. In contrast to Bowlby, however, Arieti and Bemporad emphasized the relationships between aspects of the adult personality and types of depression more than the role of early relationships.

Arieti and Bemporad, like Bowlby, also viewed depression as closely related to sadness, but a sadness that cannot be "metabolized," so that the work of sorrow cannot be completed. Sadness, a normal reaction to an adverse situation, can range from experiences of humiliation, to feeling a victim of injustice, to the loss of a loved one. Such situations demand a cognitive appraisal and a "reorganization of thoughts about life directives, and eventually different purposeful behavior" (Arieti & Bemporad, 1978, p. 121), which Arieti and Bemporad viewed as the slow activity and mental processes inherent in the sadness that facilitate this "sorrow-work." Life circumstances as well as psychological patterns have not prepared the person with depression for this reparative process: "He has no choice; he is not able to solve psychologically his sorrow or sadness, and pathological depression results" (Arieti & Bemporad, 1978, p. 128). Thus, Arieti and Bemporad viewed depression as always following a precipitating event but not as a result of that event alone. The individual's "ideology" influences the way he or she interprets and deals with the particular event. Concepts of endogenous versus reactive are meaningless in this context, because Arieti and Bemporad considered all depression to have both endogenous and reactive features. According to Arieti and Bemporad (1978, p. 7), it is the patient's ideology that "had an integrative function in the life of the patient and was used as a defense, [and] now makes him experience a state of partial or total loss, helplessness, or hopelessness which is accompanied by depression." Although Arieti and Bemporad did not negate the role of hereditary and biological factors in depression, they were primarily interested in psychological factors. Like Bowlby, they viewed negative childhood experiences, leading to maladaptive cognitive processes, as creating a vulnerability to depression. Arieti and Bemporad discussed three different types of predisposing ideologies that result in vulnerability to depression: (a) *dominant other*, (b) *dominant goal*, and (c) what might be called *self-denying*. Arieti and Bemporad did not describe distinguishing symptomatology for each type of depression (e.g., level of mood variations or nature of suicide attempts); rather, they focused on differentiating patterns of conflict and defense as well as precipitating interpersonal experiences.

An individual with a dominant-other personality relies on a highly valued other for gratification, self-esteem, and for providing meaning and purpose in life. Gratification is obtained by conforming to the expectations of the esteemed other, who also needs the patient. Clinginess, passivity, manipulativeness, and avoidance of anger characterize the relationship. The dominant-other personality has its origins in the child's compliance and submission to gain the love and approval of the parent. The child feels guilty and expects to be punished for deeds deemed wrong by the parent. The child relies on the parent for appraisal and is continuously anxious about loss of parental love. Some individuals carry this compliance with parents' wishes to an extreme and deny themselves pleasure for fear of losing parental love; similar to Bowlby's formulations, they become subservient to parental wishes to such an extent that they become compulsive caregivers. This type of depression usually follows a loss through death, divorce, or separation from or disappearance of the dominant other—a collapse of the primary interpersonal relationship in the person's life. Although the dominant other is characteristically a parent or close relative, it is also possible that a group, institution, or entire family may function as the dominant other. The deprivation of gratification from the dominant other results in guilt over the loss and feelings of depression, anger, and helplessness. The major therapeutic task with this type of patient, according to Arieti and Bemporad, involves the recognition of how the dominant other was dispensable, leading to a subsequent reappraisal of lifestyle and ideology.

A variation of the dominant-other type of depression is a claiming depression, typified by an aggressive demand for attention and gratification as well as becoming clinging and dependent. This forces significant others to establish an atmosphere of infantile indulgence, resulting in an alternating pattern of feeling guilty and making others feel guilty. Sadness develops when the gratification demanded is unavailable because of a separation from, or the loss of, the dominant other. The experience of intermittent and conditional love and the resulting excessive anaclitic dependence is similar to Bowlby's anxious–ambivalent (or preoccupied) type of attachment.

An individual with a dominant-goal personality, in contrast, relies on the achievement of a specific goal to gain and maintain self-esteem and gratification. With the attainment of this goal, the person feels loved and valued by others. Arieti and Bemporad noted that the dominant-goal personality is found more often in men and that the dominant-other personality is found more often in women. Arieti and Bemporad (1978) pointed out that, on occasion, women make the establishment of a relationship into a goal for gaining self-esteem; the emphasis then is not on the interpersonal aspects of the relationship but on its attainment per se. A dominant-goal orientation is consistent with the introjective orientation, discussed earlier, and is similar to Bowlby's anxious–avoidant type, in which an independence from interpersonal relations is defensively asserted in an arrogant self-involvement and isolation. These individuals often have obsessive features, and their depression usually follows the realization that the specific goal cannot or has not been achieved. Life consequently becomes empty and meaningless. As in the case of the dominant-other type, the acceptance of alternative and more realistic goals usually involves a complete re-evaluation of lifestyle.

Arieti and Bemporad (1978, 1980) also described a third type of personality, in which depression is a constant character style; the individual inhibits any form of gratification, does not develop intimate relationships, is aloof from everyday happenings, and as a consequence feels hopeless and empty. These individuals are often moralistic, especially hard on themselves and others, prideful, and hypochondriacal. Severe depression is often precipitated by a major change in their daily life. Like Bowlby's compulsive caregiver, many of the patients with this form of depression establish a pattern of lifelong caregiving and self-denial.

In addition to discussing differences among these three types of depression, Arieti and Bemporad (1980) stressed themes common to all three depressive personalities:

> anxiety over the direct attainment of pleasure, . . . fear that spontaneous activity will result in rejection or criticism from others, [overvaluation] of the opinions of others, and [overestimation] of their own effects on the inner lives of others [and] most significantly overwhelming inhibition [that] prevents the development of alternate modes of attaining meaning from activity. (p. 1363)

This inhibition causes despair after disruptive events, because the patient cannot formulate alternative life directions and cannot successfully integrate negative experiences. The depression can be understood "as the acute or slow realization by the patient that she or he has never developed a meaningful interpersonal bond based on love and affection and neither has he achieved any meaningful goal" (Arieti & Bemporad, 1978, p. 226). Arieti and Bemporad, from their interpersonal orientation, stressed the importance of others in the lives of all three depressive personality types. This is true even of individuals with the dominant-goal personality, who actively avoid relationships and who, from early childhood, tend to be aloof, self-involved, and oblivious to the needs of others in the pursuit of goals. Arieti and Bemporad stressed cognitive distortions as a major contributing factor to the development of psychopathology, but they viewed these distorted cognitions as the effect, not the cause, of the depression. The cause, according to Arieti and Bemporad (1978, 1980), like Bowlby, lies in childhood experiences, which lead to a maladaptive ideology and lifestyle.

Arieti and Bemporad's developmental theory differs significantly from Bowlby's formulations, despite their common focus on interpersonal relationships. Bowlby discussed the impact of significant differences in attachment that are present from early infancy, whereas Arieti and Bemporad (1978) placed the origin of the relevant personality differences at a somewhat later point in development: as a consequence of the mother's reactions when the child becomes independent and autonomous. The family environment of a depressed patient, unlike the family of a schizophrenic patient, has a quality of stability and an adherence to social conventions. During the first year, the mother is appropriately responsive to her infant and provides the nurturance and affection he or she needs. With the child's mobility and increasing interest in independence around the end of the first year, however, the mother abruptly alters the child's sense of security by beginning to give care and attention only conditionally. The child becomes fearful of the threat of the loss of mother's love and feels forced to conform to parental expectations in order to maintain her love. It is this threat that Arieti and Bemporad (1978) considered as significant in the later development of depression in adulthood. The element of loss or threat of loss and submitting to parental expectations has much in common with Bowlby's formulations of the role of insecure attachment in depression. Like Bowlby, Arieti and Bemporad (1978) postulated that the cognitive–affective structures of depression are the result of distorted early interpersonal relations. The relationship of these different cognitive–affective structures to particular forms of parenting, however, were less developed by Arieti and Bemporad than by Bowlby. Also, unlike Bowlby, Arieti and Bemporad viewed the dominant-other and the dominant-goal types of personality as having their origins in similar parenting patterns, except that in the dominant-goal type it is achievement that is originally rewarded by the parents (Arieti & Bemporad, 1980), and the child chooses to direct all his or her effort to achieving a particular goal in order to gain parental love and approval, at the exclusion of all other aspects of life.

Aaron Beck: A Cognitive–Behavioral Model

Aaron Beck's (e.g., 1983, p. 268) orientation is primarily behavioral and cognitive, and he focuses on current life events rather than the entirety of the life span—"on the here-and-now factors (without speculating. . . on the predisposing biological and psychological factors [other than cognitive patterns])." This lack of interest in long-term predisposing psychological factors distinguishes Beck from the psychodynamic investigators.

On the basis of clinical observations and research, Beck (1967b) initially concluded that the signs and symptoms of depression, such as lack of motivation or the presence of suicidal wishes, are the consequences of specific negative cognitive patterns—the *negative cognitive triad*, in which the patient views him- or herself, the future, and his or her experiences in a negative manner. These aspects of life situations are interpreted negatively more often than is warranted and are experienced by the individual as the consequence of perceived immutable inadequacies and defects in the self or in the world. Thus, the future is anticipated to be unhappy and full of hardship. On the basis of these assumptions, Beck (1983, p. 270) developed a cognitive therapy of depression designed to help the patient "identify, reality test, and correct distorted conceptualizations and the dysfunctional beliefs . . . underlying [the] cognitions." The therapist plays an active role in identifying and revising the patient's distorted cognitions through behavioral techniques such as graded task assignments and cognitive manipulations. Beck claimed that cognitive therapy is at least as effective as pharmacotherapy and certain other forms of psychotherapy in treating unipolar depression (e.g., Rush, Beck, Kovacs, & Hollon, 1977).

In his original formulation, Beck (1967a) viewed the activation of certain idiosyncratic cognitive schemas as contributing to the host of cognitive, affective, and behavioral symptoms in depression and that interventions were needed to moderate or modify these dysfunctional interpretations and beliefs. Beck later (1996) revised this theory of individual schemas in a model of linear schematic processing because it did not "fully explain many clinical phenomena and experimental findings" (p. 1) and did not adequately address a number of psychological problems. Thus, Beck (1996) proposed a major revision of his original theory of simple linear schematic processing by positing a concept of modes or networks that have cognitive, affective, motivational, and behavioral components. Modes, especially "primal modes" in psychopathology, are characterized by a prepotence of related dysfunctional beliefs, meanings, and memories that influence the processing of information. The concept of mode provides an approach to

> the relation of various psychological systems to each other, the relation of nonconscious to conscious functions, reactions to situational or endogenous variables, changes in the intensity and the quality of feelings states, and relation of personality to psychopathology and the differential responsiveness of psychological disturbances to pharmacotherapy and cognitive therapy. This addition to . . . cognitive theory can provide further clarification of normal and abnormal processes and can facilitate the refinement of interventions strategies. (p. 22)

Beck (1996) now believes that clinical disorders, including personality disorders and the cognitive organization of disorders within Axis I, can be characterized in terms of "a specific primal mode, that, when activated, draws on congruent systems to implement the 'goal' of the mode" (p. 8). These primal reactions, "although consistent in form and content, vary in intensity and threshold" (p. 8). "The cognitive component of the mode consisting of a number of interrelated elements such as core beliefs, compensatory rules, and behavioral strategies is more complex than the original simple linear model" (p. 9). Beck, however, did not specify precisely the relationships among schemas, core beliefs, automatic thoughts, compensatory rules, and personality modes (Luyten, Blatt, & Corveleyn, 2004). These primal reactions are "not necessarily dysfunctional and, indeed, may be lifesaving in certain situations" (Beck, 1996, p. 9). From an evolutionary perspective, Beck (1999, p. 413) now views depression as a reaction to loss that activates an "innate program consisting of giving up and withdrawal . . . [that] serves to reduce the individual's 'needs' until new resources were developed" (p. 413). Thus, Beck now views psychopathology as excessive or inappropriate strategies that are part of normal adaptive functioning. Beck (1996, p. 10) provided several examples of these primal modes, such as an expansive mode that includes the "evolutionary imperative of intimate bonding. . . . and other expansive modes. . . . such as acquiring wealth and property" and the total engagement of the manic mode with a "bloated self-concept," as well as a de-energized depressive mode with an impoverished self-concept.

Different from his original formulations (Beck, 1967b, 1976) of a simple linear pathway from cognition to affect, motivation and behavior, Beck now views the mode as a cognitive schema that derives from the interaction of innate patterns (proto-schemas) and congruent life experiences. The core beliefs of the self-concept and the primitive view of others are the most important components of the mode. Because of difficulty "accommodating various psychological and psychopathological phenomena to the simple schematic model of stimulus → cognitive schema → motivation, affect, and behavior" (p. 19), Beck (1996) proposed the concept of mode as "a more complete explanation of the complexity, predictability, regularity, and uniqueness of normal and abnormal reactions" (p. 19). Modes are "a composite of cognitive, affective, motivational, behavioral systems. . . . structural and operational units of personality that serve to adapt an individual to changing circumstances" (p. 19).

> It is clear that the cognitive organization in depression, for example, cannot be reduced to a few simple schemas, but consists of a complex array of schemas that vary along a number of dimensions such as accessibility (explicit or implicit) and potency or intensity. . . . The conglomerate of schemas also includes broad belief categories such as self-image, expectations, imperatives, and memories. (Beck, 1996, p. 20)

Beck's new theoretical contribution of "organizing schemas" are of a kind of algorithm that defines the conditions or circumstances necessary for activating the mode and its coordinate schemas, including affective, motivational, and behavioral components. The modes process information as individuals scan their internal and external milieus for particular conditions that fit the orienting schema of the mode. The cognitive schemas consist of rules, beliefs, and memories that organize experiences into interpretations, predictions, and images. Although the cognitive process is generally out of awareness, the products of this process are frequently in awareness. Beck (1999) elaborated further his concept of mode by noting that these specific behavioral patterns are "only the observable manifestation of adaptive and maladaptive processes. . . . functional components of a structural complex consisting of cognitive, affective, and behavioral patterns . . . [that] make up the personality organization" (p. 419). He labeled the cognitive components of these strategies as *schemas*, that include ways of "attending to, selecting, interpreting, storing, and retrieving information" (p. 420). These strategies, the "logical derivatives" of basic core beliefs, especially the self-concept, are essential for clinical formulations in which core beliefs are layered from the "underlying core belief to its representation in the conditional belief to the consequent compensatory belief and the strategy responsible for implementing the goal of the compensatory belief" (p. 426). Beck's (1996) formulation of these basic modes of organization is similar to Teasdale's (e.g., Teasdale & Barnard, 1993) concept of "interacting cognitive subsystems" (Teasdale, 1997) and my (e.g., Blatt, 1991, 1995b; Blatt & Blass, 1990, 1996; Blatt & Shichman, 1983) formulations of two primary configurations of personality development and psychopathology.

Beck (1983) also revised his original theory of depression to include the role of two major personality dimensions, which he termed *sociality* and *individuality*. *Sociality*, or the socially dependent mode, describes an emphasis on positive interaction with others, including the need for intimacy, dependence, and nurturance. A socially dependent person (the majority of whom are women) is particularly sensitive to and afraid of rejection by others because of an intense need to maintain stable relationships with others to ensure safety and gratification. The sociotropic type of depression is characterized by seeking of help, support, and reassurance; feelings of loneliness; concern about personal and social attributes; and preoccupations with, and anxiety about, the loss of gratification. Sociotropic patients are usually overly optimistic about treatment, frequently resulting in a flight into health with a temporary relief of symptoms. These patients have idealized representations of others and try to establish symbolic relationships with others in which they are demanding of attention and care. Cognitive distortions center around concerns about the irreversibility of loss and the sense of social undesirability. Suicide attempts are more often passive, such as taking an overdose of prescribed antidepressant medication (see also Blatt et al., 1982). Sociotropic depression is often precipitated by loss of a significant figure either through death or rejection.

Individuality, or the autonomous mode, refers to emphasis on independence and the attainment of self-set goals. The autonomous individual (the majority of whom are men) tends to be assertive and directive, and sensitive to demands and restrictions, particularly those that interfere with achieving goals. These individuals, according to Beck (1983), are relatively insensitive to the needs or judgments of others, although they often judge themselves harshly in comparison to others. Beck (1983) viewed autonomous or self-critical patients as isolated, pessimistic, and less reactive to environmental events. Thus, it is often difficult to identify the precipitating events associated with the onset of their depression, because it is often precipitated by internal experience, such as the feeling of having failed to live up to standards and expectations.

The autonomous type of depression is characterized by a withdrawal from people to maintain autonomy, a tendency to reject help and to blame the self for present difficulties, a high degree of self-criticism, and a fairly unremitting depressed mood (Beck, 1983). Cognitive distortions center around themes of defeat and failure because of personal incompetence. Suicide attempts are likely to be active (e.g., hanging, use of firearms; see also Blatt et al., 1982), and the expression of hostility toward the self or others is usually direct and overt. Precipitating factors for the depression are not always obvious but tend to be the perception of immutable blocking of, or failure to achieve, goals. The sociotropic individual is dependent on others for gratification, whereas gratification for the autonomous individual derives from the achievement of goals. Largely on the basis of the clarity of precipitating factors and differences in the stability of depressed mood, Beck (1983) related the autonomous type to endogenous depression (Gillespie, 1929; Kiloh & Garside, 1963) and the sociotropic type to reactive depression. Stressors, however, may be present in autonomous depression but more difficult to identify. Also, it has not been demonstrated whether symptoms differentially associated with endogenous and reactive depression (e.g., diurnal variation of mood) are different in autonomous and sociotropic types of depression.

Beck's hypotheses regarding sociotropy and autonomy derive from his general approach to psychopathology in which he regards the psychological and biological dimensions of mental illness as "two sides of the same coin" (Beck, 1983, p. 265). He discussed these two dimensions as parallel processes, and he focused primarily on psychological dimensions, especially the behavioral and cognitive aspects of depression. Beck acknowledges the presence of other possible predisposing and precipitating factors to depression, including heredity; counterproductive cognitive patterns; developmental traumas, including physical disease and loss of close relatives; and specific life stresses that impinge on particular emotional vulnerabilities associated with interpersonal relations and autonomy.

Beck's (1983) formulations of sociotropy and autonomy are similar to the psychodynamic formulations of Arieti and Bemporad, Blatt, and Bowlby discussed earlier. Beck maintains that individuals can change between the autonomous and sociotropic modes depending on specific life circumstances, although there is usually an inclination toward one mode at any particular time. This is perhaps one of the more controversial points in Beck's formulations, because it is inconsistent with personality theories that assume some degree of stability of individual personality traits.

Beck (1983) reported that two broad personality types associated with the two types of depression can be identified with his Sociotropy–Autonomy Scale (Beck, Epstein, Harrison, & Emery, 1983), but he is unclear as to whether he regarded these differences as states or traits. If an individual can be in a different mode depending on the particular life events at any given time, then individuals should report experiences in both modes, but Beck does not consider why mixtures of the two modes are seen much less often than relatively "pure" types. Beck's relative disinterest in possible predisposing factors leading to the different personality modes is consistent with his behavioral orientation, in which he affirms that a "person may present a clinical picture of a deprivation [dependent] depression after the loss of a loved one, and an autonomous depression when thwarted by adverse conditions in a vocational or professional situation" (Beck, 1983, p. 278). Beck's theory, although descriptively consistent with the earlier psychodynamic formulations, does not address the development of these different types of vulnerability but rather sees them as responses to untoward contemporary life experiences.

Theoretical Integration

Dissatisfaction with relatively ineffective classification of types of depression based on symptoms led four groups of clinical investigators, working from different theoretical perspectives, to propose that types of depression be distinguished on the basis of the life experiences or issues that lead individuals to become depressed. Consistent with Freud's (1917/1957e) formulations in *Mourning and Melancholia*, and observations in much of the classic psychoanalytic literature on depression, these investigators distinguished two major types of experiences that lead to depression: (a) disruptions of gratifying interpersonal relationships (e.g., object loss) and (b) disruptions of an effective and essentially positive sense of self (e.g., failure). These two types of experiences have been characterized by psychodynamic investigators as *anaclitic* and *introjective* (e.g., Blatt, 1974; Blatt & Shichman, 1983), or *dependent* and *self-critical* (Blatt, D'Afflitti, & Quinlan, 1976; Blatt et al., 1982), *dominant other* and *dominant goal* (Arieti & Bemporad, 1978, 1980), and *anxiously attached* and *compulsively self-reliant* (e.g., Bowlby, 1980). These formulations of depression derive from three strands of psychoanalytic theory: The contributions of Arieti and Bemporad derive primarily from an interpersonal orientation, my contributions derive primarily from an integration of psychoanalytic ego psychology with developmental cognitive theory, and Bowlby's formulations are primarily based on extensions of object relations theory. Beck's (1983) differentiation, from a cognitive–behavioral perspective, between a socially dependent (sociotropic) and an autonomous type of depression is congruent with the contemporary psychodynamic formulations about the nature of depression (Arieti & Bemporad, 1978, 1980; Blatt, 1974, 1998; and Bowlby, 1988a, 1988b). Formulations derived from both clinical experience and research findings in these four theoretical perspectives indicate an impressive degree of agreement, at least on a descriptive level, about the nature of depression.

This theoretical convergence about two types of depression defined by differential sensitivity to different types of life experiences occurred despite the fact that the four theories use different terms and involve different assumptions about the etiology of depression, especially the role of contemporary versus early life experiences. Whereas Beck (1983), for example, described differences between patients primarily in terms of current cognitive distortions, Bowlby (e.g., 1980) discussed differences in terms of the attachment patterns formed in the patient's early childhood, and Arieti and Bemporad (1978, 1980) discussed the role of somewhat later childhood experiences as the child attempts to separate and achieve a sense of independence from the mother. Despite these differences, the formulations of these four groups of investigators who have articulated these experiential dimensions of depression enable researchers to move toward a unified theory of depression that has etiological as well as therapeutic implications.

The anaclitic personality focuses on the basic relationship with the caretaking person and dominant fears of abandonment and of being unloved. Psychological functioning, primarily focused on dependency and need gratification, derives from early childhood reactions to narcissistic injury, loss of love, and the fear of impoverishment and starvation. The primary feelings in anaclitic depression are helplessness; weakness; depletion; being unloved; fears of abandonment; and intense wishes to be soothed and cared for, helped, fed, and protected. Cries for love and of hunger, and difficulty tolerating delay and postponement, are dominant and are expressed in a desperation to find satisfaction and comfort. Dominant are fears and apprehensions of being abandoned and a sense of helplessness. Object relationships are primarily consuming, relatively undifferentiated, based on need gratification, and at the early stages of separation and individuation. A temporary sense of well-being derives from experiences of love and assurance, without which the individual feels unloved, unwanted, and helpless. Thus, the individual has an inordinate fear of abandonment and an intense vulnerability to object loss and is reluctant to express anger for fear of destroying the object as a source of gratification and support.

Anaclitic (or dependent) depression is characterized by a dysphoric tone stemming from feeling unloved, unwanted, neglected, and abandoned. The individual expresses a childlike dependency; has little capacity for frustration; and desires to be fed, comforted, and soothed directly and immediately. The dependent type of depression has often been overlooked in discussions of depression, because the characteristics usually associated with clinical depression, such as a loss of self-esteem and guilt, are not marked (Blatt, 1974, 1991, 1998). Anaclitic patients are usually less reflective, which limits their articulation of associated emotions and conflicts. However, early disruptions in caring relationships, such as deprivation, inconsistency, or overindulgence, lead to an inordinate fear of loss of love, abandonment, and impoverishment (Blatt, 1974) and a feeling of helplessness about finding gratification for their hunger for love. Anaclitic depression can be expressed in a wide range of physical complaints; eating disturbances; or in suicide attempts or gestures, such as taking an overdose of prescribed antidepressants. Symptoms express that the individual feels unloved and uncared for, and thus depression is often precipitated by loss of a loved one or by childbirth (Beck, 1983; Blatt et al., 1982). A desperate need to deny loss and separation can often result in the use of primitive denial and the avoidance of unpleasant aspects of reality. Lack of gratification often leads to feelings of anger and rage, which may not be expressed directly because of fear that the anger might result in loss of contact with the gratifying other. "Interruption of a sense of being cared for . . . [often] results in a desperate clinging and seeking of substitutes with little concern for the nature of the substitute other than their providing momentary soothing" (Blatt & Shichman, 1983, p. 210). The anaclitic or infantile (dependent) individual is consequently often erratic, impulsive, and emotionally labile.

A dependent (Blatt, D'Afflitti, & Quinlan, 1976), anaclitic (Blatt, 1974), or sociotropic (Beck, 1983) type of depression is expressed in demanding and clinging behavior because of the fear of loss of love. Bowlby, and Arieti and Bemporad, like Blatt, have discussed the importance of relationships with significant others and the need for constant closeness in this type of depression, and they view the intense dependence and clinging behavior as an expression of a desperate need for nurturance. I (Blatt, 1974), however, stress the instability of the attachment in dependent depression and how the need for gratification is much more important than the commitment to a particular relationship. Patients with a dependent depression have a strong need to seek immediate replacement for a lost or unavailable object and, in contrast to Bowlby and to Arieti and Bemporad, I do not view guilt as a central theme in anaclitic depression.

Introjective (self-critical) depression, in contrast, is typified by punitive, harsh, relentless feelings of self-doubt, self-criticism, self-loathing, blame, guilt, and depression. These individuals often become involved in activities to compensate for feelings of inferiority, worthlessness, and guilt. They usually have excessively high standards; a harsh superego; a constant drive to perform and achieve; and feelings of guilt and shame over not having lived up to expectations. Often the attitudes and values of harsh and critical parental figures have been internalized (introjected). Efforts for achievement attempt to compensate for feelings of failure and inadequacy, but the capacity for enjoyment is seriously impaired. Interpersonal relationships are often intensely ambivalent, distant, and aloof. The major defenses in introjective depression are identification with the aggressor and overcompensation; strong aggressive tendencies toward the self and others are typically reflected in the violent nature of suicide attempts (Beck, 1983; Blatt, 1974, 1995a; Blatt et al., 1982). It is important to note that I view introjective depression to be at a more advanced level of psychological development than anaclitic depression, and indeed more advanced than the stages of disturbance viewed by Bowlby and by Arieti and Bemporad as significant in depression. This view of a disparity in developmental level between the two types of depression represents a notable difference between my formulations and other theories. For example, I (Blatt, 1974) consider guilt to require a relatively high developmental level in that it involves greater self-reflectivity and internality, some appreciation of cause-and-effect relationships, and an awareness of various possible forms of reparation. Beck (1983), in contrast, described the dependent or sociotropic type as more self-reflective than the autonomous type of depression.

My discussion of introjective depression parallels Bowlby's anxious–avoidant and Arieti and Bemporad's dominant-goal type of depression. The symptomatology of a self-critical (introjective) depression includes an unsatisfied drive toward achievement, relative independence or distance from interpersonal involvement, and intense self-destructive tendencies (Blatt, 1974, 1995a; Blatt et al., 1982), and it is similar to Beck's (1983) discussion of an autonomous type of depression.

Despite some inconsistencies and disagreements among these four theoretical positions describing two types of depression, one focused on disruptions of interpersonal relatedness and the other on disruptions in self-esteem, the impressive agreement among these four perspectives about the nature of depressive experiences provides new insight into depression as well as into psychopathology in general. In addition, these formulations have led to a substantial amount of clinical and empirical investigations about the etiology, nature, and treatment of depression.

In the chapters that follow, I consider various clinical expressions of these two types of depression (chap. 2), methods that have been developed for assessing these two types of depression (chap. 3), and the various empirical investigations in clinical and nonclinical settings that have derived from these methods (chap. 5).

Object Representation in Depression

The classic psychoanalytic literature on depression, as well as the more recent formulations of Bowlby (1980, 1988a, 1988b) and myself (Blatt, 1974), stress the importance of disturbances in mental representation in the etiology of depression. As suggested above, one of the primary differences between anaclitic and introjective depressions is the quality of object representation. In anaclitic depression, exemplified in my discussion of Helen, object representations are polarized, either positive or negative, and they are of insufficient strength and stability to provide support to tolerate separation and loss; thus, Helen struggled to maintain direct physical and sensory contact with people. As illustrated by the case of Helen, the representation of the object in anaclitic depression is primarily focused on experiences of frustration and gratification— of either blissful union or utter depletion, depending on the direct availability of the object. The individual has relatively little internalization of the experiences of gratification or of the object providing the satisfaction. Thus, separation and object loss are dealt with by primitive defenses such as denial, a constant demand for the visible and physical presence of objects, and a frantic search for substitutes. The representation of objects is primarily in terms of action sequences—of experiences of gratification or frustration. Because of impairments in the process of internalization and the limited development of object representations, direct, physical, sensory, need-gratifying contact with the object is constantly sought. This impairment in object representation creates a vulnerability to profound feelings of loneliness (Blatt, 1974). Thus, anaclitically depressed individuals tend to describe their parents in egocentric, sensorimotor–preoperational terms—of what parents did or failed to do for them (Blatt, 1974; Blatt et al., 1979).

George, like Helen, had traumatic experiences of object loss, but in his introjective depression he struggled to maintain contact on a developmentally more mature level by trying to establish consistent and integrated representations of significant others. His representations were initially literal, depictive, and fragmented, but as his analysis progressed his representations became more differentiated, abstract, symbolic, and integrated. It is noteworthy that introjective individuals tend to describe their parents primarily in terms of their manifest physical and functional or behavioral attributes, reflecting the more distant nature of their interpersonal relationships.

As noted earlier, Anthony (1970) presented two case illustrations of depression that also included observations that provide further clinical evidence indicating different levels of object representation in two types of depression. One patient would try to continue the session on the telephone and, on one occasion, followed Anthony in a supermarket. The end of therapy sessions provoked feelings of anxiety, depression, anger, demandingness, and a refusal to leave. Because of an inadequacy in object representation, this patient struggled to maintain direct contact with the therapist. The second patient reported that she carried a picture of Anthony in her mind that provided her with a sense of continuity and comfort. This patient was functioning on a somewhat more mature developmental level and was able to sustain a sense of contact with her therapist in a somewhat more symbolic (iconic) form.

These clinical observations, consistent with classic psychoanalytic formulations, indicate that intensely ambivalent relationships with parents in childhood are a central issue in the etiology of depression (Abraham, 1911/1927, 1924/1949; Freud, 1917/1957e). These ambivalent feelings are expressed in a wish to destroy the parent, but at the same time the child is frightened of losing the support of the dependent relationship. Because of these intense ambivalent feelings, the person is unable to establish and retain a consolidated sense of the presence of the person with feelings of affection, fondness, and respect (M. Klein, 1935). Reports that depressed patients attempt to preserve contact and to retain love and approval (Nacht & Racamier, 1960) are consistent with Freud's (1917/1957e) original formulations about impaired internalization in depression. Without internalization of adequate levels of object representation, absent objects are experienced as lost, precipitating a major crisis and depression (Blatt, 1974). The failure to establish good relations and adequate levels of internalization and representation results in vulnerability to depression. Actual, apparent, or fantasized object loss is thus often a major precipitant of depression because of these impairments in the development of object representation.

Disrupted object relations and the impaired levels of object representation in depression had been discussed extensively by Melanie Klein (1935) and her colleagues.[4] As noted earlier, Klein believes that "the structure of the personality is largely determined by the more permanent of the fantasies which the ego has about itself and the objects that it contains" (H. Segal, 1964, p. 9). Although Kleinian theory emphasizes the content of fantasies, it also notes that the level of organization of the "more permanent" fantasies (or representations) plays a major role in structuring personality development. According to H. Segal (1964), the move beyond the splitting of the paranoid position to the more organized depressive position is determined by "a predominance of good over bad experiences." The depressive position is that phase of development in which the infant recognizes the whole object and his relationship to that object. This increased differentiation and integration of object representation enables the child to perceive the mother as a whole object with diverse and even contradictory features. Disruptions in the depressive position stem from the inability to achieve this integration primarily because of the failure to resolve hostile and destructive impulses toward the object. In the depressive position, introjective processes are intensified as the child attempts to resolve ambivalence and integrate and retain the good internal object.

---

[4] Klein's formulations about depression, and the developmental sequences leading to it, can be considered independent of her formulations about specific developmental timetables, the nature and role of infantile fantasies, and the centrality of the death instinct.

H. Segal (1964) commented that "symbol formation" and the "assimilation" of the good object are outcomes of the resolution of the ambivalence of the depressive position:

> Where the depressive position has not been worked through sufficiently . . . and its capacity to regain good objects internally and externally has not been firmly established . . . the ego is dogged by constant anxiety of the total loss of good internal situations, it is impoverished and weakened, its relation to reality may be tenuous and there is a perpetual dread of, and sometimes an actual threat of regression into psychosis. (p. 67)

"It is the wish and the capacity for the restoration of the good object, internal and external, that is the basis of the ego's capacity to maintain love and relationships through conflicts and difficulties" (p. 79)—to restore and retain, in symbolic form, the lost internal objects:

> Through the repetition of experience of loss and recovery . . . the good object becomes gradually better assimilated into the ego, because, in so far as the ego has restarted and recreated the object internally, it is increasingly owned by the ego and can be assimilated by it and contribute to its growth. (p. 80)

Segal described how this is achieved by "real separation" and results in "the acceptance of the idea of separateness—the differentiation of one's own self from one's parents" and "allowing one's objects to be free, to love and restore one another without depending on oneself" (p. 89).

A number of theoretical positions, in addition to Klein's, also consider impairments in the development of object representations as an issue central to the development of a particular vulnerability to object loss and depression. In a more ego psychological orientation, adequate resolution of the Oedipal crisis leads to the capacity for symbolic representations of the objects, allowing the object to be retained internally as it is relinquished externally. Sandler and Joffe (1965), Beres (1966), Rubenfine (1968), and Roth and Blatt (1974a) all have mentioned the possibility that depression involves a failure to achieve object constancy and adequate levels of object representation. Loss of the object can be experienced and fully accepted only when adequate levels of representation have been established in the internalization achieved in the relinquishing of infantile objects and with the initial resolution of the Oedipal phase. Thus, the issue of maintaining contact with the need-gratifying object is of paramount importance in depression (Beck, 1967b; M. B. Cohen et al., 1954; Fenichel, 1945; M. Klein, 1935, 1940; Rado, 1928; Rochlin, 1965; H. Segal, 1964). Rochlin (1965) stressed a dread of abandonment and isolation in depression and the continual struggle to conserve the object. Thus, the level of interpersonal relations, internalization, and the quality of object representations determine in large measure the vulnerability to depression. Considerable clinical and empirical evidence (Abraham, 1924/1949; Anthony, 1970; Blatt, 1974; A. Freud, 1952; S. Freud, 1917/1957e; M. Klein, 1935; Rochlin, 1965) suggests that impairment in object representation creates a particular vulnerability to depression. As I discuss in detail in chapter 6, studies of children at risk (e.g., insecurely attached children and children of mothers with depression) indicate that impairment in the level of object representation appears to be important in creating a vulnerability to depression. Thus, a fuller understanding of the development of object representations could enrich our understanding of the complex phenomena of depression.

In the chapters that follow I present several methods for assessing object representation of significant others (chap. 4) as well as research that has used these methods to study aspects of parent–child relationships and their role in depression (chap. 6) and of changes in object representation during the treatment process (chap. 8).

In subsequent chapters, I explore research findings and clinical experiences relevant to the two basic hypotheses proposed in this book: (a) that depression can be effectively differentiated into two primary types—an anaclitic depression, focused on issues of loneliness, neglect, and abandonment, and an introjective depression, focused on issues of self-worth, like guilt and failure, and (b) that these two types of depression involve differential impairments in the development of mental representations of significant others—a sensorimotor level of representation focused on need gratification in anaclitic depression and an external iconic level focused on particular overstated manifest part properties or features in introjective depression.

The exploration of these two fundamental hypotheses about depression has enabled a wide range of investigators to explore more fully aspects of the etiology, current clinical expressions, and treatment of depression. In the remainder of this book, I present the results of these clinical and research explorations.

2

Clinical Expression of Anaclitic and Introjective Depression

The differentiation between dependent (anaclitic) and self-critical (introjective) depression has contributed to a fuller understanding of depression in nonclinical contexts as well as in both inpatients and outpatients. It has also increased the understanding of the nature, etiology, and treatment of depression as well as the multiple ways in which intense dysphoric affect can be expressed in disturbances that derive from depression, such as suicide, conduct disorder, somatic preoccupations, eating disorders, and substance abuse. In this chapter I present a series of clinical reports that consider various expressions of anaclitic and introjective depression in both adults and adolescents. Although many formulations of depression are based on clinical experience with severe and disabling forms, the clinical examples in this chapter indicate that much can be learned about the vicissitudes of depression that are experienced and expressed across a wide spectrum, from normality to severe psychopathology, as a function of disruptions in two major areas: (a) interpersonal relatedness and (b) self-definition. The differentiation of depression focused on loss and abandonment from a depression focused on self-criticism in both normal and clinical samples is consistent with both behavioral and psychoanalytic formulations (e.g., A. T. Beck, 1967b, 1983; Bibring, 1953; S. Freud, 1917/1957e; Seligman, 1975) that consider as two central issues in depression helplessness and dependency on the one hand and hopelessness and negative feelings about the self and reality on the other.

Anaclitic Depression

Depression that evolves from disruptions of interpersonal relatedness, primarily as a consequence of object loss, uncomplicated by feelings of guilt, has been

This chapter incorporates material from (a) "The Destructiveness of Perfectionism," by S. J. Blatt, 1995, *American Psychologist*, *50*, pp. 1003–1020. Copyright 1995 by the American Psychological Association. Reprinted with permission; (b) "Antisocial Behavior and Personality Organization," by S. J. Blatt and S. Shichman, 1981, in S. Tuttman, C. Kaye, & M. Zimmerman (Eds.), *Object and Self: A Developmental Approach*, (pp. 225–367). Copyright 1981 by International Universities Press. Reprinted with permission; and (c) "Suicide and the Representation of Transparency and Cross Sections on the Rorschach," by S. J. Blatt and B. A. Ritzler, 1974, *Journal of Consulting and Clinical Psychology*, *42*, pp. 280–287. Copyright 1974 by the American Psychological Association. Reprinted with permission.

relatively unnoticed and unexplored in both the clinical and research literature. Although the early classic psychoanalytic literature (e.g., Abraham, 1924/1949; S. Freud, 1917/1957e) discussed in detail an intense neediness (orality) in depression and observed that depression is often precipitated by object loss, most clinical accounts and research investigations have focused on superego dimensions in their formulations and explorations—on guilt and feelings of failure and worthlessness. One of the unique innovations of the investigations and formulations of depression presented in this book is the articulation and exploration of this previously relatively unrecognized, unexplored, and under-appreciated dimension (e.g., Blatt, 1974, 1998; Blatt, D'Afflitti, & Quinlan, 1976).

Several early clinical investigators reported in detail about a lethargic, apathetic, and listless neediness in their observations of what they called an *anaclitic depression* in infants during moments of abandonment and neglect. Observations by Engel and Reichsman (1956) of the gastric response of baby Monica to her mother's absence, as well as the research of Spitz and Wolf (1946) and others (e.g., Provence & Lipton, 1962) on the depleted and listless response of infants and young children in institutions that provided adequate physical care but relatively little physical contact and psychological exchange with caregivers—what they termed *hospitalism*, or *marasmus*—provide classic examples of extreme forms of anaclitic depression. These observations are consistent with the vivid reports and graphic documentation by the Robertsons (1971) of the collapse of toddlers in response to the temporary loss of their mothers due to the mothers' brief (1 to several weeks) hospitalization. These toddlers rapidly became disorganized, lethargic, and listless without contact with their mothers, even though they were participating in a well-functioning day-care facility. These reports are consistent with observations in animal research on the reactions of infant monkeys to the loss of physical contact with their mothers (e.g., Suomi & Harlow, 1977). At this time, these observations had not been extended to the consideration of depression in adults.

Clinicians and investigators did not note the relevance of these interpersonal issues for depression in adults partly because anaclitically depressed adults are usually unreflective about their personal experiences and feelings, often enacting rather than verbalizing their affective experiences, particularly their feelings of depression. Thus, the prototypical anaclitic patient presented in chapter 1, Helen, enacted her experiences of depression by constantly seeking to be close to, and held by, someone. Her sexual promiscuity was not an expression of a lack of moral standards or a defensive defiance of these standards but a simple, intense desire to be held, comforted, and soothed—to feel loved and nurtured. Her intense neediness was also expressed in somatic symptoms, especially her acne and psoriasis, which brought her frequently to physicians to receive ointments and lotions to soothe her discomfort as well as to experience their concerns about her well-being. In addition, she frequently slept during substantial portions of the analytic sessions, making me feel that she was like an infant sleeping in the safety of my arms as a refuge from a barren and neglectful world. It was partly these observations and my reactions to aspects of Helen in the psychoanalytic situation that enabled me to note similarities between aspects of her behavior, both in analysis and in her reports of her life more generally (e.g., that in her infancy she had not been held by mother), and in the earlier reports in the literature of anaclitic depression as a response to neglect in infants and young children (Blatt, 1974).

More recently, the American Psychiatric Association (1994), in the fourth edition of the *Diagnostic and Statistical Manual of Mental Disorders (DSM–IV)*, attempted to define a dependent personality disorder (DPD), with the essential features of "a pervasive and excessive need to be taken care of that leads to submissive and clinging behavior and fear of separation" (p. 665) and an urgent seeking of "another relationship as a source of care and support when a close relationship ends" (p. 669; see also Blatt, 1974; Blatt, Quinlan, Chevron, McDonald, & Zuroff, 1982; Hirschfeld, Shea, & Weise, 1995). Dependent persons can be indiscriminate in selecting partners, becoming quickly and intensely involved with grossly unreliable, undependable, and sometimes abusive partners. The weak and ineffectual sense of self of these dependent patients, and their excessive need to please others, contribute to a wide range of interpersonal difficulties (Blatt, 1974; see also Overholser, 1996). Dependent individuals are excessively concerned about maintaining interpersonal contact and are easily influenced by others, and they try to avoid disagreements and interpersonal conflict (Santor & Zuroff, 1997). Some of the basis used by the American Psychiatric Association for the articulation of DPD was the description of intensely dependent individuals with anaclitic depression (Blatt & Zuroff, 1992, p. 528) as having a "desperate need to keep in close physical contact with need-gratifying others and . . . deep longings to be loved, cared for, nurtured, and protected" (p. 528) as well as an intense reliance "on others to provide and maintain a sense of well-being, and therefore [as having] great difficulty expressing anger for fear of losing the need gratification others can provide" (p. 528). Separation, rejection, and interpersonal loss are particularly stressful and depression often occurs in response to perceived loss or rejection in social situations. The DPD described in *DSM–IV* and elsewhere (e.g., Bornstein, 1992; Millon & Kotik-Harper, 1995) is similar to Kernberg's (1984b) formulations of the infantile personality.

On the basis of a meta-analysis of 97 studies of gender differences on measures of dependency, Bornstein (1993, 1995) concluded that women consistently obtain higher dependency scores than do men. Thus, it is not surprising that anaclitic depression and DPD occur more frequently in women, because women are more often concerned "about rejection or untrustworthiness of others" (Hammen et al., 1995, p. 441). Women are especially vulnerable to changes such "as moving away from home, separation from an important relationship, and loss of a romantic partner" (Widiger & Anderson, 2003, p. 60). As Nietzel and Harris (1990, p. 291) noted, the "interaction of elevated dependency needs with negative social events is a uniquely pernicious combination." A. T. Beck (1983, p. 273), in his formulations of sociotropy and autonomy, also noted "passive–receptive wishes" (acceptance, intimacy, understanding, support, guidance) in sociotropic individuals, who, according to C. J. Robins and Block (1988, p. 848), are "particularly concerned about . . . being disapproved of by others . . . often acting in ways designed to please others . . . thereby securing their attachments." M. H. Klein, Wonderlich, and Shea (1993) called for future research on the contributions of dependent personality traits to depression in women. This vulnerability to anaclitic depression can occur through a variety of mechanisms (Bornstein, 1992; Widiger & Bornstein, 2002, p. 293).

Several other investigators (Chodoff, 1972; Hirschfeld, Klerman, Chodoff, Korchin, & Barrett, 1976; Hirschfeld et al., 1977) also have noted that dependency is an important independent dimension of depression. Also, research with the Depressive Experiences Questionnaire (DEQ; Blatt, D'Afflitti, & Quinlan, 1979), which I discuss in chapter 5, provided additional empirical conformation of the importance of this source of dysphoria and depression, as well as some of the unique ways that it can be expressed—ways very different from the more usual expressions of depression associated with severe impairments in feelings of self-worth and self-esteem. Early work with the DEQ (e.g., Blatt, 1974; Blatt, D'Afflitti, et al., 1976) indicated that anaclitic depression is often difficult for depressed individuals to articulate and communicate, and it is often difficult for clinicians to identify, because they are often distracted by the intensity of these patients' somatic symptoms (Blatt, D'Afflitti, et al., 1976) and other difficulties, including amphetamine abuse (Lidz, Lidz, & Rubenstein, 1976), alcoholism and antisocial activity (Blatt & Shichman, 1981), and chronic lethargy and fatigue (Blatt, 1974).

In chapter 5 I discuss in more detail how research with the DEQ has indicated that this interpersonal dependency dimension of depression, like the self-critical dimension, is significantly correlated with conventional measures of depression (e.g., the Beck Depression Inventory [A. T. Beck, Ward, Mendelson, Mock, & Erbaugh, 1961] and the Zung Self-Report Depression Scale [ZDS; Zung, 1965, 1971, 1972]), but only at marginal levels of significance. An analysis of the correlations of each of the 20 items of the ZDS with the Dependency (Interpersonal) and Self-Criticism Factors of the DEQ (Blatt, D'Afflitti, et al., 1976) indicated that the Self-Criticism factor of the DEQ of college students correlated significantly ($p < .05$) with the ZDS items that assess the psychological dimensions of depression (e.g., personal dissatisfaction, self-criticism, and hopelessness). The Dependency or Interpersonal factor of the DEQ, in contrast, did not correlate significantly with the total ZDS but it did correlate significantly with the few other items of the ZDS concerned with the more somatic–vegetative dimensions of depression. Thus, the Dependency or Interpersonal factor of the DEQ appears to assess a form of depression that is frequently overlooked because it is expressed primarily in bodily concerns and somatic symptoms, or in various forms of acting out, rather than in reports of feelings of being depressed, including the more usual psychological expressions of depression. Riley and McCranie (1990) also found that anaclitically depressed patients tended to not be self-reflective, particularly about affective experiences, but instead expressed their depression through somatic complaints and by seeking the care and attention of a physician. Because dependency has been a relatively neglected but an important atypical dimension of depression, relatively few clinical reports are available in the literature and only recently have empirical investigations begun to explore this type of depression. In comparison, an extensive literature, over many decades, has explored superego dimensions of depression—expressed in extensive self-criticism, guilt, and feelings of failure in attaining very high standards of perfection.

Introjective Depression

As I discussed in chapter 1, the usual formulations and measures of depression (e.g., the Beck Depression Inventory) are focused primarily on the introjective, or superego, form. Recent research on perfectionism by two independent research teams (Frost, Marten, Lahart, & Rosenblate, 1990; Hewitt & Flett, 1989, 1991) have led to further articulation of important dimensions of introjective depression and its relationship to a wide range of clinical phenomena, especially suicide.

Suicide

Research conducted by colleagues and me (Blatt et al., 1982) and by A. T. Beck (1983) indicates that patients with high levels of introjective (self-critical or autonomous) depression can be seriously suicidal; they make highly lethal suicide attempts. This serious suicidal potential provided a theoretical structure for understanding a series of detailed reports in the public media about the suicide of a highly talented and gifted individual who was intensely perfectionistic and severely self-critical.

The tragic death of Vincent Foster, a gifted and accomplished lawyer and deputy counsel to then-President Clinton, provides insight into how intense perfectionism and self-criticism could lead a very talented and highly successful individual to resort to the drastic action of killing himself—leaving family and friends at the peak of his life and career. Foster was regarded by friends and associates as a "pillar of strength," "a rock of Gibraltar." He was "one of the golden boys" (Von Drehle, 1993); "widely admired as a portrait of poise" (De Parle, 1993); a tough and effective lawyer and litigator, able to function effectively under considerable stress. He was considered by many a potential nominee to the Supreme Court. He was a leader throughout his life, from his early school years in Hope, Arkansas, to the University of Arkansas law school and from there to his partnership in the Rose Law Firm in Little Rock; he was a person of impeccable integrity, impressive intellectual capacities, intense loyalty, and powerful personal strength. His life seemed successful not only professionally but also personally. Deeply devoted to family and friends, he had a stable marriage and was the father of two sons with whom he appeared to have meaningful relationships. Hillary Rodham Clinton reportedly said, "Of a thousand people who might commit suicide, I would never pick Vince" (Rich, 1993).

Although it is inappropriate to make a clinical diagnosis without personal contact, extensive knowledge of the details of the person's life, a full psychological test assessment, or a combination of these, detailed material disseminated by the news media helps one appreciate the intensity of Foster's perfectionistic standards and his vulnerability to personal and public criticism. Extensive articles by Von Drehle in the *Washington Post* and DeParle in the *New York Times*, drawing on the troubled note that Foster wrote shortly before his death, the commencement address he delivered two months earlier at the University of Arkansas law school, memories of friends and associates, and his public record in Washington and in Little Rock provide biographic material that enable one, to some degree, to appreciate the intensity of his critical self-scrutiny, his unyielding need for perfection, and the profound anguish he experienced when he felt he had failed, especially in his responsibilities to be the "great protector" of people, to whom he felt a deep sense of loyalty. According to DeParle (1993, p. E22), "the portrait that emerges is at least partly a man stalked by his own impossible standards of perfection."

Foster was first in his class in law school, and he earned the highest score on the Arkansas bar exam. In his law firm, he was considered "the soul of the firm, . . . he researched each case extensively . . . and [would] go through 20 drafts if he had to. He could be demanding" (Von Drehle, 1993, p. A21). According to one professional associate, Foster seemed to have known only success: "I never saw a professional setback. . . . Never. Not even a tiny one . . . he seemed to glide through life" (DeParle, 1993, p. E21). He was intensely hard-working and fiercely loyal. In a commencement address to the graduates of the University of Arkansas law school a few months before his death, Foster stressed the importance of one's personal reputation:

> The reputation you develop for intellectual and ethical integrity will be your greatest asset or your worst enemy. . . . Treat every pleading, every brief, every contract, every letter, every daily task as if your career will be judged on it. . . . I cannot make this point to you too strongly. There is no victory, no advantage, no fee, no favor which is worth even a blemish on your reputation for intellect and integrity. . . . Dents to the reputation in the legal profession are irreparable. (Von Drehle, 1993, p. A20)

A series of events for which Foster felt a keen sense of responsibility occurred in the early months of the Clinton administration. Most important were matters concerning the White House travel office. He "felt he had failed to protect the President by keeping the process under control" (Von Drehle, 1993, p. A21). Another series of events at this time involved the decision of Foster and others to resign their membership in the all-White and -Christian country club of Little Rock, a decision that "really upset Vince. . . . [because] they who had tried to integrate the club . . . had to give it up," in the process abandoning friends and a way of life they loved, with the implication that the club and their friends were racist (Von Drehle, 1993, p. A21).

As the note written shortly before his death indicated, Foster was deeply upset by editorials in the *Wall Street Journal* concerning his role in the administration, editorials questioning his integrity both in Washington and back home in the Rose Law Firm. He believed that they had "tarnished his reputation." In his suicide letter, Foster wrote:

> I made mistakes from ignorance, inexperience and overwork. . . . I did not knowingly violate any law or standard of conduct. No one in the White House, to my knowledge violated any law or standard of conduct, including any action in the travel office. There was no intention to benefit any individual or specific group. . . . The FBI lied. . . . The press is covering up. . . . The

GOP has lied and misrepresented. . . . The public will never believe the innocence of the Clintons and their loyal staff. (Von Drehle, 1993, p. A21)

Believing he was disgraced in Washington and perceived as a failure in Little Rock, Foster probably felt he had nowhere to go (Von Drehle, 1993). Thus, this "tower of strength," this "rock of Gibraltar," took his own life on Tuesday, July 20, 1993, with the 1913 Colt Army service revolver he had inherited from his father, who had died several years earlier.

Foster is typical of numerous examples of talented, ambitious, and successful individuals (see Blatt, 1995a) who are driven by intense needs for perfection and plagued by intense self-scrutiny, self-doubt, and self-criticism. Powerful needs to succeed and to avoid possible public criticism and the appearance of defect force some individuals to work incessantly to achieve and accomplish but always leave them profoundly vulnerable to the criticism of others and to their own self-scrutiny and judgment. This harsh, punitive superego (S. Freud, 1917/1957e, 1923/1961b) can be a driving force for achievement, but it can also result in little satisfaction in one's accomplishments and, through a marked vulnerability to experiences of failure and criticism, in an increased susceptibility to ensuing depression and suicide. Because of the need to maintain a personal and public image of strength and perfection, such individuals are constantly trying to prove themselves; feel they are always on trial; vulnerable to any possible implication of failure or criticism; and often unable to turn to others, even the closest of confidants, for help or to share their anguish.

In attempting to understand Foster's suicide, one could evaluate whether he met the classic criteria for major depression as outlined in the *DSM–III–R* and *DSM–IV* (American Psychiatric Association, 1987, 1994): depressed mood, markedly diminished interest or pleasure, significant weight loss or gain, insomnia or hypersomnia, psychomotor agitation, fatigue, feelings of worthlessness or guilt, diminished ability to think or concentrate, and recurrent thoughts of death. Foster was clearly experiencing considerable depression. Drs. Elizabeth Hersh and Susan Lazar (1993, p. 25), arguing in a letter to the *New York Times* for the need to include adequate mental health benefits in any national health program, suggested that Foster may have been experiencing major depression, that he

did not seem to be his usual self, [his] . . . mood seemed low, [he] . . . spent weekends in bed with the shades drawn, . . . recently lost 15 pounds, and . . . sent out signals of pessimism that alarmed close friends and colleagues. (Hersh & Lazar, 1993, p. 25)

Regardless of whether Foster met the psychiatric criteria for major depression in having at least five of these designated symptoms during the 2 weeks prior to his suicide, however, tells one little about the personal vulnerabilities, environmental stresses, and mental torment that drove him to such a desperate act. It would be more productive to evaluate his life experiences and circumstances and to consider how these, interacting with his personality characteristics, could make him feel so desperate that he felt compelled to forsake family, friends, and life itself. One of the central themes in Foster appears to be his introjective personality organization with its intense level of perfectionism and severe self-criticism.

Self-Criticism (Perfectionism) and Depression

The research literature on perfectionism, or self-criticism, has grown remarkably in the past decade, and it provides further understanding of the role of introjective personality features in depression and suicide. Numerous empirical investigations, using recently developed scales, provide consistent evidence that perfectionism is a multidimensional construct that can have an important role in adaptive and maladaptive functioning, including a wide range of disorders, especially depression. Much of the initial work in this area was based on the early findings of Burns (1980a, 1980b) and on the theoretical formulations and clinical observations of Pacht (1984), Pirot (1986), and Sorotzkin (1985). Burns identified 10 items of the Dysfunctional Attitudes Scale (A. N. Weissman & Beck, 1978) that assessed perfectionism. More recently, two groups of investigators independently developed what each has called a *multidimensional perfectionism scale*. Although based on somewhat different conceptualizations, scales developed by Frost and his colleagues (e.g., Frost, Marten, Lahart, & Rosenblate, 1990) and by Hewitt and Flett (e.g., 1989, 1990, 1991) have made important contributions to the investigation of perfectionism.

Hewitt and Flett (e.g., 1990, 1991) differentiated three types of perfectionism: (a) other-oriented perfectionism, (b) self-oriented perfectionism, and (c) socially prescribed perfectionism. *Other-oriented perfectionism* involves demanding that others meet exaggerated and unrealistic standards. *Self-oriented perfectionism* involves exceedingly high, self-imposed, unrealistic standards and an intensive self-scrutiny and criticism in which there is an inability to accept flaw, fault, or failure within oneself across multiple domains. In short, it consists of an active striving to be flawless. Self-oriented perfectionism often appears to have adaptive potential—it is related, for example, to resourcefulness and constructive striving (Flett, Hewitt, Blankstein, & Mosher, 1991; Flett, Hewitt, Blankstein, & O'Brien, 1991)—but it also interacts with negative life events, especially experiences of failure, to produce depression. Thus, Hewitt and Flett (1990, see also Flett, Hewitt, & Mittelstaedt, 1991) found that self-oriented perfectionism related significantly to both the Self-Criticism ($r = .52$, $p < .001$) and Efficacy ($r = .29$, $p < .01$) scales of the DEQ (Blatt, D'Afflitti, & Quinlan, 1976). Frost, Benton, and Dowrick (1990) also found that their measure of perfectionism was significantly related to the DEQ Self-Criticism scale and that aspects of their Perfectionism scale (i.e., personal standards) also correlated significantly with the Efficacy scale of the DEQ.

Socially prescribed perfectionism is the belief that others maintain unrealistic and exaggerated expectations that are difficult, if not impossible, to meet; however, one must meet these standards to win approval and acceptance (Frost, Marten, et al., 1990; Hewitt & Flett, 1991). Because these excessive standards are experienced as externally imposed, they can often feel uncontrollable. They result in feelings of failure, anxiety, anger, helplessness, and hopelessness—feelings often associated with depression and suicidal thoughts. Whereas self-oriented perfectionism interacts primarily with achievement stressors to predict depression (Hewitt, Flett, & Ediger, 1996), socially prescribed perfectionism interacts with both interpersonal and achievement stress to predict depression (Hewitt & Flett, 1993). Self-oriented and socially prescribed perfectionism define, respectively, intra- and interpersonal dimensions of perfectionism (Flett, Hewitt, Blankstein, & O'Brien, 1991), both of which are related to psychological disturbance and distress. As earlier findings suggest (e.g., Hollender, 1965; Missildine, 1963), self-oriented and socially prescribed perfectionism are related to depression, diminished self-esteem, and suicidal ideation (Flett, Hewitt, & Mittelstaedt, 1991; Hewitt & Dyck, 1986; Hewitt & Flett, 1990; Hewitt & Flett, 1991; Hewitt, Newton, Flett, & Callander, 1997; Saddler & Sacks, 1993), as well as to scores on a well-established symptom checklist (the Hopkins SCL-90; Derogatis, 1983).

Frost, Marten, Lahart, & Rosenblate (1990) also developed a multidimensional perfectionism scale to assess dimensions of perfectionism such as excessive concern over making mistakes, high personal standards, perception of high parental expectations and parental criticism, doubting the quality of one's actions, and a preference for order and organization. Several of the subscales, especially high personal standards and a need for order and organization, are associated with good work habits, striving, and high achievement. Other subscales, especially excessive concern about making mistakes, perception of high parental standards, and doubting of one's actions, are related to a wide range of clinical disorders, especially depression.

Frost, Heimberg, Holt, Mattia, and Neubauer (1993) examined the relationships between their multidimensional perfectionism scale and those developed by Hewitt and Flett (1989). Frost et al. (1993) found that their total score correlated primarily with Hewitt and Flett's (1989) measures of self-oriented and socially prescribed perfectionism. Factor analysis of the items of both the Frost (Frost, Marten, et al., 1990) and Hewitt and Flett (1989) measures yielded two primary factors: (a) Maladaptive Evaluative Concerns and (b) Positive Achievement Striving. The dimensions most related to pathology were Frost's dimension of excessive concerns over mistakes and Hewitt and Flett's socially prescribed perfectionism. Socially prescribed perfectionism was significantly correlated with three of Frost's scales: (a) excessive concerns about mistakes, (b) high parental expectations, and (c) level of parental criticism. These findings, consistent with Hamachek's (1978) distinction of adaptive and maladaptive functions of perfectionism, indicate that perfectionism is a complex phenomenon that is linked with normal adaptive functioning as well as with psychological disturbance (W. D. Parker, 1997). In "normal perfectionism," individuals derive a sense of pleasure from painstaking effort, and they strive to excel while still feeling free to be less precise as the situation permits (Hamachek, 1978). Success brings a sense of satisfaction with a job well done (Missildine, 1963; Timpe, 1989) and feelings of self-esteem, because the individuals are able to accept both personal and environmental limitations (Pacht, 1984). Realistic and reasonable expectations and goals allow individuals to enjoy their strengths; to become emotionally invested; and to strive to function well, improve, and even excel (Flett, Hewitt, Blankstein, & Mosher, 1991). Thus, certain dimensions of perfectionism (self-oriented perfectionism [Hewitt & Flett, 1989] and high personal standards and orderliness [Frost, Marten, Lahart, & Rosenblate, 1990]) are associated with constructive striving for achievement and with other adaptive qualities, such as self-actualization (Frost, Marten, et al., 1990). Positive, supportive, and encouraging relationships with parents and teachers facilitate this desire for self-actualization (Hjelle & Smith, 1975; Nystul, 1984). College women with high personal standards, a positive type of perfectionism (Frost, Marten, et al., 1990), had mothers who reported having high standards for themselves and saw themselves as well organized. Positive perfectionistic qualities in parents are significantly related to the degree to which these positive qualities are reported by daughters (Frost, Lahart, & Rosenblate, 1991).

In response to experiences of failure, however, and especially in combination with high socially prescribed perfectionism, self-oriented perfectionism can become a neurotic perfectionism (Hamachek, 1978) that is associated with a wide range of psychological disturbances and distress (Flett, Hewitt, Blankstein, & Gray, 1998; Frost et al., 1991; Pacht, 1984), including eating disorders; depression; suicide; personality disorders; obsessive–compulsive disorders; anxiety and panic disorder; and psychosomatic disorders, including migraine headaches, sexual dysfunction, and Type A behavior (see Blatt, 1995a, for an extended review of this literature).

Neurotic perfectionism is driven by an intense need to avoid failure. Nothing seems quite good enough, and the individual is unable to derive satisfaction from what ordinarily might be considered a job well done or a superior performance. Deep-seated feelings of inferiority and vulnerability force the individual into an endless cycle of self-defeating overstriving in which each task and enterprise becomes another threatening challenge. No effort is ever satisfactory, as the individual constantly seeks approval and acceptance, and desperately tries to avoid errors and failure. Thus, ego-involving circumstances (Frost & Marten, 1990; Hewitt & Flett, 1991; Hewitt, Mittelstaedt, & Wollert, 1989) and stressful interpersonal experiences (Hewitt & Flett, 1991) create negative affect and distress. These neurotically perfectionistic individuals experience considerable negative affect before, during, and after evaluative tasks; they report that the quality of their work should have been better, and they judge their work as lower in quality than do nonperfectionists (Frost & Henderson, 1991; Frost & Marten, 1990). Extensive psychological research indicates that individuals with high levels of self-criticism and perfectionism are vulnerable to experiences of failure, to which they react with increased levels of depression (Blatt & Zuroff, 1992). Using a biochemical measure of stress (plasma homovanillic acid, a metabolite of dopamine), Gruen, Silva, Ehrlich, Schweitzer, and Friedhoff (1997) found a significant positive relationship between level of DEQ Self-Criticism and reactions to an induced-failure task in women. Excessive perfectionism and self-criticism not only create a greater vulnerability to failure; research findings indicate that these psychological qualities can also interfere with self-actualization (Flett, Hewitt, Blankstein, & Mosher, 1991).

Baumeister (1990) suggested that high personal standards (self-oriented perfectionism) and the expectations that others hold these high expectations for one (socially prescribed perfectionism) are also important dimensions in the initiation of suicidal behavior. Reports of suicidal ideation and intent have been linked to both self-oriented perfectionism (e.g., Delisle, 1990; Shaffer, 1974) and to socially prescribed perfectionism (e.g. Baumeister, 1990; Delisle, 1986, 1990; Flett & Hewitt, 2002; R. L. Hayes & Sloat, 1989; Hewitt, Flett, & Weber, 1994; Hewitt et al., 1997; Shafi, Carrigan, Whittinghill, & Derrick, 1985).

Hewitt, Flett, and Turnbull (1992; Hewitt et al., 1997) empirically examined the relationship of these two types of perfectionism to suicide threat and ideation. In a sample of psychiatric inpatients and outpatients of mixed diagnoses, they found that socially prescribed perfectionism was related significantly to increased levels of suicide potential beyond the contributions of both level of depression and feelings of hopelessness. These findings are consistent with earlier findings that socially prescribed perfectionism was elevated in patients with depression (Hewitt & Flett, 1991) and in those with borderline personality disorder (Hewitt, Flett, & Blankstein, 1991; Hewitt, Flett & Turnbull-Donovan, 1994), diagnostic groups often associated with suicidal potential. Contrary to prior findings (Ellis & Ratliff, 1986; Ranieri et al., 1987), however, Hewitt et al. (1992; Hewitt et al., 1997) found no significant relationship between self-oriented perfectionism and suicide threat. They suggested that the relationship between self-oriented perfectionism and suicidal ideation may depend on the presence of certain mediating variables, such as recent experiences of failure (Hewitt & Flett, 1993). Perfectionistic individuals are excessively concerned about making mistakes (Frost & Marten, 1990) and, therefore, are particularly vulnerable to failure experiences (Gruen et al., 1997; Hewitt & Flett, 1993) that can activate their suicidal potential (Flett, Hewitt, & Blankstein, 1991; Pacht, 1984). In a group of heterogeneous psychiatric inpatients and outpatients, however, as well as in a sample of college students, Hewitt, Flett, and Weber (1994) found that both self-oriented and socially prescribed perfectionism are associated with greater suicidal ideation and that self-oriented perfectionism moderated the link between life stress and suicidal ideation.

These significant relationships between perfectionism and suicide appear to be particularly intense among gifted adolescents (Delisle, 1986, 1990; Driscoll, 1989; Farrell, 1989; R. L. Hayes & Sloat, 1989; Weisse, 1990). As W. D. Parker and Adkins (1995; Adkins & Parker, 1996) noted, however, the evidence for this link between perfectionism and suicide in the gifted is primarily anecdotal, and further research is needed. Perfectionism may be particularly relevant to suicide in adolescents because of their tendencies toward idealism (Blos, 1979; E. H. Erikson, 1950, 1968). Garland and Zigler (1993, p. 173) noted that suicide in adolescents is often

> immediately precipitated by a shameful or humiliating experience such as an arrest, a *perceived failure* [emphasis added] at school or work, or rejection or interpersonal conflict with a romantic partner or parent (Brent, Kerr,

Goldstein, Bozigar, Wartell & Allan, 1989; Shaffer, 1974, 1988; Shaffer, Garland, Gould, Fisher, & Trautman, 1988).

Shaffer (1988) also identified a group of adolescent suicide victims who had not exhibited the usual behavioral or school problems that often accompany suicidal behavior but who were characterized as highly anxious, perfectionistic, and rigid and who appeared particularly vulnerable to major life changes. Petersen, Compas, Brooks-Gunn, Stemmler, Ey, and Grant (1993) discussed the close relation of depression to suicidal ideation and behavior in adolescents and observed that having a parent with depression is a consistent risk factor for depression. A good relationship with parents serves as a protective factor for stressful life events and the onset of depression.

Despite the impressive consistency of this extensive literature linking perfectionism to depression and suicidal ideation in both adults (e.g., Braaten & Darling, 1962; Burns, 1980a, 1980b; Davis, 1983; Hollender, 1965; Maltsberger, 1986; Marks & Haller, 1977; Orbach, Gross, & Glaubman, 1981) and adolescents (e.g., Delisle, 1986, 1990; Goldsmith, Fyer, & Frances, 1990; Hewitt et al., 1997; Shaffer, 1974) in both clinical and nonclinical samples, Hewitt, Flett, and Turnbull-Donovan (1992) pointed out that many of these findings are based on the relationship of perfectionism to suicide threat, intent, or ideation, not to actual suicidal behavior. Hewitt, Flett, & Turnbell-Donovan (1992) suggested that future work address these relationships "in individuals who have actually made serious [suicide] attempts" (p. 188). To that end, Hewitt, Flett, and Weber (1994) attempted to fill this gap by citing two very brief but striking statements describing self-oriented and socially prescribed perfectionism in two young women, each of whom made a serious suicide attempt (Berman & Jobes, 1991; Stephens, 1987). Also, the detailed reports about Vincent Foster, as well as empirical postmortem analyses of data gathered on young adults who eventually committed suicide (Apter et al., 1993), add to an increasing appreciation of the role of intense perfectionism in suicidal behavior. Apter et al. (1993) evaluated the military records of 43 Israeli male soldiers who committed suicide during their compulsory military service. Informants indicated that one of the major precipitating stressors in 28% of these soldiers involved service-related issues stemming from the perception of "humiliation or insult or a failure to live up to his own or others' expectations" (e.g., failure to perform a mission, to gain promotion, to be selected for a prestigious unit or mission). Apter et al. noted, however, that a detailed preinduction assessment failed to identify these vulnerable soldiers, even though a "significant minority" of them, in retrospect, had "previously unreported difficulties at home and at school prior to induction. . . . The need to minimize or overcome such difficulties may have been especially strong in narcissistically vulnerable subjects with unrealistically high self-expectations" (p. 142). Fazaa (2001; Fazaa & Page, 2003), extending prior research (e.g., A. T. Beck, 1983; Blatt, 1974; Blatt et al., 1982) on the relations between introjective, self-critical personality qualities and suicide, studied a large group of suicidal patients. He found that self-criticism, as assessed by the DEQ, was related to serious and lethal suicidal behavior, whereas DEQ Dependency was related primarily to suicidal gestures designed to communicate unhappiness, but without an intent to die. These findings, consistent with earlier reports, are discussed in detail in chapter 5.

A wide range of empirical and clinical research indicates that the combination of self-oriented and socially prescribed perfectionism, the sense of profound personal failure, and the belief that one has failed to meet the high standards and expectations of the people who matter most (both contemporary figures and in particular conscious and unconscious identifications with harsh, judgmental figures from the past) can create the sense that one has nowhere to turn. This can result in feelings of helplessness, hopelessness, and utter despair that lead to clinical depression and suicide (e.g., Hewitt et al., 1992; Hewitt, Flett, & Weber, 1994). These findings emphasize the central role of the introjective qualities of self-criticism and perfectionism in depression and provide the basis for understanding more fully the forces that lead some remarkably talented but exceedingly self-critical and perfectionistic individuals, such as Vincent Foster, to end their lives.

Perfectionistic individuals experience a depression focused primarily on issues of self-worth and self-criticism; they berate, criticize, and attack themselves, and they experience intense feelings of guilt, shame, failure, and worthlessness. They are driven by the danger of failing to meet stern and harshly expressed parental standards and expectations. As children, they believed that approval was contingent on meeting the parents' very strict standards, and they lived in apprehension of losing the approval and love of their parents. Intense self-criticism and the need for perfectionism seem to be an internalization of the child's relationship with his parents (Blatt, 1974), who intensely scrutinize the child's behavior; attempt to thwart the child's effort at assertion and individuation; and are intrusive, controlling, and punitive (McCranie & Bass, 1984). As I discuss in detail in chapter 6, these formulations about the relationship of parental behavior to the development of perfectionism in children are based on clinical observations, individuals' recollections about their parents, and correlational analyses—data that could possibly limit the conclusions that can be drawn about a possible causal relationship between early life experiences and the later development of intense perfectionism (Lewinsohn & Rosenbaum, 1987). Recent longitudinal research, however, indicates that these various anecdotal retrospective reports, and the correlational findings that derive from them, reflect important causal links (see also Brewin, Andrews, & Gotlib, 1993). Longitudinal studies (e.g., Gjerde, Block, & Block, 1991; Koestner, Zuroff, & Powers, 1991; Lekowitz & Tesiny, 1984; Zuroff, Koestner, & Powers, 1994) demonstrate that parental rejection and excessive authoritative control in early childhood (before age 8) is predictive of the level of the child's self-criticism in early adolescence (ages 12–13; Koestner et al., 1991) and of depression level when the child is a late adolescent or a young adult (above age 18; Gjerde et al., 1991). Also, level of self-criticism in early adolescence is predictive of less education; an occupation characterized by lower socioeconomic status; and higher levels of maladjustment, depression, and dissatisfaction with work, family, and other close relationships in later adulthood (age 31; Zuroff et al., 1994). Thus, highly perfectionistic, self-critical introjective individuals appear to view and judge themselves in the same harsh punitive fashion as they perceive that their parents had judged them (S. Freud,

1917/1957e, 1923/1961b). They struggle to meet harsh judgmental parental standards and are identified with these attitudes of their parents—attitudes that they now direct toward themselves so that whatever they accomplish is never fully sufficient (Asch, 1980; Gabbard, 1995; E. Jacobson, 1971; Meissner, 1986).

Transparent and Cross-Sectional Images as Indicators of Suicidal Potential

Roth and Blatt (1974a, 1974b) provided yet another link between vulnerability to suicide in individuals with introjective personality traits, such as self-critical perfectionism. They (Roth & Blatt, 1974a) discussed the differentiation and integration of spatial–temporal dimensions in various levels of psychological organization, including an emphasis on (a) the boundary between two independent objects, (b) the two-dimensional balance between separate elements, (c) a preoccupation with three-dimensional volume, and (d) the representation of three-dimensional objects transversing a three-dimensional field. Roth and Blatt (1974b) demonstrated in clinical reports that introjective depression, involving feelings of failure, self-loathing, self-criticism, and guilt, was associated with spatial representations of depth and volume (i.e., a concern about the properties of an object located within another object). They also found that the use of a representation of a sequence of planes, in transparent or cross-sectional views, to establish or sustain a tentative and unstable three-dimensional representation of volume or depth, was associated with negative therapeutic reactions, including suicide and self-destructive tendencies. Several empirical investigations with the Rorschach (Blatt & Ritzler, 1974; Fowler, Hilsenroth, & Piers, 2001; Hansell, Lerner, Milden, & Ludolph, 1988; Rierdan, Lang, & Eddy, 1978; K. Smith, 1981) provide systematic empirical support for the association of suicidal ideation and action with representations that contain transparent or cross-sectional elements (or both). Blatt and Ritzler (1974), in providing the initial empirical evidence for the representation of transparency and cross-sections in patients who committed suicide, cited the Rorschach responses of a very talented 35-year-old unmarried professional woman who felt worthless and had bizarre thoughts, including ideas of dissolution of her body and self-destructive fantasies. During psychiatric hospitalization, she became increasingly withdrawn and agitated and was diagnosed with a psychotic depression with thought disorder. Several months after psychological testing, this patient hung herself on the hospital unit. A postmortem review of her clinical record revealed that her Rorschach contained the following responses: On Card 2, she saw two sea animals in the upper red area and commented that the shape of the butterfly in the lower red area was "transparent like a sea creature, that's really three dimensional." When the examiner inquired further into these responses by asking her to describe the sea animals, she commented: "Red at the top could be sea animals that could be transparent. Some sea animals you can see through, I felt that way about the bottom part, also." She was asked in what way these figures were transparent and responded: "You could see other things behind them, probably red and some white in them." The examiner then asked, "anything else besides transparent?" and she replied: "The shape on the bottom looks more like the shape of a butterfly." On Card 4, her second response was: "It's something weird—sea animal. Something out of horror movies, it's transparent, too." On Card 6, she commented in her eighth response that "it's a diagram of a mine shaft with an elevator, and it's going down into the earth, it's a cross-section view."

Blatt and Ritzler (1974) also cited Rorschach responses from another female patient in her late adolescence, who committed suicide subsequent to her discharge from the hospital. Early in her hospitalization, she had been given a series of psychological tests, including the Rorschach. Her eighth response to Card 1 of the Rorschach was a "snowflake, perforated, coming to a point, flatness, thinness, and little points that don't give the effect of depth." Her first response to Card 2 was an X-ray of a chest. In response to the examiner's request to explain the ways in which it looked like an X-ray, she responded, "because of the darkness and the appearance of translucency. It is symmetrical, the light part in the middle is a big central bone structure. Darkness and translucency, light and dark ink part of it."

Her first response to Card 6 was a "cross-sectional of a pole, stuck in the ground." In response to the request to explain the ways in which it looked like a cross-section of a pole, she commented: "like a hollow pole. I could see indications in the drawing. It was as if it were sent down into a solid mass." The fourth response to Card 6 was "fish," and in response to the request to describe the fish more fully, she said there was a "sense of lightness in the center of it. The grain indicated ribs of a fish, but open and laid down flat. It has the texture of semi-translucency. Lightness and darkness, also with the grain." The third response to Card 7 was "a pot, a cross-section taken through the pot." The fourth response to Card 7 was a "piece of cheese . . . the predominant light parts are semi-translucent; that's the texture of cheese."

Transparencies and cross-sectional responses have also been noted in Rorschach protocols of patients who have made serious suicide attempts and gestures. A 25-year-old married man, for example, was seen at a Veterans Administration hospital because of severe alcoholism and several suicidal attempts in which he slashed his wrists. When he was admitted to the hospital, the clinician noted that the patient was "terrified of his own self-destructive impulses." The nursing staff, as well as his therapist, were impressed not only with his suicide attempts but with the multiple ways he tried to hurt and damage himself. The patient's Rorschach was replete with themes of death and murder. For example, his response to Card 3 of the Rorschach was: "This over here reminds me of what I would describe as Edgar Allen Poe's story of death, *Mask of Red Death*. Black, skeletal in appearance." In inquiry to this Rorschach response, he commented that it was the dark eyes and the large decaying areas of the human skull that were "hideous in appearance. I associate this with Edgar Allan Poe because I like his writing. Tantalizing horror. Eyes looking at you, but you know it's dead, and by some supernatural way, it's able to stare at you hideously." This was only one of a number of instances in which the manifest themes of death, murder, and suicide were expressed in the content of this patient's projective test responses.

In addition to this manifest content around death in some of his Rorschach responses, many responses contained representations of transparency and cross-sections. For example, his fifth response to Card 1 was "It looks like X-rays of a human pelvis." On inquiry, he commented, "Pelvic bone, rib cage, the X-ray is dark, shadowy, black and gray, and it's transparent." On Card 2, his third response to the bottom red area was "It reminds me of a microbe." On inquiry to what about the card made it look like a microbe, he commented: "The lightness of its color gives me the impression that it's transparent. From my past experiences, microbes, when seen highly magnified are so small that they are transparent." In his fourth response to Card 7, he saw a cross-sectional view of a "volcano erupting." On inquiry, he commented, "This is the internal passageway. Dark area is intensity of heat and light, area here is molten lava. Appears as if lava is flowing out of the mountain."

The representation of transparency and cross-sections in suicidal patients can occur not only in psychological test protocols and in dreams but also in a number of other forms. The gifted poetess Sylvia Plath, for example, committed suicide at age 31. Some 10 years earlier, she made a serious suicide attempt, and only by accident was she found and saved. Her autobiographical novel, *The Bell Jar*, finished and published a few months before her death, recounts her personal disintegration and first suicide attempt 10 years earlier. Frequent references to transparency and cross-sections are present in her poems and in her novel. In describing her visit to a psychiatrist, she wrote that she had not washed her clothes and hair or slept in over a week:

> I saw the days of the year stretching ahead like a series of bright, white boxes, and separating one box from another was sleep, like a black shade. Only for me, the long perspective of shades that set off one box from the next had suddenly snapped up, and I could see day after day glaring ahead of me like a white, broad, infinitely desolate avenue. (Plath, 2003, pp. 104–105)

In describing her thoughts about how to commit suicide, she wrote:

> When they asked some old Roman philosopher or other how he wanted to die, he said he would open his veins in a warm bath. I thought it would be easy, lying in the tub and seeing the redness flower from my wrists, flush after flush through the clear water, till I sank under a turf gaudy as poppies. (Plath, 2003, p. 121)

In asking a friend about suicide, she described the scene as follows:

> I rolled over onto my stomach and squinted at the view in the other direction, toward Lynn. A glassy haze ripped up from the fires in the grills and the heat on the road, and through the haze as through a curtain of clear water, I could make out a smudgy skyline of gas tanks and factory stacks and derricks and bridges.
>   It looked one hell of a mess.
>   I rolled onto my back again and made my voice casual. "If you were going to kill yourself, how would you do it?" (Plath, 2003, p. 127)

Even the title of the novel itself, *The Bell Jar*, is a transparent image—a picture of "my world and the people in it as seen through the distorting lens of a bell jar" (Plath, 1972, p. 214) that can descend at any time.

Alvarez (1972), in a scholarly, sensitive, and poignant study of suicide, *The Savage God*, begins with a memoir of Sylvia Plath. He then reviews the theories of suicide to "find out why these things happen." Alvarez described Plath's poems as having a "translucent calm" (p. 30), and he described Plath's face at the coroner's inquest as "grey and slightly transparent, like wax" (p. 33). Alvarez's use of transparent references are a testimony to his appreciation and understanding of the phenomenon of suicide. In the epilogue of his book, he described his feelings after his own suicide attempt: "I felt frail and almost transparent, as though I were made of tissue paper" (p. 232).

Transparency and cross-sectional images appear to express the desperate struggle of the individual with introjective depressive feelings to maintain an integrated sense of self. With the collapse of the capacity to experience a coherent and intact sense of self, a sense that one has substance and solidity or volume, suicide becomes a serious alternative.

Two Types of Depression in Adolescence

The distinction between anaclitic and introjective disorders enables clinicians and researchers to understand more fully some of the motivational forces that enter into disruptive adolescent behavior. Anna Freud (1949) differentiated between early disturbances of object love and disturbances that derive from later developmental phases. According to her, the former is based on early disturbances of the development of object love, in contrast to disruptions based on more structured and organized conflicts in the development and resolution of the Oedipus complex. Aichhorn (1925/1955) also distinguished between two groups of delinquency: (a) dissocial delinquents, who showed no evidence of neurotic conflict and whose struggles with the environment derived from serious frustrations of early libidinal needs, and (b) a delinquency due to more organized neurotic conflicts. Aichhorn also differentiated between two kinds of hate in delinquency: (a) an open hate, which is the result of a loss of love because of profound parental neglect, and (b) a concealed hate, which arises when the child feels that he is not loved for his own sake but is a replacement for parental lack of self-fulfillment either within themselves or with their spouse. Aichhorn also distinguished between aggressive behavior determined by an early lack of affection from aggression determined by unconscious guilt and a need for punishment. In general, Aichhorn differentiated between uninhibited, primitive delinquents who have little or no guilt and delinquents who have intense repressed guilt and are struggling with the demands of a primitive superego. Burkes and Harrison (1961) likewise distinguished between aggressive antisocial behavior as a way of avoiding depressive loneliness and aggressive behaviors that are expressions of feelings of guilt.

Blos (1957) differentiated between two types of female delinquents: One has intense ties to the pre-Oedipal mother, and the other struggles with aspects of the Oedipal complex. These two types of delinquents may commit similar offenses, but the dynamics and character structure of these two forms of delinquency are different and can be conceptualized along the anaclitic and introjective dimensions. Female delinquency can be based on a regression to the pre-Oedipal mother in which the girl has failed to achieve separation from a dependency on her mother and uses heterosexuality to protect herself against a regressive pull toward the mother. Severe deprivation or overstimulation results in a potential anaclitic regression toward the pre-Oedipal mother. Blos also discussed a second type of delinquent female, who is more introjective in quality. A prevailing Oedipal struggle never reaches sufficient resolution to result in an adequate degree of internalization. This type of delinquent girl not only experiences an Oedipal defeat at the hands of a distant, cruel, or absent father but also shares in her mother's dissatisfaction with her husband. This ambivalent bond between mother and daughter, based on a hostile or negative identification, forges a destructive relationship between them. The girl's delinquent behavior is motivated by a need for the constant possession of a partner who serves as a fantasy replacement for Oedipal defeat and provides a basis on which she can compete with the mother who hates, rejects, or ridicules the father. In her sexual delinquency, the girl expresses her wish to be desired sexually as a way of demonstrating that she is more desired than her mother. These distinctions by Aichhorn, Blos, Anna Freud, and others are consistent with my differentiation of an anaclitic and an introjective delinquency.

The distinction between anaclitic and introjective dysphoria provides a theoretical model for understanding the dynamics of some antisocial behavior. It enables one to consider delinquency in adolescence not simply as defiance of social order but as a consequence of a failure to have had positive interpersonal experiences that results in impairments in the development of particular personality structures—constructive cognitive–affective schemas of self and significant others that are essential for adaptive functioning.

Anaclitic Depression

An anaclitic or dependent personality organization in adolescence can result in depression or antisocial behavior (or both) focused around oral neediness. This form of disruptive behavior develops from fears of abandonment and experiences of neglect. Its origins are in early emotional deprivation, maternal neglect, or critical interruption in the continuity of caretaking relationships. These painful early experiences leave the adolescent with unfilled anaclitic strivings, which may be expressed in various disruptive activities.

Many early clinical investigators point to the crucial role of severe disruptions in the early parent–child relationships of disturbed adolescents, including emotional deprivation, separation from parents, loss of affection, prolonged absence or death of parents, repeated change in foster homes, institutional life, and so on, as having etiological significance in both depression and antisocial activity (e.g., Bowlby, 1952; Friedlander, 1947; Jenkins & Hewitt, 1944). Deprivation in the infantile period and critical breaks in the continuity of close personal relationships have an etiological role in the development of disturbances in adolescents. A study of 57 antisocial young children (Rexford,

1959) revealed that children who experienced very disturbed early relationships with their parents and emotionally and physically depriving environments were difficult to treat because of their very limited capacity for object relations and their tenuous grasp of reality. Burkes and Harrison (1961), in a study of aggressive children, concluded that some aggressive behavior is a means of avoiding feelings of depression, especially in children who experienced deprivations and rejection in their early years and had difficulty in forming lasting object relationships. This "deprived child syndrome" is a result of a lack of mothering, either because of prolonged separation at a crucial age or because the mother was destructive. These children had hollow interpersonal relationships, hedonistic impulsivity, and a lack of guilt. This acting out serves a self-protection function against feelings of deprivation. Burkes and Harrison noted that the character structure of these aggressive children is similar to the character structure of some patients who are depressed and that these children used aggressive behavior to avoid feelings of helplessness and powerlessness and to avoid recognizing and acknowledging their cravings for affection. Katz (1972) and D. O. Lewis and Balla (1976) also have discussed deprivation, neglect, psychological abuse, and cruelty as contributors to destructive adolescent behavior.

Friedlander (1949) discussed how any interference with the establishment of a firm mother–child relationship or with the consistent handling of primitive instinctual drives hinders ego development. Early separations, as well as inconsistent, neglectful, and rejecting caregiving, can lead to disturbances in ego development and impairments in the establishment of object relationships. Impaired ego and superego development results in impulsive behavior and little capacity for delay and planning. Anna Freud (1949) considered disruption of the mother–infant relationship a critical factor in adolescent disturbance. She considered situations in which the mother is absent, neglectful, or emotionally unstable and fails to provide steady satisfaction, or where the care is impersonal, or given by many different figures, as contributing to the development of impaired interpersonal relationships and a blunting of libidinal development that contribute to an impairment in the capacity to contain intense destructive urges that derive from the child's experiences of deprivation. Most of the conduct-disordered children studied at the Hampstead Child-Therapy Clinic had serious disruptions of the mother–child relationship. The acting out of these children often comprised distorted attempts to reach out for new objects, a search for a love object who would restore the original sense of well-being that was lost in early childhood (H. Schwartz, 1968).

Serious disruptions of relationships with parents, including the loss of a parent, are reported frequently in children with antisocial tendencies. Kaufman (1955) discussed depression after the traumatic loss of a parent as an important precipitant of antisocial behavior. Each of the cases presented by Aichhorn in his classic volume on delinquent adolescents, *Wayward Youth* (1925/1955), had a history of parental loss, often occurring in a traumatic fashion. Scharfman and Clark (1967) as well as Bowlby and Parks (1970) have identified parental loss through death, desertion, or divorce, especially premature separation from the mother, as a central factor in the formation of antisocial behavior in females. The early experiences of many antisocial adolescents are characterized by prolonged or repeated disruptions of the mother–child bond during the first years of life. Children raised in institutions often have little experience with intimate interpersonal relationships and are often asocial and experience little anxiety or guilt (Becker, 1941). They often have features of infantilism, apathy, intellectual retardation, and an inability to form object relations (Goldfarb, 1945). Various forms of deprivation (neglect and rejection, an unstable and unsatisfying mother figure, separation and loss, institutional life) during the early childhood period are associated with depression and antisocial behavior (Bender, 1947; Goldfarb, 1945).

Orality is another issue prominent in anaclitic disorders. Violent reactions to frustration have been noted in individuals with a desperate neediness for supplies from others to regulate their self-esteem. They are excessively dependent on external supplies, on being loved, on receiving care and affection (Fenichel, 1945). The primary conflict in these individuals is between a tendency to take by violence what was not given to them and a tendency to repress all aggressiveness out of a fear of losing love. They view others not as individuals but as providers and therefore interchangeable. Other people have no significance as individuals in their own right. If the necessary supplies are missing, then these anaclitic individuals become depressed, and many of their impulsive acts are attempts to fill a sense of emptiness to avoid feelings of depression. Fenichel (1945) concluded that an oral type of self-esteem regulation forms the dispositional basis for impulsive acting out, depression, and addiction. Falstein (1958) also discussed unfilled intensified oral needs and how antisocial adolescents are unable to express hostility directly toward a perceived depriving mother who fails to satisfy adequately the child's oral needs. Instead, rage is displaced onto the larger social group. Thus, considerable clinical evidence indicates that some forms of antisocial behavior are a consequence of deprivation of anaclitic needs. Severe frustration and disruptions of the infant–mother relationship result in antisocial behavior that often expresses a desperate need to fill unsatisfied cravings for care and affection. These longings can be expressed in multiple forms, including stealing supplies as a replacement for love; seeking contact, warmth, and closeness in promiscuous sexual behavior (Hollender, 1970), drug abuse (Lidz, Lidz, & Rubenstein, 1976), alcohol, or food, to fill a seemingly bottomless void; or assaulting people because of rage over feelings of deprivation and frustration. The concept of an anaclitic personality provides a theoretical structure for understanding these seemingly meaningless acts that are both self-destructive and destructive of others.

Because of a failure to achieve a sense of closeness and interpersonal relatedness in early childhood, the adolescent has an impaired capacity to experience empathy and emotional bonds, which limits his or her ability to participate in an interpersonal matrix and to experience potentially modulating affects, such as anxiety, guilt, or shame. Inconsistent caring in early childhood also creates an intolerance of delay and postponement, resulting in impulsivity and rage in response to frustration. Unpredictable caretaking experiences, with little consistency in the ways needs are satisfied, make it difficult for the child to tolerate delay and to trust the future. One impetuous act follows on another in a search for sensation and stimulation to replace a barren emptiness and loneliness.

Thus, disruptive behavior in depression can derive from an immature personality organization with an impaired capacity to tolerate delay and frustration. This antisocial behavior is often an attempt to ward off feelings of helplessness and depletion; to gratify wishes to be cared for, loved, fed, and protected; and to struggle with fears of being abandoned and an urgency to fill an inner emptiness and oral cravings. Antisocial behavior in this context can also be an expression of rage about deprivation and neglect. Early emotional deprivation leaves these individuals with profoundly impaired object relations.

AN ANACLITIC ADOLESCENT BOY. A.B., a 16-year-old, single, White male, was referred for psychiatric hospitalization after an extended history of breaking and entering, stealing, and truancy. He had been involved in these activities for about 3 years prior to hospitalization. A. also had endocrinological difficulties that resulted in significant interference with his physical growth. He appeared considerably younger than his age; his stature was significantly shorter than normal, and he looked prepubescent. He seemed to be a frightened and depressed child hiding behind a superficial bravado.

A.'s mother, Mrs. B., was the only child of divorced parents. She left school at the age of 16 to marry A.'s father because she was pregnant. Having been considered bright, she felt frustrated that she could not finish high school and continue into college. A.'s father, Mr. B., believed that his wife used her pregnancy before marriage to escape from her mother, but this possibly contrived attempt to achieve separation failed. Mrs. B. was unable to establish an independent life because her mother visited her daily and constantly intruded into her married life.

A.'s father was the youngest of four siblings. He established his own business and had remained in it for the past 15 years. He married his wife, whom he had met in high school, immediately after finishing school. Their marital relationship was poor, and after 10 years the marriage ended in divorce. Both parents had serious problems with alcohol abuse; Mrs. B. seemed to have the more severe alcohol problem, and became intoxicated whenever she confronted difficulties.

A. was the second of three children. After the birth of her first child, Mrs. B. did not want further children; A. thus was unplanned and unwanted. Mrs. B. considered A. at birth to be extremely ugly because "he had no neck, and his hair grew straight up." As soon as she brought him home from the hospital, she cut off his hair. The mother was incapable of showing affection to any of her children, but this was especially true with A. Family members reported that she had always disliked and rejected A. and was very harsh with him.

At the age of three, A. was diagnosed as having serious endocrinological problems requiring frequent hospitalization. A.'s earliest memory, from when he was age 5, had to do with his medical difficulties when he became delirious and thought that Martians were coming. His endocrinological difficulties and serious allergies required severe dietary restrictions, which A.'s father recalled as having been very difficult for his son. Because of his severe allergies, he was forbidden to eat chocolate.

During his early childhood, A. was frequently left with his aunt. She was the oldest of the father's siblings and had played a mothering role for Mr. B.

when he had been a child, extending even into his adulthood. She also often assumed primary responsibility for A.'s care, providing the affection and nurturance he did not receive from his own parents. Several times each week, A.'s mother left him with the aunt while taking her other two children with her. At one point, Mrs. B. even asked the aunt to adopt A., but the aunt refused because she already had children of her own. The aunt considered A. a lovable, warm child until age 5, when he began taking candy, small items, and change from her home without permission. This stealing coincided with the beginning of Mrs. B.'s amphetamine and alcohol abuse. A. apparently continued to steal money from relatives until approximately age 13, when he began breaking and entering homes in the neighborhood.

Mr. B. spent little time at home during A.'s early years, because he was busy establishing his business or was often drunk. The father had severe problems expressing emotion and relating to others, claiming to have had special difficulties in understanding and communicating with A. He realized that he had not established a good father–son relationship with A. and attributed this failure to A.'s frequent hospitalizations and endocrinological difficulties.

In school, A. first became a discipline problem in the fourth grade, when he was described as hyperactive. Between the ages of 5 and 8, A.'s parents separated frequently, with the father and the mother alternately leaving the home. When A. was 8, his parents finally divorced. The court awarded custody of the children to the father, because the mother was considered incapable of taking care of them. Mr. B., however, did not want them and thought of them as a burden, but he agreed to take them because they needed a home. For six months after the divorce, the children were cared for by their aunt and their paternal grandparents. The father then began a relationship with a woman who moved into the home with her children. A. and his sisters did not get along with this woman, and during this time Mr. B. began to drink more heavily.

In the first 3½ years after the divorce, A. had very little contact with his mother, seeing her occasionally on weekends. When finally the conflict between A. and the woman with whom his father was living became intolerable to the father, A. was sent to live with his mother, who was sober at the time. A.'s young sister followed him shortly to be with their mother. Mrs. B. became increasingly depressed, spending a great deal of time in her room crying. She began drinking again, and the two children were often left on their own. A. and his sister had friends who were described as "some of the worst kids in town." These friends often came over to visit with A. and his sister when there were no adults in the house. A. began stealing, and Mr. B. claimed that the mother took her children into stores to help her shoplift. At his own sister's and mother's urging, Mr. B. brought the children back into his home. Shortly afterward, A.'s younger sister ran away and was gone for two months.

A. often left the father's home to stay with his mother, where he became involved in numerous incidents of breaking and entering. His usual pattern was to skip school with a classmate to go to a good neighborhood with better homes and enter a house, looking solely for money. They would then leave without damaging the property and without stealing anything of value. A. explained that he committed these thefts simply to get money, and apparently some of this money went toward the purchase of a motorbike. Riding a motorbike became A.'s favorite pastime. Mr. B., however, believed that A. stole money primarily to support his marijuana use. When A. was 15, his father moved out of his own home into the house of a new girlfriend, and the court awarded temporary custody of A. to the paternal aunt. A. stayed with his aunt until he became a truancy problem and was returned to his father's home, where the situation had improved somewhat after the father's new girlfriend had moved in.

Eventually, A. was caught breaking and entering. The court and the probation office recommended psychiatric hospitalization. On admission and during his hospitalization, no evidence was found of thought disorder, hallucinations, or delusional thinking. A. seemed appropriate in his reactions with peers on the clinical unit; however, he had serious difficulties in his relationships with staff members. He strongly resisted authority figures, particularly women, and he responded by defying any type of limit-setting. For example, he brought marijuana into the hospital and refused to participate in the hospital activities program. His defiance eventually reached the point at which it became necessary to use seclusion to control his behavior. His unwillingness to maintain the dietary restrictions demanded by his medical difficulties also caused serious problems. At times, his defiance of these restrictions seemed to have a self-destructive intent. He maintained a massive denial of his medical problems, his depression, his disrupted family, and his personal difficulties, insisting that his problems were only legal and would be resolved if only he could find a job. He had difficulties discussing his sad and angry feelings in general but especially those toward his father, whom he saw as distant and unapproachable when sober and as unpredictable and sometimes violent when intoxicated. A. appeared to be very angry and hostile toward his father but unable to acknowledge his rage directly. Interestingly enough, A. was quite fond and protective of his mother and liked to be with her and to take care of her when she was intoxicated.

A.'s strong depressive feelings were primarily anaclitic in nature. They originated in his highly traumatic and severely deprived early experiences. In his chaotic family situation he never experienced certainty and continuity. Since childhood, he had alternately lived with his mother, father, and aunt. He never developed a capacity for communication or a sense of relatedness with any of them. His whole life was a series of severe deprivations, rejections, and neglect, which began with his unwanted birth and continued throughout his early years when he had neither a constant home nor stable parental figures. His hunger for love, concern, and a consistently caring figure left him vulnerable to feelings of depression. His delinquency was a manifestation of this depression and of his desperate attempts to find some satisfaction for his profoundly unfilled anaclitic needs. His breaking into and entering homes appeared to be desperate attempts to find some satisfaction for his cravings for a home that provided aspects of the love, care, and nurturance he had never really experienced.

AN ANACLITIC ADOLESCENT GIRL. C., a 16-year-old, White, single, female high school student, was physically and socially precocious and presented a strikingly attractive appearance. C. had engaged in multiple disruptive behaviors, including school truancy, running away from home, drug abuse, and prostitution since the age of 12. She became progressively sad, anxious, scared, and confused as her disruptive behavior became more intense. Finally, her parents referred her for psychiatric hospitalization.

C.'s father grew up in a family with extreme marital tension. His mother pressured her children to accomplish a great deal and achieve. C.'s father maintained an enmeshed relationship with his own mother. He assumed a great deal of responsibility for his mother's care, even though she was outspoken in her disapproval of his marriage. C.'s mother was from an immigrant family, and her father died at age 55 after a protracted illness. The death of the maternal grandfather, one year prior to C.'s birth, provoked a prolonged and severe mourning reaction in the mother. C. grew up in an essentially enmeshed family where generational boundaries were diffuse and relationships were eroticized, particularly with her father and brother. C.'s older brother had a history of school difficulties and violent outbursts and had been in psychotherapy for these difficulties. The family appeared to have been at war for many years; the characteristic interactional style of the family was hostile–dependent, and the predominant affect in the family was anger.

In addition to C.'s birth coinciding with the anniversary of her maternal grandfather's death, her mother had difficulty during the pregnancy with C. because of a lumbar disc, which forced her to spend the last six months of her pregnancy, and the first three months after the delivery, in bed. C.'s mother also experienced postpartum depression. C. knew that her mother had been very sick and depressed after she was born, and she recalled that her mother had a lot of physical problems throughout C.'s childhood. C. also remembered her parents constantly fighting, with her father coming home after working long hours and finding fault with everything her mother did or said.

C.'s parents disagreed about the onset of her problems; her mother stated that C. had difficulties in school virtually from the start, whereas her father maintained that no real problems had been apparent until C. was about 13, when she first began running away from home. According to C., her battle with her parents began when she was about 11 or 12 and was precipitated by her becoming increasingly uncomfortable in her intense relationship with her father, in which she was "Daddy's little girl" and "his little hostess for his friends." She had fond memories of her relationship with her father from ages 6–10. She liked to be outdoors with him, especially when her mother and brother did not take part in the outings. When C. was 11, disagreements and arguments developed with each of her parents, especially her father. The parents attempted to impose restrictions on her going out and dating or visiting with boys in her room with the door closed, smoking, using drugs, dressing up, and wearing makeup. C.'s explanation for these difficulties with her father was that he refused to accept the fact that she was no longer his little girl, and he continually attempted to tell her "how to live, how to dress, and what to do." C. became increasingly involved in activities outside the home. At home, she fought with her brother, whom she described as "jealous of my popularity" and as hating her because she "took his parents away" from him. C.'s truancy and contentiousness at home escalated; when she was 13, she and her father engaged in a physical fight which led to C.'s leaving home, getting arrested, and finally being admitted to the hospital.

After a brief crisis intervention, C. and her family were referred for family therapy. C. felt that she served as the vehicle for her parents to get into treatment, because all the therapy sessions focused on their marital relationship. C. dropped out of the family therapy, but her parents continued. At that time, C. decided that her mother could not protect her from her brother and father and that they could not continue to live together. She asked her mother to get a divorce from her father and then the two of them—C. and her mother—could live together. This was only one example of C.'s many attempts to split her family to gain her own gratification. She had difficulty sharing her mother's attention with others. After her brother left home, C.'s behavior became more problematic. The arguments with her father intensified, focusing around C.'s sexuality, provocative dress, and behavior, with C.'s father calling her "a whore." She became increasingly involved in prostitution, which culminated in her current hospitalization when she became extremely fearful that her life was being threatened by a pimp. According to C., her experiments with drugs and prostitution gave her a sense of independence and control over her own life, as well as distance from her parents. Her involvements with friends much older than herself (including the pimp) served as substitutes for her parents, whom she denounced as incompetent and intrusive and with whom she felt deeply disappointed.

Several times during her hospitalization, C. went AWOL. Each incident occurred after an experience of separation and loss. The first was precipitated by her parents' vacation plans, which she tried to thwart. The second and third instances occurred around the time of the therapist's vacation. Several weeks before the therapist's vacation, C. became increasingly depressed and broke up with her boyfriend. Shortly before the therapist was to leave on vacation, C. ran away from the hospital. She returned after the therapist had left. After the therapist returned, C. again ran away from the hospital and stayed away about as long as her therapist had been on vacation. When she returned, C. began to talk about her needs to be loved and hugged and about feeling compelled to run when she felt abandoned and alone. In a poignant moment, she stated simply, "I just wanted to be held and loved." C. struggled with the impulse to flee when her needs became overwhelming or when she feared rejection or abandonment. In her struggle to deal with feelings of loneliness and abandonment, she attempted to gain a false sense of independence, control, and autonomy.

In psychotherapy, after an initial period of mistrust, withdrawal, and superficiality, C. gradually began to talk about her sense of worthlessness, her poor self-esteem, her feelings of depression, and her experimentation with drugs and prostitution. The more she became aware of her craving for maternal care and her anguish in having to share her mother with others, the more C. experienced depression with some suicidal ideation. She articulated feelings of sadness and increasingly tried to hurt herself.

C. was very impulsive, needy, and childlike, and initially she desperately defended against recognizing her deep desires to be taken care of and her profound dependency needs. Instead she displayed a counterdependent posture and used denial, avoidance, and flight as defense mechanisms against her desperate anaclitic needs. The anaclitic personality issues underlying C.'s multiple antisocial activities seems clear. Serious deprivation of nurturance during her early childhood resulted in a desperate sense of neediness. The lack of consistent caring by her mother left C. with a profound sense of longing, which she attempted to satisfy through her acting-out behavior, especially her promiscuity. Regarding her involvement in prostitution, she denied her feelings of loneliness and loss by seeking to be taken care of by men. The sexual contact supplied her with a sense of being held and with the illusion of the intimacy and closeness for which she desperately longed. C.'s hostility against her parents—engendered by her experiences of deprivation by her mother and seductiveness by her father—contributed to her need for stimulation, which she found in drugs and sexual contact. C.'s low frustration tolerance and her inability to deal with a delay of gratification caused her to become enraged when her needs were not immediately met. Whenever she felt pain, sadness, or disappointment, she attempted to run away, both literally and metaphorically, to drugs and promiscuity. Her acting out also contained elements of the wish to punish and shame her parents. It was also an inept attempt to achieve a separation from the family and to deny her feelings of loss.

Introjective Depression

Concerns in introjective depression are primarily about feelings of being unworthy, guilty, and having failed to live up to expectations and standards. Introjective depression is characterized by exceedingly high standards and goals, ruminative self-scrutiny and evaluation, and apprehensions that one has failed to live up to perfectionistic standards. These extensive demands for perfection can lead to feelings of hopelessness about achieving approval and recognition and fears about disapproval and punishment. The child's conscious and unconscious critical feelings about him- or herself often reflect the conscious and unconscious attitudes and values of the parents.

Anger and aggression are often major issues in introjective depression, often expressed in harsh judgmental attitudes toward the self and others. Relationships are highly ambivalent, because the representations of others are usually based on negative, hostile, and aggressive aspects of the relationship, and these internalizations result in feelings of doubt, self-criticism, and guilt. The continual negative self-judgment and guilt also serves to maintain contact with the harsh, punitive, judgmental object. Disruptive behavior can develop out of the individual's preoccupations and concerns with issues of self-worth, moral standards, sexual identity, and identification. Disruptive behavior in the introjective personality usually expresses underlying superego conflicts around feelings of worthlessness, guilt, and shame.

In contrast to anaclitic acting out, which develops from feelings of abandonment and neglect, disruptive behavior in introjective adolescents derives from markedly ambivalent, demanding, depreciatory, and hostile parent–child relationships that prevent the child from developing positive self representations. At a time when the child is seeking to establish a sense of identification with his or her parents by internalizing a wide range of conscious and unconscious values—including the parents' attitudes toward the child—parents who are harsh, judgmental, critical, and punitive will be internalized with ambivalence and become part of the child's emerging identity. These intense ambivalent feelings often result in counteractive attempts to demonstrate one's power by excessively striving or by defying authority and becoming involved in antisocial acts such as drug use, aggression, and high-risk sexual activity (Blatt, 1991; Blatt, Hart, Quinlan, Leadbeater, & Auerbach, 1993; Blatt & Shichman, 1981; Blatt & Zuroff, 1992; Leadbeater, Blatt, & Quinlan, 1995; Loeber, 1990). Aichhorn (1925/1955) discussed the impairment of the ego ideal and superego as the basis for antisocial activity. An unconscious sense of guilt can become a primary motivating force for disruptive behavior. Antisocial activity is an effort to gain relief from a sense of guilt by dramatically violating the limits set by moral standards and at the same time inviting punishment for the transgression. Harsh, judgmental parental standards are directed against the self, so that the adolescent's antisocial behavior is both a defiance of these standards and at the same time a seeking of punishment and retribution for the failure to live up to these standards. A search for punishment and self-destructive activity are some of the primary manifestations of powerful, primitive, superego introjects. These primitive introjects are either externalized in disruptive behavior or internalized in depression, often accompanied by suicidal ideation.

Excessive, intense, and rigidly held parental moral codes suggest conflicts within the parents around their own unconscious temptations to violate these standards. Impairments in the child's superego development often reflect similar superego difficulties in the parents. The parents are often conflicted about their own wishes to transgress moral rules and therefore feel both danger and unconscious excitement toward the child for his or her embodiment of their own unconscious conflicts. The parents' unresolved conflicts may be expressed in their inconsistent discipline; their intense criticism can alternate with moments of excessive permissiveness that encourages the child's antisocial activity. Thus, the rigidity and instability of parental standards as well as the child's implicit recognition of the parents' unconscious wishes provide the stage and the climate for the child to begin to violate the overstated and extreme moral standards of the parents. The parents' conflicts also leave the child with rigid, severe, and conflict-laden moral standards. Without adequate internalization of modulating positive feelings of acceptance and respect, the child is left with a seriously impaired sense of self-worth. These feelings of inferiority contribute to a poor self-image and experiences of shame.

Even though the disruptive behavior may manifestly be the same in anaclitic and introjective disturbances, its motivation and meaning differ. Stealing, for example, can be related to issues of sexual identity or status within a peer culture rather than a search for oral supplies or a clinging to objects for safety and security. Sexual promiscuity can be an attempt to affirm a tenuous sexual identity rather than a seeking of warmth, closeness, affection, and body contact (Hollender, 1970). Substance abuse—of alcohol, drugs, or even food—may be a defiance of social standards or a retreat from the pressures of constantly having to achieve or prove one's self-worth rather than a seeking to fill an inner void. Truancy or running away from home can be a way of escaping feelings of inferiority and excessive and unattainable standards rather than an expression of the wish to be sought after and to know that significant people care about one and seek one's return.

AN INTROJECTIVE ADOLESCENT GIRL. D., a tall, thin, attractive, mature-appearing, 17-year-old, White, single female high school senior, had been hospitalized several times for severe drug abuse and antisocial behavior. Her history of drug abuse dated back to sixth grade, when she lost interest in school. She began to dress sloppily and "to hang around with kids" from lower socioeconomic groups. She started sniffing glue because "I didn't want to know what was going on, I was sick of the fights with my parents, I was always under attack." A few months later, she switched to "grass," feeling "tired of being told by everybody what to do. I was not worth being given a reason. I was hurt and wanted to numb out." Cannabis gave her a sense of respect in her peer group. She used it several times each week and obtained the money for its purchase by stealing from her parents. At the end of sixth grade, she had her first sexual experience with a boy she occasionally met on the beach. Thereafter she became increasingly promiscuous. She started using amphetamines, thinking that it would make it possible for her to "accept anything and do anything." Amphetamines made her feel more capable and amiable; she recalled that even her parents commented on a favorable change in her. Toward the end of that year, she became increasingly paranoid and anxious and started to use barbiturates to counter the effect of the amphetamines. She soon started to combine amphetamines with heroin, "taking amphetamines in the morning and heroin at night." Her heroin use became intense and, to obtain money, she "did everything except prostitution." She would steal from her parents and friends, break into apartments of "special friends," and engage in promiscuous sexual behavior. Her parents never became aware of her intensive drug use until about a year later, when she left home to live with an older man who was an amphetamine dealer. When she returned home after a few days, she told her parents that she had used only hash, and they did not place any restrictions on her activities. She continued her drug abuse and promiscuity and began to use cocaine to enjoy sex more fully. Her attendance at school was sporadic, and she returned only when her father threatened to send her to jail. She also entered outpatient therapy at a drug clinic "to get cleaned up." She eventually was expelled from school because of her drug abuse. She then left home to join a drug addict, who, after a few days, threw her out. She went to a drug clinic for two months but pretended to be clean by giving false urine tests. She left home once again and stayed with a "junkie friend" who had been in jail for armed assault. She was taken home by the police and hospitalized for several months. Subsequent to her discharge from the hospital, she entered a methadone program. She moved into her aunt's apartment and was happy there, feeling for the first time that she was part of a real family. However, she continued to take drugs, drank heavily, and started stealing, until finally her aunt asked her to leave the house. She was hospitalized once again.

D. came from an Irish family that had recently come into considerable wealth, reportedly gained through illegal activities. The father was the youngest of eight children of a very caring, strong mother and a cruel alcoholic father.

The father built up an extensive and highly successful business, although he had only a high school education. Despite his remarkable success, he never achieved a stable sense of self-worth and continually remained vulnerable to criticism from his wife and others, feeling impotent and seeking approval and support.

D.'s mother often had a strange appearance, frequently dressing in outlandish and inappropriate ways. Although she did remarkably well in high school, she did not go on to college, because her parents lacked sufficient funds to support her. She was married shortly after graduation from high school to a man she described in idyllic terms. He was killed in an airplane accident shortly after their marriage, and his death left her profoundly depressed. It required several years for her to get over her sorrow and grief. Several years after the death of her first husband, she met D.'s father. The relationship was tempestuous from the start, and they had constant arguments and fights throughout their marriage. She used critical comments and sarcasm to depreciate her children and her husband, especially by comparing him with her "perfect" first husband. The mother was described by the hospital staff as having psychotic features. At times, her speech was illogical, and she seemed to have a fluid and unstable sense of her self and others. She appeared very narcissistic, constantly demanding attention and gifts. She repeatedly insisted on being the center of the family and that her husband and children attend instantly to her needs. Both parents had serious personal difficulties over the years, and both drank heavily at the end of each day. Although the father's problems seemed to diminish after he began psychotherapy, the mother continued to become increasingly bizarre and depressed.

D. was born five years after her parents married. The parents argued about whether to have a child; the mother did not want one but was "forced into it" by her husband. She claimed to have cared for D., but it was actually the maternal grandmother who assumed responsibility for much of the child's care, while the mother sat and read a book or slept. The mother wanted D. to be a "soft-spoken fairy princess," but instead D. was a sturdy, gurgly, active child. The mother would buy toys for little girls and dress D. in frilly girls' clothes and expect her to sit and play quietly, but D. wanted to run around and play more active games. She never played with dolls but preferred boys' games and was considered a tomboy. One of D.'s earliest memories was how her mother made her sit and play piano, beginning around the age of 4, and hit her on the knuckles with a ruler for incorrect notes.

D. was gregarious, enjoyed being with people, and spent much of her time playing with other children—to the annoyance of her mother, who considered herself above the rest of the neighbors and constantly tried to restrain D. from playing with other children in the neighborhood. D. went to a private school because her mother thought it was the proper thing to do. D. would have preferred to stay at home and be with her friends. In her neighborhood she felt embarrassed in front of the other kids because of her parents' wealth, and at school she did not feel accepted, because her parents were considered snobbish and nouveau riche. D. was an average student and always felt that she did not live up to her parents' expectations. Her academic achievements were significantly less than those of other members of the family. D. was also ashamed of her inability to produce anything for the school newspaper, and her parents kept commenting about it. Things at which D. excelled, such as gym and athletics, did not meet with her mother's approval. Neither did her parents approve of any of D.'s friends, whom they considered to be of lower intelligence and social background. They constantly criticized D. for her selection of friends, but D. continued to meet them secretly. D. had her menarche at the age of 10. She did not confide in her mother, because she was afraid of criticism. Instead, she learned the preliminary facts from her girlfriends. D. felt different because of her early puberty and reacted in tough and rough behavior, assuming the role of a leader in her class.

The parents first noticed a change in D. when she was eight years old, after her brother's birth. Her mother had been bleeding during the pregnancy and had to have a Caesarean section. D. was frightened that her mother would die. After her brother's birth, the mother spent a great deal of time with the baby, and D. felt she was "sort of forgotten about" for awhile. The mother spent every minute with her son, effectively excluding everyone else from her life. She became involved in what her husband described as a "bizarre love relationship with her son." D. reacted to this by becoming frustrated, anxious, and overtly hostile. She was totally alienated and refused to participate in family life, often leaving the dinner table whenever she did not like something. She became sullen and quiet, spending increasing time alone in her room, often cruelly taunting and teasing her brother. The brother's birth apparently complicated an already difficult family interaction. Both D. and her mother competed for the father's attention; and whenever the father wanted to show affection to D., the mother intruded and demanded that she come first. The father tried to find compensation in D. for the irrational behavior of his wife, but his interest in his daughter only enraged his wife all the more. D., in turn, tried to use her father to get even with her mother, especially when the mother showered attention on her son. It was shortly after the birth of her brother that D.'s involvement with drugs began.

Behind a tough facade, D. seemed to be a little girl struggling desperately for some acknowledgment that she was worthwhile. The central theme of her life was the attempt, repeated again and again, to run away from a boundary-diffused family—an unavailable, overdemanding mother supported by an inconsistent father, a feeling that she never met parental expectations and was subjected to constant disapproval. D. indicated that she felt trapped and surrounded by her mother's wish that she become someone special from an early age in her life. In effect, the mother wanted D. to fulfill her own frustrated aspirations. D. was naturally active, but her goals and behavior never met her mother's definition of an ideal girl or woman. D. felt that she was always criticized, rebuked, or punished, a feeling that was augmented by her perception of utter inconsistency in her mother's motives and standards. D. was never quite sure what was expected of her. She was only aware that whatever she did usually provoked her mother's criticism and anger. She was convinced that she was evil, destructive, and sinful. D. conveyed a strong sense of having been thwarted at almost every attempt to achieve a sense of individuality. She seemed to have had to struggle to break free of her mother's rejection, intrusive attacks, and criticism in order to find some sense of self-esteem and self-worth.

Both parents were extremely moralistic and had a very rigid sense of right and wrong. Their behavior, however, was often quite inconsistent with their demands. D. was aware that she was often used by her parents in their marital battles. Both parents indirectly encouraged aspects of D.'s antisocial behavior, which they then used as a weapon against each other. The confusion, anger, ambiguity, and inconsistency of values in her parents caused considerable turmoil for D. Throughout her preadolescence, she felt that she had to go "underground" to define herself and do the things she wanted to do. Her street experiences and drug involvement were, in many ways, her attempt to separate from her mother and establish a more clearly defined image of herself as a separate person, capable of independent action and judgment, even if those actions were self-destructive. The mother offered her little as a positive figure for identification. D. viewed her mother as disturbed, phony, aggressive, and inconsistent.

D. was concerned and confused about her own identity and values. She was frightened by the intimacy of therapy and worried that the therapist would impose his values on her. She continually struggled to be independent of any control or direction. She gradually began to set her own limits rather than fighting against the possibility that others would set limits for her. Throughout the treatment, the therapist reported that he felt a need to provide D. with a context in which she could come to establish some identity and achieve some reasonable sense of limits and directions for her activities and interests.

Psychological testing revealed that D.'s disruptive behavior emerged from intense depression, rejection, loneliness, and a seething anger. What superficially appeared as thoughtless antisocial behavior and interpersonal blandness was a defense against pain, fear, and expectation of criticism and punishment. Rather than allowing herself any outward display of tenderness and warmth, D. appeared defiant and tough. She was frightened of forming relationships, because she fully expected eventually to be hurt or abandoned. To prevent this, she either isolated herself or hurt the other person, much as she felt she had been hurt in the past. Many of her Rorschach responses suggested a poignant loneliness; for example, in one card she saw an old house in the woods in which no one was at home and that had been abandoned. The major theme, however, throughout the projective testing was D.'s concept of herself as a poisonous, viperous monster who would contaminate, destroy, or injure anyone with whom she had close contact. Her Rorschach responses were dominated by themes of vampires, snakes, and biting predatory animals. Her self-concept seemed to be epitomized by her Rorschach response of a bear trap, baited with a piece of meat, waiting to snap shut on anyone who put pressure on it. D. felt herself to be evil and blackhearted, passively expecting whatever punishment the world would mete out for her recurrent "crimes." She feared and expected severe and harsh punishment to come from some external source. She seemed to have established a lifestyle based on a recurring cycle of transgressions and provocations followed by punishment, which, in turn, led to more angry and egregious transgressions. Her two modes of relating seemed to be either as a criminal being punished or as a sly, seductive con artist who would eventually betray any trust placed in her. Hostile and aggressive impulses frequently merged with sexual impulses; expressions of affection had a derisive and hostile flavor. For example, in a Rorschach response she told of two pigs sticking their tongues out at each other but later suggested that perhaps the pigs might be kissing. Thus, what appears as tenderness and warmth also involves hostile, depreciating, aggressive impulses.

AN INTROJECTIVE ADOLESCENT BOY. A defiant 18-year-old man was brought to the local state mental hospital by the state police because his friends had become apprehensive about his behavior. He had leaped from a relatively high ledge into a shallow pool without injury and was about to do it again to show his friends that he was unhurt because of skill, not luck. His friends became frightened for his well-being, restrained him, and called the police.

The young man was taken to the local state hospital, and it was about a week later that I met him for a consultation interview. During the first 50 minutes, I felt unable to establish contact with him as he regaled me with seemingly endless descriptions of his various feats and physical accomplishments. Toward the end of our hour together, he described in considerable detail how he enjoyed racing his motorcycle on the new interstate highway at high speed during rush hour traffic, darting back and forth between cars and the various lanes of traffic. Somewhat impetuously, I said, "You really don't give a damn whether you live or die!" This defiant adolescent with his intense bravado suddenly burst into tears and sobbed, "Why should I? My parents don't care whether I live or die." He quickly regained his composure and in a somewhat more subdued way said that he had been sexually involved with the girl who lived in the house next to his home and that she had become pregnant. His parents, in a state of rage, had thrown him out of the house and told him never to return. Since that time, several months earlier, he had been living with friends. He viewed this rejection by his parents as the culmination of a long series of rejections, abandonment, and severe criticism by his hostile, punitive, destructive father.

In treating this adolescent, one would have to find ways to enable him to deal with his intense underlying dysphoria and feelings of rejection and disapproval if he were going to gain control over his defiant and self-destructive behavior. Focusing primarily on the symptomatic expressions of his depression—his defiance, risk taking, and oppositionality—would be of little use without also addressing the underlying introjective depression. Prominent in this young man's difficulties seemed to be the harsh, critical, judgmental qualities of his punitive father. Introjective or self-critical features seemed central to his disturbances.

In the treatment of delinquent adolescents, the antisocial nature of their symptoms often distracts therapists, parents, teachers, and the adolescents themselves from recognizing and responding to the underlying feelings of depression. Glaser (1967) discussed how the delinquent behavior masking the depression frequently becomes the focus of treatment. Spiegel (1967) stressed the importance of responding to the depression behind the rage and the delinquent act. The success of psychotherapy with delinquents depends on the therapist's "seeking, reaching out for the underlying depression . . . in terms of the primal experiences of abandonment by the beloved" (Spiegel, 1967, p. 600). It is essential in the treatment of anaclitic delinquency that the adolescent come to recognize that his or her delinquent acts are expressions of rage over profound feelings of neglect, rejection, and abandonment as well as a seeking of replacements for feeling unloved, unfed, and unwanted. Psychotherapy with anaclitic delinquent adolescents necessitates an articulation of the deprived anaclitic needs and the underlying anaclitic depressive experiences. Because acknowledgment of these experiences is difficult, the patient will often try to avoid recognizing these threatening aspects of his or her earlier experiences by resorting to further delinquent behavior. Patients frequently can come to know and experience these painful affects and memories only gradually, and therapists must be prepared for sudden onrushes of intense depressive affect and episodes of angry and defensive antisocial behavior. Therapists must be aware of the intensity of the patients' feelings of loss and abandonment in reaction to their disrupted and difficult early life experiences and provide patients with a constructive, consistent relationship that will increasingly enable them to gain perspective on their feelings about their early experiences of deprivation and lack of love and care.

Likewise, with introjective adolescents with depression who are engaged in angry, aggressive, destructive activity, therapists need to focus on these activities as expressions of feelings of worthlessness, failure, and guilt—as defensive expressions of anger directed at the self and at critical, judgmental, controlling, punitive authority figures. Given what Winnicott (1975) called the *nuisance value* of externalizing behaviors, adolescents engaged in such activities may be more likely than adolescents with internalizing problems to come to the attention of school or community disciplinary authorities. In contrast, the less socially disruptive behavior of anaclitic adolescents with internalizing disorders is more likely to go unnoticed (Garland, 1993). Declines in academic achievement, frequent short absences from school, multiple somatic complaints (Blatt et al., 1982), and social withdrawal are among the early expressions of internalizing distress in adolescents with anaclitic depression. Thus, differences in the expression of their depression have implications for whether adolescents seek help and what types of interventions they might receive.

These four clinical examples suggest that the nature of depressive experiences is an important consideration in understanding the etiology of disruptive behavior in adolescence. Clinical and empirical research suggests complex links between depression and behavioral disruptions in adolescence; behavioral disturbances in anaclitic adolescents can be a plea for help and a seeking of care and nurturance, whereas other adolescents express their depression by antisocial acts of aggression and violence, identifying with their harsh, punitive, judgmental parents, often seeking to punish others as well as inviting others to punish them. These clinical examples and formulations provided the basis for a wide range of research assessing the relationships between these two types of depressive experiences and a variety of disruptive experiences in both nonclinical and clinical contexts. In chapter 5, I review a wide range of empirical investigations, including the hypotheses articulated in this chapter about the relationship of anaclitic and introjective issues to disruptive experiences and activity, especially in adolescence and young adulthood.

Part II

Assessment of Anaclitic and Introjective Depression and of Mental Representation

Introduction:

Assessment of Anaclitic and Introjective Depression and of Mental Representation

The chapters in this section present efforts to develop measures for assessing systematically aspects of object representation and the two dimensions of depression. In chapter 3, I present the development of the Depressive Experiences Questionnaire, which serendipitously provided a reliable and valid measure of anaclitic and introjective depressive experiences. In chapter 4, I present the development of the Object Relations Inventory, which enabled colleagues and me to assess systematically aspects of the structural organization and thematic content of the representation of caregiving relationships. These two instruments facilitated the development of a wide range of clinical and empirical investigations that have enriched the understanding of the etiology, clinical expressions, and treatment of depression. In section 3 of this book, which comprises chapters 5–7, I review this extensive research literature.

3

Measurement of Anaclitic and Introjective Depressive Experiences

The symptoms of depression are quite heterogeneous and include a combination of psychological symptoms (e.g., mood changes and pervasive loss of energy and interest) and somatic or neurovegetative symptoms (e.g., loss of sleep and appetite). This heterogeneity of symptoms (e.g., American Psychiatric Association, 1980, 1987, 1994; Feighner et al., 1972; Spitzer, Endicott, & Robins, 1978) has made it difficult to differentiate meaningful subtypes of depression. Unipolar depression, for example, is a very broad category that includes symptoms of psychotic as well as neurotic and reactive depression (e.g., Akiskal et al., 1979; Klerman, 1974). The only clinically useful distinction among various psychological and neurovegetative symptoms of depression is the presence of mania in bipolar depression (e.g. Leonhard, 1959), but even here several subtypes have been noted (Depue & Monroe, 1978; American Psychiatric Association, 1994). In addition, few consistent psychological deficits, other than those in energy or activity level, have been found among the wide range of phenomena called *depression* (e.g., W. R. Miller, 1975; Wachtel & Blatt, 1965). Studies have generally "failed to demonstrate any impairment in psychological functioning . . . unique to depression" (W. R. Miller, 1975, p. 256). Because of the remarkable heterogeneity of the symptoms of depression in both normal and clinical samples, several research teams have attempted to establish subtypes based on criteria other than clinical symptoms (e.g., Arieti & Bemporad, 1978, 1980; A. T. Beck, 1983; Blatt, 1974; Blatt, D'Afflitti, & Quinlan, 1976; Bowlby, 1988b), such as differences in personality style and the life experiences that can lead to depression.

This chapter incorporates material from (a) "Experiences of Depression in Normal Young Adults," by S. J. Blatt, J. P. D'Afflitti, and D. M. Quinlan, 1976, *Journal of Abnormal Psychology, 85,* pp. 383–389. Copyright 1976 by the American Psychological Association. Reprinted with permission; (b) "Psychometric Properties of the Adolescent Depressive Experiences Questionnaire," by S. J. Blatt, C. E. Schaffer, S. A. Bers, and D. M. Quinlan, 1992, *Journal of Personality Assessment, 59,* pp. 82–98. Copyright 1992 by Erlbaum. Reprinted with permission; (c) "Subscales Within the Dependency Factor of the Depressive Experiences Questionnaire," by S. J. Blatt, A. H. Zohar, D. M. Quinlan, D. C. Zuroff, and M. Mongrain, 1995, *Journal of Personality Assessment, 64,* pp. 319–339. Copyright 1995 by Erlbaum. Reprinted with permission; and (d) "Levels of Relatedness Within the Dependency Factor of the Depressive Experiences Questionnaire for Adolescents," by S. J. Blatt, A. H. Zohar, D. M. Quinlan, S. Luthar, and B. Hart, 1996, *Journal of Personality Assessment, 67,* pp. 52–71. Copyright 1996 by Erlbaum. Reprinted with permission.

As I discussed in chapter 1, four groups of investigators began to differentiate types of depression based on the nature of the experiences that seem to precipitate depressive episodes rather than on the nature or severity of the manifest symptoms. Although derived from somewhat different assumptions and using somewhat varying terms, each of these four theoretical positions distinguished a depression initiated by untoward interpersonal experiences, such as interpersonal loss and feelings of abandonment and loneliness, from a depression initiated by disruptions in self-esteem, achievement, or identity. Research, however, has generally not explored issues of loss and loneliness in depression as fully as issues of self-criticism, self-worth, and guilt.

The identification of an interpersonal dimension of depression involving abandonment and loss is consistent with the findings of Hirschfeld and colleagues (Hirschfeld, Klerman, Chodoff, Korchin, & Barrett, 1976; Hirschfeld et al., 1977), who have stressed the importance of dependency in depression and those investigators who have emphasized as central issues learned helplessness and the feeling of being unable to control one's life and environment (Abramson & Sackheim, 1977; Abramson, Seligman, & Teasdale, 1978; Peterson, Schwartz, & Seligman, 1981; Seligman, 1975). Individuals preoccupied with issues of interpersonal relatedness are especially vulnerable to life experiences that involve disruptions of close relationships and tend to react to these experiences with feelings of loneliness and helplessness and an intense desire to be close and intimate and to be cared for and nurtured. Females are usually more vulnerable to dysphoria in response to disruptions of interpersonal relations such as the withdrawal of affection and the unavailability of others (e.g., Chevron, Quinlan, & Blatt, 1978). This fear of abandonment, intense desire for closeness, and a marked dependency on others are often accompanied by difficulty expressing anger (Blatt, 1974; Blatt, D'Afflitti, et al., 1976; Blatt, Quinlan, Chevron, McDonald, & Zuroff, 1982) for fear of losing the love and support that others might provide. Because they are preoccupied with protecting and maintaining relationships, these individuals are much less likely to engage in aggressive and destructive activity. Disruptions of interpersonal relations potentiate these dysphoric feelings and result in exaggerated attempts to maintain relationships—for example, by attempting to engage the concern and care of others through somatic complaints, sexual promiscuity, suicidal gestures (Blatt, 1974, 1991; Blatt et al., 1982; Blatt & Shichman, 1981; Leadbeater, Blatt, & Quinlan, 1995), and the seeking of reassurance (Coyne, 1976b; Joiner, 1994).

In contrast, individuals preoccupied with issues of self-definition and self-worth, who most frequently are male, are vulnerable to experiences of failure and criticism and tend to react to these experiences with feelings of incompetence, worthlessness, and guilt. These individuals often isolate themselves from others, and the relationships they do have are often fraught with ambivalence and conflict. They are disapproving and critical of others, and they assume that others are disapproving and critical of them. Thus they feel, and often express, strong feelings of anger, which can be directed toward others as well as themselves. Dysphoria deriving from intense self-criticism creates vulnerability to life stresses that potentiate feelings of failure, guilt, and a lack of personal competence.

The formulation of two types of depression—(a) an anaclitic depression focused on interpersonal issues, such as feelings of loneliness and fears of abandonment, and (b) an introjective depression focused on issues of self-definition, such as feelings of worthlessness and fears of failure or transgression—is based not on the symptoms of depression but on the experiences that contribute to dysphoric affect. Investigations conducted from this phenomenological perspective have noted many similarities in the psychological functioning and concerns of clinically depressed patients and individuals in control samples who report feeling depressed.

Some investigators (e.g., Depue & Monroe, 1978) have argued that a similarity of college students' and patients' scores on self-report measures of depression (Carroll, Fielding, & Blashki, 1973) does not necessarily indicate a continuity between depression in nonclinical individuals and in clinical individuals. Depue and Monroe (1978), like Coyne (e.g., Coyne & Gotlib, 1983), questioned the value of research on depression based on data gathered with college students. A. T. Beck (1967a), Metcalfe and Goldman (1965), and D. C. Klein and Seligman (1974), on the other hand, have contended that the similarity of college students' and patients' scores suggests that the differences between depression in nonpatient and clinical samples is primarily a matter of degree or intensity. Studies (e.g., Blumberry, Oliver, & McClure, 1978; Hammen, 1978) have reported significant correlations between the Beck Depression Inventory (BDI; A. T. Beck, Ward, Mendelson, Mock, & Erbaugh, 1961) and independent clinical assessments of depression in college students, even though few of the students ever sought professional assistance. Also, Strober, Green, and Carlson (1981) reported a highly significant correlation ($r =. 67, p < .001$) between the BDI and global clinical ratings of depression in psychiatrically hospitalized adolescent patients. Thus, it seems that depression inventories may assess the same dimensions in clinical and nonclinical samples. Given the continuity in the nature of the experiences that lead to dysphoric affect in clinical and nonclinical samples, depression can be considered as not just a clinical disorder but a necessary, natural affective state that ranges in intensity from a mild and appropriate transient reaction to a profound and sustained disabling clinical disorder involving intense dysphoria, distorted cognition, and neurovegetative disturbances, such as sleep and weight loss and loss of libido (Blatt, 1974). Much can be gained by considering the continuity between the vicissitudes of normal psychological development and many forms of psychopathology (e.g., Blatt, 1974, 1995b), especially in depression. Brief and temporary periods of depression, for example, can have adaptive significance in providing a pause in the normal activities of everyday life that can allow individuals the time to work through and grieve disruptive life experiences, such as loss and disappointment (Blatt, 1974).

An important controversy around these matters, known as the *clinical–analogue debate*, has evolved in the last 25 years. Coyne and Gotlib (1983), in an important article entitled "The Role of Cognition in Depression: A Critical Appraisal," criticized cognitive models of depression and the research on depressive symptoms among college students. They argued (Coyne & Gotlib, 1983, 1986) that depressive symptoms among college students are considerably different from the psychiatric condition known as *major depressive disorder*

(MDD). They maintained, for example, that depressive symptoms among college students are relatively transient and have little consequences, whereas MDD is a remarkably debilitating condition with devastating consequences for patients' lives (Coyne & Gotlib, 1983). They posited further that overlooking these differences limits the external validity of studies of depressive symptoms in college students and trivializes the anguish of MDD (Coyne & Gotlib, 1983).

The position articulated by Coyne and Gotlib (1983) has not gone unchallenged. Vredenburg, Flett, and Krames (1993) published a response asserting that depressive symptoms are indeed continuous with MDD and that the study of depressive symptoms in nonclinical samples is highly relevant to the understanding of clinical depressive conditions. In a rejoinder to Vredenburg et al. (1993), Coyne (1994) reasserted his position as to the uniqueness of clinical depression, and this assertion precipitated an active debate about the continuity of depression (Coyne, 1994; Coyne & Gotlib, 1983, 1986; Coyne & Pepper, 1998; Flett, Vredenburg & Krames, 1997; Gotlib, 1984; Santor & Coyne, 2001; Segal & Shaw, 1986a, 1986b; Tennen, Hall, & Affleck, 1995; Vredenburg et al., 1993; Weary, Edwards, & Jacobson, 1995). This debate appears to have recently subsided, because emerging evidence suggests that depression is characterized by elements of both continuity and discontinuity. For example, a recent review by Flett, Vredenburg, and Krames (1997) clearly demonstrated that elevated levels of depressive symptoms, or subclinical or subthreshold levels of depression, are predictive of subsequent clinical depressive conditions (see also Judd, Rapaport, Paulus, & Brown, 1994). In particular, strong continuity has been demonstrated between elevated depressive symptoms and clinical depression in adolescence (B. E. Compas, Ey, & Grant, 1993; B. E. Compas & Hammen, 1994; Gotlib, Lewinsohn, & Seeley, 1995; Gotlib & Hammen, 1992; Lewinsohn, Solomon, Seeley, & Zeiss, 2000; Petersen, et al., 1993). Irrespective of the issue of continuity between elevated depressive symptoms and MDD, mounting evidence suggests that elevated depressive symptoms, or "psychological distress" (Coyne, 1994), although not necessarily meeting *Diagnostic and Statistical Manual of Mental Disorders* (*DSM*; e.g., American Psychiatric Association, 1994) criteria for clinical depression, is still clinically significant and therefore worthy of study in its own right. Paradoxically, among the researchers demonstrating the clinical significance of this distress were Coyne and Gotlib and their respective colleagues. Thus, Gotlib, Lewinsohn, and Seeley (1995) demonstrated that adolescents with elevated levels of depressive symptoms, but without diagnosable MDD, experienced social and interpersonal impairment comparable in magnitude to that experienced by adolescents with MDD. Similarly, Coyne, Gallo, Klinkman, and Colarco (1998) showed that elevated depressive symptoms among patients with chronic physical illness were related to impairment of self-concept and that this impairment was similar in magnitude to that experienced by patients with MDD.

Although the lexicon or taxonomy of various psychopathological states provided by the *DSM*s (e.g., *DSM–III* and *DSM–IV*; American Psychiatric Association, 1980, 1987) facilitates greater diagnostic consistency and reliability, the *DSM* is based on the assumption of clear demarcations between normal and pathological behavior. Its definitions of various independent diseases set high thresholds for identifying psychopathological states, thereby discouraging consideration of subclinical expressions of the various disorders and the exploration of possible continuities and relationships among normal and disturbed patterns of behavior. These limitations of *DSM–III* and *DSM–IV* are most evident with regard to depression. Although *DSM–III* defines MDD and a less severe form of depressed mood labeled *dysthymia*, the manual notes that "The boundaries of Dysthymia with Major Depression are unclear, particularly in children and adolescents" (American Psychiatric Association, 1980, p. 230). Thus, the failure to define a broad continuum of affect or mood disorders is especially important given the increasing evidence discussed above that depression ranges along a continuum from a normal, transient affective state to a severe, persistent, pervasive pathological disorder (cf. Blatt et al., 1982). Depression can range from a subtle and transient dysphoric experience, to an enduring characterological disorder, to a severe disabling clinical state (Blatt, 1974).

The assumption of a continuity between the nature of depressive experiences in clinical and nonclinical samples provides a number of potentially important research possibilities, including the opportunity to use continuous rather than dichotomous variables in research as well as the opportunity to study depression in a broad context, exploring distal as well as proximal events that contribute to the onset of depression. Much is to be gained by a perspective that is sensitive to the continuity between normality and pathology, because it enables investigators to study a range of variations in the intensity and quality of depressive experiences. It is noteworthy that the assumption of a continuity between normality and psychopathology has enabled a number of investigators to go beyond evaluating primarily the symptoms of depression and to focus instead on the life experiences that can lead to depression. This assumption of a continuity between normal expressions of depression and its expression in severe clinical disorders facilitated a distinction between the personal qualities, psychological experiences, and life events that characterize an anaclitic (dependent) depression and those that characterize an introjective (self-critical) depression.

In the past 25 years, four instruments have been developed that assess interpersonal or dependent and self-critical dysphoric experiences in both clinical and nonclinical settings: (a) the Depressive Experiences Questionnaire (DEQ; Blatt, D'Afflitti, & Quinlan, 1979; Blatt, D'Afflitti, et al., 1976; Blatt et al., 1982; Zuroff, Quinlan, & Blatt, 1990), (b) the Sociotropy–Autonomy Scale (SAS; A. T. Beck, Epstein, Harrison, & Emery, 1983; C. J. Robins, 1985), (c) the Dysfunctional Attitude Scale (DAS; A. N. Weissman & Beck, 1978), and (d) the Personal Style Inventory (PSI; C. J. Robins & Ladd, 1991).

Depressive Experiences Questionnaire

Because of concerns about the inadequacy of a symptom approach to depression, as well as recognition of the advantages of considering the continuities between life experiences in normal psychological states and many forms of psychopathology, especially depression, colleagues and I (Blatt, D'Afflitti, & Quinlan, 1976,

1979) constructed a 66-item questionnaire on which individuals rate themselves on a wide range of life experiences frequently associated with depression but not directly considered symptoms of depression. These items were gleaned from classic case reports of patients with affective disturbances (e.g., Bibring, 1953; M. B. Cohen, Baker, Cohen, Fromm-Reichman, & Weigert, 1954; S. Freud, 1917/1957e) that described the life experiences of depressed patients (e.g., how they relate to people, how they feel about themselves, the ways they conduct their lives). Approximately 150 statements were constructed on the basis of a review of this clinical literature on depression, and from this list 66 items that represented a relatively broad range of life experiences associated with depression were selected. Items tapped issues such as a distorted or depreciated sense of self and others, dependency, helplessness, egocentricity, fear of loss, ambivalence, difficulty in dealing with anger, self-blame, guilt, loss of autonomy, and distortions in family relations. These 66 items are presented to individuals with the request that they rate themselves on 7-point Likert-type scales that range from strongly disagree (1) to strongly agree (7). The scale includes items that are presented in both negative and positive directions. This instrument, which we labeled the Depressive Experiences Questionnaire (DEQ), was initially group-administered to 500 female and 160 male undergraduates enrolled in a local state college.

Because of significant differences between men and women on many DEQ items, the data for men and women were analyzed separately. Principal-components factor analyses (PCAs) with varimax rotations identified three orthogonal factors that appeared in both male and female college students: (a) Dependency, (b) Self-Criticism, and (c) Efficacy. Subsequent research indicated that these three factors are very stable, have high internal consistency and substantial test–retest reliability, and have been replicated in several samples (Zuroff, Quinlan, & Blatt, 1990). Additional factors had too few items (≤2) and accounted for too little variance (<5%) to have psychological or statistical consequence. The 5 DEQ items with the highest factor loadings for each of the three factors are presented in Exhibit 3.1.

The Dependency factor consists of items that are primarily externally directed; refer to interpersonal relations; and contain themes of abandonment, loneliness, and helplessness and the desire to be close to, related to, and dependent on others. High-loading items reflect concerns about being rejected, hurting or offending people, and having difficulty in managing anger and aggression for fear of losing the gratification someone could provide. The Self-Criticism factor consists of items that are more internally directed and reflect feelings of guilt, emptiness, hopelessness, dissatisfaction, and insecurity. Items with a high loading on this factor reflect concerns about a failure to meet expectations and standards, an inability to assume responsibility, feeling threatened by change, ambivalence about self and others, and a tendency to assume blame and feel critical toward oneself.

The third DEQ factor, Efficacy, involves items indicating a sense of confidence about one's resources and capacities. The items with high loadings on this factor contain themes of high standards and personal goals, a sense of responsibility, inner strength, feelings of independence, and a sense of pride and satisfaction in one's accomplishments. Individuals who score high on this

Exhibit 3.1   The Five Items With the Greatest Loading for Each of the Three
Factors of the Depressive Experiences Questionnaire

Factor I: Dependency
  1. I often think about the danger of losing someone who is close to me.
  2. After an argument, I feel very lonely.
  3. I am very sensitive to others for signs of rejection.
  4. Being alone doesn't bother me at all. (reverse scored)
  5. I worry a lot about offending or hurting someone who is close to me.

Factor II: Self-Criticism
  1. There is a considerable difference between how I am now and how I would like
     to be.
  2. I often feel guilty.
  3. The way I feel about myself frequently varies: There are times when I feel
     extremely good about myself and other times when I see only the bad in me
     and feel like a total failure.
  4. Often, I feel I have disappointed others.
  5. I often find that I don't live up to my own standards or ideals.

Factor III: Efficacy
  1. I have many inner resources (abilities, strengths).
  2. Other people have high expectations of me.
  3. I set my personal goals and standards as high as possible.
  4. I am a very independent person.
  5. What I do and say have a very strong impact on those around me.

factor are characterized by goal-oriented strivings and feelings of accomplishment, but not by extreme competitiveness.

It is important to stress that the DEQ was not developed to assess anaclitic and introjective dimensions of depression; rather, it was developed to assess the everyday life experiences of individuals with depression, and the factors of Dependency (relatedness) and Self-Criticism (self-definition) emerged, confirming the independent clinical observations and theoretical formulations of two independent dimensions (i.e., interpersonal relatedness and self-definition) as primary sources of depression (Blatt, 1974). It is also important to note that the DEQ yields factor scores: Each item, depending on its factor loading, contributes to the score on each of the three factors. Thus, a computer program is necessary to score the DEQ. The DEQ and the DEQ-A, as well as the scoring programs in the SPSS and SAS, can be obtained from S. J. Blatt, Yale University, Department of Psychiatry, 25 Park Street, New Haven, CT 06519 (sidney.blatt@yale.edu) and from D. C. Zuroff, McGill University, Department of Psychology, 1205 Dr. Penfield Avenue, Montreal, Quebec, H5A 1B1, Canada (zuroff@ego.psych.mcgill.ca).

To test initially the stability of the factor structure, the female sample ($n = 500$) was randomly divided in half, and a factor analysis was conducted in each subsample ($n = 250$). Tucker's coefficients of congruence (Harmon, 1960) were computed among the three factors of the two subsamples. The factor structure had a high degree of stability; the coefficients of congruence of each factor with its split-half duplicate were all above .900. Whereas a moderate level of congruence was found between Dependency and Efficacy (in different samples, this correlation ranges from −.30 to −.49), the congruence of Self-Criticism with the other two factors was minimal. Coefficients of congruence were also computed between each factor in the total male (n = 160) and the total female samples (n = 500). The coefficients of congruence between each factor and its counterpart in the male and female samples were again high (>.80), and again, a moderate degree of congruence emerged between Dependency and Efficacy, but only minimal congruence was observed between Self-Criticism and the other two factors. Thus, the factor structure was highly similar and stable within split halves of the female sample and between the overall female and male samples, with some tendency for Dependency and Efficacy to share a moderate degree of congruence. The DEQ's factor structure has been replicated in a number of other nonclinical samples (e.g., Beutel et al., in press; R. C. Campos, 2002; Jae Im, 1996; Jerdonek, 1980; Luyten, 2002; Priel, Besser, & Shahar, 1998; Zuroff, Quinlan, & Blatt, 1990) in several countries, including Belgium, Canada, Germany, Israel, Korea, and Portugal.

The stability of the DEQ's factor structure was also demonstrated in data from a large sample of female and male college students from introductory psychology classes at a large rural state university (Zuroff, Quinlan, & Blatt, 1990). A total of 951 female students and 650 male students completed the DEQ. The scores were subjected to a PCA with three factors extracted by means of varimax rotation. The factors that emerged not only were highly congruent with the original female factor analysis, but they also emerged in the same order as in the original sample. Scales derived from these three factors had high internal consistency (M = .78) and substantial test–retest reliability (rs ranged from .72 to .89; Zuroff, Moskowitz, Wielgus, Powers, & Franko, 1983). These factors have been replicated in several other samples, including an extensive sample with a Dutch version of the DEQ (Luyten, 2002). Luyten (2002) and colleagues (Luyten, Fontaine, Meganck, et al., 2003), using PCA with varimax and Procrustean rotations of the DEQ responses of 928 students, 253 adults, and 136 psychiatric inpatients, found evidence for the factorial invariance of the Dependency and Self-Criticism factors (see also Blaney & Kutcher, 1991; Blatt & Zuroff, 1992; Riley & McCranie, 1990). The third DEQ factor, Efficacy, was replicated by PCA with only varimax rotation. Luyten, Fontaine, Soenens, and Corveleyn (2003) also conducted a formal content analysis of the DEQ by developing an explicit category system of nine categories of DEQ items: (a) personal standards, (b) self-evaluation, (c) relational styles and beliefs, (d) expectations from others, (e) self-esteem and variations in self-esteem, (f) helplessness, (g) aggression/anger, (h) anxiety and fear, and (i) developmental history. On the basis of this content analysis, Luyten, Fontaine, Soenens, et al. (2003) differentiated between *interpersonal* and *intrapsychic* guilt. Interpersonal guilt (e.g., fear of hurting others) is associated with the Dependency factor, whereas intrapsychic guilt (e.g., not achieving or living up to moral standards) is associated with the Self-Criticism factor. In their content analyses, Luyten, Fontaine, Soenens, et al. (2003) also found that themes of helplessness, variations in self-esteem, and a fear of change appear on both the Dependency and Self-Criticism factors and thus appear to be central general issues in depression. Jae Im (1996), using PCA with varimax rotation, also replicated the DEQ factor structure in a mixed sample of Korean students, clients in a school counseling center, and psychiatric patients with a mood disorder and reported good levels of internal consistency and test–retest reliability.

The Dependency and Self-Criticism factors of the DEQ correlate significantly with traditional self-report measures of depression (e.g., the BDI [A. T. Beck et al., 1961] and the Zung Depression Scale [ZDS; Zung, 1965]). The Dependency factor usually has lower correlations than the Self-Criticism factor with these measures of depression, suggesting that it assesses an often overlooked dimension of depression. Although the Dependency and Self-Criticism factors are relatively independent in nonclinical samples, several studies (e.g., J. D. Brown & Silberschatz, 1989; Franche & Dobson, 1992; Jerdonek, 1980) found high correlations between these two factors in clinical samples. This led some researchers (e.g., Viglione, Clemmey, & Camenzuli, 1990) to question the validity of the DEQ in clinical populations. In general, however, these studies with clinical samples lacked a sufficiently large sample to test adequately the factor structure of the DEQ. Beutel et al. (in press), studying 304 participants in a community sample and 404 psychiatric ("psychosomatic") patients in Germany, replicated the three DEQ factors in their nonclinical sample but not in their clinical sample. Frank, Van Egeren, et al. (1997), however, replicated the DEQ factor structure in a large sample of adolescent inpatients using the adolescent form of the DEQ, the DEQ–A, which is discussed later in this chapter. Luyten, Blatt, & Corveleyn (in press), Luyten, Corveleyn, & Blatt (in press), in an extensive exploration of the DEQ in Belgium, concluded that the DEQ assesses primarily stable personality characteristics rather than depressed mood or other state characteristics.

In clinical samples, patients have higher Dependency and Self-Criticism scores than do nonpatients (Bagby, Schuller, et al., 1994; Blatt et al., 1982; Fairbrother & Moretti, 1998; Franche & Dobson, 1992; D. N. Klein, Harding, Taylor, & Dickstein, 1988; Lehman et al., 1997; Luyten, 2002; Rosenfarb, Becker, Khan, & Mintz, 1998). Luyten (2002) found that depressed patients scored higher on Dependency, but not on Self-Criticism, than did general psychiatric inpatients. He suggested that self-criticism (or perfectionism) may be a more general dimension in a wide range of disorders, whereas dependency may be uniquely related to depression. Lehman and colleagues (1997) found that depressed inpatients scored higher on both Dependency and Self-Criticism than did depressed outpatients, and patients with early-onset dysthymic disorder scored higher on Self-Criticism (perfectionism), but not Dependency, than did patients with major depressive disorder.

Females have higher dependency scores than males, but no gender differences are usually found for Self-Criticism or perfectionism (e.g., Blatt, Hart, Quinlan, Leadbeater, & Auerbach, 1993; Blatt et al., 1982; Brewin & Firth-Cozens, 1997; Chevron et al., 1978; Fichman, Koestner, & Zuroff, 1994, 1996, 1997; Sanfilipo, 1994; Sato & McCann, 1998; T. W. Smith, O'Keeffe, & Jenkins, 1988; R. E. Steele, 1978; Zuroff & Fitzpatrick, 1995; Zuroff, Stotland, Sweetman, Craig, & Koestner, 1995). Depression is two to three times more prevalent in women, possibly because they are as vulnerable as men to issues of self-criticism but are also much more vulnerable to feelings of loneliness, abandonment, and rejection. This combined vulnerability to feelings of loss and abandonment as well as self-criticism places women at greater risk for depression. Equally noteworthy are suggestions (Chevron et al., 1978; Sanfilipo, 1994) that gender-role characteristics, rather than gender itself, are important in the study of depression, as well as indications (e.g., Fichman et al., 1994; Mongrain & Zuroff, 1994; T. W. Smith et al., 1988) of the particular vulnerability to depression of gender-incongruent individuals, especially dependent men but also self-critical women.

Longitudinal research indicates that Dependency and Self-Criticism remain stable after clinical improvement and the remission of depression (Bagby, Schuller, et al., 1994; Franche & Dobson, 1992; Frank, Van Egeren, et al., 1997; Moore & Blackburn, 1996; Rosenfarb et al., 1998; Z. V. Segal, Shaw, Vella, & Katz, 1992; Zuroff, Blatt, Sanislow, Bondi, & Pilkonis, 1999). Bagby, Schuller, et al. (1994) conducted a 12-week follow-up study of depressed outpatients and found that recovered patients still had higher levels of Dependency and Self-Criticism than control participants but found no significant differences in these two personality dimensions between recovered and nonrecovered patients. Zuroff, Blatt, et al. (1999), based on a reanalysis of data from the National Institute of Mental Health–Treatment of Depression Collaborative Research Program (TDCRP), demonstrated that a reduction in Dependency and Self-Criticism scores does not necessarily mean that these personality dimensions are state-dependent concomitants of depression. Zuroff, Blatt, et al. (1999) found that both these personality dimensions had state and trait aspects. Several other longitudinal studies have demonstrated the predictive validity of these two dimensions, but especially self-criticism. Brewin and Firth-Cozens (1997), for example, found that Dependency and Self-Criticism in medical students predicted the severity of their depression after 2 years and 10 years. Priel and Besser (1999) found that only Self-Criticism predicted postpartum depression. Although Dependency and Self-Criticism have stability over time, the predictive validity of these two personality dimensions, especially the Dependency or interpersonal dimension, needs to be explored more fully in future research. As Luyten, Soenens, et al. (2003) noted, attempts to improve the theoretical and psychometric properties of the DEQ (e.g., Bagby, Parker, Joffe, & Buis, 1994; Flett, Hewitt, Endler, & Bagby, 1995; Fuhr & Shean, 1992; Santor, Zuroff, & Fielding, 1997; Santor, Zuroff, Mongrain, & Fielding, 1997; Viglione, Lovette, Gottlieb, & Friedberg, 1995; Welkowitz, Lish, & Bond, 1985) have generally not been successful and the original form of the DEQ still remains the most effective version of this research instrument.

A fair amount of research has investigated the relation of Dependency and Self-Criticism to dimensions of the Big Five personality model (McCrae & Costa, 1990), especially Neuroticism and Introversion. As summarized by Luyten (2002) and Luyten, Corveleyn, and Blatt (in press), findings (e.g., Cappeliez, 1993; Dunkley, Blankstein, & Flett, 1997; Mongrain, 1993; Zuroff, 1994) indicate that both Dependency and Self-Criticism are positively related to Neuroticism. Dependency is also positively related to Extraversion and Agreeableness and negatively related to Openness. Self-Criticism is negatively related to Extraversion and Agreeableness. An examination of the facets of each of the Big Five dimensions indicated that Dependency is positively associated primarily with anxiety and vulnerability and negatively associated with hostility for the facets of Neuroticism, and is positively associated with the warmth facet of Extraversion. Self-Criticism, in contrast, is mainly related to the depression and hostility facets of Neuroticism and to the low interpersonal warmth facet of the Extraversion dimension. The relationship of Self-Criticism to Conscientiousness, however, is more inconsistent (Cappeliez, 1993; Mongrain, 1993; Zuroff, 1994). These findings indicate that Dependency is related to a strong need for warm and intimate relations and reflects a fundamental interpersonal orientation in which hostility is inhibited for fear of losing the love and attention of others. Dependency is also related to a reluctance to experience change and novelty. Self-Criticism is related to egocentrism, ambivalent interpersonal relationships, and a vulnerability to depression because of constant self-scrutiny. Zuroff (1994) noted that Dependency and Self-Criticism cannot be reduced to the Big Five dimensions because they relate to different dimensions of Neuroticism: Dependency is an extraverted, agreeable form of Neuroticism, whereas Self-Criticism is a more introverted, disagreeable form of Neuroticism (Luyten, 2002; Luyten, Corveleyn, & Blatt, in press).

Bagby and Rector (1998) examined the relationship of Dependency and Self-Criticism to dimensions of the Big Five in depressed outpatients and found that although both factors were related to Neuroticism, as they are in students and nonclinical adults, they found no relationships with the other Big Five dimensions. In a factor analysis on the DEQ and the Big Five dimensions, Bagby and Rector identified three factors: (a) Self-Criticism and Neuroticism with a negative loading for Agreeableness, (b) Openness and Extraversion, and (c) Dependency and Agreeableness. Bagby and Rector (1998) concluded that although Self-Criticism appears to overlap to some degree with Neuroticism, Dependency is a more unique dimension.

Lehman et al. (1997) examined the relation between the DEQ and Tellegen's (1982) Multidimensional Personality Questionnaire and found that Dependency was positively related to Traditionalism, Social Closeness, and Harm Avoidance and negatively associated with Social Potency. Self-Criticism was positively associated with Aggression and Alienation and negatively with Social Closeness. Self-Criticism was not significantly related to the Achievement scale of the Multidimensional Personality Questionnaire, even though other investigations have consistently found that Self-Criticism is related to achievement goals (Bieling & Alden, 1998; Luyten, 2002; Mongrain & Zuroff, 1995; Zuroff & de Lorimier, 1989). Bornstein (1992) found that orality on the Rorschach was correlated with both DEQ Dependency and Self-Criticism. Kwon, Campbell, and Williams (2001) examined the relations of the SAS (A. T. Beck, 1983) to measures derived from the Thematic Apperception Test (Morgan & Murray, 1938) and found that sociotropy uniquely correlated with Need for Affiliation while autonomy uniquely correlated with Need for Achievement. Goldberg, Segal, Vella, and Shaw (1989) and Overholser and Freiheit (1994) found that Dependency in outpatients was related to dependent personality disorder, whereas Self-Criticism was related to negativistic personality disorder as measured by the Millon Clinical Multiaxial Inventory (Millon, 1997). Ouimette, Klein, Clark, & Margolis, (1992; Ouimette & Klein, 1993) with students and outpatients and K. N. Levy et al. (1995) with inpatients, evaluated personality disorders and found that Dependency was uniquely related to dependent, histrionic, and borderline personality disorders, whereas Self-Criticism was uniquely related to paranoid, obsessive–compulsive, narcissistic, schizoid, schizotypal, antisocial, and passive–aggressive personality disorders (see also, Morse, Robins, & Gittes-Fox, 2000). Southwick, Yehuda, and colleagues, in studying male veterans, found that self-criticism was an important aspect of Borderline Personality Disorder (Southwick, Yehuda, and Giller, 1995) and Post Traumatic Stress Disorder (Yehuda, Kahana, Southwick, & Giller, 1994). Wixom, Ludolph, & Westen (1993), in contrast, found that adolescent girls with a borderline diagnosis had higher scores on both the DEQ Dependency and Self-Criticism factors than depressed, non-borderline girls. Their analyses of items of the DEQ revealed that borderline girls have anaclitic fears of abandonment as well as introjective fears of being fundamentally bad or evil (Wixom et al., 1993). These findings suggest that it may be important to include gender as a dimension in investigating the role of dependency and self-criticism in various forms of psychopathology. Gunderson and colleagues (Gunderson & Phillips, 1991; Gunderson, Triebwasser, Phillips, & Sullivan, 1999) have reported that patients with major depression tend to have either avoidant and obsessive–compulsive (introjective) personality disorders or borderline and passive–aggressive (anaclitic) personality disorders. Pilkonis (1988), using prototypic descriptions, found that clinicians characterized patients with dependent depression as having dependent and borderline features (e.g., low impulsive control), whereas self-critical depression was characterized by defensive avoidance and a lack of interpersonal sensitivity.

Sanislow (1994) and Lamb (1997), using Benjamin's comprehensive method of personality assessment, the Structural Analysis of Social Behavior (SASB; L. S. Benjamin, 1974, 1988), attempted to evaluate the assumptions underlying the interpersonal (Dependency) and Self-Criticism factors of the DEQ and the theoretical formulations of anaclitic and introjective depression. Both investigators noted the conceptual similarity between the circumplex structure of the SASB that is organized around two fundamental orthogonal factors—Affiliation and Power—and the assumptions about anaclitic (dependent) and introjective (self-critical) depression and their respective concerns about interpersonal relationships and about self-definition. Sanislow theoretically mapped the two primary factors of the DEQ, Dependency and Self-Criticism, on several SASB prototypes that he identified for each of the two DEQ constructs by hypothesizing the SASB curves that he thought corresponded to each construct. Each curve was a sine wave with its highest point on the SASB cluster most representative of the DEQ construct. A cluster coefficient was computed for each participant for each of the eight SASB clusters, and then related their value to the "prototypic" curve. The resulting values are what L. S. Benjamin (1974, 1988) has called *pattern coefficients*. Sanislow identified Surface 2, "deferring and submitting to others," as relevant for the DEQ Dependency (or Interpersonal) factor and Surface 3, "self-rejecting and destroying" for the DEQ Self-Criticism factor. He found support for his hypothesis that DEQ Self-Criticism significantly correlates with the "self-rejecting and destroying" prototype on the Intrapsychic (Introjective) surface (Surface 3) in participants' ratings of themselves at their worst. He interpreted these findings as supporting the assumptions underlying the DEQ Self-Criticism factor and the formulations of the introjective personality configuration (Blatt & Shichman, 1983). He found, however, little support for his hypothesis that the DEQ Interpersonal factor would correlate with the SASB "deferring and submitting" prototype on the Interpersonal–Self-Focused surface (Surface 2).

In contrast to Sanislow (1994), Lamb (1997) did not explore the empirical relationships between the factors of the DEQ and SASB prototypes but instead evaluated his assumptions about the nature of introjective and anaclitic depression, as he hypothesized they would be expressed in SASB prototypes. Lamb assumed that introjective depression should be expressed in the SASB "attack–rejecting" prototype on the Interpersonal–Other surface (Surface 1) and that anaclitic depression would be expressed in the SASB deferring–submitting prototype on the Interpersonal–Self surface (Surface 2). Lamb assessed the validity of these hypotheses about the nature of introjective and anaclitic depression by evaluating the degree to which these two SASB prototypes correlated with several traditional measures of depression. Lamb found "virtually no support" for his assumption about the SASB expression of anaclitic depression but found "strong support" for his assumption that the attacking–rejecting SASB prototype on Surface 1 represents introjective depression. Thus, both Sanislow and Lamb found significant congruence between theoretical assumptions and the empirical assessment of aspects of introjective depression and dimensions of aggression and interpersonal isolation as assessed on the SASB. However, they found little support for their assumptions about the characteristics and measurement of anaclitic depression. Sanislow's failure to find congruence between the DEQ Dependency factor and the hypothesized SASB prototype of "submitting to others" may be a function of the fact that he did not differentiate between the two subscales recently identified (Blatt & Zohar, 1990; Blatt, Zohar, Quinlan, Zuroff, & Mongrain, 1995; Rude & Burnham, 1995) within the Interpersonal or Dependency factor of the DEQ. The identification of these two subscales within the Dependency Factor of the DEQ will be discussed shortly.

On the basis of constructs from the interpersonal problems circumplex model, Alden and Bieling (1996) and Whisman and Friedman (1998) found that the sociotropy scale of the SAS (A. T. Beck et al., 1983) is related to warmth and submissiveness (the Exploitable quadrant) and that SAS Autonomy is related to interpersonal coldness (on the border of the Avoidant and Vindictive quadrants). Likewise, Zuroff and Fitzpatrick (1995) found that DEQ Dependency and Self-Criticism were related to different patterns of insecure attachment: Self-Criticism was related to a fearful avoidant attachment style, whereas Dependency was related to preoccupied attachment.

As discussed in chapter 2, extensive research has focused on perfectionism as an important personality dimension in depression (see Flett & Hewitt, 2002). The most clinically relevant dimension of perfectionism, socially prescribed perfectionism (e.g., Hewitt & Flett, 1993), is highly correlated with DEQ Self-Criticism (Dunkley & Blankstein, 2000; Enns & Cox, 1999; Flett, Besser, et al., in press; Hewitt & Flett, 1993; Powers, Zuroff, & Topciu, in press). Given the consistent findings of the relationship of DEQ Self-Criticism to several SASB prototypes, subsequent research should explore the relationship of different aspects of perfectionism to different SASB prototypes. Future research should also be directed toward further exploration of anaclitic depression and the Interpersonal factor of the DEQ and should seek to identify the SASB prototypes that would be related to this factor as well as to the two subscales (Neediness and Relatedness) that have been recently identified within the DEQ Interpersonal factor.

Depressive Experiences Questionnaire for Adolescents (DEQ–A)

An adolescent form of the DEQ, the DEQ–A (Blatt, Schaffer, Bers, & Quinlan, 1991), was developed because some of the items of the original DEQ addressed issues not relevant to adolescents (e.g., feelings about work). Forty-three of the original 66 items of the adult DEQ were simplified and revised to make the scale appropriate for adolescents. The remainder of the items were retained in their original form. The 43 modified items were initially reviewed by a small group of adolescents to verify that the changes were clear and appropriate. The scale was then administered to a large group of male and female suburban high school students from middle or upper socioeconomic levels, ranging in age from 12 to 18 years old, and to a smaller group of male and female students in an inner-city high school who were from lower socioeconomic levels and ranged in age from 12 to 17 years. Factor analysis of these students' responses yielded three factors that were highly similar to those found with the adult DEQ. Exhibit 3.2 presents the 5 items with the highest factor loadings for each of the three factors of the DEQ–A.

A comparison between males and females on these three factors revealed coefficients of congruence above .85. In addition, in a sample of 93 college students who completed both the DEQ and the DEQ–A, the correlations between parallel factor scores on the DEQ and DEQ–A exceeded .75 for all three factors. Coefficients of congruence between each factor on both forms were .90 for Dependency, .87 for Self-Criticism, and .72 for Efficacy. An item-by-item comparison indicated that at least 40 of the 43 revised items of the DEQ–A were highly similar in terms of their factor loadings to the corresponding items of the original DEQ (Blatt et al., 1992). Each of the three DEQ–A factors had a high level of internal consistency (alpha coefficients of .90, .82, and .79, respectively) and good test–retest reliability over a period of 10 days (rs = .86, .79 and .65, respectively) and 1 year (rs = .63, .56, and .52, respectively). With the exception of a modest correlation (r = .24, p < .01) between the Interpersonal or Dependency factor at the initial evaluation and Self-Criticism factor at the 1-year retest, the correlations among the three factors over a 1-year period were low; that is, the factors remained orthogonal. In addition, the correlations of the first two factors of the DEQ–A with other measures of depression essentially replicate findings reported with the original DEQ (Blatt et al., 1992). Shahar, Henrich, Blatt, Ryan, and Little (2002), using data from a sample of 860 young adolescents in an urban, public middle school (Grades 7–9) recently replicated the factor structure of the DEQ–A and found that Self-Criticism was a more powerful predictor of the presence of negative life events and a

Exhibit 3.2   The Five Items With the Greatest Loading for Each of the Three
Factors of the Depressive Experiences Questionnaire for Adolescents

---

Factor I: Dependency
1. I often feel frightened when things change.
2. After an argument, I feel very lonely.
3. I become frightened when I feel alone.
4. I often think about the danger of losing someone close to me.
5. If I lost a very close friend it would feel like I lost an important part of myself.

Factor II: Self-Criticism
1. I am very satisfied with myself and the things I achieved.
2. There is a big difference between how I am now and how I wish I were.
3. Usually I am not satisfied with what I have.
4. I never feel safe in a close relationship with a parent or a friend.
5. I often find that I fall short of what I expect of myself.

Factor III: Efficacy
1. I set my goals at a very high level.
2. I very frequently compare myself to the goals and standards I have set for
   myself.
3. What I do and say has a very strong impact on those around me.
4. I have many inner strengths and abilities.
5. I enjoy competing with others.

---

lack of positive events than a measure of depression (BDI). Thus, the factor
structure of the DEQ–A (Blatt et al., 1992) is very stable and indicates that
interpersonal and self-critical issues also characterize the depressive concerns
of adolescents.

Luthar and Blatt (1993, 1995), focusing on an inner-city sample of adolescents, reported stronger associations for Dependency than for Self-Criticism
with assessments of diffuse tension, anxiety, worry, and sensitivity to others'
behavior (see also Alford & Gerrity, 1995). Associations with Self-Criticism
were stronger for depressive symptoms and concerns about losing the approval
of others. Consistent with findings with the DEQ in adults, both suburban and
inner-city girls scored significantly higher than boys on Dependency, but gender
differences for Self-Criticism were not significant (P. Baron & Peixoto, 1991;
Blatt et al., 1992; Chevron et al., 1978).

Frank, Van Egeren, et al. (1997), studying a large sample of adolescent
inpatients, not only replicated the factor structure of the DEQ–A in a clinical
context but also found support for the validity of the DEQ–A as a measure of
interpersonal concerns and self-criticism among seriously disturbed adolescents. Tests of the concurrent validity of the two DEQ factors indicated that
they "were related to different criterion variables or to the same criterion
variable in different ways" (Frank, Van Egeren, et al., 1997, p. 193). Consistent
with earlier studies (e.g., Nietzel & Harris, 1990), Frank, Van Egeren, et al.
(1997) found stronger and more consistent relationships between self-criticism
and depressed mood than between interpersonal concerns and depressed mood.
They concluded that their results support the predictive validity of the DEQ–A

Self-Criticism factor but that further research is needed to document the relationship between the DEQ–A Interpersonal factor and adolescents' experiences of depression. Again, research might clarify these findings with the Interpersonal factor by exploring the role of the two subscales embedded within the Interpersonal factor.

Subscales Embedded in DEQ Factor I
(Neediness and Relatedness)

As discussed earlier, the factor structures of the DEQ and the DEQ–A are robust and have been replicated in several clinical and nonclinical samples of adolescents and adults, but the Dependency Factor I usually correlates only moderately with traditional measures of depression. Thus, we (Blatt, Zohar, et al., 1995; Blatt, Zohar, Quinlan, Luthar, & Hart, 1996) examined the possibility that several different types of depressive experiences associated with interpersonal issues may not have been explicated fully in the factor analyses of the DEQ and the DEQ–A. Recent theoretical developments (e.g., Blatt, 1990, 1995b; Blatt & Blass, 1990, 1996; Blatt & Shichman, 1983) suggest that it might be possible to identify several levels of interpersonal relatedness within the Dependency factor, ranging from dependency; to cooperation; to more mature expressions of mutuality and reciprocity, including intimacy. Likewise, different levels might be identified within the development of a sense of self, ranging from a sense of separation and autonomy; to feelings of being assertive, competent, and proactive; to having a sense of identity and self-definition (Blatt & Blass, 1990, 1996). Thus, colleagues and I sought to identify different developmental levels within the Interpersonal factor (Factor I) and the Self-Criticism factor (Factor II) of the DEQ. In reviewing the items that had substantial factor loadings on Factor I, we noted that one set of items concerned feelings of helplessness, fears and apprehensions about separation and rejection, and intense concerns about the loss of gratification and support, but without a link to a particular individual or a specific relationship. Typical of these items are the following: "I become frightened when I am alone" or "Without support from others who are close to me, I would be helpless." Blatt and Zohar (1990) reviewed these items and concluded that they might assess a less mature level of interpersonal relatedness that they called *dependence* (or *neediness*). These items seemed to contrast with other items that loaded high on Factor I that assess experiences of loss and loneliness in the context of a disruption of a particular relationship with a specific person (e.g., a "loved one"), without being devastated by the possible loss. These items, such as "If someone I cared about became angry with me, I would feel threatened that he (she) might leave me," express a relational attachment to a particular person. A person endorsing this item does not feel helpless or annihilated by the loss but values the relationship and, therefore, is vulnerable to dysphoric feelings with the loss of that relationship. This interpersonal relationship is not general and undifferentiated; rather, it recognizes the unique quality of the other to whom one feels attached, and the primary issue is one of loss and loneliness; without feelings of fear, danger, apprehension, and helplessness. These items evaluate a capacity for *relatedness.* Thus, we revised the label for Factor I from Dependency to *Interpersonal Concerns*, which seemed more appropriate because it reflected the broad range of interpersonal concerns of the individuals who have elevated scores on this dimension (i.e., fears of abandonment as well as an interest in maintaining relationships). This change also avoids the misleading and negative connotation that interpersonal concerns are associated only with dependency in psychological functioning, particularly in women and adolescent girls.

To evaluate these two possible subscales within Factor I, Blatt, Zohar, et al. (1995) used (a) a theory-driven approach to empirical research, called *facet theory*, that defines theoretically potential subconstructs, or facets, within data sets, and (b) a multidimensional scaling (MDS) procedure called *smallest space analysis* (SSA; Canter, 1985; Guttman, 1968), to identify possible clusters of items that correspond to the theoretically defined facets (Guttman, 1968, 1977, 1982a, 1982b).[1] SSA represents item values as points in multidimensional space; distances between the points reflect the empirical relations among the items as measured by the correlations between them. If the theoretical model is correct, then the conceptual similarity between items will be expressed empirically, and their locations should be closer in multidimensional space. Thus, in SSA, one tests hypotheses proposed in a facet theory approach by examining whether the multidimensional space can be readily partitioned into regions that reflect the a priori theoretical clustering of items. The specified relations among the items in the various facets or clusters determine the form the partitioning is expected to take (S. Levy, 1985). Thus, the a priori definition of each of the items, according to the definition of the facets, serves as a bridge between the theory and its implementation in the empirical analyses of SSA (Schlesinger, 1978). Facet theory and SSA have been used extensively in multivariate research in the social sciences as well as in the humanities and the life sciences (Dancer, 1990).[2]

Two facets were proposed within the DEQ Dependency factor: (a) neediness (or dependence) and (b) relatedness. To explore these two possible facets within

---

[1] Professor Ruth Guttman of the Hebrew University of Jerusalem suggested the use of facet theory and SSA in these explorations.

[2] SSA (Lingoes, 1973), one of a variety of nonmetric MDS techniques for structural data analysis (Canter, 1985; Davidson, 1983; Guttman, 1968, 1977, 1982a, 1982b), presents items in Euclidean space, preserving the rank order relations among the items' intercorrelations so that more highly correlated items appear closer on the SSA map (Shye, 1978). The dimensions of SSA space can range between two and six, and the minimal dimensionality that preserves the rank order of the intercorrelations is preferred. The coefficient of alienation (J. Brown, 1985) indicates how well the rank order of the correlations is preserved by their spatial representation in a given dimensionality of SSA. In our (Blatt, Zohar, et al., 1995, 1996) analyses, SSAs of three or four dimensions were sufficient to meet the conventional criterion of coefficient of alienation of less than .20. Although the MDS axes are arbitrary, interpretations are made on the basis of the ordering of regions that are formed by clusters of theoretically related items. The Euclidean *n*-dimensional space formed by the SSA is presented in a series of two-dimensional projections. A priori specification of the items that are expected to constitute each region makes it possible to draw boundaries around the points that fill a two-dimensional SSA space. Partition boundaries may be straight or curved, as long as they yield regions having continuous boundaries that do not intersect with the boundaries of other regions (Lingoes, 1977, 1981). Regionalities are defined by the arrangements of the items in SSA space and their a priori classification according to facet theory.

this factor (Factor I) of the DEQ, SSA was applied to the 49 of the 66 DEQ items that loaded significantly (>.40) on at least one of the three factors in men or women (or both) as defined by the original DEQ factor analysis (Blatt, D'Afflitti, & Quinlan, 1979) and were clearly directional so that they could be coded in a depressive direction from high to low depressive experience. These 49 items were classified into four groups on the basis of their content by two senior PhD clinical psychologists familiar with the DEQ. They classified the items into the two proposed facets of DEQ Factor I, neediness and relatedness, as well as self-criticism and lack of efficacy. The two judges classified the items independently and agreed on 83% of the items; items classified differently were discussed until consensus was achieved. Because only 49 of the original 66 DEQ items could be included in this analysis, it was not expected that the three original DEQ factors would necessarily emerge as regions within the SSA. The primary interest in these analyses was in identifying the two potential facets or subscales within DEQ Factor I.

As discussed above, two sets of items were identified within DEQ Factor I. One set of items assesses feelings of loss and loneliness in the context of a disruption of a relationship to a specific person (e.g., a "loved one"). This set of items was labeled *Relatedness*. In contrast, items that considered feelings of helplessness, fears, and apprehensions about separation and rejection, and intense concerns about loss of gratification and general experiences of frustration without a link to a particular individual or a specific relationship, were labeled *Dependence* or *Neediness,* because they emphasize a sense of fear, danger, apprehension, and helplessness and lack any emphasis on a specific relationship (Blatt, Zohar, et al., 1995).[3]

Two large samples of undergraduate college students served as base samples for the SSA to identify these two possible facets within DEQ Factor I. There were 373 men and 780 women in Sample 1 and 310 men and 591 women in Sample 2. SSA was performed separately for men and women in both samples. The SSA projections were interpreted with reference to the a priori groupings of the items. For each of the four samples, the projections clearly showed the resolution of items within the two subscales of DEQ Factor I. For the men of Sample 1 (n = 373), the SSA map was the three-dimensional SSA projection of Axis 1 versus Axis 3. The coefficient of alienation was .198. The items of the two subscales within DEQ Factor 1 were clearly partitioned in the SSA space. The Dependence or Neediness facet was well defined, as were the Relatedness items that formed a distinct region within the Interpersonal factor. In addition, the Self-Critical region (DEQ Factor II) was distinct. Lack of Efficacy (DEQ Factor III) was also a distinct region.

---

[3]Two research groups—colleagues and I (Blatt & Zohar, 1990; Blatt, Zohar, et al., 1995; Blatt, Zohar, et al., 1996) and Rude and Burnham (1995)—independently sought to identify subscales within the Interpersonal factor of the DEQ and have used different terms to identify two subscales within DEQ Factor I. Colleagues and I have used the terms *dependence* and *relatedness*, whereas Rude and Burnham have used *neediness* and *connectedness*. Throughout this book I use a composite of these terms; I use the term *neediness* to describe concerns about interpersonal relations at a lower developmental level at which there is a wish to be taken care of, and I use the term *relatedness* to describe a more reciprocal type of interpersonal concerns.

The SSA analysis indicated that Item 22 of the DEQ ("I have difficulty breaking off a relationship even if it is making me unhappy"), which had originally been classified as a relational item, clustered with the Neediness items. On reflection, it seemed that this item indicates a less differentiated relationship. Thus, Item 22 was not included in the Relatedness facet but instead was incorporated into the Neediness facet (Blatt, Zohar, et al., 1995).

The SSA analysis based on the men of Sample 2 ($n = 310$) had a coefficient of alienation of .140. In the SSA projection of Axis 1 versus Axis 3, all eight relatedness items were clearly delineated within the Interpersonal partition.

The responses of the women of Sample 1 ($n = 780$) were best depicted in the four-dimensional SSA projection of Axis 3 versus Axis 4, which had a coefficient of alienation of .150. All eight relational items formed a distinct subregion which, like in the other samples, were within the DEQ Interpersonal region. Also, a clear regionality for lack of Efficacy, but not for Self-Criticism, was identified. For the women of Sample 2 ($n = 591$), the four-dimensional SSA projection of Axis 1 versus Axis 3 had a coefficient of alienation of .130. The eight relational items formed a subregion located partially within the Interpersonal region. Thus, the Relatedness and Neediness facets were identified in both the men and women in Samples 1 and 2. In addition, the SSA also indicated clear regions for the original three DEQ factors—Dependency, Self-Criticism, and lack of Efficacy—in three of the four samples.[4]

In summary, the differentiation of two facets within the DEQ Interpersonal factor was initially demonstrated in all four samples. The relational and neediness items, identified a priori on theoretical grounds, were located in empirically derived regionalities of the SSA. The Relatedness and Neediness items that independently clustered within the Interpersonal region and had factor loadings greater than .40 on the DEQ Interpersonal factor were retained to define two subscales within DEQ Factor I. These items are noted in Exhibit 3.3. All 8 of the initially identified Relatedness items, and 10 of the original 18 Neediness items, were retained to constitute two subscales within DEQ Factor I.

Alpha coefficients were obtained to examine the cohesion (reliability) of these two subscales, the 8 relational items and 10 neediness items, in men and women in the two samples. The alpha coefficient for the Dependence or Neediness subscale ranged from .66 to .75 ($M = .70$) for women and from .63 to .71 ($M = .70$) for men. The alpha coefficient for the Relatedness subscale ranged from .65 to .69 ($M = .68$) for women and .56 to .71 ($M = .65$) for men. The correlations between these two subscales in the samples ranged from .67 to .91 ($M = .75$) for women and from .60 to .83 ($M = .70$) for men.

These two facets within the DEQ Interpersonal factor (Neediness and Relatedness) were correlated with several independent measures of depression (BDI and ZDI as well as the DEQ Self-Criticism factor) and several measures of psychological well-being, including semantic differential ratings of self-evaluation, potency, and activity and the Masculinity and Femininity scales

---

[4]The well-replicated factor structure of the DEQ was not demonstrated in all of these SSA maps, in part because the SSAs were based on 49 of the initial 66 DEQ items (i.e., only those items that could be used in SSA).

Exhibit 3.3 Neediness and Relatedness Items Within Factor I (Dependency) of the Depressive Experiences Questionnaire

---

Neediness
 Without support from others who are close to me I would be helpless.
 I become frightened when I feel alone.
 I have difficulty breaking off a relationship that is making me unhappy.
 I often think about the danger of losing someone who is close to me.
 I am not very concerned with how other people respond to me. (reverse scored)
 I am very sensitive to others for signs of rejection.
 Even if the person who is closest to me were to leave, I could still "go it alone."
  (reverse scored)
 I am a very independent person. (reverse scored)
 Anger frightens me.
 After a fight with a friend, I must make amends as soon as possible.

Relatedness
 The lack of permanence in human relationships doesn't bother me. (reverse scored)
 I would feel like I'd be losing an important part of myself if I lost a close friend.
 I constantly try, and very often go out of my way to please people I am close to.
 I find it very hard to say "no" to the requests of friends.
 I worry a lot about offending or hurting someone who is close to me.
 If someone I cared about became angry with me, I would feel threatened that he
  (she) might leave me.
 After an argument, I feel very lonely.
 Being alone doesn't bother me at all. (reverse scored)

---

of the Bem Sex Role Inventory (BSRI; Bem, 1974), as well the DEQ Efficacy factor. To control for the high correlation between the Neediness and Relatedness subscales embedded in the DEQ Interpersonal factor, residualized scores were used to partial out the common variance. These residualized scores were correlated with the criterion measures, and their respective correlations were compared by testing for the significance of the differences between their correlations with the various criteria (McNemar, 1962).

 Collateral data from these two samples and from a smaller third sample were used to assess the construct validity of these two subscales within DEQ Factor I. The third sample consisted of 190 female and 87 male college students, enrolled in an introductory psychology course at a state university in the Southwest, who were administered the DEQ, the BDI (A. T. Beck et al., 1961); the ZDS (Zung, 1965, 1971, 1972); a semantic differential scale for rating the self on dimensions of evaluation, potency, and activity (Osgood, Suci, & Tannenbaum, 1957); and the BSRI (Bem, 1974), which assesses degree of adherence to a masculine (e.g., competence) and a feminine (e.g., warmth) gender role.[5] The BDI, ZDS, semantic differential scale, and BSRI are well-established measures with demonstrated reliability and validity.

---

[5] I am indebted to Bertha Melgoza and Samuel Roll for providing me access to this data set.

In women, the residualized Neediness subscale correlated significantly with all the depression measures, and these correlations were significantly higher than those with the residualized Relatedness subscale for two of the three measures of depression (see also Little & Garber, 2000). In fact, the correlations between the Relatedness subscale and the depression measures approached zero. The Neediness scale not only had significantly greater correlations with the measures of depression than the Relatedness scale, but it also had significantly greater correlations with the measures of depression than the original total DEQ Interpersonal factor, especially in women. The total DEQ Interpersonal factor (Factor I) for women correlated .28 and .20, respectively, ($p < .01$) with the BDI and ZDS at a significantly lower level than the correlations with the Neediness scale, $t(191) = 3.18$ and $t(187) = 4.42$, respectively, $ps < .001$. For men, the DEQ Interpersonal factor also correlated at a lower level with the BDI and ZDS (.24 [$p < .05$] and .15 [ns], respectively) than did the Neediness scale, but the difference between these correlations was significant only with the ZDS, $t(84) = 2.06$, $p < .05$.

The general pattern of these results indicates that the Neediness subscale is a more consistent measure of depression than the original DEQ Interpersonal factor, especially in women. The results with men are in the same direction but not as consistent. In general, however, the correlation of the DEQ Interpersonal factor with measures of depression appears to be reduced by the relatedness items embedded within this factor (Blatt, Zohar, et al., 1995).

In addition to the implications of these findings for the assessment of depression, the data suggest that the items of the Relatedness subscale within the Interpersonal factor assess an adaptive form of interpersonal relations. The residualized Relatedness subscale, compared with the residualized Neediness subscale, had a significantly ($p < .01$) greater correlation, especially for women, with the semantic differential dimensions of evaluation and activity; the BSRI Masculinity and Femininity scales that assess experiences of competence and warmth, respectively; and with the DEQ Efficacy factor. Again, these findings also occurred with men, although the differences between the correlations with men generally did not reach statistical significance (Blatt, Zohar, et al., 1995).

The Neediness and Relatedness subscales within the Interpersonal factor on the DEQ–A were also identified in a large sample of adolescent students (278 girls and 246 boys) enrolled in a suburban New York City high school (Blatt, Zohar, et al., 1996). An SSA was conducted on the responses of these students to the DEQ–A, and the projections were interpreted with reference to the four groups of items (Neediness, Relatedness, Self-Criticism, and Efficacy) identified in the SSA with adults (Blatt, Zohar, et al., 1995). The projections for boys and girls separately, as well as for the total sample, indicated that Neediness and Relatedness could be differentiated within the DEQ–A Interpersonal factor. For girls ($N = 278$), the SSA was the four-dimensional projection of Axis 2 versus Axis 3 with a coefficient of alienation of .150. The regionalities of the two groups of items in the partitioning of the SSA indicated that the Neediness and Relatedness items were well defined, indicating that these two groups of items form distinct subregions within the Interpersonal factor. The

Self-Critical (DEQ–A Factor II) and lack of Efficacy (DEQ–A Factor III) regions also were distinct.

In the SSA based on the male sample (N = 246), the Relatedness items were clustered within the Interpersonal region in the four-dimensional SSA projection of Axis 2 versus Axis 3, with a coefficient of alienation of .130. The Self-Critical and lack of Efficacy regions also were well delineated.

In summary, SSA differentiated the two subscales, Neediness and Relatedness, within the DEQ–A Interpersonal factor in late adolescent boys and girls. The Relatedness and Neediness items, identified a priori on theoretical grounds and empirically supported in the SSA of the DEQ with young adults (Blatt, Zohar, et al., 1995), were also clearly identified in the DEQ–A in a sample of suburban high school students. As with the adult DEQ, the Relatedness items and the Neediness items that clustered within the Interpersonal region were retained to define two subscales within the DEQ–A. The same Relatedness items and the same dependence or Neediness items identified on the DEQ with young adults (Blatt, Zohar, et al., 1995) were identified in the responses of adolescent participants to the DEQ–A (Blatt, Zohar, et al., 1996).

To examine the cohesion of the 8 Relatedness items and the 10 Neediness items in the DEQ–A, alpha reliabilities were calculated for boys and girls separately. The alpha reliability coefficient for the Neediness subscale in the DEQ–A was .73 for girls and .72 for boys; the alpha coefficient for the Relatedness subscale was .56 for girls and .67 for boys. As expected, these two subscales embedded in the DEQ Interpersonal factor of the DEQ–A were highly correlated (rs = .66 and .68 for girls and boys, respectively) in the large suburban sample and in the smaller inner-city sample (rs = .57 and .73 for girls and boys, respectively). Thus, residualized scores were used again to test the differential relations of these two subscales to various criteria (Blatt, Zohar, et al., 1996).

The students in the suburban high school had been administered the Achenbach Youth Self Report (YSR; Achenbach & Edelbrock, 1987) and the Community Epidemiological Survey for Depression (Radloff, 1977; A. N. Weissman, Orvaschel, & Padian, 1980). The Neediness subscale had significantly higher correlations with the measure of depression (Community Epidemiological Survey for Depression) than did the residualized Relatedness subscale, but only for boys. For boys and girls alike, the Neediness subscale had a significantly higher correlation with DEQ Self-Criticism and a significantly lower correlation with DEQ Efficacy than did the Relatedness subscale. The Neediness subscale also had significantly greater correlations than did the Relatedness scale with seven of the nine behavior problem scales of the Achenbach YSR (particularly the internal scales), but only with boys. With girls, however, there were no significant differences between the correlations of the two subscales with the Achenbach problem scales, except for one: Somatic Concerns. Results regarding somatic concerns in girls were in the unexpected direction; that is, Relatedness had a significantly more positive correlation with somatic problems than did Neediness.

The two subscales of residualized Neediness and Relatedness were also correlated with criterion measures in the smaller sample of 80 female and 66 male students in the inner-city high school. Findings with inner-city adolescent high school students were consistent with the findings from the suburban high school adolescents. In boys, the Neediness subscale had significantly greater correlations than did the Relatedness subscale with an independent measure of depression (Children's Depression Inventory, CDI; Kovacs, 1981) and with six of the nine problem behavior scales of the Achenbach YSR. The results with the inner-city female adolescents are also similar to the results with the suburban female adolescents: No significant differences were found between the correlations of the Neediness and the Relatedness subscales with a measure of depression or with the YSR problem scales. In fact, as with the suburban female adolescents, the significant differences are contrary to expectations: Relatedness had a significantly higher correlation with the YSR Delinquency problem scale and externalizing problems, as well as with depression on the CDI, than did neediness.

Using the DEQ–A, K. L. Bell, Tietz, Sargent, and Garrison (2002) studied undergraduate men and women and their same-sex friends and found that Dependency correlated with reports of a lack of competence in both social and academic domains. Differentiating between the Neediness and Relatedness subscales within the Dependency or Interpersonal factor, they found that only Neediness, and not Relatedness, was associated with low levels of social acceptance. Consistent with findings reported by Mongrain, Vettese, Shuster, and Kendal (1998), neediness was associated with individuals, both men and women, seeing themselves in a more positive way than did their friends. Bell et al. concluded that it is important to distinguish between immature and mature forms of interpersonal relatedness on the DEQ when studying the social relations of dependent individuals. The differentiation of two levels of interpersonal relatedness within the Dependency factor of the DEQ—one associated with psychological disturbance and distress and the other associated with more adaptive functioning—is consistent with the formulations of Bornstein (e.g., 1998) that dependency includes elements of both risk and resilience.

The identification of these two subscales within DEQ Factor I in older adolescents and adults (Blatt, Zohar, et al., 1995; Blatt, Zohar, et al., 1996) is consistent with the findings reported by Rude and Burnham (1995) who, using second-order factor analysis, also identified two subscales within the Interpersonal factor. Also consistent with the results reported by Blatt, Zohar, et al. (1995) of studies of the two subscales within DEQ Factor I with young adults, Rude and Burnham reported that "neediness was somewhat more predictive of depressive symptomatology for [young adult] women than for men" (p. 336). It is interesting, however, that these two different developmental levels of interpersonal relations identified within DEQ Factor I had different relationships to criterion measures in high school boys and girls than they did in young adults. In late adolescence, the distinction of two levels of interpersonal relations (neediness and relatedness) had significant relations with criterion measures only with boys. In young adults (Blatt, Zohar, et al., 1995; Rude & Burnham, 1995), in contrast, the distinction was effective primarily with the female participants.

In further investigating Rude and Burnham's (1995) distinctions, Zuroff, Moskowitz, and Koestner (1996) and Zuroff, Moskowitz, and Cote (1999) have suggested that neediness and connectedness have different implications for social behavior. Connectedness predicted greater psychological maturity, indicating a sensitivity to the feelings and needs of others and a regard for relationships rather than need gratification alone. Neediness, in contrast, was moderately related to dysphoria, neuroticism, anxiety over loss, introversion, and discomfort with depending on others. Connectedness was primarily related to agreeableness and conscientiousness. In both self-report and behavioral measures, neediness was associated with low scores on the dominant–submissive axis, whereas connectedness was positively related to self-reported warmth and more intimate social interactions. Individuals high on Neediness experience social interactions as less pleasant and describe themselves as less powerful. Henrich, Blatt, Kuperminc, Zohar, and Leadbeater (2001) also identified the two subscales within DEQ Factor I in a sample of early adolescent (ages 11–13) students, especially among girls. They found that Relatedness, but not Neediness, was significantly correlated with measures of interpersonal competence and the positive quality of attachment to peers. In early adolescent girls, Relatedness was significantly associated with interpersonal competence, whereas Neediness correlated negatively with measures of interpersonal competence, quality of peer attachment, number of close friends, and popularity. Girls with high Neediness scores were socially isolated and not involved in friendship groups. Thus, Neediness and Relatedness were significantly related, but in opposite directions, to interpersonal functioning in girls. Neediness was related to disrupted social functioning, whereas Relatedness was associated with the capacity to form relationships and participate in social networks. These results also indicate that in early adolescence interpersonal processes are more differentiated in girls than in boys. Although the distinction and implications of the differences between Neediness and Relatedness or connectedness need to be researched more fully, the identification of these two subscales within the Dependency or Interpersonal factor of the DEQ could prove useful in differentiating which aspects of dependency are detrimental to social functioning (e.g., Bornstein, 1998).

These findings indicate a degree of stability in the distinction of two developmental levels within the Interpersonal factor of the DEQ (Factor I). With younger and older adolescents and young adults, the subscales of Neediness and Relatedness were clearly distinguished through the MDS procedures of SSA. The results of these studies also suggest that sex and age are important issues in this distinction of two levels of interpersonal relations. Issues of interpersonal relatedness are central issues in early adolescent development, especially in girls. As Gilligan (1982) noted, teenage girls quickly develop an ethic of responsibility for attending to others' needs. The differentiation between neediness and relatedness among girls in early adolescence reflects their heightened investment in interpersonal issues. A variety of research studies (e.g., Siddique & D'Arcy, 1984; Thorbecke & Grotevant, 1982) support the theoretical view that interpersonal relationships are central in defining early adolescent girls' developing sense of identity.

The results also suggest that this interpersonal distinction becomes important for boys in later adolescence (in high school). One of the predominant concerns for boys in early adolescence is to demonstrate their strength and independence. Thus, the distinction between these two forms of relatedness becomes relevant for boys only later in their development, after they have consolidated a sense of identity. Issues of attachment and intimacy once again become more fully articulated in girls as they approach young adulthood, and thus the distinction between neediness and relatedness once again becomes salient for them.

Independent of these possible explanations of the reasons for the sex differences in the correlates of two levels of interpersonal relatedness in early and late adolescence and in young adulthood, the results indicate that the distinction between these two levels of interpersonal relatedness within DEQ Factor I is stable in adults and adolescents. This distinction may provide a more refined method for evaluating depression related to disruptions of interpersonal relatedness as well as for studying systematically the development of aspects of interpersonal relatedness in males and females in various phases of the life cycle. Subsequent research should be directed toward refining the assessment of these two facets of interpersonal relatedness on the DEQ by reducing their high degree of shared variance so that they can be used more effectively in research. Zuroff, Mongrain, and Santor (in press), on the basis of further analyses of prior data sets in which they introduced the distinction between the Neediness and Relatedness subscales, concluded that neediness occurred in "very unhappy people who badly want to be cared for and protected by others, but who expect to be hurt in relationships and have adopted submissive interpersonal styles to forestall conflict and to elicit protection and support." They found that relatedness, in contrast, occurred in "somewhat dysphoric, somewhat insecure people who have developed warm, intimate ways of relating that cement relationships by making them valued interactional partners."

The differentiation of two levels of relatedness within the Dependency or Interpersonal factor of the DEQ is consistent with recent research by Pincus and colleagues (e.g., Pincus & Gurtman, 1995; Pincus & Wilson, 2001), and Bornstein and colleagues (e.g, Bornstein, 1993, 1998; Bornstein & Cecero, 2000) demonstrating that dependency is a multidimensional construct with both adaptive and maladaptive features.

Differentiation of Levels of Self-Definition

The differentiation of two levels of interpersonal attachment within the DEQ Interpersonal factor suggests the possibility of a similar differentiation within the DEQ Self-Criticism factor. The items that contribute to the Self-Criticism factor deal primarily with feelings of failure and guilt. Although two experienced judges could reliably identify differences among some of the items of the DEQ Self-Criticism factor based on a distinction between a tendency to be evaluative and judgmental as compared to experiencing intermittent feelings of worthlessness and emptiness, SSA did not provide empirical support for this differentiation. Rather, most of the items of the DEQ Self-Criticism factor appear to assess experiences associated with a negative self-definition, and the DEQ seems to lack items that assess a less developed sense of self that might be expressed in fears of annihilation, feelings of fragmentation, and a lack of self-definition. Although colleagues and I were unable to differentiate empirically among the items of the DEQ Self-Criticism factor, the identification of two facets of interpersonal attachment—neediness and relatedness—within the DEQ Dependency factor suggests that there may be much to gain by expanding the DEQ by developing additional items to assess more fully different levels of interpersonal relatedness, as well as seeking ways to differentiate different levels of self-definition within the DEQ Self-Criticism factor. Further differentiation within the DEQ Self-Criticism factor may be especially important given the findings of the role of self-criticism in suicide (A. T. Beck, 1983; Blatt, 1995a; Blatt et al., 1982) and the serious impediment that self-criticism or perfectionism creates in the response to brief treatment of depression (Blatt, Quinlan, Pilkonis, & Shea, 1995).

A recent study indicated that Factors II and III (Self-Criticism and Efficacy) of the DEQ may be understood as assessing aspects of the self at different developmental levels (Kuperminc, Blatt, & Leadbeater, 1997). Self-Criticism assesses concerns about self-worth and failure to meet self- and externally imposed standards—items that focus on reactive issues, issues from the past that express concerns ruminative about failure and transgression. The items of the Efficacy factor, in contrast, are more positive, proactive expressions of competence and confidence in one's self and in the future. In a study of early adolescent students in a public middle school (Grades 6–8), Kuperminc et al. (1997) found that Self-Criticism and Efficacy were differentially associated with measures of maladjustment and a wide range of adaptive capacities. Self-Criticism was strongly associated with measures of maladjustment, whereas Efficacy was more strongly associated with measures of competency and the quality of interpersonal relationships. Thus, the Self-Criticism factor appears to assess dysphoric attitudes in reaction to perceived deficits and deficiencies, whereas Efficacy appears to assess proactive self-attitudes. Although the three primary factors of the DEQ (Dependency, Self-Criticism, and Efficacy) are orthogonal, Self-Criticism and Efficacy have differential relations to the two subscales (Neediness and Relatedness) within the Interpersonal factor on the DEQ–A. Specifically, Self-Criticism correlates positively with Neediness and negatively with Relatedness; that is, a maladaptive sense of self (i.e., Self-Criticism) correlates primarily with the maladaptive dimensions of interpersonal relations (Neediness). In contrast, Efficacy, an adaptive sense of self, correlates positively with adaptive dimensions of interpersonal relations (Relatedness) and negatively with the maladaptive dimensions of interpersonal relations (Neediness). In a recent longitudinal study of 860 adolescents, Shahar, Henrich, et al. (2002) used structural equation modeling and found that the occurrence of positive life events was significantly facilitated by DEQ Efficacy and impeded by DEQ Self-Criticism. These effects were fully mediated by the presence of autonomous (intrinsic) motivation, as defined and measured by Deci and Ryan (e.g., 1985). Self-Criticism in this study was associated with reduced autonomous (intrinsic) motivation and elevated levels of controlled (extrinsic) motivation, which provides further understanding of some of the mechanisms for the adverse effects of self-criticism. Thus, the DEQ appears to measure adaptive and maladaptive dimensions of interpersonal relatedness (Neediness and Relatedness) as well as adaptive and maladaptive dimensions of self-definition (Blatt & Shahar, 2003). In subsequent research, it may be productive to view Self-Criticism and Efficacy as assessing dimensions of the self at two different developmental levels. D. A. Clark and Beck (1999), like Kuperminc et al. (1997; Blatt & Shahar, 2003; Blatt, Zohar, et al., 1995, 1996), recently have begun to discuss adaptive and maladaptive modes for both sociotropy and autonomy, although they have not yet identified particular items within the SAS that might distinguish adaptive and maladaptive modes. This emphasis on identifying adaptive and maladaptive dimensions of relatedness and self-definition is consistent with the distinction between adaptive and maladaptive forms of perfectionism (e.g., Flett & Hewitt, 2002). High personal standards, for example, are not associated with depression, whereas self-criticism, another dimension of perfectionism, is associated with psychopathology (Enns, Cox, & Clara, 2002; Dunkley, Zuroff, & Blankstein, 2003).

Other Measures of Anaclitic and Introjective Depressive Experiences

In addition to the DEQ (Blatt, D'Affliti, et al., 1976), several other scales have been developed that assess these two dimensions of dysphoria, including the SAS (A. T. Beck et al., 1983) and the PSI (C. J. Robins & Luten, 1991), which attempts to integrate the DEQ and the SAS. In addition, several factor analyses indicate that two primary factors within the DAS (A. N. Weissman & Beck, 1978) also assess these dimensions of interpersonal and self-critical concerns.

Sociotropy–Autonomy Scale (SAS) and the Personal Style Inventory (PSI)

A. T. Beck et al. (1983) developed the SAS to assess the two dimensions of depression from self-reports of patients and from clinical material from therapists about patients' "sociotropic and autonomous attitudes" (A. T. Beck et al. 1983, p. 5). Factor analyses of the two 30-item self-report scales in the SAS yielded two factors. One factor, Sociotropy, consists of three subfactors or subscales reflecting (a) Concern About Disapproval (10 items; e.g., "When I am with other people, I look for signs whether or not they like being with me"), (b) Attachment Concerns (13 items; e.g., "I find it difficult to be separated from people I love"), and (c) Concerns About Pleasing Others (7 items; e.g., "I am afraid of hurting other people's feelings"). A second factor, Autonomy, also consists of three subscales: (a) Achievement (12 items; e.g., "The possibility of being rejected by others for standing up for my rights would not stop me"), (b) Freedom From Control (12 items; e.g., "It is very important that I feel free to get up and go whenever I want"), and (c) Preference for Solitude (6 items; "I like to take long walks by myself"). A. T. Beck et al. (1983) and C. J. Robins (1985) reported good levels of internal consistency (coefficient alpha) for Sociotropy (.90) and for Autonomy (.83 and .80) in both outpatients and undergraduates, respectively, although the three scales of the Autonomy factor have substantially less internal consistency (Pilon, 1987; C. J. Robins, 1985). Sociotropy and Autonomy are only marginally correlated, but only the Sociotropy factor, and not the Autonomy factor, correlates significantly with the BDI (Pilon, 1987). The total Sociotropy scale correlates significantly with the DEQ Interpersonal factor ($r = .68$; see also Flett et al., 1995), and the total Autonomy scale correlates significantly with DEQ Efficacy ($r = .39$), but not with DEQ Self-Criticism (C. J. Robins, 1985).

More recently, C. J. Robins and Luten (1991) developed the PSI, an alternative form of the SAS that appears to improve the psychometric properties of the SAS, especially the Autonomy scale, by integrating aspects of the SAS with items from the DEQ. C. J. Robins et al. (1994) later developed a 48-item revised PSI that contains 23 Sociotropy items that assess concerns about what others think, dependency, and pleasing others, and 24 items that assess self-critical perfectionism, a need for control, and interpersonal isolation. However, there have been some disagreements (e.g., Bagby, Parker, Joffe, Schuller, & Gilchrist, 1998; C. J. Robins et al., 1994) about the inclusion of the self-critical perfectionism items in the Autonomy scale. Several studies indicate that the Sociotropy and Autonomy scales of the PSI have good convergent and discriminant validity with relevant personality and vulnerability constructs (Flett, Hewitt, Garshowitz, & Martin, 1997; C. J. Robins et al., 1994; Zuroff, 1994). The Sociotropy and Autonomy scales of the PSI both correlate with measures of depression (e.g., Alden & Bieling, 1996; Kwon & Whisman, 1998; Sato & McCann, 1998). Allen, Horne, and Trinder (1996) found that PSI Sociotropy interacted with imagined rejection to produce dysphoric response as measured by physiological reactivity, but they did not find an interaction between PSI Autonomy and imagined failure. Kwon and Whisman (1998), however, did not find any interaction between the PSI scales and presumed congruent life events. Thus, the PSI appears to be a possible improvement over the SAS primarily because PSI Autonomy, compared with SAS Autonomy, now correlates with measures of depression. Zuroff (1994), however, found a moderate correlation between PSI Sociotropy and Autonomy ($rs = .35$ for men and $.30$ for women), which reduces the capacity of the PSI to identify specific vulnerability factors in depression.

Clark and colleagues (D. A. Clark & Beck, 1991; D. A. Clark, Steer, Haslam, Beck, & Brown, 1997) attempted to improve the Sociotropy and Autonomy scales of the SAS by revising 33 Autonomy items so that they now assess characteristics of the autonomous personality that were not included in the original SAS (i.e., excessively high standards of achievement, action orientation, insensitivity to the interpersonal effects of one's actions, primary focus on positive outcomes, unreflective mode of thinking, rigid and dogmatic stance on issues, and excessive striving for individual expression). Although they found that their revised SAS Sociotropy scale produced results very similar to the original 30-item SAS Sociotropy scale, their two new autonomy subscales, Solitude and Independence, are different from the original SAS Autonomy scale because they contain many new items. D. A. Clark et al. (1997) reported that initial studies with the revised SAS look promising because the new autonomy subscale, Solitude, predicted relationships with depression and other construct-related measures, and the other new autonomy subscale, Independence, correlated with measures of positive functioning and adjustment, findings that are consistent with reports by Bieling, Olshan, Brown, & Beck (1998) and Blatt and Shahar (2003), Henrich et al. (2001), and Kuperminc et al. (1997) with the DEQ. The revised SAS, however, has not been evaluated as yet with a clinically depressed sample, so it is unclear whether the revised SAS is an improvement over the original (D. A. Clark & Beck, 1999, pp. 275–276).

In an attempt to clarify the inconsistent results in the relationship of the SAS Sociotropy and Autonomy scales to depression and psychopathology, Bieling, Beck, and Brown (in press) conducted exploratory and confirmatory factor analyses of the SAS on two large samples of psychiatric patients. They found a two-factor solution for sociotropy and labeled the factors *Preference for Affiliation* and *Fear of Criticism and Rejection*, and they found that the latter had a stronger association with psychopathology. They also found a two-factor solution for autonomy and labeled the factors *Sensitivity to Others' Control* and *Independent Goal Attainment*. Although Sensitivity to Control had a positive correlation with psychopathology, Independent Goal Attainment had a negative correlation with psychopathology, and the authors speculated that it may be associated with resilience or hardiness and serve as a buffer against stress (see also Blatt & Shahar, 2003; Kuperminc et al., 1997; Shahar, Gallagher, Blatt, Kuperminc, & Leadbeater, in press).

Despite inconsistencies in the method of extraction and rotation, and a lack of cross-validation (Bieling et al., in press), the SAS has been found to predict response to treatment. Sociotropic patients do better in group therapy, whereas autonomous individuals do better in individual therapy (Zettle, Haflich, & Reynolds, 1992; Zettle & Herring, 1995). Sociotropy predicts a depressive response to negative interpersonal events and is related to dependency, lack of assertion, and introversion (Cappeliez, 1993; Gilbert & Reynolds, 1990; Moore & Blackburn, 1994; C. J. Robins, Block, & Peselow, 1989). As summarized by Bieling et al. (in press), results with the Autonomy scale have been less consistent. Although Autonomy predicts a constructive response to antidepressant medication (Peselow, Robins, Sanfilipo, Block, & Fieve, 1992; Scott, Harrington, House, & Ferrier, 1996), it has been less consistent in predicting responses to negative achievement events and other personality correlates (D. A. Clark & Beck, 1999; D. A. Clark & Oates, 1995; Hammen, Burge, & Stansbury, 1990; Hammen, Ellicott, Gitlin, & Jamison, 1989; C. J. Robins & Block, 1988; C. J. Robins et al., 1994).

Bieling et al. (in press) reviewed several recent attempts to identify clusters of items in the SAS (e.g., Bagby et al., 1998; D. A. Clark & Beck, 1991; D. A. Clark, Steer, Haslam, Beck, & Brown, 1997; Sato & McCann, 1998) and concluded that the Autonomy scale may consist of a less dysfunctional "individualistic achievement" factor and a seemingly more dysfunctional "need for control/ independence" factor. Likewise, recent research (e.g., Bagby et al., 1998; Pincus & Gurtman, 1995; Rude & Burnham, 1995; Sato & McCann, 1998) suggests that sociotropy may contain two factors: (a) Sensitivity to Others and (b) Attachment. Thus, as with the DEQ (e.g., Blatt & Shahar, 2003; Blatt, Zohar, et al., 1995; Blatt, Zohar, et al., 1996; Kuperminc et al., 1997), sociotropy as well as autonomy may have dysfunctional as well as adaptive dimensions.

Dysfunctional Attitudes Scale (DAS)

Items for the DAS (A. N. Weissman & Beck, 1978) were obtained from clinicians and based on their experiences with maladaptive (arbitrary, extreme, and rigid) attitudes of patients with depression, as originally described by A. T. Beck (1967a, 1976). DAS items are rated on a 7-point Likert-type scale that ranges from *totally agree* to *totally disagree*. The DAS was originally designed as a global measure of the dysfunctional thinking that predisposes people to depression (G. P. Brown & Beck, 2002). Investigators (e.g., Cane, Olinger, Gotlib, & Kuiper, 1986; Mongrain & Zuroff, 1989), however, have found that the DAS contains two factors that assess dependent and self-critical dysfunctional attitudes. Factor analytic studies of the DAS yielded two major and stable factors: (a) concerns about Approval by Others and Performance Evaluation or self-worth (Cane et al., 1986), or "a Need for Approval" and "Perfectionism" (e.g., Oliver & Baumgart, 1985). Blaney and Kutcher (1991), in evaluating the relationships among the two factors of the DEQ, SAS, and DAS, reported high intercorrelations among the three scales assessing concerns about interpersonal relatedness (DEQ Interpersonal factor, SAS Sociotropy, and DAS Need for Approval). The relationships among the three scales designed to assess concerns about individuality (DEQ Self-Criticism, SAS Autonomy, and the Perfectionism factor of the DAS) are more complex, primarily because the Autonomy scale of the SAS is not congruent with the other two measures. The relationship between DEQ Self-Criticism and the Perfectionism factor of the DAS, however, is substantial (Blaney & Kutcher, 1991). Powers et al. (2002) also demonstrated the convergence between DEQ Self-Criticism and the Perfectionism factor of the DAS (see also Dunkley & Blankstein, 2000; Enns & Cox, 1999; Flett, Besser, et al., in press; Hewitt & Flett, 1993). G. P. Brown and Beck (2002) presented a detailed review of research with the DAS.

Summary

In an attempt to broaden the empirical base for defining two personality prototypes that may be differentially sensitive to different types of life events leading to depression, Pilon (1987) conducted a discriminant analysis using a number of scales, including the DEQ, SAS, DAS, BDI, and the Personality Research Form. Pilon identified two fundamental dimensions: (a) relatedness to others— appealing to others for support, help, and advice, seeking to be loved and valued by others, craving affection and being overtly dependent and fearful of abandonment—and (b) feeling unsatisfied and critical of oneself, feeling a failure for not meeting expectations, needing to be outstanding and to avoid feeling inferior, and feeling ambivalent about interpersonal relationships.

The first dimension was significantly related to both the DEQ Dependency and the SAS Sociotropy factors. The second dimension did not emerge as clearly as the first. Although the second dimension was significantly related to measures of depression and to the DEQ Self-Criticism factor, it was not related to the Autonomy factor of the SAS. Pilon (1987) discussed the first dimension in terms of a sense of helplessness and the second dimension in terms of a sense of hopelessness (see also Schmale, 1972). Blaney and Kutcher (1991), who also evaluated the relationships among the two factors of the DEQ, SAS, and DAS, reported similar findings of high correlations among the three scales assessing interpersonal relatedness (Dependency, Sociotropy, and Factor I of the DAS). Blaney and Kutcher (1991), however, found that the Autonomy scale of the SAS appears to be more a measure of counterdependency than of individuality. The greater congruency between the various measures of interpersonal concerns than between the measures of self-criticism perhaps explains Nietzel and Harris's (1990) meta-analytic finding that the relations between measures of depression and the various measures of dependency are approximately equal but that DEQ Self-Criticism has substantially stronger correlations with measures of depression than does SAS Autonomy.

Luyten, Corveleyn, and Blatt (in press), in a summary of an extensive review integrating findings with the DEQ (Blatt et al., 1976), SAS (A. T. Beck et al., 1983), PSI (C. J. Robins & Ladd, 1991), and the DAS (A. N. Weissman & Beck, 1978), noted strong support for the relationship of dependency and perfectionism (self-criticism) and measures of dysphoria and depression in both clinical and nonclinical populations (e.g., Blatt, 1998; D. A. Clark & Beck, 1999; Nietzel & Harris, 1990). They found a general and consistent relationship between dependency, perfectionism (self-criticism), and traditional measures of depression, as well as with clinical ratings of depression in adolescents (e.g., Blatt, Schaffer, Bers, & Quinlan, 1992; Fichman, Koestner, & Zuroff, 1994; D. N. Klein, 1989; Luthar & Blatt, 1993), in college students and adults (e.g., Alden & Bieling, 1996; Bartelstone & Trull, 1995; Blatt et al., 1982; Brewin & Furnham, 1987; Mongrain & Zuroff, 1994; Santor & Zuroff, 1998; Sato & McCann, 1998; Shapiro, 1988; T. W. Smith, O'Keeffe, & Jenkins, 1988; Vaglum & Falkum, 1999; Welkowitz, Lish, & Bond, 1985; Zuroff, 1994; Zuroff & Fitzpatrick, 1995; Zuroff & Mongrain, 1987b; Zuroff, Stotland, Sweetman, Craig, & Koestner, 1995), and in inpatient and outpatient clinical samples (e.g., Blatt et al., 1982; J. D. Brown & Silberschatz, 1989; Fehon, Grilo, & Martino, 2000; Frank, Van Egeren, et al., 1997; D. N. Klein, 1989; D. N. Klein, Harding, Taylor, & Dickstein, 1988; Ouimette & Klein, 1993; Ouimette, Klein, Clark, & Margolis, 1992; Riley & McCranie, 1990; C. J. Robins, Bagby, Rector, Lynch, & Kennedy, 1997; Rosenfarb, Becker, Khan, & Mintz, 1998; Stein, Fruchter, & Trief, 1983).

Although all three instruments (DEQ, SAS, and DAS) have produced interesting results, psychometric problems have been identified for each (Blaney & Kutcher, 1991; Nietzel & Harris, 1990; C. J. Robins & Jacobson, 1987). For example, the DEQ may include too many items that tap state depression, the convergent validity of the SAS Autonomy scale is questionable, and the two factors of the DAS are highly correlated with one another. The use of different measures by different research groups also complicates the task of integrating findings. Of the three instruments available to assess these two types of dysphoric experiences, the psychometric properties of the DEQ are viewed as the most fully developed (Blaney & Kutcher, 1991).

The DEQ and the DEQ–A, in addition to their well-established and strong psychometric properties, have several advantages over the other scales in measuring the two primary dimensions of depression. Two levels of interpersonal relatedness have been identified within the Interpersonal factor (Factor I) that now enable investigators to differentiate a less mature and maladaptive level of neediness from a more mature and adaptive level of interpersonal relatedness. Also, research findings indicate that the Self-Criticism and Efficacy factors of the DEQ measure two different levels in the sense of self (Blatt & Shahar, 2003; Kuperminc et al., 1997). Even further, recent research findings (Blatt et al., 1982; Shahar, Gallagher, Blatt, Kuperminc, & Leadbeater, in press) indicate that the Efficacy factor (Factor III) of the DEQ moderates the effects of the other two factors of the DEQ. The fact that the third factor of the DEQ is orthogonal to the first two factors facilitates use of the Efficacy factor in data analyses to assess more fully the impact of interpersonal and self-critical concerns on psychological functioning. Recent research with the SAS (e.g., Bieling et al., in press) suggests that similar developments have taken place in which investigators are identifying functional as well as dysfunctional dimensions within the Sociotropy and Autonomy scales.

Depressive Experiences and Gender, Race, and Social Mobility

Several studies have investigated the relationship of the two types of depressive experiences (dependency and self-criticism) to gender and adherence to sex role stereotypes (Chevron et al., 1978; Golding & Singer, 1983; Rude, 1989) as well as to race, social class, and social mobility (R. E. Steele, 1978). Chevron et al. (1978) found that females scored significantly ($p \leq .05$) higher than males on the Interpersonal factor, whereas males tended to obtain higher scores than females on the Self-Criticism factor ($p \leq .10$). The difference between men and women on Efficacy was not significant. These findings were replicated by Golding and Singer (1983).

Important differences have been found between men and women in how types of depressive experiences relate to the degree of adherence to sex role stereotypes of competence and warmth–expressiveness (Broverman, Broverman, Clarkson, Rosenkrantz, & Vogel, 1970; Broverman, Vogel, Broverman, Clarkson, & Rosenkrantz, 1972). In both males and females, competence (the positively valued male stereotype) was negatively correlated with the Interpersonal factor and positively correlated with Efficacy (Chevron et al., 1978; Golding & Singer, 1983). Competency in men and women was also negatively correlated with overall depression as measured by the ZDS (Chevron et al., 1978). In contrast, men and women differed in the relationship of warmth–expressiveness (the positively valued female stereotype) to depressive experiences. Describing oneself as adhering more closely to the positively valued "feminine" trait correlated significantly ($p \leq .05$) in a positive direction with the DEQ Interpersonal factor in males (Chevron et al., 1978) but in a negative direction with Self-Criticism in females (Chevron et al., 1978; Golding & Singer, 1983).Warmth–expressiveness is a positive value for females, but for males it is related to a vulnerability to interpersonal depressive experiences. As I discuss in detail in chapter 5, research by T. W. Smith et al. (1988) elaborates these findings of the vulnerability to depressive experiences in males who emphasize the importance of interpersonal relatedness.

R. E. Steele (1978) studied the relations between depression, as measured by the ZDS and DEQ, and stressful life events in African American and White males and females. He confirmed the findings of Chevron et al. (1978) and Golding and Singer (1983) that females score higher on the Dependency factor of the DEQ. No significant differences were found for race on the two measures of depression, even though African Americans reported more stressful life events during the prior year. Individuals in a lower social class (Hollingshead's Class III as compared to Class II and I (Hollingshead & Redlich, 1958) were more depressed on the ZDS ($p < .05$). In terms of social mobility, downwardly mobile White individuals were significantly ($p < .05$) higher on the ZDS. It is interesting that a significant interaction emerged between race and social mobility in their relation to depression: Upwardly mobile African Americans and downwardly mobile Whites had higher scores on both the DEQ Interpersonal and Self-Criticism factors. Downwardly mobile White respondents were also significantly lower on DEQ Efficacy. Thus, vulnerability to depression appears to occur in response to social mobility, especially if social mobility is contrary to the implicit cultural expectations and demands that existed when Steele conducted his study (1978).

In chapter 7, I discuss in detail the fact that highly dependent and highly self-critical people are differentially sensitive to various life experiences, have different appraisal patterns regarding various conflicts and life stress, and use different coping styles in response to these stressors. Highly dependent individuals are likely to respond to disruptions of interpersonal relations by seeking compromise and avoiding direct conflict and confrontation. In contrast, highly self-critical individuals are likely to respond to disruptions of self-esteem with heightened counteractive responses to prove themselves (Batgos & Leadbeater, 1994; Blatt & Homann, 1992; Blatt & Shichman, 1983; Blatt & Zuroff, 1992; Fichman et al., 1994; Zuroff & Fitzpatrick, 1995). Evidence (T. W. Smith et al., 1988) suggests that dependent males and self-critical females (individuals in a predominantly gender-incongruent modality) are especially vulnerable to dysphoria, particularly dependent males who experience rejection and abandonment, and secondarily self-critical females confronted by failure and criticism. Thus, these distinctions of two types of depressive experiences have led to considerable empirical investigation of the characteristics of these two types of individuals as well as to some of the distal and proximal environmental experiences that contribute to the emergence of these depressive experiences. In chapters 6 and 7, I consider this extensive research on proximal and distal factors contributing to these two types of depressive experiences.

4

Assessment of Object Representation

Development of Representations

The psychoanalytic concept of mental representation (e.g., Sandler & Rosenblatt, 1962), is similar to the concept of the internal working model in attachment theory and research and to cognitive–affective schemas in social cognition. Cognitive–affective schemas, or mental representations, of self and others develop over the life cycle and have conscious and unconscious cognitive, affective, and experiential components. These schemas can involve veridical representations of consensual reality, idiosyncratic and unique constructions, or primitive and pathological distortions that suggest psychopathology (Blatt, 1995b; Blatt & Lerner, 1983a, 1983b). They provide the templates or prototypes that organize how one thinks and feels about oneself and about others. The importance of mental representations in psychoanalytic object-relations theory and attachment theory and research is consistent with the focus in developmental psychology, cognitive science, information processing, and social cognition on the role of these schemas of self and others as heuristic prototypes that provide the basis for social interaction and interpersonal behavior (e.g., Anderson, 1983; Auerbach, 1993; Horowitz, 1988; Mandler, 1988; Markus, 1977; Nelson & Grundel, 1987; Westen, 1991b).

Psychoanalytic and developmental psychology both address the development of object representation, but they assign different importance to the affective and cognitive dimensions in the development of the concept of the object. As Wolff (1960) pointed out, Piaget assumed an equal intensity for all actions regardless of the state of the organism, whereas psychoanalytic theorists assumed a hierarchy of motivations, often based on an epigenetic series

This chapter incorporates material from (a) "Levels of Object Representation in Anaclitic and Introjective Depression," by S. J. Blatt, 1974, *Psychoanalytic Study of the Child*, 29, pp. 107–157. Copyright 1974 by Yale University Press. Reprinted with permission; (b) *The Assessment of Qualitative and Structural Dimensions of Object Representations* (unpublished research manual, rev. ed.), by S. J. Blatt, E. S. Chevron, D. M. Quinlan, C. E. Schaffer, and S. Wein, 1988, Yale University; (c) *Self–Other Differentiation of Object Representations* (unpublished research manual), by D. Diamond, S. J. Blatt, D. Stayner, and N. Kaslow, 1991, Yale University; and (d) "Parent–Child Interaction in the Etiology of Dependent and Self-Critical Depression," by S. J. Blatt and E. Homann, 1992, *Clinical Psychology Review*, 12, pp. 47–91. Copyright 1992 by Elsevier. Adapted by permission.

of developmental levels (E. H. Erikson, 1950; Kestenberg, 1971), that are assumed to determine some of the categories of experience in which the development of representations occurs. Cognitive developmental psychologists, such as Piaget and Werner, have studied how the child develops cognitive schemas of primarily inanimate objects (e.g., a toy) under essentially neutral circumstances. Psychoanalytic developmental theorists and attachment investigators, in contrast, have studied the very same developmental process, but have primarily focused on how the child develops cognitive–affective schemas of the interpersonal world (concepts of self and others) in states of disequilibrium (e.g., during separation or moments of unrest), especially in caring relationships. Despite basic differences in methodology, these various approaches to the study of the development of cognitive–affective schemas describe essentially the same developmental sequence, but they differ to some degree in the specification of the time at which a particular cognitive–affective schema may first appear. Cognitive developmental theorists usually specify that a particular schema occurs somewhat later than do developmental psychoanalysts. These differences, however, are consistent with the findings (e.g., S. Bell, 1970; Ostrom, 1984) that cognitive–affective structures emerge initially in the intensity of caring interpersonal relationships and are subsequently extended as generalized schemas that the child uses to understand the inanimate world. Cognitive–affective schemas emerge first and foremost in the caring relationship and are then stabilized as generalized cognitive structures. Because these various developmental investigators and theorists describe essentially the same developmental sequence for the emergence of cognitive–affective schemas, their findings can be integrated into a consistent theoretical model that can provide considerable understanding of the development of the representational world.

Cognitive–affective schemas are established in interpersonal interactions throughout the life cycle, beginning with the infant's earliest experiences in the caring relationship with the mother. These cognitive–affective schemas are established as the child matures and experiences various developmental demands. When these perturbations are age appropriate and not severe, the child is able to alter existing cognitive schemas to accommodate the experienced perturbations, thereby leading to the development of more comprehensive and mature levels of cognitive schemas. This process usually unfolds in a natural, well-defined developmental sequence. With development, object representations become increasingly differentiated, integrated, and accurate; they proceed from amorphous, global representations, to a somewhat differentiated emphasis on part properties and functions, to representations that are highly articulated and integrated. Representations range from perceptual images of objects immediately present in the perceptual field to symbolic evocation of absent realities. Developmentally earlier forms of representation are based primarily on action sequences associated with need gratification, intermediate representations are based on specific perceptual and functional features, and later forms of object representation are more symbolic and conceptual (Blatt, 1974).

Progress in the development of object representations—the achievement of more accurate, stable, differentiated, integrated, and symbolic representations—is the result of complex developmental sequences. A new level of representation evolves from the interactions between the individual's prior developmental achievements and the patterns of the environmental responses to the child's emerging needs, capacities, and strivings during each specific developmental phase. Representations emerge initially within the mother–child relationship, in the repeated experiences of frustration and gratification with a consistent and need-gratifying object. Later stages of representation emerge out of increasingly differentiated parent–child interactions. The nature of the object relations determines the level of representations, and the establishment of more differentiated and stable representations provides a new organization for interpersonal experiences. Object relations and the development of representations are in constant interaction. Representations emerge out of the affective relationship between caregiver and child and, in turn, organize the future experiences of that relationship, leading to the next stage of representation. The level of representations indicates the level of development, such as the level of differentiation that has been achieved and the quality of the relationship with the object (H. Hartmann, Kris, & Lowenstein, 1949).

Many psychoanalytic investigators have discussed the relationship of libidinal (affective) object constancy and cognitive object constancy as defined by developmental psychologists. The development of libidinal (emotional) constancy and object representations are inextricably intertwined. As described by Anna Freud (1946), libidinal attachment shifts from the pleasurable experience, to the part property of the object providing the satisfaction, such as the breast or bottle, and eventually to the whole object itself. Emotional attachment motivates the articulation of the object, but there must be some representation (recognition) of the object to develop libidinal (emotional) attachment. Stages of representation both emerge from and facilitate the development of libidinal constancy. Thus, the emotional relationship and the levels of representation continually cause and affect one another. Without some representation of the object, there can be little emotional investment, and without emotional investment there is likely to be little progress in the development of representation. The two processes develop simultaneously in a complex transaction.

During a prerepresentational, pre-objectal stage in development, the infant initially cannot differentiate the person providing the satisfaction from the pleasurable sensations. The need-satisfying person is part of a diffuse, global, affective, sensory, physiological experience. Slowly, the infant begins to perceive that need gratification comes from a particular source, and the child's investment shifts from the satisfying experience to the need-satisfying object—from the experience of being fed to the discerned source of the pleasure (A. Freud, 1946). This is the first level of representation, a level of *sensorimotor representation*, in which the object is appreciated primarily for its need-gratifying function. The representation is relatively undifferentiated and focused primarily, if not exclusively, on the gratification being provided. Although the infant has a beginning awareness of the object, the object is still not fully separated from the experience and the event. Thus, at this level the other is experienced in terms of his or her activities; the representation is an extrapolation of the object's action pattern (Piaget, 1937/1954). The person is recognized and valued only in the specific and limited context of need gratification; he or she has little meaning or existence beyond providing comfort and alleviating pain. Behavioral indications that the infant has achieved this level of representation are the infant's recognition of the object and the infant's later capacity to search for the object, first after visible, and later after invisible, displacement.

With repeated experiences of the object disappearing and reappearing, particularly at moments of considerable discomfort, representations become more articulated and differentiated. As the need-gratifying object is encountered in a variety of contexts, it is articulated as separate from the specific experience of pleasure–pain, and the child is able to recognize the person despite variations in the surrounding situation. This stage can be characterized as *perceptual object representation*. The child has formed some conception of the person and has developed the capacity to recognize the person independent of that person's action or of the specific context. The person is recognized as an entity in its own right with a variety of features, functions, and actions, and a constant bond is maintained with the person independent of experiences of frustration–gratification. Representation is indicated by the fact that the child recognizes the person in a variety of contexts and has differentiated the person from others. This representation initially is a concrete, literal, fixed, perceptual totality, without differentiated qualities. Although the child is capable of perceptual recognition of the object, he or she still lacks the capacity to evoke a representation of the person in that person's absence. Thus, the child can be confused by extremely contradictory experiences, yet the child has consolidated his perception of the object and, as Cobliner (1965) discussed, has developed a permanent memory of the object "founded on the consolidation, on the constancy, of its corresponding percept" (p. 347).

With experience, objects become more articulated, and separate part properties and functions are differentiated within the framework of the whole object. The child begins to use these part properties as signs and symbols for the object. First, the child uses concrete signs and later uses symbols, such as a name, to represent the object. These symbols increase in their level of abstraction and begin to shift from being primarily depictive to assuming a truly representational function (Piaget, 1945/1962). For example, imitation is first based on manifest perceptual aspects of the object, such as mannerisms and gestures; later, imitation becomes increasingly symbolic and internal. Thus, the capacity for evocative memory develops initially in pictorial form; then later, in signs; and finally in more symbolic modalities.

This phase of *iconic object representation* is a transitional stage leading to conceptual representation in which the representation of the object is complex, integrated, and abstract. Iconic representations are partially symbolic and conceptual, although initially the representation is based on a concrete sign rather than an abstract symbolization of the object. Representations are based on a part property or attribute that signifies the object. The qualities and attributes are based on relatively specific, concrete, manifest part properties, functions, and interests of the object. These representations begin to reflect an appreciation of more subtle properties of the object to some degree, but initially they are primarily linked to specific manifest features or functions; are limited in scope and range; and involve vivid part properties or qualities, such as hostile and aggressive or overidealized and idyllic features. Thus, iconic representations initially are primarily denotative, depictive, concrete, fragmented, and overstated and can contain considerable contradiction and ambivalence. Subsequent iconic representations become increasingly based on more functional and symbolic features of the object (Piaget, 1945/1962).

With development, the apparent contradictions between part properties and features, as well as different experiences with the object, are resolved. The separate properties or qualities are integrated in a representation of the whole object, and this integrated representation becomes increasingly diverse, integrated, conceptual, and abstract.

At this most advanced level, *conceptual representations* integrate inner form and structure with the more manifest aspects of the object. This integration may require a resolution of apparent contradictory features of the object. The object is represented as a fully independent entity with specific and enduring characteristics, functions, values, and feelings, only some of which are relevant in any immediate situation or relationship. Object representations at this level have greater stability and continuity; contact with the actual object is no longer needed to maintain this representation. Evocative memory of objects and events is now based on images, signs, thoughts, and symbols. Eventually the individual is capable of anticipatory representations of things not previously directly perceived or experienced.

The development of conceptual or symbolic representations is achieved in the later stages of the separation–individuation process with the final resolution of the Oedipal crisis in adolescence and the relinquishing of infantile and Oedipal objects. With this achievement the child is now capable of empathy and of taking the perspective of others (Feffer, 1970). This full development of object representation is part of the development of formal operations (E. Jacobson, 1964b; Piaget, 1945/1962; Werner & Kaplan, 1983).

Thus, object representation develops epigenetically through successive developmental stages, including sensorimotor, perceptual, external and internal iconic, and conceptual levels. Later stages of representation are based on an integration and extension of earlier stages; thus, at the highest level of development, the earlier as well as the more complex levels of representation are available (Piaget, 1937/1954, 1945/1962). Aspects from earlier levels can vivify and enrich the total representation by adding affective dimensions. When developmental demands are severe, persistent, and overwhelm the child's capacities to accommodate, however, the development of these cognitive–affective schemas may be compromised (Blatt, 1991, 1995b). Various forms of psychopathology in adults are determined, in large part, by differential impairments of the schemas of the representational world that occur as a consequence of serious disruptions of the relationship between child and caregivers (Blatt, 1991, 1995b).

Mental representations of constructive caring relationships facilitate psychological development because they enable individuals to maintain a level of integration even when the usual sources of constructive environmental and interpersonal support are unavailable. Illusions and transient hallucinations of significant figures, for example, occur as part of constructive grieving (Rees, 1975) and in dealing with sensory deprivation (Heron, 1961). Throughout life, representations allow individuals to experience separations without the profound disruptions that are frequently associated with early separation, sensory deprivation, or loss. The extent to which one has access to complex, multidimensional, symbolic representations of significant caring relationships in the absence of the caregiver is also related to the capacity for affect regulation. The developmental level of object representations of relationships with significant others is an integral aspect of a mature and effective sense of self. Impairments in the capacity for object representation are associated with an intense need for close contact with others, dysregulation of affect, and an impaired sense of self (Schaffer & Blatt, 1990).

The articulation of phases in the development of object representation enables us to evaluate more fully differences in the impairment of mental representation in the two types of depression. As discussed in chapter 1, impairment in object representation appears to be an important issue in the vulnerability to depression. The level of mental representation in patients with depression is insufficient for these individuals to feel a sense of contact with the object in its absence (Blatt, 1974). The two types of depression, anaclitic and introjective, however, appear to have different types of impairment of object representations. In anaclitic depression, in which themes of helplessness and dependency predominate, object representations are primarily at a sensorimotor–preoperational level and are concerned with action sequences and the maintenance of direct, physical, sensory, need-gratifying contact with the object. Because of the insufficiency of representation, object loss is often denied by seeking an immediate replacement for the need-gratifying object. In introjective depression, in contrast, themes of self-criticism, guilt, and a sense of failure predominate. Representations of significant others are primarily at a perceptual level and iconic level; they are fragmented, isolated, static, and ambivalent. The danger is not fear of loss of the object and the need gratification the object can provide but rather an "apprehension about the loss of the object's love, acceptance and approval" (Blatt, 1974, p. 149). Excessive striving for achievement and perfection is an attempt to win love and approval; constant self-criticism and guilt are ways of maintaining contact with overstated part properties of the object expressed in fragmented, static, iconic representations. With normal development, these separate and isolated concrete perceptual images and the contradictory and fragmented part properties of iconic representations become integrated into more consolidated object representations in which ambivalence toward the object is resolved. Object loss can then be experienced without prolonged and severe depression. However, object representations at the lower developmental levels (sensorimotor–preoperational, perceptual, and external iconic) leave the person vulnerable to object loss and feelings of depression that are organized around either intense feelings of loss and loneliness or profound feelings of self-criticism and guilt (Blatt, 1974).

Object representations in patients with depression are often insubstantial; unreliable; and at a low conceptual level, focused on need gratification or manifest part features and on painful interactions. Thus, on the basis of clinical observations and theoretical considerations, it appears that anaclitic and introjective depression can be distinguished by differences in the quality of object representation. Representations in an anaclitic depression are based much more on direct sensorimotor experiences associated with need satisfaction. Because of this impaired level of representation in anaclitic depression, the patient needs to maintain direct physical contact with the need-gratifying objects. Introjective depression evolves at a higher developmental level with greater object–subject differentiation and a more complex affect structure that includes the capacity to experience guilt and to consider possible ways of atonement and reparation. Object representations in introjective depression are somewhat more developed than in anaclitic depression, because they are based on concrete perceptual characteristics and specific part properties or functions of the object. Thus, a fuller understanding of the development of object representations, as articulated in an integration of psychoanalytic theory and cognitive developmental psychology, extends our understanding of the processes of object representation and their impairment in psychopathology, particularly in the complex phenomenon of depression. As I discuss in more detail in chapter 8, progress in the treatment of depression involves the patient's resolution of intensely ambivalent feelings about the neglectful and depriving or harshly judgmental and critical aspects of the parents. Psychotherapy with patients who are depressed involves working through the intensely ambivalent feelings about these relationships, with the result that the mental representations of the parent evolve to a higher level of organization and the patient becomes increasingly less vulnerable to intense dysphoric affect.

To summarize, both anaclitic and introjective depression involve a particular impairment in the development of representation that creates particular vulnerabilities to loss and depression. Anaclitic depression is characterized primarily by sensorimotor–preoperational representations of caregiving figures; individuals with anaclitic depression need direct, immediate, physical, and need-gratifying contact with caregivers. The caregiver is not appreciated as a separate and independent entity; rather, representations center primarily on the gratification the person has provided. This sensorimotor level of representation is consistent with the observation that individuals with anaclitic depression are vulnerable to experiences of separation, abandonment, and loss (Blatt, 1974). Object representation in anaclitic depression is basically organized around sensorimotor action—around what people can do for, or to, you. Reality for these individuals is apprehended and understood primarily in action terms. The structure of thought is basically sensorimotor. In contrast, the structure of representations in introjective depression is basically organized around preoperational and iconic modes of representation. Part functions and properties (e.g., approval–disapproval, success–failure, good–bad) represent the person. The structure of thought is basically at an external iconic level at which a manifest part property or feature, in a one-sided and sometimes a distorted way, stands for the entire person. The multiple part properties are not integrated into a more conceptual mode of thought in which relationships between part properties are integrated and defined in a variety of different ways while still maintaining the basic definition and continuity of the object (Blatt, 1974). To evaluate these formulations, my colleagues and I have developed methods for assessing the structural or organizational qualities and the thematic content of mental representations.

Assessment of Object Relations and Representations

The emphasis on mental representation has had a major impact on personality assessment (Blatt, 1990b, 1999c; Leichtman, 1996a, 1996b). The recognition of the centrality of mental representation in personality organization and psychopathology, for example, has led to the development of new approaches for evaluating responses to projective techniques, such as the Rorschach (1921) and the Thematic Apperception Test (Morgan & Murray, 1938), as well as reports of early memories and dreams (e.g., Blatt, 1990b; Blatt & Auerbach, 1988; Blatt, Brenneis, Schimek, & Glick, 1976; Blatt & Lerner, 1983b; Blatt & Ritzler, 1974; Cramer, 1991; Cramer & Blatt, 1990; Cramer, Blatt, & Ford, 1988; Krohn & Mayman, 1974; Mayman, 1967; E. R. Ryan & Bell, 1984; Urist, 1977; Westen, Lohr, Silk, Gold, & Kerber, 1990). Assessment with projective methods, however, is often labor intensive in terms of gathering the data and in transforming the responses into quantitative variables. As an alternative to assessing mental representations through traditional projective techniques, several methods have been developed to assess aspects of the representations of significant caregivers, including the Object Relations Inventory (ORI), in which individuals give spontaneous descriptions of their parents (e.g., Blatt, Wein, Chevron, & Quinlan, 1979), and the Parental Bonding Instrument (PBI; G. Parker, Tupling, & Brown, 1979), a rating scale that assesses the dimensions of parental caring and overprotection. Blatt, Quinlan, and Chevron (1990) found good convergent and discriminant validity between the ORI and PBI as methods for assessing respondents' reports of their parents' behavior. In addition, each of these measures had significant correlations with aspects of the semantic differential (Osgood, Suci, & Tannenbaum, 1957), another systematic method of assessing cognitive–affective schemas of self and others. Thus, the ORI and PBI appear to provide reliable methods for obtaining retrospective accounts of caring experiences that have contributed to evaluating more fully parent–child interactions and the individual's capacity to develop coherent internal working models or representations of significant others that are particularly relevant to understanding aspects of depression.

Parental Bonding Instrument

The Parental Bonding Instrument (PBI), a 25-item questionnaire with 4-point Likert scales developed by G. Parker et al. (1979), assesses two basic dimensions of parent–child interaction: (a) caring/rejection and (b) overprotection. The caring/rejection items evaluate the expression of "affection, emotional warmth, empathy, and closeness" as contrasted with themes of rejection such as "emotional coldness, indifference and neglect" (e.g., "Spoke to me with a warm and friendly voice" vs. "Did not help me as much as I needed"). The dimension of protection evaluates themes such as "control, overprotection, intrusion, excessive contact, infantilization and prevention of independent behavior. . .[in contrast to] allowance of independence and autonomy" (e.g., "Liked me to make my own decisions" vs. "Did not want me to grow up"; G. Parker et al., 1979, p. 10). The PBI asks individuals to rate their experiences of both their mother and father during their first sixteen years. Alternate form and test–retest reliabilities are at acceptable levels, and scores on the questionnaire are consistent with judges' ratings of these dimensions as assessed in personal interviews with the respondents. Respondents' reports of their parents' behaviors of caring and overprotection are relatively independent of age, sex, and social class (G. Parker, 1981).

G. Parker et al. (1979, p. 7) identified five possible types of parent–child relationships: (a) *average* (defined statistically), (b) *optimal bonding* (high care–low overprotection), (c) *weak bonding* (low care–low overprotection), (d) *affectionate constraint* (high care–high overprotection), and (e) *affectionless control* (low care–high overprotection). Affectionless controlling parents are emotionally cold, indifferent, and neglectful (G. Parker et al., 1979) as well as overprotective, controlling, and intrusive; they seem to impede the child's development of independence and autonomy. Both the lack of caring and the tendency to overprotect and control each seem related to depression, but the combination of these two dimensions seems to be a particularly strong determinant of depression in adults (G. Parker, 1981, 1983, 1984; G. Parker & Hadzi-Pavlovic, 1984).

The validity of the PBI is suggested by the correlation between adults' ratings of their mothers and the mothers' ratings of themselves on the PBI. Although mothers rated themselves as more caring and less overprotective than their children did, the correlations between mother's self-description and child's description of mother were highly significant. Maternal care and overprotection scores, whether rated by the mothers themselves or by their children, correlated significantly with depression scores of their adult children. Biological or temperamental predispositions do not seem to be primary factors in depression, because both depression and PBI scores were independent of maternal ratings of children's childhood dependency (reports of childhood shyness and timidity).

G. Parker (1979a, 1979b) found that reports of both parental lack of caring and overprotection correlated with dependency as measured by 12 selected items from Factor I of the Depressive Experiences Questionnaire (DEQ; Blatt, D'Afflitti, et al., 1976). Reports of paternal overprotection and maternal lack of caring also correlated positively with hypochondriasis (G. Parker & Lipscombe, 1980), supporting the relationship of anaclitic depression to somatic concerns (Blatt, D'Afflitti, et al., 1976). G. Parker's findings (1979a, 1979b) indicate that depression derives from neglect and deprivation as well as from controlling and restricting overprotection that provokes feelings of anger, hopelessness, and self-criticism and thwarts experiences of autonomy (introjective depression), as well as from the anxiety it produces in making the child feel vulnerable and afraid when alone, as in anaclitic depression (see also Luthar & Blatt, 1993). The combination of low caring and high overprotection (affectionless control) was predictive of the level of depression in a sample with clinical depression, whereas low maternal caring alone was predictive of level of depression in nonclinical samples. G. Parker (1982) found that female patients with depression tended to report affectionless control in their mothers, whereas male patients tended to report affectionless control in their fathers. Parker (1982) concluded that the relative risk for depression is elevated if the patients rate one or both of their parents in ways that would place them in the group designated as expressing affectionless control. Frank, Poorman, Van Egeren, and Field (1997) found that adolescents who struggled to achieve separation from what they perceived as controlling parents were more likely to be preoccupied with issues of self-criticism, whereas adolescents who experienced fears and anxieties about separation were more likely to be preoccupied with interpersonal concerns.

Perris et al. (1986) similarly found that 64% of individuals diagnosed with unipolar depression described their fathers, and 76% described their mothers, as expressing low "emotional warmth" and high "overprotection." Gotlib, Mount, Cordy, and Whiffen (1988) found that women with postpartum depression, whose depression remitted over 2 to 4 years, reported higher parental care on the PBI than did patients whose depression did not remit. The remitted group had parental caring scores equivalent to a control group without depression. The parental overprotection scores of both the remitted and the nonremitted groups with depression, however, were significantly higher than those of control participants.

Current levels of caring seem to compensate to some degree for the effects of low parental care (G. Parker & Hadzi-Pavlovic, 1984). Women reporting low parental care but high marital affection were less depressed than those reporting high parental care and low marital affection and only slightly more depressed than those reporting high care from both sources. These findings are consistent with other studies that indicate that current uncaring family environments contribute to depression (A. G. Billings & Moos, 1982a; Garrison, 1982; Wetzel & Redmond, 1980). G. Parker and Hadzi-Pavlovic (1984) concluded that close affectional ties in adult life may modify the effects of parental deprivation. The capacity to establish meaningful interpersonal relationships, however, may be an expression of diminished depression as well as an indication of a reduced vulnerability to depression.

Object Relations Inventory

My colleagues and I (Blatt, Wein, et al., 1979) developed procedures for assessing the content and structure of representations of self and significant others, including parents, by asking individuals to describe themselves and/or each of their parents. This procedure, the Object Relations Inventory (ORI), provides a method for assessing the quality of object representation and its role in depression. It has been used with a wide range of participants, in both clinical and nonclinical samples, to assess aspects of the representation of self and significant others, including one's parents, therapist, spouse, and so on.

Using the concepts from cognitive–developmental and psychoanalytic theories about the development of representation discussed earlier, we developed three methods for evaluating aspects of these open-ended descriptions of self and significant others: (a) level of cognitive organization, or *conceptual level* (CL; Blatt, Wein, et al., 1979); (b) qualitative or thematic dimensions in descriptions of significant others (Blatt, Chevron, Quinlan, Schaffer, & Wein, 1988); and (c) level of *differentiation–relatedness* (Diamond, Blatt, Stayner, & Kaslow, 1991).

Exhibit 4.1 Conceptual Level of Self and Other Descriptions

Level and scale point	Description
Sensorimotor–preoperational: Scale point 1	People are described primarily in terms of the gratification or frustration they provide. There is little sense that others exist as entities separate and independent of their direct effect on the individual's pleasure or pain.
Concrete–perceptual: Scale point 3	People are described primarily in concrete, literal terms, usually on the basis of physical attributes and features. Emphasis is placed on external physical characteristics and appearance.
Iconic: Scale point 5	*External iconic*: People are described primarily in terms of manifest activities or functions.
Scale point 7	*Internal iconic*: People are described primarily in terms of their thoughts, feelings, and values, rather than their physical characteristics or activities. The description primarily involves psychological dimensions.
Conceptual level: Scale point 9	With a range of levels, the description integrates external appearances and activities (behavior) with internal dimensions (feelings, thoughts, and values). Apparent contradictions are resolved in an integrated, complex, coherent synthesis.

Structural Dimensions of Object Representations

STRUCTURAL DIMENSIONS: CONCEPTUAL LEVEL (CL). As discussed earlier, an integration of psychoanalytic theory and cognitive developmental psychology facilitated the identification of different levels in the cognitive development of object representations. On the basis of these theoretical formulations on the development of mental representation, a procedure was developed for assessing five levels in the developmental cognitive levels of the representation of significant others. The CL of descriptions of self and significant other can be rated on a nine-point ordinal continuum that includes sensorimotor, concrete–perceptual, external– and internal–iconic, and, finally, formal levels of representation. Definitions of each of these points are presented in Exhibit 4.1. This scale has been used extensively in prior research, and reports indicate that reliability and validity of this scoring procedure (e.g., Blatt, Wein, et al., 1979; Blatt, Chevron, et al., 1988; Bornstein & O'Neill, 1992) are at acceptable levels.

Sensorimotor–preoperational level. The person is described primarily by his or her activity in reference to the gratification or frustration he or she provides. The emphasis is on the person as an agent who causes the subject either pleasure or pain, making the subject feel good or bad. The description has a personal, subjective focus, and the person is defined primarily in terms of his or her direct effectance of pleasure and pain for the subject. There is little sense that the person is experienced or defined as a separate and independent entity. The description centers on the direct value the person has for the subject.

Concrete–perceptual level. The person is described as a separate entity, but the description is primarily concrete and literal, often characterized in terms of physical attributes. The description is literal, global, and concrete, and the emphasis is often on the person's external characteristics or physical properties.

External–iconic level. The focus is on part properties of the person in terms of his or her manifest activities, but the activities and functions (in contrast to the sensorimotor–preoperational level) are uniquely the person's and have little or no direct and explicit reference to the gratification or frustration of the subject. The activities are not directly need-gratifying for the subject; rather, the person is experienced as a separate entity in terms of his or her functional activities and attributes.

Internal–iconic level. The person is described in terms of his or her attributes and part properties, not in terms of what he or she does but rather what he or she thinks, feels, values, and so on. The description is directed more toward internal dimensions. Behavioral descriptions (e.g., "happy," "playful," "gregarious") are between external and internal iconic, with internal iconic being reserved for descriptions that convey the internal state of the person in such a way that the reader can empathize with the person's experience of reality.

At both the external– and internal–iconic levels, descriptions do not convey a complexity of actions, feelings, or values, or a development over time, or any integration of apparent contradictions. It is also important to note that iconic traits used to describe the object may have an implicit reference to the subject, particularly in descriptions given by children and adolescents, but these iconic traits give the reader a distinct sense of the person being described as separate and unique from the subject.

Conceptual level (CL). The person is described in a way that integrates all of the prior levels; the description indicates that the person is understood and experienced on a wide range of levels. The description contains an appreciation of internal dimensions of the individual in his or her own right as well as in contrast to external dimensions. Also, the presence of a timeline in the description indicates an appreciation of change and variation. A variety of dimensions are integrated in the description in ways that resolve apparent contradictions. Thus, the description may be disjunctive in that manifest, literal, and concrete features appear to contradict more internal dimensions, but the apparent contradiction is resolved in an integrated, complex synthesis. At this level, comments about the need-gratifying attributes, or physical and functional characteristics of the person can be part of a cohesive and integrated description.

Research indicates acceptable levels of interrater reliability in scoring CL on the ORI (Blatt, Wein, et al., 1979; Blatt, Chevron, et al., 1988; Bornstein & O'Neill, 1992). Blatt, Wein, et al. (1979), for example, reported that the corrected reliability correlation for the ratings of two judges of the CL of mental representation in 20 descriptions given by individuals of their parents was .78. No significant differences were found between the CL in males and females (M = 4.80, SD = 1.61 and M = 4.91, SD = 1.25, respectively) and for the descriptions of mothers and fathers (M = 4.83, SD = 1.56 and M = 4.87, SD = 1.62, respectively); neither was the Sex × Parent interaction significant. Extensive research with the ORI, more recently led us to develop another scoring procedure for assessing other structural aspects of the descriptions of self and significant others on the ORI—what we have come to call the Differentiation–Relatedness Scale (D-R).

STRUCTURAL DIMENSIONS: DIFFERENTIATION–RELATEDNESS SCALE, D-R. Drawing from theoretical formulations and clinical observations about early processes of boundary articulation (Blatt & Wild, 1976; Blatt, Wild, & Ritzler, 1975; E. Jacobson, 1964b; Kernberg, 1975, 1976), processes of separation–individuation (Coonerty, 1986; Mahler, Pine, & Bergman, 1975), the formation of the sense of self (Stern, 1985), and the development of increasingly mature levels of interpersonal relatedness and self-definition (Blatt & Blass, 1990, 1996; Blatt & Shichman, 1983), one can identify two fundamental dimensions of self- and object representation: (a) the differentiation of self from other, leading to a differentiated and integrated sense of self, and (b) the establishment of increasingly mature levels of interpersonal relatedness. To assess the level of differentiation and relatedness in descriptions of self and significant others, we (Diamond, Blatt, Stayner, & Kaslow, 1991) developed a 10-point scale on which to rate the following points: a lack of basic differentiation between self and other (Levels 1 and 2); use of mirroring (Level 3); self–other idealization or denigration (Level 4); oscillation between polarized negative and positive attributes (Level 5) as maneuvers to consolidate and stabilize representations; an emergent differentiated, constant, and integrated representation of self and other with increasing tolerance for ambiguity (Levels 6 and 7); representations of self and others as empathically interrelated (Level 8); representations of self and other in reciprocal and mutually facilitative interactions (Level 9); and reflectively constructed integrated representations of self and others in reciprocal and mutual relationships (Level 10). In general, higher ratings of differentiation–relatedness in descriptions of self and other reflect an increased articulation and stabilization of interpersonal schemas and an increased appreciation of mutual and empathetically attuned relatedness (Diamond et al., 1991).

The D-R, summarized in Exhibit 4.2, is based on the assumption that psychological development moves toward the emergence of (a) a consolidated, integrated, and individuated sense of self-definition and (b) empathically attuned, mutual relatedness with significant others (Aron, 1996; J. Benjamin, 1995; Blatt, 1991; Blatt & Blass, 1990, 1996; Jordan, 1986; J. B. Miller, 1984; Mitchell, 1988; Stern, 1985; Surrey, 1985). Differentiation and relatedness are interactive dimensions (Blatt & Blass, 1990, 1996; Blatt & Shichman, 1983;

Exhibit 4.2 Differentiation–Relatedness of Self and Object Descriptions

Level and scale point	Description
1. Self–other boundary compromise	Basic sense of physical cohesion or integrity of representations is lacking or is breached.
2. Self–other boundary confusion	Self and other are represented as physically intact and separate, but feelings and thoughts are amorphous, undifferentiated, or confused. Description may consist of a single global impressionistic quality or a flood of details with a sense of confusion and vagueness.
3. Self–other mirroring	Characteristics of self and other, such as physical appearance or body qualities, shape, or size, are virtually identical.
4. Self–other idealization	Individual attempts to consolidate representations based on unitary, unmodulated idealization or denigration. Extreme, exaggerated, one-sided descriptions.
5. Semidifferentiated, tenuous consolidation of representations through splitting (polarization) and/or by an emphasis on concrete part properties	Marked oscillation between dramatically opposite qualities or an emphasis on manifest external features.
6. Emergent, ambivalent constancy (cohesion) of self and an emergent sense of relatedness	Emerging consolidation of disparate aspects of self and other in a somewhat hesitant, equivocal, or ambivalent integration. A list of appropriate conventional characteristics but which lack a sense of uniqueness. Tentative movement toward a more individuated and cohesive sense of self and other.
7. Consolidated, constant (stable) self and other in unilateral relationships	Thoughts, feelings, needs, and fantasies are differentiated and modulated. Increasing tolerance for and integration of disparate aspects. Distinguishing qualities and characteristics. Sympathetic understanding of others.
8. Cohesive, individuated, empathically related self and others	Cohesive, nuanced, and related sense of self and others. A definite sense of identity and an interest in interpersonal relationships and a capacity to understand the perspective of others.
9. Reciprocally related integrated unfolding self and others	Cohesive sense of self and others in reciprocal relationships that transform both the self and the other in complex, continually unfolding ways.
10. Creative, integrated constructions of self and other in empathic, reciprocally attuned relationships	Integrated reciprocal relations with an appreciation that one contributes to the construction of meaning in complex interpersonal relationships.

Sander, 1984) that unfold throughout development (see also Kegan, 1982; Mitchell, 1988; Ogden, 1986). The dialectical interaction between these two developmental dimensions facilitates the emergence and consolidation of increasingly mature levels of both self-organization and intersubjectively attuned, empathic relatedness (Blatt & Blass, 1990, 1996; Blatt & Shichman, 1983). The scale assumes that, with psychological development, representations of self and other become increasingly differentiated and integrated and begin to express an increased appreciation of mutual relatedness.

As regards the dimension of differentiation, the D-R reflects, at the lowest levels, a compromise of boundaries with regard to basic body awareness, emotions, and thoughts. Subsequent scale levels reflect a unitary, unmodulated view of self and of the other as extensions of each other or as mirrored images (i.e., images in which aspects of self and other are identical). At an intermediate level, representations are organized around a unitary idealization or denigration of self or other (i.e., around an exaggerated sense of the goodness or badness of the figure described). At the next level, these exaggerated aspects of self and other alternate in a juxtaposition of polarized (i.e., all-good or all-bad) extremes. Later scale levels reflect both an increasing capacity to integrate disparate aspects of the self and other and an increased tolerance for ambivalence and ambiguity (Kernberg, 1977).

As regards the dimension of relatedness, the scale also reflects a trend toward empathically attuned mutuality in complex interpersonal relationships. At lower levels, the sense of relatedness in representations may involve being controlled by the other (e.g., trying to resist the onslaught of an other who is experienced as bad and destructive). At increasingly higher levels, relatedness may be expressed primarily in parallel interactions, in expressions of cooperation and mutuality, in understanding the other's perspective, or in expressions of empathically attuned reciprocity (Blatt & Blass, 1990, 1996). At the highest levels, descriptions reflect an awareness that one's participation in complex relational matrixes determine one's perceptions, attributions, and the construction of meaning.

These 10 levels of differentiation–relatedness were established on the basis of clinical and developmental findings and reflect what are generally regarded as clinically significant distinctions in the transition from grossly pathological to intact and even healthy object relations. The scale points are thus best regarded as discrete categories, not points on a continuum. In other words, the underlying logic of this measure is ordinal, not interval or nominal. Therefore, the various levels of this scale may not be equidistant from each other, and the specific number of scale points is to some extent arbitrary; that is, new levels of differentiation–relatedness can be added in light of new clinical observations, theoretical formulations, and research findings. Nevertheless, a clear implication of this scale is that higher differentiation–relatedness ratings reflect a greater degree of psychological health. In theory, differentiation–relatedness at Levels 8, 9, and 10 are indicative of mental health, and differentiation–relatedness at Level 7 (consolidation of object constancy) is regarded as a prerequisite for normal psychological and interpersonal functioning.

Interrater and retest reliability of this scoring procedure is at acceptable levels (Stayner, 1994), and early reports support the validity of the DR as a measure of differentiation–relatedness (e.g., Blatt, Auerbach, & Aryan, 1998; Blatt, Stayner, Auerbach, & Behrends, 1996; Diamond et al., 1991; Diamond, Kaslow, Coonerty, & Blatt, 1990).

QUALITATIVE–THEMATIC DIMENSIONS OF OBJECT REPRESENTATIONS. The descriptions of significant others can also be rated on a series of 7-point scales designed to assess each of 12 qualities that could be attributed to the person being described. These qualities are affectionate, ambitious, malevolent–benevolent, cold–warm, constructively involved, intellectual, judgmental, negative–positive, nurturant, punitive, successful, and strong–weak. In addition, the degree of ambivalence expressed in the description of the parent can be rated on a five-point scale. My colleagues and I (Blatt, Wein, et al., 1979) found that the ratings of the descriptions for each of the personal attributes of parents can be done at acceptable levels of interrater reliability (range: .69–.95, with an average corrected reliability coefficient of .84).

A principal-components factor analysis with varimax rotations identified three primary factors among the 13 qualitative features (plus an estimate of the length of the description) indicating an inherent organization to the ratings. Factor I, labeled *Nurturance*, accounted for 40% of the variance and included the following personal attributes (factor loadings are in parentheses): nurturance (.90), positive ideal (.90), benevolent (.88), warmth (.87), positive family involvement (.84), affectionate (.80), strong (.66), and successful (.65). Factor II, labeled *Striving*, accounted for 29% of the variance and included the following personal attributes: evaluative (.90), ambitious (.89), punitive (.88), intelligent (.82), ambivalent (.60), successful (.48), and strong (.48). Factor III, labeled *Verbal Fluency*, accounted for 8% of the variance and included only the number of words (.95; Blatt, Wein, et al., 1979).

The relationship between the nature of object representations and depression was initially studied in 83 female and 38 male undergraduates at a private university and at a local state teachers college (Blatt, Wein, et al., 1979). The participants were group-administered a "family interaction questionnaire" and instructed to "Describe your mother" and "Describe your father." Five minutes were allowed for each description. They were also given a version of the semantic differential (Osgood et al., 1957) for "my mother," "my father," "myself as I am" (real self), and "myself as I would like to be" (ideal self) in which they made ratings on 17 bipolar adjective scales of Osgood et al.'s (1957) three basic factors: Evaluation, Potency, and Activity.

The various scores of the descriptions of mother and father (the Nurturance and Striving factors and the number of words) correlated significantly with ratings made of each parent using the semantic differential. Particularly impressive were the correlations between the Nurturance scale of the descriptions of mother and of father and the ratings of the parents on all three dimensions of the semantic differential. The Nurturance scale had highly significant ($p \leq .001$) positive correlations with evaluation, potency, and activity on the semantic differential. The Striving scale of the description of father also correlated significantly ($p \leq .05$) with potency and activity ratings of the father on the semantic differential. No significant findings were obtained with the number of words in the parental descriptions and the dimensions of the semantic differential (Blatt, Wein, et al., 1979).

The ratings of the parental description (Nurturance, Striving, and number of words) also correlated significantly with several measures of depression—the three factors of the DEQ (Blatt, D'Afflitti, et al., 1976), the Zung Depression Scale (ZDS; Zung, 1972), and the discrepancy between real and ideal self on the evaluative dimension of the semantic differential. It was primarily the Nurturance scale of the parental descriptions that correlated significantly with measures of depression. Descriptions of both mother and father as nurturant were significantly correlated with a positive self-description on the semantic differential and with lower scores of depression as measured on the ZDS and on Factor II (Self-Criticism) of the DEQ. The Striving scale of the parental descriptions and the number of words did not relate significantly to the various measures of depression.

Based on extensive use of the ORI, the original manual for scoring these 13 qualitative dimensions of parental descriptions was refined. The refined definitions of these thematic or qualitative variables are presented in detail in Exhibit 4.3. Because some of the ratings involved substantial redefinition of the items, ratings based on the new definitions were reanalyzed for reliability and factorial composition. As discussed earlier, the descriptions of mother and father were rated by two judges on a seven-point scale for each of the following characteristics: affection, ambition, benevolence, degree of positive involvement, judgmental, intelligent, nurturant, punitive, personal strength, personal success, positive (or admired ideal), and warmth. Judges also rated on a five-point scale the degree of ambivalence expressed toward the parent. The number of lines of written description was encoded on a seven-point scale. The judges rated the descriptions of mother and father for each participant separately.

Reliability estimates of the two judges' ratings of the 13 qualitative dimensions of parental descriptions based on the new definitions were all satisfactory ($p > .70$). The 13 ratings and the estimate of length were subjected to a principal-components factor analysis with varimax rotation. Based on a limit of an eigenvalue of greater than 1.0 and a scree test, four factors, accounting for 73% of the total variance, were identified. Similar to the original factor analysis, a first factor (accounting for 34% of the total variance) included high loadings for positively valued aspects of parental behavior: benevolent, positive ideal, positive involvement, warmth, successful, nurturant, and strong. We changed the label of this factor from *Nurturance* to *Benevolent*. Two additional factors emerged that previously had been on a single factor that we had called *Striving*. In the new factor analysis, these striving items separate into two factors: One had high loadings on *ambivalent, punitive,* and *judgmental,* and the other had high loadings on *intelligent, ambitious,* and *strong*. These two new factors emerged as empirically independent, and both factors were conceptually internally consistent. The first of these two new factors was labeled *Punitive*, and the second was labeled *Ambitious*. Length of the description, as previously, emerged as a separate factor. Thus, the primary difference between the previous and the new analysis was the separation of the previous second factor (Striving) into the factors Punitive and Ambitious (Blatt, Chevron, et al., 1988;

Exhibit 4.3   The 12 Thematic Content Scales for the Description of Significant Others

Scale	Description
Affectionate	Degree to which the person is described as having and displaying overt affection or warm regard.
Ambitious	Degree to which the person is described as displaying aspirations in instrumental or occupational domains for self and others; as having an ardent desire to achieve; as aspiring, driving, or exerting pressure on self and others.
Malevolent–benevolent	Degree to which the person's intentions toward or effects on others are described as having or expressing intense ill will, spite, or hatred, rather than as doing or being disposed to doing good.
Cold–warm	Degree to which the person's interpersonal affective style is described as unemotional and impersonal rather than as warm and loving.
Degree of constructive involvement	Degree to which the person's interactions with others are described as negative (either distant and reserved, or overinvolved) rather than as positive (constructive involvement with respect for other's individuality).
Intellectual	Extent to which the person is described as emphasizing study, reflection, and speculation, interest in ideas, creative use of intellect, or capacity for rational and intelligent thought and an appreciation for complexity.
Judgmental	Degree to which the person is described as holding critical or excessively high standards rather than as being accepting and tolerant.
Negative–positive ideal	Degree to which the person is described as someone whom an individual wants to be like or emulate; the degree of admiration for qualities the person possesses.
Nurturant	Degree to which the person is described as giving care and attention without making emotional demands, rather than seeking to have one's own needs met.
Punitive	Extent to which the person is described as either physically or emotionally abusive and as inflicting suffering and pain.
Successful	Extent to which the person is described as feeling satisfied with his or her own accomplishments, whatever those accomplishments might be.
Strength (strong–weak)	Extent to which the person is described as effective, efficient, and able to resist pressure and endure; as possessing a stable sense of self; and as appearing to be a consistent figure.

Exhibit 4.4   Three Thematic Factors in Descriptions of Significant Others

Benevolent	Punitive
Affectionate	Judgmental
Benevolent	Punitive
Warm	Ambivalent
Constructive involvement	
Positive ideal	Ambitious
Nurturant	Ambitious
Successful	Intellectual
Strong	

Quinlan, Blatt, Chevron, & Wein, 1992). As indicated in Exhibit 4.4, factor analyses (Quinlan et al., 1992) of these thematic attributes revealed that the Benevolent factor comprises the attributes affectionate, benevolent, warm, constructive involvement, positive ideal, nurturant, successful, and strong. The Punitive factor includes the attributes judgmental, punitive, and ambivalent. The Ambitious factor includes the attributes ambitious and intellectual.

The correlations between the newly defined factors and the earlier Nurturant and Striving factors indicate that the new Benevolent factor and the prior Nurturant factor overlap considerably (rs = .74 and .85 for descriptions of mother and father, respectively). The new Ambitious factor was positively correlated with both the prior Nurturant and Striving factors in the description of mothers and fathers. The new Punitive factor was negatively correlated with the prior Nurturant factor in the descriptions of mothers and positively correlated with the prior Striving factor in the descriptions of fathers. The new factor structure and scales seemed preferable to the original ones, because the new factor structure separated the negatively toned dimensions of the Punitive factor from the more positively toned Ambitious factor.

The three new factor scales (Benevolent, Punitive, and Ambitious) were correlated with the semantic differential, the ZDS, and the three factors from the DEQ. In the ratings for both mother and father, the Benevolent factor correlated most highly with the semantic differential evaluation factor but also showed moderate correlations with both potency and activity. The Punitive factor, however, showed a different pattern of correlation between parents. It correlated negatively with all three semantic differential ratings for mother and only weakly correlated with evaluation for father. The Ambitious factor, on the other hand, had a complementary pattern of correlations: It was most highly correlated with the potency factor of the fathers' description on the semantic differential, and moderately correlated with the other two semantic differential scales, whereas in the mother description it was most highly correlated with semantic differential activity and correlated to a slightly lower degree with the other two semantic differential scores. Thus, the correlations of the parental description factors with the semantic differential scales supported the convergent and discriminant validity of the ratings of thematic content of the parental descriptions: The factors correlated in the expected direction for each parent on the semantic differential and had different patterns of correlations for mother and father.

The pattern of correlations of the descriptions of mother and father and depression indicate that the new Benevolent factor correlated with positive self-evaluation on the semantic differential and with DEQ Factor III (Efficacy) only for the mother's ratings. The Benevolent factor also had consistent negative correlations with ideal–real self difference on the semantic differential, the ZDS, and the Self-Criticism scale of the DEQ. The Punitive factor had expectable positive correlations with ideal–real difference on the semantic differential, the ZDS, and DEQ Self-Criticism in both mother and father. The Ambitious factor, however, had a different pattern of correlations with ratings of mother and father: Ambitious in mothers' descriptions correlated positively only with DEQ Efficacy, and in the fathers' description it correlated negatively with depression as measured by the semantic differential, ideal–real difference, ZDS, and DEQ Self-Criticism factor.

These findings indicate significant relationships between depression and several aspects of descriptions of parents in a sample of normal young adults. Perception of the parents as lacking in nurturance, support, and affection is more related to depression than the perception of parents as striving, harsh, and judgmental. These findings with college students are consistent with earlier results reported with clinical samples (S. Jacobson, Fasman, & DiMascio, 1975; Lamont, Fischoff, & Gottlieb, 1976; Lamont & Gottlieb, 1975; Raskin, Boothe, Reatig, Schutterbrandt, & Odle, 1971). The consistency of these findings provides further support for the contention (Blatt, 1974; Blatt, D'Afflitti, et al., 1976) that depression can be studied on a continuum ranging from subtle variations of normal affective states to severely disabling clinical depression. The results also indicate that parental images can be assessed with a variety of techniques in addition to the structured questionnaires used in prior research (e.g., S. Jacobson et al., 1975; Lamont & Gottlieb, 1975). These spontaneous descriptions, like the more structured semantic differential and the PBI, appear to provide valuable data for assessing the representation of parents.

An important question is whether the findings with the parental descriptions could be attributed to a general response bias characteristic of individuals who report themselves as having a negative affect such as depression. A. T. Beck (1967a), for example, offered considerable evidence that a pervasive cognitive bias exists in individuals with clinical depression. The pattern of the results with the parental descriptions, however, offers a strong argument against a general negative bias as the sole explanation of the findings. The differential correlations of the parental descriptions with the semantic differential ratings of the same as compared to the opposite sex parent cannot be a function of a general response bias.

The procedure for evaluating open-ended descriptions of parents offers interesting possibilities for the assessment of significant qualities of individuals' representations of their parents. The results of the revised scoring procedures and the new factor analysis not only essentially replicated the major findings of the previous analyses but also facilitated the differentiation of a negative disciplinary theme in the Punitive factor from a positive industriousness theme in the Ambitious factor. These findings lend added support to validity of this open-ended procedure for assessing important dimensions of individuals' representations of their parents. The results from these analyses of parental descriptions parallel the results with more structured techniques, such as the semantic differential and PBI, while adding important new content dimensions.

Scorable attributes. The extent to which a description can be scored for each of the 12 qualitative attributes—the number of scorable attributes—provides yet another structural measure: the degree of articulation of the object representation. The degree of the articulation of the object (scorable attributes) is measured by the number of these 12 qualitative attributes that can be scored in the description (0–12). The degree to which the figure has been articulated provides a third assessment of aspects of the structural organization of mental representation.

In addition, the degree of ambivalence expressed when describing the figure can be scored on a five-point scale, and the length of the description can be assessed on a seven-point scale.

Validation Studies

Research supports the validity of these scoring systems to assess structural and thematic dimensions of spontaneous descriptions of self and others. CL of descriptions of parents in nonclinical samples, for example, was found to be significantly related to experiences of depression (Blatt, Wein, et al., 1979), emotional awareness (Lane, Quinlan, Schwartz, Walker, & Zeitlin, 1990), and negotiation strategies, as well as to self-reported acting out (Schultz & Selman, 1989). In a clinical sample, Bornstein and O'Neill (1992) found that psychotic and borderline patients gave less differentiated, conceptually less complex descriptions and more negative and more ambivalent representations of both parents than did normal individuals. Moreover, Bornstein and O'Neill found that conceptual complexity (CL) was negatively related to degree of psychopathology as assessed on the Global Assessment Scale (Endicott, Spitzer, Fleiss, & Cohen, 1976), the presence and severity of hallucinations, and the impairment index on the Minnesota Multiphasic Personality Inventory (Dahlstrom, Welsh, & Dahlstrom, 1972).

Bornstein, Galley, and Leone (1986) found that the amount of oral imagery on the Rorschach was correlated with the negative description of mother as malevolent, cold, non-nurturant, weak, unsuccessful, not constructively involved with her family, and as a negative ideal. These findings are consistent with reports by Frank and colleagues (Frank, Pirsch, & Wright, 1990; Frank, Poorman, et al., 1997), as well as Baldwin (1992), that one's relationships with significant others is correlated with the quality of adjustment in adolescence. Procidano and Guinta (1989) found that the descriptions of significant others was negatively related to depressive symptoms, and Rayes et al. (1989) found the CL of the description of significant others was lower in obese participants than in individuals with normal weight. Baker, Melgoza, Roll, Quinlan, and Blatt (1997), in comparing Anglo and Chicano college students at a university in the southwestern United States, found that Chicano students had significantly lower CL in their descriptions of their mothers primarily because they emphasized the mother's actions and roles in the family rather than her independent thoughts and feelings. Anglo male respondents described their fathers at a lower CL than Chicano males, primarily because they emphasized the activity of the father's strivings. These differences in CL were not related to measures of depression and thus appear to reflect cultural differences rather than clinical issues. Sadeh, Rubin, and Berman (1993), studying Israeli college students, evaluated their descriptions of their parents as well as descriptions of their relationship with each parent. Their findings support the observations of a relationship between aspects of the representation of parents and depressive experiences. The description of the relationship to each parent provided unique findings indicating that anaclitic depressive experiences were related to aspects of the descriptions of mother and that introjective depressive experiences were related to aspects of the description of father. Sadeh et al.'s suggestion to also obtain descriptions of the relationship is a creative extension of the ORI. Marziali and Oleniuk (1990) proposed another creative innovation in evaluating the descriptions obtained with the ORI by generating scores for CL for each unit of the description, thereby creating a profile for each respondent indicating the degree to which his or her descriptions contained material at each of the five levels of CL. They compared the profiles of borderline patients with profiles of a nonclinical sample and found that the borderline patients had a greater proportion of their descriptions at the lower CLs, whereas the control groups had a greater proportion of their descriptions at the more differentiated and conceptually complex levels.

As I discuss more fully in chapter 8, changes in CL and differentiation–relatedness, as well as aspects of the qualitative dimensions in the description of significant others, significantly correlate with an independent assessment of the degree of clinical change in long-term, intensive inpatient treatment of seriously disturbed, treatment-resistant patients (Blatt & Auerbach, 2001; Blatt, Stayner, et al., 1996). Thus, the content and structure of individuals' representations of self and significant others differ in clinical and nonclinical samples and were related in clinical samples to independent assessments of level of psychopathology and clinical functioning, as well as to the degree of clinical change. In nonclinical samples, these structural and qualitative dimensions of mental representations are significantly related to aspects of general functioning, particularly the quality of interpersonal attachment (e.g., K. N. Levy, Blatt, & Shaver, 1998; Priel & Besser, 2001).

Priel and colleagues (Priel, Kantor, & Besser, 2000; Priel, Myodovnik, & Rivlin-Beniaminy, 1995; Waniel-Izhar, Besser, & Priel, in press) have modified the scoring procedures for the ORI so that it could be used with children as young as preschool age. Priel et al. (1995) demonstrated changes in the content and structural organization of description of parents in preschool children (ages 5 and 6 years) and children in the fourth grade (ages 9–10 years). They also found that developmentally more mature descriptions (higher CL) were related to more advanced conflict resolution strategies. More mature descriptions of parents in middle childhood (fourth grade) were also associated with more positive self-descriptions. Waniel-Izhar et al. (in press), studying children 9–11 years of age, found that the content and structure of representations of parents and self, as well as the quality of their relatedness, form a common underlying construct that predicts symptoms as assessed on the Teacher's Report Form (Achenbach, 1991). Also, Priel et al. (2000), using the ORI, compared the mental representation of mother among adopted and nonadopted children (average age approximately 10 years). Those children, who were adopted when they were infants, had representations of their adoptive mothers that were more concrete and less benign than the representations of nonadopted children. Among the adopted children, their representation of their birth mothers often contained "split negative aspects." Among the adoptees, greater differences between the representation of birth and adoptive mothers were associated with increased internalizing behavior on the Teacher's Report Form.

Using spontaneous descriptions of mother and father, K. N. Levy et al. (1998) assessed the relationship of the structure and content of mental representation in young adults with different attachment styles. Secure attachment was associated with more stable, consistent, positive, and integrated representations of significant others. Securely attached individuals represent their parents as trustworthy, caring, and emotionally supportive. They are less ambivalent about their parents and describe their mothers and fathers as benevolent, warm, affectionate, nonjudgmental, nonpunitive, and as providing a positive ideal who is experienced as nurturing and constructively involved. In addition, securely attached individuals appear to grasp more fully the complexity of interpersonal relationships and were able to differentiate more fully themselves from their parents while still maintaining a sense of relatedness. Conversely, insecurely attached individuals represent their parents as malevolent, punitive, and uncaring. Their descriptions were less cohesive, differentiated, and integrated.

Within the insecurely attached group, avoidant individuals described their parents as cold, judgmental, punitive, and less constructively involved. Anxious–ambivalent (preoccupied) individuals also described their parents as punitive and judgmental but, in contrast to avoidant individuals, they were more ambivalent, and thus they also described their parents as affectionate, warm, and benevolent but also as less successful, less constructively involved, and less of a positive ideal (K. N. Levy et al., 1998).

Priel and Besser (2001) found that pregnant Israeli women who were classified as securely attached had more complex, differentiated, and integrated representations of their mothers. In addition, these representations were less ambivalent and had significantly more positive characteristics than women who were classified as insecurely attached. Also, the level of complexity of the representation of mother differed significantly among the three insecure attachment groups (preoccupied, dismissing, and fearful avoidant). Priel and Besser (2001), consistent with findings reported by K. N. Levy et al. (1998), found that representations given by the fearful avoidant women were closest to the representations of the securely attached women, whereas dismissing women presented the least complex representations. Priel and Besser (2001) found that the qualities of these pregnant women's representation of their mothers was significantly related to the quality of their antenatal attachment to their infants (see also Fonagy, Steele, & Steele, 1991). These findings by K. N. Levy et al. (1998) and Priel and Besser (2001) support the assumption (e.g., Bowlby, 1980, 1988a; Main, Kaplan, & Cassidy, 1985) that attachment

Exhibit 4.5 Summary Scoring of Object Relations Inventory Protocols

Structural variables	Thematic (qualitative) factors
Conceptual level	Benevolent
Differentiation–relatedness	Punitive
Scorable attributes	Ambitious
Length	Ambivalence

styles are based on cognitive–affective schemas or internal working models of close interpersonal relationships; they also suggest that these cognitive–affective schemas may be a central issue in the etiology of anaclitic and introjective depression, because these two types of depression are associated with different types of insecure attachment (Blatt & Homann, 1992).

As discussed earlier, object representation is often insubstantial in depressed patients; the representation of the parent is often at a low developmental level and focused on painful interactions of neglect or criticism. Numerous clinical examples provide consistent evidence of important relations between aspects of an individual's representations of his or her parents and the degree and nature of depression. These findings are discussed in more detail in chapter 6 in terms of their implications for the developmental origins of depression. Also, as discussed in detail in chapter 8, progress in the treatment of depression often involves the patient's resolution of intensely ambivalent feelings about the depriving and or harshly judgmental aspects of the parents. Therapeutic progress is often expressed in significant revisions of these representations (e.g., Blatt, Auerbach, & Aryan, 1998; Blatt, Stayner, et al., 1996). Psychotherapy with patients who are depressed often involves working through intensely ambivalent feelings about significant others, with the result that the mental representations evolve to a higher level of organization. With less ambivalent and more consolidated representations, the patient becomes less vulnerable to intense dysphoric affect.

The spontaneous descriptions of self and significant others obtained with the ORI can be evaluated for several dimensions that assess the structural organization as well as aspects of the thematic content contained in these descriptions. As indicated in Exhibit 4.5, the structural dimensions of the descriptions can be assessed for the level of cognitive organization (CL), the degree to which self and other are represented as differentiated and interrelated (differentiation–relatedness), and the degree to which significant others are articulated by describing a variety of different dimensions (scorable attributes), as well as the length of the description. The thematic content of the descriptions can be assessed by three thematic factors: Benevolent, Punitive, and Ambitious, and the degree of ambivalence expressed in the descriptions also can be evaluated. Scoring manuals for these various dimensions of the ORI can be obtained from S. J. Blatt, Yale University, Department of Psychiatry, 25 Park Street, New Haven, CT 06519 (sidney.blatt@yale.edu).

Part III

Expressions of Anaclitic and Introjective Depression and Their Distal and Proximal Antecedents

Introduction:

Expressions of Anaclitic and Introjective Depression and Their Distal and Proximal Antecedents

In the chapters in this part I review research on the expressions of anaclitic and introjective depression in clinical and nonclinical settings and explore some of the distal and proximal factors that contribute to the two types of depressive experiences.

In chapter 5, I review a host of empirical studies examining the multiple ways in which the two types of dysphoric experiences and depression are expressed in clinical and nonclinical settings; in chapter 6, I review research on the developmental origins of these two types of depression. The observation of the importance of impaired or distorted representations of the self and significant others in depression has led to a wide range of studies of the distal causes (e.g., early parent–child relationships) of anaclitic and introjective depression. Other studies, reviewed in chapter 7, have examined the proximal causes (e.g., stressful life events) of depression and have found that anaclitic and introjective individuals are differentially sensitive to various types of stressful life experiences and that they construct their social context in ways that amplify the two types of depressive experiences. Thus, individuals with dysphoric experiences around abandonment or failure and guilt differ in their expression of depression, in their early experiences in caring relationships, in their sensitivity and vulnerability to different types of stressful life events, and in how they engage their environment.

5

Anaclitic and Introjective Depression in Clinical and Nonclinical Settings

Clinical Settings

The validity of the Depressive Experiences Questionnaire (DEQ; Blatt, D'Afflitti, & Quinlan, 1979) as a measure of anaclitic and introjective depression was initially assessed in two groups of psychiatric patients: (a) a heterogeneous outpatient sample of 43 men and 58 women applying for clinical services at a community mental health center, who were willing to participate in the research and were considered sufficiently intact by their clinicians to answer a questionnaire, and (b) an inpatient sample of 25 men and 71 women studied during the first three weeks of a relatively brief (30–90 days) psychiatric hospitalization. The inpatient group included all patients admitted during a 6-month period who were without indication of organic brain syndrome, who could answer a questionnaire appropriately, and who consented to participate in the research. Both outpatients and inpatients had a variety of diagnoses, but at least 90% had diagnoses of either primary or secondary depression. Approximately 15%–20% of the patients had been diagnosed as psychotic (Blatt, Quinlan, Chevron, McDonald, & Zuroff, 1982). Also studied were two nonpatient samples: (a) 87 women and 41 men in an introductory psychology course at two local colleges and (b) 65 women and 69 men employed at one of several community service agencies or participating in a local church group. The mean

This chapter incorporates material from the following sources: (a) "Interpersonal Relatedness and Self-Definition: Two Prototypes for Depression," by S. J. Blatt and D. C. Zuroff, 1992, *Clinical Psychology Review, 12*, pp. 527–562. Copyright 1992 by Elsevier. Adapted with permission. (b) "Dependency and Self-Criticism: Psychological Dimensions of Depression," by S. J. Blatt, D. M. Quinlan, E. S. Chevron, C. McDonald, and D. C. Zuroff, 1982, *Journal of Consulting and Clinical Psychology, 50*, pp. 113–124. Copyright 1982 by the American Psychological Association. Adapted with permission. (c) "The Psychodynamics of Opiate Addiction," by S. J. Blatt, B. J. Rounsaville, S. Eyre, and C. Wilber, 1984, *Journal of Nervous and Mental Disease, 172*, pp. 342–352. Copyright 1984 by Lippincott, Williams, & Wilkins. Adapted with permission. (d) "Depression and Destructive Risk-Taking Behavior in Adolescence," by S. J. Blatt, in L. P. Lipsitt & L. L. Mitnick (Eds.), *Self-Regulatory Behavior and Risk-Taking: Causes and Consequences*, pp. 285–309. Copyright 1991 by Greenwood Publishing. Adapted with permission. (e) "Gender Linked Vulnerabilities to Depressive Symptoms, Stress and Problem Behaviors in Adolescents," by B. J. Leadbeater, S. J. Blatt, and D. M. Quinlan, 1995, *Journal of Research on Adolescence, 5*, pp. 1–29. Copyright 1995 by Lawrence Erlbaum Associates, Inc. Adapted with permission.

age of the patients was 34.05 years (SD = 11.92), and the mean age of the nonpatients was 26.72 years (SD = 6.40).

All participants were administered the DEQ (Blatt, D'Afflitti, & Quinlan, 1976), the Beck Depression Inventory (BDI; A. T. Beck & Beamesderfer, 1974), the Zung Depression Scale (ZDS; Zung, 1965, 1972), and a version of the semantic differential (Osgood, Suci, & Tannenbaum, 1957). They also were administered the Minnesota Multiphasic Personality Inventory (MMPI; Hathaway & McKinley, 1943). In the semantic differential, participants were presented with four concepts ("mother," "father," "myself as I would like to be" [ideal self], and "myself as I am" [real self]) that they rated on 17 bipolar adjective scales that assess Osgood et al.'s (1957) three basic factors: (a) Evaluation, (b) Potency, and (c) Activity. The ratings of the real self on the Evaluation factor and the disparity between one's ratings of the ideal and real self are considered measures of depression (Endler, 1961; Laxer, 1964; Lohman, 1969). A comparison of the mean scores on the various measures of depression in the clinical and nonclinical groups indicated highly significant differences ($p \leq$ .001) between these two samples on every measure. Some sex differences were superimposed on patient–nonpatient differences, but with little interaction. Consistent with other findings (Chevron, Quinlan, & Blatt, 1978; Golding & Singer, 1983; R. E. Steele, 1978), men in both samples obtained lower scores than women on the DEQ Interpersonal or Dependency factor (Factor I).

The two dimensions of depression on the DEQ, especially Self-Criticism, correlated significantly with the well-established self-report measures of depression (i.e., BDI and ZDS) in both the clinical and nonclinical samples. The ZDS and the BDI were highly correlated. Self-Criticism correlates significantly with the BDI (rs = .36 for female patients and .47 for male patients) and with the ZDS for women (rs = .47 for patients and .50 for nonpatient control respondents) and for men (rs =. 41 for patients and .62 for nonpatient control respondents). In both clinical and nonclinical samples, the DEQ Self-Criticism factor also correlated significantly with the other measures of depression, including the semantic-differential ratings of self. Associations of the Interpersonal factor with the BDI and ZDS were more moderate, but still significant (for the BDI, rs = .19 for female patients and .27 for male patients; for the ZDS, rs = .20 for female patients and .24 for nonpatient control participants, and rs = .34 for male patients and for nonpatient control participants). These findings suggest that these two well-established self-report measures (i.e., the BDI and ZDS) assess depression that is primarily associated with self-criticism rather than with interpersonal issues of loss and fears of abandonment (Blatt et al., 1982; Riley & McCranie, 1990). The weaker correlations for the Interpersonal factor of the DEQ (Factor I) with standard measures of depression suggest that dependency appears to measure an unarticulated form of depression, not usually assessed by traditional measures of depression (see also Pilon, Olioff, Bryson, & Doan, 1986). Thus, the DEQ Interpersonal factor seems to assess a relatively unrecognized form of depression concerned with different issues (e.g., helplessness) and characterized by a different set of defenses—in particular, denial, repression, and displacement—than the usual self-loathing and markedly negative attitudes about the self and the world usually associated with depression. In addition, individuals high on the DEQ Interpersonal factor were not as well differentiated cognitively on the semantic differential as were individuals high on the Self-Criticism factor, suggesting that issues of depression associated with dependency may occur at a somewhat earlier and less differentiated developmental level than depressive issues associated with self-criticism (Blatt, 1974).

Several other investigators (e.g., Abramson & Sackheim, 1977; Blatt, 1974; Blatt, D'Afflitti, et al., 1976; Hirschfeld, Klerman, Chodoff, Korchin, & Barrett, 1976; Hirschfeld et al., 1977) have also noted that dependency is an important independent dimension of depression, but findings with the DEQ suggest that depression associated with dependency is often difficult for individuals to articulate and communicate and for clinicians and investigators to evaluate. Clinical and research data suggest that dysphoria associated with the interpersonal issues of dependency is often expressed in the form of somatic complaints (Beutel et al., in press; Blatt, D'Afflitti, et al., 1976), intrusive and demanding interpersonal behavior (Beutel et al., in press), amphetamine abuse (Lidz, Lidz, and Rubenstein, 1976), alcoholism, and antisocial activity (Blatt & Shichman, 1981).

For both men and women, the pattern of correlations among the various types of measures of depression in patients and nonpatient control participants was similar. With minor exceptions, correlations among the measures of depression (the DEQ Interpersonal and Self-Criticism factors, semantic differential, and the BDI and ZDS) were in the same direction and of approximately the same magnitude in both nonclinical and clinical respondents. Only DEQ Efficacy had a different pattern of correlations in the clinical and nonclinical samples (Blatt et al., 1982).

The correlation of each of the 20 ZDS items (Zung, 1965, 1971) with the Interpersonal and Self-Criticism factors of the DEQ provided important clarification about the nature of the depressive experiences assessed by the two DEQ factors. In a sample of 128 young adult college students, consistent with earlier reports (Zung, 1973), the average ZDS score was 46.20 ($SD = 9.79$), which is very close to the "morbidity index score" of 50 established by Zung as the cutoff indicating clinical depression. Only DEQ Self-Criticism correlated significantly with the total ZDS score, $r(126) = .54, p < .001$. An item analysis of the ZDS (Blatt, D'Afflitti, et al., 1976) indicated that DEQ Self-Criticism correlated significantly ($p < .05$) with 14 of the 20 ZDS items, items that Zung (1965, 1971) has labeled as assessing the "self-esteem" dimension—concerns of personal dissatisfaction, self-criticism, and hopelessness (Zung, 1965, 1971, 1972); the psychological symptoms of depression. The Interpersonal factor of the DEQ, in contrast, did not correlate significantly with the total ZDS score. The item analysis, however, indicated that the Interpersonal factor of the DEQ correlated significantly with 5 of the 20 ZDS items concerned with digestive functions, fatigue, psychomotor retardation, irritability, and indecisiveness—the more somatic–vegetative, noncognitive, or nonpsychological dimensions of depression. Thus, the Interpersonal factor of the DEQ seems to assess a form of depression that may be frequently overlooked because it is expressed primarily in the form of bodily concerns and somatic symptoms rather than the more usual psychological expressions of depression such as personal dissatisfaction, hopelessness, and emptiness. The third DEQ factor, Efficacy, in contrast, correlated significantly with 4 of the 20 ZDS items related to optimism and hopefulness (Blatt, D'Afflitti, et al., 1976).

Riley and McCranie (1990) reported similar results in their study of 107 depressed patients. They found that individuals high on the Interpersonal factor tended not to be self-reflective, particularly about affective experiences, and instead expressed their depression through somatic complaints and seeking the care and attention of a physician (see also Beutel et al., in press). Thus, dependency appears to be a relatively neglected but important dimension of depression, an observation that is consistent with results found by Seligman and his colleagues (e.g., Abramson, Seligman, & Teasdale, 1978; Peterson & Seligman, 1984; Seligman, 1975) on the cognitive, motivational, and performance deficits (Abramson et al., 1978; W. R. Miller, 1975) in depression—loss of self-esteem and sad affect as a consequence of learned helplessness and the generalized expectations of being unable to control one's life as a central etiological issue in depression. These findings are also consistent with those of Chodoff (1972) and Hirschfeld et al. (1976), who stressed the importance of dependency in depression. In general, however, dependency has not been explored as fully in research on depression as have self-criticism, self-worth, and guilt. The recent distinction of two levels of interpersonal concerns within the DEQ (Neediness and Relatedness), discussed in chapter 3, should help future investigators to evaluate more fully the role of interpersonal dimensions in psychological functioning, especially in depression.

Colleagues and I (Blatt, 1974; Blatt et al., 1982) have associated particular symptoms—including somatic complaints, crying, anxiety and phobic complaints, affective lability, and increased appetite—with a dependent, or anaclitic depression. Anhedonia, loss of interest in people and in activities, unremitting dysphoric mood, and feelings of guilt were associated with self-criticism and an introjective depression (see also Ouimette & Klein, 1993). A. T. Beck (1983) also associated several symptoms with *sociotropic depression*, a depression he viewed as a "reactive" or neurotic type of depression (Kiloh & Garside, 1963) because it involves a more reactive or labile mood, an active demand for help, an optimistic view of treatment, passive suicidal gestures, and an active onset that is clearly related to an environmental stressor. A. T. Beck (1983) viewed autonomous depression as the traditional endogenous type of depression, characterized by self-criticism, guilt, anhedonia, withdrawal, a less reactive mood, a general pessimism about treatment but a better response to medication, more active forms of suicide, and an onset determined more by internal processes than by environmental stressors.

C. J. Robins and Block (1987), using the Sociotropy–Autonomy Scale (SAS [Beck et al., 1983]) to assess these two types of dysphoria, speculated that the Sociotropy factor of the SAS was related to an "anxious" or "neurotic–reactive" type of depression, whereas the Autonomy factor of the SAS was related to issues of defeat and an "endogenous" (Kiloh & Garside, 1963) or endogenomorphic (D. F. Klein, 1974) depression. On the basis of these assumptions, C. J. Robins, Block, and Peselow (1989) studied the relationship of the two SAS factors (Sociotropy and Autonomy) to symptoms of depression in 80 patients with unipolar depression as assessed on the Hamilton Rating Scale for Depression (Hamilton, 1960, 1967) and Beck Depression Inventory (A. T. Beck

& Beamesderfer, 1974. Two symptom composites were constructed: (a) one for symptoms expected by A. T. Beck (1983) to characterize sociotropic depression and (b) one for symptoms of autonomous depression. The Sociotropy scale significantly predicted the composite score for sociotropic symptoms, but the Autonomy scale was unrelated to the composite score for autonomous symptoms. C. J. Robins et al. (1989) suggested that the disappointing results for the Autonomy scale might reflect limitations of that measure rather than of the underlying theory.

Many symptoms, however, cannot be classified as dependent or self-critical (D. A. Clark, Steer, Haslam, Beck, & Brown, 1997; C. J. Robins, Bagby, Rector, Lynch, & Kennedy, 1997). Research support for specific composites of symptoms associated with a dependent (anaclitic) and a self-critical (introjective) depression has been mixed. Peselow, Robins, Sanfilipo, Block, and Fieve (1992) found that 90.7% of 217 outpatients with depression who scored high on Autonomy and low on Sociotropy met research diagnostic criteria (RDC; Endicott & Spitzer, 1978) for endogenous depression, whereas only 19.3% of patients who scored high on Sociotropy but low on Autonomy meet these criteria. C. J. Robins and Luten (1991) used the Personal Style Inventory (Robins & Ladd, 1991) to assess sociotropy and autonomy with 50 unipolar inpatients and found that the Sociotropy scale predicted "sociotropic" symptoms and the Autonomy scale predicted "autonomous" symptoms. Exploratory analyses of individual symptoms revealed that sociotropy correlated with crying, feelings of loneliness, and variability and reactivity of mood; autonomy was significantly correlated with loss of interest or of pleasure in being with others, self-blame, irritability, and concerns about an inability to function. Luyten, Corveleyn, & Blatt (in press) found that dependency was specifically related to depression, whereas self-criticism appears to be a more general vulnerability factor (see also Cox et al., 2000). Dependency in patients with depression appears to be associated with anxiety, whereas self-criticism is related to obsessive and paranoid symptoms (Blatt, 1995a; Blatt & Shichman, 1983). It is also important to note that dependency has been associated with both positive and negative affect, whereas self-criticism is associated only with negative affect (Dunkley, Blankstein, & Flett, 1997; Jolly, Dyck, Kramer, & Wherry, 1996; Mongrain, 1993, 1998; Mongrain & Zuroff, 1995).

Klein and colleagues (D. N. Klein, 1989; D. N. Klein, Harding, Taylor, & Dickstein, 1988; D. N. Klein, Taylor, Dickstein, & Harding, 1988) have examined the temporal stability of the DEQ and its correlations with variables that assess family history, current clinical functioning, and outcome in a large sample of female outpatients, many of whom had an affective disorder. D. N. Klein, Harding, et al. (1988) found that self-criticism predicted irritability during depressive episodes and poorer social functioning at follow-up. Patients who were both dependent and self-critical also had more severe and long-standing symptoms. Self-criticism decreased in clinically improved patients but still remained significantly higher than self-criticism in nonclinical, control participants (e.g., C. J. Robins & Luten, 1991). D. N. Klein, Taylor, et al. (1988), in contrast to Robins and his colleagues, however, found relatively few significant relationships between the Interpersonal and Self-Criticism factors of the DEQ and a wide range of clinical symptoms and clinical diagnoses. Although D. N. Klein, Harding, et al. (1988) emphasized the paucity of findings between the DEQ factors and clinical symptoms and diagnoses, they provided no theoretical or clinical basis for expecting most of the clinical variables they examined to be related to the DEQ factors. The paucity of significant correlations between DEQ factors and general clinical symptoms and diagnoses is consistent with the frequent observations of the independence of psychological and biological symptoms of depression (e.g., Blatt et al., 1982) and suggests that these are relatively independent domains. Each of these domains—self-report measures and *Diagnostic and Statistical Manual of Mental Disorders* (*DSM*; e.g., American Psychiatric Association, 1994) symptoms and diagnoses—have limitations as ways of understanding central dimensions of psychopathology, especially depression.

D. N. Klein (1989), in a subsequent report, examined the validity of the DEQ in male and female outpatients with a variety of diagnoses and reported several significant and theoretically interesting findings. In both men and women, Self-Criticism was significantly related to a depressogenic attributional style (internal, global, and stable for negative outcomes) and to interviewer-rated Schneiderian signs for a depressive personality. The Interpersonal and Self-Criticism factors of the DEQ were higher in patients with primary, early-onset dysthymia than patients with major depression, suggesting that both Dependency and Self-Criticism may be important in clinical depression that has an early onset and tends to be long lasting. As suggested earlier, dependency may play a role in symptoms other than the symptoms recognized as part of affective disorders within the *DSM* system (Blatt et al., 1982). Rosenfarb, Becker, Khan, and Mintz (1998) compared unipolar and bipolar women (ages 20–63), still depressed or in remission, with nonpsychiatric control participants and found that DEQ Self-Criticism appears to be a characterological feature in both unipolar and bipolar depression but that the DEQ Interpersonal factor appears to be partly influenced by current mood state, because remitted bipolar women had lower scores on the Interpersonal factor than did the nonclinical control participants. It is possible, however, that this lower dependency score in remitted bipolar women indicated a denial of these needs, given the tendency for denial in bipolar disorders and the tendency for some bipolar women to deal with their dependency needs through reversal by compulsive caregiving (see Blatt et al., 1982).

In an effort to evaluate more fully the meaning of the three DEQ factors in clinical depression, colleagues and I (Blatt et al., 1982) studied 100 consecutive patients admitted to a psychiatric unit of a community hospital with either a primary or secondary diagnosis of depression. We evaluated several measures of depression (DEQ, BDI, ZDS, and MMPI). Each of the depression measures (DEQ Dependency and Self-Criticism), and the BDI and ZDS, correlated in the expected direction with the MMPI Depression scale. In addition, DEQ Self-Criticism and the BDI and ZDS had similar patterns of correlation with other MMPI scales: a low degree of falsification and high scores on Psychasthenia, Psychopathic Deviate,[1] Schizophrenia, and Social Introversion. The ZDS and

---

[1]Although an elevated MMPI Psychopathic Deviate scale typically is interpreted as indicative of "psychopathic" tendencies (e.g., impulsivity, nonconformity, low frustration tolerance, irresponsibility, and irritability), many of the scale items suggest concerns about low self-esteem and feelings

BDI also correlated significantly with MMPI Hysteria, Hypochondriasis, and Paranoia. The DEQ Interpersonal factor, in contrast, correlated primarily with low defensiveness, high social introversion, and the vague somatic anergic complaints assessed with the MMPI Psychasthenia scale. DEQ Efficacy was negatively correlated with Depression, Psychasthenia, Schizophrenia, and Social Introversion and, most important, it was significantly correlated in a positive direction with the MMPI Mania scale. Thus, in a clinical sample the Efficacy factor appeared to tap aspects of hypomania, including the use of denial, a defense characteristic of manic states (Blatt et al., 1982).

The various measures of depression (DEQ Dependency and Self-Criticism, ZDS, BDI, and MMPI Depression scale) were for the most part not correlated significantly with the psychiatric assessment of clinical depression in these inpatients based on Feighner et al.'s (1972) criteria (the precursor of the *DSM–III* and *DSM–IV* criteria for depression): (a) dysphoric mood; (b) neurovegetative signs, including loss of appetite, sleep disturbance, loss of energy, agitation, retardation, loss of interest, loss of libido; and (c) psychological signs, including self-reproach, guilt, concentration difficulty, and thoughts of/wishes to be dead. Correlations of the three self-report measures of depression (i.e., BDI, ZDS, and DEQ) with Feighner et al.'s criteria, individually or as a composite, were nonsignificant. A few significant correlations were found, primarily with the more psychological symptoms of Feighner et al.'s criteria: dysphoric mood correlated significantly, $r\ (89) = -.27$, $p \le .05$, in a negative direction, with DEQ Efficacy, and in a positive direction with the ZDS and the BDI, $rs(89) = .36$ and .24, respectively; and "thoughts of/wishes to be dead" correlated significantly ($p \le .05$), in a positive direction, with the DEQ Interpersonal and Self-Criticism factors as well as with the BDI, $rs(89) = .24$, .30, and .26, respectively.[2] The absence of significant correlations between self-report measures of depression and the more neurovegetative signs of Feighner et al.'s criteria is consistent with prior findings (Akiskal et al., 1979; Depue & Monroe, 1978) that indicate that the "subjective" psychological experiences and the "objective" neurovegetative signs of depression are relatively independent phenomena.

Colleagues and I (Blatt et al., 1982) also conducted a more clinical analysis in this sample of 100 consecutive inpatients by identifying patients whose depression was primarily focused on interpersonal issues, self-criticism, or both, and by comparing aspects of their independently established clinical case records. Using median splits on each of the three DEQ factors, we selected patients as exemplifying four different types of depression: (a) an interpersonal group, characterized by high (H) Dependency and low (L) Self-Criticism and Efficacy (H-L-L); (b) a self-critical group, characterized by high Self-Criticism

---

of emotional deprivation. Astin (1959), in a factor analysis of responses to the 50 items of the Psychopathic Deviate scale, identified three factors: (a) Self-Esteem, (b) Hypersensitivity, and (c) Emotional Deprivation, and two other factors that seem to assess antisocial tendencies. It is not surprising, therefore, that the depression measures correlated significantly with this scale.

[2] Significant relationships between suicidal thoughts and DEQ Self-Criticism were also found in a sample of 100 outpatients (Blatt & Quinlan, 1982). The clinical utility of the DEQ was not examined in this outpatient group, however, because the range of data and the clinical case records on these outpatients were far more limited than those available for the inpatients.

and low Dependency and Efficacy (L-H-L); (c) a mixed dependent and self-critical group, characterized by high Dependency and Self-Criticism and low Efficacy (H-H-L); and (d) a nondepressed group, characterized by low Dependency and Self-Criticism and high Efficacy (L-L-H). Approximately half of the sample fell into one of these four theoretically defined types.

The four groups differed significantly in terms of Feighner et al.'s (1972) neurovegetative criteria for clinical depression. Approximately 50% of the high dependency (H-L-L) and 50% of the high self-criticism (L-H-L) groups met all three of the Feighner criteria: (a) a minimum duration of two weeks of depressed mood or sadness; (b) a minimum number of psychological signs, such as feelings of guilt, obsessive thoughts, and disturbed sleep; and (c) a minimum number of somatic–vegetative signs, such as loss of appetite or weight, diurnal variation, and loss of interest in sexual activities. In contrast, 90% of the mixed group, those high on both Dependency and Self-Criticism (H-H-L), met all three Feighner criteria. Only 20% of the nondepressed group (L-L-H) met all three Feighner criteria. Thus, it seems that the Feighner criteria are associated equally with both a dependent and a self-critical type of depression, but the signs of severe clinical depression noted by the criteria appeared almost invariably in the group high on both the dependent and self-critical types of depression (Blatt et al., 1982). The average number of specific Feighner criteria met in the dependency, self-criticism, nondepressed, and mixed groups were 1.80, 1.83, 1.33, and 2.73, respectively. A one-way analysis of variance comparing the four groups approached statistical significance, $F(3.32) = 2.27, p \leq .06$, and the Newman–Keuls comparison of the nondepressed group (L-L-H) and the group with mixed depression (H-H-L) was statistically significant ($p \leq .05$). Thus, although Dependency and Self-Criticism each appear related to some degree to the neurovegetative disturbances of clinical depression, the presence of Feighner criteria symptoms seems to be a function primarily of the joint occurrence of both factors of depression. The lack of correlation between subjective and objective measures is important, especially because the Feighner criteria were developed as a uniform and replicable set of criteria for the diagnosis of depression that led to the *DSM–III* and *DSM–IV* (American Psychiatric Association, 1980, 1994) criteria for depression. The RDC (Spitzer, Endicott, & Robins, 1978) and the *DSM* criteria added modifications to the Feighner criteria but proceeded in an essentially similar way in defining depression and possible depressive subtypes.

Several features of the *DSM* criteria for depression are noteworthy. They do not constitute a consistent, theoretical statement about depression but are a mixed set of theoretical vegetative, psychological, and somatic clinical signs. They are not based on a single definition or even on multiple theoretical definitions of depression; neither do they explain the nature and etiology of depression, and they have no direct implications for modes of intervention. Although such descriptive classificatory systems may generate a reliable homogeneous grouping of patients, the absence of any theoretical rationale limits the contribution of such systems to the understanding of depression as compared to distinctions generated from more theoretically derived and empirically validated systems (see Blatt & Levy, 1998).

The four depression groups (high dependency, high self-criticism, high dependency and self-criticism, and denied depression) identified in the 100 consecutive inpatients on the basis of the DEQ were also compared on other test data. Highly significant differences were found among the four groups on the ZDS, BDI, and the MMPI Depression scale. The highest level of depression was reported by the mixed (H-H-L) group, the one that also showed significant elevation on Feighner et al.'s (1972) criteria. Also, although major differences in level of depression were found between the group of nondepressed inpatients— the group high on Efficacy and low on Dependency and Self-Criticism (L-L-H)—and the other three groups, there were several reasons to doubt the lower level of depression reported by the nondepressed group; namely, these individuals had significantly elevated scores on several MMPI scales, including the Lie, Defensiveness, and Mania scales, and somewhat lower scores on the MMPI Validity (F) scale.

The independently established clinical case records of these four depression groups (dependent, self-critical, mixed, and not depressed) were given to a small group of clinical investigators who were uninformed as to the groups to which the patients had been assigned. These judges reviewed these relatively brief (1–2 pages) descriptions of the patients' presenting symptoms and aspects of their lives contained in the admission notes of the hospital charts to see if they could predict the patients' DEQ grouping (Blatt et al., 1982). They predicted, in a consensus opinion, whether the patient was high on Dependency or Self-Criticism, on both, or on neither of these dimensions. They were correct in 56% of the cases (κ = .41), $z(3)$ = 4.43, $p \leq$ .001, indicating that the judges could differentiate the type of depression at a level significantly greater than chance. The most frequent error occurred in regard to the mixed group (H-H-L), where an elevation was noted on one factor (Dependency or Self-Criticism), but not the other.

The research team also specified the criteria that appeared in the case records they had used in making these differentiations (Blatt et al., 1982). Consistent with empirical findings reported by Bornstein and his colleagues (e.g., Bornstein, Galley, & Leone, 1986; Bornstein, Poynton, & Masling, 1985), the clinical records of the dependency group (H-L-L) were characterized by excesses in oral behavior (alcohol, food, or drug abuse); indications of marked dependency; a history of early object loss (e.g., parental death) or deprivation; abuse in childhood; preoccupation with issues of abandonment and loneliness; impulsive behavior; denial of anger, particularly toward caregivers, for fear of losing contact with them; use of avoidant defenses, such as denial and repression; denial of personal responsibility for their difficulties; and suicidal "gestures" (primarily through oral ingestion, such as taking an overdose of their prescribed antidepressant). Their depression was often precipitated by object loss or childbirth.

Patients in the high self-critical group (L-H-L) were described as socially isolated and intensely and critically involved with work; they felt worthless and thought of themselves as a personal and social failure, had high professional and academic strivings, and had a history of a very critical or idealized parent. They used counteractive defenses such as projection, intellectualization, and reaction formation. They had obsessive and paranoid features, anxiety and agitation, indications of aggressive acting out, and fear of loss of control, and they made serious and violent suicide attempts that had a high degree of lethality. Members of this group most often were diagnosed by the admitting psychiatrist as "depressed with psychotic features." They also had a childhood history of enuresis or bowel difficulty.

As noted above, patients in the mixed group (H-H-L) were the most difficult to differentiate. Most of the errors made by the research team in identifying the DEQ grouping of the various patients occurred with this group. The research team usually correctly identified that the patients in this group had elevated scores on one of the factors (Dependency or Self-Criticism) but failed to realize that the patients also had elevated scores on the other factor. Patients in the mixed group were characterized by features similar to those found in both of the two pure groups (H-L-L and L-H-L): experiences of loss and deprivation, excesses in oral behavior and agitation, as well as self-critical and obsessive features. In addition, they had feelings of guilt, sexual inhibitions (impotence and frigidity), and phobias. They tended to use both avoidant and counteractive defenses.

Individuals in the "nondepressed" group (L-L-H) were the easiest to identify. They were often the president of the patient government or had assumed the role of an alternate caregiver on the clinical unit. They had many features in common with the high-dependency (H-L-L) group, such as issues of orality, abandonment, and loneliness, but often in the context of denial and hyperactivity. They cared for others in the way that they wished to be cared for. Thus, they seemed to simultaneously deny and gratify their dependent cravings by assuming the role of a caregiver by being a leader on the ward or functioning as an aide to the nurses. In Bowlby's (1988b) terms, they were *compulsive caregivers*. They denied personal difficulties; had high levels of prior functioning and competence; and engaged in subtle manic behavior, such as spending sprees and making an excessive number of long distance phone calls. They also made heavy use of medication and had many somatic complaints. It is interesting that the patients in this group often were diagnosed not as manic but with a unipolar depression, like the high-dependency group. These patients often looked intact and indeed performed many caring functions on the unit. They were often discharged prematurely but were often subsequently rehospitalized with continued depressive difficulties. It is important to stress once again that although the DEQ provided important distinctions within the clinical sample, each of the three DEQ factors were essentially uncorrelated with the individual Feighner et al. (1972) neurovegetative criteria for depression.

The findings of these various studies indicate consistent and significant differences between dependent and self-critical individuals as defined by the first two factors of the DEQ. The DEQ seems to be particularly useful for assessing subjective dimensions of depression in both clinical and nonclinical samples, in differentiating distress and dysphoria focused around feelings of dependency and abandonment from those related to self-criticism and a sense of failure, worthlessness, and guilt. Frank, Poorman, Van Egeren, and Field (1997) studied 295 adolescent inpatients (ages 11–17) in an acute-care psychiatric hospital and found that both Factors I and II (Interpersonal and Self-

Critical) of the adolescent version of the DEQ, the DEQ–A, were significantly linked to depression and accounted for most of the variance in predicting depression. Beutel et al. (in press) in a mixed clinical and nonclinical sample in Germany, found that DEQ Self-Criticism was significantly associated with reduced social support, introversion, cold and rejecting interpersonal behavior, increased suicidal ideation, and recurrent depressive episodes.

The results of the various studies just discussed indicate that Dependency and Self-Criticism are also primary dimensions of depression within a clinical context. Although these factors were originally identified in nonclinical individuals (Blatt, D'Afflitti, et al., 1976), they appear to provide a typology for understanding aspects of clinical depression. Dependency and Self-Criticism had significant differential correlations with other measures of depression, and each appears to provide meaningful differentiations in a clinical context. High levels of both of these dimensions, however, can also co-occur in patients. The most severe form of clinical depression appears to result from such a combination. Depression emanating from a combination of dependency and self-criticism can lead to very intense levels of depression, because the interaction of the two sources of vulnerability creates a unique situation that is especially difficult to resolve. Intense dependency can also lead to a sense of personal weakness and failure, whereas intense strivings to compensate for feelings of inadequacy can interfere with obtaining interpersonal support for dependent longings. Thus, responding to one set of needs can create problems in the other set. An individual high on both interpersonal and self-critical concerns may be particularly vulnerable to a wide range of profound and intense experiences of depression. It may be the intensity of these difficulties in both domains that creates the neurovegetative disturbances that comprise the Feighner and the *DSM* criteria of depression.

Priel and Besser (Besser & Priel, 2003b; Priel & Besser, 1999, 2000) have investigated the role of self-criticism and dependency in postpartum depression in first-time mothers in Israel. They found that Self-Criticism, as measured by the DEQ, was associated with increased risk for postpartum depression, whereas DEQ Dependency was a protective factor that was negatively associated with depression. In the final trimester of the pregnancy, and again eight weeks after delivery, Self-Criticism was positively associated with depression as measured by the Center for Epidemiological Studies Depression Scale (CES–D; Radloff, 1977). Reports of mothers' low antenatal attachment to their babies also contributed to elevations in postpartum depression. Not only was Dependency uncorrelated with depression at both time points, but it also reduced the negative impact of self-criticism as revealed in an analysis based on structural equation modeling (SEM). In another sample of Israeli women, Priel and Besser (2000) found that social support mediated the association between both DEQ Self-Criticism and Dependency and postpartum depression, even after taking into account depression levels in the third trimester of the pregnancy. Thus, consistent findings in several samples (e.g., Besser & Priel, 2003b; Priel & Besser, 1999, 2000) indicate that self-criticism is a vulnerability factor, and dependency is a resiliency factor, for postpartum depression among first-time Israeli mothers. These findings are also partially consistent with an earlier report by Dover (1990; cited by Flett, Besser, et al., in press), who found that self-criticism, more than dependency, was associated with postpartum depression. In contradiction to Priel and Besser, however, Dover (1990) found that dependency was also significantly associated with postpartum depression. Flett, Besser, et al. (2002), consistent with Dover (1990), found that both self-criticism and dependency correlated significantly with postpartum depression in a sample of Canadian women. Also contrary to the Israeli data (Besser & Priel, 2003b; Priel & Besser, 1999, 2000), Flett, Besser, et al. (2002) did not find that dependency served as a protective factor; to the contrary, they found that dependency, like self-criticism, was associated with higher levels of depressive symptoms both during pregnancy and in the postpartum period.

Flett, Besser, et al.'s (2002) findings regarding the role of the DEQ Interpersonal factor in postpartum depression are also inconsistent with Besser and Priel's (2002) study of 120 married couples in which both partners of the marital dyad rated themselves and their spouse on the DEQ. Besser and Priel (2003a) found that DEQ Self-Criticism, reported by each member of the marital dyad, related to level of depression symptoms. Consistent with their earlier findings (Besser & Priel, 2003a; Priel & Besser, 1999, 2000), they concluded that self-criticism is an important vulnerability factor, particularly because it disrupts interpersonal relationships (e.g., Mongrain, Vettese, Shuster, & Kendal, 1998; Vettese & Mongrain, 2000). Dependency, in contrast, did not create a vulnerability to depression in Israeli women, because it seemed to facilitate the seeking of social support from the partner. Flett, Besser, et al. (in press) discussed the disparity between the findings concerning the resilient role of dependency in postpartum depression among new mothers in Israel and their own findings of its association with distress among new mothers in North America and noted that these differences may be a function of cultural differences about motherhood, attitudes of new mothers and the host society about motherhood, and the social support these societies provide new mothers. These inconsistent findings between the Israeli and Canadian samples about the role of the DEQ Interpersonal factor may be clarified by further data analyses using the recent distinction between two levels of interpersonal processes, neediness and relatedness, assessed by DEQ Factor I.

Using SEM, Flett, Besser, et al. (in press) found that reassurance seeking mediated the relationship of self-criticism—and, to a degree, dependency—to postpartum depression. Contrary to Priel and Besser's (1999) discovery of a direct link between self-criticism and postpartum depression, Flett, Besser, et al. (in press) found that almost all the effect of self-criticism on postpartum depression was mediated by reassurance seeking. Several other investigators (R. Beck, Robbins, Taylor, & Baker, 2001; Shahar, Joiner, Zuroff, & Blatt, in press) have noted the possible relationship of reassurance seeking to dependent (sociotropic) and self-critical experiences of depression. R. Beck et al. (2001) found that excessive reassurance seeking mediated the association between sociotropy, as assessed by the Personal Style Inventory (C. J. Robins et al., 1994; C. J. Robins & Luten, 1991), and depression in a cross-sectional study of 617 undergraduate students. Although sociotropy, autonomy, and reassurance seeking were all correlated significantly with depression, only sociotropy had an indirect effect on depression that was mediated by reassurance seeking. Shahar, Joiner, et al. (in press) conducted a five-week longitudinal study of

198 undergraduates using the DEQ and found a significant causal path between DEQ Self-Criticism, reassurance seeking, interpersonal stressful life events, and depressive symptoms. Although DEQ Dependency did not predict subsequent depressive symptoms, it exerted an effect on reassurance-seeking behavior that was comparable in magnitude to that of Self-Criticism. These and future studies examining the relationships between dependency (and sociotropy) and self-criticism (and autonomy) and their relationships to reassurance-seeking may further elucidate some of the mechanisms through which different types of individuals become depressed.

Carson and Baker (1996) found that a history of sexual or physical abuse (or both) and psychological maltreatment was associated with introjective, self-critical depression. Psychologically abused women were more self-critical; they reported feelings of guilt, emptiness, an inability to meet goals, and an insecurity and ambivalence about themselves and others. In a study of the impact of childhood sexual trauma on current occupational functioning, Martin (1997) found that all three DEQ factors—Dependency, Self-Criticism, and Efficacy—especially Self-Criticism, predicted a vulnerability to occupational strain. M. L. Rose (1976), in a study of moderators of childhood sexual abuse and depression in adulthood, found that DEQ Self-Criticism was a strong predictor of depression and a significant moderator of depression in adult women who had been sexually abused in childhood but who had not experienced rape in adulthood. Whereas Jarmas and Kazak (1992) found that young adults (men and women) of alcoholic fathers had higher scores on DEQ Self-Criticism than their peers, Carson and Baker (1996) found that adult women of alcoholic parents had higher scores on DEQ Efficacy than a control sample of women. Although DEQ Dependency and Self-Criticism each seem to assess important dimensions in both clinical and nonclinical samples, as discussed earlier, Efficacy appears to have a different meaning in a clinical context that indicates a hypomanic denial of difficulties and a counter-reaction to issues of dependency (Blatt et al., 1982). This may account for the apparently paradoxical findings of Carson and Baker (1994) that women of alcoholic parents had higher DEQ Efficacy scores. Many of these women of alcoholic parents may have been "parentified" children who assumed caring responsibilities for their parents, and thus their elevated scores on DEQ Efficacy may also reflect their role as compulsive caregivers. Carson and Baker (1994) also found that codependent women, who have a need to control and assume responsibility for others, are more depressed and that this depression is primarily self-critical or introjective in focus.

Leather and Mongrain (2002) studied a group of young adults with a prior episode of major depression but without evidence of bipolar illness; current substance abuse; an eating disorder; psychotic symptoms; or a borderline, antisocial, schizotypal, or schizoid personality disorder. They found that elevated DEQ Self-Criticism predicted a greater number of prior episodes of depression and that this risk increased further with elevated levels of Dependency (DEQ Factor I). These effects were maintained even after controlling statistically for current levels of neuroticism and depressive affect. Thus, both the Self-Critical and Interpersonal factors of the DEQ were associated with a more serious prior history of clinical depression, independent of current levels of depression (as measured by the CES–D) and neuroticism. In addition, the DEQ

Interpersonal factor (Factor I) was associated with the diagnosis of a prior anxiety disorder (generalized anxiety and social phobia), independent of the current level of self-criticism, depressed symptoms (CES–D), and neuroticism. Thus, individuals with elevated scores on the DEQ Interpersonal factor who had a prior episode of major depression were also more likely previously to have had an anxiety disorder (see Luthar & Blatt, 1993, 1995). Both DEQ factors were also significantly correlated with the presence of a *DSM–IV* Axis II disorder. Schulte and Mongrain (2003) explored further the relationship of the DEQ Interpersonal factor to clinical diagnosis by evaluating the two subscales within DEQ Factor I: Neediness and Connectedness (Rude & Burnham, 1995). They found that Neediness, the less mature level of interpersonal relatedness, controlling for Connectedness, predicted *DSM–IV* Axis II diagnoses in a group of young adults with a prior history of depressive illness and marginally predicted current as well as the number of previous episodes of depression. Connectedness, the more mature form of interpersonal relatedness, in contrast, was unrelated to *DSM* diagnoses once the Neediness factor was controlled for statistically. Thus, consistent with earlier reports, the relatively recent differentiation (Blatt, Zohar, Quinlan, Luthar, & Hart, 1996; Blatt, Zohar, Quinlan, Zuroff, & Mongrain, 1995; Rude & Burnham, 1995) of Neediness, a less mature level of interpersonal concerns, appears to be significantly related to measures of depression, more so than the more mature interpersonal level of relatedness (Connectedness).

DEQ data, as well as measures of levels of depression and suicidal ideation, and reports of negative and positive psychotic symptoms, were also obtained in a longitudinally studied sample of 69 psychotic patients (Shahar, Trower, et al., in press). DEQ Efficacy was associated with fewer depressive symptoms and suicidal ideation in these patients. The DEQ Interpersonal factor (Factor I) predicted more depressive symptoms on the BDI and the Calgary Depression Scale for Schizophrenia (Addington, Addington, & Maticka-Tyndale, 1993) than did DEQ Self-Criticism (Factor II). The DEQ Interpersonal factor, but not the Self-Criticism factor, also predicted the occurrence of negative symptoms. Positive symptoms, in contrast, were not predicted by any of the DEQ factors. These findings suggest that, in more disturbed psychotic patients, the Interpersonal factor of the DEQ may be a more appropriate measure than DEQ Self-Criticism, which is usually more salient in patients with depression, neuroses, or borderline personality disorder. Thus, Factor I of the DEQ may assess developmentally earlier issues that are more relevant to patients with psychoses, whereas DEQ Factor II assesses concerns seen in more organized patients. Shahar, Trower, et al. (in press) also explored the role of the two subfactors within DEQ Factor I (Neediness and Relatedness or Connectedness) within this sample of psychotic patients but found no differences in their correlations with the other measures. As discussed in chapter 3, and as indicated by the results of Schulte and Mongrain (2003), the differentiation of these two levels of interpersonal concern in the DEQ Factor I—a more primitive level of desperate neediness and a more mature level of concern for one's relationship with particularly significant others—was an important differentiation within depressed patients and nonclinical samples. It is possible that patients with psychoses do not differentiate between these two levels of interpersonal relatedness, and thus this distinction may not be as relevant with psychotic patients as it is with more organized depressed patients or individuals in nonclinical samples.

Depression and Problematic Behavior

Depression and Substance Abuse

The distinction between dependency and self-criticism has also been useful in studying the role of depression in a wide range of disruptive behavior, including substance abuse, eating disorders, and antisocial behavior, especially in adolescence. Lidz, Lidz, and Rubenstein (1976), in a detailed clinical report of five adolescent female inpatients in a long-term facility, discussed the role of anaclitic issues in amphetamine addiction. Lehman and Rodin (1989) and Bers (1988), using the DEQ, found preoccupations with dependency and self-criticism in participants with bulimia and anorexia. Hospitalized anorexic patients had substantially higher scores on the DEQ Self-Criticism and Interpersonal factors and significantly lower Efficacy scores than did nonclinical controls (Bers, 1988). Outpatients with bulimia (Lehman & Rodin, 1989) had significantly higher DEQ Self-Criticism scores (but not Factor I scores) and significantly lower Efficacy scores than a control group. It is unclear, however, whether the anorexic patients' elevated scores on the Interpersonal factor, compared with the bulimic patients, reflected differences between these two types of eating disorders or whether the hospitalized anorexic patients were more seriously disturbed than the bulimic outpatients. Steiger and colleagues (Steiger, Gauvin, Jabalpurwala, Seguin, & Stotland, 1999; Steiger, Leung, Puentes-Neuman, & Gottheil, 1992; Steiger, Puentes-Neuman, & Leung, 1991) also have found evidence of elevated DEQ Self-Criticism in individuals with eating disorders.

Depression and Opiate Addiction

Empirical investigation of opiate-addicted outpatients demonstrated the importance of self-criticism in opiate addiction (Blatt, Rounsaville, Eyre, & Wilber, 1984). Considerable controversy exists about the dynamics of drug addiction and the personality characteristics of individuals who become addicted to drugs. Part of this controversy results from considering addiction as a unitary phenomenon with little differentiation among individuals who become addicted to different substances. As Milkman and Frosch (1973) pointed out, different substances have different effects and therefore may serve different needs.

One of the more consistent findings in the numerous clinical, theoretical, and research reports on drug addiction is the centrality of depression in opiate addiction. Some investigators (e.g., Khantzian, Mack, & Schatzberg, 1974; Krystal & Raskin, 1970) have discussed opiate addiction as a maladaptive mode of managing intense affect, particularly aggression and depression. Numerous clinical case studies (e.g., Glover, 1932/1956; D. Hartmann, 1969; Krystal &

Raskin, 1970; Wishnie, 1974) and research reports (e.g., Milkman & Frosch, 1973; P. R. Robbins, 1974; Woody et al., 1983; Woody, O'Brien, & Rickels, 1975) suggest that depression is a central etiological factor in, as well as a major consequence of, opiate addiction. However, it is unclear whether the focus of this depression is derived from issues of neglect, deprivation, and loneliness or from feelings of failure, self-loathing, self-deprecation, and guilt.

Because individuals with severe depression may have difficulty with affect modulation (Khantzian et al., 1974; Wishnie, 1974), some individuals may seek opiates as an anesthetic (Krystal & Raskin, 1970). Glover (1932/1956) discussed opiate abuse as an individual's attempt to establish a symbiotic relatedness with the maternal object, with the drug serving as a replacement for the individual's failure to achieve a sense of relatedness (e.g., Khantzian, 1978; Krystal & Raskin, 1970, p. 93) with a nurturant, loving mother (Abraham, 1908/1927; Chessick, 1960; Savitt, 1963). Thus, opiate addiction has been often viewed by some investigators as an attempt to satisfy unfilled oral neediness and yearnings that are the consequence of severe maternal neglect or overindulgence (Krystal, 1974, 1977; Krystal & Raskin, 1970). The addict, unable to tolerate delay, constantly seeks infantile modes of gratification (Khantzian, 1978) because of a failure to have established adequate self-care and self-regulation. The addict feels lonely, depressed, and full of frustration and rage, and the drug is used to satisfy primitive oral cravings and to ward off intense dysphoric feelings of helplessness and dependency (Khantzian, 1978; Wurmser, 1974). Profound loneliness, sadness, hunger, and depletion result in a seeking of gratification and the soothing comfort that was never achieved in the addict's basic caring relationship with the mother.

Opiate addiction has also been conceptualized as an attempt to achieve differentiation from an intensely judgmental and harsh parental figure (C. D. Kaplan & Wogan, 1978; Krystal & Raskin, 1970). The suicidal intent inherent in opiate abuse (Simmel, 1948) is expressed as self-contempt derived from the internalized harsh, critical attitudes of the punitive parent, as well as rage felt toward the parent. Thus, guilt and shame, which are considered central to addiction (Wurmser, 1974), are often expressed in the form of depressive, obsessive, and paranoid features (Glover, 1932/1956). Addicts are plagued by profound feelings of worthlessness, hopelessness, shame, guilt, self-revulsion, and intense self-destructive impulses. Addiction is viewed as a withdrawal and isolation from interpersonal relationships because of profoundly low self-esteem and negative interpersonal expectations. The addict becomes withdrawn; angry; sullen; empty; hopeless; filled with self-blame and self-loathing; and angry at an aloof, punitive, erratic, unstable, abusive parent who made severe, unreasonable demands (Wishnie, 1974). Thus, the addict has a low tolerance for criticism and struggles to externalize blame and responsibility. A few investigators (e.g., Wishnie, 1974; Wurmser, 1974) have discussed addiction as evolving from a need to seek immediate gratification to compensate for oral deprivation from an unavailable, inconsistent mother and from feelings of guilt and shame because of a harsh, punitive, judgmental father. The differentiation between these issues of oral neediness and of self-criticism (guilt and shame) in opiate addiction suggested that the DEQ could be useful in understanding more fully the dynamics of depression in opiate addiction.

Blatt, Rounsaville, Eyre, and Wilber (1984) used the DEQ and the Hamilton (Hamilton, 1960, 1967) and Raskin Depression scales (Raskin, Boothe, Reatig, & Schulterbrandt, 1978) to compare the intensity and nature of depressive experiences in a group of outpatient opiate addicts with polydrug nonopiate substance abusers, a general psychiatric sample, and a group of normal young adults. Patients were considered as addicted to opiates if they had a history of at least one year of regular use of illicit opiates and the presence of tolerance (i.e., the need for increasing doses to obtain desired effects) or withdrawal symptoms when they attempted to reduce dosage or discontinue use. The drug abuse of the polydrug group was serious enough to necessitate treatment (an outpatient drug counseling program or a residential therapeutic community) even though an addiction to opiates had not taken place.

No significant differences were found between these two groups of substance abusers in regard to sex, race, marital status, and social class. About two thirds of the individuals in both groups were White, single men from social classes IV and V (working and lower class; Hollingshead & Redlich, 1958). The opiate and polydrug abusers were similar on many sociodemographic characteristics except that opiate addicts were somewhat older, more educated, and had a better work history. No significant differences were found between the two groups in the loss of a parent as a result of death or divorce, incidence of physical and mental illness, a history of drug abuse or legal difficulties in their immediate or extended families, or reports of family discord and quarrels. The only significant difference in an extensive examination of early life history or family patterns of the opiate and polydrug abusers was that the opiate addicts reported fewer close friends ($p \leq .008$). The number of individuals in both groups who reported that their predominant childhood recollections involved unpleasant memories of their parents (80.85% and 72.95% for the opiate and the polydrug, nonopiate groups, respectively) was impressive. Although this difference was not statistically significant, and no base rate data exist to enable one to compare these percentages to reports in other groups, the remarkably high percent of unpleasant childhood memories in both groups is noteworthy.

The opiate addicts appeared significantly more depressed than the polydrug, nonopiate addicted group. They obtained significantly higher scores on the Hamilton Somatic subscale ($p \leq .01$) and on the Self-Criticism factor of the DEQ ($p \leq .0004$). The difference between opiate and polydrug abusers on the DEQ Interpersonal factor was not significant. Thus, this depression appeared to be focused primarily around issues of self-criticism and guilt rather than themes of dependency, abandonment, rejection, and loneliness. In fact, of all the measures of depression used in this extensive study of opiate addiction, DEQ Self-Criticism provided the most effective discrimination between the opiate and the polydrug groups. Also, despite consistently significantly higher scores on many measures of psychological disturbance, opiate addicts tended to describe themselves as somewhat more effective than the polydrug abusers ($p = .067$), as measured by the DEQ Efficacy factor.

The two groups of substance abusers were compared to two reference groups: (a) a group of 134 normal adults and (b) a sample of 95 non-substance abusing inpatients in a psychiatric facility. Both the opiate and the polydrug groups had significantly ($p \leq .01$) lower scores on the DEQ Interpersonal factor than the psychiatric sample did, and even somewhat lower scores than the nonclinical participants. Opiate addicts, however, had significantly ($p \leq .0001$) higher scores on DEQ Self-Criticism than did the nonclinical participants, and even slightly higher scores than psychiatric patients. Polydrug abusers, in contrast, like the nonclinical sample, were significantly less self-critical than psychiatric patients ($p \leq .01$).

The opiate group also differed from the other groups on the DEQ Efficacy factor. Opiate addicts not only had higher efficacy scores than the polydrug group ($p \leq .07$) and the psychiatric patients ($p \leq .01$) but also somewhat higher scores than even the nonclinical participants. Polydrug abusers, in contrast, described themselves as relatively ineffective: Their scores on the DEQ Efficacy factor were significantly lower than those of nonclinical participants ($p \leq .01$) and even somewhat lower than those of the psychiatric patients.

In summary, both the opiate and the polydrug groups indicated relatively low levels of interpersonal concerns. Opiate addicts, however, were highly self-critical yet also described themselves as quite effective. Polydrug abusers, on the other hand, were not especially self-critical but described themselves as relatively ineffective. These findings suggest that self-critical depression is a central issue in opiate addiction. Opiate addicts were significantly more depressed than a group of non-opiate addicted polydrug abusers, and this depression was focused primarily around issues of self-criticism and guilt rather than around feelings of rejection, abandonment, and neglect. Opiate-addicted individuals appeared to be struggling with intensely painful problems of self-worth. Not only did they report significantly higher levels of self-criticism, but they also reported significantly greater social isolation and fewer friends. Their memories of early childhood are filled with negative images of both parents. They are estranged and isolated, feeling that they have failed and are worthless (Blatt et al., 1984). The depressive, obsessive, paranoid and self-destructive features noted in clinical reports of opiate addicts (e.g., Glover, 1932/1956; Krystal & Raskin, 1970; Rado, 1926; Simmel, 1948) is consistent with observations that psychiatric patients who have elevations primarily on the DEQ Self-Criticism scale usually have a predominantly introjective personality organization with obsessive–compulsive and paranoid features and often have difficulty modulating anger and aggression and, when intensely depressed, can become seriously self-destructive (Blatt, 1995a; Blatt et al., 1982).

Although opiate and polydrug abusers were similar in demographic characteristics and in many aspects of their early life experiences, they differed primarily in the extent of their psychopathology, especially in the intensity of depression focused primarily on issues of self-criticism. A central question, of course, is whether the depression that centers around issues of self-worth, guilt, and shame is the cause or consequence of opiate addiction. It is possible that opiate addicts' elevated self-criticism is an expression of guilt over the illicit activity associated with opiate abuse. However, if the elevated self-criticism scores were related to consumption of an illicit drug, then no differences should exist in the degree of self-criticism between the opiate-addicted and the polydrug groups, because the latter was also involved in the abuse of illicit drugs. Also, no significant correlations were found between scores on any of the three DEQ factors and aspects of the legal history of these two groups (e.g., arrests for crimes other than drug-related ones). In addition, it is particularly noteworthy that the degree of self-criticism as measured by the DEQ was predictive of the extent to which individuals in the polydrug group were using opiates. Although the members of the polydrug group were not yet addicted to opiates (i.e., they did not have a need for increasing dosages or withdrawal symptoms), the extent of their experimentation with heroin, an indication that they were likely to become addicted to opiates, was significantly correlated with their scores on the Self-Criticism factor of the DEQ. Thus, the intensity of self-criticism was not only significantly greater in opiate addicts than in polydrug abusers, but even within the polydrug, non-opiate addicted group Self-Criticism was significantly correlated with the extent to which these individuals were experimenting with heroin. These findings are consistent with Paton, Kessler, and Kandel's (1977) finding that depression severity is associated with progressive involvement with drugs. Because individuals excessively high in self-criticism usually avoid social contact, the opiate experience may provide a way for them to maintain this social isolation. It is also possible that the process of continually assaulting oneself with a needle, with the accompanying possible exposure to AIDS and other socially transmitted diseases, provides a form of self-punishment and unconscious suicidal intent that derive from the opiate addict's intense feelings of guilt and self-criticism.

A brief clinical vignette illustrates the role of guilt and self-criticism in opiate addiction. A 31-year-old married man with several children sought help for barbiturate abuse and heroin addiction. He reported a 14-year history of barbiturate and opiate abuse, and an addiction to heroin in the past two years. After detoxification, he entered both group and couples therapy. He reported an early childhood of being overindulged by his mother and her extended family. His father, disabled by back pain from a work accident and addicted to opiates, was verbally and physically abusive to both the patient and his mother. In early adolescence, the patient began spending increasing amounts of time out of the home because he could not tolerate the constant bickering between his parents and the verbal and physical harassment by his father. In his therapy, much of the first year focused on strategies to keep him free of opiates and improving his communication with his wife. Although he regularly attended group and couples therapy, he remained noticeably disturbed, but continued to deny any experiences of anxiety and depression.

After approximately one year of treatment, he became increasingly depressed, briefly returning to abusing opiates. With encouragement from his wife, he reported that this was the time of year when a friend had died in an auto accident, when he and his friend were both 17 years old. The patient reported, with much affect, that he had been the driver of the car, and has always felt deeply ashamed and guilty about the death of his friend. The patient's family denied that he was responsible for the accident and refused to talk about it, but the family of his friend would have nothing to do with the patient. He reported that his first use of opiates began shortly after this accident. He spent a number of therapy sessions painfully discussing his feelings on responsibility and guilt about the accident. His depression began to diminish and he continued to show marked improvement in his ability to communicate with his wife and friends, with no indication of any tendency to return to drug abuse.

Nonclinical Settings

In current psychiatric literature, the diagnosis of depression is usually used to designate a *syndrome* defined by a mixture of psychological states and somatic and vegetative symptoms that have been compiled by clinicians and researchers to establish a consistent set of criteria for specifying homogeneous groups that have continuity across various research studies and among different clinical diagnoses. As discussed earlier in this chapter, the criteria for depression specified in *DSM–III–R* (American Psychiatric Association, 1987) and *DSM–IV* (American Psychiatric Association, 1994) are symptomatic expressions derived from Feighner et al.'s (1972) criteria and the RDC (Spitzer et al., 1978). The nature of discourse, however, is different when discussing psychological dimensions of depression rather than clinical symptoms (Depue & Monroe, 1986). Each approach is likely to result in groups that are heterogeneous on the other dimension. The goal of *DSM* criteria, for example, is to identify groups similar in severity and in the biological or somatic–vegetative expressions of the disorder. Such groups, however, are likely to be heterogeneous on psychological dimensions. Similarly, in work with psychological dimensions, such as with the DEQ, that examines psychological and characterological qualities, individuals consistent on these psychological patterns may be heterogeneous on somatic–vegetative variables. Biological approaches seek to find homogeneity within biological variables; psychological approaches are directed at identifying consistency in psychological dimensions, including character styles, affect states, and defenses across individuals at varying levels of pathology–normality. Each approach has its strengths and purposes.

The approach to diagnosis is different in the psychological and biological perspectives. Researchers using biological criteria usually use *cut points* in attempting to define a point at which a disorder can be assumed to be present and for which biological treatment would be indicated. This categorical approach to psychopathology stands in contrast to psychological approaches, which attempt to assess individuals along a dimension that maintains continuity between nonclinical and clinical individuals. As discussed in chapter 3, psychological dimensions of depression can be studied effectively as a continuum ranging from normality to severe clinical states. Research findings indicate considerable advantage in viewing depression as a continuous dimension in which psychological disturbances are considered as deviations of normal developmental processes, the consequence of exaggerations and distortions of natural life experiences. Dependency and self-criticism repeatedly emerge as relatively stable and independent dimensions in nonclinical and clinical samples that have considerable utility in the study of psychological dimensions of depression.

DSM–III–R and *DSM–IV*, even in their narrow definition of depression as a clinical disorder, suggest a linkage between depression and disruptive behavior, especially in adolescence. For example, they note the frequent occurrence of depression in children and adolescents with conduct disorder, attention-deficit/hyperactivity disorder, and oppositional defiant disorder. The discussions of various types of conduct disorders in *DSM–III–R* and *DSM–IV* note that these disruptive behaviors are often accompanied by mood disturbances, even severe depression, as well as low self-esteem and underachievement. The co-occurrence of depression (as defined by *DSM–III–R* and *DSM–IV* criteria) and conduct disorders (e.g., school suspension, police contact, juvenile court) has been estimated to be as high as 36% (Carlson & Cantwell, 1980a; Kashani et al., 1987; Kovacs, Paulouskas, Gatsonis, & Richards, 1988; Marriage, Fine, Moretti, & Haley, 1986; Puig-Antich, 1982).

DSM–III–R and *DSM–IV*, in their discussion of depression, also note that various types of depression are associated with disruptive behavior (e.g., difficulty in school or with the legal system, substance abuse, sexually transmitted diseases, unintentional pregnancies, running away from home, accidents, fighting, homicide, suicide, truancy, stealing, vandalism, sexual promiscuity, and aggressive and reckless behavior). Likewise, the manuals note that mania, as part of a bipolar mood disturbance, may be associated with recklessness, sexual promiscuity, drug abuse, attention-deficit/hyperactivity disorder, and hyperactivity. Thus, in many ways, *DSM–III–R* and *DSM–IV* note a marked co-occurrence of mood disturbances and various types of disruptive and destructive behavior, particularly in adolescence.[3]

Although the co-occurrence of depression with a variety of untoward behavior is noted in considerable detail in the *DSM*s, especially in adolescence, these manuals assume that depression is the consequence, and not the cause, of the disordered behavior.[4] Certainly one can experience dysphoric affect in reaction to a wide range of disruptions of current life circumstances (cf. A. T. Beck, 1967a, 1999), but this reactive dysphoric response to negative current life events must be differentiated from a more pervasive and sustained dysphoria

---

[3] The following are quoted passages from *DSM–III–R* (American Psychiatric Association, 1987): "The irritability and antisocial behavior often seen in Bipolar Disorders in children or adolescence can erroneously be considered symptoms of Conduct Disorder" (p. 55). "In mood disorders there may be psychomotor agitation and difficulty in concentration that are difficult to distinguish from the hyperactivity and attention difficulties seen in Attention-deficit Hyperactivity Disorder. Therefore, it is important to consider the diagnosis of Mood Disorder before making the diagnosis of Attention-deficit Hyperactivity Disorder" (p. 52). In conduct disorder, "Self-esteem is usually low, though the person may project an image of 'toughness' . . . Symptoms of anxiety and depression are common, and may justify additional diagnoses" (p. 54). "Features of Oppositional Deficient Disorder may be seen during the course of Dysthymia or a Manic, Hypomania or Major Depressive Episode" (p. 57). "Depressed mood frequently is present" in separation anxiety disorder (p. 59). "Avoidant Disorders of childhood and adolescence are characterized by social withdrawal," which is also present in Major Depression and Dysthymia (p. 62).

[4] The following are quoted passages from *DSM–III–R* (American Psychiatric Association, 1987): "Dysthymia frequently seems to be a *consequence* [italics added] of a pre-existing chronic, nonmood Axis I or Axis III disorder, e.g., Anorexia Nervosa, Somatization Disorder, Psychoactive Substance Abuse Dependence, and Anxiety Disorder, or rheumatoid arthritis" (p. 230). "In children and adolescents, predisposing factors (for Dysthymia) are the presence of Attention-deficit Hyperactivity Disorder, Conduct Disorder, Mental Retardation, a severe Development Disorder, or an inadequate, disorganized, rejecting, and chaotic environment" (p. 231).

that expresses more enduring negative life experiences that can be a causative force in a number of behavioral disorders. Thus, it is possible that many of the behavioral disorders described in *DSM–III–R* and *DSM–IV* are symptomatic expressions of an enduring subclinical depression that has not reached a level of severity intense enough to warrant being diagnosed as either major depression or dysthymia. As discussed earlier, symptomatic expressions of depression include antisocial behavior, eating disorders, substance abuse, accidents, learning difficulty, and neglect of physical health and well-being. Glaser (1967) and Toolan (1962), for example, have discussed stealing, lying, truancy, and other destructive risk-taking behavior as symptoms of depression. Thus, many disruptive experiences in adolescents as well as in adults may be enactments of the pain and pathos of intense dysphoria and of an underlying depressive state.

Although some investigators (Geller, Chestnut, Miller, Price & Yates, 1985; Kovacs, Feinberg, Crause-Novack, Paulaskas, et al., 1984; Puig-Antich, 1982) view conduct disorder as secondary to mood disturbance, *DSM–III–R* and *DSM–IV* generally fail to consider the possibility that a wide variety of disruptive behaviors in adolescence may be the consequence of dysphoric states. In fact, various types of disruptive behavior may serve as a form of affect discharge, thereby reducing the intensity of the dysphoric affect so that the depression does not reach the necessary thresholds established by *DSM–III–R* and *DSM–IV* for the diagnosis of a mood disorder. In many ways, antisocial behavior and acting out more generally, like mania, can serve as a way of avoiding painful dysphoric affect. In addition, individuals who have a tendency to express their difficulties in behavioral activity, rather than being reflective about their experiences, may express their dysphoria in various forms of disruptive and destructive activity. Anger and rage in dysphoria and depression can be directed inwardly, through suicide, or outwardly, through violations of social norms or attacking others (the latter, of course, can result in self-destruction as well).

The literature on *masked depression* (e.g., Fisch, 1987; Glaser, 1967; Lesse, 1974) and *depressive equivalents* is relevant to understanding the relationships of depression to disruptive and destructive behavior. Disruptive behavior may "mask" the depression not only from the patient but also from the clinician and the investigator. Dysphoric experiences may be expressed in a wide range of clinical disorders, including depression as well as disruptive and destructive behavior. In fact, one might consider clinical depression as a passive yielding to intense underlying dysphoria, whereas destructive behavior, similar to mania, may be a defensive attempt to avoid and forestall experiencing intense dysphoria and a painful clinical depression. Experiences of depression may be expressed in numerous defensive maneuvers, including behavioral problems, somatic complaints, promiscuity, antisocial patterns, and delinquency (Chwast, 1967). Glaser (1967) presented several cases demonstrating that delinquent behavior can be an external expression of an underlying depression.

The observation of a relationship between disruptive behavior and underlying dysphoria was initially emphasized by Aichhorn (1925/1955), Anna Freud (1937), and subsequently a number of early psychoanalytic investigators (e.g., Blos, 1957; Burkes & Harrison, 1961; Chwast, 1967; Eissler, 1949; Falstein, 1958; Fenichel, 1945; Glaser, 1967; Lesse, 1974; Spiegel, 1967; Toolan, 1962). Greenson (1957) even suggested the term *impulsive depressives* to acknowledge the depressive core in disruptive behavior in some adolescents. Fenichel (1945) viewed most impulsive acts as a defense against experiencing depression. Anna Freud (1937) noted a parallel between the superego disturbances in depression and "ruthless" aggressive individuals. Superego disturbances may be expressed either in an external aggressive projection of anger or in introjection of guilt that leads to depression. Eissler (1949) noted that when disruptive adolescents are prevented from engaging in disruptive behaviors, they become depressed and stuporous, or they develop a panic reaction. Clinical examples presented by Aichhorn (1925/1955) illustrate well that underlying dysphoria is often seen in adolescents who have been involved in disruptive behavior. Aichhorn, in fact, commented that disruptive behavior can be a way in which an adolescent tries to escape dysphoric feelings. Toolan (1962, 1974) viewed various forms of behavioral problems in adolescence, such as acting out and delinquency, as expressions of depression that have been precipitated by object loss or a disruption of a sense of well-being. These experiences can result in depression or defensive disruptive behavior, depending on the developmental level and personality organization of the individual. In a clinical study of 121 delinquent adolescents (ages 7–16), Chwast (1967) found that 78% of the participants were at least somewhat depressed, and 46% were substantially or predominantly depressed. He concluded that a large depressive component often exists in the adolescents' disruptive behavior as they attempt to deal with a sense of emptiness and cope with demanding situations without adequate inner resources because of psychological impoverishment.

Increased reports of depressive symptoms in adolescents and young adults (Kandel & Davies, 1982, 1986; Klerman & Weissman, 1989; Rutter, 1986) have led to a burgeoning literature on the nature, etiology, and expressions of depression. However, research indicates a frequent comorbidity of affective disturbances (major depression, dysthymia, and depressed mood) with problem behaviors, particularly anxiety and conduct disorders, in children and adolescents (Carlson & Cantwell, 1980b, 1983; D. A. Cole & Carpentieri, 1990; Craighead, 1991; Kovacs et al., 1988). Clinical diagnoses of depression, as well as self-reported depressive symptoms or dysphoria, appear to be related to a range of problem behaviors in children and adolescents in community settings (Blatt, Hart, Quinlan, Leadbeater, & Auerbach, 1993; Blatt & Shichman, 1981; Colton, Gore, & Aseltine, 1991; Leadbeater, Blatt & Quinlan, 1995; Reinherz, Frost, & Pakiz, 1991; Reinherz et al., 1990; Reinherz et al., 1989). Many behavioral disturbances (e.g., conduct disorder) co-occur with reports of depression in children and adolescents (Carlson & Cantwell, 1980a; D. A. Cole & Carpentieri, 1990; Craighead, 1991; Rhode, Lewinsohn, & Seeley, 1991) in both clinical (e.g., Blatt & Shichman, 1981) and community-based samples (e.g., Achenbach & Edelbrock, 1978; Blatt et al., 1993; Blatt, Schaffer, Bers, & Quinlan, 1991; Colton et al., 1991; A. V. Horwitz & White, 1987; Reinherz et al., 1991; Reinherz et al., 1990; Reinherz et al., 1989).

The co-occurrence of depression or depressive symptoms and other problem behaviors in adolescents suggests that some common causal factors may create risks for both types of disturbances. The factors that create vulnerabilities to dysphoria and depression may also create risks for the development of other problem behaviors, particularly in adolescents. Much of the disruptive behavior noted in troubled adolescents can be understood as expressions of two types of dysphoria or depression, deriving from (a) feelings of abandonment and experiences of neglect or (b) feelings of worthlessness and failure that are the consequence of the internalization of the values and attributes of harshly judgmental and punitive parental figures. As illustrated in the clinical cases presented in chapter 2, disruptive behavior in adolescents can be a search for nurturance and soothing, or it can be an angry retaliation and retribution by seeking to hurt others, oneself, or both. Disruptive behavior can be observed in the impulsive, impetuous acts of individuals who are unaware of the danger of their behavior; in individuals who are aware of, but unconcerned about, the consequences of their actions for themselves or for others; or in individuals who consciously and unconsciously seek to hurt or even destroy others and themselves.

The differentiation of subtypes of dysphoric experiences (interpersonal distress, i.e., fears of loss of relationships and abandonment and extreme desire for closeness and dependency; or issues of self-criticism, i.e., feelings of failure or incompetence, loss of autonomy, and guilt) offers a possible approach to understanding the causal links between depression and problem behaviors in adolescents. Many of the problem behaviors found with considerable frequency in community samples of nonclinical adolescents appear to be related to these two subtypes of dysphoria. A depression characterized by dependence or loneliness appears to be a primary issue in internalizing problems, such as somatic concerns, especially in females. Self-critical dysphoria appears to be a primary issue in externalizing problems, such as delinquency and aggression, especially in males. These relationships between self-reported problem behavior and types of dysphoria persist even after the contribution of the basic level of depression is removed statistically in multiple regression analysis (Blatt et al., 1993).

Individuals with high interpersonal depressive vulnerability (DEQ Factor I) have anxious/preoccupied attachments (e.g., Zuroff & Fitzpatrick, 1995) characterized by an intense need for emotional closeness. In clinical samples, this elevated interpersonal vulnerability is associated with extreme anxiety about loss, neglect, deprivation, and abandonment in relationships. Luthar and Blatt (1993), for example, found that Self-Criticism (DEQ Factor II) in a group of inner-city adolescents had strong associations with depression and concerns about loss of approval, whereas interpersonal concerns (e.g., DEQ Factor I [Dependency]) showed stronger associations with diffuse tension, worry, and sensitivity to others' behavior. Although the association between interpersonal concerns (DEQ Factor I) and anxiety suggests that a common focus in anxiety may be issues of separation and loss of contact with others and their support (Fichman, Koestner, & Zuroff, 1997), self-critical vulnerability, in both nonclinical and clinical populations, is characterized by negative perceptions of both self (e.g., Fichman, Koestner, & Zuroff, 1996) and others and a fearful–avoidant attachment pattern (Blatt & Homann, 1992; K. N. Levy, Blatt, & Shaver, 1998; Reis & Grenyer, 2002; Zuroff & Fitzpatrick, 1995). Highly self-critical individuals are generally isolated and aloof, because they anticipate that others will be critical and untrustworthy. Self-criticism in school-age adolescents is associated with impaired attachments to both parents and peers (Batgos & Leadbeater, 1994; Fichman, Koestner, & Zuroff, 1994). As I discuss in detail in chapter 7, differential attributions of self and others that stem from the two types of depressive vulnerabilities may well create differences in interpersonal contexts that affect both available social support and the types of interpersonal events that are perceived as stressful. For example, among college women, self-criticism is associated with lower levels of trust, less self-disclosure, and unsuccessful conflict resolution.

The different vulnerability of the two types of dysphoria may partially explain the associations that have been found in adolescents between depression and the frequently dichotomized internalizing and externalizing disorders (Achenbach & Edelbrock, 1978, 1983). *Internalizing problems* generally comprise cognitive, affective, and somatic disorders, such as anxiety, depression, eating disorders, and suicidal thoughts and feelings. *Externalizing disorders*, on the other hand, typically include delinquency, aggression, drug use, high-risk sexual activity, and school problems. In community-based adolescents, general depressive symptoms correlate with broad assessments of both internalizing and externalizing disorders (Colton et al., 1991; A. V. Horwitz & White, 1987; Reinherz et al., 1990; Reinherz et al., 1989) as well as with specific problem behaviors, including conduct disorder (D. A. Cole & Carpentieri, 1990; Kovacs et al., 1988); suicidal feelings and behaviors (D. R. Robbins & Alessi, 1985); school problems, including dropout (McGrath, Keita, Strickland, & Russo, 1990); eating disorders (McGrath et al., 1990); premarital pregnancy (Yamaguchi & Kendal, 1987); and illicit drug use (Kandel, Kessler, & Margulies, 1978; Newcomb & Bentler, 1988). Females consistently show more internalizing disorders, whereas males show more externalizing disorders (Achenbach & Edelbrock, 1978; Achenbach, Howell, Quay, & Conners, 1991).

Research on disruptive behavior in community samples of adolescents suggests that anaclitic and introjective personality organizations are differentially associated with internalizing and externalizing behavior patterns. The enactments of painful affect experiences of neglect and deprivation and severely critical, judgmental parental standards result in different behavioral expression. Disruptive behavior can result from disturbances in either of these two personality styles, but the form of the disruptive behavior will differ because of differences in the nature of their preoccupations. Even when the manifest form and expression of the disruptive behavior is similar, the behavior may have different meanings for the individual. As noted in the clinical examples presented in chapter 2, disruptive behavior may in part be a defense against profound experiences of dysphoria associated with either loss or failure.

Colleagues and I (e.g., Blatt, 1991; Blatt et al., 1993; Leadbeater et al., 1995), using the DEQ–A to study community samples of adolescents, have found that interpersonal dysphoria and interpersonal stress tend to lead to internalizing problems, whereas self-critical dysphoria and threats to competence tend to lead to externalizing problems. Interpersonal concerns on the DEQ–A had strong relationships with a number of the Youth Self-Report (YSR; Achenbach, 1991) internalizing scales, including feeling unpopular, for both females and males, and with identity/suicide and somatic concerns in males. Interpersonal concerns on the DEQ–A, however, did not predict specific types of externalizing behaviors (delinquency, aggression, or the externalizing factor) in males and females. However, Self-Criticism on the DEQ–A significantly predicted these externalizing behaviors (except for delinquency in females). These significant differential relationships between DEQ Dependency and Self-Criticism, and reports of high school students about a wide variety of problem areas, as assessed by the YSR, were found after controlling for general level of depression, as measured by the Community Epidemiological Survey for Depression (Radloff, 1977). Thus, the type of dysphoria appears to determine subsequent expression of psychological disturbance and distress. Individuals with high levels of interpersonal concerns about abandonment or loss of others' support do not usually get involved in externalizing behaviors that could alienate others. On the other hand, individuals with high levels of self-critical concerns become involved in angry and disruptive behavior that both defies authority and at the same time invites the criticism and punishment they consciously and unconsciously believe they deserve (Blatt, 1991; Blatt, Hart, et al., 1993). Thus, disruptive behavior in adolescence often appears to be an expression of underlying despair and depression. The differentiation of the two types of dysphoria provides a basis for appreciating some of the dynamic factors that can lead some adolescents to become involved in particular forms of disruptive behavior. Several problem areas, such as attention disturbances, are, however, significantly correlated with both Dependency and Self-Criticism.

The significant relationships found between dependent and self-critical dysphoria and self-reports of a wide variety of problem behaviors in high school students suggest that dysphoria and behavioral disorders are closely intertwined and that involvement in particular types of problematic behavior may be an expression of different types of dysphoria. Although these correlational data are intriguing and suggestive, they do not enable one to differentiate the causal directions of these relationships or the possible influence of other, unmeasured variables. The highly significant relationships between measures of dysphoria and tendencies toward disruptive behavior in a community sample of adolescents, however, suggest that dysphoric experiences may be the cause, rather than the consequence, of disruptive behavior. Further clarification of the causal relationships between adolescent dysphoric experiences and tendencies toward problem behavior could provide the basis for the early identification of at-risk adolescents and for the development of more effective community-based intervention strategies before they become involved in serious disruptive behavior. The possible causal relationships among the two types of dysphoria and problem behaviors in a community sample of female and male adolescents were investigated in a longitudinal design that assessed these personality dimensions prior to the onset of many of these behavior disturbances.

Leadbeater, Kuperminc, Blatt, and Hertzog (1999) conducted a longitudinal study of 460 early adolescent boys and girls (ages 11–13) in an urban middle school, using SEM, and found that self-critical vulnerability, as measured by Factor II of the DEQ–A, predicted both internalizing problems (.21 for girls and .30 for boys) and externalizing problems (.15 for girls and .20 for boys). Interpersonal vulnerability, as measured by Factor I of the DEQ–A, predicted increases in internalizing problems (.14 for girls and .15 for boys). Leadbeater et al. (1999) also found that the quality of adolescents' relationships with their parents and peers influenced the adjustment of girls through both direct and indirect effects. Positive relationships with parents directly predicted lower levels of both internalizing (−.21) and externalizing (−.25) problems in girls. Girls' positive relationships with parents were also associated with fewer stressful life events (−.39) and less self-critical vulnerability on the DEQ (−.39). Good peer relations also predicted less self-critical vulnerability (−.20) in girls. For boys, positive relationships with parents were associated with less self-critical vulnerability (−.25) and fewer stressful life events (−.34) but, paradoxically, with a higher level of interpersonal vulnerability (.14). These results indicate that advances in understanding the causal directions of multivariate relationships among individual vulnerabilities, potentiating factors, and psychological disturbances depend on theoretical models that clearly specify the relationships among these variables. In chapter 7, I review research directed toward clarifying further the relationships among various proximal environmental experiences in the etiology and expression of depression.

Longitudinal research on problem behaviors in adolescents has confirmed the relationships among environmental events such as a loss of self-esteem (e.g., via failure) and dysfunctional interpersonal relationships in the development and persistence of both internalizing and externalizing disorders (B. E. Compas, 1987; B. E. Compas, Slavin, Wagner, & Vannata, 1986; Elliott, Huizinga, & Menard, 1989; Jessor & Jessor, 1977, Loeber, 1988, 1990; Luthar, 1991; L. N. Robins & Rutter, 1990). Positive interpersonal relations and personal competence in several domains (e.g., academics, sports, and community involvement) have been shown to protect against the development of depression and a wide range of disruptive behavior (e.g., Achenbach, 1991; Dishion, Patterson, Stoolmiller, & Skinner, 1991; Leadbeater, Hellner, Allen, & Aber, 1989; Luthar, 1991; Masten et al., 1988; Rutter, 1979). The interaction of impaired competence and disrupted relationships contributes to depression; this in turn augments feelings of loneliness and failure (Cicchetti & Aber, 1986; Cicchetti & Schneider-Rosen, 1984b; Cicchetti, Toth, & Bush, 1988; D. A. Cole, 1991; P. M. Cole & Zahn-Waxler, 1992; Cummings & Cicchetti, 1990). Longitudinal research has also suggested that relationships between depressive symptoms and stressful life events may be reciprocal in adolescents; symptoms not only result from, but also predict, the occurrence of stressful events (Compas, 1987; Leadbeater & Linares, 1992; Swearingen & Cohen, 1985). I discuss more fully the theoretical implication of these interactions in chapter 7.

Ryder (1997) studied coping styles of interpersonal dependent individuals in response to interpersonal and achievement losses and found that dependent individuals try to deny painful experiences, both interpersonal loss and failure, and to seek social support. Ryder, like T. W. Smith, O'Keeffe, and Jenkins (1988), also found that sex role orientation is an important variable. As I discussed in chapter 3, Henrich, Blatt, Kuperminc, Zohar, and Leadbeater (2001) and others have demonstrated the importance of differentiating two levels of concerns about interpersonal issues, Neediness and Relatedness, within the Interpersonal factor (Factor I) of the DEQ in the study of the quality of interpersonal relations in nonclinical samples. This distinction, found in young adults (Blatt, Zohar, et al., 1995) and in older (ages 15–18; Blatt, Zohar, et al., 1996) and younger adolescents (ages 11–13; Henrich et al., 2001), is associated with independent evaluations of social functioning, especially in early adolescent girls. The differentiation of Neediness and Relatedness clarifies why the original Interpersonal factor (Factor I) of the DEQ has produced paradoxical effects when used to study interpersonal behavior. Failure to differentiate between these two dimensions embedded in DEQ Factor I may mask important intrapersonal and interpersonal processes.

Luyten (2002) and Luyten, Fontaine, Soenens, et al. (2003) using a scale of values developed by S. H. Schwartz and Huismans (1995), demonstrated that DEQ Dependency and Self-Criticism in adolescents and adults have contrastingly different patterns of relationships with a wide range of values. DEQ Dependency had a significantly positive correlation with altruism (the enhancement of close relationships) and a significant negative relationship to the values of power (social status, control, and dominance) and to stimulation (excitement, novelty, and change). DEQ Self-Criticism had just the opposite relationship to these values: Self-Criticism had a significant negative relationship with altruism and significantly positive relationships with power, stimulation, and self-direction.

Summary

Self-Criticism

Self-critical individuals are more introverted (Mongrain, 1993), resentful, irritable, critical of themselves and others (Zuroff, 1994), and isolated and distant from others (Mongrain, 1998; Mongrain & Zuroff, 1994). Their interpersonal interactions are relatively unpleasant (Zuroff et al., 1995) and hostile (Mongrain et al., 1998; Zuroff & Duncan, 1999). Although they are concerned about achievement, possibly because of their apprehensions about failure, they are less agentic (Zuroff, Moskowitz, et al., 1999). As college students, these more hostile, but often passive and submissive, individuals are more frequently rejected by their roommates (Mongrain, Lubbers, & Struthers, in press). They have a fearful–avoidant attachment style and, as Mongrain et al. (in press) noted, are usually located in the hostile–submissive quadrant of the circumplex model (Laforge & Suczek, 1995; Wiggins & Trapnell, 1996).

Powers, Zuroff, and Topciu (in press) demonstrated the convergence of several measures of introjective personality features: the Self-Criticism factor of the DEQ (Blatt, D'Afflitti, et al., 1976, 1979), socially prescribed perfectionism (Hewitt & Flett, 1991), and the Perfectionism factor of the Dysfunctional Attitudes Scale (DAS; A. N. Weissman & Beck, 1978). Powers et al. labeled this construct *self-critical perfectionism*. Their data differentiated self-critical perfectionism from personal standards as assessed by Hewitt and Flett's (1989) Self-Oriented Perfectionism Scale and Frost's Personal Standards Scale (Frost, Marten, Lahart, et al., 1990). Extensive longitudinal and cross-sectional research in clinical and nonclinical samples indicates that DEQ Self-Criticism and other measures of various aspects of the introjective personality, such as socially prescribed perfectionism (Dunkley & Blankstein, 2000) and self-critical perfectionism (Dunkley, Blankstein, Halsall, Williams, & Winkworth, 2000), are associated with low self-esteem (e.g., Zuroff, Moskowitz, Wielgus, Powers, & Franko, 1983), depressive symptoms (e.g., Dunkley & Blankstein, 2000), substance abuse (Bers, 1988; Blatt et al. 1984), eating disorders (Bers, 1988; Lehman & Rodin, 1989; Steiger et al., 1999; Steiger et al., 1992; Steiger et al., 1991), excessive worry (Stober, 1998), intense negative affect and less positive affect (e.g., Mongrain, 1998; Zuroff, Moskowitz, & Cote, 1999; Zuroff, Stotland, Sweetman, Craig, & Koestner, 1995), and a tendency to assume blame (Dunkley, Zuroff, & Blankstein, 2003; Hewitt & Flett, 1991) and to be critical of oneself (Frost et al., 1997) and of others (Vettese & Mongrain, 2000). Zuroff (1994) and Dunkley et al. (1997) have found that DEQ Self-Criticism is related to Neuroticism and low Agreeableness on the NEO Personality Inventory (Costa & McCrae, 1985). Self-critical individuals have a number of negative interpersonal qualities and problems (e.g., Mongrain, 1998; Mongrain et al., 1998; Whiffen & Aubé, 1999; Whiffen, Aubé, Thompson, & Campbell, 2000; Zuroff & Duncan, 1999). For example, they are sensitive to concerns about ridicule, and they are formal, reserved, distant, and cold in their interpersonal relationships (Alden & Bieling, 1996; Mongrain & Zuroff, 1994). They avoid close intimate relationships and are dissatisfied, distrustful, and non–self-disclosing in their relationships (e.g., Mongrain, 1998; Mongrain & Zuroff, 1995). They try to manipulate others through flattery, craftiness, and deception, and they respond to stress with feelings of guilt, self-blame, and hopelessness, and they usually use maladaptive, non-problem focused coping strategies. As I discuss in chapter 6, these self-critical attitudes derive from destructive parent–child relationships. Critical, judgmental, demanding, disapproving, and punitive parents lead to negative representations of the self and others (Blatt, 1995a; Blatt & Homann, 1992; Mongrain, 1998). Self-critical individuals have unrealistic goals and stringent standards (Nietzel & Harris, 1990), react strongly to any implications of their personal failure and loss of control (Dunkley et al., 2003), and are very concerned about how others react to their mistakes (e.g., Frost et al., 1997). They are easily provoked to anger, which they direct toward others as well as themselves (Hewitt & Flett, 1991), and they can be self-destructive and suicidal (e.g., Adkins & Parker, 1996; A. T. Beck, 1983; Beutel et al., in press; Blatt, 1974, 1995a; Blatt et al., 1982; Enns, Cox, & Ineyatulla, 2003; Fazaa & Page, 2003; Hewitt, Flett, & Weber, 1994; Hewitt, Newton, Flett, & Callander, 1997). Fazaa and Page (2003), controlling for level of depression, found that suicide attempts in self-critical college students showed greater intention to die and therefore greater lethality than dependent students who had also attempted suicide. These suicide attempts were made often in response to an intrapsychic stressor. Self-critical individuals generate stressful life events involving rejection and confrontation (Beutel et al., in press; Priel & Shahar, 2000; Dunkley & Blankstein, 2000; Dunkley et al., 2000; Zuroff & Duncan, 1999), they do not elicit social support (Beutel et al., in press; Enns et al., 2003; Mongrain, 1998; Priel & Shahar, 2000), and they do not turn to others. Thus, their interpersonal relationships are characterized by pervasive negative expectations (Mongrain, 1998) and feelings of isolation, shyness, and a lack of self-esteem. They have impaired social skills (Campbell, Kwon, Reff, & Williams, 2003); Flett, Hewitt, & DeRosa, 1996) that are expressed in mistrust and a lack of intimacy (Zuroff & Fitzpatrick, 1995). They have an avoidant attachment style (Blatt & Homann, 1992; K. N. Levy, Blatt, & Shaver, 1998; Zuroff & Fitzpatrick, 1995), use avoidant coping mechanisms (Dunkley et al.,

2000; Dunkley et al., 2003), are uncomfortable socially (Norton, Buhr, Cox, Norton, & Walker, 2000), and perceive others as critical and unsupportive (Dunkley et al., 2000; Dunkley et al., 2003; Mongrain, 1998; Mongrain et al., 1998). They can spend considerable effort trying to compensate for painful feelings of inadequacy by getting involved in activities to try to inflate their sense of self-worth, but they do not feel agentic (Saragovi, Aubé, Koestner, & Zuroff, 2002).

Self-critical, socially isolated individuals (e.g., Alden & Bieling, 1996) experience less pleasure in social interactions (Zuroff et al., 1995), make fewer requests for social support, feel distant from their peers, and experience others as less expressive and forthcoming. Self-critical women were experienced by observers as less loving and more hostile toward their boyfriends (e.g., Mongrain et al., 1998) and as uncooperative (Santor, Pringle, & Israeli, 2000). They have fewer friends (Moskowitz & Zuroff, 1991; Zuroff et al., 1995) and are less liked by peers (Zuroff et al., 1983). These individuals tend to turn against others to avoid acknowledging their own sense of failure (Zuroff et al., 1983). They are less likely to accept suggestions from a friend, particularly when they feel the friend has succeeded where they have not (Santor & Zuroff, 1997), and they are likely to be quarrelsome rather than agreeable. Self-critical women report selecting their romantic partners primarily in terms of their partners' power and achievement rather than in terms of their capacity for intimacy and affection (Zuroff & de Lorimier, 1989; see also Luyten, 2002).

Self-Criticism and Dependency on the DEQ were both related to the occurrence of postpartum depression in women with high-risk pregnancies, but in different directions. High scores on Factor II (Self-Criticism) were positively related to postpartum depression; high scores on Factor I (Interpersonal), as noted earlier, were not only negatively related to the occurrence of postpartum depression but also moderated the positive relationship of Self-Criticism to postpartum depression in Israeli women (Priel & Besser, 2000).

Interpersonal Relatedness (Dependency)

Individuals with elevated scores on the DEQ Dependency (Interpersonal) factor tend to be agreeable (Mongrain, 1993); oriented to interpersonal relationships; and have more frequent, constructive, and supportive interactions with others (Mongrain, 1998; Zuroff et al., 1995). Their relationships are usually stable, secure, and harmonious (Mongrain, 1998; Mongrain & Zuroff, 1989). These individuals are usually submissive and placating (Santor & Zuroff, 1997), and thus, as college students, are more fully accepted by their roommates (Mongrain et al., in press). They attend to others and their feelings and emotions (Dunkley et al., 1997). Recent evidence (e.g., Dunkley et al., 1997; Priel & Besser, 1999, 2000, 2001) indicates that elevated scores on the DEQ Interpersonal factor also may have adaptive and protective factors because they are associated with a positive orientation to others and a seeking of social support. These individuals have an anxious–preoccupied attachment style (Zuroff & Fitzpatrick, 1995); in the circumplex model (Laforge & Suczek, 1995; Wiggins & Trapnell, 1996), they would be located in the friendly–submissive quadrant.

Interpersonal concerns, particularly neediness, are associated with less cognitive differentiation; somatic preoccupations; helplessness; and anxiety over separation, loss, and a lack of contact and support. In terms of clinical symptoms, dependency is associated with excessive oral behavior and substance abuse, especially amphetamines and alcohol, as well as with particular forms of antisocial activity involving a search for nurturance and supplies. Patients with an elevated score on the Interpersonal factor of the DEQ tend to make suicidal gestures (Blatt et al., 1982) designed to communicate their unhappiness but without serious intent to harm themselves (Fazaa, 2001; Fazaa & Page, 2003). Dependent college students usually make suicide attempts, but they tend to ensure their survival by making less lethal attempts and in ways that increase the probability of discovery. These suicide attempts often follow interpersonal life stressors and appear to be "a plea for help or nurturance" (Fazaa & Page, 2003, p. 181). They tend to be fearful, worried, and anxious, because they feel unable to cope with stress (Mongrain, 1993); and they have intense and chronic fears of being abandoned and left unprotected and uncared for (Luthar & Blatt, 1993). Initial evidence (Shahar, Trower, et al., in press) also suggests that issues of dependency, as assessed by the DEQ Interpersonal factor, may be more central to more disturbed (psychotic) patients, whereas Self-Criticism may be more central in more organized patients with depression as well as in nonclinical samples.

In future research on the clinical and nonclinical expression of interpersonal concerns it will be important to differentiate between two levels of interpersonal concerns embedded in DEQ Factor I; that is, between developmentally earlier issues of a desperate neediness and more mature or organized relatedness concerns (e.g., Blatt, Zohar, et al., 1995; Blatt, Zohar, et al., 1996; Rude & Burnham, 1995). Schulte and Mongrain (2003) found that Neediness, but not Connectedness or Relatedness, was significantly correlated with diagnoses and the presence of prior clinical episodes of depression in an outpatient sample of young adults. As recently summarized by Zuroff, Mongrain, and Santor (in press), neediness is associated with highly insecure people who want to be cared for and protected by others, but who are frightened of being abandoned and hurt, while connectedness or relatedness is associated with somewhat insecure people, but people who are capable of developing warm, intimate relationships. Although our understanding of the role of the DEQ Interpersonal factor in psychological functioning is not as extensive as our understanding of the Self-Criticism factor, research findings thus far indicate that the differentiation between Neediness and Relatedness may be an important distinction in the study of the role of interpersonal processes in psychological functioning.

Gender Differences

Although no consistent overall gender differences were found in the relations between subtypes of dysphoric experiences and problem behaviors, Leadbeater, Blatt, and Quinlan (1995) found gender differences when considering the likelihood of an individual being high (one standard deviation above the mean) on both interpersonal dysphoria and internalizing disorders or on both self-criticism and externalizing disorders. Females were six times more likely (13%) than males (2%) to be high on both interpersonal dysphoria and internalizing disorders. In contrast, no gender differences were found for elevated scores on both interpersonal dysphoria and externalizing disorders (4% of females and 2% of males). In terms of self-critical dysphoria, no gender differences were found in participants with elevated scores on both self-criticism and internalizing disorders (8% of females and 6% of males), but males were more than twice as likely (7%) as females (3%) to have elevated scores on both self-critical dysphoria and externalizing disorders. Thus, although the overall strength of the specific relations among type of dysphoria and problem behaviors does not differ by gender, the frequency of co-occurrence of more extreme levels of gender-congruent interpersonal vulnerabilities and internalizing disorders is substantially greater in females than in males, whereas the frequency of co-occurrence of more extreme levels of gender congruent self-critical vulnerability and externalizing disorders is greater in males (Leadbeater et al., 1995; see also T. W. Smith et al., 1988, for another illustration of these gender congruent effects).

Research evidence indicates that girls have higher levels of internalizing disorders and are more likely to report anaclitic depressive symptoms that express somatic preoccupations, sad affect, and loneliness. Boys, on the other hand, are more likely to have externalizing disorders and to report introjective depressive symptoms that include antagonism, aggression, and an inability to work (Achenbach & Edelbrock, 1978; Achenbach et al., 1991; Leadbeater et al., 1999; Ostrov, Offer, & Howard, 1988). Considerable differences exist in the items endorsed by girls and boys on the YSR (Achenbach, 1991). Leadbeater et al. (1995) found that all 22 internalizing items on the YSR—including somatic problems (e.g., headaches, nausea, skin problems, weight problems, overtiredness, dizziness, and eating problems), depressed mood (e.g., sadness; crying; worrying; and feeling lonely, unloved, and self-conscious), and aggression against the self (e.g., suicidal thoughts, feeling persecuted, harming oneself)— were endorsed more frequently by girls. In contrast to these more anaclitic problems in girls, boys more frequently report introjective types of problem behaviors on 12 of the 19 YSR externalizing items related to aggression (e.g., destroys things, mean to others, threatens others, swears, brags, teases, thinks about sex) and delinquent acts (e.g., destroys things, disobeys at school, fights, has bad friends, sets fires, steals outside of home). In a community-based sample, Colton et al. (1991) also found more internalizing problems (anxiety, depression, and somatic problems) among girls and more externalizing behaviors (delinquency, problem behavior at school, and poor grades) among boys (Leadbeater et al., 1995).

The prevalence of problems in adolescents and adults also reflects these gender differences (e.g., A. V. Horwitz & White, 1987; Rhode et al., 1991) in what can be considered introjective (externalizing) and anaclitic (internalizing) disorders. As summarized by Leadbeater et al. (1995), men in the United States more frequently die from violent causes (accidental death, suicides involving hanging, and homicide) than do women (Kandel, Raveis, & Davies, 1991; U.S. Bureau of the Census, 1990; Wetzel, 1989). Antisocial behavior is also more frequent among men than among women (P. Graham, 1979) and generally begins at an earlier age for boys (median age of 10) than for girls (median age of 13; Kazdin, 1987). Girls, in contrast, make more suicide attempts (Wetzel, 1989), and have more frequent referrals for clinical depression (Kashani, Sherman, Parker, & Reid, 1990), and the vast majority of cases of anorexia and bulimia occur in women (McGrath et al., 1990). These gender differences in depression begin to emerge shortly after puberty, with girls having a higher incidence of depression than boys (Nolen-Hoeksema, 1990; Nolen-Hoeksema, Girgus, & Seligman, 1991; Petersen, Sarigiani, & Kennedy, 1991).

Differences in socialization may contribute to these gender differences in the expression of psychological distress, with girls showing an internalizing pattern and boys showing an externalizing pattern (Gjerde & Block, 1991; Gjerde, Block, & Block, 1988; Horwitz & White, 1987; Kandel & Davies, 1982; A. Kaplan, 1986; Nolen-Hoeksema, 1987; Radloff & Rae, 1979; M. M. Weissman & Klerman, 1977). Kandel and Davies (1982), for example, found that the total distribution of delinquent adolescents with or without depression was the same for boys and girls but that delinquency was higher for boys (68% vs. 57%), and depressed mood was higher for girls (56% vs. 36%). In a clinic-based sample of 13- to 18-year-olds, Kashani et al. (1990) found that girls reported more anaclitic symptoms, including affective blunting (e.g., sadness, hopelessness, etc.), more concerns about appearance, and more vegetative symptoms than boys did. In an item analysis of the BDI, J. Kaplan and Arbuthnot (1985) found that girls endorsed bodily concerns, such as feeling unattractive and trying to lose weight, more often than boys. In a study of 3rd- to 12th-grade students, Worchel, Nolan, and Wilson (1987) found that girls reported more internalizing items (e.g., sadness, loneliness, fatigue, concern about doing things wrong or having bad things happen, not liking themselves, and wanting more friends), whereas boys reported more externalizing items (e.g., getting into fights and having to be pushed to do homework). Using ratings on the California Adult Q-Sort (Block, 1978), Gjerde et al. (1988) found that dysphoric men were rated as more disagreeable, aggressive, and antagonistic than were nondysphoric men, whereas dysphoric women were seen as more ego brittle, unconventional, and ruminative than were nondysphoric women. Craighead (1991) found that more female adolescents scored high on both depression and anxiety, whereas more boys scored high on both depression and sociopathy. Nolen-Hoeksema (1990) argued that the more ruminative (internalizing) coping styles of women predispose them to longer and more frequent bouts of depression, whereas men's more performance-oriented (externalizing) efforts distract them from depressive feelings, leading to shorter and less frequent experiences of depression but also to more externalizing disorders and drug use (Leadbeater et al., 1995).

Research also indicates gender differences in subtypes of depression (i.e., interpersonal and self-critical depressive vulnerabilities). Adolescent girls are more likely to have interpersonal depressive preoccupations (feelings of loss or loneliness) than are boys, but girls also are equally likely to experience self-critical depressive preoccupations (feelings of failure and lack of self-worth). Similar gender differences have been observed in adolescents' reactivity to stressful live events. Girls are particularly reactive to stressful interpersonal life events (e.g., illness in a family member) than to events that affect self-esteem (e.g., academic failure; Gore, Aseltine, & Colten, 1993; Wagner & Compas, 1990). However, girls are reactive to both types of stress, whereas boys react primarily to stressful events that affect their self-esteem. Differential vulnerabilities to interpersonal or self-critical depressive experiences, potentiated by congruent stressful life events involving either interpersonal issues or threats to self-esteem, may differentially predict higher levels of internalizing or externalizing problem behaviors in girls and boys, respectively (Leadbeater et al., 1995, 1999).

Henrich et al.'s (2001) recent findings concerning the social relations of early adolescent girls and boys indicate that girls are more vulnerable to interpersonal issues than boys are, especially in early adolescence (Brody, 1999; Gore et al., 1993; Leadbeater et al., 1995; Leadbeater et al., 1999; Zahn-Waxler, 1993). Important differences in interpersonal relationships of boys and girls suggest different possible pathways for the development of depressed affect. Research has documented the greater importance of connectedness or relatedness in adolescent girls and of status or agency in adolescent boys (see review by Buhrmester, 1996). Compared with boys, girls interact more with their same-sex friends, self-disclose more, and think more about their relationships. Girls are also more reactive to interpersonal stresses (Leadbeater et al., 1995), and they have higher scores on both DEQ Neediness and Relatedness than do boys, as well as higher scores on measures of social functioning, suggesting a greater involvement in interpersonal issues. Boys typically discourage expressions of intimacy and emotional support. Henrich et al.'s findings also suggest a greater differentiation in the quality of interpersonal relatedness in early adolescent girls. Mature interpersonal relatedness in early adolescent girls on the DEQ is associated with competent social functioning, whereas neediness is associated with less interpersonal competence. Needy girls make excessive demands on friends for reassurance and sympathy and for an inclusivity in their friendships. This can lead to rejection and social isolation (Coyne, 1976b; Joiner, 1994). These findings suggest that it is important to include gender as a factor in studying the relationships among types of depression vulnerability and internalizing and externalizing expressions of dysphoria and depression (see, e.g., T. W. Smith et al., 1988).

6

Developmental Origins
(Distal Antecedents)

Negative caring experiences create disturbances in the process of representing the self and others in caring relationships. As I discussed in detail in chapter 1, psychoanalytic formulations stress the importance in the etiology of depression of an intense ambivalent relationship with parents (Abraham, 1911/1927, 1924/1949; S. Freud, 1917/1957e). Negative caring experiences create hostile and angry feelings toward the parent, but at the same time the child is frightened of losing the support of the caring relationship. Because of these intense ambivalent feelings, the individual is unable to establish and consolidate a positive representation of the parent with feelings of affection, fondness, and respect. S. Freud (1917/1963) stressed the impairment of internalization in depression and how depressed patients struggle, in distorted ways, to preserve a sense of contact with the parent with feelings of love and approval (Nacht & Racamier, 1960). It is the failure to resolve the ambivalence and to establish relatively positive internalizations that results in the vulnerability to depression. The internalization of a loving and caring relationship reduces the vulnerability to depression; thus, actual, apparent, or fantasized object loss is often a major precipitant of depression.

Negative caring experiences create disturbances in the process of representation of the self and other in caring relationships, and these disturbances cause a vulnerability to depression. Furthermore, the developmental level of object representation appears to be related to specific types of depression. As I discussed in chapters 1 and 4, anaclitic and introjective depression appear to involve different impairments in the development of object representations. Because of these impairments, individuals with each type of depression struggle to maintain contact with the object, but in different ways—either by struggling to maintain direct physical contact or through an intensification of the processes of introjection, which is focused on partial, overstated, part properties of the object.

In an anaclitic depression, themes of helplessness and dependency predominate, and object representations are primarily at a sensorimotor–preoperational level, which emphasize action sequences of gratification and

This chapter incorporates material from "Parent–Child Interaction in the Etiology of Dependent and Self-Critical Depression," by S. J. Blatt and E. Homann, 1992, *Clinical Psychology Review*, *12*, pp. 47–91. Copyright 1992 by Elsevier. Adapted with permission.

frustration. The danger is not so much the loss of the object but of the gratification it can provide. Thus, the individual struggles to maintain direct need-gratifying contact with the object. Individuals with anaclitic depression often attempt to deny the importance of object loss by seeking immediate replacement of the need gratification. In introjective depression, representations focus primarily on fragmented, isolated part properties or qualities of the object, with little resolution of contradictions or of ambivalent feelings. The individual fears not loss of the object and the need gratification the object can provide but rather the loss of the object's acceptance and approval. This concern is often expressed in themes of self-criticism, guilt, and a sense of failure, and in excessive striving for achievement and perfection as an attempt to win love and acceptance. Constant self-criticism and feelings of guilt are often the internalization of the overstated, fragmented part properties of representations of harsh, judgmental, punitive parental figures. Thus, the experiences of guilt and self-criticism can also serve to maintain contact with the object.

Object representation is limited at these lower developmental levels, thus leaving the individual vulnerable to depression that is organized around feelings of loss and loneliness or around profound feelings of worthlessness (Blatt, 1974). In normal development, separate, isolated, manifest, fragmented, and often contradictory part properties become integrated into more consolidated object representations. Because more consolidated representation can be maintained, object loss can be experienced without prolonged and severe depression. Thus, the failure to achieve an integration and consolidation in object representation leaves an individual vulnerable to experiences of depression. Anaclitic and introjective depression differ not only in the quality of representations of others but also in the quality of the self-concept. The self in anaclitic depression is defined primarily by the quality of current interpersonal relationships (i.e., feeling unloved), whereas in introjective depression the focus is on defects and limitations of the self (Blatt & Shichman, 1983).

Thus, anaclitic and introjective depression are characterized by different impairments of cognitive schemas as well as by different symptoms and different qualities of interpersonal relatedness. Anaclitic depression involves preoccupation with the reliability, dependability, and availability of caregivers, and the primary affective experiences involve feeling uncared for, unwanted, and unloved. Themes of abandonment, rejection, and depletion abound, and these experiences create feelings of resentment, anger, and rage about being deprived and neglected. In contrast, the content of the cognitive schemas in introjective depression primarily involves preoccupations with issues of self-worth, lack of achievement, failure to meet standards and expectations, and feelings of guilt for supposed transgressions; the primary affective experiences involve feelings of being criticized, attacked, and rejected and feeling that one is a failure or bad and evil.

The differentiation of concerns about loss and abandonment from concerns about self-worth expressed in anaclitic and introjective depression, and differences in the quality of representations of self and significant others, suggests that different types of early experiences may create differential vulnerabilities to these two types of depressive experiences. Early life experiences can predispose some individuals to be especially vulnerable to experiences of abandon-ment and loss or to experiences of failure and a lack of self-worth. These vulnerabilities may be the consequence of representations of others as unrelia-ble and uncaring or as intrusive, judgmental, and punitive, and of representa-tions of the self as unloved or unworthy. Taking various theoretical perspec-tives, and using different research strategies, several independent research teams have investigated the role of the parent–child relationship in the etiology of depression and have concluded that impairments in "mental representations" (e.g., Blatt, 1974) or "internal working models" (e.g., Bowlby, 1980; Main, Kaplan, & Cassidy, 1985) of caregiving relationships are central to understand-ing the development of depression.

In one approach, researchers studied children at risk for depression, includ-ing children being raised by a mother who is depressed (e.g., Cicchetti & Aber, 1986; Gaensbauer, Harmon, Cytryn, & McKnew, 1984; Sameroff, Seifer, & Zax, 1982). Research groups (e.g., the National Institute of Mental Health [NIMH] Collaborative Project—Cytryn et al., 1984; Davenport, Zahn-Waxler, Adland, & Mayfield, 1984; Gaensbauer et al., 1984; Zahn-Waxler, McKnew, Cummings, & Radke-Yarrow, 1984; and the Rochester Longitudinal Study [RLS]—Cohn & Tronick, 1983, 1987; Field, 1984; Sameroff et al., 1982) have studied children of mothers who are depressed on the basis of the assumption that an evaluation of the caring patterns in families of children at risk for depression (Downey & Coyne, 1990; Hammen, 1991) can provide further under-standing of the role of parent–child relationships in the etiology of depression.

Other research groups (e.g., Cohn, Matias, Tronick, Connell, & Lyons-Ruth, 1986; Field, 1984; Tronick & Gianino, 1986) have studied infants and children who were insecurely attached to their caregivers (e.g., Ainsworth, 1969, 1982; Ainsworth, Blehar, Waters, & Wall, 1978; Main, 1981; Main et al., 1985) and considered how differences in attachment patterns might be related to the development of disordered behavior, including depression (Cicchetti & Aber, 1986). In a third approach (e.g., Blatt, 1974; Blatt, Wein, Chevron, & Quinlan, 1979; McCranie & Bass, 1984; Mongrain, 1998; G. Parker, 1981, 1982, 1983, 1984), researchers have studied adults' retrospective accounts of their early caring experiences and how differences in the recollections of parental caregiving patterns relate to depression.

These different research strategies have provided complementary findings. Data from the longitudinal study of normal children and children at risk, as well as adults' retrospective accounts of their childhood, suggest that parental lack of care, nurturance, or support, and parental exercise of excessive author-ity, control, criticism, or disapproval, are associated with the later development of depression (e.g., Bemporad & Romano, 1993; Blatt, 1974; Burbach & Bour-din, 1986; Gerlsma, Emmelkamp, & Arrindell, 1990; G. Parker, 1981, 1984; Rapee, 1997). These experiences of neglect or excessive control create impaired and distorted mental representations, or internal working models of caring relationships, such that children either have difficulty with separation and constantly seek reassurance and support, or they continually anticipate rejec-tion, criticism, and censure and thus avoid interpersonal involvement (Blatt & Homann, 1992). Parental caring patterns are internalized (or interiorized) in the child's mental representations of caring relationships, and the quality of these mental representations of the self and other in relationships can create a vulnerability to later depression.

Representation of Interpersonal Relationships

The concept of internal working models in attachment theory (e.g., Main et al., 1985) and Stern's (1985) concept of generalized interactive experiences are similar to the concept of mental representations discussed in the psychoanalytic literature, including the conscious and unconscious cognitive, affective, and experiential components of mental schemas of prior significant relationships and experiences (Blatt & Lerner, 1983a). The quality of the infant–parent relationship, especially early experiences surrounding attachment and separation, contributes substantially to the content and structural organization of mental representations. Constructive early caregiving experiences lead to an increasingly consolidated sense of self and of the other in various types of interactions. These generalized memory structures (which have both conscious and unconscious affective and cognitive dimensions) create expectations about subsequent interactions and determine modes of behavioral response. The importance of these cognitive–affective schemas of caring relationships in psychological development is consistent with the emphasis on person schemas and scripts in social psychology (e.g., Fiske & Linville, 1980; Hastie, 1981; Higgins, 1989; Shank & Abelson, 1977; Taylor & Crockett, 1981) and of mental representation in cognitive theory (Blatt, 1984, 1990a, 1995b).

The normal development of *evocative constancy* (a sense of the object in its absence) in the middle of the second year of life enables children to increasingly separate from their caregivers with a sense of confidence and security. The more stable and positive the mother–infant relationship, the more secure and consolidated will be the child's sense of the mother and of the self in the mother's absence. The security of the attachment relationship is closely related to the emergence of object constancy (Piaget, 1937/1954) and of visual self-recognition (Stern, 1985), both of which are early precursors of the developing sense of self (Schneider-Rosen & Cicchetti, 1984). Impairments in object constancy and in the sense of self appear to be central to experiences of depression (Blatt, 1974). Cicchetti and Aber (1986) emphasized that the tasks of the second year of life provide a crucial foundation for the future development of social and cognitive schemas and of self-regulatory skills, impairments of which are predominant in the predisposition to depression.

Fishler, Sperling, and Carr (1990) reviewed techniques for the assessment of interpersonal relatedness in adults and identified two major research approaches for assessing representations of self and significant others: (a) object-relations theory and (b) attachment theory. Assessment from an object-relations perspective tends to involve more open-ended, relatively unstructured techniques to evaluate primarily cognitive–affective dimensions of mental representation in adult clinical samples. The Object Relations Inventory, discussed in chapter 4, is an example of this type of assessment. Assessment techniques used by attachment theorists, in contrast, have generally been based on direct behavioral observation of nonclinical children; they focus on typologies of attachment behavior and apply these observations to behavior later in development—in later childhood, adolescence, and adulthood. Fishler et al. (1990) stressed how an integration of these two approaches could enrich the study of interpersonal relatedness and establish longitudinal links among early childhood experiences, the construction of cognitive–affective schemas, and behavior in adolescence and adulthood.

Main et al. (1985) and other attachment investigators have found that insecurely attached children, identified in the second year of life, have impaired mental models of attachment relationships and that these limited representations of self and other persist in later development. Consistent with these conclusions, data from the study of children raised by mothers who are depressed and children who are insecurely attached suggest that the children's difficulties in the development of adequate representations of the self and other occur because the parents struggle with similar issues from their childhood experiences with their own parents and are re-enacting these difficulties with their spouses and children (Main et al., 1985; Sroufe & Fleeson, 1986). Some parents fail to provide reliable care, nurturance, and support for their infants, whereas other parents experience difficulty managing their toddlers as they begin to assert their independence and autonomy.

Quality of Infant–Mother Attachment

Studies of Secure and Insecure Attachment

Research in the past 30 years has extensively examined the attachment relationship between infant and caregiver and how various caregiving patterns lead to differences in types of attachment and the quality of mental representations or internal working models of attachment relationships (Bowlby, 1969, 1973, 1980). An *internal working model*, as defined by Main et al. (1985), is

> a set of conscious and/or unconscious rules for the organization of information relevant to attachment and for obtaining or limiting access to that information, that is, to information regarding attachment-related experiences, feelings, and ideations. . . . Individual differences in the mental representation of the self in relation to attachment . . . [are] formed out of a history of the infant's actions, infant–parent interactions, and . . . the fate or outcome of the infant's efforts and intentions to regain the parent even in the parent's absence. The working model of the relationship to the attachment figure will reflect not an objective picture of "the parent" but rather the history of the caregiver's responses to the infant's actions or intended actions with/toward the attachment figure. (p. 75).

Disturbances in child–parent interaction patterns become evident as early as 2 to 6 months of age (Beebe & Lachmann, 1988; Cohn, Campbell, Matias, & Hopkins, 1990) and continue to emerge throughout the rapprochement phase (Mahler, Pine, & Bergman, 1975) and the development of evocative constancy (Fraiberg, 1969). Highly stable differences in the security of attachment have been noted during the first year and a half of development (e.g., Ainsworth et al., 1978; Radke-Yarrow, Cummings, Kuczyinski, & Chapman, 1985), and these differences persist into later childhood (Ainsworth et al., 1978; Main, 1983; Main et al., 1985; Main & Weston, 1981), adolescence, and adulthood. Insecure attachment, assessed between 12 and 18 months, interferes with the child's capacity to develop meaningful interpersonal relationships, to be able to trust others, and to develop a viable self-concept (Kagan, 1981; Schneider-Rosen & Cicchetti, 1984; Stern, 1985).

Attachment patterns observed in the second year of life remain remarkably stable over time, especially when the environment also remains stable (Owen, Easterbrooks, Chase-Landsdale, & Goldberg, 1984; K. C. Thompson & Hendrie, 1972; Vaughn, Egeland, Sroufe, & Waters, 1979). Qualities of the caregivers' responses are also generally quite stable over time. Changes in caregiving patterns most often occur as a function of significant changes in the level of stress in family life and in caregiving arrangements (Arend, Gove, & Sroufe, 1979; Londerville & Main, 1981; Matas, Arend, & Sroufe, 1978; Vaughn et al., 1979; Waters, Wippman, & Sroufe, 1979). Thus, the child's attachment patterns in infancy usually have an impressive continuity over the life cycle. Infants identified at 12 months of age as securely attached, for example, at 2 years of age are more enthusiastic, more cooperative with their parents, and more persistent when confronted with challenging tasks (Matas et al., 1978). Insecurely attached infants, in contrast, are rated subsequently as significantly less competent, showing little enthusiasm in problem solving, not using their parents' assistance effectively, and as less self-reliant (see also Londerville & Main, 1981). Securely attached infants at 12 months are described later in childhood as more socially confident, flexible, self-reliant, and curious than insecurely attached infants (Arend et al., 1979; Waters et al., 1979), who are described as dependent, noncompliant, and aggressive and who tend to seek attention in negative, defiant ways (see also Sroufe, 1983).

Attachment figures differ in the degree of comfort and ease they feel in physical contact with their children, in the frequency of their rejection of the infants' attempts for contact, and in the degree to which they respond harshly to their children's activities (Main, 1981; Main & Goldwyn, 1984; Main & Weston, 1981). Sensitive and responsive caretaking throughout the first year of life leads to secure attachment (Bates, Masling, & Frankel, 1985; Egeland & Sroufe, 1981; Main et al., 1985), whereas insecure attachment seems to be related to parental rejection of the infant's attempts at closeness or an insensitivity to signals from the infant (Ainsworth, Bell, & Stayton, 1971; Main et al., 1985). The caring relationships that parents establish with their children are in large part determined by the parents' own childhood experiences (Main et al., 1985), and these experiences may be expressed in the relationship with their children at different times in the child-rearing sequence. Caregivers overburdened by the young infant's dependency and demanding nature may be inconsistent, uncaring, or inattentive, thus creating conflicts around dependency in their child. Other parents may feel more stress when their children are toddlers, becoming intrusive and overcontrolling primarily in dealing with the children's assertion of independence and autonomy, creating conflict in their child around issues of assertion, self-worth, and self-definition.

Ainsworth et al. (1978), Main (1981), and Main et al. (1985) have described several different types of insecure attachment, using different measures to assess the security of attachment in infants, children, and adults. On the basis of observations of infants in the "Strange Situation" (Ainsworth et al., 1978) that give particular attention to the infants' behavior toward their parent at separation and again at reunion after a brief (three-minute) separation, Ainsworth et al. (1978) described three types of attachment behavior. *Secure* infants show some distress at separation from the caregiver but at reunion are easily comforted and interact positively with the caregiver. In one type of insecure attachment (Type A, *insecure–avoidant*), infants avoid their caregiver on reunion after the brief separation and especially do not express anger or grief about the separation. In a second type of insecure attachment (Type C, *insecure–ambivalent*, or *resistant*), infants have difficulties being comforted by their caregivers on reunion, they restrict their exploration of their environment, and they are described as impulsive and helpless (Sroufe, 1983). Main et al. (1985), in addition to identifying securely attached, insecure–avoidant, and insecure–ambivalent children (Ainsworth et al., 1978), also identified a somewhat less frequent fourth category of "Type D" infants, who demonstrate disorganized or disoriented patterns of attachment in which the infant appears to lack any clearly defined means of coping with separation and instead seems to blend contradictory features of several strategies (e.g., strong proximity seeking followed by strong avoidance), or appears dazed and disoriented when reunited with the caretaker. Disorganization is evident in disordered temporal sequences; incomplete or undirected movements; or confusion, apprehension, and depression. Main et al. tentatively concluded that children who displayed this *insecure–disorganized* pattern with their caretakers have internal working models of themselves in relation to attachment figures that are qualitatively distinct from the internal working models that guide the behaviors of the secure, insecure–avoidant, or insecure–ambivalent infants.

Main et al. (1985) assessed the internal working models of securely and insecurely attached infants at six years of age by recording the children's verbal and affective responses to a separation anxiety test consisting of 16 photographs of children experiencing separations from their parents, such as saying good night or saying goodbye to parents who are leaving for two weeks.[1] The children were asked how they felt about the separation portrayed in the pictures, and their verbal responses were scored for "emotional openness," ranging from an easy balance between self-exposure and self-containment to a variety of insecure responses, including silence and an inability to express feelings spontaneously and denial or marked disorganization. The behavior of these six-year-olds was also observed at reunions after an hour of physical separation from their parents. Children who were securely attached to the mother in infancy tended to have secure parents and were rated as emotionally open and as coping more constructively with separation at six years of age, saying, for example, that they would try to persuade their parents not to leave. This

---

[1]This instrument is the Klagsburn–Bowlby adaptation of the Hansburg Separation Anxiety Test (Klagsburn & Bowlby, 1976).

response was interpreted as indicating a relationship with parents in which the children felt that their wishes and their feelings of sadness about the separation could be communicated safely and effectively to their parents.

Children who were insecure–avoidant as infants also showed avoidant responses to family interactions at age six; they directed their attention away from the parent after a separation (perhaps even moving away from the parent) and were uncomfortable discussing their feelings about separations in the separation anxiety test. For example, they "did not know" how a child would respond to a two-week separation from the parents, and they "avoided, refused or turned around and away from . . . a presented photograph of the family" (Main et al., 1985, p. 96). The parents of these insecure–avoidant children were also rated insecure on attachment issues and often "dismissed attachment relationships as being of little concern, value or influence" (Main et al., 1985, p. 91). These parents tended not to respond to their children's request for closeness or attention. The children, in turn, were left feeling ineffective and incompetent because of their futile efforts to establish gratifying interpersonal relationships (Schaffer & Blatt, 1990).

Parents of insecure–ambivalent (Type C) infants seem "preoccupied" with their dependency on their own parents and often "still actively struggled to please them" (Main et al., 1985, p. 91).[2] Insecure–ambivalent infants display "strong and sometimes continual fear and distress, and seem constantly directed toward the parent and away from all other environmental features" (Main et al., 1985, p. 74). The lack of attention to and exploration of the environment limit the ability of these children to learn how to cope with stress or loss. These children, like their parents, seem preoccupied with maintaining contact with their parents as a source of emotional support. They seem unable to turn to others to meet their needs for affection, remaining enmeshed with their parents in an intense dependent relationship. They are unable to find sustained comfort in their primary caregivers and often lack the capacity to cope with stress or loss in adulthood.

Disorganized children (Type D) at six years display a unique form of reunion behavior in which they do not reintegrate flexibly with their parents on reunion but rather take charge of the interaction in a controlling fashion, either punitively or in a "pseudo-caretaking" manner. In responses to questions about their feelings about separation and loss they become "distressed, silent, irratio-

---

[2] Main et al. (1985) also assessed parents' internal working models of their attachment relationships with their own parents using the Adult Attachment Interview, which evaluates the coherence of descriptions of early attachment relationships and experiences, supportive and contradictory memories, and current evaluations of the experiences of early attachment relationships. They identified four major patterns. Adults rated as secure tended to see attachment relationships as influencing the development of their personality, and their descriptions of particular attachment relationships were reasonably balanced and objective. These securely attached parents tended to value attachment relationships and to discuss them freely and openly without apparent distortion. In contrast, adults rated as insecurely attached were of two types: They either discounted the importance of attachment relationships, or they seemed to overvalue relationships and to be entangled in ongoing dependency struggles with their attachment figures. A fourth group, consisting of individuals who had experienced the loss of a major attachment figure before they reached maturity and did not seem to have completed the mourning process, also was identified.

nal or occasionally self-destructive" (Main et al., 1985, p. 96). Furthermore, they were likely to have parents who had experienced a loss of their own parents before they reached maturity (43%) or the loss of a sibling or another major attachment figure, other than the parent, with whom they had been raised (52%).

The relationships of the disorganized children with their parents often seemed to be inverted—they were in a sense, parents to their parents. Yet they had no well-consolidated pattern of coping with their strong reactions to separation from their parents. The frequent history of loss of attachment figures in the parents of insecure–disorganized children, coupled with the description of depressive responses in the behavior and affect of the 12- and 18-month-old children in the Strange Situation, raises the possibility that the parents' early experience of separation and loss is a major precursor for later depressive phenomena, especially a depression focused on feelings of loneliness and loss. The data also suggest that later in development these children deal with their dependency needs by becoming a caring agent for others. They may become the overcompensating, subtly hypomanic, seemingly efficacious type of individual who deals with his or her intense depressive dependent longings through denial and reversal—as *compulsive-givers* (Bowlby, 1973)—by caring for others in ways they originally longed to be cared for (see also the findings of Blatt, Quinlan, Chevron, McDonald, & Zuroff, 1982, and others previously discussed in chapter 5).

Lyons-Ruth and her colleagues (e.g., Lyons-Ruth, 2001; Lyons-Ruth, Zeanah, & Bénoit, 2003) have distinguished two types of disorganized infants that they labeled as *Disorganized Approach* (D-Approach) and *Disorganized Avoidant* (D-Avoid). The mothers of these two types of infants differed more from each other than they differed from mothers of nondisorganized infants. Mothers of D-Avoid infants displayed role confusion and negative intrusive behavior as well as a greater contradictory mix of rejecting and attention-seeking behaviors in caring for their infants. Lyons-Ruth and Block (1996) described these mothers as hostile and self-referential in their attachment behavior. Mothers of D-Approach infants, in contrast, were more fearful, withdrawn, and inhibited, sometimes appearing as "sweet or fragile," and had higher rates of withdrawal from their infants. They were very unlikely to be overtly hostile or intrusive, but they often failed to initiate contact, or they approached the infant with hesitation. They would often initially move away or try to deflect the infant's requests before eventually giving in to the infant's concerted effort to establish contact. Lyons-Ruth et al. described these mothers as "helpless/fearful regarding attachment."

Different forms of early trauma were reported by mothers of D-Avoid and D-Approach infants. D-Avoid mothers more frequently reported a history of physical abuse or witnessing violence, and they seemed to handle their underlying fear of assault with an aggressive, hostile style of interaction. D-Approach mothers more frequently reported sexual abuse (but not physical abuse) or parental loss and were more likely to withdraw from interaction with their infant (Lyons-Ruth & Block, 1996).

D-Approach and D-Avoid infants are at equal risk for a variety of negative outcomes, such as elevated hostile–aggressive behavior toward peers in school.

They also have elevated rates of controlling attachment patterns toward parents by age six. D-Approach infants sought contact with their mothers but displayed signs of conflict, apprehension, uncertainty, helplessness, or dysphoria as well as disorganized behavior such as freezing, huddling on the floor, and apprehension. Lyons-Ruth (2001) speculated that these two infant subgroups are the precursors of punitive and caregiving stances that disorganized children use to establish control of others. These punitive hostile or solicitous caregiving–controlling behaviors become increasingly differentiated. The punitive–aggressive children exhibit more chaotic play, with themes of unresolved danger, whereas caregiving children tend to inhibit fantasy play. Lyons-Ruth speculated that these behavioral manifestations in childhood eventually become consolidated in the parental caregiving styles that she termed *hostile* and *helpless*.

Thus, Lyons-Ruth (2001) identified two very different behavioral profiles within disorganized attachment:

1. A *hostile–avoidant* subtype, in which the mother is identified with a malevolent, punitive caregiver from childhood; her hostile, distant interactions seem to be an attempt to deny her vulnerability by suppressing emotions and constantly controlling others. These mothers discipline their children by coercion, suppression of the child's anger, and prematurely encouraging the child's autonomy.

2. A *helpless/fearful* subtype, in which the mother adopts a lifelong caregiving style of attending to the needs of others, often at the expense of her own needs, resulting in a repression of her own affect. These mothers tend to be fearful and easily overwhelmed by the demands of others. They feel powerless to control their children, especially when the child's affects are aroused.

Main and colleagues (N. Kaplan, 1987; Main & Cassidy, 1988) followed low-risk, middle-class families and found that children who were identified as having disorganized attachment in infancy later expressed disorganized and dysfluent discourse and catastrophic fantasies. Main and colleagues (1985) distinguished between *controlling–punitive* behavioral responses and *controlling–caregiving* responses. Controlling–punitive children tended to harshly order the parent around or even would attempt to humiliate the parent. Controlling–caregiving children were characterized by excessive solicitousness. The development of these two types of D-Controlling behavior at age six in children judged to be disorganized during infancy has been replicated in other studies (e.g., Wartner, Grossmann, Fremmer-Bombik, & Suess, 1994; T. Jacobsen, Huss, Fendrich, Kruesi, & Ziegenhain, 1997; H. Steele, Steele, & Fonagy, 1996).

Lyons-Ruth's (e. g., 2001) and Main's (Main et al., 1985) analyses regarding two subtypes of the disorganized attachment status are highly consistent with formulations about a similar polarity—of either seeking or avoiding contact—as the fundamental dimension in the two major types of insecure attachment—the avoidant and the preoccupied styles—as well as with the formulations of the centrality of the two basic psychological dimensions of excessive attachment or isolation in anaclitic and introjective depression.

The failure of insecurely attached children to establish a secure bond with their parents, to resolve adequately the process of separation–individuation, and to establish a sense of self-definition and autonomy could lead to depression in two ways. First, the failure to achieve a consolidated differentiation between the self and a caring other and to have internalized a sense of a caring object means that even a temporary interruption of a caring relationship is experienced by the child as very disruptive. Second, failure to develop autonomy interferes with the child's confidence in being able to function independently. Thus, the child's experience of the parent as uncaring, undependable, or as harshly critical leads to a sense of the self as vulnerable, weak, and ineffective. These feelings are re-experienced in other relationships, leading to generalized feelings of helplessness and hopelessness and a lack of independence and individuality.

Parallels can be drawn between the types of insecure attachment initially identified by Ainsworth (1985) and Main (Main et al., 1985) and potential vulnerabilities to dependent and self-critical depression. Excessive dependency has been implicated as a possible risk factor in depression (Bemporad & Wilson, 1976; Blatt, 1974; Blatt, D'Afflitti, & Quinlan, 1976; Hirschfeld, Klerman, Chodoff, Korchin, & Barrett, 1976). Insecure–ambivalent infants and children who experience intensely enmeshed family relationships and have difficulty tolerating separations or in seeking support from the environment could be vulnerable to a dependent (anaclitic) type of depression in adolescence and adulthood. At age 24 months, insecure–ambivalent children express anger more directly to their attachment figures than do avoidant children, but at age 3½ years they are less enthusiastic and persistent and more dependent on their caregivers for assistance than are insecure–avoidant infants (Gove, 1982, cited in Sroufe, 1983). At age 4½ years, insecure–ambivalent children are more impulsive and helpless, and they have particularly maladaptive responses to the loss of caregivers either by death or divorce (Bowlby, 1980).

The coping patterns of insecure–avoidant children, in contrast, seem more maladaptive and more closely linked to a self-critical depression—an anhedonic, stoic, autonomous, and isolated type of depression—in adulthood (Blatt, 1974). Avoidant children express their anger indirectly, often at objects rather than people, or through subtle noncompliance (Gove, 1982). They have caregivers who provide little support and who set unclear expectations and inconsistent limits in the early parent–child interactions. These children are described by preschool teachers as hostile, isolated, disconnected (Gove, 1982), and excessively dependent (Sroufe, 1983), and by age five they are considered behavior problems (M. F. Erikson, Sroufe, & Egeland, 1985). Both ambivalent and avoidant insecurely attached children are described as being dependent, initially with their caregivers as well as later in preschool. These expressions of dependency are consistent with behavior observed in the Strange Situation, in which ambivalent infants cling to the caregivers, whereas avoidant children avoid their caregivers but may be friendly to strangers (Main, 1981). Avoidant children who are able to form relationships with adults other than their primary caregivers may have better chances for healthy relationships than avoidant children who remain "hostile, isolated and disconnected" (Gove, 1982).

Similar attachment styles have been identified in adolescents and young adults (e.g., Hazan & Shaver, 1987, 1990b; Kobak & Sceery, 1988; Shaver & Hazan, 1987; West & Sheldon, 1988; West, Sheldon, & Reiffer, 1987). Secure attachments in this older age group are characterized by mutuality and reciprocity; insecure–avoidant relationships are characterized by jealousy, resentment, and fear, whereas insecure–anxious attachments are characterized by preoccupations with the love object (Hazan & Shaver, 1987, 1990b). Anxiously attached individuals are less socially competent and more symptomatic and anxious, whereas avoidant (or dismissively) attached individuals have positive self-representations (like securely attached individuals) but are rated by others as less socially adjusted; as having more negative affect, especially hostility; and less insight and resilience (Kobak & Sceery, 1988).

Zuroff and Fitzpatrick (1995) studied attachment patterns in adults and found that a substantial percentage of male and female college students described themselves on Shaver and Hazan's (1987) measure as securely attached. Avoidant–insecure attachment was more common in men, whereas anxious attachment was more common in women. In fact, none of the 50 men in the Zuroff and Fitzpatrick sample (1995) described themselves as anxiously attached. Securely attached men and women had low scores on the Dependency and Self-Criticism factors of the Depressive Experiences Questionnaire (DEQ; Blatt, D'Afflitti, & Quinlan, 1979) and higher scores on the Efficacy factor of the DEQ. Among insecurely attached adults, avoidant women scored higher on both Dependency and Self-Criticism, especially on Self-Criticism. Anxiously attached women scored higher than control participants on Dependency and Self-Criticism, especially on Dependency. Avoidant men scored somewhat higher than control participants on Self-Criticism and lower than controls on Dependency. These findings, as well as later findings by Zuroff, Stotland, Sweetman, Craig, and Koestner (1995), lend support to the hypothesis that avoidant attachment is related to the development of self-criticism, whereas anxious attachment is expressed in excessive dependency both in childhood and later in adolescence and adulthood. As I discussed in chapter 5, K. N. Levy, Blatt, and Shaver (1998) demonstrated that young adults with different attachment styles have significant differences in the content and structure of their representations of their parents. Priel and Besser (2001) reported similar findings in a sample of Israeli women. These findings support the assumption (e.g., Bowlby, 1980, 1988b; Main et al., 1985) that attachment styles are based on cognitive–affective schemas or internal working models of close interpersonal relationships; they also suggest that these cognitive–affective structures may be a central issue in the etiology of anaclitic and introjective depression.

The theory of internal working models or mental representations of attachment relationships appears to provide a rich and promising basis for understanding how early childhood experiences set the stage for later difficulties. Early caring relationships are central in the child's development of a sense of self and the formation of perceptions and understanding of interpersonal relationships and interactions, which, when disturbed (e.g., in insecure attachment), seem to produce vulnerability to difficulties later in childhood, perhaps to depression and other disorders in adulthood. The process of prediction from childhood behavior to adult psychopathology is complex, and the processes through which internal working models of different relationships are established and generalized to new relationships are not yet understood. For example, whereas the working model of the attachment relationship with the mother seems to influence the responses of six-year-old children to measures of separation anxiety and their interpersonal behavior, 12- to 24-month-old infants distinguish between their parents in their attachment behaviors (Main et al., 1985) and often have different internal working models for different caregivers.

The complexity of the problem is compounded further when one considers the possibility that an individual may have more than one working model of the same person, or of him- or herself in different contexts (Zelnick & Buchholtz, 1990). Main (1990b) proposed that difficulties in adult relationships may arise when the child, in an effort to make sense out of confusing parental attitudes or behaviors, has internalized multiple conflicting models of the parent and his or her sense of self in relation to that parent. Thus, although one can identify a strong correspondence between parental security or insecurity and the quality of attachment observed in the child, it is not yet known what aspects of the parents' behaviors are responsible for the transmission of disturbed working models, how the child's multiple working models of different relationships combine to create expectations of new relationships, or which aspects of insecure attachment in childhood create predispositions to different forms of psychopathology in adulthood, although vulnerability seems likely to be a consequence of each of the various forms of insecure attachment.

Children of Depressed Mothers

Numerous investigators have studied the child-rearing practices of mothers with depression to identify various patterns of parent–child interaction that can disrupt the child's development. They have compared findings from the study of variations of caring patterns seen in nondepressed mothers and their infants and how distortions in caring experiences can lead to different types of insecure attachment and depression.

Children (infants to preadolescents) of parents with affective disorders are at increased risk for psychiatric disorders, especially depression (e.g., Bemporad & Wilson, 1976; Cicchetti & Aber, 1986; Cicchetti & Schneider-Rosen, 1984a, 1984b; Cytryn et al., 1984; Egeland & Sroufe, 1981; Emde, Harmon, & Good, 1986; Gaensbauer, 1982; Gaensbauer et al., 1984; Kashani et al., 1983; Klagsburn & Bowlby, 1976; Rutter, 1986). Approximately 40% of the children of parents who are depressed are diagnosed with depression or depressive symptoms (Beardslee, Bemporad, Keller, & Klerman, 1983).[3] The onset of

---

[3] Estimates of prevalence rates for depression range from 5% to 15% for adults (Boyd & Weissman, 1982) to 1% to 9% for children (Kashani et al., 1983), with various investigators indicating that depression can be diagnosed at as early as five or six years of age (Cantwell & Carlson, 1983; Rutter, Izard, & Reed, 1986). Kovacs, Feinberg, Crause-Novack, Paulaskas, and Finkelstein (1984)

depression is earlier in these children than in control participants, beginning in adolescence, and girls of mothers who are depressed are more likely to become depressed than are boys (M. M. Weissman et al., 1987). Children of parents with depression are also more likely than children of parents who are not mentally ill to have other problems, such as hyperactivity, attention-deficit/ hyperactivity disorder, anxiety disorders, delinquency, substance abuse, truancy, enuresis, mania, and bulimia (Beardslee et al., 1983; Kashani, Burk, & Reid, 1985; Orvaschel, Weissman, & Kidd, 1980; M. M. Weissman et al., 1987), and they are at increased risk for suicide attempts (Friedman et al., 1984). As I discussed in chapter 5, many of these behavioral disturbances may be expressions of depression or depressive equivalents (Blatt, 1991). The children of depressed parents often have experienced disruptive negative family environments, and they may have been abused in their homes, particularly emotional abuse (Mendelson, Robins, & Johnson, 2002). Hirsch, Moos, and Reischl (1985) found that adults with depression reported discordant family environments in their childhood and tended to create similar homes for their own children. Moon (2000), for example, in a longitudinal study of mothers' representations of their children when the children were 5 years old, found that the complexity of mothers' representation of their 5-year-old children significantly predicated the children's positive self-concept and ability to adhere to rules when the children were 12 years of age. Thus, the impaired capacity for object constancy in depressed mothers suggests that children of depressed mothers are vulnerable to many forms of psychopathology.

Davenport et al. (1984) found that affectively ill and healthy mothers did not differ in their ratings of items about their children's learning and achievement or about their patterns of teaching and disciplining their children. One exception, however, was the item "I think it's good practice for a child to perform in front of others," which mothers with depression endorsed significantly more strongly than did mothers who were not depressed. Mothers who were depressed were less likely to encourage openness to experience in their children, and they were less openly expressive of their own emotions about their children. Furthermore, depressed mothers were more likely than control participants who were not depressed to report that they had negative feelings toward their children and that they tended to be overprotective. Home observations of parent–child interactions indicated that depressed mothers were "less active in interaction with their children and more disorganized, unhappy, tense, inconsistent, and ineffective" (Cicchetti & Aber, 1986, p. 100). Sameroff et al. (1982) also noted that depressed mothers of 4-month-old infants were "less spontaneous, happy, vocal, and proximal to their child than non-mentally-ill control mothers" (pp. 96–97). Thus, in both self-report and ratings by observers,

---

and Kovacs, Feinberg, Crause-Novack, Paulaskas, et al. (1984) have found that the early onset of depression in childhood predicts a more protracted depressive illness. Depressed 3rd- to 5th-grade children reported more recent life stressors, including more major family disruptions, than did nondepressed children of the same age (S. Beck & Rosenberg, 1986), and several studies (see Lloyd, 1980) have reported higher incidences of stressful life events among adults in the year prior to onset of depression (G. W. Brown, Sklair, Harris, & Birley, 1973; Paykel et al., 1970; Paykel, Prusoff, & Myers, 1975; Paykel & Tanner, 1976; K. C. Thompson & Hendrie, 1972).

mothers with depression differ from control mothers in their child-rearing practices and their interactive style, but not in their expressed attitudes about child-rearing practices.

Although mothers with depression seem to display qualities of caretaking that are likely to be detrimental to the child, it is important to note that some mothers who are not depressed, or who have other diagnoses, may show qualities of parenting like those of mothers who are depressed, with similar effects. S. H. Goodman and Brumley (1990) compared high-risk (low socioeconomic status [SES]) schizophrenic and depressed mothers with well mothers and found that depressed mothers fell between the schizophrenic mothers and the well mothers in the quality of their parenting. Although a lack of "maternal responsiveness and affectional involvement" was strongly associated in all cases with poor social functioning in the children, regardless of maternal diagnosis, such a lack was most characteristic of schizophrenic mothers, followed by the depressed mothers and the well mothers. The authors did not speculate, however, about the specificity of low maternal responsiveness and a lack of affectional involvement as a risk factor for depression or other forms of psychopathology. It is interesting that children of depressed mothers show less adaptive behavior than children of schizophrenic mothers (Sameroff et al., 1982). Both Rutter (1990) and Beardslee and Podorefsky (1988) have pointed out that the child's ability to identify the parent as "ill" in more severe forms of mental illness, such as psychosis, may make it easier for the child to understand and adjust to bizarre or irrational behavior. Egeland and Sroufe (1981) studied a group of mothers whom they described as "psychologically unavailable." Although these women were not formally diagnosed as clinically depressed, the descriptions of their interactions with their children closely resemble the withdrawn and controlling caretaking behaviors of mothers with depression. A mother's psychological unavailability deprives the infant of a feeling of security. Even when the mother was available, her lack of encouragement and her overprotectiveness discouraged her child's exploration. Cicchetti and Aber (1986) raised the possibility that "perhaps psychological unavailability is one of the common features shared by some maltreating parents and most depressed parents which affect the security of the attachment relationship between parent and the infant" (p. 102). Data from a study of adolescent and young adult children of parents diagnosed with a unipolar affective disorder (Ouimette, Klein, Clark, & Margolis, 1992), however, found that these children did not differ from children of nondepressed parents on self-report measures of a wide range of general personality characteristics.

One avenue by which disturbed mother–child interactions may lead to later depression in the child is the mother's failure to help the infant regulate his or her affect. Tronick and Gianino (1986) described a "mutual regulation model" in which the infant uses self-regulatory behavior as well as the mother to control levels of stimulation. When the mother fails to respond to the infant's signals, the infant may become overwhelmed and disorganized; experience negative affect; and, over time, develop a conception of the self as ineffective and the mother as either unavailable or unreliable (Schaffer & Blatt, 1990). Beebe and Lachmann (1988) pointed out that the mother can be engaged with the infant, responding contingently in a temporal sense, but that regulation of the infant's affect, arousal, and attention will still fail if mother and infant are "misattuned" (i.e., if the mother increases arousal when the infant needs it decreased, or if she fails to match the infant's affective valence). Studies of moment-by-moment mother–infant interaction have shown that normal dyads meet each other in a contingent way in terms of affect, level of arousal, and attention, in a continuous cycle of interactive error and repair (Field et al., 1988; Tronick & Gianino, 1986). Failure of such matching, as in studies of simulated depression (Cohn & Tronick, 1983; Field, Healy, Goldstein, & Guthertz, 1990), leads to negative responses (protests, diverting of gaze) in the child. The level of negative affect experienced by the child of a depressed caregiver is also increased by the infant's tendency to match the mother's negativity; thus, a higher proportion of the dyad's matched states are negative (e.g., intrusive–protest, disengaged–look away; Field et al., 1990).

Continuity between disturbed early interaction patterns and later attachment has been found in several studies (see Beebe & Lachmann, 1988). Both insecure–avoidant and insecure–ambivalent children display behaviors suggestive of disrupted affect regulation—showing little or no expression of affect, punctuated by rare outbursts of anger (Main, 1981), or being overcome by distress and unable to be comforted by the caregiver. The infant–parent interactions of an insecure–ambivalent child may be characterized by a predominance of intrusive–protest interaction, whereas the interactions of an insecure–avoidant child are characterized by a predominance of disengaged–look away interactions. Disorganized–disoriented children demonstrate unusual regulation of emotion in that they appear depressed or dazed in their disjointed alternations between approach and avoidance.

Although each of these patterns represents maladaptive forms of affect expression and regulation, they may also be considered adaptive in the context of the relationship with the particular caregiver. Thus, one would expect the child later in life, especially in stressful situations, to return to these patterns, not only because it is what he or she knows best but also because these behaviors represent an attempt to achieve relative comfort or security. On a related note, Zelnick and Buchholtz (1990), following S. Freud (1900/1953) and other psychoanalytic thinkers (e.g., Blatt, 1974; Pine, 1974; Stolorow, 1978), postulated that mental representations themselves may be comforting or self-regulating in their idealizing, wish-fulfilling functions: "Imagine the functional advantages to a child of an internal representation which can be shaped to represent both wish and reality" (Zelnick & Buchholtz, 1990, p. 40).

In addition to the usual conceptualization of depression as a disturbance in affect regulation, increasing attention has been paid to the cognitive and behavioral components of adult depression. Cicchetti and Sroufe (1978) discussed the importance of the changing organization of cognition, behavior, and affect. On the basis of an integration of aspects of cognitive developmental theory (e.g., Piaget and Werner) and concepts of developmental psychoanalytic theory, I (Blatt, 1974) described these changing levels of organization as ranging from a sensorimotor–preoperational level to an integrative conceptual level. Higgins (1989), on the basis of concepts of social cognition, proposed a model of cognitive organization that ranges over five developmental levels, from an early sensorimotor level to a "later vectorial" developmental level. My (Blatt,

1974) formulations of impairments in the child's developmental level of mental representation of caregivers in depression; Higgins's (1989) formulation of the role of mental representation of caretaker interactions in affect regulation and self-evaluation; and Main's (1990b) elaboration of Bowlby's (1988a) concept of internal working models as guides to cognition (attention and memory), behavior (reunion and coping responses), and affective states (sadness and anger) in attachment-related situations can be unifying constructs for the study of the organization of behavior and affect across various developmental stages (Zelnick & Buchholtz, 1990).

The emphasis on the development of a consolidated and consistent mental representation or internal working model of attachment relationships as an important dimension of normal development is consistent with the recent emphasis in cognitive theory and research on the importance of schemas, prototypes, and scripts in psychological development. Psychological theory has moved beyond the hedonic models of associative learning and the drive-defense resolutions of psychoanalytic thought to an understanding of human behavior as being determined by the organization of meaning and memory structures that are expressed in the form of plans (e.g., G. Miller, Galanter, & Pribram, 1960), expectancies (Feather, 1966), schemas (e.g., Neisser, 1967, 1976; Piaget, 1945/1962; Werner, 1948), and scripts (e.g., Shank & Abelson, 1977). Although individuals may use different schemas and memory structures (Bartlett, 1932; Fiske & Linville, 1980; Hastie, 1981; Piaget, 1937/1954; Taylor & Crockett, 1981; Werner, 1948) in different types of situations, individuals have predominant schemes or preferred modes of organizing experiences and constructing meaning that determine their perceptions and understanding of physical and social reality (Blatt, 1974; Bruner, 1986; Gardner, 1985; N. Goodman, 1984). These cognitive schemas of the self and others, and of the actual and potential nature of interpersonal interactions, govern and regulate all human behavior, including social interaction (Beebe & Lachmann, 1988; Blatt, Auerbach, & Levy, 1997; K. N. Levy et al., 1998).

Beebe and Lachmann (1988) and Stern (1985) have described how normal infants develop a sense of the self as capable, coherent, and positive as a result of consistent interactions with a responsively attuned mother. Zelnick and Buchholtz (1990), citing Sandler, Holder, and Meers (1963), discussed the formulation that a child's model of his or her ideal self may correspond to the mother's idealized representations of the child and that

> when it does, it allows the child the gratification that he or she has complied with parental injunctions and will be loved for his or her compliance, as well as allowing the self-representation to be admired as the object that is admired. (Zelnick & Buchholtz, 1990, p. 38)

In contrast, profound untoward experiences early in life can lead to distorted, unrealistic, and disruptive schemas of the self and others because they derive from negative interactions—from relationships that are undependable or overindulgent; intrusive, judgmental, and punitive; or chaotic or unregulated and that have been internalized as distorted or impaired representations of the self and significant others. In this view, a child who is able to preserve some aspects of positive dimensions of the otherwise-disruptive caregiver might have some resilience to future pathology. Detailed study of parent–child interactions provides some understanding of how these mental representations of self and other are established.

Parent–Child Interaction

Higgins (1989) discussed how differences in caretaker–child interactions influence the development of self-regulation and self-evaluation. He noted that there are basically two types of *positive* psychological caretaking situations: (a) the presence of positive outcomes and (b) the absence of negative outcomes. Some parents attempt to minimize the likelihood that their children will experience a negative outcome, whereas other parents are oriented toward maximizing the likelihood that their children will experience a positive outcome. Likewise, two basic types of *negative* psychological caretaking situations can be differentiated: (a) the absence of positive outcomes and (b) the presence of negative outcomes. A punitive, critical disciplinary style is more likely to be associated with children experiencing negative outcomes. Higgins (1987), on the basis of self-discrepancy theory, predicted that children experiencing self–other interactions with negative outcomes would be more likely to be vulnerable to agitation-related emotions (e.g., fear, worry, edginess), whereas children experiencing self–other interactions involving the absence of positive outcomes would more likely be vulnerable to dejection-related emotions (e.g., sadness, discouragement).

The four types of caretaker–child interactions (presence of positive outcomes, absence of negative outcomes, absence of positive outcomes, presence of negative outcomes) are somewhat similar to Parker's (e. g., 1979a, 1979b) distinctions discussed in chapter 4, in that Higgins (1989) identified four caring modes, which he labeled *neglectful, abusive, spoiling,* and *overprotective.* The two "disciplinary" modes (neglectful and abusive) are likely to contribute directly to a vulnerability to the self-system, consistent with the findings that "strict/demanding" and "cold" parenting styles are related to levels of depression in undergraduates (Bohrnstedt & Fisher, 1986). Higgins (1989) speculated that extreme levels of other modes could be associated with different types of emotional problems.

Higgins (1989) also noted that the characteristics of child–caretaker interaction comprise only one source in the development of the child's self-regulatory and self-evaluative processes and that other factors have to be considered, such as family size, sex and ages of siblings, number and sex of caretakers, and so on. Also, the child's changing capacities for mental representations and experiences in later life interact with early caretaker–child relationships to influence the development of self-regulation and self-evaluation as well as emotional predispositions.

Cohn et al. (1986) described four patterns of interaction of mothers who are depressed with their infants. *Disengaged* mothers are predominantly unavailable and restricted in expression, corresponding to the traditional conception of depressed mothering patterns; *intrusive* mothers have high expressed anger and much physical poking and pulling at the infant (at least 25% of the time); *positive* mothers play with their infants and have positive expressions at least 35% of the time, and *mixed* mothers demonstrate little positive expression but show high rates of eliciting behaviors. Field et al. (1990) added a fifth pattern, *eliciting*, in which the mother spends the most time trying to elicit the infant's attention through "rapid and staccato" gestures. Field et al. (1990) compared 24 mothers who were depressed and 24 well mothers, all of whom were low-SES African American women, and found that 17% of the depressed mothers could be labeled intrusive, 29% were disengaged, 25% were eliciting, 8% were positive, and 21% were mixed, in contrast to the well mothers, of whom 2% were categorized as intrusive, 2% as disengaged, 33% as eliciting, 43% as positive, and 20% as mixed. The heterogeneity among depressed mothers suggests that as a group they were not uniformly withdrawn or disengaged, and the experience of having a depressed mother is not the same for each child. It is possible that a disengaged mother will make it difficult for her child to experience her as a dependable caregiver, whereas a controlling or punitive mother may create conditions in which the child develops more avoidant reactions to protect him- or herself from the mother's intrusions as well as an increased preoccupation with issues of self-definition, autonomy, and self-worth.

A central hypothesis of studies of mother–infant interaction has been that a mother who is depressed, unavailable, and rejecting influences her child through disruption or distortion of the child's development of normal interaction patterns, which has both affective and cognitive consequences. Beebe and Lachmann (1988) characterized the ideal mother–child relationship as one of mutual responsiveness and matching that leads to the infant feeling efficacious and understood by others (see also Schaffer & Blatt, 1990). "Derailed" interactions, in which the mother's responses do not match the infant's behaviors or do not correspond to the infant's needs, result in reduced feelings of being cared for, diminished efficacy, and a dysregulation of emotion (Tronick & Gianino, 1986) in the infant.

Studies of patterns of matching and contingent responsiveness with their infants of depressed mothers versus those who are well suggest that the patterns seem to change as the infant develops. Cohn and Tronick (1987) described three-, six-, and nine-month-old normal infants in a cross-sectional study as showing increasing differentiation and flexibility in their shared states with their mothers. Various studies of infants of depressed mothers suggest that at two to three months of age, infant–mother affective matching and contingent responsiveness most often occur around negative states (Field et al., 1990), but at six months this is less true. Depressed mother–infant dyads seldom played together, and the six-month-old infants were generally withdrawn, with little positive expression or attention to objects and a "general lack of contingent responsiveness . . . [and] little indication of turn-taking" between the mother and child (Cohn et al., 1986, p. 39). In contrast, over half of well mothers, and one third or more of their infants at age six months, tended to show evidence of contingent responsiveness. "Taken together, these findings suggest a shift [in depressed mothers] with development from contingent responsiveness at two months to an attenuated involvement with persons and objects later in the first year" (Cohn et al., 1990, p. 21). Furthermore, the response of normal three-month-old infants to the mother's simulation of depression has been shown to generalize to other, nondepressed interactions (Cohn & Tronick, 1983; Field, 1984), and this depressed response in the infants generalizes to interactions with nondepressed women (Field et al., 1990). Field et al. (1990), however, pointed out that the infant's mood improved in response to an improvement of the mother's depression at six months. Field et al. (1990) concluded that "if mood states are shared, if the mother appears to be leading these early interactions, and if the infant is resilient, it is not surprising that the infants' mood states may change as the mothers' moods change" (p. 13). Little, Robinson, Kogan, and Carter (2002) studied the relationship of maternal depressive style and emotional regulation in 12-month-old infants and found that mothers with high scores on the DEQ Interpersonal and Self-Criticism factors perceived their children as having higher levels of emotionality. Little et al. noted that more depressed mothers may have less tolerance for their children, or tend to report more depression because of raising a difficult child, or project their own difficulties onto their children. However, mothers' scores on the Self-Criticism factor of the DEQ correlated significantly with the intensity and duration of their infants' affect; that is, their infants were less able to soothe themselves without active intervention by an adult. Thus, a self-critical depressive maternal style was associated with aspects of emotional dysregulation in 12-month-old infants.

Beebe and Lachmann (1988) described how patterns of interaction between mother and child become internalized by the young infant in the form of expectations of interaction patterns. These expectations are based on the infant's experience of mutual responsiveness; contingency; and the matching of direction, affective content, and temporal patterns in interaction with the mother. Infants as young as three months of age notice and respond to changes in their mothers' behavior (Cohn & Tronick, 1987). When a nondepressed mother is instructed to simulate a depressed mood, for example, the infant responds to this change in the mother's behavior with both positive and negative eliciting behaviors, such as brief smiles and glances or crying (Cohn & Tronick, 1983; Field et al., 1990). Furthermore, infants who experienced more mutual regulation or repairs of interactive errors in normal interactions with their mothers were more persistent in trying to establish contact with their mothers who acted depressed than were infants without such experience (Tronick & Gianino, 1986). In contrast, infants of depressed mothers showed no change in behavior in response to their mothers' simulated depression (Field, 1984), suggesting that both normal infants and depressed infants establish some sort of early representation or schema of the mother's behavior that is carried over from moment to moment, such that the infant's affective and behavioral reactions to the mother's behavior are influenced by the infant's prior experiences with the mother. Such early representations were also suggested by Yarrow and Goodwin (1973), who found that a change in the mothering figure caused by moving infants of 3 to 16 months of age from a foster placement to an adoptive mother seemed to disrupt social, emotional, and cognitive capacities. These disruptions increased in frequency and severity with age and with "the stage of development of a focused relationship with the mother figure" (Yarrow & Goodwin, 1973, p. 1039).

Beebe and Lachmann (1988) cited several studies that found correspondences between mother and infant interactional tendencies in which positive infant–mother interactions at ages 2 to 4 months were associated with secure attachment at 1 year. Maternal sensitivity and contingent responsiveness in the first months of the infant's life predicted infant cognitive and social competence and secure attachment at 1 year. Looking away, fussiness, and unresponsiveness in infants at 4 months were associated with anxious attachment at 1 year (Blehar, Lieberman, & Ainsworth, 1977). A longitudinal study (Reich, 1988) found a continuity of interaction structures and patterns from 4 to 24 months. The increased instances of looking away, fussiness, and protest in young infants of mothers with depression and in infants of normal mothers who simulate depressed expressions seem similar to the behavior of avoidant and ambivalent insecurely attached infants observed in the Ainsworth (1969) Strange Situation at 12 to 18 months of age. These continuities suggest that mother–infant face-to-face interactions serve self-regulating and attachment-oriented functions for the infant; the patterns of attachment and regulation established in infancy create prototypes that shape subsequent modes of adaptation.

Intergenerational Studies

Longitudinal studies of infants and children at risk for depression facilitate evaluation of the specificity of the impact of a parent's pathology on the child's developmental processes. Although there does not seem to be a one-to-one correspondence between psychopathology in parents and in their children, certain negative parenting styles are commonly found in depressed parents, and these seem to be linked with problems experienced by the children. Extended longitudinal studies permit observation of the development of psychological symptoms, from early structures and expectations to more organized, symbolic processes. These longitudinal studies help one understand how early forms of psychopathology are transformed over the course of development into more structured forms of pathology in adults (Werner, 1948); such studies are often based on the assumption of "sensitive periods" in which differential vulnerability occurs as a consequence of various types of insult at different stages in the developmental process. Two extensive longitudinal studies of children of mothers with depression—the RLS (Sameroff et al., 1982) and the NIMH/ Colorado Collaborative Studies (Cytryn et al., 1984; Davenport et al., 1984; Gaensbauer et al., 1984; Zahn-Waxler et al., 1984)—not only suggest that having a mother who is depressed leaves a child at risk for depression (see also Cantwell, 1983; Downey & Coyne, 1990; Gershon, Bunney, Leckman, Van Eerdewegh, & DeBauche, 1976) but they also help to begin to identify critical points at which disruptions in attachment and cognitive development can occur.

The RLS research group studied four groups of children: (a) children of schizophrenic mothers ($N = 29$), (b) children of mothers who were neurotically depressed ($N = 58$), (c) children of mothers with personality disorders ($N = 40$), and (d) children of a group of mothers without evidence of mental illness ($N = 57$). They studied the impact on the children's adaptive behavior of maternal diagnosis, severity and chronicity of mother's illness, and family social status and found that family social status had stronger effects on children's early development than did mental illness variables such as diagnosis and severity and chronicity of mother's disturbance; family social status accounted for a substantial portion of the variance in the developmental quotients and home observations of the child's adaptive behavior. The mothers of low-SES Black families, in comparison to high-SES Black and low-SES White mothers, expressed less positive affect and were less interactive with their children (Sameroff et al., 1982, p. 62). With social status partialed out, the next most powerful predictor of the children's early development was the severity and chronicity of the mother's illness. The specific psychiatric diagnosis of the mother's disturbance was the least influential of the four risk factors, although, as already noted, children of mothers who were neurotically depressed did less well than children of schizophrenic mothers when compared with mothers with no mental illness.

Gaensbauer et al. (1984) compared seven male index children of parents with bipolar and unipolar depression at ages 12, 15, and 18 months with seven male children of parents without psychiatric diagnosis, matched on age, race, and SES. They observed a child's security of attachment by studying the child's behavior with the mother and with an unfamiliar adult and the child's capacity to modulate affective expression. Zahn-Waxler et al. (1984) assessed the same group of seven index and seven control boys at age 30 months in their play with a same-sex, same-age, unfamiliar peer, and with their mother and the mother of the unfamiliar peer. They also collected observations from home visits and from mothers' reports of the child's psychological problems for an entire year, beginning at age 12 months. Davenport et al. (1984) administered Q-sorts concerning the child-rearing practices of the mothers of these children when the children were 24 months old. These studies found that the children of depressed parents, as compared with the control group, seemed more fearful in free play and sadder at maternal separation and reunion at 12 months and seemed less fearful with maternal separation but more distressed during testing and at the approach of a stranger at ages 15 months and 18 months. They also seemed to have less pleasure and less interest in testing and during maternal reunion as well as more anger, displaced aggression, and distress in free play and during testing (Gaensbauer et al., 1984). Children of depressed mothers were more symptomatic; they had more severe general symptoms and more depression-related symptoms, and they were generally rated as overexcited. They were also less altruistic or sharing than control children, and this declined even further during the course of assessment. These children also experienced heightened emotional arousal while observing the argument of two adult experimenters (Zahn-Waxler et al., 1984).

Children of depressed mothers were found to differ increasingly from control children as they grew older, beginning in the second year of life, which appears to be a crucial time for the emergence of untoward behavior in children's interaction patterns. In the RLS study, children of depressed mothers did not differ from control participants on various behavioral measures at 12 months, whereas by 30 months they were rated by their mothers as "less cooperative" with family or others, "more bizarre in behavior," "more depressed," and "more often engaged in imaginary play" (Sameroff et al., 1982, p. 97) than were control children. In the NIMH study, the predominance (5/7) of the children of depressed and normal mothers were rated as securely attached to their mothers during the first year, but by 18 months only 1 of the 7 index children was rated as securely attached, versus 4 of the 7 control participants. Egeland and Sroufe (1981) and the NIMH group found a decline at 18 months in the attachment security of children whose mothers were psychologically unavailable either because of economic factors, psychological factors, or both. The percentage of securely attached infants of mothers who were "psychologically unavailable" (but not necessarily depressed) dropped from 57% at 12 months to 0% at 18 months.

Cicchetti and Aber (1986) argued that the combination of unavailability and overprotectiveness of depressed mothers is paradoxical; the challenges that mother and child face in the second year of life seem to exacerbate already-existing vulnerabilities. A mother's difficulties in managing her infant tend to appear primarily in the first half of the second year, when the infant becomes more active. As the child begins to walk and talk, and struggles to separate from the mother, these activities place stress on the maternal caretaking capacities such that the basic attachment relationship may be transformed, if it has not been already, from a secure relationship to an insecure one. The mobility of the toddler also places increased demand on the child and the mother for object constancy. Although the child probably has developed recognition or libidinal constancy at 6 to 8 months (Blatt, 1991, 1995b), he or she can separate from the mother around 16 to18 months with confidence only if he or she has developed the capacity for object (or evocative) constancy (Fraiberg, 1969). Also, although some mothers who are depressed and psychologically unavailable are able to provide the basic care and feeding, and even nurturance, required by an infant, these mothers, because of their own disturbances in evocative constancy, may be unable to tolerate the toddler's assertion for separation, independence, and autonomy. Thus, the second half of the first year, in addition to the interactional disturbances noted in the infant's first months of life, may constitute a critical period during which disturbances in the mother–infant relationship can develop.

The period around 16 to 18 months appears to be particularly critical for the etiology of depression, because the disruptions of many of the social, emotional, and cognitive competencies implicated in depression develop in late infancy and early toddlerhood. An autonomous sense of self, the affect of shame, and especially the development of object constancy as mediated by the consolidation of an internal working model (or representation) of a secure attachment relationship, all begin to develop in the second year of life. Also during the second and third years of life, the child begins to strive to meet adult standards (Kagan, 1981) and begins to become self-aware (Kagan, 1981) and self-evaluative, as expressed in the emergence of feelings of shame and guilt, and to develop self-confidence ("effectance motivation"; Harder, 1978) and a sense of pride (Sroufe, 1983). These indications of an emerging sense of self during the second and third years of life are consistent with E. H. Erikson's (1968) psychosocial formulations about the importance of issues of autonomy versus shame and initiative versus guilt in the second to fourth years of life, and with H. B. Lewis's (1990) discussion of the development of shame and guilt.

H. B. Lewis (1990, p. 239) discussed shame as a "family of feelings: humiliation, mortification, feeling ridiculous, painful self-consciousness, chagrin, shyness, and embarrassment . . . . all hav(ing) in common that the self is helpless. 'Guilt', similarly refers to a family of feelings: fault, blame, responsibility, obligation." Lewis views shame as related to the entirety of the self, whereas guilt is about things done or undone for which the self is responsible: "In shame, the self has fallen short of its respected place not only in its own eyes, but also in the eyes of others. . . . In guilt, the other is injured, or hurt, while the self . . . is able to repair it" (p. 241). The self is damaged in shame, while the self is active in guilt in the efforts to make amends. Lewis (1990, p. 246) reported that although securely attached infants respond eagerly to their mothers on the mothers' return after separation, they do so with a brief gaze aversion or a blank facial expression, which Lewis interpreted as "a mixture of pleasure and some hint of shame." In discussing the responses of disorganized and avoidant insecurely attached infants, Lewis concluded that the avoidant infants may be expressing "the forerunner of a pattern of reaction that involves bypassing the shame of being rejected" and the expression of "humiliated fury." Lewis viewed avoidance as an early expression of shame as well as a shift of attention away from the attachment figure.

Guilt and shame are central issues in adult psychopathology, particularly introjective depression (Blatt, 1974), and these issues are also part of the struggle for independence, autonomy, self-definition, and self-worth that begin to emerge during the second year of life (see also Emde et al., 1986, and Garmezy, 1987). Investigators have actively debated whether depression can exist as a distinct clinical entity in infancy or early childhood (Bemporad & Wilson, 1976; Cicchetti & Schneider-Rosen, 1984b; Garber, 1984; Rutter, 1986), in part because of the tendency to define depression primarily in terms of self-critical and deprecating views of the self (see also reviews by Arieti & Bemporad, 1978; Kashani et al., 1981). Some researchers argue that depression can begin to occur only in adolescence, because the capacity for critical self-reflective evaluation appears later in development and becomes stabilized as a psychological function sometime in early to middle adolescence. However, other forms of guilt, such as those focused on issues of separation and individuation from an insecure parent, or acceptance of responsibility for negative events, seem to occur much earlier (Zahn-Waxler, Kochanska, Krupnick, & McKnew, 1990). In addition, children experience considerable dysphoria around experiences of neglect and abandonment. In general, children are much more vulnerable to experiences of object loss than to feelings of having failed to meet internalized standards. The egocentrism of childhood often leads children, when faced with abandonment or rejection, to feel that they are unlovable. Dependence on an unreliable caretaker must be intensely frightening to a child, especially if he or she somehow feels responsible for the loss. Feeling unloved and unlovable leads to anxiety and further insecurity and expectations of further rejection.

Consistent with this conceptualization of different sources of guilt at different ages, S. Graham, Doubleday, and Guarino (1984) distinguished between guilt for feeling responsible for uncontrollable events, which seems to be experienced more often by younger children, and guilt due to feelings of responsibility for controllable events involving intentionality, which seems to be more characteristic of older children (see also S. Freud, 1930/1961a, for a distinction of guilt induced by the power of an external authority and a more internalized level of guilt derived from an inner authority). Zahn-Waxler et al. (1990) pointed to the young child's egocentrism and lack of stable differentiation between self and other as contributing to the child's vulnerability to feeling responsible (i.e., guilty) for events that occur to him or her. Zahn-Waxler et al. (1990) also found very different patterns of guilt for children of nondepressed mothers and for children of depressed mothers. Middle childhood, between ages five and nine years, seems to be a significant period for the development of guilt and patterns of internalized responsibility in normal children. Experiences of emotional involvement and guilt appear to increase concurrently with increases in concern about interpersonal relationships and the development of an empathic capacity to know the experiences of the other. Children of depressed mothers, however, seem to develop symptoms of guilt as early as five years of age (the youngest age sampled), "confirming the significance of yet an earlier period in development for internalization of responsibility" (Zahn-Waxler et al., 1990, p. 57). On the basis of both clinical interviews and semiprojective narratives about hypothetical events, Zahn-Waxler et al. (1990) found that young children of depressed mothers show high levels, relative to nondepressed children, of feelings of responsibility and emotional involvement.[4] Yet the older children of depressed mothers seem to show arrested expressions of explicit guilt. Thus, the higher levels of distress and more frequent and extreme "distortions" in the narratives of children of depressed mothers suggest that older children of depressed mothers may actually struggle to protect themselves from experiencing directly these strong feelings of guilt. Children of well and depressed mothers seem to be on "different pathways or trajectories" (Zahn-Waxler et al., 1990) in their development of patterns of guilt. Being raised by a depressed parent appears to make children more sensitive, at an earlier age, to issues of guilt and feelings of responsibility, because of the following factors: a global home climate of distress and conflict, the child's proximity to the parent's own guilt and irritability, very high demands made on a young child, guilt- and anxiety-induction techniques used by the parent, judgmental attributions about the child, use of withdrawal of love as a type of discipline, and negative attributional styles modeled by the parent and learned by the child.

Peterson and Seligman (1984), taking a cognitive–behavioral approach to depression based on a theory of learned helplessness, focused on the tendency

---

[4]Distorted responses in the narratives were those containing "violent, unusual, unrealistic, or extreme elements . . . or indexes of vulnerability, hypersensitivity, or tension" (p. 54), such as " 'The mom's leaving home because the boy wouldn't eat her peas' " or " 'The father was killed and cars kept running over the father, even the ambulance (and the mother and boy watched from the bedroom window).' "

for guilt and depression to be associated with a pessimistic explanatory style in which the individual attributes the causes of bad events to his or her own enduring negative traits rather than to external circumstances. Brewin and Furnham (1987) found that both dependency and self-criticism, but especially Self-Criticism as measured by the DEQ, were significantly associated with a negative attributional style, whereas DEQ Efficacy was significantly associated with a positive attributional style. Studies have found a convergence of mothers' and children's explanatory styles and depressive symptoms (Seligman et al., 1984). They also have found that teachers tend to criticize boys and girls for different reasons and that girls appear to learn more pessimistic explanatory styles (Dweck & Licht, 1980). A pessimistic explanatory style, in interaction with realistic aspects of a particular negative event, may produce an expectation that "no action will control outcomes in the future" (Seligman, 1975, p. 349). This pessimism, along with the loss of self-esteem and guilt, is considered sufficient to cause (self-critical) depression. The method of transmission of explanatory styles from parent or teacher to child appears to occur through the child's appropriation or internalization of the adult's values. The parent's negative attributional style, however, may be only one component of a more depressive family environment that interferes with the child's development of secure relationships and adaptive coping abilities.

Retrospective Accounts of Child-Rearing Experiences

A third approach to the study of the role of parent–child relationships in the etiology of depression has been based on individuals' recollections of their parents' caregiving behavior. Investigations of individuals' retrospective reports of their childhood caring experiences, using different methodologies, some of which were described in chapter 4, confirm and elaborate the role of these impaired levels of object representation in depression.

Numerous clinical reports indicate disrupted interpersonal relations in the childhood experiences of depressed patients (e.g., Blatt, 1974; M. B. Cohen, Baker, Cohen, Fromm-Reichman, & Weigert, 1954; Fenichel, 1945; Rado, 1928; Rochlin, 1965). M. B. Cohen et al. (1954), in their study of 12 manic–depressive patients, found that all these families thought of themselves as social outcasts, inferior, and different. The patients, as children, felt pressure to be socially proper and to live up to severe standards established by the family. Patients described their mothers as cold, fearful, contemptuous, aggressive, and ambitious, often actively blaming the failure of their husbands for the family's plight. They described their fathers as weak but lovable, acquiescent, and accepting the mothers' blame for the family's ill fortune.

Colleagues and I (Blatt, Quinlan, & Chevron, 1990; Blatt, Wein, et al., 1979) have studied the relationships between ratings of the degree of parental caring and protection, as assessed on the Parental Bonding Instrument (PBI; Parker, 1979a), and depression as assessed by the DEQ, the Beck Depression Inventory (BDI; A. T. Beck, Ward, Mendelson, Mock, & Erbaugh, 1961), and the Zung Depression Scale (ZDS; Zung, 1965). In a nonclinical sample of young adult women, caring by mother and father had a significant ($p < .05$) negative correlation with self-critical measures of depression (DEQ Self-Criticism, BDI, and ZDS). Maternal and paternal overprotection in these women also had a significant positive correlation with DEQ Self-Criticism, BDI, and ZDS, whereas mothers' overprotection also had a significant positive correlation with DEQ Dependency. These relationships, however, were not as clear in young adult men, for whom mothers' caring correlated negatively ($p < .05$) only with the BDI, and fathers' caring correlated negatively ($p < .05$) only with DEQ Self-Criticism. Maternal and paternal overprotection in men did not correlate significantly with any of the depression measures, except maternal overprotection was significantly ($p < .05$) correlated with DEQ Self-Criticism. Thus, the relationship between parental caring and protection on the PBI and types of depression seems clear in young adult women, but these relationships are less consistent for young adult men.

Studies of individuals prone to depression, but not clinically depressed at the time of testing, are consistent with these findings. Zemore and Rinholm (1989) reported that individuals who scored high on a depression-proneness scale described their parents as cold and restricting. This relationship was especially strong for the same-sex parent. Schwarz and Zuroff (1979) found that college women who were vulnerable to depression reported inconsistent affection from both parents, although inconsistent affection from the opposite-sex parent, the father, was especially important.

The findings of Zemore and Rinholm (1989), Schwarz and Zuroff (1979), and G. Parker (e.g., 1981, 1983, 1984) are consistent with the findings that the perception of adults of their "parents as lacking in nurturance, support, and affection . . . is related to depression rather than [a] perception of parents as striving, harsh and judgmental" (Blatt, Wein, et al., 1979, p. 394). Johnson, Petzel, Dupont, and Romano (1982) found that depressed patients, compared with nondepressed control participants, did not perceive their parents as setting high standards for them; rather, they perceived their parents as more critical in expressing these standards. Thus, data from these studies suggest that a lack of parental care is a predominant factor in depression and that criticism or intrusive parental control is a second, somewhat less frequent, factor.

McCranie and Bass (1984) studied parent–child relationships in individuals high on Factors I and II (Interpersonal and Self-Criticism) of the DEQ. Parent–child relationships of female nursing students were assessed with the Strict Control, Conformity, and Achievement Control scales from the Parental Behavior Form, the Parental Inconsistency of Love scale (Schwarz & Zuroff, 1979), and the Schwarz–Getter Interparental Influence Scale (Schwarz & Getter, 1980). Controlling parents

> view the child as an agent for satisfying their own needs for love and recognition rather than as an autonomous, self-willed entity. . . . Methods of controlling the child are predominantly negative, exhibiting elements of strictness combined with inconsistent expressions of love and affection reflecting conditional acceptance. (McCranie & Bass, 1984, p. 4)

DEQ Factor I was significantly correlated with perception of the mother as the dominant controlling parent who maintains strict control, insists on conformity, and impedes the child's separation. Individuals with elevations on DEQ Self-Criticism (Factor II), in contrast, described both parents as equally dominant and as inconsistent in their love and maintaining strict control, particularly by emphasizing achievement. Self-criticism seems to involve ambivalent feelings about both parents, especially about the parents' attempts to maintain control. R. Thompson and Zuroff (1998, 1999b) have found that self-critical mothers are more controlling and punitive toward their adolescent daughters, leading to their daughters' reports of insecure attachment and increased levels of self-criticism. Whiffen and Sasseville (1991) replicated McCranie and Bass's finding that self-criticism in young adult women is related to maternal emphasis on achievement and paternal control. In a clinical sample, Rosenfarb, Becker, Khan, and Mintz (1998) found that self-criticism was associated with a problematic relationship with the father and perceptions of his power and control. These findings suggest that children internalize experiences with their parents to form internal working models of self and other, and of self–other relationships, which then influence their subsequent interpersonal interactions (e.g., Baldwin, 1992; Blatt & Homann, 1992). These negative relationships then perpetuate the negative self-images of these individuals and contribute to the maintenance and extension of their self-criticism (Blatt & Homann, 1992; R. Thompson & Zuroff, 1998, 1999b). Frank, Poorman, et al. (1997) studied adolescent inpatients and found that Self-Criticism on the adolescent version of the DEQ, the DEQ–A, was associated with alienation and counterdependency from parents, whereas dependency or interpersonal concerns on the DEQ–A was associated with excessive closeness with and dependence on parents.

Perlman (1998), in a study of college women's reports of their relationship with their parents, found that the DEQ Interpersonal and Self-Criticism factors were associated with different patterns of the perceived relationship with the parents. These patterns resembled dismissive and preoccupied attachment organization. DEQ Self-Criticism was associated with perceptions of parents as both psychologically controlling and unavailable. Women high on Self-Criticism had negative models of relationships, and they seemed to emphasize separateness from their parents as a way of achieving separation–individuation. They tended to minimize the importance of closeness and expected others to be rejecting, unreliable, and unavailable. Women with elevated scores on the DEQ Interpersonal factor perceived their parents as psychologically controlling, and their relationships with their parents emphasized the maintenance of connectedness at the expense of the autonomy.

McCranie and Bass (1984) found that dependent women reported that their mothers emphasized conformity, whereas self-critical women reported parental emphasis on achievement and performance. They did not find, however, any relationship between reports of inconsistent parental love and a dependent form of depression. McCranie and Bass speculated that this might have been due to dependent individuals' inability to acknowledge dissatisfaction with, or anger at, their parents for fear of losing a relationship they feel is essential for their survival. This could also explain the unexpected findings of J. G. Parker and Lipscombe (1980); McCranie and Bass (1984); and Blatt, Quinlan, and Chevron (1990), that a dependent depression is not strongly associated with reports of inconsistent love or a lack of parental care. I (Blatt,

1974) and McCranie and Bass have suggested that anaclitically depressed individuals may have difficulty expressing anger or disappointment for fear of losing the love of people close to them, and they may instead turn to denial as a defense against both the disappointment and the fear of loss: "Individuals prone to experiences of dependency may be either less aware of or less willing to acknowledge parental rejection and inconsistent expression of affection" (McCranie & Bass, 1984, p. 7). Alternatively, individuals, especially women, who are high on dependency may have experienced neglectful or overindulgent rather than inconsistent care. Ambivalence and guilt over anger toward parents because of inconsistent parental care may be more related to a self-critical depression. The differences in these findings suggest that anaclitic and introjective depressive feelings may derive from different parental behaviors at different points in the developmental process.

The more recent differentiation of two levels of interpersonal relations on the DEQ (Neediness and Relatedness), as discussed in chapter 3, may account for some of the inconsistency in the findings of McCranie and Bass (1984) regarding the Interpersonal factor of the DEQ. Also, assessing accurately issues of dependency may be difficult, because it may involve retrospective recollections of parental behavior that occurred during early childhood rather than in middle childhood. In fact, the inconsistency scale used by McCranie and Bass seems to assess primarily inconsistent approval, an issue dominant in middle childhood, rather than inconsistent caring. It is also possible that anaclitic depressive feelings in adults is a function not of an inconsistency of caring but of a lack of parental caring or a dramatic disruption of caring as a result of parental death, divorce, stress, or illness, or of excessive caring and overprotection that thwart the child's ability to learn to care for him- or herself (see J. G. Parker & Lipscombe, 1980).

Strict control appears to be an antecedent of both dependency and self-criticism (McCranie & Bass, 1984). The difference between dependency and self-criticism, however, may be a function of how this control is maintained. Strict control achieved by manipulating the expression and availability of care and affection may result in heightened dependency, whereas control exerted through restricting autonomy and the intensive demand for achieving goals and meeting excessive standards may result in heightened self-criticism. These formulations are congruent with reports (S. Jacobson, Fasman, & DiMascio, 1975; Lamont, Fischoff, & Gottlieb, 1976; Lamont & Gottlieb, 1975; G. Parker, 1979a, 1979b; Raskin, Boothe, Reatig, Schulterbrandt, & Odle, 1971; Schwarz & Zuroff, 1979) indicating

> that depression proneness in general is influenced by parental child-rearing practices that combine elements of rejection, inconsistent expression of affection, and strict control. Such behaviors could be expected to hinder the development of normal self-esteem in the child, resulting in an increased vulnerability to generalized feelings of helplessness and failure. (McCranie & Bass, 1984, p. 7)

These formulations are also consistent with Frank, Poorman, et al.'s (1997) study, in which they found that self-critical adolescent inpatients described their relationship with their parents as distant and impeding of their autonomy, whereas high-dependent patients feared separation and perceived their relationship with their parents as close.

Focusing on possible childhood antecedents to self-criticism, Johnson et al. (1982) found that respondents with elevated scores on the BDI (a measure primarily of self-critical depression; Blatt et al., 1982) experienced their parents as evaluating them more negatively than did nondepressed respondents. Depressed individuals also rated themselves as less active and more discrepant from the ideals held for them by both their parents on dimensions of Evaluation and Activity and by their fathers on Masculinity/Femininity. No differences were found between depressed and nondepressed respondents, however, in perceptions of the parents' ideals, suggesting that depressed individuals do not have a generalized negative cognitive set and that it is not the perception of extreme ideals and excessively high standards per se that is related to depression. The difference in depression appears to be the ways these ideals are presented to the children that has an impact on them. "It may be the case, then, that depressogenic parents do not set higher goals, they may just be more critical in evaluating attempts to reach these goals" (Johnson et al., 1982, p. 61). These conclusions are consistent with reports discussed earlier (e.g., Cicchetti & Aber, 1986; Davenport et al., 1984; Sameroff et al., 1982) indicating that while depressed mothers do not differ from control mothers in their expressed attitudes about child rearing, they do differ markedly in their child-rearing practices. Parents' views of their children seem to dominate how depressed individuals feel about and evaluate themselves. The harshly critical self-evaluation of depressed individuals corresponds with how they thought their parents perceived them. Thus, the negative self-views of self-critically depressed individuals reflect the negative evaluation they experienced from their parents, and probably from others as well.

Amitay, Mongrain, and Fazaa (2002) evaluated reports from young adult women and their parents and found that self-critical mothers and fathers, as defined by the Self-Criticism factor of the DEQ, were less loving toward their daughters; in addition, self-critical fathers were also more controlling. The lack of parental love predicted self-criticism in the daughters, which in turn predicted increases in their level of depression and with their reports of having less loving and more controlling boyfriends. Amitay et al. suggested that self-critical individuals are raised in a self-critical, punitive environment and that the maintenance of their negative self-concept creates a vulnerability to depression and a predisposition to repeat these self-critical interpersonal dynamics in their own romantic relationships. The internalization (or introjection) of the cold, critical, rejecting, and controlling parental styles leads these individuals to re-create this type of interpersonal interaction in their current romantic relationships. These self-critical women will likely also repeat this faulty interaction in the next generation with their own children. Thus, early negative childhood experiences appear to create self-critical individuals who perpetuate their negative self-images by creating negative interpersonal relations that exacerbate their self-critical vulnerabilities. Amitay et al.'s findings, as well as earlier reports by R. Thompson and Zuroff (1998, 1999a, 1999b), are direct evidence that link self-criticism in mothers and fathers to their faulty parental styles and the presence of self-criticism and depression in their daughters. Mothers and fathers who are highly self-critical are less loving toward their daughters, and self-critical fathers described themselves as more controlling. These findings are consistent with reports by G. Parker and colleagues (1979b, 1981) about the importance of an "affectionless controlling" or punitive parental style and its role in depression. Thus, daughters of critical parents develop self-critical personality styles and depressed mood. It is important to note that Amitay et al.'s results directly link parental self-criticism with their daughters' depression.

These self-critical young women perceived their boyfriends as more controlling and less loving, suggesting that a self-critical personality style is passed from parents to daughters and contributes to the daughters' interpersonal difficulties and their vulnerability to depression. Self-criticism in both parents was related to a relative lack of love toward their daughters. Receiving less love from parents seemed to predict a critical style toward the self that leads to feelings of depression and to impediments in the capacity to form intimate relationships. These self-critical interpersonal dynamics in the parent–child relationship tend to repeat themselves in the current romantic relationships of these individuals. Baldwin (1992, p. 462) discussed how current patterns of interaction derive from earlier interpersonal experiences. Current relational schemas resemble the relationship these individuals had with their parents and are expressed in their reports of their relationships with their actual and ideal boyfriends. As Andrews (1989) and Swann and his colleagues (e.g., Giesler & Swann, 1999) have postulated, depressed individuals seek negative relationships to confirm their negative self-images and to maintain a sense of inter- and intrapersonal coherence. Amitay et al. (2002) found that depression associated with self-criticism predicted the degree to which such women seek a less loving, more controlling boyfriend, someone not unlike their fathers. Thus, these women maintain internal and social stability by creating a vicious cycle that makes it difficult for them to revise their overly harsh self-concepts, and they repeat these issues in the next generation, in their interactions with their own children. These findings are consistent with the results of several longitudinal studies (e.g., Gjerde, Block, & Block, 1991; Koestner, Zuroff, & Powers, 1991; Lekowitz & Tesiny, 1984), summarized below.

Descriptions of Parents

As I discussed in detail in chapter 4, colleagues and I have developed procedures to assess systematically aspects of both the organizational structure and the thematic content of descriptions of significant others (e.g., mother, father, therapist). Aspects of the structural organization that were assessed by means of these descriptions include the *conceptual level*, the degree of *articulation*, and the degree of *differentiation and relatedness* with which these figures were described. In terms of thematic content, judges were able to rate reliably the degree to which the figures were described as benevolent, punitive, and ambitious, as well as the degree of ambivalence on the descriptions. Length of the descriptions was also noted as a control variable.

In the original study (Blatt, Wein, et al., 1979), spontaneous descriptions of significant caregivers (mother and father) were used to examine differences between anaclitic and introjective depression. We found that the conceptual level of the representation of parents given by women was significantly and negatively related to measures of their depression. Higher (more conceptual) levels of representation were significantly and negatively correlated with depression as assessed by Factor I (Interpersonal) of the DEQ, the semantic differential, and the ZDS. In addition, higher conceptual levels were positively correlated ($p < .05$) with Efficacy on the DEQ. These significant correlations between conceptual level and measures of depression were not found, however, in men. In addition, the correlation between conceptual level and DEQ Self-Criticism was not significant in either women or men.

In considering the relation of the conceptual level of representation to anaclitic and introjective depression, it was important to note that the conceptual level of representations of parents in introjective depression (high DEQ Self-Criticism) theoretically should be at a moderate level (at the "perceptual and iconic level"; Blatt, 1974), whereas in anaclitic depression (high scores on the DEQ Interpersonal factor) the conceptual level should be at the lower levels (sensorimotor–preoperational). The significant correlation between conceptual level of parental descriptions and measures of depression in females but not in males may have resulted because depressive experiences in females fall predominantly along the dependency (anaclitic) dimension, whereas in males depression is more often along the self-criticism (introjective) dimension (Chevron, Quinlan, & Blatt, 1978). Thus, the relation between conceptual level of representations and measures of depression in females would more likely be linear than in males. The relation between conceptual level and DEQ Self-Criticism in males, in contrast, should be curvilinear and, therefore, not adequately assessed by a correlation analysis.

To assess further the hypotheses about the relations between conceptual level and types of depression, colleagues and I (Blatt, Wein, et al., 1979) compared the conceptual level of several groups of nonclinical participants: those whose depression was (a) primarily anaclitic (high Dependency), (b) primarily introjective (high Self-Criticism), (c) a mixture of anaclitic and introjective (high Dependency and high Self-Criticism), and (d) those who were low on both types of depression and high on Efficacy. Using median splits on each of the DEQ factors, we selected four groups of participants as exemplifying conceptually different and consistent types: (a) high Dependency and low Self-Criticism (dependent), (b) high Self-Criticism and low Dependency (self-critical), (c) high Dependency and high Self-Criticism (mixed dependent and self-critical), and (d) low Dependency and low Self-Criticism (nondepressed). A progressive increase was expected in the conceptual level, ranging from low to high in the following order across these four groups: anaclitic, mixed anaclitic–introjective, introjective, and nondepressed. A planned comparison (Winer, 1962) for the conceptual level of both mother and father across these four groups was significant ($p \leq .05$). Participants with high scores on DEQ Dependency had the lowest conceptual level, those with high scores on both Dependency and Self-Criticism were similar to the high-Dependency group, those with high scores primarily on DEQ Self-Criticism had intermediate conceptual levels, and those with low scores on both Dependency and Self-Criticism had the highest conceptual levels in their descriptions of their parents (Blatt et al., 1982).

These findings are consistent with clinical observations that the representations of patients who are introjectively depressed are at an external iconic level, focused on particular attributes that are often one sided and stated in extremely harsh and negative terms (Blatt, 1974). Although the parent is perceived as a separate entity primarily in terms of functional activities and attributes, a harsh and critical parent seems to be experienced as an intrusive inner presence that is confused with and limits the child's development of a sense of the self as independent and competent.

These results with both nonclinical and clinical samples indicate that parental descriptions can be scored reliably and that the content and structural aspects of parental representations have a significant relation to depression. Results with the PBI and the thematic and structural dimensions of the Object Relations Inventory are consistent with prior indications that neglectful, depriving, and excessively critical and punitive parents are some of the precursors of depression in adults. Parental neglect, rejection, and abuse are internalized by the child and can become elements of the representation of self and of others in caring relationships, leading some individuals to form negative cognitive schemas about themselves, their environment, and the future (A. T. Beck, 1967b). Comparisons of individuals with and without depression indicate that those who are depressed report more negative experiences with their parents (Blatt Wein, et al., 1979; Burbach & Bourdin, 1986). Most of these studies have relied on individuals' retrospective ratings and descriptions of their parents (e.g., Blatt, Wein, et al., 1979; Crook, Raskin, & Elliot, 1981; Lamont et al., 1976; Lamont & Gottlieb, 1975; G. Parker, 1981; Raskin et al., 1971; Schaefer, 1965), although a few studies have used clinicians' evaluations of patients' early childhood experiences (e.g., S. Jacobson et al., 1975). Depressed individuals recall both their mother and father as uncaring, rejecting, and excessively critical and punitive. Lewinsohn and Rosenbaum (1987), consistent with these findings, found that acutely clinically depressed individuals described their parents as more emotionally rejecting than did nondepressed control participants, but not as using more negative controlling strategies (e.g., debasement, threats of punishment, and guilt manipulation) or as being more firm or lax in their discipline. Lewinsohn and Rosenbaum also found that the issue of emotional rejection was more central to depression in females than in males.

Retrospective Accounts of Child-Rearing Practices

The use of retrospective reports and correlational data, however, raises a number of alternative possibilities beyond the conclusion that insufficient or distorted parenting creates a vulnerability to depression. It is possible, for example, that depressed characteristics of the child cause his or her parents to be less caring or that the current level of depression causes individuals to view their parents more negatively. Descriptions of parents may also reflect an individual's response set rather than actual parental attitudes and behavior.

Alternatively, it may be the specific perceptions and interpretations of the behavior of the parents, rather than the parents' actual behavior, that leave individuals vulnerable to depression. It may be individuals' experiences of the caregiving relationship, rather than the independent and objective assessment of the quality of parental behavior, that is the important dimension for understanding the causal sequences leading to depression. This problem of the validity of retrospective accounts of child-rearing practices has been addressed to some extent by G. Parker (e.g., 1981, 1982), whose investigations indicate that retrospective reports can be both reliable and valid and that parental lack of caring and psychological control are important antecedents of depression.

Lewinsohn and Rosenbaum (1987) raised the important question of whether these various reports of negative parental behavior by individuals with depression comprise an accurate description of early life experiences of individuals vulnerable to depression or whether they are a function of the current negative mood state of individuals with depression. They pointed out that a number of studies indicate that negative mood state, including depression, generally increases negative recall (Bower, 1981; Isen, Shalker, Clark, & Karp, 1978; Kuiper & MacDonald, 1982; Teasdale, Taylor, & Fogarty, 1980). Although Abrahams and Whitlock (1969) and G. Parker (1981) have found that negative reports of parents are not influenced by current depressed mood, Lewinsohn and Rosenbaum found no significant difference in parental descriptions between control participants and a group of participants with remitted depression (who were not currently depressed but had elevated scores (≥ 18) on the Center for Epidemiological Studies Depression Scale (Radloff, 1977) as well as reports of prior depressive episodes on the Schedule for Affective Disorders and Schizophrenia (Endicott & Spitzer, 1978). Patients defined as depressed according to research diagnostic criteria applied to the Schedule for Affective Disorders and Schizophrenia semistructured interview, however, recalled their parents as more rejecting than did control participants. This suggested to Lewinsohn and Rosenbaum that current negative mood states may intensify the feeling that one's parents have been emotionally rejecting. Thus, Lewinsohn and Rosenbaum called for further investigation of the degree to which memories of past events (such as parental behavior) of depressed individuals are influenced by current depressive mood. It is possible, however, that patients who are able to recover from depression have had better caring experiences in childhood than patients who are less able to recover from depressive episodes.

Several investigators, in addition to Lewinsohn and Rosenbaum (1987), have considered the possibility that negative cognitive sets may exaggerate individuals' criticisms of their parents (Bower, 1981; Gotlib, Mount, Cordy, & Whiffen, 1988; G. Parker, 1981; Perris et al., 1986). Such a pattern would be consistent with the findings that individuals who are introjectively depressed are more critical of others as well as of themselves and have more conscious ambivalent feelings about their parents (G. Parker, 1980). Johnson et al. (1982), however, found that individuals with depression do not have "a global and indiscriminant negative test-taking set" (p. 61), because they do not differ from nondepressed individuals in how they perceive what their parents expected of them. Also, Brewin, Firth-Cozens, Furnham, and Andrews (1990) found that the degree of self-criticism is related to reports of maternal lack of care and increased overprotection in women, even after controlling for the possible confounding effects of current mood state (e.g., level of happiness) and social desirability. These findings are consistent with those of McCranie and Bass (1984) and with the finding by Gotlib et al. (1988) that women with postpartum depression reported negative experiences with their parents on the PBI and that this negative report did not change when the depression remitted. In addition, in several studies (e.g., Brewin, Andrews, & Gotlib, 1993; Gold, 1986) that used structured interviews, "extreme negative self-attributions" (e.g., self-criticism) were associated with repeated physical and sexual abuse, findings consistent with the frequent courtroom testimony of guilt and self-criticism in incest and abuse victims (Gelinas, 1983). These findings indicate that reports of parental behavior from self-critical individuals accurately reflect the nature of their experiences with their parents and that these reports are not the manifestation of current depressed mood (Brewin et al., 1990).

Brewin et al. (1993) refuted the three methodological criticisms of retrospective reports, that is (a) normal limitations of memory, (b) memory deficits associated with psychopathology, and (c) distortions created by mood-congruent memory. On the basis of a review of relevant literature, they concluded that adults can accurately recall salient factual details of their childhood, that there is no consistent evidence of a general memory deficit in individuals with depression, and that only minimal evidence suggests that depressed mood distorts cognitive processes. They found, in fact, high agreement between patients' memories and external criteria. Thus, Brewin et al. (1993, p. 94) concluded that there "seems to be little reason to think that the documented relation between adverse early experience, often involving severe parental maltreatment, and later psychopathology arises from patients' distorted perceptions."

Although only a handful of prospective longitudinal studies are available, their results support the conclusion of Brewin and colleagues (1993, Brewin et al., 1993) that retrospective findings are not simply artifacts induced by current mood or memory distortions. Lekowitz and Tesiny (1984) found that paternal rejection, assessed when girls were 8 years old, predicted the girls' scores on the Minnesota Multiphasic Personality Inventory Depression scale at age 19. Depression in the 19-year-old men, however, was unrelated to the parental variables. Gjerde et al. (1991) found that depression scores as measured by the Center for Epidemiological Studies Depression Scale in 18-year-old women were predicted by maternal "positive engagement" and "authoritarian control" measured in laboratory tasks when the participants were 5 years old. Again, men's depression was not predicted by the parental characteristics. Koestner et al. (1991) found that mothers' reports of parenting practices collected when the children were 5 years old was significantly related to the children's report of self-critical tendencies at age 12. Mothers who had been rated as rejecting and restrictive by observers when their children were age 5 were more likely to have children who were self-critical at age 12. In females, this self-criticism was still evident when these children were adults (31 years). Self-critical 12-year-old boys, however, tended not to be self-critical at 31 years, but at this age they reported greater experience of aggressive impulses, although not necessarily aggressive action. Koestner et al. (1991) found that both boys' and girls' self-criticism at age 12 was predicted by rejecting, restrictive parenting in earlier childhood, especially when received from the same-sex parent. These relations remained even when the child's temperament was controlled statistically. It is interesting that all three longitudinal studies just cited found a more substantial relationship between early parenting characteristics and adult depressive tendencies in females than males. Koestner et al. (1991), for example, found that self-critical tendencies were significantly more stable from age 12 to age 31 in females than in males. Also, some inconsistency was found with regard to the relative importance of mother and father. Two studies that assessed parenting in early childhood (age five) found that the same-sex parent was more influential on later depressive tendencies; the study that assessed parenting at age eight, however, found the opposite-sex parent to be more influential, as did Schwarz and Zuroff (1979). Thus, additional factors beyond the degree of parental warmth and control contribute to the impact of caring experiences on the development of a vulnerability to depression. Evidence (e.g., Gooden & Toye, 1984; Main et al., 1985; McCranie & Bass, 1984; G. Parker, 1979a 1979b, 1982, 1983; G. Parker & Hadzi-Pavlovic, 1984) suggests that parental behavior is a complex configural effect that involves the child's sex, the characteristics of each of the parents, the quality of the parental relationship, and the age of the child when distortions and disruptions of the caring relationship occur. R. Thompson and Zuroff (1998, 1999b) found in a series of experimental studies that high-dependent mothers reacted differently to their daughters' striving for independence and autonomy as a function of competence of their daughters. With "competent" daughters, high-dependent mothers tended to be critical and controlling of their daughters' autonomy, whereas they were supportive of the autonomy in "low-competent" daughters. Highly self-critical mothers reacted in a controlling, critical way independent of the level of competence of their daughters.

Matussek, Molitor, and Seibt (1985) suggested that the behavior of the same-sex parent may be a dominant factor in a patient's psychopathology (see also Frost, Lahart, & Rosenblate, 1991; Vieth & Trull, 1999). They studied patients with neurotic depression and found that female patients seemed more affected by rejection by their mothers, whereas male patients appeared more concerned about their distant relationships with their fathers. Also, female patients with the diagnosis of endogenous unipolar depression described their mothers as demanding that they understand the mothers' worries and needs, whereas male patients described their fathers as "entirely duty-oriented, [they] knew no pleasure" (Matussek et al., 1985, p. 17). These distinctions, which have been observed across many studies (e.g., Gjerde et al., 1991; Koestner et al., 1991; Main et al., 1985; Matussek et al., 1985; McCranie & Bass, 1984; G. Parker, 1981; Zemore & Rinholm, 1989), suggest that the same-sex parent is generally more significant in the development of depression. It is possible, however, that the influence of the opposite-sex parent increases in middle childhood and adolescence (Lekowitz & Tesiny, 1984; Schwarz & Zuroff, 1979).

Matussek et al. (1985), in differentiating various diagnostic groupings of depression, described two kinds of childhood experiences, which correspond to the anaclitic–introjective distinction and which they found to be important in depression in adults. Former female patients, who had been diagnosed as neurotically depressed, reported that as children they received little attention from their mothers and little appreciation from their fathers. They felt rejected by their mothers and, as Matussek et al. concluded,

> their complaints evidence the existence of an inner concept, the imagining of a good object and a yearning for it. . . . Autonomy (in these patients) . . . is not genuine independence but an expression of a desperate struggle against feelings of need and dependence. (p. 19)

Male patients who were formerly depressed, in contrast, reported feeling distant from their fathers. Both male and female former patients felt an "intrapsychic separation" from their mothers. They reported daydreaming and keeping secrets, which Mattusek and his colleagues interpreted as the first sign of an "overcompensated, defiant autonomy" (Matussek & Feil, 1983; Matussek et al., 1985, p. 19). Parents of patients with neurotic depression were described as often in conflict with each other, each appearing as separate individuals and thus facilitating their children's individuation (Mattusek et al., 1985). In contrast, Mattusek et al. found that patients with unipolar endogenous depression were strongly bonded to demanding mothers and saw their parents as coexisting in "absolute harmony." These patients had a marked "deficiency of autonomy," manifested in a lack of opinions or interests and in an overadaptiveness (Matussek et al., 1985, p. 19). Thus, patients with unipolar endogenous depression, like anaclitic depression, seem to be dealing with issues at a lower developmental level than are patients with neurotic depression, as the latter seems more similar to introjective depression because they are dealing with issues of separation–individuation that are at a somewhat higher developmental level.

Discussion

Three major research strategies have provided complementary data supporting the relevance of the early parent–child relationship to later depression: (a) the longitudinal study of normal children, (b) the study of children at risk, and (c) the study of retrospective recollections of adults. Data from these three different research methodologies have begun to articulate some essential aspects of the parent–child relationship and their impact on current modes of adaptation. Inherent limitations exist in each of these types of research design, but the convergence of findings from multiple perspectives—from different theoretical orientations and different types of research strategies—clarifies some of the complexities of parent–child interactions and their role in psychological development (Blatt & Homann, 1992).

Inconsistent care and tendencies toward intrusive or controlling overprotection by parents stand out repeatedly as central predispositional factors for the development of depression in adulthood. The relationship of these parental caring patterns to the development of dysphoric feelings focused on intense neediness and self-criticism allows for fuller consideration of the types of representations of self and others inherent in depression. These different concerns, which derive from disruptions of the parent–child relationship, are consistent with the formulations (Blatt, 1974, 1998; Blatt, D'Afflitti, et al., 1976; Blatt et al., 1982) of two types of depression: (a) one focused on deficiencies in caring relationships (i.e., dependency) and involving representations at a sensorimotor level that center on need gratification and (b) one focused on issues of self-worth and self-definition that evolves during the second year of life during the separation–individuation phase. Issues of self-worth that derive from this second critical phase lead to patients' berating, criticizing, and attacking themselves with intense feelings of guilt, shame, and worthlessness for failing to meet stern and harsh parental standards and expectations. The child's struggles toward separation, individuation, and self-definition are thwarted by the internalized judgments of one or both parents, who are experienced as intrusive, judgmental, and controlling. The child experiences parental love as conditional, as contingent on meeting very strict parental standards, and thus he or she becomes depressed in response to perceived failure or criticism. The child's constant self-scrutiny and self-censure is a repetition of the relationship he or she had with the parents. Amitay et al.'s (2002) findings demonstrate the linkages between parents' tendencies to be self-critical and the occurrence of these tendencies in their children. This identification with parents' criticism may have the additional function of maintaining contact with them (Blatt, 1974). Because these processes of internalization occur at a time of greater psychological maturity, it is more likely that the relationship with both parents could be of issue in this type of depression.

In anaclitic depression, fear of loss of caring and nurturance is of primary concern. The mothering figure is generally unavailable or uses her love and care as a way of controlling the child, either through the withdrawal of love, or perhaps through overindulgence. The dependency and insecurity engendered by the mother's unavailability (or excessive availability) make it difficult for the child to develop a stable representation of the mother as caring or of the self as able to cope without the mother's presence. Without a stable and consolidated mental model of a caring mother, the child is unable to tolerate separation because of a failure to maintain a sense of continuity with the mother in her absence and to believe and trust that experiences of being loved and cared for can continue beyond the immediate moment. The dependent individual needs constant reaffirmation about the availability and dependability of care, desperately seeks attention and nurturance, and becomes depressed in reaction to separation or perceived abandonment. The child feels helpless and insecure in relationships, and is overwhelmed by unfulfilled longings to be cared for, but has to deny any feelings of anger for fear of further alienating the mother.

Although the analysis of parental descriptions indicates that the quality of the representations of parents is related to depression, the results do not fully address the complex issue of etiology. It is difficult, for example, to know whether representations of the parents are impaired because of depression, or whether the impaired representations reflect a general predisposition that leaves the individual vulnerable to depression, or both. Clinical (e.g., Blatt, 1974) and empirical evidence, which I discuss in detail in chapter 8 (e.g., Blatt,

Stayner, Auerbach, & Behrends, 1996), indicates that the content and the conceptual level of parental representations are central dimensions in depression and that changes in representation are paralleled by broader clinical changes. The sequence of these changes in therapy, and their relations to change in cognitive organization more generally, needs to be investigated further. Subsequent research is also needed to specify more precisely the relationships of parenting factors to the depressive experiences of dependency and self-criticism and to identify when in development these various factors have their greatest effects on children and how the different degrees and types of negative parenting by either or both parents differentially affect male and female children at various ages.

Moreover, although psychoanalytic theory suggests that the concept of the object is impaired in depression, the nature of mental representations of significant others and the role of the family in depression need further elaboration, particularly in comparison to the extensive data available on patterns of communication in families with a schizophrenic child. The cognitive processes of parents of schizophrenic patients are described as amorphous or fragmented, and often schizophrenic patients have difficulty establishing differentiation from their parents (Blatt & Wild, 1976; Lidz, 1973; Singer & Wynne, 1965b). Research findings suggest, however, that in depression the issues are not the degree of differentiation from parents but that the parents are perceived and experienced as lacking in nurturance, affection, and acceptance. Parents tend to be represented as unavailable or as harsh, critical, and judgmental. It is unclear whether the parents of patients who are depressed have been cold, unresponsive, critical, and judgmental or whether depressed individuals have less capacity for tolerating deprivation and criticism. Although we need objective assessment of parental behavior and family interactions throughout development, we also need to assess systematically the phenomenological world of the individual—how individuals experienced and remember their parents. Thus, the apparent correlations of neglectful or overprotective and controlling parenting with disrupted object constancy or unstable self-regard need to be articulated further, defining causal links and identifying intervening vulnerabilities and resiliency factors.

Study of patterns of insecure attachment, especially in children of parents who are depressed, promises to be a fruitful avenue of research, because attachment behavior provides a window into the child's representation of the parent, and this representation of the parent is correlated with parental behavior, attitudes, and history of depression (Homann, 1997). As Zuroff and Fitzpatrick (1995) noted, parallels can be drawn between types of insecure attachment (insecure–ambivalent and insecure–avoidant) and particular types of parenting styles (enmeshed and dismissive; Main et al., 1985) as well as two types of depression (anaclitic/dependent and introjective/self-critical).

The connection of insecure attachment and depression needs to be better understood, with particular attention paid to the role that depression may play as an attachment behavior itself—as a corollary to the function of attachment behaviors to modulate attachment feelings and needs (Homann, 1997). When parent–child dyads are misattuned, negative in tone, or characterized by the infant's withdrawal from social interaction, the child is likely to become depressed, to be insecurely attached—perhaps to begin to define the relationship with the parent in terms of the child's sharing the parent's depression, maybe as an attempt to use these depressed feelings to represent closeness with the parent.

An important step in understanding childhood antecedents to depression is the identification of critical periods at which certain kinds of parenting styles may be most influential. Research and theory suggest two such critical periods. The first appears to occur during the first six months of life. Cross-sectional studies indicate a shift in infants of mothers who are chronically depressed and intrusive from high levels of protest at two months to high levels of disengagement at six months, which Cohn et al. (1990) interpreted as an indication of an "attenuated" interest or a disengagement from interpersonal interaction. By six months, infants of mothers with chronic depression seem to have formed an expectation of not receiving help from the mother to regulate affect. The infants have turned away from interactive involvement. The implications of such an early critical period are important, especially given Field et al.'s (1990) assertion that infants at age six months are no longer depressed if their mothers are also no longer depressed. Mother's level of dependency facilitates, while her level of self-criticism on the DEQ impedes, her positive vocal engagement with her infant.

Another critical period appears to occur in the second year of life, in terms of the development of a vulnerability to depression (Cicchetti & Aber, 1986). Issues of control and the security of attachment are heightened at this time for both mother and child, as the toddler gains mobility and seeks autonomy yet needs a safe place to which to return. Parents who are controlling or unresponsive at a time when the child is beginning to establish a sense of autonomy, self-worth, and independence could facilitate anger and resentment in interpersonal relationships and a depreciated sense of the self with feelings of guilt, shame, and inadequacy. Children raised by mothers who are depressed and unresponsive may have greater vulnerability in separation, because they have not developed a consolidated and essentially positive sense of the mother, or of the self in effective interaction with the mother. The caretaking patterns of a depressed mother also create experiences for the child of being helpless and lonely, rather than allowing the child to experience the joy of independence that comes with separation (Schaffer & Blatt, 1990). The depressed mother's difficulty with object constancy may interfere with her ability to allow her child to achieve a sense of separation.

Yet another issue in the development of a vulnerability to depression is the gender of the psychologically unavailable or affectionless controlling parent as well as the gender of the child. Although most studies report the mother as the more influential parent (Main et al., 1985; G. Parker, 1979a, 1982, 1983; G. Parker & Hadzi-Pavlovic, 1984), this pattern is not wholly consistent with some findings indicating that paternal caring (J. G. Parker & Lipscombe, 1980), by the same-sex parent (Matussek et al., 1985) or both parents (Johnson et al., 1982; McCranie & Bass, 1984), can be primary. Many studies of children of mothers who are depressed have not examined the role of the father at all. The model of psychological development that colleagues and I have proposed (e.g., Blatt, 1995b; Blatt & Blass, 1990, 1996; Blatt & Shichman, 1983) suggests that the developmental demand for a shift in the attachment of affection from mother to father in early childhood for girls, and the developmental demand for a shift in identification from mother to father in early childhood for boys, could account for the differential tendency for females to become more often depressed around interpersonal issues (i.e., dependency) and for males to become more often depressed around issues of self-definition (i.e., self-criticism). This model also stresses the importance of the attitudes and behaviors of the same-sex parent for depression and suggests that the nature and timing of the mother's and father's untoward behavior could contribute differentially to the development of the male and female child and determine the degree and nature of subsequent vulnerability to depression—whether it is primarily focused around issues of dependency, self-worth and self-criticism, or both.

It is important for subsequent research to find ways of systematically assessing a wide variety of early life experiences, including parental affectionless control and psychological unavailability. Research also needs to be directed toward establishing further the reliability and validity of retrospective reports, recognizing that these reports provide another important perspective on the parent–child interaction—that is, how the relationship was *experienced* by the child. Researchers need to identify other potential factors in depression, including familial predispositions and possible protective or moderator variables, such as a good relationship with the other parent or other relatives, as well as support systems that may be available outside the home. The role of parent–child interaction in the etiology of depression has demonstrated the vital importance of longitudinal research designs in the study of personality development and of psychopathology. Emerging research with causal modeling has also begun to establish the reciprocal influence of characteristics of both mother and child and the importance of including both maternal and child variables in studies of the etiology of depression (Hammen, Burge, & Stansbury, 1990).

Researchers need to study less severe forms of psychological disturbance and earlier phases of psychological disorders and to examine longitudinally nonclinical samples of children, from very early in life, to appreciate the multiplicity of forces (biological, psychological, and social) that impinge on the child in the complex series of interactions that lead to different modes of adaptation. Some of these modes of adaptation are constructive, and others are distorted; some even result in the formation of serious psychopathology. Specific developmental patterns and processes need to be identified at different phases of the life cycle so that their roles in the development of psychopathology can be examined. Prototypes and precursors of pathology related to parent–child interaction may be identified in early forms of maladaptive behavior patterns or impaired cognitive structures (Blatt, 1974, 1995b; Blatt & Blass, 1996; Blatt & Shichman, 1983; Bowlby, 1969; Cicchetti & Aber, 1986; Cicchetti & Schneider-Rosen, 1984b). In considering developmental deviations, however, it is important to avoid formulations that focus on limited and specific pathogenic events, such as a single traumatic experience. It is necessary to consider the interaction between particular individual characteristics and environmental responses at a given time and over various developmental periods (Sameroff & Chandler, 1975), as well as the balance between risk factors and compensatory buffers (Cicchetti & Aber, 1986). The occurrence of depression is a result of the impact of a multiplicity of interacting factors that create a particular reaction when potentiating factors overwhelm the individual's adaptive capacities (Cicchetti & Aber, 1986). The organization of behavior into particular patterns of insecure attachment, as identified by Ainsworth et al. (1978) and Main et al. (1985), could represent a vulnerability factor for depression, especially when these patterns of insecure attachment interact with untoward contemporary life events that are congruent with the basic issues underlying the insecure attachment (Blatt & Zuroff, 1992).

A comprehensive developmental model of the etiology of depression must consider the multifaceted ways in which constitutional, organismic (Werner, 1948), and environmental factors transact to affect development and create vulnerabilities to depression, such as impairments in cognitive structures based on disturbed interpersonal experiences. Vulnerability factors may include the relatively enduring characteristics of the infant (child), the parents as individuals, the family, and the social environment, as well as of stressful life events, such as the death of a parent during the individual's childhood. Goodman and Gotlib (1999, p. 458) reviewed "a large body of literature documenting the adverse effects of maternal depression on the functioning and development of their offspring" and proposed a developmental model articulating four possible mechanisms through which risk is transmitted from the mother to her child (heritability of depression, dysfunctional neuroregulatory mechanisms, exposure to negative maternal cognitions, and the stressful context of the child's life), as well as possible factors that could moderate this transmission (the role of the father, the nature of the mother's depression, and characteristics of the child). Beyond the traditional formulations of the diathesis–stress model one must consider the hierarchies of factors that operate to create depression in an individual. Certain temperamental or biological qualities may predispose a child to insecure attachment through the impact that these temperamental dimensions have on the parents and their capacity to care adequately for their child. It is important to stress that it is not these biological or temperamental qualities of the child or the parent per se that create the insecure attachment and the vulnerability to depression; rather, it is the lack of congruence between infant and parent around these biological capacities and tendencies that has the potential for disrupting and distorting the caring relationship that influences the child's capacity for attachment and his or her development of adequate levels of mental representations or working models of caring relationships. One important disruptive factor in development may be the relative inability of parent and child to find constructive ways of resolving major temperamental differences between them that disrupts the child's development of secure attachment. Despite the individual characteristics of parent and child, it is the quality of the emotional attachments and the consequent development of mental representations of caring relationships that appear to be central to subsequent emotional and cognitive development.

Again, these conclusions indicate that the study of the antecedents and precursors of depression will proceed more effectively if researchers view depression as more than a clinical disorder, but as an affective state that varies from normality to pathology—from mild, transient, appropriate dysphoric reactions to untoward life events to severe, disabling, persistent, and intense dysphoric reactions that have little justification in current life circumstances (Blatt, 1974). In addition to studying the precursors of clinical depression, researchers need to identify the specific cognitive, emotional, interpersonal, linguistic, physiological, and other developmental processes that lead to experiences of loneliness, sadness, and feelings of worthlessness and self-criticism in children and adolescents. They also need to identify the multiple ways in which feelings of depression are expressed in children, including dysphoric mood, suicidal thoughts, sleep disturbances, and anhedonia, as well as the multiple forms of defense that children, especially adolescents, often use against experiencing depression, such as denial, mania, and displacement in various types of enactments (Blatt, 1990a). The problems are intriguing and important, with possible implications for both treatment and prevention. Continued longitudinal study of parent–child interactions and understanding of perceptions of their current as well as their past life experiences will provide further insight into some of the factors that contribute to the development of depression in childhood, adolescence, and adulthood.

Although dependent and self-critical depression both appear to involve disturbances in mental representation, it is unclear when disturbances in mental representations specifically lead to depression, or to other disorders as well (Blatt, 1995b). Thus, further research is needed to specify more precisely the relationships of these factors to anaclitic and introjective depression and to identify how and when in development different types of negative parenting, by either or both parents, differentially affect boys and girls. Research is also needed to assess the complex interaction of numerous environmental, biological, interpersonal, and intrapsychic factors and to evaluate how individuals who are exposed to difficult early and later life circumstances develop a dependent or a self-critical depression, develop other disorders, or remain relatively invulnerable to psychological disturbance.

7

Precipitating Events
(Proximal Antecedents)

A wide range of contextual experiences have been investigated as proximal causes of depression, including stressful life events, quality of social support, and the nature of interpersonal relations. Research on the proximal causes of depression was initially based on stress–diathesis models. These approaches have recently been supplemented by action-oriented models, and studies derived from this new research paradigm have greatly enhanced our understanding of the proximal causes of depressive experiences and raised a number of important theoretical issues.

Stress–Diathesis Models: Vulnerability to Depression

Many formulations of the etiology of depression (and psychopathology more generally) assume a stress–diathesis model in which individual predispositions (e.g., personality variables and cognitive schemas) interact with stressful life experiences to lead to the onset of depression (e.g., A. T. Beck, Rush, Shaw, & Emery, 1979). The study of children of mothers with depression, discussed in chapter 6, is an extension of the study of stressful life events as possible antecedents to psychopathology, especially depression. Studies of the stressful life events, particularly childhood events, of depressed adults as compared with control participants, however, are inconclusive (Cadoret, Winkur, Dorzab, & Baker, 1972; Forrest, Fraser, & Priest, 1965; Hudgeons, Morrison, & Barchha, 1967; Lloyd, 1980; Perris et al., 1986) about whether certain life events themselves cause depression or whether they cause depression because they interact with a pre-existing vulnerability (G. W. Brown & Harris, 1978; Richman & Flaherty, 1987). Hirsch, Moos, and Reischl (1985), for example, found that an interaction between having a parent who is depressed and experiencing stressful life events contributed to the occurrence of depression in adolescents. Thus, although there may be a similar incidence of stressful life events in groups

This chapter incorporates material from the following sources: (a) "Interpersonal Relatedness and Self-Definition: Two Prototypes for Depression," by S. J. Blatt and D. C. Zuroff, 1992, *Clinical Psychology Review, 12,* pp. 527–562. Copyright 1992 by Elsevier. Adapted with permission. (b) The Dialogic Self: Adaptive and Maladaptive Dimensions," by S. J. Blatt and G. Shahar, presented at "Psychoanalysis as an Empirical, Interdisciplinary Science," Austrian Academy of Science, Vienna, December 9, 2001. Copyright 2003 by the Austrian Academy of Science. Adapted with permission.

with depression and control groups, the reduced coping skills and the lack of available support networks of children of parents who are depressed may increase the likelihood of a depressive response to traumatic or stressful incidents (Cicchetti & Aber, 1986; Faravelli et al., 1986). Areas of vulnerability appear to derive from previous life events, such as insecure attachment, the death of a parent in one's childhood, or the experience of having been raised by a depressed parent. Environmental factors, however, can also facilitate the development of resilience or a resistance to depression. Resilient adolescent children of parents with depression, for example, appear to have established support systems outside their family (Beardslee & Podorefsky, 1988). Through self-awareness and understanding, these resilient adolescents are able to separate themselves from the difficulties of the parent with depression, and many of them often assume a caretaking role for their parents.

The relationship of stressful life events to dysphoric mood and depression is well documented (e.g., A. C. Billings, Cronkite, & Moos, 1983; G. W. Brown & Harris, 1978; Lloyd, 1980; Mazure & Maciejewski, 2003; Paykel, 1974) but generally accounts for only a relatively small proportion of the variance of various assessments of depression. Stress–diathesis research has attempted to address this relatively limited explanatory power of stressful life events in precipitating depression by suggesting that stress has a particularly depressogenic effect among psychologically vulnerable individuals. This elaboration of the stress–diathesis model led to the *congruency hypothesis* (see review in C. J. Robins, 1995), which posits that depression is precipitated by interactions between specific stressful life events that are congruent with the vulnerabilities of the individual—that is, particular individuals might be vulnerable to a specific set of life events. The congruency hypothesis, a logical derivative of the stress–diathesis models, stipulates that psychopathology results from a co-occurrence of a particular genetic or psychological vulnerability (i.e., diathesis) with congruent stressful life events. The ability of a particular event to trigger a depressive episode may depend on the event's resonance with the individual's particular sensitivity to issues such as self-worth, dependability of caregivers, and separation or loss (Goodyer & Altham, 1991). As Faravelli et al. (1986) noted, it may be not the event itself, but rather the meaning of the particular life event for the individual, that determines the long-term effect on depression. This more precise specification of the stress–diathesis model stipulates that not all contextual conditions activate the vulnerability of all individuals; rather, vulnerability is activated when the contextual risk factors, such as stressful life events, have specific meaning and relevance that exert a threat to individuals because of their particular personality characteristics. For example, Hammen, Marks, Mayol, and de Mayo (1985) suggested that dependent or sociotropic individuals, who are preoccupied with obtaining and maintaining close, nurturing, and protective interpersonal relations, should experience depressive symptoms especially when confronted by interpersonal stress such as rejection, discord, or separation from significant others. Self-critical or autonomous individuals, who are preoccupied with establishing and maintaining a positive sense of self, should experience depressive symptoms when faced with failure and thus be most likely to become depressed in response to experiences of failure, such as losing a job, failing an examination, or getting a poor grade.

A number of researchers, using different methods of assessing dependent and self-critical personality styles, have examined the specificity of the vulnerability of dependent and self-critical individuals to depression initiated by stressful interpersonal and achievement experiences. Hammen, Marks, Mayol, & de Mayo (1985) classified students as dependent or self-critical using a self-schema task and found that measures of depression in dependent participants were more highly correlated with negative events concerning interpersonal issues rather than with negative events concerning achievement issues. For self-critical participants, correlations were generally higher for achievement events than for interpersonal events, but few of these comparisons (i.e., between depression provoked by achievement events and that provoked by interpersonal events) were significantly different. These findings are consistent with those of Zuroff and Mongrain (1987b) that indicated a greater specificity in the vulnerability of dependent than self-critical individuals. Zuroff and Mongrain (1987b) presented audiotaped descriptions of interpersonal rejection and experiences of failure to high dependent, high self-critical, and control female college students and found that rejection and failure stimuli resulted in higher scores on the Depression scale of the Multiple Affect Adjective Check List (Zuckerman & Lubin, 1965) for both the dependent and self-critical groups as compared with control participants. Participants who scored high on the dependency factor of the DEQ (Blatt, D'Afflitti, & Quinlan, 1979) had significant increases in depression primarily in response to themes of rejection, whereas participants high on DEQ Self-Criticism reported significant increases of depression in response to both types of stimuli.

In another study, Mongrain and Zuroff (1989) asked participants to appraise the degree of stress inherent in 10 life events assumed to be relevant to interpersonal relationships and in 10 life events supposedly relevant to achievement and evaluation. The degree of stress assigned to interpersonal events was strongly related to individuals' scores on DEQ Dependency, but the degree of stress assigned to achievement events only tended to relate to scores on DEQ Self-Criticism. Mongrain and Zuroff (1989) also evaluated whether participants' descriptions of the "worst period" of depression they had "ever experienced" in their life were predominantly concerned with interpersonal, achievement, or other issues. They found that 80% of the situations described by dependent participants, and 79% of the situations described by control participants, involved interpersonal events, but less than 5% of these participants' worst periods involved achievement events. Self-critical participants, in contrast, described situations that were less concentrated in one category, with 58% reporting interpersonal situations and 37% reporting achievement-related situations. Zuroff, Igreja, and Mongrain (1990) used a longitudinal design to study female college students' retrospective reports of their worst experience of depression in the period between an initial testing with the DEQ and a follow-up testing session approximately 12 months later. Controlling for initial level of depression, Zuroff et al. (1990) found that DEQ Dependency and Self-Criticism scores at Time 1 significantly predicted, respectively, the extent of interpersonal and achievement/evaluation themes in the students' retrospective reports of the worst experience of depression in the year after the initial testing. They found, however, that over 80% of both dependent and self-critical participants reported stressful interpersonal events. The authors speculated that perhaps too few serious achievement events may have occurred for these participants over the prior 12 months to detect the self-critical individuals' vulnerability to achievement events.

Z. V. Segal, Shaw, and Vella (1989) used the two factors of the Dysfunctional Attitude Scale (A. N. Weissman & Beck, 1978) to identify "need for approval" (dependent)- and "performance evaluation" (self-critical or perfectionist)-oriented subgroups of patients with remitted depression and found that the number of negative interpersonal events during a six-month follow-up period predicted scores on the Beck Depression Inventory (BDI; A. T. Beck, Ward, Mendelson, Mock, & Erbaugh, 1961) for the need-for-approval group but that neither interpersonal nor achievement events predicted depression in the performance evaluation group. C. J. Robins and Block (1988) used the Sociotropy–Autonomy Scale (SAS; A. T. Beck, Epstein, Harrison, & Emery, 1983) to investigate the differential sensitivity of individuals primarily invested in interpersonal relatedness (sociotropy) or self-definition (e.g., autonomy) to particular types of life events. They presented nondepressed college students (BDI score < 10) with audiotaped situations of either social rejection or achievement failure. Both experimental conditions resulted in increased depressive affect in participants who were particularly concerned about separation and loss (as measured by the SAS Sociotropy scale). Participants high on the SAS Autonomy scale, however, were not significantly responsive to either the social rejection or the achievement failure tapes. They also found that concern about interpersonal relatedness (high sociotropy) was significantly associated with depression (as measured by the BDI) as a function of the negative (or positive) social life events reported during the prior three months (see also C. J. Robins & Jacobson, 1987). The relationship between the SAS Sociotropy factor and the BDI was also a function of reported negative (or positive) events that were related to issues of autonomy. SAS Autonomy, however, was not correlated with depression, or to the report of any type of negative life events in the prior three months. Thus, research by C. J. Robins and colleagues, like the other studies, has found differential sensitivity to different kinds of life events in sociotropic (dependent) but not in autonomous (self-critical) individuals.

C. J. Robins (1990) also examined these relationships in samples of depressed patients and college students who were mildly depressed. In the clinical sample, patients high on the sociotropic scale reported high levels of disruptive interpersonal life events, but not autonomy events. No evidence of congruence, however, was found for patients high on the SAS Autonomy scale. In the student sample, both the sociotropic and the autonomous groups tended to report higher levels of congruent events (interpersonal events or achievement events, respectively). Allen, Horne, and Trinder (1996), using the SAS, found that individuals high on sociotropy were vulnerable to social rejection and, to a lesser extent, to achievement failure, but they found no significant effects with SAS Autonomy. Hammen, Ellicott, Gitlin, and Jamison (1989) used the SAS to classify unipolar and bipolar patients into dependent or autonomous groups and found that symptom severity in unipolar patients over the subsequent six months was related to the experience of congruent life events, but this was not true of the bipolar group.

Although the lack of findings with the SAS Autonomy scale in these various investigations may be the consequence of limitations of that scale (see, e.g., Bartelstone & Trull, 1995; Blaney & Kutcher, 1991), this lack is consistent with reports of other investigators who used other scales to measure the vulnerability dimensions of dependency and self-criticism (e.g., Lakey & Ross, 1994). It is important to note, however, that, as discussed in chapter 2, Gruen, Silva, Ehrlich, Schweitzer, and Friedhoff (1997) used the DEQ to measure self-criticism and found a significant positive relationship in females between DEQ Self-Criticism and reactions to an induced-failure task, as measured by a biochemical measure of stress (level of plasma homovanillic acid, a metabolite of dopamine). This is consistent with reports by G. P. Brown, Hammen, Craske, and Wickens (1995) and by Blaney (2000), who have found congruency effects for both dependency and self-criticism.

Many of these studies are summarized in several reviews of research deriving from the congruency hypothesis (Blatt & Zuroff, 1992; Coyne & Whiffen, 1995; Flett, Hewitt, Endler, & Bagby, 1995; Nietzel & Harris, 1990; C. J. Robins, 1995). A general pattern emerging from these reviews is that the congruency hypothesis is more applicable to dependency than to self-criticism. Although some of the reasons for the lack of evidence supporting the congruency hypothesis in self-critical/autonomous individuals seems to be a function of difficulties with the Autonomy scale of the SAS (see, e.g., Bartelstone & Trull, 1995), in general the results indicate only partial support for the congruency hypothesis. Specifically, dependent individuals are especially vulnerable to negative interpersonal events (e.g., Bartelstone & Trull, 1995; Fichman, Koestner, & Zuroff, 1997; Hammen et al., 1989; Hammen, Marks, deMayo, & Mayol, 1985; Hammen, Marks, Mayol, & deMayo, 1985; Mongrain & Zuroff, 1994; C. J. Robins, 1990; Z. V. Segal et al., 1989; Zuroff & Mongrain, 1987a, 1987b), but the results for self-critical individuals are more equivocal in that these individuals are vulnerable to a wider range of events. Most studies have found support for an interaction between dependency/sociotropy and interpersonal stress, but not between self-criticism/autonomy and failure experiences. Self-criticism was found to interact with both interpersonal and failure-related stressful events in predicting depression (Zuroff & Mongrain, 1987b). In other studies, self-criticism interacted with neither type of stressful event, but in longitudinal studies it had a main effect on depressive symptoms (Priel & Besser, 1999, 2000; Priel & Shahar, 2000; Shahar, Blatt, Zuroff, Kuperminc, & Leadbeater, in press). These findings suggest that dependent and self-critical individuals may have differential sensitivity to environmental influence. Dependent (anaclitic) individuals appear to be responsive to a particular environmental influence, in contrast to self-critical individuals, who seem to assimilate a wide range of experiences into a well-established self-critical schema. Thus, the demonstration of the congruence hypothesis with dependent but not with self-critical individuals may indicate important differences between these individuals in the ways they are affected by, or how they engage, their environment.

Zuroff, Igreja, and Mongrain (1990) assessed DEQ Dependency and Self-Criticism and depressive symptoms in undergraduate women over a 12-month period and found that Dependency and Self-Criticism did not predict subsequent depressive symptoms as measured by the BDI. They did, however, predict congruent depressed mood; specifically, Dependency predicted anaclitic depressed mood (i.e., mood centered on loneliness and rejection), whereas Self-Criticism predicted introjective depressed mood (i.e., mood centered on guilt and self-criticism). Moreover, BDI depressive symptoms at Time 1 tended to predict self-criticism at Time 2, $F(1, 42) = 3.8$, $p < .06$. Although Zuroff, Igreja, and Mongrain interpreted these findings cautiously, they concluded that "This result hints at the existence of a reciprocal relation between depressed affect and self-criticism. Further research into more complex causal models of vulnerability may be warranted" (p. 323).

The congruency hypothesis was also evaluated in studies of the quality of interpersonal relationships of dependent and self-critical individuals. Dependency is associated with an anxious attachment style that is oriented toward a desire for close relationships and social interactions as well as a fear of loss of love (Morrison, Urquiza, & Goodlin-Jones, 1998; Zuroff & Fitzpatrick, 1995). Dependent individuals are receptive to others; report few interpersonal problems; seek help from others, including medical professionals; and try to maintain interpersonal contact by relinquishing control and minimizing disagreements. Thus, they inhibit anger and are unassertive in their relationships (Alden & Bieling, 1996; Mongrain & Zuroff, 1994; Morrison et al., 1998; Zuroff & Fitzpatrick, 1995; Zuroff, Moskowitz, Wielgus, Powers, & Franko, 1983). Dependent individuals perceive relationships as positive, loving, and supportive, but their partners have a less positive view of these relationships (Bieling & Alden, 1998; Mongrain, 1998; Mongrain, Vettese, Shuster, & Kendal, 1998). Although dependency is related to more frequent and intimate relationships, Zuroff, Stotland, Sweetman, Craig, and Koestner (1995) found that these relationships are superficial and associated with feelings of dissatisfaction and dysphoria because of the dependent individual's fear of rejection. Through their neediness, dependent individuals risk alienating others, thereby increasing their vulnerability to depression (e.g., Little & Garber, 2000). Thus, Bornstein (1992) noted that dependency has adaptive (e.g., interpersonal sensitivity and seeking of contact and assistance) as well as maladaptive features (e.g., passivity in relationships) that can leave dependent individuals at risk for distress and psychological difficulties (see also Pincus & Gurtman, 1995). These features of dependency are consistent with recent findings, discussed in chapter 3, of two levels of interpersonal relatedness (neediness and mature relatedness) within the DEQ Interpersonal factor (Blatt & Zohar, 1990; Blatt, Zohar, et al., 1995; Blatt, Zohar, et al., 1996; Rude & Burnham, 1995). Thus, dependency has elements of risk and resiliency, because it can be associated with positive experiences and social support that buffer stress and depression (S. Cohen & Wills, 1985) as well as with negative experiences that increase the individual's vulnerability to depression (Shahar & Priel, 2002).

Self-criticism is associated with an avoidant attachment style that creates cold, distant relationships characterized by hostility (Mongrain, 1998; Zuroff & Duncan, 1999), distrust, dissatisfaction with partners and children (Alden

& Bieling, 1996; Morrison et al., 1998; Zuroff, Koestner, & Powers, 1994), and feelings of isolation and loneliness (Wiseman, 1997). Wiseman (1997) found not only that loneliness among first-year college students was significantly related to higher levels of DEQ Self-Criticism and lower levels of DEQ Efficacy (see also Schacter & Zlotogorski, 1995). Wiseman also found that Self-Criticism was negatively related to frankness, sensitivity, and trust in a relationship with an intimate partner, whereas the DEQ Interpersonal factor was positively related to the quality of the attachment and the capacity for giving and trust in the relationship. Self-critical individuals remain aloof and autonomous and tend not to ask for help (Fichman, Koestner, & Zuroff, 1994; Mongrain, 1998; Morrison et al., 1998). Self-critical women, for example, try to control interpersonal situations even at the expense of disrupting a relationship with a close friend (Santor & Zuroff, 1997, 1998). They value the power and prestige of their partner rather than the partner's capacity for intimacy (Bieling & Alden, 1998; Mongrain & Zuroff, 1995; Zuroff & de Lorimier, 1989). Whiffen and Aubé (1999) found in a study of couples that self-criticism in both men and women was associated with marital complaints by the spouse, especially about their partners (Dimitrovsky, Levy-Shiff, & Schattner-Zanany, 2002; Lynch, Robins, & Morse, 2001), whereas Neediness (a subscale of the DEQ Dependency factor) was associated in women with having a spouse who was low in intimacy (Whiffen & Aubé, 1999). Self-critical individuals experience relationships as critical, hostile, and ambivalent, and their partners, in turn, perceive them as critical and less loving (Bieling & Alden, 1998; Mongrain et al., 1998; Zuroff & Duncan, 1999). Self-critical individuals also assume that their partners perceive them negatively (Fichman, Koestner, & Zuroff, 1996, 1997). They have less effective social networks because of their cold, ambivalent, disengaged interpersonal style. This lack of an effective social network as well as the fact that self-criticism is primarily associated with only negative events (Shahar & Priel, 2003) creates a vulnerability to depression. Self-criticism is a primary risk factor for depression partly because it is associated with low levels of social support (Priel & Shahar, 2000).

Thus, both dependency and self-criticism are associated with a dysfunctional interpersonal transactional cycle (Andrews, 1989; Baldwin, 1992; Safran, 1990; Wachtel, 1977) in which these interpersonal styles contribute to the very types of social context that these individuals fear and attempt to avoid (Lynch et al., 2001). The clinging interpersonal style of dependent individuals provokes the rejection and abandonment they fear, whereas the ambivalent, distrustful, disengaged interpersonal style of self-critical individuals provokes criticism and disapproval from others.[1]

---

[1]Findings by T. W. Smith, O'Keeffe, and Jenkins (1988) suggest that gender may complicate the relationships between the predisposing personality styles of dependency and self-criticism and specific types of events. Using the DEQ, Smith et al. found that men with elevated DEQ Dependency scores were particularly responsive to experiences of interpersonal loss. Women with elevated DEQ Self-Criticism scores tended to be responsive to failure experiences. These findings suggest that individuals with gender-incongruent personality styles (e.g., men high on Dependency, and women high on Self-Criticism) may have heightened vulnerability to depression initiated by dependent and self-critical issues, respectively. These findings indicate that one must consider the interaction of gender or sex role (e.g., Chevron, Quinlan, & Blatt, 1978) when studying the

Most studies of life events and depression have viewed life events as moderators in their interaction with dependency and self-criticism. These analyses have assumed that individuals are the passive recipients of their environment, but recent theory and research, as reviewed above, suggest that individuals actively influence and shape their environments, thereby contributing to their own stress, including negative life events (e.g., Hammen, 1991). Thus, dependency and self-criticism can also function as mediators (R. M. Baron & Kenny, 1986) of depression. Priel and Shahar (2000), for example, found that a mediating model best described the relationship among self-criticism, congruent negative life events, and dysphoria in students. In addition, although dependency and self-criticism both seem to generate negative life events, dependency also generates positive events that suppress the effects of dependency on dysphoria, thereby reducing the risk for depression. Thus, the identification of anaclitic and introjective groups of depression, based on the nature of their depressive experiences, has facilitated the identification of certain repetitive interactions of the person and the environment that has enabled us to understand more fully, for example, why not all depressed individuals actively seek to extract from others the message that they are truly loved (Coyne, 1976a, 1976b).

Anaclitic (dependent) and introjective (self-critical) individuals appear to be sensitive to a different range of life experiences, to have different appraisal patterns with a differential sensitivity to various conflicts and difficulties, and to use different coping mechanisms in response to different types of stressors. Individuals high on dependency are particularly responsive to disruptions of interpersonal relations and respond to these disruptions by seeking to maintain interpersonal ties by avoiding direct conflict and confrontation. Self-critical individuals, concerned about issues of self-definition, power, control, autonomy, and mastery, appear to apply their self-critical schema to a wide range of events to which they react with counteractive mechanisms. The relative lack of differentiation in self-critical individuals' responses to stimuli of loss and of failure suggests that these individuals may interpret a wide range of stressful life events as experiences of failure. These findings suggest in the future, researchers should explore how different types of individuals can experience the same event in different ways and have different modes of responding to these stressful events. Thus, future researchers will need to assess the meanings that individuals attribute to particular types of stressful life events and to evaluate their differential coping styles.

The congruency hypothesis has had a number of unique advantages, and research deriving from this hypothesis has contributed significantly to the understanding of the etiology of depression. It has allowed for the integration of a wide range of theories of depression (e.g., behavioral, cognitive, dynamic, interpersonal) and has facilitated several different approaches to focusing on the interaction between internal and external processes in the etiology of depression. The congruency hypothesis also has facilitated an important integra-

---

differential sensitivity (or vulnerability) of dependent and self-critical individuals to particular types of stressful life events. Further research should be directed toward examining the effects of gender on the congruency hypothesis.

tion of clinical theory and empirical research that led to the articulation of empirically testable hypotheses about the nature and etiology of depression. Thus, the congruency hypothesis has contributed to the development of clinical psychology as a scientific discipline (Blatt & Shahar, 2003; Shahar, 1999).

The view that psychopathology results from an activation of internal factors by congruent external events has a certain commonsense appeal and is consistent with earlier formulations of psychopathology, such as S. Freud's (1916/1957f, 1926/1959) proposal that clinical symptoms and psychological distress are the product of a "complemental series" of external trauma impinging on a relatively vulnerable ego. Despite these advantages, the congruency hypothesis rests on the premise that individuals are primarily reactive to their social context—that dependent and self-critical individuals react to life events that are particularly relevant to them. Recent research findings, however, indicate that individuals also actively contribute to the *construction* of their life events. Thus, a recent extension of the stress–diathesis model to an action theory (AT) model proposes that individuals play an active role in the construction of their environments. This more extensive theoretical model has led to a series of important studies that address the etiology of depression in more precise and complex ways. Both theory (e.g., Blatt & Zuroff, 1992; Buss, 1987; Compas, 1987; Shahar, 2001; Zuroff, 1992) and research (Mongrain & Zuroff, 1994; Priel & Shahar, 2000; Shahar & Priel, 2002) stress that the nature of personality factors, such as dependent and self-critical qualities, influence the social context (e.g., social support [Mongrain, 1998] and the quality of interpersonal relationships [Mongrain et al., 1998; Vettese & Mongrain, 2000; Zuroff & Duncan, 1999]) and how these contextual factors, in turn, influence depressive symptoms of dependent and self-critical individuals.

Action Models: How Individuals Shape Their Experiences

The distinction between an emphasis on interpersonal relatedness (e.g., dependency) and self-definition (e.g., self-criticism) and the failure to confirm consistently the congruence hypothesis, especially with self-critical or introjective individuals, has led to a wide range of investigations that have examined how environmental events and personality (or cognitive styles) reciprocally influence one another. This transactive or AT perspective has the potential for establishing a fuller integration of cognitive and interpersonal approaches in the study of depression. In reviewing the literature on stress in adolescents, Compas (1987), for example, pointed to the need to investigate the pathways from individual vulnerabilities to stressful life events by delineating the factors that make some individuals more vulnerable than others to particular stressors. Although Compas seemed to support the congruency hypothesis in his statement that "individuals with a self-critical schema may be vulnerable to negative achievement events, while others with a dependent (or interpersonal) self-schema may be vulnerable to interpersonal loss events" (p. 298), he also made the important suggestion that different depressive vulnerabilities may influence the appraisal of the significance of negative life events and result in different coping responses. He noted, for example, that disruptions in a romantic relationship can be perceived as threats to being loved and taken care of, or as a threat to a sense of personal competence in romantic relationships, or as a concern about losing the approval of peers. Similarly, failing a test may be interpreted as a threat to one's ability to please a teacher, or as losing the love and approval of one's parents, or as a failure that threatens one's ability to meet one's own expectations for success.

Thus, Compas (1987) implicitly raised an important issue about congruency research and the entire stress–diathesis model, an issue consistent with a concern expressed many years earlier by Heinrich Kluver (1961) in his experimental studies with nonhuman primates—the incorrect assumption of the "equivalence of stimuli"—that one cannot assume that a particular stimulus is equivalent across species. Compas essentially raised this same issue in noting that one cannot assume that a particular event is experienced the same way and has the same meaning for all individuals. As he noted, a disruption in a romantic relationship can be perceived and experienced as an interpersonal stress or as a threat to self-esteem. Thus, it is essential in research on stressful life events to assess the meanings that individuals construct about particular events. Even further, this view essentially questions the implicit assumption in much of the research derived from the congruency hypothesis: that individuals are passive recipients of stressful life events and that they become active only after the event has occurred. As B. E. Compas suggested, individuals have to be viewed as active agents who *construct* meaning for the events they experience (see also Blatt & Zuroff, 1992; Zuroff, 1992).

Other investigators of depression have also articulated a more transactive perspective or, a "dynamic interactionism" (Magnusson & Endler, 1977). Andrews (1989), for example, proposed a self-confirmation model of depression that described how the self-concepts of people with depression can influence their interpersonal styles, which in turn elicit feedback that confirms their negative self-concepts. Andrews discussed how individuals unconsciously engage in "self-fulfilling prophecies that support the person's initial expectations about self and experiences. . . . selectively interacting with the environment and selectively assimilating feedback from it . . . [and channeling] action and experiences in ways that are congruent with and confirmatory of their self concept" (p. 577). Andrews conceptualized interpersonal styles in terms of a circumplex model and speculated that dependency and self-criticism corresponded respectively to the warm and cold variants of a submissive style. Alden and Bieling (1996), using both the DEQ and the SAS, found that dependency is related to warmth and submissiveness, whereas self-criticism is linked to interpersonal coldness but not to submissiveness. Whisman and Friedman (1998) reported similar findings. Andrews's position is consistent with the view that dependent and self-critical individuals have different interpersonal styles that can have a differential impact on their environments. Safran's (1990) conception of cognitive–interpersonal cycles is similar to both Andrews's self-confirmation processes and to Wachtel's (1977) earlier concept of an interactional cycle.

Buss (1987) contributed further to this emerging interactive perspective by differentiating three categories or processes involved in individuals' interaction with their environment: (a) selection, (b) evocation, and (c) manipulation. *Selec-*

tion refers to the ways in which different individuals choose to participate in different environments; *evocation* refers to the tendencies of different individuals to elicit different responses from the same environment; and *manipulation* refers to the ways in which different individuals transform environments in various ways. Thus, Buss suggested that different individuals may seek different types of experiences, or provoke different types of reactions or experiences in a particular environment, or transform environments to meet their particular needs. Also, as Compas (1987) suggested, individuals can experience the same environment in different ways because of their tendency to construct different types of meaning. Thus, in contrast to the various attempts to study the congruency hypothesis that assumes that individuals' reactions are shaped by current life events (e.g., A. T. Beck, 1976, 1983) or that individuals are particularly reactive to certain contextual factors that seem to precipitate their distress, more recent formulations and findings have noted that individuals also actively contribute to generate the contextual conditions implicated in their distress (Blatt & Zuroff, 1992; Buss, 1987; B. E. Compas, 1987; Coyne, 1976b, 1998; Flett, Hewitt, Garshowitz, & Martin, 1997; Hammen, 1991, 1996; Joiner, 1994; Nelson, Hammen, Daley, Burge, & Devila, 2001; Priel & Shahar, 2000; Shahar & Priel, 2002). As Plomin and Caspi (1999) concluded, on the basis of a literature review on the role of genetic influences in a range of contextual variables,

> findings support a current shift from thinking about passive models of how environment affects individuals toward models that recognize the active role we play in selecting, modifying, and creating our own environments (Plomin, 1994). It seems likely that personality contributes importantly in this construction of experience. (p. 261)

As a consequence, investigators (e.g., Priel & Shahar, 2000) have begun to focus on the transactions of the DEQ variables of dependency and self-criticism with contextual variables such as stressful events, social support, and the quality of close relationships. For example, Shahar, Blatt, Zuroff, Kuperminc, and Leadbeater (in press) recently demonstrated in a one-year longitudinal design the reciprocal relationship between DEQ Self-Criticism and depression in young adolescent girls. Over the one-year period, self-criticism and depression reciprocally exacerbated each other.

The assumption of a dynamic interactionism is consistent not only with theoretical and empirical descriptions of individuals as "producers of their own development" (Lerner, 1982) but also with clinical research demonstrating that individuals can generate the contextual factors that contribute to their depression (Coyne, 1976a, 1976b, 1998; Depue & Monroe, 1986; Hammen, 1991, 1998; Joiner, 1994; Monroe & Simons, 1991; Monroe & Steiner, 1986; Zuroff, 1992). Action theory (AT), an emerging theoretical and empirical paradigm in social science, explores the intentional, goal-oriented, transactional nature of human behavior. As an empirical paradigm, AT-informed research examines the ways in which individuals, defined by their personality or genetic makeup, actively shape their environments and psychological development (Brandtstaedter, 1998, Lerner, 1982; Priel & Shahar, 2000; Shahar, 2001,

2002). Action theory-informed research in developmental psychology has centered on how individuals actively navigate their developmental trajectories (Lerner, 1982); in personality psychology it has focused on the impact of differences in individuals' goals (Brunstein, 1993), life tasks (Cantor, 1990), and personal strivings (Emmons, 2000).

Action theory research in clinical psychology has led to investigations of the ways individuals actively contribute to contextual factors that render them vulnerable to a host of psychopathological conditions. Investigators have examined the hypothesis that dependent and self-critical individuals actively *generate* the congruent events to which they are vulnerable. Monroe and colleagues (Depue & Monroe, 1986; Monroe & Simons, 1991; Monroe & Steiner, 1986), for example, have suggested that individuals actively contribute to the level of stressful life events and social support they experience, which in turn influences the prevalence and chronicity of their distress. Recent investigations by Hammen (1991, 1998) provide empirical support for this stress-generation model. Similarly, Coyne (1976a, 1976b, 1998) has theorized that clinical depression is formed and maintained in the context of close relations whereby patients, attempting to alleviate their distress, engage in excessive reassurance seeking that unwittingly alienates significant others, precipitating rejection and begetting more depression. Further studies conducted by Joiner and his colleagues have extended and validated the vulnerability implicated in reassurance-seeking behavior (Joiner, 1994; Joiner, Metalsky, Katz, & Beach, 1999). Recent findings (Shahar, Joiner, Zuroff, & Blatt, in press) indicate, however, that reassurance seeking does not mediate the effects of dependence and self-criticism on depression in college students.

These investigations were influenced by the implications of action or transactional models (Brandtstaedter, 1998; Buss, 1987; Lerner, 1982; Shahar, 2001; Zuroff, 1992) according to which individuals are active agents who *shape and mold* their own development and their environments. Zuroff (1992) called for the investigation of the active vulnerability of dependent and self-critical individuals. Drawing from Coyne's (1976a) interpersonal theory of depression, as well as from dynamic interactionism (Magnusson & Endler, 1977) and transactional models (Bandura, 1986) that eschew sharp distinctions in the reciprocal relations between person and situations, Zuroff (1992) proposed that dependent and self-critical individuals are frequently depressed because their personality styles contribute to the creation of disturbed relations. Subsequent research conducted by Zuroff and Mongrain and their colleagues confirmed this hypothesis. Mongrain and Zuroff (1994), using path analysis with cross-sectional data, demonstrated that stressful events partly mediate the relations between dependency and self-criticism and depressive symptoms. In another cross-sectional study, Fichman et al. (1994) found that adolescent dependency and self-criticism predicted a host of interpersonal problems that contribute to depression, although adolescent dependency also predicted a capacity for intimacy. In yet another cross-sectional study, Mongrain (1998) found that both dependency and self-criticism in young adults predicted level of social support, but in opposite directions: Self-criticism predicted reduced levels of support, whereas dependency predicted elevated levels of support. Finally, Priel and Shahar (2000) demonstrated in a longitudinal study that dependent and self-critical young adults influence their environment in different ways. They followed a large sample of Israeli young adults for nine months and found that participants' initial level of self-criticism predicted an increase of stressful events and a decrease of perceived social support over time, which in turn predicted an increase in depressive symptoms. Participants' dependency did not predict changes in stress and social support but rather was associated with elevated cross-sectional levels of social support—a finding consistent with Mongrain's (1998) results.

On the basis of findings (e.g., Monroe & Steiner, 1986; Sarason, Sarason, & Shearin, 1990) that cognitive and personality processes influence individuals' *perception* of the availability of social support, Shahar and Priel (2002) investigated the effects of dependency and self-criticism on creating negative and positive life events over 16 weeks in a large group of adolescents. They found that both dependency and self-criticism predicted elevated levels of negative events, which brought about increased depression and anxiety. Whereas self-criticism also predicted lower levels of positive events, dependency predicted elevated levels of positive events. This difference between dependency and self-criticism in terms of predicting positive events partly explains the greater levels of distress reported by self-critical individuals. The findings of Priel and Shahar (2000) and Shahar and Priel (2002) extend our understanding of an action model of vulnerability of dependent and self-critical individuals and how dependent and self-critical individuals influence their environment by constructing different types of social contexts that contribute to their distress.

Zuroff and de Lorimier (1989) demonstrated that individuals also actively *select* their environment. They found that college women high on DEQ Dependency were most interested in closeness and intimacy in their relationships and described their ideal boyfriend, for example, as someone who would have greater needs for intimacy than for power and achievement. Dependency was also significantly related to the degree to which college women experienced feelings of affection and love in their current romantic relationships (Zuroff & de Lorimier, 1989; Zuroff & Fitzpatrick, 1995). Zuroff and Fitzpatrick (1995) also found that the perception of the quality of their romantic relationships by women high on the DEQ Dependency factor was contingent on how satisfied they felt in the relationship. When dependent participants were satisfied in a relationship, both the individual and her partner were described as valuing the relationship, with each perceiving it as highly gratifying to the other. Stated differently, the relationship was perceived to have both a strong "communal" and an "exchange" dimension (M. S. Clark & Mills, 1979). When highly dependent participants were dissatisfied, the relationship was perceived as lacking communal value. Dependency in college women was also correlated with perceiving same-sex peers as friendly (Zuroff & Franko, 1986). Dependent individuals were found to use more frequent positive expressions during interactions with same-sex friends (Zuroff & Franko, 1986) and to use compromise in resolving conflicts with boyfriends (Zuroff & Fitzpatrick, 1995). Dependency in college students was also correlated with considerable discomfort about feelings of hostility (Zuroff, Moskowitz, Wielgus, Powers, & Franko, 1983). Thus, DEQ Dependency is associated not only with an elevated need for intimacy but also with difficulties in being assertive (Fichman et al., 1994) because it might disrupt relationships. Santor and colleagues (Santor, Pringle, & Israeli, 2000; Santor & Zuroff, 1997, 1998) have demonstrated the remarkable lengths to which dependent individuals will go to preserve interpersonal harmony.

Self-criticism in nonclinical and clinical samples, in contrast, has been consistently related to negative perceptions of the self and of others. Self-criticism in college women was negatively related to satisfaction in romantic relationships (Zuroff & de Lorimier, 1989; Zuroff & Fitzpatrick, 1995). Women high on DEQ Self-Criticism appear to value achievement and strength in their intimate partners, and they described their ideal boyfriends as high in the needs for achievement and masculinity rather than high in intimacy. This is consistent with other findings that self-critical women maintain romantic relationships because of a desire to attain extrinsic rewards, such as social status and respect (Rempel, Holmes, & Zanna, 1985), rather than to share satisfaction and emotional closeness. Self-critical women describe themselves as relatively unwilling to engage in self-disclosure to their boyfriends and same-sex friends, thus their relationships are often marred by unsatisfactory conflict resolution (Mongrain et al., 1998; Santor et al., 2000; Santor & Zuroff, 1997, 1998; Zuroff & Duncan, 1999; Zuroff & Fitzpatrick, 1995). They do not trust their boyfriends, and they feel that their boyfriends do not view their relationship as a source of emotional closeness. Zuroff et al. (1983) found that self-critical college women also perceived their same-sex friends to be less supportive and cooperative and that self-criticism in female college students was related to the use of turning against others as a defense during peer interactions. Self-critical women were perceived by judges as less likable than women high on dependency (Zuroff et al., 1983). The relationship of self-criticism to a vulnerability to postpartum depression (e.g., Besser & Priel, 2003a; Flett, Besser, et al., in press; Priel & Besser, 1999, 2000), as discussed in detail in chapter 5, is consistent with this wide range of studies indicating that self-critical individuals have a number of negative interpersonal characteristics and interpersonal problems (e.g., Mongrain et al., 1998; Whiffen & Aubé, 1999; Whiffen, Aubé, Thompson, & Campbell, 2000; Zuroff & Duncan, 1999).

Evidence also indicates that self-critical women *evoke* negative reactions from others. They were rated as less likable in interactions with same- and opposite-sex peers (Zuroff et al., 1983). Zuroff and Giannopoulos (1990), in an investigation of the moods of 28 heterosexual college student couples before and after 20 minutes of conversation devoted to solving the female partner's personal problem, found that women high on dependency or self-criticism reported more negative affect after the interaction than did control participants. It is interesting that these women also induced negative affect in their partners. When the woman did not have elevated scores on either dependency or self-criticism, the mood of both the woman and her boyfriend improved over the course of the conversation. Boyfriends of dependent women also reported that they provided more social support to the women.

Individuals high on dependency or self-criticism also *manipulate* their environments in different ways. Both dependent college women (Zuroff & Fitzpatrick, 1995) and dependently depressed patients (Riley & McCranie, 1990) describe themselves as unassertive and go to great lengths to maintain interpersonal relations (Mongrain et al., 1998; Santor et al., 2000; Santor &

Zuroff, 1997, 1998; Zuroff & Duncan, 1999). Self-critical women, in contrast, more readily endorse Machiavellian attitudes (Zuroff et al., 1983) and may use manipulative means to achieve their goals in many kinds of relationships. Finally, dependency in men was negatively related to the display of leadership behavior in dyadic interactions (Zuroff et al., 1983).

Amitay, Mongrain, and Fazaa (2002) used structural equation modeling (SEM) to evaluate reports from young adult women and their parents and found that the parents' level of self-criticism predicted daughters' level of self-criticism, which in turn predicted daughters' level of depression and the quality of the daughters' interpersonal relationships. Self-critical young women *selected* boyfriends who were like their critical and controlling parents, and they *created* hostile and conflictual interpersonal relationships with these boyfriends. Thus, their self-critical interpersonal dynamics, which emerged in their relationships with their parents, tended to repeat themselves in their romantic relationships (Baldwin, 1992; Blatt & Zuroff, 1992). Their relational schemas, as expressed in their descriptions of their relationship with their actual and their ideal boyfriends, resemble the relationships they had with their parents. Studies conducted by R. Thompson and Zuroff (1998, 1999a, 1999b) of the parenting behavior of dependent and self-critical mothers provide dramatic empirical evidence that the different behavioral strategies of these mothers are likely to have very different interpersonal consequences.

Another compelling example of the tendency of self-critical individuals to *generate* a negative social context that disrupts their functioning was found in analyses conducted on data from the Treatment of Depression Collaborative Research Project, a randomized clinical trial sponsored by the National Institute of Mental Health that compared three outpatient treatments for major depression: (a) cognitive–behavioral therapy (CBT), (b) interpersonal therapy, and (c) imipramine plus clinical management. These three active treatments were also compared to an inactive placebo plus clinical management condition. Original analyses of these data indicated few substantial differences in clinical outcome among the three active treatment groups (Elkin et al., 1989; Imber et al., 1990). Additional analyses conducted on this data set, however, demonstrated that patients' pretreatment perfectionism or self-criticism had a highly significant negative impact on therapeutic outcome in all three treatment conditions (Blatt, Zuroff, Bondi, Sanislow, & Pilkonis, 1998). Pretreatment self-criticism (perfectionism) impeded therapeutic progress in two thirds of the patients, primarily during the second half of the treatment, between the 9th and the 16th sessions (Blatt & Zuroff, 2002; Blatt, Zuroff, et al., 1998). Further analyses of these data (Zuroff, Blatt, et al., 2000) indicated that a significant portion of the adverse effect of pretreatment self-criticism (perfectionism) on treatment outcome was mediated through patients' impaired participation in the therapeutic alliance; pretreatment perfectionism predicted lower levels of patients' constructive participation in the therapeutic alliance. This interference with the therapeutic alliance in turn predicted poorer therapeutic outcome. Pretreatment perfectionism also had a negative impact on the patients' maintenance of close interpersonal relationships outside therapy; specifically, pretreatment self-criticism (perfectionism) predicted reduced interpersonal involvement with the therapist in treatment as well as in the patient's general social network outside of treatment, and both of these, in turn, predicted poorer therapeutic outcome (Shahar, Blatt, Zuroff, Kuperminc & Sotsky, in press). These adverse effects of pretreatment self-criticism (perfectionism) on the therapeutic alliance and on close interpersonal relations explain much of the variance of the adverse affect of self-criticism (perfectionism) on therapeutic outcome (Shahar, Blatt, Zuroff, Kuperminc, & Sotsky, 2002; Zuroff, Blatt, Krupnick, & Sotsky, 2003). Thus, self-criticism not only contributes to considerable emotional distress but also disrupts therapeutic attempts to alleviate this distress.

In summary, DEQ Dependency is correlated with investment in interpersonal relations. In nonclinical samples, it is expressed in the valuing of emotional closeness; in psychiatric patients, it is expressed as apprehensions and resentments about loss, neglect, deprivation, and abandonment. Highly dependent nonclinical participants actively seek to establish and maintain good interpersonal relationships; clinical patients with high scores on DEQ Dependency are preoccupied with past, current, and future disruptions of interpersonal relationships, such as having depriving and abandoning parents or spouses, and often their depression seems to be precipitated by object loss (Blatt, Quinlan, Chevron, McDonald, & Zuroff, 1982). In contrast, the relationships of college women high on Self-Criticism were relatively conflictual and marred by maladaptive conflict resolution (Mongrain et al., 1998; Zuroff & Duncan, 1999). Self-critical patients are socially isolated, consider themselves to be a personal and social failure, are intensely and critically involved in work rather than in relationships, and their interpersonal involvement is dominated by feelings of anger and resentment (Blatt et al., 1982), and they have difficulty participating effectively in a treatment relationship.

The interpersonal patterns of dependent and self-critical individuals, and the positive and negative contextual factors they create, reveal the sources of their vulnerability to distress as well as the defensive processes that offer them protection. Studies based on an AT model indicate that self-criticism elevates risk factors and reduces protective factors, whereas dependency elevates both protective and risk factors. Dependent individuals engage in both adaptive and maladaptive interpersonal relations. They invest considerable effort in establishing and maintaining close relations and refrain from asserting themselves in confrontational ways in their close relationships for fear of alienating their significant others. In the long term, however, the neediness of dependent individuals can leave their significant others feeling depleted (Coyne, 1976a; Joiner, 1994; Shahar, Joiner, Zuroff & Blatt, in press), thereby eliciting the rejection these dependent individuals fear and thus eventually creating increased interpersonal distress. In contrast, the interpersonal context of self-critical individuals is primarily negative. Their aloof, distinct, hostile, resentful, and manipulative interpersonal style creates confrontation and rejection, thus leading to elevated interpersonal stress. Self-critical individuals' tendency to generate a negative social environment that elevates risks and reduces protective factors is probably one of the primary factors in their relatively elevated levels of depressive symptoms and other forms of disturbance compared with more dependent individuals.

Additional studies have focused on the behavioral strategies through which dependent and self-critical individuals *influence* their environment. Dunkley,

Blankstein, Halsall, Williams, and Winkworth (2000) found that individuals with elevated self-critical perfectionism, a construct that closely corresponds to DEQ Self-Criticism, tend to engage in maladaptive coping strategies, which predicted their involvement in daily hassles. This finding was later replicated in a longitudinal study (Dunkley, Zuroff, & Blankstein, 2003) that examined both personal dispositional and situational factors that contribute to high negative and low positive affect in self-critical college men and women. Over a seven-day period, the investigators assessed daily reports of hassles, stress, social support, and coping styles. Using SEM, they found that self-criticism influenced daily emotional experiences through a number of maladaptive tendencies, including daily hassles, an avoidant coping style, low perceived social support, self-blame, and low perceived efficacy. Self-criticism also contributed to experiences of negative affect by reducing positive affect through a failure to maintain social support. Also, self-critical individuals were particularly reactive to stressors that implied personal failure, loss of control, and criticism from others, and they were relatively ineffective in using more adaptive coping strategies, such as problem-focused coping. In a cross-sectional study, Dunkley and Blankstein (2000) also found that self-critical perfectionist individuals tend to engage in maladaptive coping strategies, including low levels of task orientation and higher levels of distraction and emotion-focused coping that subsequently predicted greater involvement in daily hassles.

In a cross-sectional study, Shahar, Henrich, Blatt, Ryan, and Little (2002) sought to understand further the adverse effect of adolescent self-criticism on negative and positive life events, that is, that self-criticism predicts more negative events and less positive events, whereas dependency predicts more negative events but also more positive events (Shahar & Priel, 2003). The investigators expected that adolescent motivational orientations and behavioral strategies would mediate the effects of dependency and self-criticism on life events. Specifically, drawing from Deci and Ryan's (e.g., R. M. Ryan & Deci, 2000) distinction between intrinsic and extrinsic motivations—motivational orientations that pertain to the extent to which individuals act to realize inherently rewarding goals (i.e., intrinsic motivations) or meet expectations of significant others (i.e., extrinsic motivations)—they found that motivational orientation did not account for the effects of dependency and self-criticism on negative events, but they did account for the negative effect of self-criticism on positive events. Specifically, the investigators found that adolescents with elevated levels of self-criticism reported lower levels of intrinsic motivation in both social and academic domains. In turn, lower levels of intrinsic motivation predicted lower levels of engagement with positive life events. Thus, it seems that self-critical adolescents are characterized by an anhedonic character style that prohibits them from engaging in behaviors that are intrinsically rewarding. Since positive life events have a stress buffering effect (e.g., Shahar & Priel, 2002), the reduction of positive life events in the self-critical individuals creates a risk-related context.

Self-critical individuals seem to *generate* a risk-related social context, because they have negative representations of the self and significant others. Several investigators (e.g., Blatt, 1974; Blatt, Wein, et al., 1979; Mongrain, 1998) have demonstrated that self-critical young adults hold particularly negative representations of parental figures. These negative representations seem to organize self-critical individuals' social exchange, making it difficult for them to respond to positive interpersonal cues (Aubé & Whiffen, 1996) and forcing them to avoid intimacy and self-disclosure (Zuroff & Fitzpatrick, 1995) and to act in a hostile manner in close relationships (Zuroff & Duncan, 1999), thereby creating conflicts, confrontations, and other stressful interpersonal events (Priel & Shahar, 2000; Shahar & Priel, 1999). It seems that self-critical individuals project their own self-criticism onto others and therefore expect the condemnation from others that they inflict on themselves. It is ironic that, to the extent to which these negative representations generate a risk-related environment, this negative interpersonal environment is likely to consolidate and even exacerbate their negative representations of themselves and others, thus contributing to a reciprocal, vicious, interpersonal loop or cycle that is frequently observed by clinicians who treat patients who are depressed (Andrews, 1989; Blatt & Zuroff, 1992; Safran, 1990; Wachtel, 1994; Zuroff, 1992).

Thus, these research findings indicate that self-criticism becomes a primary instigator of depressive symptoms by generating a risk-related social environment (Dunkley, Zuroff, & Blankstein, 2003; Shahar, 2001). Specifically, elevated self-criticism interferes with close relationships; it longitudinally predicts interpersonal ruptures and tensions (Mongrain et al., 1998; Vettese & Mongrain, 2000; Zuroff & Duncan, 1999) and other stressful interpersonal events (Priel & Shahar, 2000; Shahar, Joiner, et al., in press; Shahar & Priel, 2002). Self-criticism also longitudinally predicts reduced levels of social support (Mongrain, 1998; Priel & Shahar, 2000) and fewer positive life events (Shahar & Priel, 2002). Thus, individuals with a negative sense of self (i.e., elevated self-criticism) appear to generate contextual conditions that render them vulnerable to depression and emotional distress.

In summary, dependency and self-criticism have a wide impact on the individual's social context; they affect the occurrence of negative and positive life events, levels of social support, and relationship patterns in close relations. Dependency and self-criticism exert their contextual effects through differences in motivation and behavior and thus have a different impact on the intensity of active vulnerability. Whereas self-criticism predicts a negative social context with elevated levels of risk factors and reduced levels of protective factors, dependency predicts a mixed context composed of elevated levels of both risk and protective factors.

Efficacy and Its Impact on the Social Context

Studies have only recently begun to investigate the third factor of the DEQ— Efficacy, an adaptive dimension of the self—and its impact on the individual's social context. To explore the role of the DEQ Efficacy factor on adaptation, researchers have begun to view DEQ Self-Criticism and Efficacy as negative and positive dimensions of the self, respectively (e.g., Kuperminc, Blatt, & Leadbeater, 1997), and evaluated them in respect to predicting the social contexts of young adolescents (Blatt & Shahar, 2003). They measured social context by four concurrent variables: (a) interpersonal competence and attachment to

(b) mother, (c) father, and (d) peers. They, based on SEM, found that Self-Criticism and Efficacy presented opposite patterns: Self-Criticism predicted, over one year, an increasingly negative social context, whereas Efficacy predicted an increasingly positive social context. Also, it is noteworthy that social context at Time 1 strongly predicted social context one year later (Time 2), indicating that the social context of adolescents tends to be stable over time. Given this continuity of the social content over time, the variations in the social context produced by Self-Criticism and Efficacy are impressive. Shahar, Gallagher, et al. (in press) recently found that DEQ Efficacy buffers the negative interactive impact of DEQ Dependency and Self-Criticism on adolescent adjustment. Thus, Self-Criticism and Efficacy, as measured by the DEQ, respectively assessing maladaptive and adaptive dimensions of the self, are intimately tied to social relations and generate contextual circumstances in predictable ways. Self-Criticism generates a negative, risk-related social context, whereas Efficacy generates a positive, resilience-related context.

The view of vulnerability as precipitating chronic distress is consistent with the relatively recent psychological and psychiatric literature that focuses on the clinical implications of milder forms of depression. Clinical constructs, such as subthreshold depression (Judd, Rapaport, Paulus, & Brown, 1994), minor depression (D. A. Beck & Koenig, 1996), and depressive personality disorders (Huprich, 1998), describe the presence of depressive symptoms at a level that is insufficient to warrant a *Diagnostic and Statistical Manual of Mental Disorders* (e.g., American Psychiatric Association, 1994) diagnosis of major depressive disorder (MDD) but is still highly debilitating. From the perspective of active vulnerability, these conditions might be viewed as dynamic rather than static; namely, these debilitating conditions are a dynamic process whereby, to paraphrase Lerner (1982), these individuals construct their own distress.

Another implication of this active vulnerability is that it can shed light on the clinical–analogue debate. As described in chapter 3, this debate has dominated depression research for the past 20 years (cf. Coyne, 1994; Coyne & Gotlib, 1986; Flett, Vredenburg, & Krames, 1997; Gotlib, 1984; Lewinsohn, Solomon, Seeley, & Zeiss, 2000; Pepper & Coyne, 1996; Santor & Coyne, 2001; Z. V. Segal & Shaw, 1986a, 1986b; Tennen, Hall, & Affleck, 1995; Vredenburg, Flett, & Krames, 1993; Weary, Edwards, & Jacobson, 1995). As discussed in chapter 3, two central positions have been articulated in this debate. The first is that psychological distress, as manifested by elevated levels of depressive symptoms, is continuous with clinical depression. Authors who advocate this view (e.g., Blatt, 1974; Flett, Vredenberg, et al., 1997; Lewinsohn et al., 2000) argue that psychological distress represents a mild form of depression (e.g., dysthymia), hence findings from studies of distress among community participants or college students may be generalized to patients diagnosed with MDD. In contrast, the second position holds that MDD according to the *Diagnostic and Statistical Manual of Mental Disorders* (American Psychiatric Association, 1994) is not continuous with psychological distress but rather represents a distinct and clinically relevant phenomenon (e.g., Santor & Coyne, 2001).

The links between psychological distress and depression, however, might be less problematic when viewed outside of a linear modeling framework.

Specifically, distress may predict depression only when it reaches a certain threshold, and this threshold may vary across individuals. Thus, some individuals who might have more psychological distress than others might still not meet criteria for MDD, because their distress has not reached their individual threshold (see Blatt et al., 1982). It is also in this context that the concept of *active vulnerability* may be helpful. In generating contextual risk factors, vulnerable individuals continually increase their distress and actively approach their (hypothetical) individual threshold for distress, which renders them vulnerable for MDD. Future studies should address this concept of individual thresholds for distress as well as the possibility that this threshold is actively, if unknowingly, approached by vulnerable individuals.

A third clinical implication of an AT model pertains to treatment for depression. From the point of view of AT, individuals realize conscious and unconscious goals by acting on the environment. The same processes of active vulnerability that have been demonstrated in naturalistic research are likely to be manifested in the context of therapy. In the context of treatment, the psychotherapeutic relationship is an environment shared by patient and therapist. Consequently, in an attempt to realize their goals, both patient and therapist act on each other (Blatt & Behrends, 1987; Blatt, Stayner, Auerbach, & Behrends, 1996; Shahar, 2001). As I discuss in more detail in chapter 8, self-critical individuals who generate risk factors and reduce protective factors, for example, would tend to do this also in the course of treatment, thereby disrupting the therapeutic process (Blatt & Shahar, 2003).

The various studies based on an AT model indicate that dependent and self-critical individuals actively generate different social and interpersonal contextual conditions that contribute to their distress (Blatt & Zuroff, 1992). Whereas self-criticism predicts elevated levels of contextual risk factors (i.e., negative stressful life events), as well as lower protective contextual factors (i.e., perceived social support and positive events), dependency predicts elevated levels of both risk and protective contextual factors. Thus, dependent and self-critical individuals create very different patterns of interpersonal relations involving stressful life events and social support.

These conceptualizations and findings have implications beyond research on depression: They have broad theoretical implications for psychological science. The investigations based on an AT perspective are part of a paradigm shift in psychological research. The elucidation of stress–diathesis and AT models of the transaction between individuals and their social context in contemporary psychological research, as well as in psychoanalytic theory, parallels theoretical developments in the social sciences as well as in the philosophy of science (Blatt & Shahar, 2003). In a criticism of the current state of cognitive science, Coyne (1994) argued that psychological research and cognitive science have been based on a spectator model of the self. Relying on information-processing metaphors, cognitive psychologists, for example, depict individuals as passively absorbing "data" from the environment and reacting to these data in turn. As research by Coyne and others indicates (e.g., Depue & Monroe, 1986; Hammen, 1991; Joiner, 1994; Monroe & Simons, 1991; Shahar, 2001; Zuroff, 1992), some individuals are likely to generate actively the particular context that for them is uniquely disruptive. By knowingly and unknowingly selecting their environment (Buss, 1987), and by acting to impress, influence, and shape the behavior of others, individuals actively, often unwittingly, create the particular risk and protective factors that influence their well-being.

This new view of the individual as a participant and actor, in contrast to the previous view of the individual as spectator, is an important extension of the stress–diathesis model, because it recognizes that individuals can have an active role in constructing their environment (Brandtstaedter, 1998). The main tenet of this dynamic interactionalism (Magnusson & Endler, 1977), and of AT, is that individuals shape not only their environment but also their development and, ultimately, their personality (Brandtstaedter, 1998; Lerner, 1982; Wachtel, 1994; Zuroff, 1992). Through complex interpersonal exchanges, individuals and the context reciprocally act on each other (Bandura, 1986). This shift from a spectator to an actor view of the individual is evident in the research with the DEQ. Earlier conceptualizations and investigations of the vulnerability of dependent and self-critical individuals conform to a spectator view; specifically, the congruency hypothesis assumed that dependent and self-critical individuals react specifically to interpersonal or achievement-oriented stressful events, respectively. The results of a number of recent studies that have taken an action perspective, however, indicate that dependent, self-critical, and efficacious individuals also actively shape the contextual conditions that contribute to their distress as well as to their psychological well-being (Blatt & Shahar, 2003). This elaboration and extension of the stress–diathesis model to include a dynamic interactionalism is part of a fundamental change that is occurring in scientific discourse—a shift from a Cartesian view of the individual (Descartes, 1641/1968a, 1641/1968b) as transcendentally at the center of the universe to a Hegelian (Hegel, 1807/1977) perspective in which the individual and others mutually constitute each other through their interaction (Auerbach, 1998; Auerbach & Blatt, 2001). This shift in the view of the individual in psychological research is part of a broad transition in scientific thought from a positivist, Cartesian–Newtonian cosmology to a contextualistic, relativistic Einsteinian conception of the universe in which the individual no longer stands apart in the field of observation, but is now an essential and active part of the field (Blatt, 1984, 1999a).

Part IV

Conclusions

8

Therapeutic Implications

Four Theoretical Perspectives

The formulations of the experiences of depression from the four theoretical perspectives (Arieti & Bemporad, 1980; A. T. Beck, 1983; Blatt, 1974; Bowlby, 1980) discussed in chapter 1 differ in their implications for the therapeutic process. The distinction between anaclitic and introjective depression (e.g., Blatt, 1974, 1998), with its emphasis on differences in types of defense mechanisms, instinctual preoccupations and conflicts, developmental levels, and the quality of early relationships with parents, has implications for therapy that are different from the therapeutic approaches to depression proposed by Arieti and Bemporad (1978, 1980), Beck (1983, 1996; D. A. Clark & Beck, 1999), and Bowlby (1988b). In my view, anaclitic and introjective patients differ markedly in the transference themes they enact in treatment and in the countertransference reactions they provoke in the psychotherapeutic relationship. Transference and countertransference issues with anaclitic (dependent) patients center on libidinal and affective dimensions of care, intimacy, and affection and are expressed in the therapeutic relationship around issues such as the dependability, reliability, and affection of the therapist and in fears of separation, loss, and abandonment. For introjective (self-critical) patients, the focus in treatment is usually on issues of self-definition and self-worth, characterized by concerns about power, autonomy, control, criticism, competition, and anger (Blatt & Shichman, 1983).

My approach to the therapeutic process is an extension of my understanding of the nature of the experiences of depression. The anaclitic and introjective depressive dimensions, and their associated themes of loneliness and a loss of

This chapter incorporates material from the following sources: (a) "Convergence of Psychoanalytic and Cognitive Behavioral Theories of Depression," by S. J. Blatt and C. Maroudas, 1992, *Psychoanalytic Psychology*, *9*, pp. 157–190. Copyright 1992 by Lawrence Erlbaum Associates, Inc. Adapted with permission. (b) "Change in Object and Self Representations in Long-Term, Intensive, Inpatient Treatment of Seriously Disturbed Adolescents and Young Adults," by S. J. Blatt, D. Stayner, J. S. Auerbach, and R. S. Behrends, 1996, *Psychiatry: Interpersonal and Biological Processes*, *59*, pp. 82–107. Copyright 1996 by Guilford Press. Adapted with permission. (c) "Self-Reflexivity, Intersubjectivity, and Therapeutic Change," by J. S. Auerbach and S. J. Blatt, 2001, *Psychoanalytic Psychology*, *18*, pp. 427–450. Copyright 2001 by Lawrence Erlbaum Associates, Inc. Adapted with permission. (d) "Mental Representation, Severe Psychopathology, and the Therapeutic Process," by S. J. Blatt & J. S. Auerbach, 2001, *Journal of the American Psychoanalytic Association*, *49*, pp. 113–159. Copyright 2001 by The Analytic Press. Adapted with permission.

self-esteem, define two fundamental tasks of psychological development: the development of (a) satisfying reciprocal interpersonal relatedness and (b) a differentiated, integrated, and essentially positive sense of self or of an identity (Blatt, 1995b; Blatt & Blass, 1990, 1996; Blatt & Shichman, 1983). The goals in treatment are to enable patients to appreciate and understand, as fully as possible, the early interpersonal experiences that contributed to the impairments in their capacity to develop satisfactory interpersonal relations and a realistic and effective sense of self and the multiple ways in which these impairments are currently experienced and expressed. Conscious and unconscious expressions of impairments in these two fundamental developmental processes (interpersonal relatedness and self-definition) emerge in experiences of contemporary life, in associations and dreams, as well as in transference enactments in the treatment process. Exploration of the multiple contemporary expressions of these impairments, as well as their developmental antecedents, in the context of a therapeutic relationship, helps patients revise their conceptions of self and others in their actual and potential interpersonal relationships.

Some patients, more often females, have a predominant preoccupation with issues of interpersonal relatedness. These anaclitic patients focus on issues of interpersonal relatedness early in the treatment process—on issues of trust, dependability, and love, as well as fears of loss and abandonment. Other patients, more often males, have a predominant preoccupation with issues of self-definition and self-worth. Early in treatment, these introjective patients focus on issues of separation, autonomy, control, and self-worth and on fears of criticism, disapproval, and failure. As anaclitic patients eventually begin to feel more confident and secure in their interpersonal relations, they also begin to develop and express a sense of self-definition and agency; conversely, as introjective patients eventually develop a more stable and secure sense of self, they allow themselves to experience interests in relatedness and begin to consider developing more intimate, reciprocal, interpersonal relations. Thus, conflicts around issues of interpersonal relatedness and self-definition are central in my view of therapy with all patients, but particularly with patients plagued by experiences of depression.

Therapeutic techniques with both types of depressed patients are essentially the same: exploration of the details of current and early life experiences that are related to developmental impairments in establishing an effective sense of self and in establishing satisfying reciprocal interpersonal relationships. However, the thematic foci of these explorations, as well as their expressions in the transference, differ. In anaclitic patients, treatment focuses primarily on painful and disrupted interpersonal experiences, whereas introjective patients focus primarily on their feelings of failure, worthlessness, guilt, self-loathing, and contempt.

Although A. T. Beck (1983, 1999) has described similar issues in depression (e.g., loss and dependency vs. power and competition), his therapeutic approach is different. Beck believes that sociotropic and autonomous types of depression require different therapeutic approaches. In the autonomous mode, the therapeutic focus, according to Beck, is on re-establishing a sense of self-determination, competence, and optimism regarding the achievement of goals by encouraging patients to be more flexible and adaptable, particularly regarding the setting of goals and acceptance of their limitations. For the sociotropic type of patients, the task is to change their thoughts about being unloved and unlovable.

Beck (D. A. Clark & Beck, 1999) views sociotropic patients as more responsive to interpersonal and emotionally engaging interventions and autonomous patients as more responsive to less personal and more problem-focused interventions. According to D. A. Clark and Beck (1999), sociotropic individuals prefer a close, more informal therapeutic relationship in which they look to the therapist for help and depend on the therapist to solve their personal problems. The preference of sociotropic patients for support in psychotherapy, however, may make

> treatment termination difficult . . . in that the highly sociotropic person may become either too dependent on the therapist or become preoccupied with receiving the therapist's approval and acceptance. Therapeutic work will need to focus on the sociotropic patient's dysfunctional beliefs and misinterpretations of rejection, unacceptability, abandonment, and negative reactions by others. (D. A. Clark & Beck, 1999, p. 391)

According to D. A. Clark and Beck (1999), highly autonomous individuals prefer "a more formal, detached relationship with the therapist . . . a collaborative relationship, with the patient actively engaged with the therapist in setting the agenda, homework assignments, and topics for each therapy session" (p. 391). Beck assumes that autonomous people "respond better to a therapeutic style that maintains patients' personal control, freedom, and sense of accomplishment" (D. A. Clark & Beck, 1999, pp. 391–392). Goal-directed, task, and problem-oriented interventions are "preferred over more introspective, relational, and emotive therapies. Issues involving demoralization, defeat, failure, and incompetence should be a primary focus of therapy, with treatment oriented toward restoring the autonomous person's sense of competence and accomplishment in life" (D. A. Clark & Beck, 1999, pp. 391–392). Clark and Beck (1999) noted that these theoretical formulations about the differential nature of the therapeutic process with sociotropic and autonomous patients, however, await systematic examination in empirical investigations. Blatt (1992), in fact, in further analyses of data from the Menninger Psychotherapy Research Project (MPRP), found that anaclitic patients made significantly greater therapeutic gain in 2- to 3-times weekly supportive–expressive psychotherapy than they did in 5-times weekly psychoanalysis, while introjective patients made significantly greater therapeutic gain in psychoanalysis than they did in supportive–expressive psychotherapy. This significant patient–treatment interaction will be discussed in more detail later in this chapter.

Therapy for A. T. Beck (1996) involves discharging and modifying cognitive schemas or modes—"deactivating them . . . [and] modifying their structure and content and . . . [then] priming or 'constructing' more adaptive modes to neutralize them" (p. 15). Reassurance, corrective information, and distraction create a "safety mode" (A. T. Beck, 1996, p. 16). In a very rational approach, Beck (1996) explained to patients that there is no basis for their irrational beliefs. In panic disorders, for example, "a convincing demonstration of the unrealistic nature of the fears plus the incorporation of a more realistic belief form a solid protective wall against subsequent panic attacks. This kind of corrective learning becomes structuralized in an adaptive mode" (p. 17). "Standard supportive interventions, for example, may defuse the core belief 'of being helpless or unlovable' into a more adequate 'likeable' belief" (A. T. Beck, 1996, p. 17). Beck (1996) noted, however, that this process does not permanently change the patient's dysfunctional beliefs and that "the most durable change follows from changing the . . . rules that equate, for example, a failure or a disappointment with being unlovable or powerless and substituting more precise rules regarding the meaning of a rebuff or a failure" (p. 17).

> The basic cognitive–behavioral approaches to depression, consisting of assigning a structured activity program and emphasizing "mastery" and "pleasure" (Beck et al., 1979), help to prime the productive or adaptive mode that has been dormant during the depression. . . . Activities such as graded task assignment, confronting and solving practical problems (including those created by the depression), demonstrate to the patients that they can do more than they believe and that they have more control over themselves than they realize. . . . The recognition, review, and reframing of the "automatic negative thoughts" also helps to energize reality testing as well as to modify the negative self image. (A. T. Beck, 1996, p. 17)

Other "cognitive skills, such as examining the evidence for an interpretation, exploring alternative explanations, and reinforcing . . . reality testing, are also crucial . . . in reducing the depressive mode," but this "does not necessarily change the predisposition to depression . . . it is necessary to modify the content of schemas and to apply the cognitive skills when dysfunctional interpretations arise" (A. T. Beck, 1996, pp. 17–18). It is important for the patient to learn "the basic cognitive skills during therapy and then applying them when adverse circumstances arise" (A. T. Beck, 1996, p. 18). Modifying the "structural characteristics of the depressive mode" (A. T. Beck, 1996, p. 18) involves evaluating and modifying negative evaluations by clarifying that personal success, for example, is "only one part of living and not . . . *the* measure of the individual's worth" (A. T. Beck, 1996, p. 18). These changes in the patients' value systems, such as reducing the degree of ego involvement in proving themselves successful, for example, make these events less important and lead to a stabilization of self-esteem and self-image.

Beck stresses the importance of a multifaceted approach to complex disorders such as depression, which require a combination of interventions consolidated by booster sessions to diffuse the dysfunctional mode and reinforce the adaptive mode. He believes that cognitive therapy is effective in preventing relapse because it modifies the content of the cognitive structure or mode; however, he does not consider the level of organization of the cognition structure or the role of the therapeutic relationship in any detail but focuses instead on the need for changing the patient's "definition of his lovableness and his misinterpretations of other people's negative reactions to him" (A. T. Beck, 1983, p. 275).

Beck initially devoted a chapter in his treatment manual (A. T. Beck, Rush, Shaw, & Emery, 1979) to the importance of establishing and maintaining a positive therapeutic relationship (e.g., warmth, empathy, trust, and rapport) and later stated that "the efficacy of cognitive and behavioral techniques is dependent, to a large degree, on the relationship between therapist and patient . . . the relationship requires therapist warmth, accurate empathy, and genuineness. Without these, the therapy becomes 'gimmick oriented' " (A. T. Beck, Wright, Newman, & Liese, 1993, p. 135). However, the role of the therapeutic relationship in the treatment process—how a positive therapeutic relationship, including the resolution of conflicts and ruptures of that relationship, is central to learning in cognitive therapy (e.g., Newman, 1994; Padesky, 1995; Raue & Goldfried, 1994; Safran, 1990; Safran & Muran, 1996)—is discussed in somewhat more detail only much later and primarily by other cognitive–behavioral therapists (e.g., A. T. Beck et al., 1990; Safran, 1990; Safran & Segal, 1990; Wright & Davis, 1994). According to Padesky (1996, p. 270), cognitive therapists use the therapeutic relationship as "a laboratory for testing" and revising core beliefs and their "affective, cognitive, behavioral, and relationship consequences."

Beck's formulations of the therapeutic process, in contrast to the psychodynamic formulations of Blatt (1974, 1998), Bowlby (1988b), and Arieti and Bemporad (1978, 1980), do not focus on the motivational forces and the early life experiences that may have contributed to the formation of the dysfunctional attitudes and beliefs. Also, in contrast to the formulations of Blatt, Bowlby, and Arieti and Bemporad, Beck does not discuss in detail the affective components or the structural organization of the dysfunctional attitudes and beliefs, or the role of the therapist and the therapeutic alliance or relationship as contributing to a patient's ability to revise his or her dysfunctional attitudes and beliefs. In contrast, the psychodynamic emphasis on the role of the therapist and the therapeutic alliance in the process of therapeutic change is consistent with recent empirical findings (e.g., Burns & Nolen-Hoeksema, 1992; Hayes, Castonguay, & Goldfried, 1966; Horvath & Symonds, 1991; Jones & Pulos, 1993; Krupnick et al., 1996) as well as a recent comment by Wampold (2001, p. 211) that "Clearly the person of the therapist is a critical factor in the success of therapy, more important than adherence to the protocol or the particular treatment."

Snyder and Ingram (2000) noted that it is easy to see how behavioral therapies have been viewed as minimizing the role of the therapeutic relationship in the treatment process, but they contended that contemporary behavioral therapies (e.g., dialective behavioral therapy [Linehan, 1993] and functional analytic psychotherapy [Kohlenberg & Tsai, 1991; Follette, Naugle, & Callaghan, 1996]) emphasize that the therapeutic relationship facilitates therapeutic change. Burns and Auerbach (1996), in one of the few extensive discussions of the role of the therapist in behavioral treatments, however, questioned the role of the therapist's capacity for empathy in the therapeutic process because it can be a two-way sword: "A warm and trusting therapeutic relationship can significantly enhance treatment and speed recovery, but an unsatisfactory therapeutic alliance may have a negative impact on [the] patient's self-esteem and delay recovery" (p. 161). They stressed that a focus on empathy is important because it can make therapists aware of their reactions, particularly to difficult and problematic patients, but they view the technical and the empathic dimensions of treatment as involving significantly different paradigms and requiring different personal attributes that many therapists have difficulty integrating. They did note, however, that "listening and self-expression techniques" could help cognitive–behavioral therapists improve their interpersonal skills, develop a broader range of interventions, and develop "a more compassionate and creative way" (p. 161) of dealing with difficult patients. However, Burns and Auerbach (1996), like many cognitive–behavioral therapists, do not consider empathy or the therapeutic alliance as central factors in the processes of therapeutic change.

For Bowlby (1988a), the tasks of therapy are reconnecting memories and feelings, of discovering the true targets of one's yearning and anger and the true sources of one's anxiety and pain. Understanding the basis of one's responses enables the individual to reappraise his or her reactions and possibly undertake a radical restructuring of these responses. The major aim is to help the patient understand the experiences that result in feelings of anger, fear, and yearning for love, thereby enabling him or her to alter present maladaptive modes of experiencing interpersonal relationships and of reacting to them. According to Bowlby (1988b), the therapist's task is fivefold: (a) to provide a secure base from which patients can explore the unhappy and painful aspects of their lives, past and present; (b) to assist in these explorations by encouraging patients to consider their expectations about their own feelings and behavior and those of others in their current relationships, and to help patients discover the unconscious biases that may distort their intimate relationships; (c) to encourage patients to examine the therapeutic relationship as an example of an attachment relationship; (d) to encourage patients to consider how their current perceptions, expectations, actions, and feelings may be the product of experiences of early childhood and adolescence, particularly with parental figures, and to cope with the emotions associated with these experiences; and (e) to enable patients to recognize and reappraise the mental models of self and others resulting from these early experiences. A supportive and empathic therapist is vital in this process. According to Bowlby (1988b), the therapist plays a vital role in facilitating these painful explorations, many of which would be "difficult or perhaps impossible to think about and reconsider without a trusted companion to provide support, encouragement, sympathy, and, on occasion, guidance" (p. 138). Bowlby believes that attachment theory facilitates the understanding of transference and countertransference—current and past events, experiences, and feelings, as well as unconscious conflicts that emerge in the therapeutic relationship. This view contrasts with Beck's view that the aim of therapy is to alter the patient's current "mode of construing" the world without necessarily investigating its origins.

It is important to note that Bowlby did not recommend different approaches to patients depending on their symptomatology and form of depression, beyond highlighting the need to recognize and appreciate differences in the early experiences likely to have occurred in different personality types. An interesting area of investigation deriving from Bowlby's model would be the study of the relationships between transference and countertransference issues that emerge in therapy, possible using Luborsky's (e.g., Luborsky & Crits-Cristoph,

1990) core conflictual relationship model and the types of attachment that were formed in both childhood and adulthood.

According to Arieti and Bemporad (1978, p. 295), the basic aim of therapy is to enable the patient

> to widen the horizons of his consciousness which [have] been narrowed in childhood to distort patterns of relating and a sad neglect of much that is joyful and meaningful in life. He must be made aware of his own resources for pleasure, previously unknown areas of satisfaction, and relief from the relentless feeling of guilt that accompanies each attempt at gratification. . . . this entails a cognitive restructuring in which old experiences are brought to consciousness and given new meanings. In the therapeutic relationship behavior is elicited, examined, and utilized for an alteration in the estimation of the self and others.

Like Blatt and Bowlby, but unlike Beck, Arieti and Bemporad stress understanding the patient's interpersonal world via the appraisal of early experiences in the framework of the therapeutic relationship. The therapist is supportive and reactive, because a more silent, distant therapeutic approach could further the transference distortions of an omnipotent dominant other. Arieti and Bemporad, like Blatt and Bowlby, recommend relatively few specific techniques for particular personality types; instead, they present the same basic approach for all depression, mild or severe, regardless of the patient's personality type.

Therapy is divided roughly into three stages according to Arieti and Bemporad (1978): (a) establishing the therapeutic relationship; (b) working through; and (c) applying changed cognitive structures to the patient's current, everyday life experiences. The establishment of a therapeutic relationship involves the patient changing his or her view of the therapist from that of a dominant other, either in the sense of being demanding or all-giving, to that of a significant other involved in a partnership, the common aim of which is to search for the cause of the depression and make it harmless. Arieti and Bemporad noted that it may be difficult to establish a therapeutic relationship, especially with a dominant other or claiming depression, becausethe therapist has to shift gradually from partially gratifying the patient's wishes to facilitate the development of trust, to becoming an understanding and interested, but not a dominant, other. During this process, the patient is first made aware of the maladaptive focus in his or her life, such as an inordinate need for approval or achievement, or of his or her inappropriate demands.

It is important to note that the dominant-goal and dominant-other types of depression are not viewed by Arieti and Bemporad (1978, 1980) as completely distinct; rather, they share many dynamic features. In the early stages of treatment, much anger may be expressed against the dominant other, or deep disillusionment may result from the realization of the overvaluation of the dominant goal. The focus in therapy eventually shifts from the present to the past, and the patient begins to realize the reasons for his or her maladaptive lifestyle and understand his or her childhood difficulties. The depression begins to abate, and recurs less frequently, because the patient can differentiate present from past and is able to become assertive and find fulfillment without the distortions of the past. A search for new lifestyles begins only with the awareness of how past experiences caused the sorrow. The second stage of treatment involves working through the feelings aroused by understanding and abandoning the governing maladaptive cognitive structures. Guilt feelings in a dominant-other depression may become intense in treatment with the reawakening of the guilt felt in childhood over being made to feel that one was the cause of loss of love, or as a cover for anxiety over anticipating future loss. The final stages in therapy involve encouraging patients to listen to their own individuality and not allow the dominant other or dominant goal to control their life. This requires frequent re-examination of behavior patterns and relating them to old, well-established mechanisms, so that the patients can recognize the distortions of the past and act according to their own current wishes and desires. Patients have to give up "whatever lie or impossible value has become connected with an unauthentic identity" (Arieti & Bemporad, 1978, p. 229).

Arieti and Bemporad's formulations of therapy integrate psychodynamic, cognitive, and behavioral approaches. They stress that the negative appraisals described by Beck are only part of the manifest symptomatology, and although their significance and use must be explained to the patient, "these ideas may accrue a superficial layer of depression over the deep-rooted disposition to become depressed" (Arieti & Bemporad, 1978, p. 223). Unlike Beck, Arieti and Bemporad warn therapists against getting "sidetracked" into investigating cognitive features alone. In all aspects of their formulations, Arieti and Bemporad stress the role of the interpersonal world in the etiology and treatment of depression, and therefore, share much with Blatt and Bowlby, although their terminology is different.

These formulations about the nature of the therapeutic process with anaclitic (sociotropic or dominant-other) and introjective (autonomous or dominant-goal) types of patients who are depressed raise three major issues: (a) the nature of therapeutic change in depression; (b) the nature of therapeutic change, particularly in anaclitic and introjective patients; and (c) the processes that lead to these therapeutic changes.

Therapeutic Change in the Treatment of Depression

All four theoretical approaches (Arieti & Bemporad, Beck, Blatt, and Bowlby) stress the centrality of impaired cognitive structures in depression, and the three psychodynamic approaches also emphasize the important role of the therapeutic relationship in facilitating changes in these cognitive structures. Colleagues and I, like Bowlby and Arieti and Bemporad, stress the importance of impaired cognitive structures in depression and the important role of experiences in the therapeutic relationship in contributing to changes in these cognitive structures. Thus, a fundamental assumption in my psychodynamic therapeutic approach (and those of Arieti and Bemporad and Bowlby) is that the parent–child caring relationship contributes to the formation of adaptive as well as maladaptive internal working mental models (representations or cognitive–affective schemas) of the self in caregiving relationships and that the nature of these representations expresses the quality of these early childhood attachments (Blatt, 1974, 1991, 1995b; Bowlby, 1988a, 1988b). If the early parent–child relationship and subsequent significant interpersonal experiences lead to the construction of both adaptive and maladaptive representations of self and others in childhood that are central in psychological development and functioning, then the quality of the interpersonal experiences in the therapeutic relationship should contribute to significant revisions of these maladaptive representations and to the establishment and consolidation of more adaptive cognitive schemas of self and other (Blatt, Wild, & Ritzler, 1975).

Despite the difference in emphasis between the psychodynamic and cognitive–behavioral approaches on the importance of interpersonal relations in both the etiology and treatment of depression, it is noteworthy that all four theoretical positions stress change in cognitive structures as an essential part of therapeutic change in depression. Beck, as well as Bowlby and Arieti and Bemporad, focuses on changes in the content of these cognitive structures, whereas colleagues and I emphasize primarily changes in the structural organization of mental representations. Also, as presented in chapter 4, we have developed procedures for systematically assessing both the structural organization and the thematic content of representations of self and significant others. These procedures assess the patient's level of cognitive development in the description of self and significant others; the degree to which self and other have been differentiated and are represented as both independent and as interrelated; the degree to which the descriptions of others have been articulated in dimensions of benevolent, punitive, and ambitious qualities; and the degree of ambivalence with which the significant other has been described. We also have used these procedures to study the nature of change in the therapeutic process.

Change in Mental Representations in the Therapeutic Process

The centrality of cognitive–affective schemas in psychological development and in psychopathology, as discussed in chapters 1 and 4, suggests that the assessment of these schemas may have important implications for the study of the therapeutic process. The therapeutic relationship should create a process through which impaired and or distorted interpersonal schemas are relinquished, reworked, and transformed into more adaptive cognitive–affective representations of self and other. Toward the end of treatment, representations should be more differentiated and integrated, with indications of a greater capacity for mutual interpersonal relatedness (Blatt et al., 1975).

Using procedures described in chapter 4, our research team (e.g., Blatt, Auerbach, & Aryan, 1998; Blatt, Stayner, Auerbach, & Behrends, 1996; Diamond, Blatt, Stayner, & Kaslow, 1991; Gruen & Blatt, 1990) evaluated changes in the conceptual level (CL), the degree of differentiation–relatedness (D-R), degree of articulation, and the thematic content in descriptions of self and significant others (mother, father, and therapist) given by 40 seriously disturbed, treatment-resistant adolescents and young adults at the beginning and toward the end of intensive, long-term (more than one year), psychodynamically informed inpatient treatment. Each patient's level of clinical functioning, as expressed in narrative reports in clinical case records independently prepared at admission and at discharge, was evaluated by a judge with the Global Adjustment Scale (GAS; Endicott, Spitzer, Fleiss, & Cohen, 1976), a 100-point scale for rating the severity of psychopathology. Descriptions of significant figures and the self were also obtained at admission to treatment and every six months thereafter until termination; these were scored in random order by raters blind both to the identity and clinical details of the patients and to the point in treatment from which the relevant material was sampled (Blatt, Stayner, et al., 1996; Blatt, Auerbach, et al., 1998). Using partial correlations that statistically control for differences in initial levels, we found that changes in the structural organization and content of these descriptions of the self and significant figures (i.e., mother, father, and therapist) obtained at admission and discharge were significantly correlated with independent estimates of change in psychological functioning obtained from the clinical case records.

The descriptions of all four figures (mother, father, therapist, and self) by these seriously disturbed inpatients at the beginning of treatment were generally unintegrated and involved oscillations between polarized qualities (i.e., all good or all bad) or an emphasis on concrete part properties. Clinical improvement, as independently assessed through changes in the GAS, correlated to a highly significant degree ($p < .001$) with increased differentiation–relatedness in the descriptions of mother, $r(36) = .52$; therapist, $r(36) = .50$; and self, $r(36) = .52$; as well as to a somewhat less significant degree ($p < .05$) with descriptions of father, $r(36) = .31$. An increased conceptual level of the description of father also correlated significantly with clinical improvement, $r(36) = .45$, $p < .01$. Increased conceptual level of the description of the therapist also tended to correlate with clinical improvement, $r(36) = .26, p < .10$. Statistically significant relationships were also found between the degree of clinical improvement and increased articulation (i.e., greater number of scorable attributes) in the descriptions of mother, $r(36) = .39$, $p < .01$; father, $r(36) = .28$, $p < .05$; and therapist, $r(36) = .28, p < .05$. The relationship of these changes in the structure of representations to the assessment of clinical progress was independent of change in the length of the descriptions (Blatt, Stayner, et al., 1996).

Furthermore, we (Blatt, Auerbach, & Aryan, 1998) found, over the course of long-term, psychoanalytically oriented, inpatient treatment, that this sample of seriously disturbed, treatment-resistant patients showed an increase in mean differentiation–relatedness from object representations that were initially dominated by polarization and splitting (differentiation–relatedness Level 5)—that is, by the keeping apart of good and bad aspects of an object representation—to representations at the end of treatment that involved the emergence of object constancy (differentiation–relatedness Level 6), in which there was a preliminary integration of positive and negative elements (Adler & Buie, 1979; Blatt & Auerbach, 1988; Kernberg, 1976; Mahler, Pine, & Bergman, 1975). Patients who, in independent assessment, showed the greatest clinical improvement had representations at termination that indicate a consolidation of object constancy (differentiation–relatedness Level 7) in their description of their therapists. The emergence in this sample of seriously disturbed, treatment-resistant patients of object constancy focused around the relationship with the therapist is an impressive clinical achievement.

It is also noteworthy that patients with greater therapeutic gain had higher differentiation–relatedness scores for their initial descriptions of their therapists than did patients who eventually made less therapeutic gain. Moreover, these initial differentiation–relatedness scores were usually higher for the description of the therapist than for each of the other three figures (mother, father, or self). This suggests that patients with greater therapeutic gain were initially more capable of constructing more complex and nuanced representations of a significant new figure—the therapist—suggesting that this capacity for establishing a relationship with this new figure may have a crucial role in facilitating therapeutic change (Auerbach & Blatt, 2001; Blatt & Auerbach, 2001; Blatt, Auerbach, et al., 1998).

Although we have demonstrated that the structure and content of representations change significantly during successful treatment, we need to understand more fully the processes through which treatment results in these revisions of mental representations. Further understanding of these processes of therapeutic change may be gained by observing how qualities attributed to particular figures shift over time among the people who play significant roles in the drama of therapy—among parents, therapists, and the self. Shifts in the content and structure of representations during the treatment process may provide some understanding of the mechanisms through which pathological introjects and identifications are repudiated, revised, relinquished, and eventually replaced by more adaptive representations.

In psychoanalytic therapy, for example, change is seen as a consequence of a process in which the therapeutic relationship initially mobilizes maladaptive, rigid, cognitive–affective interpersonal schemas that were established in early caring experiences with significant figures. It is assumed that expression of these schemas in the transference is essential to the therapeutic process through which these maladaptive schemas are identified and understood and eventually reworked and revised. It is possible, through qualitative analyses of the patient's descriptions of self and significant others over the course of treatment, to determine how this sequence occurs—that is, whether a patient, for example, comes to describe the therapist in terms similar to those for mother and father—and then to observe how these descriptions, of both therapist and parents, are modified as treatment proceeds.

Also of particular interest is the manner in which the patient's self-description changes. It is usually assumed, even with patients with narcissistic disturbances, that the patient starts treatment with a fundamentally negative self-concept that, through treatment, comes to be revised in a more positive direction, presumably through identification with valued aspects of the therapist, the parents, or both. Once again, qualitative analyses of these descriptions over the treatment process enabled us, for example, to see whether patients begin to describe themselves in terms previously used to describe one or the other of their parents or the therapist and whether such changes are associated with independent assessment of clinical improvement. Thus, descriptions of self and significant others throughout the treatment process provide data through which one can not only empirically assess changes in the content and structural organization of representations of self and others but also conduct qualitative analyses of the sequence of changes in the terms used in describing significant figures and the self.

A Clinical Example

To illustrate the clinical utility of our method of assessing object representations, I turn to an examination of descriptions given by a seriously disturbed, treatment-resistant, 13-year-old adolescent with introjective, psychotic depression and borderline personality disorder over the course of her 19 months of long-term, intensive, psychoanalytically oriented inpatient treatment. Her descriptions reveal changes over the course of treatment that parallel those identified in our statistical analyses of the representations of our sample of 40 patients (Blatt, Stayner, et al., 1996), including more positive descriptions of mother, therapist, and self and a more negative description of father. Her representations of each of her parents became more balanced over the course of her treatment, while the representations of her therapist became more idealized. Even further, her identification with an idealized therapist appears to have been an important vehicle for her achievement of greater self-integration. A., the elder of two children, emerged from a background of chronic bitterness between her parents, who were eventually divorced when A. was 3½. They had serious marital difficulties that began shortly after the birth of A.'s brother, when A. was 2. A.'s father was reportedly an alcoholic, and his brother experienced what was described as a "nervous breakdown." A.'s maternal uncle had been hospitalized several times for unspecified emotional disturbances. At the time of her parents' separation and divorce, A. began to have difficulty eating and had frequent temper tantrums. Psychiatric consultation was sought when A. was about four or five years old, and psychotic symptoms that emerged around age 8 had a persecutory tone, as A. began to have hallucinations of the devil's voice and face and to believe that her body was possessed by the devil. By age 10, she was having frequent arguments with her mother and brother and refusing to go to school. Her school performance deteriorated, and her relationship with her mother became increasingly hostile, turbulent, and violent. She began experimenting with cannabis and alcohol, eventually progressing to diazepam (Valium), methaqualone (Quaalude) and, eventually, intravenous heroin. Although she had minimal contact with her father during the nine years following the parents' separation and divorce, she moved to her father's home when she was age 12, because her mother found it increasingly difficult to manage her. After a suicide attempt at age 12 with an overdose of diazepam, A. was hospitalized briefly. She was discharged after a few days and continued to deteriorate during the next year. Her drug abuse worsened, as did her visual and auditory hallucinations. She remained chronically depressed, anxious, suicidal, and affectively labile, with occasional brief periods of elation and euphoria, but she refused outpatient psychotherapy. She was hospitalized briefly once again before being admitted to a small, private, long-term treatment facility. On admission to this facility, A. was diagnosed as experiencing a severe, psychotic, introjective depression with marked paranoid trends in a borderline personality disorder with mixed histrionic, compulsive, and paranoid features, and severe substance abuse.

In a clinical evaluation at admission, A. was described as depressed in appearance and behavior. Withdrawn, with poor diet and hygiene, and often distracted by internal stimuli, she was usually unable to sustain a conversation and was often unsure of what was going on around her. Her treatment team described her as enacting her depression, rather than communicating it verbally, and reported that she was obsessive, preoccupied, and ruminative, with a psychotic level of ambivalence. Her major defenses against depression were intellectualization and isolation of affect.

During the course of A.'s hospitalization, her GAS score rose from 22 at admission to 43 at discharge. Periodic reviews of A's treatment over the 19 months of hospitalization revealed that her self-esteem improved noticeably; she became less vulnerable to psychotic decompensation and intense depression and was more capable of using relationships with others to get through crises. She was also able to realize that her involvement with drugs was a substitute for the nurturance she felt she could not obtain in other ways. Although she was still considered vulnerable to psychotic regression, she was discharged from the hospital to a residential facility because of her parents' inability to continue to afford intensive treatment.

A. received multifaceted treatment in the aforementioned clinical facility, including psychoanalytically oriented individual and group psychotherapy, each three times weekly. A. had completed the Object Relations Inventory (ORI), an interview-based procedure for collecting descriptions of self and significant figures. The ORI inquires about the following significant figures in this order: mother, father, a significant other, self, and therapist. Thus, descriptions of mother, father, therapist, and self were obtained from A. shortly after her admission to the hospital and every six months thereafter until she was discharged.

Exhibit 8.1 presents the descriptions of self and significant others (mother, father, and therapist) provided by A. at various points in her treatment process.

QUANTITATIVE ANALYSIS. The various descriptions given by A. at admission and discharge were scored for the structural and thematic dimensions described in detail in chapter 4, including conceptual level, differentiation–relatedness, the number of scorable attributes, length, and the two thematic or content factors that were scorable in her protocols: benevolent and punitive. The degree of ambivalence was also scored. Table 8.1, in which A.'s scores on various structural and content scales at admission and discharge are presented, illustrates the quantitative changes in her ORI descriptions over the course of her treatment. Independent assessment of A.'s clinical functioning with the GAS based on the treatment reviews routinely prepared at intake and at termination indicated that A. made substantial therapeutic progress (from a GAS score of 22 to 43) during her 19 months of inpatient treatment. This therapeutic progress was paralleled by substantial increases in differentiation–relatedness, conceptual level, and articulation of her descriptions of self and significant others. Thus, the changes noted in A. were similar to the changes noted with

Exhibit 8.1   Patient A.: Self- and Object Representations

Admission
  Mother   Worried, aggressive, unhappy, and lonely.
               Inquiry: (*Anything else?*) No.
  Father   Outgoing, generous, considerate, understanding. That's it.
  Self   Depends on how I'm feeling. Sometimes I'm outgoing but other times
               I'm withdrawn. I don't know.
               Inquiry: (*What else?*) I don't want to describe myself. (*Why?*) 'Cause I
               get upset when I do. (*Can you tell me what upsets you?*) I'm either too
               conceited or too modest to answer something like this.
  Therapist   Sweet, supportive, trusting, and caring.

Six months
  Mother   Neurotic, irregular, stubborn, caring, overwhelming, cold. That's it.
               Inquiry: (*Neurotic?*) She's crazy. She's very edgy. The slightest thing
               may set her off. (*Irregular?*) Not consistent. Too moody. (*Stubborn?*)
               Won't budge on something she believes is right. Won't listen to reason.
               (*Caring?*) She means well. (*Overwhelming?*) Overbearing. (*Cold?*) She
               can turn herself off and be cold.
  Father   Funny, understanding, protective. He won't take enough responsibility
               for me. That's it.
               Inquiry: (*Funny?*) Has a good sense of humor. Can get me to laugh.
               (*Understanding?*) Can relate to what's going on with me and
               understand. Is considerate of my feelings. (*Protective?*) If I needed it,
               he'd protect me. (*Won't take enough. . .*) He had a daughter that
               weighed 89 pounds and was shooting dope and didn't notice.
  Self: I can't describe myself. You describe me. It's hard. No, it's easy.
               Vulnerable. Hurt. Lonely. Sort of happy. Getting more confident—no—
               please write gaining confidence. Considerate.
               Inquiry: (*Vulnerable?*) I can easily be hurt. (*Hurt?*) Can't say more.
               (*Lonely?*) I'm suffering from a lack of caring. I'm not cared about the
               way I'd like to be. (*Considerate?*) Care about others' feelings.
  Therapist   I can't describe her because I don't know her. Seems to care about me.
               That's it.

One year
  Mother   I don't want to do this . . . means well. Tries hard to be understanding.
               Overprotective. Suspicious. Alone. Insomniac. No, don't write that
               please. Cross it out. That's it. Oh yeah, curly hair, bleached. Tweezed
               eyebrows. Bad skin.
               Inquiry: (*Means well?*) Good intentions. (*Understanding?*) Self-
               explanatory. But has little conception of what my problems really are.
               (*Overprotective?*) Restricting of freedom. (*Suspicious?*) Untrusting.
               (*Alone?*) Doesn't really confide in anybody, I don't think.
  Father   Understanding. Sympathetic. Intelligent, but naive. Never really did
               what he wanted to do with his life. Friendly. Tries very hard to be
               strong. Never shows his weaknesses. Trusting. A chain smoker.
               Inquiry: (*Understanding?*) Self-explanatory. Sympathizes with my
               problems. (*Intelligent but naive?*) Never knew what was going on with
               me. Takes him a long time to catch on. (*Friendly?*) Gets along with
               others well. (*Trusting?*) Will believe you if given no reason for doubt.

Exhibit 8.1 *Continued*

Self	Depressed, suspicious, alone, manipulative, musical, artistic, sensitive, hopeless. Drug abuser, sympathetic. Can be friendly. Opinionated, withdrawn, angry, chain smoker. Can be humorous. That's it. Inquiry: (*Depressed?*) I don't enjoy life. (*Suspicious?*) Don't trust people easily. (*Sensitive?*) I take things personally. (*Hopeless?*) I'm a failure. I'll never make it. Doomed to be depressed. (*Sympathetic?*) Self-explanatory. (*Opinionated?*) I form my own opinions. (*Withdrawn?*) Keep to myself. (*Angry?*) Lots of hidden rage. Someday it will come out.
Therapist	I don't know her. I won't do it. I don't like her. Unaware, without knowing it. Has too much faith in me. (Refused inquiry.)

Eighteen months (discharge)

Mother	She's sweet, caring, opinionated. She tries hard, works hard. Sometimes overbearing. She's about 5'5", say 120 pounds, curly hair, not much up on top, sort of flat chested. Stubborn. (Inquiry): (*Overbearing?*) Sometimes she's just too much for me—all these qualities are too much for me. She doesn't like to give in.
Father	Funny, caring, good natured. Generous with me. Tries to be understanding. Can't keep a secret very well. About 5'9", 185 pounds. A little . . . chubby. Balding. A well-meaning person. Happily married at present. Inquiry: (*Happily married at present?*) Real happily married. He has a big mouth. That's all.
Self	Lonely, insecure. Hiding behind a façade. Has common sense. Abnormal opinions. One of my abnormal opinions is that people who want to kill themselves should be allowed to kill themselves—and I wasn't referring to myself either. Mature—can be mature—haven't really acted it during the psych testing. I sort of fooled around. Should have more confidence.
Therapist	I'm trying to think of a word. Tactful in approaching subjects. That wasn't the word I was thinking of—not blunt—can say things in a better fashion. She can put things in a better way that doesn't sound so intimidating or so cruel. She's sweet, generous and has high morals. She's a nice person. Has high standards.

all 40 patients in that the degree of change in the structure and content of object representation of self and significant others over treatment paralleled independent assessment of therapeutic progress. In addition to these quantitative findings, we also conducted qualitative analyses of A.'s descriptions of self and her significant others.

QUALITATIVE ANALYSIS. At admission, A. described her mother in negative and dysphoric terms. In marked contrast, she characterized her father as having positive qualities. Because these features of her father were also relational in tone, they suggested that, at least on a manifest level, A. viewed her relationship with her father as considerably more nurturant than that with

Table 8.1 Scores of Patient A. on Structural and Content Dimensions of
Descriptions of Self and Significant Others at Admission and Discharge

Dimension	Admission	Discharge (18 months)
Global Adjustment Scale	22	43
Structural dimensions		
Conceptual level		
Mother	7	5
Father	5	6
Therapist	7	7
Self	3	7
Differentiation–relatedness		
Mother	4	6
Father	4	7
Therapist	6	8
Self	5	7
Scorable attributes		
Mother	3	10
Father	7	9
Therapist	8	8
Length		
Mother	1	1
Father	1	1
Therapist	1	1
Self	1	3
Content dimensions		
Benevolent Factor		
Mother	2.00	4.50
Father	6.00	5.50
Therapist	6.00	5.33
Punitive Factor		
Mother	1.00	3.00
Father	1.00	2.00
Therapist	1.00	1.50
Ambivalence		
Mother	1.00	3.00
Father	1.00	2.00
Therapist	1.00	1.00

her mother. Although the representations of mother and father were split into
all bad and all good, this polarization also indicated a basic differentiation and
organization in A.'s thought processes.

A.'s self-description at admission, while basically negative in tone, contained perplexing polarities that suggested a beginning recognition of contradictory aspects of herself and a realization that her self-concept was highly
dependent on her affective state. Although her sensitivity to feelings of expo-

sure, shame, and grandiosity were suggestive of a narcissistic disturbance, as well as consistent with her self-critical, paranoid, introjective orientation, her recognition of some of the antecedents of her self-variability suggested that she might be capable of developing more subtle differentiations. In contrast to her polarized description of her parents, her self-description involved a higher level of differentiation. Both positive and negative images were present, as was recognition that both sets of qualities needed integration for her to understand herself. Her introspectiveness and her willingness to engage in self-description despite her reservations about the task suggested a potential to become constructively involved in psychotherapy. In general, however, her initial self-description was fragmented and unintegrated. It was organized around rudimentary polarities of attributes that were directly or indirectly stated in the descriptions of her parents.

A. characterized her therapist, like her father, in positive, idealized terms that emphasized the potential for interpersonal relatedness. Notes from the independent treatment review prepared by her therapist after three months of hospitalization described A. as very needy and as desperately hoping that her female therapist would become her wished-for, idealized mother who would care for and nurture her. A. reacted to rescheduled therapy hours and the therapist's absence during a vacation with feelings of rejection and anger. She became psychotic at times in response to these perceived losses.

At six months, A. again characterized her mother in predominantly negative terms, but this time, in contrast to her polarized description at admission, her inclusion of one positive note ("caring") made her account more differentiated. A. included not only this positive aspect but also some relational terms (e.g., "overwhelming"). Although the terms she used reflected high levels of conflict with her mother, they also implied some potential for relatedness and caring.

Parallel changes occurred in A.'s description of her father. At six months, this previously positive description now included a negatively toned quality— a sense of abandonment and neglect because her father had failed to notice her deterioration. Thus, A.'s descriptions of both parents at six months were more differentiated and, in their attempt to integrate seemingly contradictory elements, involved a higher level of complexity.

At six months, A. described herself with adjectives similiar to those she used at admission to describe her mother. These terms suggested an incipient awareness of her undifferentiated maternal identification. Although A.'s self-description continued to comprise generally contradictory images, her sense of self was no longer based solely on the juxtaposition of polarized attributes. Despite her continuing narcissistic vulnerability, she now also expressed a sense of hope and optimism—in her words, a sense of "confidence." This struggle for mastery was also enacted in her instruction to the interviewer to revise her statement "getting more confident" to "gaining confidence." This exchange around A.'s concern about the precision of her verbalizations conveyed, in word and deed, her self-reflectiveness and her increased self-esteem, as well as her ability to form a working relationship with the examiner.

A.'s description of the therapist at six months indicated that her idealized view of the therapist at admission was beginning to change. Positive adjectives at admission were now omitted, and A. now expressed some reservations about her therapist's feelings about her: "[She] seems to care about me."

Dramatic changes occurred in A.'s descriptions at one year—changes that paralleled equally important shifts in the course of her treatment. Now reluctant to describe her mother, A. first characterized her in grotesque terms and then contrasted these negative terms with her mother's good intentions. A. thus revealed both her great need for her mother, whom she regarded as depriving, and her intense fear of her mother's intrusiveness and control. The more positively toned elements in the description reflected A.'s attempt to integrate, or at least modulate, the frightening, grotesque, possibly psychotic image of her mother into a more unified, balanced representation. Through this attempt to integrate diverse facets of her mother, A. indicated that she was increasingly able to see her mother as a separate person, to experience a sense of empathy for her, and to continue to search for care and nurturance from her.

A.'s description of her father at one year also reflected increased differentiation, as A. again attempted to integrate positively and negatively toned attributes—specifically, his capacity for empathy on the one hand and his neglect and denial on the other. As with her description of her mother, A. indicated a beginning capacity to reconcile positive and negative elements of a significant other—to hold a more mature empathic appreciation of her father as a separate person with his own difficulties and limitations. However, this greater empathy for her father's difficulties did not stop her from experiencing hurt and disappointment over his neglect when she was having serious difficulties.

A.'s self-description at one year indicated a movement toward a more differentiated, unified, and coherent sense of self. The self-description contained several alternations between juxtaposed series of first negative and then positive attributes, ending with a more positive conditional note. Although some of the adjectives reflected her continuing identification with her mother's dysphoria, A.'s increased acknowledgement of these painful affects was an important part of her ability to achieve a greater cohesion in her self-description. Her growing capacity for self-reflection, and her attempts to share painful feelings and thoughts with another, paralleled an increased empathic appreciation for her parents. As a consequence of this greater empathy, she now viewed herself as "sensitive" and "sympathetic."

As significant as the changes in these three descriptions were, still more important was the change in A.'s description of her therapist. A's account at one year indicated that the therapeutic relationship had shifted dramatically from the idealization at admission. At this point, she said that she did not like her therapist and refused to describe her. These developments reflected both intense hostile feelings toward the therapist and the consolidation of a markedly negative maternal transference.

Indeed, notes from the independent treatment review at one year confirm that, in the therapist's view, an intense, psychotic, negative maternal transference had gradually developed during the previous six months. At the beginning of this review period, A. continued to put the therapist into the role of the mothering figure. She perceived her therapist's failure to gratify these wishes and the therapist's request that she put these wishes into words as a rejection.

A. became increasingly critical, oppositional, hostile, and sadistic toward the therapist. On one occasion, she had to be restrained to control her homicidal impulses toward the therapist, and for a period of time, A. discontinued her therapy sessions. Prominent attitudes of contempt and devaluation also emerged as defenses against neediness and vulnerability. This transient psychotic transference seemed to have derived in part from the emergence of very painful paranoid ideation that her mother wanted to kill her. Prior to her hospitalization, for example, A. often slept with a knife under her pillow to protect herself from her mother, who wandered around the house at night because of her insomnia. As this material was enacted and worked through in the transference, A. once again began to feel closer to her therapist and, eventually, to her mother.

Thus, significant change, reflective of considerable clinical improvement, was noted in the descriptions obtained at 18 months, at about the time of A.'s discharge from the hospital. The focus of A.'s description of her mother shifted from dysphoric to relatively nonconflictual aspects of their relationship. She described her mother in physical terms, and although she still regarded her mother as emotionally insufficient and limited in nurturance, for the first time A. used a blend of more modulated positive and negative terms that portrayed her mother as having some capacity to provide for her. Thus, at 18 months, A. was beginning to integrate more objective physical features of her mother with a more balanced, qualified, and differentiated understanding of her mother's personality.

A similar constructive change occurred in A.'s more integrated description of father. She now characterized him in positive, but not idealized, terms that also conveyed an increased sense of relatedness. As with her mother, these descriptors were moderated by qualifiers and thus seemed less polarized and absolute. She acknowledged that her father had both limitations and strengths. This description, like that of mother, was also made more objective and realistic by the introduction of his physical characteristics, even though these terms (e.g., "chubby") suggested his own neediness. A.'s use of the word *caring* to describe both her mother and father at this time indicated a greater sense of relatedness to both parents. Furthermore, A.'s move toward a more accepting view of her mother and a more critical view of her father were consistent with the patterns identified in the statistical analysis of the data gathered on all 40 patients in the overall sample discussed earlier (Blatt, Stayner, et al., 1996).

Depressive themes evident in A.'s self-description at one year were continued in her self-description at discharge, but they were less pervasive and intense. Her concern with suicide also indicated her continuing dysphoria, although she was now able to modulate this concern through intellectualization; that is, she could think about suicide as an ethical issue. The primary change at discharge, however, was her increased capacity for self-reflection. A. had finally begun to think about herself in a formal operational mode; she could clearly distinguish between her feelings of loneliness and insecurity and the façade she presented to the world.

In contrast to her refusal to describe her therapist at one year, A. now described her therapist in positive terms—her kindness, ethical standards, emotional sensitivity, and verbal facility. She emphasized the quality of relatedness with the therapist—specifically, that sharing feelings, thoughts, and experiences can enrich personal experiences. It is noteworthy that A's description of her therapist at discharge emphasized the same capacity in the therapist that A. enacted in her self-description at six months when she revised her statement "getting more confident" to the more adroit phrase "gaining confidence" and that A. herself again displayed in this description of the therapist at termination—namely, an ability to select appropriate words or phrases to communicate effectively her thoughts and feelings and especially to moderate destructive feelings and wishes. Similarly, A.'s recognition of her therapist's high moral standards paralleled her own formation of ethical beliefs, specifically about suicide. Thus, in the process of developing as an independent subject, A. unconsciously used aspects of her description of her therapist to talk about herself.

Notes from the treatment review at discharge indicated that, from the end of the first year of treatment to discharge some seven months later, A. became increasingly able not only to recognize that her hostile feelings toward her therapist derived from a long-standing sense of deprivation and rejection experienced in relation to her mother but also to verbalize her feelings of deprivation and anger. As she did, she shifted from a paranoid to a depressive organization, in which persecutory feelings and psychotic ideation were replaced by self-critical thoughts (Blatt, 1974, 1995b; Blatt & Shichman, 1983; M. Klein, 1935, 1940). Acknowledging that her view of her therapist had been distorted during much of treatment, A. was now able to express strong positive feelings for the therapist. A.'s representations of self and significant others thus reflected a clearer sense of differentiation and integration as well as an increased capacity for self-reflection and interpersonal relatedness. Although her expression of affect became increasingly moderate, balanced, and qualified, she remained dysphoric.

A.'s increased expressions of depression seemed to parallel multiple independent indications of improvement. The increase in her verbalization of depression in her self-descriptions, even when this affect was defended by intellectualization, coincided with reports in treatment reviews that she took better care of herself, sometimes attended school, was more connected to others, and appeared less psychotic. The parallel between increased dysphoria and better organized psychosocial functioning suggests that a greater capacity to experience and express self-critical feelings, rather than projecting them, was an important facet of her clinical improvement from a paranoid organization (Blatt, 1995b; Blatt & Bers, 1993; Blatt & Shichman, 1983).

Over the course of treatment, A.'s self-descriptions also increasingly emphasized interpersonal relatedness. She displayed this growing investment in the interpersonal dimensions of her experience through her recognition of the presence of the examiner (at six months), her expressions of loneliness, and her recognition of her consideration for others. Overall, therefore, A.'s descriptions were more integrated and had a greater sense of herself and others as real, substantial, and interrelated.

Of the many interesting changes in A.'s descriptions of significant figures (e.g., the transformation of A.'s psychotic maternal introject and the de-idealization of her father), perhaps most intriguing is the transformation that took place in A.'s descriptions of herself and her therapist, the way she used aspects of the therapist to find and re-appropriate positive aspects of herself. In her self-description at six months, A. manifested, as noted, a concern with verbal precision. Later, through a discussion of the therapist's ability to be tactful and precise in her statements, A.'s termination description of her therapist once again emphasized this concern with verbal skills. Also, A. did more than comment on her therapist's articulateness; she also expressed at termination her own desire and ability to find precise words and phrases to capture her feelings and thoughts about her therapist. Thus, what A. seems to have found most meaningful about her therapist—the therapist's verbal facility and tact in modulating aggressive wishes—is highly congruent with the very things that A. had enacted and verbally demonstrated much earlier in the treatment (at six months) and once again at termination.

This clinical example suggests that some patients may not only internalize the therapeutic activities, attitudes, and functions of the therapist but also actively seek to identify and construct in their therapist qualities that meet some of their own needs, the development of which had previously been thwarted by their psychological disturbances and conflicts. With the resolution of more pathological introjects earlier in the treatment process, some patients may then seek to take as their own qualities they have long sought to acquire for themselves and have now identified, or *constructed*, in their therapist.

Traditional formulations (e.g., McLaughlin, 1981) of the mutative effects of the therapeutic process stress that patients internalize "aspects of the analyst's way of looking at things . . . [which become] a self-analytic function and probably a permanent new intrapsychic representation" (p. 637). Psychological treatment produces change "through the internalization, as new psychic structures, of attitudes and values experienced in the relationship to the analyst" (p. 655) and through the "intrapsychic transformations of old transferences into new and more adaptive transferences, organized around a new object, the . . . analyst" (p. 657) However, if patients project onto the therapist aspects of their distorted and conflict-laden relationships with primary caregivers in the transference, they may also selectively construct aspects of the therapist that are congruent with their own fundamental needs and aspirations and then appropriate, through identification, elements of these constructions. Early life experiences may be expressed not only in transference enactments of pathological relationships but also in functions and experiences that patients hope adaptively to find in the therapist and in the therapeutic relationship and that, consciously and unconsciously, they eventually select to acquire for themselves.

Powerful pathological introjects may be projected onto the therapist early in the treatment process. As these transferences are identified and resolved in the therapeutic relationship, the patient may begin to project more adaptive dimensions onto the therapist. These more adaptive needs and wishes are eventually reappropriated, in a more consolidated way, through identification. Consistent with an action theory model discussed in chapter 7, in the therapeutic relationship patients discover (or construct) qualities of their therapist that they eventually take as their own because they are highly congruent with their own fundamental needs, goals, and aspirations. As Sutherland (1963, pp. 117–118) noted,

> More often . . . [an] inner object acts as a scanning apparatus which seeks
> a potential object in the outer world. . . . The general aim of psychoanalysis
> . . . in terms of an object-relations model . . . [is] initiating and maintaining
> a process whereby repressed relationship-systems are brought back within
> the organizing system of the ego that then can be subjected to learning
> and adaptation.

According to Fairbairn (1952), the ego scans the outer world for potential
objects to fulfill the role of inner objects. The experiences of external objects
are modified to conform to the characteristics of these inner objects (Meissner, 1980).

As Winnicott (1971) proposed, children construct transitional objects by
attributing qualities to the environment that have their origins in the dynamics
of inner life. The transitional object, through the interplay of projection and
introjection, is a link to the caregiving object and the gratification it provided.
This same process occurs in treatment as well. Introjection of and identification
with the therapist are therefore based not only on actual qualities of the
therapist and aspects of the therapeutic process but also on patients' perceptions of the therapist—perceptions that derive in part from the patient's pre-
existing partial introjects. Some patients seek to identify in their therapist
adaptive qualities that they have long sought to acquire from other partially
internalized objects, and then, through identification with experiences of these
qualities in the therapist and in the therapeutic relationship, patients integrate
aspects of their own qualities in a more consolidated way.

This process of adaptive projective identification (Joseph, 1981, 1983) con-
solidates, at a higher developmental level, basic adaptive qualities and capacities that the patient has long sought but has been unable to sustain because
of distorting pathological introjects. Thus, patients are active agents who seek
in the therapeutic relationship to construct and identify with personally meaningful and functionally significant aspects of the therapist; aspects that they
must obtain from someone else so that they can more fully provide these
functions for themselves. Once these functions are experienced within the
therapeutic relationship, patients can begin to make them their own and eventually become less reliant on others to provide them (Blatt & Behrends, 1987).
This complex process of externalization and internalization (projective identification), prompted by the acknowledgment and acceptance of the object's separateness and the recognition of the eventual loss of the object (Blatt & Behrends,
1987), results in more integrated psychic structure formation (Meissner, 1980).

In their efforts to understand the mutative forces in the therapeutic process, therapists and investigators often focus on aspects of the therapist's
activities, characteristics, and technique and tend to ignore important dimensions that patients bring to the treatment process. Therapists often assume
that patients seek to appropriate aspects of the treatment in which they take
pride: their therapeutic attitudes, activities, and skills; their interpretations;
and aspects of the caring therapeutic relationship. However, in their pride
and preoccupation with their therapeutic skills, therapists may overlook that
patients construct representations of their therapist on the basis of projections
not only of previous maladaptive, unattuned, relational experiences (i.e., infan-

tile needs) but also of more adaptive desires, goals, aspirations, and capacities. Because of their relative therapeutic neutrality, therapists exist as individuals for their patients in a very special way. Patients project issues onto them in the transference process, and through these projections they come to understand important aspects of their distorted life experiences. However, patients also project onto their therapists more adaptive qualities they are seeking to acquire.

In summary, a relatively simple research procedure of asking patients periodically throughout treatment to describe self and significant others has provided important data that facilitates our understanding of the therapeutic process with seriously disturbed, treatment-resistant, young adults. Detailed examination of the descriptions of mother, father, therapist, and self over long-term intensive treatment of very seriously disturbed adolescents and young adults has enabled me and my colleagues to identify important structural changes (increased articulation, differentiation, and relatedness) in descriptions of self and significant others that closely parallel independent assessment of therapeutic progress. The emergence of a more positive view of the therapist and of the mother, as well as a more negative view of the father, were related to the capacity to gain from the treatment process. These findings suggest that the development of a more constructive relationship with the mother and a greater differentiation from the father may constitute central dynamics of the treatment process, at least with seriously disturbed, treatment-resistant young adults. In a detailed qualitative analysis of the terms a particular patient attributed to various significant figures and to herself over the course of long-term intensive treatment we have also identified a potentially important aspect of the transference relationship and of the treatment process. We found that this patient not only internalized positive qualities of the therapist and the treatment process, but she also identified and constructed qualities within the therapist that she had wanted to make her own. These observations suggest that, through a complex process of positive or adaptive projective identification, some patients may attribute aspects of their own latent adaptive qualities and capacities to their therapists and then, in the course of therapy, come to re-appropriate these functions in a more consolidated and mature fashion.

These qualitative analyses of the descriptions of self and significant others provided by patient A. over the course of treatment enabled us to identify an important mechanism of therapeutic change, suggesting that intensive qualitative analyses of the descriptions provided by other patients may facilitate identification of other mechanisms of therapeutic change.

Therapeutic Change in Anaclitic and Introjective Patients

One of the major obstacles to the development of methodologically sophisticated psychotherapy research has been the assumption of a uniformity or homogeneity among patients—that patients at the start of treatment are more alike than they are different. Many psychotherapy investigators and research methodologists (e.g., Beutler, 1976, 1979; Colby, 1964; Cronbach, 1953) have stressed the need to abandon this myth and to incorporate relevant differences among patients into research designs in order to begin to address more complex questions that evaluate which therapies and therapists are most effective with which types of patients, and in what kind of ways. A major limitation in constructing this more sophisticated research design, however, has been the lack of a comprehensive theoretical framework of personality development and psychopathology that would allow investigators to identify patient characteristics that are relevant to critical aspects of the therapeutic process so that they can be introduced into the research design (Blatt & Felsen, 1993). As Harkness and Lilienfeld (1997) noted, "the last 40 years of individual differences research require the inclusion of personality trait assessment for the construction and implementation of any treatment plan that would lay claim to scientific status" (p. 349).

As Cronbach (e.g., 1953, 1975) noted many years ago, the introduction of patient variables into psychotherapy research designs must be guided by theoretically derived concepts so that investigators are not led into a "hall of mirrors" that can be created by the complexity of the potential interactions. "One can avoid entering this hall of mirrors only by exploring interactions between theoretically meaningful variables" (Beutler, 1991, p. 230). The choice of patient qualities needs to be guided by principles that are theoretically derived and supported by previous exploratory research (Beutler, 1991; Cronbach, 1975; B. Smith & Sechrest, 1991; Snow, 1991) and include dimensions thought to be relevant to the processes that are assumed to underlie psychological change (Beutler, 1991; Smith & Sechrest, 1991; Snow, 1991). The differentiation of anaclitic and introjective depression provides a theoretically grounded, empirically supported conceptual framework for introducing personality variables into psychotherapy research.

Studies of therapeutic change in long-term intensive treatment of inpatients and outpatients indicate that anaclitic and introjective patients respond differently to different types of treatment and change in different dimensions as a consequence of their participation in the treatment process. In the evaluation of long-term, intensive, psychodynamically oriented, inpatient treatment of seriously disturbed, treatment-resistant patients, colleagues and I (e.g., Blatt & Ford, 1994; Blatt, Ford, Berman, Cook, & Meyer, 1988) found that introjective patients had significantly greater overall therapeutic gain than anaclitic patients across multiple independent measures of therapeutic progress (see also Fonagy et al., 1996). Even further, we found that therapeutic change is expressed in different ways in anaclitic and introjective patients: Anaclitic patients change primarily on measures of interpersonal relatedness as assessed in clinical case reports and in psychological test protocols, whereas therapeutic change in introjective patients is expressed primarily in measures of cognitive functioning—changes in intelligence and thought disorder—and in the extent and intensity of neurotic and of psychotic symptoms. Thus, anaclitic and introjective patients change primarily in the dimensions most salient to their personality or character structure (Blatt & Ford, 1994).

Furthermore, anaclitic and introjective patients are differentially responsive to different types of therapeutic interventions. In further analyses of data gathered as part of the Menninger Psychotherapy Research Project (MPRP), which compared long-term supportive–expressive psychotherapy (SEP) and psychoanalysis, I (Blatt, 1992) found that anaclitic patients had significantly greater therapeutic gain in SEP than they did in psychoanalysis, whereas introjective patients had significantly greater therapeutic gain in psychoanalysis than in SEP. Thus, anaclitic and introjective patients are differentially responsive to different forms of treatment and change in different ways—along dimensions that are central in their personality organization.

Outpatient Treatment of Seriously Depressed Patients

Differences in therapeutic outcome and in the nature of the treatment process with patients who are anaclitically and introjectively depressed were also examined in the comparison of four different, brief (16-week) outpatient treatments for major depression. The availability of empirical data from the large-scale, multicenter study, the Treatment of Depression Collaborative Research Program (TDCRP), sponsored by the National Institute of Mental Health (NIMH), provided the opportunity to explore the role of anaclitic and introjective dimensions in the brief outpatient treatment of depression. The TDCRP was a comprehensive, well-designed, carefully conducted, collaborative, randomized clinical trial that evaluated several forms of brief (16-week) outpatient treatment for depression. Two hundred thirty-nine patients were randomly assigned to one of four treatment conditions: (a) cognitive–behavior therapy (CBT); (b) interpersonal therapy (IPT); (c) imipramine plus clinical management (IMI–CM), as a standard reference; and (d) pill–placebo plus clinical management (PLA-CM), as a double-blind control condition.

Patients were nonbipolar, nonpsychotic, seriously depressed outpatients who met research diagnostic criteria for major depressive disorder (Spitzer, Endicott, & Robins, 1978) and had a score of 14 or greater on a modified, 20-item, Hamilton Rating Scale for Depression (HRSD; Hamilton, 1960, 1967). Among patients who began treatment, 70% were female, 38% were definitely endogenous by research diagnostic criteria, and 64% had had one or more prior episodes of major depression. The average age was 35.

Patients in the TDCRP were systematically assessed at intake, at 4-week intervals until termination at 16 weeks, and again at three follow-up evaluations conducted 6, 12, and 18 months after termination. Assessments included an interview and a self-report measure of depression (HRSD [Hamilton, 1960, 1967] and Beck Depression Inventory [BDI; A. T. Beck & Beamesderfer, 1974], respectively), an interview, and a self-report measure of general clinical functioning (the GAS [Endicott et al., 1976], derived from the Schedule for Affective Disorders and Schizophrenia–Change version (SADS–C; Endicott & Spitzer, 1978), and the Hopkins Symptom Checklist [SCL-90; Derogatis, Lipman, & Covi, 1973], respectively), and an interview assessment of social adjustment (Social Adjustment Scale [SAS]; M. M. Weissman & Paykel, 1974). In addition, patients, therapists, and independent clinical evaluators rated various aspects of therapeutic progress during treatment, at termination, and at the three follow-up assessments (therapists did not participate in the follow-up assessments). Prior analyses of the TDCRP data (e.g., Elkin et al., 1989) indicated some differences in therapeutic outcome at termination among these brief treatments for depression: IMI–CM and IPT were more effective than CBT and PLA–CM, but primarily with patients who were more severely depressed. As an aside, it is important to add that, despite the frequent claim of the efficacy of the medication condition in the TDCRP (Elkin et al., 1989, Elkin, 1994; D. F. Klein & Ross, 1993), our analyses of data from the three follow-up assessments indicate that patients in the two psychotherapy conditions—CBT and IPT—reported that their treatment had a significantly greater positive effect on their life adjustment in a number of areas than did patients in the medication condition (Blatt, Zuroff, Bondi, & Sanislow, 2000). Further analyses indicate that this report of better life adjustment, what we have come to call *enhanced adaptive capacity*, six months after termination significantly reduced the subsequent vulnerability of these patients to stressful life events during the remainder of the follow-up period (Zuroff et al., 2000).

These findings not only demonstrate the constructive long-term effect of brief psychotherapy as compared to medication in the treatment of major depressive disorders, but they suggest that the frequently observed "Dodo bird effect" (Luborsky et al., 2002), in which very few differences are usually found between different types of therapeutic interventions, may be a function of the frequent focus on the reduction of manifest symptoms as the primary, if not exclusive, measure of therapeutic gain. Symptom reduction may be a ubiquitous effect that can occur to some degree in many supportive relationships. Thus, these findings of treatment differences in the TDCRP suggest that differences among treatments, and the value of psychotherapy, may become apparent primarily in measures that go beyond the assessment of symptomatic improvement to evaluate reduction in vulnerability that would facilitate the patient's ability to cope more effectively with life stresses (Blatt, Shahar, & Zuroff, 2002).

Though brief treatment can lead to significant reduction in symptoms at termination, Shea et al. (1992), in an analysis of the follow-up assessments at 6, 12, and 19 months after termination in the TDCRP, found that only approximately 20% of the patients met criteria for recovery without relapse (see also Blatt et al., 2000). Although a supportive relationship in brief treatment, as well as in post-treatment maintenance sessions (e.g., Jarrett et al.,1998), may temporarily ameliorate symptoms, particularly in dependent patients, the high rate of relapse in short-term treatment has begun to shift attention back to the value of long-term treatment (e.g., Seligman, 1995). Even further, although substantial symptom reduction can occur in brief treatment, findings indicate that short-term psychotherapy or medication do not reduce patients' level of dependency and self-criticism (Bagby, Schuller, et al., 1994; Franche & Dobson, 1992; Moore & Blackburn, 1996; Reda, Carpiniello, Secchiariolli, & Blanco, 1985; Zuroff, et al., 2000), two dimensions that create vulnerability to depression.

To introduce the anaclitic–introjective distinction into the analyses of the TDCRP data, an experienced judge reviewed the intake clinical evaluations but found that these initial clinical case reports contained primarily descriptions of the patients' neurovegetative symptoms and lacked sufficient detail about aspects of the patients' lives to allow the judge to discriminate reliably between anaclitic and introjective patients. Fortunately, the Dysfunctional Attitudes Scale (DAS; A. N. Weissman & Beck, 1978) had been included in the TDCRP protocol, primarily to assess the effects of treatment on dysfunctional cognitions. Several previous studies (e.g., Cane, Olinger, Gotlib, & Kuiper, 1986; Oliver & Baumgart, 1985), as well analyses of the DAS in the TDCRP (Imber et al., 1990), had indicated that the DAS is composed of two primary factors: (a) Need for Approval or dependency and (b) Perfectionism or self-criticism. As discussed in chapter 3, prior research (e.g., Pilon, 1987; Blaney & Kutcher, 1991) indicated that the DAS Need for Approval factor assesses primarily the relatedness or anaclitic dimension, whereas the DAS Perfectionism factor assesses primarily the self-definitional or introjective dimension. Thus, the pretreatment DAS provided the basis for introducing differences among patients on the anaclitic and introjective dimensions into the analyses of data from the TDCRP.

Although introjective patients made significant greater therapeutic change than did anaclitic patients in long-term, intensive inpatient treatment in the analysis of data from the Austen Riggs Center (Blatt & Ford, 1994), analyses of data from the TDCRP indicated that introjective outpatients had significant impairment in their therapeutic response in brief treatments (16 weeks) for depression, including medication as well as two forms of brief manual directed psychotherapy (CBT and IPT) (Blatt, Quinlan, et al., 1995). Further analyses of data from the TDCRP indicate that introjective personality traits (i.e., perfectionism) significantly interfered with therapeutic progress in approximately two thirds of the patients and that this interference occurred primarily in the latter half of the treatment process (Blatt, Zuroff, et al., 1998). These findings suggest that introjective patients may respond negatively to the imposition of an arbitrary termination date because they are dissatisfied with their progress and because the impeding arbitrary termination date threatened their need for autonomy and control (Blatt, Zuroff, et al., 1998). Further analyses of the TDCRP data indicated that introjective personality traits interfered with therapeutic progress by limiting patients' capacity to maintain a therapeutic alliance (Zuroff et al., 2000; see also Rector, Zuroff, & Segal, 1999) as well as an external social network.

Pretreatment perfectionism, as assessed on the DAS, significantly (ps = .032–.004) predicted negative outcome, as assessed by all five primary measures of clinical change in the TDCRP (HRSD, BDI, GAS, SAS, and SCL-90), across all four treatment groups (Blatt, Quinlan, Pilkonis, & Shea, 1995). Factor analysis of the residualized gain scores of these five outcome measures at termination revealed that these measures all loaded substantially ($p > .79$) on a common factor with an eigenvalue of 3.78, accounting for 75.6% of the variance (Blatt, Zuroff, Quinlan, & Pilkonis, 1996). Pretreatment Perfectionism had a highly significant ($p < .001$) negative relationship to this composite residualized gain score at termination. Need for Approval, in contrast, had a marginal, but consistently positive, relationship to treatment outcome at termination as measured by each of these five outcome measures and by the composite outcome measure ($p = .114$). Pretreatment Perfectionism also had a significant negative relationship to outcome ratings made by therapists, independent clinical evaluators, and the patients at termination (Blatt, 1999b).

This negative impact of perfectionism on therapeutic progress, independent of type of treatment, persisted even as late as the last follow-up assessment, 18 months after termination. Pretreatment Perfectionism correlated significantly with less symptom reduction and with follow-up ratings by the clinical evaluators of poorer clinical condition and a need for further treatment. Pretreatment Perfectionism also correlated significantly with ratings by patients of dissatisfaction with treatment and a reduced adaptive capacity (i.e., enhanced adaptive capacity). Thus, at follow-up, perfectionistic patients gave poorer ratings of their current condition and said that they experienced significantly less therapeutic change and that treatment had less impact on their general life adjustment (i.e., less satisfying relationships, fewer coping skills, less ability to recognize the symptoms of depression, less change in depressive attitudes).

It is important to note not only that patients with elevated pretreatment Perfectionism felt subjectively less satisfied with treatment but also that ratings by the therapists and clinical evaluators consistently indicated that greater pretreatment Perfectionism was related to significantly less improvement at termination and at the 18-month follow-up. Thus, introjective personality traits significantly interfere with patients' capacity to benefit from short-term treatment, whether the treatment involved pharmacotherapy (IMI–CM), psychotherapy (CBT or IPT), or placebo (Blatt, Quinlan, et al., 1995; Blatt, Zuroff, et al., 1996). The critical judgmental introjects and the negative cognitions of self and other of highly perfectionistic patients appear to limit markedly the effectiveness of all four brief treatment interventions in this extensive and carefully designed investigation. Conversely, patients with relatively lower levels of perfectionism were relatively responsive to all four forms of brief treatment for depression, including clinical management in conjunction with a pharmacologically inactive placebo (PLA–CM). These findings are consistent in part with a recent report by Rector, Bagby, Segal, Joffe, and Leu (2000) that although Depressive Experiences Questionnaire Self-Criticism scores did not predict response to pharmacotherapy, they were significantly associated with a poor response to cognitive therapy.

The extensive data gathered as part of the NIMH TDCRP also provided an opportunity for colleagues and me to explore some of the dynamics of brief treatment and when and how a patient's personality characteristics significantly influence the therapeutic process. Therapeutic gain in the TDCRP had been assessed every four weeks until termination, and thus it was possible to evaluate when in the treatment process pretreatment Perfectionism began to disrupt therapeutic outcome. Perfectionism disrupted therapeutic progress primarily in the last half of the treatment process. Until mid-treatment, at the eighth week, no significant differences were found in therapeutic gain between patients with different levels of perfectionism. Beginning at mid-treatment, however, only patients in the lower third of the distribution of perfectionism continued to make significant progress. Thus, when two thirds of the patients in this study, those with higher levels of perfectionism, began to confront the end of treatment, they seem to have experienced a sense of personal failure, dissatisfaction, and disillusionment with treatment (Blatt, Zuroff, et al., 1998). Even further, perfectionistic (introjective) individuals are very concerned about maintaining control and preserving their autonomy (Blatt, 1995a; Blatt & Shichman, 1983). Thus, one of the factors that may have disrupted the therapeutic progress of the more perfectionistic (introjective) patients in the TDCRP may have been the unilateral, external imposition of an arbitrary, "abrupt" (Elkin, 1994, p. 134) termination date.

Not only were colleagues and I able to identify when introjective personality qualities began to disrupt therapeutic progress, but we were also able to discover some of the mechanisms though which this disruption occurred. Krupnick et al. (1996) used a modified form of the Vanderbilt Therapeutic Alliance Scale (Hartley & Strupp, 1983) to assess the contributions of patient and therapist to the establishment of an effective therapeutic alliance in the TDCRP. Judges rated videotapes of the 3rd, 9th, and 15th treatment sessions. Krupnick et al. found that the Vanderbilt Therapeutic Alliance Scale comprised two factors: (a) a *patient factor,* which assessed the extent to which the patient was open and honest with the therapist; agreed with the therapist about tasks, goals, and responsibilities; and was actively engaged in the therapeutic work, and (b) a *therapist factor*, which assessed the extent to which the therapist committed himself and his skills to helping the patient and the degree to which he acknowledged the validity of the patient's thoughts and feelings. They found that the patient's overall contribution to the therapeutic alliance, but not that of the therapist, significantly predicted treatment outcome. Therapeutic outcome across treatment groups was predicted by the degree to which the patient became increasingly involved in the treatment process (Krupnick et al., 1996; Zuroff et al., 2000).

Using these ratings of the therapeutic alliance made by Krupnick et al. (1996), we (Zuroff et al., 2000) explored the impact of the patient's pretreatment perfectionism on the development of the therapeutic alliance and found that perfectionism significantly interfered with the patient's capacity to develop a therapeutic alliance over the course of treatment. Thus, not only were we able to identify when in the treatment process perfectionism disrupts therapeutic progress, but we were also able to identify how introjective personality traits impeded the patient's capacity to gain from the brief treatment of depression. Patients usually became increasingly involved in a constructive collaborative relationship with their therapist, but this increased involvement in the therapeutic relationship is moderated by the patient's pretreatment level of perfectionism. Increases in the therapeutic alliance, beginning at mid-treatment, were significantly less, or absent, in patients at higher levels of perfectionism. Perfectionistic individuals generally have limited capacities for developing open, collaborative relationships (Zuroff & Fitzpatrick, 1995), and therefore it may take a more extended period of time for them to establish an effective therapeutic alliance.

The effects of pretreatment perfectionism on therapeutic outcome are mediated not only by the quality of the therapeutic alliance but also by the extent to which patients are able to establish and maintain external social support during treatment and the follow-up period (Shahar, Blatt, Zuroff, Kuperminc, & Sotsky et al., in press). Thus, the disruptive effects of pretreatment perfectionism on the treatment process are primarily the consequence of perfectionism's disruption of interpersonal relatedness, both in the treatment process and in interpersonal relationships more generally. These findings of the parallel effects of pretreatment perfectionism on interpersonal relationships both within and external to the treatment process offer some support for the psychoanalytic concept of transference, in which it is assumed that the nature of the interpersonal process observed in the treatment process reflects the nature of interpersonal relations more generally.

We (Blatt, Zuroff, et al., 1996) also tried to identify aspects of the treatment process that mitigate the destructive effects of perfectionism and facilitate treatment outcome with these more difficult, highly perfectionistic patients. The TDCRP research team, using the Barrett-Lennard Relationship Inventory (B-L RI; Barrett-Lennard, 1962, 1986), asked patients at the end of the second treatment session to rate the degree to which they thought their therapist was empathic and caring. The B-L RI includes subscales that assess patients' perception of the therapist's empathic understanding, level of positive regard, and congruence—therapist qualities that Rogers (1957) believed were the "necessary and sufficient conditions" for therapeutic change. Prior studies (e.g., Barrett-Lennard, 1986; Gurman, 1977a, 1977b) demonstrate that the B-L RI was significantly related to treatment outcome at termination.

Patients' perceptions of their therapists after the second treatment hour was independent of the patients' pretreatment levels of perfectionism ($r = -.09$) and of the particular treatment group to which they had been randomly assigned, but it contributed significantly to the prediction of therapeutic gain. The contribution of the patient's early perception of the therapist to the prediction of treatment outcome, although significant, was, however, less than the contribution of pretreatment perfectionism to therapeutic progress.

Exploratory analyses of the interaction between level of perfectionism and the patient's perceptions of the therapist after the second treatment session revealed a significant quadratic interaction in predicting therapeutic outcome. At both high and low levels of perfectionism, therapeutic outcome was only marginally ($p < .15$ and $p < .10$, respectively) related to the patient's perception of the therapist as empathic and caring. Patients with high perfectionism had significantly less therapeutic gain in the brief treatment for depression, and patients with low perfectionism had significantly greater therapeutic gain, independent of the level at which they perceived their therapists as warm and supportive. A positive perception of the therapist appears to be less crucial for patients with low perfectionism, because their difficulties do not revolve around negative representations of self and other. Although patients with high perfectionism scores were able, early in the treatment process, to perceive their therapist as warm and supportive, they nevertheless were relatively less able to benefit from brief treatment (Blatt, Zuroff, et al., 1996). The intensely negative mental representations of self and others that characterize introjective perfectionistic patients appear to make it difficult for them to enter easily into a trusting therapeutic relationship even though they may initially have a positive view of their therapist. However, at the middle level of perfectionism, the patient's early view of the therapist had a highly significant ($p < .001$) impact on treatment outcome. At the middle level of perfectionism, an early view of the therapist as empathic and caring significantly reduced the disruptive effects of perfectionism on treatment outcome, whereas a negative view of the therapist significantly compounded the disruptive effects of perfectionism (Blatt, Zuroff, et al., 1996). Thus, at the middle level, the effect of perfectionism on treatment outcome is significantly contingent on the degree to which the patient initially perceives the therapist as empathic and caring.

In summary, our analyses of data from the extensive, randomized clinical trial evaluating the brief treatment of depression in the NIMH-sponsored TDCRP indicate that therapeutic outcome is significantly influenced by the quality of the therapeutic relationships and by pretreatment characteristics of the patient—by pretreatment level of perfectionism or self-criticism, that is, by introjective personality traits—independent of the type of treatment provided. This negative effect of pretreatment perfectionism on outcome occurs primarily in the second half of the treatment process, as patients approach termination. This impact occurs in large part because of interference with patients' capacity to continue to be involved in interpersonal relationships both in the therapeutic alliance, as well as external to the treatment process, particularly as the arbitrary termination date approaches. This negative impact of perfectionism on treatment outcome is significantly reduced, but only at middle levels of perfectionism, if the patient initially perceives the therapist as empathic and caring.

Although colleagues and I now have an increased understanding of the dynamics of the impact of perfectionism and self-criticism on brief treatment for depression, and some appreciation of the processes that can lead to depression and to suicide (as discussed in several prior chapters), I need to address more fully what might constitute effective treatment for highly perfectionistic, self-critical individuals. Research findings about the early life experiences of highly self-critical, perfectionistic, introjective individuals suggest that one of the primary tasks in treatment is to enable these patients to begin to relinquish aspects of their identification with harsh, judgmental, parental figures who have set excessively high standards. Treatment should also help these patients establish new or revised identifications so that they can begin to define themselves independent of their highly critical and demanding introjects while maintaining contact with the more benign and nurturant dimensions of their parental introjects.

The negative impact of perfectionism on the quality of social relationships both within and outside of the treatment process is consistent with theoretical formulations (Blatt, 1974, 1998) and extensive empirical investigations. Introjective psychopathology involves vulnerable self-esteem, especially a tendency toward hostile and harsh self-criticism, and a tendency to remain relatively distant and isolated from intimate interactions with others. As I discussed in chapters 5 and 7, self-critical individuals are distrustful and dissatisfied in their relationships and are avoidant and non-self-disclosing in close relationships (e.g., Zuroff & Fitzpatrick, 1995). Thus, it is not surprising that highly self-critical, perfectionistic patients have difficulty benefiting from brief, manual-directed treatment.

Long-Term Treatment of Anaclitic and Introjective Patients

In contrast to the indications that highly self-critical, perfectionist patients were significantly less responsive than other patients to several standard forms of brief pharmacological and psychological outpatient treatment for depression in the TDCRP, research findings from several investigations of long-term, intensive, psychodynamically oriented therapy with outpatients (Blatt, 1992) and with more seriously disturbed inpatients (Blatt & Ford, 1994; Blatt, Ford, et al., 1988) indicate that patients who are preoccupied with issues of self-definition, self-control, and self-worth (introjective patients) demonstrated significantly greater therapeutic gain than did anaclitic patients, who are preoccupied with issues of interpersonal relatedness. These data, as well as our clinical experiences with patient A., discussed earlier, indicate that seriously disturbed individuals who are excessively concerned about issues of self-definition and self-worth usually have the intellectual resources and self-reflective capacities necessary to eventually engage constructively in and benefit from extensive, long-term, intensive treatment.

Seriously disturbed, treatment-resistant, anaclitic and introjective patients responded differently to intensive psychodynamically oriented treatment in an open, inpatient treatment facility at the Austen Riggs Center in Stockbridge, MA. After an average of 15 months of long-term intensive, inpatient treatment that included at least four times weekly dynamically oriented psychotherapy, seriously disturbed introjective patients consistently demonstrated significantly greater improvement than did anaclitic patients in multiple independent assessments using various methods of evaluation (Blatt & Ford, 1994; Blatt, Ford, et al., 1988). In addition, a reanalysis of the MPRP data indicated that reliably identified introjective outpatients made significantly greater therapeutic gain in five times weekly psychoanalysis than in long-term, twice-weekly supportive–expressive psychotherapy (Blatt, 1992). The therapeutic gain of introjective patients in psychoanalysis was also significantly greater than that of anaclitic patients also treated in psychoanalysis.

The impaired response of introjective patients to the short-term treatments for depression evaluated in the TDCRP stands in contrast to the more positive response of introjective patients in the long-term, intensive treatment of seriously disturbed inpatients at the Austen Riggs Center and in the long-term, intensive, psychoanalytic treatment of outpatients in the MPRP. These findings suggest that introjective self-critical patients may require considerably longer treatment in order for them to resolve some of the negative, punitive, judgmental introjects and to begin to establish a therapeutic alliance and internalize more constructive schemas of self and significant others. A substantial period of time apparently is required for highly perfectionistic, introjective patients to allow themselves to enter into a therapeutic relationship and to begin to change deeply entrenched negative mental representations of self and others. Although perfectionistic, highly self-critical, introjective individuals, who have intense investment in issues of self-definition, self-control, and self-worth, were relatively unresponsive to a number of different forms of short-term treatment, including medication (i.e., imipramine), they were quite responsive to long-term, intensive, psychodynamically oriented therapy in both outpatient and inpatient settings.

The findings of these studies—the comparison of outpatients in two different treatments in the MPRP and the therapeutic response of two types of seriously disturbed, treatment-resistant, inpatients in long-term, intensive treatment at the Austen Riggs Center—consistent with the findings from the brief treatment of depression in the TDCRP, indicate that aspects of patients' personality determine the nature of therapeutic change and the response to different therapeutic modalities. Patients come to treatment with different types of problems, different character styles, and different needs, and they respond in different ways to different types of therapeutic intervention.

The congruence between patient and therapist, the degree to which the therapist can appreciate and be responsive to the apprehensions of the patient about dependability and support or about avoiding feelings of intimacy and closeness, are of greater potential consequence than differences among various forms of treatment. Anaclitic patients are likely to be more responsive initially to more supportive aspects of the treatment in which the therapist is more active, directive, and supportive. Introjective patients are likely to be more responsive initially to insight-oriented treatment that enables the introjective patient to maintain, at least initially, a more detached relationship with the therapist. The qualities of the therapist and of the patient, and their capacity to develop a therapeutic alliance, have a major impact on the treatment process. These findings indicate that research should be directed toward investigating aspects of the patient–therapist interaction that contribute to therapeutic progress rather than comparing the efficacy of different forms of treatments for the reduction of focal symptoms. Also, psychotherapy researchers should not only evaluate symptom reduction but also explore the reduction of long-term vulnerabilities to depression, such as patient qualities of dependency and perfectionism, that influence onset and relapse. Rather than comparing the relative efficacy and effectiveness of particular forms of treatment for a focal symptom, researchers need to address issues of the etiology and course of depression as well as more differentiated questions about the psychotherapeutic process, such as what kind of treatments are most effective for what kinds of patients, and the kinds of therapeutic gain to which different treatments lead (Blatt, Shahar, & Zuroff, 2002). Furthermore, it is important that psychotherapy researchers be aware of the impact of the research procedures on different types of patients. Repeated assessment evaluations may create particular difficulties for introjective patients because of their intense self-scrutiny and negative self-evaluation and thus may have a disruptive impact on the treatment process (Blatt, Shahar, & Zuroff, 2002). Also, externally imposed treatment constraints, such as random assignment to a treatment group and the imposition of an arbitrary termination date, not only alter the basic treatment condition (Seligman, 1995) but also, as our analyses of the TDCRP data suggest, may have particular meaning for, and impact on, different types of patients. These considerations suggest the need to conduct both naturalistic studies of the treatment process, the so-called *effectiveness* type of research (Seligman, 1995), as well as more traditional research designs, such as randomized clinical trials. Studies using more naturalistic designs or randomized clinical trials need to go beyond the study of treatment outcome and address the mechanisms or processes that contribute to therapeutic change.

Processes of Therapeutic Change

A colleague and I (Blatt & Behrends, 1987) drew a parallel between normal development and change in the therapeutic process and attempted to specify the mechanisms that lead to therapeutic progress. We discussed the role of internalization in the therapeutic process in long-term, intensive treatment and how therapeutic change, like normal psychological development, involves the development of increasingly differentiated and integrated representations of self and other. Through recognizing, experiencing, and understanding distorted modes of interpersonal relatedness in the therapeutic relationship, the therapeutic process can lead patients to relinquish maladaptive schemas of self and others and to establish increasingly mature self- and object representations and more adaptive patterns of interpersonal relatedness. We discussed revisions of these schemas of self and others in the therapeutic process as occurring through a series of gratifying involvements, at a succession of developmental levels, each of which is resolved by an experienced incompatibility, externally and/or internally induced, such that the individual no longer needs or wants to depend on the other for a particular gratifying involvement, because that function has now been appropriated (internalized) by the individual and integrated within his or her own representational repertoire. Thus, it is important to recall that, as discussed earlier in this chapter, the psychotic maternal transference in patient A. at midtreatment (at about one year) emerged when her therapist requested that she discuss, rather than enact, her intense longings for maternal care. This experienced incompatibility contributed to the emergence in the transference of an intense paranoid maternal transference that was central in A.'s difficulties. It is equally noteworthy that the more constructive identification with her therapist that appeared as a consolidation of therapeutic progress occurred at another point of experienced incompatibility: as A. approached termination of treatment and discharge from the hospital. These experienced incompatibilities resulted in therapeutic progress—to the emergence of a central conflictual issue with the mother in midtreatment and to the consolidation at termination of more differentiated, articulated, and integrated representations of self and significant others and to a constructive and adaptive identification with her therapist. However, it is important to stress that these experienced incompatibilities that resulted in therapeutic progress occurred in the context of a gratifying involvement with the therapist—within the context of a well-established therapeutic alliance.

Psychotherapy consists of two primary mutative dimensions: (a) the therapeutic relationship and (b) the interpretative process leading to insight. Therapists offer both support (the therapeutic relationship) and interpretation, and both dimensions are vital parts of the therapeutic process (Blatt & Behrends, 1987). However, different types of patients may be more responsive, at least initially, to one of these dimensions than to the other. The therapist's empathic and supportive interventions facilitate the early phases of the treatment process, especially with anaclitic patients, who are usually more attentive and responsive to aspects of the interpersonal or relational dimensions of the treatment process—the dependability and support of the therapeutic relationship. Introjective patients, in contrast, are more responsive to the interpretative aspects of the treatment process. This aspect of the treatment process is more congruent with the intellectualized cognitive style of introjective patients who initially are more comfortable with an objective, task-oriented, detached therapeutic relationship. More personal feelings about the therapist usually provoke concerns about losing control and power, possibly even precipitating feelings of distrust and suspicion. Although more alienated or distant introjective patients have the self-reflective capacities to potentially gain from long-term intensive therapy, the therapeutic process has to be more extended in order for them to begin to allow themselves to feel safe and secure with the therapist and to establish a meaningful therapeutic alliance based on feelings of trust and mutuality.

When anaclitic patients feel secure in the therapeutic relationship and are no longer threatened by apprehension of abandonment and loneliness, they can begin to consider issues of self-definition. When they feel secure in the relationship, anaclitic (dependent) patients can begin to assert a sense of agency. Thus, for example, they no longer simply seek to be loved but can begin to assert themselves and to select the type of person with whom they wish to share feelings of love and intimacy. Likewise, as introjective (self-critical) individuals begin to feel secure in their self-definition and are no longer threatened by interpersonal closeness, they can begin to allow themselves to get close to and to trust others. Thus, as anaclitic and introjective patients make therapeutic progress and resolve to some degree their respective vulnerabilities to loss and abandonment, or to impaired feelings of self-definition and self-worth, respectively, themes from the other developmental line—themes of self-definition or relatedness—begin to emerge in the treatment process. Thus, in the later stages of the treatment process, with both anaclitic and introjective patients, a normal developmental dialectic interaction between the development of relatedness and of self-definition begins to emerge in the treatment process in the "reactivation of a previously disrupted developmental process" (Blatt & Shichman, 1983, p. 249). The reactivation of this normal developmental process has its own developmental trajectory, which can now enhance the therapeutic process and eventually lead to the development of more differentiated and integrated levels of interpersonal relatedness and self-definition (see also Blatt & Blass, 1990, 1996).

Thus, in this way, the therapeutic process is different for anaclitic and introjective patients. Interpersonally oriented anaclitic patients focus initially in the therapeutic process on their difficulty managing disrupted relationships (e.g., loss and abandonment) and their fears of relinquishing particular modes of gratifying involvement. As indicated by the results of the analyses of data from the MPRP (Blatt, 1992), these patients are likely to be more responsive to the supportive and interpersonal dimensions of the therapeutic process. Although the quality of the therapeutic relationship, over a sustained period, may enable anaclitic patients to work through their intense concerns about the dependability of interpersonal relations, eventually they also have to deal with issues of self-definition and find a balance between their interpersonal needs and the emergence of a sense of self-definition and agency. As also indicated by analyses of data from the MPRP (Blatt, 1992), overly ideational introjective patients, in contrast, appear to be initially more responsive to the interpretative aspects and to the insights gained in treatment than to the relational aspects of the therapeutic process. As introjective patients become more secure in their self-definition and feelings of self-worth, they eventually must also deal with issues of interpersonal relatedness and find a balance between their concerns about self-definition and self-worth and their emerging interests in establishing close, intimate, interpersonal relationships, which have been fostered by their experiences in the therapeutic relationship. In this way, the therapeutic process eventually enables both anaclitic and introjective individuals to reinitiate a disrupted dialectical developmental process in which an integrated and coordinated development of self-definition and interpersonal relatedness proceeds, with each dimension developing in its own right as well as synergistically contributing to overall development (Blatt & Shichman, 1983). Thus, the therapeutic process, like normal development, should ultimately lead to the integration of the relatedness and self-definitional developmental lines, with the individual progressing to higher and more mature expressions in both developmental lines (Blatt & Blass, 1990, 1996), resulting in more mature representations of self and significant other. In addition, both anaclitic avoidant and introjective counteractive defenses (e.g., Blatt, 1990a; Blatt & Shichman, 1983) should become more flexible, leading to the development of the capacity for sublimation, in which well-modulated, socially appropriate, and personally meaningful behavior derives from, and in turn contributes to, the further development of a full sense of personal identity and purpose and to the development of mutually satisfying and reciprocal interpersonal relationships (Blatt, 1995b; Blatt & Shichman, 1983).

The eventual goal with both dependent (anaclitic) and self-critical (introjective) patients is to enable them to integrate increasingly mature levels of both relatedness and self-definition. Dependent and self-critical patients may approach this goal from somewhat different directions, as expressed in the different transference and countertransference issues that emerge in the earlier phases of the treatment process. These transferences derive from early life experiences that have become consolidated by means of their frequent repetition in a wide variety of situations throughout the life cycle. The re-enactment of these issues in the treatment context enables the therapist to observe the nature and power of these repetitive distorted modes of interacting and to make interventions that help the patient begin to recognize, understand, and eventually relinquish these maladaptive modes. Issues of unreliable and inconsistent caring experiences usually emerge with patients who are dependently (anaclitically) depressed, whereas patients who are self-critically (introjectively) depressed usually deal with issues of harsh, critical, punitive, intrusive, and overcontrolling early relationships. Colleagues and I, like Bowlby, assume that depression derives from insecure attachments, that dependent depression is primarily associated with anxious–ambivalent insecure attachment, whereas self-critical depression is primarily associated with avoidant, insecure attachment (Blatt & Homann, 1992; Reis & Grenyer, 2002; Zuroff & Fitzpatrick, 1995). Re-experiencing and working through these issues of attachment and separation, of relatedness and self-definition, in long-term intensive treatment facilitates the therapeutic process with both dependent and self-critical patients. The excessive concerns about relatedness in patients with anaclitic depression, in the absence of a sense of autonomy and agency, create a sense of urgent dependency on others; just as excessive autonomy in patients with introjective depression, without the context of intimate relationships, results in experiences of alienation (Bakan, 1966; L. S. Benjamin, 1988; Blatt & Blass, 1990, 1996).

In the therapeutic relationship, anaclitic or dependent patients can begin to develop a more mature sense of interpersonal relatedness, a sense of concern and sharing, leading to the development of the capacity for empathy. Transference issues in therapy with anaclitic patients initially focus on themes of dependability, affection, love, and concern, particularly as provoked by experiences of separation and loss both within and external to the treatment process. The anaclitic patient will seek reassurance that he or she is loved by frequently testing the therapist's concerns for the patient and the dependability of the therapeutic relationship. Experiences of frustration and deprivation, particularly related to separation and loss, will provoke anger and rage. However, these reactions, and the issues and experiences that provoke them, can be worked through in the treatment process. The patient comes to know and tolerate painful affects as well as pleasurable ones. Anxiety and anger, guilt and shame, become signal affects as patients begin to reflect on their feelings rather than avoiding or discharging distressing affects. Thus, the internalization of aspects of the therapeutic relationship also provides the basis through which the patient can begin to develop better affect regulation—increased tolerance for delay and postponed gratification without experiencing intense rage.

Psychopathology of the introjective personality style is organized mainly around issues of self-image involving feelings of worthlessness, guilt, and that one has failed to live up to expectations and standards. Externalizing and counteractive defenses are used to cope with these conflicts, which often are associated with issues of control and autonomy as well as more mature issues of identification and competition. Introjective patients enact these concerns about self-worth in a variety of ways, including exaggerated attempts to compensate for feelings of worthlessness and failure, or aggressive and antisocial acts in response to anger felt toward critical and punitive authority figures, or in self-destructive activity that expresses the intense feelings of worthlessness and the need for punishment for real or imagined transgressions. Some patients, often adolescents, may enact these issues through defiant antisocial behavior, as illustrated in the clinical descriptions in chapter 2, that attempts to deny introjective feelings of depression around issues of self-worth and guilt while simultaneously unconsciously inviting punishment for what are experienced as superego transgressions (e.g., failure and guilt). These conflicts around concerns about self-worth, and the patient's defensive struggles with elements of introjective depression, are the major issues that must be dealt with in the treatment process. The therapist and other significant figures in the environment can become important alternatives for the earlier figures who failed to provide an adequate basis for identification and feelings of self-worth. The therapist and other significant people become an essential part of the therapeutic process as alternate figures with whom the patient can begin to establish meaningful and constructive identifications, which are essential if the patient is to develop a stable and flexible self-definition—a sense of self-worth, an effective moral code, and appropriate and realistic personal standards and aspirations. However, these identifications can take place only in the content of a constructive therapeutic relationship. Thus, the therapeutic process with introjective patients follows the same basic principles as with anaclitic patients: dealing with the pathological introjects, always mindful of the underlying depressive issues deriving from neglect or from intense and pervasive criticism. Again, therapeutic interventions should ultimately lead to the integration of relational and self-definitional issues, with the individual progressing, as in normal development, to more mature expression of both self-definition and interpersonal relatedness (Blatt & Behrends, 1987; Blatt & Blass, 1990, 1996).

In light of our increased appreciation of the differences between the two types of depression and of the role of mental representation in psychological development and in the therapeutic process, I now return, approximately some 30 years later, to reconsider the treatment process with the two prototypic patients presented in chapter 1, who provided the experiences that led to my articulation of the two types of depression and to my appreciation of the central role of mental representations in depression and psychological development.

Helen, as discussed in detail in chapter 1, was a woman with profound anaclitic needs to be held, loved, soothed, and comforted. Her entire regard throughout treatment was her concerns about the quality of her relationships. She vividly described, for example, her anguish at an engagement party of a friend and how troubled she was by seeing a family sharing joyous moments, in contrast to the endless conflict between her parents, even at her wedding. She was so upset by the experience of seeing this joyful family that she abruptly left this party in tears. Her intense reactions to experiences of loss and abandonment were communicated in her reports about her intense reactions to the assassination of President Kennedy in which she could no longer use her contact lenses after learning about his death, even though she took considerable pride in the fact that she had only recently earned the money to purchase these lenses. She remembered vividly being left behind at age 9, when medical professionals rushed her mother to the hospital following the mother's suicide attempt.

Consistent with the research findings discussed above, Helen did not do well in psychoanalysis. She interrupted her treatment abruptly after only nine months of psychoanalytic work, and in those nine months, psychoanalytic work did little to contain her promiscuous acting out as she desperately sought to be held and soothed. Results from our study of long-term, intensive treatment of inpatients at the Austen Riggs Center indicate that anaclitic patients are not as responsive to intensive psychoanalytic interventions as are introjective patients. In addition, my analyses of data in the study of the long-term intensive treatment of outpatients at the Menninger Clinic (MPRP; Blatt, 1992) indicate that anaclitic patients are more responsive in face-to-face supportive–expressive psychotherapy than they are in intensive psychoanalysis. Helen's experiences in psychoanalysis are consistent with these findings and provide us with the opportunity to consider the ways in which psychoanalysis was not the treatment of choice for her as well as to consider whether there were pretreatment indications that psychoanalysis would be inappropriate for her.

A number of indications in the pretreatment assessment of Helen should have alerted me to Helen's potential difficulties in psychoanalysis. She reported that she had married primarily as a way of attempting to break away from what she experienced as a controlling and consuming relationship with her mother, yet she and her husband rented an apartment in direct view of her mother's home. These indications of an instability of her object ties and her diminished capacity for object constancy should have been ominous warnings about her difficulty in establishing separation and individuation as well as her inability to establish adaptive reciprocal interpersonal relationships. She had difficulty achieving an adequate level of separation–individuation from her mother and tried to use her relationship with her husband as an alternative way to separate from her mother. However, she was unable to sustain this separation and had to maintain extensive contact with her mother. Both the contrived method to try to achieve separation–individuation, as well as the failure of these efforts, should have been sufficient to discourage me from beginning psychoanalytic treatment until I had more certain evidence of the stability of Helen's separation–individuation, her level of object constancy, as well as the stability of her object ties.

Likewise, in Helen's treatment, it quickly became apparent that she was unable to tolerate the isolation of the psychoanalytic couch and that she needed more active and direct intervention. Within the first week of the analysis, Helen fell asleep for substantial parts of the analytic sessions and, as I later discovered, she used her eyeglasses as a reflecting surface to keep me in view. In retrospect, Helen should have been seen in face-to-face, supportive–expressive psychotherapy until she had made sufficient progress in her capacity for object representation so she could tolerate the isolation of the psychoanalytic process. At the very least, I should have been much more active in the psychoanalytic hours, providing her with a greater sense of my presence. These retrospective insights about the nature of Helen's difficulties, as well as the demands that the treatment process placed on her, derive from my fuller appreciation of the nature of anaclitic depression, the importance of object representation in psychological development, and how the treatment process can provide experiences that can facilitate the development of more mature levels of self and object representation.

Although George, the other patient discussed in detail in chapter 1, was initially more symptomatic and seemed to have greater functional impairment than Helen, his object representations during the evaluation sessions seemed relatively stable. Although laden with considerable introjective feelings of guilt and anger at himself and others, and recrimination, George's declaration at the beginning of his analysis that he was Raskolnikov from Dostoyevsky's *Crime and Punishment* indicated a clear and stable, although profoundly negative, self-representation. George's primary concerns were with feelings of guilt regarding his mother's death and his feelings of being a failure and unworthy. He used primarily counteractive defenses (e.g., reaction formation, intellectualization, overcompensation, and identification with the aggressor) to deal with these conflicts. George's considerable progress in psychoanalysis, as assessed at termination and in a chance encounter that I had with George many years later, is consistent with the findings in our analyses of data from the MPRP and the Riggs–Yale study that introjective patients do relatively well in long-term intensive treatment (Blatt & Zuroff, 2002), particularly in psychoanalysis (see also Fonagy et al., 1996).

It became clear in the psychoanalytic process that George's mental representations were initially at an external iconic level as he sought to construct more diverse and integrated representations of his mother, including devoting considerable energy to documenting developments in the area of her major interest during the decade in which he was with her. His recollections of his mother's interests were filled with memories of pleasant, even joyful, experiences, despite her periodic episodes of severe depression.

In addition, George's psychoanalysis dramatically illustrated the process of working through and resolution of pathological, hostile, and critical introjects and the internalization of more constructive self- and object representations. During his analysis, George often spoke of feeling like Dorian Gray—having a positive exterior appearance while feeling vile, ugly, and corrupt inside. He also spoke extensively about something dreadful inside him that had to get out in order for him to improve and, at times, feeling like a corpse on a marble slab. In the depths of his depression during his analysis, he had experiences of hearing a voice, not unlike his father's, saying "Die, boy, die." In contrast to my observations about the difficulties that Helen experienced with the relative isolation and loneliness of the psychoanalytic process, it seems that this isolation may have facilitated the therapeutic work with George. George's self-loathing and self-contempt might have made it difficult for him to explore as fully these intense negative feelings in face-to-face psychotherapy, because his profound feelings of shame and guilt may have made it difficult for him to face the therapist each day. In addition, in psychotherapy he would have probably devoted considerable effort to scanning the therapist's expressions to test the therapist's reactions to the dreadful feelings George was expressing about himself. Thus, the isolation of the psychoanalytic situation may have facilitated George's explorations of the intensely painful introjective feelings and thoughts that were so central to his difficulties. These negative self-representations diminished over the course of the analysis and were eventually replaced by more constructive self-representations in which, for example, he reported noting a sign one day that read "Today is the beginning of the rest of your life." George's closing note to me that accompanied his payment for the last month of analytic sessions reflected these marked changes in his self-representations and his representations of others. In it, he thanked me for our work together and how much I had come to mean to him. He thanked me for my "courage [and] steadfast refusal to abandon . . .faith in . . . [him] at a time when . . . [he] virtually had given up hope" and said that this "helped . . . [him] regain some measure of self-confidence and self-respect." Although the referents for these comments about my steadfast refusal to "abandon faith" in him are not clear, I believe that George was referring to the time, in the midst of his analysis, when he was feeling very suicidal and when his stepmother called and threatened me with a malpractice suit if I failed to hospitalize George to forestall a possible suicide attempt. I believe that my "steadfast" commitment to continue working with George despite his suicidal ideation and intense self-loathing provided him with experiences that facilitated the internalization of more positive intro-jects and constructive representations of self and others that were reflected in a renewed sense of belief in himself and in a trust in others. Some 25 years after George terminated his analysis, I had a chance occasion to have brief contact with him, during which he again expressed his gratitude for our work together and informed me that he was married, had three children who were in college and graduate school and doing quite well, and that he had achieved considerable recognition and success. Also, as noted in my original report of this treatment process (Blatt, 1974), much of George's therapeutic progress seemed to be the consequence of his struggles to establish more effective repre-sentations of his parents, especially of his mother, who had died when he was pre-adolescent. The developmental changes in the structure and in the thematic content of George's mental representations of self and significant others during the psychoanalytic process are consistent with research findings reported ear-lier in this chapter (Blatt, Stayner, et al., 1996) that progress in psychodynami-cally oriented treatment is accompanied by a developmental progression in the structure and content of the representations of self and significant others.

In retrospect, it is exciting to realize how much my early clinical experi-ences with these two patients, Helen and George, contributed to my under-standing of depression as a psychological phenomenon, to the importance of mental representations in psychological processes, and to my appreciation of the mechanisms of therapeutic change. Also, it has been very gratifying to realize how much the distinction of anaclitic and introjective depressive experi-ences and the recognition of the importance of object representation in psycho-logical development have contributed to advances in clinical theory, research, and practice.

Epilogue

Issues of interpersonal relatedness and self-definition define two primary foci
of depression. Extensive clinical experience and empirical investigation indicate that patients' concerns about depression are primarily focused either on
object loss and feelings of abandonment, neglect, and loneliness or on feelings of
failure, a lack of self-worth, and guilt. Recent investigations with the Depressive
Experiences Questionnaire (DEQ; Blatt, D'Afflitti, & Quinlan, 1979), however,
have indicated that at least two different developmental levels can be distinguished within each of these domains of relatedness and self-definition. Within
the interpersonal domain, we have differentiated a desperate *neediness* for
contact with a gratifying other from a more mature interpersonal level of
relatedness to particular individuals about whom one feels a sense of concern
and commitment. Neediness, as assessed with the DEQ, correlates significantly
with psychological disturbance and distress, including disrupted interpersonal
relationships, whereas relatedness correlates significantly with a wide range
of adaptive capacities. Likewise, we have been able to differentiate two levels
of self-definition within the DEQ: (a) a harsh, critical, judgmental, reflexive,
ruminative evaluation of the self as measured by the Self-Criticism factor and
(b) proactive feelings of competence as measured by the Efficacy factor. These
two qualities of self-definition also differentially relate to measures of psychological disturbance and distress and to capacities for adaptation. Extensive
research indicates that the DEQ Self-Criticism factor correlates significantly
with many psychological disturbances, whereas the Efficacy factor correlates
significantly with a range of capacities for adaptation. This identification of
several levels within the interpersonal and the self-definitional dimensions of
the DEQ should not only facilitate future research on depression but also open
possibilities for studying different levels within two primary lines of personality
development (Blatt and Blass, 1990, 1996; Blatt & Shichman, 1983)—for studying the development of capacities for interpersonal relatedness and in the
development of self-definition. Subsequent research should be directed toward
articulating further levels in the development of interpersonal relatedness
and self-definition (e.g., Feldman & Blatt, 1996). Likewise, the assessment of
different levels in the structural organization of mental representation of the
self and significant others, also considered in this book, should also facilitate
research on these developmental processes (e.g., Feldman & Blatt, 1996; K. N.
Levy, Blatt, & Shaver, 1998).

The identification of the two primary issues of interpersonal relatedness
and self-definition is not only central to understanding depression but it also

defines two primary lines of personality development in a wide range of theoretical perspectives, including psychoanalytic thought (e.g., Blatt & Blass, 1996; Blatt & Shichman, 1983; S. Freud, 1930/1961a, Loewald, 1962; Schafer, 1968), nonpsychoanalytic personality theory (e.g., Angyal, 1941, 1951; Bakan, 1966; McAdams, 1980), and in more empirical approaches to personality development (e.g., Wiggins, 1991). Even further, recent formulations (e.g., Blatt, 1990, 1995b; Blatt & Shichman, 1983) indicate that these two fundamental dimensions of personality development provide a conceptual structure for integrating many forms of psychopathology, including depression, into a comprehensive theoretical organization based on central developmental issues in various forms of psychopathology. Thus, many forms of psychopathology can be considered not only in terms of their manifest symptoms but also as disruptions of normal psychological development—not as separate and independent diseases but as interrelated modes of maladaptation. Thus the clinical observations, theoretical formulations, and empirical research findings on anaclitic and introjective dimensions in depression discussed in this volume may provide a basis to broaden our perspectives on personality development, psychopathology, and therapeutic change. Psychopathology can now be considered as evolving from a series of disruptions of the normal development of these two fundamental psychological processes, that is, the development of interpersonal relatedness and self-definition. Also, we can now consider how the therapeutic process and the therapeutic relationship can create a reparative process that enables individuals to resume a previously disrupted developmental process that moves toward more differentiated, integrated, and personally satisfying levels of interpersonal relatedness and of self-definition.

References

Abraham, K. (1916). The first pre-genital stage of the libido. In *Selected papers on psychoanalysis* (pp. 248–279). London: Hogarth Press.

Abraham, K. (1927). Notes on the psycho-analytical investigation and treatment of manic–depressive insanity and allied conditions. In *Selected papers on psychoanalysis* (pp. 137–156). London: Hogarth Press. (Original work published 1911)

Abraham, K. (1927). The psychosexual differences between hysteria and dementia praecox. In D. Bryan & A. Strachey (Trans.), *Selected papers on psychoanalysis* (pp. 64–79). London: Hogarth Press. (Original work published 1908)

Abraham, K. (1949). A short study of the development of the libido. In *Selected papers on psychoanalysis* (pp. 418–501). London: Hogarth Press. (Original work published 1924)

Abraham, K., & Freud, E. L. (1965). *The letters of Sigmund Freud and Karl Abraham 1907–1926*. New York: Basic Books.

Abrahams, M. J., & Whitlock, F. A. (1969). Childhood experience and depression. *Journal of Psychiatry, 115*, 883–888.

Abramson, L. Y., & Sackheim, H. A. (1977). A paradox in depression: Uncontrollability and self-blame. *Psychological Bulletin, 84*, 838–851.

Abramson, L. Y., Seligman, M. E. P., & Teasdale, J. D. (1978). Learned helplessness in humans: Critique and reformulation. *Journal of Abnormal Psychology, 87*, 49–74.

Achenbach, T. (1991). *Manual for Teacher's Report Form and 1991 Profile*. Burlington: University of Vermont, Department of Psychiatry.

Achenbach, T. M., & Edelbrock, C. (1978). The classification of child psychopathology: A review and analysis of empirical efforts. *Psychological Bulletin, 85*, 1275–1301.

Achenbach, T. M., & Edelbrock, C. (1983). *Manual for the Child Behavior Checklist and the Revised Child Behavior Profile*. Burlington: University of Vermont, Department of Psychiatry.

Achenbach, T. M., & Edelbrock, C. (1987). *Manual for the Youth Self-Report and Profile*. Burlington: University of Vermont, Department of Psychiatry.

Achenbach, T. M., Howell, C. T., Quay, H. C., & Conners, C. K. (1991). National survey of problems and competencies among four- to sixteen-year-olds. *Monograph of the Society for Research in Child Development, 56*(3, Serial No. 225).

Addington, D., Addington, J., & Maticka-Tyndale, E. (1993). Assessing depression in schizophrenia: The Calgary Depression Scale. *British Journal of Psychiatry, 163*, 39–44.

Adkins, K. K., & Parker, W. (1996). Perfectionism and suicidal preoccupation. *Journal of Personality, 64*, 529–543.

Adler, G., & Buie, D. H. Jr. (1979). Aloneness and borderline psychopathology: The possible relevance of child development and issues. *International Journal of Psycho-Analysis, 60*, 83–96.

Aichhorn, A. (1955). *Wayward youth*. New York: Meridian. (Original work published 1925)

Ainsworth, M. D. S. (1969). Object relations, dependency, and attachment: A theoretical review of the mother–infant relationship. *Development Psychology, 40*, 969–1025.

Ainsworth, M. D. S. (1982). Attachment: Retrospect and prospect. In C. M. Parkes & J. Stevenson-Hinde (Eds.), *The place of attachment in human behavior* (pp. 3–30). New York: Basic Books.

Ainsworth, M. S. (1985). Attachments across the life-span. *Bulletin of the New York Academy of Medicine, 61*, 792–812.

Ainsworth, M. D. S., Bell, S. M., & Stayton, D. J. (1971). Individual differences in strange-situation behavior of one-year olds. In H. R. Schaffer (Ed.), *The origins of human social relations* (pp. 17–57). London: Academic Press.

Ainsworth, M. D. S., Blehar, M. E., Waters, E., & Wall, S. (1978). *Patterns of attachment: A psychological study of the strange situation*. Hillsdale, NJ: Erlbaum.

Akiskal, H. S., Rosenthal, R. H., Rosenthal, T. L., Kashgarian, M., Khani, M. K., & Puzantian, V. R. (1979). Differentiation of primary affective illness from situational, symptomatic and secondary depressions. *Archives of General Psychiatry, 36*, 635–643.

Alden, L. E., & Bieling, P. J. (1996). Interpersonal convergence of personality constructs in dynamic and cognitive models of depression. *Journal of Research in Personality, 30,* 60–75.

Alford, B. A., & Gerrity, D. M. (1995). The specificity of sociotropy–autonomy personality dimensions to depression vs. anxiety. *Journal of Clinical Psychology, 51,* 190–224.

Allen, N. B., de L. Horne, D. J., & Trinder, J. (1996). Sociotropy, autonomy, and dysphoric emotional responses to specific classes of stress: A psychophysiological evaluation. *Journal of Abnormal Psychology, 105,* 25–33.

Alvarez, A. (1972). *The savage god.* New York: Random House.

American Psychiatric Association. (1980). *Diagnostic and statistical manual of mental disorders* (3rd ed.). Washington, DC: Author.

American Psychiatric Association. (1987). *Diagnostic and statistical manual of mental disorders* (3rd ed., rev.). Washington, DC: Author.

American Psychiatric Association. (1994). *Diagnostic and statistical manual of mental disorders* (4th ed.). Washington, DC: Author.

Amitay, O., Mongrain, M., & Fazaa, N. (2002). *Love and control: Self-criticism from parents to daughters and consequences for relationship partners.* Manuscript submitted for publication.

Anderson, J. R. (1983). *The architecture of cognition.* Cambridge, MA: Harvard University Press.

Andrews, J. D. W. (1989). Psychotherapy of depression: A self-confirmation model. *Psychological Review, 96,* 576–607.

Angyal, A. (1941). *Foundations for a science of personality.* New York: Viking Press.

Angyal, A. (1951). *Neurosis and treatment: A holistic theory.* New York: Wiley.

Anthony, E. J. (1970). Two contrasting types of adolescent depression and their treatment. *Journal of the American Psychoanalytic Association, 18,* 841–859.

Apter, A., Bleich, A., King, R. A., Kron, S., Fluch, A., Kutler, M., & Cohen, D. J. (1993). Death without warning: A clinical postmortem study of suicide in 43 Israeli adolescent males. *Archives of General Psychiatry, 50,* 138–142.

Arend, R., Gove, F. L., & Sroufe, L. A. (1979). Continuity of individual adaptation from infancy to kindergarten: A predictive study of ego resiliency and curiosity in pre-schoolers. *Child Development, 50,* 950–959.

Arieti, S., & Bemporad, J. R. (1978). *Severe and mild depression: The therapeutic approach.* New York: Basic Books.

Arieti, S., & Bemporad, J. R. (1980). The psychological organization of depression. *American Journal of Psychiatry, 137,* 1360–1365.

Aron, L. (1996). *A meeting of minds: Mutuality in psychoanalysis.* Hillsdale, NJ: Analytic Press.

Arrindell, W. A., Perris, C., Perris, H., Eisemann, M., et al. (1986). Cross-national invariance of dimensions of parental rearing behaviour: Comparison of psychometric data of Swedish depressives and healthy subjects with Dutch target ratings on the EMBU. *British Journal of Psychiatry, 148,* 305–309.

Asch, S. S. (1980). Suicide and the hidden executioner. *International Review of Psychoanalysis, 7,* 51–60.

Astin, A. W. (1959). A factor study of the MMPI Psychopathic Deviate scale. *Journal of Consulting Psychology, 23,* 550–554.

Aubé, J., & Whiffen, V. E. (1996). Depressive styles and social acuity: Further evidence for distinct interpersonal correlates of dependency and self-criticism. *Communication Research, 23,* 407–424.

Auerbach, J. S. (1993). The origins of narcissism and narcissistic personality disorder: A theoretical and empirical reformulation. In J. M. Masling & R. F. Bornstein (Eds.), *Empirical studies of psychoanalytic theories: Vol. 4. Psychoanalytic perspectives on psychopathology* (pp. 43–110). Washington, DC: American Psychological Association.

Auerbach, J. S. (1998). Dualism, self-reflexivity, and intersubjectivity: Commentary on paper by Sheldon Bach. *Psychoanalytic Dialogues, 8,* 675–683.

Auerbach, J. S., & Blatt, S. J. (2001). Self-reflexivity, intersubjectivity, and therapeutic change. *Psychoanalytic Psychology, 18,* 427–450.

Bagby, R. M., Parker, J. D. A., Joffe, R. T., & Buis, T. (1994). Reconstruction and validation of the Depressive Experiences Questionnaire. *Assessment, 1*, 59–68.

Bagby, R. M., Parker, J. D. A., Joffe, R. T., Schuller, D., & Gilchrist, E. (1998). Confirmatory factor analysis of the revised Personal Style Inventory (PSI). *Assessment, 5*, 31–43.

Bagby, R. M., & Rector, N. A. (1998). Self-criticism, dependency and the five factor model of personality in depression: Assessing construct overlap. *Personality and Individual Differences, 24*, 895–897.

Bagby, R. M., Schuller, D. R., Parker, D. A., Levitt, A., Joffe, R. T., & Schafre, M. S. (1994). Major depression and the self-criticism and dependency dimensions. *American Journal of Psychiatry, 151*, 597–599.

Bakan, D. (1966). The duality of human existence: An essay on psychology and religion. Chicago: Rand McNally.

Baker, R. C., Melgoza, B., Roll, S., Quinlan, D. M., & Blatt, S. J. (1997). Parental representations and depressive symptoms in Anglo and Chicano students. *Interamerican Journal of Psychology, 2*, 257–277.

Baldwin, M. W. (1992). Relational schemas and the processing of social information. *Psychological Bulletin, 112*, 461–484.

Bandura, A. (1986). *Social foundation of thought and action: A social cognitive theory.* Englewood Cliffs, NJ: Prentice Hall.

Barker, J., & Muenz, L. R. (1996). The role of avoidance and obsessiveness, matching patients to cognitive and interpersonal psychotherapy: Empirical findings from the TDCRP. *Journal of Consulting and Clinical Psychology, 64*, 951–958.

Barnard, P. J. (1985). Interacting cognitive systems: A psycholinguistic approach to short-term memory. In A. Ellis (Ed.), *Progress in the psychology of language* (Vol. 2, pp. 197–258). London: Erlbaum.

Baron, P., & Peixoto, N. (1991). Depressive symptoms in adolescents as a function of personality factors. *Journal of Youth and Adolescence, 20*, 493–500.

Baron, R. M., & Kenny, D. A. (1986). The moderator–mediator variable distinction in social psychological research: Conceptual, strategic, and statistical considerations. *Journal of Personality and Social Psychology, 51*, 1173–1182.

Barrett-Lennard, G. T. (1962). Dimensions of therapist responses as causal factors in therapeutic change. *Psychological Monographs, 76*(43, Whole No. 562).

Barrett-Lennard, G. T. (1986). The Relationship Inventory now: Issues and advances in theory, method, and use. In L. S. Greenberg & W. M. Pinsof (Eds.), *The psychotherapeutic process: A research handbook* (pp. 439–476). New York: Guilford Press.

Bartelstone, J. H., & Trull, T. J. (1995). Personality, life-events, and depression. *Journal of Personality Assessment, 64*, 279–294.

Bartlett, F. C. (1932). *Remembering.* Cambridge, England: Cambridge University Press.

Bates, J. E., Masling, C. A., & Frankel, K. A. (1985). Attachment security, mother–child interaction and temperament as predictors of behavior-problem ratings at age three years. *Monographs of the Society for Research in Child Development, 50*, 167–193.

Batgos, J., & Leadbeater, B. J. (1994). Parental attachment, peer relations, and dysphoria in adolescence. In M. B. Sperling & W. H. Berman (Eds.), *Attachment in adults: Clinical and developmental perspectives* (pp. 155–178). New York: Guilford Press.

Baumeister, R. F. (1990). Suicide as escape from self. *Psychological Review, 97*, 90–113.

Beardslee, W. R., Bemporad, J., Keller, M. B., & Klerman, G. L. (1983). Children of parents with major affective disorder: A review. *American Journal of Psychiatry, 140*, 825–832.

Beardslee, W. R., & Podorefsky, D. (1988). Resilient adolescents whose parents have serious affective disorders: Importance of self-understanding and relationships. *American Journal of Psychiatry, 145*, 63–69.

Beck, A. T. (1967a). *Depression: Causes and treatment.* Philadelphia: University of Pennsylvania Press.

Beck, A. T. (1967b). *Depression: Clinical, experimental, and theoretical aspects.* New York: Harper & Row.

Beck, A. T. (1976). *Cognitive therapy and emotional disorders.* New York: International Universities Press.

Beck, A. T. (1983). Cognitive therapy of depression: New perspectives. In P. J. Clayton & J. E. Barrett (Eds.), *Treatment of depression: Old controversies and new approaches* (pp. 265–290). New York: Raven.

Beck, A. T. (1996). Beyond belief: A theory of modes, personality, and psychopathology. In P. M. Salkovskis (Ed.), *Frontiers of cognitive therapy* (pp. 1–25). New York: Guilford Press.

Beck, A. T. (1999). Cognitive aspects of personality disorders and their relation to syndromal disorders: A psychoevolutionary approach. In C. R. Cloninger (Ed.), *Personality and psychopathology* (pp. 411–429). Washington, DC: American Psychiatric Press.

Beck, A. T., & Beamesderfer, A. (1974). Assessment of depression: The Depression Inventory. In P. Pichot & R. Oliver-Martin (Eds.), *Psychological measurements in psychopharmacology* (pp. 151–169). Basel, Switzerland: Karger.

Beck, A. T., Epstein, N., Harrison, R. P., & Emery, G. (1983). *Development of the Sociotropy-Autonomy Scale: A measure of personality factors in psychopathology.* Unpublished manuscript, University of Pennsylvania, Philadelphia.

Beck, A. T., & Freeman, A., Pretzer, J., Davis, D. D., Ottavani, R., Beck, J., et al. (1990). *Cognitive therapy of personality disorders.* New York: Guilford Press.

Beck, A. T., Rush, A. J., Shaw, B. F., & Emery, G. (1979). *Cognitive theory of depression.* New York: Guilford Press.

Beck, A. T., Ward, C. H., Mendelson, M., Mock, J., & Erbaugh, J. (1961). An inventory for measuring depression. *Archives of General Psychiatry, 4,* 561–571.

Beck, A. T., Wright, F. D., Newman, C. F., & Liese, B. S. (1993). *Cognitive therapy of substance abuse.* New York: Guilford Press.

Beck, D. A., & Koenig, H. G. (1996). Minor depression: A review of the literature. *International Journal of Psychiatry in Medicine, 26,* 177–209.

Beck, R., Robbins, M., Taylor, C., & Baker, L. (2001). An examination of sociotropy and excessive reassurance seeking in the prediction of depression. *Journal of Psychopathology and Behavioral Assessment, 23,* 101–105.

Beck, S., & Rosenberg, R. (1986). Frequency, quality, and impact of life events in self-rated depressed, behavioral-problem and normal children. *Journal of Consulting and Clinical Psychology, 54,* 863–864.

Becker, M. (1941). *Psychopathic personality.* Unpublished doctoral dissertation, New York University School of Social Work.

Beebe, B., & Lachman, F. M. (1988). The contribution of the mother–infant mutual influence to the origins of self- and object representations. *Psychoanalytic Psychology, 5,* 305–338.

Bell, K. L., Tietz, J. A., Sargent, S. A., & Garrison, S. A. (2002). *Self-criticism and dependency and psychosocial functioning.* Manuscript submitted for publication.

Bell, S. (1970). The development of the concept of the object as related to the infant–mother attachment. *Child Development, 41,* 291–311.

Bem, S. L. (1974). The measurement of psychological androgyny. *Journal of Consulting and Clinical Psychology, 42,* 155–162.

Bemporad, J. R., & Romano, S. (1993). Childhood experiences and adult depression: A review of studies. *American Journal of Psychoanalysis, 53,* 301–315.

Bemporad, J. R., & Wilson, A. (1976). A developmental approach to depression in childhood and adolescence. *Journal of the American Academy of Psychoanalysis, 6,* 321–352.

Bender, L. (1947). Psychopathic behavior disorders in children. In R. M. Lindner & R. V. Seliger (Eds.), *Handbook of correctional psychology* (pp. 360–377). New York: Philosophical Library.

Benjamin, J. (1988). *The bonds of love: Psychoanalysis, feminism, and the problem of domination.* New York: Pantheon.

Benjamin, J. (1995). *Like subjects, love objects: Essays on recognition and sexual differences.* New Haven, CT: Yale University Press.

Benjamin, L. S. (1974). Structural analysis of social behavior. *Psychological Review, 81,* 392–425.

Benjamin, L. S. (1988). *SASB short form users manual.* Salt Lake City, UT: INTREX Interpersonal Institute.

Beres, D. (1966). Superego and depression. In R. M. Loewenstein, L. M. Newman, M. Schur, & A. J. Solnit (Eds.), *Psychoanalysis—A general psychology.* New York: International Universities Press.

Berman, A. L., & Jobes, D. A. (1991). *Adolescent suicide: Assessment and intervention.* Washington, DC: American Psychological Association.

Bers, S. A. (1988). *The self in anorexia nervosa.* Unpublished doctoral dissertation, Yale University.

Besser, A., & Priel, B. (2003a). A multisource approach to self-critical vulnerability to depression: The moderating role of attachment. *Journal of Personality, 71,* 515–555.

Besser, A., & Priel, B. (2003b). Trait vulnerability and coping strategies in the transition to motherhood. *Current Psychology, 22,* 57–72.

Beutel, M. E., Wiltink, J., Hafner, C., Reiner, I., Bleichner, F., & Blatt, S. J. (in press). Abhangigkeit und Selbstkritik als psychologische dimensionen der depression—Validierung der deutschsprachigen vrsion des Depressive Experiences Questionnaire (DEQ) [Dependency and self-criticism as psychological dimensions in depression: Validation of the German version of the Depressive Experiences Questionnaire (DEQ)]. *Zeitschrift fur Klinische Psychologie Psychiatrie und Psychotherapie.*

Beutler, L. E. (1976, June). *Psychotherapy: When what works with whom.* Paper presented at the meeting of the Society for Psychotherapy Research, San Diego, CA.

Beutler, L. E. (1979). Toward specific psychological therapies for specific conditions. *Journal of Consulting and Clinical Psychology, 47,* 882–897.

Beutler, L. E. (1991). Have all won and must all have prizes? Revisiting Luborsky et al.'s verdict. *Journal of Consulting and Clinical Psychology, 59,* 226–232.

Bibring, E. (1953). The mechanism of depression. In P. Greenacre (Ed.), *Affective disorders* (pp. 13–48). New York: International Universities Press.

Bieling, P. J., & Alden, L. E. (1998). Cognitive–interpersonal patterns in dysphoria: The impact of sociotropy and autonomy. *Cognitive Therapy and Research, 22,* 161–178.

Bieling, P. J., Beck, A. T., & Brown, G. K. (in press). The Sociotropy Autonomy Scale: Structure and implications. *Cognitive Therapy and Research.*

Bieling, P. J., Olshan, S., Brown, G. K., & Beck, A. T. (1998). *The sociotropy-autonomy scale: Structure and implications.* Unpublished manuscript, Department of Psychiatry, University of Pennsylvania.

Billings, A. C., Cronkite, R. C., & Moos, R. H. (1983). Social environmental factors in unipolar depression: Comparisons of depressed patients and non-depressed patients. *Journal of Abnormal Psychology, 92,* 119–133.

Billings, A. G., & Moos, R. (1982a). Life stressors and social resources affect post-treatment outcomes among depressed patients. *Journal of Abnormal Psychology, 94,* 140–153.

Billings, A. G., & Moos, R. H. (1982b). Social support and functioning among community and clinical groups: A panel model. *Journal of Behavioral Medicine, 5,* 295–311.

Blaney, P. H. (2000). Stress and depression: A personality/situation interaction approach. In S. L. Johnson, A. M. Hayes, T. Field, P. McCabe, & N. Schneiderman (Eds.), *Stress, coping and depression* (pp. 89–116). Mahwah, NJ: Erlbaum.

Blaney, P. H., & Kutcher, G. S. (1991). Measures of depressive dimensions: Are they interchangeable? *Journal of Personality Assessment, 56,* 502–512.

Blatt, S. J. (1966). Review of "Neurotic Styles," by D. Shapiro. *Psychiatry: Journal for the Study of Interpersonal Processes, 29,* 426–427.

Blatt, S. J. (1974). Levels of object representation in anaclitic and introjective depression. *Psychoanalytic Study of the Child, 29,* 107–157.

Blatt, S. J. (1983). Narcissism and egocentrism as concepts in individual and cultural development. *Psychoanalysis and Contemporary Thought, 6,* 291–303.

Blatt, S. J. (with Blatt, E. S.). (1984). *Continuity and change in art: The development of modes of representation.* Hillsdale, NJ: Erlbaum.

Blatt, S. J. (1990a). Interpersonal relatedness and self-definition: Two personality configurations and their implications for psychopathology and psychotherapy. In J. L. Singer (Ed.), *Repression and dissociation: Implications for personality theory, psychopathology & health* (pp. 299–335). Chicago: University of Chicago Press.

Blatt, S. J. (1990b). The Rorschach: A test of perception or an evaluation of representation. *Journal of Personality Assessment, 54,* 236–251.

Blatt, S. J. (1991). Depression and destructive risk-taking behavior in adolescence. In L. P. Lipsitt & L. L. Mitnick (Eds.), *Self-regulatory behavior and risk-taking: Causes and consequences* (pp. 285–309). Norwood, NJ: Ablex Press.

Blatt, S. J. (1992). The differential effect of psychotherapy and psychoanalysis on anaclitic and introjective patients: The Menninger Psychotherapy Research Project revisited. *Journal of the American Psychoanalytic Association, 40,* 691–724.

Blatt, S. J. (1995a). The destructiveness of perfectionism: Implications for the treatment of depression. *American Psychologist, 50,* 1003–1020.

Blatt, S. J. (1995b). Representational structures in psychopathology. In D. Cicchetti & S. Toth (Eds.), *Rochester Symposium on Developmental Psychopathology: Vol. 6. Emotion, cognition, and representation* (pp. 1–33). Rochester, NY: University of Rochester Press.

Blatt, S. J. (1998). Contributions of psychoanalysis to the understanding and treatment of depression. *Journal of the American Psychoanalytic Association, 46,* 723–752.

Blatt, S. J. (1999a). An object relations perspective on developments in the history of art. *Psychoanalysis and Contemporary Thought, 22,* 665–685.

Blatt, S. J. (1999b). Personality factors in the brief treatment of depression: Further analyses of the NIMH sponsored Treatment for Depression Collaborative Research Program. In D. S. Janowsky (Ed.), *Psychotherapy indications and outcomes* (pp. 23–45). Washington, DC: American Psychiatric Press.

Blatt, S. J. (1999c, August). The Rorschach in the 21st century: The Assessment of Mental Representation. Plenary address to the International Rorschach Congress. Amsterdam.

Blatt, S. J., & Auerbach, J. S. (1988). Differential cognitive disturbances in three types of "borderline" patients. *Journal of Personality Disorders, 2,* 198–211.

Blatt, S. J., & Auerbach, J. S. (2001). Mental representation, severe psychopathology, and the therapeutic process. *Journal of the American Psychoanalytic Association, 49,* 113–159.

Blatt, S. J., Auerbach, J. S., & Aryan, M. (1998). Representational structures and the therapeutic process. In R. F. Bornstein & J. M. Masling (Eds.), *Empirical studies of psychoanalytic theories: Vol. 8. Empirical investigations of the therapeutic hour* (pp. 63–107). Washington, DC: American Psychological Association.

Blatt, S. J., Auerbach, J. S., & Levy, K. N. (1997). Mental representations in personality development, psychopathology, and the therapeutic process. *Review of General Psychology, 1,* 351–374.

Blatt, S. J., & Behrends, R. S. (1987). Internalization, separation–individuation, and the nature of therapeutic action. *International Journal of Psychoanalysis, 68,* 279–297.

Blatt, S. J., & Bers, S. A. (1993). The sense of self in depression: A psychodynamic perspective. In Z. V. Segal & S. J. Blatt (Eds.), *Self representation and emotional disorders: Cognitive and psychodynamic perspectives* (pp. 171–210). New York: Guilford Press.

Blatt, S. J., & Blass, R. B. (1990). Attachment and separateness: A dialectic model of the products and processes of psychological development. *Psychoanalytic Study of the Child, 45,* 107–127.

Blatt, S. J., & Blass, R. B. (1996). Relatedness and self definition: A dialectic model of personality development. In G. G. Noam & K. W. Fischer (Eds.), *Development and vulnerabilities in close relationships* (pp. 309–338). Mahwah, NJ: Erlbaum.

Blatt, S. J., Brenneis, C. B., Schimek, J. G., & Glick, M. (1976). The normal development and psychopathological impairment of the concept of the object on Rorschach. *Journal of Abnormal Psychology, 85,* 364–373.

Blatt, S. J., Chevron, E. S., Quinlan, D. M., Schaffer, C. E., & Wein, S. (1988). *The assessment of qualitative and structural dimensions of object representations* (rev. ed.). Unpublished research manual, Yale University.

Blatt, S. J., D'Afflitti, J. P., & Quinlan, D. M. (1976). Experiences of depression in normal young adults. *Journal of Abnormal Psychology, 85,* 383–389.

Blatt, S. J., D'Afflitti, J. P., & Quinlan, D. M. (1979). *Depressive Experiences Questionnaire.* Unpublished research manual, Yale University.

Blatt, S. J., & Felsen, I. (1993). "Different kinds of folks may need different kinds of strokes": The effect of patients' characteristics on therapeutic process and outcome. *Psychotherapy Research, 3,* 245–259.

Blatt, S. J., & Ford, R. Q. (1994). *Therapeutic change: An object relations perspective*. New York: Plenum.

Blatt, S. J., Ford, R. Q., Berman, W., Cook, B., & Meyer, R. (1988). The assessment of change during the intensive treatment of borderline and schizophrenic young adults. *Psychoanalytic Psychology, 5*, 127–158.

Blatt, S. J., Hart, B., Quinlan, D. M., Leadbeater, B. J., & Auerbach, J. (1993). Interpersonal and self-critical dysphoria and behavioral problems in adolescents. *Journal of Youth and Adolescence, 22*, 253–269.

Blatt, S. J., & Homann, E. (1992). Parent–child interaction in the etiology of dependent and self-critical depression. *Clinical Psychology Review, 12*, 47–91.

Blatt, S. J., & Lerner, H. D. (1983a). Investigations in the psychoanalytic theory of object relations and object representation. In J. Masling (Ed.), *Empirical studies of psychoanalytic theories* (Vol. 1, pp. 189–249). Hillsdale, NJ: Analytic Press.

Blatt, S. J., & Lerner, H. D. (1983b). The psychological assessment of object representation. *Journal of Personality Assessment, 47*, 7–28.

Blatt, S. J., & Levy, K. N. (1998). A psychodynamic approach to the diagnosis of psychopathology. In J. W. Barron (Ed.), *Making diagnosis meaningful* (pp. 73–109). Washington, DC: American Psychological Association.

Blatt, S. J., & Maroudas, C. (1992). Convergence of psychoanalytic and cognitive behavioral theories of depression. *Psychoanalytic Psychology, 9*, 157–190.

Blatt, S. J., & Quinlan, D. M. (1982). [Dependency and self-criticism in outpatients]. Unpublished research data.

Blatt, S. J., Quinlan, D. M., & Chevron, E. (1990). Empirical investigations of a psychoanalytic theory of depression. In J. M. Masling (Ed.), *Empirical studies of psychoanalytic theories* (Vol. 3, pp. 89–147). Hillsdale, NJ: Analytic Press.

Blatt, S. J., Quinlan, D. M., Chevron, E. S., McDonald, C., & Zuroff, D. (1982). Dependency and self-criticism: Psychological dimensions of depression. *Journal of Consulting and Clinical Psychology, 50*, 113–124.

Blatt, S. J., Quinlan, D. M., Pilkonis, P. A., & Shea, T. (1995). Impact of perfectionism and need for approval on the brief treatment of depression: The National Institute of Mental Health Treatment of Depression Collaborative Research Program Revisited. *Journal of Consulting and Clinical Psychology, 63*, 125–132.

Blatt, S. J., & Ritzler, B. A. (1974). Suicide and the representation of transparency and cross sections on the Rorschach. *Journal of Consulting and Clinical Psychology, 42*, 280–287.

Blatt, S. J., Rounsaville, B. J., Eyre, S., & Wilber, C. (1984). The psycho-dynamics of opiate addiction. *Journal of Nervous and Mental Disease, 172*, 342–352.

Blatt, S. J., Schaffer, C. E., Bers, S. A., & Quinlan, D. M. (1991). *The Depressive Experiences Questionnaire for Adolescents*. Unpublished research manual, Yale University.

Blatt, S. J., Schaffer, C. E., Bers, S. A., & Quinlan, D. M. (1992). Psychometric properties of the Adolescent Depressive Experiences Questionnaire. *Journal of Personality Assessment, 59*, 82–98.

Blatt, S. J., & Shahar, G. (2003). Das Dialogische Selbst: Adaptive und maladaptive Dimesionen. (The dialogic self: Adaptive and maladaptive dimensions). In P. Giampieri-Deutsh (Ed.), *Psychoanalyses im Dialog der Wissenschaften, 2*. Anglo-Amerikanische Perspektiven [Psychoanalysis as an empirical, interdisciplinary science, Vol 2. An Anglo-American perspective]. Stuttgart: Kohlammer. pp. 285–309.

Blatt, S. J., Shahar, G., & Zuroff, D. C. (2002). Anaclitic (sociotropic) and introjective (autonomous) dimensions. In J. C. Nocross (Ed.), *Psychotherapy relationships that work: Therapist contributions and responsiveness to patients* (pp. 315–333). New York: Oxford University Press.

Blatt, S. J., & Shichman, S. (1981). Antisocial behavior and personality organization. In S. Tuttman, C. Kaye, & M. Zimmerman (Eds.), *Object and self: A developmental approach: Essays in honor of Edith Jacobson* (pp. 325–367). Madison, WI: International Universities Press.

Blatt, S. J., & Shichman, S. (1983). Two primary configurations of psychopathology. *Psychoanalysis and Contemporary Thought, 6*, 187–254.

Blatt, S. J., Stayner, D., Auerbach, J., & Behrends, R. S. (1996). Change in object and self representations in long-term, intensive, inpatient treatment of seriously disturbed adolescents and young adults. *Psychiatry: Interpersonal and Biological Processes, 59*, 82–107.

Blatt, S. J., Wein, S. J., Chevron, E. S., & Quinlan, D. M. (1979). Parental representations and depression in normal young adults. *Journal of Abnormal Psychology, 88,* 388–397.

Blatt, S. J., & Wild, C. M. (1976). *Schizophrenia: A developmental analysis.* New York: Academic Press.

Blatt, S. J., Wild, C. M., & Ritzler, B. A. (1975). Disturbances in object representation in schizophrenia. *Psychoanalysis and Contemporary Science, 4,* 235–288.

Blatt, S. J., & Zohar, A. H. (1990, July). *Identifying further subtypes of depression: Application of SSA to theory refinement.* Paper presented at the International Conference on Facet Theory, Jerusalem.

Blatt, S. J., Zohar, A., Quinlan, D. M., Luthar, S. S., & Hart, B. (1996). Levels of relatedness within the dependency factor of the Depressive Experiences Questionnaire for Adolescents. *Journal of Personality Assessment, 67,* 52–71.

Blatt, S. J, Zohar, A. H., Quinlan, D. M., Zuroff, D. C., & Mongrain, M. (1995). Subscales within the dependency factor of the Depressive Experiences Questionnaire. *Journal of Personality Assessment, 64,* 319–339.

Blatt, S. J., & Zuroff, D. C. (1992). Interpersonal relatedness and self-definition: Two prototypes for depression. *Clinical Psychology Review, 12,* 527–562.

Blatt, S. J., & Zuroff, D. C. (2002). Perfectionism in the therapeutic process. In G. L. Flett & P. L. Hewitt (Eds.), *Perfectionism: Theory, research, and treatment* (pp. 393–406). Washington, DC: American Psychological Association.

Blatt, S. J., Zuroff, D. C., Bondi, C. M., & Sanislow, C. A. (2000). Short and long-term effects of medication and psychotherapy in the brief treatment of depression: Further analyses of data from the NIMH TDCRP. *Psychotherapy Research, 10,* 215–234.

Blatt, S. J., Zuroff, D. C., Bondi, C. M., Sanislow, C., & Pilkonis, P. (1998). When and how perfectionism impedes the brief treatment of depression: Further analyses of the NIMH TDCRP. *Journal of Consulting and Clinical Psychology, 66,* 423–428.

Blatt, S. J., Zuroff, D. C., Quinlan, D. M., & Pilkonis, P. A. (1996). Interpersonal factors in brief treatment of depression: Further analyses of the National Institute of Mental Health Treatment of Depression Collaborative Research Program. *Journal of Consulting and Clinical Psychology, 64,* 162–171.

Blehar, M. C., Lieberman, A. F., & Ainsworth, M. (1977). Early face-to-face interaction and its relation to later mother–infant attachment. *Child Development, 48,* 182–194.

Block, J. (1978). *The Q-sort method in personality assessment and psychiatry restored.* Palo Alto, CA: Consulting Psychologists Press.

Blos, P. (1957). Preoedipal factors in the etiology of female delinquency. *The Psychoanalytic Study of the Child, 12,* 229–249.

Blos, P. (1979). *The adolescent passage.* New York: International Universities Press.

Blumberry, W., Oliver, J., & McClure, J. (1978). Validation of the Beck Depression Inventory in a university population using psychiatric estimate as the criterion. *Journal of Consulting and Clinical Psychology, 46,* 150–155.

Bohrnstedt, G. W., & Fisher, G. A. (1986). The effects of recalled childhood and adolescent relationships compared to current role performances on young adults' affective functioning. *Social Psychology Quarterly, 49,* 19–32.

Bornstein, R. F. (1992). Parental perceptions and psychopathology. *Journal of Nervous and Mental Disease, 180,* 475–483.

Bornstein, R. F. (1993). *The dependent personality.* New York: Guilford Press.

Bornstein, R. F. (1995). Comorbidity of dependent personality disorder and other psychological disorders: An integrative review. *Journal of Personality Disorders, 9,* 286–303.

Bornstein, R. F. (1998). Depathologizing dependency. *Journal of Nervous and Mental Disease, 106,* 67–73.

Bornstein, R. F., & Cecero, J. J. (2000). Deconstructing dependency in a five-factor world: A meta-analytic review. *Journal of Personality Assessment, 74,* 324–343.

Bornstein, R. F., Galley, D. J., & Leone, D. R. (1986). Parental representations and orality. *Journal of Personality Assessment, 50,* 80–89.

Bornstein, R. F., & O'Neill, R. M. (1992). Perceptions of parents and psychopathology. *Journal of Nervous and Mental Disorders, 180,* 475–483.

Bornstein, R. F., Poynton, F. G., & Masling, J. (1985). Orality and depression: An empirical study. *Psychoanalytic Psychology*, *2*, 241–249.

Bower, G. J. (1981). Mood and memory. *American Psychologist*, *36*, 129–148.

Bowlby, J. (1952). *Maternal care and mental health*. Geneva, Switzerland: World Health Organization.

Bowlby, J. (1969). *Attachment and loss: Vol. 1. Attachment*. New York: Basic Books.

Bowlby, J. (1973). *Attachment and loss: Vol. 2. Separation, anxiety, and anger*. New York: Basic Books.

Bowlby, J. (1980). *Attachment and loss: Vol. 3. Loss: sadness and depression*. New York: Basic Books.

Bowlby, J. (1988a). Developmental psychiatry comes of age. *American Journal of Psychiatry*, *145*, 1–10.

Bowlby, J. (1988b). *A secure base: Clinical applications of attachment theory*. London: Routledge & Kegan Paul.

Bowlby, J., & Parks, C. M. (1970). Separation and loss within the family. In E. J. Anthony & C. Koupernick (Eds.), *The child in his family* (pp. 197–316). New York: Wiley.

Boyd, J. H., & Weissman, M. M. (1982). Epidemiology. In E. S. Paykel (Ed.), *Handbook of affective disorders* (pp. 109–125). New York: Guilford Press.

Braaten, L. J., & Darling, C. D. (1962). Suicidal tendencies among college students. *Psychiatric Quarterly*, *36*, 665–692.

Brandtstaedter, J. (1998). Action perspectives on human development. In W. Damon & R. M. Lerner (Eds.), *Handbook of child psychology* (pp. 807–863). New York: Wiley.

Brent, D., Kerr, M. M., Goldstein, C., Bozigar, J., Wartell, M., & Allan, M. A. (1989). An outbreak of suicide and suicidal behavior in a high school. *Journal of the Academy of Child and Adolescent Psychiatry*, *28*, 918–924.

Bretherton, I. (1985). Attachment theory: Retrospect and prospect. In I. Bretherton & E. Waters (Eds.), Growing points in attachment theory and research. *Monographs of the Society for Research in Child Development*, *50*(1–2, Serial No. 209), 3–35.

Brewerton, T. D., & George, M. S. (1993). Is migraine related to eating disorders? *International Journal of Eating Disorders*, *14*, 75–79.

Brewin, C., Andrews, B., & Gotlib, I. H. (1993). Psychopathology and early experience: A reappraisal of retrospective reports. *Psychological Bulletin*, *113*, 82–98.

Brewin, C., & Firth-Cozens, J. (1997). Dependency and self-criticism as predictors of depression in young doctors. *Journal of Occupational Health*, *2*, 242–246.

Brewin, C. R., Firth-Cozens, J., Furnham, A., & Andrews, B. (1990). Self-criticism in adulthood and perceived childhood experience. *Journal of Abnormal Psychology*, *101*, 561–562.

Brewin, C. R., & Furnham, A. (1987). Dependency, self-criticism and depressive attributional style. *British Journal of Clinical Psychology*, *26*, 225–226.

Brody, L. (1999). *Gender, emotion, and the family*. Cambridge, MA: Harvard University Press.

Broverman, I., Broverman, D., Clarkson, F. E., Rosenkrantz, P., & Vogel, S. (1970). Sex-role stereotypes and clinical judgments of mental health. *Journal of Consulting Psychology*, *34*, 1–7.

Broverman, I., Vogel, S., Broverman, D., Clarkson, F. E., & Rosenkrantz, P. (1972). Sex-role stereotypes: A current appraisal. *Journal of Social Issues*, *28*, 59–78.

Brown, G. P., & Beck, A. T. (2002). Dysfunctional attitudes, perfectionism, and models of vulnerability to depression. In G. L. Flett & P. L. Hewitt (Eds.), *Perfectionism: Theory, research, and treatment* (pp. 231–252). Washington, DC: American Psychological Association.

Brown, G. P., Hammen, C. L., Craske, M. G., & Wickens, T. D. (1995). Dimensions of dysfunctional attitudes as vulnerabilities to depressive symptoms. *Journal of Abnormal Psychology*, *104*, 431–435.

Brown, G. W., Bifulco, A., & Harris, T. O. (1987). Life events, vulnerability and onset of depression: Some refinements. *British Journal of Psychiatry*, *15*, 30–42.

Brown, G. W., & Harris, T. (1978). *Social origins of depression: A study of psychiatric disorders in women*. London: Tavistock.

Brown, G. W., Sklair, F., Harris, T. O., & Birley, J. L. T. (1973). Life events and psychiatric disorders: Part I. Some methodological issues. *Psychological Medicine*, *3*, 74–87.

Brown, J. (1985). An introduction to the uses of facet theory. In D. Canter (Ed.), *Facet theory: Approaches to social research* (pp. 17–58). New York: Springer-Verlag.

Brown, J. D., & Silberschatz, G. (1989). Dependency, self-criticism, and depressive attributional style. *Journal of Abnormal Psychology, 98,* 187–188.

Bruner, J. (1986). *Actual minds, possible worlds.* Cambridge, MA: Harvard University Press.

Brunstein, J. C. (1993). Personal goals and subjective well-being: A longitudinal study. *Journal of Personality and Social Psychology, 65,* 1061–1070.

Buhrmester, D. (1996). Need fulfillment, interpersonal competence, and the developmental context of early adolescent friendship. In W. Bukowski, A. Newcomb, & W. Hartup (Eds.), *The company they keep: Friendship in childhood and adolescence* (pp. 158–185). Cambridge, England: Cambridge University Press.

Burbach, D. J., & Bourdin, C. M. (1986). Parent–child relations and the etiology of depression: A review of methods and findings. *Clinical Psychology Review, 6,* 133–153.

Burkes, H. L., & Harrison, S. L. (1961). Aggressive behavior as a means of avoiding depression. *American Journal of Orthopsychiatry, 33,* 416–422.

Burns, D. D. (1980a). *Feeling good: The new mood therapy.* New York: New American Library.

Burns, D. (1980b, November). The perfectionist's script for self-defeat. *Psychology Today,* 34–57.

Burns, D. D., & Auerbach, A. (1996). Therapeutic empathy in cognitive–behavioral therapy: Does it really make a difference? In P. M. Salkovskis (Ed.), *Frontiers of cognitive therapy* (pp. 135–164). New York: Guilford Press.

Burns, D. D., & Nolen-Hoeksema, S. (1992). Therapeutic empathy and recovery from depression in cognitive–behavioral therapy: A structural equation model. *Journal of Consulting and Clinical Psychology, 60,* 441–449.

Buss, D. M. (1987). Selection, evocation, and manipulation. *Journal of Personality and Social Psychology, 53,* 1214–1221.

Cadoret, R. J., Winkur, G., Dorzab, J., & Baker, M. (1972). Depressive disease: Life events and onset of illness. *Archives of General Psychiatry, 26,* 133–136.

Cameron, N. (1963). *Personality development and psychopathology: A dynamic approach.* Boston: Houghton-Mifflin.

Campbell, D. G., Kwon, P., Reff, R. C., & Williams, M. G. (2003). Sociotropy and autonomy: An examination of interpersonal and work adjustment. *Journal of Personality Assessment, 80,* 206–207.

Campos, R. C. (2002). Manifestations of dependent and self-critical personality styles in Rorschach: An exploratory study. *Journal of Projective Psychology and Mental Health, 9,* 93–104.

Cane, D. B., Olinger, L. J., Gotlib, I. H., & Kuiper, N. A. (1986). Factor structure of the Dysfunctional Attitude Scale in a student population. *Journal of Clinical Psychology, 42,* 307–309.

Canter, D. (Ed.). (1985). *Facet theory: Approaches to social research.* New York: Springer-Verlag.

Cantor, N. (1990). From thought to behavior: "Having" and "doing" in the study of personality and cognition. *American Psychologist, 45,* 735–750.

Cantwell, D. P. (1983). Family genetic factors. In D. P. Cantwell & G. A. Carlson (Eds.), *Affective disorders in childhood and adolescence* (pp. 3–18). New York: Spectrum.

Cantwell, D. P., & Carlson, G. A. (1983). *Affective disorders in childhood and adolescence.* New York: Spectrum.

Cappeliez, P. (1993). The relationship between Beck's concepts of sociotropy and autonomy and the NEO Personality Inventory. *British Journal of Clinical Psychology, 32,* 78–80.

Carlson, G. A., & Cantwell, D. P. (1980a). A survey of depressive symptoms in a child and adolescent psychiatric population. *Journal of the American Academy of Child and Adolescent Psychiatry, 19,* 511–524.

Carlson, G. A., & Cantwell, D. P.(1980b). Unmasking masked depression in children and adolescents. *American Journal of Psychiatry, 137,* 445–449.

Carlson, G. A., & Cantwell, D. P. (1983). *Affective disorders in childhood and adolescence.* New York: Spectrum.

Carroll, B. J., Fielding, J. M., & Blashki, T. G. (1973). Depression rating scales: A critical review. *Archives of General Psychiatry, 28,* 361–366.

Carson, A. T., & Baker, R. C. (1994). Psychological correlates of codependency in women. *International Journal of the Addictions, 29,* 395–407.

Carson, A. T., & Baker, R. C. (1996). Depression, object relations and reality testing in women survivors of childhood abuse. *Depression, 3,* 278–285.

Chessick, R. D. (1960). The "pharmacogenic orgasm" in the drug addict. *Archives of General Psychiatry, 3*, 545–556.

Chevron, E. S., Quinlan, D. M., & Blatt, S. J. (1978). Sex roles and gender differences in the experience of depression. *Journal of Abnormal Psychology, 87*, 680–683.

Chodoff, P. (1972). The depressive personality: A critical review. *Archives of General Psychiatry, 27*, 666–673.

Chwast, J. (1967). Depressive reactions as manifested among adolescent delinquents. *American Journal of Psychotherapy, 21*, 575–589.

Cicchetti, D., & Aber, L. J. (1986). Early precursors of later depression: An organizational perspective. In L. L. Lipsett (Ed.), *Advances in infant research* (Vol. 4, pp. 87–103). Norwood, NJ: Ablex.

Cicchetti, D., & Schneider-Rosen, K. (1984a). Theoretical and empirical considerations in the investigation of the relationship between affect and cognition in atypical populations of infants: Contributions to the formulation of an integrative theory of development. In D. Izard, J. Kagan, & R. Zajoric (Eds.), *Emotions, cognitions and behavior* (pp. 366–406). New York: Cambridge University Press.

Cicchetti, D., & Schneider-Rosen, K. (1984b). Toward a transactional model of childhood depression. In D. Cicchetti & K. Schneider-Rosen (Eds.), *Childhood depression* (pp. 5–28). San Francisco: Jossey-Bass.

Cicchetti, D., & Sroufe, L. A. (1978). An organizational view of affect: Illustration from the study of Downs syndrome infants. In M. Lewis & L. Rosenblum (Eds.), *The development of affect* (pp. 309–350). New York: Plenum.

Cicchetti, D., Toth, S., & Bush, M. (1988). Developmental psychopathology and incompetence in childhood: Suggestions for intervention. In B. B. Lahey & A. E. Kazdin (Eds.), *Advances in clinical child psychology* (Vol. 11, pp. 1–71). New York: Plenum.

Clark, D. A., & Beck, A. T. (1991). Personality factors in dysphoria: A psychometric refinement of Beck's Sociotropy-Autonomy Scale. *Journal of Psychopathology and Behavioral Assessment, 13*, 369–388.

Clark, D. A., & Beck, A. T. (1999). *Scientific foundations of cognitive theory and therapy of depression*. New York: Wiley.

Clark, D. A. & Oates, T. (1995). Daily hassles, major and minor life events, and their interaction with sociotropy and autonomy. *Behavior Research and Therapy, 33*, 819–823.

Clark, D. A., Steer, R. A., Haslam, N., Beck, A. T., & Brown, G. K. (1997). Personality vulnerability, psychiatric diagnoses, and symptoms: Cluster analyses of the Sociotropy and Autonomy subscales. *Cognitive Therapy and Research, 21*, 267–283.

Clark, M. S., & Mills, J. (1979). Interpersonal attraction in exchange and communal relationships. *Journal of Personality and Social Psychology, 37*, 12–24.

Cobliner, W. G. (1965). The Geneva School of Genetic Psychology and Psychoanalysis. In R. A. Spitz (Ed.), *The first year of life* (pp. 301–356). New York: International Universities Press.

Cohen, M. B., Baker, G., Cohen, R. A., Fromm-Reichman, F., & Weigert, E. V. (1954). An intensive study of twelve cases of manic–depressive psychosis. *Psychiatry, 17*, 103–137.

Cohen, S., & Wills, T. A. (1985). Stress, social support, and the buffering hypothesis. *Psychological Bulletin, 98*, 310–357.

Cohn, J. F., Campbell, S. B., Matias, R., & Hopkins, J. (1990). Face-to-face interactions of postpartum depressed and nondepressed mother–infant pairs at 2 months. *Developmental Psychology, 26*, 15–23.

Cohn, J. F., Matias, R., Tronick, E. Z., Connell, D., & Lyons-Ruth, K. (1986). Face-to-face interactions of depressed mothers and their infants. In E. Z. Tronick & T. Field (Eds.), *New directions for child development: Vol. 34. Maternal depression and infant disturbance* (pp. 31–45). San Francisco: Jossey-Bass.

Cohn, J. F., & Tronick, E. Z. (1983). Three-month-old infants' reactions to simulated maternal depression. *Child Development, 54*, 185–193.

Cohn, J. F., & Tronick, E. Z. (1987). Mother–infant face to face interaction: The sequence of dyadic states at 3, 6, and 9 months. *Developmental Psychology, 23*, 68–77.

Colby, K. M. (1964). Psychotherapeutic processes. *Annual Review of Psychology, 15*, 347–370.

Cole, D. A. (1991). Preliminary support for a competence-based model of depression in children. *Journal of Abnormal Psychology, 100*, 181–190.

Cole, D. A., & Carpentieri, S. (1990). Social status and the comorbidity of child depression and conduct disorder. *Journal of Consulting and Clinical Psychology, 58,* 748–757.

Cole, H. E. (1991, April). *Worrying about parents: The link between preoccupied attachment and depression.* Paper presented at the biennial meeting of the Society for Research in Child Development, Seattle, WA.

Cole, P. M., & Zahn-Waxler, C. (1992). Emotional dysregulation in disruptive behavior disorders. In D. Cicchetti & S. L. Toth (Eds.), *Rochester Symposium on Developmental Psychopathology: Vol. 4. Developmental perspectives on depression* (pp. 173–209). Rochester, NY: University of Rochester Press.

Colton, M. E., Gore, S., & Aseltine, R. H. (1991). The patterning of distress and disorder in a community sample of high school aged youth. In M. E. Colton & S. Gore (Eds.), *Adolescent stress, causes and consequences* (pp. 157–181). New York: Aldine.

Compas, B. E. (1987). Stress and life events during childhood and adolescence. *Clinical Psychology Review, 7,* 275–302.

Compas, B. E., Ey, S., & Grant, K. E. (1993). Taxonomy, assessment, and diagnosis of depression during adolescence. *Psychological Bulletin, 114,* 323–344.

Compas, B. E., & Hammen, C. L. (1994). Child and adolescent depression: Covariation and co-morbidity in development. In R. J. Haggerty, L. R. Sherrod, N. Garmezy, & R. Rutter (Eds.), *Risk and resilence in children: Developmental approaches* (pp. 225–267). New York: Cambridge University Press.

Compas, B. E., Slavin, L. A., Wagner, B. M., & Vannata, K. (1986). Relationship of life events and social support with psychological dysfunction among adolescents. *Journal of Youth and Adolescence, 15,* 205–221.

Coonerty, S. (1986). An exploration of separation–individuation themes in borderline personality disorder. *Journal of Personality Assessment, 50,* 501–511.

Costa, P. T., Jr., & McCrae, R. R. (1985). *The NEO personality inventory manual.* Odessa, FL: Psychological Assessment Resources.

Cox, B. J., Rector, N. A., Bagby, R. M., Swinson, R. P., Levitt, A. J., & Joffe, R. T. (2000). Is self-criticism unique for depression? A comparison with social phobia. *Journal of Affective Disorders, 57,* 223–228.

Coyne, J. C. (1976a). Depression and the response of others. *Journal of Abnormal Psychology, 85,* 186–193.

Coyne, J. C. (1976b). Toward an interactional description of depression. *Psychiatry, 39,* 28–40.

Coyne, J. C. (1994). Self-report distress: Analog or ersatz depression? *Psychological Bulletin, 116,* 29–45.

Coyne, J. C. (1998). Thinking interactionally about depresssion: A radical restatement. In T. Joiner & J. C. Coyne (Eds.), *The interactional nature of depression* (pp. 365–392). Washington, DC: American Psychological Association.

Coyne, J. C., Gallo, S. M., Klinkman, M. S., & Colarco, M. M. (1998). Effects of recent and past major depression and distress on self-concept and coping. *Journal of Abnormal Psychology, 107,* 86–96.

Coyne, J. C., & Gotlib, I. H. (1983). The role of cognition in depression: A critical appraisal. *Psychological Bulletin, 94,* 472–505.

Coyne, J. C., & Gotlib, I. (1986). Studying the role of cognition in depression: Well-trodden paths and cul-de-sacs. *Cognitive Therapy and Research, 10,* 695–705.

Coyne, J. C., & Pepper, C. M. (1998). The therapeutic alliance in brief strategic therapy. In J. Safran & C. J. Muran (Eds.), *The therapeutic alliance in brief psychotherapy* (pp. 147–169). Washington, DC: American Psychological Association.

Coyne, J. C., & Whiffen, V. E. (1995). Issues in personality as diathesis for depression: The case of sociotropy–dependency and autonomy–self-criticism. *Psychological Bulletin, 118,* 358–378.

Craighead, W. E. (1991). Cognitive factors and classification issues in adolescent depression. *Journal of Youth and Adolescence, 20,* 311–315.

Cramer, P. (1991). *The development of defense mechanisms, theory, research, and assessment.* New York: Springer.

Cramer, P., & Blatt, S. J. (1990). Use of the TAT to measure change in defense mechanisms following intensive psychotherapy. *Journal of Personality Assessment, 54,* 236–251.

Cramer, P., Blatt, S. J., & Ford, R. Q. (1988). Defensive mechanisms in the analytic and introjective personality configuration. *Journal of Consulting and Clinical Psychology, 56,* 610–616.

Cronbach, L. J. (1953). Correlation between persons as a research tool. In O. H. Mowrer (Ed.), *Psychotherapy: Theory and research* (pp. 376–389). New York: Ronald.

Cronbach, L. J. (1975). Beyond the two disciplines of scientific psychology. *American Psychologist, 30,* 116–127.

Crook, T., Raskin, A., & Elliot, J. (1981). Parent–child relationships and adult depression. *Child Development, 52,* 950–957.

Cummings, E. M., & Cicchetti, D. (1990). Toward a transactional model of relations between attachment and depression. In M. T. Greenberg, D. Cicchetti, & E. M. Cummings (Eds.), *Attachment in the preschool years: Theory, research, and intervention* (pp. 339–372). Chicago: University of Chicago Press.

Cytryn, L., McKnew, D. H., Zahn-Waxler, C., Radke-Yarrow, M., Gaensbauer, T. J., Harmon, R. J., & Lamour, M. (1984). A developmental view of affective disturbances in the children of affectively ill parents. *American Journal of Psychiatry, 141,* 219–222.

Dahlstrom, W. G., Welsh, G. S., & Dahlstrom, L. E. (1972). *An MMPI handbook: Vol. 1. Clinical interpretation* (Rev. ed.). Minneapolis: University of Minnesota Press.

Dancer, L. S. (1990). Introduction to facet theory and its applications. *Applied Psychology, 39,* 365–377.

Davenport, Y. B., Zahn-Waxler, C., Adland, M. L., & Mayfield, A. (1984). Early childrearing practices in families with manic depressive parents. *American Journal of Psychiatry, 141,* 230–235.

Davidson, M. (1983). *Multidimensional scaling.* New York: Wiley.

Davis, P. A. (1983). *Suicidal adolescents.* Springfield, IL: Charles C Thomas.

Deci, E. L., & Ryan, R. M. (1985). *Intrinsic motivation and self-determination in human behavior.* New York: Plenum.

Delisle, J. (1986). Death with honors: Suicide among gifted adolescents. *Journal of Counseling and Development, 64,* 558–560.

Delisle, J. R. (1990). The gifted adolescent at risk: Strategies and resources for suicide prevention among gifted youth. *Journal of Education of the Gifted, 13,* 212–228.

DeParle, J. (1993, August 22). Portrait of a White House aide ensnared by his perfectionism. *New York Times,* pp. E1–E22.

Depue, R. A., & Monroe, S. M. (1978). The unipolar–bipolar distinction in the depressive disorders. *Psychological Bulletin, 85,* 1001–1029.

Depue, R. A., & Monroe, S. M. (1986). Conceptualization and measurement of human disorder in life stress research: The problem of chronic disturbance. *Psychological Bulletin, 99,* 46–51.

Derogatis, L. R. (1983). *SCL-90–R manual II: Administration, scoring and procedures.* Towson, MD: Clinical Psychometric Research.

Derogatis, L. R., Lipman, R. S., & Covi, M. D. (1973). SCL-90: An outpatient psychiatric rating scale—Preliminary report. *Psychopharmacology Bulletin, 9,* 13–28.

Descartes, R. (1968a). Discourse on the method of properly conducting one's reason and of seeking the truth in the sciences. In F. E. Sutcliffe (Trans.), *Discourse on method and the mediations* (pp. 25–91). New York: Penguin. (Original work published 1641)

Descartes, R. (1968b). Mediations on the first philosophy in which the existence of God and the real distinction between the soul and the body of man are demonstrated. In F. E. Sutcliffe (Trans.), *Discourse on method and the mediations* (pp. 93–169). New York: Penguin. (Original work published 1641)

Deutsch, H. (1933). The psychology of manic–depressive states, with particular reference to chronic hypomania. In *Neuroses and character types* (pp. 203–217). New York: International Universities Press.

Diamond, D., Blatt, S. J., Stayner, D., & Kaslow, N. (1991). *Self–other differentiation of object representations.* Unpublished research manual, Yale University.

Diamond, D., Blatt, S. J., Stayner, D., & Kaslow, N. (1992). *Differentiation, cohesion and relatedness of self and other representations: A developmental scale.* Unpublished manuscript, Yale University.

Diamond, D., Kaslow, N., Coonerty, S., & Blatt, S. J. (1990). Change in separation–individuation and intersubjectivity in long-term treatment. *Psychoanalytic Psychology, 7,* 363–397.

Dimitrovsky, L., Levy-Schiff, R., & Schattner-Zanany, I. (2002). Dimensions of depression and perfectionism in pregnant and nonpregnant women: Their levels and interrelationships and their relationship to marital satisfaction. *Journal of Psychology, 136,* 631–646.

Dishion, T. L., Patterson, G. R., Stoolmiller, M., & Skinner M. L. (1991). Family, school, and behavioral antecedents to early adolescent involvement with antisocial peers. *Developmental Psychology, 27,* 172–180.

Dover, A. (1990, June). *The influence of depression prone personality and social support on postpartum adjustment.* Paper presented at the annual convention of the Canadian Psychological Association, Ottawa, Ontario, Canada.

Downey, G., & Coyne, J. (1990). Children of depressed parents: An integrative review. *Psychological Bulletin, 108,* 50–76.

Driscoll, R. (1989). Self-condemnation: A comprehensive framework for assessment and treatment. *Psychotherapy, 26,* 104–111.

Dunkley, D. M., & Blankstein, K. R. (2000). Self-critical perfectionism, coping, hassles, and current distress: A structural equation modeling approach. *Cognitive Therapy and Research, 24,* 713–730.

Dunkley, D. M., Blankstein, K. R., & Flett, G. L. (1997). Specific cognitive–personality vulnerability styles in depression and the five-factor model of personality. *Personality and Individual Differences, 23,* 1041–1053.

Dunkley, D. M., Blankstein, K. R., Halsall, J., Williams, W., & Winkworth, G. (2000). The relation between perfectionism and distress: Hassles, coping, and perceived social support as mediators and moderators. *Journal of Counseling Psychology, 47,* 437–453.

Dunkley, D. M., Zuroff, D. C., & Blankstein, K. R. (2003). Self-critical perfectionism and daily affect: Dispositional and situational influences on stress and coping. *Journal of Personality and Social Psychology, 84,* 234–252.

Dweck, C. S., & Licht, B. (1980). Learned helplessness and intellectual achievement. In J. Garber & M. E. P. Seligman (Eds.), *Human helplessness* (pp. 197–221). New York: Academic Press.

Egeland, B., & Sroufe, L. A. (1981). Attachment and early maltreatment. *Child Development, 52,* 44–52.

Eissler, K. R. (1949). Some problems of delinquency. In K. R. Eissler (Ed.), *Searchlights on delinquency* (pp. 3–25). New York: International Universities Press.

Elicker, J., & Sroufe, L. A. (1992). Predicting peer competence and peer relationships in childhood from early parent–child relationships. In R. Parke & A. Ladd (Eds.), *Family–peer relationships: Modes of linkage* (pp. 77–106). Hillsdale, NJ: Erlbaum.

Elkin, I. (1994). The NIMH Treatment of Depression Collaborative Research Program: Where we began and where we are now. In A. E. Bergin & S. L. Garfield (Eds.), *Handbook of psychotherapy and behavior change* (4th ed., pp. 114–135). New York: Wiley.

Elkin, I., Shea, M. T., Watkins, J. T., Imber, S. D., Sotsky, S. M., Collins, J. F., et al. (1989). NIMH Treatment of Depression Collaborative Research Program: General effectiveness of treatments. *Archives of General Psychiatry, 46,* 971–983.

Elliott, D. S., Huizinga, D., & Menard, S. (1989). *Multiple problem youth: Delinquency, substance use, and mental health problems.* New York: Springer-Verlag.

Ellis, T. E., & Ratliff, K. G. (1986). Cognitive characteristics of suicidal and nonsuicidal psychiatric inpatients. *Cognitive Therapy and Research, 10,* 625–634.

Emde, R. N., Harmon, L., & Good, W. V. (1986). The development of depressive feelings in children: A transactional model for research. In M. Rutter, C. E. Izard, & P. B. Read (Eds.), *Depression in young people: Developmental and clinical perspectives* (pp. 135–160). New York: Guilford Press.

Emmons, R. A. (2000). Personality and forgiveness. In M. E. McCullough & K. E. Pargament (Eds.), *Forgiveness: Theory, research, and practice* (pp. 156–175). New York: Guilford Press.

Endicott, J., & Spitzer, R. L. (1978). A diagnostic interview: The Schedule for Affective Disorders and Schizophrenia. *Archives of General Psychology, 35,* 837–844.

Endicott, J., Spitzer, R. L., Fleiss, J. L., & Cohen, J. (1976). The Global Assessment Scale: A procedure for measuring overall severity of psychiatric disturbance. *Archives of General Psychiatry, 33,* 766–771.

Endler, N. S. (1961). Changes in meaning during psychotherapy as measured by the semantic differential. *Journal of Counseling Psychology, 8,* 105–111.

Engel, G. L., & Reichsman, F. (1956). Spontaneous and experimentally induced depressions in an infant with a gastric fistula. *Journal of the American Psychoanalytic Association, 4*, 428–452.

Enns, M. W., & Cox, B. J. (1997). Personality dimensions and depression: Review and commentary. *Canadian Journal of Psychiatry, 42*, 274–284.

Enns, M. W., & Cox, B. J. (1999). Perfectionism and depressive symptom severity in major depressive disorder. *Behavioral Research and Therapy, 37*, 783–794.

Enns, M. W, Cox, B. J., & Clara, I. (2002). Adaptive and maladaptive perfectionism: Developmental origins and association with depression proneness. *Personality and Individual Differences, 33*, 921–935.

Enns, M. W., Cox, B. J., & Inayatulla, M. (2003). Personality predictors of outcome for adolescents hospitalized for suicidal ideation. *Journal of the American Academy of Child & Adolescent Psychiatry, 42*, 720–727.

Erikson, E. H. (1950). *Childhood and society* (2nd ed.). New York: Norton.

Erikson, E. H. (1968). *Identity, youth and crisis*. New York: Norton.

Erikson, M. F., Sroufe, L. A., & Egeland, B. (1985). The relationship between quality of attachment and behavior problems in preschool in a high risk sample. *Monographs of the Society for Research in Child Development, 50*, 147–166.

Fazaa, N. (2001). *Dependency, self-criticism and suicidal behavior*. Unpublished master's thesis, University of Windsor, Windsor, Ontario, Canada.

Fazaa, N., & Page, S. (2003). Dependency and self-criticism as predictors of suicidal behavior. *Suicide and Life-Threatening Behavior, 33*, 172–185.

Fairbairn, W. R. D. (1952). *Psychoanalytic studies of the personality*. London: Routledge & Kegan Paul.

Fairbrother, N., & Moretti, M. (1998). Sociotropy, autonomy, and self-discrepancy: Status in depressed, remitted depressed, and control participants. *Cognitive Therapy and Research, 22*, 279–297.

Falstein, E. (1958). The psychodynamics of male adolescent delinquency. *American Journal of Orthopsychiatry, 38*, 613–626.

Faravelli, C., Sacchetti, E., Ambonetti, A., Conte, G., Pallanti, S., & Vita, A. (1986). Early life events and affective disorder revisited. *British Journal of Psychiatry, 148*, 288–295.

Farrell, D. M. (1989). Suicide among gifted students. *Roeper Review, 11*, 134–139.

Feather, N. T. (1966). Effects of prior success and failure on expectations of success and subsequent performance. *Journal of Personality and Social Psychology, 3*, 278–298.

Feffer, M. (1970). Developmental analysis of interpersonal behavior. *Psychology Review, 77*, 177–214.

Fehon, D. C., Grilo, C. M., & Martino, S. (2000). A comparison of dependent and self-critically depressed hospitalized adolescents. *Journal of Youth and Adolescence, 29*, 93–106.

Feighner, J. P., Robins, E., Guze, S. B., Woodruff, R. A., Winoker, G., & Munoz, R. (1972). Diagnostic criteria for use in psychiatric research. *Archives of General Psychiatry, 26*, 57–63.

Feldman, R., & Blatt, S. J. (1996). Precursors of relatedness and self-definition in mother-infant interaction. In J. Masling & R. F. Bornstein (Eds.), *Psychoanalytic Perspectives on Developmental Psychology* (pp. 1–42). Washington, DC: American Psychological Association.

Fenichel, O. (1945). *The psychoanalytic theory of neurosis*. New York: Norton.

Fichman, L., Koestner, R., & Zuroff, D. C. (1994). Depressive styles in adolescence: Assessment, relation to social functioning, and developmental trends. *Journal of Youth and Adolescence, 23*, 315–330.

Fichman, L., Koestner, R., & Zuroff, D. C. (1996). Dependency, self-criticism, and perceptions of inferiority at summer camp: I'm even worse than you think. *Journal of Youth and Adolescence, 25*, 113–126.

Fichman, L., Koestner, R., & Zuroff, D. C. (1997). Dependency and distress at summer camp. *Journal of Youth and Adolescence, 26*, 217–232.

Field, T. M. (1984). Early interactions between infants and their postpartum depressed mothers. *Infants' Behavior and Development, 7*, 527–532.

Field, T. M., Healy, B., Goldstein, S., & Guthertz, M. (1990). Behavior–state matching and synchrony in mother–infant interactions of nondepressed versus depressed dyads. *Developmental Psychology, 26*, 7–14.

Field, T. M., Healy, B., Goldstein, S., Perry S., Bendell, D., Schanberg, S., et al. (1988). Infants of depressed mothers show "depressed" behavior even with nondepressed adults. *Child Development, 59,* 1569–1579.

Fisch, R. (1987). Masked depression: Its interrelations with somatization, hypochondriasis and conversion. *International Journal of Psychiatry in Medicine, 17,* 367–379.

Fishler, P. H., Sperling, M. B., & Carr, A. C. (1990). Assessment of adult relatedness: A review of empirical findings from object relations and attachment theories. *Journal of Personality Assessment, 55,* 499–520.

Fiske, S. T., & Linville, P. W. (1980). What does the schema concept buy us? *Personality and Social Psychology Bulletin, 6,* 543–557.

Flett, G. L., Besser, A., Hewitt, P. L., Sherry, B. S., Berk, L., & Veres, F. (in press). *Personality vulnerablity factors, reassurance seeking, and postpartum depression.* Manuscript submitted for publication.

Flett, G. L., & Hewitt, P. L. (2002). Perfectionism and maladjustment: An overview of theoretical, definitional, and treatment issues. In G. L. Flett & P. L. Hewitt (Eds.), *Perfectionism: Theory, research, and treatment* (pp. 5–31). Washington, DC: American Psychological Association.

Flett, G. L., Hewitt, P. L., & Blankstein, K. R. (1991, August). *The Perfectionism Cognitions Inventory: Development, validation, and association with depression.* Paper presented at the 99th Annual Convention of the American Psychological Association, San Francisco.

Flett, G. L., Hewitt, P. L., Blankstein, K. R., & Gray, L. (1998). Psychological distress and the frequency of perfectionistic thinking. *Journal of Personality and Social Psychology, 75,* 1363–1381.

Flett, G. L., Hewitt, P. L., Blankstein, K. R., & Mosher, S. W. (1991). Perfectionism, self-actualization, and personal adjustment. *Journal of Social Behavior and Personality, 6,* 147–160.

Flett, G. L., Hewitt, P. L., Blankstein, K. R., & O'Brien, S. (1991). Perfectionism and learned resourcefulness in depression and self-esteem. *Personality and Individual Differences, 12,* 61–68.

Flett, G. L., Hewitt, P. L., & DeRosa, T. (1996). Dimensions of perfectionism, psychosocial adjustment and social skills. *Personality and Individual Differences, 20,* 143–150.

Flett, G. L., Hewitt, P. L., Endler, N. S., & Bagby, R. M. (1995). Conceptualization and assessment of personality factors in depression. *European Journal of Personality, 9,* 309–350.

Flett, G. L., Hewitt, P. L., Garshowitz, M., & Martin, T. R. (1997). Personality, negative social interactions, and depressive symptoms. *Canadian Journal of Behavioral Science, 29,* 28–37.

Flett, G. L., Hewitt, P. L., & Mittelstaedt, W. M. (1991). Dysphoria and components of self-punitiveness: A re-analysis. *Cognitive Therapy and Research, 15,* 201–219.

Flett, G. L., Hewitt, P. L., Oliver, J. M., & Macdonald, S. (2002). Perfectionism in children and their parents: A developmental analysis. In G. L. Flett & P. L. Hewitt (Eds.), *Perfectionism: Theory, research, and treatment* (pp. 89–132). Washington, DC: American Psychological Association.

Flett, G. L., Vredenburg, K., & Krames, L. (1997). The continuity of depression in clinical and nonclinical samples. *Psychological Bulletin, 121,* 395–416.

Follette, W. C., Naugle, A. E., & Callaghan, G. M. (1996). A radical behavioral understanding of the therapeutic relationship in effecting change. *Behavior Therapy, 27,* 623–641.

Fonagy, P. (2003). Some complexities in the relationship of psychoanalytic theory to technique. *Psychoanalytic Quarterly, 72,* 13–47.

Fonagy, P., Leigh, T., Steele, M., Steele, H., Kennedy, R., Mattoon, G., et al. (1996). The relation of attachment status, psychiatric classification, and response to psychotherapy. *Journal of Consulting and Clinical Psychology, 64,* 22–31.

Fonagy, P., Steele, H., & Steele, M. (1991). Maternal representations of attachment during pregnancy predict the organization of infant–mother attachment at one year of age. *Child Development, 62,* 891–905.

Fonagy, P., Steele, M., Moran, G., Steele, H., & Higgit, A. (1991). Measuring the ghost in the nursery: A summary of the main findings of the Anna Freud Center–University College London Parent–Child Study. *Bulletin of the Anna Freud Center, 14,* 115–131.

Forrest, A. D., Fraser, R. H., & Priest, R. G. (1965). Environmental factors in depressive illness. *British Journal of Psychiatry, 111,* 243–253.

Fowler, C., Hilsenroth, M., & Piers, C. (2001). An empirical study of seriously disturbed suicidal patients. *Journal of the American Psychoanalytic Association, 49,* 161–186.

Fraiberg, S. (1969). Libidinal object constancy and mental representation. *Psychoanalytic Study of the Child, 24,* 9–47.

Fraiberg, S., Adelson, E., & Shapiro, V. (1975). Ghosts in the nursery: A psychoanalytic approach to impaired infant–mother relationships. *Journal of Academy of Child Psychiatry, 14,* 387–421.

Franche, R., & Dobson, K. (1992). Self-criticism and interpersonal dependency as vulnerability factors to depression. *Cognitive Therapy and Research, 16,* 419–435.

Frank, S. J., Pirsch, L. A., & Wright, V. C. (1990). Late adolescents' perceptions of their relationships with their parents: Relationships among deidealization, autonomy, relatedness, and insecurity and implications for adolescent adjustment and ego identity status. *Journal of Youth and Adolescence, 19,* 571–588.

Frank, S. J., Poorman, M. O., Van Egeren, L. A., & Field, D. T. (1997). Perceived relationships with parents among adolescent inpatients with depressive preoccupations and depressed mood. *Journal of Clinical Child Psychology, 26,* 205–215.

Frank, S. J., Van Egeren, L. A., Paul, J. S., Poorman, M. O., Sanford, K., Williams, O. B., & Field, D. T. (1997). Measuring self-critical and interpersonal preoccupations in an adolescent inpatient sample. *Psychological Assessment, 9,* 185–195.

Freud, A. (1937). The ego and mechanisms of defense (C. Baines, Trans). New York: International Universities Press. (Original work published 1936)

Freud, A. (1946). The psychoanalytic study of infantile feeding disturbances. *The Psychoanalytic Study of the Child, 2,* 119–132.

Freud, A. (1949). Certain types and stages of social maladjustment. In K. R. Eissler (Ed.), Searchlights on delinquency (pp. 193–204). New York: International Universities Press.

Freud, A. (1952). The mutual influences in the development of ego and id. *Psychoanalytic Study of the Child, 7,* 42–50.

Freud, A. (1965). The concept of developmental lines. In A. Freud (Ed.), *Normality and pathology of childhood: Assessments of development* (pp. 62–92). Madison, CT: International Universities Press.

Freud, S. (1953). The interpretation of dreams. In J. Strachey (Ed. and Trans.), *The standard edition of the complete psychological works of Sigmund Freud* (Vols. 4 & 5, pp. 339–625). London: Hogarth Press. (Original work published 1900)

Freud, S. (1957a). Contributions to a discussion on suicide. In J. Strachey (Ed. and Trans.), *The standard edition of the complete psychological works of Sigmund Freud* (Vol. 11, pp. 231–232). London: Hogarth Press. (Original work published 1910)

Freud, S. (1957b). Draft G: On melancholia (undated, January 7, 1895). In J. Strachey (Ed. and Trans.), *The standard edition of the complete psychological works of Sigmund Freud* (Vol. 1, pp. 200–206). London: Hogarth Press. (Original work published 1895)

Freud, S. (1957c). Draft N: Notes III (May 31, 1897). In J. Strachey (Ed. and Trans.), *The standard edition of the complete psychological works of Sigmund Freud* (Vol. 1, pp. 254–257). London: Hogarth Press. (Original work published 1897)

Freud, S. (1957d). Identification. In J. Strachey (Ed. and Trans.), *The standard edition of the complete psychological works of Sigmund Freud* (Vol. 18, pp. 105–110). London: Hogarth Press. (Original work published 1921)

Freud, S. (1957e). Mourning and melancholia. In J. Strachey (Ed. and Trans.), *The standard edition of the complete psychological works of Sigmund Freud* (Vol. 14, pp. 243–258). London: Hogarth Press. (Original work published 1917)

Freud, S. (1957f). Some character-types met with in psycho-analytic work. Part II: Those wrecked by success. In J. Strachey (Ed. and Trans.), *The standard edition of the complete psychological works of Sigmund Freud* (Vol. 14, pp. 316–331). London: Hogarth Press. (Original work published 1916)

Freud, S. (1959). Inhibitions, symptoms and anxiety. In J. Strachey (Ed. and Trans.), *The standard edition of the complete psychological works of Sigmund Freud* (Vol. 20, pp. 87–174). London: Hogarth Press. (Original work published 1926)

Freud, S. (1961a). Civilization and its discontents. In J. Strachey (Ed. and Trans.), *The standard edition of the complete psychological works of Sigmund Freud* (Vol. 21, pp. 64–145). London: Hogarth Press. (Original work published 1930)

Freud, S. (1961b). The ego and the id. In J. Strachey (Ed. and Trans.), *The standard edition of the complete psychological works of Sigmund Freud* (Vol. 19, pp. 12–66). London: Hogarth Press. (Original work published 1923)

Freud, S. (1963). Introductory lectures in psycho-analysis. Part III: General theory of the neuroses. In J. Strachey (Ed. and Trans.), *The standard edition of the complete psychological works of Sigmund Freud* (Vol. 16, pp. 347, 362–365). London: Hogarth Press. (Original work published 1917)

Friedlander, K. (1947). *The psycho-analytical approach to juvenile delinquency.* New York: International Universities Press.

Friedlander, K. (1949). Latent delinquency and ego development. In K. R. Eissler (Ed.), *Searchlights on delinquency* (pp. 205–215). New York: International Universities Press.

Friedman, R. C., Corn, R., Hurt, S. W., Fibel, B., Schulick, J., & Swirsky, S. (1984). Family history of illness in the seriously suicidal adolescent: A life cycle approach. *American Journal of Orthopsychiatry, 54,* 3970–3971.

Frost, R. O., Benton, N., & Dowrick, P. W. (1990). Self-evaluation, videotape review and dysphoria. *Journal of Social and Clinical Psychology, 9,* 367–374.

Frost, R. O., Heimberg, R. G., Holt, C. S., Mattia, J. I. U., & Neubauer, A. L. (1993). A comparison of two measures of perfectionism. *Personality and Individual Differences, 14,* 119–126.

Frost, R. O., & Henderson, K. J. (1991). Perfectionism and reactions to athletic competition. *Journal of Sport Exercise Psychology, 13,* 323–335.

Frost, R. O., Lahart, C. M., & Rosenblate, R. (1991). The development of perfectionism: A study of daughters and their mothers. *Cognitive Therapy and Research, 15,* 469–489.

Frost, R. O., & Marten, P. A. (1990). Perfectionism and evaluative threat. *Cognitive Therapy and Research, 14,* 559–572.

Frost, R., Marten, P., Lahart, C., & Rosenblate, R. (1990). The dimensions of perfectionism. *Cognitive Therapy and Research, 14,* 449–468.

Frost, R. O., Trepanier, K. L., Brown, E. J., Heimberg, R. G., Juster, H. R., Makris, G. S., & Leung, A. W. (1997). Self-monitoring of mistakes among subjects high and low in perfectionistic concern over mistakes. *Cognitive Therapy and Research, 21,* 209–222.

Fuhr, S. K., & Shean, G. (1992). Subtypes of depression, efficacy, and the Depressive Experiences Questionnaire. *Journal of Psychology, 126,* 495–506.

Gabbard, G. O. (1995). General considerations in psychiatric treatment. In G. O. Gabbard (Ed.), *Treatments of psychiatric disorders* (2nd ed.), Vol. 1 (pp. 1–87). Washington, DC: American Psychiatric Press.

Gaensbauer, T. J. (1982). Regulation of emotional expression in infants from two contrasting caretaker environments. *Journal of the American Academy of Child Psychiatry, 21,* 163–170.

Gaensbauer, T. J., Harmon, R. J., Cytryn, L., & McKnew, D. H. (1984). Social and affective development in infants with a manic–depressive parent. *American Journal of Psychiatry, 141,* 223–229.

Garber, J. (1984). Classification of developmental psychotherapy: A developmental perspective. *Child Development, 55,* 30–48.

Gardner, H. (1985). *The mind's new science: A history of the cognitive revolution.* New York: Basic Books.

Garland, A. (1993). *Pathways to adolescent mental health services: Adolescent help-seeking and teacher identification and referral.* Unpublished doctoral dissertation, Yale University.

Garland, A. F., & Zigler, E. (1993). Adolescent suicide prevention: Current research and social policy implications. *American Psychologist, 48,* 169–182.

Garmezy, N. (1987). Developmental changes in response to stress. In M. Rutter, C. E. Izard, & P. B. Read (Eds.), *Depression in young people* (pp. 297–323). New York: Guilford Press.

Garrison, C. (1982). *Depression symptoms, family environment, and life change in early adolescents.* Unpublished doctoral dissertation.

Gelinas, D. J. (1983). The persisting negative effects of incest. *Psychiatry, 46,* 312–331.

Geller, B., Chestnut, B. S., Miller, D. M., Price, D. T., & Yates, B. A. (1985). Preliminary data on *DSM–III* associated features of major depressive disorder in children and adolescents. *American Journal of Psychiatry, 142,* 643–644.

George, C., & Solomon, J. (1989). Internal working models of caregiving and security of attachment at age six. *Infant Mental Health Journal, 10,* 222–237.

Gerlsma, C., Emmelkamp, P. M. G., & Arrindell, W. A. (1990). Anxiety, depression, and perception of early parenting: A meta-analysis. *Clinical Psychology Review, 10,* 251–277.

Gershon, E., Bunney, W. E., Leckman, J. F., Van Eerdewegh, M., & DeBauche, B. A. (1976). The inheritance of affective disorders: A review of data and of hypotheses. *Behavior Genetics, 6,* 227–261.

Giesler, R. B., & Swann, W. B., Jr. (1999). Striving for conformity: The role of self-verification in depression. In T. Joiner & J. C. Coyne (Eds.), *The international nature of depression: Advances in interpersonal approaches* (pp. 189–217). Washington, DC: American Psychological Association.

Gilbert, P., & Reynolds, S. (1990). The relationship between the Eysenck Personality Questionnaire and Beck's concepts of sociotropy and autonomy. *British Journal of Clinical Psychology, 29,* 319–325.

Gillespie, R. D. (1929). The clinical differentiation of types of depression. *Guy's Hospital Reports, 9,* 306–344.

Gilligan, C. (1982). *In a different voice: Psychological theory and women's development.* Cambridge, MA: Harvard University Press.

Gjerde, P. F., & Block, J. (1991). The preschool family context of 18 year olds with depressive symptoms: A prospective study. *Journal of Research on Adolescence, 1,* 63–91.

Gjerde, P. F., Block, J., & Block, J. H. (1988). Depressive symptoms and personality during late adolescence: Gender differences in the externalization–internalization of symptom expression. *Journal of Abnormal Psychology, 97,* 475–486.

Gjerde, P. F., Block, J., & Block, J. H. (1991). The preschool family context of 18 year olds with depressive symptoms: A prospective study. *Journal of Research on Adolescence, 1,* 63–91.

Glaser, K. (1967). Masked depression in children and adolescents. *American Journal of Psychotherapy, 21,* 565–574.

Glover, E. (1956). On the etiology of drug addiction. In E. Glover (Ed.), *On the early development of the mind* (pp. 187–215). New York: International Universities Press. (Original work published 1932)

Gold, E. R. (1986). Long-term effects of sexual victimization in childhood: An attributional approach. *Journal of Consulting and Clinical Psychology, 54,* 471–475.

Goldberg, J. O., Segal, Z. V., Vella, D. D., & Shaw, B. (1989). Depressive personality: Millon Clinical Multiaxial Inventory profiles of sociotropic and autonomous subtypes. *Journal of Personality Disorders, 3,* 193–198.

Goldfarb, W. (1945). Effects of psychological deprivation in infancy and subsequent stimulation. *American Journal of Psychiatry, 102,* 18–33.

Golding, J. M., & Singer, J. L. (1983). Patterns of inner experience: Daydreaming styles, depressive moods, and sex roles. *Journal of Personality and Social Psychology, 45,* 663–675.

Goldsmith, S. J., Fyer, M., & Frances, A. (1990). Personality and suicide. In S. J. Blumenthal & D. J. Kupfer (Eds.), *Suicide over the life cycle* (pp. 155–176). Washington, DC: American Psychiatric Press.

Gooden, W., & Toye, R. (1984). Occupational dream, relation to parents and depression in the early adult transition. *Journal of Clinical Psychology, 40,* 945–954.

Goodman, N. (1984). *Of mind and other matters.* Cambridge, MA: Harvard University Press.

Goodman, S. H., & Brumley, H. E. (1990). Schizophrenic and depressed parents: Relational deficits in parenting. *Developmental Psychology, 26,* 31–39.

Goodman, S. H., & Gotlib. (1999). Risk for psychopathology in the children of depressed mothers: A developmental model for understanding mechanisms of transmission. *Psychological Bulletin, 106,* 458–490.

Goodyer, I. M., & Altham, P. M. E. (1991). Lifetime exit events and recent social and family adversities in anxious and depressed school-age children and adolescents. *Journal of Affective Disorders, 21,* 219–228.

Gore, S., Aseltine, R. H., Jr., & Colten, M. E. (1993). Gender, social–relational involvement and depression. *Journal of Research on Adolescents, 3,* 101–125.

Gotlib, I. H. (1984). Depression and general psychopathology in university students. *Journal of Abnormal Psychology, 93,* 19–30.

Gotlib, I. H., & Hammen, C. L. (1992). *Psychological aspects of depression: Toward a cognitive–interpersonal integration.* New York: Wiley.

Gotlib, I. H., Lewinsohn, P. M., & Seeley, J. R. (1995). Symptoms versus a diagnosis of depression: Differences in psychosocial functioning. *Journal of Consulting and Clinical Psychology, 63,* 90–100.

Gotlib, I. H., Mount, J. H., Cordy, N. I., & Whiffen, N. E. (1988). Depression and perceptions of early parenting: A longitudinal investigation. *British Journal of Psychiatry, 152,* 24–27.

Gove, W. R. (1982). Labelling theory's explanation of mental illness: An update of recent evidence. *Deviant Behavior, 3,* 307–327.

Graham, P. (1979). Epidemiological studies. In C. Quay & J. S. Werry (Eds.), *Psychopathological disorders of childhood* (2nd ed., pp. 185–209). New York: Wiley.

Graham, S., Doubleday, C., & Guarino, P. A. (1984). The development of relations between perceived controllability and the emotions of pity, anger, and guilt. *Child Development, 55,* 561–565.

Greenson, R. (1957, December). Some clinical and theoretical considerations on acting out and the impulse disorders. Paper presented at the midwinter meetings of The American Psychoanalytic Association, New York.

Grinker, R. R., Miller, J., Sabshin, M., Nunn, R., & Nunnally, J. (1961). *The phenomena of depression.* New York: Harper & Row.

Grossmann, K., Fremmer-Bombik, E., Rudolph, J., & Grossmann, K. E. (1988). Maternal attachment representation as related to patterns of mother–infant attachment and maternal care during the first year. In R. A. Hinde & J. Stevenson-Hinde (Eds.), *Relationships within families: Mutual influences* (pp. 241–260). Oxford, England: Clarendon Press.

Gruen, R. J., & Blatt, S. J. (1990). Change in self- and object representation during long-term dynamically oriented treatment. *Psychoanalytic Psychology, 7,* 399–422.

Gruen, R. J., Silva, R., Ehrlich, J., Schweitzer, J. W., & Friedhoff, A. J. (1997). Vulnerability to stress: Self-criticism and stress-induced changes in biochemistry. *Journal of Personality, 65,* 33–47.

Gunderson, J. G., & Phillips, K. A. (1991). A current view of the interface between borderline personality disorder and depression. *American Journal of Psychiatry, 148,* 967–975.

Gunderson, J. G., Triebwasser, J., Phillips, K. A., & Sullivan, C. N. (1999). Personality and vulnerability to affective disorders. In C. R. Cloninger (Ed.), *Personality and psychopathology* (pp. 3–32). Washington, DC: American Psychiatric Press.

Guntrip, H. (1969). *Schizoid phenomena, object relations and the self.* New York: International Universities Press.

Gurman, A. S. (1977a). The patient's perception of the therapeutic relationship. In A. S. Gurman & A. M. Razin (Eds.), *Psychotherapy: A handbook of research* (pp. 503–543). New York: Pergamon.

Gurman, A. S. (1977b). Therapist and patient factors influencing the patient's perception of facilitative therapeutic conditions. *Psychiatry, 40,* 218–231.

Guttman, L. (1968). A general nonmetric technique for finding the smallest coordinate space for configuration of points. *Psychometrika, 33,* 469–506.

Guttman, L. (1977). What is not what in statistics. *The Statistician, 26,* 81–107.

Guttman, L. (1982a). Facet theory, smallest space analysis and factor analyses. *Perceptual & Motor Skills, 54,* 491–493.

Guttman, L. (1982b). What is not what in theory construction. In R. M. Hauser, D. Mechanic, & A. Haller (Eds.), *Social structure and behavior* (pp. 331–348). New York: Academic Press. (Original work published 1977)

Hamachek, D. E. (1978). Psychodynamics of normal and neurotic perfectionism. *Psychology—Quarterly Journal of Human Behavior, 15,* 27–33.

Hamilton, M. A. (1960). A rating scale for depression. *Journal of Neurology, Neurosurgery, and Psychiatry, 6,* 56–62.

Hamilton, M. A. (1967). Development of a rating scale for primary depressive illness. *British Journal of Social Clinical Psychology, 6,* 278–296.

Hammen, C. L. (1978). Depression, distortion and life stress in college students. *Cognitive Therapy and Research, 2*, 139–192.

Hammen, C. (1991). Generation of stress in the course of unipolar depression. *Journal of Abnormal Psychology, 100*, 555–561.

Hammen, C. (1996). Stress, families, and the risk for depression. In C. Mundt & M. Goldstein (Eds.), *Interpersonal factors in the origin and the course of affective disorders* (pp. 101–112). London: Gaskell Royal College of Psychiatrists.

Hammen, C. (1998). The emergence of an interpersonal approach to depression. In T. E. Joiner & J. C. Coyne (Eds.), *The interpersonal nature of depression* (pp. 21–35). Washington, DC: American Psychological Association.

Hammen, C. L., Burge, D., Daley, S. E., Davila, J., et al. (1995). Interpersonal attachment cognitions and prediction of symptomatic responses to interpersonal stress. *Journal of Abnormal Psychology, 104*, 436–443.

Hammen, C., Burge, D., & Stansbury, K. (1990). Relationship of mother and child variables to child outcomes in a high-risk sample: A casual modeling analysis. *Developmental Psychology, 26*, 24–30.

Hammen, C., Ellicott, A., Gitlin, M., & Jamison, K. R. (1989). Sociotropy–autonomy and vulnerability to specific life events in patients with unipolar depression and bipolar disorders. *Journal of Abnormal Psychology, 98*, 154–160.

Hammen, C., Marks, T., deMayo, R., & Mayol, A. (1985). Self-schemas and risk for depression: A prospective study. *Journal of Personality and Social Psychology, 49*, 1147–1159.

Hammen, C., Marks, T., Mayol, A., & deMayo, R. (1985). Depressive self-schemas, life stress, and vulnerability to depression. *Journal of Abnormal Psychology, 94*, 308–319.

Hansell, A. G., Lerner, H. D., Milden, R. S., & Ludolph, P. S. (1988). Single-sign Rorschach suicide indicators: A validity study using a depressed inpatient population. *Journal of Personality Assessment, 52*, 658–669.

Harder, S. (1978). Effectance motivation reconsidered: Toward a developmental model. *Human Development, 21*, 34–64.

Harkness, A. R., & Lilienfeld, S. O. (1997). Individual differences science for treatment planning: Personality traits. *Psychological Assessment, 9*, 349–360.

Harmon, H. (1960). *Modern factor analysis.* Chicago: University of Chicago Press.

Hartley, D. E., & Strupp, H. H. (1983). The therapeutic alliance: Its relationship to outcome in brief psychotherapy. In J. Masling (Ed.), *Empirical studies of psychoanalytic theories* (Vol. 1, pp. 1–27). Hillsdale, NJ: Analytic Press.

Hartmann, D. (1969). A study of drug-taking adolescents. *Psychoanalytic Study of the Child, 24*, 384–398.

Hartmann, H., Kris, E., & Lowenstein, R. M. (1949). Notes on the theory of aggression. *Psychoanalytical Study of the Child, 3/4*, 9–36.

Hastie, R. (1981). Schematic principles in human memory. In E. T. Higgins, P. Herman, & M. P. Zanne (Eds.), *Social cognition: The Ontario Symposium* (pp. 39–88). Hillsdale, NJ: Erlbaum.

Hathaway, S. R. and McKinley, J. C. (1943). *The Minnesota multiphasic personality inventory manual.* Minneapolis: University of Minnesota Press.

Hayes, A. M., Castonguay, L. G., & Goldfried, M. R. (1996). Effectiveness of targeting the vulnerability factors of depression in cognitive therapy. *Journal of Consulting and Clinical Psychology, 64*, 623–627.

Hayes, R. L., & Sloat, R. S. (1989). Gifted students at risk for suicide. *Roeper Review, 12*, 102–107.

Hazan, C., & Shaver, P. R. (1987). Romantic love conceptualized as an attachment process. *Journal of Personality and Social Psychology, 52*, 511–524.

Hazan, C., & Shaver, P. R. (1987). Romantic love conceptualized as an attachment process. *Journal of Personality and Social Psychology, 59*, 105–124.

Hazan, C., & Shaver, P. R. (1990). Love and work: An attachment–theoretical perspective. *Journal of Personality and Social Psychology, 59*, 270–280.

Healy, W., & Bronner, A. F. (1936). *New light on delinquency and its treatment.* New Haven, CT: Yale University Press.

Hegel, G. W. F. (1977). Hegel's phenomenology of spirit (J. N. Findlay, Ed., and A. V. Miller, Trans.). Oxford, England: Oxford University Press. (Original work published 1807)

Henrich, C. C., Blatt, S. J., Kuperminc, G. P., Zohar, A., & Leadbeater, B. J. (2001). Levels of interpersonal concerns and social functioning in early adolescent boys and girls. *Journal of Personality Assessment, 76*, 48–67.

Heron, W. (1961). Cognitive and physiological effects of perceptual isolation. In P. Solomon, P. E. Kubzansky, P. D. Leiderman, J. H. Mendelson, R. Trumbull, & D. Wexler (Eds.), *Sensory deprivation* (pp. 6–33). Cambridge, MA: Harvard University Press.

Hersh, E. K., & Lazar, S. G. (1993, August 12). Politics didn't kill Foster. New York Times, p. 25.

Hewitt, P. L., & Dyck, D. G. (1986). Perfectionism, stress, and vulnerability to depression. *Cognitive Therapy and Research, 10*, 137–142.

Hewitt, P. L., & Flett, G. L. (1989). The Multidimensional Perfectionism Scale: Development and validation. *Canadian Psychology, 30*, 339.

Hewitt, P. L., & Flett, G. L. (1990). Perfectionism and depression: A multidimensional analysis. *Journal of Social Behavior and Personality, 5*, 423–438.

Hewitt, P. L., & Flett, G. L. (1991). Perfectionism in the self and social contexts: Conceptualization, assessment, and association with psychopathology. *Journal of Personality and Social Psychology, 60*, 456–470.

Hewitt, P. L., & Flett, G. L. (1993). Dimensions of perfectionism, daily stress, and depression: A test of the specific vulnerability hypothesis. *Journal of Abnormal Psychology, 102*, 58–65.

Hewitt, P. L., & Flett, G. L. (2002). Perfectionism and stress processes in psychopathology. In G. L. Flett & P. C. Hewitt (Eds.), *Perfectionism: Theory, research, and treatment* (pp. 255–284). Washington, DC: American Psychological Association.

Hewitt, P. L., Flett, G. L., & Blankstein, K. R. (1991). Perfectionism and neuroticism in psychiatric patients and college students. *Personality and Individual Differences, 12*, 61–68.

Hewitt, P. L., Flett, G. L., & Ediger, E. (1996). Perfectionism and depression: Longitudinal assessment of a specific vulnerability hypothesis. *Journal of Abnormal Psychology, 105*, 276–280.

Hewitt, P. L., Flett, G. L., & Turnbull, W. (1992). Perfectionism and multiphasic personality inventory (MMPI) indices of personality disorder. *Journal of Psychopathology and Behavioral Assessment, 14*, 323–335.

Hewitt, P. L., Flett, G. L., & Turnbull-Donovan, W. (1992). Perfectionism and suicide potential. *British Journal of Clinical Psychology, 9*, 181–190.

Hewitt, P. L., Flett, G. L., & Turnbull-Donovan, W. (1994). Borderline personality disorder: An investigation with the Multidimensional Perfectionism Scale. *European Journal of Psychological Assessment, 10*, 28–33.

Hewitt, P. L., Flett, G. L., & Weber, C. (1994). Dimensions of perfectionism and suicide ideation. *Cognitive Therapy and Research, 18*, 439–460.

Hewitt, P. L., Mittelstaedt, W., & Wollert, R. (1989). Validation of a measure of perfectionism. *Journal of Personality Assessment, 53*, 133–144.

Hewitt, P. L., Newton, J., Flett, G. L., & Callander, L. (1997). Perfectionism and suicidal ideation in adolescent psychiatric patients. *Journal of Abnormal Child Psychology, 25*, 95–101.

Higgins, E. T. (1987). Self-discrepancy: A theory relating self and affect. *Psychological Review, 94*, 319–340.

Higgins, E. T. (1989). Continuities and discontinuities in self-regulatory and self-evaluative processes: A developmental theory relating self and affect. *Journal of Personality, 57*, 407–444.

Hirsch, B. J., Moos, R. H., & Reischl, T. M. (1985). Psychosocial adjustment of adolescent children of a depressed, arthritic or normal parent. *Journal of Abnormal Psychology, 94*, 154–164.

Hirschfeld, R. M. A., Klerman, G. L., Chodoff, P., Korchin, S. J., & Barrett, J. (1976). Dependency, self-esteem and clinical depression. *Journal of the American Academy of Psychoanalysis, 4*, 373–388.

Hirschfeld, R. M. A., Klerman, G. L., Gough, H. G., Barrett, J., Korchin, S., & Chodoff, D. (1977). A measure of interpersonal dependency. *Journal of Personality Assessment, 41*, 610–618.

Hirschfeld, R. M., Shea, T. M., & Weise, R. (1995). Dependent personality disorder. In J. W. Livesley (Ed.), *The DSM–IV personality disorders: Diagnosis and treatment of mental disorders* (pp. 239–256). New York: Guilford Press.

Hjelle, L. A., & Smith, G. (1975). Self-actualization and retrospective reports of parent–child relationships among college females. *Psychological Reports, 36,* 755–761.

Hollender, M. H. (1965). Perfectionism. *Comprehensive Psychiatry, 6,* 94–103.

Hollender, M. H. (1970). The need or wish to be held. *Archives of General Psychiatry, 22,* 445–453.

Hollingshead, A. B., & Redlich, F. C. (1958). *Social class and mental illness.* New York: Wiley.

Homann, E. (1997). *Intergenerational transmission of depression: Attachment, affect regulation and separation–individuation.* Unpublished doctoral dissertation, University of Michigan.

Horowitz, M. J. (1988). *Introduction to psychodynamics: A new synthesis.* New York: Basic Books.

Horvath, A. O., & Symonds, B. D. (1991). Relation between working alliance and outcome in psychology: A meta-analysis. *Journal of Counselling, 24,* 240–260.

Horwitz, A. V., & White, H. R. (1987). Intelligence and delinquency: A revisionist review. *American Sociological Review, 42,* 571–587.

Hudgeons, R., Morrison, J., & Barchha, R. (1967). Life events and onset of primary affective disorders. *Archives of General Psychiatry, 16,* 134–135.

Huprich, S. K. (1998). Depressive personality disorder: Theoretical issues, clinical functioning, and future research questions. *Clinical Psychology Review, 18,* 477–500.

Imber, S. D., Pilkonis, P. A., Sotsky, S. M., Elkin, I., Watkins, J. T., Collins, J. F., et al. (1990). Mode-specific effects among three treatments for depression. *Journal of Consulting and Clinical Psychology, 58,* 352–359.

Isen, A., Shalker, T., Clark, M., & Karp, L. (1978). Affect accessibility of material in memory and behavior: A cognitive loop? *Journal of Personality and Social Psychology, 36,* 1–12.

Jacobsen, T., Huss, M., Fendrich, M., Kruesi, M. J. P., & Ziegenhain, U. (1997). Children's ability to delay gratification: Longitudinal relations to mother–child attachment. *Journal of Genetic Psychology, 158,* 411–426.

Jacobson, E. (1943). Depression: The Oedipus conflict in the development of depressive mechanisms. *Psychoanalytic Quarterly, 12,* 541–560.

Jacobson, E. (1953). Contribution to the metapsychology of cyclothymic depression. In P. Greenacre (Ed.), *Affective disorders* (pp. 49–83). New York: International Universities Press.

Jacobson, E. (1954). Contribution to the metapsychology of psychotic identifications. *Journal of the American Psychoanalytic Association, 2,* 239–262.

Jacobson, E. (1964a). The effect of disappointment on ego and superego formation in normal and depressive development. *Psychoanalytic Review, 33,* 129–147.

Jacobson, E. (1964b). *The self and the object world.* New York: International Universities Press.

Jacobson, E. (1966). Problems in the differentiation between schizophrenic and melancholic states of depression. In R. M. Lowenstein, L. Newman, M. Schur, & A. J. Solnit (Eds.), Psychoanalysis—A general psychology (pp. 499–518). New York: International Universities Press.

Jacobson, E. (Ed.). (1971). *Depression: Comparative studies of normal, neurotic, and psychotic conditions.* New York: International Universities Press.

Jacobson, S., Fasman, J., & DiMascio, A. (1975). Deprivation in the childhood of depressed women. *Journal of Nervous and Mental Disease, 160,* 5–13.

Jae Im, C. (1996). *The characteristics of two depressive dimensions.* Unpublished master's thesis, University of Korea.

Jarmas, A. L., & Kazak, A. E. (1992). Young adult children of alcoholic fathers: Depressive experiences, coping styles, and family systems. *Journal of Consulting and Clinical Psychology, 60,* 244–251.

Jarrett, R. B., Basco, M. R., Risser, R., Ramanan, J., Marwill, M., Kraft, D., & Rush, A. J. (1998). Is there a role for continuation phase cognitive therapy for depressed outpatients? *Journal of Consulting & Clinical Psychology, 66,* 1036–1040.

Jarvie, H. F. (1950). On atypicality and the depressive state. *Journal of Mental Science, 96,* 208–225.

Jenkins, R. L., & Hewitt, L. (1944). Types of personality structure in child guidance clinics. *American Journal of Orthopsychiatry, 14,* 84–94.

Jerdonek, P. M. (1980). *The dimensionality and construct validity of an ego psychological measure of depressive experiences.* Unpublished doctoral dissertation, Ohio University.

Jessor, R., & Jessor, S. (1977). *Problem behavior and psychosocial development: A longitudinal study of youth.* New York: Academic Press.

Johnson, J. E., Petzel, T. P., Dupont, M. P., & Romano, B. M. (1982). Phenomenological perceptions of parental evaluations in depressed and nondepressed college students. *Journal of Clinical Psychology, 38,* 56–62.

Joiner, T. E. (1994). Contagious depression: Existence, specificity to depressed symptoms, and the role of reassurance-seeking. *Journal of Personality and Social Psychology, 67,* 287–296.

Joiner, T. E., Metalsky, G. I., Katz, J., & Beach, S. R. H. (1999). Be (re) assured: Excessive reassurance-seeking has (at least) some explanatory power regarding depression. *Psychological Inquiry, 10,* 305–308.

Jolly, J. B., Dyck, M. J., Kramer, T. A., & Wherry, J. N. (1996). The relations between sociotropy and autonomy, positive and negative affect and two proposed depression subtypes. *British Journal of Clinical Psychology, 35,* 91–101.

Jones, E. E., & Pulos, S. M. (1993). Comparing the process in psychodynamic and cognitive behavioral therapies. *Journal of Consulting and Clinical Psychology, 61,* 306–316.

Jordan, J. V. (1986). *The meaning of mutuality* (Work in progress No. 23). Wellesley, MA: The Stone Center.

Joseph, B. (1981). Defense mechanisms and phantasy in the psychoanalytic process. *Psychoanalysis in Europe, 17,* 11–28.

Joseph, B. (1983). On understanding and not understanding: Some technical issues. *International Journal of Psycho-Analysis, 64,* 291–298.

Judd, L. L., Rapaport, M. H., Paulus, M. P., & Brown, J. L. (1994). Subsyndromal symptomatic depression: A new mood disorder? *Journal of Clinical Psychiatry, 55,* 18–28.

Kagan, J. (1981). *The second year of life: The emergence of self awareness.* Cambridge, MA: Harvard University Press.

Kandel, D. B., & Davies, M. (1982). Epidemiology of depressive mood in adolescents. *Archives of General Psychiatry, 39,* 1205–1212.

Kandel, D. B., & Davies, M. (1986). Adult sequelae of adolescent depressive symptoms. *Archives of General Psychiatry, 43,* 255–262.

Kandel, D. B., Kessler, R. C., & Margulies, R. Z. (1978). Antecedents of adolescent initiation into stages of drug use: A developmental analysis. *Journal of Youth and Adolescence, 7,* 13–40.

Kandel, D. B., Raveis, V. H., & Davies, M. (1991). Suicidal ideation in adolescence: Depression, substance use, and other risk factors. *Journal of Youth and Adolescence, 20,* 289–319.

Kanzer, M. (1957). Panel report: Acting out and its relations to impulse disorders. *Journal of the American Psychoanalytic Association, 5,* 136–145.

Kaplan, A. (1986). The "self-in-relation": Implications for depression in women. *Psychotherapy, 23,* 234–242.

Kaplan, C. D., & Wogan, M. (1978). The psychoanalytic theory of addiction: A reevaluation by use of a statistical model. *American Journal of Psychoanalysis, 38,* 317–326.

Kaplan, J., & Arbuthnot, J. (1985). Affective empathy and cognitive role-taking in delinquent and nondelinquent youth. *Adolescence, 20,* 323–333.

Kaplan, N. (1987). *Individual differences in six-year-olds' thoughts about separation: Predicted from attachment to mother at age one.* Unpublished doctoral dissertation, University of California, Berkeley.

Kashani, J. H., Burk, J. P., & Reid, J. C. (1985). Depressed children of depressed parents. *Canadian Journal of Psychiatry, 30,* 265–268.

Kashani, J. H., Carlson, G. A., Beck, N. L., Hoeper, E. W., Corcoran, C. M., McAllister, J. A., et al. (1987). Depression, depressive symptoms, and depressed mood among a community sample of adolescents. *American Journal of Psychiatry, 144,* 931–934.

Kashani, J. H., Husain, A., Shokim, W. O., Hodges, K. K., Cytryn, L., & McKnew, D. H. (1981). Current perspectives on childhood depression: An overview. *American Journal of Psychiatry, 138,* 143–153.

Kashani, J. H., McGee, R. O., Clarkson, S. E., Anderson, J. C., Walton, L. A., Williams, S., et al. (1983). The nature and prevalence of major and minor depression in a sample of nine-year-old children. *Archives of General Psychiatry, 40,* 1217–1227.

Kashani, J. H., Sherman, D. D., Parker, D. R., & Reid, J. C. (1990). Utility of the Beck Depression Inventory with clinic-referred adolescents. *American Academy of Child and Adolescent Psychiatry, 29,* 278–282.

Katz, P. (1972). Patients in the development of juvenile delinquency. *Corrective Psychiatry & Journal of Social Therapy, 18,* 10–18.

Kaufman, I. (1955). Three basic sources for predelinquent character. *Nervous Child, 11,* 12–15.

Kaufman, I., Makkay, E., & Zilbach, J. (1959). The impact of adolescence on girls with delinquent character formation. *American Journal of Orthopsychiatry, 29,* 130–143.

Kazdin, A. E. (1987). *Conduct disorders in childhood and adolescence.* Newbury Park, CA: Sage.

Kazdin, A. E., & Kendall, P. C. (1998). Current progress and future plans for developing effective treatments: Comments and perspectives. *Journal of Clinical Child Psychology, 27,* 217–226.

Kegan, R. (1982). *The evolving self: Problem and process in human development.* Cambridge, MA: Harvard University Press.

Kernberg, O. F. (1975). *Borderline conditions and pathological narcissism.* New York: Aronson.

Kernberg, O. F. (1976). *Object relations theory and clinical psychoanalysis.* New York: Aronson.

Kernberg, O. F. (1977). Boundaries and structure in love relations. *Journal of the American Psychoanalytic Association, 25,* 81–114.

Kernberg, O. F. (1984a). From the Menninger Project to a research strategy for long-term psychotherapy of borderline personality disorders. In J. B. W. Williams & R. L. Spitzer (Eds.), *Psychotherapy research* (pp. 247–260). New York: Guilford Press.

Kernberg, O. F. (1984b). *Severe personality disorders: Psychotherapeutic strategies.* New Haven, CT: Yale University Press.

Kestenberg, J. S. (1971). From organ-object imagery to self and object representations. In J. B. McDevitt & C. F. Settlage (Eds.), *Separation–individuation* (pp. 75–99). New York: International Universities Press.

Khantzian, E. J. (1978). The ego, the self and opiate addiction: Theoretical and treatment consideration. *International Review of Psychoanalysis, 5,* 189–198.

Khantzian, E. J., Mack, J. F., & Schatzberg, A. F. (1974). Heroin use as an attempt to cope: Clinical observations. *American Journal of Psychiatry, 131,* 160–164.

Kiloh, L. G., & Garside, R. F. (1963). The independence of neurotic depression and endogenous depression. *British Journal of Psychiatry, 109,* 451–463.

Klagsburn, M., & Bowlby, J. (1976). Responses to separation from parents: A clinical test for young children. *British Journal of Projective Psychology, 21,* 2–27.

Klein, D. C., & Seligman, M. E. (1974). Reversal of performance deficits and perceptual deficits in learned helplessness and depression. *Journal of Abnormal Psychology, 85,* 11–26.

Klein, D. F. (1974). Endogenomorphic depression. *Archives of General Psychiatry, 31,* 447–454.

Klein, D. F., & Ross, D. C. (1993). Reanalyses of the National Institute of Mental Health Treatment of Depression Collaborative Research Program general effectiveness report. *Neuropsychopharmacology, 8,* 241–251.

Klein, D. N. (1989). The revised DEQ: A further evaluation. *Journal of Personality Assessment, 53,* 703–715.

Klein, D. N., Harding, K., Taylor, E. B., & Dickstein, S. (1988). Dependency and self-criticism in depression: Evaluation in a clinical population. *Journal of Abnormal Psychology, 97,* 399–404.

Klein, D. N., Taylor, E. B., Dickstein, S., & Harding, K. (1988). Primary early-onset dysthymia: Comparison with primary nonbipolar major depression on demographic, clinical, familial, personality, and socioenvironmental characteristics and short-term outcome. *Journal of Abnormal Psychology, 97,* 387–398.

Klein, M. (1935). A contribution to the psychogenesis of manic–depressive states. *International Journal of Psycho-Analysis, 16,* 145–174.

Klein, M. (1940). Mourning and its relation to manic–depressive states. *International Journal of Psycho-Analysis, 21,* 125–153.

Klein, M. H., Wonderlich, S., & Shea, M. T. (1993). Models of the relationship between personality and depression: Toward a framework for theory and research. In M. H. Klein, D. J. Kupfer, & M. T. Shea (Eds.), *Personality and depression* (pp. 1–54). New York: Guilford Press.

Klerman, G. L. (1974). Unipolar and bipolar depressions: Theoretical and empirical issues in establishing the validity of nosological concepts in the classification of affective disorders. In J. Argst (Ed.), *Classification and prediction of outcome of depression* (pp. 49–73). Stuttgart, Germany: F. K. Schattauer Verlag.

Klerman, G. L., & Weissman, M. M. (1989). Increasing rates of depression. *Journal of the American Medical Association, 261,* 2229–2235.

Klibinsky, R., Panofsky, E., & Saxl, F. (1964). *Saturn and melancholy: Studies in natural philosophy, religion and art.* New York: Basic Books.

Kluver, H. (1961). *Behavior mechanisms in monkeys.* Chicago: University of Chicago Press.

Kobak, R. R., & Sceery, A. (1988). Attachment in late adolescence: Working models, affect regulation and representations of self and others. *Child Development, 59,* 135–146.

Koestner, R., Zuroff, D. C., & Powers, T. A. (1991). The family origins of adolescent self-criticism and its continuity into adulthood. *Journal of Abnormal Psychology, 100,* 191–197.

Kohlenberg, R. J., & Tsai, M. (1991). *Functional analytic psychotherapy: Creating intense and curative therapeutic relationships.* New York: Plenum Press.

Kovacs, M. (1981). Rating scales to assess depression in school-aged children. *Acta Padedeopsuchiatra: International Journal of Child and Adolescent Psychiatry, 46,* 305–315.

Kovacs, M., Feinberg, T. L., Crause-Novack, M., Paulouskas, S. L., & Finkelstein, R. (1984a). Depressive disorders in childhood: I. A longitudinal perspective study of characteristics and recovery. *Archives of General Psychiatry, 41,* 229–237.

Kovacs, M., Feinberg, T. L., Crause-Novack, M., Paulouskas, S. L., Pollock, M., & Finkelstein, R. (1984). Depressive disorders in childhood: II. A longitudinal study of the risk for a subsequent major depression. *Archives of General Psychiatry, 41,* 643–649.

Kovacs, M., Paulouskas, S., Gatsonis, C., & Richards, C. (1988). Developmental stage and the expression of depressive disorders in children: An empirical analysis. In D. Cicchetti & K. Rosen-Schneider (Eds.), *Childhood depression: New directions for childhood development* (pp. 51–80). San Francisco: Jossey-Bass.

Kowal, A., & Pritchard, D. W. (1990). Psychological characteristics of children who suffer from headache: A research note. *Journal of Child Psychology & Child Psychiatry & Allied Disciplines, 31,* 637–649.

Krohn, A., & Mayman, M. (1974). Levels of object representation in dreams and projective tests. *Bulletin of The Menninger Clinic, 38,* 445–466.

Krupnick, J. L., Sotsky, S. M., Simmens, S., Moyer, J., Elkin, I., Watkins, J., & Pilkonis, P. A. (1996). The role of the therapeutic alliance in psychotherapy and pharmacotherapy outcome: Findings in the NIMH Treatment of Depression Collaborative Research Program. *Journal of Consulting and Clinical Psychology, 64,* 532–539.

Krystal, H. (1974). The genetic development of affects and affect regression. *Annual of Psychoanalysis, 2,* 98–126.

Krystal, H. (1977). Self- and object-representation in alcoholism and other drug-dependence: Implications of therapy. In J. D. Blaine & D. A. Julius (Eds.), *Psychodynamics of drug dependence* (NIDA Research Monograph No. 12, pp. 88–100). Rockville, MD: National Institute on Drug Abuse.

Krystal, H., & Raskin, H. A. (1970). *Drug dependence aspects of ego function.* Detroit, MI: Wayne State University Press.

Kuiper, N. A., & MacDonald, M. R. (1982). Self and other perception in mild depressives. *Social Cognition, 1,* 223–239.

Kuperminc, G. P., Blatt, S. J., & Leadbeater, B. J. (1997). Relatedness, self-definition and early adolescent adjustment. *Cognitive Therapy and Research, 21,* 301–320.

Kwon, P., Campbell, D. G., & Williams, M. G. (2001). Sociotropy and autonomy: Preliminary evidence for construct validity using TAT narratives. *Journal of Personality Assessment, 77,* 128–138.

Kwon, P., & Whisman, M. A. (1998). Sociotropy and autonomy as vulnerabilities to specific life events: Issues in life event categorization. *Cognitive Therapy and Research, 22,* 353–362.

Laforge, R., & Suczek, R. F. (1995). The interpersonal dimension of personality: III. An interpersonal chick list. *Journal of Personality, 24,* 94–112.

Lakey, B. R., & Ross, L. T. (1994). Dependency and self-criticism as moderators of interpersonal and achievement stress: The role of initial dysphoria. *Cognitive Therapy & Research, 18,* 581–599.

Lamb, W. K. (1997). *Evaluating the construct validity of the Structural Analysis of Social Behavior (SASB) as a measure of anaclitic and introjective depression: Two preliminary studies*. Unpublished master's thesis, University of California, Berkeley.

Lamont, J., Fischoff, S., & Gottlieb, H. (1976). Recall of parental behaviors in female neurotic depressives. *Journal of Clinical Psychology, 32,* 762–765.

Lamont, J., & Gottlieb, H. (1975). Convergent recall of parental behaviors in depressed students of different racial groups. *Journal of Clinical Psychology, 31,* 9–11.

Lane, R. D., Quinlan, D. M., Schwartz, G. E., Walker, P. A., & Zeitlin, S. B. (1990). The Levels of Emotional Awareness Scale: A cognitive–developmental measure of emotion. *Journal of Personality Assessment, 55,* 124–134.

Laxer, R. M. (1964). Self-concept changes in depressive patients in general hospital treatment. *Journal of Consulting Psychology, 28,* 214–219.

Leadbeater, B. J., Blatt, S. J., & Quinlan, D. M. (1995). Gender linked vulnerabilities to depressive symptoms, stress and problem behaviors in adolescents. *Journal of Research on Adolescence, 5,* 1–29.

Leadbeater, B. J., Hellner, I., Allen, J., & Aber, J. L. (1989). Assessment of interpersonal negotiation strategies in youth engaged in problem behaviors. *Developmental Psychology, 25,* 465–472.

Leadbeater, B. J., Kuperminc, G. P., Blatt, S. J., & Hertzog, C. (1999). A multivariate mode of gender differences in adolescents' internalizing and externalizing problems. *Developmental Psychology, 35,* 1268–1282.

Leadbeater, B. J., & Linares, L. O. (1992). Depressive symptoms in Black and Puerto Rican adolescent mothers in the first 3 years postpartum. *Development and Psychopathology, 4,* 449–466.

Leather, F., & Mongrain, M. (2002). *Dependency, self-criticism and lifetime risk for major depression.* Manuscript submitted for publication.

Lehman, A. K., Ellis, B., Becker, J., Rosenfarb, I., Devine, R., Khan, A., & Reichler, R. (1997). Personality and depression: A validation study of the Depressive Experiences Questionnaire. *Journal of Personality Assessment, 68,* 197–210.

Lehman, A. K., & Rodin, J. (1989). Styles of self-nurturance and disordered eating. *Journal of Consulting and Clinical Psychology, 57,* 117–122.

Leichtman, M. (1996a). The nature of the Rorschach task. *Journal of Personality Assessment, 67,* 478–493.

Leichtman, M. (1996b). *The Rorschach: A developmental perspective.* Hillsdale, NJ: Analytic Press.

Lekowitz, M. M., & Tesiny, E. P. (1984). Rejection and depression: Prospective and contemporaneous analyses. *Developmental Psychology, 20,* 776–785.

Leonhard, K. (1959). *Aufteilungder endogenein psychosen* (2nd ed.). Berlin, Germany: Akademie Verlag.

Lerner, R. M. (1982). Children and adolescents as producers of their own development. *Developmental Review, 2,* 305–308.

Lesse, S. (1974). *Masked depression.* New York: Aronson.

Levy, K. N., Blatt, S. J., & Shaver, P. R. (1998). Attachment style and mental representation in young adults. *Journal of Personality and Social Psychology, 74,* 407–419.

Levy, K. N., Edell, W. S., Blatt, S. J., Becker, D. F., Quinlan, D. M., Kolligan, J., & McGlashan, T. H. (1995). *Two configurations of psychopathology: The relationship of dependency, anaclitic neediness, and self-criticism to personality pathology.* Unpublished manuscript.

Levy, S. (1985). Lawful roles of facets in social theories. In D. Canter (Ed.), *Facet theory: Approaches to social research* (pp. 59–96). New York: Springer-Verlag.

Levy, S. T. (1985). Empathy and psychoanalytic technique. *Journal of the American Psychoanalytic Association, 33,* 353–378.

Lewin, B. D. (1950). *The psychoanalysis of elation.* New York: Norton.

Lewinsohn, P. M., & Rosenbaum, M. (1987). Recall of parental behavior by acute depressives, remitted depressives and non-depressives. *Journal of Personality and Social Psychology, 52,* 611–619.

Lewinsohn, P. M., Solomon, A., Seeley, J. R., & Zeiss, A. (2000). Clinical implications of "subthreshold" depressive symptoms. *Journal of Abnormal Psychology, 109*, 345–351.

Lewis, D. O., & Balla, D. A. (1976). *Delinquency and psychopathology.* New York: Grune & Stratton.

Lewis, H. B. (1990). Shame, repression, field dependency and psychopathology. In J. L. Singer (Ed.), *Repression and dissociation: Implications for personality theory, psychopathology and health* (pp. 233–257). Chicago: University of Chicago Press.

Lidz, T. (1973). *The origin and treatment of schizophrenic disorders.* New York: Basic Books.

Lidz, T., Lidz, R. W., & Rubenstein, R. (1976). An anaclitic syndrome in adolescent amphetamine addicts. *The Psychoanalytic Study of the Child, 31*, 317–348.

Linehan, M. M. (1993). *Cognitive–behavior treatment of borderline personality disorder.* New York: Guilford Press.

Lingoes, J. C. (1973). *The Guttman–Lingoes Nonmetric Program Series.* Ann Arbor, MI: Mathesis.

Lingoes, J. C. (1977). *Geometric representations of relational data.* Ann Arbor, MI: Mathesis.

Lingoes, J. C. (1981). Testing regional hypotheses in multidimensional scaling. In I. Borg (Ed.), *Multidimensional data representations: When and why* (pp. 280–310). Ann Arbor, MI: Mathesis.

Little, C., Robinson, J. L., Kogan, N., & Carter, A. (2002). *Negative emotion dysregulation in 12-month olds: Association with maternal depressive style, depressive symptoms, and reported infant social–emotional behaviors.* Manuscript submitted for publication.

Little, S. A., & Garber, J. (2000). Interpersonal and achievement orientations and specific stressors predicting depressive and aggressive symptoms in children. *Cognitive Therapy & Research, 24*, 651–670.

Lloyd, C. (1980). Life events and depressive disorders reviewed. *Archives of General Psychiatry, 37*, 541–548.

Loeber, R. (1988). Natural histories of conduct problems, delinquency, and associated substance abuse: Evidence for developmental progressions. In B. B. Lahey & A. E. Kazdin (Eds.), *Advances in clinical child psychology* (Vol. 11, pp. 73–115). New York: Plenum.

Loeber, R. (1990). Development and risk factors of juvenile antisocial behavior and delinquency. *Clinical Psychology Review, 10*, 1–41.

Loewald, H. W. (1962). Internalization, separation, mourning, and the superego. *Psychoanalytic Quarterly, 31*, 483–504.

Lohman, A. (1969). *Some relationships of self–object differentiation to empathic responsiveness and self-esteem.* Unpublished doctoral dissertation, University of Michigan.

Londerville, S., & Main, M. (1981). Security of attachment, compliance, and maternal training methods in the second year of life. *Developmental Psychology, 17*, 289–299.

Luborsky, L., & Crits-Cristoph, P. (1990). *Understanding transference: The core conflictual relationship theme.* New York: Basic Books.

Luborsky, L., Rosenthal, R., Diguer, L., Andrusyna, T. P., Berman, J. S., Levitt, J. T., Seligman, D. A., & Krause, E. D. (2002). The dodo bird verdict is alive and well—mostly. *Clinical Psychology, 9*, 2–12.

Luthar, S. S. (1991). Vulnerability and resilience: A study of high-risk adolescents. *Child Development, 62*, 600–616.

Luthar, S. S., & Blatt, S. J. (1993). Dependent and self-critical depressive experiences among inner-city adolescents. *Journal of Personality, 61*, 365–386.

Luthar, S. S., & Blatt, S. J. (1995). Differential vulnerability of dependency and self-criticism among disadvantaged teenagers. *Journal of Research on Adolescence, 5*, 431–449.

Luyten, P. (2002). *Normbesef en depressie: Aanzet tot een integratief theoretisch kader en een empirisch onderzoek aan de hand van de depressietheorie van S. J. Blatt* [Personal standards and depression: An integrative psychodynamic framework, and an empirical investigation of S. J. Blatt's theory of depression]. Unpublished doctoral dissertation, University of Leuven, Leuven, Belgium.

Luyten, P., Blatt, S. J., & Corveleyn, J. (in press). The convergence among psychodynamic and cognitive-behavioral theories of depression: Theoretical overview. In J. Corveleyn, P. Luyten, & S. J. Blatt (Eds.), *Theory and treatment of depression: Towards integration?* Leuven: Leuven University Press.

Luyten, P., Corveleyn, J., & Blatt, S. J. (in press). The convergence among psychodynamic and cognitive–behavioral theories of depression: A critical review of empirical research. In J. Corveleyn, P. Luyten, & S. J. Blatt (Eds.), *Theory and treatment of depression: Towards integration?* Leuven: Leuven University Press.

Luyten, P., Fontaine, J. R. S., Meganck, S., Jansen, B., DeGrave, C., Soenens, B., et al. (2003). *Content validity, internal structure, and reliability of the Depressive Experiences Questionnaire in students, adults and psychiatric patients.* Manuscript submitted for publication.

Luyten, P., Fontaine, J. R. J., Soenens, B., & Corveleyn, J. (2003). What you risk reveals what you value. Depressive personality styles and value priorities. Manuscript in preparation.

Luyten, P., Soenens, B., Jansen, B., Meganck, S., De Grave, C., Corveleyn, J., Maes, F., & Sabbe, B. (2003). The relationship between dependency, self-criticism, and psychopathological symptoms in students, adults, and depressed inpatients. An empirical investigation of Blatt's relative specificity hypothesis. Manuscript in preparation.

Lynch, T. R., Robins, C. J., & Morse, J. Q. (2001). Couple functioning in depression. The roles of sociotropy and autonomy. *Journal of Clinical Psychology, 57,* 93–103.

Lyons-Ruth, K. (2001). The two-person construction of defenses: Disorganized attachment strategies, unintegrated mental states and hostile/helpless relational processes. *Psychologist–Psychoanalyst, 21,* 40–45.

Lyons-Ruth, K., & Block, D. (1996). The disturbed caregiving system: Relations among childhood trauma, maternal caregiving, and infant affect and attachment. *Infant Mental Health Journal, 17,* 257–275.

Lyons-Ruth, K., Zeanah, C. H., & Bénoit, D. (2003). Disorder and risk for disorder during infancy and toddlerhood. In E. J. Mash & R. A. Barkley (Eds), *Child psychopathology* (2nd ed., pp. 589–631). New York: Guilford Press.

Magnusson, D., & Endler, N. S. (1977). Interactional psychology: Present and future prospects. In D. Magnuson & N. S. Endler, *Personality at a crossroad: Current issues in interactional psychology* (pp. 3–36). Hillsdale, NJ: Erlbaum.

Mahler, M. S. (1968). *On human symbiosis and the vicissitudes of individuation: Infantile psychosis.* New York: International Universities Press.

Mahler, M. S., Pine, F., & Bergman, A. (1975). *The psychological birth of the human infant: Symbiosis and individuation.* New York: Basic Books.

Main, M. (1981). Avoidance in the service of attachment: A working paper. In K. Immelman, G. Barlow, L. Petrinovich, & M. Main (Eds.), *Behavioral development: The Bielfeld interdisciplinary project* (pp. 651–693). New York: Cambridge University Press.

Main, M. (1983). Exploration, play, and cognitive functioning related to infant–mother attachment. *Infant Behavior and Development, 6,* 167–174.

Main, M. (1990a). Cross-cultural studies of attachment organization: Recent studies, changing methodologies, and the concept of conditional strategies. *Human Development, 33,* 48–61.

Main, M. (1990b, April). *Meta-cognitive knowledge, meta-cognitive monitoring and attachment: Some findings and some directions for future research.* Plenary address delivered to the Michigan Association for Infant Mental Health, Ann Arbor.

Main, M., & Cassidy, J. (1988). Categories of response to reunion with the parent at age 6: Predictable from infant attachment classifications and stable over a 1 month period. *Developmental Psychology, 24,* 415–426.

Main, M., & Goldwyn, R. (1984). Predicting rejection of her infant from mother's representation of her own experience: Implications for the abused–abusing intergenerational cycle. *Child Abuse and Neglect, 8,* 203–217.

Main, M., Kaplan, L., & Cassidy, J. (1985). Security in infancy, childhood and adulthood: A move to the level of representation. In I. Bretherton & E. Waters (Eds.), Growing points in attachment theory and research. *Monographs of the Society for Research in Child Development, 50*(1–2, Serial No. 209), 66–104.

Main, M., & Weston, D. R. (1981). The quality of the toddler's relationship to mother and father: Related to conflict behavior and the readiness to establish new relationships. *Child Development, 52,* 932–940.

Maltsberger, J. T. (1986). *Suicide risk.* New York: New York University Press.

Mandler, J. M. (1988). How to build a baby: On the development of an accessible representational system. *Cognitive Development, 3,* 113–136.

Marks, P. A., & Haller, D. L. (1977). Now I lay me down for keeps: A study of adolescent suicide attempts. *Journal of Clinical Psychology, 47,* 390–399.

Markus, H. (1977). Self-schemata and processing information about the self. *Journal of Personality and Social Psychology, 35,* 63–78.

Marriage, K., Fine, S., Moretti, M., & Haley, G. (1986). Relationship between depression and conduct disorder in children and adolescents. *Journal of the American Academy of Child Adolescent Psychiatry, 25,* 687–691.

Martin, M. H. (1997). *The occupational functioning of adult female survivors of childhood sexual abuse.* Unpublished doctoral dissertation, University of Memphis.

Marziali, E., & Oleniuk, J. (1990). Object representations in descriptions of significant others: A methodological study. *Journal of Personality Assessment, 54,* 105–115.

Masten, A. S., Garmezy, N., Tellegen, A., Pellegrini, D. S., Larkin, K., & Larsen, A. (1988). Competence and stress in school children: The moderating effects of individual and family qualities. *Journal of Child Psychology and Psychiatry, 29,* 745–764.

Matas, L., Arend, R., & Sroufe, L. A. (1978). Continuity and adaptation in the second year: The relationship between quality of attachment and later competence. *Child Development, 49,* 547–556.

Matussek, P., & Feil, W. B. (1983). Personality attributes of depressive patients. *Archives of General Psychiatry, 40,* 783–790.

Matussek, P., Molitor, G. A., & Seibt, G. (1985). Childhood experiences of endogenous and neurotic depressives. *European Archives of Psychiatry and Neurological Sciences, 235,* 12–20.

Mayman, M. (1967). Object-representations and object-relationships in Rorschach responses. *Journal of Projective Techniques and Personality Assessment, 31,* 17–24.

Mazure, C. M., & Maciejewski, P. K. (2003). A model risk for major depression: Effects of life stress and cognitive style vary with age. *Depression and Anxiety, 17,* 26–33.

McAdams, D. P. (1980). A thematic coding system for the intimacy motive. *Journal of Research in Personality, 14,* 413–432.

McCrae, R. R., & Costa, P. T. Jr. (1990). *Personality in adulthood.* New York: Guilford Press.

McCranie, E. W., & Bass, J. D. (1984). Childhood family antecedents of dependency and self-criticism: Implications for depression. *Journal of Abnormal Psychology, 93,* 3–8.

McGrath, E., Keita, G. P., Strickland, B. R., & Russo, N. F. (1990). *Women and depression.* Washington, DC: American Psychological Association.

McLaughlin, J. T. (1981). Transference, psychic reality, and counter-transference. *Psychoanalytic Quarterly, 50,* 637–664.

McNemar, Q. (1962). *Psychological statistics* (3rd ed.). New York: Wiley.

Mehta, V. (1993a, August 2). Casualties of Oxford. *The New Yorker,* 36–54.

Mehta, V. (1993b). *Up at Oxford.* New York: Norton.

Meissner, W. W. (1980). The problem of internalization and structure formation. *International Journal of Psychoanalysis, 61,* 237.

Meissner, W. (1986). Can psychoanalysis find itself? *Journal of the American Psychoanalytic Association, 34,* 379–400.

Mendelson, M. (1960). *Psychoanalytic concepts of depression.* Springfield, IL: Charles C Thomas.

Mendelson, T., Robins, C. J., & Johnson, C. S. (2002). Relatives of sociotropy and autonomy to developmental experiences among psychiatric patients. *Cognitive Therapy & Research, 26,* 189–198.

Metcalfe, M., & Goldman, E. (1965). Validation of an inventory for measuring depression. *British Journal of Psychiatry, 111,* 240–242.

Milkman, H., & Frosch, W. (1973). On the preferential abuse of heroin and amphetamines. *Journal of Nervous and Mental Disease, 156,* 242–248.

Miller, G., Galanter, E., & Pribram, K. (1960). *Plans and the structure of behavior.* New York: Holt, Rinehart & Winston.

Miller, J. B. (1984). *Toward a new psychology of women.* Boston: Beacon Press.

Miller, W. R. (1975). Psychological deficit in depression. *Psychological Bulletin, 82,* 238–260.

Millon, T. (Ed.). (1997). *The Millon inventories: Clinical and personality assessment.* New York: Guilford Press.

Millon, T., & Kotik-Harper, D. (1995). The relationship of depression to disorders of personality. In E. E. Beckham & W. R. Leber (Eds.), *Handbook of depression* (2nd ed., pp. 107–146). New York: Guilford Press.

Missildine, W. H. (1963). Perfectionism—If you must strive to "do better." In W. H. Missildine (Ed.), *Your inner child of the past* (pp. 75–90). New York: Pocket Books.

Mitchell, S. A. (1988). *Relational concepts in psychoanalysis: An integration*. Cambridge, MA: Harvard University Press.

Mongrain, M. (1993). Dependency and self-criticism located within the five-factor model of personality. *Personality and Individual Differences, 15*, 455–462.

Mongrain, M. (1998). Parental representations and support-seeking behavior related to dependency and self-criticism. *Journal of Personality, 66*, 151–173.

Mongrain, M., Lubbers, R., & Struthers, W. (in press). The power of love: Mediation of rejection in roommate relationships of dependents and self critics. *Personality and Social Psychology Bulletin*.

Mongrain, M., Vettese, L. C., Shuster, B., & Kendal, N. (1998). Perceptual biases, affect, and behavior in the relationships of dependents and self-critics. *Journal of Personality, 75*, 230–241.

Mongrain, M., & Zuroff, D. C. (1989). Cognitive vulnerability to depressed affect in dependent and self-critical college women. *Journal of Personality Disorders, 3*, 240–251.

Mongrain, M., & Zuroff, D. C. (1994). Ambivalence over emotional expression and negative life events: Mediators of depressive symptoms in dependent and self-critical individuals. *Personality and Individual Differences, 16*, 447–458.

Mongrain, M., & Zuroff, D. C. (1995). Motivational and affective correlates of dependency and self-criticism. *Personality and Individual Differences, 18*, 347–354.

Mongrain, M., Zuroff, D. C., & Chouinard, G. (1989, June). *The stability of personality and cognitive vulnerability markers in a sample of unipolar depressives*. Paper presented at the meeting of the Canadian Psychological Association, Halifax, Nova Scotia.

Monroe, S. M., & Simons, A. D. (1991). Diathesis–stress theories in the context of life stress research: Implications for the depressive disorders. *Psychological Bulletin, 110*, 406–425.

Monroe, S. M., & Steiner, S. C. (1986). Social support and psychopathology: Interrelations with preexisting disorder, stress, and personality. *Journal of Abnormal Psychology, 95*, 29–39.

Moon, M. Y.-K. (2000). *Longitudinal correlates of mothers' object representations of their five-year-old children: An exploratory study*. Unpublished doctoral dissertation, Columbia University.

Moore, R. G., & Blackburn, I. M. (1994). The relationship of sociotropy and autonomy to symptoms, cognition and personality in depressed patients. *Journal of Affective Disorders, 32*, 239–245.

Moore, R. G., & Blackburn, I. M. (1996). The stability of sociotropy and autonomy in depressed patients undergoing treatment. *Cognitive Therapy and Research, 20*, 69–80.

Morgan, C. D., & Murray, H. A. (1938). A method for investigating fantasies: The thematic apperception test. *Archives of Neurology and Psychiatry, 34*, 289–306.

Morrison, T. L., Urquiza, A. J., & Goodlin-Jones, B. L. (1998). Depressive experiences and romantic relationships in young adulthood. *Psychological Reports, 82*, 339–349.

Morse, J., Robins, C. J., & Gittes-Fox, M. (2000). Sociotropy, autonomy, and personality disorder criteria in psychiatric patients. *Journal of Personality Disorders, 16*, 549–560.

Moskowitz, D. S., & Zuroff, D. C. (1991, June). *Contributions of personality and environmental factors to positive and negative affect in an adult community sample*. Poster presented at the meeting of the Canadian Psychological Association, Calgary, Alberta.

Murray, C., & Lopez, A. (Eds.). (1996). *Summary: The global burden of disease*. Cambridge, MA: Harvard University Press.

Nacht, S., & Racamier, P. C. (1960). Depressive states. *International Journal of Psychoanalysis, 41*, 481–496.

Neisser, U. (1967). *Cognitive psychology*. New York: Appleton-Century-Croft.

Neisser, U. (1976). *Cognition and reality*. San Francisco: W.H. Freeman.

Nelson, D. R., Hammen, C., Daley, S. E., Burge, D., & Davila, J. (2001). Sociotropic and autonomous personality styles: Contributions to chronic life stress. *Cognitive Therapy & Research, 25*, 61–76.

Nelson, K., & Grundel, J. (1987). Generalized event representations: Basic building blocks of cognitive development. In M. Lamb & A. L. Brown (Eds.), *Advances in developmental psychology* (Vol. 1, pp. 131–158). Hillsdale, NJ: Erlbaum.

Newcomb, M. D., & Bentler, M. D. (1988). *Consequences of adolescent drug use: Impact on the lives of young adults*. Newbury Park, CA: Sage.

Newman, C. F. (1994). Understanding client resistance: Methods for enhancing motivation to change. *Cognitive and Behavioral Practice, 1*, 47–69.

Nietzel, M. T., & Harris, M. J. (1990). Relationship of dependency and achievement/autonomy to depression. *Clinical Psychology Review, 10*, 279–297.

Nolen-Hoeksema, S. (1987). Sex differences in unipolar depression: Evidence and theory. *Psychological Bulletin, 101*, 259–282.

Nolen-Hoeksema, S. (1990). *Sex differences in depression*. Stanford, CA: Stanford University Press.

Nolen-Hoeksema, S., Girgus, J. S., & Seligman, M. E. P. (1991). Sex differences in depression and explanatory style in children. *Journal of Youth and Adolescence, 20*, 233–246.

Norton, G. R., Buhr, K., Cox, B. J., Norton, P. J., & Walker, J. R. (2000). The role of depressive versus anxiety-related cognitive factors in social anxiety. *Personality and Individual Differences, 28*, 309–314.

Nystul, M. S. (1984). Positive parenting leads to self-actualized children. *Individual Psychology, 40*, 177–183.

Ogden, T. H. (1986). *The matrix of the mind: Object relations and the psychoanalytic dialogue*. New York: Aronson.

Oliver, J. M., & Baumgart, B. P. (1985). The Dysfunctional Attitude Scale: Psychometric properties in an unselected adult population. *Cognitive Theory and Research, 9*, 161–169.

Orbach, I., Gross, Y., & Glaubman, H. (1981). Some common characteristics of latency-age suicidal children: A tentative model based on case study analyses. *Suicide and Life-Threatening Behavior, 11*, 180–190.

Osgood, C. E., Suci, G. J., & Tannenbaum, P. H. (1957). *The measurement of meaning*. Urbana: University of Illinois Press.

Ostrom, T. M. (1984). The sovereignty of social cognition. In R. S. Wyer & T. K. Skrull (Eds.), *Handbook of social cognition* (Vol. 1, pp. 1–37). Hillsdale, NJ: Erlbaum.

Ostrov, E., Offer, D., & Howard, K. H. (1988). Gender differences in adolescent symptomology: A normative study. *Journal of the American Academy of Child and Adolescent Psychiatry, 28*, 394–398.

Ouimette, P. C., & Klein, D. N. (1993). Convergence of psychoanalytic and cognitive–behavioral theories of depression: A review of the empirical literature and new data on Blatt's and Beck's models. In J. Masling & R. Bornstein (Eds.), *Empirical studies of psychoanalytic theories: Vol. 4. Psychoanalytic perspectives on psychopathology* (pp. 191–223). Washington, DC: American Psychological Association.

Ouimette, P. C., Klein, D. N., Clark, D. C., & Margolis, E. T. (1992). Personality traits in offspring of parents with unipolar affective disorder: An exploratory study. *Journal of Personality Disorders, 6*, 91–98.

Orvaschel, H., Weissman, M. M., & Kidd, K. K. (1980). Children and depression: The children of depressed parents; the childhood of depressed patients; depression in children. *Journal of Affective Disorder, 2*, 1–16.

Overholser, J. C. (1996). The dependent personality and interpersonal problems. *Journal of Nervous and Mental Disease, 184*, 8–16.

Overholser, J. C., & Freiheit, S. R. (1994). Assessment of interpersonal dependency using the Millon Clinical Multiaxial Inventory—II (MCMI–II) and the Depressive Experiences Questionnaire. *Personality and Individual Differences, 17*, 71–78.

Owen, M. T., Easterbrooks, M. A., Chase-Landsdale, L., & Goldberg, W. A. (1984). The relationship between maternal employment status and stability of attachments to mother and to father. *Child Development, 55*, 1894–1901.

Pacht, A. R. (1984). Reflections on perfection. *American Psychologist, 39*, 386–390.

Padesky, C. A. (with Greenberger, D.). (1995). *Clinicians' guide to mind over mood*. New York: Guilford Press.

Padesky, C. A. (1996). Developing cognitive therapist competency: Teaching and supervision models. In P. M. Salkovskis (Ed.), *Frontiers of cognitive therapy* (pp. 266–292). New York: Guilford Press.

Panofsky, E. (1945). *Albrecht Durer*. Princeton, NJ: Princeton University Press.

Parker, G. (1979a). Parental characteristics related to depressive disorders. *British Journal of Psychiatry, 134*, 138–147.

Parker, G. (1979b). Reported parental characteristics in relation to trait depression and anxiety levels in a non-clinical group. *Australian and New Zealand Journal of Psychiatry, 13*, 260–264.

Parker, G. (1980). Vulnerability factors to normal depression. *Journal of Psychosomatic Research, 24*, 67–74.

Parker, G. (1981). Parental reports of depressives: An investigation of several explanations. *Journal of Affective Disorders, 3*, 131–140.

Parker, G. (1982). Parental representations and affective symptoms: Examination for an hereditary link. *British Journal of Medical Psychology, 55*, 57–61.

Parker, G. (1983). Parental "affectionless control" as an antecedent to depression: A risk factor delineated. *Archives of General Psychiatry, 40*, 956–960.

Parker, G. (1984). The measurement of pathogenic parental style and its relevance to psychiatric disorder. *Social Psychiatry, 19*, 75–81.

Parker, G., & Hadzi-Pavlovic, D. (1984). Modification of levels of depression in mother-bereaved women by parental and marital relationships. *Psychological Medicine, 14*, 125–135.

Parker, G., Tupling, H., & Brown, L. B. (1979). A parental bonding instrument. *British Journal of Medical Psychology, 52*, 1–10.

Parker, G., & Lipscombe, P. (1980). The relevance of early parental experiences to adult dependency, hypochrondriases and utilization of primary physicians. *British Journal of Medical Psychology, 53*, 355–363.

Parker, W. D. (1997). An empirical typology of perfectionism in academically talented children. *American Educational Research Journal, 34*, 545–562.

Parker, W. D., & Adkins, K. K. (1995). Perfectionism and the gifted. *Roeper Review, 17*, 173–176.

Paton, S., Kessler, R., & Kandel, D. B. (1977). Depressive mood and adolescent illicit drug use: A longitudinal analysis. *Journal of Genetic Psychology, 131*, 267–289.

Paykel, E. S. (1974). Recent life events and clinical depression. In E. K. E. Gunderson & R. D. Rahe (Eds.), *Life stress and illness* (pp. 134–163). Springfield, IL: Charles C Thomas.

Paykel, E. S., Myers, J. K., Dienelt, M. N., Klerman, G. L., Lindenthal, J. T., & Pepper, M. N. (1970). Life events and depression. *Archives of General Psychiatry, 21*, 753–760.

Paykel, E. S., Prusoff, B. A., & Myers, J. K. (1975). Suicide attempts and recent life events: A controlled comparison. *Archives of General Psychiatry, 32*, 327–333.

Paykel, E. S., & Tanner, J. (1976). Life events, depressive relapses and maintenance treatment. *Psychological Medicine, 6*, 481–485.

Pepper, C. M., & Coyne, J. C. (1996). The predictable instability of psychological distress in college students: A comment on Flett, Vredenburg and Krames. *Journal of Psychopathology and Behavioral Assessment, 18*, 183–186.

Perlman, J. R. (1998). *Depressive vulnerability in college-age females: Relation to separation-individuation*. Unpublished doctoral dissertation, Temple University.

Perris, C., Arrindell, W. A., Perris, H., Eismann, M., Van der Ende, J., & Van Knorring, L. (1986). Perceived depriving parental rearing and depression. *British Journal of Psychiatry, 148*, 170–175.

Peselow, E. D., Robins, C. J., Sanfilipo, M. P., Block, P., & Fieve, R. R. (1992). Sociotropy and autonomy relationship to antidepressant drug treatment response and endogenous–nonendogenous dichotomy. *Journal of Abnormal Psychology, 101*, 479–486.

Petersen, A. C., Compas, B., Brooks-Gunn, J., Stemmler, M., Ey, S., & Grant, K. E. (1993). Depression in adolescence. *American Psychologist, 48*, 155–168.

Petersen, A. C., Sarigiani, P. A., & Kennedy, R. E. (1991). Adolescent depression: Why more girls? *Journal of Youth and Adolescence, 20*, 247–272.

Peterson, C., Schwartz, S. M., & Seligman, M. E. P. (1981). Self-blame and depressive symptoms. *Journal of Personality and Social Psychology, 41*, 253–259.

Peterson, C., & Seligman, M. E. P. (1984). Causal explanations as a risk factor for depression: Theory and evidence. *Psychological Review, 91*, 347–374.

Piaget, J. (1954). *The construction of reality in the child* (M. Cook, Trans.). New York: Basic Books. (Original work published 1937)

Piaget, J. (1962). *Play, dreams and imitation in childhood* (C. Gattegno & F. M. Hodgson, Trans.). New York: Norton. (Original work published 1945)

Pilkonis, P. A. (1988). Personality prototypes among depressives: Themes of dependency and autonomy. *Journal of Personality Disorders, 2*, 144–152.

Pilon, D. (1987, August–September). *Validation of Beck's sociotropic and autonomous modes of depression*. Paper presented at the 95th Annual Convention of the American Psychological Association, New York.

Pilon, D., Olioff, M., Bryson, S. E., & Doan, B. (1986). *Relation of depressive experiences and symptoms to stress in a clinical sample*. Paper presented at the 47th annual convention of the Canadian Psychological Association, Toronto, Ontario.

Pincus, A. L., & Gurtman, M. B. (1995). The three faces of interpersonal dependency: Structural analyses of self-report dependency measures. *Journal of Personality & Social Psychology, 69*, 744–758.

Pincus, A. L., & Wilson, K. R. (2001). Interpersonal variability in dependent personality. *Journal of Personality, 69*, 223–251.

Pine, F. (1974). Libidinal object constancy: A theoretical note. *Psychoanalysis and Contemporary Science, 4*, 307–313.

Pirot, M. (1986). The pathological thought and dynamics of the perfectionist. *Individual Psychology: Journal of Adlerian Theory, Research and Practice, 42*, 51–58.

Plath, S. (2003). *The bell jar*. New York: HarperCollins.

Plomin, R. (1994). *Genetics and experience: The interplay between nature and nurture* . Newbury Park, CA: Sage.

Plomin, R., & Caspi, A. (1999). Behavioral genetics and personality. In L. A. Pervin & P. Johns (Eds.), *Handbook of personality: Theory and research* (2nd ed., pp. 251–276). New York: Guilford Press.

Powers, T. A., Zuroff, D. C., & Topciu, R. (in press). *Covert and overt expressions of self-criticism and perfectionism and their relation to depression*. Unpublished manuscript, University of Massachusetts Dartmouth.

Priel, B., & Besser, A. (1999). Vulnerability to postpartum depression symptomatology: Dependency, self-criticism and the moderating role of antenatal attachment. *Journal of Clinical and Social Psychology, 18*, 240–253.

Priel, B., & Besser, A. (2000). Dependency and self-criticism among first-time mothers: The role of global and specific support. *Journal of Social and Clinical Psychology, 19*, 437–450.

Priel, B., & Besser, A. (2001). Bridging the gap between attachment and object relations theory: A study of the transition to motherhood. *British Journal of Medical Psychology, 74*, 85–100.

Priel, B., Besser, A., & Shahar, G. (1998). *Israeli adaptation of the DEQ: Psychometric properties*. Unpublished manuscript, Ben-Gurion University of the Negev, Beer-Sheva, Israel.

Priel, B., Kantor, B., & Besser, A. (2000). Two maternal representations: A study of Israeli adopted children. *Psychoanalytic Psychology, 17*, 128–145.

Priel, B., Myodovnik, E., & Rivlin-Beniaminy, N. (1995). Parental representations among preschool and fourth-grade children: Integrating object relational and cognitive developmental frameworks. *Journal of Personality Assessment, 65*, 372–388.

Priel, B., & Shahar, G. (2000). Dependency, self-criticism, social context and distress: Comparing moderating and mediating models. *Personality and Individual Differences, 28*, 515–525.

Procidano, M. E., & Guinta, D. M. (1989). Object representations and symptomatology: Preliminary findings in young adult psychiatric inpatients. *Journal of Clinical Psychology, 45*, 309–316.

Provence, S., & Lipton, R. C. (1962). *Infants in institutions*. New York: International Universities Press.

Puig-Antich, J. (1982). Major depression and conduct disorder in prepuberty. *Journal of the American Academy of Child Psychiatry, 21*, 291–293.

Quadland, M. C. (1980). Private self-consciousness, attribution of responsibility, and perfectionistic thinking in secondary erectile dysfunction. *Journal of Sexual and Marital Therapy, 6*, 47–55.

Quinlan, D. M., Blatt, S. J., Chevron, E. S., & Wein, S. J. (1992). The analysis of descriptions of parents: Identification of a more differentiated factor structure. *Journal of Personality Assessment, 59*, 340–351.

Radke-Yarrow, M., Cummings, E. M., Kuczyinski, L., & Chapman, M. (1985). Patterns of attachment in two and three-year-olds in normal families and families with parental depression. *Child Development, 56*, 884–893.

Radloff, L. S. (1977). The CES-D Scale: A self-report depression scale for research in the general population. *Applied Psychology Measure, 3*, 385–401.

Radloff, L. S., & Rae, D. S. (1979). Susceptibility and precipitating factors in depression: Sex differences and similarities. *Journal of Abnormal Psychology, 88*, 174–181.

Rado, S. (1926). The psychic effects of intoxicants: An attempt to evolve a psychoanalytical theory of morbid cravings. *International Journal of Psychoanalysis, 7*, 396–413.

Rado, S. (1928). The problems of melancholia. *International Journal of Psycho-Analysis, 9*, 420–438.

Ranieri, W. F., Steer, R. A., Lavrence, T. I., Rissmiller, D. J., Piper, G. E., & Beck, A. T. (1987). Relationships of depression, hopelessness, and dysfunctional attitudes to suicide ideation in psychiatric patients. *Psychological Reports, 61*, 967–975.

Rapee, R. M. (1997). Potential role of childrearing practices in the development of anxiety and depression. *Clinical Psychology Review, 17*, 47–67.

Raskin, A. (1972). The NIMH collaborative depression studies: A progress report. *Psychopharmacology Bulletin, 8*, 55–59.

Raskin, A., Boothe, H., Reatig, N., & Schulterbrandt, J. G. (1978). Initial response to drugs in depressive illness and psychiatric and community adjustment a year later. *Psychological Medicine, 8*, 71–79.

Raskin, A., Boothe, H. H., Reatig, N. A., Schulterbrandt, J. G., & Odle, D. (1971). Factor analyses of normal and depressed patients' memories of parental behavior. *Psychological Reports, 29*, 871–879.

Raue, P. J., & Goldfried, M. R. (1994). The therapeutic alliance and cognitive–behavior therapy. In A. O. Horvath & L. S. Greenberg (Eds.), *The working alliance* (pp. 131–152). New York: Wiley.

Raynes, E., Auerbach, C., & Botyanski, N. C. (1989). Level of object representation and psychic structure deficit in obese persons. *Psychological Reports, 64*, 291–294.

Rector, N. A., Bagby, R. M., Segal, Z. V., Joffe, R. T., & Levitt, H. A. (2000). Self-criticism and dependency in depressed patients treated with cognitive therapy or pharmacotherapy. *Cognitive Therapy and Research, 24*, 571–584.

Rector, N. A., Zuroff, D. C., & Segal, Z. V. (1999). Cognitive change and the therapeutic alliance: The role of technical and nontechnical factors in cognitive therapy. *Psychotherapy: Theory, Research, Practice, Training, 36*, 320–328.

Reda, M. A., Carpiniello, B., Secchiaroli, L., & Blanco, S. (1985). Thinking, depression, and antidepressants: Modified and unmodified depressive beliefs during treatment with amitriptyline. *Cognitive Therapy & Research, 9*, 135–143.

Rees, W. D. (1975). The bereaved and their hallucinations. In *Bereavement, its psychosocial aspects* (pp. 66–71). New York: Columbia University Press.

Reich, A. (1988). *The prediction of social interaction at two years from mother–infant interaction at four months.* Unpublished doctoral dissertation, Yeshiva University.

Reinherz, H. Z., Frost, A. K., & Pakiz, B. (1991). Changing faces: Correlates of depressive symptoms in late adolescence. *Family and Community Health, 14*, 52–63.

Reinherz, H. Z., Frost, A. K., Stewart-Berghauer, G., Pakiz, B., Kennedy, K., & Schille, C. (1990). The many faces of correlates of depressive symptoms in adolescents. *Journal of Early Adolescence, 10*, 455–471.

Reinherz, H. Z., Stewart-Berghaver, G., Pakiz, B., Frost, A. K., Moeykens, B. A., & Holmes, W. M. (1989). The relationship of early risk and current mediators to depressive symptomology in adolescence. *Journal of the American Academy of Child and Adolescent Psychiatry, 38*, 942–947.

Reis, S., & Grenyer, B. F. S. (2002). Pathways to anaclitic and introjective depression. *Psychology and Psychotherapy: Theory, Research and Practice, 75*, 445–459.

Rempel, J. K., Holmes, J. G., & Zanna, M. P. (1985). Trust in close relationships. *Journal of Personality and Social Psychology, 49*, 95–112.

Rexford, E. N. (1959). Antisocial young children and their families. In L. Jessner & E. Pavenstedt (Eds.), *Dynamic psychopathology in childhood* (pp. 181–221). New York: Grune & Stratton.

Rhode, P., Lewinsohn, P. M., & Seeley, J. R. (1991). Comorbidity of unipolar depression: II. Comorbidity with other mental disorders in adolescents and adults. *Journal of Abnormal Psychology, 100,* 214–222.

Rich, F. (1993, September 5). Public stages. *New York Times Magazine,* p. 42.

Richman, J. A., & Flaherty, J. A. (1987). Adult psychosocial assets and depressive mood over time: Effects of internalized childhood attachments. *Journal of Nervous and Mental Disease, 175,* 703–712.

Ricks, M. H. (1985). The social transmission of parental behavior: Attachment across generations. *Monographs of the Society for Research in Child Development, 50,* 211–227.

Rierdan, J., Lang, E., & Eddy, S. (1978). Suicide and transparency responses on the Rorschach: A replication. *Journal of Consulting and Clinical Psychology, 46,* 1162–1163.

Riley, W. T., & McCranie, E. W. (1990). The Depressive Experiences Questionnaire: Validity and psychological correlates in clinical sample. *Journal of Personality Assessment, 54,* 523–533.

Robbins, P. R. (1974). Depression and drug addiction. *Psychoanalytic Quarterly, 41,* 467–475.

Robbins, D. R., & Alessi, N. E. (1985). Depressive symptoms and suicidal behavior in adolescents. *Journal of Psychiatry, 14,* 588–592.

Robertson, J., & Robertson, J. (1971). Young children in brief separation—A fresh look. *Psychoanalytic Study of the Child, 26,* 264–315.

Robins, C. J. (1985). *Effects of stimulated social reflection and achievement failure on mood as a function of sociotropy and autonomous personality characteristics.* Unpublished manuscript, Duke University.

Robins, C. J. (1990). Congruence of personality and life events in depression. *Journal of Abnormal Psychology, 99,* 393–397.

Robins, C. J. (1995). Personality–event interaction models of depression. *European Journal of Personality, 9,* 367–378.

Robins, C. J., Bagby, R. M., Rector, N. A., Lynch, T. R., & Kennedy, S. H. (1997). Sociotropy, autonomy, and patterns of symptoms in patients with major depression: A comparison of dimensional and categorical approaches. *Cognitive Therapy and Research, 21,* 285–300.

Robins, C. J., & Block, P. (1987, August–September). *Sociotropy and autonomy, depressive vulnerability and symptom profile.* Paper presented at the 95th Annual Convention of the American Psychological Association, New York.

Robins, C. J., & Block, P. (1988). Personal vulnerability, life events, and depressive symptoms: A test of a specific interactional model. *Journal of Personality and Social Psychology, 54,* 847–852.

Robins, C. J., Block, P., & Peselow, E. D. (1989). Relations of sociotropic and autonomous personality characteristics to specific symptoms in depression patients. *Journal of Abnormal Psychology, 98,* 86–88.

Robins, C. J., & Jacobson, R. (1987, November). *Problems in assessing sociotropy and autonomous personality characteristics.* Paper presented at the meetings of the Association for the Advancement of Behavior Therapy, Boston.

Robins, C. J., & Ladd, J. (1991). *Personal Style Inventory, version II.* Unpublished research scale, Duke University.

Robins, C. J., Ladd, J., Welkowitz, J., Blaney, P. H., Diaz, R., & Kutcher, G. (1994). The Personal Style Inventory: Preliminary validation studies of new measures of sociotropy and autonomy. *Journal of Psychopathology and Behavioral Assessment, 16,* 277–300.

Robins, C. J., & Luten, A. G. (1991). Sociotropy and autonomy: Differential patterns of clinical presentation in unipolar depression. *Journal of Abnormal Psychology, 100,* 74–77.

Robins, L. N., & Rutter, M. (1990). *Straight and devious pathways from childhood to adulthood.* Cambridge, England: Cambridge University Press.

Rochlin, G. (1965). *Grief and discontents.* Boston: Little, Brown.

Rogers, C. R. (1957). The necessary and sufficient conditions of therapeutic personality change. *Journal of Consulting Psychology, 21,* 95–103.

Rorschach, H. (1921). Psychodiagnostik: Methodik und ergebnisse eines wahrnemungsdianostischen experiments. Deutenlassen von zufallsformen [Psychodiagnostics]. Bern: Ernst Bircher.

Rose, G. (1962). Unconscious birth fantasies in the ninth month of treatment. *Journal of the American Psychoanalytic Association, 10,* 677–688.

Rose, M. L. (1976). *Personality configurations and adult attachment styles as moderators of the relationship between childhood sexual abuse and adulthood depression among incarcerated and college women.* Unpublished doctoral dissertation, Virginia Commonwealth University.

Rosenfarb, I. S., Becker, J., Khan, A., & Mintz, J. (1998). Dependency and self-criticism in bipolar and unipolar depressed women. *British Journal of Clinical Psychology, 37,* 409–414.

Rosenfeld, H. W. (1969). Delinquent acting out in adolescent males and the tasks of sexual identification. *Smith College Studies in Social Work, 40,* 1–29.

Roth, D., & Blatt, S. J. (1974a). Spatial representations and psychopathology. *Journal of the American Psychoanalytic Association, 22,* 854–872.

Roth, D., & Blatt, S. J. (1974b). Spatial representations of transparency and the suicide potential. *International Journal of Psychoanalysis, 55,* 287–293.

Rubenfine, D. L. (1968). Notes on a theory of depression. *Psychoanalytic Quarterly, 37,* 400–417.

Rude, S. S. (1989). Dimensions of self-control in a sample of depressed women. *Cognitive Therapy and Research, 13,* 363–375.

Rude, S. S., & Burnham, B. L. (1995). Connectedness and neediness: Factors of the DEQ and SAS dependency scales. *Cognitive Therapy and Research, 19,* 323–340.

Rush, A. J., Beck, A. T., Kovacs, M., & Hollon, S. D. (1977). Comparative efficacy of cognitive therapy and pharmacotherapy in the treatment of depressed outpatients. *Cognitive Therapy and Research, 1,* 17–37.

Rutter, M. (1979). Protective factors in children's responses to stress and disadvantage. In M. W. Kent & J. E. Rolfe (Eds.), *Primary prevention of psychopathology: Vol. 3. Social competence in children* (pp. 49–74). Hanover, NH: University Press of New England.

Rutter, M. (1986). The developmental psychopathology of depression: Issues and perspectives. In M. Rutter, C. Izard, & P. Read (Eds.), *Depression in young people: Developmental and clinical perspectives* (pp. 3–30). New York: Guilford Press.

Rutter, M. (1990). Commentary: Some focus and process considerations regarding effects of parental depression on children. *Developmental Psychology, 26,* 60–67.

Rutter, M., Izard, C. E., & Reed, P. B. (1986). *Depression in young people: Development and clinical perspectives.* New York: Guilford Press.

Ryan, E. R., & Bell, M. D. (1984). Changes in object relations from psychosis to recovery. *Journal of Abnormal Psychology, 93,* 209–215.

Ryan, R. M., & Deci, E. L. (2000). Self-determination theory and the facilitation of intrinsic motivation, social development, and well-being. *American Psychologist, 55,* 68–78.

Ryder, L. T. (1997). *An empirical investigation of the differential coping responses utilized by dependent and nondependent populations in response to interpersonal and achievement losses.* Unpublished doctoral dissertation, Washington State University.

Saddler, C. D., & Sacks, L. A. (1993). Multidimensional perfectionism and academic procrastination: Relationships with depression in university students. *Psychological Reports, 73,* 863–871.

Sadeh, A., Rubin, S. S., & Berman, E. (1993). Parental and relationship representations and experiences of depression in college students. *Journal of Personality Assessment, 60,* 192–204.

Safran, J. D. (1990). Towards a refinement of cognitive therapy in light of interpersonal theory: 1. Theory. *Clinical Psychology Review, 10,* 87–105.

Safran, J. D., & Muran, J. C. (1996). The resolution of ruptures in the therapeutic alliance. *Journal of Consulting and Clinical Psychology, 64,* 447–458.

Safran, J. D., & Segal, Z. V. (1990). *Interpersonal process in cognitive therapy.* New York: Basic Books.

Sameroff, A., & Chandler, M. (1975). Reproductive risk and the continuum caretaking casualty. In F. Horowitz (Ed.), *Review of child development research* (Vol. 4, pp. 187–244). Chicago: University of Chicago Press.

Sameroff, A. J., Seifer, R., & Zax, M. (1982). *Early development of children at risk for emotional disorder.* Chicago: University of Chicago Press.

Sander, L. W. (1984). Polarity, paradox, and the organizing process in development. In J. Call, E. Galenson, & R. Tyson (Eds.), *Frontiers of infant psychiatry* (pp. 315–327). New York: Basic Books.

Sandler, J., Holder, A., & Meers, D. (1963). The ego ideal and the ideal self. *Psychoanalytic Study of the Child, 18,* 139–158.

Sandler, J., & Joffe, W. G. (1965). Notes on childhood depression. *International Journal of Psychoanalysis, 46,* 88–96.

Sandler, J., & Rosenblatt, B. (1962). The concept of the representational world. *Psychoanalytic Study of the Child, 17,* 128–145.

Sanfilipo, M. P. (1994). Masculinity, femininity, and subjective experiences of depression. *Journal of Clinical Psychology, 50,* 144–157.

Sanislow, C. A. (1994). *Bridging sociotropy and autonomy with dependency and self-criticism: Structural analysis of interpersonal perception.* Unpublished doctoral dissertation, Duke University.

Santor, D. A., & Coyne, J. C. (2001). Evaluating the continuity of symptomatology between depressed and nondepressed individuals. *Journal of Abnormal Psychology, 110,* 216–225.

Santor, D. A., Pringle, J. D., & Israeli, A. L. (2000). Enhancing and disrupting cooperative behavior in couples: Effects of dependency and self-criticism following favorable and unfavorable performance behavior. *Cognitive Therapy and Research, 24,* 379–397.

Santor, D. A., & Zuroff, D. C. (1997). Interpersonal responses to threats to status and interpersonal relatedness: Effects of dependency and self-criticism. *British Journal of Clinical Psychology, 36,* 521–542.

Santor, D. A., & Zuroff, D. C. (1998). Controlling shared resources: Effects of dependency, self-criticism, and threats to self-worth. *Personality and Individual Differences, 24,* 237–252.

Santor, D. A., Zuroff, D. C., & Fielding, A. (1997). Analysis and revision of the Depressive Experiences Questionnaire: Examining scale performance as a function of scale length. *Journal of Personality Assessment, 69,* 145–163.

Santor, D. A., Zuroff, D. C., Mongrain, M., & Fielding, A. (1997). Validating the McGill revision of the Depressive Experiences Questionnaire. *Journal of Personality Assessment, 69,* 164–182.

Saragovi, C., Aubé, J., Koestner, R., & Zuroff, D. (2002). Traits, motives, and depressive styles as reflections of agency and communion. *Personality & Social Psychology Bulletin, 28,* 563–577.

Sarason, I. G., Sarason, B. R., & Shearin, E. N. (1990). Social support as an individual difference variable: Its stability, origins, and relational aspects. *Journal of Personality and Social Psychology, 50,* 845–855.

Sato, T., & McCann, D. (1998). Individual differences in relatedness and individuality: An exploration of two constructs. *Personality and Individual Differences, 24,* 847–859.

Savitt, R. A. (1963). Psychoanalytic studies on addiction: Ego structure in narcotic addiction. *Psychoanalytic Quarterly, 32,* 43–57.

Schachter, E. P., & Zlotogorski, Z. (1995). Self-critical and dependent aspects of loneliness. *Israel Journal of Psychiatry & Related Sciences, 32,* 205–211.

Schaefer, E. S. (1965). Childrens' reports of parental behavior: An inventory. *Child Development, 36,* 413–424.

Schafer, R. (1968). *Aspects of internalization.* New York: International Universities Press.

Schaffer, C. E., & Blatt, S. J. (1990). Interpersonal relationships and the experience of perceived efficacy. In R. J. Sternberg & J. Kolligian Jr. (Eds.), *Competency considered* (pp. 229–245). New Haven, CT: Yale University Press.

Scharfman, M. A., & Clark, R. W. (1967). Delinquent adolescent girls. *Archives of General Psychiatry, 17,* 441–447.

Schlesinger, I. M. (1978). On some properties of the mapping sentence. In S. Shye (Ed.), *Theory construction and data analysis in the behavioral sciences* (pp. 181–191). San Francisco: Jossey-Bass.

Schmale, A. H. (1972). Depression as affect, character style and symptom formation. In R. Holt & E. Peterfreund (Eds.), *Psychoanalysis and contemporary science* (pp. 327–351). New York: Macmillan.

Schneider-Rosen, K., & Cicchetti, D. (1984). The relationship between affect and cognition in maltreated infants: Quality of attachment and the development of self recognition. *Child Development, 55,* 648–658.

Schulte, F., & Mongrain, M. (2003, August). *Distinguishing between mature and immature forms of dependency.* Presentation at the annual convention of the American Psychological Association, Toronto, Canada.

Schultz, L. H., & Selman, R. L. (1989). Bridging the gap between interpersonal thought and action in early adolescence: The role of psychodynamic processes. *Development and Psychopathology, 1,* 133–152.

Schwartz, H. (1968). Contribution to symposium on acting out. *International Journal of Psychoanalysis, 49,* 179–181.

Schwartz, S. H., & Huismans, S. (1995). Value priorities and religiosity in four Western religions. *Social Psychology Quarterly, 58,* 88–107.

Schwarz, J. C., and Getter, H. (1980). Parental conflict and dominance in late adolescent maladjustment: A triple interaction model. *Journal of Abnormal Psychology, 89,* 573–580.

Schwarz, J. C., & Zuroff, D. (1979). Family structure and depression in female college students: Effects of parental conflict, decision making power, and inconsistency of love. *Journal of Abnormal Psychology, 88,* 398–406.

Scott, J., Harrington, J., House, R., & Ferrier, I. N. (1996). A preliminary study of the relationship among personality, cognitive vulnerability, symptom profile, and outcome in major depressive disorder. *Journal of Nervous and Mental Disease, 184,* 503–505.

Segal, H. (1964). *Introduction to the work of Melanie Klein.* London: Heinemann.

Segal, Z. V., & Shaw, B. F. (1986a). Cognition in depression: A reappraisal of Coyne and Gotlib's critique. *Cognitive Therapy and Research, 10,* 671–693.

Segal, Z. V., & Shaw, B. F. (1986b). When cul-de-sacs are more mentality than reality: A rejoinder to Coyne and Gotlib. *Cognitive Therapy and Research, 10,* 707–714.

Segal, Z. V., Shaw, B. F., & Vella, D. D. (1989). Life stress and depression: A test of congruency hypothesis for life event content and depressive subtype. *Canadian Journal of Behavioral Science, 21,* 389–400.

Segal, Z. V., Shaw, B. F., Vella, D. D., & Katz, R. (1992). Cognitive and life stress predictors of relapse in remitted unipolar depressed patients: Test of the congruency hypothesis. *Journal of Abnormal Psychology, 101,* 26–36.

Seligman, M. E. P. (1975). *Helplessness: On depression, development, and death.* San Francisco: Freeman.

Seligman, M. E. P. (1995). The effectiveness of psychotherapy: The Consumer Reports study. *American Psychologist, 50,* 965–974.

Seligman, M. E. P., Peterson, C., Kaslow, N. J., Tanenbaum, R. L., Alloy, L. B., & Abramson, L. Y. (1984). Explanatory style and depressive symptoms among children. *Journal of Abnormal Psychology, 93,* 235–238.

Shaffer, D. (1974). Suicide in childhood and early adolescence. *Journal of Child Psychology and Psychiatry and Allied Disciplines, 15,* 275–291.

Shaffer, D. (1988). The epidemiology of teen suicide: An examination of risk factor. *Journal of Clinical Psychiatry, 49,* 36–41.

Shaffer, D., Garland, A., Gould, M., Fisher, P., & Trautman, P. (1988). Preventing teenage suicide: A critical review. *Journal of the American Academy of Child and Adolescent Psychiatry, 27,* 675–687.

Shafi, M., Carrigan, S., Whittinghill, J. R., & Derrick, A. (1985). Psychological autopsy of completed suicide in children and adolescents. *American Journal of Psychiatry, 15,* 275–291.

Shahar, G. (1999). *Interrelations between various measures of personality vulnerability to depression.* Unpublished manuscript, Ben-Gurion University of the Negev, Beer-Sheva, Israel.

Shahar, G. (2001). Commentary on "Shame and Community: Social Components of Depression." *Psychiatry, 64,* 228–239.

Shahar, G. (2002). *Excessive evaluative concerns complicate the diagnosis and treatment of unipolar depression.* Manuscript submitted for publication.

Shahar, G., Blatt, S. J., & Ford, R. Q. (2003). Mixed anaclitic–introjective psychopathology in treatment-resistant inpatients undergoing psychoanalytic psychotherapy. *Psychoanalytic Psychology, 20,* 84–102.

Shahar, G., Blatt, S. J., Zuroff, D. C., Kuperminc, G. P., & Leadbeater, B. J. (in press). Reciprocal relations between personality vulnerability and depressive symptoms among early adolescent girls and boys. *Cognitive Theory and Research.*

Shahar, G., Blatt, S. J., Zuroff, D. C., Kuperminc, J. L.., & Sotsky, S. M. (in press). Perfectionism impedes social relations and response to brief treatment of depression. *Journal of Social and Clinical Psychology.*

Shahar, G., Gallagher, L. F., Blatt, S. J., Kuperminc, G. P., & Leadbeater, B. J. (in press). An interactive-synergetic approach for the assessment of personality vulnerability to depression: Illustration with the adolescent version of the depressive experiences questionnaire. *Journal of Clinical Psychology.*

Shahar, G., Henrich, C. C., Blatt, S. J., Ryan, D. C., & Little, T. D. (2002). Interpersonal relatedness, self-definition, and their motivational underpinning during adolescence: A theoretical and empirical integration. *Developmental Psychology, 39,* 470–483.

Shahar, G., Joiner, T. E., Zuroff, D. C., & Blatt, S. J. (in press). Co-occurrence of stress-specific mediating and moderating effects of personality on depression. *Personality and Individual Differences.*

Shahar, G., & Priel, B. (1999, Boston). *Self-critical perfectionism, life events and emotional distress in adolescence.* Poster presented at the 107th Annual Convention of the American Psychological Association, Boston.

Shahar, G., & Priel, B. (2002). *Self-criticism predicts a distress-related social context: Dependency predicts a mixed context: Further support of an action model of personality vulnerability.* Manuscript submitted for publication.

Shahar, G., & Priel, B. (2003). Active vulnerability, adolescent distress, and the mediating/ suppressing role of life events. *Personality and Individual Differences, 35,* 199–218.

Shahar, G., Trower, P., Iqbal, Z., Birchwood, M., Davidson, L., & Chadwick, P. (in press). The person in recovery from acute and severe psychosis: The role of dependency, self-criticism, and efficacy. *American Journal of Orthopsychiatry.*

Shank, R. C., & Abelson, R. (1977). *Scripts, plans, goals and understanding.* Hillsdale, NJ: Erlbaum.

Shapiro, J. P. (1988). Relationships between dimensions of depressive experience and perceptions of the lives of people in general. *Journal of Personality Assessment, 52,* 297–308.

Shaver, P. R., & Hazan, C. (1987). Being lonely, falling in love: Perspectives from attachment theory. *Journal of Social Behavior and Personality, 2,* 105–124.

Shea, T., Elkin, I., Imber, S. D., Sotsky, S. M., Watkins, J. T., Collins, J. F., et al. (1992). Course of depressive symptoms over follow-up: Findings from the National Institute of Mental Health Treatment of Depression Collaborative Research Program. *Archives of General Psychiatry, 49,* 782–787.

Shye, S. (1978). *Theory construction and data analysis in the behavioral sciences.* San Francisco: Jossey-Bass.

Siddique, C. M., & D'Arcy, C. (1984). Adolescence, stress, and psychological well-being. *Journal of Youth and Adolescence, 13,* 459–473.

Simmel, E. (1948). Alcoholism and addiction. *Psychoanalytic Quarterly, 17,* 6–31.

Singer, M. T., & Wynne, L. C. (1965a). Thought disorder and family relations of schizophrenics: III. Methodology using projective techniques. *Archives of General Psychiatry, 12,* 187–200.

Singer, M. T., & Wynne, L. C. (1965b). Thought disorders and family relations of schizophrenics: IV. Results and implications. *Archives of General Psychiatry, 12,* 201–212.

Slade, A., & Aber, L. J. (1992). Attachment, drives and development: Conflicts and convergences in theory. In J. Barron, M. Eagle, & D. Wolitsky (Eds.), *Interface of psychoanalysis and psychology* (pp. 154–185). Washington, DC: American Psychological Association.

Smith, B., & Sechrest, L. (1991). The treatment of Aptitude × Treatment interactions. *Journal of Consulting and Clinical Psychology, 59,* 233–244.

Smith, K. (1981). Using a battery of tests to predict suicide in a long-term hospital: A quantitative analysis. *Journal of Clinical Psychology, 37,* 555–563.

Smith, T. W., O'Keeffe, J. C, & Jenkins, M. (1988). Dependency and self-criticism: Correlates of depression or moderators of the effects of stressful events? *Journal of Personality Disorders, 2,* 160–169.

Snow, R. E. (1991). Aptitude–treatment interactions as a framework for research on individual differences in psychotherapy. *Journal of Consulting and Clinical Psychology, 59*, 205–216.

Snyder, C. R., & Ingram, R. E. (2000). *Handbook of psychological change: Psychotherapy and processes and practices for the 21st century.* New York: Wiley.

Sorotzkin, B. (1985). The quest for perfection: Avoiding guilt or avoiding shame? *Psychotherapy, 22*, 564–571.

Southwick, S. M., Yehuda, R., & Giller, E. L. (1995). Psychological dimensions of depression in borderline personality disorder. *American Journal of Psychiatry, 152*, 789–791.

Spiegel, R. (1967). Anger and acting out. *American Journal of Psychotherapy, 21*, 597–606.

Spitz, R. A. (1965). *The first year of life.* New York: International Universities Press.

Spitz, R. A., & Wolf, K. M. (1946). Anaclitic depression. *Psychoanalytic Study of the Child, 2*, 313–342.

Spitzer, R. L., Endicott, J., & Robins, E. (1978). Research diagnostic criteria: Rationale and reliability. *Archives of General Psychiatry, 35*, 773–782.

Sroufe, L. A. (1983). Infant–caregiver attachment and patterns of attachment in pre-school: The roots of maladaptive competence. In M. Perlmutter (Ed.), *Minnesota Symposium on Child Psychology* (Vol. 16, pp. 41–83). Hillsdale, NJ: Erlbaum.

Sroufe, L. A., & Fleeson, J. (1986). Attachment and the construction of relationships. In W. W. Harups & Z. Rubin (Eds.), *Relationships and development* (pp. 51–71). Hillsdale, NJ: Erlbaum.

Stayner, D. (1994). *The relationship between clinical functioning and changes in self and object representations in the treatment of severely impaired inpatients.* Unpublished doctoral dissertation, Teachers College, Columbia University.

Steele, H., Steele, M., & Fonagy, P. (1996). Associations among attachment classifications of mothers, fathers, and their infants. *Child Development, 67*, 541–555.

Steele, R. E. (1978). Relationship of race, sex, social class and social mobility to depression in normal adults. *Journal of Social Psychology, 104*, 37–47.

Steiger, H., Gauvin, L., Jabalpurwala, S., Seguin, J. R., & Stotland, S. (1999). Hypersensitivity to social interactions in bulimic syndromes: Relationship to binge eating. *Journal of Consulting and Clinical Psychology, 67*, 765–775.

Steiger, H., Leung, F. Y., Puentes-Neuman, G., & Gottheil, N. (1992). Psychosocial profiles of adolescent girls with varying degrees of eating and mood disturbances. *International Journal of Eating Disorders, 11*, 121–131.

Steiger, H., Puentes-Neuman, G., & Leung, F. Y. (1991). Personality and family features of adolescent girls with eating symptoms: Evidence for restricter/binger differences in nonclinical population. *Addictive Behaviors, 16*, 303–314.

Stein, N., Fruchter, H. J., & Trief, P. (1983). Experiences of depression and illness behavior in patients with intractable chronic pain. *Journal of Clinical Psychology, 39*, 31–33.

Stephens, B. J. (1987). Cheap thrills and humble pie: The adolescence of female suicide attempters. *Suicide and Life-Threatening Behavior, 17*, 107–118.

Stern, D. N. (1985). *The interpersonal world of the infant: A view from psychoanalysis and developmental psychology.* New York: Basic Books.

Stober, J. (1998). The Frost Multidimensional Perfectionism Scale revisited: More perfect with four (instead of six) dimensions. *Personality and Individual Differences, 24*, 481–491.

Stolorow, R. D. (1978). The concept of psychic structure: Its metapsychological and clinical psychoanalytic meanings. *International Review of Psychoanalysis, 5*, 313–320.

Strober, M., Green, J., & Carlson, G. (1981). Utility of the Beck Depression Inventory with psychiatrically hospitalized adolescents. *Journal of Consulting and Clinical Psychology, 49*, 482–483.

Suomi, S. J., & Harlow, H. F. (1977). Depression: Production and alleviation of depressive behaviors in monkeys. In J. D. Maser & M. Seligman (Eds.), *Psychopathology: Experimental models. A series of books in psychology* (pp. 131–173). San Francisco: Freeman.

Surrey, J. L. (1985). *Self-in-relation: A theory of women's development.* Unpublished manuscript, Stone Center for Developmental Services and Studies, Wellesley College.

Sutherland, J. (1963). Object relations and the conceptual model of psychoanalysis. *British Journal of Medical Psychology, 36*, 109–124.

Swearingen, E. M., & Cohen, L. H. (1985). Life events and psychological distress: A prospective study of young adolescents. *Developmental Psychology, 24,* 103–109.

Taylor, S. E., & Crockett, J. (1981). Schematic bases of social information processing. In E. T. Higgins, C. P. Herman, & M. P. Zanna (Eds.), *Social cognition: The Ontario Symposium on Personality and Social Psychology* (pp. 89–134). Hillsdale, NJ: Erlbaum.

Teasdale, J. D. (1983). Negative thinking in depression: Cause, effect, or reciprocal relation? *Advances in Behaviour Research and Therapy, 5,* 3–25.

Teasdale, J. D. (1997). The transformation of meaning: The interacting cognitive subsystems approach. In M. J. Powers & C. R. Brewin (Eds.), *The transformation of meaning in psychological therapies: Integrating theory and practice* (pp. 141–156). New York: Wiley.

Teasdale, J. D., & Barnard, P. (1993). *Affect, cognition, and change.* Hove, England: Erlbaum.

Teasdale, J. D., Taylor, R., & Fogarty, S. J. (1980). Effects of induced elation–depression on the accessibility of memories of happy and unhappy experiences. *Behaviour Research and Therapy, 8,* 339–346.

Tellegen, A. (1982). *Brief manual for the Differential Personality Questionnaire.* Unpublished manuscript, University of Minnesota, Minneapolis.

Tennen, H., Hall, J. A., & Affleck, G. (1995). Depression research methodologies in the *Journal of Personality and Social Psychology*: A review and critique. *Journal of Personality and Social Psychology, 68,* 870–884.

Thompson, K. C., & Hendrie, H. C. (1972). Environmental stress in primary depressive illness. *Archives of General Psychiatry, 26,* 130–132.

Thompson, R., & Zuroff, D. C. (1998). Dependent and self-critical mothers' responses to adolescent autonomy and competence. *Personality and Individual Differences, 24,* 311–324.

Thompson, R., & Zuroff, D. C. (1999a). Dependent and self-critical mothers' responses to adolescent sons' autonomy and competence. *Journal of Youth and Adolescence, 28,* 365–385.

Thompson, R., & Zuroff, D. C. (1999b). Development of self-criticism in adolescent girls: Roles of maternal dissatisfaction, maternal coldness, and insecure attachment. *Journal of Youth and Adolescence, 28,* 197–210.

Thorbecke, W., & Grotevant, H. D. (1982). Gender differences in adolescent interpersonal identity formation. *Journal of Youth and Adolescence, 11,* 479–492.

Timpe, R. L. (1989). Perfectionism: Positive possibility or personal pathology? *Journal of Psychology and Christianity, 8,* 23–24.

Toolan, J. M. (1962). Depression in children and adolescents. *American Journal of Orthopsychiatry, 32,* 404–415.

Toolan, J. M. (1974). Masked depression in children and adolescents. In S. Lesse (Ed.), *Masked depression* (pp. 141–164). New York: Jason Aronson.

Tronick, E. Z., & Gianino, A. (1986). The transmission of maternal disturbance to the infant. In E. Z. Tronic & T. Field (Eds.), *Maternal depression and infant disturbance* (pp. 5–12). San Francisco, CA: Jossey-Bass.

U.S. Bureau of the Census. (1990). *Statistical abstracts of the United States, 1990* (110th ed.). Washington, DC: Author.

Unwin, J. R. (1970). Depression in alienated youth. *Journal of the Canadian Psychiatric Association, 15,* 83–86.

Urist, J. (1977). The Rorschach test and the assessment of object relations. *Journal of Personality Assessment, 41,* 3–9.

Vaglum, P., & Falkum, E. (1999). Self-criticism, dependency and depressive symptoms in a nationwide sample of Norwegian physicians. *Journal of Affective Disorders, 52,* 153–159.

Vaughn, B., Egeland, B., Sroufe, L. A., & Waters, E. (1979). Individual differences in infant mother attachment at twelve and eighteen months: Stability and change in infant mother attachment in families under stress. *Child Development, 50,* 971–975.

Vettese, L. C., & Mongrain, M. (2000). Communication about the self and partner in the relationships of dependents and self-critics. *Cognitive Therapy and Research, 24,* 609–626.

Vieth, A. Z., & Trull, T. J. (1999). Family patterns of perfectionism: An examination of college students and their parents. *Journal of Personality Assessment, 72,* 49–67.

Viglione, D. J., Clemmey, P. A., & Camenzuli, L. (1990). The Depressive Experiences Questionnaire: A critical review. *Journal of Personality Assessment, 55,* 52–64.

Viglione, D. J., Lovette, G. J., Gottlieb, R., & Friedberg, R. (1995). Depressive Experiences Question-naire: An empirical exploration of the underlying theory. *Journal of Personality Assessment*, *65*, 91–99.

Von Drehle, D. (1993, August 15). The crumbling of a pillar in Washington. *The Washington Post*, pp. A20–A21.

Vredenburg, K., Flett, G.L., & Krames, L. (1993). Analogue versus clinical depression: A critical reappraisal. *Psychological Bulletin*, *113*, 327–344.

Wachtel, P. L. (1977). *Psychoanalysis and behavior therapy*. New York: Basic Books.

Wachtel, P. L. (1994). Cyclical processes in personality and psychopathology. *Journal of Abnormal Psychology*, *103*, 51–66.

Wachtel, P. L., & Blatt, S. J. (1965). Energy deployment and achievement. *Journal of Consulting Psychology*, *29*, 302–308.

Wagner, B. M., & Compas, B. E. (1990). Gender, instrumentality, and expressivity: Moderators of the relation between stress and psychological symptoms during adolesence. *American Journal of Community Psychology*, *18*, 383–406.

Wampold, B. E. (1997). Methodological problems in identifying efficacious psychotherapies. *Psychotherapy Research, 7*, 21-43.

Wampold, B. E. (2001). The great psychotherapy debate: Models, Methods, and Findings. Mahwah, NJ: Erlbaum.

Waniel-Izhar, A., Besser, A., & Priel, B. (in press). Preadolescent symptomatology: The role of internal representations of self, mother, and relatedness. *Journal of Personality*.

Wartner, U. G., Grossman, K., Fremmer-Bombik, E., & Suess, G. (1994). Attachment patterns at age six in south Germany: Predictability from infancy and implications for preschool behavior. *Child Development*, *65*, 1014–1027.

Waters, E. (1978). The reliability and stability of individual differences in infant–mother attachment. *Child Development*, *50*, 821–829.

Waters, E., Wippman, J., & Sroufe, L. A. (1979). Attachment, positive affect and competence in the peer group: Two studies in construct validation. *Child Development*, *50*, 821–829.

Weary, G., Edwards, J. A., & Jacobson, J. A. (1995). Depression research in the *Journal of Personality and Social Psychology*: A reply. *Journal of Personality and Social Psychology*, *68*, 885–891.

Weiss, E. (1944). Clinical aspects of depression. *Psychoanalytic Quarterly*, *13*, 445–461.

Weisse, D. E. (1990). Gifted adolescents and suicide. *School Counselor*, *37*, 351–358.

Weissman, A. N., & Beck, A. T. (1978, August–September). *Development and validation of the Dysfunctional Attitudes Scale: A preliminary investigation*. Paper presented at the 86th Annual Convention of the American Psychological Association, Toronto, Ontario, Canada.

Weissman, A. N., Orvaschel, H., & Padian, N. (1980). Children's symptoms and social functioning on self report scales. *Journal of Nervous and Mental Disorders*, *168*, 736–740.

Weissman, M. M., Gammen, G. D., John, K., Merikangas, K. R., Warner, V., Prusoff, B. A., & Sholomskas, D. (1987). Children of depressed mothers: Increased psychopathology and early onset of depression. *Archives of General Psychiatry*, *44*, 847–853.

Weissman, M. M., & Klerman, G. L. (1977). Sex differences in epidemiology of depression. *Archives of General Psychiatry*, *34*, 98–111.

Weissman, M. M., & Paykel, E. S. (1974). *The depressed women: Study of social relationships*. Chicago: University of Chicago Press.

Welkowitz, J., Lish, J. D., & Bond, R. N. (1985). The Depressive Experiences Questionnaire: Revision and validation. *Journal of Personality Assessment*, *49*, 89–94.

Werner, H. (1948). *Comparative psychology of mental development*. New York: International Universities Press.

Werner, H., & Kaplan, B. (1983). *Symbol formation: An organismic–developmental approach to language and the expression of thought*. New York: Wiley.

West, M., & Sheldon, A. E. R. (1988). Classification of pathological attachment patterns in adults. *Journal of Personality Disorders*, *2*, 153–159.

West, M., Sheldon, A., & Reiffer, L. (1987). An approach to the delineation of adult attachment: Scale development and reliability. *Journal of Nervous and Mental Disease*, *175*, 738–741.

Westen, D. (1991a). Clinical assessment of object relations using the TAT. *Journal of Personality Assessment*, *56*, 56–74.

Westen, D. (1991). Social cognition and object relations. *Psychological Bulletin, 109,* 429–455.

Westen, D., Lohr, N. E., Silk, K., Gold, L., & Kerber, K. (1990). Object relations and social cognition in borderlines, major depressives, and normals: A Thematic Apperception Test analysis. *Psychological Assessment, 2,* 355–364.

Wetzel, J. W. (1989). *American youth: A statistical snapshot.* Washington, DC: Youth and America's future: The William T. Grant Commission on Work, Family, and Citizenship.

Wetzel, J. W., & Redmond, P. C. (1980) A person–environment study of depression. *Social Service Review, 54,* 363–375.

Whiffen, V. E., & Aubé, J. A. (1999). Personality, interpersonal context, and depression in couples. *Journal of Social and Personal Relationships, 16,* 369–383.

Whiffen, V. E., Aubé, J. A., Thompson, J. M., & Campbell, T. L. (2000). Attachment beliefs and interpersonal contexts associated with dependency and self-criticism. *Journal of Social and Clinical Psychology, 19,* 184–205.

Whiffen, V. E., & Sasseville, T. M. (1991). Dependency, self-criticism, and recollections of parenting: Sex differences and the role of depressive affect. *Journal of Social and Clinical Psychology, 10,* 121–133.

Whisman, M., & Friedman, M. A. (1998). Interpersonal problem behaviors associated with dysfunctional attitudes. *Cognitive Therapy and Research, 22,* 149–160.

Widiger, T. A., & Anderson, K. G. (2003). Personality and depression in women. *Journal of Affective Disorders, 74,* 59–66.

Widiger, T. A., & Bornstein, R. F. (2002). Histrionic, narcissistic, and dependent personality disorders. In H. E. Adams & P. Sutker (Eds.), *Comprehensive handbook of psychopathology* (3rd ed., pp. xxx–xxx) New York: Plenum.

Wiggins, J. S. (1991). Agency and communion as conceptual coordinates for the understanding and measurement of interpersonal behavior. In W. W. Grove, & D. Cicchetti (Eds.), *Thinking clearly about psychology, Vol. 2: Personality and psychotherapy* (pp. 89–113). Minneapolis: University of Minnesota Press.

Wiggins, J. S., & Trapnell, P. D. (1996). A dyadic–interactional perspective on the five-factor model. In J. S. Wiggins (Ed.), *The five-factor model of personality: Theoretical perspectives* (pp. 88–162). New York: Guilford Press.

Winer, B. J. (1962). *Statistical principles in experimental design.* New York: Wiley.

Winnicott, D. W. (1954). The depressive position in normal emotional development. *British Journal of Medical Psychology, 28,* 89–100.

Winnicott, D. W. (1971). Mirror-role of mother and family in child development. In *Playing and reality* (pp. 111–118). London: Tavistock.

Winnicott, D. W. (1975). *The antisocial tendency: Through pediatrics to psychoanalysis.* New York: Basic Books.

Wiseman, H. (1997). Interpersonal relatedness and self-definition in the experience of loneliness during the transition to university. *Personal Relationships, 4,* 285–299.

Wishnie, H. (1974). Opiate addiction: A masked depression. In S. Lesse (Ed.), *Masked depression* (pp. 330–367). New York: Aronson.

Wixom, J., Ludolph, P., & Westen, D. (1993). The quality of depression in adolescents with borderline personality disorder. *Journal of the American Academy of Child & Adolescent Psychiatry, 32,* 1172–1177.

Wolff, P. H. (1960). *The developmental psychologies of Jean Piaget and psychoanalysis.* New York: International Universities Press.

Woody, G. E., Luborsky, L., McLellan, A. T., O'Brien, C. P., Beck, A. I., Blaine, J., et al. (1983). Psychotherapy for opiate addicts. *Archives of General Psychiatry, 40,* 639–645.

Woody, G. E., O'Brien, C. P., & Rickels, K. (1975). A placebo-controlled study of doxepin in combination with methadone. *American Journal of Psychiatry, 132,* 447–450.

Worchel, F. F., Nolan, B., & Wilson, V. (1987). New perspectives on child and adolescent depression. *Journal of School Psychology, 25,* 411–414.

Wright, J. H., & Davis, D. (1994). The therapeutic relationship in cognitive behavioral therapy: Patient perceptions and therapist responses. *Cognitive and Behavioral Practice, 1,* 25–45.

Wurmser, L. (1974). Psychoanalytic considerations of the etiology of compulsive drug use. *Journal of the American Psychoanalytic Association, 22*, 820–843.

Yamaguchi, K., & Kendal, D. (1987). Drug use and other determinants of premarital pregnancy and its outcomes: A dynamic analysis of competing life events. *Journal of Marriage and the Family, 49*, 257–270.

Yarrow, L. J., & Goodwin, M. S. (1973). The immediate impact of separation: Reactions of infants to a change in mother figures. In J. Stone, H. T. Smith, & C. B. Murphy (Eds.), *The competent infant* (pp. 1032–1040). New York: Basic Books.

Yehuda, R., Kahana, B., Southwick, S. M., & Giller, E. L. (1994). Depressive features in Holocaust survivors with post-traumatic stress disorder. *Journal of Traumatic Stress, 7*, 699–704.

Zahn-Waxler, C. (1993). Caregivers' interpretations of infant emotions: A comparison of depressed and well mothers. In R. N. Emde, J. D. Osofsky, et al. (Eds.), *The IFEEL pictures: A new instrument for interpreting emotions* (pp. 175–184). Madison, CT: International Universities Press.

Zahn-Waxler, C., Kochanska, G., Krupnick, J., & McKnew, D. (1990). Patterns of guilt in children of depressed and well mothers. *Developmental Psychology, 26*, 51–59.

Zahn-Waxler, C., McKnew, D. H., Cummings, E. M., & Radke-Yarrow, M. (1984). Problem behaviors and peer interactions of young children with a manic depressive parent. *Child Development, 55*, 112–122.

Zeanah, C., Benoit, D., Hirshberg, L., Barton, M., & Regan, C. (1991). *Classifying mothers' representations of their infants: Results from structured interviews.* Paper presented at the annual meeting of the American Academy of Child and Adolescent Psychiatry, San Francisco.

Zelnick, L., & Buchholtz, E. S. (1990). The concept of mental representations in light of recent infant research. *Psychoanalytic Psychology, 7*, 29–58.

Zemore, R., & Rinholm, J. (1989). Vulnerability to depression as a function of parental rejection and control. *Canadian Journal of Behavioural Science, 21*, 364–376.

Zettle, R. D., Haflich, J. L., & Reynolds, R. A. (1992). Responsivity to cognitive therapy as a function of treatment format and client personality dimensions. *Journal of Clinical Psychology, 48*, 787–797.

Zettle, R. D., & Herring, E. L. (1995). Treatment utility of the sociotropy/autonomy distinction: Implications for cognitive therapy. *Journal of Clinical Psychology, 51*, 280–289.

Zetzel, E. R. (1953). The depressive position. In P. Greenacre (Ed.), *Affective disorders* (pp. 84–116). New York: International Universities Press.

Zetzel, E. R. (1960). Introduction to the symposium on "depressive illness." *International Journal of Psycho-Analysis, 41*, 476–480.

Zetzel, E. R. (1965). Depression and the incapacity to bear it. In *Drives, affects, behavior* (Vol. 2, pp. 243–274). New York: International Universities Press.

Zuckerman, M., & Lubin, B. (1965). *Manual for the Multiple Affect Adjective Checklist.* San Diego, CA: Educational and Industrial Testing Service.

Zung, W. W. (1965). Self-rating depression scale. *Archives of General Psychiatry, 12*, 63–70.

Zung, W. W. (1971). Depression in the normal adult population. *Psychosomatics, 12*, 164–167.

Zung, W. W. (1972). How normal is depression? *Psychosomatics, 13*, 174–178.

Zung, W. W. (1973). From art to science: The diagnosis and treatment of depression. *Archives of General Psychiatry, 29*, 328–337.

Zuroff, D. C. (1980). Distortion of memory in depressed, formerly depressed, and never depressed college students. *Psychological Reports, 46*, 415–425.

Zuroff, D. C. (1992). New directions for cognitive models of depression. *Psychological Inquiry, 3*, 274–277.

Zuroff, D. C. (1994). Depressive personality styles and the five-factor model of personality. *Journal of Personality Assessment, 63*, 453–472.

Zuroff, D.C., & Blatt, S. J. (2002). Vicissitudes of life after the short-term treatment of depression: Roles of stress, social support, and personality. *Journal of Social and Clinical Psychology, 21*, 473–496.

Zuroff, D. C., Blatt, S. J., Krupnick, J. L., & Sotsky, S. M. (2003). When brief treatment is over: Enhanced adaptive capacities and stress reactivity after termination. *Psychotherapy Research, 13*, 99–115.

Zuroff, D. C., Blatt, S. J., Sanislow, C. A., Bondi, C. M., & Pilkonis, P. A. (1999). Vulnerability to depression: Reexamining state dependence and relative stability. *Journal of Abnormal Psychology, 108,* 76–89.

Zuroff, D. C., Blatt, S. J., Sotsky, S. M., Krupnick, J. L., Martin, D. J., Sanislow, C. A., & Simmens, S. (2000). Relation of therapeutic alliance and perfectionism to outcome in brief outpatient treatment of depression. *Journal of Consulting and Clinical Psychology, 68,* 114–124.

Zuroff, D. C., & de Lorimier, S. (1989). Ideal and actual romantic partners of women varying in dependency and self-criticism. *Journal of Personality, 57,* 825–846.

Zuroff, D. C., & Duncan, N. (1999). Self-criticism and conflict resolution in romantic couples. *Canadian Journal of Behavioral Science, 31,* 137–149.

Zuroff, D. C., & Fitzpatrick, D. (1995). Depressive personality styles: Implications for adult attachment. *Personality and Individual Differences, 18,* 253–265.

Zuroff, D. C., & Franko, D. L. (1986, April). Depressed and test anxious students' interactions with friends: Effects of dependency and self-criticism. Paper presented at the meeting of the Eastern Psychological Association, New York.

Zuroff, D. C., & Giannopoulos, C. (1990, June). *Negative affect in the romantic relationships of dependent and self-critical women.* Poster presented at the meeting of the Canadian Psychological Association, Ottawa, Ontario.

Zuroff, D. C., Igreja, I., & Mongrain, M. (1990). Dysfunctional attitudes, dependency, and self-criticism as predictors of depressive mood states: A 12-month longitudinal study. *Cognitive Therapy and Research, 14,* 315–326.

Zuroff, D. C., Koestner, R., & Powers, T. A. (1994). Self-criticism at age 12: A longitudinal study of adjustment in later adolescence and adulthood. *Journal of Cognitive Therapy and Research, 18,* 367–385.

Zuroff, D. C., & Mongrain, M. (1987a). *Attributions of dependent and self-critical women for interpersonal rejection and achievement failure.* Unpublished manuscript, McGill University, Montreal, Quebec, Canada.

Zuroff, D. C., & Mongrain, M. (1987b). Dependency and self-criticism: Vulnerability factors for depressive affective states. *Journal of Abnormal Psychology, 96,* 14–22.

Zuroff, D. C., Mongrain, M., & Santor, D. (in press). Conceptualizing and measuring personality vulnerability to depression: Revisiting issues raised by Coyne and Whiffen (1995). *Psychological Bulletin.*

Zuroff, D. C., Moskowitz, D. S., & Cote, S. (1999). Dependency, self-criticism, interpersonal behaviour, and affect: Evolutionary perspectives. *British Journal of Clinical Psychology, 38,* 231–250.

Zuroff, D. C., Moskowitz, D. S., & Koestner, R. (1996, August). Differentiating the construct of Dependency: Rude and Burnham's Neediness and Connectedness factors. Poster presented at the 104th Annual Convention of the American Psychological Association, Toronto, Ontario, Canada.

Zuroff, D. C., Moskowitz, D. S., Wielgus, M. S., Powers, T. A., & Franko, D. L. (1983). Construct validation of the Dependency and Self-Criticism scales of the Depressive Experiences Questionnaire. *Journal of Research in Personality, 17,* 226–241.

Zuroff, D. C., Quinlan, D. M., & Blatt, S. J. (1990). Psychometric properties of the Depressive Experiences Questionnaire. *Journal of Personality Assessment, 55,* 65–72.

Zuroff, D. C., Stotland, S., Sweetman, E., Craig, J., & Koestner, R. (1995). Dependency, self-criticism, and social interactions. *British Journal of Clinical Psychology, 34,* 543–553.

Index

About the Author

Sidney J. Blatt received his PhD in personality development and psychopathology from the University of Chicago in 1957, where he interned with Dr. Carl Rogers. He was a post-doctoral fellow in the joint program at the University of Illinois Medical School and Michael Reese Hospital in Chicago. He joined the faculty of the psychology department at Yale University in 1960, and in 1964 also assumed the post of chief of the psychology section in the Department of Psychiatry. Dr. Blatt was a fellow of the Foundations Fund for Research in Psychiatry for psychoanalytic training at the Western New England Institute for Psychoanalysis, graduating in 1972. He has also held a Senior Fulbright Research Fellowship.

Dr. Blatt has published extensively (approaching some 200 publications) in a wide range of journals in psychology, psychiatry, and psychoanalysis. He is also coauthor of several books—*The Interpretation of Psychological Tests* (1968/1988; with J. Allison & C. N. Zimet), *Schizophrenia: A Developmental Analysis* (1976; with C. M. Wild), *Continuity and Change in Art: The Development of Modes of Representation* (1984; with E. S. Blatt), and *Therapeutic Change: An Object Relations Perspective* (1994; with R. Q. Ford) and is coeditor of several volumes—*The Self in Emotional Distress: Cognitive and Psychodynamic Perspectives* (1993; with Z. V. Segal), three volumes on psychoanalytic theory and attachment research (1999, 1999, 2003; with D. Diamond), and *Theory and Treatment of Depression: Toward Integration* (in press; with J. Corevelyn & P. Luyten). He is on the editorial board of a number of journals in psychology, psychiatry, and psychoanalysis and has received citations from professional organizations for distinguished contributions to research, teaching, and clinical practice. He has also been visiting professor at a number of universities, including the Hebrew University of Jerusalem, University College London, Catholic University of Lueven, and Ben Gurion University of the Negev, as well as at the Menninger Foundation.